Speech Analysis

Automatic Speech and Speaker Recognition, *Edited by N. R. Dixon and T. Martin*

The Engineer in Transition to Management, *I. Gray*

Multidimensional Systems: Theory & Application, *Edited by N. K. Bose*

Analog Integrated Circuits, *Edited by A. B. Grebene*

Integrated-Circuit Operational Amplifiers, *Edited by R. G. Meyer*

Modern Spectrum Analysis, *Edited by D. G. Childers*

Digital Image Processing for Remote Sensing, *Edited by R. Bernstein*

Reflector Antennas, *Edited by A. W. Love*

Phase-Locked Loops & Their Application, *Edited by W. C. Lindsey and M. K. Simon*

Digital Signal Computers and Processors, *Edited by A. C. Salazar*

Systems Engineering: Methodology and Applications, *Edited by A. P. Sage*

Modern Crystal and Mechanical Filters, *Edited by D. F. Sheahan and R. A. Johnson*

Electrical Noise: Fundamentals and Sources, *Edited by M. S. Gupta*

Computer Methods in Image Analysis, *Edited by J. K. Aggarwal, R. O. Duda, and A. Rosenfeld*

Microprocessors: Fundamentals and Applications, *Edited by W. C. Lin*

Machine Recognition of Patterns, *Edited by A. K. Agrawala*

Turning Points in American Electrical History, *Edited by J. E. Brittain*

Charge-Coupled Devices: Technology and Applications, *Edited by R. Melen and D. Buss*

Spread Spectrum Techniques, *Edited by R. C. Dixon*

Electronic Switching: Central Office Systems of the World, *Edited by A. E. Joel, Jr.*

Electromagnetic Horn Antennas, *Edited by A. W. Love*

Waveform Quantization and Coding, *Edited by N. S. Jayant*

Communication Satellite Systems: An Overview of the Technology, *Edited by R. G. Gould and Y. F. Lum*

Literature Survey of Communication Satellite Systems and Technology, *Edited by J. H. W. Unger*

Solar Cells, *Edited by C. E. Backus*

Computer Networking, *Edited by R. P. Blanc and I. W. Cotton*

Communications Channels: Characterization and Behavior, *Edited by B. Goldberg*

Large-Scale Networks: Theory and Design, *Edited by F. T. Boesch*

Optical Fiber Technology, *Edited by D. Gloge*

Selected Papers in Digital Signal Processing, II, *Edited by the Digital Signal Processing Committee*

A Guide for Better Technical Presentations, *Edited by R. M. Woelfle*

Career Management: A Guide to Combating Obsolescence, *Edited by H. G. Kaufman*

Energy and Man: Technical and Social Aspects of Energy, *Edited by M. G. Morgan*

Magnetic Bubble Technology: Integrated-Circuit Magnetics for Digital Storage and Processing, *Edited by H. Chang*

Frequency Synthesis: Techniques and Applications, *Edited by J. Gorski-Popiel*

Literature in Digital Processing: Author and Permuted Title Index (Revised and Expanded Edition), *Edited by H. D. Helms, J. F. Kaiser, and L. R. Rabiner*

Data Communications via Fading Channels, *Edited by K. Brayer*

Nonlinear Networks: Theory and Analysis, *Edited by A. N. Willson, Jr.*

Computer Communications, *Edited by P. E. Green, Jr. and R. W. Lucky*

Stability of Large Electric Power Systems, *Edited by R. T. Byerly and E. W. Kimbark*

Automatic Test Equipment: Hardware, Software, and Management, *Edited by F. Liguori*

Key Papers in the Development of Coding Theory, *Edited by E. R. Berkekamp*

Technology and Social Institutions, *Edited by K. Chen*

Key Papers in the Development of Information Theory, *Edited by D. Slepian*

Computer-Aided Filter Design, *Edited by G. Szentirmai*

Laser Devices and Applications, *Edited by I. P. Kaminow and A. E. Siegman*

Integrated Optics, *Edited by D. Marcuse*

Laser Theory, *Edited by F. S. Barnes*

Digital Signal Processing, *Edited by L. R. Rabiner and C. M. Radar*

Minicomputers: Hardware, Software, and Applications, *Edited by J. D. Schoeffler and R. H. Temple*

Semiconductor Memories, *Edited by D. A. Hodges*

Power Semiconductor Applications, Volume II: Equipment and Systems, *Edited by J. D. Harnden, Jr. and F. B. Golden*

Power Semiconductor Applications, Volume I: General Considerations, *Edited by J. D. Harnden, Jr. and F. B. Golden*

A Practical Guide to Minicomputer Applications, *Edited by F. F. Coury*

Active Inductorless Filters, *Edited by S. K. Mitra*

Clearing the Air: The Impact of the Clean Air Act on Technology, *Edited by J. C. Redmond, J. C. Cook, and A. A. J. Hoffman*

24330
191180

ML

£19·25

R4

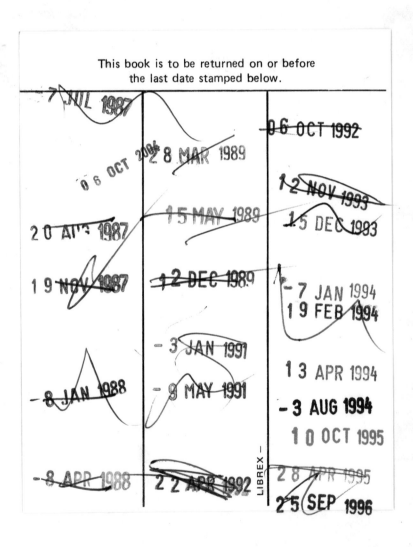

Speech Analysis

Edited by

Ronald W. Schafer
Professor of Electrical Engineering
Georgia Institute of Technology

John D. Markel
President
Signal Technology, Inc.

A volume in the IEEE PRESS Selected Reprint Series,
prepared under the sponsorship of the IEEE
Acoustics, Speech, and Signal Processing Society.

IEEE
PRESS

The Institute of Electrical and Electronics Engineers, Inc. New York

Contents

Foreword

The compilation of this collection of reprints on speech analysis was initiated as a project of the Speech Processing Committee of the Acoustics, Speech, and Signal Processing Society. The goal of this project was to make available in a convenient form a set of important papers in the field of speech analysis that would provide: (1) historical perspective, (2) convenient tutorial discussions of the fundamentals of speech modeling and analysis, and (3) discussion of the latest state-of-the-art methods of speech analysis.

In selecting the papers for this book we attempted to emphasize fundamental principles that continue to be widely used in speech analysis. Our approach to the selection of papers was to define the scope of our project by selecting a sizable number of papers which were then organized into a number of subareas of speech analysis. This initial selection was based upon those papers that we had found useful in our own work in speech processing. Our preliminary outline was then sent to a number of active workers in the speech processing field, asking them to rate each paper as to whether it should be included in our collection. The response that we received was very gratifying. Many people took our request very seriously—thoughtfully commenting on many of the papers and offering numerous suggestions of papers that we had overlooked. We found that there was general agreement on the importance of many of the papers that we had listed, and these formed the nucleus of the present book. The rest of the papers were selected to fill the gaps between the major ideas.

In making our final selections we were faced with many difficult choices. Page limitations forced us to omit many papers that we wanted to include. We very much regret that many fine papers had to be excluded and we regret that there are many people who have contributed to the field of speech analysis whose work is not *directly* represented in this collection of papers. We hope that these authors will understand that we were motivated solely by a desire to produce the most useful and comprehensive collection of papers, consistent with economic limitations.

In conclusion, we wish to acknowledge the efforts of the following people who reviewed our initial outline: S. J. Campanella, J. L. Flanagan, J. N. Holmes, D. Klatt, J. Makhoul, T. B. Martin, M. Medress, P. Mermelstein, E. P. Neuberg, L. R. Rabiner, A. E. Rosenberg, M. R. Sambur, T. Skinner, H. Wakita, C. J. Weinstein, and D. Y. Wong.

Although the comments and suggestions of these individuals had an important impact on the final form of this book, the ultimate responsibility for its form and content is ours.

Introduction

In the production of speech, sound is generated in the vocal system either by vibration of the vocal cords or by the creation of turbulent air flow at a constriction. The sounds thus produced are spectrally shaped by the transmission characteristics of the vocal tract which consists of the pharynx and oral cavity. In some cases the nasal tract is also involved. This process can be modeled as a slowly time-varying linear system that is excited by a source which is a quasi-periodic pulse signal for voiced speech or a flat spectrum random signal for unvoiced speech. *Speech analysis* is simply the process of estimating the (time-varying) parameters of the model for speech production from a speech signal that is assumed to be the output of that model. *Speech synthesis* is the process of producing an acoustic signal by controlling the model for speech production with an appropriate set of parameters. If the model is sufficiently accurate and the parameters are accurately determined, the resulting output of the model is in some cases indistinguishable from natural speech.

Speech analysis is a fundamental ingredient of almost all the important technical problems of speech communication. A speech analysis system when coupled to a corresponding speech synthesis system comprises a vocoder. Such systems can provide a means of efficient transmission or storage of speech signals. Speech analysis systems usually serve as the "front end" for systems for automatic speech recognition (or speech understanding) and for automatic speaker verification (or speaker identification) systems. Speech analysis is also involved in many aids-to-the-handicapped such as speeded speech for the blind and visual training aids for teaching the deaf to speak. Still another area where speech analysis plays a fundamental role is in enhancing the quality of speech signals that have been degraded by noise, reverberation, or by production in an unusual atmosphere (diver's speech).

Just as there are many areas of application, there are also many different speech analysis techniques, each based upon a particular speech production model, and each applicable to a particular set of problems. The papers of this collection are organized so as to lead from the basic speech model (Part I) to general principles of speech analysis (Part II) to techniques for estimating specific speech parameters (Parts III and IV). Finally, Part V is concerned with systems for analysis and synthesis of speech. This is one of the major areas of application of speech analysis techniques, and it is an area that can be reasonably well summarized by such a limited number of papers. It should again be emphasized that the material of Parts I–IV is basic to many other applications and aids-to-the-handicapped. However, it is impossible to do justice to these areas in the limited space available to us. Indeed any one of these applications areas is worthy of its own collection of reprints.

The papers collected here span a period of almost 40 years. It is extremely interesting to note, however, that the basic principles of speech analysis have not changed dramatically in that time. What has changed is the technology that can be applied to speech communication problems. As recently as 20 years ago, speech analysis was done almost exclusively with analog hardware. Then in the 1960's speech researchers turned to digital computers to facilitate the design of complicated systems through simulations. As computers became increasingly more capable and less expensive, it became clear that digital processing had many advantages over analog techniques. Today digital techniques are predominant in both research and technology in speech communication. The future promises many new and exciting developments in the applications areas mentioned above. Underlying these advances will be new methods of speech analysis, grounded in the basic speech model but incorporating new knowledge about speech production and latest technical advances in computation and signal processing. We hope that this volume of reprints will serve to summarize where we are and point the way to new advances.

Part I
Properties of the Speech Signal

As discussed in the introduction, speech analysis is concerned with the estimation, from the speech signal, of the parameters of a model for speech production consisting of a slowly time-varying linear system excited by either quasi-periodic (glottal) pulses or random noise. Thus, the basic problems of speech analysis are: voiced/unvoiced classification; pitch period estimation for voiced speech; estimation of the glottal pulse shape; and estimation of vocal tract transmission properties. In this part we have selected a set of papers that describe the basic speech model. The first paper, by Flanagan, provides a very readable introduction to the speech model. This paper also suggests how speech models can be used in speech synthesis, i.e., to provide machines with voices. The second paper, by Fant, gives a discussion of the acoustic theory of speech production in the style of his classic book [1]. This paper introduces the relationship between vocal tract shape and the frequency response of the vocal system. This concept is further discussed in the third paper by Dunn which focuses on the relationship between vowel resonances (or formants) and vocal tract shape. The fourth paper by Peterson and Barney also is concerned with properties of vowel sounds. This paper is widely referenced and it is the source of much valuable data on average formant frequencies of vowels. This paper also discusses the use of the sound spectrograph in speech analysis.

The fifth paper, by Fujimura, is concerned with a study of the properties of nasal sounds. The differences between nasals and vowels are studied in detail both through models and through measurements. The sixth paper, by Heinz and Stevens, describes the properties of voiceless fricative sounds. In this paper, the authors present an acoustic model for production of fricative sounds and they compare this model to experimental measurements previously obtained by Hughes and Halle [2].

The final paper, by Flanagan and Cherry, describes a model for both voiced and unvoiced excitation in speech production. Recent research [3] has carried this excitation model much further; however, this brief paper provides a very good introduction to the properties of the glottal waveform in voiced speech and the random excitation for fricatives.

The papers of this part are representative of a large body of basic research on modeling of the speech production process. Our purpose here was not to be exhaustive—this would require another book—but to portray the essential components of the basic speech model. The material presented in these papers provides adequate background to understand the methods of speech analysis discussed in the remaining papers. Further detail is available in the books cited below [1, 4, 5].

References

1. G. Fant, *Acoustic Theory of Speech Production*, Mouton, The Hague, 1970.
2. G. W. Hughes and M. Halle, "Spectral properties of fricative consonants," *J. Acoust. Soc. Am.*, vol. 28, pp. 303-310, Mar. 1956.
3. K. Ishizaka and J. L. Flanagan, "Synthesis of voiced sounds from a two-mass model of the vocal cords," *Bell Syst. Tech. J.*, vol. 50, pp. 1233-1368, July-Aug. 1972.
4. J. L. Flanagan, *Speech Analysis, Synthesis and Perception*, 2nd ed., Springer-Verlag, New York, 1972.
5. L. R. Rabiner and R. W. Schafer, *Digital Processing of Speech Signals*, Prentice-Hall, Englewood Cliffs, NJ., 1978.

Received 6 March 1972

Voices of Men and Machines*

J. L. FLANAGAN

Bell Telephone Laboratories, Murray Hill, New Jersey 07974

Talking computers are likely to become a fixture in modern society. The range of information services that can be provided by voice from computers depends largely upon how clever computers become at imitating human speech. This, in turn, depends upon the fundamental acoustic and linguistic knowledge that can be imparted to the machine. This article summarizes the principles of human speech generation, traces some historical interests in speaking machines, and indicates present capabilities of talking computers.

Machines which, with more or less success, imitate human speech, are the most difficult to construct, so many are the agencies engaged in uttering even a single word—lungs, larynx, tongue, palate, teeth, lips—so many are the inflections and variations of tone and articulation, that the mechanician finds his ingenuity taxed to the utmost to imitate them.

Scientific American **24**, 32
(14 Jan. 1871)

I. COMMUNICATION BY SPEECH

Man's primary means of communication is speech. He is unique among life forms in his ability to acquire and use speech. It is even more remarkable that he has derived the ability from physiological apparatus designed for other purposes—the vital functions of breathing and eating.

Because man evolved in an air atmosphere, it is not surprising that he learned to signal by producing longitudinal vibrations (acoustic waves) in the air medium. At the acoustic level, speech consists of rapid and deterministic fluctuations in air pressure. These sound pressures are generated and radiated by man's vocal apparatus; they are detected by his ear and apprehended by his brain.

The specialized, acoustic code of speech did not develop overnight. Passage of untold time probably witnessed the progress of human speech from the grunt and bark level of man's fellow creatures. At least one speculation holds that early man's first means of communication probably were hand signals. Speech perhaps evolved when man discovered he could supplement his hand signals by audible and distinctive "gestures" of his vocal tract. As Sir Richard Paget[1] put

it, "What drove man to the invention of speech was, as I imagine, not so much the need of expressing his thoughts as the difficulty of 'talking with his hands full.' It was the continual use of man's hands for craftsmanship, the chase, and the beginnings of art and agriculture, that drove him to find other methods of expressing his ideas—namely, by a specialized pantomine of the tongue and lips."

Throughout history man's voice has been a source of interest and wonderment. Ancient man often took his ability of speech as a symbol of divine origin. Not unnaturally, he sometimes ascribed the same ability to his gods. Zealous priests, not insensitive to the opportunity, frequently tried to make their idols speak directly to the people. Talking statues, miraculous voices, and oracles were well known in the Greek and Roman civilizations—the voice usually coming to the artificial mouth through cleverly concealed speaking tubes (Fig. 1).[2,3]

As the world entered the Renaissance, superstition yielded to scientific curiosity. Man began to inquire more seriously into the nature of things. Human life and physiology were fair targets of study, and the mechanism of speech belonged in this sphere. Attempts were made to imitate man's voice with mechanical contrivances, and some were exceedingly clever in design. This approach to vocal modeling even today affords insight into the acoustic nonlinearities which attend speech production.

II. MAN'S VOICE

Through the developments of modern acoustic theory, the understanding of human voice production is beginning to be complete. The fundamental principles

Reprinted with permission from *J. Acoust. Soc. Am.*, vol. 51, pp. 1375–1387, Mar 1972.

FIG. 1. Artist's conception of a speaking idol.

of sound generation in the vocal tract and the acoustic filtering behavior of the tract are essentially established, although some of the nonlinearities in vocal-cord vibration and in source–tract interaction remain to be studied and quantified. This acoustic understanding forms the basis for all present-day efforts in speech synthesis.[4]

In contrast, knowledge is incomplete about the linguistic rules which dictate the ordered motions of the vocal system. Studies of speech prosody, relating to stress, pause, and pitch assignment, and studies of the dynamical properties of articulatory motions are all current topics of speech research.[5–8]

A. Functions of the Vocal Tract

Acoustic understanding of voice production can be indicated with the help of Fig. 2, which is a sagittal-plane x ray of a man's head. Main parts of the vocal apparatus are shown. The vocal tract proper is a nonuniform acoustic tube about 17 cm in length. It is terminated at one end by the vocal cords (or by the opening between them, the glottis) and at the other by the lips. The cross-sectional area of the tract is determined by placement of the lips, jaw, tongue, and velum, and can vary from zero (complete closure) to about 20 cm².

An ancillary cavity, the nasal tract, can be coupled to the vocal tract by the trap-door action of the velum. The nasal tract begins at the velum and terminates at the nostrils. In man, the cavity is about 12 cm long and has a volume of about 60 cm³. During non-nasal sounds the velum seals off the nasal cavity and no sound is radiated from the nostrils.

Sound can be generated in the vocal system in three ways. Voiced sounds are produced by elevating the air pressure in the lungs, forcing a flow through the vocal-cord orifice (the glottis) and causing the cords to vibrate. The interrupted flow produces quasiperiodic, broad-spectrum pulses which excite the vocal tract. The physiological structure of the vocal cords, which produce this pulsive air flow, is shown in Fig. 3. The vibrating ligaments of the vocal cords are about 18 mm long and the mean glottal opening is typically 5 mm².

Fricative sounds of speech are generated by forming a constriction at some point in the tract and forcing air through the constriction at a sufficiently high Reynolds' number to produce turbulence. A noise source of sound pressure is thereby created. Plosive sounds result from making a complete closure, again usually toward the front, building up pressure behind the closure, and abruptly releasing it. Fricative noise (or aspiration) typically follows the transient release.

All these vocal sources—for periodic voiced sounds and for aperiodic voiceless sounds—are relatively broad in spectrum. The vocal system acts as a time-varying filter to impose its resonant characteristics on the sources.

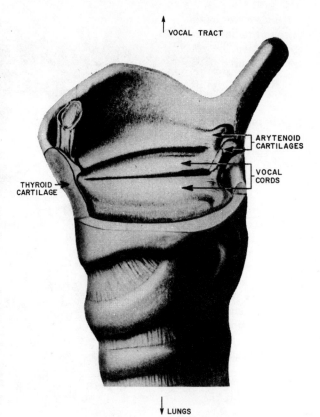

FIG. 3. Schematic view of the human larynx.

B. A Model of Speech-Sound Generation

Because of the relatively loose interaction between the vocal system and the sound sources, these can be approximately represented as linearly separable. In this form, their individual acoustic properties can be conveniently examined. Figure 4(top) represents the vocal tract as a time-varying filter which is excited by broad-

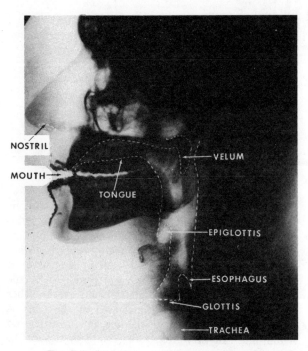

FIG. 2. Sagittal-plane x ray of the vocal system.[4]

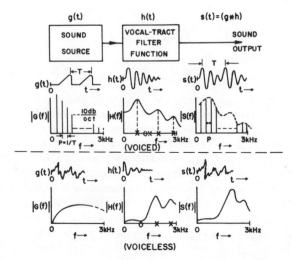

FIG. 4. Source-system model of speech production.[21]

The Journal of the Acoustical Society of America

spectrum sources having relatively fixed characteristics. The sound radiated from the mouth $s(t)$ can, to a first approximation, be considered the convolution of the excitation source $g(t)$ and the transmission characteristic $h(t)$.

For voiced sounds, the excitation source is the acoustic volume velocity at the vocal cords. This is typically pulsive and periodic, and has a line spectrum whose harmonics diminish in amplitude approximately as $1/f^2$ [sketched as $|G(f)|$ in Fig. 4(middle)]. The vocal-tract filter function [sketched as $|H(f)|$] has transmission poles corresponding to the acoustic resonances (or formants) of the vocal tract. The tract length is comparable to a wavelength at the frequencies of interest. It is essentially open at the mouth end and closed at the glottal end, and its eigenfrequencies correspond roughly to the odd quarter-wave resonances of such a pipe. For a straight pipe of 17-cm length, the first three frequencies are 500, 1500, and 2500 Hz.

For vowel sounds the pipe is excited at the glottal (vocal-cord) end, and it has no side-branch resonators. Its transmission consequently has only poles (shown by the ✕'s). Nasal sounds typically exhibit an additional pole and zero in the frequency range below 3 kHz (shown by the dashed ✕–0). The output magnitude spectrum $|S(f)|$ is therefore a line spectrum which has imposed upon it the resonances of the vocal transmission. As the vocal tract takes on the shapes for different sounds, the frequencies of these resonances change.

In a similar manner, the unvoiced sounds are excited from a noise source which is relatively flat in spectrum [Fig. 4(lower)]. This source is typically positioned at some point along the tract, and the transmission function is, to first order, approximated by a couple of poles and a zero. Again the radiated sound reflects these resonances.

In continuous speech the formant resonances move around as the vocal tract changes shape. Figure 5 shows a sound spectrogram (a time–frequency-intensity plot) of a sentence in which the first three formant frequencies are traced. These parameters vary slowly (compared to the pressure fluctuations in the speech wave) because of the physical limitations on how quickly the vocal tract can change in shape. (That is, the tongue, jaw, lips, etc., have significant mass, and their accelerations are limited by the forces which the articulatory muscles can generate.)

On the basis of these relations, a simple, reasonable, and approximate model of speech generation includes a time-varying filter, whose resonances and antiresonances can change continuously to simulate the vocal-tract transmission, and whose excitation is derived from two kinds of signal sources: a periodic pulse generator of variable period to simulate voiced sounds, and a broad-band noise generator to simulate voiceless sounds.

C. Aid for Man's Voice—the Artificial Larynx

Sometimes man's voice fails. Mishaps of accident or disease can impair the ability to generate sound with the vocal-cord structure shown in Fig. 3. The impairment may take the form of paralysis of the cords or of a complete loss of the larynx, In such cases speech is impossible unless a substitute can be supplied for the vocal cords. Again, modern understanding of the acoustic principles of speech production suggests alternatives.

Following a laryngectomy, major parts of the larynx structure, including the vocal cords, may be missing. The trachea is typically terminated in an opening at the base of the throat, and breathing is accomplished through this port. The esophagus and pharynx are normally intact.

Some laryngectomees can learn to talk with esophageal speech. In this process air is swallowed into the esophagus and stomach. It is expelled so as to produce a vibration of the entry folds of the esophagus. The vibration interrupts the air stream in a fashion similar to

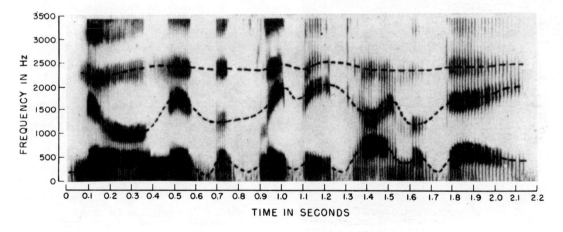

"NOON IS THE SLEEPY TIME OF DAY"

FIG. 5. Sound spectrogram of a sentence showing the time variation of the first three vocal resonances, or formants.

Volume 51   Number 5 (Part 1)   1972

that of the natural vocal cords. This is an adequate substitute voice for laryngectomees who can learn esophageal speech. Some persons, however, find it difficult, if not impossible to learn. For these, other methods are necessary.

One of the earliest mechanical voice aids was the Western Electric model 2 artificial larynx.[9] This device introduces a sound similar to that of the natural vocal cords into the vocal tract. It is shown schematically in Fig. 6. A tube conducts the breath stream from the tracheal outlet to a cylindrical chamber. A tuned reed is located in the chamber and controls the air flow into a mouth tube. Vibration of the reed interrupts the air flow into the mouth tube (much as the natural vocal cords "chop up" the breath stream), and pulses of air are introduced into the vocal tract.

This early device had the advantage that control of voicing and, to a certain extent, pitch could be effected by the user's own breath. Also, the flow of the breath into the mouth could be used to produce sibilants. The device has the obvious disadvantages that it is conspicuous and nonhygienic. The mouth tube also interferes with movement of the articulators, and introduction of the voiced excitation at a point forward in the tract results in undesired sound properties.

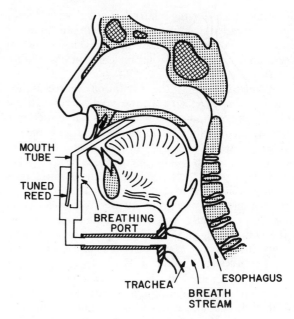

Fig. 6. Early mechanical artificial larynx.[9]

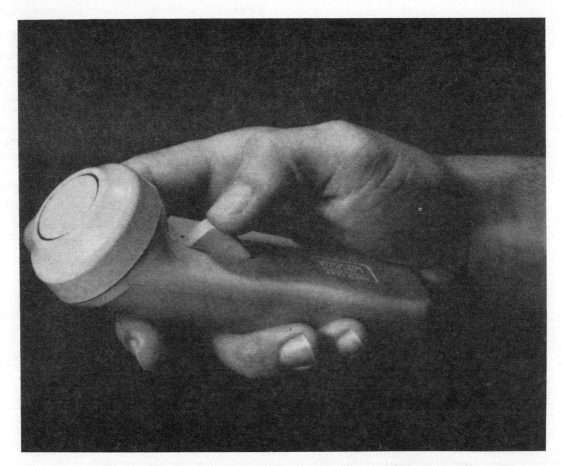

Fig. 7. Modern electronic artificial larynx (courtesy of Western Electric Company).

The Journal of the Acoustical Society of America

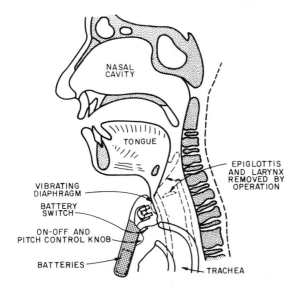

FIG. 8. Use of the electronic artificial larynx.

Nevertheless, this early mechanical aid has served for over 30 years, and more than 5000 were manufactured and distributed.

Electronic advances have led to prosthetic devices which are more convenient and satisfactory. Representative of these is the Western Electric model 5 artificial larynx shown in Fig. 7.[10] This device is a self-contained, battery-powered electronic pulser which actuates a telephone transducer. Transistor circuitry permits reliable and physically small construction. Frequency control of the multivibrator pulse, accomplished by means of the thumb lever, simulates changes in voice pitch. The transducer is placed against the lower throat so that pulses of acoustic volume velocity are produced at a place in the tract proximate to the normal location of the vocal cords (Fig. 8). Consonant sounds are produced from air trapped in the mouth and expelled by movement of the tongue and throat. The electronic instrument has distinct hygienic and cosmetic advantages, and over the past several years, more than 20 000 have been manufactured and distributed.

III. MACHINES THAT SPEAK

Although talking automata may have had their inception with the desire to sway superstitious man, other motivations eventually prevailed. A genuine drive to understand the nature of man's speech accounts for more scientific progress than the efforts toward novelty or entertaining deceptions. Fundamental understanding still motivates today's efforts, as do the important applications of voice answerback from computers and the efficient transmission of speech signals. Early efforts to imitate man's speech invariably took the form of mechanical devices. Modern efforts invariably develop in electrical terms.

A. Mechanical Speaking Machines

Much treachery lies in trying to model nature verbatim, rather than in terms of underlying physical principles. And while man has been notably unsuccessful in making flying machines which flap their wings like birds, he has been somewhat better at building mechanical contrivances which behave acoustically like the human vocal tract.

One of the earliest documented efforts at speech simulation was by one Christian Gottlieb Kratzenstein.[1] In the year 1779 the Imperial Academy of St. Petersburg put the following questions as the subject of their annual prize. "(1) What is the nature and character of the sounds of the vowels *a, e, i, o, u*, (that make them) so different from one another? (2) Can an instrument be constructed like the *vox humana* pipes of an organ, which shall accurately express the sounds of the vowels?"

The winning solution was offered by Kratzenstein, who constructed a set of acoustic resonators similar in form and dimensions to the human mouth. He activated the resonators, shown in Fig. 9, with a vibrating reed (like the reed of a mouth organ—of which type he apparently was the inventor) which, like the human vocal cords, interrupted an air stream. The resonators are said to have imitated "with tolerable accuracy" the five vowels, but they provided little indication of the acoustic principles underlying vowel formation.

A more successful imitation of vowel sounds and an imitation of many consonants was made about the same time by Wolfgang von Kempelen of Vienna.[1] His apparatus consisted of a conical resonator, like the bell of a clarinet, fitted with a reed which was enclosed in a box supplied with air from a bellows. A few years later—in 1791—von Kempelen constructed and demonstrated a more elaborate machine for generating connected utterances.[11] Although the machine was ingenious and received considerable publicity, von Kempelen was not taken seriously by his scientific colleagues. The reason was that this truly brilliant gentleman had earlier perpetrated a deception in the form of a mechanical chess-playing machine. The principal "mechanism" of the machine was the concealed, legless, excommander of the Polish regiment at Riga, named Worouski—a master chess player.[2]

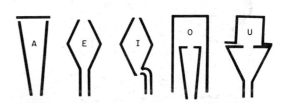

FIG. 9. Kratzenstein's resonators for synthesis of vowel sounds. The resonators are actuated by blowing through a free, vibrating reed into the lower end. The I sound is produced simply by blowing into the lower pipe without a reed.[1]

Von Kempelen's speaking machine, however, was a completely legitimate device.[12] It used a bellows to supply air to a reed which, in turn, excited a single, hand-varied resonator that produced voiced sounds. Consonants, including nasals, were simulated by four separate constricted passages, controlled by the fingers of the other hand. An improved version of the machine, built by Sir Charles Wheatstone from von Kempelen's description, is shown in Fig. 10.

Von Kempelen's efforts probably had a more far-reaching influence than is generally appreciated. During Alexander Graham Bell's boyhood in Edinburgh, Scotland (late 1800s), Bell had an opportunity to see the reproduction of von Kempelen's machine, which had been construted by Wheatstone. He was greatly impressed with the device. With stimulation from his father (Alexander Melville Bell, an elocutionist like his own father), and his brother Melville's assistance, Bell set out to construct a speaking automaton of his own.

Following their father's advice, the boys attempted to copy the vocal organs by making a cast from a human skull and molding the vocal parts in guttapercha. The lips, tongue, palate, teeth, pharynx, and velum were represented. The lips were a framework of wire, covered with rubber which had been stuffed with cotton batting. Rubber cheeks enclosed the mouth cavity, and the tongue was simulated by wooden sections—likewise covered by a rubber skin and stuffed with batting. The parts were actuated by levers controlled from a keyboard. A larynx "box" was constructed of tin and had a flexible tube for a windpipe. A vocal-cord

orifice was made by stretching a slotted rubber sheet over tin supports.[13]

Bell says the device could be made to say vowels and nasals and could be manipulated to produce a few simple utterances (apparently well enough to attract the neighbors). It is interesting to speculate about how this background may later have been influential in creating U. S. Patent No. 174,465, dated 14 February 1876—perhaps one of the most valuable in history.

Interest in mechanical analogs continues to the present day. The movtiation is mainly to simulate and measure nonlinear vocal effects. The latter are generally difficult to analyze computationally. One of the difficult parameters to measure in the real vocal tract is the location, intensity, spectrum, and internal impedance of the sound source for unvoiced sounds. One way of gaining knowledge about this source is with a mechanical analog.

B. Electrical Synthesizers of Speech

The evolution of electronic technology caused interest in speech synthesis to assume a broader basis. Academic interest in the physiology and acoustics of speech production was supplemented by the potential for communicating at a distance. In modern terms, this takes the form of efficient digital encoding of speech information and the important applications of voice response from computers. Toward these ends the acoustic principles of speech production must be converted into electrical terms—much along the lines indicated in Sec. II-B and in Fig. 4.

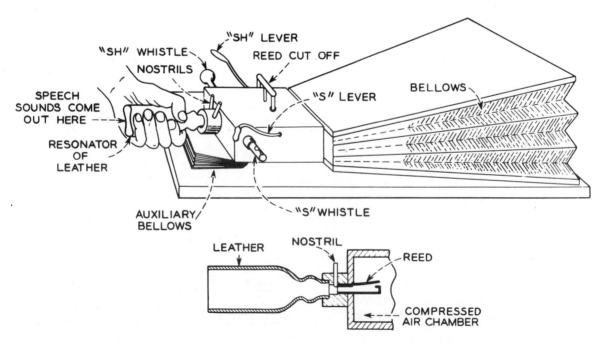

Fig. 10. Wheatstone's reconstruction of von Kempelen's speaking machine.[1]

The Journal of the Acoustical Society of America

One of the first electrical synthesizers which attempted to produce connected speech was the Voder (for *Voice Operation Demonstrator*).[14] Following the principles of source–tract separation, this device used electrical networks which could be selected by finger-actuated keys and whose resonances were similar to those of individual speech sounds. The device is shown in Fig. 11.

The "resonance control" box of the device contains ten contiguous bandpass filters which span the speech frequency range and are connected in parallel. All the filters receive excitation from either the noise source or the buzz (relaxation) oscillator. The wrist bar selects the excitation source, and a foot pedal controls the pitch of the buzz oscillator. The outputs of the bandpass filters pass through potentiometer gain controls and are added. Ten finger keys operate the potentiometers. Three additional keys provide a transient excitation of selected filters to simulate stop-constant sounds.

This speaking machine was demonstrated by trained operators at the World's Fairs of 1939 (New York) and 1940 (San Francisco). Although the training required was quite long (on the order of a year or more), the operators were able to "play" the machines—literally as though they were organs or pianos—and to produce intelligible speech.

The Voder and related early developments led to other analog electronic synthesizers of speech. These ranged from analog circuitry that duplicated the vocal resonances to bilateral transmission-line simulations of the vocal tract. The efforts were largely characterized by two motivations: first, as before, a fundamental interest in speech production; and second, the new

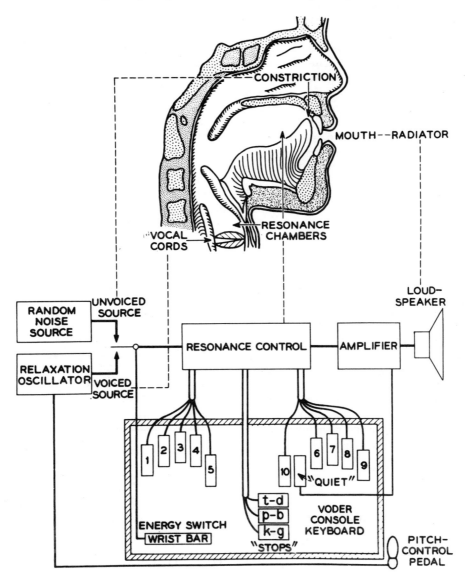

Fig. 11. Schematic diagram of the electrical speaking machine Voder.[14]

Volume 51   Number 5 (Part 1)   1972

promise of highly efficient voice communication. In the latter case the techniques of speech analysis and speech synthesis pointed ways to conserve significantly the transmission bandwidth used for speech signals.

On the first count, good progress continued in understanding speech production. On the second count, complete band-compression systems, based upon the principles of speech analysis and synthesis, were devised and tested. The most notable of these was the Vocoder, invented by H. Dudley,[15] which spawned a subfield of communication engineering.[16] Although the Vocoder and its many relatives typically operate with some quality impairment, some of the devices have been used for a number of years for special communications applications. No civil telephone use has yet been made of analysis–synthesis devices, but bandsavings are accomplished in simpler ways with time-division switching methods.[17] One consideration in the use of analysis–synthesis techniques is the complexity of terminal equipment needed to achieve bandsaving with good quality. Such processing is economically attractive only for expensive long-haul channels, or for applications where bandwidth is at a premium.

The advent of sampled-data theory, digital computers, and integrated circuits has caused speech analysis and synthesis to take on some new dimensions. Sampled-data theory tells us how to represent continuous physical systems in terms of discrete numerical operations. Digital computers are able to perform the arithmetic of these operations fast and accurately, and are able to store large quantities of numbers—which can represent speech signals. Integrated circuitry allows us to build small, inexpensive, complex electrical components, among them the digital circuitry which makes computers.

Along with these developments, and with the emerging understanding of speech acoustics, the focuses of fundamental and applied interests have shifted somewhat. On the fundamental side, linguistic and semantic problems of speech are coming under scrutiny through the power of digital machines.[5–8,18,19] On the applied side, an overwhelming motivation is to provide voices for computers.[20] Voice answer-back capability would open new possibilities for automatic information services, computer-based instruction, and simple inexpensive computer terminals. Further on the applied side, integrated digital circuitry makes complex processing for high-quality analysis–synthesis telephony more attractive, and applications to satellite communication, deep-space exploration, and mobile radiotelephone appear possibilities.[21]

C. Talking Computers

If computers could speak their answers, as well as print them on a typewriter or display them on an oscilloscope, their capabilities could be applied in new ways. Automatic information services—such as medical

DIGITAL SYNTHESIZER

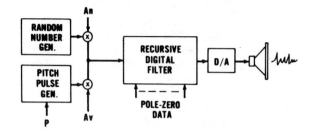

FIG. 12. Digital circuit model of speech generation.[21]

data, inventory accounting, travel information, and the like—would only be as far away as the nearest telephone. In effect, the ordinary pushbutton telephone could become a computer terminal.

There are well-known techniques for prerecording natural voice utterances and storing these messages in a computer memory.[22] For good results such messages can be used only in the context in which they were recorded. Therefore, if the computer is to speak with a large, sophisticated vocabulary, and if it is expected to use this vocabulary to form a wide variety of messages and contexts, the simple technique of prerecorded natural speech is ruled out. Economical storage of large amounts of speech data, in a form flexible enough to generate arbitrary messages, implies a speech synthesis approach.[20]

Synthesis of a meaningful speech signal by a computer program requires a description, in some form, of the vocal-tract resonances corresponding to that speech signal. Following the source-system representation of the vocal tract, as discussed in Fig. 4, leads to a digital synthesis system made up of the components shown in Fig. 12. A random number generator simulates the source for voiceless sounds. Its variance is controlled as a function of time by the noise amplitude signal A_n.

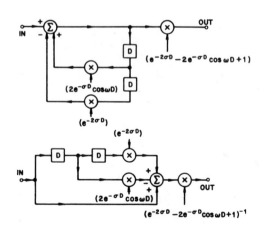

FIG. 13. Recursive relations for sampled data (digital) approximation of (a) a continuous simple resonance, and (b) a simple antiresonance.[4]

The Journal of the Acoustical Society of America

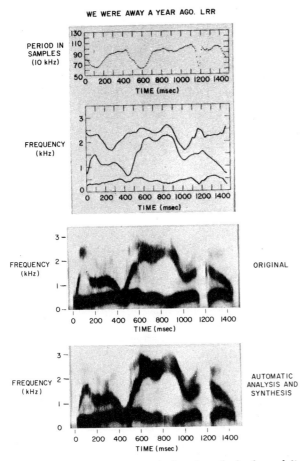

WE WERE AWAY A YEAR AGO. LRR

PERIOD IN SAMPLES (10 kHz)

TIME (msec)

FREQUENCY (kHz)

TIME (msec)

FREQUENCY (kHz)

ORIGINAL

TIME (msec)

FREQUENCY (kHz)

AUTOMATIC ANALYSIS AND SYNTHESIS

TIME (msec)

FIG. 14. Automatic formant analysis and synthesis of speech.[24]

Similarly, a counter is used to produce pulses at the pitch frequency P to simulate the vocal-cord source used for voiced sounds. Its amplitude is determined by the voicing intensity parameter A_v. These sources are

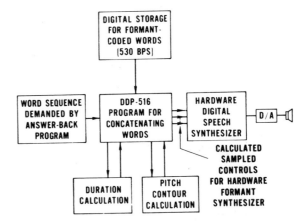

FIG. 15. Bell Laboratories implementation of an experimental computer voice response system. A Honeywell DDP-516 laboratory computer is used for calculating the synthetic speech.[20]

filtered by a recursive filter whose coefficients are determined by the speech formants as they change with time. Three variable resonances, as shown in Fig. 4, are typically used for voiced sounds, and a pole–zero combination for voiceless sounds. Digital-to-analog (D/A) conversion yields an audible output.

The recursive digital filter generates quantized samples of the speech signal and it represents these samples by binary numbers. The filter can be implemented by discrete (digital) operation in a number of ways. An especially convenient approach is to represent the resonances and antiresonances individually by second-order difference equations.[4] The recursion relations for a single resonance and a single antiresonance are diagrammed in the upper and lower parts, respectively, of Fig. 13. The time between samples is D, and the radian frequency and bandwidth of the resonance (or antiresonance) are ω and σ, respectively.

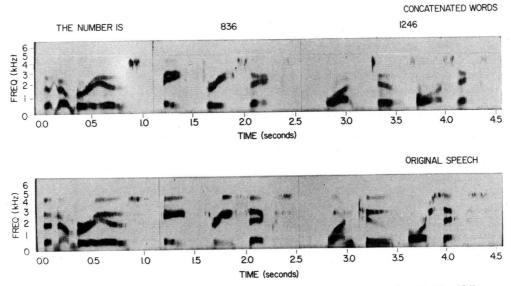

FIG. 16. Synthesis of seven digit telephone numbers from the computer system shown in Fig. 15.[25]

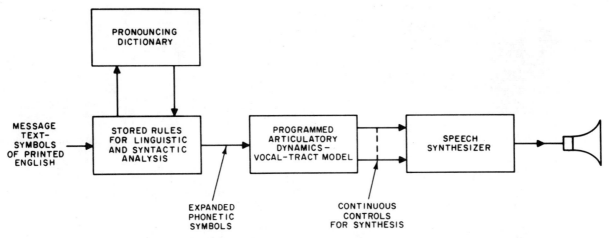

FIG. 17. Block diagram of speech synthesis from printed English text.[7]

These recursion relations can be realized by programmed instructions in the computer,[4] or they can be accomplished by special digital hardware.[23]

The control functions which specify the resonances, antiresonances, and excitation of the filter must be supplied externally. Two computer techniques for obtaining these controls are available.[20] In one, called formant synthesis, the data are measured from natural speech utterances. In another, called text synthesis, the data are calculated from programmed knowledge of the speech process. We can indicate the nature of both methods.

The formant synthesis method depends upon a computer program that analyzes natural speech to obtain the variation of three formants and the voice pitch. A typical output of this program is shown at the top of Fig. 14.[4] These data, when provided to a synthesizer as in Fig. 12, produce synthetic speech similar to the original natural utterance, as shown by the spectrograms in the lower part of Fig. 14. Although this example is an all-voiced utterance, similar operations are applied for voiceless sounds.

In formant synthesis, economical storage and vocabulary flexibility are achieved by storing a library of formant-coded words. Individual, naturally uttered words are formant analyzed, and their formant functions are stored. (The recorded bit rate for these data is 530 bits/sec, or 1/100 of that required to store the natural speech waveform). When a given word sequence (message) is specified by an answer-back program, the computer accesses the formant functions in the prescribed sequence. By a stored program it calculates the duration and the pitch inflection for each word in that prescribed context. It then calculates smooth transitions of the formant functions at the word boundaries to effect a realistic concatenation of the words. Finally, the computer issues the resulting control functions to a digital synthesizer.

Such a system has been implemented at Bell Laboratories on a Honeywell DDP-516 computer, as shown in Fig. 15.[25] In this case the synthesizer is a hardware digital filter, external to the computer. As a consequence, the synthesis operations run about ten times faster than real time, hence one computer can serve ten external synthesizers. This system has been applied experimentally to the automatic generation of seven-digit telephone numbers, and to the synthesis of spoken wire lists for the wiring of telephone circuits. A typical

ENGLISH TEXT	SYNTAX AND PROSODIC RULES OUTPUT
the	4dh 4a
north	6n $4aw 2er 6th
wind	6w *qq51 4n 4d
and	4aa -n -d
the	-dh 4a
sun	6s *qq5uh 6n

FIG. 18. Automatic conversion of printed English symbols into expanded phonetic symbols for text synthesis.[7]

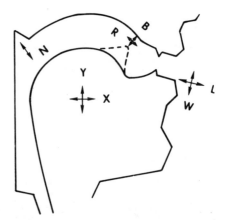

FIG. 19. Articulatory model of the human vocal tract. This vocal model, also programmed in a DDP-516 computer, is used for speech synthesis from printed text. The figure is identical to the computer scope display which shows the vocal motions during synthetic speaking.[5]

The Journal of the Acoustical Society of America

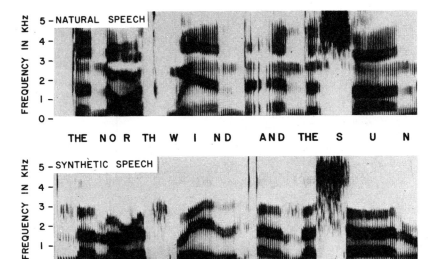

THE NOR TH W I ND AND THE S U N

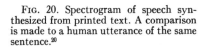

FIG. 20. Spectrogram of speech synthesized from printed text. A comparison is made to a human utterance of the same sentence.[20]

result of a digit synthesis produced by the system is shown in Fig. 16.

The storage economy and vocabulary flexibility achieved by formant synthesis appear attractive for "middle-sized" vocabularies such as inventory reporting, flight information, and computer instruction. Voice readout of encyclopedic amounts of information requires even more economy of storage, and hence a more elaborate synthesis system. Text synthesis is such.

In text synthesis, the computer stores a pronouncing dictionary, as shown in Fig. 17. The dictionary contains for each entry just what one finds in ordinary desk dictionaries—a phonemic transcription of each word, indication of word stress, some rudimentary grammatical information (whether the word is a noun, adjective, verb, etc.) and information about endings and derived forms. The message to be converted into speech is supplied as the printed English text. Each word is looked up in the dictionary and the resulting information passed to a program which incorporates linguistic and syntactic rules for English. In this program a strategy for the stress and phrasing of each sentence is formed, pauses are inserted where necessary, and the duration and pitch of individual phonemes are assigned. The result is an output of discrete symbols representing the sequence of phonemes and their individual pitch and duration calculated for the prescribed context.[7] This symbol string represents a 2:1 or 3:1 expansion over the input discrete alphabetic symbols, and is illustrated in Fig. 18.

The expanded symbol set constitutes "commands" which are given to a dynamic (programmed) model of the vocal tract.[5] The model represents the shape of a man's vocal tract after the fashion shown in Fig. 19. The seven articulatory parameters define the shape of the vocal tract. They assume values dictated by the discrete symbol set, but in responding to these discrete commands they impose their own, physiologically realistic time constants. Periodically (typically at 100

sec^{-1}), the eigenfrequencies (or formants) of the model vocal tract are computed as the tract deforms, and the results, along with calculated excitation information, are issued to a hardware synthesizer of the type discussed previously.

In this scheme the machine synthesizes the output speech with no recourse to any vestige of human speech. The storage economy and flexibility in synthesis approaches the order of 1000:1 when compared to a facsimile recording of the natural speech signal.

A typical output of the text synthesis system also implemented on a DDP-516 computer, is shown in Fig. 20. As might be expected, the machine displays its own accent (which, incidentally, can be varied by changing the linguistic rules). Present stage of development is such that its intelligibility is beginning to be acceptable. This technique, and the formant synthesis method described previously, both appear promising for giving voices to computers.[20]

IV. SUMMARY

Interest in simulating the human voice began in antiquity. Motivation has ranged from superstitiously influencing man, to amusing man, aiding man to communicate and, more recently, to providing man sophisticated means for obtaining information from computers—information in a form (namely speech) which is easily transportable (by telephone) and is easily assimilated (by the human ear). In the modern context, fundamental understanding of human voice production and of the structure of language promises new communication and information capabilities for the service of man.

* This paper draws upon material prepared for an article "The Synthesis of Speech," Sci. Amer. (Feb. 1972).

[1] Richard Paget, *Human Speech: Some Observations, Experiments, and Conclusions as to the Nature, Origin, Purpose and Possible Improvement of Human Speech* (Harcourt, New York, 1930).

[2] Charles Wheatstone, *Scientific Papers of Sir Charles Wheatstone* (Physical Society of London, London, 1879). One famous

oracle was the head of Orpheus on the Isle of Lesbos. This idol is supposed to have predicted—albeit in equivocal terms—the violent death of Cyrus the Great, which terminated his expedition against the Scythians.

[3] David Brewster, *Letters on Natural Magic* (Harper, New York, 1832). Another account holds that ". . . in the fourth century, when Bishop Theophilus broke to pieces the statues at Alexandria, he found some which were hollow, and which were so placed against a wall that the priest could conceal himself behind them and address the ignorant spectators through their mouths."

[4] J. L. Flanagan, *Speech Analysis, Synthesis and Perception* (Springer Verlag, New York, 1965). 2nd ed., 1972.

[5] C. H. Coker, "Speech Synthesis with a Parametric Articulatory Model," Proc. Speech Symp., Kyoto, Japan, paper A-4, Aug. 1968.

[6] L. R. Rabiner, "Speech Synthesis by Rule: An Acoustic Domain Approach," Bell System Tech. J. 47, 17–37 (1968).

[7] C. H. Coker, N. Umeda, and C. Browman, "Automatic Synthesis from Text," Digest of IEEE Int. Commun. Conf., New York, March 1971.

[8] N. Umeda, "Linguistics and Speech Science," Science (in preparation).

[9] R. R. Riesz, "An Artificial Larynx," J. Acoust. Soc. Amer. 1, 273–279 (1930).

[10] H. L. Barney, F. E. Haworth, and H. K. Dunn, "An Experimental Transistorized Artificial Larynx," Bell System Tech. J. 38, 1337–1356 (1959).

[11] H. Dudley and T. H. Tarnoczy, "The Speaking Machine of Wolfgang von Kempelen," J. Acoust. Soc. Amer. 22, 151–166 (1950).

[12] Anon., "Talking Machines," Sci. Amer. 24, 32 (1871).

[13] A. G. Bell, "Prehistoric Telephone Days," Nat. Geograph. Mag. 41, 223–242 (1922).

[14] H. Dudley, R. R. Riesz, and S. A. Watkins, "A Synthetic Speaker," J. Franklin Inst. 227, 739–764 (1939).

[15] H. Dudley, "The Vocoder," Bell Labs. Record 17, 122–126 (1939b).

[16] M. R. Schroeder, "Vocoders: Analysis and Synthesis of Speech," Proc. IEEE 54, 720–734 (1966).

[17] E. E. O'Neil, TASI Bell Labs. Record 37, 83–87 (1959).

[18] F. S. Cooper, J. H. Gaitenby, I. G. Mattingly, and N. Umeda, "Reading Aids for the Blind: A Special Case of Machine-to-Man Communication," IEEE Trans. Audio Electroacoust. AU-17, 266–270 (1969).

[19] J. Allen, "Machine-to-Man Communication by Speech, Part 2: Synthesis of Prosodic Features of Speech by Rule," 1968 Spring Joint Computer Conf., Washington, D. C., AFIPS Proc. 32, 339–344 (1968).

[20] J. L. Flanagan, C. H. Coker, L. R. Rabiner, R. W. Schafer, and N. Umeda, "Synthetic Voices for Computers," IEEE Spectrum 7, No. 10, 22–45 (1970).

[21] J. L. Flanagan, "Digital Representation of Speech Signals," BTL Symp. Digital Tech. Commun., Murray Hill, N. J., 12–13 Nov. 1970.

[22] These techniques are already in use for computer voice response.

[23] L. R. Rabiner, L. B. Jackson, R. W. Schafer, and C. H. Coker, "Digital Hardware for Speech Synthesis," Proc. Int. Congr. Acoust., 7th, Budapest, Hungary, Aug. 1971.

[24] R. W. Schafer and L. R. Rabiner, "System for Automatic Formant Analysis of Voiced Speech," J. Acoust. Soc. Amer. 47, 634–648 (1970).

[25] L. R. Rabiner, R. W. Schafer, and J. L. Flanagan, "Computer Synthesis of Speech by Concatenation of Formant-Coded Words," Bell System Tech. J. 50, 1541–1558 (1971).

The Acoustics of Speech

G. FANT

Inst. of Telegraphy and Telephony, Royal Institute of Technology, Stockholm (Sweden)

The acoustics of speech includes in a broad sense both the theory of speech as wave motion and how speech waves are produced and heard. This is a field of study which has intrigued researchers of various specialities during the last centuries and it has ancient traditions.

Classical phonetics has been and is still articulatory phonetics dealing with an inventory of speech sounds defined from their production within the vocal tract. The speech research of communication engineers is more concerned with the speech wave which we will define by the sound pressure variations at a point in front of the speaker.

With modern sound recording and analysis techniques it is possible to undertake rather complete specifications of the speech wave. However, a maximally detailed description is unmanageably complex and the great problem is to find useful approximation. The physiology of the speaking mechanism on the other hand cannot be studied and described with the same exactness. When it comes to hearing, there are even less possibilities to make complete specifications. The neurophysiology of speaking and hearing are the least accessible links of the complete communication system but they carry the key to many interesting problems.

The following presentation concentrates on the structure of speech waves and the theory of speech production.

SPECTROGRAPHIC ANALYSIS

The "Visible Speech" spectrographic techniques [1], introduced by the Bell Telephone Laboratories some fifteen years ago, are still our most important means of studying the characteristics of speech waves. The most useful records are the well-known spectrograms with time in horizontal direction, frequency in vertical direction, and intensity of time-frequency bounded areas displayed by the relative blackness or brightness of the picture marking.

The spectrograms of Fig. 1 were obtained with the Sona-Graph-analyzer which is a commercial development of the original Bell Telephone Laboratories speech spectrograph. This is a heterodyne analyzer with a fixed filter of alternative 45 c/s or 300 c/s bandwidth. A piece of speech maximally 2.4 sec long is analyzed by repetitive analysis with frequency increments of 15 c/s between successive closed loop repetitions of a stored piece of speech. A doubling of the broad or narrow bandwidths can be accomplished by the trick of replaying the speech material from a tape-recorder to the Sona-Graph storage loop at half the normal speed as is exemplified in Fig. 1. Adjustments have been made in the frequency scale in order to retain the same frequency scale (expanded) as in the normal speech processing.

The overall intensity as a function of time has to be recorded by means of supplementary instrumentation to the spectrograph, in the form of an amplitude display curve on the same sheet as the spectrogram or as a separate display on an oscillograph[2].

The spectral distribution of intensity or energy within a specific short time interval of the speech wave is defined by an intensity (db amplitude) *vs.* frequency curve. A

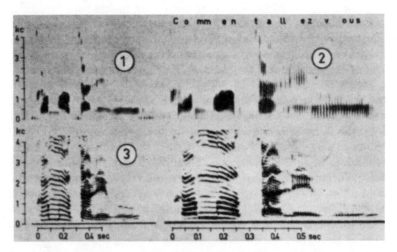

Fig. 1. Time–frequency–intensity spectrograms illustrating the effects of various analysis bandwidths 300 c/s in 1, 600 c/s in 2, 45 c/s in 3, 90 c/s in 4.

spectrum section of this type may be produced on a spectrograph by synchronous sampling of the separate frequency channels. In case the sound to be analyzed is produced in a sustained form it may be convenient to utilize a sweep-frequency method of analysis. The spectra of Fig. 2 pertain to synthetic and human vowels each of 3 sec duration analyzed by means of a filter of 32 c/s width moving at constant speed of 1.3 kc/s through the frequency range of 0–4000 c/s.

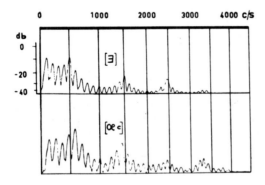

Fig. 2. Harmonic spectra obtained from narrow bandwidth sweep frequency analysis of sustained sound œ, and of the synthetic reference sound [ɜ].

Vowels and other voiced sounds possess periodic or rather quasi-periodic wave forms and accordingly display harmonic spectra. This fine structure originates from the opening and closing movements of the vocal cords periodically modulating the volume of the exhaled air during phonation at a rate of F_0 c/s, which is the voice fundamental frequency[3, 4]. In narrow-band spectrograms F_0 is the harmonic spacing and in broad-band spectrograms $1/F_0$ is the time interval between successive striations each reflecting a single voice cycle. The time variation of F_0 is the physical basis of intonation.

The train of successive airpulses emerging from the vibrating glottis is the primary source of voiced sounds. The air cavities within the vocal tract act as a multiresonant filter on the transmitted sound and impress upon it a corresponding formant structure superimposed on the harmonic fine structure. This can be clearly seen in Fig. 2. The frequencies of the three lowest formants, F_1, F_2, F_3, are the main determinants of the phonetic quality of a vowel.

The resonance frequencies of the vocal tract F_1, F_2, F_3, F_4, conceptually contained in the term F-pattern, vary more or less continuously across the often sharply time localized breaks in the spectrographic time-frequency-intensity picture. Such breaks may for instance indicate shifts from voice to noise source or vice versa. Each position of the articulatory organs has its specific F-pattern. Some ambiguities do exist due to compensatory forms of articulation but these are not very important in normal speech. The time-variation of the F-pattern across one or several adjacent sound segments, which may be referred to as the F-formant transitions, are often important auditory cues for the identification of a consonant supplementing the cues inherent in the composition of the sound segments traditionally assigned to the consonant.

In general, the continuous elements of speech are due to the continuity of the position of the articulators. The discrete breaks are mainly due to a shift in manner of production, that is a change in type of source (fine structure), or a radical change in the active resonator system through which the sound is filtered (open/closed mouth passage with and without a lateral or a nasal by-pass of the sound). A sudden shift in the F-pattern and in the overall intensity following the step from a closed to an open mouth passage may thus be regarded as a discontinuity.

Spectrographic pictures convey an overflow of data which are non-essential for descriptive purposes. This redundancy is in part a matter of interrelations, repetitions, and continuities within the signal structure, in part the presence of a fine structure the details of which carry very little or no information. Any description of the speech wave, for speech typewriter coding purposes or for speech bandwidth compression applications or merely for the study of acoustic correlates to phonetic categories, must be based on approximations. Binary coded pattern aspects as well as quantized parameter data belong to the inventory of such specifications.

When processing the spectrographic data on connected speech the first object is to identify the boundaries of successive sound segments. A sound segment generally carries information on more than one phoneme of a sequence. Conversely, each phoneme may be physically encoded to a smaller or greater extent in the pattern aspect of several adjacent sound segments. The number of successive sound segments of a piece of connected speech is generally larger than the number of phonemes. Stop sounds, for instance, can be considered to be made up of at least two typical sound segments, the occlusion and the burst, and the latter phase may in some instances be split up into three successive and partly overlapping phases, the explosion transient, a short fricative, and an h-sound. The description of a sound segment for the purpose of identification may be based on the following parameters, previously mentioned and summarized below.

1. Duration
2. Intensity
3. Energy (Area under the intensity-time curve)
4. Voice fundamental frequency, F_0
5. The F-pattern ($=F_1, F_2, F_3, F_4$, etc.)
6. The formant structure (Frequency-intensity distribution)
7. The fine structure; referring to speech production, the source (Voiced, unvoiced, mixed, or silence)

In addition there enter the dynamical aspects of speech patterns[5] in terms of the time variation of each of the variables 2-7. The identification of a phoneme from the physical data contained in successive sound segments involves first a phonetical categorization, essentially with regard to "manner of production", and then within each category, a choice related to "position of articulators", for instance the choice of one of [b], [d], [g] when the phoneme has been identified as a voiced stop.

The techniques of automatic speech recognition are still in an initial phase of development. Instrumental problems are severe and specificational theory is not fully established. The main difficulty in any speech writing coding scheme[6] is the variability of human speech. However, this area of research is developing rapidly.

THEORY OF SPEECH PRODUCTION

Acoustic theory of speech production[7, 8] in its present form is largely based on equivalent circuit concepts. As visualized in Fig. 3 any speech sound is regarded as the filtered output of a network in which a sound source is inserted. The characteristics of any

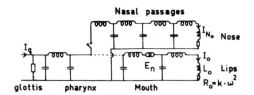

Fig. 3. Equivalent circuit representation of human and synthetic speech production applied to voiced sounds. The coils and condensers of the circuit should be regarded as distributed elements rather than lumped elements pertaining to specific cavities.

quasi-stationary sound segment thus contains the characteristics of the source and those of the network, the latter referred to as the vocal tract transfer function or filter function. In terms of Laplace transforms

$$P(s) = S(s)T(s) \qquad (1)$$

where $P(s)$ pertains to the radiated sound, $S(s)$ to the source, $T(s)$ to the vocal tract transfer function, and $s = \sigma + j\omega$ to the complex frequency variable.

The transfer function $T(s)$ of voiced sounds is defined as the ratio of the Laplace transforms of the sound pressure at a distance l cm from the speaker to the volume velocity of the pulsating airflow passing the vocal cords. If the coupling to the nasal cavities is negligible this function has no other zero than that at the origin of the complex frequency plane. This differentiation approximates the transfer from volume velocity at the lips to the sound pressure in the radiated wave. The ideal transfer function of voiced sounds,

$$T(s,l) = \frac{s}{4\pi l} \cdot \prod_{n=1}^{\infty} \frac{1}{(1 - s/\hat{s}_n)(1 - s/\hat{s}_n^*)}$$ (2)

is thus essentially an infinite pole product, where

$$\hat{s}_n = \sigma_n + j\omega_n \quad \text{and} \quad \hat{s}_n^* = \sigma_n - j\omega_n$$

are conjugate complex poles. For synthesis applications the infinite product is substituted for a finite (3, 4, or 5) number of poles and a "higher pole correction"[8].

The air-filled cavities within the vocal tract constitute a continuously inhomogeneous transmission line with low losses, and the equivalent network may thus be described in terms of the distributed series inductance and parallel capacitance per length unit along the vocal tract. Series and parallel resistances representing finite losses enter a complete representation. A lumped element representation of a series inductance for a constriction and a capacitance for the volume of a specific cavity is not permissible, except for very low frequencies.

Each resonance of the vocal cavities may be described in terms of its frequency F_n and bandwidth B_n which are related to the conjugate complex poles of $T(s)$ as follows

$$\left. \begin{aligned} F_n &= \omega_n/2\pi \\ B_n &= -\sigma_n/\pi \end{aligned} \right\}$$ (3)

The average spacing within the frequency scale of these resonances is of the order of 1000 c/s or more specifically $c/2l_v$ were l_v is the effective length of the vocal tract and c the velocity of sound. This inverse dependency of formant frequencies on vocal cavity length dimensions explains the higher formant frequencies of females compared to males, and of children compared to adults.

The two constituents of a pole, the frequency and the bandwidth, may be studied by various means of exciting the vocal cavities. One is merely to thump the outside of the throat with a finger and measure the damped exponential, the decay characteristics of which provide a measure of the bandwidth according to (3). The vocal tract response to any transient excitation must contain as a component a damped oscillation

$$p_n(t) = A_n e^{-\pi B_n t} \cdot \cos(2\pi F_n t + \varphi_n)$$ (4)

which is the inverse transform of a formant number n.

The same frequencies and bandwidths may be obtained from the sine-wave response of the vocal tract as determined experimentally from driving the vocal tract with a larynx microphone utilized as a sound source and a pickup microphone close to the lips. This is exemplified by Fig. 4. Typical values of resonance bandwidths are shown in Fig. 5. They are of the order of 50 c/s in the frequency region occupied by the first and second formant. Formant bandwidths are slightly greater than resonance bandwidths due to additional losses through the glottis slit.

The equivalent circuit theory of speech production suggests a convenient method[9] of deriving the properties of the vocal source[4] without bringing any probes into the vocal cavities. This is the inverse filtering technique of passing the speech wave through anti-resonance circuits, one for each formant. The first step is to integrate the speech wave thus removing the radiation zero of $T(s)$.

Some results of this technique are illustrated in Fig. 6*. It may be observed that integration alone provides a first approximation to the voice flow. The apparent starting point of the damped oscillations appears to coincide with the offset of the flow, *i.e.* the closing phase. These curves display the well-known facts that increased

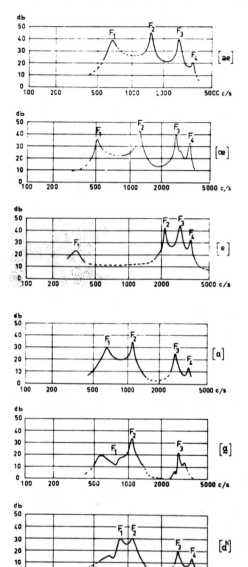

Fig. 4. Sine-wave response curves of the vocal tract driven externally from the pharynx and measured 2 cm in front of the lips. The effect of lowering the soft palate as in a nasalized vowel and of opening the vocal cords as in h-sounds is illustrated for the vowel [ɑ].

---

* These illustrations of inverse filtering originate from a thesis work by C. CEDERLUND of the Speech Transmission Laboratory, Royal Institute of Technology, Stockholm (Sweden).

voice efforts sharpen the wave shape of the vocal airpulses. At low voice intensities the closure phase is relatively short and the wave form is rounded. A tendency of a double peaked voice flow period has been found for one of the subjects.

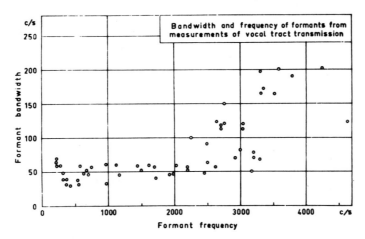

Fig. 5. Frequency dependency of the bandwidth of vocal resonances under conditions of closed glottis.

Another aspect of the Laplace transform representation is the frequency domain decomposition of vowels into elementary resonance curves. This is illustrated in Fig. 7, which pertains to idealized vowels. A shift of F_1 one octave up in frequency is apparently followed by an increase in the spectrum envelope level of 12 db at all frequencies well above F_1. When any two relatively close lying formants approach in frequency there occurs an increase in intensity of each which is 6 db per halving of their distance. These and other rules relating spectrum shape and spectrum levels to formant frequencies, *i.e.* to the F-pattern may be observed from Fig. 8, which illustrates the effects of changing F_1 and F_2 and also F_3 within the spectra of synthetic

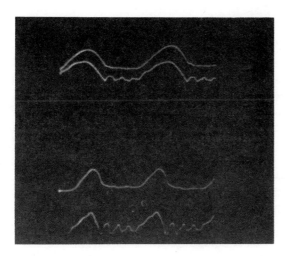

Fig. 6. Wave forms of the regenerated voice flow and, for comparison, the merely integrated speech wave. The upper pair of curves pertains to the vowel [æ] produced with a low voice effort and the bottom pair pertains to the same vowel produced with a high voice effort. The first four formants were filtered out in the top curve of each pair, but appear as damped oscillations in the merely integrated wave.

vowels. Most of these are close to Swedish vowels, the articulatory positions of which are shown in Fig. 9. Here as well as in Fig. 8 the vowels are arranged in terms of increasing F_1 to the right and increasing F_2 upwards in the diagram.

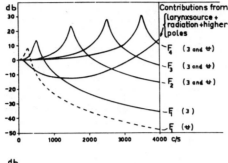

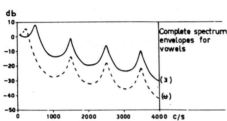

Fig. 7. Spectrum decomposition of ideal vowels in terms of elementary resonance curves, one for each formant plus additional constant characteristics. The latter include a voice source spectrum sloping —12 db/octave and a high frequency emphasis representing the residual contribution from formants higher than the fourth. The effect of shifting F_1 down one octave is indicated by the broken line. Each elementary resonance curve is analogous to a low-pass filter of 12 db/octave attenuation above its cutoff frequency.

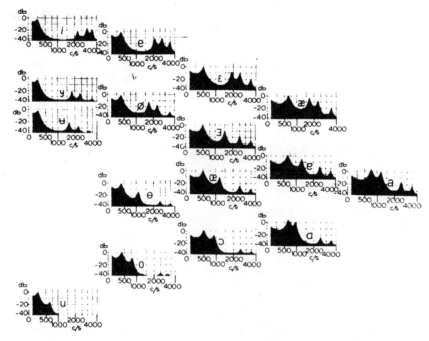

Fig. 8. Spectra on an approximate mel scale of synthetic vowels ordered according to the particular F_1 and F_2. The changes in spectrum shape and in formant levels following a shift in one or more of the formant frequencies should be observed.

The main articulatory variables are
1. the location,
2. the degree of constriction of the main narrowing between the tongue and the opposite wall of the vocal cavities, and
3. the degree of constriction and lengthening of the lip passage. The generalized relation suggested in older phonetics literature, that F_1 is due to the cavity behind the tongue constriction and F_2 to the cavity in front of the constriction is an impermissible oversimplification, sometimes contradicting actual relations. All parts of the vocal cavities have some influence on all formants and each formant is dependent on the entire shape of the complete system[7, 10]. The general rules are that a tongue constriction located in the middle of the mouth cavity is optimal for a high F_2 and that a maximally high F_1 requires the main constriction to be located just above the larynx and the mouth cavity to be wide-open. A constriction location slightly advanced from that of maximum F_2 provides maximal F_3.

A decrease of the lip-opening area or increase of the length of the lip passage

Fig. 9. X-ray tracings of Swedish vowels arranged as in Fig. 8 according to increasing F_1, right, and increasing F_2, up.

causes a lowering of the frequencies of all formants. F_1 is maximally low when the mouth cavity is constricted and F_2 is maximally low when the tongue constriction is in the upper part of the pharynx.

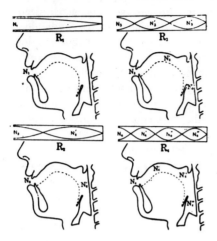

Fig. 10. Distribution of volume velocity at the frequencies of each of the first four resonances of an ideal neutral articulation in which the vocal tract simulates a tube of constant cross-sectional area. (After CHIBA and KAJIYAMA[12].)

All these relations observed when correlating articulatory and spectrographic data and corroborated model experiments[7, 11] may be inferred from a simple consideration of the distribution of pressure of volume velocity inside a neutral state idealized model of the vocal tract defined by a tube of constant cross-sectional area open at the lip end and closed at the larynx end. As shown in Fig. 10 there is a volume velocity maximum at the lips and a minimum at the glottis independent of the particular resonance frequency. The second resonance has an additional volume velocity maximum at $1/_3$ of the vocal tract length above the glottis and a volume velocity minimum at a place $1/_3$ of the total tube length from the lip end. The homogeneous tube has resonance frequencies at 500, 1500, 2500, 3500 c/s, etc.

If this neutral tube is constricted at a volume velocity maximum, *i.e.* at a pressure minimum, there results a shift down in the frequency of the particular resonance[12, 13]. This is to be expected since the minimum pressure at the constriction implies that the distributed capacitance in this region is small compared to the inductance and that an area change thus is effectively an inductance change[7]. The simple rule may thus be stated that a constriction of the vocal cavities at the place of a volume velocity maximum causes a shift down in the particular resonance frequency and that a constriction at a volume velocity minimum causes a shift up of the particular resonance frequency.

CONSONANT SPECTRA AND THEIR DETERMINANTS IN SPEECH PRODUCTION

Some of the sounds referred to as consonants, *e.g.* [j], [w], [v], [r], and [1] are often produced as voiced continuants with little or insignificant noise added. Sound segments of the speech wave belonging to this category, except [1] in a strict sense, may be analytically treated as vowels, *i.e.* formant intensities are only dependent on the F-pattern of resonance frequencies (poles) and on the particular source spectrum. In all other categories of sound segments, *i.e.* nasal consonants, unvoiced stops, fricatives and affricates, and the unvoiced parts of the corresponding "voiced" sound segments, there enters in addition a 0-pattern of anti-resonances (zeroes) as an additional determinant of formant levels. This is also true of [l] but to a lesser extent.

The common denominator of all non-nasal speech sounds, voiced or not, is the F-pattern defining the frequencies where formants may be found. In some instances the bandwidths of the higher resonances are so broad that adjacent formants merge into a single formant area. Thus, typically for the [s]-sound, the formants $F1$, $F2$, $F3$, $F4$ are very weak and the main spectral energy is contained in $F5$, $F6$, $F7$, $F8$, $F9$ generally seen in the spectrogram as a single or two formant areas. In the sound segment of nasal consonants there are more resonances (poles) than those of the F-pattern in which case the F-pattern is defined to comprise those frequencies which show the greatest continuity with the F-positions of orally open, adjacent sound segments. The F-pattern of nasalized vowels is similarly defined from a continuity to non-nasalized sound segments disregarding those resonances introduced by the nasal coupling.

The zero function of a vocal tract transfer function is due to the cavity system behind the source (typical for all noise sounds) or to the presence of a cavity system in front of the source shunting the main path of wave propagation (typical for nasal consonants, nasalized vowels, and laterals).

When discussing the spectral effects of poles and zeroes, it is convenient to distinguish between free poles and zeroes and bound poles and zeroes, the latter comprising pairs of a pole and a close lying zero, providing small combined spectral contributions only. In a frequency region of low coupling between a front cavity and a back cavity or between a shunting cavity and a main outlet, all the poles of the back cavities or of the shunt are bound. This is the reason for the low intensity of formants lower than $F5$ in the spectrum of the [s]-sound and the low intensity of $F2$

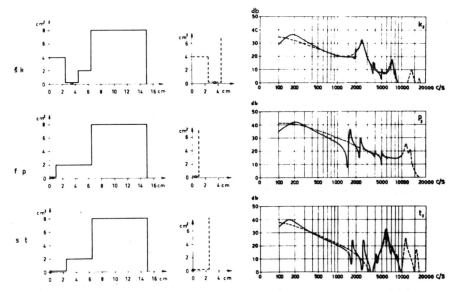

Fig. 11. Simple idealized vocal tract models and corresponding spectra of the sounds [k], [p] and [t]. Coarticulation with a front vowel is suggested by the relatively narrow mouth cavity. Broken line figures and curves pertain to models involving front resonators only and the corresponding spectra.

in the spectrum of most nasal consonants. The free poles are generally due to the cavities in front of the source and have a considerable association with the back cavities only when the coupling is great. When approximating a sound spectrum in terms of poles and zeroes it is evidently possible to discard the bound poles and zeroes. Those bound poles entering the F-pattern are, however, of specificational importance as the starting points of formant transitions towards adjacent sound segments.

Pole-zero patterns of palatal, labial, and dental sounds, derived from idealized cavity configurations, are shown in Fig. 11. The spectrum of the stop [k] is dominated by a free pole which is the first resonance of the front cavity. The labial consonant [p] has no free poles and no free zeroes unless the tongue is in a high palatal position, and the dental consonant [t] has a free zero in the region of 3000 c/s and a free pole at 6000 c s originating from the narrow tongue passage which contribute to the relative emphasis of the spectrum above 4000 c/s. In natural speech there is an additional free pole originating from the resonance of the cavity in front of the teeth.

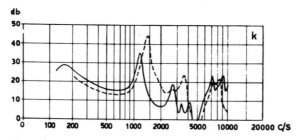

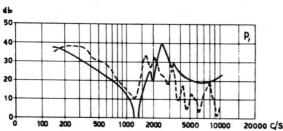

Fig. 12. Calculated spectra (solid lines) derived from X-ray studies of vocal tract dimensions, and spectra of the same sound sampled from the subject's connected speech (broken lines). The tongue articulation of [k] was postvelar and for [p] palatal. The sampling pertains to the first 10 msec of the explosion.

The accuracy which can be achieved in predicting the spectrum of a stop consonant of a subject's connected speech from X-ray pictures of his stationary articulation of the "same" sound is illustrated by Fig. 12 which pertains to the explosion phase of a [k]-sound of velar articulation and a palatalized [p]-sound. The predictability is good considering the apparent difficulties.

SPEECH SYNTHESIS*

Depending on how well the synthesis instrumentation preserves the general properties of speech, various levels of naturalness may be reached from very machine-like qualities to a rather natural sounding speech. Synthesis is made either to simulate a human model or to generate an impersonal speech by rule. Systematic synthesis experiments

---

* A review of synthesis methods may be found in ref. 2 (chapter 3.3).

are generally directed towards the evaluation of the relative importance of various pattern aspects. An important contribution to our understanding of the distinctive sound cues stems from the investigations at the Haskins Laboratories[14]. Their classical investigations were based on a constant pitch harmonic synthesizer, which provides a high degree of approximation of the speech wave. The results obtained from their studies should be checked by similar experiments with formant coded synthesizers capable of producing a more natural speech. Such studies are under way or are planned now in several laboratories in U.S.A., England, and in Sweden. Much of this work is directed to the realization of analysis-synthesis telephone systems enabling bandwidth reductions greater than those of a channel vocoder[15]. The signals extracted at the transmitting end and controlling the synthesis at the receiving end are of a parametric nature and have a low information rate. The formant coding implies an extensive use of Laplace transforms for the parametric decomposition. One example of such a synthesis scheme is shown in Fig. 13.

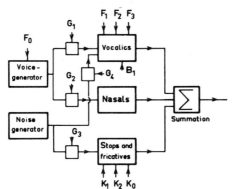

Fig. 13. Block diagram of the Swedish formant coded speech synthesizer OVE II.

Formant coded speech synthesis may be adopted as a supplement to analysis for expressing speech spectra in terms of pole-zero patterns providing a synthetic copy approximating the natural sample. This procedure has been called analysis by synthesis and is a promising approach to descriptive problems.

REFERENCES

1. R. K. POTTER, A. G. KOPP AND H. C. GREEN, *Visible Speech*, Van Nostrand, New York, 1947.
2. G. FANT, *Acta Polytechnica Scand.*, 246 (1958) 1.
3. J. W. VAN DEN BERG, *J. Speech and Hearing Research*, 1 (1958) 227.
4. J. L. FLANAGAN, *J. Speech and Hearing Research*, 1 (1958) 99.
5. H. M. TRUBY, *Acta Radiol.*, (1959) Suppl. 182.
6. D. B. FRY AND P. DENES, *Language and Speech*, 1 (1958) 35.
7. G. FANT, *Acoustic Theory of Speech Production*, RIT Div. of Telegraphy-Telephony, Report No. 10, 1958; to be published by Mouton & Co., 's-Gravenhage, 1960.
8. G. FANT, *Ericsson Technics*, 15 (1959) 3.
9. R. MILLER, *J. Acoust. Soc. Am.*, 31 (1959) 667.
10. H. K. DUNN, *J. Acoust. Soc. Am.*, 22 (1950) 740.

11. K. N. STEVENS AND A. S. HOUSE, *J. Acoust. Soc. Am.*, 27 (1955) 484, and 28 (1956) 578.
12. T. CHIBA AND M. KAJIYAMA, *The Vowel, its Nature and Structure*, Kaiseikan Publ. Co., Tokyo, 1941.
13. G. UNGEHEUER, *Z. Phonetik allgem. Sprachwiss.*, 11 (1958) 35.
14. A. M. LIBERMAN, P. DELATTRE AND F. S. COOPER, *J. Acoust. Soc. Am.*, 29 (1957) 117.
15. M. R. SCHROEDER, *Recent Progress in Speech Coding at the Bell Telephone Laboratories*, this book, p. 201.

The Calculation of Vowel Resonances, and an Electrical Vocal Tract*

H. K. Dunn

Bell Telephone Laboratories, Inc., Murray Hill, New Jersey

(Received April 20, 1950)

By treating the vocal tract as a series of cylindrical sections, or acoustic lines, it is possible to use transmission line theory in finding the resonances. With constants uniformly distributed along each section, resonances appear as modes of vibration of the tract taken as a whole. Thus, the fundamental mode of the smaller cavity may be affected considerably by a higher mode of the larger; and in addition, higher resonances are found without postulating additional cavities. This is an advantage over the lumped constant treatment, where it is necessary to postulate a different cavity for each resonance, and where the interaction terms in the equation do not include the higher modes of vibration. Under the distributed treatment, dimensions for each vowel may be taken from x-ray photographs of the vocal tract. The calculations then yield at least three resonances which lie in the frequency regions known for the vowel, from analyses of normal speech. Dependence of the different resonances upon the different cavities is discussed in some detail in the paper.

An electrical circuit based on the transmission line analogy has been made to produce acceptable vowel sounds. This circuit is useful in confirming the general theory and in research on the phonetic effects of articulator movements. The possibility of using such a circuit as a phonetic standard for vowel sounds is discussed.

INTRODUCTION

IT has been known for more than two hundred years[1] that the different vowels have associated with them different frequency regions, in which the sound is more intense than elsewhere in the spectrum. The name "formant" has been applied to these regions, and will be used in this paper. Early investigators thought that each vowel had one formant. Better methods of analysis showed two formants, while it is now known that four or more may be found. Just how many of these are necessary for vowel recognition is a point which has not been entirely established, and is not of primary importance in this paper. However, it seems likely that two are essential for good quality in most vowels, while the third adds somewhat to this quality, and may be essential in some sounds (the General American ɚ,[2] as in "bird," for example).

Data on the frequency positions of the vowel formants have been accumulating gradually,[3–5] and at an accelerated pace[6] since the development of the sound spectrograph.[7,8] Figure 1 shows sections from the spectrograms of a series of steady state vowels, from the voice of a male speaker. The dark bars in the pattern show the frequency positions of the formants of each vowel. While the positions in this figure are typical, not all speakers have the same formant frequencies for the same vowels. In particular, the voices of women tend to show somewhat higher frequency positions, and those of small children higher still.[6] The exact relations between formants, necessary for a given phonetic quality, is another point not yet fully established.

It has also been recognized for more than a century that the vowel formants arise in some way from resonances in the vocal tract. Although there are different ways of approaching the subject, which in the past were somewhat controversial, there will probably now be no objection to the viewpoint taken in this paper: that the vibrating vocal cords produce a periodic interruption of the air flowing through them, the volume velocity having a wave form such that harmonics of the fundamental are present up to high values; and that these harmonics are selectively transmitted by the vocal tract, the transmission characteristic varying from vowel to vowel. The peaks of the transmission curve may be called the resonance frequencies, and the harmonics near such a peak (none need be exactly at the peak) together make up a formant.

The vocal tract dimensions, upon which a theoretical prediction of the frequency positions of the formants must be based, have been rather difficult to obtain. This was especially true of the cavity in the throat, behind the tongue, and dimensions for this part of the tract were at one time based very largely on conjecture. The use of x-rays has helped this situation a great deal. The best set of dimensions known to the

* An abridged version of this paper was presented at the 38th meeting of the Acoustical Society at St. Louis, November 18, 1949. Parts of it were also given, together with a demonstration of the electrical vocal tract, at the Speech Communication Conference at Massachusetts Institute of Technology, May 31, 1950.

[1] G. Oscar Russell, *The Vowel* (Ohio State University Press, Columbus, 1928). The first three chapters give a historical summary of vowel theories.

[2] International Phonetic Symbols for the vowels will be used, as follows;

i eat	æ at	o obey	ɚ bird
ɪ it	a ask	u boot	
e hate	ɑ father	ʊ foot	
ɛ let	ɔ lost	ə about	

[3] Harvey Fletcher, *Speech and Hearing* (D. Van Nostrand Company, Inc., New York, 1929).

[4] Sir Richard Paget, *Human Speech* (Harcourt, Brace and Company, Inc., New York, 1930).

[5] John C. Steinberg, "Application of sound measuring instruments to the study of phonetic problems," J. Acous. Soc. Am. 6, 16 (1934).

[6] R. K. Potter and G. E. Peterson, "The representation of vowels and their movements," J. Acous. Soc. Am. 20, 528 (1948).

[7] Koenig, Dunn, and Lacy, "The sound spectrograph," J. Acous. Soc. Am. 18, 19 (1946).

[8] Potter, Kopp, and Green, *Visible Speech* (D. Van Nostrand Company, Inc., New York, 1947).

author are those given by Russell,[1] in which x-ray photographs in the median plane of the head were supplemented with cross measurements by means of "palatograms" and the "laryngoperiskop." Other excellent x-ray photographs have been published by Curry,[9] and by Parmenter and Treviño.[10] They all show that the tongue diagrams proposed by Lloyd,[11] and used by many others, are incorrect in certain details. In particular, these diagrams did not show the extension of the tongue constriction down toward the larynx, which occurs in several vowels.

When one examines the x-rays, it is obvious that a mathematical treatment that would take into account all the small variations in shape would be an extremely complex and difficult matter. A simplification of some kind is necessary; yet the treatment of the vocal tract as a double Helmholtz resonator, using only the volumes of the cavities and the conductivities of the passages between them and to the open air, is too great a simplification. This "lumped constant" type of treatment properly applies only for frequencies such that all dimensions are small compared with one-fourth wave-length, and in speech we are definitely interested in frequencies much higher than this. The author has not been able to find in the literature any lumped constant calculations, based on actual vocal tract dimensions.* Crandall[12] did the reverse: that is, he calculated volumes and conductivities necessary to produce two known formants in the different vowels. When he built corresponding models (not trying to match the actual shapes of the vocal cavities), his results were only partly successful. Benton[13] also developed the equations for the double Helmholtz resonator, and pointed out

the limitations, without applying the equations to real cases. He also treated the case of a shape like a fat bottle with a long neck, and allowed for the presence of standing waves in the neck. This was applied to some plasticine models of front vowels, with good results. In the real vocal tract, however, it is the large back cavity which has the greater length in these front vowels, and therefore requires the distributed treatment more than the "neck," even where the bottle shape is approximately correct. To say that the higher formant is due to the small cavity, or neck, is not an answer to this objection: it is unsafe to neglect any large dimension at the higher frequencies, because of the interaction of the higher modes of the larger cavity with the fundamental mode of the smaller.

This failure of older efforts to find a satisfactory theoretical tie between formant frequencies and cavity dimensions has been particularly stressed by Russell.[1,14,15] He mentions several possible factors other than cavity size, among them variations in the spectrum of the glottal tone and in the softness of the cavity walls.[16] In considering the damping of vowel formants and their relative amplitudes, both of these possible parameters would have to be considered. The author believes that they are relatively unimportant if formant frequencies alone are wanted, and that the greatest step toward making theory fit the facts can be taken by considering the distributed nature of the acoustic masses and compliances in the cavities and passages of the tract. This means, of course, taking shape as well as size into consideration.

In this paper the vocal tract will be treated as a series of cylindrical sections placed end to end. There

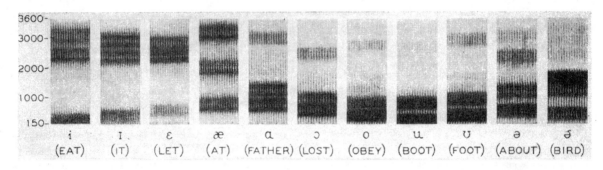

FIG. 1. Sections from the spectrograms of a series of vowels, all from the same male speaker. A frequency scale in cycles per second is given at the left. The analyzing band width used was 300 cycles per second.

[9] R. Curry, J. Physiol. **91**, 254 (1937): Arch. Sprach. Stimmhk. **2**, 1 (1938).
[10] C. E. Parmenter and S. N. Treviño, "Vowel positions as shown by x-ray," Quar. J. Speech **18**, 351 (1932).
[11] R. J. Lloyd, "The genesis of vowels," J. Anat. Physiol. **31**, 233 and Plate IX (1896).
* May 10, 1950. Since this paper was written, the author has had the opportunity of examining *The Vowel, Its Nature and Structure*, by T. Chiba and M. Kajiyama (Tokyo-Kaiseikan Publishing Company, Ltd., Tokyo, 1941). These authors made x-ray studies, and used dimensions so obtained in calculating the resonances of several vowels. Lumped constants were used for a, o, and ɯ (a Japanese variation of the English u). For e and i, the shape assumed was that of two cylindrical tubes of different diameters, joined by a tapering section, and a distributed treatment was used. For an approach to the calculation and interpretation of vowel formants, different from that of the present paper, the book should be consulted.
[12] I. B. Crandall, "Dynamical study of the vowel sounds, II," Bell Sys. Tech. J. **6**, 100 (1927).
[13] W. E. Benton, Appendix I of reference 4.
[14] G. Oscar Russell, "The mechanism of speech," J. Acous. Soc. Am. **1**, 83 (1929).
[15] G. Oscar Russell, *Speech and Voice* (The Macmillan Company, Inc., New York, 1931).
[16] See especially reference 1, pp. 164, 165.

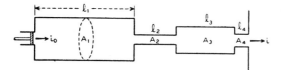

FIG. 2. Model of vocal tract assumed for the calculations.

is considerable justification for this in Russell's x-ray photographs,[1,15] particularly where the cavities become large, and the errors of using lumped constants therefore greater. This model is still a simplification, but a much less radical one than the reduction to volumes and conductivities only. The advantage lies in the possibility of taking the acoustical masses and compliances as uniformly distributed throughout the length of each cylindrical section. One result is more accurate values for the frequencies of the first two resonances; but another is the finding of additional resonances, even though the model may still be considered as made up of two cavities and two constrictions only. These additional resonances are higher modes of vibration, arising from reflections at the points of impedance change in the tract.

THEORY

Figure 2 shows the shape assumed for the calculations. The piston in this figure represents the source in the vocal cords. It is assumed to be of high impedance, and delivers a volume velocity i_0, which is constant with impedance changes in the tract, but may be different at different frequencies. The vocal tract is assumed to be made up of four cylindrical sections, representing (from left to right) the throat cavity, the constriction caused by the hump of the tongue, the mouth cavity, and the constriction due to the lips. A volume velocity i is delivered to the open air, from a baffle representing the speaker's face. No nose cavity is considered, because the passage into this cavity is usually closed by the velum, in good English vowels. The x-rays show it to be so closed in most cases, and it is believed that most of the formant measurements, with which the calculations will be compared, were taken with it closed.

A uniform cylindrical section, such as is shown in Fig. 3, having a plane wave passing through it, is analogous to a section of transmission line. That is, the acoustical resistance, mass and compliance are distributed along the cylinder in the same way that resistance, inductance, and capacitance are distributed along the line. Furthermore, the uniform line section in a steady state may be replaced, as far as effects observable outside the section are concerned, by the T-network of impedances shown in Fig. 3, and described by Eqs. (1) to (4).[17,18] These impedances are quite

[17] W. P. Mason, *Electromechanical Transducers and Wave Filters* (D. Van Nostrand Company, Inc., New York, 1942, 1948), pp. 62, 119.
[18] K. S. Johnson, *Transmission Circuits for Telephonic Communication* (D. Van Nostrand Company, Inc., New York, 1924), pp. 133, 144.

independent of how the line section is terminated at either end.

$$Z_1 = Z_0 \tanh(\Gamma l/2), \tag{1}$$

$$Z_2 = Z_0 \operatorname{csch} \Gamma l, \tag{2}$$

$$Z_0 = \left\{ \frac{R+j\omega L}{G+j\omega C} \right\}^{\frac{1}{2}}, \tag{3}$$

$$\Gamma = [(R+j\omega L)(G+j\omega C)]^{\frac{1}{2}}. \tag{4}$$

In these equations l is the length of the section, ω is 2π times the frequency, and j is the imaginary unit, while R, L, G, and C are, respectively, the distributed resistance, inductance, "leakance," and capacitance, each *per unit length* of the line. Z_0 is called the characteristic impedance of the line, and Γ the propagation constant.

R and G are dissipative terms, representing in the acoustical case the viscous resistance and the absorption of energy by the walls of the cylinder. We will neglect both of them, with confidence that this will not greatly change the frequency positions of the resonances. The acoustical equivalents of L and C are given by

$$L = \rho/A, \quad C = A/\rho c^2, \tag{5}$$

where ρ is the density of air, c the velocity of sound, and A the area of cross section of the cylinder.[19] The length l will remain the same in the electrical and acoustical cases. Making these omissions and substitutions,

$$Z_0 \approx \rho c/A, \quad \Gamma \approx j\omega/c, \tag{6}$$

$$Z_1 \approx (\rho c/A) \tanh j(\omega l/2c) = j(\rho c/A) \tan(\omega l/2c), \tag{7}$$

$$Z_2 \approx (\rho c/A) \operatorname{csch} j(\omega l/c) = -j(\rho c/A) \csc(\omega l/c). \tag{8}$$

The reduction to circular functions was made possible by neglecting R and G. The impedances are reduced to reactances, and we shall write

$$X_1 = (\rho c/A) \tan(\omega l/2c), \quad X_2' = (\rho c/A) \csc(\omega l/c), \tag{9}$$

$$Z_1 = jX_1, \qquad Z_2 = -jX_2. \tag{10}$$

The complete vocal tract of Fig. 2 can now be replaced by the circuit of Fig. 4. A high impedance generator, representing the source in the glottis, delivers a current i_0 to the first of four T-sections, each representing one of the cavities or constrictions of the tract. The output current i, representing the volume velocity from the lips, passes through a radiation re-

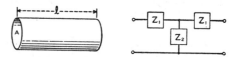

FIG. 3. A cylindrical section with a plane wave passing through it may be represented by a T-section of impedances, which are hyperbolic functions of frequency.

[19] It is understood that a circular cross section is not necessary to the argument.

sistance and a radiation reactance, given by[20]

$$R_r = \rho\omega^2/2\pi c, \quad L_r = 8\rho/3\pi^2 r, \tag{11}$$

where r is the radius of a circular orifice having the same area as the lip opening.

The circuit of Fig. 4 may be simplified by neglecting some of the circuit elements. Thus, the first X_{11} is in series with the high impedance generator, and should be negligible. Since X_{22} and X_{24} depend upon the very small volumes of the constrictions, they represent very high shunt reactances, and can be removed. Then R_r, although responsible for the energy radiated, is small compared with ωL_r in its effect upon i, at frequencies of interest. The circuit is simplified to that of Fig. 5, where X_{C1} and X_{C2} are the same as X_{21} and X_{23}, i.e. the compliance reactances from the throat and mouth cavities. X_{L1}, however, is the sum of X_{11}, $2X_{12}$, and X_{13}, thus combining mass terms from the tongue constriction and from the cavities on either side; while X_{L2} is the sum of X_{13}, $2X_{14}$, and ωL_r, combining mass terms from the lip constriction, from the mouth cavity on one side, and from the radiation reactance on the other. Referring to (9) and (11)

$$X_{C1} = \frac{\rho c}{A_1} \csc\frac{\omega l_1}{c}, \tag{12}$$

$$X_{C2} = \frac{\rho c}{A_3} \csc\frac{\omega l_3}{c}, \tag{13}$$

$$X_{L1} = \frac{\rho c}{A_1}\tan\frac{\omega l_1}{2c} + 2\frac{\rho c}{A_2}\tan\frac{\omega l_2}{2c} + \frac{\rho c}{A_3}\tan\frac{\omega l_3}{2c}, \tag{14}$$

$$X_{L2} = \frac{\rho c}{A_3}\tan\frac{\omega l_3}{2c} + 2\frac{\rho c}{A_4}\tan\frac{\omega l_4}{2c} + \frac{8\rho\omega}{3\pi^2 r}. \tag{15}$$

When the product of frequency by length is small, the tangents can be replaced by their arguments, and the cosecants by the reciprocals of their arguments. This may be done for the middle term of (15), since the length l_4 of the lip constriction is small. The same is often true for the length l_2 of the tongue constriction. The process is equivalent to using lumped elements to represent the corresponding parts.

The transmission characteristic of the circuit of Fig. 5, expressed as the ratio of output current to

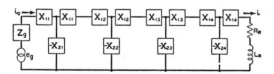

FIG. 4. Electrical analog of the vocal tract model of Fig. 2.

[20] I. B. Crandall, *Theory of Vibrating Systems and Sound* (D. Van Nostrand Company, Inc., New York, 1927), pp. 147, 148. The mechanical quantities given by Crandall are reduced here to acoustical.

FIG. 5. Circuit of Fig. 4 simplified by the omission of certain elements and the combination of others.

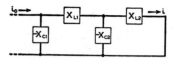

input current, is

$$\frac{i}{i_0} = \frac{X_{C1}/X_{L2}}{(X_{L1}-X_{C1})[(1/X_{C2})-(1/X_{L2})]-1}. \tag{16}$$

When Eqs. (12) to (15) are substituted in (16), it becomes the ratio of volume velocities in the output and input of the vocal tract (with the limitations that neglect of dissipation has imposed). Resonances are found by setting the denominator equal to zero, and solving for frequency.

$$(X_{L1}-X_{C1})[(1/X_{C2})-(1/X_{L2})]=1. \tag{17}$$

Equation (17) is the condition for resonance, with the exception that X_{L2} must not be infinite at the same time. When this happens, a closer examination shows that i/i_0 does not have a maximum at the point. The value of X_{C1} will not give us trouble, since it is a cosecant function, and cannot become zero. If one wishes an unexceptional form for the resonance condition, (16) may be reduced to

$$\frac{i}{i_0} = \frac{1}{[(X_{L1}/X_{C1})-1][(X_{L2}/X_{C2})-1]-X_{L2}/X_{C1}}. \tag{18}$$

The denominator of (18) is now equated to zero, and (12) to (15) substituted in it, with the additional substitutions

$$a = (2A_1/A_2)\tan(\omega l_2/2c), \tag{19}$$

$$b = A_3[(2/A_4)\tan(\omega l_4/2c)+(8\omega/3\pi^2 rc)]. \tag{20}$$

(If the constrictions are lumped, a and b are both proportional to frequency.) The condition for resonance becomes

$$\sin(\omega l_1/c)\{a[b\sin(\omega l_3/c)-\cos(\omega l_3/c)]$$
$$-(A_1/A_3)[b\cos(\omega l_3/c)+\sin(\omega l_3/c)]\}$$
$$-\cos(\omega l_1/c)[b\sin(\omega l_3/c)-\cos(\omega l_3/c)]=0. \tag{21}$$

This has no exceptions, and the curve of the function never goes to infinity, as it frequently does with (17). However, (17) will be used in this paper because it permits certain relationships between the cavities and the formants, not so easily seen from (21), to be pointed out.

EXAMPLES

Dimensions for the calculations were taken as far as possible from Russell's x-rays. In particular, his "Subject 236" was chosen, because the vocal tract is so clearly delineated in the figures for this subject in the book, and also because tables of measurements are given which include volumes of the cavities.[21] The

[21] See reference 1, pp. 110–112, 167–181.

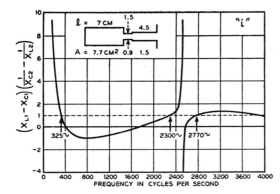

FIG. 6. Configuration assumed for the vowel i (eat), and curve giving resonances.

subject was a man, and although he was French, only those vowels are used here which appear also in English.

It was necessary to estimate the horizontal widths of the constricted parts, in order to get cross-sectional areas, since this dimension is not given in the book. For the cavities, areas could be obtained from the

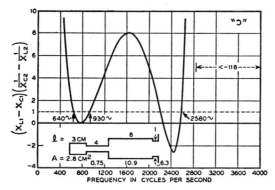

FIG. 7. Configuration and curve for the vowel ɔ (lost).

volumes and lengths. There was some ambiguity in choosing lengths for cavities, when they tapered at the ends. Also, there should be end corrections where one cylinder meets another of a different size, but these have been ignored since they would surely be smaller than the uncertainties involved in changing the actual shape into a cylinder. The end correction at the lips

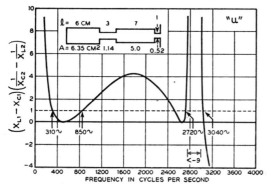

FIG. 8. Configuration and curve for the vowel u (boot).

is taken care of by the radiation reactance. It is admitted that some of the results given were obtained only after dimensions first chosen were altered. The alterations, however, were kept within what seemed to be a reasonable interpretation of the photographs, in terms of our model.

The density of air and velocity of sound were taken at the temperature of the human body: $\rho = 1.14 \times 10^{-3}$ g/cm^3, and $c = 3.53 \times 10^4$ cm/sec. From these and the dimensions, the X's of (12) to (15) were calculated for different frequencies, and the product on the left of (17) was plotted against frequency. Resonances are looked for where the ordinate one is crossed, with the exception noted above.

In Figs. 6–8, curves are shown for the vowels i, ɔ, and u. The shape assumed for each vowel is also shown, with dimensions. The actual configurations shown by the x-rays are given in Fig. 9, together with a scale also taken from one of the prints. In the curve for each vowel, there is one crossing of ordinate one that arises from an infinite value of X_{L2}, and which is not a resonance. The resonances are marked with their frequencies. Since we are dealing with circular functions of frequency, we would expect to find recurring solutions as frequency increases, as many as we wish to find. These are the higher modes of vibration mentioned previously. For i and ɔ, three are found below 4000 cycles per second, while for u there are four.

COMPARISON WITH MEASURED FORMANTS

The actual values of the formant frequencies, present in the vowels spoken as the x-rays were taken, are not known to us. We have, however, Russell's designation of the vowel in each case, and can compare the calculated resonances with a range of values measured when the same vowel is spoken by a number of different speakers. Such data, covering 33 male speakers, have been supplied by G. E. Peterson and H. L. Barney,[22] and it is found that the calculations fall within the range of observed values in all cases except those for the third and fourth resonances of u. In this case, the third formant is lower and the fourth (where observed) higher, than the calculated resonances given in Fig. 8. Since the first and second resonances are well placed, and since the third and fourth formants are rather unimportant in the u (being low in amplitude), it is quite possible that they were actually near to the points calculated. It would still be a good u if they were. It is interesting to note that by lengthening the mouth cavity 1 cm, shortening the throat cavity by the same amount, but changing the cross sections of both so as to keep the volumes as they were, the four resonances of the u are changed to 298, 860, 2450, and 3580 cycles per second. The first two have been changed very little, being relatively insensitive to length changes at these low frequencies, if volume remains constant. The third

[22] To be published.

 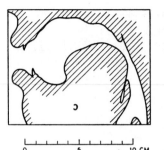 

FIG. 9. Actual configurations from which the dimensions in Figs. 6–8 were taken (from *The Vowel* by G. Oscar Russell, Figs. 111, 108, and 105).

and fourth are quite sensitive to length, and have moved to normal positions. The changes suggested, however, are hardly within the "reasonable" range for the example used.

Obviously, too many factors have been neglected (irregularities in shape, end corrections, dissipation, elastic yielding of the walls, compliances of the constricted parts, finite glottal impedance, cross modes of vibration) for it to be expected that exact formant frequencies would be calculated in a particular case. On the other hand, it is very interesting that the three examples tried come out so nearly in the expected places. In fact, *it seems probable that the first three formants of a non-nasal vowel arise very largely in the manner indicated by the cylindrical model.* The fourth is much less certain, since some of the neglected factors, such as irregularities in shape (including minor cavities) or cross modes of vibration, could be expected to produce resonances in the same frequency region where the fourth resonance of the uniform cylinders is found.

A comparison with lumped constant calculations will show how much has been gained by the distributed treatment. The circuit elements of Fig. 5 were lumped by the method explained just after Eq. (15). Even here, however, the mass values obtained profited greatly by the cylindrical assumption, since it made it possible to calculate not only the masses in the constrictions themselves, but also the additional masses added, due to the cavities on either side. The compliance terms did not profit in this way, since they depend, when lumped, on volume only. The results of the calculations on the three vowels are given in Table I, along with those found by the distributed method.

The first resonances are not much different, but the second resonances are raised appreciably by the distributed method. This is particularly true for the i, where it makes all the difference between an inacceptable and an acceptable value. In addition, the lumped treatment yields but two resonances, while a third is added by the distributed treatment.

If the validity of the cylindrical model be taken as largely substantiated, some interesting conclusions can be drawn as to how the formants depend upon the different cavities and constrictions.

ORIGIN OF FORMANTS ONE AND TWO

Confining our attention at present to the first two formants only, let us examine the low frequency ends of the curves of Figs. 6 to 8. The curve always starts from plus infinity. Since the ordinate is the product of $X_{L1}-X_{C1}$ and $(1/X_{C2})-(1/X_{L2})$, it is zero when each of these quantities is zero. These zeros are both points where a mass reactance is equal to a compliance reactance, and therefore represent the natural frequencies of these systems, each taken alone. Thus, the point where $X_{L1}=X_{C1}$ is the natural frequency of the throat cavity taken with the tongue constriction, although the outside mass encountered is not that of the open air, but the half-mass of the mouth cavity (note the third term of (14)). When $X_{L2}=X_{C2}$, we have the frequency of the mouth cavity taken with the lip constriction, and working into the open air, but with the back of the cavity closed off. With these stipulations, let us call the zeros of the curves the *uncoupled frequencies* of the two cavities. For i, Fig. 6, the uncoupled frequencies are far apart, while for both ɔ and u they are close together. Note again that resonances in the coupled system occur where the ordinate is *one*. We can then make the general statement that *both uncoupled frequencies of the cavities lie between the first and second formants of the vowel.* An exception may occur when the mouth cavity becomes very short, in which case the curve, after approaching zero a second time, from below, turns and goes to minus infinity; then in coming back from plus infinity it produces a second resonance just a little below the second zero.

Either the throat cavity or the mouth cavity may have the lower uncoupled frequency, or they may be exactly equal, in which case the curve just touches zero; but the curve cannot cross *one* twice without at least touching zero between. Therefore *the first two formants never completely coincide in a continuing sound.* This conclusion and that of the preceding paragraph can be reached also through lumped constant equations, and have been mentioned by Benton.[13]

When the uncoupled frequencies are widely separated, it is possible to speak of each of the two low formants as being chiefly dependent on one or the other of the two cavities, since the *one* crossings of the curve may be roughly paired with the zeros. This chief dependence, however, can be exchanged between the two formants without their ever being equal. This only means that in the middle, where the uncoupled frequencies are close together, the dependence upon the cavities is very much mixed. If everything else could be kept constant,

TABLE I. Resonance frequencies found by two methods.

	Lumped	Distributed
i	322, 1950 c.p.s.	325, 2300, 2770 c.p.s.
ɔ	625, 873	640, 930, 2580
u	305, 794	310, 850, 2720

while the tongue hump is moved gradually from a far forward position to a far back position, the first two formants would draw together up to a point, then separate again. There is no good sequence of vowels in English to illustrate this, although an approximation may be had in the series i, u, ə, particularly if the lips are more closed than normally in i and ə. The u represents the close approach of the formants in this series.

Although the uncoupled frequencies are nearly equal in the u (Fig. 8), the two resonances are still some distance apart. In the ɔ (Fig. 7) the uncoupled frequencies are also close together, and the resonances closer than in the u, due to the curve's having a steeper slope as it approaches and leaves zero. The throat cavity for ɔ is much smaller than for u, and the tongue constriction longer, while the mouth cavity is larger and the lips wider. This tends to keep the uncoupled frequencies (where $X_{L1}=X_{C1}$ and $X_{L2}=X_{C2}$) about equal in both cases. In the ɔ, however, the X_{L1} and X_{C1} are much larger than the X_{L2} and X_{C2}, hence both $X_{L1}-X_{C1}$ and $(1/X_{C2})-(1/X_{L2})$ increase in magnitude more rapidly as frequency departs from that of the uncoupled resonances, and the curve of their product is steeper. This point also can be shown by lumped constant equations.

Extending the above considerations, it can be said that the series of English "back" vowels, u, o, ɔ, ɑ, are all produced in this manner. The tongue hump moves back from the u position, but the uncoupled frequencies are kept nearly equal by opening the lips at the same time. The first two formants draw closer together, as shown in Fig. 1, and *the dependence of these formants on the two cavities cannot be separated for any of these vowels.* The uncoupled frequency also moves upward during the sequence. That is, while the volume of the throat cavity is decreasing and the mass of the tongue constriction increasing, their product (the reciprocal square root of which is proportional to the uncoupled frequency, on a lumped constant basis) is decreasing; and while the volume of the mouth cavity is increasing and the mass of the lip constriction decreasing, their product is also decreasing, and keeping about equal to the other product.

The vowel ʊ is not included in the above sequence. While its tongue position is farther back than for the u,[15] the passage becomes less constricted rather than more, while the lip opening also becomes somewhat larger. The uncoupled frequencies move apart, and the first formant becomes somewhat more dependent on the mouth cavity, the second on the throat cavity. Although the formants may not be much farther apart than in u,

both have moved higher. In the ə, the tongue constriction moves still farther back, and the lips are slightly more open. Both formants are higher than in ʊ, and a little farther apart.

To look further into the question of how closely formants one and two may approach each other, several assumed configurations for the vowel ɑ are given in Fig. 10, together with the resonances found from them. Figure 10a approximates the most common shape. In the manner described above, the first two resonances can be brought still closer by diminishing the throat cavity further, while at the same time lengthening or narrowing (or both) the constriction. Supposing that the throat cavity has completely disappeared, Fig. 10b shows the corresponding configuration and resonances. Some x-rays for the ɑ show an approach to this condition, though not with so extreme a narrowing of the passage. Formants one and two, in Fig. 10b, are only a little more than 100 cycles per second apart. Further narrowing would bring them still closer, but complete merging would require complete closure of the passage, which would stop the flow of sound.

It is quite probable that, with a high fundamental frequency, formants one and two of the ɑ sometimes get as close as or closer than the separation between harmonics. In this case the ear would probably not distinguish the condition from that of a single broad resonance. Even a Fourier spectrum would not show a clear separation. Still, if the transmission of the tract could be explored with a sine wave, the separation would be found.

If a single resonance will suffice to give the ɑ quality, in place of the usual two, then a configuration like that of Fig. 10c would produce the vowel. This single tube, closed at one end, resonates for $l=\lambda/4, 3\lambda/4, 5\lambda/4$, and so on, where λ is the wave-length. For a first resonance of 1000 cycles per second, the length including the end correction is 8.8 cm. An artificial cavity of this size, or one shorter with a constricted opening, may produce the vowel, particularly if the tube is well damped (the author has not tried it). However, a real voice cannot produce it in this way, for even a small child has a vocal tract much longer than that required. It can also be said that if a gradual change from 10a or 10b to 10c were possible, the resonances would separate instead of coming together, thus producing some other vowel in the intermediate stage. That is to say, the two formants cannot be made to merge, except (as mentioned above) by a complete closure, and cessation of sound.

The tongue hump usually extends farthest back for the ɑ, although its position may be about the same in the ɔ on one side, and the æ on the other. A typical change from ɑ to æ may be seen in Fig. 11, taken from Russell's "Subject 271," a woman. The change may be described as consisting chiefly in a large reduction of the tongue constriction. This raises the uncoupled frequency of the throat cavity, while leaving that of the mouth cavity not much different. The second formant is pushed up ahead of the uncoupled frequency, and is therefore higher than for ɑ, as seen in Fig. 1. It becomes mainly due to the throat cavity, while the first formant depends much more upon the mouth cavity. The New England "a" represents an intermediate position between the ɑ and æ.

From æ to ɛ the change in formants shown in Fig. 1 is small, but the change in configuration shown in Fig. 11 is rather large. The constriction disappears from the throat and reappears in the mouth. If this were accomplished by a continuous upward movement of the constriction, unchanged in magnitude, the second formant would be found first to drop toward the first formant, then rise again to a higher position than at the start. This has been confirmed by means of the electrical vocal tract (to be described later), and provides a good illustration of the process explained earlier: the approach of the two formants while the chief dependence on the two cavities is being exchanged between them. The uncoupled frequencies would cross during the change. In the real voice, however, the change is probably accomplished by pulling the base of the tongue away from the back of the throat, simultaneously with an upward movement in the mouth. The effort necessary would be small, as it actually seems to be. The intermediate stage in this case would approach the condition of a single uniform tube, for which the second resonance is three times the first. Since formant measurements show that this ratio for æ is generally less than three, while that for ɛ is generally greater, the formants in the intermediate stage would also be intermediate, as actual trial on a real voice shows them to be. The end result is the same, in that the chief dependence of the first formant has changed from the mouth cavity to the throat cavity, that of the second formant in the reverse direction. This change has come through a different process, however, than that outlined above. Here the division between the two cavities has disappeared in one position, and reappeared in another. In the intermediate stage we cannot speak of the uncoupled frequencies, except in terms of a constriction of no magnitude and arbitrary position. What we do, then, is to shift this position some distance while there is no constriction, and when the uncoupled frequencies reappear they are in new places, reversed from the old. Another possible (and perhaps more likely) intermediate configuration is one in which *both* constrictions are partly present. This would also result in a smooth rise in the second formant.

Not all x-rays of the æ show a configuration like that in Fig. 11, some appearing closer to the ɛ position. These may or may not have been phonetically identical with the others, for there seems to be a considerable range in the phonetic values of sounds identified by this symbol. In either case the shift from back to front has probably occurred earlier in the series, in the manner that has been suggested.

For the rest of the "front" vowels, ɛ, e, ɪ, and i, the

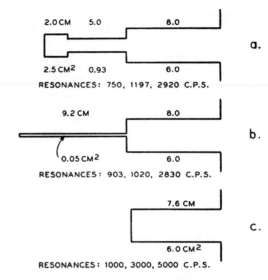

FIG. 10. Three assumed configurations for the vowel ɑ (father), with corresponding resonances.

tongue hump moves forward, while the constriction increases, but the lips remain rather open. The uncoupled frequencies get farther apart, separating the first two formants more and more, as shown in Fig. 1. The chief dependence of the first formant remains with the throat cavity, while that of the second is on the mouth cavity, except that it begins to be affected by the second resonance of the throat cavity. This point will be examined in the next section.

THE THIRD FORMANT

The third formant can usually be described as the second resonance of the longer cavity. This conclusion first appeared likely when the calculations, for the examples given and for a number of other examples in which dimensions were changed arbitrarily, showed the third resonance lying between those frequencies for which the longer cavity was one-half and three-fourths wavelengths long. This is exactly where the second resonance of a single cylindrical tube, closed at one end and mass loaded at the other, must be found. In Fig. 12 such a tube is shown, in which the constriction at the open end is short enough to be lumped as an acoustical mass, m. Treating the tube as a section of transmission line without dissipation, and assuming that a constant volume velocity is introduced at the closed end, the condition for resonance is

$$\cot(\omega l/c) = \cot(2\pi l/\lambda) = (Am/\rho c)\omega. \qquad (22)$$

Resonances occur where the curve of $\cot \omega l/c$, in Fig. 12, intersects the straight line $Am\omega/\rho c$. If $m=0$ the resonances are at $l=\lambda/4$, $3\lambda/4$, and so on. (Actually m cannot be reduced entirely to zero, but the radiation mass remaining is usually taken care of by a correction to the tube length.) As m increases, the second resonance approaches the $l=\lambda/2$ position, but cannot go below it.

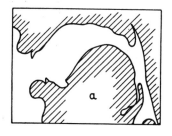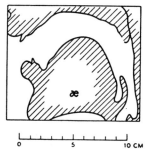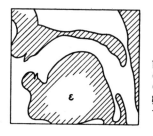

FIG. 11. Configurations used by a speaker for the vowels ɑ (father), æ (at), and ε (let) (from tables of measurements given in *The Vowel* by G. Oscar Russell, pp. 220–222).

In the second place, it is true that the effects of the two cavities are more easily separated as we go to higher frequencies. The condition for resonance (21) may be changed to

$$-[a^2+(A_1/A_3)^2]^{\frac{1}{2}}\sin(\omega l_1/c)$$
$$\times\{b\cos[(\omega l_3/c)+\varphi]+\sin[(\omega l_3/c)+\varphi)]\}$$
$$-\cos(\omega l_1/c)[b\sin(\omega l_3/c)-\cos(\omega l_3/c)]=0 \quad (23)$$

where

$$\tan\varphi=(A_3/A_1)a=(2A_3/A_2)\tan(\omega l_2/2c). \quad (24)$$

Depending upon how much larger the cross section of the mouth cavity is than that of the tongue constriction ($A_3 > A_2$), φ will approach $\pi/2$ at a much lower frequency than that required for $\omega l_2/2c$. It may, in fact, be nearly $\pi/2$ for a considerable range of moderately large values of frequency. If it is put equal to $\pi/2$, we note from (24) that $a \gg A_1/A_3$, and (23) becomes

$$[a\sin(\omega l_1/c)-\cos(\omega l_1/c)]$$
$$\times[b\sin(\omega l_3/c)-\cos(\omega l_3/c)]=0. \quad (25)$$

Or,

$$\cot(\omega l_1/c)=a, \quad \cot(\omega l_3/c)=b. \quad (26)$$

The two cavities are separated, and each has a condition for resonance like that of (22), since a and b are almost proportional to frequency.

It is true, of course, that the condition $\varphi \approx \pi/2$ is not always satisfied at the frequency of the third formant. In that case, the exact position of the resonance is influenced by the shorter cavity. This probably happens in the front vowels, where A_3 may not be a great deal larger than A_2, and the length of the mouth cavity, l_3, becomes short. In this way a slight rise in the third formant, from ε to i, may be explained, even though the longer cavity is increasing in length. It is even possible for the third formant to become chiefly dependent upon the shorter cavity, in which case the second formant becomes chiefly the second resonance of the longer cavity. This can happen when the mouth cavity becomes very short, shorter than in the normal i. The exchange of dependence (as in the case of the first and second formants) takes place as the second and third formants approach each other and then separate again, without ever being equal.

When a front vowel is terminated by a k or g, spectrograms show the second and third formants merging just as the stop occurs (several examples may be found in *Visible Speech*[8]). The motion of the tongue in this case is such as to shorten the mouth cavity, as well as close the passage between the cavities. The closure reduces the second resonance of the throat cavity to the $\lambda/2$ position, while the shortening of the mouth cavity tends to raise the second formant to this point or above. Complete coincidence probably cannot happen except at complete closure of the passage.

A sound which requires a different description of the third formant is the ɚ of General American speech. Here this formant takes a relatively low position, only a little above the second. In the author's case, and probably in the usual case, the sound can be made by first forming the neutral ə, then raising the tip of the tongue nearly to the hard palate. This subdivides the mouth cavity, making a total of three cavities. From calling the third formant the second resonance of the mouth cavity in the ə, it must be described in terms of three cavities in the ɚ. The motion of the formant during the change is smooth and continuous, and calculations on the effect of gradually introducing a constriction into a previously uniform cylinder, show that the original second resonance of the cylinder should fall in just this way. Confirmation of the above description of the ɚ has been obtained from the electrical vocal tract. No x-ray photographs for the sound have been discovered.

VARIATIONS IN CONFIGURATION

There is no doubt that the same sound, or at least nearly enough the same to be acceptable to the ear, can be produced by somewhat different configurations. Some of these variations have been suggested in the preceding sections. If one were limited in adjustment to the lips, tongue constriction, and tongue position only, there are already more variables than needed to place two formants in required positions, and just enough for three. When variations in cross sections of the two cavities are added, the possibilities increase. It must also be stated that many x-rays show some signs of three cavities. The added constriction produced by the tip of the tongue in ɚ has been cited, and the epiglottis also appears to constrict the throat somewhat in some cases; or there may be two constrictions produced by the base and middle portion of the tongue. Even a slight added constriction may serve to shift the formants, particularly the third. In any case, it seems probable that careful consideration of both shape and size of all parts of the vocal tract (assuming the mathematics can be handled) will yield resonant frequencies close to the positions of the formants.

EFFECTS OF TRACT SIZE

Small children have appreciably shorter vocal tracts than adults. It has also been noted that the formant frequencies for children are higher.[6] In Eqs. (12) to (15), which define the quantities in the resonance condition (17), note that if all lengths are decreased in the same proportion, we have only to increase ω in the same proportion to keep all terms the same except the last term of (15), and this is usually a small part of X_{L2}. *The resonant frequencies are then almost inversely proportional to the lengths, provided all are changed at once.* If all the areas are changed in the same proportion, again neglecting the last term of (15), we find that the two factors of the left side of (17) are changed in opposite directions, their product remaining unchanged. *The resonant frequencies are then almost independent of cross sections, provided all are changed at once.* A change of areas does affect the characteristic impedance, however, as may be seen from the Z_0 of (6). If lengths and diameters are changed together, all in the same proportion, then even the last term of (15) contributes to the above rules, since it may be written $8\rho\omega r/3\pi A_4$.

The higher formants of small children are at least understandable on the above basis, although the reasons for their acceptance as giving the same vowels as the lower formants of adults must be looked for in the hearing process. The result of filling the vocal tract with hydrogen or helium[23] is also a rise in formant frequencies.[24] In this case the velocity c has increased, and it may be seen from the Eqs. (12) to (15) that the effect on the resonant frequencies is the same as a decrease in all the lengths.

In accordance with the statements of the preceding section, it must be expected that a moderate difference in length may sometimes be compensated by other changes, keeping the essential formants unchanged.

DAMPING

If the R and G of Eqs. (3) and (4) are retained, we are confronted not only with a much more difficult mathematical problem, but also with the problem of choosing values for these constants, which may be different in different parts of the tract. Until it is done, it may not be possible to predict very accurately, either the band widths or the relative amplitudes of the formants in a vowel. However, some idea of relative amplitudes may be obtained from positions.

The transmissions for i and u, as given by Eqs. (16) or (18), have been plotted in Figs. 13 and 14. The main

[23] Helium is recommended for this experiment because of the greater safety, although the effect is not quite as large as with hydrogen.

[24] Ernst Bárány, "Transposition of speech sounds," J. Acous. Soc. Am. **8**, 217 (1937).

effect of dissipation will be the reduction of the transmission at the resonances to finite values. At frequencies not near the resonances, we would not expect the real value of transmission to be much different from the calculated. The dotted curves of Figs. 13 and 14 therefore show approximately possible real transmission curves.

Also shown in each of these figures is a "base curve." This was obtained as follows. Let us suppose that the poles of (18) have all been found (zeros of the denominator), and let us designate the positive ones as $\omega_1, \omega_2, \cdots \omega_n$, in order of increasing frequency. For every positive pole there will be a negative one of the same magnitude (since all quantities in (12) to (15) change sign when the sign of ω is changed, their ratios remain the same). Equation (18) can then be written

$$\frac{i}{i_0} = \frac{K}{(\omega^2-\omega_1^2)(\omega^2-\omega_2^2)\cdots(\omega^2-\omega_n^2)}, \quad (27)$$

where K is a constant. From (18) we get $i/i_0=1$ when $\omega=0$ (X_{L1} and X_{L2} are both zero, while X_{C1} and X_{C2} are both infinite). Since (27) must have the same value at the same frequency,

$$\frac{i}{i_0} = \frac{(-1)^n \omega_1^2 \omega_2^2 \cdots \omega_n^2}{(\omega^2-\omega_1^2)(\omega^2-\omega_2^2)\cdots(\omega^2-\omega_n^2)}. \quad (28)$$

From (28), we can see that if ω is much smaller than ω_1, and therefore much smaller than all the other poles, the transmission is flat at the value 1. If ω^2 becomes large enough to make ω_1^2 negligible in comparison, but is still much smaller than ω_2^2, the transmission will be approximately,

$$i/i_0 \approx -\omega_1^2/\omega^2. \quad (29)$$

Plotted on decibel and log-frequency scales (ignoring the negative sign), this is a straight line with a downward slope of 40 db per decade (12 db per octave).

Moving the frequency up between ω_2 and ω_3, again

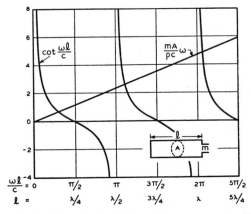

FIG. 12. A single cylindrical tube, closed at one end and **mass** loaded at the other, has resonances given by the intersections **of** the cotangent curve with the diagonal line.

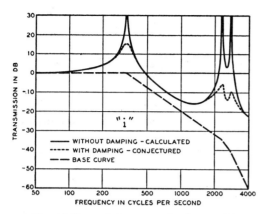

FIG. 13. Transmission curves for the vowel i.

assuming it is far from either, the transmission becomes

$$i/i_0 \approx \omega_1^2 \omega_2^2/\omega^4, \qquad (30)$$

which has a downward slope of 80 db per decade, as frequency increases. Continuing this process, the line increases its downward slope by 40 db per decade each time a resonance is passed.

If the lines represented by (29) and (30) are extended toward each other, they intersect at exactly the frequency of ω_2, and any other two adjacent sections will intersect at the resonance between them. The "base lines" of Figs. 13 and 14 are drawn by following zero db as far as the first resonance, turning downward 40 db per decade, and an additional 40 db per decade as each successive resonance is passed. The actual transmission curve will approach this line only where the frequency is far from any resonance, and the closer the resonances are together, the greater the height of the intermediate transmission curve above the base line.

The advantage of the base line is that it shows the general trend of the curve. If we compare the curves for i and u, we see that this trend provides one reason (for example) for the lower magnitude of the third formant in u than in i. Although the −40 db per decade slope starts at about the same frequency, the −80 db per decade slope begins much earlier for the u than for the i. The values of the dissipation constants in different parts of the vocal tract will also affect the relative heights of the resonance peaks.

To obtain the envelope of the pressure spectrum, measured at a distance from the lips, there would have to be applied to the transmission curves two other frequency characteristics: the radiation from the lips, which would essentially tilt the curve toward higher amplitudes at higher frequencies, at a rate of 20 db per decade (6 db per octave); and the spectrum of the volume velocity delivered by the vocal cords, which is not known exactly, but is certainly lower at higher frequencies, and probably at a rate of between −20 and −30 db per decade. If it were −20 db per decade, then the pressure spectrum should look nearly like the transmission curve.

Damping constants in db per second have been measured by Fletcher,[3] Steinberg[5] and Lewis and Tuthill.[25,26] They found it necessary to apply a correction spectrum to the observed pressure spectra, in order to make the formant curves (especially the first) look more like simple resonance curves. The correction used in each case was an increase in the amplitudes at higher frequencies, at a rate of 30 db per decade. If the transmission curves of Figs. 13 and 14 have added to them the radiation characteristic, then the slope is 20 db per decade at low frequencies, and approaches −20 db per decade at frequencies well above the first resonance but below the second. The first formant would then have nearly the form of a simple resonance curve. That is, the pressure spectrum would have this simple resonance shape in the first formant, if the source spectrum were flat. The correction found empirically by the above investigators would then be the inverse of the source spectrum, and the latter could be described as having harmonic amplitudes proportional to the −1.5 power of the harmonic number. This is the way Fletcher interpreted the correction (reference 3, p. 50), although the present author would prefer to speak of the "volume velocity spectrum," rather than "the force which is acting on the resonant cavity." It should be added that all of the above authors made it clear that the correction was only approximate.

The finding of a damping constant for each formant would seem to involve the assumption that the source spectrum is applied separately to a different simple resonator for each of the formants. This may be a helpful concept for some purposes, but should not be taken as representing actual conditions. If it did, each resonator would have a transmission curve approaching 20 db per decade on the low side, −20 db per decade on the high side; or, if the radiation characteristic were removed, the slopes approached would be zero and −40 db per decade. An addition of such curves, even

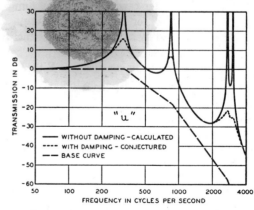

FIG. 14. Transmission curves for the vowel u.

[25] Don Lewis, "Vocal resonance," J. Acous. Soc. Am. 8, 91 (1936).

[26] D. Lewis and C. Tuthill, "Resonant frequencies and damping constants of resonators involved in the production of sustained vowels 'O' and 'Ah,'" J. Acous. Soc. Am. 11, 451 (1940).

with each resonator given an independent attenuation factor, could not be made to look like the curve of Fig. 14. For one thing, the tail of the second resonance would overshadow the third and higher resonances. Actually a product of the transmissions of simple resonators, rather than their addition, would be indicated by the form of Eq. (28). It has been found, in fact, by those who have made artificial vowels through the use of resonant circuits in parallel, that additional suppression is necessary between and above the resonances in order to get acceptable vowel quality.[27]

AN ELECTRICAL VOCAL TRACT (EVT)

The use of transmission line theory in calculating vowel resonances has led naturally to the setting up of a transmission line vocal tract model in the laboratory.[28] Figure 15 shows the schematic circuit. A line with distributed constants is approximated through the use of 25 lumped sections, each representing a cylinder 0.5 cm long and 6 cm² in cross section. The whole is then divided into two "cavities" by the use of a lumped, but variable inductance, which can be inserted between any two sections of the line. This represents the "tongue hump" constriction. Another variable inductance at the end of the line represents the constriction at the lips. A high impedance complex-wave generator is applied to the input. The wave shape used to date is essentially that of a condenser discharge repeated before the discharge has progressed too far, so that the harmonic amplitudes are nearly inversely proportional to harmonic number (−20 db per decade). The radiation characteristic is introduced by taking, as the output, the voltage across a small inductance. This voltage then represents pressure in the air outside the lips. A "whisper" can be produced by the substitution of white noise for the periodic source.

A photograph of the EVT is shown in Fig. 16. The coils and condensers of the line are mounted in the rear. The panel in the center carries the tongue hump inductance and a control for its magnitude. Its position in the tract is changed by sliding the whole panel back and forth. A fixed panel at the right carries a control for the magnitude of the lip constriction. Either cavity can be shortened by cutting out sections at the ends, by means of the sliders at the upper corners.

The whole series of English vowels can be produced by this apparatus—not perfectly, but distinctly better than we were able to make with three independent tuned circuits without additional suppression between and above the resonances. A series of spectrograms of vowels made by the EVT is reproduced in Fig. 17,

[27] K. W. Wagner, "Ein neues elektrisches Sprechgerät zur Nachbildung der menschlichen Vokale," Preuss. Akad. Wiss., Berlin, Ab. 2, 44 pp. (1936).

[28] A summary of previous methods of making artificial speech sounds is given by Homer Dudley and T. H. Tarnoczy in "The speaking machine of Wolfgang von Kempelen," J. Acous. Soc. Am. 22, 151 (1950).

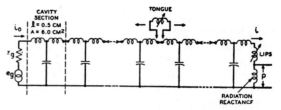

FIG. 15. Schematic circuit of the electrical vocal tract.

where they may be compared with the natural vowels of Fig. 1.

Some observers have called some of the vowels "nasal," which is surprising in view of the fact that the device has no "nose." The effect can probably be explained on the basis that some of the formants are too wide, due to too much resistance in the circuit. The analogs of the acoustical units of mass and compliance were taken as the practical units of inductance and capacitance. This gave the right frequencies, but resulted in a very low electrical impedance for the circuit ($Z_0 = 6.7$ ohms). The resistances of contacts and connecting wires are therefore too important, resulting in a Q of not more than two or three at the lowest formant frequencies. The only resistor added to the circuit is a variable one across the tongue hump inductance, and it is seldom used. A higher impedance circuit should be tried.

Another limitation of the EVT in its present form is that there is no way of controlling the cross sections of the cavities. This is probably important in the front vowels, where the mouth cavity is smaller than the 6 cm² used. A trade between length and area can be made, to a certain extent, but it is probable that the third formant could be better located by closer adherence to the real situation.

In spite of the limitations, the EVT is of considerable value in checking the theory and in investigating the phonetic effects of the independent movements of the different articulators. Some strange sounds are produced with certain settings, although many of them appear in foreign languages. Recently the American ɝ was added to the vocabulary by setting first for the neutral ə, then adding a second "hump" in the proper position and magnitude, between the first hump and the lips. The sound is recognized at once by all who hear it. It is also found possible to improve some of the other vowels a little by a small amount of a second hump.

The acceptability of the artificial vowels is considerably improved by the introduction of a pitch inflection, a change in the fundamental frequency during the vowel production. This is only putting into the sound some of the variability which is nearly always present in the human voice. It is well known that even a human vowel may be hard to recognize if it is recorded in an even monotone, and then reproduced continuously, as from a concentric phonograph groove. It is probable that

Russell[29] would have been better satisfied with the results from his own clay models, if he had introduced a pitch inflection.

It is possible that a perfected cricuit, of the general type described, could be used as a phonetic standard. A vowel could be specified in terms of electrical constants (including those required for generating the input spectrum), and reproduced at any time or place without the variability associated with the human voice. At present, phonograph records of spoken sounds are the nearest approach to a phonetic standard. If generally accepted, such records would serve the purpose of distributing the standard and preserving it in time. It might be easier, however, to get a jury of phoneticians to agree on sounds produced by an impersonal machine, than on the pronunciation by any one real voice. In addition, by imitating on the EVT one's own pronunciation of a sound, and comparing the settings with the standard settings for that sound, it should be possible to learn how to correct the articulator positions.

SUMMARY OF CONCLUSIONS

1. The frequencies of the first three formants of most non-nasal vowels may be approximately calculated from vocal tract dimensions, by treating the tract as a series of cylindrical sections, with acoustical mass and compliance uniformly distributed along each section.

2. The uncoupled natural frequencies of the separate throat and mouth cavities, each taken with the constriction adjoining it on the side toward the open air, both lie between the first two resonances of the coupled system.

3. The first two formants in a continuing vowel cannot completely coincide, although they may sometimes lie so close that the separation is not apparent in a Fourier analysis, if the fundamental frequency is high.

4. Only when the first two formants are well separated is it possible to say that the first depends more upon one cavity, the second upon another. In the vowels u, o, ɔ, and ɑ, the dependence of both formants lies almost equally upon both cavities. In ʊ, ə, and sometimes æ, the first formant depends more upon the mouth cavity, the second upon the throat cavity. In ɛ, e, and ɪ, the reverse is true. In i, the first formant depends very much upon the throat cavity, but the second formant is strongly affected by the second resonance of the throat cavity, as well as by the first resonance of the mouth cavity.

5. The third vowel formant can usually be described as the second resonance of the longer cavity. In i, however, it is affected by the first resonance of the shorter cavity. In ɚ it must be described in terms of three cavities, and in some examples of other vowels it may be affected by a partial formation of a third cavity.

6. The formant frequencies are inversely proportional to the lengths of the cylindrical sections, and independent of cross-sectional areas, provided the changes in either case are proportionate in the different parts of the vocal tract.

7. While the relative amplitudes of formants must depend to a large extent upon dissipation constants, there is also a general trend which makes the amplitude of one formant dependent upon the frequency spacing of those that lie below it.

8. An electrical circuit built like a transmission line, but divided into "cavities" by a lumped inductance, and terminated with another inductance, will produce vowel sounds when supplied with energy from a suitable complex source.

WORK REMAINING UNFINISHED

Dissipation constants should be added to the theory, and a completely predicted transmission curve obtained

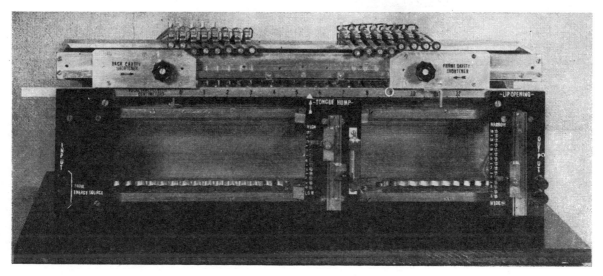

FIG. 16. Front view of the electrical vocal tract.

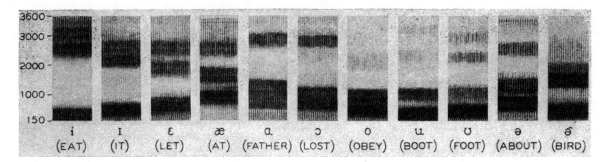

FIG. 17. Spectrograms of vowels produced by the electrical vocal tract. Compare with Fig. 1.

for one or two cases. The case of three cavities in line should be solved. A nose cavity should be added, both to the theory and to the electrical vocal tract. The theory should be applied to many more sounds, including some consonants, and to transitions between sounds. The EVT should be improved and used to check and extend the theory. Effects of changes in the source spectrum should be investigated. An attempt should be made to measure the real vocal tract transmission for different vowel configurations, perhaps by introducing a known volume velocity spectrum into the throat cavity and measuring the external pressure spectrum. By comparing this with the sound when the vocal cords are used, the spectrum of the volume velocity from the cords could be obtained. Another large field of study is that of the factors responsible for differences in voice quality, between individuals. Some of these factors may arise from transmission differences.

ACKNOWLEDGMENTS

The author is indebted to many of his colleagues in Bell Telephone Laboratories. He particularly wishes to thank Messrs. R. K. Potter, J. C. Steinberg, R. L. Miller and H. T. O'Neil for very helpful suggestions, and Mr. L. O. Schott for the mechanical design of the electrical vocal tract, and for the automatic pitch inflection circuit used with it.

Control Methods Used in a Study of the Vowels

Gordon E. Peterson and Harold L. Barney
Bell Telephone Laboratories, Inc., Murray Hill, New Jersey
(Received December 3, 1951)

Relationships between a listener's identification of a spoken vowel and its properties as revealed from acoustic measurement of its sound wave have been a subject of study by many investigators. Both the utterance and the identification of a vowel depend upon the language and dialectal backgrounds and the vocal and auditory characteristics of the individuals concerned. The purpose of this paper is to discuss some of the control methods that have been used in the evaluation of these effects in a vowel study program at Bell Telephone Laboratories. The plan of the study, calibration of recording and measuring equipment, and methods for checking the performance of both speakers and listeners are described. The methods are illustrated from results of tests involving some 76 speakers and 70 listeners.

INTRODUCTION

CONSIDERABLE variation is to be found in the processes of speech production because of their complexity and because they depend upon the past experience of the individual. As in much of human behavior there is a self-correcting, or servomechanism type of feedback involved as the speaker hears his own voice and adjusts his articulatory mechanisms.[1]

In the elementary case of a word containing a consonant-vowel-consonant phoneme[2,3] structure, a speaker's pronunciation of the vowel within the word will be influenced by his particular dialectal background; and his pronunciation of the vowel may differ both in phonetic quality and in measurable characteristics from that produced in the word by speakers with other backgrounds. A listener, likewise, is influenced in his identification of a sound by his past experience.

Variations are observed when a given individual makes repeated utterances of the same phoneme. A very significant property of these variations is that they are not random in a statistical sense, but show trends and sudden breaks or shifts in level, and other types of nonrandom fluctuations.[4] Variations likewise appear in the successive identifications by a listener of the same utterance. It is probable that the identification of repeated sounds is also nonrandom but there is little direct evidence in this work to support such a conclusion.

A study of sustained vowels was undertaken to investigate in a general way the relation between the vowel phoneme intended by a speaker and that identified by a listener, and to relate these in turn to acoustical measurements of the formant or energy concentration positions in the speech waves.

In the plan of the study certain methods and techniques were employed which aided greatly in the collection of significant data. These methods included randomization of test material and repetitions to obtain sequences of observations for the purpose of checking the measurement procedures and the speaker and listener consistency. The acoustic measurements were made with the sound spectrograph; to minimize measurement errors, a method was used for rapid calibration of the recording and analyzing apparatus by means of a complex test tone. Statistical techniques were applied to the results of measurements, both of the calibrating signals and of the vowel sounds.

These methods of measurement and analysis have been found to be precise enough to resolve the effects of different dialectal backgrounds and of the nonrandom trends in speakers' utterances. Some aspects of the vowel study will be presented in the following paragraphs to illustrate the usefulness of the methods employed.

EXPERIMENTAL PROCEDURES

The plan of the study is illustrated in Fig. 1. A list of words (List 1) was presented to the speaker and his utterances of the words were recorded with a magnetic tape recorder. The list contained ten monosyllabic words each beginning with [h] and ending with [d] and differing only in the vowel. The words used were *heed, hid, head, had, hod, hawed, hood, who'd, hud,* and *heard.* The order of the words was randomized in each list, and each speaker was asked to pronounce two different lists. The purpose of randomizing the words in the list was to avoid practice effects which would be associated with an unvarying order.

If a given List 1, recorded by a speaker, were played back to a listener and the listener were asked to write down what he heard on a second list (List 2), a comparison of List 1 and List 2 would reveal occasional

[1] Bernard S. Lee, J. Acoust. Soc. Am. **22**, 824 (1950).
[2] B. Bloch, Language **24**, 3 (1948).
[3] B. Bloch, Language **26**, 88 (1950).
[4] R. K. Potter and J. C. Steinberg, J. Acoust. Soc. Am. **26**, 807 (1950).

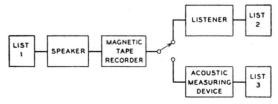

Fig. 1. Recording and measuring arrangements for vowel study.

Reprinted with permission from *J. Acoust. Soc. Am.,* vol. 24, pp. 175–184, Mar. 1952.

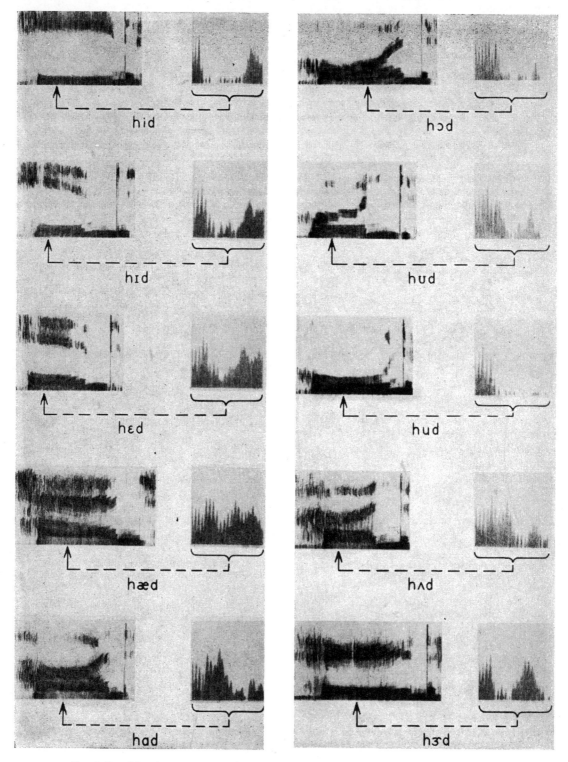

Fig. 2. Broad band spectrograms and amplitude sections of the word list by a female speaker.

differences, or disagreements, between speaker and listener. Instead of being played back to a listener, List 1 might be played into an acoustic measuring device and the outputs classified according to the measured properties of the sounds into a List 3. The three lists will differ in some words depending upon the characteristics of the speaker, the listener, and the measuring device.

A total of 76 speakers, including 33 men, 28 women and 15 children, each recorded two lists of 10 words, making a total of 1520 recorded words. Two of the speakers were born outside the United States and a few others spoke a foreign language before learning English. Most of the women and children grew up in the Middle Atlantic speech area.[5] The male speakers represented a much broader regional sampling of the United States; the majority of them spoke General American.[5]

The words were randomized and were presented to a group of 70 listeners in a series of eight sessions. The listening group contained only men and women, and represented much the same dialectal distribution as did the group of speakers, with the exception that a few observers were included who had spoken a foreign language throughout their youth. Thirty-two of the 76 speakers were also among the 70 observers.

The 1520 words were also analyzed by means of the sound spectrograph.[6,7]

Representative spectrograms and sections of these words by a male speaker are shown in Fig. 3 of the paper by R. K. Potter and J. C. Steinberg;[4] a similar list by a female speaker is shown here as Fig. 2.[8] In the spectrograms, we see the initial [h] followed by the vowel, and then by the final [d]. There is generally a part of the vowel following the influence of the [h] and preceding the influence of the [d] during which a practically steady state is reached. In this interval, a section is made, as shown to the right of the spectrograms. The sections, portraying frequency on a horizontal scale, and amplitude of the voiced harmonics on the vertical side, have been measured with calibrated Plexiglass templates to provide data about the fundamental and formant frequencies and relative formant amplitudes of each of the 1520 recorded sounds.

LISTENING TESTS

The 1520 recorded words were presented to the group of 70 adult observers over a high quality loud speaker system in Arnold Auditorium at the Murray Hill Laboratories. The general purpose of these tests was to obtain an aural classification of each vowel to supplement the speaker's classification. In presenting the words to the observers, the procedure was to reproduce at each of seven sessions, 200 words recorded by 10 speakers. At the eighth session, there remained five men's and one child's recordings to be presented; to these were added three women's and one child's recordings which had been given in previous sessions, making again a total of 200 words. The sound level at the observers' positions was approximately 70 db re 0.0002 dyne/cm², and varied over a range of about 3 db at the different positions.

In selecting the speakers for each of the first seven

[5] C. K. Thomas, *Phonetics of American English*, The Ronald Press Company (New York, 1947).
[6] Koenig, Dunn, and Lacy, J. Acoust. Soc. Am. **17**, 19 (1946).
[7] L. G. Kersta, J. Acoust. Soc. Am. **20**, 796 (1948).
[8] Key words for the vowel symbols are as follows: [i] heed, [ɪ] hid, [ɛ] head, [æ] had, [ɑ] father, [ɔ] ball, [ʊ] hood, [u] who'd, [ʌ] hud, [ɝ] heard.

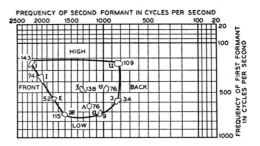

FIG. 3. Vowel loop with numbers of sounds unanimously classified by listeners; each sound was presented 152 times.

sessions, 4 men, 4 women, and 2 children were chosen at random from the respective groups of 33, 28, and 15. The order of occurrence of the 200 words spoken by the 10 speakers for each session was randomized for presentation to the observers.

Each observer was given a pad containing 200 lines having the 10 words on each line. He was asked to draw a line through the one word in each line that he heard. The observers' seating positions in the auditorium were chosen by a randomizing procedure, and each observer took the same position for each of the eight sessions, which were given on eight different days.

The randomizing of the speakers in the listening sessions was designed to facilitate checks of learning effects from one session to another. The randomizing of words in each group of 200 was designed to minimize successful guessing and the learning of a particular speaker's dialect. The seating positions of the listeners were randomized so that it would be possible to determine whether position in the auditorium had an effect on the identification of the sounds.

DISCUSSION OF LISTENING TEST RESULTS

The total of 1520 sounds heard by the observers consisted of the 10 vowels, each presented 152 times. The ease with which the observers classified the various vowels varied greatly. Of the 152 [i] sounds, for instance, 143 were unanimously classified by all observers as [i]. Of the 152 sounds which the speakers intended for [ɑ], on the other hand, only 9 were unanimously classified as [ɑ] by the whole jury.

These data are summarized in Fig. 3. This figure shows the positions of the 10 vowels in a vowel loop in which the frequency of the first formant is plotted against the frequency of the second formant[9] on mel scales;[10] in this plot the origin is at the upper right. The numbers beside each of the phonetic symbols are the numbers of sounds, out of 152, which were unanimously classified as that particular vowel by the jury. It is of interest in passing that in no case did the jury agree unanimously that a sound was something other than what the speaker intended. Figure 3 shows that

[9] R. K. Potter and G. E. Peterson, J. Acoust. Soc. Am. **20**, 528 (1948).
[10] S. S. Stevens and J. Volkman, Am. J. Psychol. 329 (July, 1940).

[i], [ɜ], [æ], and [u] are generally quite well understood.

To obtain the locations of the small areas shown in Fig. 3, the vowels were repeated by a single speaker on twelve different days. A line enclosing all twelve points was drawn for each vowel; the differences in the shapes of these areas probably have little significance.

When the vowels are plotted in the manner shown in Fig. 3, they appear in essentially the same positions as those shown in the tongue hump position diagrams which phoneticians have employed for many years.[11] The terms "high, front, low back" refer to the tongue positions in the mouth. The [i], for instance, is made with the tongue hump high and forward, the [u] with the hump high and back, and the [ɑ] and [æ] with the tongue hump low.

It is of interest that when observers disagreed with speakers on the classification of a vowel, the two classifications were nearly always in adjacent positions of the vowel loop of Fig. 3. This is illustrated by the data shown on Table I. This table shows how the observers classified the vowels, as compared with the vowels intended by the speakers. For instance, on all the 152 sounds intended as [i] by the speakers, there were 10,267 total votes by all observers that they were [i], 4 votes for [ɪ], 6 votes for [ɛ], and 3 votes for [ɔ]. Of the 152 [ɑ] sounds, there was a large fraction of the sounds on which some of the observers voted for [ɔ]. [ɪ] was taken for [ɛ] a sizable percentage of the time, and [ɛ] was called either [ɪ] or [æ] (adjacent sounds on the vowel loop shown in the preceding Fig. 3) quite a large number of times. [ɑ] and [ɔ], and [ʌ] and [ɑ] were also confused to a certain extent. Here again, as in Fig. 2, the [i], [ɜ], [æ], and [u] show high intelligibility scores.

It is of considerable interest that the substitutions shown conform to present dialectal trends in American speech rather well,[12] and in part, to the prevailing vowel shifts observable over long periods of time in most languages.[13] The common tendency is continually to shift toward higher vowels in speech, which correspond to smaller mouth openings.

The listener, on the other hand, would tend to make the opposite substitution. This effect is most simply described in terms of the front vowels. If a speaker produces [ɪ] for [ɛ], for example [mɪn] for [mɛn] as currently heard in some American dialects; then such an individual when serving as a listener will be inclined to write *men* when he hears [mɪn]. Thus it is that in the substitutions shown in Table I, [ɪ] most frequently became [ɛ], and [ɛ] most frequently became [æ]. The explanation of the high intelligibility of [æ] is probably based on this same pattern. It will be noted along the

vowel loop that a wide gap appears between [æ] and [ɑ]. The [a] of the Romance languages appears in this region. Since that vowel was present in neither the lists nor the dialects of most of the speakers and observers the [æ] was usually correctly identified.

The [i] and the [u] are the terminal or end positions in the mouth and on the vowel loop toward which the vowels are normally directed in the prevailing process of pronunciation change. In the formation of [i] the tongue is humped higher and farther forward than for any other vowel; in [u] the tongue hump takes the highest posterior position in the mouth and the lips are more rounded than for any other vowel. The vowels [u] and [i] are thus much more difficult to displace, and a greater stability in the organic formation of these sounds would probably be expected, which in turn should mean that these sounds are recognized more consistently by a listener.

The high intelligibility of [ɜ] probably results from the retroflexion which is present to a marked degree only in the formation of this vowel; that is, in addition to the regular humping of the tongue, the edges of the tongue are turned up against the gum ridge or the hard palate. In the acoustical pattern the third formant is markedly lower than for any other vowel. Thus in both physiological and acoustical phonetics the [ɜ] occupies a singular position among the American vowels.

The very low scores on [ɑ] and [ɔ] in Fig. 3 undoubtedly result primarily from the fact that some members of the speaking group and many members of the listening group speak one of the forms of American dialects in which [ɑ] and [ɔ] are not differentiated.

When the individuals' votes on the sounds are analyzed, marked differences are seen in the way they classified the sounds. Not only did the total numbers of agreements with the speakers vary, but the proportions of agreements for the various vowels was significantly different. Figure 4 will be used to illustrate this point. If we plot total numbers of disagreements for all tests, rather than agreements, the result is shown by the upper chart. This shows that [ɪ], [ɛ], [ɑ], [ɔ], and [ʌ] had the most disagreements. An "average" observer would be expected to have a distribution of disagreements similar in proportions to this graph. The middle graph illustrates the distribution of disagreements given by observer number 06. His chief difficulty was in distinguishing between [ɑ] and [ɔ]. This type of distribution is characteristic of several observers. Observer 013, whose distribution of disagreements is plotted on the bottom graph, shows a tendency to confuse [ɪ] and [ɛ] more than the average.

The distributions of disagreements of all 70 observers differ from each other, depending on their language experience, but the differences are generally less extreme than the two examples shown on Fig. 4. Thirty-two of the 70 observers were also speakers. In cases where an observer such as 06 was also a speaker, the remainder of the jury generally had more disagreements

[11] D. Jones, *An Outline of English Phonetics* (W. Heffer and Sons, Ltd., Cambridge, England, 1947).

[12] G. W. Gray and C. M. Wise, *The Bases of Speech* (Harper Brothers, New York, 1946), pp. 217–302.

[13] L. Bloomfield, *Language* (Henry Holt and Company, New York, 1933), pp. 369–391.

with his [ɑ] and [ɔ] sounds than with the other sounds he spoke. Thus it appears that if a speaker does not differentiate clearly between a pair of sounds in speaking them, he is unlikely to classify them properly when he hears others speak them. His language experience, as would be expected, influences both his speaking and his hearing of sounds.

Since the listening group was not given a series of training sessions for these tests, learning would be expected in the results of the tests.[14] Several pieces of evidence indicate a certain amount of practice effect, but the data are not such as to provide anything more than a very approximate measure of its magnitude.

For one check on practice effect, a ninth test was given the jury, in which all the words having more than 10 disagreements in any of the preceding eight tests were repeated. There was a total of about 175 such words; to these were added 25 words which had no disagreements, picked at random from the first eight tests. On the ninth test, 67 words had more disagreements, 109 had less disagreements, and 24 had the same number of disagreements as in the preceding tests. The probability of getting this result had there been no practice or other effect, but only a random variation of observers' votes, would be about 0.01. When these data are broken down into three groups for the men, women and children speakers, the largest differences in numbers of disagreements for the original and repeated tests was on the childrens' words, indicating a larger practice or learning effect on their sounds. The indicated learning effect on men's and women's speech was nearly the same. When the data are classified according to the vowel sound, the learning effect indicated by the repetitions was least on [i], [ɝ], and [u], and greatest on [ɑ] and [ɔ].

Another indication that there was a practice effect lies in the sequence of total numbers of disagreements by tests. From the second to the seventh test, the total number of disagreements by all observers diminished consistently from test to test, and the first test had considerably more disagreements than the eighth, thus strongly indicating a downward trend. With the speakers randomized in their order of appearance in the eight tests, each test would be expected to have approximately the same number of disagreements. The probability of getting the sequence of numbers of total disagreements which was obtained would be somewhat less than 0.05 if there were no learning trend or other nonrandom effect.

It was also found that the listening position had an effect upon the scores obtained. The observers were arranged in 9 rows in the auditorium, and the listeners in the back 4 rows had a significantly greater number of disagreements with the speakers than did the listeners in the first 5 rows. The effect of a listener's position

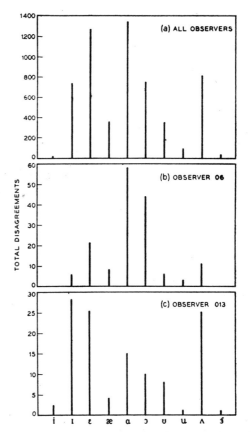

FIG. 4. Observer disagreements in listening tests.

within an auditorium upon intelligibility has been observed previously and is reported in the literature.[15]

ACOUSTIC MEASUREMENTS

Calibrations of Equipment

A rapid calibrating technique was developed for checking the over-all performance of the recording and analyzing systems. This depended on the use of a test tone which had an envelope spectrum that was essentially flat with frequency over the voice band. The circuit used to generate this test tone is shown schematically in Fig. 5. It consists essentially of an overloading amplifier and pulse sharpening circuit. The wave shapes which may be observed at several different points in the test tone generator are indicated in Fig. 5.

The test tone generator may be driven by an input sine wave signal of any frequency between 50 and 2000 cycles. Figure 6(a) shows a section of the test tone with a 100 cycle repetition frequency, which had been recorded on magnetic tape in place of the word lists by the speaker, and then played back into the sound spectrograph. The departure from uniform frequency response of the over-all systems is indicated by the shape of the envelope enclosing the peaks of the 100

[14] H. Fletcher and R. H. Galt, J. Acoust. Soc. Am. 22, 93 (1950).

[15] V. O. Knudsen and C. M. Harris, *Acoustical Designing in Architecture* (John Wiley and Sons, New York, 1950), pp. 180–181.

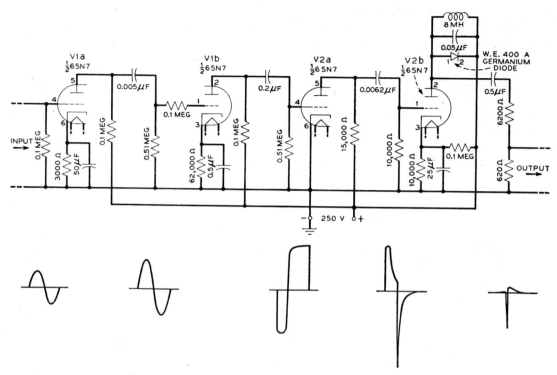

FIG. 5. Schematic of calibrating tone generator.

cycle harmonics. With the 100 cycles from the Laboratories standard frequency oscillator as the drive signal, the frequency calibration of the systems may be checked very readily by comparison of the harmonic spacing on the section with the template scale. The amplitude scale in 6(a) is obtained by inserting a pure tone at the spectrograph in 5 db increments. The frequency scale for spectrograms may also be calibrated as shown in Fig. 6(b). The horizontal lines here are representations of the harmonics of the test tone when the test tone generator is driven by a 500 cycle standard frequency. These lines further afford a means of checking the amount of speed irregularity or wow in the over-all mechanical system. A calibration of the time scale may be obtained by using the test tone generator with 100 cycle drive and making a broad band spectrogram as shown in Fig. 6(c). The spacings between vertical striations in this case correspond to one-hundredth of a second intervals.

In the process of recording some of the word lists, it was arranged to substitute the calibrating test tone circuit for the microphone circuit, and record a few seconds of test tone between the lists of words. When the word lists were analyzed with the spectrograph, the accompanying test tone sections provided a means of checking the over-all frequency response of the recorder and analyzer, and the frequency scale of the sectioner.

The effect of speed variations in either the recorder or the sound spectrograph is to change the frequency scale. A series of measurements with the 100 cycle test tone showed that the tape recorder ran approximately one percent slower when playing back than it did on recording.

The speed variations on the sound spectrograph were measured with the test tone applied directly, and the maximum short time variations were found to be ±0.3 percent. Such direct calibrations of the frequency scale of the spectrograph, during a period of four weeks when most of the spectrographic analysis was done, showed maximum deviations of ±30 cycles at the 31st harmonic of the 100 cycle test tone. During that period a control chart[16] of the measurements of the 3100 cycle component of the test tone showed a downward trend of about 10 cycles, which was attributed to changes in the electonic circuit components of the spectrograph. As a result of these calibration tests, it was concluded that the frequency scale of the sound spectrograph could be relied upon as being accurate within ±1 percent.

Formant Measurements

Measurements of both the frequency and the amplitude of the formants were made for the 20 words recorded by each of the 76 speakers. The frequency position of each formant was obtained by estimating a weighted average of the frequencies of the principal components in the formant. (See reference 4 for a discussion of this procedure.) When the principal components in the formant were symmetrically distributed about a dominant component, such as the second formant of [ʌ] *hud* in Fig. 2, there is little ambiguity

[16] "A.S.T.M. manual on presentation of data," Am. Soc. Testing Materials (Philadelphia, 1945), Appendix B.

in choosing the formant frequency. When the distribution is asymmetrical, however, as in the first formant of [ɜ] *heard* in Fig. 2, the difference between estimated formant frequency and that assigned by the ear may be appreciable.

One of the greatest difficulties in estimating formant frequencies was encountered in those cases where the fundamental frequency was high so that the formant was poorly defined. These factors may account for some, but certainly not all, of the differences discussed later

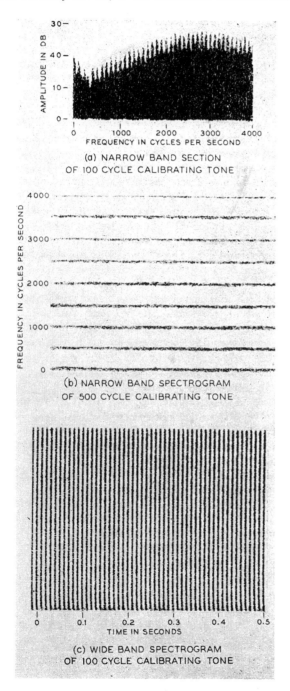

FIG. 6. Spectrograms and section of calibrating tone.

(a) NARROW BAND SECTION
OF 100 CYCLE CALIBRATING TONE

(b) NARROW BAND SPECTROGRAM
OF 500 CYCLE CALIBRATING TONE

(c) WIDE BAND SPECTROGRAM
OF 100 CYCLE CALIBRATING TONE

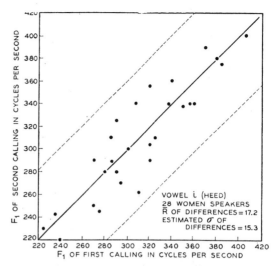

VOWEL i (HEED)
28 WOMEN SPEAKERS
$\bar{R}$ OF DIFFERENCES = 17.2
ESTIMATED σ OF
DIFFERENCES = 15.3

FIG. 7. Accuracy-precision chart of first formant frequencies of [i] as spoken by 28 women.

between vowel classification by ear and by measured values of formant frequencies.

Amplitudes were obtained by assigning a value in decibels to the formant peak. In the case of the amplitude measurements it was then necessary to apply a correction for the over-all frequency response of the system.

The procedure of making duplicate recordings and analyses of the ten words for each of the speakers provided the basis for essential checks on the reliability of the data.

One method by which the duplicate measured values were used is illustrated by Fig. 7. This is a plot of the values for the first formant frequency F_1 of [i] as in *heed*, as spoken by the 28 female subjects. Each point represents, for a single speaker, the value of F_1 measured for the *heed* in the first list, *versus* the value of F_1 for the *heed* in the second list. If the F_1 for the second list or calling was greater than that for the first calling, the point lies above a 45-degree line; if it is less, the point lies below the 45-degree line. The average difference $\bar{R}$ between the paired values of F_1 for first and second callings, was 17.2 cycles. The estimated standard deviation σ derived from the differences between pairs of F_1 values was 15.3 cycles. The dotted lines in Fig. 7 are spaced $\pm 3\,\sigma$ cycles from the 45-degree line through the origin. In case a point falls outside the dotted lines, it is generally because of an erroneous measurement.

Each of the three formant frequencies for each of the 10 vowels was plotted in this way. There were 760 such points for each formant, or a total of 2280 points plotted on 90 accuracy-precision charts like Fig. 7. Of these 2280 points, 118 fell outside the $\pm 3\,\sigma$ limits. On checking back over the measurements, it was found that 88 of the points were incorrect because of gross measurement errors, typographical errors in transcribing the data, or because the section had been made during the influence period of the consonants instead of in the

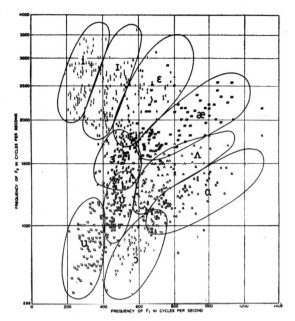

FIG. 8. Frequency of second formant *versus* frequency of first formant for ten vowels by 76 speakers.

fore it is assumed that the data are not statistically random, but that there are statistically significant differences between speakers. Since the measurements for pairs of callings were so nearly alike, as contrasted with the measurements on the same sound for different speakers, this indicated that the precision of measurements with the sound spectrograph was sufficient to resolve satisfactorily the differences between the various individuals' pronunciations of the same sounds.

RESULTS OF ACOUSTIC MEASUREMENTS

In Fig. 3, as discussed previously, are plotted areas in the plane of the second formant F_2 *versus* the first formant F_1. These areas enclose points for several repetitions of the sustained vowels by one of the writers. It is clear that here the vowels may be separated readily, simply by plotting F_2 against F_1; that is, on the F_2-F_1 plane, points for each vowel lie in isolated areas, with no overlapping of adjacent areas, even though there exists the variation of the measured values which we have discussed above.

The variation of the measured data for a group of speakers is much larger than the variation encountered in repetitions with the same speaker, however, as may be shown by the data for F_1 and F_2 for the 76 speakers. In Fig. 8 are plotted the points for the second calling by each speaker, with the points identified according to the speaker's word list. The closed loops for each vowel have been drawn arbitrarily to enclose most of the points; the more extreme and isolated points were disregarded so that in general these loops include about 90 percent of the values. The frequency scales on this and Fig. 9 are spaced according to the approximation to an aural scale described by Koenig, which is linear to 1000 cps and logarithmic above.[17]

Considerable overlapping of areas is indicated, particularly between [ɝ] and [ɛ], [ɝ] and [ʊ], [ʊ] and [u], and [ɑ] and [ɔ]. In the case of the [ɝ] sound, it may be easily distinguished from all the others if the third formant frequency is used, as the position of the third formant is very close in frequency to that of the second.

The data of Fig. 8 show that the distribution of points in the F_1-F_2 plane is continuous in going from sound to sound; these distributions doubtless represent

steady state period of the vowel. When corrected, these 88 points were within the $\pm 3\sigma$ limits. Of the remaining 30 points which were still outside the limits, 20 were the result of the individuals' having produced pairs of sounds which were unlike phonetically, as shown by the results of the listening tests.

The duplicate measurements may also be used to show that the difference between successive utterances of the same sound by the same individual is much less significant statistically than the difference between utterances of the same sound by different individuals. An analysis of variance of the data in Fig. 7 shows that the differences between callings of pairs are not significant. However, the value for the variance ratio when comparing speakers is much larger than that corresponding to a 0.1 percent probability. In other words, if the measurements shown in Fig. 7 for all callings by all speakers were assumed to constitute a body of statistically random data, the probability of having a variance ratio as high as that found when comparing speakers would be less than one in a thousand. There-

TABLE I. Classifications of vowels by speakers and by listeners. Vowels as classified by listeners.

		i	ɪ	ɛ	æ	ɑ	ɔ	ʊ	u	ʌ	ɝ
	i	10267	4	6	...	...	3	...	...	...	...
	ɪ	6	9549	694	2	1	1	...	...	...	26
	ɛ	...	257	9014	949	1	3	...	...	2	51
	æ	...	1	300	9919	2	2	...	...	15	39
Vowels intended by speakers	ɑ	...	1	...	19	8936	1013	69	...	228	7
	ɔ	...	...	1	2	590	9534	71	5	62	14
	ʊ	...	...	1	1	16	51	9924	96	171	19
	u	...	...	1	...	2	...	78	10196	...	2
	ʌ	...	1	1	8	540	127	103	...	9476	21
	ɝ	...	...	23	6	2	3	...	...	2	10243

[17] W. Koenig, Bell Labs. Record **27**, (August, 1949), pp. 299–301.

TABLE II. Averages of fundamental and formant frequencies and formant amplitudes of vowels by 76 speakers.

		i	ɪ	ɛ	æ	ɑ	ɔ	ʊ	u	ʌ	ɝ
Fundamental frequencies (cps)	M	136	135	130	127	124	129	137	141	130	133
	W	235	232	223	210	212	216	232	231	221	218
	Ch	272	269	260	251	256	263	276	274	261	261
Formant frequencies (cps)											
F_1	M	270	390	530	660	730	570	440	300	640	490
	W	310	430	610	860	850	590	470	370	760	500
	Ch	370	530	690	1010	1030	680	560	430	850	560
F_2	M	2290	1990	1840	1720	1090	840	1020	870	1190	1350
	W	2790	2480	2330	2050	1220	920	1160	950	1400	1640
	Ch	3200	2730	2610	2320	1370	1060	1410	1170	1590	1820
F_3	M	3010	2550	2480	2410	2440	2410	2240	2240	2390	1690
	W	3310	3070	2990	2850	2810	2710	2680	2670	2780	1960
	Ch	3730	3600	3570	3320	3170	3180	3310	3260	3360	2160
Formant amplitudes (db)	L_1	−4	−3	−2	−1	−1	0	−1	−3	−1	−5
	L_2	−24	−23	−17	−12	−5	−7	−12	−19	−10	−15
	L_3	−28	−27	−24	−22	−28	−34	−34	−43	−27	−20

large differences in the way individuals speak the sounds. The values for F_3 and the relative amplitudes of the formants also have correspondingly large variations between individuals. Part of the variations are because of the differences between classes of speakers, that is, men, women and children. In general, the children's formants are highest in frequency, the women's intermediate, and the men's formants are lowest in frequency.

These differences may be observed in the averaged formant frequencies given on Table II. The first formants for the children are seen to be about half an octave higher than those of the men, and the second and third formants are also appreciably higher. The measurements of amplitudes of the formants did not show decided differences between classes of speakers, and so have been averaged all together. The formant amplitudes are all referred to the amplitude of the first formant in [ɔ], when the total phonetic powers of the vowels are corrected so as to be related to each other by the ratios of powers given by Fletcher.[18]

Various methods of correlating the results of the listening tests with the formant measurements have been studied. In terms of the first two formants the nature of the relationship is illustrated in Fig. 9. In this figure measurements for all vowels of both callings are plotted in which all members of the listening group agreed with the speaker. Since the values for the men and the children generally lie at the two ends of the distributions for each vowel, the confusion between vowels is well illustrated by their data; thus the measurements for the women speakers have been omitted.

The lines on Fig. 9 are the same as the boundaries drawn in Fig. 8. As indicated previously, some vowels received 100 percent agreement much more frequently than others.

[18] H. Fletcher, *Speech and Hearing* (D. Van Nostrand Company, Inc., New York, 1929), p. 74.

The plot has also been simplified by the omission of [ɝ]. The [ɝ] produces extensive overlap in the [ʊ] region in a graph involving only the first two formants. As explained previously, however, the [ɝ] may be isolated from the other vowels readily by means of the third formant.

When only vowels which received 100 percent recognition are plotted, the scatter and overlap are somewhat reduced over that for all callings. The scatter is greater, however, than might be expected.

If the first and second formant parameters measured from these words well defined their phonetic values; and if the listening tests were an exact means of classifying the words, then the points for each vowel of

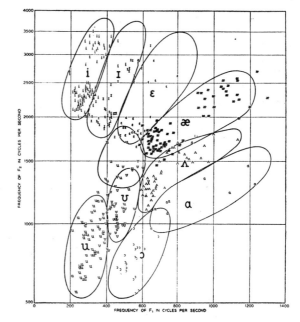

FIG. 9. Frequency of second formant *versus* frequency of first formant for vowels spoken by men and children, which were classified unanimously by all listeners.

Fig. 9 should be well separated. Words judged intermediate in phonetic position should fall at intermediate positions in such a plot. In other words, the distributions of measured formant values in these plots do not correspond closely to the distributions of phonetic values.

It is the present belief that the complex acoustical patterns represented by the words are not adequately represented by a single section, but require a more complex portrayal. The initial and final influences often shown in the bar movements of the spectrograms are of importance here.[19] The evaluation of these changing bar patterns of normal conversational speech is, of course, a problem of major importance in the study of the fundamental information bearing elements of speech.

A further study of the vowel formants is now nearing completion. This study employs sustained vowels, without influences, obtained and measured under controlled conditions. The general objectives are to determine further the most fundamental means of evaluating the formants, and to obtain the relations among the various formants for each of the vowels as produced by difference speakers. When this information has been obtained it is anticipated that it will serve as a basis for determining methods of evaluating and relating the changing formants within words as produced by various speakers.

SUMMARY

The results of our work to date on the development of methods for making acoustic and aural measurements on vowel sounds may be summarized as follows.

1. Calibration and measurement techniques have been developed with the sound spectrograph which make possible its use in a detailed study of the variations that appear in a broad sample of speech.

2. Repeated utterances, repeated measurements at various stages in the vowel study, and randomization in test procedures have made possible the application of powerful statistical methods in the analysis of the data.

3. The data, when so analyzed, reveal that both the production and the identification of vowel sounds by an individual depend on his previous language experience.

4. It is also found that the production of vowel sounds by an individual is not a random process, i.e., the values of the acoustic measurements of the sounds are not distributed in random order. This is probably true of many other processes involving individuals' subjective responses.

5. Finally, the data show that certain of the vowels are generally better understood than others, possibly because they represent "limit" positions of the articulatory mechanisms.

ACKNOWLEDGMENTS

The work which we have discussed has involved the contributions of a number of people. We should like to acknowledge the guidance of Mr. R. K. Potter and Mr. J. C. Steinberg in the plan of the experiment, and the contribution of Dr. W. A. Shewhart who has assisted in the design and interpretation of the study with respect to the application of statistical methods. We are indebted to Miss M. C. Packer for assistance in statistical analyses of the data. We wish to acknowledge also the assistance given by Mr. Anthony Prestigiacomo, Mr. George Blake, and Miss E. T. Leddy in the recording and analysis of the sounds and in the preparation of the data.

---

[19] Potter, Kopp, and Green, *Visible Speech* (D. Van Nostrand Company, Inc., New York, 1947).

Analysis of Nasal Consonants

Osamu Fujimura

University of Electro-Communications, Chofu, Tokyo, Japan

(Received September 5, 1962)

The sound spectra of nasal murmurs in various vowel contexts have been studied by use of an analysis-by-synthesis scheme. The acoustic characteristics are described in terms of format–antiformant distributions (pole–zero locations of the transfer function for the articulatory system) in the frequency domain. It is shown that the location of the antiformant characterizes the murmur of each consonant within the class. The spectral structures are discussed with reference to the articulatory features, and acoustical interpretations of the observed characteristics of the formants and antiformant are given. Also suggested is the existence of certain gross spectral features that are characteristic of nasals as a class.

THE generation of nasal sounds is characterized by two essential features. One is the participation of the nasal passages in the formation of the spectral characteristics of the sound output, and the other is the characteristic condition in the vocal tract proper and its change as a function of time. The latter feature of nasal consonants resembles, to some extent, the feature characterizing the production of stop consonants.[1] The former feature reveals itself most predominantly in the spectral pattern of the nasal murmur, i.e., the sound produced with a complete closure at a point in the oral cavity, and with an appreciable amount of coupling of the nasal passages to the vocal tract.

The present study gives the results of a detailed analysis of a number of samples of nasal murmurs occurring in various vowel contexts. The speech material consisted of natural utterances of nonsense syllables generated by talkers of American English. The experimental data were obtained with a computer, using an analysis–synthesis scheme.[2] An interpretation of the acoustic data is given in terms of the articulation of nasal consonants, following theoretical principles similar to those enunciated by Fant.[3]

I. THEORETICAL CONSIDERATIONS

The entire articulatory system for the production of nasal murmurs, which is shown in the upper part of Fig. 1, consists of three subsystems: (a) the pharynx extending from the glottis to the velum, (b) the oral cavity, with a complete closure at the anterior end, and (c) the nasal tract including the nasopharynx and nasal passages that are terminated by radiation impedances. For discussion of signal components in the frequency range of primary interest, say 200 to 2500 cps, we can assume that these three parts are acoustically coupled to one another only at their ends at the velum. The dimension of the part of the system that serves for this coupling is assumed to be small compared to the wavelengths of the sound components of interest. The transmission through the wall is also assumed to be negligible.

A simplified model for the acoustic system is shown in the lower part of Fig. 1.

Let us represent the volume velocity at the glottis by the time function $u_s(t)$ and the volume velocity at the nostrils by $u_0(t)$. Their Laplace transforms $U_s(s)$ and $U_0(s)$ are related to each other by the transfer function $T(s)$ through the equation

$$U_0(s) = T(s) \cdot U_s(s), \qquad (1)$$

where s is the complex frequency. The transfer function $T(s)$ can be expressed in terms of its poles, represented by s_i, and zeros, represented by s_j, as follows:

$$T(s) = \frac{\prod_{i=1}^{n} \left(1 - \frac{s}{s_j}\right)\left(1 - \frac{s}{s_j^*}\right)}{\prod_{i=1}^{m} \left(1 - \frac{s}{s_i}\right)\left(1 - \frac{s}{s_i^*}\right)} H(s), \qquad (2)$$

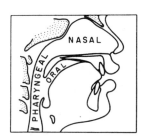

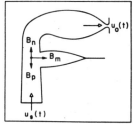

FIG. 1. The upper figure is a tracing from a radiograph showing a midsagittal section of the vocal and nasal tracts during production of the nasal consonant /n/. The structure of the articulatory system is schematized in the lower figure as a joined three-tube model. The figure also indicates the source and output volume velocities $u_s(t)$ and $u_0(t)$, and shows the velopharyngeal coupling point where the susceptances B_p, B_m, and B_n looking into the pharynx, mouth, and nose are defined.

[1] O. Fujimura, J. Speech Hearing Research 4, 233–247 (1961).

[2] C. G. Bell, H. Fujisaki, J. M. Heinz, K. N. Stevens, and A. S. House, J. Acoust. Soc. Am. 33, 1725–1736 (1961).

[3] C. G. M. Fant, *Acoustic Theory of Speech Production* (Mouton and Company, 's-Gravenhage, The Netherlands, 1960).

Reprinted with permission from *J. Acoust. Soc. Am.*, vol. 34, pp. 1865–1875, Dec. 1962.

where m and n are appropriately selected numbers, for example five and one, respectively (see *infra*). The correction term $H(s)$ represents the effect of poles and zeros of frequency higher than those accounted for in the products.[3] Except for this correction term, which is considered to be a relatively smooth function of frequency, the characteristics of the transfer function are specified completely within the frequency range of interest by the locations of the limited number of m poles and n zeros.

In order to estimate the essential structure of the transfer function $T(s)$, it is profitable to begin discussion by assuming a nondissipative system. The poles and zeros of the transfer function for the lossless case lie on the imaginary axis of the s plane, and their frequencies can be estimated semiquantitatively by a graphical method.[3] If we assume that the three subsystems— pharyngeal, nasal, and oral—can be approximated by three acoustic tubes that transmit plane waves and in general have varying cross-section areas along the direction of sound transmission, then we can find the locations of the poles and zeros of $T(s)$ by examining the driving-point susceptances looking into the three tubes from the coupling point. These susceptances are defined in Fig. 1 as B_p, B_n, and B_m, as shown. The locations of the poles of $T(s)$, i.e., the formant frequencies, are in general given by the frequencies where the sum of the susceptances looking in all possible directions at any arbitrary point in the system is zero. Thus at the coupling point, in particular, the internal susceptance $B_i = B_p + B_n$ must be equated to the negative of the driving-point susceptance B_m looking into the mouth cavity to obtain the formant frequencies. The zeros of $T(s)$ occur at frequencies for which $B_m = \infty$, since at these frequencies the mouth cavity short-circuits transmission to the nose.

Figure 2 gives sketches of the susceptance curves for articulatory configurations that are considered to represent typical productions of /m/ and /n/. From the general theory of linear lossless networks, a driving-point susceptance is always a monotonically increasing function of frequency except at singularities. The locations of the zero-crossing points and the singularities of the susceptance curves can be estimated grossly from the geometrical configurations of the tracts corresponding to the given articulation. Since the oral cavity is terminated by a complete closure and the nostrils are open for normal articulations of nasal murmurs, the susceptance curve for B_m starts from the origin and the internal susceptance B_i starts from minus infinity.

If the mouth cavity is not coupled to the main tube (viz., the pharyngo-nasal tract), as in the case of /ŋ/ approximately, the axis-crossing points (i.e., the zeros) of the internal susceptance B_i give the formant frequencies. These frequencies are designated by arrows in Fig. 2. When coupling to the mouth cavity is introduced, the normal modes are perturbed and a shift in

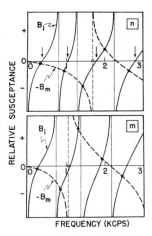

FIG. 2. Frequency characteristics of the susceptances B_i and B_m, assuming the acoustic system to be lossless. The internal susceptance B_i is the sum of the susceptance B_p and B_n shown in Fig. 1. The upper graph was drawn for the /n/ configuration and the lower graph for the /m/ configuration, based on the analysis data of utterances by a male speaker (KS). The arrows in the upper graph indicate the zeros of B_i, which coincide approximately with the formants observed during the production of /ŋ/. The open circles identify the first singularity of B_m and hence show the locations of antiformants. The solid points identify the points of intersection of the curves, corresponding to the resonance condition $B_i + B_m = 0$, and thus predict the frequencies of the formants.

the formant frequencies is observed. The altered formant frequencies are given by the locations of the intersections of the two curves (closed circles in the figure), where the condition $B_m + B_n + B_p = 0$ is satisfied. The density of the zero-crossing points of B_i depends on the acoustical length of the composite main tube extending from the glottis to the nostrils. The average spacing of these formants of the uncoupled system along the frequency axis is about 800 cps for a typical male speaker. This value is appreciably smaller than the average spacing of about 1000 cps for vowels, and the difference is ascribed to the unequal lengths of the nasal and oral cavities.

The location of the first pole of B_m, i.e., the first resonant frequency of the mouth cavity when it is open to a free field at its posterior end, is usually not lower than 700 cps, and is lower for /m/ than for /n/ (see *infra*). This antiresonance observed in the output, or "antiformant" as it may be called, probably constitutes the only zero of $T(s)$ in the low- to middle-frequency ranges. The second singularity of B_m usually seems to occur near 3000 cps or higher for /m/, and is much higher for /n/.

Once we know the essential structure of the transfer function for the lossless case in which the poles and zeros lie on the imaginary axis, we can account for the effect of damping on the output spectrum in an approximate manner by adding appropriate real parts to the poles and zeros. The amount of damping is not necessarily the same for each pole or zero, nor is it well established in the available data reported so far. There are some estimations, however, both from analyses of the spectra of natural utterances and from analog-synthesis experiments.[3-5] The present study supplies further information on the damping factors for the poles and zeros of $T(s)$.

The acoustic output that is of most interest is the sound pressure $P_d(s)$ picked up at a distance d from the speaker's face. If the radiation from the nostrils is approximated by that from a simple spherical source,[6] then the sound pressure is related to the output-volume velocity $U_0(s)$ by

$$P_d(s) = (s\rho/4\pi d)\cdot\exp(-sd/c)\cdot U_0(s), \qquad (3)$$

where ρ is the density of air and c is the velocity of sound in air.

In our simplified model of the articulatory system, an assumption is made that the nasal tract consists of a single acoustic tube. In reality, of course, the nasal system at a central point branches into two separate tubes, each of which opens at one of the nostrils. If the system is symmetric with respect to the point at which the sound is measured, this geometrical branching is acoustically immaterial. In this case, we can legitimately interpret the output signal $U_0(s)$ in (1) as representing the total volume velocity from the nostrils, and we can predict the frequency characteristics of the susceptance B_n on the basis of the simple tube model.

When the two nasal passages are appreciably different in their acoustical dimensions, we may define a virtual output-volume velocity $U_0(s)$ by the formula (3), $P_d(s)$ being an observable quantity. In such a case, however, the volume velocity, which may be interpreted as a total output at the nostrils, no longer represents the output from a single nasal tube, and the effective transfer function $T_e(s) = U_0(s)/U_s(s)$ may contain additional pole–zero pairs in a relatively high-frequency region. We can assume, however, that the effect of these pole–zero pairs on the spectrum within the frequency range of interest is small, and can be represented by a smoothly changing function of frequency. This deviation function can be absorbed into the over-all correction term (see *infra*).

By combining (1), (2), and (3), we obtain

$$P_d(s) = (s\rho/4\pi d)\exp(-sd/c)$$

$$\times\frac{\displaystyle\prod_{j=1}^{n}\left(1-\frac{s}{s_j}\right)\left(1-\frac{s}{s_j{}^*}\right)}{\displaystyle\prod_{i=1}^{m}\left(1-\frac{s}{s_i}\right)\left(1-\frac{s}{s_i{}^*}\right)}H(s)\cdot U_s(s). \qquad (4)$$

Since we are interested in comparing the calculated spectrum to the observed spectrum, we shall take the

absolute value of (4) and put $s = j\omega$, ω being the radian frequency. The amplitude spectrum of the source $|U_s(j\omega)|$ contains the so-called harmonic structure when the system is excited by a periodic glottal source. If we take the envelope of the spectrum, however, the peaks and valleys in the spectrum are consequences of the product terms of the poles and zeros[7] in Eq. (4). Both $|H(j\omega)|$ and the envelope of $|U_s(j\omega)|$ can be represented by slowly varying functions of frequency, and they contribute only to the gross slope of the spectrum. As a first approximation, the envelope of $|U_s(j\omega)|$ can be represented by a constant slope of -12 dB/octave on a logarithmic frequency scale, i.e., by a term proportional to ω^{-2}. The first term of (4), which represents the transfer characteristic of the radiation, is proportional to ω and introduces a constant slope of $+6$ dB/octave. We now transfer these major effects of the source and the radiation to the left-hand side of the formula, and we introduce a new over-all correction term $K(\omega)$, which takes care of the possible deviations of these two functions from the first approximations above as well as the magnitude of the higher-pole correction term $H(j\omega)$. The factor $K(\omega)$ may also contain correction terms representing the effects of the asymmetry of the nasal passages, and possibly the effects of the nonrigid walls of the cavities and the nonrigid termination at the glottis. Thus we obtain the following relation between the spectrum envelope $E(\omega)$ and the poles and zeros of the transfer function:

$$\kappa\omega E(\omega) = K(\omega)\left|\frac{\displaystyle\prod_{j=1}^{n}\left(1-\frac{j\omega}{\sigma_j+j\omega_j}\right)\left(1-\frac{j\omega}{\sigma_j-j\omega_j}\right)}{\displaystyle\prod_{i=1}^{m}\left(1-\frac{j\omega}{\sigma_i+j\omega_i}\right)\left(1-\frac{j\omega}{\sigma_i-j\omega_i}\right)}\right|, \qquad (5)$$

where κ is a constant which varies according to the absolute signal level at the point where the sound is observed. In deriving (5) from (4), we have put $s_i = \sigma_i + j\omega_i$ and $s_j = \sigma_j + j\omega_j$.

II. EXPERIMENTAL PROCEDURE

Preparation of the Speech Materials

The speech materials used in the experimental study were drawn from a large group of nonsense utterances generated by three talkers.[8] These utterances were all of the form /hə'CVC/, i.e., a stressed consonant–vowel–consonant syllable preceded by an unstressed syllable. In the case of syllables with /m/ and /n/, the initial and final consonants were identical. The consonant /ŋ/ occurred in final position only, in utterances of the form

[4] K. Nakata, J. Acoust. Soc. Am. **31**, 661–666 (1959).
[5] A. S. House, J. Speech Hearing Disorders **22**, 190–204 (1957).
[6] Experimental evidence supporting this approximation is found in J. L. Flanagan, J. Acoust. Soc. Am. **32**, 1613–1620 (1960).

[7] Furthermore, depending on the particular waveform of the glottal vibration, the envelope of the source spectrum may be represented by a number of zeros which are densely distributed in the frequency domain; cf., M. V. Mathews, J. E. Miller, and E. E. David, Jr., J. Acoust. Soc. Am. **33**, 179–186 (1961).
[8] A. S. House, J. Acoust. Soc. Am. **33**, 1174–1178 (1961).

/hə'rVŋ/. For each of these syllables a variety of vowels was used.

In preparation for further analysis, quantized intensity–frequency–time representations of all of these utterances were obtained in a form suitable for processing by a digital computer.[2] The speech was passed through a bank of 36 filters, covering the frequency range 100 to 7200 cps, the filter outputs were rectified, smoothed, and sampled periodically at 8.3-msec intervals, and the sampled outputs were quantized in 1-dB steps. The "digital spectrogram" for each utterance was stored on punched tape, and these data were then available to be read into the memory of the computer in preparation for further processing by the analysis-by-synthesis techniques.

General Method of Spectrum Reduction

A previous paper has described a procedure utilizing a digital computer for obtaining accurate data on the pole–zero distributions for the vocal-tract transfer function from spectral samples of natural utterances.[2] In the present study this procedure, with minor modifications, has been used for the analysis of spectral samples of nasal murmurs.

The basic steps in the analysis procedure are the following: (a) the operator specifies the locations of a set of poles and zeros in the complex-frequency plane, viz., the poles and zeros of the right-hand side of Eq. (5), including a set of poles and zeros to approximate the

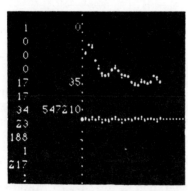

FIG. 3. Photograph of display on the cathode-ray tube of the digital computer when the pole and zero locations have been adjusted to match a spectral sample of /n/. On the graph, the points on the vertical axis represent 5-dB steps in amplitude; each point on the horizontal axis represents one of the 36 filter outputs. These curves are displayed: the input speech spectrum (upper curve of light points), the comparison spectrum (upper curve of heavy points), and the difference curve. The three numbers 17, 34, and 23 at the left show the magnitude of the absolute, variation, and squared-error scores over 24 filter points, that is, up to about 3050 cps. The number 35 appearing near the center of the display represents the sample number (the time location of the sampled spectrum) within the utterance. The other numbers are not relevant to this discussion. The frequencies (bandwidths) in cps of the poles and zeros used to construct the comparison spectrum in this example are: poles at 300 (30), 1050 (120), 1450 (100), 2000 (200), 2650 (100), 3300 (200), 3600 (200); zero at 1600 (450), plus a correction for higher poles. See reference 2 for a discussion of this type of display.

correction factor $K(\omega)$; (b) a trial spectrum corresponding to this configuration of poles and zeros is computed internally in the analyzer; (c) this spectrum is compared with the speech spectrum to be analyzed, and measures of the goodness of fit between the two spectra are computed; (d) the pole and zero locations are modified by the operator until a satisfactory match is obtained between the trial spectrum and the spectrum under analysis. The set of poles and zeros that yields the best-fitting spectrum is then assumed to characterize the input spectrum. The computation of each trial spectrum includes a calculation that takes into account the characteristics of the filters that perform the initial processing of the speech, and the spectrum is then specified at 36 points corresponding to the center frequencies of the 36 filters. The difference between input and trial spectra is thus calculated at each of 36 points. These calculations are performed after the over-all level of the trial spectrum in relation to the input spectrum is adjusted so that the sum of the difference values over the frequency range of interest is zero.

The calculated and input spectra are displayed on the cathode-ray tube of the computer, together with the difference values. An example of such a display is shown in Fig. 3. The display also indicates three measures of the goodness of fit, calculated from the error curve. One of these error scores, to which reference will be made in the later discussions, is the sum of the squares of the difference values (square sum). In the present study, visual inspection of the curves displayed on the cathode-ray tube provided the principal basis for the judgment as to whether the calculated spectrum gave a satisfactory match with the input spectrum. The error scores were also taken into consideration, and these were recorded to provide a quantitative description of the goodness of fit. The frequency range over which the error scores were calculated could be selected by the experimenter; for most of the study, the lowest 24 channels (up to 3100 cps) were used for fitting of spectra of /n/ and /ŋ/, and 20 channels (up to 2300 cps) were used for /m/.

In general, a number of spectral samples at 8.3-msec intervals was analyzed successively for a given nasal consonant. When a satisfactory match for a given spectral sample was obtained, i.e., when no appreciable improvement in the accuracy of the data in terms of the pole–zero distribution was expected for further adjustments of the poles and zero(s), then the locations of the poles and zero(s) that gave the match were recorded, and the next spectral sample was tried. It was sometimes necessary to make many adjustments of the poles and zeros before a reasonable match with a given input spectrum was obtained.

Matching of Spectra of Nasal Murmurs

The strategy that prescribes how to adjust the pole–zero locations in order to find a best match is **not** necessarily simple or mechanical. Limitations have to be imposed on the choice of the pole–zero distributions, since it is possible that different distributions provide a good fit with a given spectral sample. One constraint governing the selection of pole–zero distributions is imposed by the requirement that the frequencies of the poles and zeros must change continuously with time within the murmur period and cannot perform discontinuous jumps during the few milliseconds between spectral samples. Another requirement is, of course, that the pole–zero distributions must be compatible with the theoretical considerations that are given above and are epitomized in the graphs of Fig. 2.

In order to predict the approximate locations of the poles for spectral samples of /m/ or /n/ it is necessary first to find the approximate frequencies of the zeros of B_i in Fig. 2. These can be determined empirically by examining spectral samples of utterances of /ŋ/. The poles required for matching spectra of /ŋ/ should be almost the same as the zeros of B_i, since the length of the mouth cavity for the /ŋ/ configuration is short, and hence no antiformants are to be expected in the frequency region below 3000 cps. Thus as a preliminary to a study of /m/ and /n/ spectra, matches were obtained for a number of spectral samples of /ŋ/ uttered by three talkers in several vowel contexts. Four conjugate pairs of poles were required below 3000 cps to obtain these matches; the frequency ranges of the poles were 250–400 cps, 950–1150 cps, 1700–2200 cps, and 2300–3000 cps. For a given talker these ranges were more limited. For talker KS, whose utterances were most intensively analyzed in the study, the frequencies of the four formants for /ŋ/ were typically 350, 1050, 1900, and 2750 cps, and the dependence on vowel context was rather small. Since these values are in agreement with previously reported data[3,5,9] and are also reasonable in view of the dimensions of the articulatory system, they were used to indicate the average positions of the zeros of B_i, and hence to determine the approximate shape of the B_i curves.

In addition to the B_i curve in Fig. 2, it is necessary to know roughly the frequency of at least the first pole of B_m for the /m/ and /n/ configurations in order to predict the approximate pole–zero distributions for the spectra of these sounds. Some previous studies have provided data on this antiformant frequency, and it is known that the first singularity of B_m occurs at about 1000 cps or lower for /m/, and in the range of 1500–2000 cps for /n/.[3,5,9,10]

Keeping these values and the graphical structures shown in Fig. 2 in mind, we examined a number of spectral samples of /m/ and /n/ in a preliminary way, in order to gain experience with the matching technique and to determine the approximate frequency ranges to

be expected for the formants and antiformants. Practical representations of the correction curve $K(\omega)$ in terms of distributions of a set of poles and/or zeros in the complex-frequency domain were also tested before proceeding to a systematic collection of data. In matching the spectra of /n/, it was determined that a suitable correction curve could be constructed by locating fixed poles at 4500, 5000, 5500, and 7000 cps and two "buffer poles" in the range 3000–4000 cps. The buffer poles were adjusted, if necessary, to improve the fit in the upper part of the frequency range under consideration. Thus it was necessary to adjust the frequencies and bandwidths of seven poles (the five poles shown in Fig. 2 plus the two buffer poles) and one zero in order to obtain a spectrum that matched a spectral sample of /n/.

In the case of /m/, the frequency range within which a match was to be obtained was restricted to 100–2300 cps, corresponding to 20 filter channels, in order to avoid the necessity of including a second antiformant. Two fixed zeros on the negative real axis, located at 1000 cps and 2000 cps, served to represent the average effect of the higher poles and zeros. This simpler specification of the correction curve was found to be quite appropriate as far as its influence on the pertinent frequency range was concerned. Again the frequencies and bandwidths of seven poles and one zero were adjusted in order to obtain a match for each spectral sample of /m/.

With the practical procedure thus established, the accuracy of the spectral matches in terms of the square sum was typically 20 to 40 dB^2 for the lowest 20–24 filter channels, although occasionally it was not possible to obtain such a good match. In some utterances, an additional pole–zero pair above the main frequency range was inserted to match the spectrum near the high-frequency end of the pertinent range. Likewise, an auxiliary pole–zero pair (mostly in the frequency range 0 to 500 cps) was inserted in order to improve the match at low frequencies, presumably representing a deviation of the source spectrum from the ideal slope of −12 dB/octave.

III. RESULTS

Examples of intervocalic nasal consonants occurring in 14 different words of the type described previously were closely studied by the matching techniques just outlined. Ten of these words were spoken by KS, and provided versions of /m/ and /n/ before each of the five stressed vowels /iɛæɑu/. The remaining four, spoken by JM, contained /m/ and /n/ followed by /ɛ/ and by /ɑ/. For each of these intervocalic nasal consonants, matches were obtained for every spectral sample throughout the nasal murmur. Many other spectral samples in both intervocalic and final /m/ and /n/ and in final /ŋ/, in various vowel contexts, were matched for portions of the murmur periods. These supplemental materials

[9] S. Hattori, K. Yamamoto, and O. Fujimura, J. Acoust. Soc. Am. **30**, 267–274 (1958).

[10] S. Horiguti, Japan. Z. Oto-Rhino-Laryngol. **49**, 551–575 (1943) (in Japanese).

consisted of utterances by three speakers, two of whom were KS and JM.

Movements of the Formants and Antiformants

Since spectral matches were made throughout the entire duration of the nasal murmurs, it was possible to

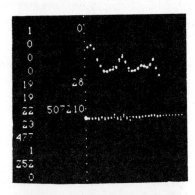

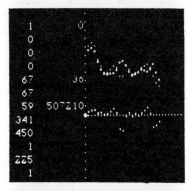

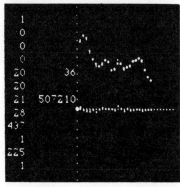

FIG. 4. Three photographs of computer display showing typical changes that occur in the spectrum during an utterance of /m/ in intervocalic position. The upper photograph shows the results of matching a spectral sample (No. 28) near the beginning of the /m/. The frequencies (bandwidths) in cps of the poles and zero at frequencies below 2500 cps are: poles at 280 (60), 940 (30), 1240 (30), 1950 (300), 2560 (50); zero at 980 (50). The middle photograph shows the result obtained when the same comparison spectrum is matched against a spectral sample (No. 36) 67 msec later in the utterance. The square-sum-error score is 341 dB², as compared to 23 dB² in the match above. In the lower photograph the frequencies (bandwidths) of the poles and zero of the comparison spectrum have been adjusted to: poles at 290 (30), 980 (40), 1360 (50), 1950 (300), 2300 (120); zero at 1170 (50). This comparison spectrum provides a better fit (square sum 28 dB²) to spectrum No. 36.

trace the movements of the poles and zeros continuously during these intervals. An example of the changes that occur in the pole–zero configuration is demonstrated in Fig. 4, which gives the cathode-ray tube display for two spectral samples in the intervocalic nasal /m/ in the syllable /hə'mim/. The first sample (No. 28) occurred approximately 35 msec after the beginning of the /m/, and the second sample (No. 36) occurred about 65 msec later, or about 40 msec before the explosion into the front vowel. The poles and zeros were adjusted to give a reasonable match to the first sample, as shown in the upper part of Fig. 4. When the same trial spectrum was compared with the second sample (Fig. 4, middle portion), a large error score (341 dB²) was obtained, indicating that the poles and zero had shifted. When the frequencies and bandwidths of the poles and zero were readjusted, the match shown in the lower portion of Fig. 4 was obtained. It is interesting to note that the two spectra have quite different appearances, particularly in the central frequency region, even though the framework of the pole–zero distribution is not altered (see infra).

This variability that is observed in the spectrum for a relatively restricted kind of change in the formant–antiformant structure indicates that it may be difficult to describe the characteristics of individual nasal consonants in terms of their spectra. As a matter of fact, the uppermost sample of /m/ in Fig. 4 apparently resembles the spectral sample from /n/ shown in Fig. 3 more closely than it does the lower /m/ sample of Fig. 4.

The change of the pole–zero distribution throughout the entire intervocalic nasal murmur in the word /hə'mim/ is shown in the upper portion of Fig. 5. The interval from samples 25 to 40 corresponds to the time during which the lips are closed. For the first four samples the zero is located very close to one of the poles, with the result that the effect of this pole–zero pair on the spectrum is minimized. Toward the later part of the murmur period the zero shifts upward and the frequency of the pole immediately above it rises gradually at the same time.

In the lower portion of Fig. 5 similar data are plotted for the intervocalic /n/ in the utterance of /hə'nɑn/ by the same speaker. The most conspicuous change occurs in the portion close to the boundary of the following vowel, where the zero shifts downward in frequency and the pole immediately below it also moves downward. At the last sample, the zero apparently overtakes the pole. The frequency of the second pole gradually increases over the entire interval, and there are slight changes in the first, fourth, and fifth poles.

Comparison of Nasals in Different Vowel Environments

Data for each of the two nasals in five vowel environments for speaker KS are summarized in Fig. 6; similar utterances of words containing the vowel /ε/ by the

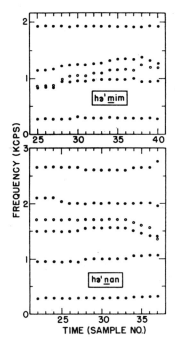

FIG. 5. Frequencies of formants (closed circles) and antiformants (open circles) for typical utterances of intervocalic /m/ (upper graph) and /n/ (lower graph) plotted against time throughout the murmur periods. Time samples are 8.3 msec apart. The data are illustrative of transitions that occur as a result of articulatory movement during the production of nasal murmurs. Sample 35 in the lower portion of the figure corresponds to the spectrum in Fig. 3; samples 28 and 36 in the upper portion correspond to the spectra in Fig. 4.

speaker JM are shown for comparison. In addition, the locations of poles for the uncoupled nasal /ŋ/ are indicated by arrows for each of the two speakers. Of the three points connected by lines, the point at the left corresponds to the second sample within the consonant, the middle point represents the sample at the center of the interval, and the point at the right represents the next-to-last sample within the interval.

When we compare the upper and lower portions of Fig. 6, we see a clear difference in the location of the antiformant (zero) for the two nasals /m/ and /n/. The zero is located between 750 cps and 1250 cps for /m/ and between 1450 cps and 2200 cps for /n/. Since the zero for /ŋ/ is above 3000 cps, it can be said that the nasals /m/, /n/, and /ŋ/ are characterized by low, medium, and high positions of the antiformant, respectively. Furthermore, the antiformant changes its position appreciably from word to word and also within the same utterance, depending on the change in the configuration of the oral cavity. The antiformant seems to have a considerable influence on the formants in its immediate vicinity, but other formants within the frequency range of interest remain relatively constant, at least for the same speaker. Thus for /m/, the first and the fourth formants are almost invariant and the second and third formants with the antiformant form a variable "cluster." For /n/, on the other hand, the variable cluster consists of

the third and fourth formants and the antiformant, and the first, second, and fifth formants are relatively stable. The structure of the cluster can change radically, i.e., the order of the two formants and one antiformant on the frequency axis is not always the same (see *infra*).

The variability is, however, limited only to that in local structures, and the location of the antiformant normally falls within a distinctly defined range for the individual consonant, as described above. In other words, the difference between the murmur sounds of the three nasal consonants may be described in the following way: /ŋ/ has four formants in the main frequency range (up to about 3000 cps), /n/ is obtained when the third of the formants is replaced by a cluster consisting of two formants and one antiformant, /m/ is obtained when the second formant is replaced by a similar cluster.

Damping

The damping of the resonance or antiresonance is another important factor that may characterize nasal sounds when compared with oral sounds.[4,5] This study has supplied quantitative data on the bandwidths of the formants and antiformant, but unfortunately the accuracy of the data in this respect is not as high as that of the data on the frequencies of the formants or antiformant. Certain errors can stem in part from the

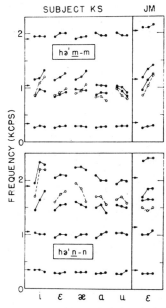

FIG. 6. Data on formant (closed circles) and antiformant (open circles) locations for examples of /m/ (upper graph) and /n/ (lower graph) in intervocalic position preceding the different vowels identified on the abscissa. In each case the three joined points represent samples in a given nasal consonant; from left to right the points represent a spectral sample located close to the beginning of the nasal murmur, a centrally located sample, and a sample close to the end of the nasal murmur. Each right-hand sample, therefore, reflects an immediate influence of the following vowel. Data for two subjects are shown. For each subject the arrows at the left represent the locations of the formants for utterances of /ŋ/ (cf., Fig. 2).

TABLE I. Values of half-power bandwidths in cps of formants and antiformants for various intervocalic nasal consonants. Averages are taken for spectral samples throughout the nasal murmur in five vowel contexts; data for one talker (KS).

	/m/	/n/	/ŋ/
Formant 1	60	40	80
2	60	100	100
3	90	110	230
4	280	170	100
5	170	100	...
Antiformant	80	600	...

approximate method used to calculate the comparison spectrum, in part from the harmonic structure of the observed spectrum, and in part and probably most unpredictably from the lack of precise knowledge concerning the voice–source characteristic $|U_s(\omega)|$. Reliable conclusions can, however, be drawn from some characteristics that are consistently observed in the data. On the average, bandwidths of formants observed in the samples of nasal murmurs are comparable to or greater than those observed in vowels. Individual formants, however, have different amounts of damping, and the bandwidths are not necessarily constant nor monotonically related to the frequency of the formant. Table I shows the average values of the half-power bandwidths corresponding to each of the poles and zeros. The averages were taken for /m/ and /n/ separately over the entire periods of the intervocalic nasals in the five words containing different vowels. In the case of /n/, the second, third, and fifth formants have comparable bandwidth values on the average, and the fourth, which is normally located slightly above 2000 cps, has an appreciably higher damping. The tendency is the same in /m/, but the fourth formant seems to have still wider bandwidths than those of /n/, and the second and third formants have appreciably narrower bandwidths than the corresponding formants of /n/. More notable, however, is the very wide bandwidth of the antiformant of /n/ as compared with the rather sharp antiformant of /m/. In the case of /ŋ/, the third formant, somewhat below 2000 cps, always had a wider bandwidth than the second and the fourth formants.

The tendencies observed above for the frequencies and bandwidths of the formants and antiformant for speaker KS were consistently seen for other speakers also. There seems little doubt, therefore, that the above findings illustrate typical features of the nasal consonants. The present data indicate, however, that certain details, particularly the location of the highest pole within the frequency region considered above, are quite dependent on individual speakers.

IV. DISCUSSION

The data of Figs. 5 and 6, which were obtained by examining the acoustic spectra of nasal murmurs, can be used to infer the nature of the articulatory configurations that gave rise to the sounds. The analysis is made by comparing the data on pole–zero locations with susceptance sketches of the type shown previously in Fig. 2.

Frequency and Bandwidth of Antiformant

Figure 6 shows that the frequency of the antiformant for /m/ is relatively high when the consonant precedes a front vowel such as /i/, and is lower when the context is a back vowel. A simple calculation shows that this antiformant would occur at about 1000 cps if the mouth cavity were a uniform tube of length 8 cm. When /m/ precedes a front vowel, the anterior part of the oral cavity during the /m/ is narrowed in anticipation of the vowel, and acoustical theory would predict a consequent rise in the frequency of the first pole of B_m. In the case of the back vowel context (/ɑ/ and /u/ in Fig. 6), the anticipatory tongue position results in a large mouth cavity with a comparatively narrow neck, with a consequent decrease in the frequency of the antiformant.

Similar effects of the adjacent vowel are noted in the case of /n/, although now the mouth cavity is smaller than for /m/, and the antiformant occurs at a higher frequency. The average value of the antiformant frequency for /n/ in various vowel contexts is about 1700 cps. If a uniform tube were assumed as a crude model of the oral acoustic system, the effective length would be about 5 cm. In a similar fashion, a mouth tube less than 3 cm in length would give rise to an antiformant frequency above 3000 cps, and would correspond to the generation of /ŋ/.

It was mentioned in the preceding section that the antiformant of /n/ has considerably more damping than that of /m/. In the case of /n/, the wedge-shaped termination of the oral cavity causes a gradual change in characteristic impedance and hence results in relatively large absorption of sound energy at the termination. The configuration of the oral cavity for /m/, on the other hand, has a rather abrupt termination, and the mouth cavity has a smaller ratio of surface area to volume. The acoustic losses in the oral cavity are, therefore, less appreciable, and the bandwidth of the antiformant is smaller.

Interpretation of Formants

The interpretation of the poles of the transfer function, viz., the formants of nasal consonants, is more complex than the interpretation of the zeros because, in general, we have to consider the effects of all three of the constituent tracts (see *supra*). The behavior of the formant–antiformant distribution as a consequence of a change in the articulatory conditions can be understood most easily if we interpret the acoustic characteristics of the articulatory system in terms of the singularities of the three driving-point admittances looking into the oral, pharyngeal, and nasal cavities from the velum.

Let us consider a frequency range that lies between two adjacent singularities of the internal admittance B_i, for example, the frequency range 800–1300 cps in the upper portion of Fig. 2. The curve B_i has always one zero-crossing point within such a range, and this point gives the frequency of a formant of the uncoupled system. If the antiformant is not within this range, we can always find one and only one formant of the coupled system, and its frequency is generally different from the formant frequency of the uncoupled system. In particular, if the frequency range is below the frequency of the lowest antiformant, the formant of the coupled system is always lower in frequency than that of the uncoupled system. The amount of the shift is generally small if the formant is located far away from the antiformant, or if the pertinent frequency range is very narrow, i.e., if the two singularities of B_i are closely located. In the present data, in good conformity with the statement above, the first formants of /m/ and /n/ were found to be somewhat lower than that of /ŋ/ in general. The second formant of /n/ also was generally lower than that of /ŋ/.

If an antiformant is located within the frequency range between two singularities of B_i, then two formants as well as the antiformant occur within the region, replacing the formant of the uncoupled system. Their locations and the degree of concentration of the cluster change considerably from case to case. The formants are always located on either side of the antiformant, however, and they also lie on either side of the formant frequency of the uncoupled system. In other words, there cannot be a singularity of B_i immediately next to the antiformant without having a formant in between. (There is always one singularity of B_i between any two adjacent formants when no antiformant lies between the formants.) When the formant and antiformant are located close to each other, the singularity is also close to the formant. If the antiformant shifts continuously toward a singularity of B_i, then the formant–antiformant pair tends toward the latter, and finally the order of the antiformant and the formant is inverted as the antiformant crosses the singularity of B_i. Thus an annihilation of a formant–antiformant pair can occur if and only if the antiformant frequency coincides with the frequency of a singularity of B_i, i.e., coincides with a characteristic frequency of either the pharyngeal or nasal cavity. Therefore, by observing an annihilation or a crossing of such a pair in the output spectrum, we can conclude that a singularity of the internal admittance exists at that frequency. It should be mentioned, however, that the location of this annihilated pair can be determined only when the movement of the pair is traced continuously for a considerable period of an utterance. Examples are seen in Figs. 5 and 6.

In the upper portion of Fig. 5, a superposition of the second formant and the antiformant is observed in the beginning portion of /m/, and hence there is a singularity of B_i at this frequency, i.e., at about 800 cps. For the reasons given below, this lowest (except one at the origin) singularity of B_i is considered to correspond to the lowest short-circuit resonance of the nasal cavity. In the lower portion of Fig. 5, toward the end of /n/, a similar annihilation is observed for the third formant and the antiformant at about 1400 cps. The singularity of B_i at this frequency is probably the lowest short-circuit resonance of the pharynx cavity. The marked descent of the antiformant in this case is caused by the retraction of the tongue in anticipation of the back vowel.

In Fig. 6, the antiformant for /m/ is generally found in the vicinity of the second formant. If we inspect this frequency region in the light of the rules given above, we conclude that the location of the lowest singularity of B_i is relatively constant (just below 1000 cps) regardless of the coarticulation. The next higher singularity of B_i, on the other hand, seems to shift its location considerably depending on the tongue position (probably near 1000 cps before /u/ and around 1500 cps before front vowels). When the tongue is retracted in anticipation of the high back vowel /u/, the pharyngeal cavity must be narrowed significantly at its upper end (near the coupling point), and hence the location of the singularity of B_p (the susceptance looking into the pharynx) must be lowered. Conversely, a higher position of this singularity is expected for an /m/ anticipating a front vowel. The data for /m/ depicted in Fig. 6, therefore, provide evidence that the lowest singularity of B_i is a singularity of B_n, and the next is a singularity of B_p. The singularity of B_n is always around 850–1000 cps for the data of the speaker KS. Other data of different speakers, however, indicate somewhat less stability of this singularity of B_n. It is expected that this frequency generally shifts from utterance to utterance, to some extent randomly depending on the height of the velum, and of course from subject to subject depending on the individual nasal-tract configuration. It is theoretically not impossible, in an extreme case, that the singularity of B_p descends so much (in the case of a coarticulation of a high back vowel) that it becomes lower than the singularity of B_n.

The data of Fig. 6 show in general that there are some formants that remain relatively unaffected by the change of articulatory conditions. The second formant of /n/, for example, is located always around 1000 cps for all samples of /n/. This relatively constant location of the second formant for /n/ is partially explained by the relatively constant location of the next lower singularity, which is a singularity of B_n. Probably the susceptance looking into the pharynx for the articulation of /n/ is comparatively high (and positive) in this frequency range. (Consequently, as seen in the upper diagram of Fig. 2, the curve of B_i rises rapidly from minus infinity, and the formant is bound close to the singularity of B_i.) If this is true, we can regard the second formant for /n/ approximately as a resonance of the nasal-tract proper. Since at this frequency the nasal tract opens into a low impedance at its posterior end, the formant will remain unchanged unless the position of the velum is altered significantly.[11]

Also at a relatively fixed position is the fourth formant of /m/, which for speaker KS is at about 2000 cps. For /n/, on the other hand, the fourth formant varies considerably with the context, being as high as 2300 cps before the vowel /i/, while the fifth formant is relatively fixed at 2600–2700 cps. The particularly wide bandwidth of the fourth formant of /m/ may be interpreted as an indication that this formant is affiliated to the nasal cavity. At this frequency, probably all of the three susceptances have small magnitudes, and consequently the nasal tract may be regarded as having nearly an open-circuit resonance.

V. COMMON CHARACTERISTICS OF NASAL MURMURS

As was discussed in the preceding sections, the appearance of the spectra of nasal murmurs may vary considerably from one sample to another, depending on the individual nasal consonant and its context; the spectra also depend on the individual speaker who utters the sound, or even his temporary physiological state. The spectrum envelope can be altered significantly by a slight modification of the pole–zero pattern. The structure of the cluster, in particular, is of primary importance in determining the relative levels of the local spectral peaks in the middle-frequency range. The variability of the relative levels even within one nasal murmur presumably causes an inherent difficulty for an automatic recognition scheme that is based on a straightforward analysis.

The perceptual impression of nasal sounds is somehow substantially different from that of other speech sounds. It is reasonable, therefore, to assume that there are some gross acoustic features that characterize the nasals as a class. In view of our data concerning the structure of the spectral envelope, it may be said that the following three features characterize the spectra of nasal murmurs in general: (1) the existence of a very low first formant that is located at about 300 cps and is well separated from the upper formant structure; (2) relatively high damping factors of the formants; and (3) high density of the formants in the frequency domain (and the existence of the antiformant).

In gross terms, the latter two characteristics in combination give rise to an even distribution of the sound energy in the middle-frequency range between, say, 800 cps and 2300 cps. There is neither a prominent

energy concentration nor an appreciably wide and deep spectral "valley" in any portion of this frequency range. This feature, when combined with the very low location of the first spectral peak, cannot be found in other vocalics. Diffuse vowels, for example, have similar low first formant frequencies, but there is an apparent concentration of the sound energy either toward the low end or high end of the middle-frequency range depending on the grave-acute distinction.[3,12,13]

The first general feature results in a relatively well-defined low concentration and a consistent lack of energy in the range just above it (around 600 cps). This frequency range in the vicinity of 600 cps can be influenced by a low antiformant of /m/, but it is not likely to have strong components, for the following reason. The location of the lowest singularity of B_i, which is considered to represent the short-circuit resonance of the nasal cavity, is relatively constant regardless of the tongue articulation; it cannot be very low in frequency during the phonation of a nasal murmur because the back opening of the cavity has to be open. When the antiformant frequency is very low, there can be a formant below the singularity of B_n, but, according to the rules stated in the previous section, the antiformant has to be below the formant in this case. Thus, even for the lowest possible antiformant frequency, say 700 cps, there cannot be a predominant influence of the next higher formant upon the frequency range around 600 cps.

This relatively stable spectral characteristic in the low-frequency range may be of some practical value in the formulation of criteria for identifying nasal consonants as a class. A preliminary experiment has suggested that the murmur samples of the nasals in various contexts always give a good match with a standard curve when the comparison of the spectra is made in a limited range such as 200 to 1000 cps. A combination of this feature with the above-mentioned gross feature in the middle-frequency range may constitute a reliable criterion for the automatic recognition of the class of nasal consonants.

VI. CONCLUDING REMARKS

It has been shown that the spectral structure of nasal murmurs can be described in a unified and compact form in terms of the pole–zero distribution of the transfer function of the articulatory system. Through semiquantitative consideration of the admittance curves the task of finding the pole–zero distribution was made feasible, and reconstruction of the spectra using the theory as a guide has resulted in satisfactory fits between the calculated spectra and the measured spectra.

---

[11] This interpretation agrees with the description of the formant given by Fant.[3] The location of the formant also compares very well with Fant's data and with the data reported by House.[5]

[12] R. Jakobson and M. Halle, *Fundamentals of Language* (Mouton and Company, 's-Gravenhage, The Netherlands, 1956).
[13] K. N. Stevens and A. S. House, J. Speech Hearing Research **4**, 303–320 (1961).

The procedure used to achieve the matches is by no means simple or mechanical, however; the strategy of finding better fits is rather involved, and a machine could hardly replace the human operator at the stage of this study. Since the manual operation was so complex and time-consuming, the amount of spoken material which could be examined in this experiment was quite limited.

In order to automatize the matching process, it is desirable to find a set of variables that incorporates some of the constraints imposed on the pole–zero structures of nasal murmurs. One possibility is that the frequencies of the poles and zero(s) be computed from plausible sets of values of the locations of the singularities (and zero crossings) of the susceptances B_p, B_n, and B_m, assuming appropriate relations between the admittance levels. Perhaps even more desirable is a procedure that tracks articulatory rather than acoustic parameters. In such a scheme, the articulation of the sound is specified in terms of several articulatory variables, the output spectrum is computed from the articulatory description, and the computed spectrum is compared with the observed spectrum.[14] In a recognition scheme of the analysis-by-synthesis type, it is very advantageous to control a set of variables that is directly linked to the speech-production mechanism because then we can immediately exploit our knowledge about the physical restrictions of the motor activities and also about the linguistic or phonetic rules that govern the utterance of the language the speaker talks. The principle of continuity of articulatory movements between a vowel and a nasal when they are adjacent

may, for example, be of great help in finding parameter values that yield spectral matches for nasal murmurs.

In the present study we have discussed only one portion of the acoustic continuum that is influenced by a nasal consonant, namely, the nasal murmur. Although it is possible within the class of nasals to separate /m/, /n/, and /ŋ/ on the basis of the location of the antiformant, there is no doubt that the formant transitions of the adjacent vowels often play a more important or even dominant role in the recognition of the individual nasals.[15]

ACKNOWLEDGMENTS

This study was made possible by the use of a computer program for pole–zero matching and of speech material, both prepared by the Speech Communication Group at the Research Laboratory of Electronics, MIT. Thanks are due to the members of the group, in particular to John M. Heinz and Hiroya Fujisaki for their advice and assistance concerning the use and modifications of the program. Many stimulating discussions and helpful suggestions contributed by Kenneth N. Stevens and Arthur S. House, as well as the constant and understanding encouragement of Morris Halle, are most sincerely appreciated. The spectrum matching was performed on the TX-O computer, a facility of the Research Laboratory of Electronics, MIT.

This work was performed while the author was on the staff of the Research Laboratory of Electronics, Massachusetts Institute of Technology. The work was supported in part by the U. S. Army Signal Corps, the Air Force Office of Scientific Research, and the Office of Naval Research; in part by the Air Force Cambridge Research Laboratories under Contract AF 19(604)-6102; and in part by the National Science Foundation under Grant G-7364.

---

[14] J. M. Heinz, "Reduction of Speech Spectra to Descriptions in Terms of Vocal-Tract Area Functions," Quart. Progr. Rept. 64, Research Laboratory of Electronics, MIT (January 15, 1961), pp. 198–203. Also, J. M. Heinz, "Analysis of Speech Spectra in Terms of a Model of Articulation," Proceedings of the IVth International Congress on Acoustics, Copenhagen, Denmark, August 1962, and Proceedings of the Speech Communication Seminar, Stockholm, Sweden, August 1962.

[15] A. M. Liberman, P. C. Delattre, F. S. Cooper, and L. J. Gerstman, Psychol. Monograph No. 8, 1–13 (1954).

On the Properties of Voiceless Fricative Consonants*

JOHN M. HEINZ AND KENNETH N. STEVENS

*Department of Electrical Engineering and Research Laboratory of Electronics,
Massachusetts Institute of Technology, Cambridge, Massachusetts*

According to an acoustical theory of speech production, the spectra of voiceless fricatives can be characterized by poles and zeros whose frequency locations are dependent on the vocal-tract configuration and on the location of the source of excitation within the vocal tract. The locations of the important poles and zeros in the spectra of fricatives can be determined by a matching process whereby comparison spectra synthesized by electric circuits are matched against the spectra under analysis. This method has been used to determine the frequencies and bandwidths of the important poles and zeros for several versions of /f/, /s/, and /ʃ/. Based on these findings, a simplified electrical model is developed for the synthesis of voiceless fricatives. The model consists of a noise-excited electric circuit characterized by a pole and a zero whose frequency locations can be varied. Stimuli generated by this model, both in isolation and in syllables, are presented to listeners for identification. The results of the listening tests are consistent with the data from the acoustic analyses and with the findings of other investigators.

A T the present time, the production, the perception, and the acoustical properties of the voiceless fricative consonants are only partially understood. At the level of speech production it is known that the sounds are generated as a result of turbulence and other nonlinear processes in a vocal tract of fairly complicated shape,[1,2] but a satisfactory quantitative theory that describes this situation in detail has yet to be developed. At the level of the acoustical signal, some analyses of fricatives have been made,[2–5] but a detailed discussion of significant acoustical features of fricatives and of their statistical distributions in various contexts has not been given. The perception of fricatives has been studied by various methods, particularly by synthesis techniques,[6–8] but our understanding of the important cues is far from complete.

The study to be reported here reviews the acoustic theory of the production of fricative consonants. This theory is then used as a point of departure for an analysis of the acoustic spectra of a small sample of fricatives and for an experimental investigation of the synthesis and perception of this class of consonants. Thus, the present study represents an attempt to follow a unified approach, based at the articulatory level, for the examination of fricatives at the acoustical and perceptual levels.

ACOUSTICAL PROPERTIES OF FRICATIVE CONSONANTS

A mid-sagittal section through the vocal tract during production of a typical fricative is shown in Fig. 1. The articulatory configuration is characterized by a rather narrow constriction, the position of which depends upon the particular consonant. Air is forced through this constriction at high velocity, and turbulent flow occurs in the vicinity of the constriction and possibly also at the teeth. Noise is generated as a result of the turbulent flow, and this noise acts as excitation for the acoustic tube that forms the constriction and for the cavities anterior to the constriction. There may also be some acoustical coupling through the constriction to the rear cavities.

Experimental studies suggest that the equivalent plane-wave noise source within the vocal tract has a low internal acoustical impedance and a relatively broad spectrum.[2,9,10] Thus, an equivalent-circuit representation of the production of fricative consonants would have the form shown in Fig. 2. This equivalent circuit differs from the usual vowel circuit representation in several respects: (1) the source is a constant-

* This work was supported in part by the U. S. Army (Signal Corps), the U. S. Air Force (Office of Scientific Research, Air Research and Development Command), and the U. S. Navy (Office of Naval Research); and in part by the U. S. Air Force under contract.

[1] W. Meyer-Eppler, Z. Phonetik, usw. **7**, 196 (1953).

[2] G. Fant, *Acoustic Theory of Speech Production* (Mouton and Company, The Hague, 1960); also Tech. Rept. No. 10, Speech Transmission Laboratory, Royal Institute of Technology, Stockholm, Sweden, 1958.

[3] T. Tarnoczy, Acta Linguistica (Budapest) **4**, 313 (1954).

[4] G. W. Hughes and M. Halle, J. Acoust. Soc. Am. **28**, 303 (1956).

[5] P. Strevens, Language and Speech **3**, 32 (1960).

[6] K. S. Harris, Language and Speech **1**, 1 (1958).

[7] G. Rosen, "Dynamic analog speech synthesizer," Sc.D. thesis, Massachusetts Institute of Technology, January, 1960; also Tech. Rept. No. 353, Research Laboratory of Electronics, Massachusetts Institute of Technology, February, 1960.

[8] K. Nakata, J. Radio Research Lab. (Japan) **7**, 319 (1960).

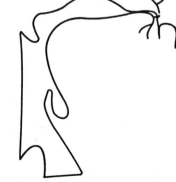

FIG. 1. Midsagittal section illustrating an articulatory configuration appropriate to the fricative consonant /s/ (adapted from Fant[2]).

[9] J. M. Heinz, Mass. Inst. Technol. Acoustics Lab., Quart. Rept. (October–December 1956) p. 5.

[10] J. M. Heinz, Mass. Inst. Technol. Research Lab. Electronics, Quart. Progr. Rept. (July 15, 1958), p. 146.

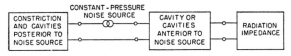

FIG. 2. An equivalent circuit representation of the production of fricative consonants.

pressure noise source rather than a periodic constant-velocity source; (2) the source is located within the vocal tract rather than at the glottis; (3) additional damping is introduced by turbulence losses at the constriction and also by losses at the glottis and below, since the glottis remains somewhat more open than during vowel production in order that air may flow continuously through the tract. These differences indicate that, for fricative consonants, the energy-density spectrum of the acoustic output signal is continuous and is characterized by approximately the same poles (or resonances) as those that characterize a vowel spectrum produced with the same vocal-tract configuration.[11] The poles are simply the natural frequencies of the vocal tract and do not depend on the location of the source.[12] In the case of fricatives, however, usually some of the poles are more heavily damped

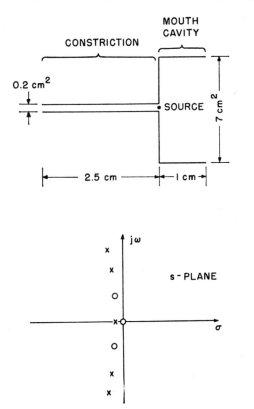

FIG. 3. An idealized model of the vocal tract for the production of the fricative consonant /s/, together with a pole-zero plot of the transfer ratio appropriate to this configuration and source location.

[11] C. G. M. Fant, Mass. Inst. Technol. Acoustics Lab., Tech. Rept. No. 12 (January, 1952).

[12] For a discussion of this property of linear systems, see, for example, E. A. Guillemin, *Synthesis of Passive Networks* (John Wiley & Sons, Inc., New York, 1957), Chap. 1.

because of the additional losses. Zeros (or antiresonances) characterize the output spectra of fricatives at frequencies for which the driving-point impedance of the portion of the vocal tract posterior to the noise source is infinite, i.e., at poles of that impedance. At these frequencies the source is decoupled from the front cavities.

The transfer function relating the sound pressure produced at a distance in front of a speaker to the equivalent source sound pressure (expressed as a function of the complex frequency $s = \sigma + j\omega$) can be described by the product

$$T(s) = [P(s) \cdot R(s)]Z(s), \qquad (1)$$

where $P(s)$ is a function containing the poles that represent the natural frequencies of the vocal tract, $R(s)$ is the radiation characteristic, and $Z(s)$ is a function containing the zeros of the transfer function. The first two factors are approximately the same as those constituting the transfer function for a vowel produced with the same vocal-tract configuration as the fricative. (The vowel transfer function relates the sound pressure at a distance to the volume velocity of the glottal source.) The last factor in Eq. (1), containing the zeros, is dependent on the position of the noise source, and does not occur in the vowel transfer function. Quantitatively, $T(s)$ is of the form

$$T(s) \propto \left[s \cdot \prod_i \frac{s_i s_i^*}{(s-s_i)(s-s_i^*)} \right] \cdot \prod_j \frac{(s-s_j)(s-s_j^*)}{s_j s_j^*}(s-s_g),$$

where $\prod$ denotes a product of terms, s^* denotes the complex conjugate of s, s_i are the poles of the transfer function, s_j are the zeros of the transfer function, and s_g is a real-axis zero dependent upon glottal losses.

A male vocal tract is approximately 17 cm in length, giving rise to resonances spaced, on the average, 1000 cps apart. Since, in a particular example, the source may be posterior to the mouth opening, the average spacing of the antiresonances is more than 1000 cps. If a long narrow constriction is formed in the vocal tract near the mouth opening, some of the resonances and antiresonances tend to move together in pairs in such a way as to cancel any net effect on the spectrum of the output. Since the average spacing of the antiresonances is greater than that of the resonances, this cancellation cannot obtain throughout the entire frequency range, but is usually effective below the frequency for which the length of the constriction is a quarter wavelength. Above this frequency, there is a region in which there are more poles than zeros and these are sufficiently well separated to permit each to have its individual effect on the spectrum. Thus, a definite formant structure appears, and typically several formants are prominent. In addition, the first formant normally is heavily damped and the bandwidths of the first few formants reflect the presence of losses greater than those typical of vowel production.[2]

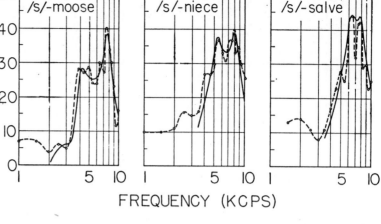

FIG. 4. Comparison of spectra measured by Hughes and Halle[4] for the fricative /s/ as spoken by one subject in different contexts (dashed curves), and spectra obtained as the output of appropriate electric networks (solid curves).

The pole-zero cancellation may also be viewed differently: the cancellation may be considered to occur because the coupling between the source and back cavities is small. Thus, for a vocal-tract configuration with a narrow constriction the output spectrum is approximately unchanged if the back cavities are neglected. The prominant formants in the spectrum are very nearly those arising from the natural frequencies of the front cavities and possibly the constriction. The antiresonances in this approximation are then contributed solely by the constriction. If the constriction is not sufficiently narrow or long, this approximation may not adequately describe the output spectrum.

As an example, consider the highly idealized representation of the /s/ configuration, shown in Fig. 3. The acoustical output of the configuration is characterized by poles whose frequencies are the natural frequencies of the front cavity and of the constriction and by zeros at frequencies for which the impedance looking back from the source is large. For the idealized structure depicted in Fig. 3, there are two poles and one zero in the frequency range below 10 000 cps, at the relative locations shown in the diagram of the s-plane in the figure. The frequency locations for the two poles correspond closely to frequencies for which the length of the constriction

is $\lambda/2$ (one-half wavelength) and the length of the front cavity is $\lambda/4$, i.e., 6800 and 8600 cps, respectively. The zero is located at a frequency for which the length of the constriction is $\lambda/4$, in this case 3400 cps. In this example, it is possible to associate specific resonances with specific cavities because the impedance levels or cross-sectional areas of the two cavities are quite different, and consequently there is relatively little interaction between the two cavities.

Although a model of the type shown in Fig. 3 is highly idealized, it gives results that are in general agreement with measured spectra of spoken fricative consonants. An electrical analog of such a model would be a linear electric circuit whose transfer function is characterized by an appropriate set of poles and zeros.

In Fig. 4 measured spectra[4] for the fricative /s/ as produced by one speaker in several different words are shown as dashed lines. The solid lines show the spectra that were obtained at the output of an appropriate electric circuit when excited by white noise; the transfer function of the circuit from source to output is characterized by two conjugate pairs of poles and by a conjugate pair of zeros. By proper selection of the center frequencies and bandwidths of the poles and zeros, it was possible

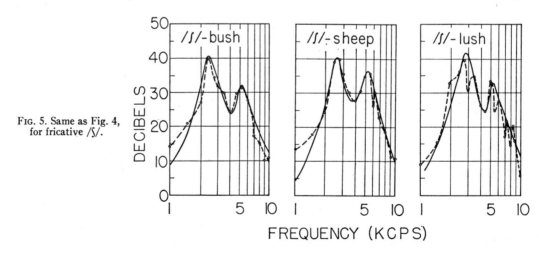

FIG. 5. Same as Fig. 4, for fricative /ʃ/.

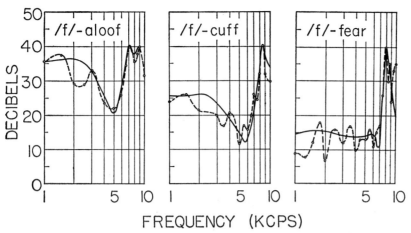

FIG. 6. Same as Fig. 4, for fricative /f/.

to obtain a reasonably good fit to each of the measured spectra, as the figure demonstrates.

Measured spectra for /ʃ/ and /f/ in several contexts are shown as dashed lines in Figs. 5 and 6, respectively. The solid lines are again spectra obtained from simple electric circuits. A circuit having two conjugate pairs of poles and a conjugate pair of zeros was used to generate the /ʃ/ spectra. In addition, the noise source had a spectrum with a slope of +18 db/octave up to 3000 cps and a flat characteristic above 3000 cps. This low-frequency rising characteristic compensates in part for an actual pole-zero pair that occurs in the speech spectrum, typically a zero near 900 cps and a pole (corresponding to the second vowel formant) near 2000 cps. The presence of this pole-zero pair has been verified in close examination of /ʃ/ spectra.[13] The two poles and zero of the circuit for /ʃ/ are located at frequencies higher than the simulated pole-zero pair, but in general they are at lower frequencies than the poles and zero for /s/.

A circuit and source similar to that used for the /s/ spectra was used in the generation of the /f/ spectra in Fig. 6. The frequencies of the principal poles and zeros for /f/ are considerably higher than those for /s/, since the lengths of the constriction and of the cavity anterior to the constriction for /f/ are quite short, of the order of 1 or 2 cm depending to some extent upon whether the adjacent vowel is rounded or unrounded. The half-wavelength resonance (correponding to a pole in the output spectrum) for a tube of length 2 cm, for example, is about 8000 cps. It was found that some of the /f/ spectra were characterized by broad low-frequency noise in addition to the high-frequency peaks; for these sounds it was necessary to add low-frequency noise electrically in order to obtain good agreement with the measured spectra. A possible source of this low-frequency noise is turbulence at the lips beyond the constriction; this source is relatively uncoupled to the vocal-tract cavities.

[13] J. M. Heinz, J. Acoust. Soc. Am. **32**, 1517 (A) (1960).

Table I presents a summary of data for several examples of /ʃ/, /s/, and /f/ in different contexts. The table shows that the variation in pole and zero locations from one version of a fricative to another is often quite large. This variation is evidence of appreciable influence of the adjacent vowel on the articulation of a fricative; additional differences are to be expected from one subject to another. The natural speech spectra shown here were measured with filters having bandwidths of 100 cps, and hence exhibit resonances which have greater bandwidths than do the resonances of actual speech. A more accurate procedure would be to pass the sounds generated by electric circuits through the same filters that are used to measure the speech spectra before comparing the two.

TABLE I. Frequencies and bandwidths (in cps) of poles and zeros of the transfer functions of electric circuits that were used to generate spectra providing good matches with spectra of /ʃ/, /s/, and /f/ spoken in the words shown at the left. The speech spectra are from the data of Hughes and Halle,[4] and are samples of utterances of one speaker. Two poles and one zero were used to match all the spectra. In order to match the spectra of /ʃ/ an additional circuit was added to provide a relatively sharp cut-off for frequencies below 3000 cps, as explained in the text; low-frequency noise was added to the synthesized spectra in order to match some of the /f/ spectra at low frequencies.

Sample	First pole frequency	First pole band width	Second pole frequency	Second pole band width	Zero frequency	Zero band width
/ʃ/-sheep	2400	400	5400	1100	3400	1800
/ʃ/-shack	2200	600	5100	1000	3900	1500
/ʃ/-sure	2500	500	4300	1100	3400	1400
/ʃ/-bush	2200	400	4900	1100	3800	1400
/ʃ/-leash	2400	500	4800	900	3700	1400
/ʃ/-lush	2700	600	5400	900	4400	1600
/s/-sect	6400	900	8000	1400	2900	1100
/s/-soothe	3500	600	8100	700	2700	1100
/s/-salve	5700	800	8000	1200	2900	1100
/s/-moose	4000	600	8000	600	3300	1000
/s/-niece	4900	700	8400	1100	2400	1300
/s/-bus	4600	800	8000	800	2300	1100
/f/-fear	7900	900	8200	900	6800	600
/f/-cuff	8400	1000	12200	1000	5900	1100
/f/-aloof	6800	1000	9000	1100	4600	1000

The general procedure of matching speech spectra with spectra generated by simple linear circuits in order to obtain data on frequency locations of poles and zeros in speech spectra has much to recommend it.[14] Since a match is found over the entire spectrum rather than just at the peaks, it is possible to obtain data that are more accurate than those found by a method that locates spectral peaks or valleys. This is particularly true if the spectrum is noisy so that the formants are not well defined, or if two formants lie close together with the result that the spectrum does not have two separate peaks. In these cases, the additional information gained by considering the effect of a pole or zero over the whole spectrum is quite important.[2] The method also lends itself to an unambiguous definition of a formant frequency as a resonant frequency or pole of the vocal tract which produced the sound.[15,16] A natural frequency of the vocal tract may not always be identical with the frequency of a peak in the spectrum, especially if two formants lie close together. A procedure that takes the entire spectrum shape into account, however, allows a formant frequency to be determined in many cases in which the spectrum does not show an obvious or distinct peak in the vicinity of that frequency.

SYNTHESIS AND PERCEPTION OF FRICATIVE CONSONANTS

Reasonably good approximations to the fricative spectra in Figs. 4–6 could be obtained by white noise excitation of circuits that are characterized by one (conjugate-pair) zero and by only one (conjugate-pair) pole instead of two. The output spectra for such circuits would have the same shapes as the spectra plotted in Figs. 4–6, at least up to a frequency somewhat above the frequency of the first major peak. Examination of a number of spectra from the Hughes-Halle paper[4] suggest that the best simple fit is obtained when the frequency of the zero of the circuit is roughly an octave below the pole frequency. A basic circuit having this property was used for the generation of all stimuli in the perceptual tests to be described here. A typical output spectrum of the circuit when excited by white noise is shown by the solid curve of Fig. 7.

In order to allow for examples of /f/ and /θ/ which may have additional broad low-frequency energy, as mentioned earlier, low-frequency noise was added electrically to some of the basic stimuli that have resonant frequencies above 6500 cps. Typical spectra of the low-frequency noise are shown by the dashed lines in Fig. 7, in which the values 0, −7, and −14 db represent the level of the low-frequency noise relative to the level of the noise in the unmodified stimulus.

[14] One of the early attempts to use this technique was reported by D. Lewis [J. Acoust. Soc. Am. 8, 91 (1936)], who matched simple resonance curves to vowel spectra in the vicinity of the spectral peaks.

[15] L. Hermann, Arch. Physiol. 58, 264 (1894).

[16] J. L. Flanagan and A. S. House, J. Acoust. Soc. Am. 28, 1099 (1956).

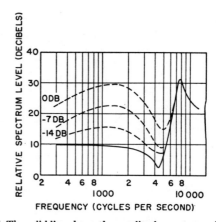

Fig. 7. The solid line shows the amplitude spectrum of a typical stimulus used in the fricative identification tests. When the resonant frequency was 6500 or 8000 cps, some stimuli were modified by the addition of low-frequency noise, yielding spectra like those shown by dashed lines. The parameter is the level of the low-frequency noise relative to the level of the noise in the unmodified stimulus.

The purpose of the perpetual tests to be described here is to determine whether a highly idealized analog circuit characterized by one pole and one zero can generate stimuli that elicit appropriate responses from human listeners, and to establish ranges of pole-zero locations that are associated with particular fricative responses.

Identification of Isolated Synthetic Fricatives

In the first perceptual test, which was an exploratory experiment, sounds of the type described above were generated in isolation. The resonant frequency of the circuit was varied through several values from 2000 to 8000 cps. As noted above, the frequency of the anti-resonance was constrained to lie one octave below the frequency of the resonance. For each resonant frequency, the resonance bandwidth was given three different values that encompassed the range of bandwidths observed in the spectra of fricatives reported by Hughes and Halle. At 2000 cps, the half-power bandwidth values were 170, 300, and 500 cps, and at 8000 cps they were 1000, 1500, and 2000 cps. When the resonant frequency was 6500 or 8000 cps, additional stimuli with three values of low-frequency noise were generated: the levels of low-frequency noise were those shown in Fig. 7.

The stimuli were tape recorded in random order and were presented over a high-quality loudspeaker in a sound-treated studio to a group of six subjects who were asked to identify each by making one of the responses /ʃ,ç,s,θ,f/. Each stimulus was presented four times to each subject in the course of the test. The level of each sound was the same, as measured with a VU meter, and the duration of each sound was fixed at about 200 msec. The subjects were members of the speech research group at the Massachusetts Institute of Technology.

No significant differences in response were obtained over the range of bandwidths used, and consequently

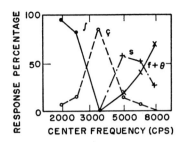

FIG. 8. Results of identification test for isolated synthetic fricative consonants. The abscissa represents the resonant frequency of the electric circuit used to generate the stimuli. Responses of /f/ and /θ/ are combined.

the responses for the three bandwidth values were averaged. In Fig. 8, the response percentages are plotted as a function of the center frequency of the noise for the stimuli that contained no additional low-frequency energy (solid line of Fig. 7, for example). A consistent shift in responses from /ʃ/ to /ç/ to /s/ to /f,θ/ is obtained as the resonant frequency is increased. Distinctions between /f/ and /θ/ could not, apparently, be made for these isolated stimuli, and hence these responses are lumped together. Addition of low-frequency noise to the stimuli with resonant frequencies at 6500 and 8000 cps did not cause an appreciable shift in the pattern of responses; the /f,θ/ responses increased slightly at the expense of /s/ responses.

The results of the exploratory test demonstrate that a consistent pattern of responses is obtained with isolated stimuli. It is reasonable to expect, however, that the identification of a fricative consonant may be dependent not only on the spectrum of the steady-state portion of the sound but also on the formant transitions of the adjacent vowel or vowels and on the intensity of the fricative relative to that of the vowel. In order to examine the role of these cues, it is necessary to generate stimuli consisting of syllables.

Identification of Fricative-Vowel Syllables

The fricative portions of the stimuli in the fricative-vowel syllable test were synthesized in the same manner as those in the test of isolated stimuli. Fricatives with the following five values of resonant frequency were generated: 2500, 3500, 5000, 6500, and 8000 cps. When the resonant frequency was 6500 or 8000 cps, additional stimuli with two levels of low-frequency noise were used, designated 0 and −10 db (cf. Fig. 7). Thus, nine noise spectra were tested, four of which were characterized by additional low-frequency noise. Only one value of bandwidth was selected for each resonant frequency, since the test of isolated fricatives showed that the responses were relatively independent of bandwidth over a 2:1 range in bandwidth. The resonance bandwidths at 2500, 3500, 5000, 6500, and 8000 cps were 400, 600, 800, 1000, and 1500 cps, respectively.

The test syllables consisted of each of the nine noise spectra followed by the synthetic vowel /ɑ/. A schematized intensity-frequency-time pattern of a typical stimulus, together with graphs showing the modulating signals controlling the synthesizer, are shown in Fig. 9.

The vowel was generated by a resonance synthesizer.[17] Timing of fricative onset and decay, vowel onset and decay, and formant transitions was accomplished by a timer and control apparatus designed by Rosen.[7] The over-all level of the fricative relative to the vowel (at the input to the tape recorder) was given three values: −5, −15, and −25 db. The resonant frequencies of the synthesizer were controlled to execute piecewise-linear transitions from a set of starting frequencies or loci[18] to frequencies appropriate to the vowel /ɑ/. The starting frequency for the first-formant transition was 200 cps, and the starting frequency for the second-formant transition was 900, 1700, or 2400 cps; there was no third-formant transition. The time at which the formant frequencies began moving in a piecewise-linear fashion from these starting frequencies was 25 msec prior to the onset of buzz excitation. Stimuli with no vowel transitions were also tested. The 108 stimuli (nine spectra, three levels, four transition values) were tape-recorded in random order and presented twice to a group of listeners. Eight listeners participated, and thus the total number of judgments per stimulus was 16. The stimuli were presented under PDR-8 earphones at a

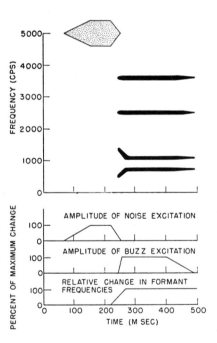

FIG. 9. Schematized description of a typical stimulus used in the identification test for fricative-vowel syllables. The solid bars in the upper part of the figure show how the formant frequencies change as a function of time in the vowel portion of the syllable, including typical transitions at the onset of buzz excitation and the steady formants corresponding to the vowel /ɑ/. The shaded area preceding the vowel depicts the fricative portion of a typical syllable. The lower part of the figure shows the form of the signals used to control the excitation and formant parameters in the synthesizer.

[17] K. N. Stevens, J. Audio Eng. Soc. 4, 2 (1956)
[18] P. C. Delattre, A. M. Liberman, and F. S. Cooper, J. Acoust. Soc. Am. 27, 769 (1955).

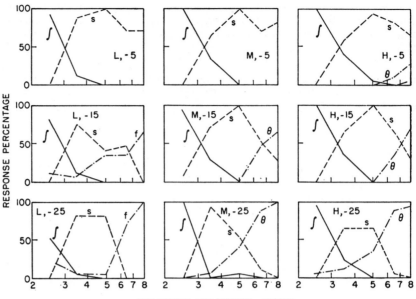

FIG. 10. Results of the identification test for synthetic fricative-vowel syllables. Percentage of responses for eight listeners is plotted as a function of the resonant frequency of the electric circuit used to generate the initial (fricative) portion of the syllable. Three starting frequencies for the transition of the second formant are denoted by L (900 cps), M (1700 cps), and H (2400 cps); the numbers -5, -15, and -25 indicate the over-all level, in decibels, of the fricative portion relative to the vowel portion of the syllable.

comfortable listening level.[19] The subjects were instructed to identify the initial consonant in each syllable as one of /f,θ,s,ʃ/. For the second presentation of the material, they were also instructed to indicate which stimuli they judged to be "natural versions" of the syllables.

The results of the fricative identification test for stimuli with formant transitions are summarized in Fig. 10. The percentages for each consonant response are plotted as a function of the resonant frequency of the synthesizing circuit. For stimuli with no formant transitions the maximum response percentages for each fricative were almost always lower than the best percentages shown in the figure.

Stimuli with resonant frequencies of 6500 or 8000 cps usually yielded /f/ and /θ/ responses, particularly for the lower noise levels. In general, the addition of low-frequency noise to the basic stimuli with these resonant frequencies (see Fig. 7) did not greatly influence the responses, although the response percentages for /f/ and /θ/ were slightly higher when low-frequency noise was present. The points at 6500 and 8000 cps in the curves in Fig. 10 represent data for the 0-db level of low-frequency noise.

Analysis of the "naturalness" responses showed that, in general, stimuli with high response percentages in a particular class were also judged to be "natural" syllables. It may be significant to note, however, that two of the stimuli were judged unanimously to be natural versions of /f/ and /θ/, respectively, whereas no version of /s/ or /ʃ/ received such a unanimous vote.

[19] Calibration curves of the PDR-8 earphones used in this experiment (measured with a 6-cc coupler) show that there may be fluctuations in the frequency response as great as ±8 db in the frequency range 7000–9000 cps. Since the relative levels described above were measured before the stimuli were transduced, caution should be exercised in applying precise interpretation to certain of the data for stimuli having a resonant frequency of 8000 cps.

The data of Fig. 10 for relative fricative levels of -5 and -25 db are replotted and smoothed in Fig. 11. For each fricative level, these response maps indicate regions of resonant frequencies and formant transitions associated with each of the four responses.

Figures 10 and 11 demonstrate that /ʃ/ responses are always associated with resonant frequencies in the vicinity of 2500 cps. These results are in good agreement with the analysis of the Hughes-Halle data in Table I, which shows the frequency of the first major resonance for /ʃ/ to be in the range 2200 to 2700 cps. Responses of /s/ are obtained when the resonant frequency of the stimulus is above 3000 cps, and /f/ and /θ/ responses are obtained for very high frequency resonances,

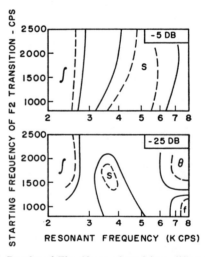

FIG. 11. Results of Fig. 10 are plotted in a different way for over-all levels of the fricative portion relative to the vowel portion of the syllable of -5 and -25 db. The contours show ranges of $F2$ transitions and resonant frequencies for fricative portions of syllables within which each fricative response is greater than 75% (solid lines) and greater than 90% (dashed lines).

especially when the intensity of the fricative is low. The data of Table I are in agreement with these results, since they indicate that the frequency of the first major pole for /s/ is in the range 3500 to 6400 cps and for /f/ is in the range 6800 to 8400 cps. As noted above, the listeners were not unanimous in judging any stimulus to be a "natural" version of /s/ or /ʃ/. It is suggested that a circuit with more than one pole and zero may be necessary if highly natural versions of these fricative consonants are to be synthesized.

The general features of the results shown in Figs. 10 and 11 are similar to those reported by Nakata[8] who studied the synthesis and perception (by Japanese listeners) of the fricative consonants /ʃ,s,f/. The resonant frequencies for greatest /ʃ/ and /s/ responses for Japanese listeners were, however, somewhat higher than the corresponding frequencies in the present experiment, and formant transitions had less influence on the responses of Nakata's listeners.

The effects of the transitions of adjacent vowel formants on the identification of fricative consonants in the present experiment are consistent with the results of fricative identification tests reported by Harris.[6] Harris' stimuli were constructed by combining the noise from one spoken fricative-vowel syllable with the voiced portion of another; the stimuli were presented to listeners for identification as one of the voiceless fricatives of American English. She argued from her results that the important cues for the fricatives /s/ and /ʃ/ are given by the noise, but that differentiation of /f/ and /θ/ is accomplished primarily on the basis of cues contained in the vocalic part of the syllable. The present data lead to similar conclusions: /f/ is distinguished from /θ/ apparently on the basis of the transition of the second formant in the adjacent vowel, whereas formant transitions do not have an appreciable effect on /s/ and /ʃ/ responses, particularly when the intensity of the fricative is high.

It is well known that the locus or apparent starting frequency for the second formant ($F2$) of a vowel preceded by a consonant such as a stop or fricative gives some indication of the articulatory configuration used to generate the consonant.[18,20,21] In general, tests with synthetic speech and studies with vocal-tract analogs have shown that $F2$ loci of low frequency (1000 cps or less) are associated with bilabial or labio-dental configurations; $F2$ loci in the middle frequency range (1500 to 2000 cps) are associated with alveolar configurations; and $F2$ loci above 2000 cps are associated with palatal configurations. These loci are probably influenced to some extent by the adjacent vowel and are only approximate. The present data relating to formant transitions appropriate to the articulation of fricative consonants are in general agreement with these findings, although precise comparisons are, of course, not possible since the scope of the present experiment is rather limited.

SUMMARY AND CONCLUSIONS

In this paper an acoustical theory of the production of voiceless fricative consonants is reviewed, and it is shown that the results of analyses of spectra of these consonants are consistent with the theory. Simplified versions of fricative consonants, generated in accordance with the theory, are demonstrated to elicit responses that are in agreement with the results of the spectral analyses. Although the data presented here are not of sufficient scope to be considered as general descriptions of fricative consonants as they occur in all phonetic contexts and as they are produced by many different talkers, they nevertheless suggest a method of approach for further study of these and other classes of speech sounds.

ACKNOWLEDGMENTS

The authors wish to express their appreciation to Jane Arnold and Kazuo Nakata, who administered the listening tests, and to Arthur House, who provided helpful comment and discussion during the course of the work.

[20] R. K. Potter, G. A. Kopp, and H. C. Green, *Visible Speech* (D. Van Nostrand Company, Inc., Princeton, New Jersey, 1947).
[21] K. N. Stevens and A. S. House, J. Acoust. Soc. Am. **28**, 578 (1956).

Excitation of Vocal-Tract Synthesizers*

J. L. Flanagan and L. Cherry

Bell Telephone Laboratories, Incorporated, Murray Hill, New Jersey 07974

A method is described for representing voiced and voiceless excitation in the vocal tract. Three physiological factors suffice for synthesis of nonnasal speech: subglottal pressure, vocal-cord tension, and vocal-tract shape. Voiced excitation is obtained from an oscillator model of the cords. Voiceless excitation is produced by elements that approximate turbulent flow in the tract. These elements are controlled automatically by factors related to the acoustic volume velocity in the tract and the tract shape. Voiced, voiceless, and voiced-fricative sounds are synthesized from a vocal tract incorporating these sources. The whole system is computer simulated.

A DESCRIPTION of speech in physiological terms promises one route to improved synthesis. The physiological description should embrace the mechanism of sound generation in the vocal tract, as well as the tract geometry and its transmission properties. Toward this objective, we have made a computer simulation of the vocal tract, and of the mechanisms of voiced and voiceless excitation, at least as we presently understand them. Our aim is to synthesize all sounds in terms of three physiological factors: namely, subglottal pressure, vocal-cord tension, and vocal-tract shape. This report describes preliminary experiments to test the feasibility of this approach.

I. VOICED EXCITATION

For calculation of voiced excitation, we represent the vibrating vocal cords as a second-order mechanical system. The components are shown in Fig. 1. Air from the lungs on the left passes through the glottal constriction formed by the cords and into the vocal tract on the right. The acoustic volume velocity through the glottis is U_g, and the subglottal air pressure is P_s. The vibrating vocal cords are represented by the single mass M, the stiffness K, and the viscous loss B. The cords have thickness d and length l. Vertical displacement x, of the mass changes the glottal area A_g, and varies the flow U_g. At rest, the glottal opening has the phonation neutral area A_{g0}.

The mechanical oscillator is forced by a function of the subglottal pressure and the Bernoulli pressure in

---

* Based upon material presented at the 6th International Congress on Acoustics, Tokyo, Japan, August 1968.

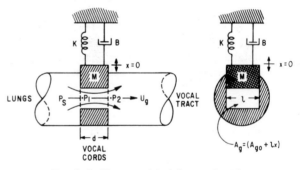

FIG. 1. Oscillator model of the vocal cords.

the orifice. The Bernoulli pressure is dependent upon U_g^2, which, in turn, is conditioned by the nonlinear, time-varying acoustic impedance of the glottal opening. In qualitative terms, the operation is as follows: the cords are set to the neutral or rest area, and the sub-

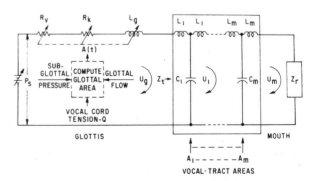

FIG. 2. Network representation of the vocal system for voiced sounds.

Reprinted with permission from *J. Acoust. Soc. Am.*, vol. 45, pp. 764–769, Mar. 1969.

VOCAL-TRACT SHAPE: /ɑ/

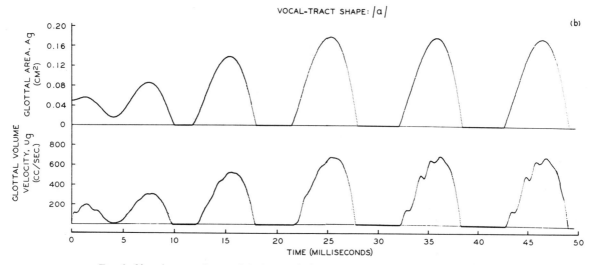

FIG. 3. Glottal area and acoustic volume velocity calculated from the vocal-cord model.

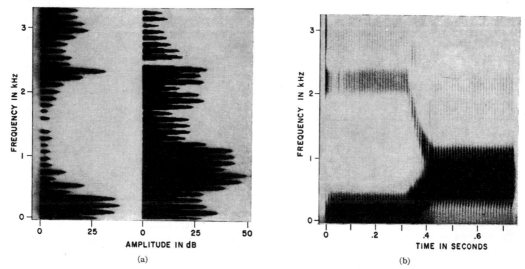

(a)   (b)

FIG. 4. Sound spectrogram of the synthesizer output. The sound corresponds to a linear transition from vowel /i/ to the vowel /ɑ/. Amplitude sections are shown for the central portion of each vowel.

glottal pressure applied. As the flow builds up, so does the negative Bernoulli pressure. The latter draws the mass down to interrupt the flow. As the flow diminishes, so does the Bernoulli pressure, and the spring acts to retrieve the mass. Under appropriate conditions, stable oscillation results.[1]

The undamped natural frequency of the oscillator is proportional to $(K/M)^{\frac{1}{2}}$. It is convenient for us to define a vocal-cord tension parameter Q, which scales the natural frequency by multiplying the stiffness and dividing the mass. This is analogous to the physiological tensing of the cords, which stiffens them and reduces their distributed mass.

Using this formulation for glottal behavior, the complete vocal system, for voiced nonnasal sounds, may be represented by the network in Fig. 2.

The tract is represented as a nonuniform transmission line whose sections correspond to plane-wave propagation in abutting cylindrical elements. The tract configuration is described by the cross-sectional area values $(A_1 - - - A_m)$. In our present case, $m=10$. The radiation load at the mouth is Z_r and is taken as the radiation impedance of a piston in a plane baffle. The acoustic volume velocity through the mouth, and hence into the radiation impedance, is U_m. The acoustic driving-point impedance seen by the glottis is Z_t.

The acoustic impedance of the glottal orifice is characterized by two loss elements, R_v and R_k, and an inertance, L_g.[1] The values of these impedances depend upon the time-varying glottal area $A_g(t)$. In addition,

---

[1] Computational details of this formulation are described in J. L. Flanagan and L. Landgraf, "Self-Oscillating Source for Vocal-Tract Synthesizers," IEEE Trans. Audio Electroacoust. **AU-16**, 57–64 (1968).

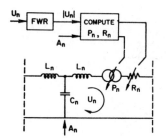

FIG. 5. Network modification for simulating the properties of turbulent flow in the vocal tract.

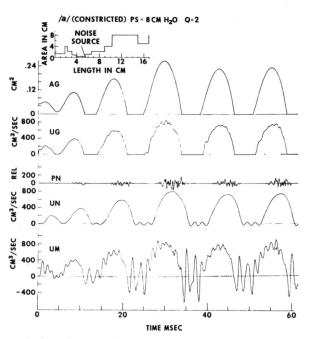

FIG. 6. Waveforms of functions calculated for a voiced fricative articulation corresponding to the constricted vowel /ɑ/.

R_k is dependent upon $|U_g|$. The glottal area is linked to P_s and to U_g through the differential equation that describes the vocal-cord motion and its forcing function. The value of the tension parameter Q is also introduced into this equation. In other words, the dashed box of Fig. 2 represents iterative solutions to the differential equation for the system described in Fig. 1.

This continuous system can be represented by $(m+2)$ differential equations, which, in turn, can be approximated by difference equations. We have programmed these difference equations for simultaneous solution on a GE 645 digital computer. The program accepts as input data time-varying samples of the subglottal pressure P_s, the cord tension Q, and the vocal tract areas $(A_1 --- A_m)$, and it computes sampled values of all volume velocities, including the glottal flow and mouth output. The results can be plotted for visual display and D/A converted for audible output. A typical glottal area and volume velocity, plotted by the computer for a vocal-tract shape corresponding to the vowel /ɑ/, is shown in Fig. 3. This Figure shows the initial 50 msec of voicing.

The top curve is the glottal area result, and the lower curve the glottal flow. The calculation is for a subglottal pressure of 8 cm H_2O and a tension value that places the cord oscillation in the pitch range of a man. One notices that by about the fourth period a steady state is achieved. One sees, in this case, irregularities in the glottal flow that are caused by acoustic interaction at the first formant frequency of the tract. One also notices that this temporal detail in the volume flow is not noticeably reflected in the mechanical behavior, that is in the area wave.

We have examined the behavior of the vocal-cord model for a wide range of glottal conditions and the results suggest that it duplicates many of the features of human speech (for example, the variation of fundamental frequency with P_s).[2–6] One of the best ways to

assess the behavior is to listen to the sound quality resulting from the program. A spectrogram of the audible output for a linear transition from the vowel /i/ to the vowel /ɑ/ is shown in Fig. 4. The glottal conditions in this case are constant and are: $P_s=8$ cm H_2O and $Q=2.0$. The resulting fundamental frequency of these sounds is not only a function of the glottal parameters, but also of the tract shape; that is, a function of the acoustic loading that the tract presents to the vocal cords. The spectral sections indicate realistic formant and pitch values.

II. VOICELESS EXCITATION

With slight modification, and with no additional control data, the synthesis can be arranged to include fricative and stop excitation. Fricative excitation is generated by turbulent air flow at a constriction, and stop excitation is produced by making a complete closure, building up pressure and abruptly releasing it. The stop release is frequently followed by a noise excitation owing to turbulence generated at the constriction after the release.

Experimental measurements indicate that the noise sound pressure generated by turbulence is proportional to the square of the Reynolds number for the flow.[7] To the extent that a one-dimensional wave treatment is valid, the noise sound pressure can be taken as

[2] Data on the behavior of the model as a function of its parameters are given in Ref. 1. Variation of fundamental frequency, mean glottal flow and glottal duty cycle are given as functions of subglottal pressure and cord tension. These calculated functions can be compared to corresponding data for natural speech in Ref. 3–6.

[3] J. W. van den Berg, J. T. Zantema, and P. Doornenbal, Jr., "On the Air Resistance and the Bernoulli Effect of the Human Larynx," J. Acoust. Soc. Amer. 29, 626–631 (1957).

[4] J. W. van den Berg, "Direct and Indirect Determination of the Mean Subglottal Pressure," Folia Phoniat. 8, 1–24 (1956).

[5] S. Öhman and J. Lindqvist, "Analysis and Synthesis of

Prosodic Pitch Contours," Speech Transmission Lab., Roy. Inst. Tech., Stockholm, Quart. Progr. Status Rep. (Apr. 1965):

[6] P. Lieberman, "Intonation, Perception and Language" (MIT Res. Monogr. 38, 1967).

[7] W. Meyer-Eppler, "Zum Erzeugungsmechanismus der Geräuschlaute," Z. Phonetik 7, 196–212 (1953).

766   Volume 45   Number 3   1969

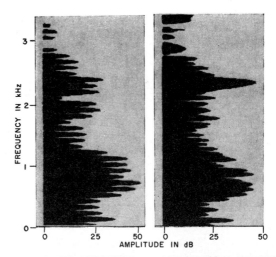

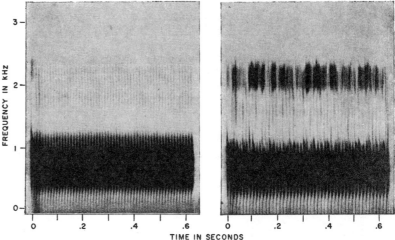

FIG. 7. Spectrograms of the synthesized output for normal vowel /ɑ/ and the constricted /ɑ/ shown in Fig. 6. Amplitude sections are shown for the central portion of each vowel.

proportional to the square of the volume velocity and inversely proportional to the constriction area. Measurements also suggest that the noise source is spatially distributed, but generally can be located at, or immediately downstream of the closure. Its internal impedance is primarily resistive, and it excites the vocal system as a series pressure source. Its spectrum is broadly peaked in the midaudio range and falls off at low and high frequencies.[8]

The transmission-line vocal tract can be modified to approximate the nonlinearities of turbulent flow. Figure 5 shows a single section of the transmission line so modified. A series noise source P_n, with internal resistance R_n is introduced into each section of the line. The area of the section is A_n and the volume current circulating in the right branch is U_n. The level of the noise source and the value of its internal resistance are functions of U_n and A_n. The noise source is modulated in amplitude by a function proportional to the squared Reynolds number, namely, U_n^2/A_n. The source resist-

ance is a flow-dependent loss similar to the glotta resistance. To first order, it is proportional to $|U_n|$ and inversely proportional to A_n^2. The diagram indicates that these quantities are used to determine P_n and R_n on a sample-by-sample basis.

By continually noting the magnitudes of the volume currents in each section, and knowing the corresponding areas, the synthesizer detects conditions suitable to turbulent flow. Noise excitation and loss are therefore introduced automatically at any constriction. Small constrictions and low Reynolds numbers produce inaudible noise. The square-law dependence of P_n upon U_n has the perceptual effect of a noise threshold. (A real threshold switch can be used on the noise source, if desired.) The original control data, namely, vocal-tract shape, subglottal pressure, and cord tension, in effect, determine the place of the constriction and the loss and noise introduced there.

For the P_n source, we have used Gaussian noise, bandpassed between 500 and 4000 Hz. Also, to ensure stability, the volume flow U_n is low-pass filtered to 500 Hz before it modulates the noise source. In other

[8] J. M. Heinz, "Model Studies of the Production of Fricative Consonants," MIT Res. Lab. Electron. Quart. Progr. Rep. (15 July 1968).

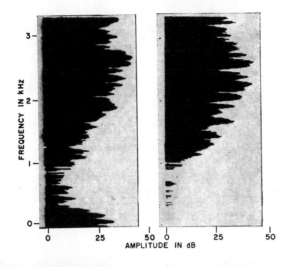

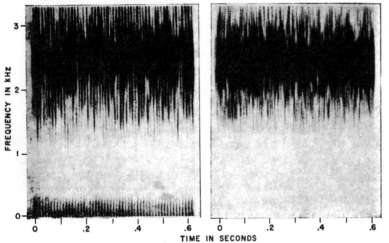

FIG. 8. Sound spectrograms for the voiced–voiceless cognates /ʒ/ and /ʃ/. Amplitude sections are shown for the central portion of each sound.

words, the noise is produced by the low-frequency components of U_n, including the dc flow.

This noise excitation works equally well for both voiced and unvoiced sounds. The operation for voiced fricatives includes all features of the formulation, and is a good vehicle for explanation. For example, consider what happens in a vowel when the constriction is made substantially smaller, giving rise to conditions favorable for turbulent flow. Since we have already shown results for the vowel /ɑ/, consider the same vowel with the constriction narrowed. (This configuration is not proposed as a realistic English sound, but merely to illustrate the effect of tightening the vowel constriction.) The situation is shown in Fig. 6. All glottal conditions are the same as before, but the constriction is narrowed to less than half the normal vowel constriction (namely, to 0.3 cm²).

The top trace shows the glottal area, and one notices that it settles to a periodic oscillation in about four periods—the final pitch here is somewhat less than that in Fig. 3 because the acoustic load is different. The second trace from the top shows the glottal flow. The glottal flow is about the same in peak value as before and is conditioned primarily by the glottal impedance and not by the tract constriction. At about the third period, noise that has been produced at the constriction by the flow buildup has propagated back to the glottis and influences the U_g flow. Note, too, that noise influence on the mechanical oscillator (i.e., the area function) is negligible.

The third trace shows the output of the noise source at the constriction. This output is proportional to the constriction current squared, divided by the constriction area. The fourth trace shows the low-passed constriction current that produces the noise. One sees that the tendency is for the noise to be generated in pitch-synchronous bursts, corresponding to the pulses of glottal volume flow. The result is a combined excitation in which the voicing and noise signals are multiplicatively related, as they are in the human.

The final trace is the volume flow at the mouth, and one can notice noise perturbations in the waveform. Note, too, that the epoch of greatest formant excitation corresponds to the falling phase of the glottal flow. A

Volume 45   Number 3   1969

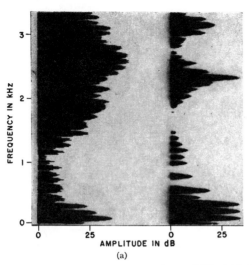
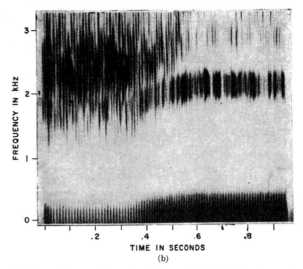

FIG. 9. Spectrogram for the synthesized syllable /ʒi/. Amplitude sections are shown for the central portion of each sound.

spectrogram of this audible output is compared with that for a normal /ɑ/ in Fig. 7. Note in the constricted, noisy /ɑ/ that: (1) the first formant has been lowered in frequency, (2) the fundamental frequency is slightly lower, and (3) pitch-synchronous noise excitation is clearly evident, particularly at the higher frequencies.

The voiceless sounds are produced simply by setting the neutral area of the vocal cords to a relatively large value, for example 1 cm². This change can be signaled by the cord tension parameter. As this is done, the Bernoulli pressure in the glottal orifice diminishes, the oscillations of the vocal cords decay, and the cord displacement assumes the steady large value. Measurements on real speech suggest this kind of effect in passing from voiced to voiceless sounds.[9,10] Corresponding exactly to this change, spectrograms of the audible output for the voiced–voiceless cognates /ʒ/ and /ʃ/ are compared in Fig. 8. The vocal-tract shape is the same for both sounds. One sees a pronounced voice bar in /ʒ/ that, of course, is absent in /ʃ/. The eigenfrequencies of the two systems are similar but not exactly the same because of the difference in glottal termination. Lower resonances are not strongly evident in the /ʃ/ output, because its transmission function, from point of constriction to mouth, exhibits low-frequency zeros.

---

[9] M. Sawashima, "Observation of the Glottal Movements," Proc. Speech Symp., Kyoto (Aug. 1968), Paper C-2-1.

[10] M. Sawashima, H. Hirose, S. Kiritani, and O. Fujimura, "Articulatory Movements of the Larynx," Proc. Int. Congr. Acoust., 6th, Tokyo (Aug. 1968), Paper B-1.

The dynamics of continuous synthesis can be illustrated by a consonant–vowel syllable. Figure 9 shows the syllable /ʒi/ synthesized by the system. In this case, the subglottal pressure and cord tension are held constant and the area function is changed linearly from the configuration for /ʒ/ to that for /i/. Heavy noise excitation is apparent during the tightly constricted /ʒ/, and the noise diminishes as the articulation shifts to /i/. Also in this case, the high, front vowel /i/ is characterized by a relatively tight constriction and a small amount of noise excitation continues in the /i/. This same effect can be seen in human speech.

The present model also appears capable of treating sounds such as glottal stops and the glottal aspiration that accompanies /h/. In the former, the tension control can cause an abrupt glottal closure and cessation of voicing. Restoration to a normal tension and quiescent glottal opening permits voicing to again be initiated. In the latter, the flow velocity and area at the glottis can be monitored just as is done along the tract. When conditions suitable for turbulence exist, a noise excitation can be introduced at the glottal location.

In summary, the work suggests that nonnasal speech (including vocal system and its excitation) can be described in terms of the physiological factors subglottal pressure, cord tension, and tract shape. Voiced sounds are produced from these data by an oscillator model of the cords. Voiceless sounds are obtained automatically, in a physiologically realistic way, from the same data. The excitation technique appears to have potential for vocal-tract synthesizers and for speech synthesis in computer answer-back systems.

Part II
Speech Analysis Methods

The papers in this part are concerned with general approaches to speech analysis; i.e., the methods discussed in this section are not restricted to the estimation of a specific speech parameter.

The first paper, by Schafer and Rabiner, is a survey of digital techniques for speech processing. This paper discusses almost all of the basic digital techniques that are represented in this book. In this paper it is seen that an important assumption in most speech analysis techniques is that the parameters of the underlying speech model change slowly with time. This leads to a variety of "short-time" analysis methods in which parameters are estimated from short segments of the speech signal. The second paper, by Bell *et al.*, introduces the important concepts of short-time Fourier analysis and analysis-by-synthesis in which the parameters of a model for speech production are systematically adjusted so as to obtain a match between the output of the model and the Fourier spectrum of a segment of a speech signal. These basic principles are augmented further in the third paper, by Mathews, Miller, and David, which introduces the concept of pitch synchronous analysis; i.e., the estimation of speech parameters from individual "pitch periods."

The fourth paper, by Oppenheim and Schafer, provides a theoretical basis for the application of homorphic filtering to speech analysis. In this approach, the speech signal is viewed as the convolution of an excitation signal with a vocal tract impulse response. A basic ingredient of homomorphic processing is the cepstrum, a representation of the speech signal which has been found to be very useful in pitch detection and in analysis/synthesis.

The last paper, by Makhoul, serves as a comprehensive summary of the basic techniques of linear predictive analysis. This approach, often called linear predictive coding (LPC), is no doubt the most widely used method of speech analysis. The reader will find this approach used as the basis for estimating all the parameters of speech and as the basis for a number of analysis/synthesis schemes. Indeed, all of the basic principles illustrated by the papers of this section are to be found throughout the remaining papers of the book. More detail on LPC analysis is given in papers 5, 6, and 7 of Part IV and in [1].

Reference

1. J. D. Markel and A. H. Gray, *Linear Predictive Analysis of Speech*, Springer–Verlag, New York, 1976.

Digital Representations of Speech Signals

RONALD W. SCHAFER, SENIOR MEMBER, IEEE, AND LAWRENCE R. RABINER, MEMBER, IEEE

Invited Paper

Abstract—This paper presents several digital signal processing methods for representing speech. Included among the representations are simple waveform coding methods; time domain techniques; frequency domain representations; nonlinear or homomorphic methods; and finally linear predictive coding techniques. The advantages and disadvantages of each of these representations for various speech processing applications are discussed.

I. Introduction

THE NOTION of a *representation* of a speech signal is central to almost every area of speech communication research. Often the form of representation of the speech signal is not singled out for special attention or concern but yet it is implicit in the formulation of a problem or in the design of a system. A good example of this situation is in telephony, where speech is, in fact, represented by fluctuations in electrical current for purposes of long distance transmission. In other situations, however, we must often pay strict attention to the choice and method of implementation of the representation of the speech signal. This is true, for example, in such diverse areas as speech transmission, computer storage of speech and computer voice response, speech synthesis, speech aids for the handicapped, speaker verification and identification, and speech recognition. In all of these areas, digital representations; i.e., representations as sequences of numbers, are becoming increasingly dominant. There are two basic reasons for this. First, through the use of small general purpose digital computers, speech researchers have been able to apply a wide variety of digital signal processing techniques to speech communication problems. These techniques cover a range of complexity and sophistication that is impossible to match with analog methods. Second, the recent and predicted future developments in integrated circuit technology make it possible to realize digital speech processing schemes economically as hardware devices having the same sophistication and flexibility as a computer program implementation.

The purpose of this paper is to survey the important and most useful methods for obtaining digital representations of speech signals. This is a formidable task since the number and variety of such methods is great. Thus we must begin by disclaiming any pretentions to completeness; we shall only try to point out the methods that in our view are the most useful in the technical and research areas of speech communication.

The organization of this paper is as follows. In Section II, we briefly review the speech production process and show how it can be modeled with a simple digital representation. We then discuss a class of waveform coding methods for representing

speech in Section III. Included in this class are linear pulse-code modulation (PCM), delta modulation (DM), differential PCM, adaptive delta modulation, and finally adaptive differential PCM (DPCM). It is shown at the end of this section that if an adaptive predictor is incorporated in these models, the waveform coding technique becomes quite similar to the linear predictive coding method to be discussed in Section VII.

In Section IV, we discuss various time-domain representations of speech. Included in this section are the concepts of zero crossing analysis, autocorrelation functions, "peak-to-peak" type estimations, and the use of "energy" functions. In Section V, we discuss frequency domain representations of speech for which the concept of short-time spectrum analysis is dominant. Several examples of systems based on short-time spectrum analysis are given in this section.

In Section VI, we discuss the topic of homomorphic analysis of speech. In this section the concept of the cepstrum is introduced. Finally, in Section VII, we discuss the two basic methods of linear prediction analysis, explain their similarities and differences and discuss the basic concepts which are derivable from them including the spectrum, cepstrum, and autocorrelation function.

II. A Digital Model for Production of the Speech Signal [1]–[3]

A schematic diagram of the human vocal apparatus is shown in Fig. 1. The vocal tract is an acoustic tube that is terminated at one end by the vocal cords and at the other end by the lips. An ancillary tube, the nasal tract, can be connected or disconnected by the movement of the velum. The shape of the vocal tract is determined by the position of the lips, jaw, tongue, and velum.

Sound is generated in this system in three ways. Voiced sounds are produced by exciting the vocal tract with quasi-periodic pulses of air pressure caused by vibration of the vocal cords. Fricative sounds are produced by forming a constriction somewhere in the vocal tract, and forcing air through the constriction, thereby creating turbulence which produces a source of noise to excite the vocal tract. Plosive sounds are created by completely closing off the vocal tract, building up pressure, and then quickly releasing it. All these sources create a wide-band excitation of the vocal tract which in turn acts as a linear time-varying filter which imposes its transmission properties on the frequency spectra of the sources. The vocal tract can be characterized by its natural frequencies (or formants) which correspond to resonances in the sound transmission characteristics of the vocal tract.

A typical speech waveform is shown in Fig. 2, which illustrates some of the basic properties of the speech signal. We see, for example, that although the properties of the waveform change with time, it is reasonable to view the speech waveform as being composed of segments during which the signal properties remain

Manuscript received September 18, 1974; revised November 25, 1974.
R. W. Schafer was with the Bell Laboratories, Inc., Murray Hill, N.J. He is now with the Department of Electrical Engineering, Georgia Institute of Technology, Atlanta, Ga. 30332.
L. R. Rabiner is with the Bell Laboratories, Inc., Murray Hill, N.J. 07974.

Reprinted from *Proc. IEEE*, vol. 63, pp. 662–677, Apr. 1975.

SCHAFER AND RABINER: SPEECH SIGNALS

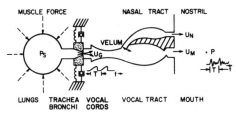

Fig. 1. Schematic diagram of mechanism of speech production. (After Flanagan *et al.* [2].)

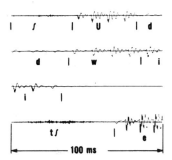

Fig. 2. An illustration of a speech waveform, corresponding to the utterance *"Should we chase"*.

rather constant. Such segments are demarked in Fig. 2 below the waveform. These sample segments have the appearance either of a low-level random (unvoiced) signal (as in ∫ or t∫ in Fig. 2) or a high-level quasi-periodic (voiced signal) (as in U or w or i) with each period displaying the exponentially decaying response properties of an acoustic transmission system. We note that the dynamic range of the waveform is large; i.e., the peak amplitude of a voiced segment is much larger than the peak amplitude of an unvoiced segment.

Because the sound sources and vocal tract shape are relatively independent, a reasonable approximation is to model them separately, as shown in Fig. 3. In this digital model, samples of the speech waveform are assumed to be the output of a time-varying digital filter that approximates the transmission properties of the vocal tract and the spectral properties of the glottal pulse shape. Since, as is clear from Fig. 2, the vocal tract changes shape rather slowly in continuous speech (likewise its sound transmission properties) it is reasonable to assume that the digital filter in Fig. 3 has fixed characteristics over a time interval of on the order of 10 ms. Thus the digital filter may be characterized in each such interval by an impulse response or a set of coefficients for a digital filter. For voiced speech, the digital filter is excited by an impulse train generator that creates a quasi-periodic impulse train in which the spacing between impulses corresponds to the fundamental period of the glottal excitation.[1] For unvoiced speech, the filter is excited by a random number generator that produces flat spectrum noise. In both cases, an amplitude control regulates the intensity of the input to the digital filter.

This model is the basis of a wide variety of representations of speech signals. These are conveniently classified as either waveform representations or parametric representations depending upon whether the speech waveform is represented directly or whether the representation is in terms of time-varying parameters of the basic speech model. These representations range in complexity from simply samples of the speech wave-

[1] It is assumed that the effects of the glottal pulse shape are included in the digital filter.

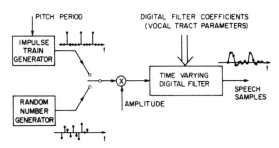

Fig. 3. Digital processing model for production of speech signals.

form taken periodically in time to estimates of the parameters of the model in Fig. 3. The choice of the digital representation is governed by three major considerations: processing complexity, information (bit) rate, and flexibility. By complexity, we mean the amount of processing required to obtain the chosen representation. In many cases processing complexity is a measure of cost of implementation of the system in hardware. A simple representation can generally be implemented more economically than a complex representation. Thus complexity is often the overriding consideration in some transmission applications where low terminal cost is crucial. Information or bit rate is a measure of the redundancy in the speech signal which has been removed by the processing. A low bit rate means that the digital representation of the speech signal can be transmitted over a low capacity channel, or stored efficiently in digital memory. Finally flexibility is a measure of how the speech can be manipulated or altered for applications other than transmission, e.g., voice response, speech recognition, or speaker verification. In general, greater complexity is the price paid to lower the bit rate and increase the flexibility. However, tradeoffs can generally be made among these three factors. In transmission and voice response applications the quality and intelligibility of the reconstituted speech are also prime considerations. Most of the techniques we will discuss are capable of producing good quality, highly intelligible speech, although some of the techniques are primarily analysis methods, and as such are limited to applications where the speech signal need not be reconstructed.

In the remainder of this paper, we will discuss a number of of digital representations that span the spectrum of possibilities in each of the above areas of concern. We shall begin with the simplest, least efficient and least flexible representation of speech and progress to more complex ones which have the greatest flexibility and lowest bit rate.

III. DIGITAL WAVEFORM CODING

Conceptually, the simplest digital representations of speech are concerned with direct representation of the speech waveform. Such schemes as PCM, DM, and DPCM are all based on Shannon's sampling theorem, which says that any bandlimited signal can be exactly reconstructed from samples taken periodically in time if the sampling rate is twice the highest frequency of the signal. We begin with a discussion of the simplest waveform coding technique; i.e., PCM.

A. PCM

In applying the sampling theorem to a digital representation of speech there are two main concerns. These are depicted in Fig. 4. If the signal bandwidth is W hertz, then the sampling period must be $T \leqslant 1/(2W)$. Since the samples $x(nT)$ of the signal generally take on a continuous range of values, they must be quantized for transmission or digital storage. If we repre-

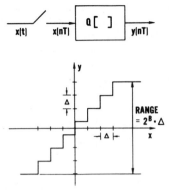

Fig. 4. Sampling and quantizing of an analog signal.

sent the samples as B-bit binary words, then the bit rate is $2BW$ bits/s. The value of W required for speech signals depends on the ultimate use of the samples. We know from measurements and theoretical studies that speech sounds such as fricatives have rather wide bandwidths (on the order of 10 kHz). On the other hand much of the information required for speech intelligibility is contained in the variation of the first three formant frequencies of voiced speech and these are typically below 3 kHz. Thus, a sampling rate between 6 kHz and 20 kHz is generally used. No matter what the sampling rate is, the speech signal must be suitably low-pass filtered prior to the sampling process to eliminate undesired high frequencies of the speech and high frequency noise.

The choice of the number of bits per sample B is also dependent upon the intended use of the samples. If our purpose is transmission or computer storage followed by conversion back to an analog signal, we are only concerned that the resulting analog signal be perceptually acceptable. Also, the sampling process just described is generally the first step in any digital speech analysis techniques. Since errors incurred in the sampling process will propagate to more refined digital representations, we are often justified in a very generous allotment of bits and sampling rate if the sampled speech wave is to undergo further processing. However it should be noted that the amount of processing required to implement most systems is proportional to sampling rate. Thus we should try to keep the sampling rate as low as possible, consistent with other objectives.

One objective measure of the fidelity of the PCM representation is the ratio of the signal power to the quantization noise power. If we define the quantization noise in Fig. 4 as the following:

$$e(nT) = x(nT) - Q[x(nT)] = x(nT) - y(nT)$$

then it can be shown [4], [7] that about 11 bits are required in order that the signal-to-noise ratio (SNR) be 60 dB. (This is often referred to as "toll quantity".) It is easily shown that the addition of one bit changes the SNR by 6 dB.

The preceding discussion can be summarized by stating that an adequate PCM representation for most purposes requires from 66 000 bits/s (11 bits × 6 kHz) to 220 000 bits/s (11 bits × 20 kHz). This is a very significant consideration in transmission or storage for processing on a computer.

Since we generally have little flexibility in lowering the sampling rate, as this is governed by other considerations, the main hope for lowering the overall bit rate is in reducing the number of bits/sample. The key to such reductions lies in considering one of the basic properties of the speech signal;

namely, that speech has a wide dynamic range. We see from Fig. 4 that if B is fixed, then the step size Δ must be chosen so that $\Delta \cdot 2^B$ spans the maximum peak-to-peak range of the signal. Thus the quantizer step size is determined by the amplitude of the voiced segments of speech whereas a good representation of unvoiced segments requires a much smaller step size.

One solution to this problem is to use a nonlinear quantizer characteristic which distributes the quantization levels more densely for lower amplitudes than for high amplitudes. Based on empirical determinations of the amplitude distribution of speech signals, a logarithmic quantizer characteristic has been found to be nearly optimum [9]. Using a logarithmic quantizer, 7 bits/sample are sufficient to obtain toll quality. An alternative approach is the use of a time varying step size [5]–[7], i.e., an adaptive quantizer. When the signal level is low, a small step size is used; and when the signal amplitude is large, an appropriate large step size is used. The adjustment of the step size may be done by logical operations on the sequence of samples arising from adaptive quantization process [5]–[7].

B. Differential Quantization

Further reductions in bit rate for waveform quantization methods can be obtained by considering more of the detailed properties of the speech signal. Specifically, it is clear from Fig. 2 that there is a great deal of redundancy in the speech signal. Removal of some of this redundancy can yield a concomitant reduction in bit rate, at the expense of increased complexity in the signal processing algorithms. Fig. 5 depicts a general differential quantization scheme. The scheme is based on the fact that even for sampling at just the Nyquist rate $(T = 1/(2W))$, the correlation between successive samples is quite high and, as the sampling rate increases, the sample-to-sample correlation increases, approaching unity for very high sampling rates.

In the system of Fig. 5, let us assume that $\tilde{x}(n)$ is an estimate of the value of the speech sample $x(n) = x(nT)$. Then if the estimate is good, the variance of the difference $\delta(n) = x(n) - \tilde{x}(n)$ should be small, and thus the variance of the quantization error should be smaller than that incurred in quantizing the speech samples $x(n)$. The quantized difference signal $\hat{\delta}(n)$ when added to $\tilde{x}(n)$ produces a reconstructed signal $\hat{x}(n)$ which differs from $x(n)$ by only the quantization error of the difference signal; i.e.,

$$e(n) = \delta(n) - \hat{\delta}(n)$$
$$= [x(n) - \tilde{x}(n)] - [\hat{x}(n) - \tilde{x}(n)]$$
$$= x(n) - \hat{x}(n).$$

Due to the redundancy in the speech signal, it seems plausible that a given sample could be predicted as a linear combination of previous samples. In fact even the simplest linear combination may suffice; i.e., a constant times the previous sample. Therefore if the quantization error is small, $\hat{x}(n)$ will be a good approximation to $x(n)$ and

$$\tilde{x}(n) = a\hat{x}(n-1), \quad a \approx 1 \qquad (1)$$

will be a good estimate of $x(n)$. The z transform of (1) is

$$\tilde{X}(z) = az^{-1}\hat{X}(z).$$

Thus the predictor is characterized by the polynomial

$$P(z) = \frac{\tilde{X}(z)}{\hat{X}(z)} = az^{-1} . \qquad (2)$$

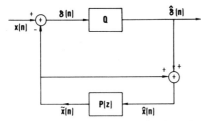

Fig. 5. General differential quantization scheme.

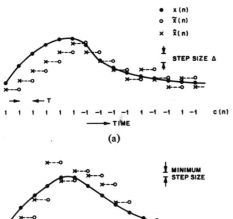

Fig. 6. Illustration of delta modulation. (a) Fixed step size. (b) Adaptive step size.

A more general predictor polynomial is of the form

$$P(z) = \sum_{k=1}^{p} a_k z^{-k}. \qquad (3)$$

The basic principle of linear prediction is applied in more generality in Section VII.

In using differential quantization, we are free to choose the sampling rate, the quantizer and the predictor so as to reduce the bit rate. If the sampling rate is much higher than the Nyquist rate, the correlation between adjacent samples is very close to one and it is possible to use a 1-bit quantizer to obtain a good approximation to the input samples. This case, illustrated in Fig. 6(a), is called DM. In Fig. 6(a), we have illustrated how $x(n)$, $\tilde{x}(n)$, and $\hat{x}(n)$ vary with time. (We have shown the case where $a = 1$.) The quantized difference signal has the form

$$\hat{\delta}(n) = \Delta \cdot c(n)$$

where

$$c(n) = \begin{cases} +1, & \text{if } \delta(n) \geqslant 0 \\ -1, & \text{if } \delta(n) < 0 \end{cases}$$

and Δ is the fixed step size. Fig. 6(a) shows the two types of errors that are inherent in differential quantization schemes. On the left of the figure, the slope of the waveform is greater than the maximum rate of increase of the staircase approximation; i.e., for this choice of sampling period, Δ is too small to follow rapid changes in the waveform. This is called slope overload. On the right side of the figure, we see that in slowly

varying parts of the waveform there is a tendency to oscillate up and down about the waveform. This is called granular distortion. In such regions we would like to have a smaller step size to reduce the magnitude of the quantization error.

One solution to this dilemma is to let the step size vary so that Δ becomes large during slope overload and small during granular distortion. This can be done by searching for patterns in the code word sequence $c(n)$. For example a run of $+1$'s or -1's means slope overload, while an alternating pattern means granularity. A simple logic for varying the step size is [6]

$$\Delta(n) = \begin{cases} P\Delta(n-1), & \text{if } c(n) = c(n-1) \\ Q\Delta(n-1), & \text{if } c(n) \neq c(n-1). \end{cases}$$

The quantized difference signal is now

$$\hat{\delta}(n) = \Delta(n) \cdot c(n).$$

An optimum choice of the parameters is [6]

$$P = 1.5, \qquad Q = 1/P.$$

This scheme is illustrated by Fig. 6(b). (Here, for simplicity we have assumed $P = 2$ and $a = 1$.) It can be seen that this adaptive delta modulator (ADM) is able to follow rapid increases in slope and also it is able to use a smaller step size in regions of granularity. In practice, limits are placed on the step size variation so that $\Delta_{\min} \leqslant \Delta(n) \leqslant \Delta_{\max}$. This prevents the step size both from becoming unreasonably large and from being driven to zero when the input to the differential quantizer is zero.

If we use a multibit quantizer in Fig. 5, then a lower sampling rate can be used. This case is DPCM. If the sampling rate is the Nyquist rate, then we can use two bits less in the quantizer than required for straight PCM for the same SNR [8]. Furthermore, we can adapt the quantizer step size to obtain further improvements. Schemes similar to the ADM system just described have been implemented for multi-bit quantizers. These are called adaptive DPCM (ADPCM) systems [5].

Such a representation has been used for storage of speech at 24 kbits/s for a computer voice response system [10], [11]. An interesting result of this work is the observation that the adaptive quantizing provides a simple means of finding the beginning and end of a speech utterance [10]. This is a problem that arises in many situations, including speech recognition, speaker verification and computer voice response.

IV. TIME DOMAIN ANALYSIS METHODS

The objective of digital waveform coding is to represent the speech waveform as accurately as possible so that an acoustic signal can be reconstructed from the digital representation. In many speech processing problems, however, we are not interested in reconstructing an acoustic signal but rather we are concerned with representing the speech signal in terms of a set of properties or parameters of the model discussed in Section II. Some rather simple, but useful, characterizations can be derived by simple measurements on the waveform itself; i.e., upon a PCM representation of the waveform.

The key to these, and, indeed, the key to all parametric representations, is the concept of short-time analysis. We note from Fig. 2 that if we select an arbitrary segment of the speech waveform of about 10- to 30-ms duration, then it is quite probable that the properties of the waveform remain roughly invariant over that interval. For example, we may select a voiced interval in which the speech signal is characterized by the fundamental period and the amplitude of each basic period. On the other hand, we may select an unvoiced segment where the signal is characterized by the lack of periodicity and the amplitude of the waveform. Since these properties vary from segment-to-segment, it is common to analyze speech on a time-varying basis by carrying out an analysis on short segments of speech selected at uniformly spaced time intervals.

A. Peak Measurements

It is only necessary to glance at Fig. 2 to see that during voiced intervals, the speech signal is characterized by a sequence of peaks that occur periodically at the fundamental frequency of the speech signal. In contrast, during unvoiced intervals the peaks are relatively smaller and do not occur in any discernible pattern. Thus the maximum peak amplitude during an analysis interval can serve as a simple indication of the amplitude of the signal and as an aid in distinguishing between voiced and unvoiced speech segments.

The time between corresponding peaks is, of course, equal to the fundamental period for voiced speech. This principle has been used in a number of schemes for determining the fundamental period or pitch period. A difficulty with this approach is that even over a short analysis interval, the speech signal is not exactly periodic. Since each period has a number of peaks, it is possible to make several different estimates of the period. A method for logically combining the results of several simple measurements of this kind to improve accuracy has been discussed by Gold and Rabiner [12], [13]. By careful choice of the basic measurements and careful design of the logic, the accuracy of the combined results is much greater than the accuracy of any of the individual estimates.

B. Energy Measurements

One of the simplest representations of a signal is its energy. In the case of a real discrete-time signal $x(n)$, the energy is defined in general as

$$E = \sum_{n=-\infty}^{\infty} x^2(n). \qquad (4)$$

For nonstationary signals such as speech, it is often more appropriate to consider a time-varying energy calculation such as the following:

$$E(n) = \sum_{m=0}^{N-1} [w(m)x(n-m)]^2 \qquad (5)$$

where $w(m)$ is a weighting sequence or window which selects a segment of $x(n)$, and N is the number of samples in the window. For the simple case of $w(m) = 1$, $E(n)$ is the sum of the squares of the N most recent values of $x(n)$. Fig. 7(a) shows how the energy measurement of (5) can be viewed in terms of filtering the sequence $x^2(n)$ by a finite impulse response (FIR) filter with impulse response $w^2(n)$.

It is to be expected that the function $E(n)$ would display the time varying amplitude properties of the speech signal. However, the definition of (5) requires careful interpretation. First there is the choice of window. The purpose of the window is to attach lower weight to speech samples which occurred further back in time, thus $w(m)$ generally tends to 0 monotonically as m gets larger. When one wants to apply equal weight to the entire interval, a rectangular window is used. The

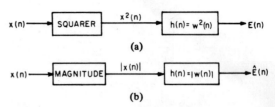

(a)

(b)

Fig. 7. (a) Implementation of short-time energy calculation using a finite impulse response digital filter. (b) An alternative definition of energy.

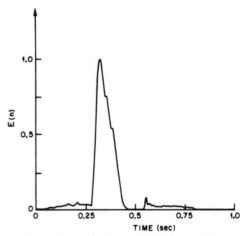

Fig. 8. Normalized energy for the word /six/.

second difficulty involves choice of measurement interval N. If N is too small, i.e., less than a pitch period, $E(n)$ of (6) will fluctuate very rapidly depending on exact details of the waveform. If N is too large, i.e., several pitch periods, $E(n)$ will have very little variation, and will not reflect the changing properties of the speech signal. A suitable practical choice of N is on the order of 100–200 for a 10-kHz sampling rate (i.e., 10–20 ms of speech).

The major significance of $E(n)$ is that it provides a good measure for separating voiced speech segments from unvoiced speech segments. $E(n)$ for unvoiced segments is much smaller than for voiced segments. Also the smaller the value of N, the less smearing there is in locating the exact instant at which unvoiced speech becomes voiced and vice versa. Furthermore, for very high quality speech, the energy can be used to separate unvoiced speech from silence.

One difficulty with energy measurements is that they are very sensitive to large signal levels (because they enter the computation as a square), thereby emphasizing large sample-to-sample variations in $E(n)$. One relatively simple way of alleviating this problem is to use as a measure of energy, the function

$$\hat{E}(n) = \sum_{m=0}^{N-1} |w(m)x(n-m)| \qquad (6)$$

where the sum of absolute values is computed instead of the sum of squares. Fig. 7(b) shows an interpretation of (6) as a linear filtering operation on $|x(n)|$. Fig. 8 shows the energy function for the word six for a 10-ms rectangular window. It is easy to see the low energy fricative regions at the beginning and end of six, and the stop gap region during the /k/ for which the energy is almost zero. An example of the application of energy measurements is the speech recognition work of Reddy [14].

C. Zero Crossing Measurements

Another very simple time domain analysis method is based on zero crossing measurements. In the context of a digital implementation, a zero crossing can be said to occur between sampling instants n and $n - 1$ if

$$\text{sign } [x(n)] \neq \text{sign } [x(n - 1)] . \qquad (7)$$

This measurement is trivial to implement and is often used as a gross estimate of the frequency content of a speech signal. Its use is motivated by the observation that if the signal is a sinusoid of frequency f_0, then the average number of zero crossings is

$$n_z = 2f_0 \text{ crossings/s.} \qquad (8)$$

However, the interpretation of zero crossing measurements for speech is much less precise, because of the broad frequency spectrum of most speech sounds. Nevertheless, very crude estimates of spectrum properties such as this may often suffice.

For example, it is well known that the energy of voiced speech tends to be concentrated below 3 kHz, whereas the energy of fricatives generally is concentrated above 3 kHz. Thus, zero crossing measurements (along with energy information) are often used in making a decision about whether a particular segment of speech is voiced or unvoiced. If the zero crossing rate is high, the implication is unvoiced; if the zero crossing rate is low, the segment is most likely to be voiced. Zero crossing measurements, coupled with a pitch detection scheme, provide a useful approach to estimation of excitation parameters [34]. Zero crossing measurements have also been useful as representations of speech signals for speech recognition [14].

In implementing zero crossing measurements digitally, there are a number of important considerations. Although the basic algorithm requires only a comparison of signs of two successive samples, special care must be taken in the sampling process. Noise, dc offset, and 60-Hz hum have disastrous effects on zero crossing measurements. Thus for zero crossing measurements a bandpass filter rather than a low-pass filter may be necessary prior to sampling to avoid the said difficulties. Also, the sampling period T determines the time resolution of the zero crossing measurements; thus fine resolution requires a high sampling rate. However, very crude quantization (1 bit in fact) is all that is necessary to preserve the zero crossing information.

D. Short-Time Autocorrelation Analysis

The autocorrelation function of a discrete-time signal $x(n)$ is defined as

$$\varphi(m) = \lim_{N \to \infty} \frac{1}{2N + 1} \sum_{n=-N}^{N} x(n) \, x(n + m) .$$

The autocorrelation function is useful for displaying structure in any waveform, speech being no exception. For example, if a signal is periodic with period P, i.e., $x(n + P) = x(n)$ for all n, then it is easily shown that

$$\varphi(m) = \varphi(m + P). \qquad (9)$$

Thus periodicity in the autocorrelation function indicates periodicity in the signal. Also, an autocorrelation function that is sharply peaked around $m = 0$ and falls off rapidly to zero as m

increases indicates a lack of predictable structure in the signal.

As we have observed, speech is not a stationary signal. However, the properties of the speech signal remain fixed over relatively long time intervals. As we have already seen, this leads to the notion of short-time analysis techniques that operate on short segments of the speech signal. For example consider a segment of N samples of the signal

$$x_l(n) = x(n + l), \qquad 0 \leq n \leq N - 1 \qquad (10)$$

where l denotes the beginning of the segment. Then the short-time autocorrelation function can be defined as

$$\varphi_l(m) = \frac{1}{N} \sum_{n=0}^{N'-1} x_l(n) x_l(n + m), \qquad 0 \leq m \leq M_0 - 1 \quad (11)$$

where M_0 denotes the maximum lag that is of interest. For example, if we wish to observe periodicity in a waveform, then we would require $M_0 > P$. The integer N' is for the moment unspecified.

We can interpret (11) as the autocorrelation of a segment of the speech signal of length N samples beginning at sample l. If $N' = N$, then data from outside the segment $l \leq n \leq N + l - 1$ is used in the computation. If $N' = N - m$, then only data from that interval is required. In this case, the segment is often weighted by a "window" function that smoothly tapers the ends of the segment to zero. In using the autocorrelation function to detect periodicity in speech, either choice is satisfactory; however, we shall see in Section VII that the distinction is important in analysis methods based on linear prediction. In either case, the direct computation of $\varphi_l(m)$ for $0 \leq m \leq M_0 - 1$ requires computational effort proportional to $M_0 \cdot N$. This can be a significant overhead factor.

Short-time analysis methods typically are applied to estimate parameters of the speech model discussed in Section II. The normal assumption is that although a sampling rate ranging from 6 kHz to 20 kHz may be necessary to preserve the essential features of the speech signal in a PCM representation, much lower sampling rates suffice for the slowly varying parameters of the model (50 to 100 Hz is typical). Suppose for example that the sampling rate of the speech signal is 10 kHz and the short-time autocorrelation is to be computed 100 times/s. The estimate of the autocorrelation is generally based upon from 20- to 40-ms segments of the speech signal. (For estimates of periodicity, the window must be long enough to encompass at least two periods of the speech signal.) Thus, for a 10-kHz sampling rate $200 \leq N \leq 400$, and the autocorrelation estimates must be computed by moving in increments of 100 samples.

In using the short-time autocorrelation function for pitch period estimation, it is desirable that the correlation function be sharply peaked so that a strong peak will stand out at multiples of P, the period. The correlation function of speech is not sharply peaked because there is a great deal of predictable structure in each period of the speech waveform. Sondhi [15] has given several methods of sharpening the peaks in the autocorrelation function. One of these called center clipping is illustrated in Fig. 9. The nonlinear operation of clipping out the middle of the speech waveform is very effective in reducing the sample to sample correlation of the signal. This is illustrated in Fig. 10 which shows a succession of short-time

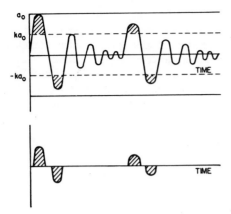

Fig. 9. Illustration of center clipping.

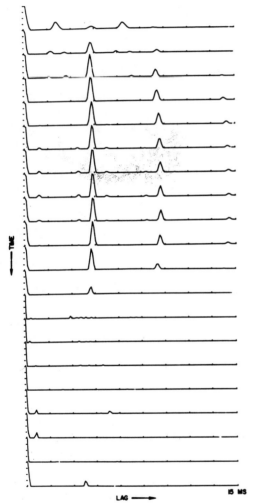

Fig. 10. Sequence of autocorrelation functions for center-clipped speech.

autocorrelation functions each estimated from 30-ms segments of center-clipped speech which are selected at intervals of 15 ms ($66\frac{2}{3}$-Hz sampling rate).

From a set of correlation functions of this type it is possible to estimate the pitch period simply by locating the strong peak that is in evidence during voiced intervals. Sondhi [15] gives a decision algorithm that formalizes this process. This scheme has been found to perform very well in situations where the speech is voiced but the wave shape is almost sinusoidal or when the fundamental frequency is missing [15].

V. Short-Time Spectrum Analysis

Short-time spectrum analysis has traditionally been one of the most important speech processing techniques. As we have previously stated, the fundamental assumption underlying any short-time analysis method is that over a long-time interval, speech is nonstationary but that over a sufficiently short-time interval it can be considered stationary. Thus, the Fourier transform of a short segment of speech should give a good spectral representation of the speech during that time interval. Measurement of the short-time spectrum is the basic operation in the channel vocoder [19], [26] the phase vocoder [18], spectrogram displays [21], [23], and some speech recognition systems [20]. Two methods are commonly used for implementing short-time Fourier analysis. The first uses a bank of bandpass filters. This method was originally used with analog filters and it can be implemented with even greater precision and flexibility with digital filters. The second method uses a fast Fourier transform (FFT) algorithm. This method is fundamentally digital and has no analog counterpart. When implemented on a computer, the FFT method is generally computationally superior to the bank-of-filters model.

A. Filter Banks for Short-Time Spectrum Analysis

Fig. 11 shows a simple way of implementing a short-time spectrum analyzer using a bank of bandpass filters. If the filter passbands are chosen to cover the speech band, then, roughly speaking, the outputs can be thought of as a Fourier representation of the input speech signal. If the filters are carefully designed, the sum of all the filter outputs will be a good approximation to the original speech signal [24]. This is the basis for communication systems such as the channel vocoder and the phase vocoder.

Based on some fundamental ideas of spectrum analysis, the discrete short-time spectrum of $x(n)$ is defined as

$$X_l(\omega) = \sum_{n=-\infty}^{l} x(n)\, h(l-n)\, e^{-j\omega n} \tag{12a}$$

$$= |X_l(\omega)|\, e^{j\theta_l(\omega)} \tag{12b}$$

$$= a_l(\omega) - jb_l(\omega). \tag{12c}$$

Equation (12) can be interpreted in a number of ways. As shown in Fig. 12, one interpretation is that $X_l(\omega)$ is the Fourier transform of a sequence $x(n)$ that is weighted by a "window" $h(l-n)$. Thus the short-time Fourier transform is a function of both frequency ω and the discrete time index l. A second interpretation follows if we assume that $h(n)$ is the impulse response of a low-pass digital filter. Assume that we wish to evaluate the short-time transform at frequency ω. Then $X_n(\omega)$ is seen to be the output of the low-pass filter with input $x(n)\, e^{-j\omega n}$. This is depicted in Fig. 13(a). To avoid complex arithmetic, the system of Fig. 13(a) is generally implemented as shown in Fig. 13(b) where the output parameters are $a_n(\omega)$ and $b_n(\omega)$, the real and imaginary parts of the spectrum. The bandwidth of the low-pass filter determines the frequency resolution. Typically, this bandwidth is on the order of 50 Hz. Thus the spectrum signals can be sampled at a much lower rate ($\sim$100 Hz) than the speech signal itself.

Using digital filters, it has been shown [24], [25] that the short-time Fourier transform can be a very good representation of the speech signal in the sense that the output obtained by summing appropriately modulated bandpass channels can be made indistinguishable from the input. This requires a bit

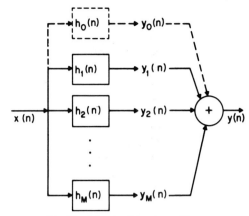

Fig. 11. A bank of bandpass filters.

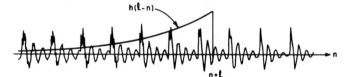

Fig. 12. Illustration of computation of the short-time Fourier transform.

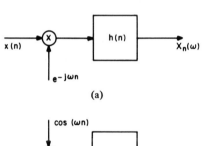

(a)

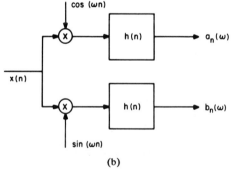

(b)

Fig. 13. Short-time Fourier analysis and synthesis for one channel centered at ω.

rate on the order of the bit rate required for comparable PCM representation. However, the resulting representation of the speech signal permits greater flexibility in the sense that the spectral parameters $a_n(\omega)$ and $b_n(\omega)$ provide information about the parameters of the speech model in a convenient and useful form. For example the time and frequency dimensions of a speech signal can be independently manipulated through simple manipulations of the spectral parameters [18].

B. Use of the FFT for Short-Time Spectrum Analysis

The FFT is a set of highly efficient algorithms for evaluating the discrete Fourier transform (DFT) expressions

$$F(k) = \sum_{n=0}^{M-1} f(n) \exp\left(-j\frac{2\pi}{M}kn\right), \qquad k = 0, 1, \cdots, M-1 \quad (13)$$

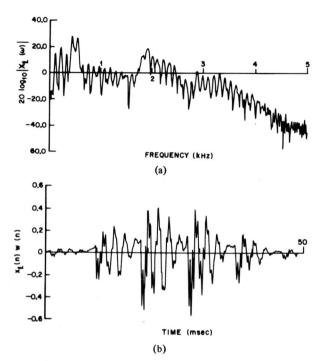

Fig. 14. (a) Log magnitude of the short-time transform. (b) Corresponding windowed speech segment. ($N = 500$.)

and

$$f(n) = \frac{1}{M} \sum_{k=0}^{M-1} F(k) \exp\left(j\frac{2\pi}{M}kn\right), \qquad n = 0, 1, \cdots, M-1. \quad (14)$$

For using these expressions, it is convenient to define the short-time transform as

$$X_l(\omega) = \sum_{n=0}^{N-1} x_l(n) \, w(n) \, e^{-j\omega n} \quad (15a)$$

where

$$x_l(n) = x(n+l), \quad n = 0, 1, \cdots, N-1, \quad l = 0, L, 2L, \cdots. \quad (15b)$$

As in the case of the short-time autocorrelation function, we interpret (15a) as the Fourier transform of a segment of speech N samples long (weighted by a window $w(n)$), beginning at l. The frequency resolution of the spectrum measurement is inversely proportional to the window length N. This is illustrated in Fig. 14. Fig. 14(a) shows the short-time transform and Fig. 14(b) shows the corresponding windowed segment of speech data. A Hamming window [17] of length 50 ms was used. ($N = 500$ samples at a 10-kHz sampling rate.) Note that the individual harmonics of the pitch period are resolved in the short-time transform. Figs. 15(a) and (b) show the short-time transform and the windowed speech for $N = 50$ samples. (The speech segment is the first 50 samples of the segment shown in Fig. 14(b).) In this case the frequency resolution is much less than in Fig. 14. We note that the spectrum of Fig. 14 could be considered comparable to a conventional narrow-band spectrogram measurement while Fig. 15 is comparable to a conventional wide-band spectrogram analysis. In particular, Figs. 14 and 15 show typical spectral cross-sections at a particular time. In the first case, both the pitch information and vocal tract transfer function information is present while in the latter case only the general shape of the vocal tract transfer function is preserved.

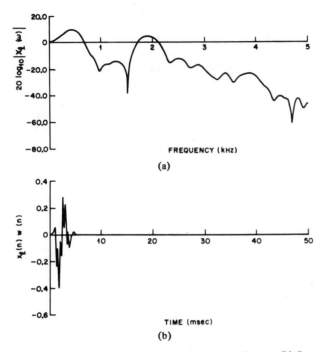

(a)

(b)

Fig. 15. (a) Log magnitude of the short-time transform. (b) Corresponding windowed speech segment. ($N = 50$.)

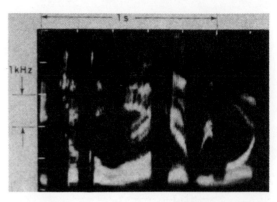

Fig. 16. An example of a spectrogram produced using digital spectrum analysis and computer graphics display. (After Oppenheim [23].)

An FFT algorithm can be used to compute (15) at equally spaced frequencies $\omega_k = 2\pi k/M$, for $k = 0, 1, \cdots, M - 1$. If $M \geqslant N$, then the sequence $x_l(n) w(n)$ must be augmented with $M - N$ zero valued samples to form a sequence of length M. In this case we can compute

$$X_l\left(\frac{2\pi}{M} k\right) = \sum_{n=0}^{N-1} x_l(n) w(n) e^{-j2\pi kn/M},$$

$$k = 0, 1, \cdots, M - 1 \quad (16)$$

using an FFT algorithm.

On the other hand if $M < N$, we can take advantage of the periodicity of the complex exponential $\exp(-j2\pi kn/M)$ to express (15a) as

$$X_l\left(\frac{2\pi}{M} k\right) = \sum_{n=0}^{M-1} g(n) e^{-j2\pi kn/M},$$

$$k = 0, 1, \cdots, M - 1 \quad (17a)$$

where

$$g(n) = \sum_{r=0}^{[N/M]} x_l(n+r) w(n+r) \quad (17b)$$

and $[N/M]$ means the largest integer in N/M. This latter feature of FFT spectrum analysis is useful whenever one wishes to only evaluate the transform at intervals of $\omega = 2\pi/M$ but at the same time wishes to obtain the better frequency resolution corresponding to a window of length N. Using the preceding approach, it is also possible to use the FFT to compute the outputs of a uniformly spaced bank of filters as required in a phase vocoder analyzer [24].

An important consequence of the definition of the short-time spectrum in (15) is that $|X_l(\omega)|^2/N$ is the Fourier trans-

form of the short-time autocorrelation function

$$R_l(m) = \frac{1}{N} \sum_{n=0}^{N-1-m} x_l(n) w(n) x_l(n+m) w(n+m). \quad (18)$$

That is,

$$R_l(m) = \frac{1}{2\pi} \int_{-\pi}^{\pi} \frac{|X_l(\omega)|^2}{N} e^{j\omega m} d\omega. \quad (19)$$

Furthermore, it can be shown that if $X_l(2\pi k/M)$ is computed with $M \geqslant 2N$, then $R_l(m)$ is the inverse of $|X_l(2\pi k/M)|^2/N$; i.e.,

$$R_l(m) = \frac{1}{M} \sum_{k=0}^{M-1} \frac{|X_l(2\pi k/M)|^2}{N} e^{j2\pi kn/M},$$

$$0 \leqslant m \leqslant N - 1. \quad (20)$$

If we suppose that $R_l(m)$ is required for $0 \leqslant m \leqslant M_0 - 1$, where M_0 is a large number, as in pitch detection, it may be most efficient to first compute the short-time transform using (16), and then compute the autocorrelation function using (20).

C. Short-Time Spectrum Representations of Speech

The short-time spectrum can serve directly as a representation of the speech signal as is the case in many vocoder systems [18], [19], [25], [26] and in some speech recognition systems [20]. In many cases, however, the short-time spectrum is computed as an intermediate step in the estimation of one or more of the time varying parameters of the speech model. In the narrow-band short-time spectrum as in Fig. 14(a), both pitch and vocal tract transfer function information are clearly in evidence, while the wide-band analysis, as in Fig. 15(a), does not preserve the pitch information. Thus there are a variety of methods for estimating fundamental frequency directly from the narrow-band short-time spectrum [22], [27]. Similarly there are a wide variety of methods of estimating parameters such as formant frequencies from the short-time spectrum [16], [26].

One of the most useful tools in speech science is the sound spectrograph. This device produces a plot of energy as a function of time and frequency; i.e., a display of the short-time spectrum. The basis analysis techniques of this section have been used to generate spectrographic displays that are similar to, but in many cases more elaborate and flexible than, con-

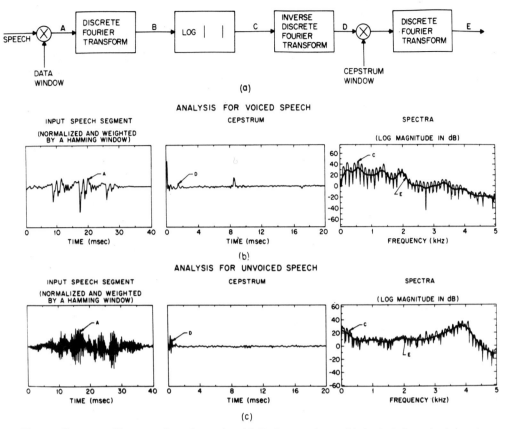

Fig. 17. Homomorphic processing of speech. (a) Basic operations. (b) Analysis for voiced speech. (c) Analysis for unvoiced speech.

ventional spectrograms [21], [23], [28]. As we have pointed out, there is great flexibility for computer spectral analysis in window length and shape or equivalently frequency resolution. Also, the spectrum can be shaped in a manner to enhance it for display, and it is possible to precisely correlate the speech waveform with the spectrographic display.

Such schemes have been implemented in a variety of ways but most of them use (15) to compute a set of short-time spectra at equally spaced time intervals. This set of spectra can be thought of as samples of the two dimensional function $X_l(\omega)$ which can be plotted as a frequency-time-intensity plot on an oscilloscope or television monitor. Using such techniques it has been possible to produce on-line spectrogram displays that are equal in quality to conventional spectrograms and far surpass them in flexibility and innovation. An example of one approach is shown in Fig. 16 [23].

VI. HOMOMORPHIC SPEECH PROCESSING

Homomorphic filtering is a class of nonlinear signal processing techniques that is based on a generalization of the principle of superposition that defines linear systems. Such techniques have been applied in separating signals that have been combined by multiplication and convolution [31]. The application of these techniques to speech processing is again based on the assumption that although speech production is a time varying process, it can be viewed on a short-time basis as the convolution of an excitation function (either random noise or a quasi-periodic pulse train) with the vocal tract impulse response. Thus methods for separating the components of a convolution are of interest.

A. Fundamentals

A homomorphic system for speech analysis is shown in Fig. 17(a). We assume that the signal at A is the discrete convolution of the excitation and the vocal tract impulse response. Then the short-time Fourier transform (i.e., the spectrum of the windowed signal), computed using the FFT method of the previous section, is the product of the Fourier transforms of the excitation and the vocal tract impulse response. Taking the logarithm of the magnitude of the Fourier transform, we obtain at C the sum of the logarithms of the transforms of the excitation and vocal tract impulse response. Since the inverse discrete Fourier transform (IDFT) is a linear operation, the result at D (called the cepstrum of the input at A) is an additive combination of the cepstra of the excitation and vocal tract components. Thus, the effect of the operations, windowing, DFT, log magnitude, and IDFT is to approximately transform convolution into addition. The value of this transformation can be seen from Fig. 17(b), which depicts the results of such an analysis for voiced speech. The curve labeled A is the input speech segment that has been multiplied by a Hamming window. The rapidly varying curve labeled C is the log-magnitude of the short-time transform. It consists of a slowly varying component due to the vocal tract transmission, and a rapidly varying periodic component due to the periodic excitation. The slowly varying part of the log magnitude produces the low-time part of the cepstrum (D), and the rapidly varying periodic component of the log magnitude manifests itself in the strong peak at a time equal to the period of the input speech segment. If we assume that the vocal tract transfer function in the model of Fig. 3 is of the form of an all-pole model,

$$H(z) = \frac{A}{1 - \sum_{k=1}^{p} a_k z^{-k}} = A \prod_{k=1}^{p} \frac{1}{1 - z_k z^{-1}} \qquad (21)$$

then the cepstrum of the vocal tract component of the convolution can be shown [30], [47] to be

$$\hat{h}(n) = \begin{cases} 0, & n < 0 \\ \log A, & n = 0 \\ \sum_{k=1}^{p} \frac{z_k^n}{n}, & n > 0. \end{cases} \qquad (22)$$

If we assume that the excitation component is a periodic train of impulses, then it can be shown [30] that the cepstrum of the excitation component will also be a train of impulses with the same spacing as the input impulse train. This is clearly reflected in the cepstrum for voiced speech in Fig. 17(b). The important point is that the cepstrum consists of an additive combination in which (due to the $1/n$ falloff) the vocal tract and excitation components essentially do not overlap. The situation for unvoiced speech, shown in Fig. 17(c), is much the same with the exception that the random nature of the excitation component of the input speech segment (A) causes a rapidly varying random component in the log magnitude (C). Thus in the cepstrum (D), the low time components correspond as before to the slowly varying vocal tract transfer function; however, since the rapid variations of the log magnitude are not, in this case, periodic, there is no strong peak as for the voiced speech segment. Thus, the cepstrum serves as an excellent basis for estimating the fundamental period of voiced speech and for determining whether a particular speech segment is voiced or unvoiced [29].

The vocal tract transfer function, often called the spectrum envelope, can be obtained by removing the rapidly varying components of the log magnitude spectrum by linear filtering. One approach to this filtering operation involves computing the IDFT of the log magnitude spectrum (to give the cepstrum), multiplying the cepstrum by an appropriate window that only passes the short-time components, and then computing the DFT of the resulting windowed cepstrum. This method corresponds to the fast convolution method [45]–[49], in this case being applied to filter a function of frequency rather than a function of time. The results for voiced and unvoiced speech segments are labeled E in Figs. 17(b) and (c), respectively.

The smoothed spectrum obtained by the above method is in many respects comparable to a short-time spectrum obtained by direct analysis using a short data window. The major difference, however, is that the cepstrum method is based upon the initial computation of a narrow-band spectrum, which involves a wide time window, while the wide-band spectrum is computed using a very narrow-time window. The smoothing is done upon a narrow-band log-magnitude spectrum rather than upon the short-time Fourier transform itself, as is the case for wide-band analysis. Thus, for speech segments in which the basic parameters such as pitch period and formant frequencies are not changing, we should expect the cepstrum method to produce superior results to direct spectrum analysis. When the speech spectrum is changing rapidly, as in the case of a voiced/unvoiced boundary, the direct method may produce a better representation than the cepstrum method due to its shorter averaging time.

B. Estimation of Formant Frequencies and Pitch Period

The results depicted in Fig. 17 suggest algorithms for estimating basic speech parameters such as pitch period and formant frequencies. Specifically, voiced/unvoiced classification of the excitation is indicated by the presence or absence of a strong peak in the cepstrum [29]. The presence of a strong peak for voiced speech is dependent upon there being many harmonics present in the spectrum. In cases where this is not true, such as voiced stops, zero crossing measurements are helpful in distinguishing voiced from unvoiced speech [34]. If a strong peak is present, its location is a good indicator of the pitch period.

The smoothed spectrum retains peaks at the vocal tract resonances or formant frequencies. One approach to estimating the formants is to search the smooth spectra for peaks and then decide which peaks correspond to formants [34]. Another approach uses iterative methods to adjust the parameters of a model similar to (21) until a good match to the smooth spectrum is obtained [33].

An illustration of the use of homomorphic processing is given in Fig. 18. On the left are shown a sequence of cepstra computed at 20-ms intervals. The strong peak indicates that the speech is voiced during the entire interval. On the right are successive short-time spectra and homomorphically smoothed short-time spectra. The lines connecting the peaks of the smooth spectra show the formant frequencies automatically estimated from the spectrum peaks. The peak-picking approach is relatively simple except when two formants merge as in the third and fourth frames from the top and the last 4 frames from the bottom. In this case it is useful to evaluate the vocal tract transfer function on a contour which passes closer to the poles thereby sharpening the resonances [34].

Speech can be synthesized from formant and pitch data by using the estimated parameters to vary the parameters of the model of Fig. 3. With efficient coding of the parameters, speech is thus represented by about 1000 bits/s [2]. In addition to this high efficiency, the formant representation offers great flexibility in manipulating basic speech parameters. Also, since so much of the speech model is built into the representation, these parameters are very useful for other purposes such as speech recognition and speaker verification.

C. The Cepstrum as a Representation of Speech

The low-time samples of the cepstrum contain mostly information about the vocal tract transfer function $H(z)$ of (21). It can be shown [31], [47], that the following recurrence formula relates the vocal tract impulse response $h(n)$ to the cepstrum $\hat{h}(n)$ of (22):

$$h(n) = \begin{cases} \hat{h}(n)h(0) + \sum_{k=0}^{n-1} \left(\frac{k}{n}\right) \hat{h}(k)h(n-k), & 1 \leq n \\ e^{\hat{h}(0)}, & n = 0. \end{cases} \qquad (23)$$

Also using (23) it is easily shown that the coefficients a_n in (21) are related to the cepstrum by

$$a_n = \hat{h}(n) - \sum_{k=0}^{n-1} \left(\frac{k}{n}\right) \hat{h}(k)a_{n-k}, \qquad 1 \leq n \leq p. \qquad (24)$$

CEPSTRA   SPECTRA

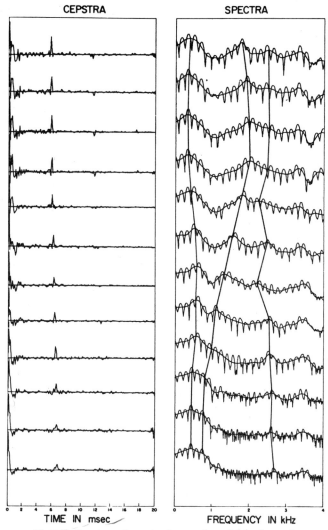

TIME IN msec

FREQUENCY IN kHz

Fig. 18. Cepstra and spectra for a region of voiced speech.

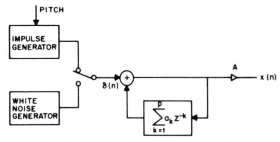

Fig. 19. Digital model for speech production.

Since the cepstrum contains all of the information of the short-time spectrum, it can be viewed as still another representation of the speech signal. This principle has been applied in a speech analysis synthesis scheme called the homomorphic vocoder [32]. In this system, the low-time cepstrum values and an estimate of pitch period serve as a representation of the speech signal from which an acoustic wave can be reconstructed.

VII. LINEAR PREDICTIVE ANALYSIS

Among the most useful methods of speech analysis are those based upon the principle of linear prediction. These methods are important because of their accuracy and their speed of computation. In this section, we present a formulation of linear predictive analysis and discuss some of the issues which are involved in using it in practical speech applications.

The basic idea behind linear predictive coding (LPC) is that a sample of speech can be approximated as a linear combination of the past p speech samples. By minimizing the square difference between the actual speech samples and the linearly predicted ones, one can determine the predictor coefficients; i.e., the weighting coefficients of the linear combination. The basic philosophy of this scheme is reminiscent of and, in fact, related to the waveform quantization methods discussed in Section III [35]. There it was mentioned that a linear pre-

dictor can be applied in a differential quantization scheme to reduce the bit rate of the digital representation of the speech waveform. In this case, as in linear predictive analysis, the predictor coefficients must be adapted (i.e., updated regularly) to match the time-varying properties of the speech signal.

A. Fundamental Principles

The use of linear predictive analysis is suggested by the digital model of Section II. Assume that samples of the speech signal are produced by the model of Fig. 3, where over a short time interval the linear system has the transfer function

$$H(z) = \frac{A}{1 - \sum_{k=1}^{p} a_k z^{-k}}. \tag{25}$$

For voiced speech, the system is excited by an impulse train and for unvoiced speech it is excited by random white noise as depicted in Fig. 19. Linear prediction analysis is based on the observation that for such a system the speech samples $x(n)$ are related to the excitation $\delta(n)$ by the following difference equation:

$$x(n) = \sum_{k=1}^{p} a_k x(n-k) + \delta(n). \tag{26}$$

Suppose that we process the speech signal with a linear predictor; i.e.,

$$\tilde{x}(n) = \sum_{k=1}^{p} \alpha_k x(n-k).$$

Then the predictor error is defined as

$$\epsilon(n) = x(n) - \tilde{x}(n) = x(n) - \sum_{k=1}^{p} \alpha_k x(n-k). \tag{27}$$

Note that in this case the prediction is based on the unquantized samples $x(n)$, whereas in Section III, the prediction was based on quantized samples $\hat{x}(n)$. It can be seen by comparing (26) and (27) that if $\alpha_k = a_k$, and if the speech signal really does obey the model of (26), then $\epsilon(n) = \delta(n)$. Therefore, between the excitation impulses of voiced speech, the prediction error should be very small if the predictor coefficients α_k are equal to the parameters a_k of the vocal tract transfer function. Thus the predictor polynomial

$$P(z) = 1 - \sum_{k=1}^{p} \alpha_k z^{-k}$$

is a good approximation to the denominator of the vocal tract transfer function.[2]

One approach for obtaining the predictor coefficients is based on minimizing the average squared prediction error over a short segment of the speech waveform. That is, we search for the values of α_k that minimize

$$E_l = \sum_{n=0}^{N-1} (x_l(n) - \tilde{x}_l(n))^2$$

$$= \sum_{n=0}^{N-1} \left(x_l(n) - \sum_{k=1}^{p} \alpha_k x_l(n-k) \right)^2 \qquad (28)$$

where $x_l(n)$ is a segment of speech that has been selected in the vicinity of sample l; i.e.,

$$x_l(n) = x(n+l).$$

There are two basic ways of choosing $x_l(n)$ each leading to procedures that are somewhat different in the details of their implementation and the results that are obtained. Leaving $x_l(n)$ unspecified for now, we can find the values of α_k that minimize E_l in (28) by setting $\partial E_l / \partial \alpha_i = 0$, $i = 1, 2, \cdots, p$, thus obtaining the equations

$$\sum_{n=0}^{N-1} x_l(n-i)x_l(n) = \sum_{k=1}^{p} \alpha_k \sum_{n=0}^{N-1} x_l(n-i)x_l(n-k),$$

$$1 \leqslant i \leqslant p. \qquad (29)$$

If we define

$$\varphi_l(i, k) = \sum_{n=0}^{N-1} x_l(n-i)x_l(n-k) \qquad (30)$$

then (29) can be written more compactly as

$$\sum_{k=1}^{p} \alpha_k \varphi_l(i, k) = \varphi_l(i, 0), \qquad i = 1, 2, \cdots, p. \qquad (31)$$

This set of p equations in p unknowns can be solved for the unknown predictor coefficients that minimize the average squared prediction error for the segment $x_l(n)$. To do this, the quantities $\varphi_l(i, k)$ must be computed for $1 \leqslant i \leqslant p$ and $1 \leqslant k \leqslant p$. The details of this computation depend upon how $x_l(n)$ is defined.

By a simple substitution of variables, (30) can be written as

$$\varphi_l(i, k) = \sum_{n=-i}^{N-1-i} x_l(n)x_l(n+i-k)$$

$$= \sum_{n=-k}^{N-1-k} x_l(n)x_l(n+k-i). \qquad (32)$$

Clearly, $\varphi_l(i, k) = \varphi_l(k, i)$. We observe from (32) that values of $x_l(n)$ are required outside the interval $0 \leqslant n \leqslant N-1$. If we choose to supply the values outside this interval we note that we then require

$$x_l(n) = x(n+l), \qquad -p \leqslant n \leqslant N-2 \qquad (33)$$

to evaluate $\varphi_l(i, k)$. This method and its attendant details was proposed by Atal [36] and has come to be called the *covariance*

---

method because of the similarity of the matrix $\varphi_l(i, k)$ to a covariance matric.

If we choose not to supply values of the signal outside the interval $0 \leqslant n \leqslant N-1$, then we must resort to using a finite duration window $w(n)$ to reduce the end effects thereby obtaining,

$$x_l(n) = \begin{cases} x(n+l)w(n), & 0 \leqslant n \leqslant N-1 \\ 0, & \text{otherwise.} \end{cases}$$

Using this definition of $x_l(n)$, (32) becomes

$$\varphi_l(i, k) = \sum_{n=0}^{N-1-(i-k)} x_l(n)x_l(n+i-k).$$

$$= \sum_{n=0}^{N-1-(k-i)} x_l(n)x_l(n+k-i)$$

$$\equiv r_l(i-k) = r_l(k-i). \qquad (34)$$

In this case (31) becomes

$$\sum_{k=1}^{p} \alpha_k r_l(|i-k|) = r_l(i), \qquad i = 1, 2, \cdots, p. \qquad (35)$$

From (34) and (18), it is clear that $r_l(n) = NR_l(n)$; i.e., $r_l(n)$ is equal (to within a constant multiplier) to the short-time autocorrelation function, which in turn is related to the short-time Fourier transform $X_l(\omega)$. Thus the method based on (35) is called the *autocorrelation method*. Methods of this type have been proposed by Itakura [38] (the maximum likelihood method) and Markel [41]–[43] (the inverse filter formulation).

The basic difference between the covariance method and the autocorrelation method is the necessity to use a window for the autocorrelation method. For the covariance method the section length is increased by augmenting p samples to enable the first p samples of the section ($x_l(n)$, $0 \leqslant n \leqslant p-1$) to be predicted from speech samples outside the section. Thus an equal number of samples go into the computation of $\varphi(i, j)$ for all indices i and j, and no window is required. For the autocorrelation method one is trying to predict the first p samples from speech samples outside the section. Since these samples are arbitrarily zero, a large error may result. To reduce the error a window is applied which smoothly tapers the signal to zero at the ends of the window.

At this point it is worth noting the mathematical and physical interpretations of using windows in the autocorrelation method. The process of multiplication of a signal by a window is equivalent to a circular convolution of the frequency response of the window with the speech spectrum. Thus a smearing occurs in the speech spectrum. The extent of this smearing depends on the section length N and the actual window used. However, it is clear that with the autocorrelation method, parameters such as formant bandwidths may not be accurately estimated. In many practical applications this is of little or no consequence; however, for vocoder applications it may be significant.

B. Details of Implementation

Both (31) and (35) are a set of p equations in p unknowns that can be expressed in matrix form as

$$\Phi \cdot a = \Psi. \qquad (36)$$

These equations may be solved for the predictor coefficients using any general procedure for solving linear equations. However, if computational efficiency is important, as it usually is, some special properties of the matrix Φ can be exploited to reduce computation. In the case of (31) (the covariance method) Φ is symmetric and positive definite. Utilization of this fact leads to an efficient procedure for solving for the vector *a* of predictor coefficients that is based on matrix factorization. This method is called the square root method, or the Cholesky decomposition [37].

Similarly, for the autocorrelation method the matrix Φ is symmetric and positive definite and also has the property that the elements along any diagonal are equal. Such a matrix is called a Toeplitz matrix and in this case an even more efficient method for solving the equations can be found [43]. This method is called the Levinson method.

Since computational efficiency is an important consideration in any practical speech analysis scheme, it is worthwhile comparing these two methods of linear prediction in this sense. The square root method for solving the covariance method formulation requires on the order of p^3 operations (multiplications) whereas the Levinson method for solving the autocorrelation formulation requires on the order of p^2 operations. Thus the solution of the equation for the autocorrelation formulation is inherently faster computationally than for the covariance formulation. In particular, for $p = 14$, Makhoul and Wolf [39] note a ratio in computation time of 3.2 to 1 in favor of the autocorrelation method. However, this savings in computation is not significant when viewed in the total framework of the method for two reasons. First the time required to compute the matrix of correlations is significantly greater than the time to solve the matrix equation. For example, for $N = 150$, Makhoul and Wolf [39] note that it takes ten times longer to compute the matrix then to solve the matrix equations using the autocorrelation method. Thus the savings in computation of the Levinson method becomes much less significant. As a second consideration the value of N required for both methods is not the same. For the autocorrelation method (for 10-kHz sampling) a value of N in the range 150 to 300 is generally required. For the covariance method a much smaller value of N can be used if care is taken to begin the section after a pitch pulse. In fact, Atal reports using values of N on the order of 30 with good results [36]. Thus there are many factors which determine computational efficiency.

Another difference between the two methods concerns the roots of the predictor polynomial which are the poles of the digital filter that accounts for the vocal tract transmission properties. For stability of this system, the roots must be inside the unit circle of the z plane. This is not guaranteed by the covariance method [36]; however, given *sufficient computational accuracy* the autocorrelation method guarantees stability [39], [43].

Another consideration in using these two methods is the numerical stability of the matrix inversion. Wilkinson [44] has shown that the square-root method is very stable numerically; no such statement has been made for the Levinson method. Markel [43] has pointed out that when implemented with finite precision arithmetic, the Levinson method requires careful scaling, and it is beneficial if the speech spectrum has been equalized by a simple first-order network.

Until now we have dealt with considerations which can be easily quantified and for which definitive statements can be made. When one becomes seriously interested in using linear predictive methods, several other considerations are involved. These include the necessity for spectrum equalization prior to analysis; the effects of the analog prefilter prior to analog-to-

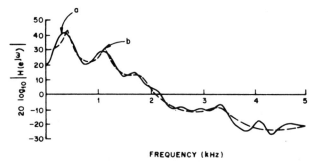

Fig. 20. Comparison of speech spectra. (a) Obtained by cepstrum smoothing. (b) Obtained by linear prediction.

digital (A/D) conversion; the effects of finite word length on the analysis; the desirability of various structures for implementing the system; and finally the ease of building the various alternatives in digital hardware. Markel [43] has provided some excellent insights into several of these issues but most of them are as yet unresolved.

C. Uses of Linear Prediction Analysis

Once the predictor coefficients have been obtained, they can be used in various ways to represent the properties of the speech signal.

1) Spectrum Estimation: If the predictor polynomial is assumed to represent the denominator of the vocal tract transfer function, we can obtain the frequency response of the vocal tract (for a particular segment of the speech signal) as

$$H(e^{j\omega T}) = \frac{A}{1 - \sum_{k=1}^{p} \alpha_k e^{-j\omega kT}}. \tag{37}$$

An example is shown in Fig. 20, where the spectrum obtained using (37) with the predictor coefficients estimated by the autocorrelation method is compared to that obtained by cepstrum smoothing for the same segment of speech. The formant frequencies are clearly in evidence in both plots, however, Fig. 20(b) has fewer extraneous peaks. This is because p was chosen so that at most 6 ($p = 12$) resonance peaks could occur. To determine the appropriate value of p for a given sampling rate, a good rule of thumb is to allow one pair of poles to account for radiation and glottal effects, and one pair of poles for each formant frequency expected in the frequency range $0 \leqslant \omega \leqslant \pi/T$. Thus, for a 10-kHz sampling rate we expect not more than 5 formant frequencies so $p = 12$ should give a good representation of the spectrum. For unvoiced speech it has been shown that a reasonably small prediction error can be obtained with a value of p on the order of 12 [36], [43].

Another point to notice is that the spectrum peaks in Fig. 20(a) are much broader than the peaks in Fig. 20(b). This is an inherent property of the homomorphic method since the Fig. 20(a) was obtained by smoothing the short-time log spectrum.

2) Formant Frequency Estimation: Smooth spectra such as Fig. 20(b) have been used in a peak picking algorithm to estimate formant frequencies in much the same manner as spectra such as Fig. 20(a) were used [41].

If p is chosen as discussed here, it can be assumed that the roots of the predictor polynomial will in general correspond to the formant frequencies. These roots can be obtained by factoring the predictor polynomial. An example is shown in Fig. 21. It is clear by comparing the plot of Fig. 21(b) to the spec-

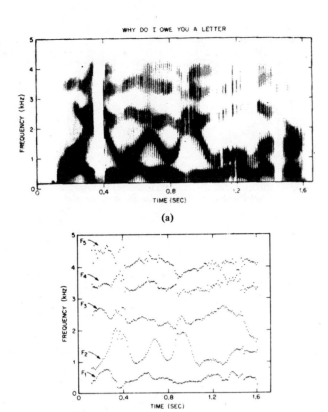

WHY DO I OWE YOU A LETTER

(a)

(b)

Fig. 21. (a) Spectrogram of predictor polynomial. (b) Roots of predictor polynomial (after Atal [36]).

trogram that the roots of the predictor polynomial are generally very good estimates of the formant frequencies. As with all formant analysis problems the difficulty in the problem lies in giving a particular formant label to a pole. Several reliable algorithms exist for doing this job [34], [41].

3) Pitch Detection: We recall that if we use the predictor coefficients as in our original formulation, then the prediction error

$$\epsilon(n) = x(n) - \sum_{k=1}^{p} \alpha_k x(n-k) \qquad (38)$$

should appear very much like the excitation function $\delta(n)$ in Fig. 19. Thus it might be expected that the prediction error signal might be useful as a starting point for determining properties of the excitation; i.e., pitch period and voiced/unvoiced decision. Several procedures of this type have been suggested [40], [42].

4) Relation to the Cepstrum and Autocorrelation Function: In addition to the aforementioned, the basic linear prediction coefficients can be transformed directly into a number of other representations of the speech signal. For example by solving (24) for $\hat{h}(n)$, we obtain the recurrence formula

$$\hat{h}(n) = a_n + \sum_{k=0}^{n-1} \left(\frac{k}{n}\right) \hat{h}(k) a_{n-k} \qquad (39)$$

relating the cepstrum of the vocal tract impulse response to the coefficients a_n in (25). Similarly it can be shown [35] that the autocorrelation function of the vocal tract impulse re-

sponse defined as

$$r(m) = \sum_{n=0}^{\infty} h(n) h(n+m) \qquad (40)$$

satisfies the recurrence formula

$$r(m) = \begin{cases} \sum_{k=1}^{p} a_k r(i-k), & m \geq 1 \\ \sum_{k=1}^{p} a_k r(k) + 1, & m = 1. \end{cases} \qquad (41)$$

5) Speech Synthesis: Finally, the predictor coefficients and excitation information can be used in the model of Fig. 19 to reconstruct a speech waveform [36]. In this case it is necessary to estimate the constant A in (25) as well as the parameters of the predictor polynomial. This can be done as part of the computation of the predictor coefficients [43] but in most cases A is simply chosen to match the energy of the synthetic speech to the energy of the original speech [36].

D. Discussion

The underlying structure of linear prediction analysis is that over short sections of speech one can accurately predict the current speech sample from the preceding p samples. Although a wide variety of different formulations of this method have arisen, the inherent similarities between methods are much larger than the supposed differences. To make all the decisions as to which particular method to use, what section duration etc., one must pay strict attention to the ultimate application of the method. Thus for most speech recognition applications, for example, the differences between formulations are *not* significant. For other more stringent applications, such as analysis/synthesis, the differences may indeed be quite significant and may mean the difference between an acceptable and a nonacceptable system.

VIII. SUMMARY

In this paper, we have discussed a wide variety of digital representations of speech signals. These representations have varied in complexity, information rate, and flexibility from simple waveform coding schemes to analysis schemes such as homomorphic filtering and linear prediction analysis which are directed toward the estimation of the parameters of a detailed model of speech production. We have focused our attention almost exclusively on analysis techniques that are of wide applicability. The results of most of these techniques can be applied in a variety of speech processing applications including speech recognition, speech synthesis, and speaker verification.

REFERENCES

General

[1] G. Fant, *Acoustic Theory of Speech Production.* The Hague, The Netherlands: Mouton, 1970.
[2] J. L. Flanagan, C. H. Coker, L. R. Rabiner, R. W. Schafer, and N. Umeda, "Synthetic voices for computers," *IEEE Spectrum,* vol. 7, pp. 22–45, Oct. 1970.
[3] J. L. Flanagan, *Speech Analysis, Synthesis and Perception,* 2nd ed. New York: Springer-Verlag, 1972.

Waveform Coding

[4] H. S. Black, *Modulation Theory.* Princeton, N.J.: Van Nostrand, 1953.

[5] P. Cummiskey, N. S. Jayant, and J. L. Flanagan, "Adaptive quantization in differential PCM coding of speech," *Bell Syst. Tech. J.*, pp. 1105–1118, Sept. 1973.

[6] N. S. Jayant, "Adaptive delta modulation with a one-bit memory," *Bell Syst. Tech. J.*, pp. 321–342, Mar. 1970.

[7] ——, "Digital coding of speech waveforms," *Proc. IEEE.*, vol. 62, pp. 611–632, May 1974.

[8] R. A. McDonald, "Signal-to-noise and idle channel performance of DPCM systems—particular application to voice signals," *Bell Syst. Tech. J.*, pp. 1123–1151, 1966.

[9] J. Max, "Quantizing for minimum distortion," *IRE Trans. Inform. Theory*, vol. 1T- pp. 7–12, Mar. 1960.

[10] L. H. Rosenthal, R. W. Schafer, and L. R. Rabiner "An algorithm for locating the beginning and end of an utterance using ADPCM coded speech," *Bell Syst. Tech. J.*, vol. 53, pp. 1127–1135, July-Aug. 1974.

[11] L. H. Rosenthal, L. R. Rabiner, R. W. Schafer, P. Cummiskey, and J. L. Flanagan, "A multiline computer voice response system utilizing ADPCM coded speech," *IEEE Trans. Acoust., Speech, and Sig. Processing*, vol. ASSP-22, pp. 339–352, Oct. 1974.

Time-Domain Methods

[12] B. Gold, "Note on buzz–hiss detection," *J. Acoust. Soc. Amer.*, vol. 36, pp. 1659–1661, 1964.

[13] B. Gold and L. R. Rabiner, "Parallel processing techniques for estimating pitch periods of speech in the time domain," *J. Acoust. Soc. Amer.*, vol. 46, no. 2, pp. 442–449, Aug. 1969.

[14] D. R. Reddy, "Computer recognition of connected speech," *J. Acoust. Soc. Amer.*, vol. 42, no. 2, pp. 329–347, Aug. 1967.

[15] M. M. Sondhi, "New methods of pitch detection," *IEEE Trans. Audio Electroacoust.*, vol. AU-16, pp. 262–266, June 1968.

Short-Time Spectrum Analysis

[16] C. G. Bell, H. Fujisaki, J. M. Heinz, K. N. Stevens, and A. S. House, "Reduction of speech spectra by analysis-by-synthesis techniques," *J. Acoust. Soc. Amer.*, vol. 33, pp. 1725–1736, Dec. 1961.

[17] R. B. Blackman and J. W. Tukey, *The Measurement of Power Spectra.* New York: Dover, 1959.

[18] J. L. Flanagan and R. M. Golden, "Phase vocoder," *Bell Syst. Tech. J.*, vol. 45, pp. 1493–1509, Nov. 1966.

[19] B. Gold and C. M. Rader, "Systems for compressing the bandwidth of speech," *IEEE Trans. Audio Electroacoust.*, vol. AU-15, pp. 131–135, Sept. 1967; and "The channel vocoder," *IEEE Trans. Audio Electroacoust.*, vol. AU-15, pp. 148–160, Dec. 1967.

[20] T. Martin, "Acoustic recognition of a limited vocabulary in continuous speech," Ph.D. dissertation, Univ. Pennsylvania, Philadelphia, 1970. (Available from Univ. Microfilms, Ann Arbor, Mich.)

[21] P. Mermelstein, "Computer generated spectrogram displays for on-line speech research," *IEEE Trans. Audio Electroacoust.*, vol. AU-19, pp. 44–47, Mar. 1971.

[22] A. M. Noll, "Pitch determination of human speech by the harmonic product spectrum, the harmonic sum spectrum, and a maximum likelihood estimate," in *Computer Processing in Communications Proceedings*, J. Fox, Ed. New York: Polytechnic Press, 1969.

[23] A. V. Oppenheim, "Speech spectrograms using the fast Fourier transform," *IEEE Spectrum*, vol. 7, pp. 57–62, Aug. 1970.

[24] R. W. Schafer and L. R. Rabiner, "Design of digital filter banks for speech analysis," *Bell Syst. Tech. J.*, vol. 50, no. 10, pp. 3097–3115, Dec. 1971.

[25] ——, "Design and simulation of a speech analysis-synthesis system based on short-time Fourier analysis," *IEEE Trans. Audio Electroacoust.*, vol. AU-21, pp. 165–174, June 1973.

[26] M. R. Schroeder, "Vocoders: Analysis and synthesis of speech," *Proc. IEEE*, vol. 54, pp. 720–734, May 1966.

[27] M. R. Schroeder, "Period histogram and product spectrum: New methods for fundamental-frequency measurement," *J. Acoust.*

Soc. Amer., vol. 43, no. 4, pp. 829–834, Apr. 1968.

[28] H. R. Silverman and N. R. Dixon, "A parametrically controlled spectral analysis system for speech," *IEEE Trans. Acoustics, Speech, and Sig. Processing*, vol. ASSP-22, pp. 362–381, Oct. 1974.

Homomorphic Speech Analysis

[29] A. M. Noll, "Cepstrum pitch determination," *J. Acoust. Soc. Amer.*, vol. 41, pp. 293–309, Feb. 1967.

[30] A. V. Oppenheim and R. W. Schafer, "Homomorphic analysis of speech," *IEEE Trans. Audio Electroacoust.*, vol. AU-16, pp. 221–226, June 1968.

[31] A. V. Oppenheim, R. W. Schafer, and T. G. Stockham, Jr., "Nonlinear filtering of multiplied and convolved signals," *Proc. IEEE*, vol. 56, pp. 1264–1291, Aug. 1968.

[32] A. V. Oppenheim, "A speech analysis-synthesis system based on homomorphic filtering," *J. Acoust. Soc. Amer.*, vol. 45, pp. 458–465, Feb. 1969.

[33] J. Olive, "Automatic formant tracking in a Newton–Raphson technique," *J. Acoust. Soc. Amer.*, vol. 50, pt. 2, pp. 661–670, Aug. 1971.

[34] R. W. Schafer and L. R. Rabiner, "System for automatic formant analysis of voiced speech," *J. Acoust. Soc. Amer.*, vol. 47, no. 2, pp. 634–648, Feb. 1970.

Linear Prediction Analysis

[35] B. S. Atal and M. R. Schroeder, "Adaptive predictive coding of speech signals," *Bell Syst. Tech. J.*, vol. 49, 1970.

[36] B. S. Atal and S. L. Hanauer, "Speech analysis and synthesis by linear prediction of the speech wave," *J. Acoust. Soc. Amer.*, vol. 50, pt. 2, pp. 637–655, Aug. 1971.

[37] D. K. Faddeev and V. N. Faddeeva, *Computational Methods of Linear Algebra.* San Francisco, Calif.: Freeman, 1963.

[38] F. Itakura and S. Saito, "An analysis-synthesis telephony system based on maximum likelihood method," *Electronics Commun. Japan*, vol. 53A, pp. 36–43, 1970.

[39] J. I. Makhoul and J. J. Wolf, "Linear prediction and the spectral analysis of speech," Bolt, Beranek, and Newman Inc., Boston, Mass., BBN Rep. 2304, Aug. 31, 1972.

[40] J. N. Maksym, "Real-time pitch extraction by adaptive prediction of the speech waveform," *IEEE Trans. Audio Electroacoust.*, vol. AU-21, pp. 149–153, June 1973.

[41] J. D. Markel, "Digital inverse filtering—A new tool for formant trajectory estimation," *IEEE Trans. Audio Electroacoust.*, vol. AU-20, pp. 129–137, June 1972.

[42] J. D. Markel, "The sift algorithm for fundamental frequency estimation," *IEEE Trans. Audio Electroacoust.*, vol. AU-20, pp. 367–377, Dec. 1972.

[43] J. D. Markel, A. H. Gray, Jr., and H. Wakita, "Linear prediction of speech-theory and practice," Speech Communications Res. Lab., Santa Barbara, Calif., SCRL Monograph 10, Sept. 1973.

[44] J. H. Wilkinson, *Rounding Errors in Algebraic Processes.* Englewood Cliffs, N.J.: Prentice-Hall, 1963.

Digital Signal Processing

[45] B. Gold and C. M. Rader, *Digital Processing of Signals.* New York: McGraw-Hill, 1969.

[46] H. D. Helms, "Fast Fourier transform method of computing difference equations and simulating filters," *IEEE Trans. Audio Electroacoust.*, vol. AU-15, no. 2, pp. 85–90, June 1967.

[47] A. V. Oppenheim and R. W. Schafer, *Digital Signal Processing.* Englewood Cliffs, N.J.: Prentice-Hall, 1975.

[48] L. R. Rabiner and B. Gold, *Theory and Application of Digital Signal Processing.* Englewood Cliffs, N.J.: Prentice-Hall, 1975.

[49] T. G. Stockham, Jr., "High speed convolution and correlation," *AFIPS Proc.*, pp. 229–233, 1966.

Reduction of Speech Spectra by Analysis-by-Synthesis Techniques

C. G. Bell,* H. Fujisaki,† J. M. Heinz, K. N. Stevens, and A. S. House

Research Laboratory of Electronics, Massachusetts Institute of Technology, Cambridge, Massachusetts

(Received September 6, 1961)

Procedures are described for reducing the speech wave to a specification in terms of the time-varying vocal-tract resonances and source characteristics. The basic method, which has been called analysis by synthesis, involves the comparison of speech spectra with a series of spectra that are synthesized within the analyzer. Each comparison spectrum is generated according to a set of rules based on an acoustical theory of speech production. The result of the analysis of each input spectrum is a set of parameters that describes the synthesized spectrum providing the best match. In one version of the method convergence, towards the best match is controlled by the experimenter; in another version convergence to a match is accomplished automatically without the intervention of the experimenter. All the operations have been programmed on a general-purpose digital computer and have been applied to the analysis of vowels and some consonants. The advantages of the analysis techniques are discussed.

THE problem of representing speech events in terms of low-information-rate signals that describe the essential features of the speech wave is one of the central problems in the area of speech communication. To the student of phonemics and phonetics it is important to be able to describe in a simple way the acoustical features associated with the various allophones of the phonemes. For the engineer concerned with problems of communication, an efficient description of speech signals is needed for the development of systems for speech bandwidth compression and for the realization of procedures for machine recognition and generation of speech.

The development of the sound spectrograph[1] represented a significant contribution to speech analysis, since it displays the speech events in a way that brings into clear focus certain of the essential features of the signal such as the formant movements. The three-dimensional intensity-frequency-time representation, together with the procedure for displaying spectral sections, provides a means for isolating significant features for certain classes of sounds, although the techniques are less successful for other classes, particularly certain types of consonants.

During the past few years, there have been two developments which suggest that it is now possible to bring more powerful techniques to bear on problems of speech analysis. The first has been the significant advance that has occurred in our understanding of the acoustics of speech production. The second has been the increasing availability of high-speed digital computers for applications such as speech analysis. Theoretical studies have led to a clearer understanding of the constraints imposed on the speech signal by the vocal mechanism, and have suggested means whereby speech signals can be represented in terms of parameters that have a definite and rigorous relation to articulation. Digital computers have made it possible to use the results of the acoustical studies in such a way that rapid and precise reduction of speech signals can be accomplished.

This paper describes an attempt to utilize the findings of the acoustical theory to develop procedures for the analysis and reduction of speech signals by computer techniques. Since the method is based on an acoustical theory of speech production, it is appropriate to outline the essential features of such a theory before proceeding to a description of the analysis techniques.

ACOUSTICAL THEORY OF SPEECH PRODUCTION

The generally accepted theory of speech production[2-4] views the speech wave as the result of acoustic excitation of the vocal tract by one or more sources. In the case of voiced sounds, there is a source at the glottis, and this glottal source is a quasi-periodic volume-velocity wave whose spectrum envelope decreases with increasing frequency at a rate of about 12 db/octave in the range 300–2500 cps. The characteristics of the glottal source are to a large extent independent of the vocal-tract configuration anterior to the glottis. For some classes of sounds there may be a source of excitation of the vocal tract as a result of a sudden pressure release or as a result of turbulent air flow through a constriction or past the teeth or other obstructions. Such a source can be considered as a differential-pressure source, usually located in the vicinity of a vocal-tract constriction, and this source generally has a relatively broad and smooth spectrum. The spectrum $P(s)$ of the sound pressure measured at a distance from the lips as a result of a source of excitation whose spectrum is given by $S(s)$ can be written

$$P(s) = S(s) \quad T(s) \quad R(s). \qquad (1)$$

In this equation $T(s)$ is the transfer function of the vocal tract; for voiced sounds, $T(s)$ is the ratio of the volume

* Present address: Digital Equipment Corporation, Maynard, Massachusetts.

† Present address: University of Tokyo, Tokyo, Japan.

[1] W. Koenig, H. K. Dunn, and L. Y. Lacy, J. Acoust. Soc. Am. 17, 19 (1946).

[2] H. Dudley, Bell System Tech. J. 19, 495 (1940).

[3] T. Chiba and M. Kajiyama, *The Vowel, Its Nature and Structure* (Tokyo-Kaiseikan Publishing Company, Ltd., Tokyo, 1941).

[4] G. Fant, *Acoustic Theory of Speech Production* (Mouton and Company, 's-Gravenhage, 1960).

Reprinted with permission from *J. Acoust. Soc. Am.*, vol. 33, pp. 1725–1736, Dec. 1961.

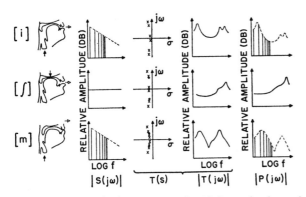

FIG. 1. A nonquantitative representation of the production and acoustic characteristics of speech sounds. In the left column are sketches of articulatory configurations in the midsagittal plane for three phones as indicated, together with source (solid arrows) and output (open arrows) locations. In addition each row of the figure shows the magnitude of the source spectrum $|S(j\omega)|$, the pole and zero locations in the complex frequency plane for the vocal-tract transfer function $T(s)$, the magnitude of the transfer function $|T(j\omega)|$, and the magnitude of the sound pressure at a distance in front of the face $|P(j\omega)|$, respectively, for each representative articulation. In cases with periodic (glottal) excitation, incomplete sets of harmonics are shown together with spectrum-envelope curves.

velocity at the mouth opening (and at the nostrils if there is coupling to the nasal cavities) to the source volume velocity, whereas for a noiselike or transient source at a constriction, $T(s)$ is the ratio of the volume velocity at the mouth opening to the sound pressure of the source. The radiation characteristic $R(s)$ is the ratio of the sound pressure at distance r in front of the talker to the volume velocity at the lips, and in the frequency range up to about 4000 cps is given approximately by the result for a simple source

$$R(s) = (s\rho/4\pi r)e^{-(sr/c)}, \qquad (2)$$

where ρ = density of air and c = velocity of sound in air. In all of these relations, s is the complex frequency, and can be replaced by $j\omega$ to obtain Fourier spectra, where ω is the angular frequency.

When the source is at the glottis and when there is no coupling to the nasal cavities, $T(s)$ is characterized by a number of poles, and can be written

$$T(s) = \frac{s_1 s_1^* s_2 s_2^* \cdots}{(s-s_1)(s-s_1^*)(s-s_2)(s-s_2^*)\cdots}, \qquad (3)$$

where the asterisks designate complex conjugates and s_1, s_2, $\cdots$ are the poles corresponding to the various vocal-tract resonances or formants. The frequencies and bandwidths for the poles are, of course, dependent on the vocal-tract configuration. For an idealized source spectrum envelope with a decreasing slope of 12 db/octave, i.e., a spectrum envelope proportional to $1/\omega^2$, and for a radiation characteristic proportional to ω [cf. Eq. (2)], the magnitude of the spectrum envelope $|P_E(j\omega)|$ of the sound pressure for a nonnasal vowel

is given by

$$|P_E(j\omega)| \propto (1/\omega)|T(j\omega)|. \qquad (4)$$

Thus if the idealized source spectrum is assumed, the envelope $|P_E(j\omega)|$ is characterized by a pole in the vicinity of $\omega=0$ and by a set of conjugate-complex pairs of poles, corresponding to the poles of $T(s)$ in Eq. (3). Alternatively, if the sound pressure is transduced and passed through a circuit with a frequency characteristic that rises at 6 db/octave, the spectrum envelope of the resulting signal is characterized by the poles of $T(s)$ and only those poles, assuming the idealized shape for the source spectrum envelope.

When there is coupling between the vocal tract and the nasal tract, or when the vocal-tract excitation is at a point other than the glottis, the transfer function $T(s)$ is characterized by zeros as well as poles, and can, in general, be written

$$T(s) = K\frac{(s-s_a)(s-s_a^*)(s-s_b)(s-s_b^*)\cdots}{(s-s_1)(s-s_1^*)(s-s_2)(s-s_2^*)\cdots}, \qquad (5)$$

where s_a, s_a^*, s_b, s_b^*, $\cdots$ are the zeros and K is a real quantity independent of frequency. The frequencies and bandwidths for the zeros depend both on the vocal-tract configuration and on the location of the source in the vocal tract, whereas for a given vocal-tract configuration the poles of $T(s)$ are independent of the location of the source.

Relations between the speech spectra and the articulatory processes that produce them are summarized by the sketches in Fig. 1 for three classes of speech sounds. For each class of sounds, the figure shows a typical articulatory configuration and source location, and approximate source spectrum, a representation of the poles and zeros of the transfer function, a plot of the magnitude of the transfer function vs frequency, and the output spectrum. The spectra for the vowel and for the nasal consonant are, of course, line spectra, whereas the fricative has a continuous spectrum. In each case, the output spectrum (in decibels) is obtained by adding the spectra of the source and the transfer function, and then applying a 6 db/octave correction for the radiation characteristic, as explained above.

The acoustical theory may be summarized, therefore, as follows. The spectrum of the vocal-tract output (in decibels) is the sum of a source spectrum, a transfer function and a radiation characteristic. For a given class of speech sounds, the source spectrum and the radiation characteristic are relatively invariant from one talker to another, and are largely independent of the articulatory configuration. The transfer function is determined by the articulatory configuration and the source location, and is completely described in terms of a set of poles in the case of nonnasal vowel and vowel-like sounds, and by a set of poles and zeros for other classes of sounds.

ANALYSIS-BY-SYNTHESIS MODEL

The term *analysis by synthesis* is used to refer to an active analysis process that can be applied to signals that are produced by a generator whose properties are known.[5,6] The heart of an analysis-by-synthesis system is a signal generator capable of synthesizing all and only the signals to be analyzed. The signals synthesized by the generator are compared with the signals to be analyzed, and a measure of error is computed. Different signals are generated until one is found that causes the error to reach some smallest value, at which time the analyzer indicates the properties of the internally generated signal. It has been suggested[6,7] that a scheme of this type has applications in the analysis of linguistic phenomena at various levels of representation: acoustic, graphic, phonological, morphological, and syntactic. Of concern in the present discussion is the analysis of linguistic events at the acoustic level.

The procedure used to accomplish analysis by synthesis at the acoustic level[7] is shown schematically in Fig. 2. The speech is passed first through a peripheral element in this case a *filter set*, the outputs of which are recitfied, smoothed, sampled at prescribed time intervals, and then stored. (The techniques used to process the speech by the filter system and to store the spectra in the computer memory are described in the Appendix.) The component labeled *spectrum generator*, when given appropriate instructions, can generate outputs that are compatible with the original stored speech data. In the present case, this component generates speechlike spectra when provided with information on the poles and zeros of the vocal-tract transfer function and on the type of vocal-tract excitation. The *comparator* computes a measure of the difference between the input speech spectra and spectra generated by the model. The order in which different trial spectra are synthesized by the model is prescribed by a control or *strategy* component that makes decisions on the basis of (1) previous error scores for the spectral sample under analysis, (2) the results of analyses of adjacent spectral samples, and (3) possibly the results of preliminary direct measure-

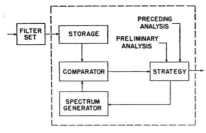

FIG. 2. Paradigm of an analysis-by-synthesis process for the reduction of speech spectra.

[5] D. M. Mackay, Brit. J. Philo. Sci. **2**, 105 (1951).
[6] M. Halle and K. N. Stevens, "Analysis by synthesis," Proc. Sem. Speech Compression and Processing, edited by W. Wathen-Dunn and L. E. Woods, AFCRC–TR–59–198, December 1959, Vol. II, Paper D7.
[7] K. N. Stevens, J. Acoust. Soc. Am. **32**, 47 (1960).

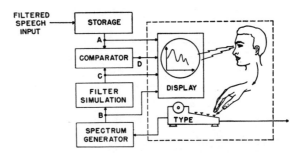

FIG. 3. Paradigm of the mode of the analysis-by-synthesis reduction scheme in which the experimenter controls the selection of parameters of the comparison spectra. The strategy or control element of Fig. 2 is realized by the contents of the dashed box at the right. The nodes A–D show points where functions can be selected and displayed on the cathode-ray tube output. The process is described fully in the text.

ments on the spectral sample. When a synthesized spectrum that provides minimum error is obtained, the analyzer indicates (or stores) the pole-zero locations and source characteristics of that spectrum.

Five operations, therefore, are performed in the analyzer: (a) storage of the speech data processed by the input filter set, (b) generation of speech spectra, (c) instruction of the spectrum generator by a control system, (d) calculation of measures of the difference between the input speech spectra and the spectra computed internally, and (e) display, in some form, of the parameters of the generator that yield minimum error.

The success and utility of the analysis-by-synthesis technique in comparison with other analysis methods depends largely upon the speed and accuracy with which speech spectra can be analyzed, and it is important, therefore, that the number of trial spectra that need to be synthesized in order to obtain a minimum error be kept as small as possible. Thus one of the central problems in the design of an analysis-by-synthesis scheme is that of devising a strategy to be used by the control component to assure rapid convergence to the desired result.

In the analysis procedures described here, two different methods have been used to implement the operations in the strategy component of Fig. 2. In one case, the control function is performed by the experimenter, and hence the problem of specifying a strategy for automatic analysis is circumvented. In the other case a rudimentary strategy that permits automatic analysis of speech spectra is employed. The former method is slower than the automatic procedure, but leads to greater accuracy of analysis, and can be used in the development of strategies that might ultimately be incorporated into a more sophisticated automatic procedure. The two analysis methods will be discussed in detail in the following sections.

EXPERIMENTAL MATCHING OF VOWEL AND CONSONANT SPECTRA

When control of the internal spectrum generator is placed in the hands of the experimenter, the analysis-by-

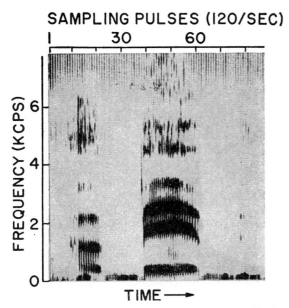

FIG. 4. Sound spectrogram of a nonsense utterance, [hə'bɪb]. The time sampling pulses (high-pass filtered) appear at the top of the spectrogram.

synthesis procedure takes the form shown in Fig. 3. In this figure all operations indicated in the blocks, except the decisions and actions of the operator, are performed within the digital computer or its peripheral equipment. Instructions are communicated to the spectrum generator through a typewriter that is operated by the experimenter. The locations (in the complex frequency plane) of a trial set of poles and zeros are typed, and the spectrum generator and filter simulation portions of the system compute a spectrum to be compared with the input speech spectrum that is under analysis. Measured or computed functions existing at various points in the analysis process can be displayed on a cathode-ray tube, as shown in the figure. The task of the operator is to adjust the positions of the poles and zeros until a "best fit" is obtained between the spectrum under analysis and the internally generated spectrum. The experimenter can use both a set of numerical error scores and visual examination of the displayed functions to determine how to adjust the set of poles and zeros in order to improve the match and to decide when a best fit has been obtained.

As indicated in the Appendix, the speech spectra in the present analysis scheme are obtained by passing the speech signal through a pre-emphasis circuit with a rising characteristic of 6 db/octave and then through a bank of 36 filters. Each filter output is rectified and smoothed by a low-pass filter with a time constant of about 10 msec. The rectified and smoothed outputs are sampled periodically at intervals of 8.3 msec, processed by an analog-to-digital converter, converted to logarithmic values (to the nearest decibel), and stored in the computer memory. The spectral data are also stored on punched tape and are thus available for future analysis.

In order to facilitate analysis of specific components of the utterances, conventional sound spectrograms of the speech materials are made. A spectrogram of a typical dissyllabic utterance used in one experimental study is shown in Fig. 4. Time pulses indicating the instants at which the filter outputs are sampled by the computer are high-pass filtered and mixed with the speech signal before the spectrograms are made, and appear as closely spaced vertical lines across the top of the spectrogram. The numerical identification of the pulses shown on the spectrogram corresponds to the way successive spectra are labeled in the computer memory. Thus the experimenter can, if he wishes, use the spectrogram as a guide in the selection of a particular spectrum or group of spectra from the computer memory. The selection is achieved by a simple instruction to the computer identifying the spectrum to be displayed and analyzed.

The manner in which the speech spectra are displayed is shown by the example in Fig. 5, which was taken from the utterance whose spectrogram is given in Fig. 4. The number at the upper right of the display indicates that the spectrum number is 48, and reference to the spectrogram shows that the spectrum occurred during the stressed vowel [ɪ]. The points along the abscissa represent successive filters in the analyzing bank, and the ordinate is the amplitude in decibels. In terms of the processes portrayed by Fig. 3, this spectrum is found at node A.

As described above, the experimenter specifies the locations of a set of poles and zeros and the internal spectrum generator computes the corresponding spectrum that is to be compared with a speech spectrum such as that shown in Fig. 5. Computation of the synthesized spectrum is carried out in two steps. The first step is to calculate the logarithm of the magnitude of the transfer function as a function of frequency and the second step is to compute the effective spectrum that would be measured if a signal with a spectrum corresponding to this transfer function were processed by the analyzing filter bank. The second step is necessary since the original speech signal itself is, of course, processed by a bank of relatively broad filters, and thus a

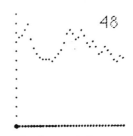

FIG. 5. Photograph of a spectral representation of an input speech sample (at node A in Fig. 3) displayed on the face of the output cathode-ray tube. Each point on the horizontal axis represents one of the 36 filter outputs; the points on the vertical axis represent 5-db steps in amplitude. The input speech has received a 6 db/octave pre-emphasis. The number 48 identifies a sample in the vowel [ɪ] in the word shown in Fig. 4.

valid comparison can be made only if both the inputsignal and the internally generated signal undergo the same sequence of operations.

For a single conjugate pair of poles at frequency F_n with bandwidth ΔF_n the function to be computed in the internal spectrum generator during the first step is[8]

$$20 \log|T_n| = 20 \log\left\{\frac{F_n{}^2+(\tfrac{1}{2}\Delta F_n)^2}{[(f-F_n)^2+(\tfrac{1}{2}\Delta F_n)^2]^{\frac{1}{2}}[(f+F_n)^2+(\tfrac{1}{2}\Delta F_n)^2]^{\frac{1}{2}}}\right\}, \tag{10}$$

where f is the frequency variable and T_n is the portion of the system function associated with the nth pair of poles. The logarithm of the magnitude of the system function for a zero is, of course, the negative of that for a pole with the same frequency and bandwidth. For a real-axis pole at a frequency minus F_a, the function to be computed is

$$20 \log\{F_a/(f^2+F_a{}^2)^{\frac{1}{2}}\}. \tag{11}$$

These functions are computed to the nearest $\frac{1}{8}$ db at 100-cps intervals of f. When more than one pole or zero is specified, the logarithm of the system function is obtained by adding the logarithms of the system functions corresponding to the individual poles and zeros. A result of this calculation for a typical set of poles appropriate for a vowel is shown in Fig. 6, which is a photograph of the cathode-ray tube display obtained from node B in Fig. 3. Although values up to 10 kc are displayed here, usually only the spectrum up to about 3000 cps is of interest for vowels. In this type of display a logarithmic scale is used for the abscissa.

The second step in the computation of comparison spectra is the evaluation of the effect of the filter bank on the computed transfer function. If the magnitude of the transfer function of a filter is designated as $|A_i(f)|$, where i represents the filter number from 1 to 36, then the magnitude of the square-law rectified and smoothed output of the filter when the input spectrum has a magnitude $|H(f)|$ is proportional to

$$\left[\int_0^\infty |H(f)|^2 |A_i(f)|^2 df\right]^{\frac{1}{2}}. \tag{12}$$

The difference between the result of this computation and the result of processing the data by full-wave recitfication can be expected to be less than 1 db. Thirty-six such integrals are evaluated in the computer to obtain the hypothetical rectified filter outputs corresponding to a given input spectrum. These numbers are expressed in decibels to permit direct comparison with the spectra that are under analysis.

The result of the filter calculation for the spectrum given in Fig. 6 is shown as one of the curves in Fig. 7. Figure 7 is an example of the display of the events at nodes A, C, and D in the system schematized previously

in Fig. 3. The original speech spectrum (the one previously given in Fig. 5) and the difference curve (node D) are shown in addition to the internally synthesized spectrum (node C). The numbers at the left are three numerical measures of the error.

In all of the spectrum matching procedures described in this report, three different error scores were computed and were available as measures of the goodness of fit between the speech spectra and the internally synthesized spectra. The error curve is represented by 36 values (corresponding to the 36 filters) that will be designated as a set of numbers e_i. The error curve is always adjusted automatically such that the weighted mean of e_i is zero over the entire range of values of i. The three error measures are the following:

$$\text{Absolute error} = \sum_{i=1}^{36} |w_i e_i|\,;$$

$$\text{Variation} = \sum_{i=1}^{35} |w_{i+1}e_{i+1} - w_i e_i|\,;$$

$$\text{Square of error} = \sum_{i=1}^{36} w_i{}^2 e_i{}^2\,;$$

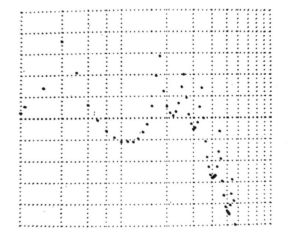

FIG. 6. Photograph of a computed spectrum (at node B in Fig. 3) displayed on the face of the output cathode-ray tube. The horizontal axis is a logarithmic frequency scale from 200 cps to 10 000 cps. The vertical axis represents amplitude in decibels, the small points indicating 1-db steps. The spectrum shown is characterized by resonant frequencies (bandwidths), in cps, of 430 (30), 1770 (80), 2580 (150), plus resonances every 1000 cps from 3500 cps to 9500 cps with bandwidths gradually increasing to 300 cps. Datum points are plotted every 100 cps. For convenience, the datum points at 100 and 200 cps are both plotted close to the 200-cps line.

---

[8] More precisely, ΔF_n is $1/\pi$ times the real part of the complex frequency of the pole (i.e., $1/\pi$ times the distance of the pole from the $j\omega$ axis in the s plane). When ΔF_n is small compared with F_n, then ΔF_n is very nearly equal to the bandwidth.

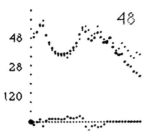

FIG. 7. Photograph of output display showing superposition of input spectrum (upper curve of light points) and comparison spectrum (upper curve of heavy points) obtained at node C of Fig. 3. The lower curve is the difference curve, obtained at node D of Fig. 3. The three numbers at the left show, from top to bottom, the magnitude of the absolute, variation, and squared error scores (see text) over 24 filter points, that is, up to about 3050 cps. The input spectrum is sample 48 shown in Fig. 5; the comparison spectrum is that shown in Fig. 6 after processing by the simulated filters. The error curve is typical of a situation in which a resonance in the comparison spectrum is improperly located.

where w_i represents arbitrary weighting factors which may be assigned depending on the frequency range considered to be important for matching a particular class of spectra. For example, it has been found convenient to match vowel spectra over the values of i from 1 to 24, corresponding to a frequency range of 100 to 3050 cps. A simple way of weighting the error in this case is to put $w_i=1$ over $i=1$ to 24, and $w_i=0$ over $i=25$ to 36. More sophisticated schemes for assigning weighting factors can, of course, be adopted. The variation, being a sum of first differences of the weighted error curve, provides an indication of the amount of fluctuation in the error curve, while the other two numbers provide measures of the amount of deviation of the curve from the zero axis. The significance of the different measures of error will be of particular interest in the discussion of automatic matching procedures in the next section. For experimental matching of various types of speech spectra the square of the error has been used more frequently than the other measures.

For the spectral match shown in Fig. 7, the square of the error, summed over 24 points in frequency, is 120 db². The error curve in this case has an irregularity at frequencies in the vicinity of the second resonance. This irregularity is due, apparently, to an incorrect selection of the frequency position of the second pole. When this frequency is adjusted upwards, the match between the two spectra would be expected to become better.

Some indication of the sensitivity of the error scores to small changes in the resonant frequency in this example is given by the upper curve in Fig. 8. This curve has a reasonably sharp minimum of 30 db² for a resonant frequency of 1870 cps. Evidently this error score is quite sensitive to small changes in the resonant frequency, and an accuracy better than 30 cps is to be expected in this case. The minimum for the variation error score generally is not as sharp as that for the squared error. Figure 8 also shows the squared error as a function of the frequency of $F2$ for a second formant in a lower frequency range, the second formant of the

vowel [ɑ]. Curves of form similar to those of Fig. 8 have been obtained for variations in both bandwidth and resonant frequency in the process of matching a large number of vowel spectra.

When the second resonant frequency of the internally generated spectrum of Fig. 7 is given the value that yields minimum squared error in Fig. 8, the spectral match shown in Fig. 9 is obtained. It is to be noted that a good match to the vowel spectrum shown in Fig. 9 was obtained in the frequency range 100–3050 cps by synthesizing a spectrum characterized by three conjugate pole pairs in this frequency range together with a group of poles at higher frequencies. The high-frequency poles must be included simply to provide the proper levels for the lower resonances.[9] Since the original speech spectrum was pre-emphasized with a slope of 6 db/octave, then, as noted previously, the spectrum envelope of the resulting signal is characterized simply by the set of conjugate pairs of poles of $T(s)$, if an idealized source spectrum envelope with a falling characteristic of 12 db/octave is assumed. As a matter of fact, any significant deviation of the synthesized spectrum from the speech spectrum of Fig. 9 would indicate that the shape of the actual source spectrum differed from this ideal shape. The fact that a good match is obtained in this case indicates that a −12 db/octave slope is a reasonable approximation for the spectrum envelope of the glottal source.[10]

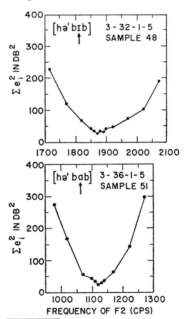

FIG. 8. Examples of the effect on the squared error score of varying the frequency of a single resonance of the comparison spectrum through a range of values in the vicinity of the actual vowel formant frequency. The upper graph refers to a sample taken centrally in a vowel characterized by a high-frequency second formant (sample 48, as in Figs. 4, 5, 7). The lower graph illustrates the same result for a sample from a vowel with a second formant at a lower frequency.

[9] G. Fant, "On the predictability of formant levels and spectrum envelopes from formant frequencies," *For Roman Jakobson*, edited by M. Halle *et al.* (Mouton and Company, 's-Gravenhage, 1956), pp. 109–120.

[10] The matching of a large number of spectral samples in voiced speech sounds has shown the same general results. These analysis procedures, however, are not highly sensitive to local variations in the shape of the glottal spectrum since the analog filters used in processing the speech materials are not very selective. Thus the form of the glottal spectrum derived by this method cannot be compared in detail with that derived from time-domain analyses.

By the procedure discussed above, matches have been obtained for a number of spectra associated with vowel and consonant portions of utterances by several male talkers. Systematic studies of the pole-zero patterns for various time locations through these utterances have been made[11] and detailed reports are in preparation. Examples of the matches obtained for three classes of speech sounds other than nonnasal vowels are shown in Fig. 10. In all cases it was possible to select a set of poles and zeros such that good fits were obtained with the data. In the matching of a spectrum such as one of these, the initial step was to determine the approximate locations of the poles and zeros from theoretical considerations and by examination of the general shape of the spectrum. Convergence to pole and zero locations yielding an optimum fit was achieved through a trial-and-error process, always with the constraint that the locations be consistent with known theoretical relations between vocal-tract configurations and the acoustic signal.

AUTOMATIC MATCHING OF VOWEL SPECTRA; THE STRATEGY PROBLEM

Although application of the spectrum-matching technique described above usually resulted in good agreement between the speech spectra and the synthesized spectra, and, presumably, in reasonably accurate values for spectral poles and zeros, the method has the disadvantage that it is tedious and is not completely automatic. Attempts have been made, therefore, to reduce the time required for the generation of comparison spectra and to program the computer to perform the function of the experimenter in the analysis scheme of Fig. 3. The task of developing an optimum strategy whereby rapid convergence to a best-fitting vowel spectrum is achieved is by no means trivial, and is an example of the hill-climbing problem that has received considerable attention in the field of pattern recognition.[12] The strategy that is used in the present automatic

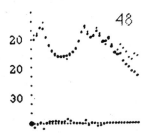

FIG. 9. Photograph of a display such as that described in Fig. 7, showing a good match between the input and comparison spectra. To obtain this match to the vowel [ɪ] the values of the lowest four resonant frequencies (bandwidths), in cps, of the comparison spectrum were 430 (30), 1870 (80), 2580 (150), and 3400 (120); additional resonances were spaced at 1000-cps intervals from 4500 to 9500 cps with gradually increasing bandwidths up to 300 cps.

[11] A. S. House, K. N. Stevens, and H. Fujisaki, J. Acoust. Soc. Am. **32**, 1517 (1960); J. M. Heinz, J. Acoust. Soc. Am. **32**, 1517 (1960); O. Fujimura, J. Acoust. Soc. Am. **32**, 1517 (1960).

[12] M. Minsky, Proc. Inst. Radio Engrs. **49**, 8 (1961).

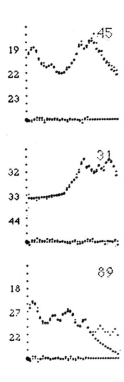

FIG. 10. Photographs of matches similar to that of Fig. 7 for spectra of speech sounds other than nonnasal vowels. The upper photograph shows a match to a (nasalized) vowel [i] occurring in the phonetic environment [m-m]. The comparison curve was constructed from three poles (and their conjugates) up to 3200 cps, a correction for higher poles, and a pole-zero pair in the vicinity of 1200 cps; the error scores were computed over 24 filters.[16] The middle photograph is a match to the fricative [ʃ] in initial position in a stressed syllable. In this case the error score was computed over 36 filters up to 7000 cps and the comparison curve was constructed from seven poles, three zeros, and three real-axis zeros close to zero frequency.[11] In the lower photograph the speech spectrum was sampled from an [n] in word final position and the error score was computed over 24 filters. The comparison curve was constructed from five poles and a zero up to 3000 cps, plus a higher-pole correction.[11]

matching scheme is a rather elementary one; more complex strategies are being developed to obtain more accurate and rapid analyses.[13,14] The automatic method to be described is applicable only to the analysis of the spectra of nonnasal vowels.

Generation of Comparison Spectra

In the experimental analysis procedure described above, each internally generated spectrum is computed as needed, and the integrations to simulate the effect of the filter bank are performed for each trial spectrum. The calculation of each pole factor and the simulation of the filtering of the synthesized spectra are the most time-consuming portions of the above method, however, and automation of the matching procedure would not be practical unless the time required for these operations was reduced. A more rapid (but less precise) procedure for the generation of comparison spectra was therefore adopted. In this procedure the comparison spectra are assembled from a limited set of elemental spectra that are stored within the computer memory.

Five elemental spectra are added to obtain the spectrum envelope of a vowel (in decibels) in the frequency range that includes the first three vocal-tract resonances (up to about 3000 cps for adult male voices). Four of these spectra are simple resonance curves each of which corresponds to a conjugate pair of poles of the vocal-tract transfer function. An inventory of 78 simple resonance curves is stored in the computer memory with resonant frequencies spaced every 20 cps from 160 to

[13] A. Paul, S.M. thesis (unpublished), M.I.T. (1961).

[14] M. V. Mathews (personal communication, 1961).

500 cps, every 50 cps from 500 to 3000 cps, and every 100 cps from 3000 to 4000 cps. The bandwidth of the resonance associated with each of these curves is fixed at a value suggested by measured data on formant bandwidth; it is 60 cps for the low-frequency resonances and increases to 180 cps for the high-frequency resonances. Vowel spectra with various combinations of resonances can be assembled by selection of appropriate groups of four such curves. The fifth elemental spectrum is a curve that, in the frequency range of the first three vocal-tract resonances, accounts for the source spectrum, the radiation characteristic, and poles of the vocal-tract transfer function higher than the fourth. This "correction" spectrum is a relatively smooth curve, and its shape is not expected to change markedly from one adult male speaker to another or from one vowel to another, although some variation in the slope of the curve may occur. An inventory of six such correction spectra is stored in the computer memory, and one of these is always added to the group of four resonance curves to synthesize a complete vowel spectrum.

The 84 elemental spectra that are stored in the computer memory are actually the curves that would be obtained if each of the simple resonance spectra and correction spectra were processed by the filter bank in the manner discussed above [Eq. (12)]. The elimination of the necessity of spectrum calculation and filter simulation greatly reduces the time required for the generation of comparison spectra (by a factor of about 50 in the present case), but it inevitably leads to some error in the synthesized spectra, especially at high frequencies where the filter bandwidths are not constant. Correction for the primary effect of the filter bandwidths can be made, and is actually included in the above procedure. It can be shown, however, that compensation for this error cannot be made exactly, especially for cases in which two resonances are closely spaced. Consequently this procedure for assembling vowel spectra has some inherent error, although this error is usually quite small.

Description of Strategy

From the 84 stored elemental curves, it is possible to assemble about 5×10^5 vowel-like spectra, if reasonable assumptions are made concerning the frequency range for each of the first four formants. Since in the analysis of a given speech spectrum it is impractical to make a comparison with each of these synthesized spectra, it is essential to devise a strategy whereby only a small subset of comparison spectra needs to be assembled and tested before convergence to the best-fitting spectrum is achieved. It is possible to distinguish two situations that require different strategies. One situation arises when no prior information is available concerning the formant frequencies for the vowel spectrum under analysis, and/or when no previous data have been obtained for the talker who generated the utterance in

which this spectrum occurs. Such a case would occur when, in the analysis of the formant frequencies during the vowel portion of a syllable, one spectrum is selected to be examined first. Here the basic task of the analyzer is to establish a good first approximation to the input spectrum. In the second situation, which occurs much more frequently than the first, approximate data concerning the formant frequencies and the appropriate correction spectrum are already available in the analyzer. These data may have been obtained either from analysis of a spectrum sample located adjacent to the spectrum to be analyzed or from a preliminary approximate analysis of the spectrum. In this case, the task of the analyzer is to optimize the match between the input and the synthesized spectra.

When there is no prior knowledge of the locations of the formants, one method that has been used to establish the approximate values of the formant frequencies consists of the following steps: (1) Elemental spectra corresponding to formant frequencies in the expected range of F_1 (plus a standard F_4 curve and a standard correction curve) are each compared with the speech spectrum to be analyzed, and the curve yielding the minimum variation error is selected tentatively as identifying F_1. (2) Elemental spectra corresponding to formant frequencies in the expected range of F_2 are each added in turn to the curve found in (1) and the composite curve yielding the minimum variation error is selected tentatively as identifying F_2. (3) Step (2) is repeated to find tentative values for F_3. (4) After approximate values for the first three formant frequencies are found in this way, elemental spectra corresponding to formant frequencies in the expected range of F_4 are each added in place of the standard F_4 curve adopted in previous steps, and the one yielding the minimum error score is found. (5) Step (4) is repeated to find the correction curve yielding the minimum error score. (6) The set of first four formant frequencies and the correction curve found by the above procedures are then used as starting points for the more exact analysis procedure that is employed when approximate data of this type are available.

It is to be noted that in the first step above, no elemental spectra corresponding to F_2 and F_3 are included in the synthesized spectrum. It can be shown, nevertheless, that the variation error score can serve to locate the approximate position of the lowest resonance in the input spectrum. The squared error score can give reliable results only after a reasonable approximation to the input spectrum is established, and is not a good criterion at this stage of the preliminary analysis. Throughout the automatic procedures pertaining to the analysis of vowels produced by adult male talkers error scores were computed with equal weighting for the 24 filters in the frequency range 100–3050 cps.

In the process of developing the preliminary analysis procedure outlined above, various alternative schemes for obtaining a first approximation to the formant frequencies were tried. In one such scheme the spectrum of a neutral vowel, i.e., $F_1 = 500$ cps with subsequent formants occurring at intervals of 1000 cps, was used as the zero-order approximation, and the frequency positions of the formants were revised successively within appropriate ranges. Another scheme involved the matching of the input spectrum against members of a small stored set of standard vocalic spectra and the selection of the best approximation. A third procedure obtained estimates of approximate values of formant frequencies from direct measurements of certain gross features of the input spectrum.[15] Further studies with a large number of talkers and utterances will be required before the over-all performance of these various preliminary analysis procedures (or possibly combinations of them) can be compared quantitatively.

When approximate values for the formant frequencies and correction spectrum are available, an iterative procedure is employed, and the sequence of operations is the following: (1) With F_2, F_3, F_4, and the correction spectrum fixed at the given values, curves with resonant frequencies in the vicinity of the given F_1 are used to form a series of spectra that are compared with the speech spectrum to be analyzed. The value of F_1 yielding the minimum squared error is selected and used in subsequent steps. (2) Step (1) is repeated but with F_1, F_3, F_4, and the correction spectrum at the given values and F_2 as the variable. (3) Step (1) is repeated to find, in turn, revised values for F_3, F_4 and the correction spectrum. (4) Steps (1)–(3) are repeated. If the results are the same as those obtained after the first set of trials, the analysis of the given spectrum is terminated; otherwise the process is repeated until no improvement in the fit is obtained.

The automatic method for the analysis of vowels has been used to obtain data on the variation with time of the formant frequencies of stressed vowels in a number of dissyllabic utterances. The computer has been programmed to perform the analysis on each spectral sample in turn within a designated region of the utterance. The initial step in the procedure is to prescribe the range of spectral samples over which the analysis is to be performed and to select a sample located centrally within this range. The analysis is first carried out on the centrally located sample, following one of the procedures that require no *a priori* knowledge of the approximate formant frequencies. The more precise iterative procedure is then applied to this sample to locate the formant frequencies and correction spectrum more exactly. These values of formant frequencies and correction spectrum are used as first approximations in the analysis of the following spectral sample. In this manner the analysis is performed on each spectral sample in turn until the end of the designated interval is reached. Then the program returns to the centrally located sample, and uses the results previously obtained

[15] F. Poza, S.M. thesis (unpublished), M.I.T. (1959).

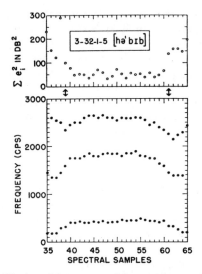

FIG. 11. Display of data on vowel formant frequencies derived by the automatic analysis procedure. The utterance is the same as that shown in Fig. 4. Time is on the horizontal axis and is indicated in terms of samples which occur at 8.3-msec intervals. The solid points represent the lowest three vowel formants in each sample as determined by the automatic procedure. The open points at the top of the figure give a measure of the error of fit between the input and comparison spectra. The arrows indicate points in time where study of the spectrogram of the utterance (see Fig. 4) suggests the locations of vocalic boundaries.

for this sample as first approximations to the next preceding sample. The analysis is carried out on each preceding sample moving toward the beginning of the designated time interval. The results for each spectral sample are stored in the computer memory. After the analysis of all samples is completed, an instruction can be given to the computer to print or punch out the results of the analysis of each sample in order, or to display the results on the oscilloscope in various ways.

Typical Results

Figure 11 displays typical results of the automatic vowel analysis program for a portion of the utterance whose spectrogram is shown in Fig. 4. The first three formant frequencies found by the program are plotted for each spectral sample in the stressed vowel. The squared error score for each sample is also shown in the upper part of the figure. The arrows indicate the "vowel" boundaries suggested by study of the spectrogram. It is noted that the error score increases sharply at these boundaries, since it is not possible, of course, to obtain good matches with consonant spectra by assembling a set of simple resonance curves by a procedure based on a theory of vowel production.

Several limitations of the automatic procedure have already been pointed out, and further studies will be necessary to overcome these limitations. The automatic analysis procedure in its present form requires that many trials be made before convergence to a set of resonant frequencies is achieved, and consequently the analysis takes a considerable amount of time (order of 1000 times real time for the computer and the programs used in these studies). Furthermore, small but systematic errors in formant locations occur as a result of (a) the incomplete correction for the effect of the filters in the construction of the comparison spectrum and (b) the inability to vary the bandwidths of the formants. Both of these types of errors can be eliminated if a more complex and time-consuming procedure is used to assemble the spectra, similar to the procedure used in the experimental method described in connection with Fig. 3. If, however, formant bandwidth were a variable in the matching process, then a more detailed strategy would be necessary to converge to both the frequencies and the bandwidths appropriate to a given spectral sample.[13]

Remarks on Extension of Automatic Analysis Procedure to Other Classes of Speech Spectra

The automatic speech reduction procedure just described is applicable only to spectra of nonnasal vowels or vowel-like sounds for which the vocal-tract transfer function is characterized by a set of conjugate pairs of poles. Thus for the matching of these types of spectra the internal spectrum generator in Fig. 2 need be instructed simply to synthesize spectra corresponding to a product of terms each of which represents a conjugate pair of poles. On the other hand, completely automatic procedures for reduction of spectra other than those of vowels or vowel-like sounds have not yet been developed. This lack of progress stems largely from the fact that the generation of these other classes of sounds is not yet understood in detail. While it is known, for example, that spectra occurring during the production of nasal, stop, and fricative consonants are characterized by zeros as well as poles, the numbers of zeros and poles required and the frequency ranges to be expected for each cannot be specified easily and systematically on the basis of present knowledge.

The spectrum of a nasalized vowel, for example, is characterized by about four poles and one zero in the frequency range up to 3000 cps,[16,17] but the problem of devising a strategy that would lead to automatic matching of such a spectrum is a formidable one. If the positions of the four poles and zero were varied independently, a large number of combinations would have to be tried, but in order to avoid erroneous results these should include only those combinations that could in fact represent outputs of a vocal tract. To meet this requirement constant reference to articulation would have to be made during the process of searching for suitable pole-zero combinations.

In view of these complications it is suggested that the strategy in an automatic analysis-by-synthesis procedure that is applicable to all types of spectra should consist of a search for parameters that are more directly related to articulation than are the pole-zero locations. In effect, the proposed strategy would require a search through a set of articulatory configurations. For each trial configuration the pole-zero locations, and hence the over-all spectrum, would be computed and compared with the spectrum under analysis. Different articulatory configurations would be tried until a spectrum yielding a best fit with the input spectrum was obtained. Thus in the case of matching the spectrum of a nasalized vowel, the strategy would try different vowel configurations and different amounts of coupling to the nasal cavities until an optimum spectral match was obtained.

The realization of this type of analysis scheme requires that a model be developed for specifying articulatory configurations in a simple yet meaningful way. Although various simple models have already been proposed[18–20] it is clear that much must be learned concerning articulatory constraints and the relations between articulation and the acoustic output before a suitable strategy for the automatic reduction of all kinds of speech spectra is developed.

DISCUSSION

Analysis-by-synthesis procedures for the reduction of speech spectra have been used in one form or another by several investigators. Early attempts to use a spectrum matching technique were reported by Steinberg[21] and by Lewis,[22] who matched simple resonance curves to vowel spectra in the vicinity of the spectral peaks. The method was carried much further by Fant,[4,23] who demonstrated how the spectra associated with simple linear circuits can be matched against vowel and consonant spectra. In Fant's studies, the experimenter can be said to have been situated within the feedback loop (as in Fig. 3 above) and the comparison spectra were either computed or measured from simple analog circuits. The goodness of fit was assessed by visual examination of the curves. Similar procedures were used by Heinz and Stevens[24] for the matching of the spectra of fricative consonants. Matching of the spectra of several vowels was achieved by Mathews, Miller, and David,[25] who used digital computer techniques for the analysis

[16] O. Fujimura, "Analysis of nasalized vowels," Quart. Progr. Rept. **62**, Research Laboratory of Electronics, M.I.T. (1961). pp. 191–192.

[17] Reference 4, pp. 148 ff.

[18] Reference 4, pp. 71 ff.

[19] K. N. Stevens and A. S. House, J. Acoust. Soc. Am. **27**, 484 (1955).

[20] O. Fujimura (personal communication, 1960).

[21] J. C. Steinberg, J. Acoust. Soc. Am. **6**, 16 (1934).

[22] D. Lewis, J. Acoust. Soc. Am. **8**, 91 (1936).

[23] C. G. M. Fant, "Transmission properties of the vocal tract, II." Quart. Progr. Rept. Acoustics Laboratory, M.I.T. (Oct.–Dec. 1950), pp. 14–19.

[24] J. M. Heinz and K. N. Stevens, J. Acoust. Soc. Am. **33**, 589 (1961).

[25] M. V. Mathews, J. E. Miller, and E. E. David, Jr., J. Acoust. Soc. Am. **33**, 179 (1961).

of spectra computed from individual periods of the glottal output. They devised procedures for finding a set of poles corresponding to the vocal-tract transfer function and zeros to approximate the detailed form of the glottal spectrum such that best fits were obtained with the spectra under analysis. By performing a "pitch synchronous" analysis, they were able to obtain a rather detailed picture of the characteristics of the glottal excitation as well as the vocal-tract resonances, although the procedure was complicated by the necessity for adjusting a large number of parameters in order to converge to a best fit. The principles of the active speech analysis procedure have also been enunciated by Inomata,[26] who, in connection with a program concerned with automatic speech recognition, has used computer techniques to search for a set of poles that yield a spectrum that matches a given vowel spectrum.

Whereas the methods just summarized, as well as those described in this paper, involve the matching of speech spectra and thus are carried out in the frequency domain, analysis procedures based on the same principle can also be applied in the time domain. The "inverse filtering" techniques described by Miller[27] involve the processing of the vowel sounds by a cascaded set of filters that are characterized by a set of conjugate pairs of zeros. When the frequencies of the zeros are adjusted to coincide with those of the poles that describe the vocal-tract transfer function for the vowel, then the output of the filters represents the waveform of the glottal source. Since the general shape of the glottal pulse is known, then a procedure can be devised for adjusting the zeros until the expected shape is obtained. The processing of the signal by a cascaded sequence of filters in the time domain is analogous to subtracting elemental resonance spectra (in decibels) from the speech spectrum. It would appear difficult, however, to devise an automatic analysis procedure based on time-domain methods, since criteria for optimum cancellation of a pole by a zero might be difficult to devise.

The various versions of analysis-by-synthesis or feedback methods of speech spectrum analysis such as those that have been described here and by others are considered to have important advantages over other analysis schemes. For the feedback analysis method, once a set of parameters is found such that a good replica of the input signal is generated when these parameters are applied as instructions to the internal generative model, then there is little question that this set constitutes an adequate representation of the input. In contrast to this method are the passive or open-loop analysis procedures in which simple attributes of the spectra, such as the major spectral peaks, are measured directly and are used to provide a simple representation of the speech signal. There is no assurance in these cases that important data have not been discarded or that an error has not been made in the extraction of a particular parameter.

Other potential advantages of the feedback analysis procedure stem from the fact that it permits certain quasi-invariant features of the speech signal to be accounted for in a relatively straightforward manner. Thus, in principle, once certain properties of a given talker, such as the spectrum of the glottal output or the approximate range of variation of his formant frequencies, have been evaluated, then these properties can be assumed to remain relatively unchanged over a period of time, and the strategy during this period is simplified. In a sense, the method is geared to the extraction of features of the signal that are changing, and spends little time on the extraction of features that do not change or that change only slowly.

The similarity between an analysis-by-synthesis procedure and certain aspects of human perception have led several investigators to speculate that man manipulates sensory data such as speech by an active internal replication process.[5-7,26,28,29] If there is any basis for such speculation, then analysis techniques of the type described here would have the additional advantage that they bear at least some resemblance to the process of human speech reception.

ACKNOWLEDGMENTS

The authors have profited from stimulation, counsel and technical assistance contributed by their associates. Discussions with Osamu Fujimura have particularly influenced the course of the research. Ideas contributed by George Rosen and Fausto Poza are also acknowledged with gratitude, as is the criticism and encouragement of Morris Halle, the programming aid of Paul T. Brady and the technical assistance of Jane Arnold. Finally, the work would not have been possible without the availability of the TX-O computer, a facility of the Department of Electrical Engineering, M.I.T., and the cooperation and help of its technical staff.

This work was supported in part by the U. S. Army Signal Corps, the Air Force Office of Scientific Research, and the Office of Naval Research; and in part by the Air Force Cambridge Research Laboratories.

APPENDIX: SPEECH INPUT SYSTEM

Sampled speech data are introduced into the computer in spectral form using equipment the block diagram of which is shown in Fig. 12. Speech is recorded on one channel of a two-channel magnetic tape loop and sampling pulses are recorded on the other channel. The speech is played back through a pre-emphasis network into a

[26] S. Inomata, Bull. Electro-Tech. Lab. (Tokyo) 24, 597 (1960).
[27] R. L. Miller, J. Acoust. Soc. Am. 31, 667 (1959).
[28] G. A. Miller, E. Galanter, and K. H. Pribram, *Plans and the Structure of Behavior* (Henry Holt and Company, New York, 1960).
[29] L. A. Chistovich, Soviet Phys.—Acoustics 6, 393 (1961); [Akust. Zhur. 6, 392 (1960)].

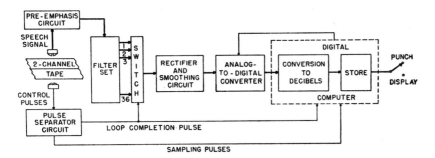

FIG. 12. Block diagram of the procedure used in preparing speech materials for computer analysis.

bank of 36 simple-tuned filters. The pre-emphasis network has a rising frequency characteristic of 6 db/octave. The center frequencies of the filters range from 150 to 7025 cps and are selected so that the half-power points of adjacent filters are coincident. The filter bandwidths are constant at 100 cps for center frequencies up to 1550 cps and then increase gradually until reaching a value of 475 cps for a center frequency of 7025 cps. During the read-in process, the outputs of the filters are selected in sequence by a stepping switch that steps after each cycle of the tape loop. Thus the loop is played 36 times to obtain a complete spectral analysis of the speech sample. The selected filter output is full-wave rectified and smoothed before being converted from analog to digital form. A commercial analog-to-digital encoder performs this conversion.

The second tape channel contains recorded control pulses. A pulse train of positive polarity in which the pulses occur every 8.3 msec is used to indicate times at which the data are to be sampled. A train of opposite polarity marks the end of the tape loop and initiates the stepping switch. These control pulses enter two light-pen flip-flop registers of the computer, so that the sampling can then be controlled by the computer.

The computer is programmed to search the light-pen flip-flop registers for "sample" pulses and to transfer data from the encoder when such a pulse appears. The filter outputs are encoded into 10 bits and are read into the computer, where the data are then converted into decibels, encoded into six bits, and rearranged so that three samples are stored in each 18-bit memory register. Thus each group of 12 registers contains outputs of the 36 filters at one sample time. Successive groups of 12 registers contain speech spectra at successive 8.3-msec intervals. With the present 8192-word memory, 3648 registers are used for data storage, and thus approximately 2.5 seconds of speech can be processed. The program provides routines that allow the data to be displayed on an oscilloscope or punched out on paper tape for later use. In addition, several error-checking routines are built into the program to maintan the accuracy of the read-in process.

Pitch Synchronous Analysis of Voiced Sounds[1]

M. V. Mathews, Joan E. Miller, and E. E. David, Jr.

Bell Telephone Laboratories, Inc., Murray Hill, New Jersey

(Received November 18, 1960)

A study of vowel sounds by means of a spectral analysis keyed synchronously to the voice pitch has been carried out. Spectra are obtained by Fourier analysis of individual pitch periods which were established by visual inspection of oscillograms. A digital computer served as the analyzer. The spectra are represented by a pattern of zeros and poles obtained by a process of successive approximation, again carried out by computer. The contributions from vocal tract and glottal source can be uniquely separated and examined. These results show that vowel sounds can be represented by a sequence of poles arising from the vocal tract and a sequence of zeros charactering the izglottal excitation. The frequencies of the vocal tract poles agreed with previous measurements, but the damping factors were not entirely consistent with earlier estimates. The zeros showed approximately uniform frequency spacing, particularly at high frequencies. A theoretical development indicated that this characteristic was to be expected from the known structure of the glottal excitation. The zero pattern was used to estimate the ratio of open-to-closed time for the glottis during voicing.

SPEECH is the acoustic result of certain events in the vocal apparatus. Indeed, many of the characteristics of these events can be deduced from the acoustical properties of the speech itself. For instance, it has been long realized that speech formants are a reflection of vocal tract resonances, and that the quasi-periodic nature of vocalized speech can be attributed directly to the vocal cord excitation. Usually, such features have been studied with the aid of the sound spectrograph and other special instruments. Though of great utility, these instruments have limitations, both in the range and flexibility of their analysis parameters, and in the dynamic range and resolution of their output displays. With the advent of digital computers as analysis tools, much more sophisticated processing and display have become possible.[2,3] This paper presents a basic speech spectrum analysis[4,5] which takes advantage of the greater resources of the computer. The results indicate that this analysis leads to a much more precise acoustic representation of the speech wave than heretofore feasible. Consequently, this representation can be tied quite accurately to vocal tract events.

In the first step of the analysis the speech time waveform is segmented into pitch periods which are then subjected to a Fourier expansion. The resulting spectrum is approximated by a number of resonances (poles) and antiresonances (zeros). Utilizing the assumption that each period is one of an infinite sequence of identical periods, this "pitch synchronous" representation can be related easily and precisely to vocal characteristics. In particular, the physical constraints imposed by the known structure of the vocal tract permit the poles and zeros to be assigned uniquely to either the vocal tract itself of the vocal cord excitation. The salient properties of these contributions to speech production can then be established. This method is applied here to vowel sounds but may be generalized to other voiced sounds as well.

Throughout the paper, the positions of the poles and zeros are specified by complex numbers. These can be considered as Cartesian coordinates in a "complex" plane on which the axes are σ, the real component, and ω, the imaginary component. The former determines the damping factor of the poles or zero, while the ω coordinate specifies its frequency. Such a geometrical presentation is an aid in comprehending the significance of a pole-zero representation.

MATHEMATICAL CHARACTERIZATION OF VOCALIC SOUNDS

Fourier Analysis and Glottal-Vocal Tract Spectrum

For pitch-synchronous analysis, the vocal tract will be represented as shown in Fig. 1. A sequence of glottal pulses $g(t)$ is the volume velocity input to a vocal tract which has a transfer characteristic $V(j\omega)$. The resulting sound pressure wave $f(t)$ is measured at a point in front of the mouth and forms the basic data for deducing both the parameters of $V(j\omega)$ and the properties of the glottal source. In the analysis it will be assumed that $f(t)$ is periodic. Then the Fourier coefficients of a period are computed according to the relation

$$\alpha_m - j\beta_m = \frac{2}{T} \int_{-T/2}^{T/2} f(t)e^{-jm\omega_0 t}dt \quad m = 1, 2, \cdots, \quad (1)$$

[1] This paper is the written version of a talk given at the 58th Meeting of the Acoustical Society of America held at Cleveland, Ohio, October 22–24, 1959. See J. E. Miller, M. V. Mathews, and E. E. David, Jr., J. Acoust. Soc. Am. **31**, 1564(A) (1959).

[2] E. E. David, Jr., M. V. Mathews, and H. S. McDonald, Proc. I.R.E. West. Joint Computer Conf. 354 (1959).

[3] E. E. David, Jr., Proc. I.R.E. **49**, 319 (1961).

[4] E. E. David, Jr., IBM J. Research Develop. **2**, 294 (1958). (See particularly pp. 3–6, 207, and Fig. 16.)

[5] E. E. David, Jr., M. V. Mathews, and Joan E. Miller, *Proceedings of the III International Congress on Acoustics* (Elsevier Publishing Company, Amsterdam, 1960).

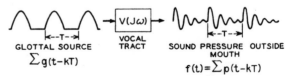

FIG. 1. Vocal tract representation.

Reprinted with permission from *J. Acoust. Soc. Am.*, vol. 33, pp. 179–186, Feb. 1961.

where T is the period, $\omega_0 = 2\pi/T$, and α_m and β_m are the usual cosine and sine coefficients. It is then necessary to develop the relationship between α_m and β_m and the generator properties, $V(j\omega)$ and $g(t)$. As will be seen, α_m and β_m do not completely specify $V(j\omega)$ and $g(t)$ and the nature of this uncertainty will be apparent from the analysis. The vocal tract response to a single glottal pulse is designated $p(t)$. Thus

$$P(j\omega) = V(j\omega)G(j\omega),$$

where

$$P(j\omega) = \int_{-\infty}^{+\infty} p(t)e^{-j\omega t}dt$$

and

$$G(j\omega) = \int_{-\infty}^{+\infty} g(t)e^{-j\omega t}dt.$$

The periodic sound pressure $f(t)$ is then

$$f(t) = \sum_{k=-\infty}^{+\infty} p(t-kT). \tag{2}$$

With the substitution of $f(t)$ from Eq. (2), Eq. (1) becomes

$$\alpha_m - j\beta_m = \frac{2}{T}\int_{-T/2}^{T/2}\left[\sum_{k=-\infty}^{+\infty} p(t-kT)\right]e^{-jm\omega_0 t}dt$$

which, using the definition of a Fourier transform, reduces to

$$\alpha_m - j\beta_m = (2/T)P(jm\omega_0)$$
$$= (2/T)V(jm\omega_0)G(jm\omega_0). \quad m=1, 2, \cdots. \tag{3}$$

Equation (3) is the desired relation between the Fourier coefficients and the product $V(j\omega)G(j\omega)$. From the equation it can be seen that only values of this function at harmonic frequencies $jm\omega_0$, $m=1, 2, \cdots$, are specified by the Fourier coefficients. Intermediate values of $V(j\omega)G(j\omega)$ can be changed arbitrarily without effecting $f(t)$. Therefore, it is not possible to compute $V(j\omega)G(j\omega)$ for all values of ω without further assumptions about the forms of $V(j\omega)$ and $G(j\omega)$.

Antiresonances, or Zeros, of $G(j\omega)$

It is shown in Appendix A using certain reasonable assumptions about the glottal pulse that $G(j\omega)$ will have only zeros at finite frequencies, that these zeroes are typically more numerous than the poles of $V(j\omega)$, and that at high frequencies they tend to be equally spaced along a line parallel to the imaginary axis. A sufficient set of requirements on the glottal pulse is that a complete closure occur for each pulse, i.e., that $g(t)$ be nonzero only for $0 < t < T_c$, that a discontinuity in the first derivative $g'(t)$ occur at $t=0$ and $t=T_c$, and that $g(t)$ be smooth to the extent that for $0 < t < T_c g''(t)$ exists and is of bounded variation. Motion picture

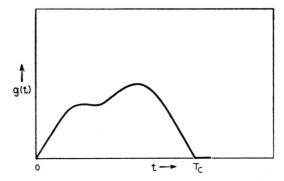

FIG. 2. Glottal wave.

studies of the glottis[6] seem to show that although closure does not always occur, there is at least an important class of voicing for which it does. In addition, Miller's work[7] indicates that most high frequencies are generated by opening and closing discontinuities. Hence, our idealization of the glottal waveform appears to be reasonable. A wave illustrating the requirements is shown on Fig. 2. For such a wave the spectrum $G(j\omega)$ will have only zeros and at sufficiently high frequencies they will be equally spaced along a locus parallel to the imaginary axis having a real part σ,

$$\sigma = \ln\left[-\frac{g'(T_c-)}{g'(0+)}\right], \tag{4}$$

where $g'(T_c-)$ is the slope of $g(t)$ just before closure and $g'(0+)$ is the slope just after opening. The locus may either be in the right or left half plane depending on whether $|g'(T_c-)|$ is greater or less than $|g'(0+)|$.

The imaginary component of the zero locations at high frequencies is

$$\omega = (\pi/T_c)(1\pm 2n) \quad n=m, m+1, \cdots. \tag{5}$$

Thus the asymptotic spacing of the zeros is $2\pi/T_c$ rad/sec. Since the pitch period is T, harmonics occur at $2\pi/T$ rad/sec and therefore, the ratio of asymptotic zeros to harmonics is T_c/T which is the duty factor of the glottis. Photographic evidence indicates values of $\frac{1}{3}$ to $\frac{1}{2}$ may be typical for the duty factor. Therefore, there are a half to a third as many zeros as harmonics. Of course, this result applies only to zeros at large ω, however, the studies described below of actual data indicate that the asymptotic spacing obtains to quite low frequencies.

Resonances, or Poles, of $V(j\omega)$

It has been shown by Fant[8] and Weibel[9] that when the nasal cavity is sealed off by the velum, the vocal

[6] J. L. Flanagan, J. Speech and Hearing Research 1, 99 (1958).
[7] R. L. Miller, J. Acoust. Soc. Am. 31, 667 (1959).
[8] C. G. M. Fant, Tech. Rept. No. 12, Mass. Inst. Tech. Acoustics Lab., Cambridge, Massachusetts (1952).
[9] E. S. Weibel, J. Acoust. Soc. Am. 27, 858 (1955).

tract transfer function can be characterized by an infinite number of poles located near the imaginary axis and *no* zeros. In addition, $V(j\omega)$ has a zero at zero frequency and a pole on the negative real axis to account for radiation effects. The absence of other zeros in $V(j\omega)$ is particularly fortunate since it enables us to separate $P(j\omega)$ into $V(j\omega)$ and $G(j\omega)$ simply by separating poles and zeros.

The pole-zero representation of the spectrum of $P(j\omega)=V(j\omega)G(j\omega)$ can be written in the form

$$P(j\omega)=K\frac{(j\omega)}{(j\omega+R)}\frac{\prod_{n=1}^{\infty}\left(1-\frac{j\omega}{Z_n}\right)}{\prod_{n=1}^{\infty}\left(1-\frac{j\omega}{P_n}\right)}, \quad (6)$$

where K sets the spectrum amplitude; $(j\omega)/(j\omega+R)$ specifies the radiation effects; Z_n, $n=1, 2, \cdots$, are locations of zeros introduced by the glottis; and P_n, $n=1, 2, \cdots$, are locations of vocal tract poles. This characterization makes explicit the parameters used in the sequel to fit the pitch-synchronous spectral data derived from speech waveforms.

SPECTRAL FITTING TECHNIQUE

The determination of the parameters of $P(j\omega)$ [Eq. (6)] from the Fourier coefficients α_m, β_m [Eq. (1)] of a period appears to be possible only by an approximation process. A straightforward technique is to guess a set of parameters for $P(j\omega)$, compute values of $P(jm\omega_0)$, $m=1, 2, \cdots$, evaluate some error function between $P(jm\omega_0)$ and $\alpha_m-j\beta_m$, and adjust the parameters in a systematic way so as to minimize the error. Such a technique is known generally as the method of successive approximations. Whether it is at all successful depends critically on the nature of the problem, the error function selected, and the rules for adjusting parameters.[10]

As a result of these factors three different error criteria were used. For most of the parameters a weighted mean-square-error

$$\text{SQ ER}=\sum_{m=1}^{M} W(m-m_0)[\log|P(jm\omega_0)|$$
$$-\log(\alpha_m^2+\beta_m^2)^{\frac{1}{2}}]^2 \quad (7)$$

was minimized, where m_0 is the harmonic number of the spectral component nearest the pole or zero being considered. This expression was used for poles and zeros near the imaginary axis. $W(m-m_0)$ is a weighting function having the values in Table I which stresses the error near the singularity. Such a weighting tends to position the poles and zeros so as to fit the local fluctua-

---

[10] See, for example, C. G. Bell, F. Poza, and K. N. Stevens, Proc. of Seminar on Speech Compression and Processing, Air Force Cambridge Research Center, Bedford, Massachusetts, 28 (1959).

TABLE I. Error weighting function.

m	≤ -5	-4	-3	-2	-1	0	$+1$	$+2$	$+3$	$+4$	$\geq +5$
$W(m)$	0	0.25	0.5	0.75	1	1	1	0.75	0.5	0.25	0

tions in the speech spectrum. M is the number of harmonics in the frequency range of interest. The logarithmic measure of spectrum amplitude was chosen to assure equal sensitivity to movements of both poles and zeros.

For poles and zeros far from the imaginary axis, (such as the radiation pole at $-R$), an expression similar to Eq. (7) was chosen but with $W(m)=1$ for all m thus evaluating the error uniformly over the entire spectrum. The average spectrum amplitude, K, was computed so as to equate the average value of $\log|P(jm\omega_0)|$ with the average of $\log(\alpha_m^2+\beta_m^2)^{\frac{1}{2}}$. K was reevaluated each time any of the other parameters were changed.

The rules for varying parameters were quite simple. Each zero or pole was specified by a real and an imaginary part. A fixed incremental magnitude was specified for each part (the increments were not necessarily equal for the two parts). The imaginary part was first incremented so as to reduce the error. Next a similar process was carried out for the real part. All the zeros and poles were varied in turn, this whole process constituting one cycle or approximation. A specified number of cycles could be carried out in a computation. The rate of variation of any zero or pole could be controlled through its increment magnitude, and poles or zeros could be fixed by making their increments zero.

One modification to $P(j\omega)$ is necessary before carrying out the approximation. As written in Eq. (6), $P(j\omega)$ contains an infinite number of parameters, a somewhat impractical number for computations. Consequently, only the first few zeros and poles are chosen for adjustment while for higher frequencies both zeros and poles are assumed to lie equally spaced along the imaginary axis. This spacing is a reasonable approximation to their asymptotic behavior presented above. Thus $P(j\omega)$ can be separated into two parts:

$$P(j\omega)=\left[K\frac{(j\omega)}{(j\omega+R)}\frac{\prod_{n=1}^{N_z}\left(1-\frac{j\omega}{Z_n}\right)\left(1-\frac{j\omega}{\bar{Z}_n}\right)}{\prod_{n=1}^{N_p}\left(1-\frac{j\omega}{P_n}\right)\left(1-\frac{j\omega}{\bar{P}_n}\right)}\right][H(j\omega)], \quad (8)$$

where $H(j\omega)$ is the contribution of the high-frequency poles and zeros, and N_p and N_z are, respectively, the number of low-frequency pole and zero pairs which will be adjusted. ($\bar{P}_n$ and $\bar{Z}_n$ are conjugates of P_n and Z_n.)

The high-frequency correction is evaluated in Appendix B and the first order approximation to it is

$$H(j\omega)=\exp(-K_1\omega^2),$$

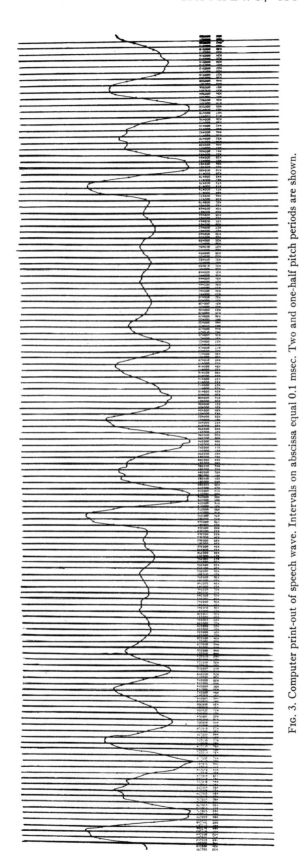

Fig. 3. Computer print-out of speech wave. Intervals on abscissa equal 0.1 msec. Two and one-half pitch periods are shown.

where

$$K_1 = \frac{1}{d_z{}^2} \sum_{n=1}^{\infty} \frac{1}{(N_z+n-\frac{1}{2})^2} - \frac{1}{d_p{}^2} \sum_{n=1}^{\infty} \frac{1}{(N_p+n-\frac{1}{2})^2}.$$

This estimate results from zeros and poles regularly spaced respectively d_z and d_p units apart on the imaginary axis. Thus the zeros occur at $\omega = \pm(N_z+n-\frac{1}{2})d_z$ $n=1, 2, \cdots$, and the poles occur at $\omega = \pm(N_p+n-\frac{1}{2})d_p$ $n=1, 2, \cdots$.

The effect of these zeros and poles is manifested through a constant K_1. Since this constant is generally not known in advance, it, too, is included as one of the parameters which is adjusted to minimize the error.

RESULTS

The spectral fitting program was applied to twenty utterances from the set of vowel sounds /i/, /e/, /a/, /ʌ/, /ɜ/, /ɔ/, /O/ and /u/ which span the vowel triangle. Each sound was sustained for about 1 sec by a male speaker at normal intensity. Recordings were made on an Ampex 300 tape recorder at 15 in/sec from a Western Electric 633A microphone located 6 in. from the speakers mouth in a sound treated room. The magnetic tape was played back through a 4kc low-pass filter and rerecorded on a digital recorder[2] sampling 10 000 times/sec and uniformly quantizing each sample into 2048 levels. Twelve of the 20 sounds were played into the digital recorder at $7\frac{1}{2}$ in./sec, thus effecting a sampling rate of 20 000/sec with respect to the original utterances. It was subsequently established that there were no significant differences between spectra computed from data taken at the two rates.

Samples near the center of the sustained sounds were plotted on the computer tabulator for pitch detection. One example is shown on Fig. 3. From these plots the beginning and end of a pitch period were established by visual inspection to the nearest sample. These points were defined as coincident with the zero crossing before the principal peak in the period. The computer then interpolated between samples to locate the zero crossing to an estimated accuracy of $\frac{1}{10}$ sampling interval. Estimates of α_m and β_m were then computed by first interpolating a set of equally spaced points in the pitch period, then multiplying the samples by appropriate sine and cosine functions and summing over the period.[11]

Four typical pitch-synchronous spectra for the sounds /i/, /ʌ/, /u/, and /e/ are presented by the solid line graphs in Fig. 4. The spectra show both peaks due to poles and small oscillations resulting from glottal zeros. For example, as established by the approximation process, the /e/ spectra has poles at about the 4th, 17th, 24th, and 32nd harmonics. The oscillations from the glottal zeros are most prominent between the 5th and 15th harmonics and between the 25th and 32nd harmonics. Also, there is a dimple on the low-frequency

[11] E. Guillemin, *The Mathematics of Circuit Analysis* (John Wiley & Sons, Inc., New York, 1950), 2nd printing, pp. 445–447.

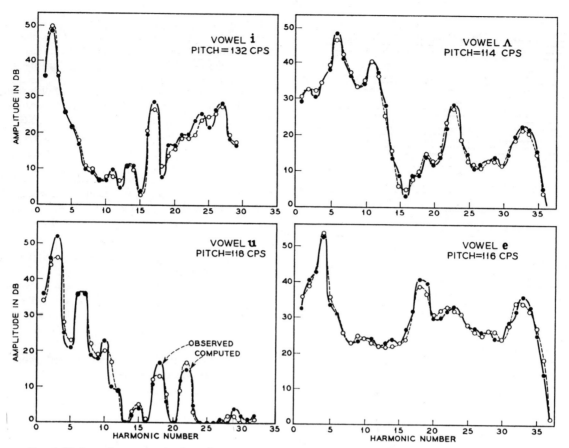

FIG. 4. Pitch synchronous spectral matches. Solid lines show observed spectra. Dotted lines show fitted spectra.

side of the first formant peak resulting from a zero near the second harmonic.

A conventional spectrogram section of the /e/ sound is shown for comparison on Fig. 5. The section was made with a 45~ filter. It compares reasonably well with the pitch-synchronous spectrum, the differences being attributable to a 6 db/octave high-frequency emphasis in the spectrograph and the fixed integration time of the spectrograph which is not related to the pitch period. However most of the features in the pitch-synchronous spectrum can be seen in the section. The poles are, of course, quite obvious. The zero oscillations are visible in places, though they are not as uniform as in the pitch-synchronous spectrum. In addition the section shows spectral fluctuations which arise from the non-pitch-synchronous nature of the analysis. These are as large as those arising from the glottal zeros. Therefore, it would be difficult to locate the glottal zeros accurately from a spectrogram.

The process for fitting the spectrum with poles and zeros was initiated by guessing a set of poles and zeros using the major peaks to position poles, and the small oscillations to estimate the spacing of an approximately periodic zero pattern. The initial damping factors on both poles and zeros placed them about 100 cps left of the imaginary axis. The radiation pole was fixed at

3500 cycles on the negative real axis. The fitting program then executed 10 to 20 complete cycles, each of which consisted of a perturbation of each parameter in every pole and zero (except the zero at the origin) and an adjustment of K_1. If a good fit was not so obtained the result was examined visually, suitable adjustments in the pole-zero pattern made, and another set of cycles commenced. Two trials were almost always sufficient to obtain fits as good as those shown by the dashed curves on Fig. 4.

The pole-zero patterns producing the curves of Fig. 4 are shown on Fig. 6. All points are indicated in the left

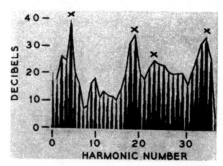

FIG. 5. Spectrogram section of sound /e/. Crosses mark pole positions from Fig. 6.

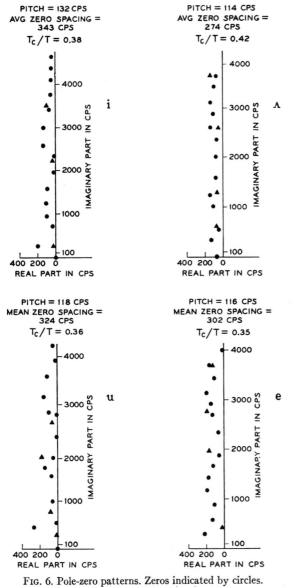

FIG. 6. Pole-zero patterns. Zeros indicated by circles.
Poles indicated by triangles.

higher poles have an average bandwidth two to three times greater than the House-Stevens' averages and are close to Bogert's[14] results. The source of this variance is by no means established. Perhaps the high-frequency pole positions with the glottis open are sufficiently shifted when it is closed to widen the effective bandwidth when averaged over a period.

The zeros of Fig. 6 are approximately equally spaced in the imaginary direction, this arrangement agreeing with the asymptotic theory developed in Appendix A. In addition, the real part of the zero locations varies so as to present a scalloped appearance. Just what the significance, if any, of this regularity is not known. A distribution for the real part of the zeros in terms of equivalent bandwidth (2X real part) is also given on Fig. 7. As can be seen, it is comparable to that of the poles. Thus the minima due to zeros should be as sharp as the peaks produced by the poles. The prominence of the pole peaks compared with the zero oscillations on the spectrograms arises from the close, uniform spacing of the zeros. Thus the minima are too close together to produce large oscillations.

half plane, though some of the zeros might well lie in the right half plane. We have no basis, however, for deciding between left and right alternatives from spectrum amplitude data alone.

The frequency positions of the poles agree well for the particular sounds with the Peterson-Barney[12] vowel data. Distributions of the damping factors of the poles are given in Fig. 7 as equivalent bandwidths. The average bandwidths for the first four poles are 73, 204, 270, and 208 cps, respectively. The figure for the first pole is comparable with that obtained by House and Stevens[13] for three male subjects with open glottis. The

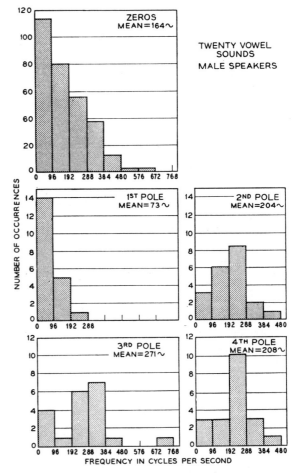

FIG. 7. Distribution of equivalent bandwidths for poles and zeros.

[12] G. E. Peterson, and H. L. Barney, J. Acoust. Soc. Am. 24, 175 (1952).
[13] A. S. House and K. N. Stevens, J. Speech and Hearing Research 1, 309 (1958).
[14] B. P. Bogert, J. Acoust. Soc. Am. 25, 791 (1953).

If the average spacing of the zeros is taken as a measure of T_c, then the duty factor of the glottis can be estimated. Fig. 8 shows a distribution function for T_c/T for the 20 sounds analyzed. Most of the duty factors lie between 0.3 and 0.4.

The analyses presented here give a measure of the success and characteristics of the approximation program. The program is inconveniently sensitive to the accuracy of the initial setting, and the rates at which the pole-zero pattern was allowed to change. If the initial setting is close to the final answer, the process converges quickly. Convergence is measured both by the appearance of a small error between the fitted and original spectra, and by stable oscillation of pole and zero positions on successive trials. However, for poor initial conditions the approximation failed to converge in some cases.

The error function is more sensitive to the frequency locations of the poles and zeros than their location in the real direction. Consequently, real parts are undoubtedly less accurate. One of the most difficult conditions to satisfy is the selection of poles and zeros to fit local fluctuations in the spectrum while at the same time obtaining the correct overall spectrum slope. Simultaneously satisfying both these requirements is good evidence that an appropriate set of poles and zeros has been found.

CONCLUSION

The use of digital computers for speech analysis is justifiable only if data not readily available by simpler methods can be so obtained. Spectral analysis keyed to the voice pitch is a case which fits this criterion. Being normalized with respect to the voice pitch, the pitch-synchronous analysis produces uniformly interpretable spectra over a wide range of voices independent of their pitch.[4,15] In addition, this analysis can be related rigorously to events in the vocal tract. This relation is at best difficult to establish for the usual filter bank or spectrograph analysis.

The pitch-synchronous analysis used in this paper leads to characterization of the glottal excitation in terms of spectral zeros. These tend to be uniformly spaced at high frequencies, and the distance between them is a measure of the ratio of open-to-closed time of the glottis during voicing. This characterization is based on three factors: (1) according to the best estimates of the glottal waveform, a spectrum with only zeros, these being uniformly spaced at high frequencies should result, (2) oscillations from the zeros are clearly evident in pitch-synchronous spectra and can be seen in regular spectrogram sections, (3) a good fit to pitch synchronous spectra is obtained using zeros and poles which conform to those expected from an acoustic theory of speech production. The spectral oscillations due to the zeros are usually rather small, on the order of 2 to 5 db. Thus,

[15] G. E. Peterson, J. Speech and Hearing Research **2**, 173 (1959).

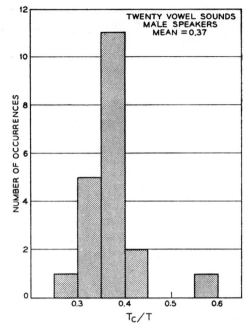

Fig. 8. Distribution of duty factor for glottis.

though they may be important determinants of spectral detail, they do not greatly change the gross spectral shape. For example, glottal zeros may introduce spurious local maxima, but would not restrict the average slope.

The approximation process which was used to fit the spectra with poles and zeros converged satisfactorily providing the human operator inserted suitable initial conditions. The spectral fits so obtained were about $\pm 2-3$ db over the 4 kc frequency range. These data provide accurate estimates of formant bandwidths and glottal waveform properties.

The analysis described involves a good deal of human intervention. For determining basis speech properties, this feature is not objectionable. As a speech analyzer for voice coding or recognition purposes, an entirely automatic scheme is required. Schemes for automatic pitch detection and formant tracking have been demonstrated both digitally and in analog circuitry with, however, only partial success. Perhaps better automatic procedures can be derived as truncations and refinements are applied to our analysis method. In any case, a systematic investigation of speech representations will undoubtedly hold important implications for automatic speech processing.

APPENDIX A. ZEROS OF THE TRANSFORM OF A GLOTTAL PULSE

The transform $G(j\omega)$ of a glottal pulse of the type shown on Fig. 2 may be written

$$G(j\omega) = \int_0^{T_c} g(t)e^{-j\omega t}dt.$$

Since the range of both the integration and $g(t)$ are finite, and for finite ω, $e^{-j\omega t}$ is finite, it is immediately apparent that $G(j\omega)$ must be finite and hence can have no poles but only zeros at finite frequencies. Further, if we integrate the expression for $G(j\omega)$ twice by parts noting that $g(0) = g(T_c) = 0$, we obtain

$$G(j\omega) = \frac{1}{\omega^2}[g'(T_c-)e^{-j\omega T_c} - g'(0+)]$$
$$- \frac{1}{\omega^2}\int_0^{T_c} g''(t)e^{-j\omega t}dt.$$

If $g''(t)$ exists and is of bounded variation in the interval $0 < t < T_c$, the integral will be of order $1/\omega$ or less. Hence the second term will be of order $1/\omega^3$ or less and will become insignificant compared to the first term as ω becomes large. Thus at high frequencies the zeros of $G(j\omega)$ will occur where

$$[g'(T_c-)e^{-j\omega T_c} - g'(0+)] = 0.$$

By extending ω into the complex plane as

$$s = \sigma + j\omega,$$

the asymptotic zeros of $G(j\omega)$ are seen to occur at

$$\sigma = \ln\left[-\frac{g'(T_c-)}{g'(0+)}\right]$$

$$\omega = (\pi/T_c)[1\pm 2n] \quad n = m, m+1, \cdots.$$

This result is the source of Eqs. (4) and (5) in the body of the paper.

APPENDIX B. CORRECTION TERM FOR HIGH FREQUENCY POLES AND ZEROS

In the body of the paper, the transform of the vocal tract output $P(j\omega)$ was divided into two parts, see Eq. (8). The left-hand term contains the N_z zeros and N_p poles which will be adjusted by the fitting process. The right-hand term $H(j\omega)$ is the ratio of an infinite product of zeros divided by an infinite product of poles:

$$H(j\omega) = IP_{\text{zeros}}(j\omega)/IP_{\text{poles}}(j\omega).$$

If the zeros in the infinite product are assumed to lie along the imaginary axis at $\omega = \pm(N_z + n - \frac{1}{2})d_z$ $n = 1, 2, \cdots$, where d_z is their spacing, then

$$IP_{\text{zeros}} = \prod_{n=N_z+1}^{\infty}\left[1 - \left(\frac{j\omega}{j(n-\frac{1}{2})d_z}\right)^2\right].$$

A series approximation for products of this type has been worked out by Fant,[16] and we will follow his technique. The logarithm of IP_{zeros}

$$\ln IP_{\text{zeros}}(j\omega) = \sum_{n=1}^{\infty}\ln\left(1 - \frac{\omega^2}{(N_z+n-\frac{1}{2})^2 d_z^2}\right)$$

may be rewritten by a series expansion of the logarithm in the form

$$\ln IP_{\text{zeros}}(j\omega)$$
$$= -\sum_{n=1}^{\infty}\left[\frac{\omega^2}{(N_z+n-\frac{1}{2})^2 d_z^2} + \frac{\omega^4}{2(N_z+n-\frac{1}{2})^4 d_z^4} + \cdots\right].$$

An approximation is simply the first term of the expansion. Thus

$$IP_{\text{zeros}}(j\omega) \cong \exp\left[-\frac{\omega^2}{d_z^2}\sum_{n=1}^{\infty}\frac{1}{(N_z+n-\frac{1}{2})^2}\right].$$

A similar argument applies to $IP_{\text{poles}}(j\omega)$. Therefore, an estimate of $H(j\omega)$ is

$$H(j\omega) = \exp(-K_1\omega^2),$$

where

$$K_1 = \frac{1}{d_z^2}\sum_{n=1}^{\infty}\frac{1}{(N_z+n-\frac{1}{2})^2} - \frac{1}{d_p^2}\sum_{n=1}^{\infty}\frac{1}{(N_p+n-\frac{1}{2})^2},$$

and d_z and d_p are the asymptotic zero and pole spacings, N_z and N_p are the number of zeros and poles explicitly included in the spectrum.

[16] C. G. M. Fant, Rept. No. 10, Division of Telegraphy-Telephony, Royal Institute of Technology, Stockholm, Sweden, 73 (1958).

Homomorphic Analysis of Speech

ALAN V. OPPENHEIM, MEMBER, IEEE
RONALD W. SCHAFER, MEMBER, IEEE

Abstract—Classes of systems which satisfy a generalized principle of superposition have been previously proposed and termed "homomorphic systems," emphasizing their interpretation as homomorphic (i.e., algebraically linear) transformations. One such class appears suited to the separation of signals that have been convolved. In this paper, an approach to deconvolution of speech, based on these ideas, is discussed.

INTRODUCTION

IT IS GENERALLY accepted that a reasonable model for the speech waveform consists of a convolution of components representing the contributions of vocal cord timing, glottal pulse, and vocal tract impulse response. Both for speech bandwidth compression and for basic studies of the nature of the speech wave, it is desirable to isolate the effects of each of these components.

In this paper, a procedure for separating the components of speech is proposed and discussed. The procedure is based on an approach to nonlinear filtering of signals which have been nonadditively combined, that has been termed generalized linear filtering. In its realization for the deconvolution of speech, it is similar in some respects to cepstral analysis,[1] with the primary difference resulting from its application to the separation of the components rather than detection. The motivation for applying these ideas to speech processing was a direct result of the success of cepstral pitch detection, as discussed by Noll.[2]

HOMOMORPHIC DECONVOLUTION

Consider a signal $s(t)$ consisting of the convolution of two components $s_1(t)$ and $s_2(t)$ so that $s(t) = s_1(t) \otimes s_2(t)$, where $\otimes$ denotes convolution. In a manner similar to the linear filtering problem, we can restrict the class of filters to those having the property that, if ϕ denotes the transformation of the filter, then

$$\phi[s_1(t) \otimes s_2(t)] = \phi[s_1(t)] \otimes \phi[s_2(t)]. \tag{1}$$

In other words, the filter satisfies a principle of superposition under an operation (convolution) which is matched to the way in which the signals to be separated have been combined, in the same way that linear filters are matched to signals which have been added. The general class of systems satisfying a principle of superposition under some rule of combination for the inputs and outputs, has been termed homomorphic systems.[3] The particular class of homomorphic systems represented by (1) has been studied in detail. A canonic representation for this class of filters is shown in Fig. 1, in which

Fig. 1. Canonic form for homomorphic deconvolution.

the system D is invertible and has the property that

$$D[s_1(t) \otimes s_2(t)] = D[s_1(t)] + D[s_2(t)] \tag{2}$$

and the system D^{-1} is the inverse of the system D. The system L is a linear system. Thus, any system having the property specified by (1) can be decomposed in the form of Fig. 1, and any system of this form will have the property of (1).

Manuscript received September 6, 1967. The work at the M.I.T. Research Lab. of Electronics was supported in part by the Joint Services Electronics program. This paper was presented at the 1967 Conference on Speech Communication and Processing, Cambridge, Mass.

A. V. Oppenheim is with the Dept. of Electrical Engineering and Lincoln Laboratory, Massachusetts Institute of Technology, Lexington, Mass. (Operated with support from the U. S. Air Force.)

R. W. Schafer is with the Dept. of Electrical Engineering and the Research Laboratory of Electronics, Massachusetts Institute of Technology, Cambridge, Mass.

Reprinted from *IEEE Trans. Audio Electroacoust.*, vol. AU-16, pp. 221-226, June 1968.

There are several possible equivalent representations of the system D. The most straightforward and most generally applicable is shown in Fig. 2. In this representation, the response $\hat{s}(t)$ of the system D is related to the excitation $s(t)$ through the equation

$$\hat{S}(j\omega) = \log S(j\omega) = \log |S(j\omega)| + j\theta(j\omega)$$

where $S(j\omega)$ and $\hat{S}(j\omega)$ are the complex Fourier transforms of $s(t)$ and $\hat{s}(t)$, respectively, and $\theta(j\omega)$ is the phase associated with $S(j\omega)$. We note that $\hat{s}(t)$ is similar to the cepstrum in that it results from a spectral transformation on the log spectrum. The differences result from the fact that the cepstrum incorporates only spectral magnitude information, whereas $\hat{s}(t)$ uses both spectral magnitude and phase. For this reason, it has been convenient to refer to $\hat{s}(t)$ as the complex cepstrum, emphasizing the use of the complex Fourier transform and the complex logarithm.

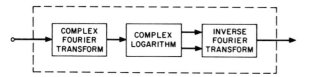

Fig. 2.   Realization of the transformation $D(\cdot)$ of Fig. 1.

PROPERTIES OF THE COMPLEX CEPSTRUM

In realizing the transformation D, it is necessary to use a digital computer; consequently, the input and output are viewed as discrete sequences, and the Fourier transformation is replaced by the z-transform evaluated on the unit circle. Thus, we will represent the input sequence as $s(n)$, the complex cepstrum as $\hat{s}(n)$, and their z-transforms as $S(z)$ and $\hat{S}(z)$, respectively, so that

$$\hat{S}(z) = \log S(z).$$

The phase associated with $S(z)$ evaluated on the unit circle is considered as a continuous and odd function of ω in the range $-\pi < \omega < \pi$.

If we restrict $S(z)$ to be of the form

$$S(z) = |k| z^r \frac{\prod_{i=1}^{m_0}(1 - a_i z^{-1}) \prod_{i=1}^{m_1}(1 - b_i z)}{\prod_{i=1}^{p_0}(1 - c_i z^{-1}) \prod_{i=1}^{p_1}(1 - d_i z)}$$

where a_i and c_i are the zeros and poles, respectively, inside the unit circle, and $(1/b_i)$ and $(1/d_i)$ are the zeros and poles respectively outside the unit circle, then it can be shown[1] that

$$\hat{s}(n) = \frac{r}{n}\cos \pi n - \frac{1}{2\pi j n} \oint_c \left[z \frac{S'(z)}{S(z)} \right] z^{n-1} dz \quad n \neq 0 \quad (3)$$

[1] The complex cepstrum $\hat{s}(n)$ is given by the inverse z-transform of $\log S(z)$, i.e., $\hat{s}(n) = (1/2\pi j)\oint \log S(z)z^{n-1} dz$. Equation (3) is derived by integrating this equation by parts for z on the unit circle. Since the phase is considered as a continuous and odd function of ω, it is discontinuous at $\omega = n\pi$ if $r \neq 0$, resulting in the first term in (3).

where the contour of integration c is taken to be the unit circle. If $s(n)$ has no poles or zeros outside the unit circle (including poles or zeros at infinity), corresponding to an input sequence which is minimum phase, then $r = 0$ and (3) becomes

$$\hat{s}(n) = \frac{1}{2\pi j n} \oint \left[-z \frac{S'(z)}{S(z)} \right] z^{n-1} dz \quad n \neq 0. \quad (4)$$

However, the poles of the factor $z(S'(z)/S(z))$ occur at values of z for which $S(z)$ has either poles or zeros, which, for the case of a minimum phase sequence, are entirely within the unit circle in the z-plane. Under this condition, then, $\hat{s}(n) = 0$ for $n < 0$; in other words, the complex cepstrum of a minimum phase sequence is zero for $n < 0$. In a similar manner, we can consider sequences for which $S(z)$ has all its poles and zeros outside the unit circle. Such sequences could appropriately be termed maximum phase sequences. In this case, the complex cepstrum is zero for $n > 0$.

Because of the restriction placed on the phase of $S(z)$, namely, that it is an odd function of ω, the complex cepstrum will always have zero imaginary part, i.e., it is always a pure real function. This is seen by observing that

$$\hat{s}(n) = \frac{1}{2\pi j} \oint \log S(z)z^{n-1} dz$$

or, with the contour of integration taken to be the unit circle,

$$\hat{s}(n) = \frac{1}{2\pi} \int_{-\pi}^{\pi} [\log |S(e^{j\omega})| + j\theta(\omega)]e^{j\omega n} d\omega.$$

With $\log |S(e^{j\omega})|$ an even function of ω, and $\theta(\omega)$ an odd function of ω,

$$\hat{s}(n) = \frac{1}{2\pi} \int_{-\pi}^{\pi} \log |S(e^{j\pi})| \cos \omega n d\omega$$

$$- \frac{1}{2\pi} \int_{-\pi}^{\pi} \theta(\omega) \sin \omega n d\omega.$$

If the sequence $s(n)$ is minimum phase, then it is possible to obtain the complex cepstrum from the inverse transform of the logarithm of the spectral magnitude. Let $EV[\hat{s}(n)]$ denote the even part of $\hat{s}(n)$, i.e.,

$$EV[\hat{s}(n)] = \frac{1}{2}[\hat{s}(n) + \hat{s}(-n)].$$

Since $\hat{s}(n)$ is zero for $n < 0$ if $s(n)$ is minimum phase, then

$$\hat{s}(n) = 2u(n)EV[\hat{s}(n)]$$

where

$$u(n) = \begin{cases} 1 & n > 0 \\ \frac{1}{2} & n = 0 \\ 0 & n < 0 \end{cases}$$

IEEE TRANSACTIONS ON AUDIO AND ELECTROACOUSTICS   JUNE 1968

but

$$EV[\hat{s}(n)] = Z^{-1}[\log |S(e^{j\omega})|]$$ (5)

and, therefore,

$$\hat{s}(n) = 2u(n) \cdot Z^{-1}[\log |S(e^{j\omega})|]$$ (6)

where Z^{-1} denotes the inverse z-transform.

Determining the complex cepstrum on the basis of (6) corresponds to reconstructing the phase associated with the magnitude of the spectrum by using the Hilbert transform. We observe also from (5) that $EV[\hat{s}(n)]$ corresponds to the cepstrum.[2] For minimum phase sequences, the cepstrum and the complex cepstrum will be identical (except for a factor of 2) for $n > 0$.

THE COMPLEX CEPSTRUM OF SPEECH

We assume that samples of the speech waveform can be considered as the discrete convolution of sequences representing pitch, glottal pulse, and vocal tract, denoted by $p(n)$, $g(n)$, and $v(n)$, respectively. Furthermore, a sequence to be processed will consist of a portion of the speech waveform as viewed through a window $w(n)$, so that

$$s(n) = [p(n) \otimes g(n) \otimes v(n)]w(n).$$ (7)

If we assume that the term $g(n) \otimes v(n)$ has an effective duration of N samples, and $w(n)$ is smooth compared with this term so that $w(n_1) \cong w(n_1 + N)$ for any n_1, then (7) can be approximated as

$$s(n) \cong [p(n)w(n)] \otimes g(n) \otimes v(n).$$

Let us first consider the term $p(n)w(n)$ which we abbreviate as $p_1(n) = p(n)w(n)$. Treating the sequence of pitch pulses $p(n)$ as a train of equally spaced unit samples with spacing of τ samples, then the z-transform of $p_1(n)$, denoted by $P_1(z)$, is

$$P_1(z) = \sum_{k=-\infty}^{\infty} w(k\tau)(z^\tau)^{-k}.$$

Let $w_\tau(n)$ be defined as the window compressed in time by τ, so that $w_\tau(n) = w(n\tau)$ with $W_\tau(z)$ and $\hat{w}_\tau(n)$ denoting the z-transform and complex cepstrum, respectively, of $w_\tau(n)$. Then,

$$P_1(z) = W_\tau(z^\tau)$$

and

$$\log P_1(z) = \log W_\tau(z^\tau)$$

so that $\hat{p}_1(n)$, the complex cepstrum of $p_1(n)$, is given by

$$\hat{p}_1(n) = \hat{w}_\tau\left(\frac{n}{\tau}\right) \quad n = 0, \pm\tau, \pm 2\tau, \cdots$$
$$= 0 \quad \text{otherwise.}$$ (8)

[2] As discussed in Noll,[2] there has been a variety of definitions of the cepstrum. In the present context, the cepstrum is considered as the inverse Fourier transform of the log magnitude of the Fourier transform.

In other words, the complex cepstrum of a train of pitch samples weighted with a window can be determined by compressing the window by a factor τ corresponding to the spacing between pitch samples, determining the complex cepstrum, and expanding the result by a factor τ.[3] We observe that $\hat{p}_1(n)$ as expressed by (8) consists of a train of samples with spacing τ, in which the mth sample has a weighting $\hat{w}_\tau(m)$.

If we assume that the original window $w(n)$ is a minimum phase window, i.e., that all poles and zeros of its z-transform lie inside the unit circle, then all poles and zeros of the z-transform of $w_\tau(n)$ lie inside the unit circle, and, hence, $\hat{w}_\tau(n)$ is zero for $n < 0$. For a minimum phase window, then, the complex cepstrum of $\hat{p}_1(n)$ will be zero for $n < 0$. Similarly, if $w(n)$ is maximum phase, such that all poles and zeros of its z-transform lie outside the unit circle, then $\hat{p}_1(n)$ will be zero for $n > 0$. If the window is symmetric then $\hat{p}_1(n)$ will be symmetric.

The complex cepstrum of the sequence $v(n)$ corresponding to the vocal tract impulse response can be derived, if we assume that it is representable as a cascade of damped resonators. In this case, $v(n)$ is minimum phase and $V(z)$ is of the form

$$V(z) = \frac{K}{\displaystyle\prod_{i=1}^{M}(1 - a_iz^{-1})(1 - a_i^*z^{-1})} \quad |a_i| < 1.$$

Since all poles of $V(z)$ are inside the unit circle, $\hat{v}(n)$ is determined from (4), and is given by

$$\hat{v}(n) = -\frac{1}{2\pi j n}\oint\left[z\frac{V'(z)}{V(z)}\right]z^{n-1}dz \quad n \neq 0.$$

Evaluating the integrand,

$$z\frac{V'(z)}{V(z)} = -\sum_{i=1}^{M}\frac{a_iz^{-1}}{(1 - a_iz^{-1})} - \sum_{i=1}^{M}\frac{a_i^*z^{-1}}{(1 - a_i^*z^{-1})}$$

and

$$\hat{v}(n) = +\frac{1}{2\pi j n}\sum_{i=1}^{M}\left[\oint\frac{a_iz^{-1}}{1 - a_1z^{-1}}z^{n-1}dz\right.$$
$$\left. + \oint\frac{a_i^*z^{-1}}{1 - a_i^*z^{-1}}z^{n-1}dz\right]$$
$$= \frac{1}{n}\sum_{i=1}^{M}[(a_i)^n + (a_i^*)^n] \quad n > 0$$
$$= 0 \quad n < 0$$

or

$$\hat{v}(n) = \sum_{i=1}^{M}\frac{|a_i|^n}{n}\cos\omega_i n \quad n > 0$$
$$= 0 \quad n < 0$$ (9)

[3] The derivation of this result assumes that the phase associated with the window is zero at $\omega = \pm\pi$.

OPPENHEIM AND SCHAFER: HOMOMORPHIC ANALYSIS OF SPEECH

where

$$a_i = |a_i| e^{j\omega_i}.$$

An accurate analytical representation of the glottal pulse $g(n)$ is not known and, consequently, it is difficult to make any specific statements regarding $\hat{g}(n)$. If we assume that it is a time-limited pulse, then its z-transform is representable entirely by zeros (with the exception of poles at $z=0$). We can expect, in general, that $G(z)$ will contain zeros both inside and outside the unit circle, in other words will be nonminimum phase.[4] We can express $g(n)$ as the convolution of a minimum phase sequence and a maximum phase sequence, so that

$$g(n) = g_1(n) \otimes g_2(n)$$

where $g_1(n)$ is minimum phase, and $g_2(n)$ is maximum phase. The complex cepstrum of $v_1(n)$ will be zero for $n<0$, and will be dominated for large n by the zeros closest to the unit circle. If e^{σ_1} represents the distance from the origin in the z-plane to the zero of $v_1(n)$ closest to the unit circle, then for large positive n, $\hat{v}_1(n)$ behaves as $e^{n\sigma_1}/n$. Similarly, if e^{σ_2} represents the distance from the origin in the z-plane to the zero of $v_2(n)$ closest to the unit circle, then for large negative n, $\hat{v}_2(n)$ behaves as $e^{n\sigma_2}/n$. Consequently, the duration of the complex cepstrum of the glottal pulse will be governed by the zeros of its z-transform which are closest to the unit circle. We will assume that e^{σ_1} and e^{σ_2} are such that the complex cepstrum of the glottal pulse has an effective duration which is less than a pitch period.

From the above arguments, we can consider dividing the complex cepstrum into three regions. Comparing (8) and (9), the complex cepstrum of the vocal tract decays rapidly relative to the contribution from pitch. Consequently, for the magnitude of n greater than or equal to a pitch period, the primary contribution is due to pitch. For positive values of n less than a pitch period, the contribution is from the vocal tract and the minimum phase component of the glottal pulse. For negative n, the contribution is from the maximum phase component of the glottal pulse.

To recover $p_1(n)$, we wish to keep only those points in $\hat{s}(n)$ for n greater than, or equal to, a pitch period. If the number of points in a pitch period is n_p, then the linear filter corresponds to multiplying $\hat{s}(n)$ by zero for $|n| < n_p$ and by unity for $|n| > n_p$. To recover the term $g_1(n) \otimes v(n)$, we multiply $\hat{s}(n)$ by zero for $n<0$ and $n \geq n_p$, and to recover $g_2(n)$, we retain only those values of $\hat{s}(n)$ for $-n_p < n < 0$. After filtering, the result is transformed by the inverse of the system D.

Since no clear statements can be made about the relative importance of the maximum and minimum phase components of the glottal pulse, the notion of recover-

[4] Mathews, Miller, and David[4] have argued that the asymptotic zeros of the glottal pulse lie in the right half of the s-plane, if the slope of the leading edge plus the slope of the trailing edge is negative. In such cases, then, the glottal pulse is nonminimum phase.

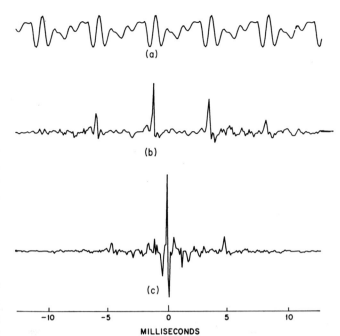

Fig. 3. (a) Sample of the vowel "ah." (b) Resulting output due to pitch. (c) Complex cepstrum of (a).

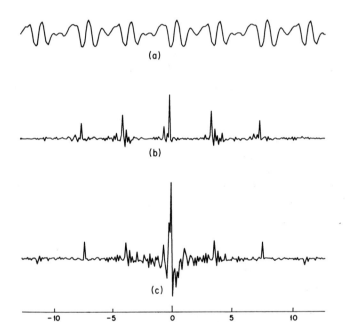

Fig. 4. (a) The speech sample of Fig. 3 resynthesized with alternating pitch. (b) and (c) Output due to pitch and the complex cepstrum, respectively.

ing the maximum phase component has no obvious implications. However, if we retain values in the complex cepstrum for small positive and negative values of n, then combined vocal tract and glottal pulse information can be recovered with the appropriate phase relations.

An an example of the recovery of pitch, consider the vowel "ah" as in father, shown in Fig. 3(a). The speech was sampled at 10 kHz and weighted with a Hanning window 25.6 ms in duration. The complex cepstrum is shown in Fig. 3(c), and the weighted output due to the pitch pulses is shown in Fig. 3(b).

To investigate the method for cases of varying pitch, a single pulse was obtained by "low time filtering" the complex cepstrum to recover the term $v(n) \otimes g(n)$. The speech wave was then resynthesized by convolving this pulse with a train of unit samples with alternating spacing. Fig. 4 shows the resynthesized speech, weighted output due to the pitch pulses, and complex cepstrum for alternating pitch.

From Fig. 3, it appears that for constant pitch there is no particular advantage in carrying out pitch detection on the recovered pitch pulses rather than the complex cepstrum, and in many similar examples tried, the peak is as evident in the cepstrum as in the complex cepstrum. Thus, for examples of this type, where pitch is constant, the inclusion of phase information and processing by the inverse of the system D seems to offer no advantage over cepstral pitch detection, as discussed by Noll. From Fig. 4, however, it appears that this processing places in evidence individual variations between pitch periods. These conclusions, however, are based on a small number of examples, and must be considered as tentative without further experimental verification.

A METHOD FOR INVERSE FILTERING

In the previous discussion, the approach taken was to transform the convolved components of speech into additive components in the complex cepstrum, and attempt to separate them by linear filtering. An alternative approach is to remove the unwanted components by subtracting them, and processing the result by means of the system D^{-1}. This approach is entirely equivalent to processing the original waveform with a linear filter whose frequency response is the reciprocal of the Fourier transform of the unwanted components, i.e., inverse filtering. This approach to filtering requires an accurate representation of the components to be removed.

For the recovery of source information, corresponding to a train of glottal pulses, the signal to be removed is the vocal tract impulse response, or formant structure of the speech. R. Miller[5] and others[6],[7] have successfully used the method of inverse filtering, determining the parameters of the inverse filter by trial and error. In the work by J. Miller, the parameters are determined by matching the speech spectrum. In general, it appears to be difficult to locate the formant frequencies and bandwidths accurately in the presence of the spectral fine structure, due to pitch. In the spectral matching carried out by J. Miller, this fine structure was removed by using single pitch periods.

From the previous discussion, it is clear that the vocal tract and glottal pulse information can be separated from the spectral fine structure or pitch by retaining only those values of the cepstrum for values of $|n|$ less than a pitch period. This corresponds to linear smoothing of the log spectrum to obtain the spectral envelope. Vocal tract parameters can then be obtained by match-

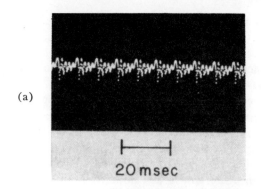

(a)

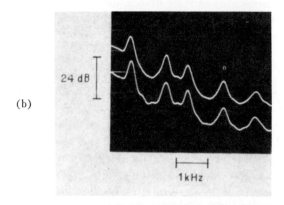

(b)

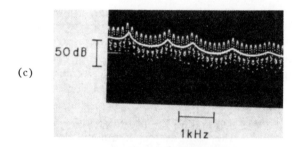

(c)

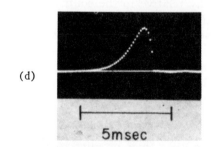

(d)

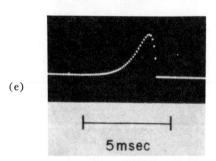

(e)

Fig. 5. (a) Synthetic vowel used to illustrate spectral matching and inverse filtering. (b) Lower trace: log spectral envelope of speech sample. Upper trace: smoothed log spectrum of ideal resonators. (c) Log spectrum of speech sample, and unsmoothed log spectrum of resonators superimposed. (d) Recovered "glottal" pulse. (e) Original pulse used to generate the synthetic speech.

ing the smoothed log spectrum with the log spectrum of a set of ideal cascade resonators. Since smoothing of the log spectrum introduces some distortion into the spectral envelope, it is desirable to do the same linear smoothing on the log spectrum of the ideal resonators. Equation (9) specifies an analytic expression for the cepstrum of the resonators, and, therefore, it is a straightforward procedure to generate the cepstrum directly, weighting with the same window used on the cepstrum of the original speech for smoothing of the log spectrum. When a reasonable match has been obtained, the complex cepstrum of the ideal resonators is subtracted from that for the original speech, and the output of the system D^{-1} is determined. To illustrate the procedure, consider the synthetic vowel "ah" of Fig. 5(a), which has been sampled at 10 kHz. To obtain the smoothed log spectrum, the cepstral values for $n < 36$ were used. The resulting smoothed log spectrum consists of both vocal tract and glottal pulse information. In Fig. 5(b), the lower trace represents the smoothed log spectrum of the synthetic speech, and the upper trace is the smoothed log spectrum of a set of resonators, together with a double order pole to represent the glottal spectrum (a term to approximate the glottal spectrum

is included only to facilitate the matching). In Fig. 5(c), the unsmoothed log spectrum of the original and the matching spectrum are superimposed. The resonator frequencies and bandwidths are identical for Fig. 5(b) and (c). The log spectrum of the glottal pulses are obtained by subtracting the resonator spectrum from the unsmoothed speech spectrum. The "glottal" pulse obtained for this example is shown in Fig. 5(d). For comparison, the original pulse used to generate the synthetic speech is shown in Fig. 5(e).

REFERENCES

[1] B. P. Bogert, M. Healy, and J. Tukey, "The quefrency alanysis of time series for echoes: cepstrum, pseudo-autocovariance, cross-cepstrum and saphe cracking," in *Proc. Symp. on Time Series Analysis*, M. Rosenblatt, Ed. New York: Wiley, 1963, ch. 15, pp. 209–243.

[2] A. M. Noll, "Cepstrum pitch determination," *J. Acoust. Soc. Am.*, vol. 41, pp. 293–309, February 1967.

[3] A. V. Oppenheim, "Superposition in a class of nonlinear systems," *1964 IEEE Internat'l Conv. Rec.*, pt. 1, pp. 171–177.

[4] M. V. Mathews, J. E. Miller, and E. E. David Jr, "Pitch synchronous analysis of voiced sounds," *J. Acoust. Soc. Am.*, vol. 33, pp. 179–186, February 1961.

[5] R. Miller, "Nature of the vocal cord wave," *J. Acoust. Soc. Am.*, vol. 31, pp. 667–677, June 1959.

[6] J. E. Miller, private communication.

[7] P. B. Carr and D. Trill, "Long-term larynx-excitation spectra," *J. Acoust. Soc. Am.*, vol. 36, pp. 2033–2040, November 1964.

Linear Prediction: A Tutorial Review

JOHN MAKHOUL, MEMBER, IEEE

Invited Paper

Abstract—This paper gives an exposition of linear prediction in the analysis of discrete signals. The signal is modeled as a linear combination of its past values and present and past values of a hypothetical input to a system whose output is the given signal. In the frequency domain, this is equivalent to modeling the signal spectrum by a pole-zero spectrum. The major part of the paper is devoted to all-pole models. The model parameters are obtained by a least squares analysis in the time domain. Two methods result, depending on whether the signal is assumed to be stationary or nonstationary. The same results are then derived in the frequency domain. The resulting spectral matching formulation allows for the modeling of selected portions of a spectrum, for arbitrary spectral shaping in the frequency domain, and for the modeling of continuous as well as discrete spectra. This also leads to a discussion of the advantages and disadvantages of the least squares error criterion. A spectral interpretation is given to the normalized minimum prediction error. Applications of the normalized error are given, including the determination of an "optimal" number of poles. The use of linear prediction in data compression is reviewed. For purposes of transmission, particular attention is given to the quantization and encoding of the reflection (or partial correlation) coefficients. Finally, a brief introduction to pole-zero modeling is given.

I. Introduction

A. Overview

THE MATHEMATICAL analysis of the behavior of general dynamic systems (be they engineering, social, or economic) has been an area of concern since the beginning of this century. The problem has been pursued with accelerated vigor since the advent of electronic digital computers over two decades ago. The analysis of the outputs of dynamic systems was for the most part the concern of "time series analysis," which was developed mainly within the fields of statistics, econometrics, and communications. Most of the work on time series analysis was actually done by statisticians. More recently, advances in the analysis of dynamic systems have been made in the field of control theory based on state-space concepts and time domain analysis.

This paper is a tutorial review of one aspect of time series analysis: linear prediction (defined here). The exposition is based on an intuitive approach, with emphasis on the clarity of ideas rather than mathematical rigor. Although the large body of related literature available on this topic often requires advanced knowledge of statistics and/or control theory concepts, this paper employs no control theory concepts *per se* and only the basic notions of statistics and random processes. For example, the very important statistical concepts of *consistency* and *efficiency* [74], [75] in the estimation of parameters will not be dealt with. It is hoped this paper will serve as a simple introduction to some of the tools used in time series analysis, as well as be a detailed analysis of those aspects of linear prediction of interest to the specialist.

Manuscript received July 21, 1974; revised November, 1974. This work was supported by the Information Processing Techniques Branch of the Advanced Research Projects Agency under Contract DAHC15-17-C-0088.

The author is with Bolt Beranek and Newman, Inc., Cambridge, Mass. 02138.

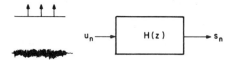

Fig. 1. Discrete speech production model.

B. Current Applications

Before we delve into signal analysis, we shall give three examples of the types of problems that are of current interest.[1] These examples will then serve to illustrate some of the concepts that are developed.

Neurophysics [15], [32], [36], [102]: The spontaneous electrical brain activity is normally measured by means of electrodes placed on the patient's scalp. The recordings, known as electroencephalograms (or EEG signals), show certain periodicities (sharp resonances) accompanied by some randomness. These signals are believed to carry information about the medical status of the brain and are used by physicians as a means of diagnosis. It is of interest to detect the presence, position, and strength of the different resonances, known as rhythms. The three most common rhythms are known as the alpha, beta, and delta rhythms. Therefore, the basic interest here is to describe the spectrum in a simple mathematical manner that would yield the characteristics of the different rhythms.

Geophysics [84]–[87], [114]: In one of the successful methods of oil exploration, a charge of dynamite is exploded in the earth, and the resulting vibrations at various points on the surface of the ground are recorded by a seismograph as seismic traces. The job of the geophysicist is to use these traces in the determination of the structure of the sedimentary rock layers. Such information is then used to decide on the presence of oil in that area. Of interest here are the direct arrival times and strengths of the deep reflections of the explosion, which are then used to determine the layered structure. If somehow one is able to remove (deconvolve) the impulse response of the structure from the seismic trace, the desired arrival times should appear as impulses of different phases and amplitudes.

Speech Communication [10], [33], [47], [50], [51], [62], [68], [89]: In EEG analysis, the spectrum of the recorded signal was of interest. In seismic analysis, the spectral properties of the seismic trace were of interest only to facilitate the deconvolution process in order to obtain the desired impulses. In the analysis of speech, both types of information are of interest.

Fig. 1 shows a rather successful model of speech production. The model consists of a filter that is excited by either a quasi-periodic train of impulses or a random noise source. The periodic source produces voiced sounds such as vowels and

[1] For applications to economic and industrial time series, see for example [17].

Reprinted from *Proc. IEEE*, vol. 63, pp. 561–580, Apr. 1975.

nasals, and the noise source produces unvoiced or fricated sounds such as the fricatives (f, th, s, sh). The parameters of the filter determine the identity (spectral characteristics) of the particular sound for each of the two types of excitation.

Given a particular speech signal, it is of interest to determine the general type of sound it is, voiced or fricated, and if voiced what the pitch period is (i.e., distance between pitch pulses). In addition, one is interested in the identity of the sound which can be obtained from the spectrum. Such derived information can then be used in an automatic speech recognition system or a speech compression system.

C. Linear Prediction

In applying time series analysis to the aforementioned applications, each continuous-time signal $s(t)$ is sampled to obtain a discrete-time[2] signal $s(nT)$, also known as a time series, where n is an integer variable and T is the sampling interval. The sampling frequency is then $f_s = 1/T$. (Henceforth, we shall abbreviate $s(nT)$ by s_n with no loss in generality.)

A major concern of time series analysis [6], [11], [12], [14], [17], [43], [45], [46], [54], [105], [112] has been the estimation of power spectra, cross-spectra, coherence functions, autocorrelation and cross-correlation functions. A more active concern at this time is that of system modeling. It is clear that if one is successful in developing a parametric model for the behavior of some signal, then that model can be used for different applications, such as prediction or forecasting, control, and data compression.

One of the most powerful models currently in use is that where a signal s_n is considered to be the output of some system with some unknown input u_n such that the following relation holds:

$$s_n = -\sum_{k=1}^{p} a_k s_{n-k} + G \sum_{l=0}^{q} b_l u_{n-l}, \qquad b_0 = 1 \qquad (1)$$

where a_k, $1 \leqslant k \leqslant p$, b_l, $1 \leqslant l \leqslant q$, and the gain G are the parameters of the hypothesized system. Equation (1) says that the "output" s_n is a linear function of past outputs and present and past inputs. That is, the signal s_n is *predictable* from *linear* combinations of past outputs and inputs. Hence the name *linear prediction*.

Equation (1) can also be specified in the frequency domain by taking the z transform on both sides of (1). If $H(z)$ is the transfer function of the system, as in Fig. 1, then we have from (1):

$$H(z) = \frac{S(z)}{U(z)} = G \frac{1 + \sum_{l=1}^{q} b_l z^{-l}}{1 + \sum_{k=1}^{p} a_k z^{-k}} \qquad (2)$$

where

$$S(z) = \sum_{n=-\infty}^{\infty} s_n z^{-n} \qquad (3)$$

is the z transform of s_n, and $U(z)$ is the z transform of u_n. $H(z)$ in (2) is the general *pole-zero model*. The roots of the

numerator and denominator polynomials are the zeros and poles of the model, respectively.

There are two special cases of the model that are of interest:
1) all-zero model: $a_k = 0$, $1 \leqslant k \leqslant p$
2) all-pole model: $b_l = 0$, $1 \leqslant l \leqslant q$.

The all-zero model is known in the statistical literature as the *moving average* (MA) model, and the all-pole model is known as the *autoregressive* (AR) model [17]. The pole-zero model is then known as the *autoregressive moving average* (ARMA) model. In this paper we shall use the pole-zero terminology since it is more familiar to engineers.

The major part of this paper will be devoted to the all-pole model. This has been, by far, the most widely used model. Historically, the first use of an all-pole model in the analysis of time series is attributed to Yule [115] in a paper on sunspot analysis. Work on this subject, as well as on time series analysis in general, proceeded vigorously after 1933 when Kolmogorov laid a rigorous foundation for the theory of probability. Later developments by statisticians, such as Cramér and Wold, culminated in the parallel and independent work of Kolmogorov [58] and Norbert Wiener [107] on the prediction and filtering of stationary time series. For a bibliography on time series through the year 1959, see the encyclopedic work edited by Wold [113]. For a discussion of all-pole (autoregressive) models see, for example, [17], [45], [105], [112].

Much of the recent work on system modeling has been done in the area of control theory under the subjects of estimation and system identification. Recent survey papers with extensive references are those of Åström and Eykhoff [8] and Nieman *et al.* [73]. The December 1974 issue of the IEEE TRANSACTIONS ON AUTOMATIC CONTROL is devoted to the subject of system identification. Another relevant survey paper is that of Kailath [55] on linear filtering theory. Related books are those of Lee [60], Sage and Melsa [88], and Eykhoff [30].

D. Paper Outline

Sections II–V deal exclusively with the all-pole model. In Section II, the estimation of model parameters is derived in the time domain by the method of least squares. The resulting normal equations are obtained for deterministic as well as random signals[3] (both stationary and nonstationary). Direct and iterative techniques are presented for the computation of the predictor coefficients, and the stability of the all-pole filter $H(z)$ is discussed. The response of the all-pole filter is then analyzed for two important types of input excitation: a deterministic impulse and statistical white noise.

In Section III, the all-pole modeling of a signal is derived completely in the frequency domain. The method of least squares translates into a spectral matching method where the signal spectrum is to be matched or fitted by a model spectrum. This formulation allows one to perform arbitrary spectral shaping before modeling. This viewpoint has special relevance today with the availability of hardware spectrum analyzers and fast Fourier transform techniques [21]. (We point out that all-pole modeling by linear prediction is identical to the method of maximum entropy spectral estimation [18], [96].)

Section IV gives a detailed discussion of the advantages and disadvantages of the least squares error criterion. The properties of the normalized error are reviewed. Its use is discussed

---

[2] See [80] for an exposition of the terminology in digital signal processing.

[3] See [12] for a description of deterministic and random signals.

in measuring the ill-conditioning of the normal equations, and in determining an optimal number of poles.

Section V discusses the use of linear prediction in data compression. Alternate representations of the linear predictor are presented and their properties under quantization are discussed. Particular emphasis is given to the quantization and encoding of the reflection (or partial correlation) coefficients.

Finally, in Section VI, a brief discussion of pole-zero modeling is given, with emphasis on methods presented earlier for the all-pole case.

II. PARAMETER ESTIMATION

A. All-Pole Model

In the all-pole model, we assume that the signal s_n is given as a linear combination of past values and some input u_n:

$$s_n = -\sum_{k=1}^{p} a_k s_{n-k} + G u_n \qquad (4)$$

where G is a gain factor. This model is shown in Fig. 2 in the time and frequency domains. The transfer function $H(z)$ in (2) now reduces to an all-pole transfer function

$$H(z) = \frac{G}{1 + \sum_{k=1}^{p} a_k z^{-k}}. \qquad (5)$$

Given a particular signal s_n, the problem is to determine the predictor coefficients a_k and the gain G in some manner.

The derivations will be given using an intuitive least squares approach, assuming first that s_n is a deterministic signal and then that s_n is a sample from a random process. The results are identical to those obtained by the method of maximum likelihood [6], [74], [75] with the assumption that the signal is Gaussian [60], [73]. The reader is reminded of the existence of more general least squares methods such as weighted and a priori least squares [16], [90].

B. Method of Least Squares

Here we assume that the input u_n is totally unknown, which is the case in many applications, such as EEG analysis. Therefore, the signal s_n can be predicted only approximately from a linearly weighted summation of past samples. Let this approximation of s_n be $\tilde{s}_n$, where

$$\tilde{s}_n = -\sum_{k=1}^{p} a_k s_{n-k}. \qquad (6)$$

Then the error between the actual value s_n and the predicted value $\tilde{s}_n$ is given by

$$e_n = s_n - \tilde{s}_n = s_n + \sum_{k=1}^{p} a_k s_{n-k}. \qquad (7)$$

e_n is also known as the residual. In the method of least squares the parameters a_k are obtained as a result of the minimization of the mean or total squared error with respect to each of the parameters. (Note that this problem is identical to the problem of designing the optimal one-step prediction digital Wiener filter [85].)

The analysis will be developed along two lines. First, we assume that s_n is a deterministic signal, and then we give

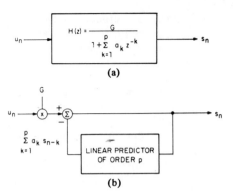

Fig. 2. (a) Discrete all-pole model in the frequency domain. (b) Discrete all-pole model in the time domain.

analogous derivations assuming that s_n is a sample from a random process.

1) Deterministic Signal: Denote the total squared error by E, where

$$E = \sum_n e_n^2 = \sum_n \left(s_n + \sum_{k=1}^{p} a_k s_{n-k} \right)^2. \qquad (8)$$

The range of the summation in (8) and the definition of s_n in that range is of importance. However, let us first minimize E without specifying the range of the summation. E is minimized by setting

$$\frac{\partial E}{\partial a_i} = 0, \qquad 1 \leqslant i \leqslant p. \qquad (9)$$

From (8) and (9) we obtain the set of equations:

$$\sum_{k=1}^{p} a_k \sum_n s_{n-k} s_{n-i} = -\sum_n s_n s_{n-i}, \qquad 1 \leqslant i \leqslant p. \qquad (10)$$

Equations (10) are known in least squares terminology as the *normal equations*. For any definition of the signal s_n, (10) forms a set of p equations in p unknowns which can be solved for the predictor coefficients $\{a_k, 1 \leqslant k \leqslant p\}$ which minimize E in (8).

The minimum total squared error, denoted by E_p, is obtained by expanding (8) and substituting (10). The result can be shown to be

$$E_p = \sum_n s_n^2 + \sum_{k=1}^{p} a_k \sum_n s_n s_{n-k}. \qquad (11)$$

We shall now specify the range of summation over n in (8), (10), and (11). There are two cases of interest, which will lead to two distinct methods for the estimation of the parameters.

a) Autocorrelation method: Here we assume that the error in (8) is minimized over the infinite duration $-\infty < n < \infty$. Equations (10) and (11) then reduce to

$$\sum_{k=1}^{p} a_k R(i - k) = -R(i), \qquad 1 \leqslant i \leqslant p \qquad (12)$$

$$E_p = R(0) + \sum_{k=1}^{p} a_k R(k) \qquad (13)$$

where

$$R(i) = \sum_{n=-\infty}^{\infty} s_n s_{n+i} \qquad (14)$$

is the autocorrelation function of the signal s_n. Note that $R(i)$ is an even function of i, i.e.,

$$R(-i) = R(i). \qquad (15)$$

Since the coefficients $R(i - k)$ form what often is known as an autocorrelation matrix, we shall call this method the *autocorrelation method*. An autocorrelation matrix is a symmetric Toeplitz matrix. (A Toeplitz matrix is one where all the elements along each diagonal are equal [42].)

In practice, the signal s_n is known over only a finite interval, or we are interested in the signal over only a finite interval. One popular method is to multiply the signal s_n by a *window* function w_n to obtain another signal s_n' that is zero outside some interval $0 \leqslant n \leqslant N - 1$:

$$s_n' = \begin{cases} s_n w_n, & 0 \leqslant n \leqslant N - 1 \\ 0, & \text{otherwise.} \end{cases} \qquad (16)$$

The autocorrelation function is then given by

$$R(i) = \sum_{n=0}^{N-1-i} s_n' s_{n+i}', \qquad i \geqslant 0. \qquad (17)$$

The shape of the window function w_n can be of importance. The subject is discussed further in Section III.

b) Covariance method: In contrast with the autocorrelation method, here we assume that the error E in (8) is minimized over a finite interval, say, $0 \leqslant n \leqslant N - 1$. Equations (10) and (11) then reduce to

$$\sum_{k=1}^{p} a_k \varphi_{ki} = -\varphi_{0i}, \qquad 1 \leqslant i \leqslant p \qquad (18)$$

$$E_p = \varphi_{00} + \sum_{k=1}^{p} a_k \varphi_{0k} \qquad (19)$$

where

$$\varphi_{ik} = \sum_{n=0}^{N-1} s_{n-i} s_{n-k} \qquad (20)$$

is the covariance of the signal s_n in the given interval. The coefficients φ_{ki} in (18) form a covariance matrix, and, therefore, we shall call this method the *covariance method*. From (20) it can be easily shown that the covariance matrix φ_{ik} is symmetric, i.e., $\varphi_{ik} = \varphi_{ki}$. However, unlike the autocorrelation matrix, the terms along each diagonal are not equal. This can be seen by writing from (20)

$$\varphi_{i+1, k+1} = \varphi_{ik} + s_{-i-1} s_{-k-1} - s_{N-1-i} s_{N-1-k}. \qquad (21)$$

Note from (21) also that values of the signal s_n for $-p \leqslant n \leqslant N - 1$ must be known: a total of $p + N$ samples. The covariance method reduces to the autocorrelation method as the interval over which n varies goes to infinity.

We point out here that the covariance method is similar to the method of Prony [49], [71] where a signal is approximated by the summation of a set of damped exponentials.

2) Random Signal: If the signal s_n is assumed to be a sample of a random process, then the error e_n in (7) is also a sample of a random process. In the least squares method, we minimize the expected value of the square of the error. Thus

$$E = \mathscr{E}(e_n^2) = \mathscr{E}\left(s_n + \sum_{k=1}^{p} a_k s_{n-k}\right)^2. \qquad (22)$$

Applying (9) to (22), we obtain the normal equations:

$$\sum_{k=1}^{p} a_k \mathscr{E}(s_{n-k} s_{n-i}) = -\mathscr{E}(s_n s_{n-i}), \qquad 1 \leqslant i \leqslant p. \qquad (23)$$

The minimum average error is then given by

$$E_p = \mathscr{E}(s_n^2) + \sum_{k=1}^{p} a_k \mathscr{E}(s_n s_{n-k}). \qquad (24)$$

Taking the expectations in (23) and (24) depends on whether the process s_n is stationary or nonstationary.

a) Stationary case: For a stationary process s_n, we have

$$\mathscr{E}(s_{n-k} s_{n-i}) = R(i - k) \qquad (25)$$

where $R(i)$ is the autocorrelation of the process. Equations (23) and (24) now reduce to equations identical to (12) and (13), respectively. The only difference is that here the autocorrelation is that of a stationary process instead of a deterministic signal. For a stationary (and ergodic) process the autocorrelation can be computed as a time average [12]. Different approximations have been suggested in the literature [54] for estimating $R(i)$ from a finite known signal s_n. One such approximation is given by (17).[4] Using this estimate in the stationary case gives the same solution for the coefficients a_k as the autocorrelation method in the deterministic case.

b) Nonstationary case: For a nonstationary process s_n, we have

$$\mathscr{E}(s_{n-k} s_{n-i}) = R(n - k, n - i) \qquad (26)$$

where $R(t, t')$ is the nonstationary autocorrelation between times t and t'. $R(n - k, n - i)$ is a function of the time index n. Without loss of generality, we shall assume that we are interested in estimating the parameters a_k at time $n = 0$. Then, (23) and (24) reduce to

$$\sum_{k=1}^{p} a_k R(-k, -i) = -R(0, -i) \qquad (27)$$

$$E_p' = R(0, 0) + \sum_{k=1}^{p} a_k R(0, k). \qquad (28)$$

In estimating the nonstationary autocorrelation coefficients from the signal s_n, we note that nonstationary processes are not ergodic, and, therefore, one cannot substitute the ensemble average by a time average. However, for a certain class of nonstationary processes known as *locally stationary processes* [12], [92], it is reasonable to estimate the autocorrelation function with respect to a point in time as a short-time average. Examples of nonstationary processes that can be considered to be locally stationary are speech and EEG signals.

---

[4] Usually the estimate given by (17) is divided by N, but that does not affect the solution for the predictor coefficients.

In a manner analogous to the stationary case, we estimate $R(-k, -i)$ by φ_{ik} in (20). Using this approximation for the nonstationary autocorrelation leads to a solution for the parameters a_k in (27) that is identical to that given by (18) in the covariance method in the deterministic case.

Note that for a stationary signal: $R(t, t') = R(t - t')$, and therefore, the normal equations (27) and (28) reduce to (12) and (13).

3) Gain Computation: Since in the least squares method we assumed that the input was unknown, it does not make much sense to determine a value for the gain G. However, there are certain interesting observations that can be made.

Equation (7) can be rewritten as

$$s_n = -\sum_{k=1}^{p} a_k s_{n-k} + e_n. \tag{29}$$

Comparing (4) and (29) we see that the only input signal u_n that will result in the signal s_n as output is that where $Gu_n = e_n$. That is, the input signal is proportional to the error signal. For any other input u_n, the output from the filter $H(z)$ in Fig. 2 will be different from s_n. However, if we insist that whatever the input u_n, the energy in the output signal must equal that of the original signal s_n, then we can at least specify the total energy in the input signal. Since the filter $H(z)$ is fixed, it is clear from the above that the total energy in the input signal Gu_n must equal the total energy in the error signal, which is given by E_p in (13) or (19), depending on the method used.

Two types of input that are of special interest are: the deterministic impulse and stationary white noise. By examining the response of the filter $H(z)$ to each of these two inputs we shall gain further insight into the time domain properties of the all-pole model. The input gain is then determined as a by-product of an autocorrelation analysis.

a) Impulse input: Let the input to the all-pole filter $H(z)$ be an impulse or unit sample at $n = 0$, i.e. $u_n = \delta_{n0}$, where δ_{nm} is the Kronecker delta. The output of the filter $H(z)$ is then its impulse response h_n, where

$$h_n = -\sum_{k=1}^{p} a_k h_{n-k} + G\delta_{n0}. \tag{30}$$

The autocorrelation $\hat{R}(i)$ of the impulse response h_n has an interesting relationship to the autocorrelation $R(i)$ of the signal s_n. Multiply (30) by h_{n-i} and sum over all n. The result can be shown to be [10], [62]:

$$\hat{R}(i) = -\sum_{k=1}^{p} a_k \hat{R}(i-k), \quad 1 \le |i| \le \infty \tag{31}$$

$$\hat{R}(0) = -\sum_{k=1}^{p} a_k \hat{R}(k) + G^2. \tag{32}$$

Given our condition that the total energy in h_n must equal that in s_n, we must have

$$\hat{R}(0) = R(0) \tag{33}$$

since the zeroth autocorrelation coefficient is equal to the total energy in the signal. From (33) and the similarity between (12) and (31) we conclude that [62]

$$\hat{R}(i) = R(i), \quad 0 \le i \le p. \tag{34}$$

This says that the first $p + 1$ coefficients of the autocorrelation of the impulse response of $H(z)$ are identical to the corresponding autocorrelation coefficients of the signal. The problem of linear prediction using the autocorrelation method can be stated in a new way as follows. Find a filter of the form $H(z)$ in (5) such that the first $p + 1$ values of the autocorrelation of its impulse response are equal to the first $p + 1$ values of the signal autocorrelation, and such that (31) applies.

From (32), (34), and (13), the gain is equal to

$$G^2 = E_p = R(0) + \sum_{k=1}^{p} a_k R(k) \tag{35}$$

where G^2 is the total energy in the input $G\delta_{n0}$.

b) White noise input: Here the input u_n is assumed to be a sequence of uncorrelated samples (white noise) with zero mean and unit variance, i.e., $\mathcal{E}(u_n) = 0$, all n, and $\mathcal{E}(u_n u_m) = \delta_{nm}$. Denote the output of the filter by $\hat{s}_n$. For a fixed filter $H(z)$, the output $\hat{s}_n$ forms a stationary random process:

$$\hat{s}_n = -\sum_{k=1}^{p} a_k \hat{s}_{n-k} + Gu_n. \tag{36}$$

Multiply (36) by $\hat{s}_{n-i}$ and take expected values. By noting that u_n and $\hat{s}_{n-i}$ are uncorrelated for $i > 0$, the result can be shown [17] to be identical to (31) and (32), where $\hat{R}(i) = \mathcal{E}(\hat{s}_n \hat{s}_{n-i})$ is the autocorrelation of the output $\hat{s}_n$. Therefore, (31) and (32) completely specify an all-pole random process as well. Equations (31) are known in the statistical literature as the *Yule–Walker equations* [17], [98], [115].

For the random case we require that the average energy (or variance) of the output $\hat{s}_n$ be equal to the variance of the original signal s_n, or $\hat{R}(0) = R(0)$, since the zeroth autocorrelation of a zero-mean random process is the variance. By a reasoning similar to that given in the previous section, we conclude that (34) and (35) also apply for the random case.

From the preceding, we see that the relations linking the autocorrelation coefficients of the output of an all-pole filter are the same whether the input is a single impulse or white noise. This is to be expected since both types of input have identical autocorrelations and, of course, identical flat spectra. This dualism between the deterministic impulse and statistical white noise is an intriguing one. Its usefulness surfaces very elegantly in modeling the speech process, as in Fig. 1, where both unit impulses as well as white noise are actually used to synthesize speech.

C. Computation of Predictor Parameters

1) Direct Methods: In each of the two formulations of linear prediction presented in the previous section, the predictor coefficients a_k, $1 \le k \le p$, can be computed by solving a set of p equations with p unknowns. These equations are (12) for the autocorrelation (stationary) method and (18) for the covariance (nonstationary) method. There exist several standard methods for performing the necessary computations, e.g., the Gauss reduction or elimination method and the Crout reduction method [49]. These general methods require $p^3/3 + O(p^2)$ operations (multiplications or divisions) and p^2 storage locations. However, we note from (12) and (18) that the matrix of coefficients in each case is a covariance matrix. Covariance matrices are symmetric and in general positive semidefinite, although in practice they are usually positive definite. Therefore, (12) and (18) can be solved more efficiently by the square-root or Cholesky decomposition method [31], [39], [59], [110]. This method requires about half the computation $p^3/6 + O(p^2)$ and about half the storage $p^2/2$ of the general methods. The numerical stability properties of this method are well understood [109], [111]; the method is considered to be quite stable.

Further reduction in storage and computation time is possible in solving the autocorrelation normal equations (12) because of their special form. Equation (12) can be expanded in matrix form as

$$
\begin{bmatrix}
R_0 & R_1 & R_2 & \cdots & R_{p-1} \\
R_1 & R_0 & R_1 & \cdots & R_{p-2} \\
R_2 & R_1 & R_0 & \cdots & R_{p-3} \\
\cdot & \cdot & \cdot & & \cdot \\
\cdot & \cdot & \cdot & \cdot & \cdot \\
\cdot & \cdot & \cdot & & \cdot \\
R_{p-1} & R_{p-2} & R_{p-3} & \cdots & R_0
\end{bmatrix}
\begin{bmatrix}
a_1 \\ a_2 \\ a_3 \\ \cdot \\ \cdot \\ \cdot \\ a_p
\end{bmatrix}
= -
\begin{bmatrix}
R_1 \\ R_2 \\ R_3 \\ \cdot \\ \cdot \\ \cdot \\ R_p
\end{bmatrix}.
$$

(37)

Note that the $p \times p$ autocorrelation matrix is symmetric and the elements along any diagonal are identical (i.e., a Toeplitz matrix). Levinson [61] derived an elegant recursive procedure for solving this type of equation. The procedure was later reformulated by Robinson [85]. Levinson's method assumes the column vector on the right hand side of (37) to be a general column vector. By making use of the fact that this column vector comprises the same elements found in the autocorrelation matrix, another method attributed to Durbin [25] emerges which is twice as fast as Levinson's. The method requires only $2p$ storage locations and $p^2 + O(p)$ operations: a big saving from the more general methods. Durbin's recursive procedure can be specified as follows:

$$E_0 = R(0) \tag{38a}$$

$$k_i = - \left[R(i) + \sum_{j=1}^{i-1} a_j^{(i-1)} R(i-j) \right] \bigg/ E_{i-1} \tag{38b}$$

$$a_i^{(i)} = k_i$$
$$a_j^{(i)} = a_j^{(i-1)} + k_i a_{i-j}^{(i-1)}, \quad 1 \leqslant j \leqslant i-1 \tag{38c}$$

$$E_i = (1 - k_i^2) E_{i-1}. \tag{38d}$$

Equations (38b)–(38d) are solved recursively for $i = 1, 2, \cdots, p$. The final solution is given by

$$a_j = a_j^{(p)}, \quad 1 \leqslant j \leqslant p. \tag{38e}$$

Note that in obtaining the solution for a predictor of order p, one actually computes the solutions for all predictors of order less than p. It has been reported [78] that this solution is numerically relatively unstable. However, most researchers have not found this to be a problem in practice.

It should be emphasized that, for many applications, the solution of the normal equations (12) or (18) does not form the major computational load. The computation of the autocorrelation or covariance coefficients require pN operations, which can dominate the computation time if $N \gg p$, as is often the case.

The solution to (37) is unaffected if all the autocorrelation coefficients are scaled by a constant. In particular, if all $R(i)$ are normalized by dividing by $R(0)$, we have what are known

as the *normalized autocorrelation coefficients* $r(i)$:

$$r(i) = \frac{R(i)}{R(0)} \tag{39}$$

which have the property that $|r(i)| \leqslant 1$. This can be useful in the proper application of scaling to a fixed point solution to (37).

A byproduct of the solution in (38) is the computation of the minimum total error E_i at every step. It can easily be shown that the minimum error E_i decreases (or remains the same) as the order of the predictor increases [61]. E_i is never negative, of course, since it is a squared error. Therefore, we must have

$$0 \leqslant E_i \leqslant E_{i-1}, \quad E_0 = R(0). \tag{40}$$

If the autocorrelation coefficients are normalized as in (39), then the minimum error E_i is also divided by $R(0)$. We shall call the resulting quantity the *normalized error* V_i:

$$V_i = \frac{E_i}{R(0)} = 1 + \sum_{k=1}^{i} a_k r(k). \tag{41}$$

From (40) it is clear that

$$0 \leqslant V_i \leqslant 1, \quad i \geqslant 0. \tag{42}$$

Also, from (38d) and (41), the final normalized error V_p is

$$V_p = \prod_{i=1}^{p} (1 - k_i^2). \tag{43}$$

The intermediate quantities k_i, $1 \leqslant i \leqslant p$, are known as the *reflection coefficients*. In the statistical literature, they are known as *partial correlation coefficients* [6], [17]. k_i can be interpreted as the (negative) partial correlation between s_n and s_{n+i} holding $s_{n+1}, \cdots, s_{n+i-1}$ fixed. The use of the term "reflection coefficient" comes from transmission line theory, where k_i can be considered as the reflection coefficient at the boundary between two sections with impedances Z_i and Z_{i+1}. k_i is then given by

$$k_i = \frac{Z_{i+1} - Z_i}{Z_{i+1} + Z_i}. \tag{44}$$

The transfer function $H(z)$ can then be considered as that of a sequence of these sections with impedance ratios given from (44) by

$$\frac{Z_{i+1}}{Z_i} = \frac{1 + k_i}{1 - k_i}, \quad 1 \leqslant i \leqslant p. \tag{45}$$

The same explanation can be given for any type of situation where there is plane wave transmission with normal incidence in a medium consisting of a sequence of sections or slabs with different impedances. In the case of an acoustic tube with p sections of equal thickness, the impedance ratios reduce to the inverse ratio of the consecutive cross-sectional areas. This fact has been used recently in speech analysis [10], [52], [97]. Because of the more familiar "engineering interpretation" for k_i, we shall refer to them in this paper as reflection coefficients.

2) Iterative Methods: Beside the direct methods for the solution of simultaneous linear equations, there exist a number of iterative methods. In these methods, one begins by an initial guess for the solution. The solution is then updated by adding a correction term that is usually based on the gradient of some error criterion. In general, iterative methods require more computation to achieve a desired degree of convergence than the direct methods. However, in some applications [100] one often has a good initial guess, which might lead to the solution in only a few iterations. This can be a big saving over direct methods if the number of equations is large. Some of the iterative methods are the gradient method, the steepest descent method, Newton's method, conjugate gradient method and the stochastic approximation method [81], [108].

Up till now we have assumed that the whole signal is given all at once. For certain real time applications it is useful to be able to perform the computations as the signal is coming in. Adaptive schemes exist which update the solution based on every new observation of the signal [106]. The update is usually proportional to the difference between the new observation and the predicted value given the present solution. Another application for adaptive procedures is in the processing of very long data records, where the solution might converge long before all the data is analyzed. It is worth noting that Kalman filtering notions [56] are very useful in obtaining adaptive solutions [60].

3) Filter Stability: After the predictor parameters are computed, the question of the stability of the resulting filter $H(z)$ arises. Filter stability is important for many applications. A causal all-pole filter is stable if all its poles lie inside the unit circle (in which case it is also a filter with minimum phase). The poles of $H(z)$ are simply the roots of the denominator polynomial $A(z)$, where

$$A(z) = 1 + \sum_{k=1}^{p} a_k z^{-k} \qquad (46)$$

and

$$H(z) = \frac{G}{A(z)}. \qquad (47)$$

$A(z)$ is also known as the *inverse filter*.

If the coefficients $R(i)$ in (12) are positive definite [79] (which is assured if $R(i)$ is computed from a nonzero signal using (17) or from a positive definite spectrum[5]), the solution of the autocorrelation equation (12) gives predictor parameters which guarantee that all the roots of $A(z)$ lie inside the unit circle, i.e., a stable $H(z)$ [42], [85], [104]. This result can also be obtained from orthogonal polynomial theory. In fact, if one denotes the inverse filter at step i in iteration (38) by $A_i(z)$, then it can be shown that the polynomials $A_i(z)$ for $i = 0, 1, 2, \cdots$, form an orthogonal set over the unit circle [35], [42], [93]:

$$\frac{1}{2\pi} \int_{-\pi}^{\pi} P(\omega) A_n(e^{j\omega}) A_m(e^{-j\omega}) d\omega = E_n \delta_{nm},$$

$$n, m = 0, 1, 2, \cdots \qquad (48)$$

where E_n is the minimum error for an nth order predictor, and $P(\omega)$ is any positive definite spectrum whose Fourier transform results in the autocorrelation coefficients $R(i)$ that are used in (12). The recurrence relation for these polynomials is

as follows:

$$A_i(z) = A_{i-1}(z) + k_i z^{-i} A_{i-1}(z^{-1}) \qquad (49)$$

which is the same as the recursion in (38c).

The positive definiteness of $R(i)$ can often be lost if one uses a small word length to represent $R(i)$ in a computer. Also, roundoff errors can cause the autocorrelation matrix to become ill-conditioned. Therefore, it is often necessary to check for the stability of $H(z)$. Checking if the roots of $A(z)$ are inside the unit circle is a costly procedure that is best avoided One method is to check if all the successive errors are positive. In fact, the condition $E_i > 0$, $1 \leq i \leq p$, is a necessary and sufficient condition for the stability of $H(z)$. From (38d) and (40) it is clear that an equivalent condition for the stability of $H(z)$ is that

$$|k_i| < 1, \qquad 1 \leq i \leq p. \qquad (50)$$

Therefore, the recursive procedure (38) also facilitates the check for the stability of the filter $H(z)$.

The predictor parameters resulting from a solution to the covariance matrix equation (18) cannot in general be guaranteed to form a stable filter. The computed filter tends to be more stable as the number of signal samples N is increased, i.e., as the covariance matrix approaches an autocorrelation matrix. Given the computed predictor parameters, it is useful to be able to test for the stability of the filter $H(z)$. One method is to compute the reflection coefficients k_i from the predictor parameters by a backward recursion, and then check for stability using (50). The recursion is as follows:

$$k_i = a_i^{(i)}$$

$$a_j^{(i-1)} = \frac{a_j^{(i)} - a_i^{(i)} a_{i-j}^{(i)}}{1 - k_i^2}, \qquad 1 \leq j \leq i - 1 \qquad (51)$$

where the index i takes values $p, p - 1, \cdots, 1$ in that order. Initially $a_j^{(p)} = a_j$, $1 \leq j \leq p$. It is interesting to note that this method for checking the stability of $H(z)$ is essentially the same as the Lehmer–Schur method [81] for testing whether or not the zeros of a polynomial lie inside the unit circle. An unstable filter can be made stable by reflecting the poles outside the unit circle inside [10], such that the magnitude of the system frequency response remains the same. Filter instability can often be avoided by adding a very small number to the diagonal elements in the covariance matrix.

A question always arises as to whether to use the autocorrelation method or covariance method in estimating the predictor parameters. The covariance method is quite general and can be used with no restrictions. The only problem is that of the stability of the resulting filter, which is not a severe problem generally. In the autocorrelation method, on the other hand, the filter is guaranteed to be stable, but problems of parameter accuracy can arise because of the necessity of windowing (truncating) the time signal. This is usually a problem if the signal is a portion of an impulse response. For example, if the impulse response of an all-pole filter is analyzed by the covariance method, the filter parameters can be computed accurately from only a finite number of samples of the signal. Using the autocorrelation method, one cannot obtain the exact parameter values unless the whole infinite impulse response is used in the analysis. However, in practice, very good approximations can be obtained by truncating the impulse response at a point where most of the decay of the response has already occurred.

III. SPECTRAL ESTIMATION

In Section II, the stationary and nonstationary methods of linear prediction were derived from a time domain formulation. In this section we show that the same normal equations can be derived from a frequency domain formulation. It will become clear that linear prediction is basically a correlation type of analysis which can be approached either from the time or frequency domain. The insights gained from the frequency domain analysis will lead to new applications for linear predictive analysis. This section and the following are based mainly on references [62]–[64].

A. Frequency Domain Formulations

1) Stationary Case: The error e_n between the actual signal and the predicted signal is given by (7). Applying the z transform to (7), we obtain

$$E(z) = \left[1 + \sum_{k=1}^{p} a_k z^{-k}\right] S(z) = A(z) S(z) \qquad (52)$$

where $A(z)$ is the inverse filter defined in (46), and $E(z)$ and $S(z)$ are the z transforms of e_n and s_n, respectively. Therefore, e_n can be viewed as the result of passing s_n through the inverse filter $A(z)$. Assuming a deterministic signal[6] s_n, and applying Parseval's theorem, the total error to be minimized is given by

$$E = \sum_{n=-\infty}^{\infty} e_n^2 = \frac{1}{2\pi} \int_{-\pi}^{\pi} |E(e^{j\omega})|^2 \, d\omega \qquad (53)$$

where $E(e^{j\omega})$ is obtained by evaluating $E(z)$ on the unit circle $z = e^{j\omega}$. Denoting the power spectrum of the signal s_n by $P(\omega)$, where

$$P(\omega) = |S(e^{j\omega})|^2 \qquad (54)$$

we have from (52)–(54)

$$E = \frac{1}{2\pi} \int_{-\pi}^{\pi} P(\omega) A(e^{j\omega}) A(e^{-j\omega}) \, d\omega. \qquad (55)$$

Following the same procedure as in Section II, E is minimized by applying (9) to (55). The result can be shown [64] to be identical to the autocorrelation normal equations (12), but with the autocorrelation $R(i)$ obtained from the signal spectrum $P(\omega)$ by an inverse Fourier transform

$$R(i) = \frac{1}{2\pi} \int_{-\pi}^{\pi} P(\omega) \cos(i\omega) \, d\omega. \qquad (56)$$

Note that in (56) the cosine transform is adequate since $P(\omega)$ is real and even. The minimum squared error E_p can be obtained by substituting (12) and (56) in (55), which results in the same equation as in (13).

2) Nonstationary Case: Here the signal s_n and the error e_n are assumed to be nonstationary. If $R(t, t')$ is the nonstationary autocorrelation of s_n, then we define the nonstationary two-dimensional (2-D) spectrum $Q(\omega, \omega')$ of s_n by [12], [64], [67], [79]

$$Q(\omega, \omega') = \sum_{t'=-\infty}^{\infty} \sum_{t=-\infty}^{\infty} R(t, t') \exp[-j(\omega t - \omega' t')]. \qquad (57)$$

---

[6] A similar development assuming a random signal gives the same results.

$R(t, t')$ can then be recovered from $Q(\omega, \omega')$ by an inverse 2-D Fourier transform

$$R(t, t') = \left(\frac{1}{2\pi}\right)^2 \int_{-\pi}^{\pi} \int_{-\pi}^{\pi} Q(\omega, \omega') \exp[j(\omega t - \omega' t')] \, d\omega \, d\omega'. \qquad (58)$$

As in the time domain formulation, we are interested in minimizing the error variance for time $n = 0$, which is now given by [64]

$$E = \left(\frac{1}{2\pi}\right)^2 \int_{-\pi}^{\pi} \int_{-\pi}^{\pi} Q(\omega, \omega') A(e^{j\omega}) A(e^{-j\omega'}) \, d\omega \, d\omega'. \qquad (59)$$

Applying (9) to (59) results in equations identical to the nonstationary normal equations (27), where $R(t, t')$ is now defined by (58). The minimum error is then obtained by substituting (27) and (58) in (59). The answer is identical to (28).

B. Linear Predictive Spectral Matching

In this section we shall examine in what manner the signal spectrum $P(\omega)$ is approximated by the all-pole model spectrum, which we shall denote by $\hat{P}(\omega)$. From (5) and (47):

$$\hat{P}(\omega) = |H(e^{j\omega})|^2 = \frac{G^2}{|A(e^{j\omega})|^2} \qquad (60)$$

$$= \frac{G^2}{\left|1 + \sum_{k=1}^{p} a_k e^{-jk\omega}\right|^2}.$$

From (52) and (54) we have

$$P(\omega) = \frac{|E(e^{j\omega})|^2}{|A(e^{j\omega})|^2}. \qquad (61)$$

By comparing (60) and (61) we see that if $P(\omega)$ is being modeled by $\hat{P}(\omega)$, then the error power spectrum $|E(e^{j\omega})|^2$ is being modeled by a flat spectrum equal to G^2. This means that the actual error signal e_n is being approximated by another signal that has a flat spectrum, such as a unit impulse, white noise, or any other signal with a flat spectrum. The filter $A(z)$ is sometimes known as a "whitening filter" since it attempts to produce an output signal e_n that is white, i.e., has a flat spectrum.

From (53), (60), and (61), the total error can be written as

$$E = \frac{G^2}{2\pi} \int_{-\pi}^{\pi} \frac{P(\omega)}{\hat{P}(\omega)} \, d\omega. \qquad (62)$$

Therefore, minimizing the total error E is equivalent to the minimization of the integrated ratio of the signal spectrum $P(\omega)$ to its approximation $\hat{P}(\omega)$. (This interpretation of the least squares error was proposed in a classic paper by Whittle [103]. An equivalent formulation using maximum likelihood estimation has been given by Itakura [50], [51].) Now, we can back up and restate the problem of linear prediction as follows. Given some spectrum $P(\omega)$, we wish to model it by another spectrum $\hat{P}(\omega)$ such that the integrated ratio between the two spectra as in (62) is minimized. The parameters of the model spectrum are computed from the normal equations (12), where the needed autocorrelation coefficients $R(i)$ are easily computed from $P(\omega)$ by a simple Fourier transform. The gain factor G is obtained by equating the total energy in the two

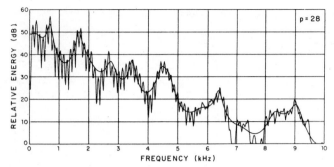

Fig. 3. A 28-pole fit to an FFT-computed signal spectrum. The signal was sampled at 20 kHz.

spectra, i.e., $\hat{R}(0) = R(0)$, where

$$\hat{R}(i) = \frac{1}{2\pi} \int_{-\pi}^{\pi} \hat{P}(\omega) \cos(i\omega)\, d\omega. \tag{63}$$

Note that $\hat{R}(i)$ is the autocorrelation of the impulse response of $H(z)$, which is given by (31) and (32). As then, the gain is computed from (35).

The manner in which the model spectrum $\hat{P}(\omega)$ approximates $P(\omega)$ is largely reflected in the relation between the corresponding autocorrelation functions. From (34), we have $\hat{R}(i) = R(i)$, $0 \le i \le p$. Since $P(\omega)$ and $\hat{P}(\omega)$ are Fourier transforms of $R(i)$ and $\hat{R}(i)$, respectively, it follows that increasing the value of the order of the model p increases the range over which $R(i)$ and $\hat{R}(i)$ are equal, resulting in a better fit of $\hat{P}(\omega)$ to $P(\omega)$. In the limit, as $p \to \infty$, $\hat{R}(i)$ becomes identical to $R(i)$ for all i, and hence the two spectra become identical:

$$\hat{P}(\omega) = P(\omega), \qquad \text{as } p \to \infty. \tag{64}$$

This statement says that we can approximate any spectrum arbitrarily closely by an all-pole model.

Another important conclusion is that since linear predictive analysis can be viewed as a process of spectrum or autocorrelation matching, one must be careful how to estimate the spectrum $P(\omega)$ or the corresponding autocorrelation that is to be modeled. Since the signal is often weighted or windowed[7] before either the autocorrelation or the spectrum is computed, it can be quite important to properly choose the type and width of the data window to be used. The choice of window depends very much on the type of signal to be analyzed. If the signal can be considered to be stationary for a long period of time (relative to the effective length of the system impulse response), then a rectangular window suffices. However, for signals that result from systems that are varying relatively quickly, the time of analysis must necessarily be limited. For example, in many transient speech sounds, the signal can be considered stationary for a duration of only one or two pitch periods. In that case a window such as Hamming or Hanning [14] is more appropriate. See [13], [14], [26], [54], [64], [99], [101] for more on the issue of windowing and spectral estimation in general.

An example of linear predictive (LP) spectral estimation is shown in Fig. 3, where the original spectrum $P(\omega)$ was obtained by computing the fast Fourier transform (FFT) of a 20-ms, Hamming windowed, 20-kHz sampled speech signal.

[7] Note that here we are discussing *data* windows which are applied directly to the signal, as opposed to *lag* windows, which statisticians have traditionally applied to the autocorrelation.

The speech sound was the vowel [æ] as in the word "bat." The harmonics due to the periodicity of the sound are evident in the FFT spectrum. Fig. 3 also shows a 28-pole fit ($p = 28$) to the signal spectrum. In this case the autocorrelation coefficients needed to solve the normal equations (12) were computed directly from the time signal. The all-pole spectrum $\hat{P}(\omega)$ was computed from (60) by dividing G^2 by the magnitude squared of the FFT of the sequence: $1, a_1, a_2, \cdots, a_p$. Arbitrary frequency resolution in computing $\hat{P}(\omega)$ can be obtained by simply appending an appropriate number of zeros to this sequence before taking the FFT. An alternate method of computing $\hat{P}(\omega)$ is obtained by rewriting (60) as

$$\hat{P}(\omega) = \frac{G^2}{\rho(0) + 2 \sum_{i=1}^{p} \rho(i) \cos(i\omega)} \tag{65}$$

where

$$\rho(i) = \sum_{k=0}^{p-i} a_k a_{k+i}, \qquad a_0 = 1, \quad 0 \le i \le p \tag{66}$$

is the autocorrelation of the impulse response of the inverse filter $A(z)$. From (65), $\hat{P}(\omega)$ can be computed by dividing G^2 by the real part of the FFT of the sequence: $\rho(0), 2\rho(1), 2\rho(2), \cdots, 2\rho(p)$. Note that the slope of $\hat{P}(\omega)$ is always zero at $\omega = 0$ and $\omega = \pi$.

Another property of $\hat{P}(\omega)$ is obtained by noting that the minimum error $E_p = G^2$, and, therefore, from (62) we have

$$\frac{1}{2\pi} \int_{-\pi}^{\pi} \frac{P(\omega)}{\hat{P}(\omega)}\, d\omega = 1. \tag{67}$$

(This relation is a special case of a more general result (48) relating the fact that the polynomials $A_0(z), A_1(z), \cdots, A_p(z), \cdots$, form a complete set of orthogonal polynomials with weight $P(\omega)$.) Equation (67) is true for all values of p. In particular, it is true as $p \to \infty$, in which case from (64) we see that (67) becomes an identity. Another important case where (67) becomes an identity is when $P(\omega)$ is an all-pole spectrum with p_0 poles, then $\hat{P}(\omega)$ will be identical to $P(\omega)$ for all $p \ge p_0$. Relation (67) will be useful in discussing the properties of the error measure in Section IV.

The transfer functions $S(z)$ and $H(z)$ corresponding to $P(\omega)$ and $\hat{P}(\omega)$ are also related. It can be shown [62] that as $p \to \infty$, $H(z)$ is given by

$$H_\infty(z) = \frac{G}{1 + \sum_{k=1}^{\infty} a_k z^{-k}} = \sum_{n=0}^{N-1} h_\infty(n) z^{-n}, \qquad p \to \infty \tag{68}$$

where $h_\infty(n)$, $0 \le n \le N - 1$, is the minimum phase sequence corresponding to s_n, $0 \le n \le N - 1$. Note that the minimum phase sequence is of the same length as the original signal. Fig. 4 shows a signal ($N = 256$) and its approximate minimum phase counterpart, obtained by first performing a LP analysis for $p = 250$, and then computing the sequence $h(n)$ by long division.

C. Selective Linear Prediction

The major point of the previous section was that LP analysis can be regarded as a method of spectral modeling. We had tacitly assumed that the model spectrum spans the same frequency range as the signal spectrum. We now generalize the

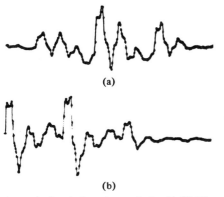

(a)

(b)

Fig. 4. (a) A 256-sample windowed speech signal. (b) The corresponding approximate minimum phase sequence obtained using a linear predictor of order $p = 250$.

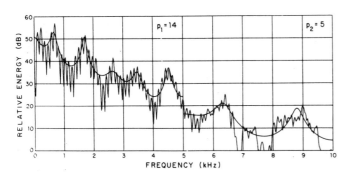

Fig. 5. Application of selective linear prediction to the same signal spectrum as in Fig. 3, with a 14-pole fit to the 0–5 kHz region and a 5-pole fit to the 5–10 kHz region.

LP spectral modeling method to the case where we wish to fit only a selected portion of a given spectrum.

Suppose we wish to model the spectrum $P(\omega)$ only in the region[8] $\omega_\alpha \leqslant \omega \leqslant \omega_\beta$ by an all-pole spectrum given by (60). Call the signal spectrum in that region $P'(\omega)$. In order to compute the parameters of the model spectrum $\hat{P}(\omega)$, we first perform a linear mapping of the given region onto the upper half of the unit circle in the z plane. This can be accomplished by the mapping $\omega' = \pi(\omega - \omega_\alpha)/(\omega_\beta - \omega_\alpha)$, so that the given region is mapped onto $0 \leqslant \omega' \leqslant \pi$. In addition, let $P'(-\omega') = P'(\omega')$ define the spectrum over the lower half of the unit circle. The model parameters are then computed from the normal equations (12), where the autocorrelation coefficients are obtained by a Fourier transform with $P'(\omega')$ replacing $P(\omega)$ and ω' replacing ω in (56).

Selective linear prediction has had applications in speech recognition and speech compression [63]. An example of its usage is shown in Fig. 5. For speech recognition applications, the 0–5 kHz region is more important than the 5–10 kHz. Even when the 5–10 kHz region is important, only a rough idea of the shape of the spectrum is sufficient. In Fig. 5, the signal spectrum is the same as in Fig. 3. The 0–5 kHz region is modeled by a 14-pole spectrum, while the 5–10 kHz region is modeled independently by only a 5-pole model.

An important point, which should be clear by now, is that since we assume the availability of the signal spectrum $P(\omega)$, any desired frequency shaping or scaling can be performed directly on the signal spectrum before linear predictive modeling is applied.

D. Modeling Discrete Spectra

Thus far we have assumed that the spectrum $P(\omega)$ is a continuous function of frequency. More often, however, the spectrum is known at only a finite number of frequencies. For example, FFT-derived spectra and those obtained from many commercially available spectrum analyzers have values at equally spaced frequency points. On the other hand, filter bank spectra, and, for example, third-octave band spectrum analyzers have values at frequencies that are not necessarily equally spaced. In order to be able to model these discrete spectra, only one change in our analysis need be made. The error measure E in (62) is defined as a summation instead of an integral. The rest of the analysis remains the same except that the autocorrelation coefficients $R(i)$ are now computed from

$$R(i) = \frac{1}{M} \sum_{m=0}^{M-1} P(\omega_m) \cos(i\omega_m) \qquad (69)$$

where M is the total number of spectral points on the unit circle. The frequencies ω_m are those for which a spectral value exists, and they need not be equally spaced. Below we demonstrate the application of LP modeling for filter bank and harmonic spectra.

Fig. 6(a) shows a typical 14-pole fit to a spectrum of the fricative [s] that was FFT computed from the time signal. Fig. 6(b) shows a similar fit to a line spectrum that is typical of filter bank spectra. What we have actually done here is to simulate a filter bank where the filters are linearly spaced up to 1.6 kHz and logarithmically spaced thereafter. Note that the all-pole spectrum for the simulated filter bank is remarkably similar to the one in the top figure, even though the number of spectral points is much smaller.

The dashed curve in Fig. 7(a) is a 14-pole spectrum. If one applied LP analysis to this spectrum, the all-pole model for $p = 14$ would be identical to the dashed spectrum. The situation is not so favorable for discrete spectra. Let us assume that the dashed spectrum corresponds to the transfer function of a 14-pole filter. If this filter is excited by a periodic train of impulses with fundamental frequency F_0, the spectrum of the output signal will be a discrete line spectrum with spectral values only at the harmonics (multiples of F_0). The line spectrum for $F_0 = 312$ Hz is shown in Fig. 7(a). Note that the dashed spectrum is an envelope of the harmonic spectrum. The result of applying a 14-pole LP analysis to the harmonic spectrum is shown as the solid curve in Fig. 7(a). The discrepancy between the two all-pole spectra is obvious. In general, the types of discrepancies that can occur between the model and original spectra include merging or splitting of pole peaks, and increasing or decreasing of pole frequencies and bandwidths. Pole movements are generally in the direction of the nearest harmonic. As the fundamental frequency decreases, these discrepancies decrease, as shown in Fig. 7(b) for $F_0 = 156$ Hz.

It is important to note in Fig. 7 that the dashed curve is the *only* possible 14-pole spectrum that coincides with the line spectrum at the harmonics.[9] It is significant that the all-pole spectrum resulting from LP modeling does not yield the spectrum we desire. The immediate reason for this is that the solution for the model parameters from (12) depends on the values of the signal autocorrelation, which for the periodic signal are

---

[8] The remainder of the spectrum is simply neglected.

[9] In general this is true only if the period between input impulses is greater than twice the number of poles in the filter.

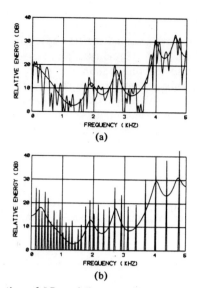

Fig. 6. Application of LP modeling to a filter bank spectrum. (a) A 14-pole fit to the original spectrum. (b) A 14-pole fit to the simulated filter bank spectrum.

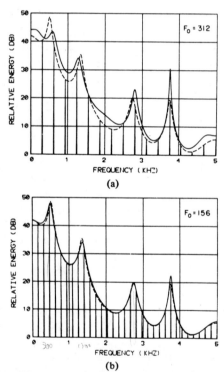

Fig. 7. Application of LP modeling to harmonic spectra. Dashed curve: 14-pole filter spectrum. Vertical lines: Corresponding harmonic spectrum for (a) and (b). (a) $F_0 = 312$ Hz. (b) $F_0 = 156$ Hz. Solid curve: 14-pole fit to the discrete harmonic spectrum. (For display purposes, the energy in the model spectrum (solid curve) was set equal to the energy in the filter spectrum (dashed curve).)

different from that for the single impulse response. However, the major underlying reason lies in the properties of the error measure used. This is the topic of the next section.

IV. ERROR ANALYSIS

An important aspect of any fitting or matching procedure is the properties of the error measure that is employed, and whether those properties are commensurate with certain objectives. In this section we shall examine the properties of the error measure used in LP analysis and we shall discuss its

strengths and weaknesses in order to be able to fully utilize its capabilities. The analysis will be restricted to the stationary (autocorrelation) case, although the conclusions can be extrapolated to the nonstationary (covariance) case.

The error measure used in Section II-B to determine the predictor parameters is the least squares error measure due to Gauss, who first reported on it in the early 1800's. This error measure has been used extensively since then, and is quite well understood. Its major asset is its mathematical tractability. Its main characteristic is that it puts great emphasis on large errors and little emphasis on small errors. Purely from the time domain, it is often difficult to say whether such an error measure is a desirable one or not for the problem at hand. Many would probably agree that it does not really matter which error measure one uses as long as it is a reasonable function of the magnitude of the error at each point. For the linear prediction problem, we are fortunate that the error measure can also be written in the frequency domain and can be interpreted as a goodness of fit between a given signal spectrum and a model spectrum that approximates it. The insights gained in the frequency domain should enhance our understanding of the least squares error criterion.

A. The Minimum Error

For each value of p, minimization of the error measure E in (62) leads to the minimum error E_p in (13), which is given in terms of the predictor and autocorrelation coefficients. Here we derive an expression for E_p in the frequency domain, which will help us determine some of its properties. Other properties will be discussed when we discuss the normalized minimum error.

Let

$$\hat{c}_0 = \frac{1}{2\pi} \int_{-\pi}^{\pi} \log \hat{P}(\omega) \, d\omega \qquad (70)$$

be the zeroth coefficient (quefrency) of the cepstrum (inverse Fourier transform of log spectrum) [38], [77] corresponding to $\hat{P}(\omega)$. From (60), (70) reduces to

$$\hat{c}_0 = \log G^2 - \frac{1}{2\pi} \int_{-\pi}^{\pi} \log |A(e^{j\omega})|^2 \, d\omega. \qquad (71)$$

$A(z)$ has all its zeros inside the unit circle. Therefore, the integral in (71) is equal to zero [64], [69], [103]. Since $G^2 = E_p$, we conclude from (71) that

$$E_p = e^{\hat{c}_0}. \qquad (72)$$

From (72) and (70), E_p can be interpreted as the geometric mean of the model spectrum $\hat{P}(\omega)$. From (40) we know that E_p decreases as p increases. The minimum occurs as $p \to \infty$, and is equal to

$$E_{min} = E_\infty = e^{c_0} \qquad (73)$$

where c_0 is obtained by substituting $P(\omega)$ for $\hat{P}(\omega)$ in (70).[10] Therefore, the absolute minimum error is a function of $P(\omega)$ only, and is equal to its geometric mean, which is always positive for positive definite spectra.[11] This is a curious result, because it says that the minimum error can be nonzero even

---

[10] If $P(\omega)$ is a p_0-pole spectrum then $E_p = E_{min}$ for all $p \geq p_0$.

[11] E_{min} is equal to zero only if $P(\omega)$ is zero over a noncountable set of frequencies (i.e., over a line segment). In that case, the signal is perfectly predictable and the prediction error is zero [107].

when the matching spectrum $\hat{P}(\omega)$ is identical to the matched spectrum $P(\omega)$. Therefore, although E_p is a measure of fit of the model spectrum to the signal spectrum, it is not an absolute one. The measure is always relative to $E_{\min}$. The nonzero aspect of $E_{\min}$ can be understood by realizing that, for any p, E_p is equal to that portion of the signal energy that is not predictable by a pth order predictor. For example, the impulse response of an all-pole filter is perfectly predictable *except* for the initial nonzero value. It is the energy in this initial value that shows up in E_p. (Note that in the covariance method one can choose the region of analysis to exclude the initial value, in which case the prediction error would be zero for this example.)

B. Spectral Matching Properties

The LP error measure E in (62) has two major properties:[12] a global property and a local property.

1) Global Property: Because the contributions to the total error are determined by the *ratio* of the two spectra, the matching process should perform uniformly over the whole frequency range, irrespective of the general shaping of the spectrum.

This is an important property for spectral estimation because it makes sure that the spectral match at frequencies with little energy is just as good, on the average, as the match at frequencies with high energy (see Fig. 3). If the error measure had been of the form $\int |P(\omega) - \hat{P}(\omega)| \, d\omega$, the spectral matches would have been best at high energy frequency points.

2) Local Property: This property deals with how the match is done in each small region of the spectrum.

Let the ratio of $P(\omega)$ to $\hat{P}(\omega)$ be given by

$$E(\omega) = \frac{P(\omega)}{\hat{P}(\omega)}. \tag{74}$$

Then from (67) we have

$$\frac{1}{2\pi} \int_{-\pi}^{\pi} E(\omega) \, d\omega = 1, \quad \text{for all } p. \tag{75}$$

$E(\omega)$ can be interpreted as the "instantaneous error" between $P(\omega)$ and $\hat{P}(\omega)$ at frequency ω. Equation (75) says that the arithmetic mean of $E(\omega)$ is equal to 1, which means that there are values of $E(\omega)$ greater and less than 1 such that the average is equal to 1.[13] In terms of the two spectra, this means that $P(\omega)$ will be greater than $\hat{P}(\omega)$ in some regions and less in others such that (75) applies. However, the contribution to the total error is more significant when $P(\omega)$ is greater than $\hat{P}(\omega)$ than when $P(\omega)$ is smaller, e.g., a ratio of $E(\omega) = 2$ contributes more to the total error than a ratio of $1/2$. We conclude that:

after the minimization of error, we expect a better fit of $\hat{P}(\omega)$ to $P(\omega)$ where $P(\omega)$ is greater than $\hat{P}(\omega)$, than where $P(\omega)$ is smaller (on the average).

For example, if $P(\omega)$ is the power spectrum of a quasi-periodic signal (such as in Fig. 3), then most of the energy in $P(\omega)$ will exist in the harmonics, and very little energy will reside between harmonics. The error measure in (62) insures that the

approximation of $\hat{P}(\omega)$ to $P(\omega)$ is far superior at the harmonics than between the harmonics. If the signal had been generated by exciting a filter with a periodic sequence of impulses, then the system response of the filter must pass through all the harmonic peaks. Therefore, with a proper choice of the model order p, minimization of the LP error measure results in a model spectrum that is a good approximation to that system response. This leads to one characteristic of the local property:

minimization of the error measure E results in a model spectrum $\hat{P}(\omega)$ that is a good estimate of the *spectral envelope* of the signal spectrum $P(\omega)$.

Fig. 6 shows that this statement also applies in a qualitative way when the excitation is random noise. It should be clear from the above that the importance of the local property is not as crucial when the variations of the signal spectrum from the spectral envelope are much less pronounced.

In the modeling of harmonic spectra, we showed an example in Fig. 7(a) where, although the all-pole spectrum resulting from LP modeling was a reasonably good estimate of the harmonic spectral envelope, it did not yield the unique all-pole transfer function that coincides with the line spectrum at the harmonics. This is a significant *disadvantage* of LP modeling, and is an indirect reflection of another characteristic of the local property: *the cancellation of errors.* This is evident from (75) where the instantaneous errors $E(\omega)$ are greater and less than 1 such that the average is 1. To help elucidate this point, let us define a new error measure E' that is the logarithm of E in (62):

$$E' = \log \left[\frac{1}{2\pi} \int_{-\pi}^{\pi} \frac{P(\omega)}{\hat{P}(\omega)} \, d\omega \right] \tag{76}$$

where the gain factor has been omitted since it is not relevant to this discussion. It is simple to show that the minimization of E' is equivalent to the minimization of E. For cases where $P(\omega)$ is smooth relative to $\hat{P}(\omega)$ and the values of $P(\omega)$ are not expected to deviate very much from $\hat{P}(\omega)$, the logarithm of the average of spectral ratios can be approximated by the average of the logarithms, i.e.,

$$E' \cong \frac{1}{2\pi} \int_{-\pi}^{\pi} \log \frac{P(\omega)}{\hat{P}(\omega)} \, d\omega. \tag{77}$$

From (77) it is clear that the contributions to the error when $P(\omega) > \hat{P}(\omega)$ *cancel* those when $P(\omega) < \hat{P}(\omega)$.

The above discussion suggests the use of an error measure that takes the magnitude of the integrand in (77). One such error measure is

$$E'' = \frac{1}{2\pi} \int_{-\pi}^{\pi} \left[\log \frac{P(\omega)}{\hat{P}(\omega)} \right]^2 \, d\omega$$

$$= \frac{1}{2\pi} \int_{-\pi}^{\pi} [\log P(\omega) - \log \hat{P}(\omega)]^2 \, d\omega. \tag{78}$$

E'' is just the mean squared error between the two log spectra. It has the important property that the minimum error of zero occurs if and only if $\hat{P}(\omega)$ is identical to $P(\omega)$. Therefore, if we use (the discrete form of) E'' in modeling the harmonic spectrum in Fig. 7(a), the resulting model spectrum (for $p = 14$) will be identical to the dashed spectrum, since the minimum error of zero is achievable by that spectrum. However, while the error measure E'' solves one problem, it introduces an-

---

[12] Itakura [50], [51] discusses a maximum likelihood error criterion having the same properties.

[13] Except for the special case when $P(\omega)$ is all-pole, the condition $E(\omega) = 1$ for all ω is true only as $p \to \infty$.

other. Note that the contributions to the total error in (78) are equally important whether $P(\omega) > \hat{P}(\omega)$ or vice versa. This means that if the variations of $P(\omega)$ are large relative to $\hat{P}(\omega)$ (such as in Fig. 3), the resulting model spectrum will *not* be a good estimate of the spectral envelope. In addition, the minimization of E'' in (78) results in a set of nonlinear equations that must be solved iteratively, thus increasing the computational load tremendously.

Our conclusion is that the LP error measure in (62) is to be preferred in general, except for certain special cases (as in Fig. 7(a)) where an error measure such as E'' in (78) can be used, provided one is willing to carry the extra computational burden.

The global and local properties described here are properties of the error measure in (62) and do not depend on the details of $P(\omega)$ and $\hat{P}(\omega)$. These properties apply *on the average* over the whole frequency range. Depending on the detailed shapes of $P(\omega)$ and $\hat{P}(\omega)$, the resulting match can be better in one spectral region than in another. For example, if $\hat{P}(\omega)$ is an all-pole model spectrum and if the signal spectrum $P(\omega)$ contains zeros as well as poles, then one would not expect as good a match at the zeros as at the poles. This is especially true if the zeros have bandwidths of the same order as the poles or less. (Wide bandwidth zeros are usually well approximated by poles.) On the other hand, if $\hat{P}(\omega)$ is an all-zero spectrum then the preceding statement would have to be reversed.

C. The Normalized Error

The normalized error has been a very useful parameter for the determination of the optimal number of parameters to be used in the model spectrum. This subject will be discussed in the following section. Here we shall present some of the properties of the normalized error, especially as they relate to the signal and model spectra.

1) Relation to the Spectral Dynamic Range: The normalized error was defined in Section II as the ratio of the minimum error E_p to the energy in the signal $R(0)$. Keeping in mind that $R(0) = \hat{R}(0)$, and substituting for E_p from (72), we obtain

$$V_p = \frac{E_p}{R(0)} = \frac{e^{\hat{c}_0}}{\hat{R}(0)}. \qquad (79)$$

Also, from (73), we have in the limit as $p \to \infty$:

$$V_{\min} = V_\infty = \frac{e^{c_0}}{R(0)}. \qquad (80)$$

Therefore, the normalized error is always equal to the normalized zero quefrency of the model spectrum. From (40) and (79) it is clear that V_p is a monotonically decreasing function of p, with $V_0 = 1$ and $V_\infty = V_{\min}$ in (80). Fig. 8 shows plots of V_p as a function of p for two speech sounds (sampled at 10 kHz) whose spectra are similar to those in Figs. 3 and 6.

It is instructive to write V_p as a function of $\hat{P}(\omega)$. From (63) and (70), (79) can be rewritten as

$$V_p = \frac{\exp\left[\dfrac{1}{2\pi}\displaystyle\int_{-\pi}^{\pi} \log \hat{P}(\omega)\, d\omega\right]}{\dfrac{1}{2\pi}\displaystyle\int_{-\pi}^{\pi} \hat{P}(\omega)\, d\omega}. \qquad (81)$$

It is clear from (81) that V_p depends completely on the shape of the model spectrum, and from (80), $V_{\min}$ is determined solely by the shape of the signal spectrum. An interesting way

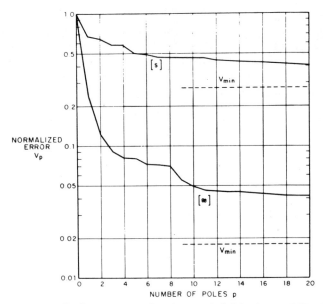

Fig. 8. Normalized error curves for the sounds [s] in the word "list" and [æ] in the word "potassium."

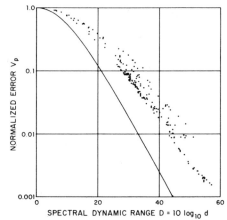

Fig. 9. Two-pole normalized error versus spectral dynamic range for 200 different two-pole models. The solid curve is V_a, the absolute lower bound on the normalized error.

to view (81) is that V_p is equal to the ratio of the geometric mean of the model spectrum to its arithmetic mean. This ratio has been used in the past as a measure of the spread of the data [22], [48]. When the spread of the data is small, the ratio is close to 1. Indeed, from (81) it is easy to see that if $\hat{P}(\omega)$ is flat, $V_p = 1$. On the other hand, if the data spread is large, then V_p becomes close to zero. Again, from (81) we see that if $\hat{P}(\omega)$ is zero for a portion of the spectrum (hence a large spread), then $V_p = 0$. (Another way of looking at V_p is in terms of the flatness of the spectrum [40].)

Another measure of data spread is the dynamic range. We define the spectral dynamic range d as the ratio of the highest to the lowest amplitude points on the spectrum:

$$d = H/L$$

where

$$H = \max_\omega \hat{P}(\omega) \qquad L = \min_\omega \hat{P}(\omega). \qquad (82)$$

The relation between the normalized error and the spectral dynamic range is illustrated in Fig. 9. The dark dots in the figure are plots of the normalized error versus the spectral dynamic range (in decibels) for 2-pole models of 200 different speech spectra. The solid curve in Fig. 9 is an absolute lower bound on the geometric-to-arithmetic mean ratio for *any* spectrum with a given dynamic range. The curve is a plot of the following relation [22], [64]

$$V_a = \gamma e^{(1-\gamma)} \tag{83}$$

where

$$\gamma = \frac{\log d}{d-1} \tag{84}$$

and V_a stands for the absolute lower bound on V_p for a given d. The overall impression from Fig. 9 is that the normalized error generally decreases as the dynamic range of the spectrum increases. This is apparent in Fig. 8 where V_p for the vowel [æ] is less than that for the fricative [s], and [æ] has a much higher spectral dynamic range than [s].

2) A Measure of Ill-Conditioning: In solving the autocorrelation normal equations (12), the condition of the autocorrelation matrix is an important consideration in deciding the accuracy of the computation needed. An ill-conditioned matrix can cause numerical problems in the solution. An accepted measure of ill-conditioning in a matrix is given by the ratio

$$d' = \lambda_{\max}/\lambda_{\min} \tag{85}$$

where $\lambda_{\max}$ and $\lambda_{\min}$ are the maximum and minimum eigenvalues of the matrix [27], [81]. Grenander and Szegö [41], [42] have shown that all the eigenvalues of an autocorrelation matrix lie in the range $\lambda_i \in [H, L]$, $1 \leqslant i \leqslant p$, where H and L are defined in (82). In addition, as the order of the matrix p increases, the eigenvalues become approximately equal to $\hat{P}(\omega)$ evaluated at equally spaced points with separation $2\pi/(p+1)$. Therefore, the ratio d' given in (85) can be well approximated by the dynamic range of $\hat{P}(\omega)$:

$$d' \cong d. \tag{86}$$

Therefore, the spectral dynamic range is a good measure of the ill-conditioning of the autocorrelation matrix. The larger the dynamic range, the greater is the chance that the matrix is ill-conditioned.

But in the previous section we noted that an increase in d usually results in a decrease in the normalized error V_p. Therefore, V_p can also be used as a measure of ill-conditioning: the ill-conditioning is greater with decreased V_p. The problem becomes more and more serious as $V_p \to 0$, i.e., as the signal becomes highly predictable.

If ill-conditioning occurs sporadically, then one way of patching the problem is to increase the values along the principal diagonal of the matrix by a small fraction of a percent. However, if the problem is a regular one, then it is a good idea if one can reduce the dynamic range of the signal spectrum. For example, if the spectrum has a general slope, then a single-zero filter of the form $1 + az^{-1}$ applied to the signal can be very effective. The new signal is given by

$$s'_n = s_n + a s_{n-1}. \tag{87}$$

An optimal value for a is obtained by solving for the filter $A(z)$ that "whitens" (flattens) s'_n. This is, of course, given by the first order predictor, where

$$a = -\frac{R(1)}{R(0)}. \tag{88}$$

$R(1)$ and $R(0)$ are autocorrelation coefficients of the signal s_n. The filtered signal s'_n is then guaranteed to have a smaller spectral dynamic range. The above process is usually referred to as *preemphasis*.

One conclusion from the above concerns the design of the low-pass filter that one uses before sampling the signal to reduce aliasing. In order to ensure against aliasing, it is usually recommended that the cutoff frequency of the filter be lower than half the sampling frequency. However, if the cutoff frequency is appreciably lower than half the sampling frequency, then the spectral dynamic range of the signal spectrum increases, especially if the filter has a sharp cutoff and the stop band is very low relative to the pass band. This increases problems of ill-conditioning. Therefore, if one uses a lowpass filter with a sharp cutoff, the cutoff frequency should be set as close to half the sampling frequency as possible.

D. Optimal Number of Poles

One of the important decisions that usually has to be made in fitting of all-pole models is the determination of an "optimal" number of poles. It is a nontrivial exercise to define the word "optimal" here, for as we have seen, the fit of the model "improves" as the number of poles p increases. The problem is where to stop. Clearly we would like the minimum value of p that is adequate for the problem at hand, both to reduce our computation and to minimize the possibility of ill-conditioning (which increases with p since V_p decreases).

If the signal spectrum is an all-pole spectrum with p_0 poles, then we know that $V_p = V_{p_0}$, $p \geqslant p_0$, and $k_p = 0$, $p > p_0$, i.e., the error curve remains flat for $p > p_0$. Therefore, if we expect the signal spectrum to be an all-pole spectrum, a simple test to obtain the optimal p is to check when the error curve becomes flat. But, if the signal is the output of a p_0-pole filter with white noise excitation, then the suggested test will not work, because the estimates of the poles are based on a finite number of data points and the error curve will not be flat for $p > p_0$. In practice, however, the error curve will be almost flat for $p > p_0$. This suggests the use of the following threshold test

$$1 - \frac{V_{p+1}}{V_p} < \delta. \tag{89}$$

This test must succeed for several consecutive values before one is sure that the error curve has actually flattened out.

The use of the ratio V_{p+1}/V_p has been an accepted method in the statistical literature [6], [17], [112] for the determination of the optimal p. The test is based on hypothesis testing procedures using maximum likelihood ratios. A critical review of hypothesis testing procedures has been given recently by Akaike [5]. Akaike's main point is that model fitting is a problem where multiple decision procedures are required rather than hypothesis testing. The fitting problem should be stated as an estimation problem with an associated measure of fit. Akaike suggests the use of an information theoretic criterion that is an estimate of the mean log-likelihood [3], [5].[14] This is given by

$$I(p) = -2 \log (\text{maximum likelihood}) + 2p. \tag{90}$$

The value of p for which $I(p)$ is minimum is taken to be the optimal value. In our problem of all-pole modeling, if we assume that the signal has a Gaussian probability distribution,

---

[14] An earlier criterion used by Akaike is what he called the "final prediction error" [1], [2], [37].

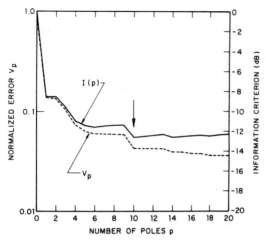

Fig. 10. A plot of Akaike's information criterion versus the order of the predictor p. Here, $I(p) = 10 \log_{10} V_p + (8.686p/0.4N)$, ($N$ = 200, Hamming windowed). The "optimal" value of p occurs at the minimum of $I(p)$, shown by the arrow at $p = 10$.

then (90) reduces to (neglecting additive constants and dividing by N) [6], [17], [51]

$$I(p) = \log V_p + \frac{2p}{N_e} \qquad (91)$$

where N_e is the "effective" number of data points in the signal. The word "effective" is used to indicate that one must compensate for possible windowing. The effective width of a window can be taken as the ratio of the energy under the window relative to that of a rectangular window. For example, for a Hamming window, $N_e = 0.4N$.

Note that the first term in (91) decreases as a function of p, and the second term increases. Therefore, a minimum can occur. In practice, there are usually several local minima, then the value of p corresponding to the absolute minimum of $I(p)$ is taken as the optimal value. Usually $I(p)$ is computed up to the maximum value of interest,[15] and the minimum of $I(p)$ is found in that region.

Fig. 10 shows an example of the application of Akaike's criterion. The dotted curve is the usual error curve and the solid curve is a plot of $I(p)$ in (91) multiplied by $10 \log_{10} e$ to obtain the results in decibels. In Fig. 10, the optimal predictor order is $p = 10$. Note that $I(p)$ for $p > 10$ slopes upward, but very gently. This indicates that the actual absolute minimum is quite sensitive to the linear term in (91). In practice, the criterion in (91) should not be regarded as an absolute, because it is based on several assumptions which might not apply for the signal of interest. For example, the assumptions of uncorrelated noise excitation and Gaussian distributions might not hold. Therefore, the experimenter should feel free to adjust the criterion to suit one's application. One simple way of "tuning" the criterion is to multiply N_e by an appropriate factor.

V. Data Compression by Linear Prediction

The methods outlined in Section II for the modeling of the behavior of a signal can be very useful in data compression. The process of signal or system modeling is essentially one of redundancy removal, which is the essence of data compression.

[15] Akaike informed me that he usually recommends $p_{max} < 3N^{1/2}$ as the maximum value of p that should be used if one is interested in a reliable estimate.

The idea of attempting to predict the value of a signal from previous sample values has been labeled in communications as "predictive coding" [28]. Adaptive linear prediction has been used extensively in speech and video transmission [7], [9], [23], [44], [50], [57], [83]. For the purposes of transmission one must quantize and transmit the predictor parameters or some transformation thereof. It has been known for some time that the quantization of the predictor parameters themselves is quite inefficient since a large number of bits is required to retain the desired fidelity in the reconstructed signal at the receiver [72]. Below, several equivalent representations of the predictor are presented and their quantization properties are discussed. We shall continue to assume that $H(z)$ is always stable, and hence minimum phase. $A(z)$ is, of course, then also minimum phase.

A. Alternate Representations of Linear Predictor

The following is a list of possible sets of parameters that characterize uniquely the all-pole filter $H(z)$ or its inverse $A(z)$.

1) (a) Impulse response of the inverse filter $A(z)$, i.e., predictor parameters a_k, $1 \leqslant k \leqslant p$.

   (b) Impulse response of the all-pole model h_n, $0 \leqslant n \leqslant p$, which is defined in (30). Note that the first $p + 1$ coefficients uniquely specify the filter.

2) (a) Autocorrelation coefficients of a_k, $\rho(i)$, $0 \leqslant i \leqslant p$, as defined in (66).

   (b) Autocorrelation coefficients of h_n, $\hat{R}(i)$, $0 \leqslant i \leqslant p$, as defined in (31) and (32).

3) Spectral coefficients of $A(z)$, Γ_i, $0 \leqslant i \leqslant p$ (or equivalently spectral coefficients of $H(z)$, G^2/Γ_i):

$$\Gamma_i = \rho(0) + 2 \sum_{j=1}^{P} \rho(j) \cos \frac{2\pi ij}{2p+1}, \qquad 0 \leqslant i \leqslant p \qquad (92)$$

where $\rho(i)$ are as defined in (66). In other words, $\{\Gamma_i\}$ is obtained from $\{\rho(i)\}$ by a discrete Fourier transform.

4) Cepstral coefficients of $A(z)$, c_n, $1 \leqslant n \leqslant p$ (or equivalently cepstral coefficients of $H(z)$, $-c_n$):

$$c_n = \frac{1}{2\pi} \int_{-\pi}^{\pi} \log A(e^{j\omega}) e^{jn\omega} \, d\omega. \qquad (93)$$

Since $A(z)$ is minimum phase, (93) reduces to [38], [77]

$$c_n = a_n - \sum_{m=1}^{n-1} \frac{m}{n} c_m a_{n-m}, \qquad 1 \leqslant n \leqslant p. \qquad (94)$$

Equation (94) is an iterative method for the computation of the cepstral coefficients directly from the predictor coefficients.

5) Poles of $H(z)$ or zeros of $A(z)$, z_k, $1 \leqslant k \leqslant p$, where $\{z_k\}$ are either real or form complex conjugate pairs. Conversion of the roots to the s plane can be achieved by setting each root $z_k = e^{s_k T}$, where $s_k = \sigma_k + j\omega_k$ is the corresponding pole in the s plane, and T is the sampling period. If the root $z_k = z_{kr} + jz_{ki}$, then

$$\omega_k = \frac{1}{T} \arctan \frac{z_{ki}}{z_{kr}}$$

$$\sigma_k = \frac{1}{2T} \log (z_{kr}^2 + z_{ki}^2) \qquad (95)$$

where z_{kr} and z_{ki} are the real and imaginary parts of z_k, respectively.

6) Reflection coefficients k_i, $1 \leqslant i \leqslant p$, which are obtained as a byproduct of the solution of the autocorrelation normal equations, as in (38), or from the backward recursion (51).

Some of the preceding sets of parameters have $p + 1$ coefficients while others have only p coefficients. However, for the latter sets the gain G needs to be specified as well, thus keeping the total number of parameters as $p + 1$ for all the cases.

For purposes of data transmission, one is usually interested in recovering the predictor coefficients from the parameters that are chosen for transmission. The required transformations are clear for most of the above parameters, except perhaps for the parameters $\rho(i)$ and Γ_i. Through an inverse DFT, the spectral coefficients Γ_i can be converted to autocorrelation coefficients $\rho(i)$. One method of recovering the predictor parameters from $\{\rho(i)\}$ is as follows. Apply a DFT to the sequence $\{\rho(i)\}$ after appending it with an appropriate number of zeros to achieve sufficient resolution in the resulting spectrum of $A(z)$. Divide G^2 by this spectrum to obtain the spectrum of the filter $H(z)$. Inverse Fourier transformation of the spectrum of $H(z)$ yields the autocorrelation coefficients $\hat{R}(i)$. The first $p + 1$ coefficients $\hat{R}(i)$, $0 \leqslant i \leqslant p$, are then used to compute the predictor coefficients via the normal equations (12) with $R(i) = \hat{R}(i)$.

B. Quantization Properties

Although the sets of parameters given above provide equivalent information about the linear predictor, their properties under quantization are different. For the purpose of quantization, two desirable properties for a parameter set to have are: 1) filter stability upon quantization and 2) a natural ordering of the parameters. Property 1) means that the poles of $H(z)$ continue to be inside the unit circle even after parameter quantization. By 2), we mean that the parameters exhibit an inherent ordering, e.g., the predictor coefficients are ordered as $a_1, a_2, \cdots, a_p$. If a_1 and a_2 are interchanged then $H(z)$ is no longer the same in general, thus illustrating the existence of an ordering. The poles of $H(z)$, on the other hand, are not naturally ordered since interchanging the values of any two poles does not change the filter. When an ordering is present, a statistical study on the distribution of individual parameters can be used to develop better encoding schemes. Only the poles and the reflection coefficients insure stability upon quantization, while all the sets of parameters except the poles possess a natural ordering. Thus only the reflection coefficients possess both of these properties.

In an experimental study [63] of the quantization properties of the different parameters, it was found that the impulse responses $\{a_k\}$ and $\{h_n\}$ and the autocorrelations $\{\rho(i)\}$ and $\{\hat{R}(i)\}$ are highly susceptible to causing instability of the filter upon quantization. Therefore, these sets of parameters can be used only under minimal quantization, in which case the transmission rate would be excessive.

In the experimental investigation of the spectral and cepstral parameters, it was found that the quantization properties of these parameters are generally superior to those of the impulse responses and autocorrelation coefficients. The spectral parameters often yield results comparable to those obtained by quantizing the reflection coefficients. However, for the cases when the spectrum consists of one or more very sharp peaks (narrow bandwidths), the effects of quantizing the spectral coefficients often cause certain regions in the reconstructed spectrum (as described in the previous section) to become negative, which leads to instability of the computed filter.

Quantization of the cepstral coefficients can also lead to instabilities. It should be noted here that the quantization properties of these parameters give better results if the spectral dynamic range of the signal is limited by some form of preprocessing.

Filter stability is preserved under quantization of the poles. But poles are expensive to compute, and they do not possess a natural ordering.

The conclusion is that, of the sets of parameters given in the preceding, the reflection coefficients are the best set to use as transmission parameters. In addition to ease of computation, stability under quantization, and natural ordering, the values of the reflection coefficients k_i, $i < p$, do not change as p is increased, unlike any of the other parameters. In the following, we discuss the optimal quantization of the reflection coefficients.

C. Optimal Quantization [53], [65]

Optimal quantization of the reflection coefficients depends on the fidelity criterion chosen. For many applications, it is important that the log spectrum of the all-pole model be preserved. In this case, it is reasonable to study the sensitivity of the log spectrum with respect to changes in the reflection coefficients. In a recent study [65], a spectral sensitivity curve was plotted versus each of the reflection coefficients k_i for many different all-pole models obtained by analyzing a large number of speech samples. The results of the study show that each sensitivity curve versus k_i has the same general shape, irrespective of the index i. Each sensitivity curve is U-shaped; it is even-symmetric about $k_i = 0$, with large values when $|k_i| \to 1$, and small values when $|k_i|$ is close to zero. These properties indicate that linear quantization of the reflection coefficients is not desirable, especially if some of them take values very close to 1, which happens when the spectrum contains sharp resonances. Nonlinear quantization of k_i is equivalent to a linear quantization of another parameter, say g_i, which is related to k_i by a nonlinear transformation. The requirement that the spectral sensitivity of the new parameters be flat resulted in the following optimal transformation [65]:

$$g_i = \log \frac{1 + k_i}{1 - k_i}, \qquad \text{all } i. \tag{96}$$

It is interesting to note from (45) that g_i is simply the logarithm of the hypothetical impedance ratios corresponding to k_i.

The optimality of the preceding transformation was based on a specific spectral fidelity criterion. Other transformations would result if other quantization fidelity criteria were adopted.[16]

The transmission rate can be reduced further without affecting the fidelity by proper encoding of each parameter. Variable word length encoding [34] (such as Huffman) can be used for this purpose if the statistical distributions of each of the parameters is known. These distributions can be obtained very simply from a representative sample of signals.

VI. POLE-ZERO MODELING

Given the spectrum of some arbitrary signal, it is generally not possible to determine for certain the identity of the system that generated the signal in terms of a set of poles and

---

[16] Using a log likelihood criterion, Itakura informed me that a transformation proportional to arcsin (k_i) is optimal.

zeros. The problem is inherently nondeterministic, for a zero can be approximated arbitrarily closely by a large number of poles and vice versa. Indeed, we have seen in this paper that the all-pole model spectrum can approximate the signal spectrum arbitrarily closely by simply increasing the number of poles. However, if there are a number of influential zeros in the signal spectrum, the number of model poles can become very large. For data compression applications, this is an undesirable situation. Also, there are applications where the identification of the zeros is important. Therefore, it is useful to be able to model a spectrum in terms of poles and zeros.

Much effort is currently being expended on the problem of pole-zero modeling [8], [17], [19], [20], [29], [30], [88], [91]. Most of these methods are purely in the time domain. However, there seems to be a growing interest in frequency domain methods [4], [46], [94], partly due to the speed offered by the FFT. Add to this the market availability of spectrum analyzers and special hardware FFT processors. Of course, the time and frequency domain approaches should give similar results since LP analysis is actually performed in the autocorrelation domain.

The beauty of all-pole modeling is that it is relatively simple, straightforward, well understood, inexpensive, and "always" works. Unfortunately, none of these properties apply to pole-zero modeling. The main difficulty is that the pole-zero problem is nonlinear. We show this below for the stationary case. Then, we sketch out representative schemes for iterative and noniterative estimation of the pole and zero parameters. No exhaustive analysis is attempted; the reader is referred to the aforementioned references.

A. Normal Equations

The transfer function of the pole-zero model is given by $H(z)$ in (2). The corresponding model spectrum is given by

$$\hat{P}(\omega) = |H(e^{j\omega})|^2 = G^2 \frac{|B(e^{j\omega})|^2}{|A(e^{j\omega})|^2} = G^2 \frac{N(\omega)}{D(\omega)} \qquad (97)$$

where $B(z)$ and $A(z)$ are the numerator and denominator polynomials in $H(z)$, and the all-zero spectra $N(\omega)$ and $D(\omega)$ form the numerator and denominator of $\hat{P}(\omega)$ and are given by

$$N(\omega) = \left| 1 + \sum_{l=1}^{q} b_l e^{-jl\omega} \right|^2 \qquad (98)$$

and

$$D(\omega) = \left| 1 + \sum_{k=1}^{p} a_k e^{-jk\omega} \right|^2. \qquad (99)$$

The matching error between the signal spectrum $P(\omega)$ and $\hat{P}(\omega)$ is given by (62), and from (97) is equal to

$$E = \frac{1}{2\pi} \int_{-\pi}^{\pi} P(\omega) \frac{D(\omega)}{N(\omega)} d\omega. \qquad (100)$$

E can be interpreted as the residual energy obtained by passing the signal through the filter $A(z)/B(z)$. The problem is to determine $\{a_k\}$ and $\{b_l\}$ such that E in (100) is minimized.

In the sequel we shall make use of the following two relations:

$$\frac{\partial N(\omega)}{\partial b_i} = 2 \sum_{l=0}^{q} b_l \cos(i-l)\omega, \qquad b_0 = 1 \qquad (101)$$

$$\frac{\partial D(\omega)}{\partial a_i} = 2 \sum_{k=0}^{p} a_k \cos(i-k)\omega, \quad a_0 = 1. \qquad (102)$$

In addition, we shall use the notation $R_{\alpha\beta}(i)$ to represent the autocorrelation defined by

$$R_{\alpha\beta}(i) = \frac{1}{2\pi} \int_{-\pi}^{\pi} P(\omega) \frac{[D(\omega)]^{\beta}}{[N(\omega)]^{\alpha}} \cos(i\omega) d\omega. \qquad (103)$$

Thus, $R_{00}(i)$ is simply the Fourier transform of $P(\omega)$.[17] Taking $\partial E/\partial a_i$ in (100) one obtains

$$\frac{\partial E}{\partial a_i} = 2 \sum_{k=0}^{p} a_k R_{10}(i-k), \qquad 1 \leqslant i \leqslant p. \qquad (104)$$

Similarly, one can show that

$$\frac{\partial E}{\partial b_i} = -2 \sum_{l=0}^{q} b_l R_{21}(i-l), \qquad 1 \leqslant i \leqslant q. \qquad (105)$$

In order to minimize E, we set $\partial E/\partial a_i = 0$, $1 \leqslant i \leqslant p$, and $\partial E/\partial b_i = 0$, $1 \leqslant i \leqslant q$, simultaneously. These, then, comprise the normal equations.

From (103), it is clear that $R_{10}(i-k)$ is not a function of a_k. Therefore, setting (104) to zero results in a set of linear equations, identical in form to the autocorrelation normal equations (12). However, $R_{21}(i-l)$ in (105) is a function of b_l, as can be deduced from (103) with $\alpha = 2$ and $\beta = 1$. Therefore, setting (105) to zero results in a set of nonlinear equations in b_l. If one wishes to solve for $\{a_k\}$ and $\{b_l\}$ simultaneously, then one solves a set of $p + q$ nonlinear equations.

Note that if the signal is assumed to be nonstationary, the above analysis can be modified accordingly in a manner similar to that in Section III-A for the all-pole case. The resulting equations will be very similar in form to the preceding equations, with nonstationary autocorrelations replacing the stationary autocorrelations.

B. Iterative Solutions

Since the minimization of E in (100) leads to a set of nonlinear equations, the problem of minimizing E must then be solved iteratively. There are many methods in the literature for finding the extrema of a function [30], [108], many of which are applicable in our case. In particular, gradient methods are appropriate here since it is possible to evaluate the error gradient, as in (104) and (105). One such method was used by Tretter and Steiglitz [94] in pole-zero modeling. Other schemes, such as the Newton–Raphson method, require the evaluation of the Hessian (i.e., second derivative). This can be very cumbersome in many problems, but is straightforward in our case. This is illustrated below by giving a Newton–Raphson solution.

Let $x' = [a_1 a_2 \cdots a_p b_1 b_2 \cdots b_q]$ be the transpose of a column vector x whose elements are the coefficients a_k and b_l. If $x(m)$ is the solution at iteration m, then $x(m+1)$ is given by

$$x(m+1) = x(m) - J^{-1} \frac{\partial E}{\partial x} \bigg|_{x=x(m)} \qquad (106)$$

where J is the $(p+q) \times (p+q)$ symmetric Hessian matrix

---

[17] For a discrete spectrum $P(\omega_n)$ the integrals in (100) and (103) are replaced by summations.

given by $J = \partial^2 E / \partial x \partial x'$. Setting $a' = [a_1 a_2 \cdots a_p]$ and $b' = [b_1 b_2 \cdots b_q]$, (106) can be partitioned, with $x' = [a'b']$, as

$$
\begin{bmatrix} a(m+1) \\ b(m+1) \end{bmatrix} = \begin{bmatrix} a(m) \\ b(m) \end{bmatrix} - \begin{bmatrix} \dfrac{\partial^2 E}{\partial a \partial a'} & \dfrac{\partial^2 E}{\partial a \partial b'} \\ \dfrac{\partial^2 E}{\partial b \partial a'} & \dfrac{\partial^2 E}{\partial b \partial b'} \end{bmatrix}^{-1}_{\substack{a=a(m) \\ b=b(m)}} \begin{bmatrix} \dfrac{\partial E}{\partial a} \\ \dfrac{\partial E}{\partial b} \end{bmatrix}_{\substack{a=a(m) \\ b=b(m)}} .
$$

(107)

The elements of the first-order partial derivatives in (107) are given by (104) and (105). The elements of the second partial derivatives can be shown to be equal to

$$
\frac{\partial^2 E}{\partial a_i \partial a_j} = 2 R_{10}(i - j) \tag{108}
$$

$$
\frac{\partial^2 E}{\partial a_i \partial b_j} = -2 \sum_{k=0}^{p} \sum_{l=0}^{q} a_k b_l
$$
$$
\cdot [R_{20}(j + i - l - k) + R_{20}(j - i - l + k)] \tag{109}
$$

$$
\frac{\partial^2 E}{\partial b_i \partial b_j} = -2 R_{21}(i - j) + 4 \sum_{k=0}^{p} \sum_{l=0}^{q} b_k b_l
$$
$$
\cdot [R_{31}(j + i - l - k) + R_{31}(j - i - l + k)]. \tag{110}
$$

Given the estimates $a(m)$ and $b(m)$, one can compute $N(\omega)$ and $D(\omega)$ from (98) and (99) using FFT's, and then use (103) to compute the autocorrelations R_{10}, R_{20}, R_{21}, and R_{31}, which can then be used in (107)–(110) to compute the new estimates $a(m+1)$ and $b(m+1)$. The iterations are halted when the error gradient goes below some prespecified threshold. The minimum error is then computed from (100).

The Newton–Raphson method works very well if the initial estimate is close to the optimum. In that case, the Hessian J is positive definite and the convergence is quadratic [30]. In the next section we discuss noniterative methods which can be used to give these good initial estimates.

C. Noniterative Solutions

One property that is common to noniterative methods is that a good estimate of the number of poles and zeros seems to be necessary for a reasonable solution. Indeed, in that case, there is not much need to go to expensive iterative methods. However, in general, such information is unavailable and one is interested in obtaining the best estimate for a given p and q. Then, noniterative methods can be used profitably to give good initial estimates that are necessary in iterative methods.

1) Pole Estimation: Assume that the signal s_n had been generated by exciting the pole-zero filter $H(z)$ in (2) by either an impulse or white noise. Then it is simple to show that the signal autocorrelation obeys the autocorrelation equation (31) for $i > q$. Therefore, the coefficients a_k can be estimated by solving (31) with $q + 1 \leqslant i \leqslant q + p$.

The effect of the poles can now be removed by applying the inverse filter $A(z)$ to the signal. In the spectral domain this can be done by computing a new spectrum $P_1(\omega) = P(\omega) D(\omega)$. The problem now reduces to the estimation of the zeros in $P_1(\omega)$.

2) Zero Estimation: A promising noniterative method for pole-zero estimation is that of *cepstral prediction* [76], [95]. The basic idea is that the poles of nc_n, where c_n is the complex cepstrum, comprise the poles and zeros of the signal

[77]. Therefore, for zero estimation, the problem reduces to finding the poles of nc_n which can be computed by the method just described above, where c_n here is the cepstrum corresponding to $P_1(\omega)$.

Another method for zero estimation is that of *inverse LP modeling* [63]. The idea is quite simple: Invert the spectrum $P_1(\omega)$ and apply a q-pole LP analysis. The resulting predictor coefficients are then good estimates of b_l. This method gives good results if $P_1(\omega)$ is smooth relative to the model spectrum. Problems arise if the variations of the signal spectrum about the model spectrum are large. The reason is that LP modeling attempts to make a good fit to the spectral envelope, and the envelope of the inverted spectrum is usually different from the inverse of the desired spectral envelope. One solution is to smooth the spectrum $P_1(\omega)$ before inversion. Spectral smoothing is usually performed by applying a low-pass filter to the spectrum (autocorrelation smoothing) or to the log spectrum (cepstral smoothing). Another method is all-pole smoothing. Indeed, all-pole modeling can be thought of as just another method of smoothing the spectrum, where the degree of smoothing is controlled by the order of the predictor p, which is usually chosen to be much larger than the number of zeros in the model q. We point out that zero estimation by inverse LP modeling with all-pole smoothing is similar to the method of Durbin [24], [25] in the time domain.

VII. Conclusion

Linear prediction is an autocorrelation-domain analysis. Therefore, it can be approached from either the time or frequency domain. The least squares error criterion in the time domain translates into a spectral matching criterion in the frequency domain. This viewpoint was helpful in exploring the advantages and disadvantages of the least squares error criterion.

The major portion of this paper was devoted to all-pole modeling. This type of modeling is simple, inexpensive and effective; hence its wide applicability and acceptance. In contrast, pole-zero modeling is not simple, generally expensive, and is not yet well understood. Future research should be directed at acquiring a better understanding of the problems in pole-zero modeling and developing appropriate methodologies to deal with these problems.

Acknowledgment

The author wishes to thank the following friends and colleagues who have read and commented on earlier versions of this paper: H. Akaike, R. Barakat, C. Cook, T. Fortmann, F. Itakura, G. Kopec, A. Oppenheim, L. Rabiner, R. Viswanathan, and V. Zue. He is especially grateful to R. Viswanathan for the fruitful discussions they have had throughout the writing of the paper and for his help in supplying many of the references. He also wishes to thank B. Aighes, C. Williams, and R. Schwartz for their assistance in the preparation of the manuscript.

References

[1] H. Akaike, "Power spectrum estimation through autoregressive model fitting," *Ann. Inst. Statist. Math.*, vol. 21, pp. 407–419, 1969.

[2] ——, "Statistical predictor identification," *Ann. Inst. Statist. Math.*, vol. 22, pp. 203–217, 1970.

[3] ——, "Information theory and an extension of the maximum likelihood principle," in *Proc. 2nd Int. Symp. Information Theory* (Supplement to Problems of Control and Information Theory), 1972.

[4] ——, "Maximum likelihood identification of Gaussian autoregressive moving average models," *Biometrika*, vol. 60, no. 2, pp. 255–265, 1973.

[5] ——, "A new look at statistical model identification," *IEEE Trans. Automat. Contr.*, vol. AC-19, pp. 716–723, Dec. 1974.

[6] T. W. Anderson, *The Statistical Analysis of Time Series.* New York: Wiley, 1971.

[7] C. A. Andrews, J. M. Davies, and G. R. Schwartz, "Adaptive data compression," *Proc. IEEE*, vol. 55, pp. 267–277, Mar. 1967.

[8] K. J. Åström and P. Eykhoff, "System identification—A survey," *Automatica*, vol. 7, pp. 123–162, 1971.

[9] B. S. Atal and M. R. Schroeder, "Adaptive predictive coding of speech signals," *Bell Syst. Tech. J.*, vol. 49, no. 6, pp. 1973–1986, Oct. 1970.

[10] B. S. Atal and S. L. Hanauer, "Speech analysis and synthesis by linear prediction of the speech wave," *J. Acoust. Soc. Amer.*, vol. 50, no. 2, pp. 637–655, 1971.

[11] M. S. Bartlett, *An Introduction to Stochastic Processes with Special Reference to Methods and Applications.* Cambridge, England: Cambridge Univ. Press, 1956.

[12] J. S. Bendat and A. G. Piersol, *Random Data: Analysis and Measurement Procedures.* New York: Wiley, 1971.

[13] C. Bingham, M. D. Godfrey, and J. W. Tukey, "Modern techniques of power spectrum estimation," *IEEE Trans. Audio Electroacoust.*, vol. AU-15, pp. 56–66, June 1967.

[14] R. B. Blackman and J. W. Tukey, *The Measurement of Power Spectra.* New York: Dover, 1958.

[15] T. Bohlin, "Comparison of two methods of modeling stationary EEG signals," *IBM J. Res. Dev.*, pp. 194–205, May 1973.

[16] S. F. Boll, "*A priori* digital speech analysis," Computer Science Div., Univ. Utah, Salt Lake City, UTEC-CSC-73-123, 1973.

[17] G. E. Box and G. M. Jenkins, *Time Series Analysis Forecasting and Control.* San Francisco, Calif.: Holden-Day, 1970.

[18] J. P. Burg, "The relationship between maximum entropy spectra and maximum likelihood spectra," *Geophysics*, vol. 37, no. 2, pp. 375–376, Apr. 1972.

[19] C. S. Burrus and T. W. Parks, "Time domain design of recursive digital filters," *IEEE Trans. Audio Electroacoust.*, vol. AU-18, pp. 137–141, June 1970.

[20] J. C. Chow, "On estimating the orders of an autoregressive moving-average process with uncertain observations," *IEEE Trans. Automat. Contr.*, vol. AC-17, pp. 707–709, Oct. 1972.

[21] W. T. Cochran *et al.*, "What is the fast Fourier transform?," *IEEE Trans. Audio Electroacoust.*, vol. AU-15, pp. 45–55, June 1967.

[22] H. Cox, "Linear versus logarithmic averaging," *J. Acoust. Soc. Amer.*, vol. 39, no. 4, pp. 688–690, 1966.

[23] L. D. Davisson, "The theoretical analysis of data compression systems," *Proc. IEEE*, vol. 56, pp. 176–186, Feb. 1968.

[24] J. Durbin, "Efficient estimation of parameters in moving-average models," *Biometrika*, vol. 46, Parts 1 and 2, pp. 306–316, 1959.

[25] ——, "The fitting of time-series models," *Rev. Inst. Int. Statist.*, vol. 28, no. 3, pp. 233–243, 1960.

[26] A. Eberhard, "An optimal discrete window for the calculation of power spectra," *IEEE Trans. Audio Electroacoust.*, vol. AU-21, pp. 37–43, Feb. 1973.

[27] M. P. Ekstrom, "A spectral characterization of the ill-conditioning in numerical deconvolution," *IEEE Trans. Audio Electroacoust.*, vol. AU-21, pp. 344–348, Aug. 1973.

[28] P. Elias, "Predictive coding, Parts I and II," *IRE Trans. Inform. Theory*, vol. IT-1, p. 16, Mar. 1955.

[29] A. G. Evans and R. Fischl, "Optimal least squares time-domain synthesis of recursive digital filters," *IEEE Trans. Audio Electroacoust.*, vol. AU-21, pp. 61–65, Feb. 1973.

[30] P. Eykhoff, *System Identification: Parameter and State Estimation.* New York: Wiley, 1974.

[31] D. K. Faddeev and V. N. Faddeeva, *Computational Methods of Linear Algebra.* San Francisco, Calif.: Freeman, 1963.

[32] P. B. C. Fenwick, P. Michie, J. Dollimore, and G. W. Fenton, "Mathematical simulation of the electroencephalogram using an autoregressive series," *Bio-Med. Comput.*, vol. 2, pp. 281–307, 1971.

[33] J. L. Flanagan, *Speech Analysis Synthesis and Perception*, 2nd Edition. New York: Springer-Verlag, 1972.

[34] R. G. Gallager, *Information Theory and Reliable Communication.* New York: Wiley, 1968.

[35] L. Y. Geronimus, *Orthogonal Polynomials.* New York: Consultants Bureau, 1961.

[36] W. Gersch, "Spectral analysis of EEG's by autoregressive decomposition of time series," *Math. Biosci.*, vol. 7, pp. 205–222, 1970.

[37] W. Gersch and D. R. Sharpe, "Estimation of power spectra with finite-order autoregressive models," *IEEE Trans. Automat. Contr.*, vol. AC-18, pp. 367–369, Aug. 1973.

[38] B. Gold and C. M. Rader, *Digital Processing of Signals.* New York: McGraw-Hill, 1969.

[39] G. H. Golub and C. Reinsch, "Singular value decomposition and least squares solutions," *Numer. Math.*, vol. 14, pp. 403–420, 1970.

[40] A. H. Gray and J. D. Markel, "A spectral-flatness measure for studying the autocorrelation method of linear prediction of speech analysis," *IEEE Trans. Acoust., Speech, Signal Processing*, vol. ASSP-22, pp. 207–216, June 1974.

[41] R. M. Gray, "On the asymptotic eigenvalue distribution of Toeplitz matrices," *IEEE Trans. Inform. Theory*, vol. IT-18, pp. 725–730, Nov. 1972.

[42] U. Grenander and G. Szegö, *Toeplitz Forms and Their Applications.* Berkeley, Calif.: Univ. California Press, 1958.

[43] U. Grenander and M. Rosenblatt, *Statistical Analysis of Stationary Time Series.* New York: Wiley, 1957.

[44] A. Habibi and G. S. Robinson, "A survey of digital picture coding," *Computer*, pp. 22–34, May 1974.

[45] E. J. Hannan, *Time Series Analysis.* London, England: Methuen, 1960.

[46] ——, *Multiple Time Series.* New York: Wiley, 1970.

[47] J. R. Haskew, J. M. Kelly, R. M. Kelly, Jr., and T. H. McKinney, "Results of a study of the linear prediction vocoder," *IEEE Trans. Commun.*, vol. COM-21, pp. 1008–1014, Sept. 1973.

[48] R. L. Hershey, "Analysis of the difference between log mean and mean log averaging," *J. Acoust. Soc. Amer.*, vol. 51, pp. 1194–1197, 1972.

[49] F. B. Hildebrand, *Introduction to Numerical Values.* New York: McGraw-Hill, 1956.

[50] F. Itakura and S. Saito, "Analysis synthesis telephony based on the maximum likelihood method," in *Rep. 6th Int. Congr. Acoustics*, Y. Kohasi, Ed., pp. C17–C20, Paper C-5-5, Aug. 1968.

[51] ——, "A statistical method for estimation of speech spectral density and formant frequencies," *Electron. Commun. Japan*, vol. 53-A, no. 1, pp. 36–43, 1970.

[52] ——, "Digital filtering techniques for speech analysis and synthesis," in *Conf. Rec., 7th Int. Congr. Acoustics*, Paper 25 C 1, 1971.

[53] ——, "On the optimum quantization of feature parameters in the Parcor speech synthesizer," in *IEEE Conf. Rec., 1972 Conf. Speech Communication and Processing*, pp. 434–437, Apr. 1972.

[54] G. M. Jenkins and D. G. Watts, *Spectral Analysis and Its Applications.* San Francisco, Calif.: Holden-Day, 1968.

[55] T. Kailath, "A view of three decades of linear filtering theory," *IEEE Trans. Inform. Theory*, vol. IT-20, pp. 146–181, Mar. 1974.

[56] R. E. Kalman, "A new approach to linear filtering and prediction problems," *Trans. ASME, J. Basic Eng.*, Series D82, pp. 35–45, 1960.

[57] H. Kobayashi and L. R. Bahl, "Image data compression by predictive coding I: Prediction algorithms," *IBM J. Res. Dev.*, pp. 164–171, Mar. 1974.

[58] A. Kolmogorov, "Interpolation und Extrapolation von stationären zufälligen Folgen," *Bull. Acad. Sci., U.S.S.R., Ser. Math.*, vol. 5, pp. 3–14, 1941.

[59] K. S. Kunz, *Numerical Analysis.* New York: McGraw-Hill, 1957.

[60] R. C. K. Lee, *Optimal Estimation, Identification, and Control*, Research Monograph no. 28. Cambridge, Mass.: M.I.T. Press, 1964.

[61] N. Levinson, "The Wiener RMS (root mean square) error criterion in filter design and prediction," *J. Math. Phys.*, vol. 25, no. 4, pp. 261–278, 1947. Also Appendix B, in N. Wiener, *Extrapolation, Interpolation and Smoothing of Stationary Time Series.* Cambridge, Mass.: M.I.T. Press, 1949.

[62] J. Makhoul, "Spectral analysis of speech by linear prediction," *IEEE Trans. Audio Electroacoust.*, vol. AU-21, pp. 140–148, June 1973.

[63] ——, "Selective linear prediction and analysis-by-synthesis in speech analysis," Bolt Beranek and Newman Inc., Cambridge, Mass., Rep. 2578, Apr. 1974.

[64] J. Makhoul and J. J. Wolf, "Linear prediction and the spectral analysis of speech," Bolt Beranek and Newman Inc., Cambridge, Mass., NTIS AD-749066, Rep. 2304, Aug. 1972.

[65] J. Makhoul and R. Viswanathan, "Quantization properties of transmission parameters in linear predictive systems," Bolt Beranek and Newman Inc., Cambridge, Mass., Rep. 2800, Apr. 1974.

[66] H. B. Mann and A. Wald, "On the statistical treatment of linear stochastic difference equations," *Econometrica*, vol. 11, nos. 3 and 4, pp. 173–220, 1943.

[67] W. D. Mark, "Spectral analysis of the convolution and filtering of non-stationary stochastic processes," *J. Sound Vib.*, no. 11, pp. 19–63, 1970.

[68] J. D. Markel, "Digital inverse filtering—A new tool for formant trajectory estimation," *IEEE Trans. Audio Electroacoust.*, vol. AU-20, pp. 129–137, June 1972.

[69] J. D. Markel and A. H. Gray, "On autocorrelation equations as applied to speech analysis," *IEEE Trans. Audio Electroacoust.*, vol. AU-20, pp. 69-79, Apr. 1973.

[70] E. Matsui *et al.*, "An adaptive method for speech analysis based on Kalman filtering theory," *Bull Electrotech. Lab*, vol. 36, no. 3, pp. 42-51, 1972 (in Japanese).

[71] R. N. McDonough and W. H. Huggins, "Best least-squares representation of signals by exponentials," *IEEE Trans. Automat. Contr.*, vol. AC-13, pp. 408-412, Aug. 1968.

[72] S. K. Mitra and R. J. Sherwood, "Estimation of pole-zero displacements of a digital filter due to coefficient quantization," *IEEE Trans. Circuits Syst.*, vol. CAS-21, pp. 116-124, Jan. 1974.

[73] R. E. Nieman, D. G. Fisher, and D. E. Seborg, "A review of process identification and parameter estimation techniques," *Int. J. Control*, vol. 13, no. 2, pp. 209-264, 1971.

[74] R. H. Norden, "A survey of maximum likelihood estimation," *Int. Statist. Rev.*, vol. 40, no. 3, pp. 329-354, 1972.

[75] ——, "A survey of maximum likelihood estimation, Part 2," *Int. Statist. Rev.*, vol. 41, no. 1, pp. 39-58, 1973.

[76] A. Oppenheim and J. M. Tribolet, "Pole-zero modeling using cepstral prediction," Res. Lab. Electronics, M.I.T., Cambridge, Mass., QPR 111, pp. 157-159, 1973.

[77] A. V. Oppenheim, R. W. Schafer and T. G. Stockham, "Nonlinear filtering of multiplied and convolved signals," *Proc. IEEE*, vol. 56, pp. 1264-1291, Aug. 1968.

[78] M. Pagano, "An algorithm for fitting autoregressive schemes," *J. Royal Statist. Soc., Series C (Applied Statistics)*, vol. 21, no. 3, pp. 274-281, 1972.

[79] A. Papoulis, *Probability, Random Variables, and Stochastic Processes.* New York: McGraw-Hill, 1965.

[80] L. R. Rabiner *et al.*, "Terminology in digital signal processing," *IEEE Trans. Audio Electroacoust.*, vol. AU-20, pp. 322-337, Dec. 1972.

[81] A. Ralston, *A First Course in Numerical Analysis.* New York: McGraw-Hill, 1965.

[82] A. Ralston and H. Wilf, *Mathematical Methods for Digital Computers*, vol. II. New York: Wiley, 1967.

[83] M. P. Ristenbatt, "Alternatives in digital communications," *Proc. IEEE*, vol. 61, pp. 703-721, June 1973.

[84] E. A. Robinson, *Multichannel Time Series Analysis with Digital Computer Programs.* San Francisco, Calif.: Holden-Day, 1967.

[85] ——, *Statistical Communication and Detection.* New York: Hafner, 1967.

[86] ——, "Predictive decomposition of time series with application to seismic exploration," *Geophysics*, vol. 32, no. 3, pp. 418-484, June 1967.

[87] E. A. Robinson and S. Treitel, *The Robinson-Treitel Reader*, 3rd ed. Tulsa, Okla.: Seismograph Service Corp., 1973.

[88] A. P. Sage and J. L. Melsa, *System Identification.* New York: Academic Press, 1971.

[89] R. W. Schafer and L. R. Rabiner, "Digital representations of speech signals," this issue, pp. 662-677.

[90] F. C. Schweppe, *Uncertain Dynamic Systems.* Englewood Cliffs, N.J.: Prentice-Hall, 1973.

[91] J. L. Shanks, "Recursion filters for digital processing," *Geophysics*, vol. XXXII, no. 1, pp. 33-51, 1967.

[92] R. A. Silverman, "Locally stationary random processes," *IRE Trans. Inform. Theory*, vol. IT-3, pp. 182-187, Sept. 1957.

[93] G. Szegö, *Orthogonal Polynomials.* New York: Amer. Math. Soc. Colloquium Publ., vol. XXIII, N.Y., 1959.

[94] S. A. Tretter and K. Steiglitz, "Power-spectrum identification in terms of rational models," *IEEE Trans. Automat. Control*, vol. AC-12, pp. 185-188, Apr. 1967.

[95] J. M. Tribolet, "Identification of linear discrete systems with applications to speech processing," Master's thesis, Dep. Elec. Eng., M.I.T., Cambridge, Mass., Jan. 1974.

[96] A. Van den Bos, "Alternative interpretation of maximum entropy spectral analysis," *IEEE Trans. Inform. Theory*, vol. IT-17, pp. 493-494, July 1971.

[97] H. Wakita, "Direct estimation of the vocal tract shape by inverse filtering of acoustic speech waveforms," *IEEE Trans. Audio Electroacoust.*, vol. AU-21, pp. 417-427, Oct. 1973.

[98] G. Walker, "On periodicity in series of related terms," *Proc. Royal Soc.*, vol. 131-A, p. 518, 1931.

[99] R. J. Wang, "Optimum window length for the measurement of time-varying power spectra," *J. Acoust. Soc. Amer.*, vol. 52, no. 1 (part 1), pp. 33-38, 1971.

[100] R. J. Wang and S. Treitel, "The determination of digital Wiener filters by means of gradient methods," *Geophysics*, vol. 38, no. 2, pp. 310-326, Apr. 1973.

[101] P. D. Welch, "A direct digital method of power spectrum estimation," *IBM J. Res. Dev.*, vol. 5, pp. 141-156, Apr. 1961.

[102] A. Wennberg and L. H. Zetterberg, "Application of a computer-based model for EEG analysis," *Electroencephalogr. Clin. Neurophys.*, vol. 31, no. 5, pp. 457-468, 1971.

[103] P. Whittle, "Some recent contributions to the theory of stationary processes," Appendix 2, in H. Wold, *A Study in the Analysis of Stationary Time Series.* Stockholm, Sweden: Almqvist and Wiksell, 1954.

[104] ——, "On the fitting of multivariate autoregressions, and the approximate canonical factorization of a spectral density matrix," *Biometrika*, vol. 50, nos. 1 and 2, pp. 129-134, 1963.

[105] ——, *Prediction and Regulation by Linear Least Square Methods.* London, England: English Universities Press, 1963.

[106] B. Widrow, P. E. Mantey, L. J. Griffiths, and B. B. Goode, "Adaptive antenna systems," *Proc. IEEE*, vol. 55, pp. 2143-2159, Dec. 1967.

[107] N. Wiener, *Extrapolation, Interpolation and Smoothing of Stationary Time Series With Engineering Applications.* Cambridge, Mass.: M.I.T. Press, 1949.

[108] D. J. Wilde, *Optimum Seeking Methods.* Englewood Cliffs, N.J.: Prentice-Hall, 1964.

[109] J. H. Wilkinson, "Error analysis of direct methods of matrix inversion," *J. Ass. Comput. Mach.*, vol. 8, no. 3, pp. 281-330, 1961.

[110] ——, "The solution of ill-conditioned linear equations," in Ralston and Wilf, *Mathematical Methods for Digital Computers*, pp. 65-93, 1967.

[111] J. H. Wilkinson and C. Reinsch, *Linear Algebra*, vol. II. New York: Springer-Verlag, 1971.

[112] H. Wold, *A Study in the Analysis of Stationary Time Series.* Stockholm, Sweden: Almqvist and Wiksell, 1954.

[113] H. O. A. Wold, *Bibliography on Time Series and Stochastic Processes.* Cambridge, Mass.: M.I.T. Press, 1965.

[114] L. C. Wood and S. Treitel, "Seismic signal processing," this issue, pp. 649-661.

[115] G. U. Yule, "On a method of investigating periodicities in disturbed series, with special reference to Wolfer's sunspot numbers," *Phil. Trans. Roy. Soc.*, vol. 226-A, pp. 267-298, 1927.

Part III
Estimation of Excitation Parameters

This part is concerned with estimation of the excitation signal in the model for speech production. The papers are divided into two groups. The first group is concerned with schemes for estimating the "pitch period" or equivalently the fundamental frequency of voiced speech and for distinguishing between voiced and unvoiced speech. The second group of two papers is concerned with determining the glottal waveform for voiced speech in contrast to the more common approach of simple estimating the periodicity.

A. Pitch and Voicing Estimation

The first paper, by Gold and Rabiner, describes a pitch detection algorithm that introduces the principle of parallel processing in speech analysis. The basic idea of this scheme is that good performance can be obtained from crude measurements by combining a number of such measurements. The particular scheme presented in this paper requires little computation and thus the method is attractive for real-time operation.

The second paper, by Sondhi, focuses on the use of the short-time autocorrelation function for pitch detection. Specifically, Sondhi gives techniques for spectrum flattening; i.e., turning the speech waveform into a train of pulses whose autocorrelation function shows the periodicity in an unambiguous way. The basic principle of center clipping outlined here has been extensively studied [1] and utilized in a real-time hardware pitch detector [2]. The third paper, by Ross et al., describes a modification of the autocorrelation method called the average magnitude difference function (AMDF). Because the AMDF requires little computation it has been widely used in real-time digital systems.

The fourth paper, by Noll, details a pitch detection scheme based on the cepstrum (inverse Fourier transform of the logarithm of the magnitude of the short time Fourier transform). This method has been widely used, although its implementation requires considerable computation. The fifth paper, by Markel, describes an algorithm based upon spectrum flattening using an inverse filter obtained by linear predictive analysis. This paper gives a number of computational simplifications that facilitate real-time operation. A similar approach was described in [3]. The last of the pitch detection papers is by Rabiner et al. This paper describes an extensive experimental comparison and evaluation of all the pitch detection schemes described in this section (and others). The paper is a very useful guide to limitations and strengths of the various pitch detectors studied.

A fundamental problem of excitation analysis is the classification of speech as voiced or unvoiced. Generally this classification is built into the pitch detection algorithm as in all of the algorithms described by the papers of this section. Another approach is to consider the voiced/unvoiced decision separately from the pitch period estimation. An example of this approach is given in [4].

B. Estimation of the Glottal Waveform

In some cases it is of interest to obtain an estimate of the glottal waveform not just its period. This is the case, for example, in vocal pathology studies and in situations where it is desirable to separate the filtering effect of the vocal pulse shape from the filtering effect of the vocal tract transmittance.

In this area there are not nearly as many published papers as in pitch detection. The two papers given below, by Miller and Holmes respectively, are the basic papers in this field. Both papers describe inverse filtering approaches in which an inverse filter is obtained which cancels estimated formant resonances.

A paper by Rosenberg [5], is relevant to the topic of this section. That paper describes the use of the pitch synchronous analysis techniques of Mathews, Miller, and David (third paper of Part II) to obtain (and modify) the glottal wave shape. This paper, which is not included because it emphasizes perceptual effects rather than the analysis techniques, should be consulted by those interested in the importance of the glottal wave in speech analysis.

References

1. L. R. Rabiner, "On the use of autocorrelation analysis for pitch detection," *IEEE Trans. Acoust., Speech, and Signal Proc.,* vol. ASSP-25, pp. 22–33, Feb. 1977.
2. J. J. Dubnowski, R. W. Schafer, and L. R. Rabiner, "Real-time digital hardware pitch detector," *IEEE Trans. Acoust., Speech, and Signal Proc.,* vol. ASSP-24, pp. 2–8, Feb. 1976.
3. J. N. Maksym, "Real-time pitch extraction by adaptive prediction of the speech waveform," *IEEE Trans. Audio Electroacoust.,* vol. AU-21, pp. 149–153, June 1973.
4. B. S. Atal and L. R. Rabiner, "A pattern recognition approach to voiced-unvoiced classification with applications to speech recognition," *IEEE Trans. Acoust., Speech, and Signal Proc.,* vol. ASSP-24, pp. 201–212, June 1976.
5. A. E. Rosenberg, "Effect of glottal pulse shape on the quality of natural vowels," *J. Acoust. Soc. Am.,* vol. 49 (Pt. 2), pp. 583–590, Feb. 1971.

Received 3 February 1969

Parallel Processing Techniques for Estimating Pitch Periods of Speech in the Time Domain

B. Gold

MIT Lincoln Laboratory, Lexington, Massachusetts 02173

L. Rabiner

Bell Telephone Laboratories, Incorporated, Murray Hill, New Jersey 07974

A computational algorithm for estimating pitch periods of speech in the time domain is presented, and two recent modifications of the algorithm are discussed in detail. The algorithm and its modifications have been found to be relatively accurate and efficient in tests on real and synthetic speech.

INTRODUCTION

H. Dudley's[1-3] invention of the vocoder in the mid-1930's initiated work in the still expanding technical area of speech analysis–synthesis systems. Dudley described the speech signal in terms of an excitation function and the shape of the short time spectrum. In this formulation, an important excitation parameter is fundamental voice frequency, or its inverse, which is called the pitch period.

A major obstacle to the use of vocoders in practical systems has been the accurate estimation of pitch period. Precise estimation of the voice fundamental frequency appears to be necessary to synthesize speech of acceptable quality. Hundreds of pitch-period estimation schemes have been proposed and tested; an excellent survey of much of this work appears in McKinney.[4] The need for an accurate and versatile pitch-period measurement was recognized for many years at the Bell Telephone Laboratories and led to the development of voice-excited vocoder techniques,[5-7] wherein improved excitation was attained at the cost of increased bandwidth.

A. Parallel Estimates

In the early 1960's, the idea of designing a pitch-period estimator based on parallel processing techniques was developed at Lincoln Laboratory.[8,9] The basic idea in parallel processing was that an improvement in accuracy could be obtained by suitably combining the outputs of more than one elementary pitch-period estimator. Parallel processing also seemed appropriate because it appeared similar to the human processing associated with estimation of pitch period from visual inspection of the speech wave. Selfridge (in a personal communication to Gold) and Doyle[10] were strong advocates of parallelism in electronic decision-making equipment, and Minsky (in an unpublished internal MIT report) performed some early experiments on parallel processing for pitch-period estimation. Gill[11] developed a pitch-period measurement based on correlation and joined three such systems in parallel to form a pitch-

[1] H. Dudley, "Remaking Speech," J. Acoust. Soc. Amer. 11, 169–177 (1939).
[2] H. Dudley, "The Vocoder," Bell Lab. Record 18, 122–126 (1939).
[3] H. Dudley, "The Carrier Nature of Speech," Bell System Tech. J. 19, 495–515 (1940).
[4] N. P. McKinney, "Laryngeal Frequency Analysis for Linguistic Research," Rep. No. 14, Univ. of Michigan, Commun. Sci. Lab. (1965).
[5] M. R. Schroeder, "Recent Progress in Speech Coding at Bell Telephone Laboratories," Proc. Int. Congr. Acoust., 3rd, Stuttgart, 201–210 (1959).
[6] E. E. David, Jr., M. R. Schroeder, B. F. Logan, and A. J. Prestigiacomo, "New Applications of Voice Excitation to Vocoders," Speech Commun. Seminar, Stockholm (1962).
[7] B. Gold and J. Tierney, "Digitized Voice-Excited Vocoder for Telephone-Quality Inputs Using Bandpass Sampling of the Baseband Signal," J. Acoust. Soc. Amer. 37, 753–754 (1965).
[8] B. Gold, "Computer Program for Pitch Extraction," J. Acoust. Soc. Amer. 34, 916–921 (1962).
[9] B. Gold, "Description of a Computer Program for Pitch Detection," Proc. Int. Congr. Acoust., 4th, Copenhagen (1962), Paper G34.
[10] W. Doyle, "Recognition of Sloppy, Hand Printed Characters," Fall Joint Computer Conf., 133–142 (1960).
[11] J. S. Gill, "Estimation of Larynx-Pulse Timing During Speech," Proc. Int. Congr. Acoust., 4th, Copenhagen (1962), Paper G33.

Reprinted with permission from *J. Acoust. Soc. Am.*, vol. 46, pp. 442–448, Aug. 1969.

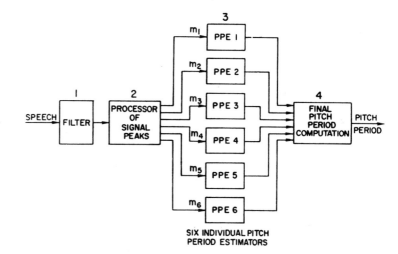

FIG. 1. Block diagram of pitch-period estimation algorithm.

period estimator. In both the above schemes, however, processing following the parallel pitch-period measurements was rudimentary. In distinction, the schemes to be described in this paper tend to simplify the parallel detectors, but employ relatively sophisticated algorithms to process the parallel pitch-period outputs.

The first parallel processing scheme developed by Gold[8] was a computer program using three parallel pitch-period estimators. This scheme processed a full band speech waveform, and used peakedness and regularity tests to estimate pitch periods. A relatively elementary combiner algorithm was used to determine the final pitch-period estimate.

Following this first attempt, a pitch-period estimator based on combinations of six simple pitch-period estimators and suitable majority logic was developed at Lincoln Laboratory.[9,12] This parallel processing scheme differed significantly from the earlier one in almost all aspects. A low-pass-filtered waveform is processed rather than the full-band speech; the measurements of the individual detectors are of the peak-to-peak and peak-to-valley type; and a sophisticated coincidence detector is used as part of the final decision algorithm. This scheme was both simulated on a digital computer, and built into a hardware device. This device has been used successfully in several Lincoln vocoder systems[13,14] and outside of Lincoln,[15] but is generally considered to be too intricate and costly a device for general usage. Recent advances in integrated circuit components, however, appear to be eliminating this problem.

B. Computer Estimation of Pitch Period

Recently there has arisen need for fast, efficient pitch-period estimation schemes for use on a digital computer to aid in the investigation of pitch contours of speech.[16,17] In order to process large numbers of data on a digital computer, real-time (or close to it) operation of such an algorithm is a necessity. Powerful pitch-period measurements based on spectral analyses of speech have been invented,[18,19] but computer simulations of these techniques require 100 or more times real time to run and hence are unsuitable for these intended applications. With these problems in mind, the search for a fast computer program and an efficient hardware realization led to two modified, and appreciably simpler, versions of Gold's second parallel processing algorithm (henceforth referred to as the original algorithm). It is the intent of this paper to describe in detail the original algorithm, to describe the two simplified modifications, and to show the results of some measurements.

I. ORIGINAL ALGORITHM

The algorithm can be conveniently divided into four parts, as shown in Fig. 1.

1. Filtering of the speech signal.
2. Generation of six functions of the peaks of the filtered speech signal.
3. Six identical "simple" pitch-period estimators, each working on one of the above six functions.
4. Final pitch-period computation, based on examination of the results from each "simple" pitch-period estimator.

[12] N. L. Daggett, "A Computer for Vocoder Pitch Extraction," Tech. Note 1966-3, Lincoln Laboratory, Lexington (1966).
[13] J. Tierney et al., "Channel Vocoder with Digital Pitch Extractor," J. Acoust. Soc. Amer. 36, 1901–1905 (1964).
[14] J. Tierney and J. N. Harris, "The Lincoln Laboratory Experimental Terminal Channel Vocoder," IEEE Comm. Conv. Boulder, Colorado, 531–534 (1965).
[15] Final Rep., "Digital Pitch Vocoder," Prime Contract No. AF19 (628)-5167, Subcontract No. 361, Philco N. 2452 prepared for MIT Lincoln Lab. (1968).

[16] H. Levitt and L. R. Rabiner, "Analysis of Fundamental Frequency Contours," J. Acoust. Soc. Amer. 45, 317 (A) (1969).
[17] R. J. Scholes, "On the Spoken Disambiguation of Superficially Ambiguous Sentences," Bell Lab. Memorandum (1968) (unpublished).
[18] A. M. Noll, "Cepstral Pitch Determination," J. Acoust. Soc. Amer. 41, 293–309 (1967).
[19] M. R. Schroeder, "Period Histogram and Product Spectrum: New Methods for Fundamental Frequency Measurement," J. Acoust. Soc. Amer. 43, 829–834 (1968).

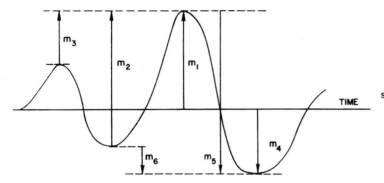

FIG. 2. Basic measurements made on the filtered speech.

Referring to Fig. 1, the primary purpose of the filter is to select approximately the first formant region. No other information is necessary, and peaks caused by higher formants tend to reduce the accuracy of subsequent pitch detection. If the input speech contains the fundamental frequency, a low-pass filter with 36 dB per octave falloff beyond 600 Hz works well, although the precise cutoff and specific filter design are not critical. Of course, care should be taken to eliminate 60- and 120-Hz hum, for example, with a high-pass filter of about 100-Hz cutoff. In the event that no fundamental is expected to be present (the speech having previously been sent through a telephone cable, for example), a bandpass filter from 300 to 900 Hz is suitable, so that at least two higher harmonics of the speech are processed. For applications (with fundamental present) where the highest fundamental frequency to be processed is lower than 600 Hz, the low-pass filter cutoff can be reduced. However, if the cutoff frequency is reduced to about 250 Hz, a noticeable change appears in the estimated pitch periods and this has been shown to produce vocoded speech with a rough quality.[20] Also, in the case when no fundamental is present and nonlinear elements are used to regenerate the fundamental, these same effects occur; i.e., the vocoder speech has a noticeably rough quality.

The second block in Fig. 1 is explained by reference to Fig. 2. Pulses of height m_1, m_2, and m_3 are generated at every positive peak of the filtered speech while pulses of height m_4, m_5, and m_6 are generated at each negative peak. Measurements m_1 and m_4 are simple peak (positive and negative) measurements, whereas measurements m_2, m_3, m_5, and m_6 depend on previous peaks of the speech. Measurements m_2 and m_5 are peak-to-valley and valley-to-peak measurements whereas m_3 and m_6 are peak-to-previous-peak and valley-to-previous-valley measurements. All the m's are converted into positive pulse trains. Measurements m_3 and m_6 are not permitted to become negative. Hence, if a current peak (or valley) is not as large as the previous peak (or valley) measurement m_3 (or m_6) is set to zero.

[20] A. J. Goldberg, "Vocoded Speech in the Absence of the Laryngeal Fundamental," MS thesis, MIT (1967).

The choice of this particular set of measurements was based on consideration of two extreme cases as seen in Fig. 3. For the case when only the fundamental is present [Fig. 3(a)], measurements m_3 and m_6 fail but measurements m_1, m_2, m_4, and m_5 provide strong indications of the period. For the case when a very strong second harmonic, and some fundamental, are present [Fig. 3(b)], measurements m_3 and m_6 will probably be correct; whereas m_1, m_2, m_4, and m_5 will incorrectly provide indications of half the period. Although measurements m_1, m_2, m_4, and m_5 may fail, it is shown below how the final computation has high probability of being correct.

To estimate the pitch period accurately enough for a vocoder requires that the positions of the peaks of the filtered speech be accurate to within 100 μsec. Thus if the algorithm were performed digitally, a 10-kHz sampling rate would be required.

The six sets of pulse trains are applied to the six individual pitch detectors as shown in Fig. 1. The operation of the detector is illustrated in Fig. 4. In essence, each simple pitch-period estimator is a peak-detecting rundown circuit. As seen in Fig. 4, following each detected pulse there is a blanking interval (during which no pulses can be detected) followed by a simple exponential decay. Whenever a pulse exceeds the level of the rundown circuit (during the decay), it is detected

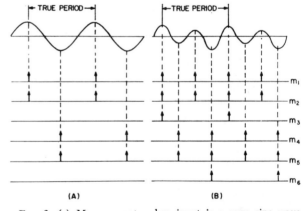

FIG. 3. (a) Measurements when input is a pure sine wave. Measurements m_1, m_2, m_4, and m_5 are correct. (b) Measurements when input contains a strong second harmonic and some fundamental. Measurements m_3 and m_6 are correct, whereas m_1, m_2, m_4, and m_5 are incorrect.

and the rundown circuit is reset. It should be noted that both the rundown time constant and the blanking time of each detector are functions of the smoothed estimate of pitch period, P_{av}, of that detector. P_{av} is derived from the iteration

$$P_{av}(n) = [P_{av}(n-1) + P_{new}]/2,$$

where P_{new} is the most recent estimate of pitch period; $P_{av}(n)$ is the current smoothed estimate of pitch period; $P_{av}(n-1)$ is the previous smoothed estimate of pitch period. Each time a new peak is detected, P_{av} is updated according to the iteration. To prevent extremes of value of blanking time or rundown time constant, P_{av} is limited to be greater than 4 msec and less than 10 msec. Within these limits, the dependence of blanking time τ and rundown time constant β on P_{av} is given by

$$\tau = 0.4 P_{av},$$

$$\beta = P_{av}/0.695.$$

The final computation of pitch period is performed by Block 4 of Fig. 1, which may be thought of as a special purpose computer, with a memory, an arithmetic algorithm and control hardware to steer all the incoming signals. At any time t_0 an estimate of pitch period is made by:

1. Forming a 6×6 matrix of estimates of pitch period. The columns of the matrix represent the individual detectors and the rows are estimates of period. The first three rows are the three most recent estimates of period. The fourth row is a sum of the first and second rows; the fifth row is the sum of the second and third rows; and the sixth row is a sum of the first three rows. The technique for forming the matrix is illustrated in Fig. 5. The reason for the last three rows of the matrix is that sometimes the individual detectors will indicate second or third harmonic rather than fundamental and it will be entries in the last three rows which are correct rather than the three most recent estimates of pitch period.

2. Comparing each of the entries in the first row of the matrix to the other 35 entries of the matrix and counting the number of coincidences. (A precise definition of coincidence is given below.) That particular $P_{i1} (i=1,2,3,4,5,6)$ that is most popular (greatest number of coincidences) is used as the final estimate of pitch period.

Now, a few words about "coincidence." *First*, to determine whether two pitch-period estimates "coin-

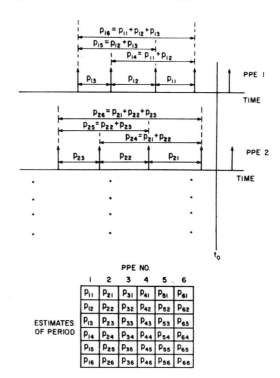

FIG. 5. Final estimation of pitch period. A matrix of estimates of pitch period is formed from the outputs of the six individual pitch-period estimators. Each of the entries of the first row of the matrix is a candidate for the final estimate.

cide" it seems more appropriate to observe their ratios rather than their differences. However, the ratio measurement can be very approximate to avoid the need of a divide computation. *Second*, because during many parts of the speech there are sizable variations of successive pitch-period measurements, it is useful to include several threshold values to define coincidence, and then try to select, for each over-all pitch-period computation, the threshold which yields the most consistent answer. With this explanation, we now define the computation of Block 4 of Fig. 1.

Figure 6 shows a table of 16 coincidence window widths. As indicated in Fig. 5, only the most recent estimated pitch period from a given detector is a "candidate" for final choice. This candidate is thus one of six possible choices for the "correct" pitch period. To determine the "winner," each candidate is numerically compared with all of the remaining 35 pitch numbers. This comparison is repeated four times, corre-

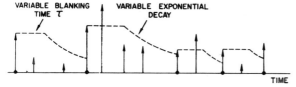

FIG. 4. Operation of the detection circuit which consists of a variable blanking time during which no pulses are accepted, followed by a variable exponential rundown.

FIG. 6. Table of coincidence window widths as a function of pitch period and bias.

PITCH PERIOD RANGE (msec)	BIAS			
	1	2	5	7
1.6–3.1	1	2	3	4
3.1–6.3	2	4	6	8
6.3–12.7	4	8	12	16
12.7–25.5	8	16	24	32

COINCIDENCE WINDOW WIDTH IN HUNDREDS OF MICROSECONDS

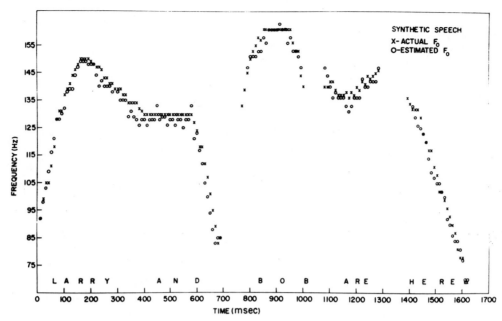

FIG. 7. Comparison between fundamental frequency estimates obtained using the modified algorithm and the true values for synthetic speech.

sponding to each column in the table of Fig. 6. From each column, the appropriate window width is chosen as a function of the estimate associated with the candidate. Thus, if this estimate, for example, were 4 msec, coincidence between the candidate and any compared interval would mean that their difference was less than or equal to $\pm 200 \mu$sec. After the number of coincidences is tabulated, a bias of 1 is subtracted from that number. The measurement is then repeated for the second column; this time the windows are wider, increasing the probability of coincidence, but, in compensation, a bias of 2 is subtracted from the compilation. After the computation has been repeated in this way for all four columns, the largest biased number is used as the number of coincidences that represents that particular pitch-period estimate. The entire procedure is now repeated for the remaining five candidates, and the winner is chosen to be that number with the greatest number of biased coincidences. In the course of this computation, a total of $6 \times 4 \times 35$ coincidence measurements (comparison of the magnitude of a difference with a fixed number) has to be made. Repetition of the complete computation every 5 msec suffices to follow even rapid pitch-period variations. The use of this computation for the voiced–unvoiced decision has been discussed in a previous paper.[21] It is interesting to note that the algorithm described above can operate effectively even when the background acoustic noise level is very high. In one informal but striking experiment, the level on a white-noise generator was turned up so that the speaker could not hear himself talk into the handset connected

to the vocoder; yet his conversation was completely intelligible to the listener. Unfortunately, in this experiment, no quantitative measurements were made.

II. MODIFICATION TO PITCH ALGORITHM

A. First Modification

The approximate execution time of the algorithm described above was about 50 times real time on a moderately fast computer (Lincoln Lab. TX-2). Since it was desired to speed up the program and limit the range of fundamental frequency to about 220 Hz (thus implying that male speech will be best suited for analysis), the following modifications were made:

1. Replace the sampled-data low-pass filter with an analog filter and, instead, sample the low-pass filtered

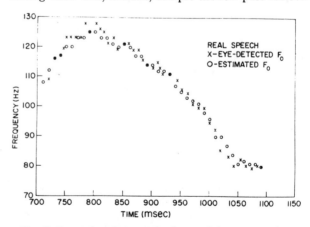

FIG. 8. Comparison between fundamental frequency estimates obtained using the modified algorithm and values detected by eye for natural speech.

[21] B. Gold, "Note on Buzz–Hiss Detection," J. Acoust. Soc. Amer. 36, 1659–1661 (1964).

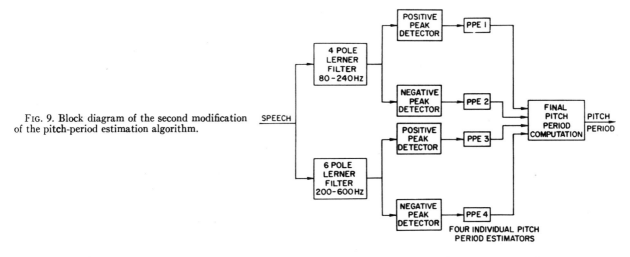

FIG. 9. Block diagram of the second modification of the pitch-period estimation algorithm.

speech at 10 kHz. A standard Allison 2BR filter (36 dB/oct rolloff) with low-frequency cutoff of 70 Hz and high-frequency cutoff of 600 Hz was used.

2. Use a fixed blanking-time and rundown-time constant independent of the smoothed estimate of pitch period. Values used for this modification were 3 msec blanking time and 5.2 msec as the rundown-circuit time constant. These values were chosen to yield good results for an anticipated average fundamental frequency of 125 Hz.

3. Use only a single set of coincidence measurements, based on differences in period rather than ratios. Since the range of pitch period allowed was much smaller than the original algorithm was designed for, a single coincidence measurement was experimentally shown capable of providing good results over the interval of interest. A coincidence measurement of ± 300 μsec was used. The range of pitch periods considered was about 5–14 msec (corresponding to F_0 values from 70 to 200 Hz). Using a single coincidence measurement eliminated the complicated search procedure for the current estimate of period.

These modifications were programmed into the original algorithm and tested on many examples of real and synthetic speech. The program was written in FORTRAN IV for a GE 635 computer and was found to be exceedingly fast in operation. The execution time of the program was about 1.3 to 1.5 times real time. This feature and the accuracy in estimating pitch period are the strong points of the algorithm which make it extremely attractive from a research standpoint. For those projects where the efficient extraction of an F_0 contour is of importance[16,17] the speed of computation of this modified algorithm is much faster than comparable techniques for extracting fundamental frequency such as the cepstrum[18] or autocorrelation techniques.[22]

Examples of fundamental frequency estimation using this modified algorithm are shown in Figs. 7 and 8.

[22] B. S. Atal, "Automatic Speaker Recognition Based on Pitch Contours," J. Acoust. Soc. Amer. 45, 309 (A) (1969).

Figure 7 shows an example of fundamental frequency estimation from synthetic speech. The reason for using synthetic speech is that values of F_0 are known in advance and this provides a measure of the accuracy of the algorithm. Figure 7 shows that the algorithm does a good job in tracking values of F_0 over a fairly wide range (70 to 150 Hz). Estimates of F_0 are generally within ± 2 Hz of the true values, although occasionally the differences get larger. Another observation from Fig. 7 is that at the start (and occasionally at the cessation) of voicing, there is often no estimate of F_0 indicating that the number of coincidences is small. An unvoiced indication is the result until voicing has occurred long enough for the number of coincidences to exceed the threshold for voicing. This usually occurs within 20–30 msec after the initiation of voicing. Figure 8 shows a comparison between F_0 estimated by the modified algorithm and an eye-detected version from real speech. A single voiced interval of 0.4 sec duration was used as a basis of comparison. Clearly, the eye-detected and estimated values of F_0 are in good agreement throughout the interval. No quantitative estimates can be made on the basis of Fig. 8 as there are no estimates as to the accuracy of eye-detected pitch periods. In fact, in one experiment it was reported that pitch-period data automatically extracted using the original algorithm was favored over eye-detected pitch periods by about 2 to 1, in a preference test when listening to speech synthesized on the Lincoln Laboratory vocoder.[20]

B. Second Modification

If it is required only to measure fundamental frequencies below 300 Hz, another simplification of the basic algorithm is possible, along the following lines:

1. The filtering of the speech signal is made more selective.

2. The number of pitch-period estimators is reduced to four.

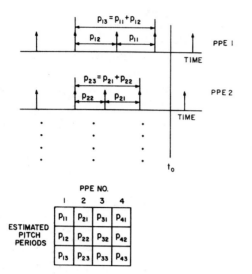

FIG. 10. Final estimation of pitch period for the second modification.

3. The blanking-time and rundown-time constants are fixed as in the first modification.

4. Two, rather than three pitch intervals are saved from each estimator.

5. The biasing system shown in Fig. 6 is eliminated, so that only one of the columns shown is necessary, as for the first modification.

Following is a description of how these changes were effected.

Lerner filters are designed by specifying the pole positions and residues.[23,24] Thus, the four-pole filter in Fig. 9 has the pole positions 80, 120, 200, and 240 Hz, each 80 Hz to the left of the $j\omega$ axis with the corresponding residues of $\frac{1}{2}$, -1, $+1$, $-\frac{1}{2}$. The six-pole filter has pole positions at 200, 250, 350, 450, 550, 600 Hz with damping frequency 100 Hz and residues $\frac{1}{2}$, -1, $+1$, -1, $+1$, $-\frac{1}{2}$. The peak detectors shown in Fig. 9 merely locate and measure the heights of the negative and positive peaks of the two incident waveforms.

[23] R. M. Lerner, "Band-Pass Filters with Linear Phase," Proc. IEEE 52, 249–268 (1964).

[24] P. R. Drouilhet, Jr., and L. M. Goodman, "Pole-Shared Linear Phase Band-Pass Filter Bank," Proc. IEEE 54, 701–703 (1966).

Pitch periods are estimated from the four pulse trains by four identical detectors which operate in the same manner as those of Fig. 1 but are now simplified to have a fixed 2-msec blanking time and a fixed rundown with time constant adjusted to run down to half the initial value in 5 msec. (Note that rundown does not begin until blanking has terminated.) Also, each detector is reset if the rundown time exceeds 16 msec, to a level of about 20 dB below the maximum permissible rundown signal.

The basic memory store for the final computation consists of 12 pitch-period estimates, three from each detector, as shown in Fig. 10. There are now only four "candidates." Selection is again made on the basis of the most "popular" candidate, but the bias system is removed and coincidence is defined by the inequality $|p_c - p_i| < \frac{1}{8} p_i$.

Buzz–hiss information is obtainable on the basis of two measurements. If, during the coincidence measurements, two or more of the candidate periods are 16 msec (which implies that they have been reset), a hiss decision is made. Also, if the number of coincidences attained by the winner is fewer than four, a hiss decision is made.

III. CONCLUSION

A parallel processing algorithm (and two modifications) for estimating pitch periods of speech was presented and explained in detail. One of the main features of this algorithm is that the outputs of individual pitch-period estimators are combined to produce highly accurate results. The original algorithm appears to work quite well when the speaker is in a noisy environment. Furthermore, performance remains good when the voice fundamental frequency is not present.

The execution time for a programmed version of the first modification is very much less than other standard techniques for estimating pitch periods. This modification appears to be as effective as the original algorithm provided that the voice fundamental frequency is present and is lower than about 220 Hz. The second modification leads to an appreciably simpler hardware realization than the original algorithm, and performs comparably provided that the voice fundamental frequency remains below 300 Hz.

New Methods of Pitch Extraction

MAN MOHAN SONDHI

Abstract—Three new methods will be described for the extraction of the fundamental pitch from a speech signal. These are: 1) spectrum flattening followed by a minimum phase correction to synchronize harmonics, 2) spectrum flattening followed by autocorrelation, and 3) nonlinear distortion followed by autocorrelation.

The last two methods will be shown to be exceptionally rugged, in that they can tolerate a considerable amount of high-pass filtering and additive noise with little degradation in performance.

Manuscript received September 28, 1967. This paper was presented at the 1967 Conference on Speech Communication and Processing, Cambridge, Mass.

The author is with Bell Telephone Laboratories Inc., Murray Hill, N. J.

I. Introduction

A LARGE proportion of present-day vocoders are based upon the analysis of a speech signal into an excitation signal and a vocal tract transfer function. Both the excitation and the transfer function are then described in terms of a small number of slowly varying parameters, from which an estimate of the original speech wave is synthesized. There is need for improvement in our descriptions of both the transfer function as well as the excitation. However, the remarkably small degradation of speech quality in a voice-excited vocoder[1] indicates that the greater need is for an improved parametric representation of the excitation.

Traditionally, the excitation is regarded as consisting of intervals that are either voiced (v) or unvoiced (uv). Such a v/uv dichotomy is clearly an oversimplification, as indicated, for instance, by the existence of voiced fricatives. However, it is generally accepted that many improvements in our methods of deriving the excitation signal are possible, even without the embellishment of partial voicing.

We will use the term pitch extractor for a device or algorithm which makes a v/uv decision, and, during periods of voicing, gives an indication of the pitch period (or the fundamental frequency). In this paper, we describe three out of a number of pitch extractors considered by the author during the past few years. Our only apology for adding to the already large list of methods for pitch extraction described in the literature[2] is that the methods described here are based upon promising new ideas not previously reported.

The basic notion common to all three pitch extractors described here is the following. If the harmonics of the fundamental frequency could be made equal in amplitude and put into phase synchronism with each other, the resulting waveform would be a train of highly peaked pulses, and the interval between these pulses would correspond to the current pitch period. During unvoiced intervals, no such pulse train would obtain and, thus, a v/uv decision could be based upon the presence or absence of the pulse train.

We turn now to a method for equalizing amplitudes of the harmonics. This will form the basic element for the first two of our pitch extractors.

II. The Spectrum Flattener

Due to the variability of the fundamental frequency and of the formants, no fixed equalizer can adequately equalize the amplitudes of the harmonics. What is needed is a system that dynamically adapts to the varying spectrum. A block diagram of one such scheme is shown in Fig. 1. The speech signal is filtered through a bank of n band-pass filters (approximately 100-Hz wide) $F_1, \cdots, F_n$, which span the bandwidth of the

Reprinted from *IEEE Trans. Audio Electroacoust.*, vol. AU–16, pp. 262–266, June 1968.

153

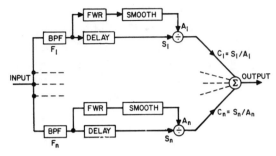

Fig. 1.   Schematic of spectrum flattener.

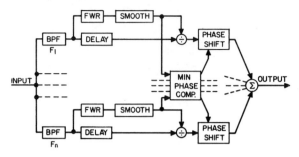

Fig. 3.   Schematic of spectrum flattener with minimum phase compensation.

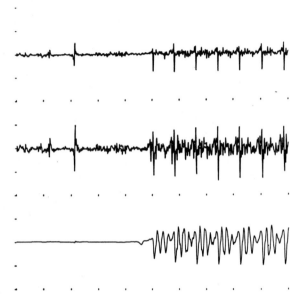

Fig. 2.   Example of spectrum flattening (middle trace), spectrum flattening and minimum phase compensation (upper trace). The lowest trace is the original speech. The total duration is 100 ms.

signal. The output of the filter F_i is fed to a full-wave rectifier and to a delay line. The full-wave rectifier output is smoothed to give a short-time estimate A_i of the amplitude of the output of F_i. The signal S_i is the output of F_i delayed by an amount D to compensate for the delay of the smoothing filter. The signal $C_i = S_i/A_i$ is, thus, the output of F_i normalized to unit amplitude. The processing of the channels 1 through n is identical. The signals C_i are summed to give the desired flat spectrum signal. An example of such a spectrum flattening is shown in Fig. 2, where the lowermost trace is the original speech input, and the middle trace is the spectrum flattened version. The voiced intervals, as expected, show up as trains of rather peaked pulses. No such peaking occurs in unvoiced intervals.

The basic objective of spectrum flattening can be achieved in ways other than the one shown in Fig. 1. Thus, for example, the Hilbert envelopes of the signals S_i can be used as estimates of amplitude A_i; or the signals S_i can be infinitely clipped and refiltered through filters identical to the F_i.

III. PITCH EXTRACTION BY MINIMUM PHASE COMPENSATION OF SPECTRUM FLATTENED SPEECH

As remarked in Section I, the fundamental periodicity would be rendered much more detectable if the equal-amplitude harmonics could be phase synchronized. The following method suggests itself. The amplitude estimates A_i $(i=1, \cdots, n)$ provide n equally spaced samples of the short-time spectrum of the speech signal. There exists a unique minimum phase network which has this amplitude response, and whose phase response can be readily computed.[3] Approximate synchronization can be achieved by phase shifting each of the signals C_i by an amount equal and opposite to the minimum phase computed for the ith channel. This is illustrated in Fig. 3. The phase shifting may be implemented by adding the proper proportions of C_i and a signal in phase quadrature to C_i. (The signal $dC_i/d(w_{0i}t)$ is a good approximation to the quadrature signal, where w_{0i} is the center frequency of the ith filter.)

The uppermost trace in Fig. 2 is an example of speech processed this way. The pitch markers turned out to be much sharper than we had anticipated. We must hasten to add, however, that the method is not always as successful. It is clear that the minimum phase assumption is not always valid, e.g., for nasalized vowels and whenever the glottal pulse shapes are not well approximated by the impulse response of a minimum phase network. Therefore, this method does not appear to be well suited for use as a part of a vocoder system. Nevertheless, it is an interesting approach, and could be a useful laboratory tool for providing synchronous pitch markers.

IV. PITCH EXTRACTION BY AUTOCORRELATION OF SPECTRUM FLATTENED SPEECH

Another method that we have successfully used to synchronize the harmonics is autocorrelation of the output of a spectrum flattener. The idea of autocorrelation is not new, and has been used both for pitch extraction as well as various other applications where an indication of periodicity is desired. However, the preprocessing by the spectrum flattener makes this type of pitch ex-

obtained in this manner is shown in Fig. 4. (To make a better visual display, the correlation functions were half-wave rectified and squared before plotting.[1])

The peaks in the correlation function corresponding to the pitch period are readily picked up. However, to ensure that peaks are not missed during rapid vocal tract transitions and during the trailing portions of voiced intervals, a decision algorithm is used. This algorithm and the method used for generating slowly varying parameters to describe the v/uv decision and the pitch will be discussed after a description of the third pitch extractor.

V. Pitch Extraction by Center Clipping and Autocorrelation

As shown in Section IV, autocorrelation of a speech signal, after removal of the formant structure, is a powerful method of pitch extraction. We have successfully tried another way of removing formant structure, namely, center clipping. The center clipped speech signal is obtained in the manner illustrated in Fig. 5. In every 5-ms interval, the maximum absolute value a_0 of the signal is found, and all portions of the signal between $\pm k a_0$ are removed. Typically, k is chosen to be about 0.3. Autocorrelation functions for this center clipped signal are then computed as in Section IV. A sample of traces of correlation functions obtained from center-clipped speech is shown in Fig. 6.

Center clipping of speech was first used by Licklider and Pollack[6] in an experiment in which they showed that, whereas speech that has been infinitely peak-clipped is highly intelligible, even a few percent of center clipping drastically reduces intelligibility. The explanation is not hard to find. Whereas infinite peak-clipping retains the formants of the speech signal (although it introduces a few secondary "formants"), center clipping destroys formant structure, while retaining the periodicity. It is the removal of formant structure that is so important for a good pitch extractor.

Center clipping, as seen from Fig. 6, is an efficient and exceedingly simple way of formant removal. In conjunction with an autocorrelator and the decision algorithm (to be described in Section VI), it provides a very good pitch extractor. In at least one type of situation, it works more reliably than spectrum flattening, or even the more elaborate cepstrum pitch extractor. This is the case when a voiced segment of speech becomes almost sinusoidal. (This occurs, for example, if the speech signal is the sound /i/ spoken by a female and high-pass filtered with a cutoff at about 200 or 300 Hz. This is not a very unusual situation if the speech has traveled over an ordinary telephone circuit.) Since the success of both the cepstrum and the spectrum

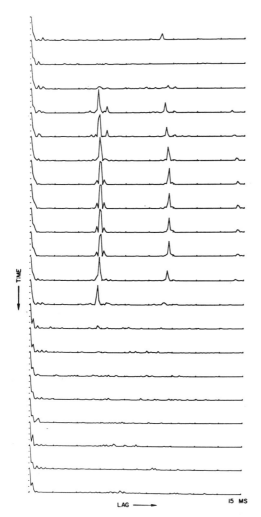

Fig. 4. Sample of correlation functions. Each trace is the correlation function of a 30-ms segment of spectrum flattened speech with a 15-ms overlap with the preceding and succeeding segments.

tractor highly reliable. To our knowledge, the only other type of preprocessing tried with autocorrelation pitch extractors is infinite peak-clipping.[4] This results in a binary signal which considerably simplifies the implementation of the correlator. However, as is well known, infinite peak clipping does not remove the formant structure of the speech, and the peaks in the correlation function due to formants are difficult to distinguish from those due to the fundamental periodicity. The spectrum flattened signal is, on the other hand, virtually devoid of formant structure, and its correlation function has no discernible peaks due to formants.

The correlation function is computed as follows. A 30-ms segment of the spectrally flattened speech signal is isolated and multiplied by a Hamming window.[5] The autocorrelation of this truncated segment is computed for lags up to 15 ms and normalized to unity for zero lag. Another 30-ms segment of the signal is selected with a 15-ms overlap with the previous segment, and the process continued. A sample of successive traces

[1] The length of the analysis intervals is not critical. We have successfully tried 40-ms analysis intervals with a 30-ms overlap between consecutive intervals.

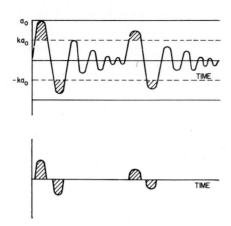

Fig. 5. Illustration of the process of center clipping.

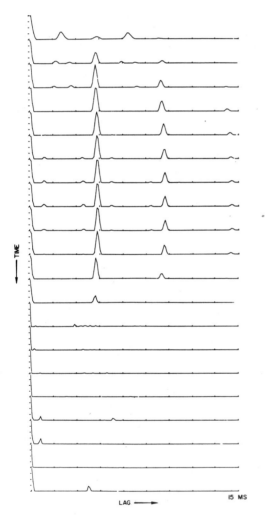

Fig. 6. Sample of correlation functions. Each trace is the correlation function of a 30-ms segment of center clipped speech with a 15-ms overlap with the preceding and succeeding segments.

flattener depends upon the presence of a large number of harmonics, these types of pitch extractors are prone to error in such cases. The absence of a large number of harmonics clearly is not a serious problem for the center-clipping method.

VI. THE DECISION ALGORITHM

A relatively simple algorithm suffices to pick the correlation peaks corresponding to the pitch period during voiced intervals, and to make the v/uv decision. The algorithm is adapted from the one used by Noll for his cepstrum pitch extractor.[7] Since it has been described in detail in his paper, only the main points are summarized here.

1) Each correlation trace of the type shown in Figs. 4 and 6 is the basis of a decision which applies to 15 ms of the speech.

2) The correlation functions are weighted to emphasize peaks at large lags (mainly to offset the effect of the Hamming window). The weighting function was determined by trial and error, and is essentially a linear weighting.

3) A threshold is preset, and the location of the first peak in the correlation function exceeding this threshold is accepted as the pitch for the corresponding 15-ms interval. (No acceptable peak indicates an unvoiced interval.)

4) The decision for the current interval (say B) is modified by the decisions for the preceding and succeeding intervals (say A and C, respectively). If A and C are voiced (unvoiced), then B is forced to be declared voiced (unvoiced). If A and C have approximately equal pitch, and the pitch for B differs by more than 60 percent, then the pitch for B is declared to be the average of A and C. If two successive intervals show a large departure from the pitch for preceding intervals, it is accepted as a genuine large change.

5) If a pitch peak is found for one 15-ms interval, the threshold for the succeeding intervals is lowered by a factor of 2 over a ± 1-ms region around the peak. The original threshold is restored if the pitch changes or the voicing interval ends.

These features eliminate the occasional errors of pitch doubling, spurious voicing, and spurious unvoicing that would otherwise arise.

VII. TESTS AND CONCLUSIONS

It is clear that the two preceding pitch extractors can tolerate considerable high-pass filtering of the input signal, as well as addition of broadband noise. In fact, the traces of Fig. 4 were obtained from speech filtered through a band-pass filter from 250 to 3250 Hz, and those of Fig. 6 were obtained from speech similarly filtered with additive white noise at a signal-to-noise ratio of about 18 dB.

As a test of the use of these pitch extractors in vocoder systems, the output of the decision algorithm was converted to two vocoder signals. The first signal had a value 0 during unvoiced intervals, and 1 during voiced intervals. The second signal had a constant value for each 15-ms interval, corresponding to the pitch for that interval. These two signals were low-pass filtered to

SONDHI: PITCH EXTRACTION

about 33 Hz. These low-pass signals (*A* and *B*, respectively) were then converted to an excitation signal as follows. Whenever *A* exceeded $\frac{1}{2}$ (indicating an unvoiced interval), the excitation consisted of white Gaussian noise. In the voiced intervals, pitch pulses were obtained by means of a ramp signal of constant slope. Whenever the ramp reached the level of signal *B*, a pitch pulse was generated, the ramp was reset to zero, and the sequence was repeated as often as necessary until the end of the voiced interval. Excitation signals generated in this manner were used with a 13-channel vocoder simulated by Golden.[8]

The resulting resynthesized speech was judged excellent by listeners in informal listening tests. None of the usual troubles of pitch doubling and loss of the trailing portions of voiced intervals was noticeable.

In conclusion, we might mention that we have tested the pitch extractors by computer simulation. We have tested them on a number of male and female voices, with speech signals that have been high-pass filtered and have additive white noise, and with signals that have been recorded over a telephone line. Computer simulation is not an entirely adequate test of these systems; however, the success so far indicates them to be worthy of extensive study on hardware models based upon the simulations.

REFERENCES

[1] M. R. Schroeder, E. E. David, B. F. Logan, and A. J. Prestigiacomo, "Voice-excited vocoders for practical speech-bandwidth reduction," *Proc. Internat'l Symp. on Information Theory* (Belgium, August 1962).

[2] N. P. McKinney, "Laryngeal frequency analysis for linguistic research," Communication Sciences Lab., University of Michigan, Ann Arbor, Rept. 14, September 1965. Chapter 4 gives a comprehensive bibliography.

[3] H. W. Bode, *Network Analysis and Feedback Amplifier Design.* New York: Van Nostrand, 1947, ch. 14.

[4] J. S. Gill, "Automatic extraction of the excitation function of speech," *Proc. 3rd Internat'l Cong. on Acoustics*, vol. 1. Amsterdam: Elsevier, 1961, pp. 217–220.

[5] R. B. Blackman and J. W. Tukey, *The Measurement of Power Spectra.* New York: Dover, 1959.

[6] J. C. R. Licklider and I. Pollack, "Effects of differentiation, integration, and infinite peak clipping upon the intelligibility of speech," *J. Acoust. Soc. Am.*, vol. 20, pp. 42–50, January 1948.

[7] A. M. Noll, "Cepstrum pitch determination," *J. Acoust. Soc. Am.*, vol. 41, pp. 293–309, February 1967.

[8] R. M. Golden, "Digital computer simulation of a sampled-data voice-excited vocoder," *J. Acoust. Soc. Am.*, vol. 35, pp. 1358–1366, September 1963.

Average Magnitude Difference Function Pitch Extractor

MYRON J. ROSS, MEMBER, IEEE, HARRY L. SHAFFER, ANDREW COHEN, MEMBER, IEEE,
RICHARD FREUDBERG, MEMBER, IEEE, AND HAROLD J. MANLEY

Abstract—This paper describes a method for using the average magnitude difference function (AMDF) and associated decision logic to estimate the pitch period of voiced speech sounds. The AMDF is a variation on autocorrelation analysis where, instead of correlating the input speech at various delays (where multiplications and summations are formed at each value of delay), a difference signal is formed between the delayed speech and the original and, at each delay, the absolute magnitude of the difference is taken. The difference signal is always zero at delay = ϕ, and exhibits deep nulls at delays corresponding to the pitch period of voiced sounds. Some of the reasons the AMDF is attractive include the following. 1) It is a simple measurement which gives a good estimate of pitch contour, 2) it has no multiply operations, 3) its dynamic range characteristics are suitable for implementation on a 16-bit machine, and 4) the nature of its operations makes it suitable for implementation on a programmable processor or in special purpose hardware.

The implementation of the AMDF pitch extractor (nonreal-time simulation and real-time) is described and experimental results presented to illustrate its basic measurement properties.

I. INTRODUCTION

IN RECENT years, digital speech compression techniques, which model the human mechanism for generating speech sounds, have been very successful for information rates of 7200 bits/s and below [1], [2]. These schemes generally comprise a synthesizer filter (referred to as the vocal tract filter) which performs spectral shaping on an excitation signal much the same way the vocal tract shapes the air stream generated by the lungs and respiratory muscles, and modulated by the vocal chords (see Fig. 1). During voiced synthesis, the digital equivalent of an impulse carrier (sometimes referred to as a buzz source) operating at the measured pitch rate is convolved with the vocal tract impulse response to produce the synthetic output speech. A noise carrier is used to excite the vocal tract response filter during unvoiced synthesis. The vocal tract impulse response used in this process is a discretely time-varying function whose parameters are updated at the frame updating rate. The problem of generating the pitch impulse carrier (or unit sample pitch carrier) is primarily one of determining the points in time at which unit sample pitch pulses occur. Since the human ear is sensitive to small variations in this carrier, a method for generating an acceptable pitch contour is critical to the scheme if high quality speech is to be generated.

Manuscript received November 26, 1973; revised April 24, 1974. This work was supported by the Narrowband Systems Group, Electronics Command, Fort Monmouth, N. J. under Contract DAAB07-71-C-0207.

M. J. Ross is with CNR, Newton, Mass. 02159.

H. L. Shaffer, A. Cohen, R. Freudberg, and H. J. Manley are with GTE Sylvania, Needham, Mass.

II. AUTOCORRELATION AND CROSS-CORRELATION ANALYSIS

It is well known that the autocorrelation function (ACF) of a speech signal (of suitable length) can be used for pitch detection [see Fig. 2(c)]. It is generally not necessary to compute the entire autocorrelation function for each L second segment of speech; values of delay (or shift) falling in a search range of approximately 3–15 ms are usually computed. Since values of pitch frequency generally fall within the range of 70–300 Hz, (corresponding to the search range of 3–15 ms), much data processing can be eliminated in ACF pitch detection by obviating the need to compute the entire ACF of each L second analysis interval for shifts outside this range.[1] This portion of the ACF is then "scanned" for a strong peak. Assuming that various voicing criteria are satisfied in the pitch logic, the pitch period is then taken to be the location or delay value of the "strong" peak relative to zero delay or the true origin of the ACF.

A further reduction in data processing can be achieved by computing over a portion of the analysis interval L' [Fig. 2(b)] where $L' < L$ is cross correlated with the full L second interval [Fig. 2(d)]. This is the cross-correlation function (CCF). A truncated version of this function [Fig. 2(e)] is quite suitable for the detection of pitch.

The length L' is chosen in accordance with the expected pitch period, e.g., it may be approximately equal to two pitch periods of the normal male speakers (i.e., 100 Hz). Under these conditions, L is about 20 ms and L might typically be 36 ms, resulting in a pitch search range of $L-L'$ or about 16 ms. Experimental results have shown that L' can be as low as 8–9 ms and L as low as 23 ms without causing severe deterioration in the pitch estimation process. An advantage of the CCF method is that the relative sizes of the correlation peaks tend to remain constant as a function of delay. In this regard, an essentially linear decrease in correlation peak size versus delay can be observed in the ACF method. On the other hand, the constancy of correlation peak size in Fig. 2(e) occurs since there is always full overlap of data between the two segments being cross correlated in the CCF method. This is not the case in the ACF method since data overlap falls off linearly with delay. Because the correlation peaks tend to remain relatively large in the CCF, they are more easily discernable in the detection of pitch.

Mathematically, the autocorrelation function of an L second segment of digitized speech is defined as

[1] Also, only one-half of the ACF need be computed since it is an even function.

Reprinted from *IEEE Trans. Acoust., Speech, and Signal Process.*, vol. ASSP-22, pp. 353–362, Oct. 1974.

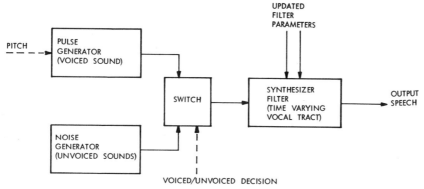

Fig. 1. Model of the speech production mechanism.

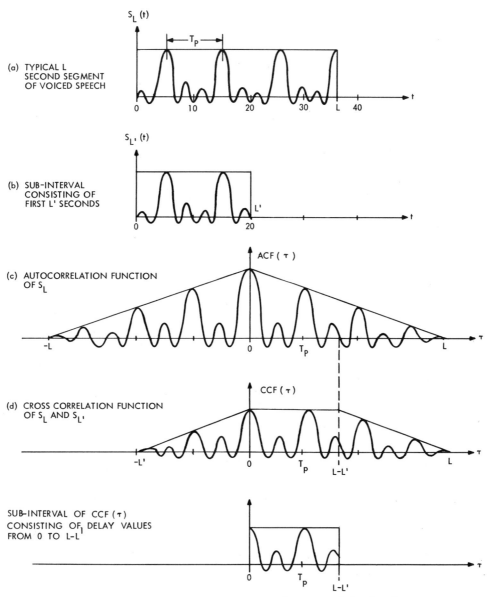

Fig. 2. Comparison of autocorrelation and cross-correlation functions.

$$\mathrm{ACF}_\tau = \frac{1}{L} \sum_{j=1}^{L} S_j S_{j-\tau}, \qquad \tau = 0,1,\cdots\tau_{\max} \qquad (1)$$

where

$S_j = j$th sample of the speech waveform vector

$$(S_j) = (S_1, S_2, \cdots, S_L)$$

$L =$ size of the speech segment

$\tau =$ delay value

$\tau_{\max} =$ maximum delay shift $(\tau_{\max} = L)$

while that of the cross correlation function is given as

$$CCF_\tau = \frac{1}{L'} \sum_{j=1}^{L'} S_j' S_{j-\tau}, \qquad \tau = 0,1,\cdots\tau_{\max} \qquad (2)$$

where

S_j = jth sample of the speech waveform vector
$$(S_j) = (S_1, S_2, \cdots, S_L)$$
S_j' = jth sample of the speech waveform subvector
$$(S_j') = (S_1, S_2, \cdots, S_{L'})$$
L' = portion of speech segment
τ = delay value
$\tau_{\max}$ = maximum delay shift ($\tau_{\max} \leq L - L'$).

If L and L' are chosen judiciously, the truncated CCF minimizes computational requirements yet contains sufficient data to yield accurate pitch estimation.

III. AVERAGE MAGNITUDE DIFFERENCE FUNCTION (AMDF) [3], [4]

A variation of autocorrelation analysis for measuring the periodicity of voiced speech uses the AMDF, defined by the relation

$$D_\tau = \frac{1}{L} \sum_{j=1}^{L} |S_j - S_{j-\tau}|, \qquad \tau = 0,1,\cdots\tau_{\max} \qquad (3)$$

where S_j are the samples of input speech

$$(S_j) = (S_1, S_2, \cdots, S_L)$$

and $S_{j-\tau}$ are the samples time shifted τ seconds.

The vertical bars denote taking the magnitude of the difference $S_j - S_{j-\tau}$. Thus a difference signal D_τ is formed by delaying the input speech various amounts, subtracting the delayed waveform from the original, and summing the magnitude of the differences between sample values. The difference signal [Fig. 4(b)] is always zero at delay = ϕ, and is observed to exhibit deep nulls at delays corresponding to the pitch period of a voiced sound having a quasi-periodic structure.

An approximate expression that provides a useful relationship between the AMDF and the ACF of a sampled sequence will now be developed. This relationship is based on the well known bound,

$$\frac{1}{N} \sum_{k=\phi}^{N-1} |X_k| \leq \left(\frac{1}{N} \sum_{k=0}^{N-1} X_k^2\right)^{1/2}. \qquad (4)$$

In (4), the left side is the average magnitude of the samples sequence $\{X_k\}$ while the right side of the equation is the rms value of the sequence. The bound represented by (1) is readily established by Schwarz's inequality [5], [6].

The AMDF for a sequence of samples $\{S_k\}$ is defined by the relation

$$D_n \equiv \frac{1}{N} \sum_{k=0}^{N-1} |S_k - S_{k-n}| \qquad (5)$$

where the delay index n ranges from $-(N-1)$ to $+(N-1)$ (i.e., $n = -(N-1),\cdots-1,0,1,2,3,\cdots, N-1$) to generate the complete AMDF. In implementing

(5), the summing index k ranges from $k = n$ to $k = N - 1$ for $n \geq 0$. That is, the AMDF is formed only in the region of overlap of the sequences S_k and S_{k-n}. Thus for $n < 0$, the summing index k ranges from 0 to $N - 1 + n$. It is seen that D_n is an even function (i.e., $D_n = D_{-n}$) according to the above definitions.

Using (4) we can approximate D_n in the form

$$D_n = \frac{1}{N} \sum_k |S_k - S_{k-n}| \cong \beta_n \left(\frac{1}{N} \sum_k (S_k - S_{k-n})^2\right)^{1/2}. \qquad (6)$$

In (6), the coefficient β_n is a scale factor. For Gaussian sequences it is possible to determine a value for β_n (analytically) that would achieve equality on the average between the average magnitude and rms sums. For other distributions, a value for β_n can be determined experimentally by testing a large number of sequences. It is evident that β_n depends upon the joint probability density function (pdf) of S_k and S_{k-n}. Since the joint pdf of S_k and S_{k-n} will in general vary with the delay index n, the coefficient β_n will therefore be a function of n. Our experience is that β_n can vary from about 0.6 to 1.0 depending upon the sampled sequence but is not a rapidly varying function of the delay index n.

By expanding the squared term in braces under the square root sign in (6) we can express D_n in the form,

$$D_n \cong \beta_n \left(\frac{1}{N} \sum_k S_k^2 + \frac{1}{N} \sum_k S_{k-n}^2 - \frac{2}{N} \sum_k S_k S_{k-n}\right)^{1/2}. \qquad (7)$$

By defining the ACF of the sequence $\{S_k\}$ as

$$R_n = \frac{1}{N} \sum_k S_k S_{k-n} \qquad (8)$$

it is seen that the third sum in the braces is $-2R_n$. Assuming that the sequence $\{S_k\}$ corresponds to a stationary process it is evident that the first two sums in (7) are simply the ACF evaluated at $n = 0$. That is

$$R_0 = \frac{1}{N} \sum_k S_k^2 \cong \frac{1}{N} \sum_k S_{k-n}^2 \qquad (9)$$

under the assumption of stationarity. Using (8) and (9) in (7) yields D_n as

$$D_n \cong \beta_n [2(R_0 - R_n)]^{1/2}. \qquad (10)$$

The properties of the AMDF are accurately characterized by (10). Specifically, the AMDF is seen to be zero at zero delay ($n = 0$) and varies as the square root of the ACF that has been negated and "dc shifted" by R_0. This is precisely the character of the AMDF that has been observed experimentally in actual computations using the definitions of (5). Nulls will appear in D_n at those points where R_n is large compared with R_0. This occurs when the sequence $\{S_k\}$ is taken from a voiced speech sound containing two or more pitch periods in the sequence. The separation of the nulls is a direct measure of the pitch period.

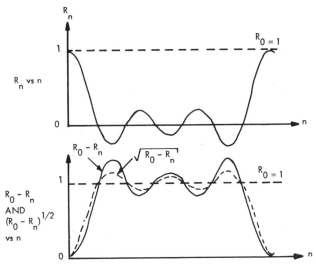

Fig. 3. Sketches of R_n, $R_0 - R_n$ and $(R_0 - R_n)^{1/2}$ for a typical periodic ACF.

Reference is made to Fig. 3 showing sketches of a typical (periodic) ACF, R_n, followed by the negated and shifted ACF, $(R_0 - R_n)$. This latter function is compared with a sketch of its square root, $(R_0 - R_n)^{1/2}$. It is interesting to note that the effect of the square root is to sharpen the nulls (i.e., reduce their width). This effect is helpful in increasing the resolution of pitch measurement (when comparing the AMDF with the ACF) in that the reduced width of the nulls enables greater accuracy in determining their locations.

These characteristics of the AMDF predicated by (10) can be observed in the oscilloscope pictures of Fig. 4. The experimental results that have been observed indicate that (10) not only provides an accurate characterization of the AMDF in terms of the ACF but could be used to compute the ACF from AMDF[2] with many fewer multiplies than are required in computing the ACF directly.

Fig. 4 compares oscilloscope patterns of the ACF and AMDF for 36 ms of the voiced sound "aw". D_τ is zero at $\tau = \phi$, corresponding to the peak of the ACF. D_τ also exhibits deep nulls at time spacings equal to the pitch period, corresponding to the highest peak of the ACF, and thus provides an indication of the periodic structure of the voiced sound.

In Fig. 6, for the unvoiced segment "sh," neither an ACF secondary peak nor an AMDF null is observed, since a periodic structure does not exist for this sound. Fig. 5 shows that the spacing between pitch peaks for the "aw" sound is still evident despite a 10 dB signal-to-noise ratio.

The AMDF is a variation of ACF analysis where, instead of correlating the input speech at various delays (where multiplications and summations are formed at each value of delay), a difference signal is formed between the delayed speech and the original, and at each delay value the absolute magnitude is taken. Unlike the autocorrelation

[2] With acceptable accuracy for many speech processing applications.

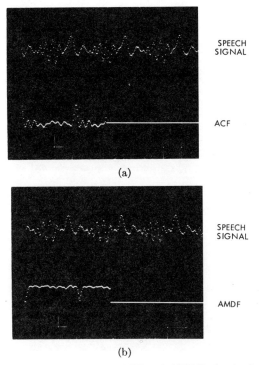

Fig. 4. Oscilloscope pictures of ACF and AMDF of voiced speech sound "aw" for high SNR. (a) Speech signal (top trace) and its ACF (bottom trace) for high SNR. (b) Speech signal (top trace) and its AMDF for high SNR.

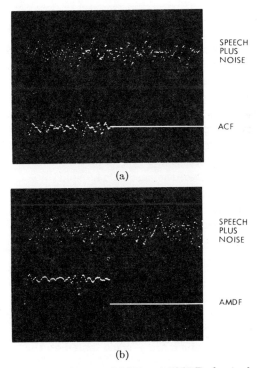

Fig. 5. Oscilloscope pictures of ACF and AMDF of voiced speech sound "aw" for 10 dB SNR. (a) Speech signal (top trace) and its ACF (bottom trace) for 10 dB SNR. (b) Speech signal (top) and its AMDF (bottom) for 10 dB SNR.

or cross-correlation function, however, the AMDF calculations require no multiplications, a desirable property for real-time applications.

For each value of delay, computation is made over an integrating window of L' samples, similar to the procedure

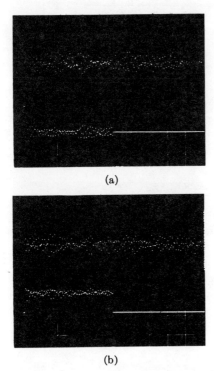

(a)

(b)

Fig. 6. Oscilloscope pictures of ACF and AMDF of unvoiced speech sound "sh" for high SNR. (a) Speech signal (top) and its ACF (bottom) for high SNR. (b) Speech signal (top) and its AMDF (bottom) for high SNR.

used to obtain the truncated cross-correlation function of Fig. 2(e). To generate the entire range of delays, the window is "cross differenced" with the full analysis interval. An advantage of this method is that the relative sizes of the nulls tend to remain constant as a function of delay. This is because there is always full overlap of data between the two segments being cross differenced.

In extractors of this type, the limiting factor on accuracy is the inability to completely separate the fine structure from the effects of the spectral envelope. For this reason, decision logic and prior knowledge of voicing are used along with the function itself to help make the pitch decision more reliable.

IV. PITCH DETECTION LOGIC

Fig. 7 shows the set of logical rules developed for extraction of pitch information from the AMDF. It is comparable in complexity to the logic you might find in an ACF pitch extractor. There are five separate logic paths, each of which are selected, based on the three most recent voiced/unvoiced (VUV) decisions. The parameter LOGIC is the weighted number obtained by treating the three consecutive decisions as a binary number, i.e.,

$$\text{LOGIC} = \text{VUV}\,(n) + 2\,\text{VUV}\,(n-1) + 4\,\text{VUV}\,(n-2)$$

$$(11)$$

where

VUV $(n) = \phi$ if the nth interval was unvoiced.
VUV $(n) = 1$ if the nth interval was voiced.

The range of values that LOGIC can assume is 0–7. Thus, there are eight possible conditions that the pitch logic is designed to handle. Thresholds indicated in the flow were determined empirically by examining speech data for many different utterances and speakers.

In path A, the present VUV decision is unvoiced and the logic asks whether this decision should be changed to voiced. A change is justified by the presence of a strong periodic waveform within the analysis interval.

In path B, the present VUV decision is voiced. Normally the pitch should equal the minimum position of the AMDF in the search range. However, an unvoiced decision can occur if either the maximum AMDF value is not sufficiently strong or the ratio of the maximum to minimum value is below the specified threshold.

In path C, the nth and $(n-1)$th VUV decisions are voiced but the $(n-2)$th interval was unvoiced. This is an indication of the onset of voicing; the pitch extractor changes to voiced and chooses the minimum value of the AMDF as the pitch.

In path D, we extend voicing an additional frame when the VUV decision indicates unvoicing after an extended period of voicing. If the frame should actually be unvoiced at this point, the speech waveform, typically, is of such low amplitude that it makes little difference to the synthesizer. More importantly, though, in the event that the extractor is in error and the interval should be voiced, this extension eliminates the possibility of an unvoiced interval somewhere in the middle of a voiced sound.

Path E is the normal path for sustained voicing and employs a feature for locking onto the true pitch and tracking it. A tracking window of ± 12 samples about the last measured pitch period is defined within which the logic looks for a minimum. This minimum is then compared with the minimum in the entire AMDF search range. Normally, the tracking minimum is selected as the pitch but the logic will change to the nontracking position if the amplitude of the minimum outside the tracking range is less than $1/2$ the tracking amplitude minimum. For higher frequencies, more nulls are present in the AMDF so a null outside the tracking window is required to be less than $1/8$ the minimum in the tracking window to be chosen. There is also a path for changing the VUV decision from voiced to unvoiced, and for extending the previous pitch value.

For all UV intervals, as well as the first voiced interval, the samples of the input segment are reversed in time. This is introduced to overcome a serious problem related to the onset of voicing. For this analysis interval, the waveform is partially unvoiced and partially voiced with the integrating window falling on the UV portion. A correlation of these samples will not exist for any calculated data value. Reversing the time function places the samples from the voiced portion of the speech waveform in the integrating window. If the interval is basically voiced, the AMDF will have a low amplitude null; if less than 50 percent of the interval is voiced, then the decision would be an unvoiced output.

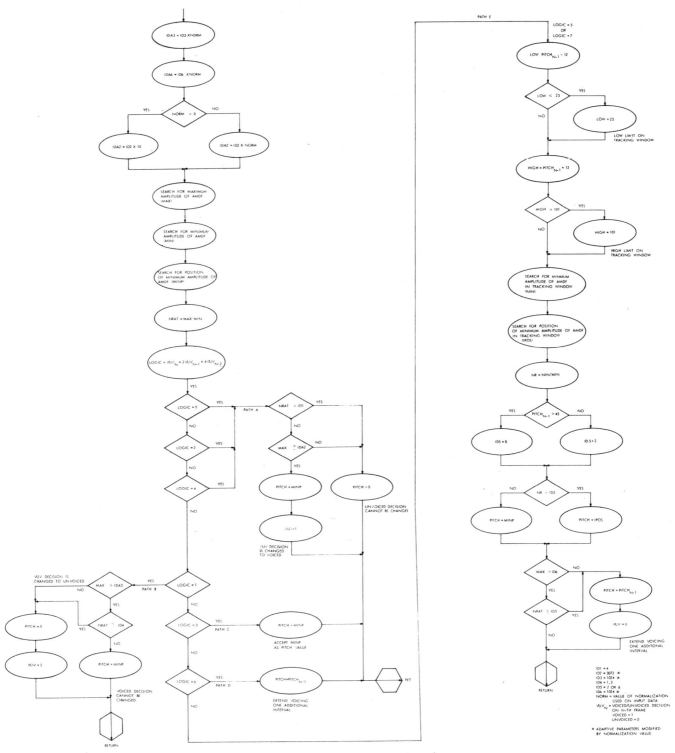

Fig. 7.   AMDF pitch extraction logic flow chart.

For all voiced intervals other than at the onset of voicing, the samples in the analysis window are not reversed. At the trailing end of voicing this has the same advantage that reversing the time function had at the onset of voicing, i.e., the periodic portion is contained in the integrating window, and it is possible to track the pitch more accurately to the completion of the voiced sound.

V. EXPERIMENTAL RESULTS

Fig. 8 shows the pitch period contour for the utterance "health suffers when food goes bad" measured by an AMDF and ACF pitch extractor, each with appropriate decision logic and VUV detection. The frames where the ACF extractor differed from the decision of the AMDF extractor are indicated by a circle.

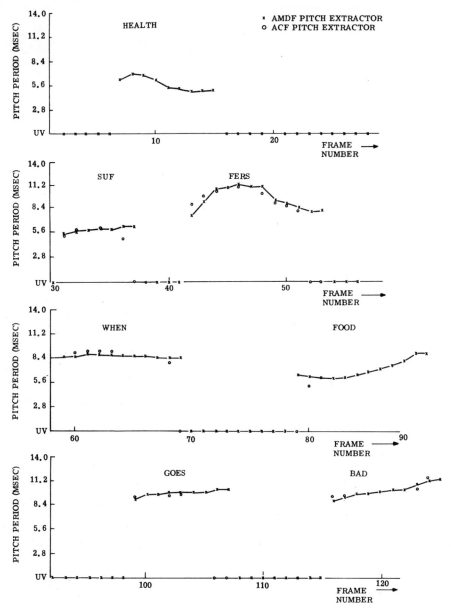

Fig. 8.   Pitch period contour for "health suffers when food goes bad."

The curves are in good general agreement, differing mainly at the onset or trailing end of voicing. It is reasonable to assume that, at these points, the signal amplitude is so small that it makes little difference to a synthesizer whether they are voiced or unvoiced.

In the simulation of the AMDF logic, the voicing decision could be arbitrarily changed. Errors were thus introduced in the voicing decision and the effects on the measured pitch contour were noted. Fig. 9 is a plot of the fundamental frequency for the words "health suffers" and the degradations which occurred when the voicing decisions were constrained to be, respectively, all voiced, all unvoiced, or voiced/unvoiced randomly with equal probability of occurrence. The results show that the logic will attempt to lock onto the correct pitch period in spite of errors which try to offset it. Also evident is a bias toward

voicing since the case where the voicing decisions were forced to be unvoiced produced the most serious degradation.

Adding noise to the input signal caused pitch errors to be generated. These errors were speaker dependent but appeared to consist mostly of pitch doublings occurring at the onset or central portion of voiced sounds. Few dropouts were evident; for the most part, the extractor tended to maintain voicing. As the signal-to-noise ratio was varied from 30 dB to 10 dB, the number of errors increased, although not a substantial amount. A more substantial increase in error was found in going from the uncorrupted speed to a high S/N (30 dB) than in decreasing the S/N appreciably. Some evidence is available which shows that the AMDF remains suitable for pitch extraction down to a ϕ dB S/N [7]. However, more extensive evaluation on a

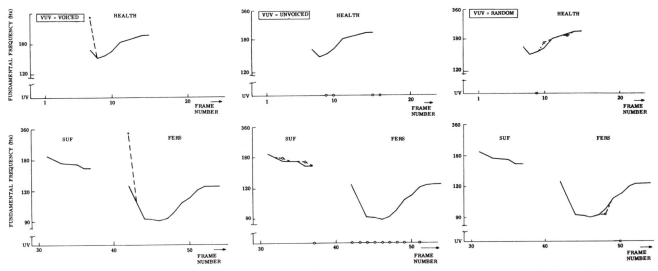

Fig. 9. Fundamental frequency for the utterance "health suffers" with the introduction of errors in the voicing decision.

wide variety of sounds and speakers is required in order to completely evaluate the lowest S/N at which the AMDF pitch extractor will successfully operate.

VI. REAL-TIME IMPLEMENTATION

A. Run-Time Estimates

The ability to implement an AMDF pitch extractor in real time is a direct consequence of the number of operations necessary and the computational speed of the available machine.

A flow chart of the instruction code which would generate samples of the AMDF in real time on a GTE Sylvania programmable signal processor (PSP) is depicted in Fig. 10. For this particular machine (shown in Fig. 11), a multiply instruction takes 750 ns while additions, subtractions, and manipulations of data generally take 250 to 375 ns apiece. For each set of operations included in the dashed block of Fig. 10, 1.875 μs of time are required. This includes 500 ns each for the load, subtract, test, and negate instructions and an additional 375 ns for storing the partial sum. For each analysis interval, there are 64 computations (equal to the number of samples in the integrating window[3]) in order to calculate a single point of the AMDF. Thus, the time interval is 64 × 1.875 μs or 120.0 μs. Since 77 samples of the AMDF are generated within each frame, the total time required is about 9.24 ms. These 77 samples are adequate to allow pitch analysis in the range of 70 Hz to 300 Hz at a 7040 Hz sampling rate. The time estimate should also include the required loop control to maintain accuracy in the AMDF generation. This accounts for approximately 250 μs. The total time interval, with the inclusion of approximately 0.2 ms for the decision logic is the running-time estimate for pitch extraction on this machine. Actual system times were approximately 10 ms for generation of

[3] This corresponds to about 9 ms of speech sampled at a 7040 Hz rate.

the AMDF and an average of 0.25 ms to perform the decision logic.

B. Conservation of Dynamic Range

In order to preserve accuracy in performing the summations of (3), the calculation of each point of the AMDF is divided into four partial summations, each dealing with 16 terms, i.e.,

$$D_\tau = \{ \tfrac{1}{4} \sum_{j=1}^{16} |S_j - S_{j-\tau}| + \tfrac{1}{4} \sum_{j=17}^{32} |S_j - S_{j-\tau}|$$

$$+ \tfrac{1}{4} \sum_{j=33}^{48} |S_j - S_{j-\tau}| + \tfrac{1}{4} \sum_{j=49}^{64} |S_j - S_{j-\tau}|\}$$

$$\tau = 0, 1, \cdots, \tau_{\max}. \quad (12)$$

The input data are scaled so the largest value obtainable is $\pm(2^{10} - 1)$. A factor of 2 is required since each difference sample is the result of combining two input samples yielding a maximum of $2(2^{10} - 1) = 2^{11} - 2$. Since 64 difference samples (2^6) are summed in the integrating window, the accuracy required to calculate each point of the AMDF is $(2^6)(2^{11} - 2) = 2^{17} - 2^7$. This will overload in a 16-bit computer. The accuracy required in summing 16 points is $2^4(2^{11} - 2)$ or $2^{15} - 2^5$. Each partial sum is factored by 2^{-2}; the four partial sums can then be combined to generate one point of the AMDF. This is suitable for calculation on a 16-bit machine.

C. Methods for Reducing Run-Time Requirements

There are several ways to reduce the time for pitch extraction. One possibility is to generate the AMDF function in an external hardwired device and feed the results into the computer via an I/O channel. Pitch extraction logic on the AMDF signal would require a complex hardware design but would represent a minor load on the processor; thus, a reasonable approach would be to perform the logic inside the processor. The hardware interface to an external AMDF generator could be quite simple. For input, the

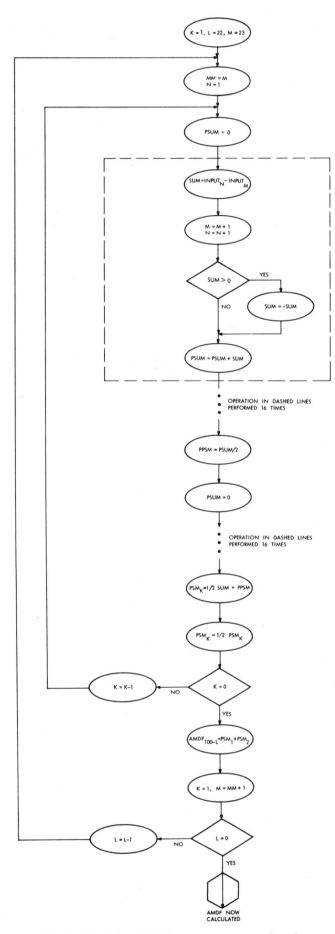

Fig. 10.   Real-time AMDF generator program flow chart.

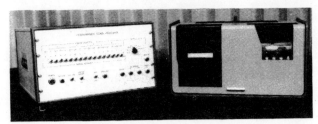

Fig. 11.   GTE Sylvania programmable signal processor (PSP) with card reader.

AMDF function generator would use the processor's A/D converter, and for output the AMDF function would be transmitted to the main processor at the sampling rate. An alternate input scheme is to use a sign-magnitude A/D converter, thus eliminating the magnitude test instruction within the dashed block of Fig. 10. This would reduce the AMDF generating time from 9.24 ms to 6.8 ms.

Another possibility for faster operation, is to develop special instructions to decrease the computation. An instruction that added to the magnitude of the accumulator into a 20-bit precision register in one instruction cycle would decrease time for the inner loop and the time for scaling the intermediate sums. Such an instruction would reduce the AMDF generation from 9.24 ms to about 5.44 ms.

Other interesting approaches include such ideas as band-limiting the input signal to 1000 Hz and resampling at one-fifth the sampling rate [8]. This can provide a reduction in the number of computations necessary to obtain the AMDF. Some success was found with the simple scheme of generating every second or third point of the AMDF, while restricting the decision logic to ignore points which have not been calculated. In both these cases, however, it should be recognized that a cruder version of the AMDF is generated which could result in a possible loss of accuracy.

Implementation of the ACF or CCF requires multiplies in place of the sum and magnitude instructions. In general, for a machine with a fast multiply, it takes no more time to generate an ACF or CCF than it does to generate an AMDF. However, fast multiply hardware is somewhat expensive. Also, more scaling is required to handle the large dynamic range associated with the multiply operation than would be for an equivalent summation process. Thus the use of the AMDF, which requires no multiply instructions and does not have restrictive dynamic range constraints, has an advantage over the ACF or CCF with respect to machine complexity.

REFERENCES

[1] M. R. Schroeder, "Vocoders: analysis and synthesis of speech," *Proc. IEEE*, vol. 54, pp. 720–734, May 1966.
[2] J. L. Flanagan, *Speech Analysis, Synthesis, and Perception.* New York: Academic, 1965, 2nd ed., 1972.
[3] "Narrow band autocorrelation study," GTE Sylvania, Inc., Needham, Mass., Final Rep.,[4] Contract DAAB07-71-C-0207, July 1972.
[4] H. L. Shaffer, M. J. Ross, and A. Cohen, "AMDF pitch ex-

[4] Requests for this document must be referred to: Commanding General, U. S. Army Electronics Command, Attn: AMSEL-NL-Y-4, Fort Monmouth, N. J. 07703.

tractor," presented at the 85th meeting of the Acoustical Society of America, Boston, Mass., Apr. 10–13, 1973.

[5] R. L. Freudberg, "A comparison of the averages

$$\frac{1}{N} \sum_{k=1}^{N} |X_k| \quad \text{and} \quad \left(\frac{1}{N} \sum_{k=1}^{N} X_k{}^2\right)^{1/2},"$$

GTE Sylvania, Inc., Needham, Mass., Res. Note, Sept. 1970.

[6] J. M. Wozencraft, *Principles of Communication Engineering*, I. M. Jacobs, Ed. New York: Wiley, 1965.

[7] H. L. Shaffer and C. Howard, "Real-time generation of the cross-correlation function and difference magnitude function," GTE Sylvania, Inc., Needham, Mass., Res. Note, July 1970.

[8] J. D. Markel, "The SIFT algorithm for fundamental frequency estimation," *IEEE Trans. Audio Electroacoust.*, vol. AU-20, pp. 367–377, Dec. 1972.

The SIFT Algorithm for Fundamental Frequency Estimation

JOHN D. MARKEL

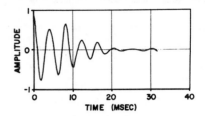

Fig. 1. Normalized autocorrelation results from a test segment of the vowel /i/ spoken in the phrase: "We were."

Abstract—In this paper a new method for estimating F_0, the fundamental frequency of voiced speech versus time, is presented. The algorithm is based upon a simplified version of a general technique for fundamental frequency extraction using digital inverse filtering. It is demonstrated that the simplified inverse filter tracking algorithm (hereafter referred to as the SIFT algorithm) encompasses the desirable properties of both autocorrelation and cepstral pitch analysis techniques. In addition, the SIFT algorithm is composed of only a relatively small number of elementary arithmetic operations. In machine language, SIFT should run in several times real time while with special-purpose hardware it could easily be realized in real time.

I. Autocorrelation, Cepstral, and Inverse Filter Analysis

One of the oldest digital methods for estimating the fundamental frequency (F_0) of voiced speech is autocorrelation analysis. A window or frame of data of N samples, encompassing several pitch periods, is used to calculate the short-term autocorrelation sequence specified by

$$\rho_j = \sum_{n=0}^{N-1-|j|} s_n s_{n+|j|},$$

where $\{s_n\} = \{s_0, s_1, \cdots, s_{N-1}\}$ defines the input sequence obtained from the continuous-speech signal by sampling above the Nyquist frequency and $j = 0,1, \cdots, N-1$. The N-length sequence $\{\rho_j\}$ can be efficiently calculated for large N if N is an integer power of two by applying a fast Fourier transform (FFT) in the following manner. Define $\{s'_n\}$ as the $N' = 2N$-length sequence obtained by appending N zeros to the end of the sequence $\{s_n\}$. Then: 1) calculate $\{S'_k\} =$ FFT $\{s'_n\}$, 2) replace $\{S'_k\}$ by $\{|S'_k|^2\}$, and 3) calculate $\{\rho'_j\} = $ FFT $\{S'_k\}/N'$. Finally, $\rho_j = \rho'_j$, $j = 0$, 1, $\cdots$, $N-1$. (Note that $\rho'_j - \rho'_{N'-j} = 0$, 1, $\cdots$, $N'/2$.) Since $\{s_n\}$ is real, the computation time can be further reduced by one half. F_0 is defined over the sequence of N samples as the reciprocal of the estimated pitch period P, where P is the location in time of the maximum ρ_j within some specified interval. An important property is that if P is known to lie within a specified interval, it is only necessary to search this interval of the autocorrelation sequence. Furthermore, the dynamic range of the pitch period peaks in the autocorrelation sequence is usually less than 10 dB. In contrast, pitch extraction from the acoustic wave itself, a common approach to tracking with analog devices, requires the detection of peaks over a dynamic range sometimes exceeding 30 dB.

The acoustic speech waveform can be modeled as the convolution of terms that includes a periodic component due to the glottal waveform and a term representing the vocal tract impulse response. The resonances or formants of the vocal tract have narrow enough bandwidths (50–80) Hz for the autocorrelation sequence to frequently have several high-amplitude oscillations that interact with the component due to the pitch period. Fig. 1 shows the autocorrelation sequence obtained from a 32 ms segment of the vowel /i/ spoken in the context: "We were." This segment has been analyzed under different conditions for comparative purposes and will hereafter be referred to as the test segment. The zero-time sample is always the largest amplitude term and therefore, an autocorrelation sequence can always be normalized to unity at the origin. The pitch period can be seen by the slight increase in the third positive peak. In general, the pitch peak detection is nontrivial, and in addition, the estimate will be somewhat in error due to the interaction of the glottal wave component and the damped sinusoidal term due predominantly to the first formant [2].

The single property $\log ab = \log a + \log b$ leads to what has been termed cepstral analysis, a suggested solution to the fundamental frequency extraction problem. The cepstrum is calculated identically as the autocorrelation previously described using two FFT's except that in step 2), instead of replacing $\{S'_k\}$ by $\{|S'_k|^2\}$, $\{S'_k\}$ is replaced by $\{\log |S'_k|^2\}$. With this trivial modification, dramatically different results are obtained. Fig. 2 shows the cepstrum for the test segment. Fig. 2(a) shows the cepstrum normalized to unity at the origin while Fig. 2(b) shows the cepstrum normalized to the pitch peak after the first two milliseconds were zeroed out. The sharp peak at 8.3 ms is due to the pitch period. To the right of the first few samples, the pitch period in a voiced segment can usually be uniquely defined by the largest peak in the cepstrum. The effects of the vocal tract impulse response are contained largely within the first few milliseconds of the origin [3]. Thus

Manuscript received May 8, 1972. This work was supported by the Office of Naval Research under Contract N00014-67-C-0118.

The author is with Speech Communications Research Laboratory, Inc. (SCRL), Santa Barbara, Calif. 93101.

Reprinted from *IEEE Trans. Audio Electroacoust.*, vol. AU–20, pp. 367–377, Dec. 1972.

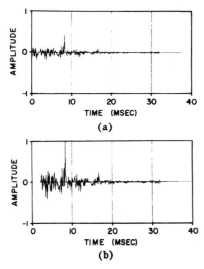

Fig. 2. Cepstral analysis results. (a) Normalized to unity at origin. (b) Normalized to unity at peak where first two milliseconds have been zeroed out.

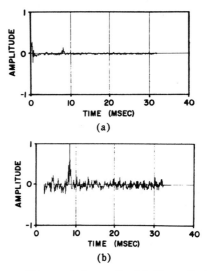

Fig. 3. Inverse filter analysis results. (a) Normalized to unity at the origin. (b) Normalized to unity at peak where first two milliseconds have been zeroed out.

the problem of interaction between the formants and fundamental frequency has been largely solved. Unfortunately, because of the nonlinear logarithmic operation, two undesirable results are obtained: 1) the peak at the origin can no longer be used as a reference for normalization, and 2) the actual amplitude of the spike is a function not only of the number of pitch periods within the window, but also of the spectral shape. The zero-time value of the peak is dependent only upon the mean value of the log magnitude spectrum. Spectral shaping is dependent largely upon the formant values and to a first order approximation can be considered independent of the fundamental frequency.

If F_0 tracking is accomplished manually or if the speech segment is completely voiced, these criticisms are irrelevant. Generally, however, it is desirable to automatically determine whether the segment is voiced (in which case F_0 is to be calculated) or unvoiced (in which case F_0 does not exist). It has been stated that voicing is detected by a sharp spike at the pitch period while unvoicing is detected by the absence of a sharp spike [4]. Although this statement when used as an algorithm works extremely well for manual calculation, automatic implementation is not trivial for the two reasons stated above.

What is proposed in this paper is a simplified analysis technique, based upon an inverse filter formulation [1] which retains the advantages of both the autocorrelation and cepstral analysis techniques. The results from an inverse filter analysis of the test segment are shown in Fig. 3. Fig. 3(a) shows the output normalized to unity at the origin, while Fig. 3(b) shows the output normalized to the pitch peak after the first 2 ms were zeroed out. This output sequence is defined as the autocorrelation of the inverse filter output and thus can be

normalized so that the units on the ordinate correspond to correlation values from -1.0 to 1.0. There is a sharp peak corresponding to a correlation value of 0.43 at 8.3 ms. The pitch period is defined as the location of this peak, and generally it will have the largest correlation over all samples except at the origin. Since it is always possible to normalize the output, and since the data values have the physical interpretation of correlation, it should be possible to define a simple voiced-unvoiced decision based upon a fixed threshold value.

In Figs. 2(b) and 3(b), the waveforms are normalized to the pitch peak so that the peak signal-to-noise ratios can be compared over the interval (2, 32) ms. Since negative correlation values can never be possible candidates for pitch estimators, the peak undesired noise amplitude is 0.30 in the autocorrelation sequence. For the cepstrum in the interval (2, 32) ms, the maximum undesired peak is 0.25. Note that the first few milliseconds of the cepstrum can have very large positive or negative terms. One additional comment pertaining to the cepstrum is in order. Squaring of the cepstral samples has been suggested in the literature [5]. By squaring the samples, certainly a much more attractive representation is obtained. Unfortunately, this does not accomplish any desirable goal, since the dynamic range over which detection must be accomplished is also squared. The results for the SIFT algorithm to be developed in this paper are shown in Fig. 4 for the test segment. The properties are quite similar to the inverse filter analysis shown in Fig. 3. The major differences are: 1) the peak is broadened slightly; 2) the higher frequency terms in the undesired portion of the output are suppressed; 3) the harmonics of the pitch period are more apparent since a Hamming window was not applied to the input data; and 4) the desired signal-peak-to-undesired-noise-peak ratio is increased.

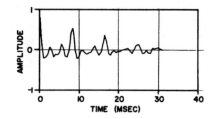

Fig. 4. SIFT algorithm results for the analysis of the test segment.

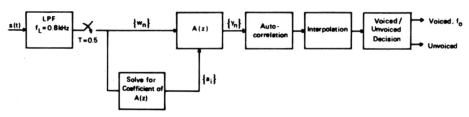

Fig. 5. Block diagram of the SIFT algorithm.

II. The SIFT Algorithm

A Block Diagram Description

A block diagram of the SIFT analysis system is shown in Fig. 5. The speech waveform $s(t)$ is first prefiltered by a low-pass filter with a cutoff at 0.8 kHz. After sampling the filter output at a 2-kHz rate, the first five terms $\rho_j, j = 0, 1, \cdots, 4$, of the short-term autocorrelation sequence are calculated for an appropriate input length (as a representative number $N = 64$ was chosen corresponding to a 32-ms window). The set of linear equations $\sum_{i=1}^{4} a_i \rho_{i-j} = -\rho_j, j = 1, 2, \cdots, 4$, is then solved for the inverse filter coefficients $\{a_i\}$, where the inverse filter is defined by $A(z) = 1 + \sum_{i=1}^{4} a_i z^{-1}$. Knowing $\{a_i\}$, the inverse filter output $\{y_n\}$ can be calculated. The output autocorrelation sequence $\{r_n\}$ from which F_0 is estimated is then calculated as the autocorrelation sequence of $\{y_n\}$. After $\{r_n\}$ is obtained, the largest peak within specified limits is found. Interpolation is applied in the region of the peak and then a voiced-unvoiced decision is made based upon the interpolated peak. If the segment is voiced, the reciprocal of the location of the interpolated peak defines F_0. Each of these operations, along with computational considerations, will be discussed in detail.

Prefiltering

A sampling frequency of 10 kHz is often used in digital speech analysis to insure that all significant frequency components of voiced speech are accurately represented. This sampling rate also insures adequate time scale resolution (0.1 ms) for accurate estimation of P. By deriving a sampling theorem that corresponds to a form of trignometric interpolation, accurate estimation of P will be shown possible even with a 2-kHz sampling rate chosen for the analysis. By using this low sampling frequency, the total number of necessary operations is greatly reduced.

To insure against folding over of frequency components (aliasing) into the (0, 1) kHz range, it is necessary that the input signal be bandlimited to 1 kHz. Aliasing problems are minimal for voiced speech since the spectrum of a voiced sample will always have a maximum peak in the range (0, 1) kHz with the largest peak outside the range, generally 5–10 dB below the first peak. For unvoiced speech, however, such a situation will not usually exist. For example, the peak during an /s/ may be located at 5 kHz with an amplitude 30 dB above the low-frequency components. Unless rather elaborate (and time-consuming) digital filtering is employed, the filter cutoff must be chosen as somewhat less than 1 kHz. A cutoff at 0.8 kHz is a reasonable choice for including most of the low-frequency range while providing sufficient attenuation at 1.0 kHz. To demonstrate the fact that extremely sharp cutoff filters are not necessary and that phase and group delay characteristics are not critical, a Chebyshev 3-pole 2-dB ripple filter specification has been used.

Actually, for the simulation a digital version was implemented, since a 10-kHz sampling rate was most readily available. The digital filter is specified by $u_n = a_1 s_n + a_2 u_{n-1}$ and $x_n = a_3 u_n + a_4 x_{n-1} + a_5 x_{n-2}$ where

$$a_1 = 1 - e^{-\alpha_1 T}$$

$$a_2 = e^{-\alpha_1 T}$$

$$a_3 = 1 - 2e^{-\alpha_2 T} \cos \beta_2 T + e^{-2\alpha_2 T}$$

$$a_4 = 2e^{-\alpha_2 T} \cos \beta_2 T$$

$$a_5 = -e^{-2\alpha_2 T}$$

$$\alpha_1 = (0.3572)2\pi f_c$$

$$\alpha_2 = (0.1786)\pi f_c$$

$$\beta_2 = (0.8938)\pi f_c$$
$$u_n = 0, \qquad n < 0$$
$$x_n = 0, \qquad n < 0.$$

and $\{s_n\}$ and $\{x_n\}$ are the input and output sequences, respectively, $f_c = 0.8$ kHz, and $T = 0.1$ ms. To convert the samples to a 2-kHz rate, assuming the input is sampled at 10 kHz, a new sequence $\{w_n\}$, made up of every fifth sample of $\{x_n\}$, is defined.

Fig. 6 shows the discrete frequency response of the digital filter. Some aliasing obviously occurs since the response is down only about 10 dB at the folding frequency. If a sharper cutoff filter is applied, less aliasing will occur and slightly better results will be obtained. Nonetheless, it is demonstrated that accurate simulation results are obtained even with this filter.

Determination of the Inverse Filter

The general form of the inverse filter $A(z) = 1 + \sum_{i=1}^{\overline{M}} a_i z^{-i}$ is defined by determining the coefficients $\{a_i\}$ such that the difference between a constant and the filter output, $Y(z)$, is minimized in the least squares sense. Using this criterion the inverse filter will attempt to transform the input spectrum into a white noise, or a constant, spectrum. To within an irrelevant gain constant, this criterion is equivalent to minimizing the energy output of the filter $A(z)$. Thus the coefficients can be determined from

$$\frac{\partial}{\partial a_k} \sum_{n=1}^{L_1} y_n^2 = \frac{\partial}{\partial a_k} \sum_{n=0}^{L_1} \left(x_n + \sum_{i=1}^{\overline{M}} a_i x_{n-i} \right)^2 = 0,$$
$$k = 1, 2, \cdots, \overline{M}$$

with the solution given by the autocorrelation equations

$$\sum_{i=1}^{\overline{M}} a_i p_{i-j} = -p_j, \qquad i = 1, 2, \cdots, \overline{M}$$

where the autocorrelation coefficients p_j are calculated from $\{w_n\}$ by $p_j = \sum_{n=0}^{N-1-j} w_n w_{n+j}$, $j = 0, 1, \cdots, \overline{M}$, and $L_1 = N + \overline{M} - 1$. The success of the method is strongly dependent upon a proper choice of $\overline{M}$ the number of undetermined filter coefficients and N the number of data samples. If $\overline{M}$ is too small, very poor estimation of the resonance structure within the range $(0, F_s/2)$ is obtained, where F_s is the sampling frequency. If $\overline{M}$ is too large, then the fine-grain structure (due to the pitch periods) is estimated along with the resonance structure (in the limit, if $\overline{M}$ is large enough, the input will be transformed into a Kronecker delta function at the origin). What is desired is to obtain a close estimation only of the resonance structure, and to ignore the finegrain structure. N should be large enough to include several pitch periods but small enough to insure that significant pitch period variations do not occur.

For this study $\overline{M} = 4$ and $N = 64$ have been chosen. With $\overline{M} = 4$, either zero, one, or two resonances can be accurately represented. The minimum number of resonances possible within $(0, 1)$ kHz is zero (due to un-

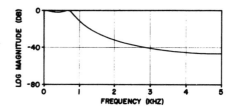

Fig. 6. Frequency response of 3-pole 2-dB ripple Chebyshev filter used in SIFT.

voiced speech) while the maximum is two (due to voiced speech with close first and second formants). With $N = 64$, a maximum interval of 32 ms can be represented, corresponding to approximately three pitch periods of a normal male voice. Additional considerations in the choice of N and $\overline{M}$ are presented elsewhere [6]. The set of autocorrelation equations is most efficiently solved for general $\overline{M}$ by use of Levinson's method [7]. With four coefficients, however, it is possible to quite easily obtain a closed form solution for the $\{a_i\}$. The set of linear equations to be solved is

$$a_1 p_0 + a_2 p_1 + a_3 p_2 + a_4 p_3 = -p_1$$
$$a_1 p_1 + a_2 p_0 + a_3 p_1 + a_4 p_2 = -p_2$$
$$a_1 p_2 + a_2 p_1 + a_3 p_0 + a_4 p_1 = -p_3$$
$$a_1 p_3 + a_2 p_2 + a_3 p_1 + a_4 p_0 = -p_4.$$

By adding the first equation to the last, and the second equation to the next to last,

$$\alpha_{14}(p_0 + p_3) + \alpha_{23}(p_1 + p_2) = -(p_1 + p_4)$$
$$\alpha_{14}(p_1 + p_2) + \alpha_{23}(p_0 + p_1) = -(p_2 + p_3)$$

where $\alpha_{14} = a_1 + a_4$ and $\alpha_{23} = a_2 + a_3$. If instead of adding, the corresponding equations are subtracted,

$$\beta_{14}(p_0 - p_3) + \beta_{23}(p_1 - p_2) = -(p_1 - p_4)$$
$$\beta_{14}(p_1 - p_2) + \beta_{23}(p_0 - p_1) = -(p_2 - p_3)$$

where $\beta_{14} = a_1 - a_4$ and $\beta_{23} = a_2 - a_3$.

Solving each of the two sets of second-order equations gives the $\{a_i\}$ as

$$a_1 = (\alpha_{14} + \beta_{14})/2$$
$$a_2 = (\alpha_{23} + \beta_{23})/2$$
$$a_3 = (\alpha_{23} - \beta_{23})/2$$
$$a_4 = (\alpha_{14} - \beta_{14})/2.$$

Since $|A(e^{i\omega T})|^2 = |1 + \sum_{i=1}^{\overline{M}} a_i e^{-i\omega T}|^2$ defines the spectrum of the inverse filter, $|D(e^{i\omega T})|^2 = |1/A(e^{i\omega T})|^2$ defines the estimate of the resonance behavior of the inverse filter input spectrum. The reciprocal of the inverse filter spectrum, $|D(e^{i\omega T})|^2$, is shown with the input spectrum on an expanded logarithmic scale for the test segment in Fig. 7. The first formant peak is clearly predicted. The primary peaks every 120 Hz under the smooth envelope are due to the periodicity of the waveform, while the secondary peaks every 31 Hz are due to the 32-ms length of data.

After the inverse filter is specified for a particular

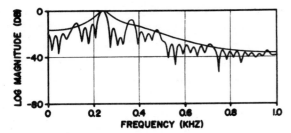

Fig. 7. Spectrum of SIFT inverse filter input and reciprocal of inverse filter.

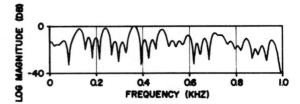

Fig. 8. Spectrum of SIFT inverse filter output.

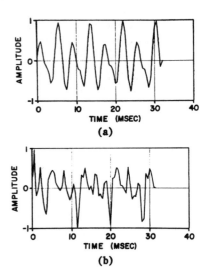

Fig. 9. Inverse filter waveforms from SIFT. (a) Input waveform. (b) Output waveform.

frame, the output $\{y_n\}$ corresponding to the error or deviation from a white noise sequence is calculated as

$$y_n = w_n + \sum_{i=1}^{4} a_i w_{n-i} \quad n = 0, 1, \cdots, 63,$$

$$\text{where } w_n = 0, n < 0.$$

Although $\{y_n\}$ will have nonzero values out to $n = N + \overline{M}$, they will not contribute to the pitch estimates and are thus ignored. Fig. 8 shows the spectrum of the inverse filter output for the test segment. The major resonance behavior has been completely removed leaving only the fundamental frequency information superimposed upon a constant. Thus, the inverse filter can be considered as a prewhitening filter which attempts to whiten the input spectrum by eliminating the trend characteristics or spectral shaping (due predominantly to the vocal tract resonances or formants) while retaining the fine structure due to the glottal pulses. Note that since the length of the inverse filter is constrained to a small value, it would probably be more correct to say the inverse filter acts as a pseudo-prewhitening filter since the output obviously does not have a purely constant spectrum. Actually, the glottal pulses also have trend characteristics which are removed by the inverse filter. Thus if the input waveform were synthesized according to Fant's [8] model, the acoustic speech wave at the output to the inverse filter would be transformed into Kronecker delta functions at the initiation of each pitch period. Fig. 9 illustrates results for the SIFT algorithm as seen at the output of the inverse filter, compared with the input test segment. It is seen that the formant structure (the damped sinusoidal characteristic) has been removed and fairly sharp pulses at the initiation of each pitch period are obtained at the inverse filter output. (It is easily shown that the width of the pitch period spike will be approximately $1/f_c$ ms where f_c is the filter cutoff in kilohertz.) Although an attempt could be made to estimate the pitch period directly from the inverse filter output, it is not recommended for the same reasons that direct pitch estimation from the acoustic waveform is not recommended, as discussed earlier.

The pitch period estimates are finally obtained by a standard autocorrelation method, only the input signal now has the resonance structure or formant information eliminated. The autocorrelation sequence $\{r_n\}$ calcu-

lated at the output of the inverse filter is of length $M = 2N$ and is given by

$$r_n = \begin{cases} \sum_{j=0}^{N-1-n} y_j y_{j+n}, & n = 0, 1, \cdots, M/2-1 \\ 0, & n = M/2 \\ r_{M-n}, & n = M/2+1, M/2+2, \cdots, M-1. \end{cases}$$

It is assumed that the initial pitch period estimate is known within ± 4 ms. Thus for each frame, a total of 16 autocorrelation samples are necessary (including r_0, used for normalization). When a peak $\hat{r}$ is obtained at $n = \hat{N}$, r_n is evaluated for $n = \hat{N}-7$, $\hat{N}-6$, $\cdots$, $\hat{N}$, $\cdots$, $\hat{N}+6$, $\hat{N}+7$, and $n = 0$ in the following frame.

If an unvoiced decision is made, $\hat{N}$ is reset to the initial value chosen. For most speech, an 8 ms range is quite sufficient. For a male speaker with an average 8 ms pitch period, calculation of 15 autocorrelation values encompasses a range of 83–250 Hz. Because the pitch samples are tracked from frame to frame, a much larger range of F_0 is effectively obtained. If, however, a greater range of uncertainty exists on F_0, it is only necessary to calculate additional autocorrelation terms from the inverse filter output.

Interpolation

Accurate measurement of fundamental frequency requires a time scale resolution of approximately 0.1 to 0.15 ms. If T had been chosen as 0.125 ms, and the true pitch P were 6 ms for example, the maximum quantization error would be approximately $T/2P^2$ =1.74 Hz. For the chosen value of $T=0.5$ ms, the maximum quantization error of 7.0 Hz is large enough to be quite noticeable in synthetic speech. The straightforward approach to this problem of decreasing the sampling period greatly increases the computation time, and also then makes it necessary to eliminate the resonance effects of the higher formants by designing a considerably larger filter. This approach is discussed elsewhere [1]. A simplified solution to this problem can be obtained by deriving a trigonometric interpolation function for $\{r_n\}$, the autocorrelation sequence obtained from the inverse filter. For simplicity it is assumed that M is a power of 2. Then the $M=2N$ length sequence $\{r_n\}$ has a discrete Fourier transform (DFT) given by

$$R_k = \sum_{n=0}^{M-1} r_n e^{-j2\pi nk/M}, \qquad k = 0, 1, \cdots, M-1.$$

But since $\{r_n\}$ is an autocorrelation sequence, it must be real symmetric in the sense that $r_n = r_{M-n}$, $n=0, 1, \cdots, M/2$, and thus, $\{R_k\}$ must be real and symmetric, resulting in

$$R_k = 2 \sum_{l=0}^{M/2-1} u_l \cos \frac{2\pi lk}{M}, \quad k = 0, 1, \cdots, M-1 \quad (1)$$

where

$$u_l = \begin{cases} \frac{1}{2}r_0, & l = 0 \\ r_l, & l = 1, 2, \cdots, M/2 - 1. \end{cases} \quad (2)$$

The inverse relationship is

$$r_n = \frac{1}{M} \sum_{k=0}^{M-1} R_k e^{j2\pi nk/M}$$

$$= \frac{1}{M}\left[R_0 + R_{M/2}e^{j\pi n} + 2 \sum_{k=1}^{M/2-1} R_k \cos (2\pi nk/M) \right]. \quad (3)$$

Now, if a new sequence $\{\hat{R}_k\}$ of length $M'=2^I M$ is defined as

$$\hat{R}_k = \begin{cases} R_k, & k = 0, 1, \cdots, M/2 \\ 0, & k = M/2 + 1, \cdots, M' - M/2 \\ R_{M'-k}, & k = M' - M/2 + 1, \cdots, M' - 1 \end{cases} \quad (4)$$

where I is a positive integer, then $\hat{r}_n$ is given by

$$\hat{r}_n = \frac{1}{M'} \sum_{k=0}^{M'-1} \hat{R}_k \exp\left(\frac{j2\pi kn}{M'}\right), \quad n = 0, 1, \cdots, M' - 1$$

$$\frac{1}{M'}\left[R_0 + R_{M/2}\exp\left(\frac{j\pi nM}{M'}\right) + 2 \sum_{k=1}^{M/2-1} R_k \right.$$

$$\left. \cdot \cos\left(\frac{2\pi k}{M}\frac{nM}{M'}\right)\right]$$

$$= \frac{M}{M'} r_{\frac{nM}{M'}}, \qquad n = 0, 1, \cdots, M' - 1. \quad (5)$$

Thus $\{r_n\}$ can be interpolated efficiently with the use

of two FFT's. The interpolated sequence $\{\hat{r}_n\}$ can also be derived explicitly in terms of $\{r_n\}$. Substituting (1) into (5),

$$r_a = \frac{1}{M}\left[2 \sum_{l=0}^{M/2-1} u_l + 2e^{j\pi a} \sum_{l=0}^{M/2-1} u_l(-1)^l \right.$$

$$\left. + 4 \sum_{k=1}^{M/2-1} \sum_{l=0}^{M/2-1} \mu_l \cos \frac{2\pi lk}{M} \cos \frac{2\pi ak}{M} \right]$$

where $a = nM/M'$. It is reasonable to assume that the folding frequency term $R_{M/2}$ does not substantially contribute to the final results if $M \gg 1$. By interchanging the summations on k and l and writing the cosines in exponential form, geometric progressions are obtained which result in

$$r_a = \frac{1}{M}\left\{ 2 \sum_{l=0}^{M/2-1} \mu_l + \sum_{l=0}^{M/2-1} \mu_l \right.$$

$$\cdot\left[\frac{\sin \alpha(M-1)/2 - \sin \alpha/2}{\sin \alpha/2}\right.$$

$$\left.\left. + \frac{\sin \beta(M-1)/2 - \sin \beta/2}{\sin \beta/2}\right]\right\}.$$

This equation reduces very neatly into the interpolation formula

$$r_a = \frac{1}{M} \sum_{l=0}^{M/2-1} \mu_l \left[\frac{\sin \alpha(M-1)/2}{\sin \alpha/2} + \frac{\sin \beta(M-1)/2}{\sin \beta/2}\right] \quad (6)$$

where

$$\alpha = \frac{2\pi}{M}(l + a)$$

$$\beta = \frac{2\pi}{M}(l - a)$$

$$a = \frac{nM}{M'}, \qquad n = 0, 1, \cdots, M' - 1.$$

$M=2N$ and u_l is defined by (2). If interpolation over the full range of the term a is desired, it is much faster to use the FFT twice, as indicated by (1)–(5). For this application, however, the characteristics of the resulting autocorrelation sequence allow a much faster solution by the direct application of (6). For voiced speech, the largest peak away from the origin at $n = \hat{N}$ will generally define the pitch period within ± 1 sample. Since the peak is usually about three samples wide (assuming $f_c = 0.8$ kHz and $T = 0.5$ ms), a very reasonable approximation to the interpolated values between $\hat{N} - 1$ and $\hat{N} + 1$ can be accomplished by using only $r_{\hat{N}-1}$, $r_{\hat{N}}$, and $r_{\hat{N}+1}$ and considering all other terms as zero. This is possible because of the rather rapid decay of the interpolation function (assuming $\hat{N} > 3$ or 4 which will be the case except for extremely high F_0). Fig. 10 is a graph of r_a versus a for $r_n = \delta_{n,16}$ on a normalized time scale where $a = n/4$, $n = 0, 1, 2, \cdots, N$. The distance between zero crossings, away from the main peak, precisely defines

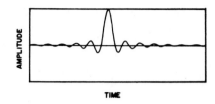

Fig. 10. Representation of interpolation function. Zero crossings occur at sampling interval.

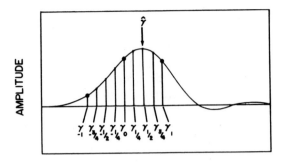

TIME

Fig. 11. Illustration showing 4/1 interpolation about the points γ_{-1}, γ_0, γ_1, $\hat{\gamma}$ indicates the interpolated peak estimate.

the sampling period. It is seen from (6) that the exact values of the interpolation function are dependent upon l. In the region 2–16 ms, however, the differences are relatively small. By referring $\hat{N}$ to some fixed point and defining the interpolation ratio M'/M, it is possible to obtain a considerably simplified set of algebraic equations. If a 4 to 1 interpolation ratio is used, discrete samples will be calculated at intervals of 0.125 ms. By defining $n = 16$ in (6) as the reference point (corresponding to 8 ms), and noting symmetry relationships, the simplified interpolation equations can by written in matrix form as

$$[\gamma_{\pm 3/4} \quad \gamma_{\pm 1/2} \quad \gamma_{\pm 1/4}]^T = A [\gamma_{\pm 1} \quad \gamma_0 \quad \gamma_{\mp 1}]^T \quad (7)$$

where

$$A = \begin{bmatrix} 0.879124 & 0.321662 & -0.150534 \\ 0.637643 & 0.636110 & -0.212208 \\ 0.322745 & 0.878039 & -0.158147 \end{bmatrix}$$

and $\gamma_a = r_{\hat{N}+a}/r_0$.

An example of 4/1 interpolation using (7) is shown in Fig. 11 on a normalized time scale. The discrete samples with large dots indicate the uninterpolated pitch peak estimate and adjacent terms from the autocorrelation calculation $\{r_n\}$, normalized by r_0. The interpolated samples are indicated by the small dots, while the solid line indicates the continuous curve obtained by evaluating the general interpolation equation (6). The peak value over the seven samples $\gamma_{i/4}$, $i = 0, \pm 1, \pm 2, \pm 3$, is defined as $\hat{\gamma}$.

In practice $\gamma_{\pm 3/4}$ will never be the peak value $\hat{\gamma}$ and thus need not be calculated. The slope measured from γ_0 will indicate the direction of the peak and thus only three terms must be calculated per frame ($\gamma_{\pm 1/4}$ and $\gamma_{1/2}$ if $\gamma_{1/4} > \gamma_{-1/4}$ or $\gamma_{\pm 1/4}$ and $\gamma_{-1/2}$ if $\gamma_{1/4} < \gamma_{-1/4}$). The interpolated F_0 measurement is finally given by $F_0(\text{kHz}) = 1/P$ where $P = (\hat{N}+\hat{a})/2$ and $\hat{a}$ is the index corresponding to $\hat{\gamma}$.

Decision Criteria

If the pitch period were constant over a very large number of input samples, pitch detection would be trivial since the autocorrelation calculation would average out the undesired terms (defined as noise) to essentially zero value. Assuming the noise to be Gaussian in nature, it is possible to predict a threshold value to assure that the probability of any noise sample in the

autocorrelation sequence is less than some specified value, as a function of the number of samples N [1]. The result for $N = 64$, assuming an error probability of 0.001, is 0.378 for the threshold. It is shown in the section on experimental results that a threshold setting of 0.378 to 0.400 is quite realistic.

If the inverse filter output is modeled as a periodic Kronecker delta train, the normalized autocorrelation sequence is described by a linear function of the period with a decreasing slope. For the parameters suggested, we have found that the estimated pitch period peak $\hat{\gamma}$ for voiced speech can be reasonably well described by $\hat{\gamma} = -0.03P + 0.9$ in many cases, where $2 \leq P \leq 16$ ms. This equation assumes, of course, that within the 64-point window, pitch period variations are small. With a threshold setting of 0.4, pitch period estimates of up to 16 ms can therefore be obtained. (In the actual implementation P is estimated from $(\hat{N}+\hat{a})/2$.)

Under most conditions, a voiced-unvoiced decison can be made by simply testing to see if $\hat{\gamma}$ is greater than some predefined threshold. If so, the segment is defined as voiced. Otherwise, it is defined as unvoiced. However, anomalies can occur, such as a peak in a voiced segment being slightly below the threshold, whereas the preceding and following segments cross the threshold.

A simple decision algorithm for determining whether a particular frame is voiced or unvoiced is shown in Fig. 12. Whenever a peak exceeds the threshold value of 0.4, frame k is defined as voiced. Occasionally it is possible for a voiced frame to be incorrectly defined as unvoiced due to either considerable variation in the pitch period values or phonetic variations within the window. If this isolated condition is detected, frame $k-1$ is redefined as voiced with a pitch period equal to the mean of frame k and frame $k-2$.

If the peak in frame k does not cross the threshold, it is tested to see if the previous two frames are unvoiced. If so, frame k is unvoiced. If the previous two frames are voiced, then the threshold is lowered by 25 percent. At the end of a voiced phrase, part of the segment may be voiced and part unvoiced. This decision algorithm favors the voiced portion. In addition, fairly rapid changes in the pitch period values within a window can cause the peak correlation value to be decreased

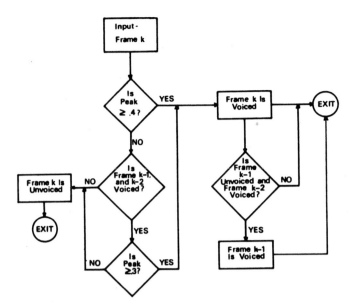

Fig. 12. Decision algorithm for voiced-unvoiced decision.

by 15–20 percent. If the peak still does not cross the threshold, frame k is defined as unvoiced. Otherwise it is defined as voiced.

Calculation of Necessary Operations

Let t_a and t_m denote the computer add and multiply times, respectively, in microseconds. It is reasonable to assume for simplicity that a subtract operation is equivalent to an add and a divide is roughly equivalent to a multiply. Calculation of the five correlation coefficients from the 64-point input sequence requires 320 $(t_a + t_m)$ µs. Calculation of the inverse filter coefficients requires $20t_a + 16t_m$ µs if the terms are efficiently grouped. Performing the inverse filtering of the input signal requires $256t_m + 320t_a$ µs. The autocorrelation calculation of the inverse filter output requires $1024(t_a + t_m)$ µs. Finally, the interpolation and peak picking require roughly $69t_a + 9t_m$ µs (for simplicity, a comparison is assumed equivalent to an addition). Thus, for real time total arithmetic computation $1750t_m + 1625t_a \leq 1000P_f$, where P_f (ms) is the time interval between frames of data. If $P_f = 15$ ms, $t_m = 5$ µs and $t_a = 3$ µs, real-time processing can be accomplished (assuming that overhead functions such as fetching and storing are included in the add and multiply times). Thus, it should be possible to operate in close to a real time environment even with the popular minicomputers if programming is done in assembler language and inefficient software floating point subroutines can be avoided. With the design of special-purpose hardware, it should be possible to easily attain a real time digital fundamental frequency tracker using the SIFT algorithm. As a further advantage of the method, the algebra involved is quite simple and requires only the four basic arithmetic operations without any table lookups.

In contrast, the cepstral analysis method as described by Schafer and Rabiner [9] uses two 1024-point real FFT's that require at least $(3t_a + 2t_m)10^4$ µs. Thus, the SIFT algorithm is greater than an order of magnitude faster than the cepstral analysis pitch extraction method for the assumed conditions of $t_m = 5$ µs and $t_a = 3$ µs. With both algorithms programmed in Fortran on an IBM 1800, the SIFT algorithm was found to be approximately 20 times faster, even with efficient real FFT computation.

III. Experimental Results

To illustrate the capability of the SIFT algorithm for voiced speech, the exclamatory "oh" with a sharply rising and falling F_0 was spoken and analyzed. The data was also cepstrally analyzed for comparison purposes. The input data was analyzed at 16 ms intervals using a 32 ms sliding window.

The cepstral estimates were obtained by multiplying the data by a 32-ms Hamming window. A sampling rate of 10 kHz was used, to allow a 0.1 ms time scale resolution. Since the utterance is all voiced, the cepstral estimate for F_0 was defined by $F_0 = 1/P$ where P is the location of the cepstral peak in the range (2, 16) ms. The SIFT algorithm estimates for this example were also made by simply searching the output sequence for a peak in the range (2, 16) ms.

Results are shown in Fig. 13 where the triangles indicate cepstral estimates and the dots indicate SIFT estimates. The points are shown at 32 ms increments. The analysis covers an extremely wide range of fundamental frequency, from approximately 70–330 Hz. This range encompasses the vast majority of fundamental frequency range from adult male speech to children's speech. With the exception of a few frames of data, the results are seen to be quite close. There is one gross error due to the cepstral analysis at frame zero and one due to the SIFT analysis at frame 20, where the second harmonic of the pitch period had slightly higher amplitude than the fundamental. The average deviation between the two curves (excluding the two gross errors) is approximately 3 Hz. These results are obtained in spite of the fact that the second formant frequency F_2 varies from slightly above to slightly below the folding frequency in the SIFT algorithm. For several frames of data, namely frames 12–21, a component due to F_2 occurs in the autocorrelation of the inverse filter output. If sharper input filtering is applied, the results at the high fundamental frequency will compare favorably with the cepstral results.

To demonstrate typical results obtainable from SIFT where both voiced and unvoiced sounds occur, the phrase "put she can," spoken with each word emphasized, was analyzed. Again, for comparative purposes, cepstral analysis was performed on the same frames of input data. Within any range, say (2, 16) ms, a peak can be found for cepstral output. So that no difficulties would be encountered in the voiced-unvoiced decision using cepstral analysis, the decision was made manu-

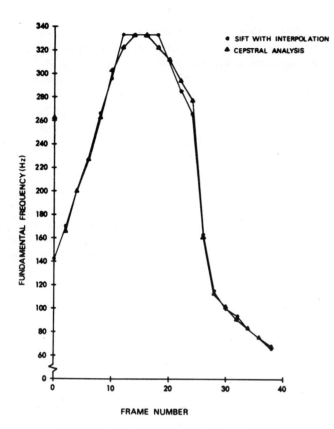

Fig. 13. F_0 analysis for the utterance "oh."

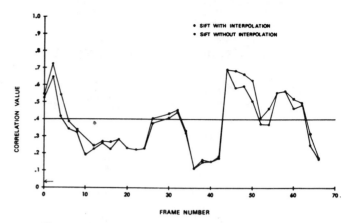

Fig. 14. Peak correlation values measured from SIFT for the phrase "put she can."

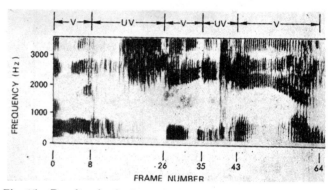

Fig. 15. Results of voiced-unvoiced decision from SIFT algorithm shown on spectrogram of utterance "put she can."

ally by inspection of the cepstral output data for each frame. If a reasonably sharp peak occurred with respect to the noise level, the segment was defined as voiced with $F_0 = 1/P$, where P is the location of the maximum peak in the range (2, 16) ms. Otherwise, the segment was defined as unvoiced and P was not used.

The fundamental frequency and voiced-unvoiced decision with the SIFT algorithm were obtained automatically. First, it is of interest to observe the character of the normalized peak amplitude within each frame as a function of the frame number. The peak uninterpolated and interpolated values versus even frame numbers are shown in Fig. 14. Based upon the previously discussed model, the peak correlation value excluding the origin would be expected to vary from around 0.30 to 0.70, depending upon the number of pitch periods per window and the variation between pitch period values within the window.

For unvoiced speech, the correlation between samples is small, with the actual value depending upon the number of samples analyzed. The peak correlation (excluding the origin) for unvoiced speech is usually less than 0.35 if $N \geq 60$. In fact, within a 99.9 percent confidence interval the peak amplitude in an unvoiced portion will be less than 0.378. Thus, with good theoretical justification it is possible to use a fixed threshold to make voiced-unvoiced decisions, using the SIFT algorithm. As a conservative value, 0.4 is chosen as the threshold. Although this value effectively guarantees that an unvoiced segment will not be defined as voiced,

it does not guarantee that voiced segments will not occasionally be mistaken for unvoiced segments. Detection of these conditions and their correction is accomplished automatically by the flow chart presented previously in Fig. 12. For visual comparison, the automatically estimated boundaries are shown on a spectrogram of the utterance in Fig. 15. Note that the actual phrase analyzed has nearly all of the initial plosive /p/ missing and thus the analysis defines the beginning as voiced. All of these boundaries are within ±1 frame (16 ms) of those estimated manually from cepstral analysis output data. Representative time series from which the voiced-unvoiced decisions and fundamental frequency estimates were obtained are compared along with the input data in Fig. 16. Every other frame of data, from frame 22 through frame 46 is shown. The leftmost series is the cepstral output data from 2 to 16 ms. A single normalization factor was applied to all frames of data for plotting purposes. The middle series is the output data from the SIFT algorithm just before the peak peaking and interpolation. On the right is shown the corresponding frames of input data from which the cepstral and SIFT algorithm results were obtained.

By inspection of the input data, it can be seen that frames 22–24 are unvoiced while voicing is beginning in frame 26. Frames 28–32 are clearly voiced, while frame

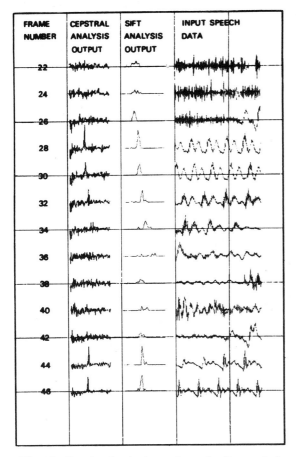

FRAME NUMBER	CEPSTRAL ANALYSIS OUTPUT	SIFT ANALYSIS OUTPUT	INPUT SPEECH DATA

Fig. 16.   Input and output waveforms for the cepstral and SIFT algorithm.

34 shows a voiced segment ending. Frames 36–42 are clearly unvoiced, while frames 44–46 are clearly voiced.

The voiced-unvoiced decisions can also be easily made by visual inspection of the cepstral data. Frames 28–32 and 44–46 are voiced. All other frames are unvoiced.

The SIFT results shown in these frames correspond to the data calculated within the tracking window of length 8 ms with initial center location chosen as 6 ms. At frame 26, the algorithm starts tracking the voiced portion. Tracking is continued with the center location of the window equal to the previous pitch period estimate until frame 36 at which time an unvoiced decision is made and the window is shifted back down to the initial location for frame 38. Only positive correlation values can be candidates for pitch peaks and thus negative values were set to zero for plotting purposes. Frames 28–34 and 44–46 were automatically defined as voiced. It is interesting to note that for these frames of data the relative values of the peak amplitudes in both the cepstral and SIFT output are quite similar.

Referring to Fig. 14, one additional advantage of performing interpolation can be seen. For the regions in which voicing occurs, interpolation significantly increases the peak values, while for unvoiced portions interpolation makes very little difference. Thus, the effective desired peak to undesired signal ratio is increased, allowing for somewhat easier discrimination between voiced and unvoiced sounds.

In Fig. 17, the estimated fundamental frequency versus even frame numbers has been presented for several situations. The triangles denote cepstral analysis results (resolution of 0.1 ms) which will be considered as reference values. The circles indicate F_0 estimates from SIFT without interpolation (that is, estimates with a resolution of 0.5 ms) and the solid dots indicate F_0 estimates with interpolation (corresponding to a resolution of 0.125 ms).

The results just shown are extremely close for each voiced segment. Note that the interpolated values do generally lie much closer to the cepstral analysis estimates than noninterpolated estimates.

IV. Summary

A new algorithm for efficient accurate automatic extraction of fundamental frequency from speech has been developed. Experimental results have been presented to demonstrate the accuracy of the SIFT algorithm with respect to the widely used cepstral analysis method.

Rather difficult analysis examples were purposely chosen to illustrate both the capabilities and limitations of the method. The algorithm does not guarantee error-free analysis; in one example, a gross error was shown. Also, it was shown that in practice, a few more tests in addition to a simple "yes-no" threshold decision are necessary to determine whether a segment is voiced or unvoiced.

Furthermore, it has been experimentally demonstrated that the difficult problem of detecting voicing during the transition from a voiced to unvoiced interval is not completely resolved. An illustration of this problem can be seen from close inspection of the vicinity of frame 35 in Fig. 15. (It should be pointed out, however, that whenever the SIFT algorithm failed to extract correct voicing, cepstral analysis also failed.)

Even with these possible limitations, the SIFT algorithm is believed to be a very worthwhile approach for consideration as a fundamental frequency extraction technique in automated digital speech analysis systems for the following reasons: 1) the unvoiced-voiced decision algorithm is quite simple; 2) implementation requires only the four elementary arithmetic operations, without any table lookups or complex indexing (such as necessary for FFT implementations); 3) the algorithm is very efficient computationally; and 4) informal listening tests of synthetic speech show no significant perceptual differences when cepstral analysis and the SIFT analysis F_0 contours were compared.

The SIFT algorithm is conservatively an order of

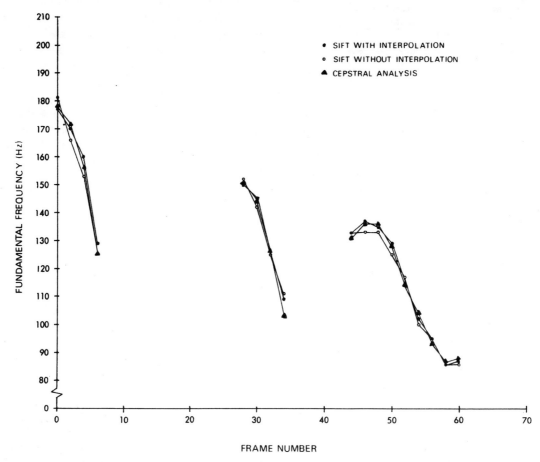

Fig. 17. Estimated fundamental frequency curves versus frame number for utterance "put she can."

magnitude faster than cepstral analysis, if prefiltering is done with an analog filter. It was demonstrated that the filter response characteristics are generally not critical since all results presented here were accomplished by digitally simulating a low-order Chebyshev filter. Even with general purpose minicomputers it should be possible to accurately analyze fundamental frequency contours within ten or twenty times real time using the SIFT algorithm. Presently techniques are being considered for implementing a real-time hardware version of the SIFT algorithm.

Acknowledgment

The author wishes to thank Dr. D. Broad for several discussions and many suggestions. He is also grateful for the careful reading and constructive criticisms of the reviewer.

References

[1] J. D. Markel, "Automatic formant and fundamental frequency extraction from a digital inverse filter formulation," in *Conf. Rec. 1972 Int. Conf. Speech Commun. and Processing*, 1972, Paper B9, pp. 81–84.
[2] M. R. Schroeder, "Vocoders: Analysis and synthesis of speech," *Proc. IEEE*, vol. 54, pp. 720–734, May 1966.
[3] A. M. Noll, "Cepstrum pitch determination," *J. Acoust. Soc. Amer.*, vol. 41, pp. 293–309, Feb. 1967.
[4] M. R. Schroeder, "Parameter estimation in speech: A lesson in unorthodoxy," *Proc. IEEE*, vol. 58, pp. 707–712, May 1970.
[5] A. M. Noll, "Short-time spectrum and 'cepstrum' techniques for vocal-pitch detection," *J. Acoust. Soc. Amer.*, vol. 36, pp. 296–302, Feb. 1964.
[6] J. D. Markel, "A linear least-squares inverse filter formulation for formant trajectory estimation," Speech Commun. Res. Lab., Santa Barbara, Calif., SCRL Monograph 7, Aug. 1971.
[7] N. Levinson, "The Wiener RMS (root-mean square error) criterion in filter design and prediction," Appendix in N. Wiener, *Extrapolation and Smoothing of Stationary Times Series*, Cambridge, Mass.: M.I.T. Press, 1966, pp. 129–148.
[8] G. C. M. Fant, *Acoustic Theory of Speech Production*. 's-Gravenhage: Mouton, 1960, pp. 42–46.
[9] R. W. Schafer and L. R. Rabiner, "System for automatic analysis of voiced speech," *J. Acoust. Soc. Amer.*, vol. 47, pp. 634–648, Feb. 1970.

Received 24 August 1966

Cepstrum Pitch Determination

A. Michael Noll

Bell Telephone Laboratories, Murray Hill, New Jersey 07971

The cepstrum, defined as the power spectrum of the logarithm of the power spectrum, has a strong peak corresponding to the pitch period of the voiced-speech segment being analyzed. Cepstra were calculated on a digital computer and were automatically plotted on microfilm. Algorithms were developed heuristically for picking those peaks corresponding to voiced-speech segments and the vocal pitch periods. This information was then used to derive the excitation for a computer-simulated channel vocoder. The pitch quality of the vocoded speech was judged by experienced listeners in informal comparison tests to be indistinguishable from the original speech.

INTRODUCTION

VOICED-speech sounds result from the resonant action of the vocal tract on the periodic puffs of air admitted through the vocal cords. For pitch-period determination, the time periodicity of the source signal must be obtained from the observed speech signal. Also, voiced–unvoiced decisions require accurate determination of the presence or absence of such periodic puffs in the source signal. This deceptively simple problem has been the object of considerable research over the past few decades. Aside from its obvious use in analysis of speech sounds from a pure research standpoint, an accurate pitch detector must also perform adequately as an integral part of most speech-bandwidth compression schemes. The design of an accurate pitch detector that works satisfactorily with band-limited, noisy speech signals remains one of the challenging areas of speech processing research.

In a previous paper, a new method for obtaining the fundamental frequency or pitch of human speech was described.[1] Since the logarithm of the amplitude spectrum of a periodic time signal with rich harmonic structure is itself "periodic" in frequency, the new method consisted of spectrum analyzing this log amplitude spectrum. Adopting some new terminology proposed by Tukey, the method was called "cepstrum" pitch detection, where the term cepstrum refers to the spectrum of the log-amplitude spectrum. Computer programs were written to perform short-time cepstrum analyses of

speech, and the resultant pitch information was used to obtain the excitation for computer-simulated vocoders. The synthesized speech was quite encouraging as demonstrated by tapes played at the sixty-seventh meeting of the Acoustical Society.[2]

The early computer programs written to simulate the cepstrum analyzer have since undergone a number of changes towards simplicity and efficiency. The results of analyses of speech cepstra were used to design an automatic method for determining the pitch periods from the cepstral peaks. This automatic peak picker, though not previously described, was used to obtain the excitation signals for the computer-simulated vocoders. Some interesting and unexpected pitch fluctuations and pitch doubling have been discovered during the observations of speech cepstra required to develop the algorithms for the cepstral peak picker. These topics and new approaches to explaining and justifying cepstrum pitch determination were not reported in the previous papers; and now is also a good time to present the historical background leading to the concept of short-time cepstrum analysis for vocal-pitch detection. This paper treats all these topics and concludes with descriptions of some possible hardware implementations of cepstrum analyzers.

I. HISTORICAL BACKGROUNDS

In the fall of 1959, Bogert (of Bell Telephone Laboratories) noticed banding in spectrograms of seismic signals. He realized that this banding was caused by

---

[1] A. M. Noll, "Short-Time Spectrum and 'Cepstrum' Techniques for Vocal-Pitch Detection," J. Acoust. Soc. Am. **36**, 296–302 (1964).

[2] A. M. Noll and M. R. Schroeder, "Short-Time 'Cepstrum' Pitch Detection," J. Acoust. Soc. Am. **36**, 1030 (1964).

Reprinted with permission from *J. Acoust. Soc. Am.*, vol. 41, pp. 293–309, Feb. 1967.

"periodic" ripples in the spectra and that this was characteristic of the spectra of any signal consisting of itself plus an echo. The frequency spacing of these ripples equals the reciprocal of the difference in time arrivals of the two waves. Tukey (of both Princeton University and Bell Telephone Laboratories) suggested that this frequency difference might be obtained by first taking the logarithm of the spectrum, thereby making the ripples nearly cosinusoidal. A spectrum analysis of the log spectrum then could be performed to determine the "frequency" of the ripple. In early 1960, Bogert programmed Tukey's suggestion on a computer and proceeded to analyze numerous earthquakes and explosions. Tukey, noticing similarities between time series analysis and log-spectrum series analysis, introduced a new set of paraphrased terms. The spectrum of the log spectrum was called the "cepstrum," and the frequency of the spectral ripples were referred to as "quefrency." Bogert, Tukey, and Healy published their ideas in an article with perhaps one of the weirdest titles ever encountered in the scientific literature: "The Quefrency Alanysis of Time Series for Echoes: Cepstrum, Pseudo-Autocovariance, Cross-Cepstrum and Saphe Cracking."[3] In the article, they very clearly expressed a pessimistic view for achieving adequate classification of seismic events by cepstral techniques. In fact, no definitive indication of focal depth was found.

Their article was issued as an internal Bell Laboratories memorandum before publication in Rosenblatt's book. Schroeder read the memorandum and realized that voiced speech spectra also have ripples, and hence cepstrum analysis might be suitable for vocal-pitch determination. In June 1962, Schroeder suggested cepstrum-pitch determination as an area worthy of further study. At that time, he and Atal had just completed a paper on methods for performing short-time spectrum analyses.[4] Thus, the atmosphere was perfect for the concept of short-time cepstrum analysis that then developed.

Seismic signals consist of a single event, and therefore only one cepstrum is obtained. Speech, however, changes with time, and a single cepstrum of a long speech signal would be meaningless. Hence, a series of cepstra for short segments of the speech signal are required—a short-time cepstrum. A scheme was devised for performing such short-time cepstral analyses utilizing delay lines and multipliers as shown in Fig. 1. A computer program was written with a special-purpose block-diagram language to simulate this method, and the short-time spectra and cepstra were automatically plotted by the computer on microfilm.[5] The cepstra for voiced speech intervals had strong peaks corresponding to the pitch period. The conclusion was quite definite: Although a single cepstrum analysis of seismic events was not promising for seismic classification, short-time cepstrum analysis of speech performed excellently as a new means for vocal-pitch determination.

In recent papers, the heutristics of cepstrum analysis for extracting echoed signals from noise has been developed by Bogert and Ossanna.[6] Also, a more general formalism of separating convolved signals and its relation with cepstrum analysis has been treated by Oppenheim.[7]

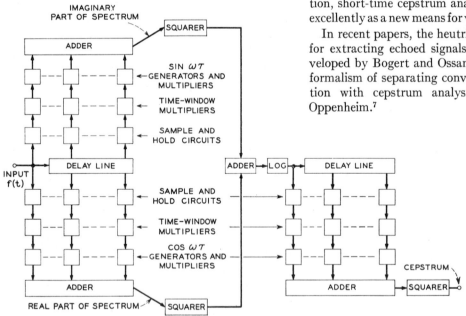

FIG. 1. Block diagram of sampled-data device for performing short-time cepstrum analysis.

[3] B. P. Bogert, M. J. R. Healy, and J. W. Tukey, in *Proceedings of the Symposium on Time Series Analysis*, by M. Rosenblatt, Ed. (John Wiley & Sons, Inc., New York, 1963), Chap. 15, pp. 209–243.

[4] M. R. Schroeder and B. S. Atal, "Generalized Short-Time Power Spectra and Autocorrelation Functions," J. Acoust. Soc. Am. **34**, 1679–1683 (1962).

[5] J. L. Kelly, Jr., Carol Lochbaum, and V. A. Vyssotsky, "A Block Diagram Compiler," Bell System Tech. J. **40**, 669–677 (1961).

[6] B. P. Bogert and J. F. Ossanna, "The Heuristics of a Stationary Complex Echoed Gaussian Signal in Stationary Gaussian Noise," IEEE Trans. Information Theory **IT-12**, No. 3, 343 (1966).

[7] A. V. Oppenheim, "Nonlinear Filtering of Convolved Signals," Mass. Inst. Technol. Res. Lab. Electron. Quart. Progr. Rept. No. 80, 168–175 (January 1966).

II. CESTRUM-PITCH DETERMINATION

In its most basic form, the system for producing voiced speech sounds consists only of the vocal source and the vocal tract as shown in Fig. 2. The source signal $s(t)$ is the periodic puffs of air admitted through the vocal cords. The effect of the vocal tract is completely specified by its impulse response $h(t)$ such that the output speech signal $f(t)$ equals the convolution of $s(t)$ and $h(t)$. Alternatively, if $S(\omega)$ is the spectrum of the vocal source and $H(\omega)$ is the transfer function or spectrum of the vocal tract, then the spectrum of the speech signal equals the product of $S(\omega)$ and $H(\omega)$. Expressed algebraically,

$$f(t) = s(t)*h(t), \tag{1}$$

$$F(\omega) = S(\omega) \cdot H(\omega), \tag{2}$$

with

$$F(\omega) = \mathfrak{F}[f(t)], \tag{3}$$

$$S(\omega) = \mathfrak{F}[s(t)], \tag{4}$$

$$H(\omega) = \mathfrak{F}[h(t)], \tag{5}$$

where $*$ denotes convolution, $\mathfrak{F}$ denotes Fourier transformation, and the Fourier transforms of $s(t)$ and $h(t)$ are assumed to exist.

The source signal and, therefore, the speech signal, are quasiperiodic for voiced-speech sounds. If the period is T seconds, then the power spectrum $|F(\omega)|^2$ of the speech signal consists of harmonics spaced T^{-1} Hz. Thus, the power spectrum of a voiced speech signal is "periodic" along the frequency axis with "period" equal to the reciprocal of the period of the time signal being analyzed. The obvious way to measure this "period" in the power spectrum is to take the Fourier transform of the spectrum that will have a peak corresponding to the "period." This spectrum of the power spectrum is more commonly known as the autocorrelation function of the original time signal. Mathematically, the autocorrelation function $r(\tau)$ is defined as

$$r(\tau) \equiv \mathfrak{F}[|F(\omega)|^2]. \tag{6}$$

The speech power spectrum equals the product of the spectra of the vocal source and the vocal tract. But the Fourier transform of a product equals the convolution of the Fourier transforms of the two multiplicands. Thus,

$$r(\tau) = \mathfrak{F}[|S(\omega)|^2|H(\omega)|^2] \tag{7}$$

$$= \mathfrak{F}[|S(\omega)|^2]*\mathfrak{F}[|H(\omega)|^2] \tag{8}$$

$$= r_s(\tau)*r_h(\tau), \tag{9}$$

where $r_s(\tau)$ and $r_h(\tau)$ are the autocorrelation functions of $s(t)$ and $h(t)$, respectively. The effects of the vocal source and vocal tract are therefore convolved with each other in the autocorrelation functions. This results in broad peaks and in some cases multiple peaks in the autocorrelation function; thus, an autocorrelation

FIG. 2. Basic system for the production of voiced speech sounds. $h(t)$ is the impulse response of the vocal tract.

approach to pitch determination is, in general, unsatisfactory.[8]

The solution is to devise a new function in which the effects of the vocal source and vocal tract are nearly independent or easily identifiable and separable. The Fourier transform of the *logarithm* of the power spectrum is such a new function and, indeed, separates the effects of the vocal source and tract. The reason for this is that the logarithm of a product equals the sum of the logarithms of the multiplicands:

$$\log|F(\omega)|^2 = \log[|S(\omega)|^2 \cdot |H(\omega)|^2] \tag{10}$$

$$= \log|S(\omega)|^2 + \log|H(\omega)|^2. \tag{11}$$

The Fourier transform of the logarithm power spectrum preserves the additive property and is

$$\mathfrak{F}[\log|F(\omega)|^2] = \mathfrak{F}[\log|S(\omega)|^2] + \mathfrak{F}[\log|H(\omega)|^2]. \tag{12}$$

The source and tract effects are now additive rather than convolved as in the autocorrelation. The importance of this can be intuitively explained with the assistance of Fig. 3. The effect of the vocal tract is to produce a "low-frequency" ripple in the logarithm spectrum, while the periodicity of the vocal source manifests itself as a "high-frequency" ripple in the logarithm spectrum. Therefore, the spectrum of the logarithm power spectrum has a sharp peak corresponding to the high-frequency source ripples in the logarithm spectrum and a broader peak corresponding to the low-frequency formant structure in the logarithm spectrum. The peak corresponding to the source periodicity can be made more pronounced by squaring the second spectrum. This function, the square of the Fourier transform of the logarithm power spectrum, is called the "cepstrum," borrowing Tukey's terminology.

To prevent confusion between the usual frequency components of a time function and the "frequency" ripples in the logarithm spectrum, Tukey has used the paraphrased word *quefrency* in describing the "frequency" of the spectral ripples. Quefrencies have the units of cycles per hertz or, simply, seconds. Adopting this terminology, the cepstrum consists of a peak occurring at a high quefrency equal to the pitch period in seconds and low-quefrency information corresponding to the formant structure in the logarithm spectrum.

Thus far, no mention has been made about the time length of the signal under analysis. As mentioned before, for seismic signals, a single cepstrum analysis is performed for the whole seismic event. But speech param-

[8] M. R. Schroeder, "Vocoders: Analysis and Synthesis of Speech," Proc. IEEE 54, No. 5, 720–734 (1966).

The Journal of the Acoustical Society of America

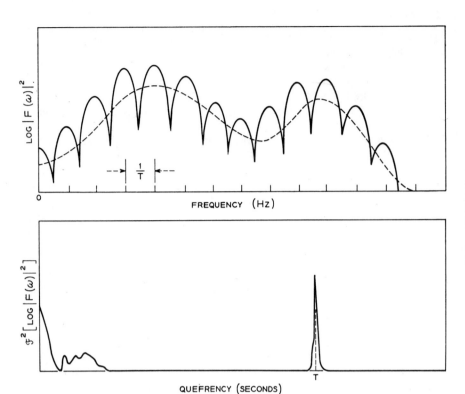

FIG. 3. Logarithm power spectrum (top) of a voiced speech segment showing a spectral periodicity resulting from the pitch periodicity of the speech. The power spectrum of the logarithm spectrum, or cepstrum (bottom), therefore has a sharp peak corresponding to this spectral periodicity.

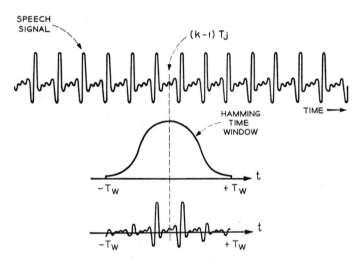

FIG. 4. Basic operations required for obtaining the short-time cepstrum of a speech signal. The hamming time window of length T_w sec moves in jumps of T_J sec.

K^{TH} SHORT–TIME SPECTRUM:

$$F_K(\omega) \equiv \int_{-T_W}^{T_W} \left[\mathord{\sim}\mathord{\uparrow}\mathord{\uparrow} \right] e^{-j\omega t}\, dt$$

K^{TH} LOG POWER SPECTRUM:

$$\mathrm{LOG}\left| F_K(\omega) \right|^2 = \mathrm{LOG}\left[\mathcal{R}e^2 F_K(\omega) + \mathcal{J}m^2 F_K(\omega) \right]$$

K^{TH} SHORT–TIME CEPSTRUM:

$$C_K(q) \equiv \left| \int_0^{\omega_C} \mathrm{LOG}\left| F_K(\omega) \right|^2 \cos \omega q\, dq \right|^2$$

Volume 41   Number 2   1967

eters—and, in particular, pitch—change with time; therefore a series of cepstra for short time segments of the signal are required. This is accomplished by multiplying the time signal by a function that is zero outside some finite time interval. The function performs something like a window through which the time signal is viewed, and its effects are discussed later in more detail. As shown in Fig. 4, the time-limited signal is spectrum analyzed once to obtain the log spectrum and then again to produce the cepstrum. A new portion of the time signal then enters the window and is similarly analyzed to produce another cepstrum. This process, when performed repetitively, results in a series of short-time cepstra. The time window, if desired, could also look at overlapping portions of the signal.

The resultant cepstra are automatically examined to determine the maximum peaks corresponding to voiced speech intervals and the frequency of these peaks. This information is used to decide if the speech segment is voiced or unvoiced and, if voiced, to determine the pitch period.

Both the effects of the time window and a mathematical justification for the spectral ripples were neglected in the preceding discussion and are now taken up. The time-limited signal to be analyzed is

$$g(t) = [s(t)*h(t)] \cdot w(t) \qquad (13)$$

from Eq. 1, where $w(t)$ is the time window, defined to be zero for $|t| > T_W$. But, the periodic source signal $s(t)$ can be represented as the superposition of an infinite series of identical signals $s_0(t)$ repeated every T seconds:

$$s(t) = \sum_{n=-\infty}^{\infty} s_0(t-nT) \qquad (14)$$

$$= s_0(t) * \sum_{n=-\infty}^{\infty} \delta(t-nT). \qquad (15)$$

Substitution into Eq. 13 gives

$$g(t) = \left\{\left[s_0(t) * \sum_{n=-\infty}^{\infty} \delta(t-nT)\right] * h(t)\right\} w(t). \qquad (16)$$

The Fourier transform or complex spectrum $G(\omega)$ of $g(t)$ is

$$G(\omega) = \left\{\left[s_0(\omega) \sum_{n=-\infty}^{\infty} \delta\left(\omega - n\frac{2\pi}{T}\right)\right] H(\omega)\right\} * W(\omega) \qquad (17)$$

$$= \left[\sum_{n=-\infty}^{\infty} H(\omega)S_0(\omega)\delta\left(\omega - n\frac{2\pi}{T}\right)\right] * W(\omega) \qquad (18)$$

$$= \left[\sum_{n=-\infty}^{\infty} H\left(n\frac{2\pi}{T}\right)S_0\left(n\frac{2\pi}{T}\right)\delta\left(\omega - n\frac{2\pi}{T}\right)\right] * W(\omega), \qquad (19)$$

where $S_0(\omega)$, $H(\omega)$, and $W(\omega)$ are the Fourier transforms of $s_0(t)$, $h(t)$, and $w(t)$, respectively.

The results of the preceding show that if the original speech signal $s(t)*h(t)$ is not time-limited, then the complex spectrum consists of an infinite series of impulses spaced T^{-1} Hz and with amplitude $H(n2\pi/T) \times S_0(n2\pi/T)$. If the non-time-limited signal is band-limited, the complex spectrum would be frequency limited or zero for $|\omega| > \omega_{max}$. The effect of time limiting the speech signal with a multiplicative time window $w(t)$ is a convolution of the corresponding spectral window $W(\omega)$ with the spectral impulses of the non-time-limited complex spectrum. Thus, the impulses are broadened and assume the shape of $W(\omega)$. The complex spectrum is now no longer frequency-limited, since $W(\omega)$ is the transform of a time-limited function and, therefore, cannot be zero over any finite frequency interval. Hence, the complex spectrum is not strictly frequency-limited, but can be described as being approximately frequency-limited if $W(\omega)$ has very small side lobes. Also, the main lobe of $W(\omega)$ determines the spectral resolution, and therefore a $W(\omega)$ with low-amplitude side lobes and a narrow main lobe is required. Although these requirements are mutually exclusive, a good compromise is the hamming time window,[9]

$$w(t) = 0.54 + 0.46 \cos(\pi t/T_W); \quad |t| \leq T_W \qquad (20)$$
$$= 0; \quad |t| > T_W.$$

The hamming spectral window has a maximum side lobe 44 dB below its peak response.

III. NUMERICAL COMPUTATION OF CEPSTRA

The Fourier transform $F(\omega)$ of some function of time $f(t)$ is defined as

$$F(\omega) \equiv \int_{-\infty}^{\infty} f(t)e^{-j\omega t}dt. \qquad (21)$$

If $f(t)$ is time limited by some multiplicative time window $w(t)$ such that $w(t) = 0$ for $|t| > T_W$ and if complex exponentiation is separated into real and imaginary parts, Eq. 21 becomes

$$F(\omega) = \int_{-T_W}^{T_W} w(t)f(t)\cos(\omega t)dt$$

$$- j\int_{-T_W}^{T_W} w(t)f(t)\sin(\omega t)dt. \qquad (22)$$

Furthermore, since $F(\omega)$ has a time-limited transform, namely, $w(-t)f(-t)$, then by Nyquist's sampling theorem applied to the frequency domain, ω can be represented as $\omega = m\Delta\omega$, where $\Delta\omega \leq 2\pi/(2T_W)$. Also, since $f(t)$ is band-limited to 0 to $\omega_c/(2\pi)$ Hz, t can be represented as $t = l\Delta t$, where $\Delta t = 2\pi/(2\omega_c)$. Thus, the integrations in Eq. 22 can be replaced by summations,

[9] R. B. Blackman and J. W. Tukey, *The Measurement of Power Spectra* (Dover Publications, Inc., New York, 1959).

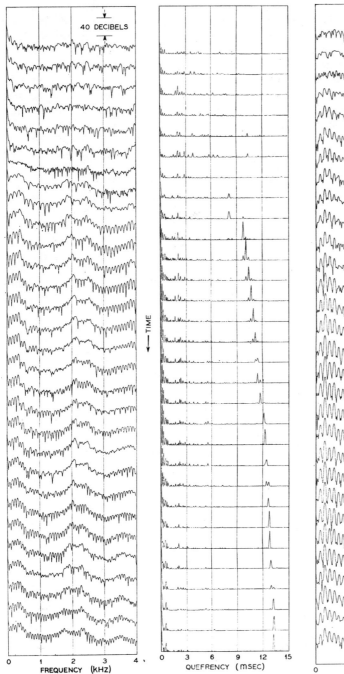

FIG. 5. Short-time logarithm spectra (left) and short-time cepstra (right) for a male talker (L.G.) recorded with a condenser microphone. The 40 msec-long hamming time moved in jumps of 10 msec.

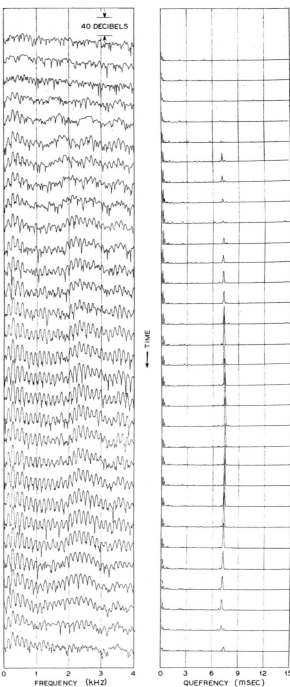

FIG. 6. Short-time logarithm spectra (left) and short-time cepstra (right) for a male talker (F.L.C.) recorded from a 500-type telephone set with carbon microphone.

so that $F(\omega)$ becomes

$$F(m\Delta\omega) = \Delta t \sum_{l=-L}^{L} w(l\Delta t) f(l\Delta t) \cos(lm\Delta t\Delta\omega)$$

$$- j\Delta t \sum_{l=-L}^{L} w(l\Delta t) f(l\Delta t) \sin(lm\Delta t\Delta\omega), \quad (23)$$

where $L = T_W \Delta t$.

This equation led to the concept of a delay line for storing $2L+1$ samples of the input signal (sample and hold circuits at the taps of the delay line) so that the signal being analyzed remains constant during the analysis (window multipliers, function generators for cosine and sine, and adders as shown in Fig. 1). The real and imaginary parts of the spectrum produced by

Volume 41   Number 2   1967

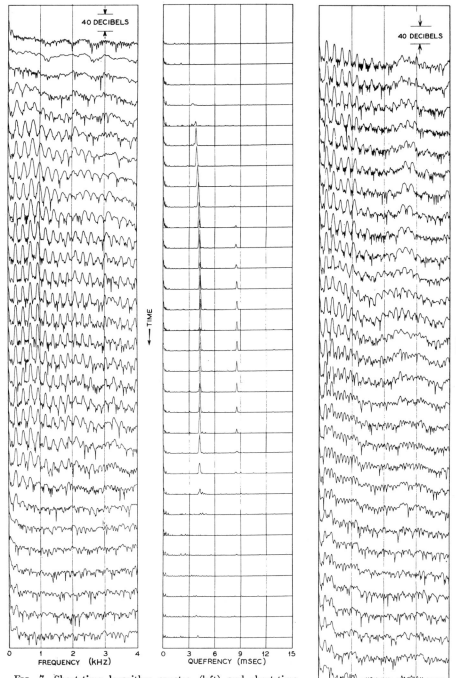

FIG. 7. Short-time logarithm spectra (left) and short-time cepstra (right) for a female talker (S.S.) recorded with a condenser microphone.

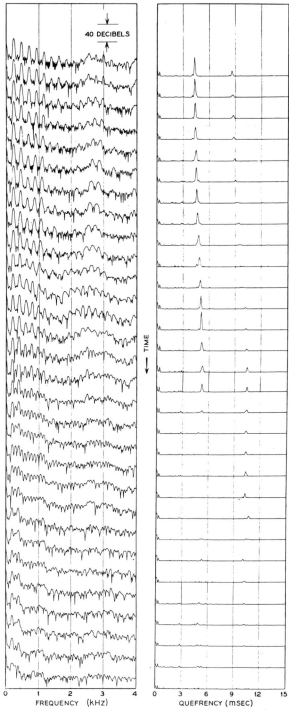

FIG. 8. Short-time logarithm spectra (left) and short-time cepstra (right) of "(scr)eaming," spoken by a female talker (S.S.) and recorded with a condenser microphone. A doubling in pitch period occurs at the end of the utterance.

this sampled-data spectrum analyzer are squared and added to generate the power spectrum. The logarithm of the power spectrum is used as the input to a similar power-spectrum analyzer whose output is the cepstrum.

This sampled-data analyzer was simulated on an IBM–7094 digital computer by using the BLODI compiler. The input speech to the computer was band-limited to 4 kHz, sampled every 10^{-4} secs, and digitized;

the time window extended from -15 to $+15$ msec. The results reported in the previous paper were obtained with this computer simulation, which consumed nearly 2 h of computer time to analyze only 2 sec of speech.

The Journal of the Acoustical Society of America

The program was extremely unwieldy and changes in any parameters were difficult. Obviously, some streamlining of the program was required if further progress in cepstrum-pitch detection were to be accomplished.

Only a single spectrum in a series of spectra is defined by Eq. 22. If the time window moves in jumps of T_J sec, then the kth short-time spectrum $F_k(m)$ is defined as

$$F_k(m) = \sum_{l=-L}^{L} w(l) f[(k-1)K+l] \cos(lm\Delta t\Delta\omega)$$
$$- j \sum_{l=-L}^{L} w(l) f[(k-1)K+l] \sin(lm\Delta t\Delta\omega), \quad (24)$$

where $L = T_W/\Delta t$, $K = T_J/\Delta t$ and $m = 0, 1, \cdots, \omega_c/\Delta\omega$.

The kth short-time power spectrum is the magnitude squared of the kth short-time spectrum:

$$|F_k(m)|^2 = \{ \sum_{l=-L}^{L} w(l) f[(k-1)K+l] \cos(lm\Delta t\Delta\omega) \}^2$$
$$+ \{ \sum_{l=-L}^{L} w(l) f[(k-1)K+l] \sin(lm\Delta t\Delta\omega) \}^2.$$
$$(25)$$

Although the complex spectrum may be sampled at $\Delta\omega \leq 2\pi/(2T_W)$, the power spectrum should be sampled at $\Delta\omega \leq 2\pi/(4T_W)$. This is because the Fourier transform of the power spectrum is the autocorrelation function that for a signal time limited to $\pm T_W$ sec is itself time-limited to $\pm 2T_W$ sec. By Nyquist's sampling theorem, the power spectrum therefore must be sampled at $\Delta\omega \leq 2\pi/(4T_W)$. Strictly speaking, if the Fourier transform of the power spectrum is time-limited, then the Fourier transform of the logarithm power spectrum is generally not time-limited. But from experience that the aliasing is negligible, the log power spectrum is sampled at the same interval as the power spectrum. Since the computer is used in taking logarithms, the logarithm of zero is forced to be noninfinite.

The cepstrum $C(\tau)$ is now formally defined as the power spectrum of the logarithm power spectrum. Since the log power spectrum is an even function, this definition is equivalent to the square of the cosine transform of the log power spectrum, or

$$C(\tau) \equiv \left\{ \int_0^\infty \log|F(\omega)|^2 \cos(\omega\tau) d\omega \right\}^2. \quad (26)$$

For $C(\tau)$ to be sampled, the Fourier transform of $C(\tau)$ must be band-limited. However, $C(\tau)$ is the product of two cosine transforms, and therefore the Fourier transform of $C(\tau)$ is the convolution of the Fourier transforms of the individual cosine transforms. But, since the cosine transform of $\log|F(\omega)|^2$ is also an even function, the Fourier transform of the cosine transform

of $\log|F(\omega)|^2$ simply gives $\log|F(\omega)|^2$. Thus, the Fourier transform of $C(\tau)$ equals the convolution of $\log|F(\omega)|^2$ with itself. Since $\log|F(\omega)|^2$ is very small for $|\omega| > \omega_c$, the convolution is very nearly limited to the interval $|\omega| \leq 2\omega_c$. Nyquist's theorem can therefore be applied, and the cepstrum can be sampled so that $\tau = n\Delta\tau$ with $\Delta\tau \leq 2\pi/(4\omega_c)$. Thus, the kth short-time cepstrum $C_k(n)$ can be calculated as

$$C_k(n) = \sum_{m=0}^{M} \log|F_k(m)|^2 \cos(mn\Delta\tau\Delta\omega), \quad (27)$$

where $\Delta\omega \leq 2\pi/(4T_W)$, $M = \omega_c/\Delta\omega$, $n = 0, 1, \cdots, N$ with N some arbitrary upper limit on the desired quefrencies in the cepstrum.

The numerical operations indicated by Eqs. 25 and 27 were programmed in the FORTRAN language. To conserve execution time, all sine and cosine operations were performed as table lookups from calculated sine and cosine tables. Also, the computation of the sine and cosine transforms utilized even and odd symmetry in the input signal to reduce further the number of calculations. Nevertheless, the program was still very lengthy and required about 0.8 h to compute the cepstra for about 2 sec of speech. Recently, an algorithm has been developed by Cooley and Tukey for performing fast numerical Fourier transformations.[10] This algorithm has been incorporated into the cepstrum program and has resulted in a program about eight times faster than the previous one.

A very important factor in the computer calculation of short-time cepstra has been facilities for the automatic plotting of the spectra and cepstra. These facilities consist of a cathode-ray tube and camera, both under the direct control of the digital computer.

IV. EXAMPLES OF SPEECH SPECTRA AND CEPSTRA

The computer technique described in the preceding portions of this paper was used to analyze a few selected sentences and words. The speech was low-pass filtered to 4 kHz and sampled every 10^{-4} sec. The hamming time window was 40 msec long and moved in jumps of 10 msec. The spectral components were calculated at frequency intervals of 12.5 Hz up to a maximum frequency of 4 kHz; the cepstral components were calculated at intervals of 0.0625 msec up to a maximum quefrency of 15 msec. The results of the calculations were automatically plotted on microfilm by the computer with corresponding spectra and cepstra shown adjacent to each other. Time progresses downwards in jumps of 10 msec.

Figure 5 shows the spectra and cepstra of a male talker (L.G.) recorded with a condenser microphone; Fig. 6 is for a different male talker (F.L.C.) recorded

---

[10] J. W. Cooley and J. W. Tukey, "An Algorithm for the Machine Calculation of Complex Fourier Series," Math. of Computation **19**, 297–301 (1965).

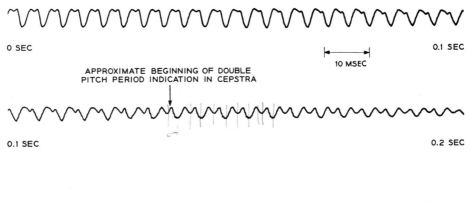

FIG. 9. Speech waveform of the "ing" portion of "(scr)eaming," showing the approximate location of the switch to double pitch period indicated by the cepstra.

from a 500-type telephone set with carbon transmitter; Fig. 7 is female speech (S.S.) recorded from a condenser microphone. In all three examples, the voiced-speech intervals are clearly indicated by the sharp peaks in the cepstra. The cepstral peaks in Fig. 5 for the voiced-speech intervals of Curves 11–15 are particularly interesting since they consist of a major peak with two smaller peaks on either side. This occurred because the pitch was changing rapidly such that each 40-msec analysis interval contained different pitch periods. Actually, the 40-msec hamming window looks mostly at only the center 20 msec since the tails of the window are strongly weighted down in amplitude. Thus, very little smoothing is actually present, and the largest cepstral peak corresponds to the dominant pitch period mostly within the 20-msec center interval.

Figure 8 shows the spectra and cepstra of the utterance (scr)eaming spoken by a female talker (S.S.) into a condenser microphone. At about the 12th cepstrum, a second "rahmonic" appears and gradually grows in amplitude until, at about the 17th cepstrum, its amplitude exceeds the fundamental peak at about 5.2 msec. The fundamental peak then disappears, leaving only the cepstral peak at 10.4 msec. This would imply a doubling of pitch period at the end of the "··· ing" sound, and, indeed, speech synthesized with the doubled excitation sounds natural and compares better with the original than excitation that does not double in period at the "··· ing" portion. The spectra corresponding to this transition show the alternate harmonics gradually growing in amplitude until they fill in the gaps between the harmonics corresponding to the lower pitch period. The actual speech waveform is shown in Fig. 9, and the point of transition is indicated. Although the doubling is discernible towards the end of the signal, the cepstrum gives an indication of doubling earlier than would be determined by visual inspection of the waveform.

The spectra and cepstra of the word *chase* spoken by

a famale talker (B.M.) and recorded with a condenser microphone is shown in Fig. 10. The 12th, 13th, and 14th cepstra have small second rahmonics at about 8.8 msec that are smaller in amplitude than the fundamental cepstral peak at about 4.4 msec. However, the 19th through 21st cepstra have second rahmonics with amplitudes exceeding the fundamental. This type of doubling of pitch period imbedded in voiced speech sounds wrong when used as excitation for a vocoder and is therefore considered as undesirable. The spectra for the double pitch consist of harmonics corresponding to the 4.4-msec pitch period with interlaced harmonics that fade in and out across the spectrum. This type of spectrum is caused by minute jitter in the pitch-pulse timing.[11] If the vocal source signal $s(t)$ is assumed to consist of air puffs at $\cdots 0, T+\epsilon, 2T, 3T+\epsilon, \cdots$, then

$$s(t) = \sum_{n=-\infty}^{\infty} \left[s_0(t-2nT) + s_0(t-\epsilon-2nT-T) \right]$$

(28)

$$= s_0(t)* \sum_{n=-\infty}^{\infty} \left[\delta(t-2nT) + \delta(t-2nT-T-\epsilon) \right].$$

The Fourier transform of the summation portion corresponding to the jittered pulses is

$$J(\omega) = \left[1 + e^{-j\omega(T+\epsilon)} \right] \sum_{n=-\infty}^{\infty} \delta\left(\omega - n\frac{2\pi}{2T} \right). \quad (29)$$

But,

$$\left| 1 + e^{-j\omega(T+\epsilon)} \right|^2 = 2[1 + \cos\omega(T+\epsilon)], \quad (30)$$

so that the power spectrum consists of impulses every $1/2T$ Hz with an amplitude fluctuation of $[1+\cos \omega(T+\epsilon)]$. If there is not jitter, then $\epsilon=0$; and, since $[1+\cos\omega T]=0$ for $\omega=(\pi/T)n$ (where $n=1,3,5,\cdots$),

[11] B. Gold and J. Tierney, "Pitch-Induced Spectral Distortion in Channel Vocoders," J. Acoust. Soc. Am. **35**, 730–731 (1963).

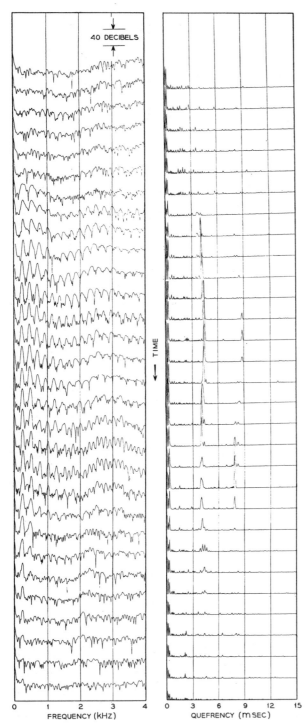

FIG. 10. Short-time logarithm spectra (left) and short-time cepstra (right) of "chase," spoken by a female talker (B.M.) and recorded with a condenser microphone. The 19th through 21st cepstra have second rahmonics that exceed the fundamental and that would result in an undesired indication of pitch-period doubling.

the odd harmonics disappear, thereby leaving impulses every $1/T$ Hz. However, if ϵ is not zero, the spectrum starts with impulses spaced $1/T$ Hz, but gradually

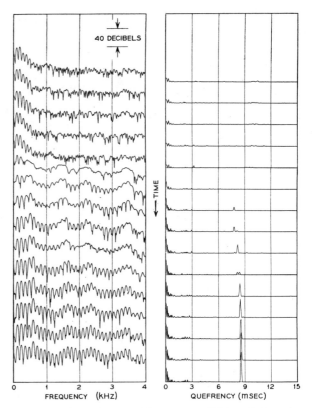

FIG. 11. Short-time logarithm spectra (left) and short-time cepstra (right) of "(o)be(y)," spoken by a male talker (R.C.L.) and recorded with a condenser microphone. The explosion occurs at the sixth spectrum and cepstrum.

impulses appear at $1/2T$-Hz intervals and then periodically fade in and out across the spectrum. The jitter can be calculated from the frequency in the spectrum at which the amplitude of the impulses are first equal, since at this frequency the Nth cosine wave with period $1/(T+\epsilon)$ Hz has a maximum situated exactly between two adjacent impulses. For the spoken word *chase*, this occurred at 3 kHz corresponding to an $\epsilon \approx 0.08$ msec, which is smaller than the accuracy of one previous measurement of pitch perturbations.[12]

The spectra and cepstra shown in Figs. 11–13 are for a male speaker (R.C.L.) recorded with a condenser microphone. These speech utterances were chosen by O. Fujimura in his investigations at Bell Telephone Laboratories of speech sounds. The first set of spectra and cepstra show the explosion in the word *obey* (occuring at the sixth line of Fig. 11) as exemplified by a completely ripple-free spectrum. Figure 13 shows the spectra and cepstra for the voiced fricative portion of the word *razor* at the sixth through ninth lines.

V. AUTOMATIC TRACKING OF CEPSTRAL PEAKS

The cepstral peaks corresponding to voiced speech intervals can easily be picked visually. However, these

[12] P. Lieberman, "Perturbations in Vocal Pitch," J. Acoust. Soc. Am. 33, 597–603 (1961).

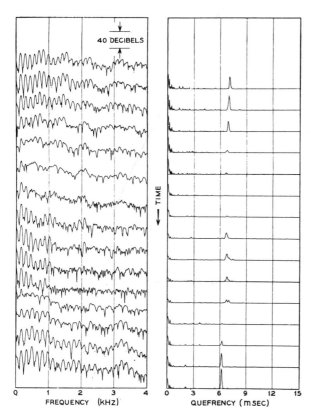

FIG. 12. Short-time logarithm spectra (left) and short-time cepstra (right) of "(b)abbl(ed)," spoken by a male talker (R.C.L.) and recorded with a condenser microphone. The explosion occurs at the sixth spectrum and cepstrum.

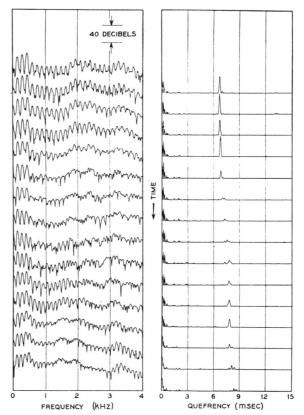

FIG. 13. Short-time logarithm spectra (left) and short-time cepstra (right) of "(r)azor," spoken by a male talker (R.C.L.) and recorded with a condenser microphone. The voiced fricative occurs at the sixth through ninth spectra and cepstra.

peaks must be picked automatically if cepstrum techniques are to be used in a pitch detection scheme. This section of the paper describes the heuristic development of an algorithm for picking the cepstral peak that best describes the pitch of the speech for that time interval. The criterion of "best" was evaluated by using the pitch data as excitation of a computer-simulated vocoder and then comparing the vocoded speech with the original speech.

The examples of cepstra indicate that the cepstral peaks are clearly defined and are quite sharp. Hence, the peak-picking scheme is to determine the maximum value in the cepstrum exceeding some specified threshold. Since pitch periods of less than 1 msec are not usually encountered, the interval searched for the peak in the cepstrum is 1–15 msec.

Since the cepstral peaks decrease in amplitude with increasing quefrency, a linear multiplicative weighting was applied over the 1–15-msec range. The weighting was 1 at 1 msec and 5 at 15 msec. The Fourier transform of the power spectrum of the time window equals the convolution of the time window with itself,

$$\mathfrak{F}[|W(\omega)|^2] = \mathfrak{F}[W(\omega)W(-\omega)] \qquad (31)$$
$$= w(t) * w(-t).$$

Thus, the higher-quefrency components in the power spectrum decrease as the time window convolved with itself. Although the mathematics becomes unwieldy for an exact solution, it is reasonable to expect the higher-quefrency components in the logarithm of the power spectrum to decrease similarly, thereby explaining the need of weighting of the higher quefrencies in the cepstrum. The linear weighting with range of 1–5 was chosen empirically by using periodic pulse trains with varying periods as input to the cepstrum program.

The cepstral peaks at the end of a voiced-speech segment usually decrease in amplitude and would fall below the peak threshold. The solution is to decrease the threshold by some factor (2) over a quefrency range of ± 1 msec of the immediately preceding pitch period when tracking the pitch in a series of voiced-speech segments. The threshold reverts to its normal value over the whole cepstrum range after the end of the series of voiced segments.

There is also the possibility that an isolated cepstral peak might exceed the threshold, thereby resulting in a false indication of a voiced speech segment. In fact, some isolated flaps of the vocal cords have been observed as the cause of such an isolated cepstral peak. In any event, such peaks should not be considered as

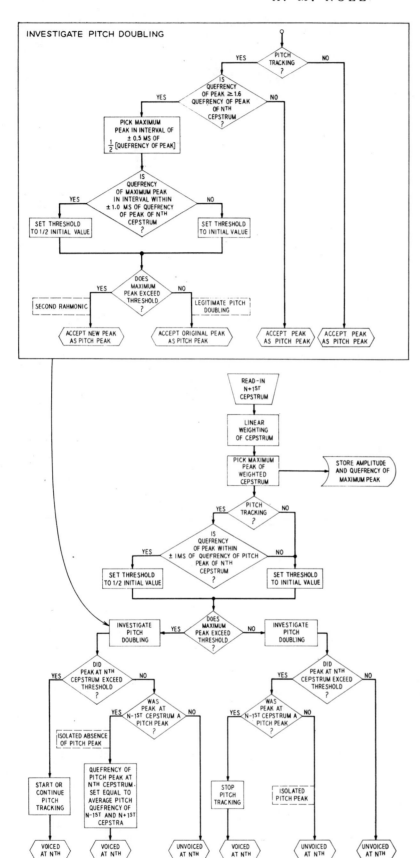

Fig. 14. Flow chart of the algorithm used to decide if the Nth cepstrum represents a voiced speech interval.

voiced, and this is accomplished by disregarding any cepstral peaks exceeding the threshold if the immediately preceding cepstrum and immediately following cepstrum indicate unvoiced speech. This means that the immediately following cepstrum must be peak searched before a decision can be made about the present cepstrum. Hence, a delay of one cepstrum must be introduced to eliminate this requirement of knowledge about the future. Before deciding about the "present" cepstrum, however, knowledge about the preceding and following cepstrum is also required for the algorithm used to eliminate another problem, namely, pitch doubling.

An example of legitimate pitch doubling occurred at the end of the word *screaming*, as shown in Fig. 8. However, the second rahmonic of a cepstral peak sometimes exceeds the fundamental, and the second rahmonic should not be chosen as representing the pitch period. Thus, the peak picking algorithm should eliminate false pitch doubling caused by a second rahmonic but should also allow legitimate pitch doubling. For legitimate doubling, there is no cepstral peak at a one-half quefrency, but for erroneous doubling, there is such a peak at one-half quefrency since this is the fundamental. The algorithm capitalizes upon this observation by looking for a cepstral peak exceeding the threshold in an interval of ±0.5 msec of one-half the quefrency of the double-pitch peak. If such a peak is found, then it is assumed that it represents the fundamental, and the double-pitch indication is wrong. The threshold is reduced by a factor of 2 if the maximum peak in the ±0.5-msec interval falls within ±1.0 msec of the immediately preceding pitch period. Pitch doubling has occurred whenever the cepstral peak exceeding the threshold is at a quefrency of ≥1.6 times the immediately preceding pitch period.

A flow chart of the peak-picking algorithm is shown in Fig. 14. The algorithm determines whether the cepstral peak of the Nth cepstrum represents a voiced speech segment. Information about the $N-1$th cepstrum is stored, and the $N+1$th cepstrum is peak picked before deciding about the Nth cepstrum. The $N+1$th cepstrum is read in, linear weighting is applied, and the maximum peak is picked. If the preceding two cepstra represented voiced-speech segments, then pitch tracking is in effect, and the threshold is reduced to $\frac{1}{2}$ its initial value if the quefrency of the peak is within ±1.0 msec of the quefrency of the pitch peak of the Nth cepstrum. The previously determined peak in the $N+1$th cepstrum is now compared with the threshold. Pitch doubling is investigated whether the peak exceeds or does not exceed the threshold. Both cases are checked since the peak might represent pitch doubling and yet not exceed the initial value of the threshold. But, the fundamental peak could still exceed the $\frac{1}{2}$ initial value threshold. If the maximum peak exceeds the threshold, it is tentatively chosen as a pitch peak representing a voiced-speech segment at the $N+1$th cepstrum. The

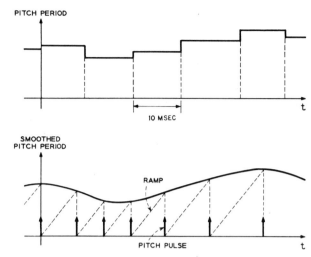

FIG. 15. Method for deriving pitch pulses from pitch period data supplied by cepstral peak picker.

information about the $N+1$th cepstrum and $N-1$th cepstrum is then used to decide if the Nth cepstral peak represents an isolated voiced segment or an isolated absence of voicing in a series of voiced-speech segments. The final result is an indication of whether the Nth cepstrum represents a voiced or an unvoiced speech segment. If the segment is voiced, the pitch period is also given.

A computer program was written to perform the operations required by the algorithm. The voicing and pitch-period information were both printed on paper and written on magnetic tapes for later processing.

VI. VOCODER EXCITATION

The final judge of any vocal-pitch detection scheme is its ability to perform satisfactorily in determining the excitation for a vocoder. Vocodor excitation in the form of pitch pulses during voicing and white noise during nonvoicing thus had to be derived from the results of the cepstral peak picking.

The cepstral peak picker produced two outputs on digital magnetic tape. The first tape contained voicing information as two dc levels corresponding to a voiced or unvoiced speech interval. The levels were constant for the 10-msec corresponding to the speech time jumps. The second tape contained the pitch period as dc level signals that also were constant for 10 msec. These two tapes formed the input to the excitation generator.

The voicing and pitch-period signals are first each smoothed by a pair of 33-Hz low-pass filters. The pitch pulses are derived from the smoothed pitch signal as shown in Fig. 15 by running a counter up until it equals the smoothed pitch signal. An impulse is then emitted, and the counter is reset to zero before again starting its count. If the smoothed pitch signal is measured in tenths of a millisecond and the counter counts in tenths of a millisecond, then the timing between the emitted

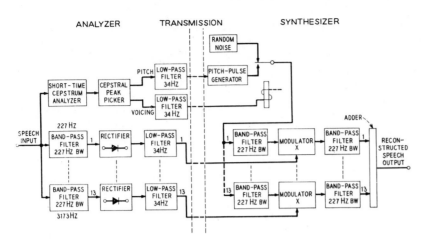

FIG. 16. Block diagram of 13-spectrum channel vocoder with excitation derived from a cepstrum pitch detector.

impulses equals the pitch period. The smoothed voicing signal is used to control a double-throw switch for choosing either pitch pulses or white noise as a final excitation output.

This technique was devised and simulated on the computer by M. M. Sondhi using the BLODI programming language. The output of the program was still another digital magnetic tape, which was then used as the excitation input to a 13-spectrum channel vocoder designed by Golden.[13] The vocoder was also simulated on the computer using the BLODI programming language. The spectrum channel information was derived from a computer-simulated vocoder analyzer and, together with the excitation, they formed the input to the computer-simulated synthesizer. The whole operation from speech signal to simulated vocoder output is shown in Fig. 16. The digital computer generated numerous visual outputs on microfilm including the short-time spectra and cepstra, the voicing and pitch-period variations, the original speech signal, and the vocoded speech signal. These visual outputs were extremely valuable in devising the final versions of all the different portions of the chain making up the complete pitch-detection scheme.

The complete scheme, including the vocoder, was used to modify and improve all portions of the chain by comparing the vocoded speech with the original speech. In particular, the pitch-period doubling at the end of the word *screaming* was determined to be aurally correct by such a comparison of original with vocoded speech.

The synthetic speech from the computer-simulated cepstrum-excitation channel vocoder was compared both with the original speech and with the synthetic speech from a computer-simulated voice-excited vocoder and the same computer-simulated channel vocoder, but with the full-band speech as excitation. Although only a few sentences spoken by four talkers were used in these informal paired-comparison tests, the

pitch quality of the channel vocoder with cepstrum pitch detection was judged to be excellent by experienced vocoder critics. This optimism was sufficient to initialize construction of a real-time cepstrum pitch detector.[14]

VII. IMPLEMENTATION OF CEPSTRUM ANALYZERS

In its most basic form, cepstrum-pitch detection requires two spectrum analyses with logic circuitry for picking the cepstral peak corresponding to the pitch period of a voiced-speech segment. Thus, a means for performing two spectrum analyses in real time is required for a hardware implementation of a cepstrum-pitch detector. The requirements of real-time operation and good frequency resolution in the spectrum analyzers are somewhat difficult to satisfy and have therefore resulted in the correct opinion that a hardware cepstrum analyzer would be difficult to construct.

However, techniques are available for performing real-time spectrum analyses that could be adapted to cepstrum analysis. One such method performs the spectrum analysis by a circulating delay line with a time-variable phase shifter operating upon a heterodyned version of the time signal. This method, described by Bickel and Bernstein[15] has been successfully used by Weiss, Vogel, and Harris in an implementation of a cepstrum analyzer.[16,17] Still another method, similar to a spectrum analyzer described by Gill, uses a heterodyne filter operating on a time-swept version of the input signal.[18] Kelly and Kennedy have utilized this

[13] R. M. Golden, "Digital Computer Simulation of a Sampled-Data Voice-Excited Vocoder," J. Acoust. Soc. Am. **35**, 1358–1366 (1963).

[14] J. M. Kelly and R. N. Kennedy, "An Experimental Cepstrum Pitch Detector for Use in a 2400-bit/sec Channel Vocoder," presented at the *72nd* meeting of Acoustical Society of America (Nov. 1966), Paper 1H3.
[15] H. J. Bickel and R. I. Bernstein, U. S. Patent No. 3,013,209.
[16] H. J. Bickel, "Spectrum Analysis with Delay-Line Filter," IRE WESCON Conv. Rec. **1959** (Part 8), 59–67 (1959).
[17] M. R. Weiss, R. P. Vogel, and C. M. Harris, "Implementation of a Pitch Extractor of the Double-Spectrum-Analysis Type," J. Acoust. Soc. Am. **40**, 657–662 (1966).
[18] J. S. Gill, "A Versatile Method for Short-Term Spectrum Analysis in 'Real-Time,'" Nature **189**, No. 4759, 117–119 (14 Jan. 1961).

method in yet another successful implementation also including logic circuitry to track the cepstral peak.[14] They have also derived vocoder excitation from their cepstra and have produced excellent-quality vocoded speech utilizing a complete hardware system of cepstrum analyzer and vocoder.

Both methods utilize analog-circuit techniques during all or part of the spectrum analysis. Digital techniques, however, have progressed to the state where a completely digital implementation should be possible. The Cooley–Tukey algorithm greatly reduces the number of multiplications and additions, and might be of practical use in such a completely digital cepstrum analyzer.

Another promising method utilizes the spectrum analyzing properties of a lens.[19,20] A lens forms at its focal plane an image that is the Fourier transform of the image at the object plane. Since this is a *spatial* Fourier transform, the signal must be frozen in time with light intensity made proportional to signal amplitude. A coherent light source is required to illuminate the spatial representation of the signal, and there are some questions concerning the most efficient way to convert the time signal into such a spatial signal. But, the technique seems particularly promising (since parallel processing is very convenient), so that thousands of signals could be analyzed almost simultaneously.

VIII. PSEUDO-AUTOCOVARIANCE OR CEPSTRUM?

In their article in Rosenblatt's book, Bogert et al.,[3] define the cepstrum as "autocovariance and Fourier transformation . . . [of] the log spectrum of the original process." Since the Fourier transform of the autocovariance of some function is identical with the power spectrum of the same function, the cepstrum should be equivalent to the power spectrum of the log power spectrum of the original process. Furthermore, since the log power spectrum is an even function of frequency, the cepstrum should equal the square of the cosine transform of the log power spectrum.

Later in the article, Bogert et al. define a pseudo-autocovariance as "the Fourier transform of [the] log··· power spectrum." The "pseudo" prefix is logically used since the Fourier transform of the non-logged power spectrum is the usual autocovariance. Thus, the cepstrum should equal the square of the pseudo-autocovariance. But, in their definition of the cepstrum, Bogert et al. had meant to assume that the log spectrum existed for all positive frequencies (private communication). As a result, their cepstrum equals the sum of the squares of the sine transform and the cosine transform of the log power spectrum. Stated mathematically, their definition of the cepstrum is

$$C_{\text{Bogert}}(\tau) = \{\mathfrak{F}_{\sin}[\log|F(\omega)|^2]\}^2 + \{\mathfrak{F}_{\cos}[\log|F(\omega)|^2]\}^2, \quad (32)$$

where $\mathfrak{F}_{\sin}$ and $\mathfrak{F}_{\cos}$ denote Fourier sine transformation and Fourier cosine transformation, respectively; $F(\omega)$ is the complex Fourier transform of the original process; and $F(\omega) \equiv 0$ for $\omega < 0$. The pseudo-autocovariance is

$$R_c(\tau) = \mathfrak{F}_{\cos}[\log|F(\omega)|^2] \quad (33)$$

and its square is identical with the definition of the cepstrum used in this paper. A pseudoquadrature auto-covariance can be defined as

$$R_s(\tau) = \mathfrak{F}_{\sin}[\log|F(\omega)|^2], \quad (34)$$

so that

$$C_{\text{Bogert}}(\tau) = [R_c(\tau)]^2 + [R_s(\tau)]^2. \quad (35)$$

Two different definitions of the cepstrum can certainly lead to some confusion, but in this paper the cepstrum has consistently been defined as the square of the cosine transform of the log power spectrum.

The digital computer was programmed to calculate the following short-time functions: the square of the cosine transform of the one-sided log power spectrum (pseudo-autocovariance squared), the square of the sine transform of the one-sided log power spectrum (pseudoquadrature autocovariance squared), and the sum of the squares of the cosine and sine transforms of the one-sided log power spectrum (Bogert's cepstrum). The input signal was a male talker recorded from a 500-type telephone handset with additive white noise (signal-to-noise ratio approximately 12 dB). The three short-time functions with the corresponding log power spectrum are shown in Fig. 17 for a voiced speech segment. The pseudoquadrature autocovariance is very noisy, so that Bogert's cepstrum does not have peaks as sharp as the pseudo-autocovariance alone. Clearly, in retrospect, these results are good justification for using only the pseudo-autocovariance for speech pitch detection.

IX. CONCLUSION

Some of the advantages claimed for cepstrum pitch detection and confirmed by computer simulation are, first, that the fundamental frequency component need not be present in the time signal, since the spectral ripples or fine structure caused by the harmonics give rise to the cepstral peak. For this reason, cepstrum pitch detection is particularly well suited to such bandpass-filtered signals as telephone speech. Since only the power spectrum is used, phase is completely ignored. Additive white noise is not too degrading if it does not destroy the spectral ripples. Actually, a clearly defined cepstral peak has been obtained for speech signals with a 6-dB signal-to-noise ratio over the 40-msec analysis interval.

[19] L. J. Cutrona, E. N. Leith, C. J. Palermo, and L. J. Porcello, "Optical Data Processing and Filtering Systems," IRE Trans. Information Theory IT-6, 386–400 (1960).

[20] B. Julesz, A. M. Noll, and M. R. Schroeder, "Optical Cepstrum Analysis" (unpublished morandum).

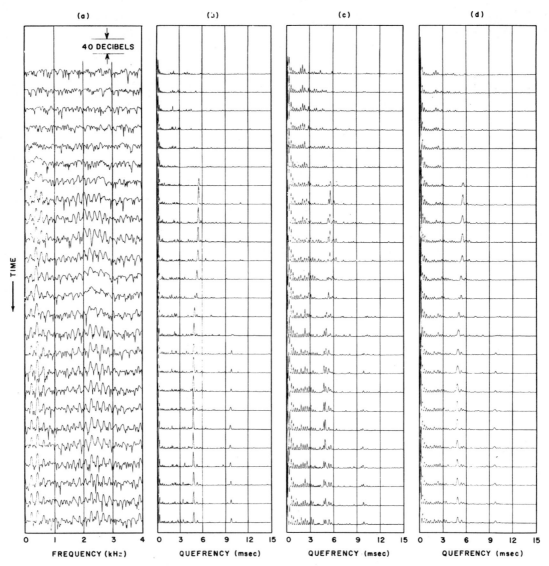

FIG. 17. (a) Short-time logarithm spectra, (b) pseudo-autocovariance squared, (c) pseudoquadrature autocovariance squared, and (d) Bogert's cepstra (defined as the sum of the squares of the cosine and sine transforms of the logarithm spectra) for a male talker (F.L.C.) recorded from a 500-type telephone handset and with additive white noise (signal-to-noise ratio ≈ 12 dB).

Of course, cepstrum pitch detection is insensitive to narrow-band white noise, since such noise would at most obscure only a few spectral ripples.

Cepstrum pitch detection has to some extent changed our over-all concept of a vocoder. Previously, most diagrams of a channel vocoder showed considerable detail about the channel filters while the pitch detector was usually shown as a small block at the bottom, although the pitch detector itself was sometimes quite elaborate. However, the spectrum-channel information is obtained as an intermediate step during the cepstrum-analysis process. Thus, our new concept of a vocoder analyzer shows an involved diagram of a pitch detector with the spectrum-channel information obtained as a by-product! (See Fig. 18.) Perhaps this is more realistic,

because it has long been recognized that accurate pitch information is the most challenging aspect of vocoder design. The spectrum-channel information has perhaps been reduced to its true relative importance.

But where does all this effort lead us?. It seems that vocoder design is becoming conceptually more complicated with asymptotic, though not necessarily insignificant, improvements in quality. The vocoder schemes and pitch detectors are becoming increasingly exotic, as exemplified by cepstrum pitch detection. Also, such new speech transmission methods as microwave, satellites, and the promise of light communication over laser beams might someday change the present restrictions on available bandwidth. The future of vocoders for speech bandwidth compression might seem bleak. Why

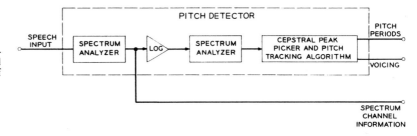

FIG. 18. New concept of spectrum channel vocoder in which the spectrum channel information is obtained as a by-product of the cepstrum pitch detector.

continue, then, with vocoder development, and—in particular—why be concerned with pitch detectors?

Special-purpose vocoders can be useful in removing certain types of speech distortion. For example, the "Donald Duck" quality of speech spoken in the helium environment used in certain underwater quarters such as Sealab can be eliminated by frequency shifting of the vocoder channel signals.[21] The transmission of speech can be made private or secure by the use of vocoders.[8] An accurate pitch-detection scheme would become a

very important tool in speech research by fostering research in pitch fluctuations and patterns. Thus, further research and development of pitch detectors is warranted not only to produce speech bandwidth-compression vocoders but also as a fundamental tool for speech research and for special-purpose vocoders.

As mentioned previously, cepstrum analysis performs remarkably well as a vocal-pitch detector. However, a more general conclusion has evolved from the concept of cepstrum analysis: that the spectrum itself can be regarded as a signal and can be processed by standard signal-analysis techniques. With such a viewpoint, cepstrum analysis and other signal processing of the spectrum do not seem quite so exotic.

[21] R. M. Golden, "Improving Naturalness and Intelligibility of Helium–Oxygen Speech Using Vocoder Techniques," J. Acoust. Soc. Am. 40, 621–624 (1966).

A Comparative Performance Study of Several Pitch Detection Algorithms

LAWRENCE R. RABINER, FELLOW, IEEE, MICHAEL J. CHENG, STUDENT MEMBER, IEEE,
AARON E. ROSENBERG, MEMBER, IEEE, AND CAROL A. McGONEGAL

Abstract—A comparative performance study of seven pitch detection algorithms was conducted. A speech data base, consisting of eight utterances spoken by three males, three females, and one child was constructed. Telephone, close talking microphone, and wideband recordings were made of each of the utterances. For each of the utterances in the data base, a "standard" pitch contour was semiautomatically measured using a highly sophisticated interactive pitch detection program. The "standard" pitch contour was then compared with the pitch contour that was obtained from each of the seven programmed pitch detectors. The algorithms used in this study were 1) a center clipping, infinite-peak clipping, modified autocorrelation method (AUTOC), 2) the cepstral method (CEP), 3) the simplified inverse filtering technique (SIFT) method, 4) the parallel processing time-domain method (PPROC), 5) the data reduction method (DARD), 6) a spectral flattening linear predictive coding (LPC) method, and 7) the average magnitude difference function (AMDF) method. A set of measurements was made on the pitch contours to quantify the various types of errors which occur in each of the above methods. Included among the error measurements were the average and standard deviation of the error in pitch period during voiced regions, the number of gross errors in the pitch period, and the average number of voiced–unvoiced classification errors. For each of the error measurements, the individual pitch detectors could be rank ordered as a measure of their relative performance as a function of recording condition, and pitch range of the various speakers. Performance scores are presented for each of the seven pitch detectors based on each of the categories of error.

I. Introduction

A PITCH DETECTOR is an essential component in a variety of speech processing systems. Besides providing valuable insights into the nature of the excitation source for speech production, the pitch contour of an utterance is useful for recognizing speakers [1], [2], for speech instruction to the hearing impaired [3], and is required in almost all speech analysis-synthesis (vocoder) systems [4]. Because of the importance of pitch detection, a wide variety of algorithms for pitch detection have been proposed in the speech processing literature (e.g., [5]-[11]). In spite of the proliferation of pitch detectors, very little formal evaluation and comparison among the different types of pitch detectors has been attempted. There are a wide variety of reasons why such an evaluation has not been made. Among these are the difficulty in selection of a reasonable standard of comparison; collection of a comprehensive data base; choice of pitch detectors for evaluation; and the difficulty in interpreting the results in a meaningful and unbiased way. This paper is a report on an attempt to provide such a performance evaluation

Manuscript received March 3, 1976; revised June 7, 1976.
The authors are with Bell Laboratories, Murray Hill, NJ 07974.

of seven pitch detection algorithms. Although a wide variety of alternatives were available in almost every aspect of this investigation, several arbitrary (but hopefully reasonable) decisions were made to limit the scope of the performance evaluation to a reasonable size.

In this section we provide an overview of the investigation. We begin with a discussion of the general problems and issues in pitch detection. Then we discuss the various types of pitch detection algorithms which have been proposed and review their general characteristics. We conclude with a discussion of the types of performance measures which would be suitable for various applications.

In Section II the detailed implementations of the seven pitch detectors used in this study are reviewed. Included in this section is a brief discussion of the method of operation of the pitch detector and the method used to make a voiced-unvoiced classification. In Section III we discuss the data base selected for evaluating the seven pitch detectors. In Section IV the method used to measure the standard pitch contour is outlined. Section V presents the results of several error analyses. Section VI provides a discussion of the error analyses and Section VII discusses the computational considerations in the implementation of each of the algorithms.

A. Problems in Pitch Detection

Accurate and reliable measurement of the pitch period of a speech signal from the acoustic pressure waveform alone is often exceedingly difficult for several reasons. One reason is that the glottal excitation waveform is not a perfect train of periodic pulses. Although finding the period of a perfectly periodic waveform is straightforward, measuring the period of a speech waveform, which varies both in period and in the detailed structure of the waveform within a period, can be quite difficult. A second difficulty in measuring pitch period is the interaction between the vocal tract and the glottal excitation. In some instances the formants of the vocal tract can alter significantly the structure of the glottal waveform so that the actual pitch period is difficult to detect. Such interactions generally are most deleterious to pitch detection during rapid movements of the articulators when the formants are also changing rapidly. A third problem in reliably measuring pitch is the inherent difficulty in defining the exact beginning and end of each pitch period during voiced speech segments. The choice of the exact beginning and ending locations of the pitch period is often quite arbitrary. For example, based on the acoustic waveform alone, some candidates for defining the

Reprinted from *IEEE Trans. Acoust., Speech, and Signal Process.*, vol. ASSP-24, pp. 399–417, Oct. 1976.

beginning and end of the period include the maximum value during the period, the zero crossing prior to the maximum, etc. The only requirement on such a measurement is that it be consistent from period-to-period in order to be able to define the "exact" location of the beginning and end of each pitch period. The lack of such consistency can lead to spurious pitch period estimates. Fig. 1 shows two possible choices for defining a pitch marker directly based on waveform measurements. The two waveform measurements shown in Fig. 1 can (and often will) give slightly different values for the pitch period. The pitch period discrepancies are due not only to the quasiperiodicity of the speech waveform, but also the fact that peak measurements are sensitive to the formant structure during the pitch period, whereas zero crossings of a waveform are sensitive to the formants, noise, and any dc level in the waveform. A fourth difficulty in pitch detection is distinguishing between unvoiced speech and low-level voiced speech. In many cases transitions between unvoiced speech segments and low-level voiced speech segments are very subtle and thus are extremely hard to pinpoint.

In addition to the difficulties in measuring pitch period discussed above, additional complications occur when one is faced with the problem of pitch extraction of speech that has been transmitted through the telephone system. Many systems, in which pitch detection is required, must process telephone-quality speech. The effects of the telephone system on speech include linear filtering, nonlinear processing, and the addition of noise to the speech signal. With regard to linear filtering, the telephone system acts like a bandpass filter (low-frequency cutoff of approximately 200 Hz, high-frequency cutoff of approximately 3200 Hz) which can significantly attenuate the fundamental pitch frequency and many of the higher pitch harmonics. The result is that the periodicity of the signal is much harder to detect. Nonlinear contributions of the telephone system to the speech signals can, depending on the particular transmission system used, include the following.

1) Phase distortion.
2) Fading or amplitude modulation of the speech signal.
3) Crosstalk between two or more messages.
4) Clipping or distortion of extremely high-level sounds.

(It should be noted that one would *not* expect all the above listed effects to occur simultaneously.) Thus the overall effect of the telephone line is to obscure the periodic structure of the speech waveform such that the pitch period becomes more difficult to detect.

B. Types of Pitch Detectors

As a result of the numerous difficulties in pitch measurements, a wide variety of sophisticated pitch detection methods have been developed. Basically, a pitch detector is a device which makes a voiced–unvoiced decision, and, during periods of voiced speech, provides a measurement of the pitch period. However, some pitch detection algorithms just determine the pitch during voiced segments of speech and rely on some other technique for the voiced–unvoiced decisions. Pitch detection

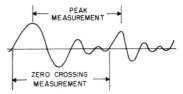
Fig. 1. Two waveform measurements which can be used to define pitch markers.

algorithms can roughly be divided into the following three broad categories.

1) A group which utilizes principally the time-domain properties of speech signals.
2) A group which utilizes principally the frequency-domain properties of speech signals.
3) A group which utilizes both the time- and frequency-domain properties of speech signals.

Time-domain pitch detectors operate directly on the speech waveform to estimate the pitch period. For these pitch detectors the measurements most often made are peak and valley measurements, zero-crossing measurements, and autocorrelation measurements. The basic assumption that is made in all these cases is that if a quasiperiodic signal has been suitably processed to minimize the effects of the formant structure, then simple time-domain measurements will provide good estimates of the period.

The class of frequency-domain pitch detectors use the property that if the signal is periodic in the time domain, then the frequency spectrum of the signal will consist of a series of impulses at the fundamental frequency and its harmonics. Thus simple measurements can be made on the frequency spectrum of the signal (or a nonlinearly transformed version of it as in the cepstral pitch detector [5]) to estimate the period of the signal.

The class of hybrid pitch detectors incorporates features of both the time-domain and the frequency-domain approaches to pitch detection. For example, a hybrid pitch detector might use frequency-domain techniques to provide a spectrally flattened time waveform, and then use autocorrelation measurements to estimate the pitch period.

In this investigation four time-domain, one frequency-domain, and two hybrid pitch detectors were studied. Detailed discussions of the algorithms which were used will be given in Section II.

C. Criteria for Evaluating Pitch Detectors

One of the most difficult problems in comparing and evaluating the performance of pitch detectors is choosing a meaningful objective performance criterion. The basic problem is that a criterion suitable for one application may not be suitable for a different application of pitch detectors.

There are many characteristics of pitch detection algorithms which influence the choice of a set of performance criteria. Among these factors are the following.

1) Accuracy in estimating pitch period.
2) Accuracy in making a voiced–unvoiced decision.
3) Robustness of the measurements, i.e., they must be

modified for different transmission conditions, speakers, etc.

4) Speed of operation.
5) Complexity of the algorithm.
6) Suitability for hardware implementation.
7) Cost of hardware implementation.

Depending on the specific application, various weights must be given to each of the above factors in choosing a single objective performance criterion. In this paper we will present results based on factors 1 and 2 in the above list, i.e., only those factors which are most amenable to numerical tabulations. However, whenever possible, we will try to discuss how factors 3–7 enter into an overall assessment of the pitch detectors discussed in this paper.

There is one major factor which was omitted from the above list and which, for many applications, is the dominant factor in evaluating pitch detectors. This factor is the perceptual accuracy of the pitch detectors, i.e., the question of how faithfully the pitch contour measured by the pitch detector matches the natural excitation pitch contour in terms of synthetic speech quality. We have omitted this factor from the list because it is not an objective performance criterion, but is instead a subjective criterion that can only be assessed through a series of extensive perceptual tests using synthetic speech samples. Such a companion investigation is being undertaken by the authors and will be reported on at a later date.

II. PITCH DETECTION ALGORITHMS

As stated earlier, seven distinct algorithms for detecting pitch were investigated. These algorithms were the following.

1) Modified autocorrelation method using clipping (AUTOC) (Dubnowski [11]).
2) Cepstrum method (CEP) (Schafer [12]).
3) Simplified inverse filtering technique (SIFT) (Markel [8]).
4) Data reduction method (DARD) (Miller [9]).
5) Parallel processing method (PPROC) (Rabiner [2]).
6) Spectral equalization LPC method using Newton's transformation (LPC) (Atal, unpublished).
7) Average magnitude difference function (AMDF) (NSA version, [10]).

The names in parentheses are the individual (or group) responsible for providing Fortran code for the computational parts of each algorithm, and the code following the name of the method is the abbreviation which will be used to refer to the pitch detector throughout this paper.

The choice of pitch detectors was based on both practical considerations (i.e., availability of reasonably portable Fortran code) as well as the desire to choose a good cross section of recent examples of each of the three types of pitch detectors discussed in Section I. Thus, included in this study were two time-domain (waveform) pitch detectors (4 and 5), two autocorrelation pitch detectors (1 and 7), one frequency-domain pitch detector (2), and two LPC hybrid pitch detectors (3 and 6).

In the following section we provide a summary of the method of operation of each of the seven pitch detectors.

Whenever possible, exact values of parameters of the pitch detector (e.g., section length, window, etc., will be given).

A. Modified Autocorrelation Method (AUTOC)

The modified autocorrelation pitch detector is based on the center-clipping method of Sondhi [7]. Fig. 2 shows a block diagram of the pitch detection algorithm. The method requires that the speech be low-passed filtered to 900 Hz. (A 99-point linear phase, finite impulse response (FIR) digital filter is used to low-pass filter the speech. Detailed characteristics of this low-pass filter, which is used for several of the pitch detectors, are given in [13].)

The low-pass filtered speech signal is digitized at a 10-kHz sampling rate and sectioned into overlapping 30-ms (300 samples) sections for processing. Since the pitch period computation for all pitch detectors is performed 100 times/s, i.e., every 10 ms, adjacent sections overlap by 20 ms or 200 samples.

The first stage of processing is the computation of a clipping level c_L for the current 30-ms section of speech. The clipping level is set at a value which is 64 percent of the smaller of the peak absolute sample values in the first and last 10-ms portions of the section. Following the determination of the clipping level, the 30-ms section of speech is center clipped, and then infinite peak clipped, resulting in a signal which assumes one of three possible values—+1 if the sample exceeds the positive clipping level, –1 if the sample falls below the negative clipping level, and 0 otherwise.

Following clipping the autocorrelation function for the 30-ms section is computed over a range of lags from 20 samples to 200 samples (i.e., 2-ms–20-ms period). Additionally, the autocorrelation at 0 delay is computed for appropriate normalization purposes. The autocorrelation function is then searched for its maximum (normalized) value. If the maximum (normalized value) exceeds 0.3, the section is classified as voiced and the location of the maximum is the pitch period. Otherwise, the section is classified as unvoiced.

In addition to the voiced–unvoiced classification based on the autocorrelation function, a preliminary test is carried out on each section of speech to determine if the peak signal amplitude within the section is sufficiently large to warrant the pitch computation. If the peak signal level within the section is below a given threshold,[1] the section is classified as unvoiced (silence) and no pitch computations are made. This method of eliminating low-level speech sections from further processing was also used for pitch detectors 2 (CEP), 3 (SIFT), and 5 (PPROC).

B. Cepstral Method (CEP)

Fig. 3 shows a flow diagram of the cepstral pitch detector described in [12]. Each block of 512 samples (51.2 ms) is weighted by a 512-point Hamming window, and then the cepstrum of that block is computed. The peak cepstral value and its location is determined and if the value of this peak exceeds a fixed threshold, the section is called voiced and the pitch period is the location of the peak. If the peak does not

---

[1] The threshold chosen is 1/15 of the peak absolute signal value within the utterance.

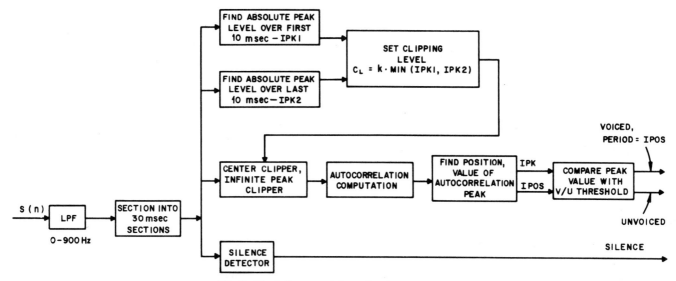

Fig. 2. Block diagram of the AUTOC pitch detector.

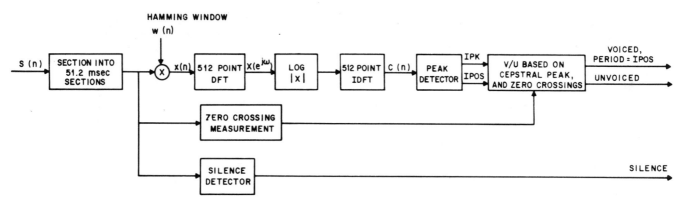

Fig. 3. Block diagram of the CEP pitch detector.

exceed the threshold, a zero-crossing count is made on the block. If the zero-crossing count exceeds a given threshold, the block is called unvoiced. Otherwise it is called voiced and the period is the location of the maximum value of the cepstrum.

As in the modified autocorrelation method, a preliminary silence detector (based on the signal level) is used to classify all low-level blocks as silence (unvoiced speech) prior to the cepstral computation. It should also be noted that the cepstral pitch detector uses the full-band speech signal for processing.

C. Simplified Inverse Filtering Technique (SIFT)

Fig. 4 shows a block diagram of the SIFT method of pitch detection [8]. A block of 400 speech samples (40 ms at a 10-kHz rate) is low-pass filtered to a bandwidth of 900 Hz, and then decimated (down sampled) by a 5 to 1 ratio. The coefficients of a 4th-order inverse filter are obtained using the autocorrelation method of LPC analysis [14]. The 2-kHz speech signal is then inverse filtered to give a spectrally flattened signal which is then autocorrelated. The pitch period is obtained by interpolating the autocorrelation function in the neighborhood of the peak of the autocorrelation function. A voiced–unvoiced decision is made on the basis of the amplitude of the peak of the autocorrelation function. The threshold

used for this test is a normalized value of 0.4 for the autocorrelation peak.

As with the previous two pitch detectors, a preliminary silence detector is used to classify low-level sections as silence and eliminate them from further consideration.

D. Data Reduction Method (DARD)

Fig. 5 shows a block diagram of the data reduction pitch detector of Miller [9]. This pitch detector places pitch markers directly on a low-pass filtered (0–900 Hz) speech signal and thus is a pitch synchronous pitch detector.

To obtain the appropriate pitch markers, the data reduction method first detects excursion cycles in the waveform based on intervals between major zero crossings. The remainder of the algorithm tries to isolate and identify the principal excursion cycles, i.e., those which correspond to true pitch periods. This is accomplished through a series of steps using energy measurements and logic based on permissible pitch periods and anticipated syllabic rate changes of pitch. An error correction procedure is used to provide a reasonable measure of continuity in the pitch markers.

Since there is no inherent voiced–unvoiced calculation within this pitch detector, regions of unvoiced speech are identified by the lack of pitch markers.

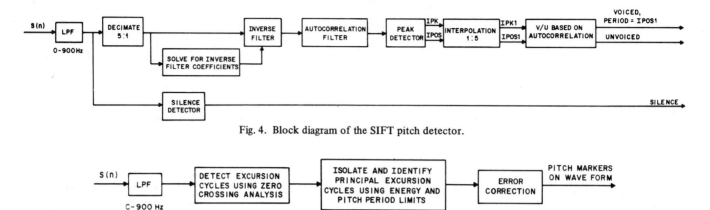

Fig. 4. Block diagram of the SIFT pitch detector.

Fig. 5. Block diagram of the DARD pitch detector.

E. Parallel Processing Method (PPROC)

Fig. 6 shows a block diagram of the parallel processing pitch detector [6]. The speech signal is first low-pass filtered to a bandwidth of 900 Hz. Then a series of measurements are made on the peaks and valleys of the low-pass filtered signal to give six separate functions. Each of these six functions is processed by an elementary pitch period estimator (PPE), giving six separate estimates of the pitch period. The six pitch estimates are then combined by a sophisticated decision algorithm which determines the pitch period. A voiced–unvoiced decision is obtained based on the degree of agreement among the six pitch detectors. Additionally, the preliminary silence detector described in Section II-A is used to classify low-level segments as silence.

F. Spectral Equalization LPC Method Using Newton's Transformation (LPC)

Fig. 7 shows a block diagram of an LPC pitch detector proposed by Atal (unpublished). The first step in this pitch detector is a voiced–unvoiced detector which uses a pattern-recognition technique to classify each 10-ms interval of speech as voiced or unvoiced [15]. If the speech section is classified as voiced, the 10-kHz sampled speech is digitally low-pass filtered to a bandwidth of about 900 Hz, and then decimated by 5 to 1 to a 2-kHz sampling rate. A 41-pole LPC analysis is performed on a 40-ms frame of speech to give a good representation of the speech spectrum in terms of the pitch harmonics. A Newton transformation is used to spectrally flatten the speech, i.e., to transform the signal into one which has sharp peaks at the pitch impulses, and is approximately zero everywhere else. A peak picker is used to determine the pitch period at the 2-kHz rate and a simple interpolation network is used to obtain higher resolution in the value of the pitch period.

It should be pointed out that the voiced–unvoiced pattern recognition algorithm uses a training set which provides a statistical description of the measurements used in the algorithm for each of classes. The success of this method of making a voiced–unvoiced decision depends heavily on how well the training set of data characterizes the different speech classes.

With careful training, voiced–unvoiced accuracies on the order of 99 percent have been obtained [15].

G. Average Magnitude Different Function (AMDF)

Fig. 8 shows a block diagram of the AMDF pitch detector [10]. (The version used in this study was kindly supplied by M. Malpass of the Massachusetts Institute of Technology Lincoln Laboratory, based on the NSA version of the AMDF method. Details of implementation differ somewhat from those of [10].) The speech signal, initially sampled at 10 kHz, is decimated to a 6.67-kHz rate using a system of the type discussed in [16]. A zero-crossing measurement (NOZ) is made on the full-band speech file, and an energy measurement (ENG) is made on a low-pass filtered version (0–900 Hz) of the signal. The average magnitude difference function is computed on the low-pass filtered speech signal at 48 lags running from 16 to 124 samples. The pitch period is identified as the value of the lag at which the minimum AMDF occurs. Thus a fairly coarse quantization is obtained for the pitch period. Logic is used to check for pitch period doubling, etc., and to check on continuity of pitch periods with previous pitch estimates (a type of nonlinear smoothing). In addition to the pitch estimate, the ratio between the maximum and minimum values of AMDF (MAX/MIN) is obtained. This measurement, along with NOZ and ENG is used to make a voiced–unvoiced decision using logical operations.

III. DATA BASE FOR EVALUATION

In order to evaluate the performance of these seven pitch detectors, an appropriately chosen data base was required to span the range of pitch, types of utterances, and recording and transmission environments which are normally encountered in speech processing. In this section we describe the data base used in this study.

A. Speakers

The set of seven speakers for this study included the following.

1) Low-pitched male (LM).
2) Male speaker 1 (M1).
3) Male speaker 2 (M2).

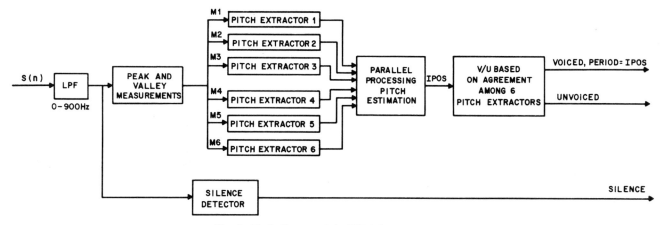

Fig. 6. Block diagram of the PPROC pitch detector.

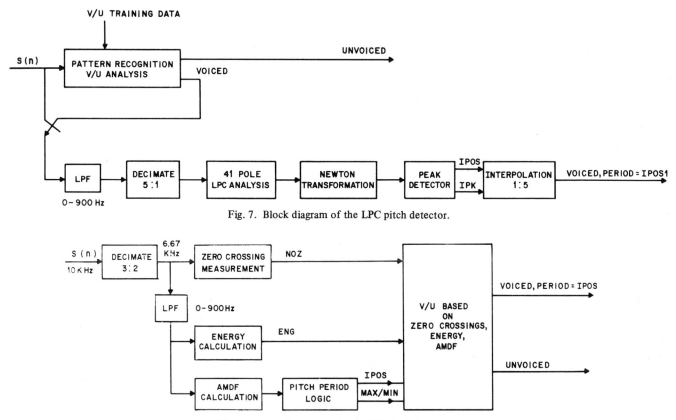

Fig. 7. Block diagram of the LPC pitch detector.

Fig. 8. Block diagram of the AMDF pitch detector.

4) Female speaker 1 (F1).

5) Female speaker 2 (F2)

6) Child (4 year old) (C1).

7) Diplophonic speaker (D1).

Diplophonia is a condition in which a person's alternate glottal pulses are more strongly correlated (both in length and amplitude) than adjacent glottal pulses. Thus, it is extremely difficult to detect the pitch of a diplophonic speaker—even under the best of conditions. Fig. 9 shows a section of waveform from the diplophonic speaker. It is hard to detect, even by eye, the correct pitch periods. For diplophonic speakers, many pitch detectors calculate the pitch period as the distance between major peaks, and not the distance between major and minor peaks. As a result, the pitch contour for a diplophonic speaker often exhibits a large amount of pitch period doubling.

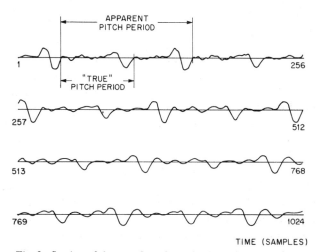

Fig. 9. Section of the waveform from the diplophonic speaker.

To illustrate the range of pitch (both period and frequency) for the speakers in the data base, Fig. 10 shows a plot of the pitch variation for each of the seven speakers for the utterances used in this evaluation (see Section III-B). It can be seen that a wide range of pitch is encompassed by these seven speakers. Additionally, Fig. 11 shows the individual histograms for each of these speakers. It can be seen from this figure that the low-pitched (long period) speakers used in this study (i.e., LM, M1, M2) had a much larger range of pitch period variation than the high-pitched speakers. The histogram for the low-pitched male (LM) shows that on several occasions his pitch period exceeded 200 samples (i.e., the pitch frequency fell below 50 Hz). Since this was outside the anticipated range of pitch variation, all the pitch detectors made errors during these regions.

B. Recorded Utterances

The utterances used in this study included the four monosyllabic nonsense words:

1) Hayed
2) Heed
3) Hod
4) Hoed

and the four sentences:

5) We were away a year ago.
6) I know when my lawyer is due.
7) Every salt breeze comes from the sea.
8) I was stunned by the beauty of the view.

Sentences 5 and 6 are all voiced (except for the stop gaps) whereas sentences 7 and 8 contain both voiced and unvoiced speech.

C. Recording Conditions

The three types of recording conditions that were used in this study included:

1) Close-talking microphone (M). ⎫
2) Standard telephone transmission (T). ⎬ simultaneous recording
3) High-quality microphone (W). ⎭

The close-talking microphone recordings were made simultaneously with the telephone recordings since this was the most convenient method of providing a good-quality signal (during voiced regions) for manual pitch detection which could be time aligned with the telephone recordings and which did not interfere with using a standard telephone handset in a natural manner. However, because of its placement close to the mouth of the speaker, the close-talking microphone was quite sensitive to breath noise, plosives, and other unvoiced transients. The telephone recordings were made over the local PBX using an ordinary telephone handset. The close-talking microphone recordings were band-limited to about 3 kHz, as were the telephone recordings. The recordings made on the high-quality microphone were wideband recordings which were filtered at 4 kHz prior to digitization.

IV. Measurement of the Standard Pitch Contour

The method used to measure the standard pitch contour for each of the utterances in the data base was the semiautomatic

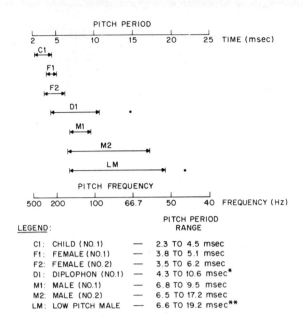

LEGEND:

		PITCH PERIOD RANGE
C1:	CHILD (NO.1)	— 2.3 TO 4.5 msec
F1:	FEMALE (NO.1)	— 3.8 TO 5.1 msec
F2:	FEMALE (NO.2)	— 3.5 TO 6.2 msec
D1:	DIPLOPHON (NO.1)	— 4.3 TO 10.6 msec*
M1:	MALE (NO.1)	— 6.8 TO 9.5 msec
M2:	MALE (NO.2)	— 6.5 TO 17.2 msec
LM:	LOW PITCH MALE	— 6.6 TO 19.2 msec**

*AT TWO ISOLATED POINTS THE PITCH PERIOD WAS 14.7 msec
**AT TWO ISOLATED POINTS THE PITCH PERIOD WAS 21.8 msec

Fig. 10. Pitch variation for each of the speakers used in this study.

pitch detector of McGonegal *et al.* [13] which was developed for this study. This method is a highly sophisticated, user-interactive, pitch detector which estimated pitch on a 10-ms frame-by-frame basis. Extensive analysis of the results obtained from this semiautomatic pitch detector across several users on the same utterances showed this method to be highly reliable [13].

Using the semiautomatic method the analysis time for an experienced user was about 30 min to process 1 s of speech (i.e., 100 frames). For the data base used in this study, a total of 60 h of computer processing was required to estimate the standard pitch contours for the entire data base.

V. Error Analysis Results

The way in which objective comparisons of the performance of each of the individual pitch detectors were made was as follows. For each of the utterances in the data base, a standard pitch contour was obtained using the semiautomatic method of Section IV. We denote the standard pitch contour as $p_s(m)$ were m goes from 1 to M, and M is the number of 10-ms frames in the utterance. The contour $p_s(m)$ has the value 0 if the mth frame is unvoiced; otherwise it has the value of the pitch period for the mth frame.

Next, each of the utterances was used as input to each of the seven pitch detectors and a set of pitch contours was obtained as output. We denote the pitch contour from the jth pitch detector ($j = 1, 2, \cdots, 7$) as $\{p_j(m), m = 1, 2, \cdots, M\}$. Of course, special attention had to be given in the Fortran code to compensate the processing delay of each pitch detector to ensure that the pitch contours from each of the seven pitch detectors registered properly with the standard pitch contour.

To quantitatively measure the performance of each of the pitch detectors relative to the semiautomatic analysis, a series of error measurements was defined for each utterance. In Sec-

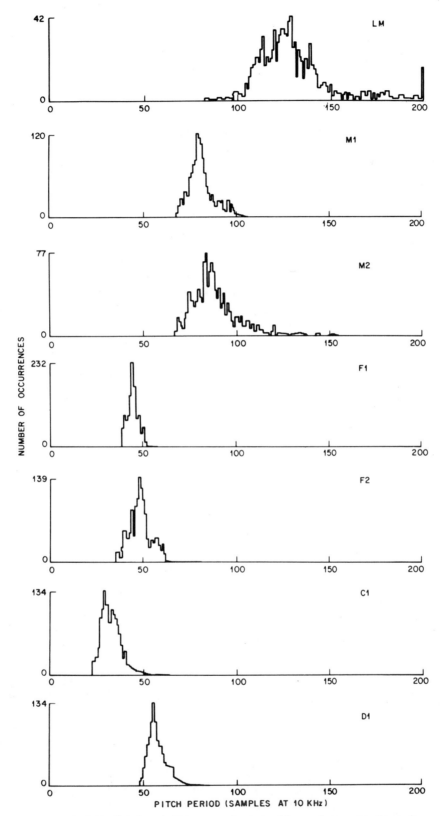

Fig. 11. Individual pitch period histograms for each of the speakers used in this study.

tion V-A we discuss the problems associated with defining these error measurements and attaching physical significance to their values.

The result of the error measurements was a set of scores of the performance of each pitch detector for each utterance, for each recording condition, and for each speaker. Due to the excessive amount of data, the individual results were averaged over the utterances of a single speaker, for each recording condition. A complete set of these results for all the performance classes is given in Section V-B. Finally, where appropriate, the results were averaged over recording conditions and an absolute ranking of each of the pitch detectors for each speaker was given. Such rankings provided a good picture of the performance strengths and weaknesses of each of the seven pitch detectors.

Before proceeding to the discussion of the error measurements, an additional dimension to the error analysis should be mentioned. This added dimension was the application of nonlinear smoothing (error correcting) methods to detect and correct several types of errors which occur in pitch detection [17]. Such a nonlinear smoother was incorporated into this investigation to see what the effects would be on this data base. Extensive examples of the applications of nonlinear smoothers to speech processing are given in [17].

A. Definition of Error Parameters

As mentioned above, for every utterance in the data base there is a standard pitch contour, $p_s(m)$, and a pitch contour for each pitch detector, $p_j(m)$, where j denotes the pitch detector used in the comparison, i.e., $j = 1$ is the AUTOC method, $j = 2$ is the CEP method, etc. By comparing $p_s(m)$ to $p_j(m)$, (for each value of j) it can be seen that four possibilities can occur for each value of m. These four possibilities are the following.

1) $p_s(m) = 0$, $p_j(m) = 0$ in which case both the standard analysis and the pitch detector classified the mth interval as unvoiced. No error results here.

2) $p_s(m) = 0$, $p_j(m) \neq 0$ in which case the standard analysis classified the mth interval as unvoiced, but the pitch detector classified the mth interval as voiced. An unvoiced-to-voiced error results here.

3) $p_s(m) \neq 0$, $p_j(m) = 0$ in which case the standard analysis classified the mth interval as voiced, but the pitch detector classified the mth interval as unvoiced. A voiced-to-unvoiced error results here.

4) $p_s(m) = P_1 \neq 0$, $p_j(m) = P_2 \neq 0$ in which case both the standard analysis and the pitch detector classified the mth interval as voiced. For this case two types of errors can exist, depending on the values of P_1 and P_2, the pitch periods from the standard analysis and from the pitch detector. If we define the voiced error $e(m)$ as

$$e(m) = P_1 - P_2,$$ (1)

then, if $|e(m)| \geqslant 10$ samples (i.e., more than 1-ms error in estimating the pitch period), the error was classified as a *gross* pitch period error. For such cases, the pitch detector has failed dramatically in estimating the pitch period. Possible causes of such gross pitch errors are pitch period doubling or tripling, inadequate suppression of formants so as to effect pitch measurements, etc. The second type of pitch error was the *fine* pitch period error in which case $|e(m)| < 10$ samples. For such cases the pitch detector has estimated the pitch period sufficiently accurately to attribute the errors (primarily) to the measurement techniques.

Based on the above four possibilities for comparing each frame of the reference pitch contour to each frame of each pitch detector contour, five distinct measurements of the performance of each pitch detector were derived. These five error measurements are the following.

1) Gross Error Count: For this measurement the number of

gross pitch period errors (as defined above) per utterance was tabulated.

2) Mean of the Fine Pitch Errors: The mean $\bar{e}$ is defined as

$$\bar{e} = \frac{1}{N_i} \sum_{j=1}^{N_i} e(m_j)$$ (2)

where m_j is the jth interval in the utterance for which $|e(m)| < 10$ (fine pitch error), and N_i is the number of such intervals in the utterance. Thus $\bar{e}$ is a measure of the bias in the pitch measurement during voiced intervals.

3) Standard Deviation of the Fine Pitch Errors: The standard deviation, σ_e, is defined as

$$\sigma_e = \sqrt{\frac{1}{N_i} \sum_{j=1}^{N_i} e^2(m_j) - \bar{e}^2}.$$ (3)

The standard deviation of the fine pitch errors is a measure of the accuracy of the pitch detector in measuring pitch period during voiced intervals.

4) Voiced-to-Unvoiced Error Rate: This measurement shows the accuracy in correctly classifying voiced intervals.

5) Unvoiced-to-Voiced Error Rate: This measurement shows the accuracy in correctly classifying unvoiced intervals.

Although other error analyses are possible, it was felt that these five error measurements provided a good description of the performance strengths and weaknesses of each of the seven pitch detectors. The results of these error analyses are given in Section V-B. Before presenting these results, we first show some examples of the individual pitch contours for three of the utterances used in this study. Figs. 12–14 show typical sets of pitch contours for the seventh utterance of Section III-B, for the wideband condition, for speakers LM, M2, and C1. The curve of the upper left in each figure is the result of the semiautomatic analysis (i.e., the standard pitch contour). It can be seen from these figures that each of the types of errors discussed above occurs in these examples. Finally, Fig. 15 shows the result of processing each of the pitch contours of Fig. 13 by a nonlinear smoother (a combination of running medians of length 7 and some simple logic). The overall similarity among the smoothed pitch contours is startlingly evident in Fig. 15. As will be seen later, a good nonlinear smoother (error correcter) is able to correct a large number of the errors in pitch detection and considerably improve the performance of a pitch detector. However, if the error rate is too high, no amount of nonlinear smoothing will suffice.

B. Results of Error Analysis

The complete set of error analyses discussed in Section V-A was performed on the entire data base of Section III, and the major results are presented in Tables I–XX, along with corresponding performance scores for each error category. Several points about the analysis should first be noted before discussing the individual tables and the resulting performance scores. First it must be pointed out that for the microphone and telephone recording conditions all eight sentences were processed, whereas for the wideband case only the four sentences were processed (i.e., the four nonsense words were not used).

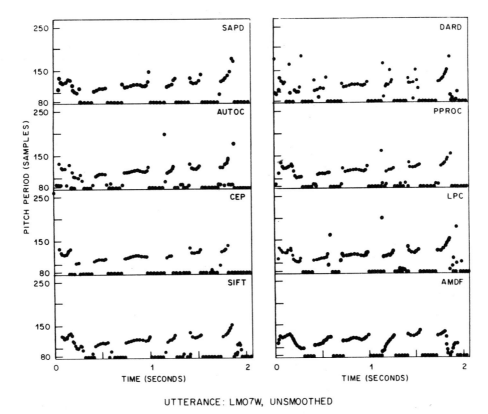

Fig. 12. Representative set of raw pitch contours for utterance 7, speaker LM, recording condition W.

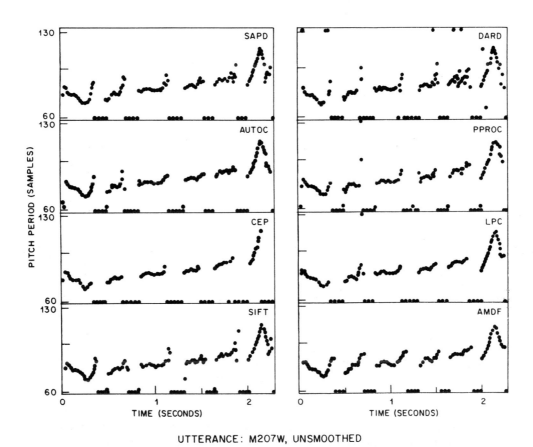

Fig. 13. Representative set of raw pitch contours for utterance 7, speaker M2, condition W.

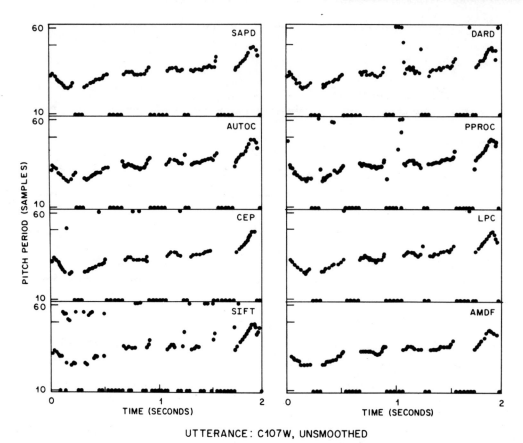

UTTERANCE: C107W, UNSMOOTHED

Fig. 14. Representative set of raw pitch contours for utterance 7, speaker C1, condition W.

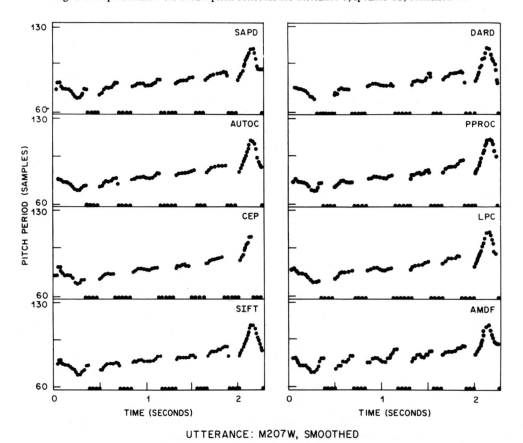

UTTERANCE: M207W, SMOOTHED

Fig. 15. Representative set of nonlinearly smoothed pitch contours for utterance 7, speaker M2, condition W.

Second, the results obtained for the diplophonic speaker (D1) were omitted entirely from the error analysis because of the universal difficulties of all the pitch detectors (including the semiautomatic method) in estimating the correct pitch period for this speaker. Some of the raw analysis results for speaker D1 are presented in the M.S. thesis of Cheng [18]. Finally, because of the large number of factors involved in the analysis, each of the error measurements was averaged over the utterances of each speaker. This is justified in that it is not anticipated that the sentence material is a factor in the performance evaluation of any pitch detector.

The format for the results presented in Tables I–XX is as follows. First we present the average (over utterances) error scores for each category for each speaker, recording condition, and pitch detector. Also included in the tables is a sum of the raw averages across the three recording conditions. Each table of raw data is followed by one (or sometimes two) table(s) of performance rankings based on an empirical (but hopefully physically justifiable) evaluation of the average scores for each pitch detector and for each speaker. From these performance rankings for each error category the performance strengths and weaknesses of each pitch detector can readily be seen and evaluated. Following the tables of unsmoothed raw averages, the results obtained after nonlinear smoothing are presented. Comparisons between the unsmoothed and smoothed performance rankings show cases where the error rate is too high to be properly corrected with simple nonlinear smoothing techniques. We now proceed to discuss the results for each of the five error categories of Section V-A.

1) Gross Pitch Errors: Tables I–IV present the results obtained for the gross pitch error measurements. From Table I it can be seen that, for the most part, a great deal of homogeneity existed between the scores for the three recording conditions, although in some cases there were fairly substantial differences in the average gross error scores. Table II shows the performance rankings based on the sum of the average gross error scores across the three recording conditions. The best rankings are the lowest scores in Table II, i.e., 1 is the best score, 5 is the worst score. Rank 1 was given to a score of from 0 to 6; rank 2 for a score from 6 to 18; rank 3 for a score from 18 to 42; rank 4 for a score from 42 to 90; and rank 5 for scores over 90. The scale in this case is logarithmic because the difficulty in detecting and correcting such gross errors inherently appears to be logarithmically related to the number of such errors per utterance. Based on these assumptions, the rankings of Table II show that each pitch detector performed better for some speakers (i.e., range of pitch variation) than for others. For example, the AUTOC pitch detector performed much worse on the two low-pitch speakers (LM and M2) than on the three higher pitch speakers (F1, F2, C1); whereas the CEP pitch detector performed much better on the lower pitch speakers than on the higher pitch speakers. An overall ranking score for each pitch detector (i.e., the sum of the rankings over the speakers) is given at the bottom of Table II, and the ranking scores in the rightmost column of Table II (the sum of the rankings over the pitch detector) is a measure of the difficulty of detecting pitch for a given speaker. Table II shows that the overall ranking scores for five of the seven pitch detectors were comparable, and that the two others were

TABLE I
NUMBER OF GROSS PITCH ERRORS—UNSMOOTHED

Speaker		AUTOC	CEP	SIFT	DARD	PPROC	LPC	AMDF
LM	M	15.3	0.5	0.6	5.8	10.0	4.4	12.8
	T	26.1	1.1	4.5	5.8	11.0	5.6	15.6
	W	19.5	1.3	4.5	13.8	23.8	13.0	23.8
	Sum	60.9	2.9	9.6	25.4	44.8	23.0	52.2
M1	M	0.6	0.1	0.0	5.9	2.0	0.1	0.3
	T	3.4	0.1	0.8	6.3	3.0	0.8	0.8
	W	2.8	0.5	3.0	23.5	6.0	0.8	2.8
	Sum	6.8	0.7	3.8	35.7	11.0	1.7	3.9
M2	M	6.1	0.4	1.3	15.9	4.9	2.9	7.3
	T	9.9	0.6	3.4	4.0	5.8	4.0	9.8
	W	7.3	1.3	5.3	26.8	12.3	5.5	8.5
	Sum	23.3	2.3	10.0	46.7	23.0	12.4	25.6
F1	M	1.9	9.1	4.4	7.3	4.0	2.4	0.5
	T	1.6	8.5	1.8	6.3	2.8	1.4	0.0
	W	0.0	29.0	8.0	0.8	4.0	2.0	0.0
	Sum	3.5	46.0	14.2	14.4	10.8	5.8	0.5
F2	M	0.4	1.4	2.1	7.1	2.4	1.6	0.6
	T	0.6	2.0	1.5	5.6	1.5	1.5	1.0
	W	2.0	2.5	3.8	8.5	5.0	2.0	1.8
	Sum	3.0	5.9	7.4	21.2	8.9	5.1	3.4
C1	M	1.0	13.6	65.3	6.1	7.8	8.3	10.6
	T	1.9	14.8	62.6	12.9	9.0	12.3	9.1
	W	0.0	12.5	40.8	3.0	7.3	5.5	6.5
	Sum	2.9	40.9	168.7	22.0	24.1	26.1	26.2

TABLE II
PERFORMANCE SCORES BASED ON SUM OF GROSS PITCH ERRORS—UNSMOOTHED

Speaker	AUTOC	CEP	SIFT	DARD	PPROC	LPC	AMDF	Sum
LM	4	1	2	3	4	3	4	21
M1	2	1	1	3	2	1	1	11
M2	3	1	2	4	3	2	3	18
F1	1	4	2	2	2	1	1	13
F2	1	1	2	3	2	1	1	11
C1	1	3	5	3	3	3	3	21
Sum	12	11	14	18	16	11	13	

Code: $(0-6) = 1$, $(6-12) = 2$, $(12-42) = 3$, $(42-90) = 4$, $(90-\ ) = 5$.

somewhat inferior for this error category. Additionally, it is seen that the speakers with the most extreme pitch (LM, C1) presented the most difficulty in terms of this error category.

Tables III and IV present the results for the gross pitch error category after processing by a nonlinear smoother. This type of error is most easily detected and corrected by the nonlinear smoother used in this study as verified by Tables III and IV. It can be seen from Table IV that only 12 out of the 42 pairs in Table IV were not given the best ranking of 1. These 12 represent cases where the gross error rate was too high to be corrected entirely by a nonlinear smoother. The overall ranking scores for the smoothed results showed all seven pitch detectors (with the exception of speaker C1 for pitch detector SIFT) to be essentially identical in their overall performance in this error category.

2) Fine Pitch Error–Average Value: The results of the analysis of the average value of the fine pitch error indicated that all seven pitch detectors yielded average values of $\bar{e}$ on the order of ± 0.5 samples across all utterances, speakers, and re-

TABLE III
Number of Gross Pitch Errors—Smoothed

Speaker		AUTOC	CEP	SIFT	DARD	PPROC	LPC	AMDF
LM	M	5.3	2.3	2.0	3.5	5.8	3.6	9.4
	T	6.1	1.6	2.0	2.0	6.0	3.1	10.8
	W	3.8	5.0	6.8	5.0	13.3	9.5	17.3
	Sum	15.2	8.9	10.8	10.5	25.1	16.2	37.5
M1	M	0.3	0.4	0.5	0.8	1.3	0.4	0.6
	T	0.0	0.1	0.0	0.5	0.1	0.3	0.5
	W	0.3	0.5	0.5	2.8	1.5	0.8	2.8
	Sum	0.6	1.0	1.0	4.1	2.9	1.5	3.9
M2	M	0.8	1.5	1.5	6.0	2.9	3.5	6.4
	T	1.3	1.8	1.4	2.3	3.0	3.6	7.4
	W	2.3	2.3	3.0	8.3	7.0	5.0	5.3
	Sum	4.4	5.6	5.9	16.6	12.9	12.1	19.1
F1	M	0.0	0.8	0.0	0.1	0.0	0.0	0.0
	T	0.0	0.0	0.0	0.1	0.0	0.0	0.0
	W	0.0	0.0	0.0	0.0	0.0	0.0	0.0
	Sum	0.0	0.8	0.0	0.2	0.0	0.0	0.0
F2	M	0.0	0.1	0.0	0.4	0.3	0.0	0.1
	T	0.1	0.0	0.1	0.6	0.0	0.3	0.3
	W	0.8	0.0	1.3	0.3	1.3	0.0	0.0
	Sum	0.9	0.1	1.4	1.3	1.6	0.3	0.4
C1	M	0.0	0.0	57.4	0.1	0.0	0.0	0.5
	T	0.0	0.0	55.8	0.3	0.0	0.0	1.8
	W	0.0	0.0	15.8	0.0	0.0	0.0	0.0
	Sum	0.0	0.0	129.0	0.4	0.0	0.0	2.3

TABLE V
Standard Deviation of Fine Pitch Errors—Unsmoothed

Speaker		AUTOC	CEP	SIFT	DARD	PPROC	LPC	AMDF
LM	M	1.0	0.9	0.9	1.1	1.8	1.1	2.3
	T	1.0	1.0	0.9	1.2	1.9	1.2	2.1
	W	0.8	1.0	0.9	1.1	1.6	1.1	2.1
	Sum	2.8	2.9	2.7	3.4	5.3	3.4	6.5
M1	M	0.7	0.5	0.7	0.9	0.9	0.6	1.1
	T	0.6	0.5	0.7	0.8	0.6	0.6	1.0
	W	1.0	0.8	0.8	1.3	1.1	0.7	1.3
	Sum	2.3	1.8	2.2	3.0	2.6	1.9	3.4
M2	M	0.7	0.7	0.7	1.0	1.1	0.8	1.5
	T	0.6	0.7	0.8	1.0	1.0	0.9	1.3
	W	1.0	0.9	1.0	1.2	1.4	0.9	1.6
	Sum	2.3	2.3	2.5	3.2	3.5	2.6	4.4
F1	M	0.6	0.5	0.7	1.1	0.8	0.6	1.0
	T	0.6	0.6	0.7	1.0	0.9	0.6	1.1
	W	0.5	0.5	0.7	0.9	0.8	0.5	0.9
	Sum	1.7	1.6	2.1	3.0	2.5	1.7	3.0
F2	M	0.6	0.6	0.6	0.8	0.8	0.4	1.1
	T	0.6	0.5	0.7	0.9	0.8	0.5	1.3
	W	0.6	0.5	0.7	0.8	0.7	0.6	1.1
	Sum	1.8	1.6	2.0	2.5	2.3	1.5	3.5
C1	M	0.4	0.5	0.8	0.7	0.6	0.5	0.9
	T	0.4	0.5	0.8	0.8	0.6	0.5	1.0
	W	0.5	0.4	0.9	0.8	0.7	0.5	1.0
	Sum	1.3	1.4	2.5	2.3	1.9	1.5	2.9

TABLE IV
Performance Scores Based on Sum of Gross Pitch Errors—Smoothed

Speaker	AUTOC	CEP	SIFT	DARD	PPROC	LPC	AMDF	Sum
LM	2	2	2	2	3	2	3	16
M1	1	1	1	1	1	1	1	7
M2	1	1	1	2	2	2	2	11
F1	1	1	1	1	1	1	1	7
F2	1	1	1	1	1	1	1	7
C1	1	1	5	1	1	1	1	11
Sum	7	7	11	8	9	8	9	

Code same as Table II.

TABLE VI
Performance Scores Based on Sum of Standard Deviations of Fine Pitch Errors—Unsmoothed

Speaker	AUTOC	CEP	SIFT	DARD	PPROC	LPC	AMDF	Sum
LM	2	2	2	3	4	3	5	21
M1	2	2	2	2	2	2	3	15
M2	2	2	2	3	3	2	3	17
F1	2	2	2	3	2	2	3	15
F2	2	2	2	2	2	1	3	14
C1	1	1	2	2	2	1	2	11
Sum	11	11	12	15	15	11	18	

Code: $(0–1.5) = 1$, $(1.5–3) = 2$, $(3–4.5) = 3$, $(4.5–6) = 4$, $(6–\ ) = 5$.

cording conditions. No consistent bias (either positive or negative) in the value of $\bar{e}$ was noted in the data. Thus for all practical purposes the average value of the fine pitch error was essentially 0 in all cases and, therefore, no results are tabulated here.

3) Fine Pitch Error–Standard Deviation: Tables V–VIII present the results of the analysis of the standard deviation of the fine pitch error. The units of the standard deviation are samples. The results here were quite homogeneous across recording conditions and thus the sum of the standard deviations over recording conditions was used as the performance measure in Tables VI (raw averages) and VIII (smoothed averages). Based on the analysis results, a standard deviation of less than 0.5 samples per condition, or 1.5 samples for the sum was given a score of 1. A linear scale was used for this measurement —thus a standard deviation sum from 1.5 to 3 samples was given the next best score (2), etc.

As seen in Table VI, four of the pitch detectors (AUTOC, CEP, SIFT, and LPC) performed almost uniformly across all speakers, and had comparably high overall performance scores.

The two simple time-domain pitch detectors (DARD and PPROC) had somewhat higher scores (poorer performance) due to the lower resolution which is obtained in estimating a pitch period directly on the waveform due to effects discussed earlier. Finally, the worst performance in this category was for the AMDF pitch detector. This result is due to the lack of resolution in the AMDF measurement which is made only every third or fourth sample—thus the pitch period is only estimated to within a couple of samples.

Tables VII and VIII for the smoothed standard deviations show that the nonlinear smoother does not strongly affect the raw results presented in Tables V and VI. Slight differences in the overall performance scores do exist both because of the gross pitch period errors which are detected and corrected to fine pitch period errors, and because of the smoothing of the fine pitch errors themselves.

4) Voiced-to-Unvoiced Errors: Tables IX–XIV present the results of the voiced-to-unvoiced errors for each pitch detector. Table IX gives the raw average scores for each recording condi-

TABLE VII
STANDARD DEVIATION OF FINE PITCH ERRORS—SMOOTHED

Speaker		AUTOC	CEP	SIFT	DARD	PPROC	LPC	AMDF
						Pitch Detector		
LM	M	1.1	1.1	1.0	1.2	1.5	1.1	1.9
	T	1.0	1.2	1.0	1.3	1.6	1.3	1.9
	W	1.2	1.3	0.9	1.2	1.5	1.0	2.0
	Sum	3.3	3.6	2.9	3.7	4.6	3.4	5.8
M1	M	0.6	0.6	0.6	0.8	0.7	0.5	1.2
	T	0.6	0.6	0.6	0.7	0.6	0.5	1.0
	W	0.8	0.9	0.9	1.1	0.9	0.7	1.3
	Sum	2.0	2.1	2.1	2.6	2.2	1.7	3.5
M2	M	0.8	0.8	0.8	1.0	1.0	0.8	1.5
	T	0.8	0.9	0.9	0.9	0.8	0.9	1.6
	W	0.9	1.1	1.1	1.2	1.3	0.8	1.5
	Sum	2.5	2.8	2.8	3.1	3.1	2.5	4.6
F1	M	0.5	0.5	0.6	0.8	0.6	0.5	0.9
	T	0.5	0.6	0.6	0.9	0.7	0.5	1.0
	W	0.5	0.5	0.8	0.7	0.6	0.4	0.8
	Sum	1.5	1.6	2.0	2.4	1.9	1.4	2.7
F2	M	0.6	0.6	0.6	0.9	0.7	0.4	1.0
	T	0.5	0.5	0.6	0.8	0.7	0.5	1.2
	W	0.6	0.5	0.6	0.7	0.6	0.5	1.0
	Sum	1.7	1.6	1.8	2.4	2.0	1.4	3.2
C1	M	0.4	0.6	1.1	0.6	0.6	0.5	0.9
	T	0.5	0.5	0.7	0.7	0.5	0.6	1.1
	W	0.5	0.5	0.9	0.6	0.7	0.4	0.8
	Sum	1.4	1.6	2.7	1.9	1.8	1.5	2.8

TABLE VIII
PERFORMANCE SCORES BASED ON SUM OF STANDARD DEVIATIONS OF FINE
PITCH ERRORS—SMOOTHED

Speaker	AUTOC	CEP	SIFT	DARD	PPROC	LPC	AMDF	Sum
				Pitch Detector				
LM	3	3	2	3	4	3	4	22
M1	2	2	2	2	2	2	3	15
M2	2	2	2	3	3	2	4	18
F1	1	2	2	2	2	1	2	12
F2	2	2	2	2	2	1	3	14
C1	1	2	2	2	2	1	2	12
Sum	11	13	12	14	15	10	18	

Code same as Table VI.

tion as well as the sum of the scores across recording conditions. Each of the scores is given as a ratio of the number of voiced-to-unvoiced errors to the number of voiced intervals for each condition. As might be anticipated, there is a great lack of homogeneity of the results across recording conditions, especially for the LPC pitch detector.

Table X gives a performance evaluation of the pitch detectors for the raw data of the voiced-to-unvoiced error rate averaged over the three recording conditions. The scores at the top of this table are the percentage of voiced-to-unvoiced errors for each pitch detector. A ranking of 1 was given to a pitch detector with an average error rate less than 5 (percent). A linear scale was used for these performance scores as shown in Table X.

Based on the overall rankings, it can be seen that five of the pitch detectors (AUTOC, DARD, PPROC, LPC, and AMDF) had essentially equivalent performance scores and all tended to be homogeneous across speakers. The SIFT pitch detector

had a somewhat poorer performance than the top five, and the CEP pitch detector had a poor performance for this error category. We defer a discussion of these results to Section VI.

Because of the lack of homogeneity across recording conditions, a second set of performance ratings was made for this error category based solely on the wideband recordings. These results are presented in Table XI. From this table it can be seen that four of the pitch detectors (AUTOC, PPROC, LPC, and AMDF) performed extremely well on this condition. The SIFT and DARD methods had somewhat poorer performance scores, while the CEP method had the worst score.

Tables XII–XIV show the error scores and performance rankings for voiced-to-unvoiced errors for the smoothed pitch contours. The effect of the smoother is to change slightly the number of voiced-to-unvoiced errors. The performance rankings for the data averaged over recording conditions (Table XIII) shows slightly different results than for the raw data; however, the rankings for the wideband condition (Table XIV) are quite similar to the raw data rankings of Table XI.

The results of Tables IX–XIV also show that the most difficult speakers were the two low-pitched speakers (LM, M2) and the high-pitched speaker (C1).

5) Unvoiced-to-Voiced Errors: The last set of tables (Tables XV–XX) show the results of the unvoiced-to-voiced error analysis. The form of the data in these tables is identical to that used in the voiced-to-unvoiced error category. A performance ranking of 1 was given to an unvoiced-to-voiced error rate of less than 10 percent. The remaining ranking scores were assigned linearly as shown in Table XVI. The overall performance scores for the raw data averaged across recording conditions showed the CEP pitch detector to have a very low score (high performance), in contrast to the very high scores it obtained in the previous error category. The AUTOC, SIFT, DARD, PPROC, and AMDF pitch detectors all had similar performance rankings and the LPC pitch detector had a very poor score. (Again we defer discussion of these results to Section VI.)

Table XVII (for the raw wideband data only) shows the performance of the LPC pitch detector to be substantially improved and comparable to all but the CEP pitch detector.

As seen in Tables XVIII–XX, the nonlinear smoother substantially helps almost all the pitch detectors for the unvoiced-to-voiced error category. The performance rankings for all but the LPC pitch detector are almost comparable for the smoothed data averaged over recording conditions (Table XIX); for the wideband smoothed data (Table XX) all seven pitch detectors had comparable performance scores.

VI. DISCUSSION OF ERROR ANALYSIS RESULTS

The error analysis and performance evaluation presented in Section V points up the strengths and weaknesses of each of the pitch detectors used in the study. No single pitch detector was uniformly top ranked across all speakers, recording conditions, and error measurements. In this section we discuss the results presented in Section V with a view towards explaining the general trends in the performance scores and how they relate back to the specific methods of pitch detection used in this study.

TABLE IX
VOICED-TO-UNVOICED ERRORS—UNSMOOTHED

Speaker		AUTOC	CEP	SIFT	DARD	PPROC	LPC	AMDF
					Pitch Detector			
LM	M	32/631	168/631	58/631	66/631	16/631	1/631	27/631
	T	36/631	235/631	105/631	66/631	37/631	78/631	40/631
	W	33/533	130/533	46/533	77/533	18/533	4/533	15/533
	Sum	101/1795	533/1795	209/1795	209/1795	71/1795	83/1795	82/1795
M1	M	19/703	54/703	11/703	30/703	25/703	3/703	28/703
	T	45/703	75/703	37/703	75/703	51/703	36/703	57/703
	W	6/654	88/654	7/654	39/654	14/654	14/654	5/654
	Sum	70/2060	217/2060	55/2060	144/2060	90/2060	53/2060	90/2060
M2	M	48/772	89/772	38/772	65/772	28/772	1/772	40/772
	T	60/772	123/772	60/772	104/772	67/772	194/772	67/772
	W	27/660	123/660	12/660	37/660	15/660	26/660	16/660
	Sum	135/2204	335/2204	110/2204	196/2204	110/2204	221/2204	113/2204
F1	M	10/762	99/762	45/762	15/762	18/762	6/762	21/762
	T	38/762	97/762	42/762	40/762	45/762	148/762	26/762
	W	7/603	70/603	28/603	18/603	14/603	1/603	17/603
	Sum	55/2127	266/2127	115/2127	73/2127	77/2127	155/2127	64/2127
F2	M	18/810	62/810	36/810	14/810	17/810	3/810	23/810
	T	46/810	67/810	37/810	32/810	41/810	68/810	36/810
	W	16/670	68/670	30/670	49/670	33/670	12/670	30/670
	Sum	80/2290	197/2290	103/2290	95/2290	91/2290	83/2290	89/2290
C1	M	38/935	93/935	130/935	27/935	20/935	5/935	21/935
	T	68/935	100/935	137/935	58/935	52/935	43/935	52/935
	W	9/568	66/568	139/568	18/568	12/568	5/568	13/568
	Sum	115/2438	259/2438	406/2438	103/2438	84/2438	53/2438	86/2438

TABLE X
PERFORMANCE SCORES BASED ON SUM OF VOICED-TO-UNVOICED
ERRORS—UNSMOOTHED

Speaker	AUTOC	CEP	SIFT	DARD	PPROC	LPC	AMDF
				Pitch Detector			
LM	5.6	29.7	11.6	11.6	4.0	4.6	4.6
M1	3.4	10.5	2.7	7.0	4.4	2.6	4.4
M2	6.1	15.2	5.0	8.9	5.0	10.0	5.1
F1	2.6	12.5	5.4	3.4	3.6	7.3	3.0
F2	3.5	8.6	4.5	4.1	4.0	3.6	3.9
C1	4.7	10.6	16.7	4.2	3.4	2.2	3.5

(a) Percentage Error Rate

Speaker	AUTOC	CEP	SIFT	DARD	PPROC	LPC	AMDF	Sum
LM	2	5	3	3	1	1	1	16
M1	1	3	1	2	1	1	1	10
M2	2	4	2	2	2	3	2	17
F1	1	3	2	1	1	2	1	11
F2	1	2	1	1	1	1	1	8
C1	1	3	4	1	1	1	1	11
Sum	8	20	13	10	7	9	7	

(b) Performance Scores

Code: (0–5) = 1, (5–10) = 2, (10–15) = 3, (15–20) = 4, (20–) = 5.

TABLE XI
PERFORMANCE SCORES BASED ON VOICED-TO-UNVOICED ERRORS—
WIDEBAND DATA—UNSMOOTHED

Speaker	AUTOC	CEP	SIFT	DARD	PPROC	LPC	AMDF
				Pitch Detector			
LM	6.2	24.4	8.6	14.4	3.4	0.8	2.8
M1	0.9	13.5	1.1	6.0	2.1	2.1	0.8
M2	4.1	18.6	1.8	5.6	2.3	3.9	2.4
F1	1.2	11.6	4.6	3.0	2.3	0.2	2.8
F2	2.4	10.1	4.5	7.3	4.9	1.8	4.5
C1	1.6	11.6	24.5	3.2	2.1	0.9	2.3

(a) Percentage Error Rate

Speaker	AUTOC	CEP	SIFT	DARD	PPROC	LPC	AMDF	Sum
LM	2	5	2	3	1	1	1	15
M1	1	3	1	2	1	1	1	10
M2	1	4	1	2	1	1	1	11
F1	1	3	1	1	1	1	1	9
F2	1	3	1	2	1	1	1	10
C1	1	3	5	1	1	1	1	13
Sum	7	21	11	11	6	6	6	

(b) Performance Scores

Code same as Table X.

The results on the gross pitch period errors (Tables I–IV) showed that the time-domain and hybrid pitch detectors had greatest difficulty with the low-pitched speakers (LM, M2) whereas the spectral pitch detector (CEP) had the greatest difficulty with the high-pitched speakers (C1, F1). The difficulties of time-domain methods for low-pitched speakers are due to the fixed 30–40-ms analysis frame which is generally in- adequate for low-pitched speakers. The difficulties of spectral methods for high-pitched speakers are due to the small number of harmonics which are present in their spectra, leading to analysis difficulties in choosing the correct pitch. The poor performance of the SIFT pitch detector on speaker C1 is related to the problem of reliably spectrally flattening (by in- verse filtering) a signal in which generally only one harmonic occurs.

TABLE XII
VOICED-TO-UNVOICED ERRORS—SMOOTHED

Speaker		AUTOC	CEP	SIFT	DARD	PPROC	LPC	AMDF
					Pitch Detector			
LM	M	112/626	137/626	48/626	56/626	31/626	6/626	34/626
	T	213/626	226/626	135/626	60/626	60/626	79/626	85/626
	W	69/512	97/512	28/512	61/512	18/512	6/512	11/512
	Sum	404/1764	460/1764	211/1764	117/1764	109/1764	91/1764	130/1764
M1	M	20/706	43/706	8/706	33/706	26/706	0/706	24/706
	T	64/706	65/706	42/706	91/706	67/706	25/706	60/706
	W	9/657	74/657	7/657	44/657	17/657	14/657	5/657
	Sum	93/2069	182/2069	57/2069	168/2069	110/2069	39/2069	89/2069
M2	M	90/782	80/782	47/782	86/782	45/782	0/782	46/782
	T	134/782	104/782	86/782	114/782	89/782	213/782	85/782
	W	32/660	116/660	9/660	43/660	25/660	15/660	16/660
	Sum	256/2224	300/2224	142/2224	243/2224	159/2224	228/2224	147/2224
F1	M	7/769	119/769	50/769	32/769	16/769	2/769	19/769
	T	40/769	92/769	34/769	53/769	45/769	157/769	22/769
	W	7/607	81/607	22/607	24/607	18/607	2/607	21/607
	Sum	54/2145	292/2145	106/2145	109/2145	79/2145	161/2145	62/2145
F2	M	13/815	61/815	29/815	17/815	8/815	4/815	32/815
	T	44/815	70/815	34/815	43/815	46/815	47/815	48/815
	W	15/676	72/676	28/676	83/676	38/676	12/676	32/676
	Sum	72/2306	203/2306	91/2306	143/2306	92/2306	63/2306	112/2306
C1	M	40/941	99/941	198/941	44/941	31/941	31/941	86/941
	T	70/941	107/941	175/941	107/941	65/941	85/941	97/941
	W	8/600	70/600	230/600	26/600	15/600	5/600	33/600
	Sum	118/2482	276/2482	603/2482	177/2482	111/2482	121/2482	216/2482

TABLE XIII
PERFORMANCE SCORES BASED ON SUM OF VOICED-TO-UNVOICED
ERRORS—SMOOTHED

Speaker	AUTOC	CEP	SIFT	DARD	PPROC	LPC	AMDF
			Pitch Detector				
LM	22.9	26.1	12.0	10.0	6.2	5.2	7.4
M1	4.5	8.8	2.8	8.1	5.3	1.9	4.3
M2	11.5	13.5	6.4	10.9	7.1	10.3	6.6
F1	2.5	13.6	4.9	5.1	3.7	7.5	2.9
F2	3.1	8.8	3.9	6.2	4.0	2.7	4.9
C1	4.8	11.1	24.3	7.1	4.5	4.9	8.7

(a) Percentage Error Rate

Speaker	AUTOC	CEP	SIFT	DARD	PPROC	LPC	AMDF	Sum
LM	5	5	3	3	2	2	2	22
M1	1	2	1	2	2	1	1	10
M2	3	3	2	3	2	3	2	18
F1	1	3	1	2	1	2	1	11
F2	1	2	1	2	1	1	1	9
C1	1	3	5	2	1	1	2	15
Sum	12	18	13	14	9	10	9	

(b) Performance Scores

Code same as Table X.

TABLE XIV
PERFORMANCE SCORES BASED ON VOICED-TO-UNVOICED ERRORS—
WIDEBAND DATA—SMOOTHED

Speaker	AUTOC	CEP	SIFT	DARD	PPROC	LPC	AMDF
			Pitch Detector				
LM	13.5	18.9	5.5	11.9	3.5	1.2	2.1
M1	1.4	11.3	1.1	6.7	2.6	2.1	0.8
M2	4.8	17.6	1.4	6.5	3.8	2.3	2.4
F1	1.2	13.3	3.6	4.0	3.0	0.3	3.5
F2	2.2	10.7	4.1	12.3	5.6	1.8	4.7
C1	1.3	11.7	38.3	4.3	2.5	0.8	5.5

(a) Percentage Error Rate

Speaker	AUTOC	CEP	SIFT	DARD	PPROC	LPC	AMDF	Sum
LM	3	4	2	3	1	1	1	15
M1	1	3	1	2	1	1	1	10
M2	1	4	1	2	1	1	1	11
F1	1	3	1	1	1	1	1	9
F2	1	3	1	3	2	1	1	12
C1	1	3	5	1	1	1	2	14
Sum	8	20	11	12	7	6	7	

(b) Performance Scores

Code same as Table X.

The results on the fine pitch period errors (Tables V–VIII) showed that (aside from the AMDF method which inherently lacked pitch resolution) the time-domain waveform pitch detectors (DARD, PPROC) had somewhat lower resolution than the other methods. This is due to the sensitivity of waveform peaks, valleys, and zero crossings to formant changes, noise, distortion, etc.

The error measurements of voiced-to-unvoiced and unvoiced-to-voiced errors provided several interesting results. These categories *cannot* be examined separately because they are often intimately related. For example, a voiced–unvoiced detector which is biased towards the category voiced will generally have a low voiced-to-unvoiced error rate, but in compensation will have a high unvoiced-to-voiced error rate. There are three types of voiced–unvoiced decision methods used in the seven pitch detectors. One method is the use of a

TABLE XV
UNVOICED-TO-VOICED ERRORS—UNSMOOTHED

Speaker		AUTOC	CEP	SIFT	DARD	PPROC	LPC	AMDF
					Pitch Detector			
LM	M	44/277	16/277	45/277	24/277	52/277	165/277	48/277
	T	35/277	5/277	46/277	25/277	71/277	133/277	69/277
	W	32/180	3/180	33/180	25/180	29/180	46/180	31/180
	Sum	111/734	24/734	124/734	74/734	152/734	344/734	148/734
M1	M	32/292	5/292	52/292	27/292	25/292	73/292	35/292
	T	26/292	5/292	52/292	36/292	74/292	96/292	68/292
	W	14/132	9/132	22/132	9/132	16/132	11/132	18/132
	Sum	72/716	19/716	126/716	72/716	115/716	180/716	121/716
M2	M	42/324	19/324	55/324	88/324	65/324	226/324	43/324
	T	39/324	13/324	59/324	11/324	52/324	141/324	38/324
	W	20/128	4/128	30/128	19/128	26/128	22/128	24/128
	Sum	101/772	36/772	144/772	118/772	143/772	389/772	105/772
F1	M	40/219	9/219	50/219	56/219	48/219	68/219	29/219
	T	30/219	8/219	47/219	25/219	43/219	51/219	29/219
	W	21/125	5/125	31/125	8/125	13/125	15/125	6/125
	Sum	91/563	22/563	128/563	89/563	104/563	134/563	64/563
F2	M	86/400	20/400	91/400	147/400	128/400	254/400	126/400
	T	51/400	23/400	84/400	71/400	107/400	188/400	89/400
	W	16/160	11/160	27/160	3/160	9/160	15/160	13/160
	Sum	153/960	54/960	202/960	221/960	244/960	457/960	228/960
C1	M	43/312	7/312	73/312	29/312	51/312	89/312	37/312
	T	35/312	10/312	57/312	43/312	74/312	102/312	43/312
	W	15/132	7/132	21/132	17/132	15/132	11/132	9/132
	Sum	93/756	24/756	151/756	89/756	140/756	202/756	89/756

TABLE XVI
PERFORMANCE SCORES BASED ON SUM OF UNVOICED-TO-VOICED
ERRORS—UNSMOOTHED

Speaker	AUTOC	CEP	SIFT	DARD	PPROC	LPC	AMDF
				Pitch Detector			
LM	15.1	3.3	16.9	10.0	20.7	46.9	20.2
M1	10.1	2.7	17.6	10.1	16.1	25.1	16.9
M2	13.1	4.7	18.7	15.3	18.5	50.4	13.6
F1	16.2	3.9	22.7	15.8	18.5	23.8	11.4
F2	15.9	5.6	21.0	23.0	25.4	47.6	23.8
C1	12.3	3.2	20.0	11.8	18.5	26.7	11.8

(a) Percentage Error Rate

Speaker	AUTOC	CEP	SIFT	DART	PPROC	LPC	AMDF	Sum
LM	2	1	2	2	3	5	3	18
M1	2	1	2	2	2	3	2	14
M2	2	1	2	2	2	5	2	16
F1	2	1	3	2	2	3	2	15
F2	2	1	3	3	3	5	3	20
C1	2	1	3	2	2	3	2	15
Sum	12	6	15	13	14	24	14	

(b) Performance Scores

Code: (0–10) = 1, (10–20) = 2, (20–30) = 3,
(30–40) = 4, (40–) = 5.

TABLE XVII
PERFORMANCE SCORES BASED ON UNVOICED-TO-VOICED ERRORS—
WIDEBAND DATA—UNSMOOTHED

Speaker	AUTOC	CEP	SIFT	DARD	PPROC	LPC	AMDF
				Pitch Detector			
LM	17.8	1.7	18.3	13.9	16.1	25.6	17.2
M1	10.6	6.8	16.7	6.8	12.1	8.3	13.6
M2	15.6	3.1	23.4	14.8	20.3	17.2	18.8
F1	16.8	4.0	24.8	6.4	10.4	12.0	4.8
F2	10.0	6.9	16.9	1.9	5.6	9.4	8.1
C1	11.4	5.3	15.9	12.9	11.4	8.3	6.8

(a) Percentage Error Rate

Speaker	AUTOC	CEP	SIFT	DARD	PPROC	LPC	AMDF	Sum
LM	2	1	2	2	2	3	2	14
M1	2	1	2	1	2	1	2	11
M2	2	1	3	2	3	2	2	15
F1	2	1	3	1	2	2	1	12
F2	2	1	2	1	1	1	1	9
C1	2	1	2	2	2	1	1	11
Sum	12	6	14	9	12	10	9	

(b) Performance Scores

Code same as Table XVI.

simple threshold on one or more measurements to classify an interval as voiced or unvoiced. For example, the preliminary voiced–unvoiced detector used in the AUTOC, CEP, SIFT, and PPROC methods used a waveform threshold to remove intervals of silence. The second type of voiced–unvoiced detector is the periodicity measurement. For example, the AUTOC, AMDF, and SIFT methods used a threshold on the autocorrelation peak to decide if the interval was periodic whereas the CEP method used a threshold on the cepstral peak for this purpose. The third type of voiced–unvoiced detector is the pattern recognition statistical approach used in the LPC pitch detector. Each of these methods has some advantages and disadvantages. For example, the periodicity measurement tends to be extremely robust with regard to noise, distortion, and spurious transients in the signal. Thus methods like the AUTOC and AMDF pitch detectors tended to work uni-

TABLE XVIII
UNVOICED-TO-VOICED ERRORS—SMOOTHED

Speaker		AUTOC	CEP	SIFT	DARD	PPROC	LPC	AMDF
					Pitch Detector			
LM	M	5/282	3/282	6/282	18/282	24/282	95/282	51/282
	T	3/282	0/282	9/282	11/282	25/282	59/282	64/282
	W	3/201	2/201	17/201	11/201	20/201	43/201	35/201
	Sum	11/765	5/765	32/765	40/765	69/765	197/765	150/765
M1	M	19/289	3/289	45/289	17/289	9/289	55/289	35/289
	T	3/289	5/289	33/289	5/289	29/289	65/289	54/289
	W	8/129	7/129	20/129	5/129	3/129	9/129	15/129
	Sum	30/707	15/707	98/707	27/707	41/707	129/707	104/707
M2	M	5/314	13/314	18/314	45/314	21/314	225/314	31/314
	T	4/314	8/314	5/314	2/314	13/314	131/314	37/314
	W	17/128	4/128	20/128	9/128	16/128	20/128	24/128
	Sum	26/756	25/756	43/756	56/756	50/756	376/756	92/756
F1	M	31/212	5/212	34/212	3/212	21/212	33/212	15/212
	T	19/212	1/212	44/212	2/212	19/212	19/212	18/212
	W	17/121	5/121	20/121	0/121	6/121	11/121	6/121
	Sum	67/545	11/545	98/545	5/545	46/545	63/545	39/545
F2	M	34/395	5/395	52/395	42/395	48/395	82/395	44/395
	T	26/395	11/395	64/395	35/395	55/395	132/395	44/395
	W	8/154	10/154	20/154	0/154	7/154	6/154	9/154
	Sum	68/944	26/944	136/944	77/944	110/944	220/944	97/944
C1	M	16/306	4/306	31/306	4/306	16/306	10/306	13/306
	T	10/306	6/306	18/306	3/306	15/306	3/306	9/306
	W	13/130	5/130	10/130	0/130	7/130	10/130	7/130
	Sum	39/742	15/742	59/742	7/742	38/742	23/742	29/742

TABLE XIX
PERFORMANCE SCORES BASED ON SUM OF UNVOICED-TO-VOICED
ERRORS—SMOOTHED

Speaker	AUTOC	CEP	SIFT	DARD	PPROC	LPC	AMDF
			Pitch Detector				
LM	1.4	0.7	4.2	5.2	9.0	25.8	19.6
M1	4.2	2.1	13.9	3.8	5.8	18.2	14.7
M2	3.4	3.3	5.7	7.4	6.6	49.7	12.2
F1	12.3	2.0	18.0	0.9	8.4	11.6	7.2
F2	7.2	2.8	14.4	8.2	11.7	23.3	10.3
C1	5.3	2.0	8.0	0.9	5.1	3.1	3.9

(a) Percentage Error Rate

Speaker	AUTOC	CEP	SIFT	DARD	PPROC	LPC	AMDF	Sum
LM	1	1	1	1	1	3	2	10
M1	1	1	2	1	1	2	2	10
M2	1	1	1	1	1	5	2	12
F1	2	1	2	1	1	2	1	10
F2	1	1	2	1	2	3	2	12
C1	1	1	1	1	1	1	1	7
Sum	7	6	9	6	7	16	10	

(b) Performance Scores

Code same as Table XVI.

TABLE XX
PERFORMANCE SCORES BASED ON UNVOICED-TO-VOICED ERRORS—
WIDEBAND DATA—SMOOTHED

Speaker	AUTOC	CEP	SIFT	DARD	PPROC	LPC	AMDF
			Pitch Detector				
LM	1.5	1.0	8.5	5.5	10.0	21.4	17.4
M1	6.2	5.4	15.5	3.9	2.3	7.0	11.6
M2	13.3	3.1	15.6	7.0	12.5	15.6	18.8
F1	14.0	4.1	16.5	0.0	5.0	9.1	5.0
F2	5.2	6.5	13.0	0.0	4.5	3.9	5.8
C1	10.0	3.8	7.7	0.0	5.4	7.7	5.4

(a) Percentage Error Rate

Speaker	AUTOC	CEP	SIFT	DARD	PPROC	LPC	AMDF	Sum
LM	1	1	1	1	2	3	2	11
M1	1	1	2	1	1	1	2	9
M2	2	1	2	1	2	2	2	12
F1	2	1	2	1	1	1	1	9
F2	1	1	2	1	1	1	1	8
C1	2	1	1	1	1	1	1	8
Sum	9	6	10	6	8	9	9	

(b) Performance Scores

Code same as Table XVI.

formly well across recording conditions, whereas a method like the LPC pitch detector, which used a pattern recognition voiced–unvoiced detector, worked much better for wideband recordings than for microphone or telephone recordings. The distortions (especially high-level transients) and band-limiting in both the microphone and telephone recordings made reliable voiced–unvoiced decisions almost impossible for the

pattern recognition approach (of the LPC method) using the five parameters discussed in [15]. However, for the wideband recordings, this method worked quite well.

The only method which had no formal voiced–unvoiced detector was the DARD method. This method just identified pitch period markers directly on the speech waveform. The method used to classify an interval as voiced was to measure the spacing between adjacent markers centered around the interval and to call the interval as unvoiced if the marker spacing exceeded 200 samples (20-ms period). This method provided surprisingly good results yielding a reasonable voiced-unvoiced error rate.

Finally, it can be seen that the CEP pitch detector had a strong tendency to classify voiced intervals as unvoiced. In compensation the unvoiced-to-voiced error rate for the CEP method was very low. Readjustment of the cepstral peak threshold and the following zero-crossing threshold would yield a tradeoff in these scores.

VII. COMPUTATIONAL CONSIDERATIONS

Since none of the pitch detectors used in this study are commercially available, another factor in comparing these pitch detectors is their speed of execution on the computer (a Data General NOVA 800 minicomputer[2]) on which all the simulations were run. Table XXI shows such a comparison along with other computational considerations for implementing the various algorithms. The execution times given in the table are the time required to process 1 s of speech. It can be seen that the two waveform time-domain pitch detectors (DARD and PPROC) ran the fastest, whereas all the others were on the order of 1 to 2 orders of magnitude slower. The AMDF pitch detector would take about four times longer if the resolution in the measurement were increased to 1 sample at a 6.67-kHz rate. The AUTOC pitch detector is a factor of 2 or more faster than the SIFT, LPC, and CEP pitch detectors because of the simplified autocorrelation function which is computed using a counter rather than a multiplier and an adder.

Table XXI also includes some of the details of how the various pitch detection algorithms were implemented on the NOVA 800 computer. The numerical method of realization (i.e., fixed or floating point) is indicated in the column labeled "arithmetic type." Three of the algorithms were realized in integer arithmetic (DARD, PPROC, and AUTOC); three were realized in floating-point arithmetic (AMDF,[3] SIFT, and LPC): the CEP method used both integer arithmetic [for windowing and fast Fourier transforms (FFT's)], and floating arithmetic (for the log magnitude operation). The next column indicates whether or not downsampling (i.e., reduction of the sampling rate of the signal to a lower rate) was used in the realization to reduce the computation. Although not used for the AMDF and AUTOC methods, it could easily be incorporated into these methods to speed up the realization. Finally, the last column shows the dependence of the computation on the sampling rate of the input. As seen in this table, all the methods are approximately linearly or quadratically dependent on the sampling rate, assuming all the parameters of the

TABLE XXI
COMPUTATIONAL CONSIDERATIONS FOR THE SEVEN PITCH DETECTORS ON THE NOVA 800 MINICOMPUTER

Pitch Detector	Speed/s of Speech	Arithmetic Type	Down-sampling Used	Dependence on Sampling Rate
DARD	5 s	Integer	No	Linear
PPROC	7.5 s	Integer	No	Linear
AMDF	50 s	Floating point	No[a]	Quadratic
AUTOC	120 s	Integer	No[a]	Quadratic
SIFT	250 s	Floating point	Yes	Quadratic
LPC	300 s	Floating point	Yes	Quadratic
CEP	400 s	Mixed	No	Linear

[a]These algorithms could easily incorporate downsampling.

analysis (i.e., analysis section length, pitch range, etc.) remain the same.

VIII. SUMMARY

This paper has reported on the results of a rather extensive performance evaluation of seven pitch detection algorithms. Using a variety of error measurements, the performance strengths and weaknesses of each of the pitch detectors for different speakers and different recording conditions were highlighted.

A major issue which arises when trying to understand the results of this study is how to interpret the various error scores. This is one problem for which we have no simple answer other than it all depends on the intended application of the pitch analysis. For example, classifying a low-level voiced speech interval as unvoiced may be perfectly acceptable for a vocoder, but may cause great problems for a recognition system. Similarly, the level at which various types of errors become significant also depends strongly on the application. We have presented performance scores based on a criterion related to the applications with which the authors are most familiar, i.e., speaker verification systems [2] and digit recognition systems [17].

Finally, an important consideration in interpreting the results presented here is the perceptual effect of each of the types of errors discussed in Section V. A parallel series of investigations is required to provide perceptual comparisons among the seven pitch detectors. Such an investigation is currently being made by the authors.

REFERENCES

[1] B. S. Atal, "Automatic speaker recognition based on pitch contours," *J. Acoust. Soc. Amer.*, vol. 52, pp. 1687–1697, Dec. 1972.

[2] A. E. Rosenberg and M. R. Sambur, "New techniques for automatic speaker verification," *IEEE Trans. Acoust., Speech, Signal Processing*, vol. ASSP-23, pp. 169–176, Apr. 1975.

[3] H. Levitt, "Speech processing aids for the deaf: An overview," *IEEE Trans. Audio Electroacoust. (Special Issue on 1972 Conference on Speech Communication and Processing)*, vol. AU-21, pp. 269–273, June 1973.

[4] J. L. Flanagan, *Speech Analysis, Synthesis, and Perception.* New York: Springer-Verlag, 1972.

[5] A. M. Noll, "Cepstrum pitch determination," *J. Acoust. Soc. Amer.*, vol. 41, pp. 293–309, Feb. 1967.

---

[2]Cycle time 800 ns, add time of 1.6 μs, multiply time of 3.6 μs. The machine also had floating-point hardware.

[3]The AMDF algorithm as provided to us was implemented in integer arithmetic. However the 16-bit integer representation of the NOVA 800 is inadequate for this implementation. Consequently, the computations were converted to floating point.

[6] B. Gold and L. R. Rabiner, "Parallel processing techniques for estimating pitch periods of speech in the time domain," *J. Acoust. Soc. Amer.*, vol. 46, pp. 442–448, Aug. 1969.

[7] M. M. Sondhi, "New methods of pitch extraction," *IEEE Trans. Audio Electroacoust. (Special Issue on Speech Communication and Processing—Part II)* vol. AU-16, pp. 262–266, June 1968.

[8] J. D. Markel, "The SIFT algorithm for fundamental frequency estimation," *IEEE Trans. Audio Electroacoust.*, vol. AU-20, pp. 367–377, Dec. 1972.

[9] N. J. Miller, "Pitch detection by data reduction," *IEEE Trans. Acoust., Speech, Signal Processing (Special Issue on IEEE Symposium on Speech Recognition)*, vol. ASSP-23, pp. 72–79, Feb. 1975.

[10] M. J. Ross, H. L. Shaffer, A. Cohen, R. Freudberg, and H. J. Manley, "Average magnitude difference function pitch extractor," *IEEE Trans. Acoust., Speech, Signal Processing*, vol. ASSP-22, pp. 353–362, Oct. 1974.

[11] J. J. Dubnowski, R. W. Schafer, and L. R. Rabiner, "Real-time digital hardware pitch detector," *IEEE Trans. Acoust., Speech, Signal Processing*, vol. ASSP-24, pp. 2–8, Feb. 1976.

[12] R. W. Schafer and L. R. Rabiner, "System for automatic formant analysis of voiced speech," *J. Acoust. Soc. Amer.*, vol. 47, pp. 634–648, Feb. 1970.

[13] C. A. McGonegal, L. R. Rabiner, and A. E. Rosenberg, "A semi-automatic pitch detector (SAPD)," *IEEE Trans. Acoust., Speech, Signal Processing*, vol. ASSP-23, pp. 570–574, Dec. 1975.

[14] J. D. Markel and A. H. Gray, *Linear Prediction of Speech*. New York: Springer, 1976.

[15] B. S. Atal and L. R. Rabiner, "A pattern recognition approach to voiced–unvoiced–silence classification with applications to speech recognition," *IEEE Trans. Acoust., Speech, Signal Processing*, vol. ASSP-24, pp. 201–212, June 1976.

[16] R. E. Crochiere and L. R. Rabiner, "Optimum FIR digital filter implementations for decimation, interpolation, and narrow-band filtering," *IEEE Trans. Acoust., Speech, Signal Processing*, vol. ASSP-23, pp. 444–456, Oct. 1975.

[17] L. R. Rabiner, M. R. Sambur, and C. E. Schmidt, "Applications of a nonlinear smoothing algorithm to speech processing," *IEEE Trans. Acoust., Speech, Signal Processing*, vol. ASSP-23, pp. 552–557, Dec. 1975.

[18] M. J. Cheng, "A comparative performance study of several pitch detection algorithms," M. S. thesis, Mass. Inst. Technol., Cambridge, June 1975.

[19] L. R. Rabiner and M. R. Sambur, "Some preliminary experiments in the recognition of connected digits," *IEEE Trans. Acoust., Speech, Signal Processing*, vol. ASSP-24, pp. 170–182, Apr. 1976.

Nature of the Vocal Cord Wave*

R. L. Miller

Bell Telephone Laboratories, Inc., Murray Hill, New Jersey

(Received March 9, 1959)

The shape of the vocal cord wave is an important parameter in a true analog representation of the vocal mechanism, since the final speech wave is a function of both the generator wave shape and the transfer impedance of the vocal tract. The shape of this wave has been determined by two independent methods: (1) by the derivation and use of a network having a characteristic which is the inverse of the first vocal resonance, and (2) by measuring the area of the vocal cord opening as a function of time through the use of motion picture studies. Harmonic analysis of some of the typical shapes obtained indicate that a uniform distribution of harmonic amplitudes is a rarity; instead there is a tendency for the distribution to have a cyclical variation of the form $(\sin kn/kn^2)$. The results obtained through the use of the inverse network indicate that the main excitation of the higher resonances occurs at the point of vocal cord closure and that the magnitude of this excitation can be controlled by the talker over wide ranges.

INTRODUCTION

THE exact nature of the vocal cord wave and the part it plays in speech production has long been the subject of speculation as well as much theoretical and experimental effort. Early discussion by Wheatstone, Helmholtz, Herman, Koenig, Scripture, and many others revolved around the way this wave entered in with the vocal resonances to determine vowel character. However, even though Wheatstone, as early as 1837, proposed that the vocal cords act as a harmonic generator, very little information as to its exact nature has been obtained, the usual description being that it is a "pulsed" or "sawtooth" wave which has many harmonics falling off according to a power law.

The reason for this lack of information is fairly obvious since the vocal cords are located in a rather inaccessible place as far as making measurements is concerned, particularly when they are in operation. Secondly, the output waves which are generated by them have been thoroughly hidden by the complex acoustical nature of the vocal tract.

The shapes of these waves are, of course, of considerable interest in many problems of speech analysis and speech synthesis. Since the final speech wave must be given by a product of both the generator components and the transfer impedance of the vocal tract, the frequency content of the generator is obviously very important.

Chronologically, the work to be reported here began in 1948 and was first centered about area measurements of the vocal cord opening made in connection with the high-speed motion picture of the vocal cords.[1] This original work actually gave a very good picture of the nature of the waves and the resulting implications. Nevertheless, at the time one was faced with the fact that its conclusions were based on assumptions which,

although probably correct, could not be substantiated. For this reason, the report on this work was never published. Some of the results are included, however, in a later section of this paper, since it has a bearing on the more recent work.

The later phase of this work, which is felt to give a reasonably accurate picture of the vocal cord wave, has been based on the increasing realization in recent years that the transmission characteristics of the vocal tract itself can be duplicated as accurately as desired, assuming a certain knowledge of the parameters. If this is possible, then by network theory it should also be possible to reconstruct the generator (vocal cord) wave from the output wave. The approach used was to develop a network which was inverse to the transfer characteristic of the vocal tract. This network was limited to a frequency range for which the parameters could be obtained with considerable accuracy.

THEORETICAL CONSIDERATIONS

In recent years a considerable amount of excellent analysis of the vocal tract as an acoustical system has been carried out by such workers as Dunn,[2] Stevens, Kasowski, Fant,[3,4] Weibel,[5] and others. Of particular interest as a background to the present work is that of Dunn and Weibel. There is general agreement that by treating the vocal tract as a series of cylindrical sections or acoustical lines, and with constants uniformly distributed along each section, then a very accurate representation of the tract can be obtained. There is also agreement that as one restricts himself to the lower frequency region (wavelengths large compared to cavity dimensions), the lumped circuit representation also becomes quite accurate. Dunn shows an error of only 2% for a first resonance located at 640 cps when com-

---

* An abridged version of this paper was presented at the 50th meeting of the Acoustical Society, Providence, Rhode Island, December 16, 1955 [abstract in J. Acoust. Soc. Am. 28, 159 (1956)] and at the International Voice Conference, Chicago, Illinois, May 22, 1957.

[1] D. W. Farnsworth, Bell Labs. Record 18, 203 (1940).

[2] H. K. Dunn, J. Acoust. Soc. Am. 22, 740–753 (1950).
[3] C. G. M. Fant, "Transmission properties of the vocal tract," Mass. Inst. Technol. Acoustics Lab. Tech. Rept. No. 12, January, 1952.
[4] Stevens, Kasowski, and Fant, J. Acoust. Soc. Am. 25, 734–742 (1953).
[5] E. S. Weibel, J. Acoust. Soc. Am. 27, 858–865 (1955).

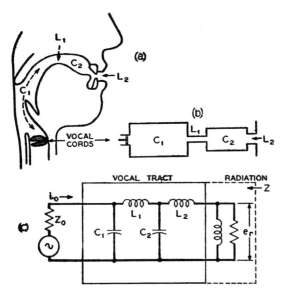

FIG. 1. Vocal tract analogs. (a) Actual vocal tract. (b) Equivalent acoustical analog. (c) Equivalent electrical analog.

puted by the lumped representation as compared to that obtained by the distributed representation.

Figure 1 illustrates the vocal tract, the generally accepted acoustical analog, and the lumped electrical equivalent. This latter circuit is in agreement with the lumped circuit developed by Dunn. It is also similar to that shown by Olson.[6] The lumped elements have been identified with the corresponding parts of the vocal tract and acoustical analog by the same symbols. This is not to infer that this would be an accurate representation from the distributed standpoint.

It will be found that a circuit of the type shown in Fig. 1 will have two points of resonance in its transmission characteristic. As has been demonstrated by Dunn, it is necessary to take into account the distributed nature of the system to obtain the third and higher formants (resonances). However, since it is our intention to confine our operations to the first resonance alone, it will be primarily the presence of the second which can lead to any substantial error and hence the lumped circuit representation will be adequate.

In the front vowel series [i, ɪ, ɛ, æ], one finds that there is a relatively large spacing between the first and second formants. For example, in the sound [i] (formants at 325 and 2300 cps), one finds that the front cavity (C_2) becomes very small and at the same time C_1 is larger. This gives rise to the first resonance being given primarily by C_1 resonating with $L_1 + L_2$ while the second resonance is given primarily by L_2 with C_2 (radiation reactance enters in as a part of L_2). If one redraws this circuit in the form given in Fig. 2, it becomes more readily apparent that the first resonance

[6] H. F. Olson, *Elements of Acoustical Engineering* (D. Van Nostrand Company, Inc., Princeton, 1940), first edition, p. 62, Fig. 44.

is in the form of a parallel resonant circuit and the output voltage (sound pressure) appears essentially as a voltage division of the voltage across the resonant circuit. C_2 is shown dotted, since it plays only a minor role in determining the parameters of the first resonance which will be our main concern; however, it is the source of a possible error and its effect will be treated later.

We may then show our basic first resonance by the circuit at the left side of Fig. 3. Dissipation must be introduced in connection with both elements, since it is not known exactly how this occurs in the natural system.

The generator impedance Z_0 (acoustical impedance of the vocal cord slit) is undoubtedly a complex quantity. Since the dimensions of the vocal cord slit are much smaller than those of the vocal cavities, it is essentially a high impedance source probably having the form of a large resistance and an inductance in series. However, it is a well-known principle in network theory that one can consider the source as a constant current generator (a very high resistance) and, therefore, one deals in terms of the wave shape of the current into the network rather than that of the voltage. Current would represent the volume velocity in acoustical terms. Any reactance term present in the actual generator impedance is thus reflected in the wave shape of the generator current.

In a different approach to the problem of accurately representing the transmission characteristic of a complex acoustical system, such as the vocal tract, Weibel[5] has demonstrated that the transfer impedance may be expanded in a series of partial fractions. The result of such an expansion is that each normal mode of the vocal cavities, in other words each formant, is represented by one term in this series. Again by taking a large number of terms, as accurate a representation of the transfer impedance can be obtained as desired; however, with only a limited number of terms extending over the range of interest, an excellent representation can be obtained. Of particular interest to the present work is the fact that each term of the expansion takes the exact form of the damped resonant circuit given in Fig. 3. Likewise, in an expansion of this type, the main error to our representation of the first resonance is the "skirt" of the second resonance which overlaps it, and the further away the resonance, the smaller the error

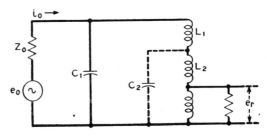

FIG. 2. Electrical analog of Fig. 1 redrawn.

which results. This is analogous to the error caused by C_2 in the first portrayal.

INVERSE NETWORK

The problem of developing an inverse network to the structure of the first resonance is generally well known and is covered in most textbooks on network theory.[7,8] The form it takes is shown in the right-hand part of Fig. 3. The general relation of its components is given by the expression

$$Z_v Z_x = \frac{L_v}{C_x} = \frac{L_x}{C_v} = R_{1v} R_{1x} = R_{2v} R_{2x} = R^2. \quad (1)$$

If we can correctly determine the values of such an inverse network, then the wave form of the voltage developed across the inverse network Z_x is a replica of the current i_0. Assuming that the coupling resistor R_c is very large, we can write

$$e_v = i_0 Z_v \quad \text{and} \quad i_x = \frac{e_v}{R_c} = \frac{i_0 Z_v}{R_c}. \quad (2)$$

From Eqs. (1) and (2),

$$e_x = i_x Z_x = \frac{i_0 Z_x Z_v}{R_c} = \frac{i_0 R^2}{R_c}. \quad (3)$$

The problem then resolves itself into that of deducing the four unknown quantities of the inverse network. This is not as difficult as it might appear on the surface. First, since we are not interested in absolute values but only ratios, we can select a fixed value for one of the elements, here shown as the inductance. This is equivalent to multiplying the expression Z_x by an additional constant. By making a careful spectrographic analysis of the sound, we can determine the frequency position of the first formant with reasonable accuracy. This allows the determination of C. Likewise by a study of the spectrogram, we can obtain an approximate value for the Q of the resonance.

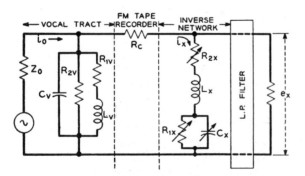

FIG. 3. Equivalent electrical circuit of first resonance associated with its inverse network.

---

[7] T. E. Shea, *Transmission Networks and Wave Filters* (D. Van Nostrand Company, Inc., Princeton, 1929), p. 124.

[8] *Motion Picture Sound Engineering* (D. Van Nostrand Company, Inc., Princeton, 1929), p. 223.

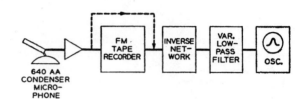

FIG. 4. Schematic of experimental circuit.

This gives a series of possible combinations between R_{1x} and R_{2x}, all of which give the same Q. We are then left with one more parameter to determine, the ratio between R_{1x} and R_{2x}. This last theoretical stumbling block was finally solved in a rather interesting manner. It is well known from observations of the motion pictures of vocal cord action that most people have a considerable period of closure of the vocal cords during each operating cycle. If this is so, then the volume velocity wave must become zero during this period. We can then, as a final adjustment, vary the ratios of the two damping resistors until this part of the wave represents zero current on our measuring instrument. This, of course, assumes that the region of closure can be readily identified. Fortunately this turned out to be true in the experimental investigation.

EXPERIMENTAL IMPLEMENTATION

The experimental system that was constructed to carry out experiments of this nature is shown in Fig. 4. There are several rigid requirements that must be observed in such a system. One of the main ones is that the apparatus must be carefully designed to maintain constant gain and linear phase relations over the entire frequency range of interest. This is a necessary requirement for maintaining exact wave shape. Since, in the outline under theoretical consideration, one must start with the pressure wave as radiated from the mouth, then a high quality condenser microphone, such as the 640AA, is an excellent pickup device.

Since the sound wave must be analyzed in order to find out the frequency of the first resonance and the Q associated with it, it becomes necessary to record the wave. The usual types of magnetic tape recorders are very unsatisfactory for this purpose since they are poor from a standpoint of maintaining linear phase relations. However, a recorder which utilizes frequency modulation can fulfill the requirements for amplitude response and phase linearity. The particular one used (Ampex-Model 306) has a flat response between 0 and 5000 cps.

Since it is required that we restrict ourselves to the frequencies of only the first resonance, a variable low-pass filter must be supplied to eliminate those components falling above. A requirement is that it have a good transient response to essentially square waves. The type utilized in these experiments was one having essentially a Gaussian cutoff characteristic with its inherent good phase linearity in the cutoff region.

As will be discussed later this filter only has the

effect of slightly rounding the corners of a square wave of the lower fundamental frequencies encountered. This fortunately is also in the direction to compensate for the small error introduced by the capacitance C_2 of Fig. 2.

EXPERIMENTAL PROCEDURE

One of the first steps in the experimental work was to calibrate the over-all system. This was done by coupling a calibrated condenser microphone used as a source through a small coupling unit to the microphone used in the system. The test consisted of applying a 100-cps square voltage wave to this microphone and observing the wave shape at other points in the system. It was determined in this manner that, except for the expected rounding due to the variable low-pass filter, distortion of the square wave was negligible. It is necessary in this test, of course, to replace the inverse network by a suitable resistance.

A second step, which was felt necessary in order to get the feel of the sensitivity of the various adjustments, was to actually set up an approximate simulation of the vocal tract as given in Fig. 2 and apply sawtooth and triangular waves of the form that might be expected. It was determined by this technique that the most sensitive adjustment was that of the value of the capacitance C_x. Fortunately, as was determined by these exploratory tests, there is a very accurate way of determining the correct setting. If the value of C_x is incorrect by only a few percent, then a pronounced ripple appears on the slope of the reconstructed triangular or sawtooth wave at the periodicity of the first resonance. This ripple decreases to zero as the correct value is reached and reappears in the opposite phase if one overcorrects. The Q adjustment is not particularly sensitive. For low values of Q, it is important to have the correct ratios between the two resistances; for high values of Q this becomes less important.

In the first series of tests, the subjects used were males having fairly low pitches. This was desirable for two reasons: (1) more harmonics are obtained in the limited frequency band, and thus define the shape of the vocal wave more exactly, and (2) voices of this category tend to have longer closure times which gives a better setting of the ratios of the two dissipative resistances. Samples of steady vowels were recorded through the condenser microphone onto the FM tape recorder. In the initial tests, vowels were limited to the front vowel series which have the best spacing between the first and second formant.

These recordings were first processed by means of a sound spectrograph. The narrow band analysis was used primarily for computing the resonance frequency and the approximate Q. In applying the results of the analysis to the inverse network, the values were put in directly without recourse to the figure on the oscillo-

scope. This was to avoid any tendency for the operator to "juggle" values in order to make the figure take on a preconceived shape. The only adjustment allowed at this point was to select the ratio of resistances to give the best horizontal adjustment to the region of closure, which was quite clearly defined at this stage for most subjects. The results of these first tests were quite convincing that this approach to the solution of the problem is essentially correct, uniformly and logically shaped pulses being obtained directly without further adjustments.

Although the previous procedure was necessary to show that one could arrive at logical pulse shapes by a controlled and direct procedure, later work indicated that several short cuts could be taken to obtain the same results more directly: (1) The technique to determine the value of C_1 by tuning until the first resonance ripple disappears is an even more accurate method of measuring the frequency of this formant than by spectrograph. (2) The value of Q is sufficiently high (of the order of 15) that the adjustment is neither critical in itself nor particularly sensitive to whether it is obtained from R_{1x} or R_{2x}.

While it was stated under theoretical considerations that in order to determine the last unknown, one could vary the ratio of R_{1x} and R_{2x} to make the closure appear properly, it was found in practice that changes of this ratio within the indicated ranges of Q produced only

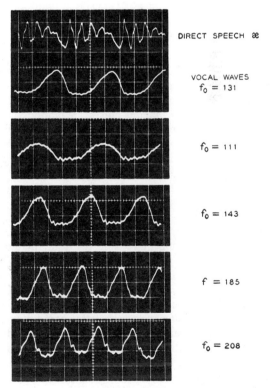

DIRECT SPEECH æ

VOCAL WAVES
$f_0 = 131$

$f_0 = 111$

$f_0 = 143$

$f = 185$

$f_0 = 208$

Fig. 5. Vocal cord waves obtained from male speaker for the sound [æ] at different pitches.

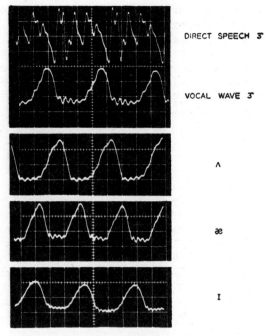

FIG. 6. Same as Fig. 5 except for different sounds.

at the higher pitches. The ratio of the second formant energy to the total also increases somewhat.

An interesting phenomenon which is due to the experimental setup becomes increasingly apparent for the higher pitched waves. This is the apparent start of the second formant energy before closure point is reached. This is difficult to explain from the natural excitation of a resonant circuit by a sudden change in the excitation wave. It is explainable, however, by the fact that a low-pass filter is used in the transmission path to eliminate the second formant energy. Although this filter eliminates this energy to a large extent, the envelope delay of such a filter is less in the cutoff region than it is in the pass-band region, thus allowing this energy to reach the oscilloscope a little before the energy which is being transmitted in the pass-band region and used to define the vocal cord wave.

In Fig. 6 are shown other sounds made by the same speaker as the sounds of Fig. 5. The same general shaped wave occurs for all of these sounds.

Figure 7 is perhaps the most revealing of all of the results in portraying the action of the vocal cords and the resulting wave. Here the data have been portrayed in a somewhat different way. In the top trace of each

limited changes in the shape and slope of the closure period.

With these principles in mind, it was possible for an operator to adjust the inverse network directly while a subject made a sustained vowel, thus bypassing the need for a recording device and spectrographic analysis.

EXPERIMENTAL RESULTS

Some of the resulting wave forms obtained in these experiments are illustrated in the following several figures. Figure 5 shows the resulting wave forms obtained for a male speaker saying the sound [æ] for several pitches. This sound is one of the more desirable since it has a reasonably high first formant at 660 cps and a second formant at about 1800 cps. This gives a large number of harmonics under the first resonance, and at the same time gives a reasonable spacing for the use of the low-pass filter to remove most of the energy in the second formant. The top two traces show the direct speech wave and the vocal cord wave for the speaker's normal pitch. As can be seen, there is a closure period of not quite half the total period, a gradual rising, and then a more abrupt closure. While there is no evidence of the frequency of the first formant, there is a slight ripple left due to a small amount of the second formant energy and an even smaller amount of third. It is interesting to note that the main excitation of the second formant starts at the point of sudden closure. This will be demonstrated more clearly in a later figure. If one interpolates by eye what the wave shape would be without the small ripple, it appears very probable that the closure is really a well-defined sharp corner. The wave becomes a little more triangular

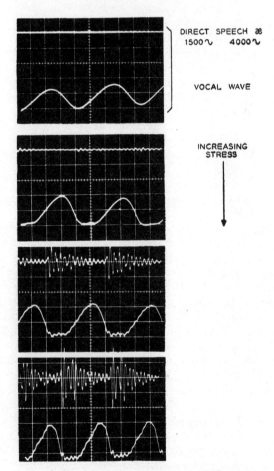

FIG. 7. Vocal cord waves of the sound [æ] spoken with increasing stress.

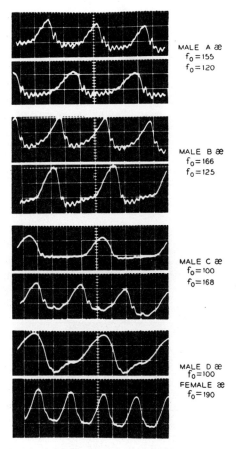

MALE A æ
$f_0 = 155$
$f_0 = 120$

MALE B æ
$f_0 = 166$
$f_0 = 125$

MALE C æ
$f_0 = 100$
$f_0 = 168$

MALE D æ
$f_0 = 100$
FEMALE æ
$f_0 = 190$

FIG. 8. Vocal cord waves of the sound [æ] for different speakers.

vocal wave is portrayed the speech energy above 1500 cps. This was obtained by the use of a high-pass filter in a separate path. The speaker made the same phonetic sound in each case, but with increasing stress, starting with a fairly softly spoken sound. As can be seen, the initial vocal cord wave is almost sinusoidal with practically no indication of a closure. With increasing stress, there is a very marked increase in the rate of closure, and only a small change in the rate of opening. Since no change was made in the measuring circuits during this series, then the amplitudes are significant when compared with each other. The energy in the first formant, which defines the vocal cord wave, has remained almost constant in amplitude, while that occurring in the second and higher formants has increased by an amplitude ratio of 10:1 (20 db) in the last three waves alone. The amount in the first wave is barely perceptible. This illustrates very graphically that a person can, at will, change the ratio of the energy in the first and higher formants over a very large range. It also demonstrates very graphically that the main excitation of the formants occurs primarily in phase with the rapid closure of the vocal cords. This is diametrically opposite to the usual supposition that it is given by the sudden opening of the vocal cords. As will

be demonstrated later under the section on harmonic analysis, the sharpness of the closure is directly related to the increase in high-frequency energy.

Figure 8 includes some other interesting shapes encountered in different subjects. In speaker A, there is some indication that the closure is not particularly good over the region where it normally occurs. This speaker is also of interest in that as the pitch is varied his wave shape over a cycle appears to stay uniform. This is in contrast with speakers B and C where the pulse during the opening phase remains essentially the same in shape and time duration while the pitch is varied, and instead the time of closure varies.

These two characteristics have a special significance in speech production in relation to the overtone structure. In the first case, the individual harmonics keep the same amplitude relations as pitch varies. In the second case, the distribution of energy as a function of frequency stays constant as the harmonic spacing varies under the distribution envelope.

Speaker B shows a characteristic shape which appears almost as commonly as a wave with a flat closure. This would appear to be a broad closure period in which there occurs a slight and gradual opening and then the more abrupt. Speaker D shows a special case of this in which a very short closure occurs and a second phase in which there would be a small opening remaining fairly steady. These waves which have a closure other than the characteristic flat type are not susceptible to significant changes with variations of the Q controls over their possible ranges.

The high-pitched case of speaker C ($f_0 = 168$) illustrates the effect of a small error in the tuning of C. Here it was caused by a slight shift in first resonance frequency of the speaker in going to a higher pitch, after having been adjusted correctly for the lower pitched case. The female voice illustrates a case where the opening and closing have about equal steepness.

Figure 9 shows another rather interesting result which was obtained by this technique. In this illustration the voiced fricatives [z] and [v] have been made by a speaker while the inverse network was adjusted. As has been brought out by previous workers, this type of sound is made up of a combination of voiced or harmonic energy in the low-frequency region and quasi-random energy in the high-frequency region. The random energy is created by the turbulence of the air passing through a constriction. The air passing through the constriction is, of course, derived from that passing through the vocal cords. The arrangements for portraying the high-frequency energy by the top trace and the vocal cord wave by the lower trace is similar to that used for Fig. 7. Although it was more difficult to obtain a smooth vocal cord wave because, in part, of the turbulence, the same general shape is evident.

The relation of the amplitude of high-frequency energy to the volume velocity of the vocal cord wave is of particular interest. In the sound [z] where the

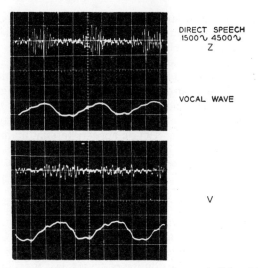

DIRECT SPEECH
1500∿ 4500∿
Z

VOCAL WAVE

V

FIG. 9. Vocal cord waves for voiced fricative sounds [z] and [v].

constriction is formed by essentially rigid teeth and the tongue, the low amplitude occurs in phase with the zero amplitude portion of the vocal cord velocity wave. In the sound [v] the low amplitude of the high-frequency energy lags behind the zero amplitude of the vocal cord wave. The reason for this is not particularly obvious although the result was obtained consistently. One speculation is that it is associated with the fact that the constriction is partially formed with an essentially massive lip which vibrates under influence of the vocal cord wave.

ACCURACY CONSIDERATIONS

As has been pointed out earlier, one of the main possible sources of error in the inverse network technique is the failure to take the capacitance C_2 of Fig. 1 into account, or looked at another way, the "skirt" of the second resonance overlaps the first resonance. The presence of C_2 has two effects as follows.

(1) It lowers the frequency of the first resonance somewhat by virtue of the combination of its reactance with that of L_2; however, this is automatically corrected for in the inverse network adjustment to the true resonance that exists.

(2) The presence of the "skirt" causes a gradual rise in the transmission characteristic of the first resonance, the amount of the rise becoming more pronounced as the second resonance is approached. However, the low-pass filter whose cutoff point is placed midway between the two resonances has a gradually increasing loss up to the point of cutoff.

These two effects are thus in the opposite direction and, for the orders of Q involved in the resonances, also of the same order of magnitude thus tending to compensate for each other. It is already known that the distortion of the filter itself to such waves is small so that of the combination should be even less. This

was borne out in the tests with the simulated vocal tract in which any apparent distortion by these two effects was overshadowed by the residual energy of the second formant itself. The magnitude of the energy is apparent in the various figures of the vocal wave.

Another possible source of error which must be considered is the effect of other paths of sound transmission to the microphone than that of the main vocal tract which has been considered. The most likely source is that of the nasal passage. In the typical sounds utilized in the measurements this passageway is closed off by the soft palate, so that a relatively small proportion of the total energy should be obtained by this path. Other possible paths are radiation from the chest and throat.

The effect of the large nasal cavity on the main vocal tract when closed off by the soft palate can be represented essentially by a capacitive reactance in series with a large resistance. In our equivalent circuit this would appear in shunt across the capacitance C_v. To a first approximation this can be viewed as a modification of the values of C_v and R_{2v}, and will be taken into account in the adjustment of the inverse network. There will, of course, be some small residual error due to it.

An estimate of the maximum amount of energy which could reach the microphone from other sources than that of the vocal tract itself can be obtained by a measurement of harmonic spectra of vowels as given by spectrographs. If one compares the energy falling under the well defined first resonance to that appearing at the edges, it will be found to measure somewhat over 20 db greater and even a part of the energy at the edges comes through the vocal tract itself. Thus one would appear justified in concluding that the error due to this type of energy could not be more than a 10% amplitude variation at worst, and probably much less.

One of the best demonstrations of the general accuracy of the method is the portrayal of the various waves of Fig. 7. Here, a very consistent and logical series of wave shapes are obtained which, as demonstrated later by harmonic analysis, correlate very well with the high-frequency energy obtained in the higher formants.

A main virtue of the inverse network technique is that it bypasses any need for making assumptions as to the physical construction, dynamics, pressures, and other features involved in the action of the vocal cords themselves, but simply gives the effective generator wave regardless of how it is originated.

HARMONIC ANALYSIS

One of the most important results of being able to obtain the general shape of the vocal cord wave is that it allows the determination of the type of harmonic spectra available for shaping by the vocal tract. In Fig. 10 is given the actual harmonic analysis obtained

222

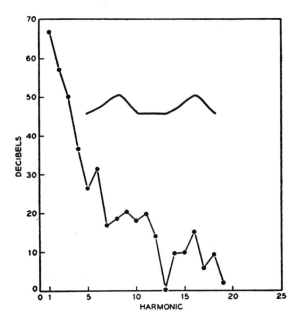

FIG. 10. Harmonic analysis of typical vocal cord wave.

by electro-optical means of a wave typical of the shapes given in Figs. 5 and 7.

The analysis shows the rate at which the amplitudes decrease. It also demonstrates that the distribution is far from uniform. From the harmonic analysis of many wave forms of the type shown in the various patterns, it appears that the one shown is quite typical but, of course, they are not ever quite the same. There is a tendency in many for the variation to be cyclical, that is, there will be a dip about every 4th or 5th harmonic.

In Fig. 11 an analysis is made of an essentially triangular wave. This wave was actually taken from the vocal cord area waves discussed later, but could equally well apply to some of those that appear on Figs. 5, 6, or 8. The harmonic analysis as obtained from the actual wave by electro-optical means is shown by the solid curve. If we were to assume that the wave is triangular (without the rounding of corners), then it is straightforward to carry out a mathematical Fourier analysis. The dashed curve shows the amplitudes of harmonics from such an assumption. This curve with the systematic variation arises from the fact that the harmonic amplitude coefficients are given by the expression,

$$A_n = K\left[\frac{\sin(\pi n l_1/T)}{\pi n l_1/T}\right]^2. \quad (4)$$

The measured curve follows very much the same general shape, except that the rounding of corners has dropped the relative levels of the higher frequencies.

Another example of how the harmonic amplitudes of the vocal wave can vary for a speaker is given in Fig. 12. In this example the second, third, and fourth vocal cord waves of Fig. 7 have been mathematically analyzed for their Fourier terms. To make this feasible,

the assumption was made that the waves were triangular (no rounding of corners) but otherwise followed the same slopes of the waves shown. The resulting harmonics have been plotted against frequency, with the actual fundamental period being taken into account. The assumption that the waves are triangular will, of course, affect the amplitudes of the higher harmonics in much the same manner as illustrated in Fig. 11; however the relative changes in amplitudes due to changes in slopes and widths will be indicated.

Inspection of this figure shows several effects emerging:

(1) Each wave shows a distinct cyclic nature, but differing from each other. This is due primarily to the change in length and shape of the pulse.

(2) There is an increase in amplitude of about 8–10 db for the higher harmonics. A part of this is due to the steepening of the slopes, and the rest is due to the increase in fundamental frequency which causes a given harmonic to fall higher in frequency.

(3) Since the actual increase in energy shown in Fig. 6 is approximately 20 db, then the additional 10 db must be attributed to the increase in sharpness of the corners, and as evidenced by the wave forms this effect is most pronounced at the closure point. This same order of change in amplitude is evidenced by the analyses of Figs. 10 and 11.

VOCAL CORD AREA WAVES

As mentioned in the introduction, early investigations were carried out by means of measurements made on motion pictures of vocal cord action. The main measurement utilized in this work was the area of the vocal

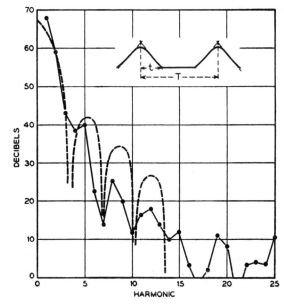

FIG. 11. Actual harmonic analysis of a vocal cord wave and mathematical Fourier analysis of nearest triangular wave (dashed curve).

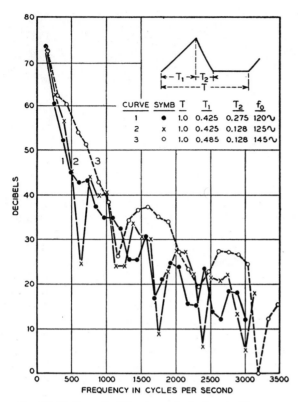

FIG. 12. Mathematical Fourier analysis of sawtooth waves approximating those of Fig. 7.

cord opening as a function of time. Figure 13 shows a number of typical waves obtained in this manner.

In order to apply these waves directly to depicting the generator of the vocal system, we would have to be able to say that either the pressure or velocity wave was some function of the area of the vocal cord opening. Most of the work done on this type of problem indicates that there is a nonlinear relation between the area of opening and the wave produced. R. Clark Jones[9] in the treatment of the variable orifice of sirens considers the variable area orifice as mainly a resistance, although it has some inductance in series with it, the value of the resistance being given approximately by the following relations:

$$G = \frac{P}{V} = \frac{1}{2}\rho \frac{V}{A^2} = \frac{1}{2}\rho \frac{\mu}{A}. \qquad (5)$$

In these relations P is the pressure difference across the orifice, V the volume velocity, G the resistance, ρ the air density, A the effective area[†] of opening, and μ the linear velocity. This general form for the variation of the resistance of small orifices has also been given by L. J. Sivian[10] and checked experimentally on orifices having the same order of size and velocities as exist in the glottis. We can see that the resistance is not only

[9] R. Clark Jones, J. Acoust. Soc. Am. **18**, 371–386 (1946).

[†] Area of *vena contracta* which is related to the actual area by a constant.

[10] L. J. Sivian, J. Acoust. Soc. Am. **7**, 94–101 (1935).

inversely proportional to the area but is also proportional to the linear velocity which is not necessarily a constant. Since the dimensions of the vocal cord opening are considerably smaller than those of the vocal tract, it should then be possible to consider the vocal cords as essentially a constant current source. By solving the above expression (5) for V, which is the acoustic equivalent of current, we obtain

$$V = A(2P/\rho)^{\frac{1}{2}} = KAP^{\frac{1}{2}}. \qquad (6)$$

Thus we find the volume velocity is proportional to the area and that it is also a function of the pressure across the glottis.

It is, of course, very difficult to say exactly what the pressure is across the vocal cord opening. The lungs act to apply a fairly constant pressure to the vocal cords and since the vocal cords are operating into the vocal cavities at nearly atmospheric pressure, it would not appear that the variation in pressure would be of a great magnitude. Thus this variation would not be a controlling factor in the wave shape, but rather would enter in as a distortion of the area wave.

If the area waves are compared to those obtained by the inverse network method, considerable similarity will be found. As a matter of fact, there is a greater variation between the various area waves than there is between many of the waves obtained by the two methods.

Probably the outstanding difference which appears in the two types of waves is that in the area waves the opening phase is usually the most abrupt, only one wave showing the opposite characteristic. In those obtained by the inverse method, the closing phase is characteristically the most abrupt. These findings are not necessarily incompatible since there are a number of

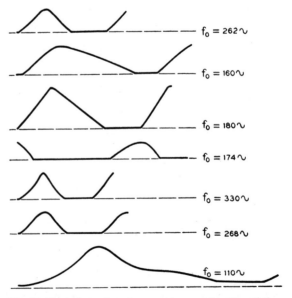

FIG. 13. Typical vocal cord area waves as a function of time obtained from motion pictures of several speakers.

R. L. MILLER

factors relating the two waves which are not too well known, such as the pressure gradient across the glottis and the impedance of the glottal opening. Another factor is that the motions of the vocal cords and the forces involved, as can be observed from motion pictures, are extremely complex. In many cases there is a complicated three-dimensional rolling motion associated with the closure and opening, thus making difficult a true evaluation of the area wave as the generator source.

There has become available in recent years a considerable amount of vocal cord data beyond that of the Bell Telephone Laboratories film which was the basis of the above study. One important source has been the work at Northwestern University by Fletcher,[11] von Leden, Moore,[12] and Timcke.[13] In general these more recent data show similar characteristic area waves to those of Fig. 13.

Flanagan[14] in an analysis utilizing the area wave data of Fletcher[11] has shown that there should be some steepening of the leading and trailing edges of the volume velocity wave when compared to the area wave. This is due to a nonlinear relation between volume velocity and vocal cord area for small areas of opening. Since this effect applies equally to both the opening and closing phases, it could not account for the difference in waves as obtained by the two methods.

Timcke, von Leden, and Moore[13] have pointed out an effect which could be a partial explanation of the differences appearing in the two methods. They show that as the intensity of a sound increases a point is reached where the closing phase of the wave becomes steeper than the opening phase. This same general effect is apparent in Fig. 7; here, however, even the softly spoken sound shows a tendency for the closing phase to be steeper. The fact that the main excitation of the resonances invariably occurs during the closure period appears to be one incontravertible bit of evidence. A method of checking this apparent anomaly in the two approaches would be to carry out both types of measurements on the same person and sound.

It is of considerable interest to note that harmonic analysis of either type wave results in very much the same distribution of harmonics.

SIGNIFICANCE OF RESULTS TO SPEECH PRODUCTION

Perhaps the most important result which emerges from this work is the knowledge that a uniform harmonic distribution in the glottal wave is a rarity.

Studies of the analyses of a large number of varying wave forms of this type indicate that one can expect variations of the order of ±3 to 6 db from a mean value. Extreme variations such as the actual disappearance of a harmonic will be found. There is a decided tendency for the distribution to have a cyclical variation. This is particularly true in the lower harmonics, while for the high-order harmonics, the variation becomes more nearly random. This factor undoubtedly accounts for the presence of what often appears to be secondary or spurious resonances in the voice spectra obtained by spectrographic analysis. Their presence has long puzzled and hampered people making spectrographic analysis and formant measurements. A cyclical variation of about every fourth or fifth harmonic appears to be a typical result for male voices.

The wide variation of the upper harmonics with stress and similar factors change the relative amplitudes of formants without changing the phonetic evaluation greatly. This undoubtedly accounts for the fact that formant amplitude is not a closely controlled factor in speech discrimination.[15]

It is extremely hard to generalize any mathematical rules for such Fourier analysis of the many shapes encountered, without carrying each out individually. Perhaps the closest approach could be based on the fact that most vocal cord waves are distinguished usually by a period of closure, with some smoothly varying function falling between. Inspection of textbooks[16] which list Fourier analysis of similar standard types such as triangular, partial sine, and sawtooth, show that they are nearly always characterized by terms of the form $(\sin nx/n^2x^2)$ or $(\sin^2 nx/n^2x^2)$.

Another result that has an important bearing on speech parameters has to do with the slope of the harmonic distribution. Because of the gyrations of the spectrum it would be extremely difficult to give a figure for the slope in any limited region. However, if we refer to the simple idealized case illustrated in Fig. 11, one finds that the slope of the harmonics is defined by Eq. (4); and the slope of the peaks in the distribution is proportional to $1/n^2$. The numerator of the equation determines how the harmonics vary within a peak but since its value varies cyclically through the value of 1 for each peak, it does not enter into the over-all slope. If we take into account the rounding of corners we find that the slope of the measured curve is proportional to $1/_n2.35$.

Applying this same criterion to the measurement of the slopes of the distributions of Fig. 12, we find that the slopes are proportional to $1/_n1.92$, $1/_n1.86$, and $1/_n1.75$, respectively. If we were to add the indicated 10 db due to rounding, the slope of $1/_n1.92$ would change to approximately $1/_n2.4$. The correction for the

[11] W. W. Fletcher, "A study of internal laryngeal activity in relation to vocal intensity," Ph.D. thesis, Northwestern University (1950).
[12] P. Moore and H. von Leden, "Sound film—The larynx and voice—the function of the normal larynx," 1956.
[13] Timcke, von Leden, and Moore, A.M.A. Arch. Otolaryngol. 68, 1–19 (July, 1958).
[14] J. L. Flanagan, J. Speech and Hearing Research 1, 99–116 (1958).
[15] G. E. Peterson and H. L. Barney, J. Acoust. Soc. Am. 24, 175–184 (1952).
[16] Reference Data for Radio Engineers (Federal Telephone and Radio Corporation, New York, 1955), third edition.

latter two waves would, of course, be less because of the increase in sharpness of the closure. Measured curves obtained by electro-optical means for such waves as $C(f_0=100)$ of Fig. 8 and Fig. 13 ($f_0=174$) have also been found to give slopes of the order of $1/_n 1.8$. If we went back to the first vocal wave of Fig. 7, the value would be at least $1/_n 2.9$. Thus we can see the indicated range over which the harmonics may vary, even by a single speaker.

The fact that an individual will have his own characteristic distributions raises the question as to just how much he makes use of it in forming his vocabulary, and how it enters into the individuality of his voice. Another factor along this same line, which may give a clue as to how some people solve this problem, is the fact that they tend to keep the pulse shape and width constant, and it is primarily the closure period that varies. This keeps the frequency-energy distribution essentially constant as the pitch varies, thus presumably having less effect on the formant values.

Several other aspects emerge as further possible uses of the inverse network technique as follows.

(1) Since it is necessary only to pick up the person's voice by a microphone in order to observe a measure of his vocal cord operation, the technique could have possibilities as a clinical tool to observe pathological cases.

(2) The method offers an accurate way of measuring the natural period of the first formant independent of the effect of the harmonic spectrum itself. This difficulty is encountered in spectrographic analysis.

(3) A further refinement of the technique offers the possibility of obtaining accurate measurement of the Q of the resonances of the vocal tract. There were indications in the present measurements that the actual Q was somewhat higher than the present generally accepted values.[17] It might also be pointed out that a distribution of harmonics such as indicated by Figs. 9, 10, and 11 could have serious repercussions on the value of Q as computed from a spectrogram unless taken into account.

ACKNOWLEDGMENTS

The author is indebted to many of his colleagues in Bell Telephone Laboratories. He particularly wishes to thank Mr. H. K. Dunn, Mr. E. S. Weibel, and Mr. M. R. Schroeder for their helpful suggestions and Mr. R. K. Potter who obtained the original area data from the Bell film and encouraged the study.

---

[17] A. S. House and K. N. Stevens, J. Speech and Hearing Research **1**, 309 (1958).

An Investigation of the Volume Velocity Waveform at the Larynx during
Speech by Means of an Inverse Filter

J.N. Holmes (Joint Speech Research Unit of the British Post Office,
Eastcote)

Introduction

In recent years there has been much interest in the nature of the vibration of the
vocal chords. This interest has arisen from various applications in the fields of
medicine, phonetics, and communications engineering.

There are various methods of study available, of which high speed cine-photography
has been the most widely used.[1,2,3] This method is expensive if a lot of data is
required, but it gives very detailed information about the form of the larynx vibration
It has the disadvantage that ordinary speaking conditions cannot be studied because of
the necessity for a laryngoscope mirror in the mouth.

In the field of communications, where one is primarily interested in the acoustic
output from the larynx, the inverse filtering method[4,5] is preferable because the
results are cheaply and easily obtainable during normal speech and are obtained
directly in the form of volume velocity waveforms.

In addition certain features of the vocal chord wave, such as the time instants
when the main pulsings of the vocal cavities occur, are very clearly shown by this
method. It has been stated by Miller[4] that in general the main instant of excitation
of the second formant is at the closure of the glottis, but it will be shown here that
in many cases there are also well defined instants of excitation of the second and
higher formants at other points in the larynx wave.

Experimental Method

It has been shown by Fant[6] that for non-nasalized vowels the transfer function of
the vocal tract can be closely approximated in the range up to 5000 c/s by a function
having four or five suitably chosen conjugate pole pairs, a correction for higher poles
and a zero at zero frequency to represent the effect of radiation from the mouth.
Similarly an inverse network can be made with a few suitably placed zeros, a higher
zero correction, and a pole at zero frequency. In practice it will suffice if the
transfer function has the correct amplitude and phase characteristic in the range 50
c/s to 5000 c/s, and so the pole need not be at the origin, provided the effect of its
displacement from the origin is compensated in the frequency range required.

The inverse filter used in the experiments described here consists of five cascaded
similar networks whose transfer functions each have one complex conjugate zero pair
adjustable in frequency and bandwidth, together with a higher pole pair which is well
above the frequency range of interest. The correction for higher zeros is included in
the inter-network couplings. The low frequency pole which corrects for the radiation
at the mouth is included in the formant-one zero circuit, and may be switched out if
the differentiated larynx wave is required. Each adjustable zero network is arranged
to give a low frequency transmission which is independent of the frequency of the zero,
and to have facilities for disconnecting the zero circuit without affecting the low
frequency gain. This latter facility is useful for showing the effect of inverse
filtering all except one of the formants, so that the excitation pattern of each
formant can be seen separately.

The sounds are magnetically recorded and replayed repeatedly from a tape loop into
the inverse filter. An oscilloscope, whose time-base is synchronized to the loop, is
used for studying the filter output. The frequencies and bandwidths of the zeros are
then adjusted to produce minimum formant-frequency ripple in the output waveform.
During vowels this condition is usually well defined, and provides, incidentally, an
accurate measure of the formant frequencies. The waveform with all the formant ripple
removed represents the volume velocity at the larynx.

Precautions to minimize errors

The required inverse filter settings are normally well defined, but the correct larynx waveforms will not be obtained unless all the conditions assumed in the theoretical model are met. The serious danger here is that if these conditions are not quite met there may be a setting of the inverse filter controls which will give a waveform which is at least credible as a larynx wave, but which will have a shape very different from that of the volume velocity wave at the larynx.

It is thus essential to take many precautions to prevent errors. As non-nasalized vowels are assumed it was necessary to avoid those near to nasal consonants. A good anechoic chamber was used to achieve free field radiation, and a condenser microphone to reproduce the sound pressure waveform accurately.

It was impossible to avoid the presence of very low frequency noise in the microphone output due to slight variations in room air pressure, and air movements caused by breathing and slight body movements. This noise made it essential to limit the low frequency response of the system by means of A.C. couplings in the amplifiers, but even so some remaining noise, mainly in the region of 10 c/s, caused slight variations of the base line on the measured larynx waves.

In the electrical equipment the combined effect of phase distortion in all amplifier A.C. couplings was corrected, and extreme precautions were taken to avoid distortion and noise in the magnetic recorder.

Fortunately it was possible to test the overall performance of the complete electrical system. A test waveform was generated consisting of a 50 c/s square wave feeding an all-pole network similar to that needed to synthesize a neutral vowel. This waveform was fed into the microphone amplifier through a capacitor equal in value to the microphone capacitance. The zeros of the inverse filter were adjusted to the frequencies of the poles of the test network, and the waveform was displayed without the low frequency pole of the inverse filter in operation. The quality of the square wave so obtained is shown in fig. 1. As can be seen it is not a perfect square wave, but the errors are not sufficient to make an appreciable difference to the measured larynx waveforms.

Fig. 1. Test waveform

Results

Study of several different examples of larynx waves show results similar to those already published[2,4,5,7,8] but with quite large differences in waveshape and in length of the closed period for different talkers, different degrees of stress, and different frequency of vibration. Two typical such waveforms are shown in figs. 2 and 3. Further study of the sample in fig. 3 was made to see how the formants are excited. This was done by differentiating the larynx wave to emphasize the higher frequencies, and removing the zero from the inverse filter for one formant at a time. The results for the first three formants are shown in figs. 4, 5 and 6. It can be seen from these figures that the first formant is excited once per cycle at the closure of the larynx. The second formant has two main excitation points of nearly equal intensity, one at the closure and another at the re-opening of the larynx. The third formant has the same two excitation points, but in this case the opening pulse is of much less intensity than the closure. This sort of variation between formants is typical of a large number of samples examined, and the more complicated patterns of excitation are noticed most in the higher formants. It will be seen from these figures, and it has been found to be generally true for most speakers, that successive larynx wave cycles are almost identical, even in fine detail. It is well known, however, that considerable variations between successive cycles occur frequently for some talkers, and on some occasions for almost all talkers. The vibrations of a habitually irregular larynx have not yet been studied, but several cases have been investigated in which the behaviour of a normal larynx is changing. Fig. 7 shows a vowel starting from a glottal stop, and it can be seen that the three cycles shown are of very different form. The step on the opening phase of the third cycle persisted for the remainder of the

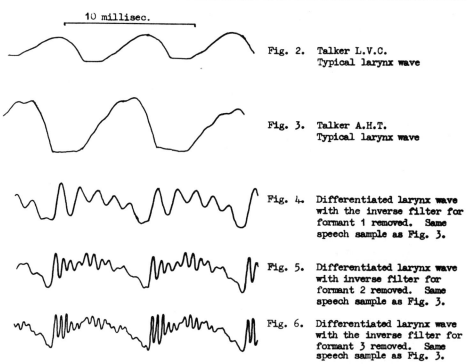

10 millisec.

Fig. 2. Talker L.V.C.
Typical larynx wave

Fig. 3. Talker A.H.T.
Typical larynx wave

Fig. 4. Differentiated larynx wave
with the inverse filter for
formant 1 removed. Same
speech sample as Fig. 3.

Fig. 5. Differentiated larynx wave
with inverse filter for
formant 2 removed. Same
speech sample as Fig. 3.

Fig. 6. Differentiated larynx wave
with the inverse filter for
formant 3 removed. Same
speech sample as Fig. 3.

vowel, and was found to be a frequently seen characteristic of that speaker. Several other cases of initiation and cessation of voicing have been examined, both with a glottal stop and with an open glottis condition adjoining. After an initial glottal stop about three cycles of vibration are generally needed to achieve full amplitude, and sometimes a few more to establish a repetitive pattern. Voicing starting from an open glottis has been observed to take about twice as many cycles to build up.

Examination of one sample of an /h/ sound between two vowels shows voicing with a volume velocity wave whose peak-to-peak amplitude is not significantly different from in the vowels but which does cease to have a completely closed period. Successive cycles of the vibration to differ appreciably during the /h/. Examination of the excitation of the formants shows that the first and second formants derived their excitation mainly from the larynx vibration, whereas the higher formants were mainly excited by friction, which appeared to be continuously present through each larynx cycle. It is assumed that the mean volume velocity during the /h/ is much higher than in the vowels, but this would not be shown because the apparatus response is not maintained below 50 c/s.

Several other examples of larynx vibration have been studied by this method but space limitation prevents any more being shown here.

Conclusions

The main facts brought out by this investigation are:-
(i) The fine detail of the larynx wave is normally very complicated, in particular in its effect in exciting the higher formants. The lack of this complexity in the excitation normally used in speech synthesis leads one to suspect that this may be a partial cause of unnaturalness in synthetic speech.
(ii) For most speakers the period, form, and even fine detail, of vibration do not often change suddenly except in regions near intentional changes in larynx behaviour.

References

1. FARNSWORTH, D.W., "High-speed motion pictures of the human vocal chords". Bell Laboratories Record, 18, 203-208 (1940).

2. MOORE, P. and LEDEN, von H., "Dynamic variations of the vibratory pattern in the normal larynx". Folia Phoniatrica, 10, 205-238 (1958).

3. GILL, J.S., "Estimation of vocal excitation during speech with particular reference to the requirements of analysis-synthesis telephony". Ph.D. Thesis, University of London (1961).

4. MILLER, R.L., "Nature of the Vocal Chord Wave". J. Acoust. Soc. Amer. 31, 667-677, (1959).

5. SPEECH TRANSMISSION LABORATORY QUARTERLY PROGRESS AND STATUS REPORT, Royal Institute of Technology, Stockholm, (July-September 1960).

6. FANT, C.G.M., "Acoustic Theory of Speech Production". Mouton & Co. (1960).

7. FLANAGAN, J.L., "Some properties of the glottal sound source". J. Speech and Hearing Research, 1, 99-116 (1958).

8. SONESSON, B., "On the anatomy and vibratory pattern of the human vocal folds", Acta-Oto-Laryngologica, Supplementum 156, (1960).

Fig. 7. Talker J.N.H. Larynx wave after a glottal stop.

Fig. 8. Talker L.V.C. Differentiated larynx wave with the inverse filter for formant 4 removed

(a) during a voiced /h/ sound, showing mainly fricative excitation.

(b) during the preceding vowel, showing excitation mainly from the larynx closure.

10 millisec.

Part IV
Estimation of Vocal Tract Parameters

The papers in this part are concerned with the problems of obtaining a representation of the effect of the vocal tract transmission properties directly from the speech signal. We have divided the papers into two groups. The first group is focused on the problem of estimating formant frequencies and other representations of the vocal tract frequency response. The second group is concerned with estimating the vocal tract shape from the acoustic waveform.

A. Spectrum and Formant Frequency Estimation

The first paper in this part, by Flanagan, describes an analog approach to estimating formants in continuous speech. This paper describes the use of peak-picking on a short-time Fourier representation to obtain the formant frequency estimates. This same principle appears in the fourth and seventh papers discussed below.

The second paper, by Dunn, deals with sound spectrograph measurements of vowel formant bandwidths. Although more flexible methods of measuring formant bandwidths are now possible with digital techniques, this paper remains a source of fundamental data. The third paper, by Pinson, describes a pitch-synchronous time-domain analysis-by-synthesis method in which the speech wave is approximated by a sum of complex exponential signals. The results of the analysis are estimates of both the formant frequencies and the bandwidths.

The fourth paper, by Schafer and Rabiner, describes the application of homomorphic processing to the estimation of the vocal tract frequency response (spectral envelope) and the use of peak picking to estimate formant frequencies. This paper also introduces the idea of sharpening formant resonances by evaluating the discrete spectrum estimate off the unit circle (or equivalently, off the $j\omega$-axis), so as to facilitate the separation of closely spaced poles. An analysis-by-synthesis approach based upon homomorphic spectral smoothing is discussed in [1].

The next three papers, by Atal and Hanauer, Itakura and Saito, and Markel, respectively, are concerned with linear predictive analysis methods for estimating the vocal tract transfer function and formant frequencies. These papers, together with the tutorial paper by Makhoul in Part II, and the book by Markel and Gray [2], are basic references describing the many ways that linear predictive methods can be applied to estimating speech parameters. Although the authors of these papers take different points of view in formulating the analysis methods, the resulting methods have much in common, and the results obtained are very comparable.

The last two papers describe a peak-picking algorithm based upon an LPC spectrum estimate. In these papers we find combined many of the ideas introduced in the previous papers; i.e., peak-picking, resonance sharpening, and linear predictive spectrum estimation.

B. Estimation of Vocal Tract Area Functions

Techniques for estimating the vocal tract area function directly from the speech signal are of interest in studies of the speech production process and as the basis for efficient coding of the speech signal. This is a difficult problem, beset with uniqueness problems, and a problem which is far from solved. The two papers in this section are representative of published progress to date.

The first paper, by Mermelstein, describes a technique for computing a smoothed area function from the low frequency formant frequencies. A related paper, by Schroeder [3], uses the same mathematical frame work in estimating the vocal tract shape from direct acoustic measurements (i.e., in a nonspeaking situation). Another more recent approach of this kind is discussed in [4]. These papers are not included because we have limited our scope to direct analysis of the speech signal.

The second paper, by Wakita, is based upon the fact that a recursion formula exists that relates the linear predictive parameters estimated from the speech signal to the areas of a set of concatenated lossless acoustic tubes. A similar result is noted in the paper by Atal and Hanauer in Part IV-A.

References

1. J. P. Olive, "Automatic formant tracking by a Newton–Raphson Technique," *J. Acoust. Soc. Am.*, vol. 50 (Pat. 2), pp. 661–670, Aug. 1971.
2. J. D. Markel and A. H. Gray, Jr., *Linear Prediction of Speech*, Springer--Verlag, New York, 1976.
3. M. R. Schroeder, "Determination of the geometry of the human vocal tract by acoustic measurements," *J. Acoust. Soc. Am.*, vol. 41 (Pt. 2), pp. 1002–1010, Apr. 1967.
4. M. M. Sondhi and B. Gopinath, "Determination of vocal tract shape from impulse response at the lips," *J. Acoust. Soc. Am.*, vol. 49 (Pt. 2), pp. 1867–1873, June 1971.

Automatic Extraction of Formant Frequencies from Continuous Speech*

JAMES L. FLANAGAN

Acoustics Laboratory, Massachusetts Institute of Technology, Cambridge, Massachusetts, and
Air Force Cambridge Research Center, Cambridge, Massachusetts

(Received September 7, 1955)

Two electronic devices for automatically extracting the first three formant frequencies from continuous speech are described. Both devices are designed to yield three continuous dc output voltages whose magnitudes, as functions of time, represent the formant frequencies of the input speech. The principles of operation and the design features of both devices are discussed, and typical examples of the operation of each are presented.

I. INTRODUCTION

EXPERIMENTS in the analysis and perception of speech[1-4] have shown that certain speech sounds, notably the vowels, may be identified and synthesized principally from a knowledge of the formant frequencies.[5] The formant frequencies, therefore, appear to be important information-bearing elements of speech.

In fact, analytical analysis of the vocal mechanism[6] has shown that the acoustic output during vowel production may be specified rather accurately from a knowledge of the formant frequencies and the fundamental vocal frequency. These facts, together with the recent and considerable advances in the synthesis of speech with synthesizers controlled by formant information,[7-11] have made a device for automatically extracting the formant frequencies from continuous speech very desirable. Such a device would constitute the main component of a speech analyzer for a band-width compression system operating upon formant-coding principles.

---

* This paper is based on material in "A speech analyzer for a formant-coding compression system," Sc.D. thesis, Electrical Engineering Department, Massachusetts Institute of Technology (1955). The thesis is available in published form as Scientific Report No. 4, Acoustics Laboratory, Massachusetts Institute of Technology, May 1955.

[1] R. K. Potter and J. C. Steinberg, J. Acoust. Soc. Am. 22, 807–820 (1950).
[2] G. E. Peterson and H. L. Barney, J. Acoust. Soc. Am. 24, 175–184 (1952).
[3] G. E. Peterson, J. Acoust. Soc. Am. 24, 629–637 (1952).
[4] F. S. Cooper *et al.*, J. Acoust. Soc. Am. 24, 597–606 (1952).
[5] Formant frequency may be defined in at least three ways: (1) as the frequency of the maximum of a gross concentration of energy in the spectrum of a speech sound, (2) as the frequency of the centroid of a gross concentration of spectral energy, or (3) as a normal mode of vibration of the vocal mechanism. These definitions are related but are not identical. For the purpose of the present discussion we shall use the first definition.

[6] C. G. M. Fant, Transmission Properties of the Vocal Tract, Technical Report No. 12, Acoustics Laboratory, Massachusetts Institute of Technology (1952).
[7] W. A. Munson and H. G. Montgomery, J. Acoust. Soc. Am. 22, 678 (A) (1950).
[8] C. G. M. Fant, IVA (Stockholm) 24, 331–337 (1953).
[9] W. Lawrence, Chap. 34 in *Communication Theory*, edited by W. Jackson (Butterworth Scientific Publications, London, 1953).
[10] Meeks, Borst, and Cooper, J. Acoust. Soc. Am. 26, 137 (A) (1954).
[11] Stevens, Bastide, and Smith, J. Acoust. Soc. Am. 27, 207 (A) (1955).

Reprinted with permission from *J. Acoust. Soc. Am.*, vol. 28, pp. 110–118, Jan. 1956.

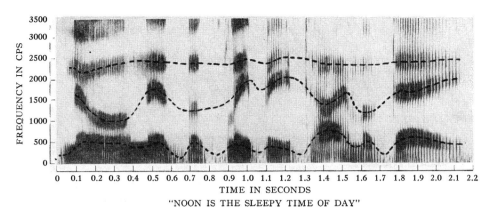

FIG. 1. Continuous curves representing the frequencies of the first three formants of a conversational utterance of speech. The curves are extrapolated continuously across the silent and unvoiced intervals of the utterance.

It would also provide an interesting tool for clinical and therapeutical speech work.

For the purposes of the speech compression system the formant-extracting device should be able to accept continuous speech at its input and to yield output voltages whose magnitudes, as functions of time, represent the frequencies of the formants. During the silent and unvoiced intervals of the speech utterances the output voltages should be extrapolated continuously and usually with continuity of slope.[12] A set of such formant signals is illustrated in Fig. 1 by curves drawn through the center frequencies of the formant bars on a sound spectrogram produced by a *Sonograph* (Kay Electric Company). A device that would provide formant data in this manner is assumed, therefore, to be the ideal formant extractor.

There are two obvious facets to the problem of developing such a device for the automatic analysis of speech. The first is designing and engineering the apparatus, and the second is quantitatively evaluating the performance of the device when speech is the input. The first usually proceeds according to idealized and simplified specifications derived from a limited knowledge of the ensemble of possible inputs. The second involves a statistical evaluation of the operation of the device, ideally for all possible speech inputs. Both of these steps are necessary in arriving at an acceptable solution to the problem.

At least two attempts have been made previously to develop devices for extracting the frequencies of the first and second formants from continuous speech.[13,14]

Both of these approaches were based upon determining the density of zero axis-crossings of grossly filtered speech. The hypothesis was that the density of the axis-crossings either of normal speech or of speech appropriately low-pass filtered is a good approximation to the frequency of the first formant, while the density of the axis-crossings of differentiated speech or of speech appropriately high-pass filtered is a good approximation to the frequency of the second formant. The success of these devices as extractors of precise formant information was rather limited. The indications of formant frequency were, in general, not very accurate and the operation was not very reliable. The foregoing principle of approximate formant detection has been used with success, however, in a device designed to recognize spoken digits.[14]

Two methods for obtaining formant information in the form illustrated in Fig. 1 have been investigated and are reported here. The design of the apparatus for both methods was guided by the results of psychoacoustic experiments and both of the formant-extracting devices have been evaluated by a technique devised for quantitatively rating the performance. The present paper, however, will discuss only the principles and typical operation of the formant extractors, while the evaluation procedure and the results of the evaluation will be discussed in a companion paper.[15]

II. THE SPECTRUM-SAMPLING FORMANT EXTRACTOR

The first method for formant extraction is based upon a periodic sampling of the short-time spectrum of speech to obtain successive time functions representing the spectrum. Appropriate circuitry operates upon these time functions to determine the frequencies of the spectral maxima, or formants. The method has been designated, therefore, the spectrum-sampling method.[16]

---

[12] The continuity of the formant signals can be argued in the following manner. The formant tuning is a continuous function of the displacement of the articulators and generally has a continuous first derivative with respect to articulator displacement. The articulators, i.e., the tongue, lips, jaw, etc., are massive elements. The human muscles are capable of exerting only a finite force, hence the acceleration of the articulators must be finite and their velocity and displacement must be continuous. The formant tuning, therefore, must also be a continuous function of time. An exception to the continuous first derivative occurs when a complete closure is made in the vocal tract, for example, during the production of a stop consonant.

[13] E. Peterson, J. Acoust. Soc. Am. **23**, 668–674 (1951).

[14] Davis, Biddulph, and Balashek, J. Acoust. Soc. Am. **24**, 637–642 (1952).

[15] J. L. Flanagan, J. Acoust. Soc. Am. **28**, 118 (1956).

[16] The circuit details and engineering data for this formant extractor are given in: J. L. Flanagan, "A speech analyzer for a formant-coding compression system," Scientific Report No. 4, Acoustics Laboratory, Massachusetts Institute of Technology (1955).

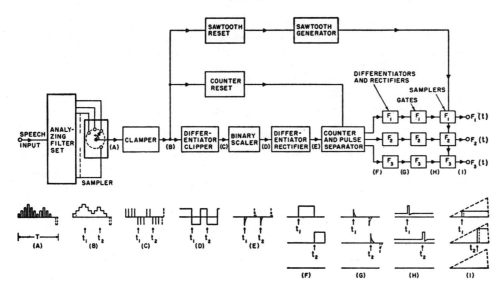

FIG. 2. Block diagram showing the principles of operation of the spectrum-sampling formant extractor.

The first step in the formant-extracting procedure is to make a gross Fourier transformation of the input speech to obtain a short-time amplitude spectrum. A set of analyzing filters is used to accomplish this transformation. The filter set is composed of 36 contiguous band pass filters, all having a common input but separate outputs. Each channel of the set includes a simple-tuned circuit, an amplifier, a full-wave rectifier, and a smoothing network with a time constant of 10 milliseconds. Choice of the center frequencies and band widths of the filters represents a compromise: the band widths are greater than the just discriminable differences in formant frequency[17] but are smaller than differences in formant frequency which are phonemic.[2] The center frequencies of the filter channels are set on a Koenig frequency scale[18] extending from 150 cps to 7000 cps.[19] The half-power band widths of the filter channels are 100 cps each for frequencies below 1000 cps, and increase logarithmically above 1000 cps to a band width of 450 cps at 7000 cps. Adjacent channels overlap at the half-power frequencies. The gain and band width of each channel may be adjusted independently and the useful dynamic range of each channel is greater than 30 db.

Since the spectrum of speech slopes downward on the average at about 10 db/octave, it is desirable to perform a frequency equalization that permits all filter channels to operate at about the same signal level. It is also desirable to obtain a spectral output in which all the maxima are approximately of the same amplitude. Equalization of the spectral maxima alleviates the problem of dynamic range in the formant-analyzing equipment to follow. A driver amplifier employing an equalizing network is used therefore to supply the input to the filter set. The equalizing network has a frequency

response which rises at approximately 10 db/octave between 750 cps and 3000 cps and is essentially flat outside this range. The network and the driver amplifier are an integral part of the filter set and any reference to the filter set in the remainder of this discussion assumes that the input speech is equalized according to the frequency characteristic just mentioned.

Principles of Operation

The principles of operation of the spectrum-sampling system are shown in Fig. 2. Speech is transduced and passed into the filter set at the left of the figure. The outputs of the filters are scanned periodically 60 times a second by a sampling switch. The output of the sampling switch is a time function of voltage samples representing values of the short-time amplitude spectrum of the input speech. The wave form at (A) in Fig. 2 shows the time function obtained during one scan of the sampling switch for a spectrum having only two maxima (or formants). The single, dotted, negative sample at the end of the scan is utilized for resetting and synchronizing the equipment.

The output samples from the sampling switch are sent through a clamper circuit[20] to produce the stairstep wave form shown at (B). This wave form is differentiated and peak clipped to yield the wave form at (C). The differentiation produces a train of pulses which change polarity at the times the spectral maxima are passed, namely, t_1 and t_2; the peak clipping renders the apparatus reasonably insensitive to changes in the level of the input speech. These pulses trigger a binary scaler circuit which changes state each time the derivative

[17] J. L. Flanagan, J. Acoust. Soc. Am. **27**, 613–617 (1955).
[18] W. Koenig, Bell Labs. Record **27**, 299 (1949).
[19] The channels above 3650 cps are not used when extracting only the first three formants.

[20] A clamper is an active low-pass filter circuit having an impulse response whose Laplace transform is:

$$(1/s)(1 - e^{-sT}),$$

where T is a constant sampling period in seconds. In the present case this response is realized by connecting a storage capacitor across the sampling arm of the nonshorting sampling switch.

pulses change sign, and the output of the scaler is wave form (D). The output of the scaler is differentiated and rectified to produce individual pulses indicating the times t_1 and t_2 within the sampling interval, as shown at (E).

The pulses marking the maxima are separated into individual channels to facilitate the conversion of the times t_1 and t_2 into voltages. This separation is accomplished by allowing the pulses (E) to trigger a scale-of-ten counter which is reset each sampling period (i.e., 60 times/sec). The trigger pulses cause conduction to move successively from one cathode to the next in a multicathode, glow-transfer tube that is part of the counter circuit. The wave forms (F) are obtained respectively at the first three cathodes of the glow-transfer tube when the counter is triggered by (E). The individual outputs from the counter are differentiated and rectified to obtain (G), which represents an effective separation of the pulses in (E). The separated pulses, still indicating t_1 and t_2, trigger one-shot multivibrators and independently generate accurate gate pulses of 500 microseconds duration, as shown at (H). The gates are allowed to sample a calibrating (or sweep) wave form generated in synchronism with the sampling switch. The calibrating wave form is shown as a linearly increasing (sawtooth) voltage at (I). The amplitude values of the calibrating wave are "read" by the gates at times t_1 and t_2 and these values are stored in the sampler circuits until the next sampling interval. The voltages stored by the samplers are illustrated by the wave forms (I). These stored voltages are made available as outputs. The output of each sampler is smoothed by a low-pass network having a cut-off frequency of about 10 cps, the approximate band width of the formant signal. The outputs of the formant-extracting device therefore are smoothed voltages whose magnitudes as functions of time represent the formant frequencies.

At the cessation of the speech input to the filter set the sampler circuits are left with the final values of the formant frequencies. The storage circuits lose these values relatively slowly (with a time constant of approximately $\frac{1}{4}$ second) and the output voltages return slowly to predetermined "neutral" values of the formant frequencies.[21]

The Calibrating Wave Form and Its Constraints

If a linear calibrating or sweep wave form is employed, the formant output voltages are linearly related to frequency on a Koenig scale because the center frequencies of the filter channels are arranged on a Koenig scale. For comparison purposes, it is desirable to have the calibration of the formant tracker correspond to the frequency scale of the sound spectrograph which is essentially linear. Provisions have been made in the

sweep circuits, therefore, to generate a nonlinear calibrating wave form to yield formant output voltages which are directly proportional to frequency on a linear scale.

The effect of errors in formant detection can be minimized by properly constraining the sweep voltages sampled by the sampler units for the first formant (F1), the second formant (F2), and the third formant (F3), respectively. It is known that the formants characteristically occupy certain frequency ranges which overlap to some extent. Consideration of formant frequency data[2] shows that for male voices the probability is small that F1 will exceed 1050 cps, F2 will be found outside the range 750–2400 cps, and F3 will fall below 2000 cps.[22] Consequently the sweep voltages of the individual samplers are constrained with additional nonlinear circuit elements to correspond to these figures.

Typical Results Obtained with the Spectrum-Sampling System

The output voltages from the formant extractor were recorded on an oscillographic pen recorder. The calibration of the over-all system and the tape speed of the recorder were adjusted to correspond to the time-frequency calibration of the sound spectrograph. This permitted the formant voltages recorded for a particular speech sample to be traced directly from the recording tape and superimposed on the sound spectrogram of the speech sample. Typical comparisons of the outputs of the formant extractor with expanded range spectrograms are shown for two conversational utterances in Fig. 3. While the outputs of the formant extractor do not correspond precisely to the functions previously postulated as ideal, they do in general follow the formants with reasonable accuracy and are extrapolated across the unvoiced and silent intervals in a fashion to yield reasonably proper transitions. A detailed discussion of the accuracy and reliability of this formant extractor is given in a companion paper.[15]

Advantages and Disadvantages of the Spectrum-Sampling System

The chief advantage of the spectrum-sampling system is that its manner of formant detection does not necessarily require the formant frequencies to be constrained to any fixed ranges. The formants may occupy frequency ranges which can overlap even to the extent of being identical. The choice of sweep voltage constraints, however, has restricted this overlap to more practical, though generally adequate, values.

The machine is relatively insensitive to input level due to its peak-clipping and scaling features. In the present equipment the input level may vary over a range of approximately 30 db.

---

[21] The neutral or quiescent values for the present arrangement of the equipment are: zero cps, 1500 cps, and 2500 cps for the first, second, and third formant channels, respectively.

[22] Exceptions to this constraint are r-colored sounds which may have F3's as low as 1700 cps.

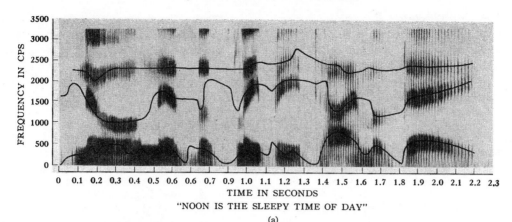

"NOON IS THE SLEEPY TIME OF DAY"

(a)

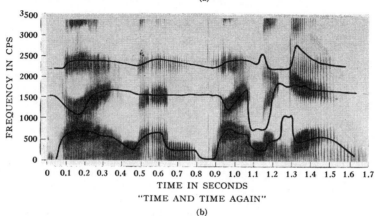

"TIME AND TIME AGAIN"

(b)

FIG. 3. Comparison of the outputs of the spectrum-sampling formant extractor with the sound spectrograms for two conversational utterances. (Speaker: J. M.)

The calibration stability is dependent chiefly upon the stability of the sweep voltage that is sampled by each sampler unit and, up to a certain point, can be made as good as one cares to make the stability of the sweep. For the present arrangement of the equipment the stability of the frequency calibration is approximately two percent.

The main disadvantage of the spectrum-sampling system is that its operation is based upon differentiation of the sampled spectrum and detection of the points having zero slope. The only effective discrimination against spurious formants, or local maxima in the short-time spectrum, is provided by the grossness of the Fourier transformation, that is, the band widths of the analyzing filters. If a spurious or false formant is not sufficiently "covered up" by the filter set, the machine may detect the maximum causing, for example, the $F1$ sampler to respond erroneously. The $F2$ and $F3$ indications, therefore, generally will be in error also, because the machine labels the maxima in succession as it finds them in any single scan of the filter outputs. In other words, the proper detection of a particular formant is contingent upon the proper detection of all lower formants.

Another source of error exists in the machine because of the finite scan time of the sampling switch. If a speech input is applied at a time when the sampling switch has already passed the first formant, but has not completed its scan, the machine will, in completing the scan, label the first maximum found from that point on as $F1$; clearly an error. One can estimate the likelihood of this "initial scan error" by considering the distribution of the contacts of the sampling switch (or filter channels) over the approximate frequency ranges of the formants. On the basis of the distribution of contacts, the set of conditional probabilities expressing the probability of an initial scan error, when the frequency of $F1$ is known, can be written down. If it is assumed that the probability of finding $F1$ in any filter channel in the frequency range of $F1$ is the same, then the probability of an initial scan error can be determined by computing the expectation value of the set of conditional probabilities. This computation has been made for the contact arrangement used with the present equipment and the probability of an initial scan error is found to be 0.7.

The latter disadvantage could be eliminated by incorporating into the equipment an "inhibiting circuit" that recognizes the appearance of an input and prevents the system from operating until the sampling switch reaches the number one contact, i.e., the lowest frequency channel. The inhibiting action could be accomplished by a coincidence circuit that permits the machine to start analyzing only after an output has appeared from the filter set *and* the scan synchronizing pulse has occurred. The secondary importance and the moderate complexity of an inhibiting circuit, however, did not appear to justify its inclusion in the first design of the apparatus.

One further improvement might be the increasing of the scan speed, from 60 cps to upwards of 100 cps. Increasing the scan speed would not lessen the probability of an initial error but it would improve the time resolution which is now limited to 1/60 second. The present speed, however, is generally sufficient for formant analysis of vowels, since vowels usually persist for 50 milliseconds or longer.

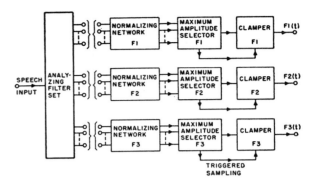

Fig. 4. Block diagram of the spectrum-segmentation formant extractor.

III. THE SPECTRUM-SEGMENTATION FORMANT EXTRACTOR

In the second formant-extracting method the speech spectrum is divided into frequency ranges characteristically occupied by the formants, and electronic circuits determine and indicate the frequency of the maximum within each spectral segment. The method has been termed, therefore, the spectrum-segmentation method.[16] The spectrum-segmentation method is based upon the fact that the first three formants occupy frequency ranges which, on the average, do not overlap greatly. Examination of formant data for adult male speakers[2] shows that, on the average, a division can be made between the ranges of $F1$ and $F2$ at a frequency of approximately 800 cps. The division between $F2$ and $F3$ is not quite so definite, but a compromise division at 2280 cps can be made. This compromise results in a slight restriction of the upper end of the frequency range of $F2$, i.e., that part of the range associated with extreme front vowels, and also eliminates that part of the frequency range of $F3$ usually associated with *r*-colored vowels.

Like the spectrum-sampling method the basic operation in the spectrum-segmentation method is to obtain an appropriate short-time spectrum of the input speech. The set of analyzing filters described in Sec. II is used, therefore, also with the spectrum-segmentation system.

Principles of Operation

A block diagram of the spectrum-segmentation system is shown in Fig. 4. The channels of the analyzing filter set are segmented into contiguous groups to cover the $F1$, $F2$, and $F3$ frequency ranges, respectively. The constraints imposed on the frequency ranges of the formants are those mentioned above, namely: (1) the first formant indicated by the system will fall below 800 cps, (2) the second formant will fall between 800 cps and 2280 cps, and (3) the third formant will fall above 2280 cps.[23] The constraints are imposed with the realiza-

---

[23] These constraints on the frequency ranges of the formants are for adult male speakers. The constraints are different for adult female speakers and for speakers who are children.

tion that errors in formant frequency will result, but also with the intention of determining how serious the errors are. The outputs of each group of filter channels allocated to cover a given formant range are monitored electronically and the channel having the maximum output within each group is selected and indicated at a rate of 60 times per second. This indication within each formant group is taken as an indication of the formant frequency.

The Normalizing Network

As shown in Fig. 4 each set of filter output voltages constituting a formant group is sent first through an "amplitude-normalizing" network. The normalizing circuit computes the mean value of its set of input voltages (i.e., the filter output voltages) and subtracts this mean value from each member of the input set. It provides one-half of this difference at each corresponding output. For example, if e_k is the voltage input to the normalizing circuit from the kth filter channel of a group of channels of total number, N, then the normalized kth channel voltage is:

$$e_k' = \frac{1}{2}\left[e_k - \frac{1}{N} \sum_{n=1}^{N} e_n \right].$$

This operation of constraining the mean value of the set of voltages to zero without altering the relative amplitudes permits reliable selection of the maximum voltage over a range of mean amplitudes greater than 30 db.

The Maximum Amplitude Selector

The normalized set of voltages of any one group is sent to a thyratron maximum-amplitude selector. The maximum selector contains a shield-grid thyratron tube for each channel of the set, and each normalized voltage is led to a corresponding thyratron control grid. The set of thyratron tubes have a common plate load resistor and are simultaneously enabled and disabled by effectively switching the plate supply voltage on and off at a rate of 60 times per second. The thyratron

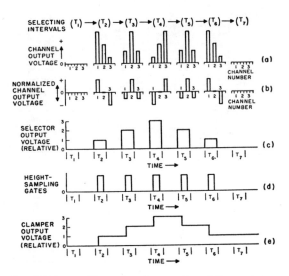

FIG. 5. Diagram illustrating the operation of the spectrum-segmentation formant extractor.

having the maximum positive grid voltage will fire when the set is enabled. Since the set has a common plate load, the firing of one tube precludes the firing of any other tube during the enabling time. A potentiometer is connected as the cathode resistor of each thyratron and the output is taken from the arm of the potentiometer. The arm of the potentiometer is set so that the output voltage (when the tube fires) is proportional to the frequency of the channel that the tube is monitoring (or else proportional to some desired frequency calibrating function). All the potentiometer arms are connected to a resistive summation network to provide a single common output from the selector. The output voltage from the selector, therefore, is a series of rectangular pulses whose heights correspond to the frequency of the channel selected as having the maximum output. The heights of the output pulses consequently represent the frequency of the formant, within the segmentation limits imposed.

The operation of the maximum selector is illustrated in Fig. 5 at (a), (b), and (c). Figure 5 (a) represents the output voltages of three arbitrary filter channels during seven successive selecting time intervals. In the first time interval, no output has appeared. In the second interval, a filter output has appeared and channel number one has the maximum value. In the following intervals, the maximum moves successively from channel one to two, from two to three, from three back to two, and from two back to one. Figure 5 (b) shows the normalized values of these channel voltages during the same successive selecting intervals. Figure 5 (c) assumes that the maximum selector is selecting from these three channels and shows its output voltage as a function of time for the same succession of selecting intervals.

The Clamper Circuit

The final component in the block diagram of Fig. 4 is a clamper circuit. The clamper is an active filter that has an impulse response whose Laplace transform is: $(1/s)(1-e^{-sT})$, where T is the selecting or firing period of the selector. (The selecting period and enabling-disabling period are different to the extent that the thyratrons may or may not fire or select during any given enabling time.) The selector output pulses, whose heights represent formant frequency, are fed into the clamper for smoothing. A gate pulse is generated in the clamper by a one-shot multivibrator that is triggered each time a thyratron in the selector fires. The gate pulse is allowed to "read" the heights of the successive output pulses from the selector. This height-reading gate is illustrated in Fig. 5 (d). The voltage read is stored and held in the clamper circuit until the next reading occurs and each stored value is made available at the output. The clamper output therefore is a "staircase" smoothing of the output pulses from the selector, and is shown in Fig. 5 (e).

When the thyratrons cease selecting, the clamper holds the value of voltage read during the final selection. It loses this value relatively slowly, returning to zero or to a neutral voltage with a time constant of approximately a quarter of a second.[21] Storage of the final selection provides an extrapolation of the formant voltages across the silent and unvoiced intervals of a speech utterance. The staircase output from the clamper is smoothed further by a passive low-pass network having a cut-off frequency of approximately 10 cps.

Typical Results Obtained with the Spectrum-Segmentation System

The calibration of the spectrum-segmentation system was adjusted so that the formant output voltages were recorded on an oscillographic pen recorder with the same time and frequency scale as the sound spectrograph. Tracing these recordings permitted direct comparison of the formant outputs with a sound spectrograph of the input speech. Two such comparisons are shown for conversational utterances in Fig. 6. The comparisons in Fig. 6 indicate that the extractor follows the formant structure of continuous speech with fairly good accuracy. A detailed discussion, however, of the accuracy and reliability of this formant extractor is given in a companion paper.[15]

Advantages and Disadvantages of the Spectrum-Segmentation System

The most appealing feature of the spectrum-segmentation system is its simplicity. The system is extremely stable and its calibration can be matched to essentially any single-valued function relating formant frequency and output voltage. The system exhibits no "initial sampling error" as was encountered in the spectrum-

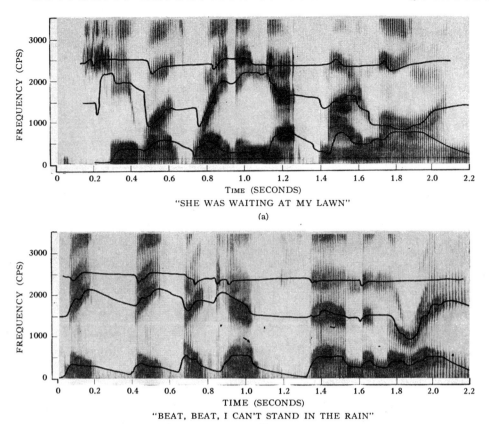

FIG. 6. Comparison of the outputs of the spectrum-segmentation formant extractor with the sound spectrograms for two conversational utterances. [Figure 6(a), speaker: J. F.; Fig. 6(b), speaker: J. M.]

sampling system. The time resolution is approximately the same as the spectrum-sampling system, but it can be increased by simply increasing the enabling-disabling frequency of the thyratron selectors. Selections of $F1$, $F2$, and $F3$ are made simultaneously and not in time sequence. The likelihood of selection of spurious formants is much less than in the spectrum-sampling system since the selection is made on the basis of spectral amplitude and not on the basis of the frequency derivative of the spectrum.

The chief disadvantage of the spectrum-segmentation system arises from the constraints imposed upon the frequency ranges of the formants. Since very little overlap exists between the frequency ranges of $F1$ and $F2$ for male voices the $F1$ range is restricted negligibly. The restriction of the upper end of the range of $F2$ and the lower end of the range of $F3$, however, is not negligible for extreme front vowels and central retroflex vowels, respectively. The limited data in Fig. 6 suggest that the error in formant detection due to restriction of the frequency ranges is generally small and relatively inconsequential. This indication, however, can be quantified only by detailed evaluation of the system with "controlled" speech material.

A scheme has been devised to partially overcome the difficulty arising from the overlap of the ranges for $F2$

and $F3$, but it has not yet been incorporated into the apparatus. The basic idea is to automatically adjust the "boundary" between the ranges of $F2$ and $F3$ according to the frequency of $F2$. First, sufficient range is allowed for $F2$ by curtailing the lower end of the $F3$ range. Then, $F1$ and $F2$ are selected synchronously, while $F3$ is selected 1/60 of a second later, during the disabling time of the $F1$ and $F2$ selectors. If $F2$ is found to be low the lower end of the $F3$ range is extended by automatically switching several of the higher $F2$ channels into the $F3$ group. If $F2$ is found to be high the lower end of the $F3$ range is maintained in its restricted condition.

IV. DISCUSSION

The qualitative data shown in Figs. 3 and 6 on the typical operation of the two formant extractors indicate that both devices meet the design objectives to a reasonable degree. A comparison of the data, however, suggests that the spectrum-segmentation system is generally more accurate and reliable than the spectrum-sampling system. A detailed evaluation of the two systems has been made, and the procedure and technique for the evaluation and the results of the evaluation are topics of a companion paper.[15] The results of the evaluation substantiate, in general, the foregoing indications of the relative merits of the two systems.

As mentioned previously a formant-extracting device constitutes an important component of a speech compression system based upon formant-coding principles. The spectrum-segmentation formant extractor discussed above is presently being used in the analyzing apparatus for such a band-width compression system.[16] The formant extractor and allied analyzing equipment are arranged to transmit continuous formant and vocal excitation data to a terminal analog type of speech synthesizer.[11] The control information transmitted specifies the frequencies of the first three formants, the amplitude of voicing excitation, the amplitude of fricative excitation and the fundamental vocal frequency. Intelligible vowel sounds can be transmitted over this preliminary system in a total transmission band width of approximately 30 cps. The intelligibility of connected speech transmitted over the presently existing system is rather low and does not yet compare favorably with the conventional telephone channel. It is expected, however, that the perfection of an additional channel for the transmission of consonant data may result in an acceptable speech transmission system requiring a total band width of the order of 50 cps.

In conclusion, one other interesting application of the same formant extractor deserves mention. The extractor has been used to provide a visual display of $F1$ vs $F2$ on the screen of an oscilloscope. By placing a mask corresponding to the "vowel triangle" (on the $F1$–$F2$ plane) on the screen of the oscilloscope, one is able to identify certain vowels and sequences of vowels from the visual cues alone. Such an arrangement might provide a useful tool for clinical speech work in that it appears to constitute a transformation which permits replacement of the normal aural feedback in man with an equivalent visual feedback, at least for vowel sounds.

V. ACKNOWLEDGMENTS

The author wishes to thank his associates in the Speech Group of the Acoustics Laboratory of the Massachusetts Institute of Technology for their invaluable assistance, suggestions, and criticisms.

Methods of Measuring Vowel Formant Bandwidths

H. K. Dunn

Bell Telephone Laboratories, Inc., Murray Hill, New Jersey

(Received September 12, 1961)

The damping constants of vowel formants, as expressed in the half-power bandwidths, have been studied from the reports of several investigators. The accuracies of methods of measurement used have been estimated through application of the same methods to an electrical analog of the vocal tract. Two new sets of measurements are presented, one on spectrograms of real speech, the other making use of an artificial larynx, applied to real subjects. It is concluded that, while wide individual variations occur, the average bandwidths for male voices probably lie in the lower range of those which have been reported.

INTRODUCTION

THE human vocal tract has long been recognized as a resonant system, and efforts have been made to measure the resonant frequencies and the damping constants associated with them. One form of expressing the damping is by means of the half-power bandwidths, that is, the widths of the resonant peaks, in cycles per second, at approximately three decibels below the peaks. This is the quantity which will be discussed in this paper. Where results of others have been expressed in a different form, they are reduced here to the bandwidths. Some theoretical considerations and mathematical relationships are discussed briefly in the Appendix.

While the formant frequencies associated with the different vowels are quite well known, and can be measured with considerable accuracy in any given case, it has been found much more difficult to make accurate measurements of bandwidth. The Fourier analysis of a vowel sound yields a set of harmonics spaced at frequency intervals equal to the fundamental frequency, and even with a male fundamental of 100 cps or somewhat lower, the harmonics are too far apart to define accurately the shape of the formant envelope. The situation is worse for a woman's voice, and most investigators have confined their attention to male voices. In addition to the spacing difficulty, the spectrum of the glottal sound source, which forms the input for the natural vowel, is not known precisely enough to permit determination of the tract characteristics from the output spectrum alone.

The first mention of a specific damping constant for a natural vowel, as far as the author is aware, was by Fletcher[1] in 1929. He gave 500 as a "typical" value for the damping (in nepers per second) of the first formant of /ɑ/. The corresponding bandwidth is 159 cps. It is interesting to note that in 1922 Stewart,[2] making synthetic vowels by means of electrical resonators, used bandwidths as low as 16 cps for the first formants of /u/, /ε/, and /i/, and as high as 250 cps for the first and second formants of /æ/. He did not find these values critical, however, for the recognition of the vowels.

Average bandwidths found in seven more recent investigations are given in Table I, plus two new sets of measurements to be described later. In all cases there were considerable variations in individual results, and only average values are given for comparison. Some notion of their worth as averages may be obtained from the numbers of voices and vowels used. No claim is made for completeness in the table, but the sets of measurements included will illustrate the methods that have been used.

ANALYSES OF OSCILLOGRAMS

The first four sets of measurements, at the top of Table I, came from Fourier analysis by measurements on enlarged curves of single periods, in oscillograms of the vowel waves. Those of Steinberg[3] are for a single male voice speaking the sentence "Joe took Father's shoe bench out." Enough periods were analyzed (seven to ten for each vowel) that the variation of damping throughout the course of each vowel could be shown. The labor involved in such an analysis of one short sentence is considerable, since each period analyzed requires 2–3 hr. The averages shown in Table I were made by the author, from central values chosen from each of the seven vowels. No values for the third formant were given by Steinberg. As compared with

TABLE I. Average half-power bandwidths of three vowel formants (cps).

	Year	Number of Voices	Vowels	First formant	Second formant	Third formant
Steinberg[3]	1934	1	7	83	118	...
Lewis[4]	1936	1	5	39	51	80
Lewis and Tuthill[5]	1940	6	2	45	50	93
Tarnóczy[6]	1943	?	4 to 9	110	190	260
Bogert[7]	1953	33	10	130	150	185
van den Berg[15]	1955	1	11	54	66	89
House and Stevens[16]	1958	3	8	54	65	70
New spectrogram measurements	1961	20	10	50	64	115
30 pps measurements	1961	2	12	47	75	106

[1] H. Fletcher, *Speech and Hearing* (D. Van Nostrand Company, Inc., Princeton, New Jersey, 1929, 1953), p. 50.

[2] J. Q. Stewart, "An electrical analogue of the vocal organs," Nature **110**, 311–312 (1922).

[3] J. C. Steinberg, "Application of sound measuring instruments to the study of phonetic problems," J. Acoust. Soc. Am. **6**, 16–24 (1934).

Reprinted with permission from *J. Acoust. Soc. Am.*, vol. 33, pp. 1737–1746, Dec. 1961.

the Lewis results, those of Steinberg are probably subject to greater errors arising from the wide harmonic spacing.

Lewis[4] also used single periods of oscillograms, analyzed in his case by an Henrici analyzer to 40 harmonics. His vowels were sung, and by analyzing several periods in a vibrato cycle he could obtain several sets of harmonics for the same vowel, with slightly different fundamental frequencies. Thus the formant envelope was much better defined than it would be with a single pitch for the vowel. Only one voice and five vowels, /i, ɛ, ɑ, o, u/, are included in the average. Lewis and Tuthill[5] used the same technique, extending the measurements for two of the vowels, /ɑ, o/, to six voices each. The use of vibrato undoubtedly gave increased accuracy for these samples and for the singing type of vowel production. Conceivably, the damping of spoken vowels could be different. It was necessary for Lewis and Tuthill to assume a falling off of source harmonics at a 9-db per octave rate, in order to get an approximate fit to a resonance curve, in the lower formants. Even then some of the harmonics do not fit the curve well, perhaps due to irregularities in the source spectrum.

It is not clear how many voices Tarnóczy[6] used for each of his vowels. He mentions the use of seven male and seven female voices, but it is uncertain whether any of the female voices are included in the published results. Average results for one of his vowels came from only six examples, one or two of which were omitted in the result for each of the three formants. Makeup of the other vowel averages is not specified. The number of vowels used is also variable, nine being included in the first formant average, four in the second, and six in the third.

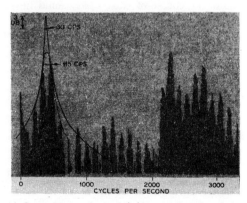

Fig. 1. Spectrogram of vowel /e/ by a male voice. An envelope drawn by eye over the harmonics of a formant may indicate a higher bandwidth than one which also follows the law for a simple resonance.

The bandwidths given by Tarnóczy are mostly the highest found by any observer. This may arise partly from his vowels having been sung "stepwise" in pitch, in order to fill in the formant envelopes. He found it necessary to adjust amplitudes of harmonics by the integral of the whole curve, in order to fit harmonics from the different pitches into the same envelopes. Even so, any variations between utterances would tend to widen the formants. One would have more confidence in the vibrato technique of Lewis for keeping the frequency and width of the formant constant as well as the amplitude. One notices also that Tarnóczy did not find the second formant of /u/, /o/, and /ɑ/. Most observers do find two close but distinct low formants in these vowels. Tarnóczy apparently has included harmonics of both formants in a single assumed resonance, which would then appear wider than the true formants. His failure to separate these formants also casts doubt on the general accuracy of his analyses.

ANALYSES OF SOUND SPECTROGRAMS

Bogert's Measurements

A more rapid method of collecting data on bandwidths was introduced by Bogert.[7] He made use of the type of analysis obtained from the sound spectrograph,[8] and more particularly from the sectioner[9] which forms a part of this instrument. The spectrum at any point of time in a recorded speech sample can be obtained in a few minutes, as compared with hours by the methods discussed above. It will not, however, correspond to a single fundamental period as the previous analyses do, because of the electric filtering used. With a nominal 45- to 50-cps filter, the spectrum is integrated over two or more fundamental periods of a man's voice.

Bogert's vowel samples were taken from those collected earlier by Peterson and Barney,[10] each of 10 vowels being spoken in a word beginning with /h/ and ending with /d/. Bogert chose 100 of these recorded vowels, spoken by 33 different male voices. Thus each of the 10 vowels appears 10 times in the average, but each speaker only about three times. On the spectrograms from these samples he drew envelopes by eye over the harmonics of the formants, and measured widths 3 db below the peaks.

Figure 1 illustrates a probable source of error in Bogert's measurements, arising mainly from the wide spacing of harmonics. This is the spectrogram of an /e/, spoken by a male voice at a fundamental frequency of 130 cps. A curve drawn by eye over the first formant might look like the dashed curve, which has a bandwidth

[4] D. Lewis, "Vocal resonance," J. Acoust. Soc. Am. **8**, 91–99 (1936).

[5] D. Lewis and C. Tuthill, "Resonant frequencies and damping constants of resonators involved in the production of sustained vowels 'O' and 'Ah'," J. Acoust. Soc. Am. **11**, 451–456 (1940).

[6] T. v. Tarnóczy, "Resonanzdaten der Vokalresonatoren," Akust. Z. **8**, 22–31 (1943).

[7] B. P. Bogert, "On the band width of vowel formants," J. Acoust. Soc. Am. **25**, 791–792 (1953).

[8] W. Koenig, H. K. Dunn, and L. Y. Lacy, "The sound spectrograph," J. Acoust. Soc. Am. **18**, 19–49 (1946).

[9] L. G. Kersta, "Amplitude cross-section representation with the sound spectrograph," J. Acoust. Soc. Am. **20**, 796–801 (1948).

[10] G. E. Peterson and H. L. Barney, "Control methods used in a study of the vowels," J. Acoust. Soc. Am. **24**, 175–184 (1952).

of 115 cps. This could have been obtained by Bogert's method. The solid curve passes through most of the same harmonics, but at the same time obeys the law for a simple resonance. It is only 30 cps wide.

New Spectrogram Measurements

An attempt has been made to remeasure the spectrograms with greater attention to the shape of the envelope curves while retaining the advantage of relatively rapid collection of data. For this purpose a number of true resonance curves of different widths were calculated according to Eq. (7) (Appendix), and carefully inscribed on a sheet of transparent acetate, in the amplitude and frequency scales of the spectrograms. By placing this sheet over the spectrogram, the curve which fits each formant best can be found. The actual bandwidths used were 30 to 100 cps in steps of 10, 100 to 200 in steps of 20, one curve for 240 cps, and one for 300 cps.

The vowel samples used were taken from the same Peterson and Barney archives which Bogert had used.

TABLE II. Bandwidths of formants (cps) by curve-fitting on spectrogram sections. From 40 examples of each vowel.

Vowels	First formant Av Extremes			Second formant Av Extremes			Third formant Av Extremes		
i	38	30	80	66	30	120	171	60	300
ɪ	42	30	100	71	40	120	142	60	300
ɛ	42	30	120	72	30	140	126	50	300
æ	65	30	140	90	40	200	156	50	300
ɑ	60	30	160	50	30	80	102	40	300
ɔ	47	30	120	50	30	200	98	40	240
u	50	30	120	58	30	200	107	50	200
ʊ	51	30	100	61	30	140	90	40	200
ʌ	56	30	140	63	30	140	102	50	300
ɜ	46	30	80	59	30	120	58	40	120
Av	49.7			64.0			115.2		

Instead of the latter's 100, 400 samples were measured, consisting of 10 vowels spoken twice each by 20 male voices. The average results are given in the "New spectrogram measurements" of Table I. They are much smaller than Bogert's averages.

Results are given in greater detail in Table II, where the average bandwidths for each vowel are given, along with the extremes of the individual measurements.

Formant frequencies were also measured, and averaged for each vowel, and the vowel bandwidths are plotted against these frequencies in Fig. 2. Points are labeled with the symbols of the vowels. A trend of the variation is suggested by the dashed straight lines, one for each formant. These could easily be welded into a continuous curve through the first and second formants, but the change in slope is sharp in passing to the third formant. If the individual measurements were plotted, the spread of points would be so great that the suggested trend would be much more difficult to see.

In Fig. 3 the same data are plotted in terms of the formant Q, found by dividing formant frequency by

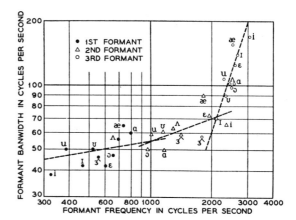

FIG. 2. Bandwidths by fitted curves on spectrograms. When the averages from 20 male voices on each vowel are plotted against the average formant frequencies, trends are suggested.

bandwidth. There is a continuous rise in average Q with frequency through the first and second formants, but a sharp fall through the third.

There are a number of sources of error in the new spectrogram measurements. Along with other analyses of natural vowels, they suffer from wide harmonic spacing, from the effects of other formants, and from the unknown input spectrum. For example, the low amplitudes of the fifth and sixth harmonics of Fig. 1 may well be due to an irregularity of the source spectrum.[11] The measurements also suffer (along with Bogert's) from the imperfections of the sound spectrograph.[8,9] These include some unevenness of the recording paper, slight variations in contact resistance in the switching operations, and a tendency of the circuits to overload and produce spurious harmonics unless great care is taken in the signal levels used. It might also be argued that bandwidths of the order of 30 to 40 cps could not be measured after passing through the

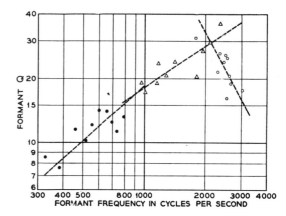

FIG. 3. The data of Fig. 2 are plotted in terms of Q instead of bandwidth.

[11] R. L. Miller, "Nature of the vocal cord wave," J. Acoust. Soc. Am. **31**, 667–677 (1959).

spectrograph filter of about 50 cps. For widely spaced harmonics, as in natural speech, this objection does not seem to hold. The filter of the spectrograph has much sharper cutoffs than a simple resonance of this width would have, so that a weak harmonic is never overwhelmed by the skirts of a neighboring strong one. However, one must use only the peaks of the harmonic traces, in drawing an envelope.

There are also some uncertainties especially connected with the curve-fitting methods used. Equation (7) (see Appendix), used for the curve calculations, pertains to a series-resonant relation. This would be correct (as explained in the Appendix) for an input of constant amplitude and an output measured as pressure outside the lips of the speaker. It is not correct to make the curves symmetrical about the peak frequency, as was done in this experiment, and as illustrated by the solid curve of Fig. 1. On a linear frequency scale, the curve should fall off faster on the low-frequency side, not so fast on the high side. The skewness, however, is a function of frequency, being greatest at low frequencies. To include it in the curves drawn would require a whole

family of curves at each frequency, which would result in losing much of the rapid-measurement advantage.

There is another reason why the symmetrical curves may even be an advantage. The source harmonics of the human voice decrease in amplitude with increasing frequency. Fletcher,[1] Steinberg,[3] and Lewis[4] all found 9 db per octave to be a reasonable rate to assume for this falling off. Flanagan[12] finds 10 to 12 db per octave. If we assume the smallest of these rates, and further take account of a 6-db per octave rise in the response of the sound spectrograph ("high shaping" introduced to make the high formants more nearly comparable with the low), we have left at least a 3-db per octave falling off in the spectrogram input harmonics. By calculation and plotting of several assumed resonances in the lower range, it is found that a 3-db per octave drop in input, applied to an accurate series resonance curve, results in a rather close approach to the symmetrical curve used in these measurements.

The actual fit obtained with the curves is considerably dependent on the judgment of the person making the fitting. For example, it may not be easy to decide whether the 50-, 60-, or 70-cps curve fits a given formant best. The fact that in Table II the first formant of each of the 10 vowels was given a least width of 30 cps indicates lack of accuracy in measuring these low formants. The author feels, however, that it would be useless to attempt to use finer gradations of width in this area. The wide spread of extremes in Table II shows, for the most part, real differences among individual speakers. Even the same speaker sometimes showed a considerable difference between his two utterances of the same vowel.

Comparison of Methods by the EVT

The electrical vocal tract (EVT)[13,14] is a transmission-line analogue of the real tract, in which a multiplicity of formants is generated similar to those of real, non-nasal vowels. The EVT formants can be measured, not only by the methods used for real vowels, but also by a more exact method in which sine-wave inputs are used. Thus, without any assumption as to the correctness of absolute values, we have a check on the reliability of other methods of measurement.

This network was set to produce each of the ten vowels of the spectrogram measurements, and for each setting the sine-wave bandwidth was obtained. A sawtooth input of 120 cps fundamental was then applied, and spectrograms of the 10 synthetic vowels made. These spectrograms were then measured by the two methods: the author's estimate of Bogert's method, and the new curve-fitting method. The results are given in Table III.

TABLE III. Bandwidths of synthetic vowels from EVT. In cps, 3 db below peaks.

Vowel	By sine wave	From spectrogram envelopes			
		Fitted curves		Eye curves	
		Width	Error	Width	Error
First formant					
i	16	30	+14	60	+44
ɪ	31	40	+ 9	110	+79
ɛ	64	60	− 4	100	+36
æ	85	60	−25	100	+15
ɑ	91	40	−51	120	+29
ɔ	62	40	−22	120	+58
u	24	30	+ 6	100	+76
ʊ	40	30	−10	60	+20
ʌ	65	30	−35	100	+35
ɝ	38	30	− 8	70	+32
Av	51.6	39	−12.6	94	+42.4
Second formant					
i	100	80	−20	150	+50
ɪ	100	50	−50	130	+30
ɛ	80	80	00	130	+50
æ	90	60	−30	110	+20
ɑ	73	40	−33	100	+27
ɔ	46	40	− 6	100	+54
u	24	30	+ 6	100	+76
ʊ	44	30	−14	100	+56
ʌ	53	40	−13	90	+37
ɝ	52	50	− 2	100	+48
Av	66.2	50	−16.2	111	+44.8
Third formant					
i	170	180	+ 10	180	+ 10
ɪ	150	100	− 50	160	+ 10
ɛ	120	100	− 20	110	− 10
æ	90	120	+ 30	120	+ 30
ɑ	110	100	− 10	120	+ 10
ɔ	90	80	− 10	110	+ 20
u	200	100	−100	130	− 70
ʊ	110	100	− 10	300	+190
ʌ	100	120	+ 20	110	+ 10
ɝ	50	40	− 10	100	+ 50
Av	119	104	− 15	144	+ 25

[12] J. L. Flanagan, "Some properties of the glottal sound source," J. Speech and Hearing Research 1, 99–116 (1958).

[13] H. K. Dunn, "The calculation of vowel resonances and an electrical vocal tract," J. Acoust. Soc. Am. 22, 740–753 (1950).

[14] L. O. Schott, "An electrical vocal system," Bell Lab. Record 28, 549–555 (1950).

Assuming that the sine-wave bandwidths are accurate, errors in the EVT spectrogram measurements can be calculated, and these have been added to Table III. The envelopes drawn by eye are too wide in all cases except two in the third formant. Average errors are 42.4, 44.8, and 25.0 cps for the three formants. The fitted curves, on the other hand, are too narrow, except for the first formant of three vowels, the second of one, and the third formant of three. Averages are too narrow by 12.6, 16.2, and 15.0 cps.

It can probably be concluded that the Bogert bandwidths of Table I are larger than the true average widths of male vowels; also that those given under "New spectrogram measurements" are closer to the correct average values, but are probably a little too small. The large errors shown for some of the vowels in Table III, however, do not inspire confidence in the curve-fitting as a quick method of getting accurate bandwidths for a given vowel sample.

For example, the largest first formant error with the fitted curves in Table III was in /ɑ/, measured 51 cps too small. This spectrogram is illustrated in Fig. 4. The dashed curve is the resonance of 40 cps width which was selected as the best fit for the first formant. The sine-wave measurements, at 3 db below the peaks of the network response, were 91, 73, and 110 cps, at frequencies of 843, 1266, and 2818 cps. If we make the assumption that these are the bandwidths and frequencies of three separate resonances, and combine them as explained in the Appendix, with allowance also for a 6 db per octave rise which is built into the EVT output, and for the measured input spectrum, the result is the solid curve. The closeness of the fit of this curve to the harmonics is added proof that the error is present in the use of the fitted simple curve.

The solid envelope of Fig. 4 was obtained through the use of a sine-wave guide. In real vowels we do not have such a guide, and it is seen that the choice of the right simple resonance can be difficult. It should not be concluded, however, that all examples of a given vowel would be fitted with the same errors as are shown in Table III. In forty natural examples of /ɑ/, first formant widths were found from 30 to 160 cps (see Table II), which is some evidence against a systematic large error and in favor of a more nearly correct average for the vowel. If this reasoning is correct, then the trends shown in Figs. 2 and 3 can be accepted more readily.

USE OF SUBSTITUTE SOUND SOURCES

Since the unknown spectrum of the volume velocity at the glottis is the largest source of error in observation of the tract characteristics in vowel production, the replacement of the vocal cords by a source of known spectrum is an attractive possibility. The most obvious difficulties are those of applying such a source at the tract input, and ensuring that the tract is the same as for a natural vowel.

FIG. 4. Spectrogram of a synthetic /ɑ/, from the electrical vocal tract. A fitted single resonance on the first formant is in considerable bandwidth error. Curve calculated from the combination of sine-wave bandwidths is also shown.

van den Berg's Measurements

The most direct kind of measurement has been made by van den Berg.[15] His subject had had a partial laryngectomy, an operation which left an opening to the pharynx near the larynx position. A small calibrated sound source could be inserted here, and a sine-wave input swept through the frequency range as the man held his articulators in a given vowel position. Output from the lips was measured for 11 different vowels.

The measurements should be accurate. They are, of course, limited to the one subject and the question may arise whether his vowel positions were representative of those of a normal vocal tract. Although this method is not generally available, it is interesting to have this one direct measurement, which is included in Table I. It agrees particularly well with the House and Stevens results.

House and Stevens Spark Method

The substitute source used by House and Stevens[16] was a spark set off inside the mouth of a subject as he held his articulators in a given vowel position. As a result of this impulse excitation, the observer must deal with a decaying wave rather than the nearly steady state of other investigations. This also leads to a bandwidth measurement, if means are found for separating the different formants effectively [see Appendix, Eqs. (11), (6)]. The means used by House and Stevens was to record the decaying sound on tape, then play it back repeatedly into a filter of simple resonant form, tuned to the frequency of each formant in turn. The filter was always greater in bandwidth than the formant being measured, and its effect on the decay rate of the formant was held to be negligible.

There are two theoretical reasons for expecting the House and Stevens results to be somewhat on the small

[15] J. van den Berg, "Transmission of the vocal cavities," J. Acoust. Soc. Am. 27, 161–168 (1955).

[16] A. S. House and K. N. Stevens, "Estimation of formant band widths from measurements of transient response of the vocal tract," J. Speech and Hearing Research 1, 309–315 (1958).

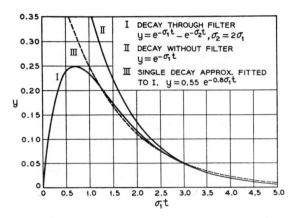

FIG. 5. Curve (III) fitted to the falling portion of a filtered decaying signal (I) indicates a lower damping constant than the actual decay of the signal (II).

side. One of these has to do with neglect of the filter constant. The solution of the differential equation which expresses the application of a decaying wave to a simple resonant filter has the form

$$i = A_1 e^{-\sigma_1 t} \sin(\omega_1 t + \varphi_1) + A_2 e^{-\sigma_2 t} \sin(\omega_2 t + \varphi_2),$$

where i is current in the filter, σ_1 and ω_1 are constants of the decaying input, and σ_2 and ω_2 are constants of the filter. A_1, A_2, φ_1, and φ_2 are complicated functions of the four constants.

Under the House and Stevens conditions, some assumptions can be made which greatly simplify this equation. Since the filter was tuned to the formant frequency, ω_2 is the same as ω_1. Then σ_2 was always greater than σ_1, and almost certainly ω_1 was considerably greater than either σ_2 or σ_1. With these assumptions the filter current equation reduces to

$$i = A(e^{-\sigma_1 t} - e^{-\sigma_2 t})\cos\omega_1 t.$$

If σ_2 is enough greater than σ_1, $e^{-\sigma_2 t}$ will become negligible while σ_1 is still measurable in the decaying wave, and apparently House and Stevens made this assump-

tion. However, σ_2 is limited to a size which will still permit suppression of the other formants of the vowel.

In Fig. 5 an assumed case is shown in which σ_2 is twice σ_1. Envelopes only of the decay are plotted. Curve II applies to the input alone, having the desired constant σ_1. Curve I, however, is actually observed. In fitting exponential curves to the decay portion of curve I it is not likely that curve II would be chosen, but more likely that a curve like III would be selected. This curve has a decay constant (and therefore a bandwidth) 20% too small. Of course this error could be avoided by inclusion of the known filter constant in the trial curves. This increases the labor of a measurement.

Another source of difference between the House and Stevens results and the conditions during actual speech comes from the application of the spark in the mouth rather than in the pharynx. This does not change the frequencies of resonance appreciably, but it does introduce antiresonances which usually have the effect of narrowing the resonances near them.

Figure 6 shows the steady state response of the electrical vocal tract, set for the vowel /o/, with both throat and mouth inputs. The 3 db widths of both first and second formants are decreased appreciably by the mouth application. In this case there is also a large increase in amplitude of the third formant, which would make it easier to separate out for decay measurement, but would increase the difficulty of measuring the second formant.

It is not possible to specify the size of errors from the above sources, in the House and Stevens measurements. We can examine, however, what errors arise in a few cases with the electrical vocal tract. The spark excitation was simulated with a square pulse 100 to 150 μsec long, so that the first zero in its spectrum of harmonics was 6700 to 10 000 cps, well above our range of measurement. This pulse could be applied to either the throat or the mouth of the analog circuit. A filter of simple resonant structure, adjustable in frequency and damping, was connected to the output of the EVT and to an oscilloscope.

To make the trace persistent enough to be photographed, the pulse was repeated 10 times per second.

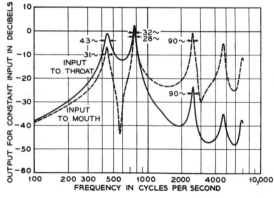

FIG. 6. Steady state measurements of EVT /o/ show decreased bandwidths of first and second formants when the input is applied to the mouth instead of the throat.

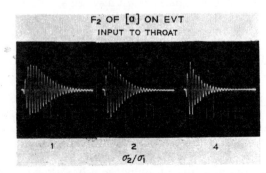

FIG. 7. Decay of second formant of a synthetic /a/ from EVT. The shape of the envelope depends upon the ratio of filter and formant decay constants.

246

At this rate, practically complete decay was realized between pulses, in all cases.

Examples of the decay of artificial vowel formants are shown in Figs. 7 and 8. Figure 7 shows the effect of changing the filter constant on the second formant of an /ɑ/. The damping constants of filter and formant are represented by σ_2 and σ_1, and their ratio is shown. When they are equal, the effect of the filter is too great, as shown by the excessive rounding. At a ratio of 2, the decay is measurable, but at 4 the decay is too irregular for accurate measurement due to insufficient suppression of the first formant.

Figure 8 is for the third formant of /ɑ/, at two constant ratios and with application of input to both throat and mouth. Here the mouth application gives a much smoother decay picture because of the increased amplitude of the third formant (see Fig. 6). The ratio of 4 is better here for accurate damping-rate measurement.

With the EVT there was no difficulty connected with applying the source, as there must have been in the real vowels when the mouth cavity was small. In many cases, however, no good filter adjustment could be found which would produce measurable decay pictures.

In Table IV some results are given. Results from "fitted single decay" curves are shown, and also from "fitted double decay," in which the known filter constant is taken into account. In all cases the latter result was in closer agreement with the sine-wave widths, which are shown for comparison. The first two pairs of measurements show better accuracy of the "single" results when a higher ratio of filter-to-formant decay constants is used. The throat and mouth input comparisons of the last three pairs show decreased widths for mouth input in two of the three cases. The sine-wave widths are also smaller for mouth input, but it is the throat-input case that should be taken for the closest relation with real vowels. Thus, the mouth result for the second formant of /ɑ/, 46 cps by the single decay curve, would have to be compared with 94 cps. Even taking account of the filter constant brings it only to 54. Most errors, however, are less than these.

TABLE IV. Bandwidths of electrical vocal tract from filtered decay curves.

Vowel	Formant	Input point	σ_2/σ_1	Fitted single decay	Fitted double decay	By sine wave
i	2	Throat	2	99 cps	118	120
i	2	Throat	4	116	118	120
ɑ	3	Mouth	2	93	105	120
ɑ	3	Mouth	4	103	108	120
i	1	Throat	4	24	25	26
i	1	Mouth	4	25	26	27
ʌ	1	Throat	4	62	67	74
ʌ	1	Mouth	4	59	60	63
ɑ	2	Throat	2	74	83	94
ɑ	2	Mouth	2	46	54	54

The values quoted in Table I from House and Stevens are for three male subjects in the "closed glottis" condition. This is probably closer to the conditions during speech than the open glottis would be. Their eight vowels do not cover the field. In particular, the omission of /i/ probably lowers the average for the third formant.

Artificial Larynx Source

As still another use of a substitute for the vocal cords, a few measurements have been made in which a pulse generator operating at thirty pulses per second was connected to the transducer of an electronic artificial larynx.[17] This transducer is a modified telephone receiver, which, when held with its diaphragm against the outside of the throat, produces a sound source inside the pharynx. The use of the low-frequency input provided a spectrum of harmonics only 30 cps apart, thus defining the peak of a resonance much more accurately than the natural voice frequencies do.

A different method of analysis was used, also, rather than the standard spectrogram or the Fourier analysis of an oscillogram. The subject was asked to hold a vowel constant for three or four seconds, while a tape record was made. Since he could hear the vowel being produced, constancy was not too difficult in most cases. The playback of the tape, in a closed loop, was then analyzed for each harmonic by means of a wave analyzer with a filter 4 cps wide.

The pulse length was 150 μsec, and the input spectrum to the transducer almost flat to 5000 cps. Unfortunately, however, the spectrum of sound produced inside the throat was not accurately known. From the appearance of the output analysis, the input spectrum had considerable irregularity. Figure 9 shows such an analysis for the vowel /i/ from a male subject. The

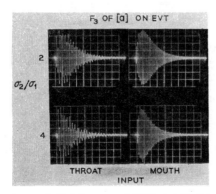

FIG. 8. Decay of third formant of EVT /ɑ/. In this case, the application of the input in the mouth gives a more regular filtered decay.

[17] H. L. Barney, F. E. Haworth, and H. K. Dunn, "An experimental transistorized artificial larynx," Bell System Tech. J. 38, 1337–1356 (1959).

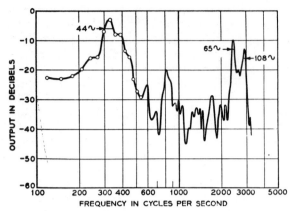

FIG. 9. Analysis, by a four-cps filter, of a male /i/ produced by an artificial larynx at thirty pulses per second.

measured 30 cps points are shown through the first formant, but omitted from the upper frequencies because of crowding on this logarithmic scale. The upper formant bandwidths were measured, however, by plotting on a more extended scale.

The irregularity in the curve of Fig. 9 is apparent. What we would like to know is, what degree of accuracy remains in the bandwidths 3 db below the peaks? Some notion of the answer may be obtained from an experiment with the electrical vocal tract. The artificial larynx, with its 30-pps input, was pressed against a sheet of porous rubber $\frac{3}{16}$ in. thick. A microphone picked up the sound about an inch from the back surface of the rubber, and it was recorded. The rubber sheet was intended to represent the wall of the throat, and while the spectrum of sound transmitted through it would not be the same as that produced in the throat, it is similarly irregular. This recorded tape was used to supply an input to the EVT.

The result is shown in Table V, with the EVT set to produce the vowel /ʌ/. The first column gives the sine-wave measurement, while the second used the 4-cps analysis, with the input to the EVT direct from the pulse generator. The closeness of these two columns is a check on the analyzing procedure. Bandwidths with the irregular input, in the last column, are 9 cps too wide in the first formant, 7 cps too small in the second and third. If similar accuracy were obtained with real tracts, the result would not be too unsatisfactory, but of course this cannot be guaranteed.

With this uncertainty, results are presented in the bottom line of Table I for 12 vowels each on two male subjects, both with closed glottis. The results are well below the Bogert figures; fairly close to van den Berg and House and Stevens in the first formant, a little higher in the second and third; and they are comparable with the new spectrogram measurements.

DISCUSSION

Natural vowels are usually studied by observing the pressure wave outside the lips of the speaker, and analyzing for the spectrum of this wave. Assuming that a correct envelope can be drawn, how nearly will bandwidths measured 3 db below the peaks of this curve represent the actual constants of the individual resonances of the vocal tract?

It is explained in the Appendix, and illustrated in Fig. 10, how separate resonances are combined. A vowel spectrum envelope is similar to the dashed curve of Fig. 10, except that in the real case the input spectrum is not flat.

It is also shown in the Appendix that the upward slope of 6 db per octave introduced by radiation, applied to a single resonance of the type found in vowels, rarely changes the bandwidth by as much as 1%. (A peak already distorted by the effects of neighboring formants may have its bandwidth changed more than this amount, by the 6 db per octave shift.) A steady falling off of glottal harmonics with increasing frequency works in the opposite direction, and if it were the 9 db or more per octave which has been found probable, it would more than counteract the radiation rise, and leave little net change in the bandwidth.

The effects of combinations of formants on the individual bandwidths may be appreciable. As may be seen from the curves of Fig. 10, it is the lower amplitudes of a single resonance that are affected most by the presence of the other resonances. Within 3 db of the peak, the effect is much less, but there may still be an effect, especially where a neighboring formant is close in frequency. In the calculated case of the /ɔ/ of Fig. 10, the first three individual resonances have bandwidths of 57, 57, and 79 cps ($Q=11$, 17, 32), while the combined curve gives 3-db widths of 61, 59, and 81 cps. The largest of these three changes is about 7%, and probably larger shifts are possible.

However, the greatest uncertainty remaining, in the direct measurement of bandwidths from natural vowel spectra, lies in the irregularities of the spectrum of the glottal source (arising from "zeros," in the complex mathematical sense). Given the frequency and damping of the resonators, a combined transfer impedance can be calculated, as was done in Fig. 10. Given also the frequency and damping constants of the zeros of an input spectrum, these can be included in the calculation, giving an output spectrum. One can imagine trying many sets·of such constants until a match is obtained for any given vowel spectrum.

TABLE V. Bandwidths of EVT /ʌ/, with 30 pps input, and 4 cps output analysis.

Formant	By sine wave	By 30 pps direct	By 30 pps through rubber sheet
1	61 cps	62	70
2	50	50	43
3	92	90	85

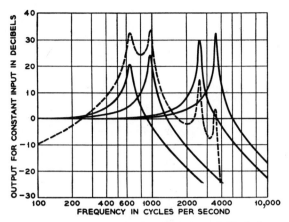

FIG. 10. Four simple parallel resonances, and (dashed curve) their combination in tandem plus a six db per octave upward shift.

An approach to such a method has already been made by Mathews, Miller, and David,[18] a digital computer being used for making the many calculations. They succeeded in following most of the minor fluctuations of the real vowel spectra, as well as the major peaks, but in the matter of formant bandwidths it is probable that appreciable errors arise from the remaining discrepancies at the harmonic points. In fact, it may be concluded that their trial bandwidths are on the large side, since curves through the synthetic points, in many of the peaks of the four examples shown, are flatter than those through the real points.

It is probable that this or some other computer method can be perfected to the point where accurate bandwidths can be obtained from real vowel examples. Then, if costs are not prohibitive, a survey covering a large number of voices and conditions might be made. It seems likely that such a survey will disclose considerable differences among individuals, and perhaps in the same individual with different types of speaking or singing.

Certainly none of the sets of results presented in Table I can be taken as an accurate average of the formant bandwidths. The various tests are not accurate enough in the individual measurement or they do not cover enough voices, or both. Perhaps the best that can be said now is that the real averages for male voices probably tend toward the lower end of the range shown in Table I.

Aside from the desire to know, probably the best present reason for measuring bandwidths is to be able to supply synthetic vowels with the correct values. It has been known at least from the time of Stewart[2] that bandwidth values are not critical for the recognition of synthetic vowels. Somewhat more exact values are probably necessary for greatest naturalness. In this

connection House[19] has conducted preference tests for synthetic vowels given different sets of formant widths. Although these showed greatest listener preference when the first-second-third widths were in the 40-50-60- to 70-85-100-cps region, he actually had some preference votes for his widest combination, 220-260-300. Perhaps this would be as good a way as any to determine the best bandwidths, except that many more combinations than the seven used by House would have to be tried in order to establish the best value for each formant.

It will also have to be decided whether, for best synthetic vowels, a single set of bandwidths or perhaps a single set of dissipative elements will suffice; or whether changes from vowel to vowel must be used. It is questionable whether such refinements will be found necessary.

APPENDIX

The transmission characteristic of the human vocal tract for nonnasal vowels, as a function of frequency, has been shown to be like that of several independent resonators so arranged that the signal must pass from one to the next, in tandem.[13,20] If we designate by i_0 and i_1 the steady state amplitudes of input and output volume velocities of the first of these resonators, in response to a radian frequency ω, their ratio may be expressed reasonably well as

$$\frac{i_1}{i_0} = \frac{\omega_1^2}{[(\omega_1^2 - \omega^2)^2 + 4\sigma_1^2\omega^2]^{\frac{1}{2}}}, \qquad (1)$$

where ω_1 is a resonant radian frequency, and σ_1 a damping constant.

An electrical analog of this first resonator is the circuit of Fig. 11 (a), with ω_1 defined as $(1/LC)^{\frac{1}{2}}$ and σ_1 as $R/2L$. This may be called a low-pass resonance, since at low frequencies the ratio i_1/i_0 approaches the constant value 1. As frequency increases, i_1/i_0 reaches a peak at

$$\omega_p = (\omega_1^2 - 2\sigma_1^2)^{\frac{1}{2}}. \qquad (2)$$

For a moderately high Q, $2\sigma_1^2$ is small compared with ω_1^2, and the peak frequency is close to ω_1 [see Eq. (9)]. As frequency increases above ω_1, i_1/i_0 approaches a falloff rate of 12 db per octave. In the analog circuit, a voltage proportional to i_1 may be passed on by taking it across R.

FIG. 11. A simple electrical resonator in (a) a parallel connection and (b) a series connection.

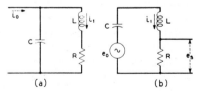

[18] M. V. Mathews, J. E. Miller, and E. E. David, Jr., "Pitch synchronous analysis of voiced sounds," J. Acoust. Soc. Am. 33, 179–186 (1961).

[19] A. S. House, "Formant band widths and vowel preference," J. Speech and Hearing Research 3, 3–8 (1960).
[20] Gunnar Fant, *Acoustic Theory of Speech Production* (Mouton & Company, 's-Gravenhage, The Hague, Netherlands, 1960).

In the vocal tract characteristic there are a large number of such resonances, each having a transfer impedance like Eq. (1), but with different constants. The complete transmission characteristic, i.e., the ratio of volume velocity amplitude at the lips to that at the glottis, is the product of the transfer impedances of all the individual resonances.

If, instead of volume velocity at the lips we wish to deal with pressure measured outside the lips, a factor for the radiation characteristic must be included. Over the frequency range important for vowels the radiation is approximately proportional to frequency, i.e., a 6-db increase in amplitude for each octave increase in frequency.

In Fig. 10 four separate resonances are shown, each plotted according to Eq. (1), with different sets of constants. These four sounded together would be heard as the vowel /ɔ/. Also in Fig. 10 is a combined curve found by multiplying together the four transfer impedances and applying the 6 db per octave radiation characteristic. If more resonances were present, they would each have an effect on the combined curve, but as their resonant frequencies become higher and higher, their effects in a limited range at the low frequency end become more and more negligible.

The radiation characteristic can be applied only once to the full combination of resonances. Near each peak, however, in a range over which the effects of the other resonances are almost constant, the shape of the peak will be changed by the 6 db per octave shift almost as if that resonance were standing alone.

Supposing a single resonance were involved, the amplitude ratio of output pressure to input volume velocity can be found from Eq. (1) by introducing a factor ω in the numerator. If we also apply a constant factor $2\sigma_1/\omega_1^2$ the shape of the curve will not be changed.

$$\frac{p}{i_0} = \frac{2\sigma_1\omega}{[(\omega_1^2-\omega^2)^2+4\sigma_1^2\omega^2]^{\frac{1}{2}}}. \tag{3}$$

Examination of the series circuit, Fig. 11(b), for the amplitude ratio of e_s to a series input voltage e_0, leads to the same Eq. (3), ω_1 and σ_1 being defined as with Fig. 11(a). This is the justification for trying to fit a formant envelope to a series resonance curve, *insofar as the formant stands alone*, and attributing the departure from such a curve to the spectrum of the glottal input.

The peak of (3) comes at exactly ω_1, and its value is 1. As the frequency is changed in either direction from ω_1, the curve of (3) approaches a falling slope of 6 db per octave. If we let r be the ratio of the peak amplitude to that at any other point, then (3) may be set equal to $1/r$. Solving then for ω,

$$\omega = [\omega_1^2+(r^2-1)\sigma_1^2]^{\frac{1}{2}}\pm\sigma_1(r^2-1)^{\frac{1}{2}}. \tag{4}$$

For any value of r there are two values of ω, both given by (4). The difference between them, divided by 2π to reduce to cycles per second, may be called the bandwidth β.

$$\beta = (\sigma_1/\pi)(r^2-1)^{\frac{1}{2}}. \tag{5}$$

Designate by B the bandwidth at the half-power point, i.e., very nearly 3 db below the peak. At this point, $r^2=2$, and (5) becomes

$$B=\sigma_1/\pi. \tag{6}$$

Equation (5) may then be written

$$\beta = B(r^2-1)^{\frac{1}{2}}. \tag{7}$$

Equations (3) to (7) apply to the series type of resonance, illustrated in Fig. 11(b). The peak frequency and bandwidth of the parallel circuit of Fig. 11(a) can be equated to those of the series circuit, times a factor involving the Q of the resonance. Q may be defined as the quotient of resonant frequency divided by half-power bandwidth, or in terms of ω_1 and σ_1,

$$Q=\omega_1/2\sigma_1. \tag{8}$$

Let this definition (8) apply to both types of circuit, then for the parallel circuit (2) becomes

$$\omega_p=\omega_1[1-(1/2Q^2)]^{\frac{1}{2}}.$$

Or, for moderately large values of Q, approximately,

$$\omega_p=\omega_1[1-(1/4Q^2)]. \tag{9}$$

By treating (1) as we did (3), and making approximations for a large Q, the half-power bandwidth of the parallel circuit is

$$B=(\sigma_1/\pi)[1+(1/4Q^2)]. \tag{10}$$

The Q of a vowel formant is rarely less than 5. Assuming this value, the peak frequency of the parallel circuit is 1% less than that of the series circuit, while the half-power bandwidth is 1% greater. For larger Q's the differences are smaller.

If either circuit, 11(a) or 11(b), is excited by an impulse, the instantaneous i_1 of the circuit will undergo damped oscillations, given by

$$i_1=Ke^{-\sigma_1t}\cos[(\omega_1^2-\sigma_1^2)^{\frac{1}{2}}t+\varphi], \tag{11}$$

where the amplitude K and the phase φ are dependent on the nature of the impulse. The frequency of free oscillation, $(\omega_1^2-\sigma_1^2)^{\frac{1}{2}}$, is intermediate between ω_1, the frequency of maximum response of the series circuit, and ω_p, that of the parallel circuit. The position of σ_1 in the exponential is the reason for calling this quantity a damping constant.

Pitch-Synchronous Time-Domain Estimation of Formant Frequencies and Bandwidths

Elliot N. Pinson

Bell Telephone Laboratories, Inc., Murray Hill, New Jersey
(Received 14 March 1963)

A technique for the measurement of vocal-tract formant frequencies and bandwidths during voiced speech is described. A theoretical justification for the method is presented, based on a model of the vocal tract that is linear and stationary over time intervals of the order of one pitch period (approximately 0.01 sec). In brief, the technique consists of selecting a portion of one pitch period of a speech waveform during which the glottis is closed. This finite-duration signal is approximated in a weighted-least-squares sense by a function of the form

$$\hat{f}(t) = \sum_{i=1}^{N} e^{-\pi B_i t}(a_i \cos 2\pi F_i t + c_i \sin 2\pi F_i t) + a_0,$$

where a_i, c_i, F_i, and B_i are selected to minimize the weighted-squared error between $\hat{f}(t)$ and the actual speech signal of interest, $f(t)$. B_i and F_i are estimates of the bandwidth and frequency, respectively, of the ith formant. A digital-computer program was used to perform the minimization. The program was used to determine the bandwidths and frequencies of the first four formants of the vowels /i/, /ɔ/, and /ɑ/ in the context b(vowel)t. Two male speakers produced most of the speech waveforms. The technique seems to be most reliable for the first two formants. It yields results that appear to have a smaller variance than those obtained by previously reported methods, although the variance is still substantial.

INTRODUCTION

$\mathbf{A}$CCURATE determination of the resonant frequencies of the vocal tract (i.e., formant frequencies) in various articulatory configurations is of interest both in the synthesis and in the analysis of speech. For vowel sounds, in particular, the formant frequencies (especially the first and second formants) play a dominant role in determining which vowel is produced by a speaker and which vowel is perceived by a listener.[1-4] Formant bandwidths, on the other hand, affect speech quality and, in any synthesis procedure, must be selected properly to achieve natural-sounding speech. In speech analysis, the formant bandwidths may affect the accuracy attainable by formant-frequency locating procedures.

Several methods have been used to estimate the formant frequencies of vowels. Almost all of these tech-

niques have as a common starting point the transformation of the acoustic data into spectral form. The methods used to obtain the spectrum have included use of the sound spectrograph,[5] banks of bandpass filters,[6] and pitch-synchronous Fourier analysis.[7] From the spectrum, initial coarse estimates for formant frequencies can be obtained by observing the frequencies of the principal spectral peaks. Improvements may be made by interpolation or by fitting to the observed spectrum a synthesized spectrum in which the formant frequencies are adjustable parameters.

Measurements have also been made of the bandwidths of vocal-tract resonances for vowel sounds. Again, most investigators depend upon an initial transformation of the acoustic data into spectral form. The techniques then applied to yield numerical bandwidth values are well-summarized by Dunn.[8] In general, the

[1] G. E. Peterson and H. L. Barney, J. Acoust. Soc. Am. **24**, 175 (1952).
[2] G. E. Peterson, J. Acoust. Soc. Am. **24**, 629 (1952).
[3] G. E. Peterson, Language **27**, 541 (1951).
[4] G. Fairbanks and P. Grubb, J. Speech Hearing Res. 4, 203 (1961).

[5] W. Koenig, H. K. Dunn, and L. Y. Lacy, J. Acoust. Soc. Am. **18**, 19 (1946).
[6] C. G. Bell, H. Fujisaki, J. M. Heinz, K. N. Stevens, and A. S. House, J. Acoust. Soc. Am. **33**, 1725 (1961).
[7] M. V. Mathews, J. E. Miller, and E. E. David, J. Acoust. Soc. Am. **33**, 179 (1961).
[8] H. K. Dunn, J. Acoust. Soc. Am. **33**, 1737 (1961).

Reprinted with permission from *J. Acoust. Soc. Am.*, vol. 35, pp. 1264–1273, Aug. 1963.

bandwidths were estimated by fitting resonance curves to the observed spectrum and choosing that bandwidth that minimized the error in fit. One exception to the heavily traveled spectral route is the technique described by House and Stevens,[9] in which the vocal tract was excited by a spark at the tip of a probe that was inserted into the mouth. The spark acted as an impulsive source, and the damping of the vocal tract was estimated by measuring the rate of decay of the transient that occurred. Bandpass filters were used to separate the various formants prior to measuring decay rates.

Three effects are of major importance in limiting the accuracy with which formant frequencies and bandwidths of vowels can be estimated from spectral data. These are: (1) the effect of source periodicity on the spectrum; (2) the effect of the source-spectrum envelope; and (3) the effect of time averaging over both closed- and open-glottis conditions. These effects are discussed in more detail in the following paragraphs.

Because of the periodicity of the source (i.e., the puffs of air flowing through the glottis that excite the vocal tract), the spectrum of the acoustic waveform consists roughly of lines at a fundamental (pitch) frequency and its harmonics (see Fig. 1). Little information about the spectrum between pitch harmonics is available, so the frequencies of spectral peaks must be interpolated between these lines. Bandwidth estimates are even more difficult to obtain. The dashed line in Fig. 1 is a curve that might be drawn by hand to estimate the shape of the continuous spectrum; the solid line is the standard resonance curve, selected from a set of templates of resonances having bandwidths up to 300 cps, which appears to give the best fit to the measured spectrum. The dashed curve leads to a bandwidth estimate of 115 cps, while the solid curve results in an estimated bandwidth of 30 cps. This is certainly a sizeable spread, and illustrates the effect of harmonic spacing on bandwidth estimation.

A further complication arises if the envelope of the source spectrum exhibits rapid variations with frequency. Since the measured spectrum is the product of the spectrum of the glottal source and the spectrum of the transfer function of the vocal tract, the effect of the source spectrum is to "distort" the features of interest. In particular, it is very difficult to estimate bandwidth accurately because of this interaction if the source spectrum has zeros near the resonant frequencies of the vocal tract.

Finally, consider the effect of the relatively long averaging times used in any analog-spectrum measuring device. Because of this, the output at any time depends upon both open- and closed-glottis portions of the speech waveform. This difficulty is encountered even in pitch-synchronous Fourier analysis, since the spectrum is

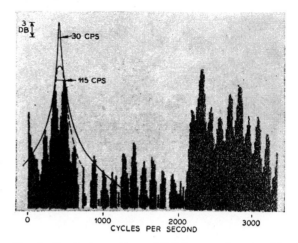

FIG. 1. Spectrogram of vowel [e] by a male voice. Fitted true-resonance curve (30 cps) and envelope drawn by eye (115 cps). [From Dunn.[8]]

computed from a complete pitch period of the acoustic waveform, including both open- and closed-glottis segments. It is well-known that vocal-tract resonances are different in the open- and closed-glottis conditions. Bandwidths, in particular, tend to be larger when the glottis is open and there is coupling to the lower vocal tract.

The remainder of this paper describes a pitch-synchronous time-domain method for determining both the frequencies and bandwidths of vowel formants. It is pitch-synchronous because it operates on individual pitch periods of the acoustic waveform to obtain its estimates. It operates in the time domain (as opposed to the frequency domain) because it operates directly on the acoustic time waveform without transforming it into spectral form before proceeding with an estimation procedure. It (hopefully) operates only on portions of the acoustic waveform produced when the glottis is closed and the lower vocal tract is decoupled from the system. The method is of particular interest for the estimation of bandwidths. Since it is only indirectly affected by the three difficulties mentioned above, its results should be more accurate than spectral-bandwidth estimates.

I. OUTLINE OF TIME-DOMAIN APPROXIMATION METHOD

The technique is based upon the acoustic theory of speech production,[10] which leads to the model of speech production shown in Fig. 2. In Fig. 2(a), the vocal tract is represented by a tube of varying cross-sectional area. The configuration at any instant of time t can be specified by an area function $A(x,t)$, where x is the distance from the glottal source to the cross section of of the vocal tract being specified. If we assume that the configuration of the vocal tract changes very little

---

[9] A. S. House and K. N. Stevens, J. Speech Hearing Res. **1**, 309 (1958).

[10] C. G. M. Fant, *Acoustic Theory of Speech Production* (Mouton and Company, The Hague, 1960).

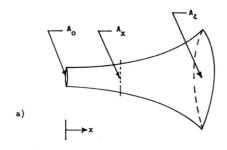

a)

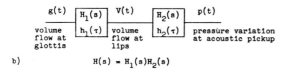

b)

$$H(s) = H_1(s)H_2(s)$$

Fig. 2. Vocal tract as represented by (a) an acoustic resonator and (b) a transfer function.

during a time interval of one pitch period, then the system can be approximated on this short-term basis by a linear, time-invariant set of equations and can be represented by the transfer functions $H_1(s)$ and $H_2(s)$, shown in Fig. 1(b). $H_1(s)$ is the transfer function relating volume flow at the glottis to volume flow at the lips. $H_2(s)$ is the transfer function between volume flow at the lips and pressure variations at an acoustic pickup (e.g., a microphone).

Figure 3 illustrates what the time waveforms $g(t)$ and $p(t)$ are during a typical sustained vowel sound. The glottal pulses are produced at the pitch frequency of the speaker. The feature of interest in the present application is the pulselike character of the glottal wave. A pitch period of duration T_p seconds can be subdivided into intervals T_c and T_0, during which the glottis is substantially closed and open, respectively. Since the model of the vocal tract shown in Fig. 2(b) is linear and time-invariant, it follows that, during any interval when the glottis is closed and the vocal tract unexcited,

the system response is completely determined by the following information: (1) the initial conditions at the beginning of the unexcited interval and (2) the system transfer function $H_1(s)H_2(s)$. If the system transfer function is of the form

$$H_1(s)H_2(s) = \prod_{i=1}^{k} \frac{N(s)}{s - s_i}, \qquad (1)$$

then the time response during the glottis-closed interval T_c is of the form

$$p(t) = \sum_{i=1}^{k} c_i e^{s_i t}, \qquad (2)$$

where $N(s)$ represents the numerator polynominal in the transform variable s, s_i the poles of the transfer function (in general, complex quantities), and c_i the complex amplitude coefficients [functions of $N(s)$, the poles of the transfer function, and initial conditions]. It should be emphasized that, if the assumptions about the vocal-tract transfer function (i.e., that it is linear and time invariant) and the glottal source [i.e., that $g(t)$ is zero over sometime interval] are valid, the frequencies present in the time response characterized by Eq. (2) are completely independent of the source. The principal poles of the transfer function are located at the resonant frequencies of the vocal tract. If such a pole is located at

$$s_i = -\sigma_i + j\omega_i, \qquad (3)$$

the bandwidth and frequency of that resonance are, respectively,

$$B_i = \sigma_i/\pi = \text{bandwidth of } i\text{th formant (cps)}; \quad (4)$$

$$F_i = \omega_i/2\pi = \text{frequency of } i\text{th formant (cps)}. \quad (5)$$

In order to obtain estimates of the formant frequencies and bandwidths, a weighted-least-squares-fitting procedure was used. A function of the form

$$f(t) = a_0 + \sum_{i=1}^{N} e^{-\pi B_i t}(a_i \cos 2\pi F_i t + b_i \sin 2\pi F_i t) \quad (6)$$

was generated. The parameters

$$a_0, a_i, b_i, B_i, F_i (i = 1, \cdots, N)$$

were adjusted to minimize the error defined by Eq. (7):

$$E = \sum_{M=1}^{K} W_M^2 (p_M - f_M)^2, \qquad (7)$$

where

$$W_M = \text{error-weighting function} \qquad (8)$$

$$p_M = p(t) \quad \text{for } t = M\Delta, \qquad (9)$$

$$f_M = f(t) \quad \text{for } t = M\Delta, \qquad (10)$$

$\Delta = \text{sampling interval} = 0.0001 \text{ sec, and } K = \text{number of}$

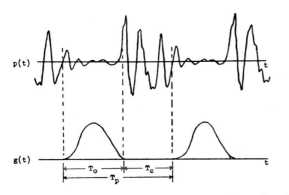

Fig. 3. Example of possible acoustic pressure waveform $p(t)$ and its associated glottal volume velocity $g(t)$.

samples over which the fit is attempted. A summation is used rather than an integral in Eq. (7) because all mathematical operations were performed in a digital computer on sampled data. Two different procedures for minimizing (7) were programmed and are described in the Appendix. The values of F_i and B_i that minimize E are the desired estimates of the formant frequencies and bandwidths.

The form of Eq. (6) warrants comment. Note that $f(t)$ includes contributions from the first N formant frequencies and a constant bias term. N was taken to be either 3 or 4 during the analysis. These choices lead to a thirteen- and a seventeen-parameter nonlinear least-squares-fitting problem, respectively. All other poles contributing to the output waveform have been neglected in order to keep the complexity of the problem to a minimum.

If the fitting procedure used an orthogonal sequence of approximating functions, the omission of additional terms would not affect the answers obtained for the principal formant bandwidths and frequencies. Unfortunately, the sequence of damped sinusoids is not orthogonal and the omitted terms are a cause of error in our estimates. Among the poles that have been omitted in Eq. (6) are the higher-order formant poles and the singularity due to radiation impedance. All poles of the 4-kc/sec low-pass filter and 120-cps high-pass filter through which the input-speech waveform was passed are also neglected. Since the contribution of these additional terms to the input time function in the frequency range of interest is small, their effect on the results should also be small.

II. RESULTS

The method described in Sec. I was used to determine formant bandwidths and frequencies for the three vowels /ɔ/, /i/, and /ɑ/. The test vocabulary consisted of two utterances by each of two speakers of the words "bought," "beet," and "bottle." Thus, a total of twelve words was analyzed. Several pitch periods from each of the words were examined in detail.

These words are a subset of a larger vocabulary that had been recorded for use in this and other speech-processing experiments. In order to obtain high-quality data, the recordings were made in an anechoic chamber, using a condenser microphone. The acoustic waveform was sampled at a 10-kc/sec rate, converted into 11-bit digital form, and recorded directly on digital tape. The analog acoustic signal was band-limited to a frequency range between 120 and 4000 cps prior to digital conversion. Thus, 60-cps pickup was largely eliminated, as were the effects of signal-frequency components above the 5-kc/sec Nyquist frequency.

The results presented below were all obtained by using the linearized-approximation technique described in the Appendix. The weighting function $W(M)$ was trapezoidal; it increased linearly from 0.1 to 1.0 over

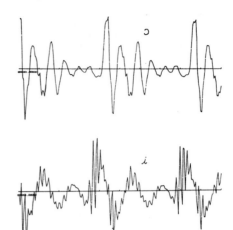

FIG. 4. Typical acoustic waveforms for the 3 vowel sounds examined.

the first ten samples and decreased linearly from 1.0 to 0.1 over the last ten samples being fitted. K, the number of samples over which the fit was accomplished, was set equal to 57. This meant the fit was over slightly more than one-half a pitch period. (It should be mentioned that, in the early stages of this investigation, values of K of 50, 55, and 60 were also used. There did not appear to be any significant difference in results when K was varied over this small range.)

Figure 4 shows samples of the waveforms that were used in this investigation. These are typical of the waveforms that occur in the central portion of the vowels ɔ, i, and ɑ. Figures 5 and 6 show the way in which it is possible to fit the input waveforms by a sum of damped sinusoids. The upper half of these two figures presents the original input data as a solid line and the approximation to the input data as a line with + marks at each of the sample points. The curves have been normalized so that the maximum amplitude on the figures has a value of 1.0. The lower half of each figure shows the weighted-error curve, i.e., the difference between the two curves in the upper half of the figure multiplied by the appropriate weighting function $W(M)$. The curves are normalized so that the maximum amplitude plotted has a magnitude equal to the number plotted below the leftmost portion of the horizontal axis. Thus, in Fig. 6, the maximum value of the weighted error is 0.08186; in other words, the error curve is plotted at about 12 times the scale of the speech waveform in this case.

Table I summarizes the results that were obtained for the three vowels studied. The numbers in this Table

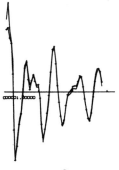

a
N = 3

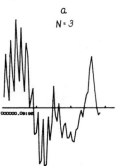

FIG. 5. Typical results of least-squares-fitting procedure for the vowel |ɑ|. *Upper graph:* Input data (solid line) and approximation achieved by using 3 formants (line with + marks). *Lower graph:* Magnified view of the weighted difference between the upper two curves.

TABLE I. First- and second-formant bandwidths; first-, second-, and third-formant frequencies (3 vowels, 2 speakers, 2 utterances per speaker).

Vowel	Speaker	Utterance	B_1	B_2	F_1	F_2	F_3
ɔ	A	1	57.	51.	626.	918.	2525.
		2	58.	34.	641.	975.	2569.
	B	1	23.	53.	600.	1008.	2263.
		2	34.	40.	590.	981.	2309.
i	A	1	74.	76.	326.	2104.	2604.
		2	63.	47.	307.	2156.	2663.
	B	1	67.	?	302.	2115.	2758.
		2	68.	53.	311.	2096.	2655.
ɑ	A	1	59.	98.	738.	1123.	2479.
		2	56.	75.	748.	1160.	2511.
	B	1	55.	69.	658.	1135.	2281.
		2	31.	67.	629.	1114.	2211.

are not averages, but are values obtained from single pitch periods taken from the central portion of the vowel sounds. Notice that there is considerable variation in the numbers presented, even between utterances by the same speaker.

There are several reasons why this might be anticipated. First, since the vowels being examined were extracted from words, rather than from sustained

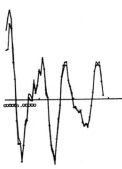

ɔ
N = 4

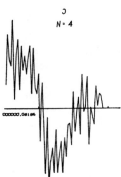

FIG. 6. Typical results of least-squares-fitting procedure for the vowel |ɔ|. *Upper graph:* Input data (solid line) and approximation achieved by using 4 formants (line with + marks). *Lower graph:* Magnified view of the weighted difference between the upper two curves.

vowels, steady-state conditions were not reached. That formant transitions are taking place is apparent from Table II. Note particularly the systematic shift in all formant frequencies. Second, there is some variation in the estimates obtained from a single pitch period if the interval (within the pitch period) over which the fit is attempted is varied. The percentage variation is much more significant in the estimates of bandwidth than it is in the frequency estimates. Curves illustrating this source of variance are shown in Figs. 7 and 8. In some of the pitch periods examined, the variation was even larger than that shown in these figures.

Pitch periods from other sources have also been analyzed. I report only on two cases that are of particular interest. The first was produced using an artificial larynx for a source. The male speaker was instructed to shape his articulators for the vowel ɑ. The artificial larynx was placed against the throat near the larynx to provide a buzz source. The drive signal for the artificial-larynx diaphragm was a train of short pulses (of about 1- to 2-msec duration) whose repetition frequency, the pitch of the source, was set to 30 cps. Thus, the waveforms produced had pitch periods over 30 msec long, during all of which time the glottis was closed. Furthermore, the source was inactive over a large portion of the pitch period.

TABLE II. First- and second-formant bandwidths; first-, second-, and third-formant frequencies (3 vowels, speaker A, 3 consecutive pitch periods).

Vowel	Pitch period	B_1	B_2	F_1	F_2	F_3
ɔ	1	57.	34.	634.	968.	2579.
	2	58.	34.	641.	975.	2569.
	3	58.	34.	647.	987.	2555.
i	1	66.	61.	318.	2110.	2613.
	2	63.	47.	307.	2156.	2663.
	3	66.	71.	297.	2165.	2763.
ɑ	1	59.	79.	745.	1141.	2534.
	2	56.	75.	748.	1160.	2511.
	3	55.	70.	748.	1170.	2481.

A least-squares fit was made to four segments 150 samples long (15 msec) taken near the center of a single pitch period. The initial samples of the four segments differed by as much as 5.9 msec. Results for the first two formant bandwidths were 30 and 40 cps, respectively, when averaged over the four intervals. Individual results for the first two bandwidths were always within 10% of the average. This is much less variation than that observed when real speech was used as the input. The third-formant bandwidth, averaged over the four analyses, was 74.5 cps. Here, single measurements were always within 15% of the average. The first three formant frequencies were 584, 1245, and 2675 cps, with all measurements within 0.2% of the averaged values.

The self-consistency of these results has been stressed to show that the variance obtained when using real speech may be due to real differences in the signal rather than errors in the measurement process. The most important factor here is probably the effect of fitting over an interval where the glottis is not completely closed, or where the area of the opening is changing. It is well-known that the formant frequencies and,

TABLE III. Results for pitch periods from a female speaker.[a]
Case 1: "high altitude"; case 2: "young outlaw."

| Time of starting sample | Case 1 | | Case 2 | | |
	$t=0$	$t=35$ (msec)	$t=0$	$t=36$	$t=57$ (msec)
B_1 (cps)	28	59	78	67	65
B_2 (cps)	153	184	126	99	81
F_1 (cps)	625	757	991	998	965
F_2 (cps)	2506	2355	1568	1487	1449

[a] See text for discussion.

especially, bandwidths are dependent upon the glottal-source impedance, and this is a strong function of the area of the glottal opening.

Finally, I should like to mention some results obtained using a female speaker. Typically, female pitch is so high that a pitch period is too short for accurate results to be obtained. However, in samples of connected speech made by one particular female speaker, it was observed (from spectrograms) that there were several instances where she apparently skipped glottal pulses. This meant that the response due to the previous glottal pulse continued undisturbed for at least twice as long as normal, and it was possible to fit over these intervals with confidence.

Two separated sounds were analyzed. Both occurred during relatively rapid phonemic transitions. The first interval occurred in the phrase "high altitude" and was in the transition between the diphthong /ai/ and the vowel /æ/. The second interval was in the phrase "young outlaw" and occurred at the beginning of the transition into the diphthong /au/. In both intervals, there were several consecutive long periods, and

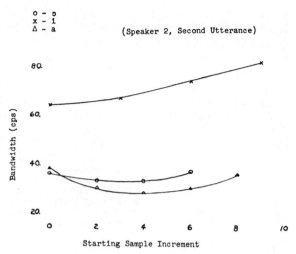

FIG. 7. Variation of first-formant bandwidths as a function of starting sample within one pitch period.

analyses were made of a few consecutive periods in each case.

The results are shown in Table III. A word of caution is necessary regarding the second-formant bandwidth and frequency estimates of case 1. The amplitude of this formant was quite small, and the estimates are not very reliable. However, all the other numbers in the table are probably quite reliable.

CONCLUSIONS

There are several reasons to expect that the time-domain technique described in this paper provides estimates of formant frequencies and bandwidths that compare favorably in terms of accuracy with other methods that have been used. First, the speech wave-form is approximated only during an interval during

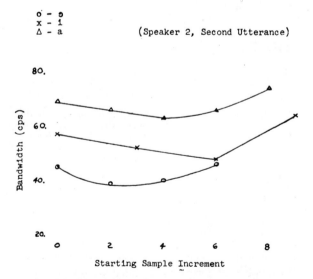

FIG. 8. Variation of second-formant bandwidths as a function of starting sample within one pitch period.

which the glottis is closed, thus eliminating the misleading effects of the source spectrum. Second, a sophisticated fitting procedure is used, thus eliminating the necessity of first separating individual formants before measuring their rates of decay. The effect of such formant-separating filters on the observed apparent decay rates can be misleading.[8] Finally, natural speech is used rather than an artificially excited vocal tract. This should insure that the articulator configuration is indeed the natural one for the various vowels examined.

The method leads to good estimates of the first two formant bandwidths of the vowels to which it has been applied and to good estimates of the first three formant frequencies. Because the amount of speech analyzed by this method is small, it is not possible to state whether there is a significant difference between the results described here and previously published work. There certainly is no large difference, however. A limitation of the approach is that it is applicable only to speakers with relatively low pitch (i.e., below about 140 cps) because, for high-pitched speech, the interval over which a fit can be attempted becomes too small for accurate results to be obtained.

ACKNOWLEDGMENTS

Many thanks are due Dr. H. K. Dunn for Fig. 1, which originally appeared in Ref. 8.

APPENDIX

Details of Least-Squares-Fitting Procedure

Two different techniques were programmed for a 7090 computer to carry out the parameter estimation of interest. These are described separately in parts A and B below. The methods have as a common goal the approximation of an input-speech waveform $p(t)$ by a function $f(t)$, which is a function of several adjustable parameters. Since a finite piece of data is to be approximated and the computation is to be performed in a digital computer, only a finite number K of input samples of the continuous time functions are considered. Without loss of generality, it is assumed that the first sample in this sequence occurs at time $t=0$, and successive samples occur every Δ sec thereafter. Thus, the approximating function is written as

$$f_M = f(t=M\Delta) \quad M=0, \cdots, K-1$$

$$= a_0 + \sum_{i=1}^{N} e^{-\mu_M B_i}(a_i \cos 2\mu_M F_i + b_i \sin 2\mu_M F_i), \quad (A1)$$

where $B_i = i$th-formant bandwidth in cps, $F_i = i$th-formant frequency in cps, $a_0, a_i, b_i =$ amplitude coefficients, $N =$ number of formants included in the fitting procedure, and $\mu_M = \pi \Delta M$.

The error function is

$$E = \sum_{M=0}^{K-1} W^2{}_M (p_M - f_M)^2, \quad (A2)$$

where W_M is the weighting coefficient for Mth error sample; $p_M = p(t=M\Delta) =$ amplitude of Mth sample of input-speech waveform; and K is the number of samples over which a fit is attempted.

The fit is accomplished by selecting the parameters $a_0, a_1, b_1, B_1, F_1, \cdots, a_N, b_N, B_N, F_N$ such that E is a minimum. In the case of an approximating function utilizing three formants $(N=3)$, this leads to a 13-parameter nonlinear least-squares-fitting problem. For $N=4$, the problem involves 17 parameters. Both programs to be described require, as input data, the K samples, p_M, and initial estimates of the $2N$ parameters B_i and $F_i (i=1, \cdots, N)$.

A. Modified Steepest-Descent Method

The problem is broken into two parts: (1) determination of the a_0, a_i, and b_i to achieve a minimum weighted-squared error holding the B_i and F_i constant; (2) making incremental changes in the B_i and F_i, holding the a_i and b_i constant, to further decrease the error. Steps 1 and 2 are iterated again and again until a good fit is achieved and no further decrease in the error is achieved.

Since the lower-case parameters enter the problem linearly, step 1 is accomplished by the solution of a set of linear algebraic equations.

At this point, a change of notation is necessary or the algebra gets out of hand. Define the vector $\boldsymbol{\beta}$ by

$$\boldsymbol{\beta} = \begin{bmatrix} \beta_1 \\ \beta_2 \\ \vdots \\ \beta_{2N} \\ \beta_{2N+1} \end{bmatrix} = \begin{bmatrix} a_1 \\ b_1 \\ \vdots \\ b_N \\ a_0 \end{bmatrix}, \quad (A3)$$

and the quantities Φ_{Mi} by

$$\Phi_{M,2i-1} = e^{-\mu_M B_i} \cos 2\mu_M F_i \quad i=1, \cdots, N \quad (A4)$$

$$\Phi_{M,2i} = e^{-\mu_M B_i} \sin 2\mu_M F_i \quad i=1, \cdots, N \quad (A5)$$

$$\Phi_{M,2N+1} = 1. \quad (A6)$$

Then, Eq. (A1) becomes

$$f_M = \sum_{i=1}^{2N+1} \beta_i \Phi_{Mi}. \quad (A7)$$

To obtain the minimum of E with respect to any parameter β_i, take the partial derivative of Eq. (A2) with respect to that parameter and set it equal to zero. Since the variable parameters enter only through the function f_M, it follows that

$$\frac{\partial E}{\partial \beta_i} = 0 = -2 \sum_{M=0}^{K-1} W^2_M (p_M - f_M) \frac{\partial f_M}{\partial \beta_i}, \quad \text{(A8)}$$

or

$$\sum_{M=0}^{K-1} W^2_M f_M \frac{\partial f_M}{\partial \beta_i} = \sum_{M=0}^{K-1} W^2_M p_M \frac{\partial f_M}{\partial \beta_i}. \quad \text{(A9)}$$

But,

$$\frac{\partial f_M}{\partial \beta_i} = \Phi_{Mi}. \quad \text{(A10)}$$

Substituting Eqs. (A7) and (A10) into Eq. (A9) and changing the order of summation leads to the result

$$\sum_{j=1}^{2N+1} \left[\sum_{M=0}^{K-1} W^2_M \Phi_{Mj} \Phi_{Mi} \right] \beta_j = \sum_{M=0}^{K-1} W^2_M p_M \Phi_{Mi}$$

$$i = 1, \cdots, 2N+1. \quad \text{(A11)}$$

In matrix notation, this result is

$$\mathbf{D}\boldsymbol{\beta} = \boldsymbol{\gamma}, \quad \text{(A12)}$$

where

$$d_{ij} = d_{ji} = \sum_{M=0}^{K-1} W^2_M \Phi_{Mi} \Phi_{Mj} \quad i, j = 1, \cdots, 2N+1, \quad \text{(A13)}$$

and

$$\gamma_i = \sum_{M=0}^{K-1} W^2_M p_M \Phi_{Mi} \quad i = 1, \cdots, 2N+1. \quad \text{(A14)}$$

Solving for the unknown variables in $\boldsymbol{\beta}$ gives

$$\boldsymbol{\beta} = \mathbf{D}^{-1}\boldsymbol{\gamma}. \quad \text{(A15)}$$

This solves the first half of the problem; i.e., given an assumed set of formant frequencies and bandwidths, a solution has been found for the set of amplitude coefficients, which minimizes the squared error.

A further change of notation is now desirable. Define the $2N$ dimensional vector $\boldsymbol{\xi}$ by its elements

$$\begin{aligned} \xi_{2i-1} &= B_i \\ &\qquad\qquad i = 1, \cdots, N. \quad \text{(A16)} \\ \xi_{2i} &= F_i \end{aligned}$$

Now compute the partial derivatives of E with respect to each of the ξ_i. From Eq. (A2) it follows that

$$\frac{\partial E}{\partial \xi_i} = -2 \sum_{M=0}^{K-1} W^2_M (p_M - f_M) \frac{\partial f_M}{\partial \xi_i}. \quad \text{(A17)}$$

From Eqs. (A4), (A5), (A7), and (A16), it follows that

$$\frac{\partial f_M}{\partial \xi_i} = \begin{cases} -\mu_M (\beta_i \Phi_{Mi} + \beta_{i+1} \Phi_{M,i+1}) & i \text{ odd} \quad \text{(A18)} \\ -2\mu_M (\beta_{i-1} \Phi_{Mi} - \beta_i \Phi_{M,i-1}) & i \text{ even.} \quad \text{(A19)} \end{cases}$$

The final equation for obtaining the gradient of E is,

thus,

$$\frac{\partial E}{\partial \xi_i} = \begin{cases} 2 \sum_{M=0}^{K-1} \mu_M W^2_M (p_M - f_M)(\beta_i \Phi_{Mi} + \beta_{i+1} \Phi_{M,i+1}) \\ \qquad\qquad\qquad\qquad\qquad i \text{ odd} \quad \text{(A20)} \\ 4 \sum_{M=1}^{K-1} \mu_M W^2_M (p_M - f_M) \\ \qquad\qquad \times (\beta_{i-1} \Phi_{Mi} - \beta_i \Phi_{M,i-1}) \quad i \text{ even.} \end{cases}$$

In a standard "steepest-descent" procedure, each ξ_i would be incremented by an amount proportional to the negative of the gradient of E with respect to that variable; i.e., a new vector $\boldsymbol{\xi}'$ would be formed such that

$$\xi_i' = \xi_i - \text{const} \times \frac{\partial E}{\partial \xi_i}. \quad \text{(A21)}$$

The new values ξ_i' replace the old values ξ_i. This technique was tried and failed miserably. Convergence to a stable minimum rarely occurred. After some experimentation, a satisfactory stratagem based on steepest descent was found. A set of increments λ_i was specified as part of the input data, and the values of ξ_i were changed according to the rule

$$\xi_i' = \begin{cases} \xi_i - \lambda_i & \text{if } \partial E/\partial \xi_i > 0 \\ \xi_i & \text{if } \partial E/\partial \xi_i = 0 \\ \xi_i + \lambda_i & \text{if } \partial E/\partial \xi_i < 0. \end{cases} \quad \text{(A22)}$$

In addition, the values of the λ_i were increased or decreased automatically according to the following rule. If the sign of $\partial E/\partial \xi_i$ did not change during four consecutive iterations, the value of λ_i was doubled. If the sign of $\partial E/\partial \xi_i$ on any iteration differed from its previous value, the value of λ_i was halved. Thus, the formant bandwidths and frequencies were changed by decreasing amounts as a minimum in the squared error was approached. An upper limit of 128 cycles was imposed on the allowable step size. Initial values of the λ_i varied from 1 to 32 cycles under different circumstances.

The iteration on the bandwidth and frequency parameters ξ_i was repeated four or five times before a new set of optimum amplitude coefficients β_i was computed.

B. Linearized-Approximation Method

In this approach, it is assumed that the true optimum fit to the input data is given by Eq. (A1). Instead of having the correct parameter values a_0, a_1, b_1, $\cdots$, b_N, B_1, F_1, $\cdots$, F_N, however, only parameters a_{00}, a_{01}, b_{01}, $\cdots$, F_{0N} are available. These parameters are called the "nominal" parameters here. Incremental parameters are defined by the following set of equations:

$$\begin{aligned} a_i &= a_{0i} + \delta a_i \\ b_i &= b_{0i} + \delta b_i \\ B_i &= B_{0i} + \delta B_i \quad i = 1, \cdots, N. \quad \text{(A23)} \\ F_i &= F_{0i} + \delta F_i \\ a_0 &= a_{00} + \delta a_0 \end{aligned}$$

It is now possible to make a Taylor-series expansion of f_M about the nominal parameter values. Let

$\bar{f}_M = f_M$ if all parameters are at their
nominal values.　　(A24)

Then,

$$f_M = \bar{f}_M + \delta a_0 + \sum_{i=1}^{N} e^{-\mu_M B_i} [\delta a_i \cos 2\mu_M F_{0i} + \delta b_i \sin 2\mu_M F_{0i}$$

$$+ 2\mu_M(-a_{0i} \sin 2\mu_M F_{0i} + b_{0i} \cos 2\mu_M F_{0i})\delta F_i$$

$$-\mu_M(a_{0i} \cos 2\mu_M F_{0i} + b_{0i} \sin 2\mu_M F_{0i})\delta B_i]$$

$$+ \text{(terms of second or higher order)}. \quad \text{(A25)}$$

This expression can be linearized by neglecting terms of second or higher order. If this is done, it is possible to write Eq. (A25) as

$$f_M = \bar{f}_M + \sum_{i=1}^{4N+1} C_{Mi}\alpha_i, \quad \text{(A26)}$$

where

$$C_{M,4N+1} = 1$$
$$C_{M,4i} = e^{-\mu_M B_{0i}} \sin 2\mu_M F_{0i}$$
$$C_{M,4i-1} = e^{-\mu_M B_{0i}} \cos 2\mu_M F_{0i}$$
$$C_{M,4i-2} = 2\mu_M(-a_{0i}C_{M,4i} + b_{0i}C_{M,4i-1})$$
$$C_{M,4i-3} = -\mu_M(a_{0i}C_{M,4i-1} + b_{0i}C_{M,4i})$$
$$\alpha_{4N+1} = \delta a_0, \quad \alpha_{4i} = \delta b_i, \quad \alpha_{4i-1} = \delta a_i,$$
$$\alpha_{4i-2} = \delta F_i, \quad \alpha_{4i-3} = \delta B_i \quad (i=1, \cdots, N). \quad \text{(A27)}$$

Substituting Eq. (A26) into the error Eq. (A2) gives

$$E = \sum_{M=0}^{K-1} W^2_M(p_M - \bar{f}_M - \sum_{j=1}^{4N+1} C_{Mj}\alpha_j)^2. \quad \text{(A28)}$$

To obtain the set of $\alpha_i(i=1, \cdots, 4N+1)$, which minimizes the error, we take the partial derivatives of E with respect to the α_i and set them equal to zero.

$$\frac{\partial E}{\partial \alpha_i} = 0 = 2 \sum_{M=0}^{K-1} W^2_M(p_M - \bar{f}_M - \sum_{j=1}^{4N+1} C_{Mj}\alpha_j)C_{Mi}$$

$$i=1, \cdots, 4N+1, \quad \text{(A29)}$$

or

$$\sum_{j=1}^{4N+1} (\sum_{M=0}^{K-1} W^2_M C_{Mi} C_{Mj})\alpha_j = \sum_{M=0}^{K-1} W^2_M C_{Mi}(p_M - \bar{f}_M)$$

$$i=1, \cdots, 4N+1. \quad \text{(A30)}$$

For convenience, define the matrix $\mathbf{S}$ (having K rows and $4N+1$ columns) by

$$\mathbf{S} = \{s_{Mi}\} = \{W_M C_{Mi}\} \quad \begin{matrix} M=0, \cdots, K-1 \\ i=1, \cdots, 4N+1, \end{matrix} \quad \text{(A31)}$$

and the K-dimensional vector $\boldsymbol{\varepsilon}$ by

$$\epsilon_M = W_M(p_M - \bar{f}_M) \quad M=0, \cdots, K-1, \quad \text{(A32)}$$

and the matrix $\mathbf{A}$ by

$$\mathbf{A} = \mathbf{S}^T\mathbf{S}, \quad \text{(A33)}$$

where $\mathbf{S}^T$ denotes the transpose of $\mathbf{S}$. Then, in matrix notation, Eq. (A30) becomes

$$\mathbf{A}\boldsymbol{\alpha} = \mathbf{S}^T\boldsymbol{\varepsilon}, \quad \text{(A34)}$$

and, solving for the unknown vector $\boldsymbol{\alpha}$,

$$\boldsymbol{\alpha} = \mathbf{T}^T\boldsymbol{\varepsilon}, \quad \text{(A35)}$$

where

$$\mathbf{T} = \mathbf{S}\mathbf{A}^{-1}. \quad \text{(A36)}$$

The matrix $\mathbf{T}$ will be called the "sensitivity" matrix since it relates the weighted error $\boldsymbol{\varepsilon}$ between the input-speech waveform and the nominal waveform to changes $\boldsymbol{\alpha}$ in the nominal parameter values.

Since it is difficult to make initial guesses as to the values of the nominal amplitude coefficients a_{00}, a_{01}, $\cdots$, b_{0N}, the first part of the modified steepest-descent method (described in part A of this Appendix) is also used in the linearized method; i.e., initial estimates of formant frequencies and bandwidths are made and initial estimates of the amplitude coefficients are made, using Eq. (A15). Then, the matrix $\mathbf{T}$ is computed using the initial formant estimates and initial amplitude coefficients as "nominal" values. The increments α_i are computed from Eq. (A35) and are used to improve the formant estimates via Eq. (A23) [and the last two relationships in Eq. (A27)]. Then these two steps are repeated again and again.

Usually, about four iterations of this type were necessary for the solution to converge. If the initial estimates were very bad, the method would not converge, and this was immediately apparent because the α_i would be given very large values. The error, using the newly computed nominal values, would increase substantially rather than decrease. The Barney–Peterson values for formant frequencies for a particular vowel were used as initial estimates. Initial bandwidth estimates from 50 (for the first formant) to 160 cps (for the fourth formant) were made, and convergence was usually not a problem. When the solution did not converge, changes were made in the initial estimates in an *ad hoc* manner until satisfactory convergence was obtained.

A final comment is in order on the accuracy of the estimates obtained in this way. Equation (A35) has an interesting interpretation that leads directly to an estimate of the expected inaccuracy due to noise in the input-speech signal. From Eq. (A35) it follows that

$$\alpha_i = \sum_{M=0}^{K-1} t_{Mi}\epsilon_M, \quad \text{(A37)}$$

and

$$\alpha_i\alpha_j = \sum_{M=0}^{K-1} \sum_{L=0}^{K-1} t_{Mi}t_{Li}\epsilon_M\epsilon_L, \quad \text{(A38)}$$

where the t_{Mi} are defined by the equation

$$\mathbf{T}^T = \{t_{Mi}\} \quad M = 0, \cdots, K-1;$$
$$i = 1, \cdots, 4N+1. \quad \text{(A39)}$$

Considering both the ϵ_M and the α_i to be random variables, take the expected value of Eqs. (A37) and (A38). Thus,

$$E(\alpha_i) = \sum_{M=0}^{K-1} t_{Mi} E(\epsilon_M), \quad \text{(A40)}$$

and

$$E(\alpha_i \alpha_j) = \sum_{M=0}^{K-1} \sum_{L=0}^{K-1} t_{Mi} t_{Lj} E(\epsilon_M \epsilon_L). \quad \text{(A41)}$$

The variance of the estimate α_i is labeled σ_i^2 and is given by

$$\sigma_i^2 = \sum_{M=0}^{K-1} \sum_{L=0}^{K-1} t_{Mi} t_{Li} [E(\epsilon_M \epsilon_L) - E(\epsilon_M) E(\epsilon_L)]. \quad \text{(A42)}$$

But the bracketed expression is simply the covariance of the random variables ϵ_M and ϵ_L and is denoted by η^2_{ML}. Thus,

$$\sigma^2_i = \sum_{M=0}^{K-1} \sum_{L=0}^{K-1} t_{Mi} t_{Li} \eta^2_{ML}. \quad \text{(A43)}$$

If something is known about the covariance matrix of the weighted errors ϵ_M, then an estimate of the variance of the estimates of formant frequencies and bandwidths is readily obtainable. For example, if it is assumed that the ϵ_M are independent random variables having the constant variance η^2, if follows that

$$\eta_{ML} = \begin{cases} \eta^2 & \text{for} \quad M = L \\ 0 & \text{for} \quad M \neq L, \end{cases} \quad \text{(A44)}$$

and, for this simple case, Eq. (A43) leads to the result

$$\sigma_i = \left(\sum_{M=0}^{K-1} t^2_{Mi} \right)^{\frac{1}{2}} \eta \quad \text{(A45)}$$

$$= C_i' \eta, \quad \text{(A46)}$$

where

$$C_i' = \left(\sum_{M=0}^{K-1} t^2_{Mi} \right)^{\frac{1}{2}}. \quad \text{(A47)}$$

The values obtained for C_i' for the three vowels under consideration varied considerably. Values for the first three formant frequencies averaged over both speakers and all vowels are given below for the first three formant frequencies:

$$C_i \approx \begin{cases} 70 & \text{for first formant frequency} \\ 240 & \text{for second formant frequency} \\ 950 & \text{for third formant frequency.} \end{cases} \quad \text{(A48)}$$

The values of C_i' for the first three formant bandwidths are very close to double the values for the corresponding formant frequencies. Very roughly, the normalized standard deviation η of the noise in the data used for this paper was $\eta \cong 0.03$. Thus, the standard deviation of the formant-frequency estimates would be, roughly, 2, 7, and 29 cps for the first-, second-, and third-formant-frequency estimates, respectively. The standard deviations due to additive random noise would be roughly 4, 14, and 58 cps for the first-, second-, and third-formant bandwidths, respectively. Unfortunately, errors due to other causes, such as inaccuracies in the model, undoubtedly are more important.

Received 17 July 1969

System for Automatic Formant Analysis of Voiced Speech

Ronald W. Schafer and Lawrence R. Rabiner

Bell Telephone Laboratories, Incorporated, Murray Hill, New Jersey 07974

A system for automatically estimating the lowest three formants and the pitch period of voiced speech is presented. The system is based on a digital computation of the cepstrum (defined as the inverse transform of the log magnitude of the z-transform). The pitch period estimate and smoothed log magnitude are obtained from the cepstrum. Formants are estimated from the smoothed spectral envelope using constraints on formant frequency ranges and relative levels of spectral peaks at the formant frequencies. These constraints allow the detection of cases where two formants are too close together in frequency to be resolved in the initial spectral envelope. In these cases, a new spectral analysis algorithm (the chirp z-transform algorithm) allows the efficient computation of a narrow-band spectrum in which the formant resolution is enhanced. Formant and pitch period data obtained by the analysis system are used to control a digital formant synthesizer. Results, in the form of spectrograms, are presented to illustrate the performance of the system.

INTRODUCTION

The acoustic theory of speech production[1] is the basis for most speech analysis–synthesis systems. The essence of this theory is that the speech waveform can be modeled as the output of a lumped parameter, linear, quasi-time-invariant system in response to an excitation which is either random noise (unvoiced sounds), a quasi-periodic pulse train (voiced sounds), or in some cases, a mixture of these sources (voiced fricatives). The implication of the model is that speech can be produced by proper excitation of a series or parallel connection of resonators whose complex natural frequencies vary slowly and continuously with time so as to approximate the time-varying eigenfrequencies of the vocal tract. These frequencies are called the formant frequencies, or simply formants.

This paper describes a system for automatically estimating pitch period and the lowest three formants of (nonnasal) voiced speech. By restricting the class of speech sounds to be analyzed, we have been able to develop a fully automatic system for estimating the desired parameters. It should be noted that the system presented here can be viewed as part of a larger system that would operate on a wider class of speech sounds. Such a system would incorporate a scheme for classifying speech sounds into several classes, each of which would then be analyzed by a different system.

The techniques presented in this paper may find application in a wide range of speech-processing problems. For example, if fully automatic analysis techniques can be developed for the other classes of speech sounds such as voiced and unvoiced fricatives, stops, and nasals; these can be combined into a formant–vocoder system. More immediate applications are foreseen in the areas of speaker recognition and speech recognition. Another area of application, which in a sense was the original motivation for studying the problem of automatic formant estimation, is as a tool in the evaluation and design of systems using synthetic speech as an output—such as a computer voice-response device. For example, in development of a system for speech synthesis-by-rule, automatic means for estimating formants and pitch could be used to analyze the utterances of a cross section of speakers each speaking a given utterance. These data could be compared to the formants and pitch generated by the synthesis-by-rule system. Such comparisons would provide a means for designing new synthesis strategies and for improving existing ones.

In the remainder of this section, some of the details of the model for production of voiced speech are reviewed, and the relationship of our work to previous research on the estimation of formant frequencies is discussed. The remaining sections discuss details of the approach and results that have been obtained.

---

[1] C. G. M. Fant, *Acoustic Theory of Speech Production* (Mouton and Co., 's-Gravenhage, The Netherlands, 1960).

A. Model for Voiced-Speech Waveforms

The model upon which the analysis is based is shown in Fig. 1(a). The samples of the speech waveform (10-kHz sampling rate) are viewed as the output of the discrete-time system of Fig. 1(a). Since a digital computer is used to perform both analysis and synthesis, it is preferable to think in terms of a discrete-time model and discrete-time-analysis techniques rather than the more familiar analog model and corresponding analysis methods.

In Fig. 1(a), the box labeled "Impulse Train Generator" provides a train of unit samples whose spacing is τ, the pitch period, which is a function of time. The multiplier A is a gain control, which varies with time and controls the intensity of the output. The cascade of networks $G(z)R(z)$ is an approximation to the combination of the glottal-source spectrum and the radiation load spectrum. This cascade is a discrete linear time-invariant network of the form

$$G(z)R(z) = \left(\frac{1-e^{-aT}}{1-z^{-1}e^{-aT}}\right)\left(\frac{1+e^{-bT}}{1+z^{-1}e^{-bT}}\right), \quad (1)$$

where a and b are constants that characterize the speaker (and possibly the utterance). Representative values of a and b are 400π and 5000π, respectively. More accurate values for a given speaker may be determined from a long-term average spectrum for that speaker. For the work presented in this paper, fixed values for a and b have been used throughout. Figure 2 shows a plot of the spectrum for the network $G(z)R(z)$ using these values for a and b.

The system labeled $V(z)$ in Fig. 1(a) is a linear quasi-time-invariant discrete system which consists of a cascade connection of digital resonators as shown in

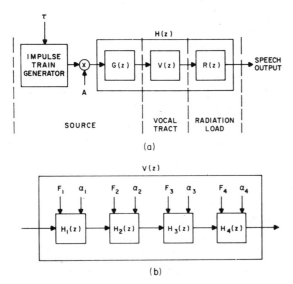

FIG. 1. (a) Digital model for voiced speech. (b) Detailed diagram of model for vocal tract transmission.

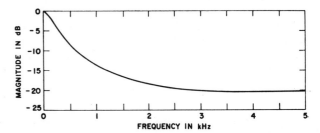

FIG. 2. Evaluation of the fixed system function $G(z)R(z)$ on the unit circle.

Fig. 1(b). That is,

$$V(z) = \prod_{k=1}^{4} H_k(z), \quad (2)$$

where

$$H_k(z) = \frac{(1-2e^{-\alpha_k T}\cos\omega_k T + e^{-2\alpha_k T})}{[1-(2e^{-\alpha_k T}\cos\omega_k T)z^{-1} + e^{-2\alpha_k T}z^{-2}]} \quad (3)$$

and $\omega_k = 2\pi F_k$, and $T = 0.0001$ sec.

The purpose of the system $V(z)$ is to model the vocal tract transmission characteristics. In synthesizing speech or in modeling the speech waveform, the formant frequencies F_k and bandwidths $2\alpha_k$ vary with time, corresponding to the fact that the vocal tract changes shape as different sounds are produced. Since these parameters vary slowly with time, the spectrum of a short segment of speech is characterized, to a good approximation, by Eqs. 1–3 with fixed values of F_k and α_k. Over long time intervals, these equations should be interpreted as specifying the sequence of numerical operations required to compute the samples of an approximation to the speech waveform. Because the input speech is filtered sharply to contain no frequencies above 4 kHz, it is only necessary for $V(z)$ to consist of three time-varying digital resonators and a fourth fixed resonator to ensure proper spectral balance at high frequencies.

According to the acoustic theory,[1] another pole and a zero in series with the configuration of Fig. 1(a) are required to represent nasal consonants. In the system described in this paper, no provision is made for estimating this pole and zero. Preliminary synthesis results indicate that this extra pole and zero may not be necessary for acceptable synthetic speech.

The analysis of the speech waveform involves the determination of the time-varying parameters of the model: i.e., the formant frequencies F_k, the source-radiation parameters a and b, the formant bandwidths $2\alpha_k$, the pitch period τ, and the gain A. The analysis system discussed here determines, as a function of time, only the lowest three formants, the pitch period and the gain. In resynthesizing the speech for comparison with the original speech, F_4, a, b, and all the α_k's are held fixed.

The Journal of the Acoustical Society of America

It has been shown[2] that the model of Fig. 1(a) is at least as effective in approximating the spectral properties of speech signals as the more conventional continuous-time models that employ higher pole-correction networks. Figure 3 shows the results of evaluating the z-transform

$$H(z) = G(z)V(z)R(z) \qquad (4)$$

on the unit circle, i.e., for $z = e^{j\omega T}$, where T is the sampling period. As noted in the figure, the peaks in spectral envelope $|H(e^{j\omega T})|$ occur at frequencies which are generally quite close to the formant frequencies. The basic approach of the analysis scheme is to estimate the formant frequencies from the peaks in a computed approximation to $|H(e^{j\omega T})|$. To facilitate the estimation of the formant frequencies, constraints on formant frequency ranges and relative levels of the formant peaks are imposed. The method of cepstral analysis and a new spectral-analysis algorithm are techniques employed in the analysis scheme.

B. Previous Research on Formant Estimation

Since the pitch period and formant frequencies are the essential parameters in the acoustic model for the production of voiced speech, it is not surprising that a great deal of previous research has been directed toward estimation of these parameters from the acoustic waveform. Generally, the estimation of pitch period and the estimation of formant frequencies have been treated as two distinct problems. However, since the main emphasis of this paper is on estimation of the formant frequencies, and since estimation of pitch period and formant frequencies do not require independent analyses in the system proposed here, there is no need to review work on pitch period estimation. In contrast, some of the principles upon which the present system is based are basic to many of the previous schemes for estimation of formant frequencies. Therefore, it seems worthwhile to review some of the major efforts in this area that have influenced the work presented here. It should be emphasized that this section is not meant to be a comprehensive review of the literature on formant estimation. Its purpose is simply to place the present work in context.

Although virtually all methods of formant estimation have been based on essentially a continuous-time version of the model discussed earlier, the techniques for estimating formants have differed widely. A majority of the previous systems have used frequency domain techniques. One such approach could be termed "peak picking," i.e., finding the location of spectral peaks in the short-time amplitude spectrum. For example,

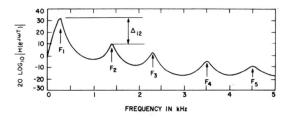

FIG. 3. An example of the evaluation of the system function $G(z)R(z)V(z)$ on the unit circle. Arrows mark the formant frequencies.

Flanagan[3-5] proposed two formant vocoder systems of this type in which a short-time spectrum was computed using an analog filter bank. The first three formants were estimated by locating spectral peaks in frequency ranges appropriate for the first three formants.

In another frequency-domain approach, termed "analysis by synthesis,"[6-9] a spectrum was computed using a filter bank[6-8] or pitch synchronously (i.e., using only a single period of the speech of the speech waveform) using a digital computer.[9] The computer synthesized a "best" spectral match (i.e., minimum mean-square error) by systematically varying the formant frequencies and bandwidths. The success of this technique depends on the accuracy of the speech model. Therefore, its performance is theoretically best for vowels.

A formant vocoder system employing analysis-by-synthesis techniques was discussed by Coker.[10] In this system, the differences between individual speakers were accounted for by recording an average curve of the difference between the measured and synthesized spectra. This difference curve was then used as a correction to improve spectral balance. Formant continuity constraints were also incorporated into the system as an aid in searching for the formants.

The use of low-order spectral moments[11] is another

[2] B. Gold and L. R. Rabiner, "Analysis of Digital and Analog Formant Synthesizers," IEEE Trans. Audio Electroacoust. AU-16, 81–94 (1968).

[3] J. L. Flanagan, "Automatic Extraction of Formant Frequencies from Continuous Speech," J. Acoust. Soc. Amer. 28, 110–118 (1956).

[4] J. L. Flanagan, "Evaluation of Two Formant-Extracting Devices," J. Acoust. Soc. Amer. 28, 118–125 (1956).

[5] J. L. Flanagan, Speech Analysis Synthesis and Perception (Academic Press, Inc. New York, 1965).

[6] C. G. Bell, F. Poza, and K. N. Stevens, "Automatic Resolution of Speech Spectra into Elemental Spectra," Proceedings of the Seminar on Speech Compression and Processing, W. Wathen-Dunn and L. E. Woods, Eds., AFCRC-TR-59-198, Vol. 1. Paper A-6, Dec. 1959.

[7] C. G. Bell, H. Fujisaki, J. M. Heinz, K. N. Stevens, and A. S. House, "Reduction of Speech Spectra by Analysis-by-Synthesis Techniques," J. Acoust. Soc. Amer. 33, 1725–1736 (1961).

[8] A.P. Paul, A. S. House, and K. N. Stevens, "Automatic Reduction of Vowel Spectra; an Analysis-by-Synthesis Method and its Evaluation," J. Acoust. Soc. Amer. 36, 303–308 (1964).

[9] M. V. Mathews, J. E. Miller, and E. E. David, Jr., "Pitch Synchronous Analysis of Voiced Sounds," J. Acoust. Soc. Amer. 33, 179–186 (1961).

[10] C. H. Coker, "Real Time Formant Vocoder, Using a Filter Bank, a General-Purpose Digital Computer, and an Analog Synthesizer," J. Acoust. Soc. Amer. 38, 940(A) (1965).

[11] J. Suzuki, Y. Kadokawa, and K. Nakata, "Formant-Frequency Extraction by the Method of Moment Calculations," J. Acoust. Soc. Amer. 35, 1345–1353 (1963).

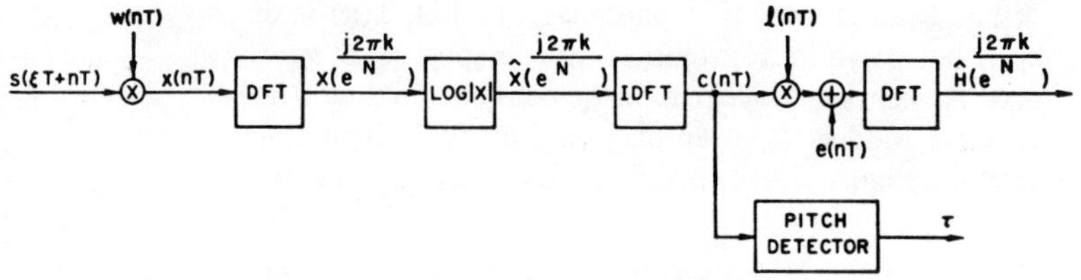

FIG. 4. Block diagram of the system for estimating formant frequencies and pitch period.

frequency-domain approach that has been tried. Although this approach did not produce very accurate formant data, it did yield approximations that were useful in more refined analyses.

One example of a time domain technique for estimating formants was the application of the analysis-by-synthesis approach directly to the acoustic waveform.[12] By systematic variation of the amplitudes, phases, damping and oscillation frequencies of a sum of complex exponential functions, a portion of the acoustic waveform was approximated in a minimum mean-square error sense. This technique was applied to the estimation of the formants of vowels.

The systems discussed in this section are not the only ones which have been proposed. However, they illustrate many of the basic principles involved in estimation of formant frequencies. It seems reasonable to state that none of the previous systems represents a completely successful solution to the problem of automatic estimation of formant frequencies of voiced speech. It may also be said, however, that no matter how sophisticated the analysis, the validity of the results reflects the validity of the model upon which the analysis is based. Although the model which has been discussed is not as good for voiced stops, voiced fricatives, and nasals as for vowels, glides, and semivowels, it was felt that the flexibility and efficiency of the formant representation of voiced speech justified a further effort toward a fully automatic formant-estimation system. The system proposed in this paper incorporates many of the principles just discussed. In addition, new spectral-analysis techniques and constraints based on a digital-speech model have been combined into a system which has produced accurate formant data for vowels, glides, and semivowels, and provided a good spectral match in the case of voiced stops, voiced fricatives, and nasals.

I. DESCRIPTION OF THE ANALYSIS SYSTEM

In this section, an asynchronous system for determining (as a function of time) the pitch period, the gain, and the lowest three formants of voiced-speech sounds is presented. Since the system is asynchronous, exact determination of a "pitch period" is not required. Instead, the analysis is applied to several periods of speech at a time. This has the advantage of eliminating the

difficult problem of accurately determining pitch periods in the acoustic waveform. A disadvantage of this method, however, is that formant and pitch period estimates are in a sense "averaged" over the analysis window. As is demonstrated by the results, this "averaging" is not significant for the formant transitions and pitch period changes which are encountered in normal male speech. The analysis involves two basic parts:

(1) The estimation of pitch period and the computation of the spectral envelope,

(2) the estimation of formants from the spectral envelope.

Each of these procedures is discussed in detail in the following two sections.

A. Estimation of Pitch Period and Spectral Envelope

The pitch period and the spectral envelope are estimated from the cepstrum of a segment of the speech waveform. Since a variety of definitions of the cepstrum exists,[13] it is important to state our definition here. In this paper, the cepstrum of a segment of a sampled speech waveform is defined as the inverse transform of the logarithm of the z-transform of that segment.

Cepstral techniques for pitch period estimation have been discussed by Noll.[13] Oppenheim and Schafer[14] and Oppenheim[15] have discussed cepstral analysis techniques and their application to speech analysis within the context of a theory of generalized linear filtering. These previous investigations have shown that the logarithm of the Fourier transform (the z-transform evaluated on the unit circle for sampled data) of a segment of voiced speech consists of a slowly varying component attributable to the convolution of the glottal pulse with the vocal-tract impulse response, plus a rapidly varying periodic component due to the repetitive nature of the acoustic waveform. These two additive components can be separated by linear filtering of the logarithm of the transform. The assumption that the log magnitude is composed of two separate components is supported by the model for the speech waveform given previously. A

[12] E. N. Pinson, "Pitch Synchronous Time-Domain Estimation of Formant Frequencies and Bandwidths," J. Acoust. Soc. Amer. **35**, 1264–1273 (1963).

[13] A. M. Noll, "Cepstrum Pitch Determination," J. Acoust. Soc. Amer. **41**, 293–309 (1967). Research at Bell Telephone Laboratories I, Proc. Int. Congr. Acoust., 5th, Liège, 1965, Paper A21.

[14] A. V. Oppenheim and R. W. Schafer, "Homomorphic Analysis of Speech," IEEE Trans. Audio Electroacoust. **AU-16**, 221–226 (1968).

[15] A. V. Oppenheim, "A Speech Analysis Synthesis System Based on Homomorphic Filtering," J. Acoust. Soc. Amer. **45**, 458–465 (1969).

The Journal of the Acoustical Society of America

detailed analysis of such a discrete model is given by Oppenheim and Schafer.[14]

The details of the computation of the cepstrum are summarized in Fig. 4. A segment of speech $s(\xi T+nT)$ is weighted by a symmetric window function $w(nT)$ such that

$$x(nT)=s(\xi T+nT)w(nT)$$
$$=[p(\xi T+nT)*h(nT)]\cdot w(nT), \quad 0\leq n \quad M, \quad (5)$$

where $*$ denotes discrete convolution, and ξT is the starting sample of a particular segment of the speech waveform.

In Eq. 5, $p(\xi T+nT)$ represents a quasiperiodic impulse train appropriate for the particular segment being analyzed, and $h(nT)$ represents the triple convolution of the vocal-tract impulse response with the glottal pulse and the radiation load impulse response [i.e., $h(nT)=v(nT)*r(nT)*g(nT)$, where $v(nT)$ is the inverse z-transform of $V(z)$, $r(nT)$ is the inverse z-transform of $R(z)$, and $g(nT)$ is the inverse z-transform of $G(z)$ in Fig. 1(a)].

The window function $w(nT)$ tapers to zero at each end in order to minimize the effects due to the inclusion of a nonintegral number of pitch periods within the window. Since $w(nT)$ varies slowly with respect to variations in $s(nT)$, $x(nT)$ is given approximately by[14]

$$x(nT)\approx h(nT)*p_w(nT), \quad (6)$$

where

$$p_w(nT)=p(\xi T+nT)w(nT). \quad (7)$$

That is, the purpose of multiplication of the speech by the window is to improve the approximation that a segment of voiced speech can be represented as a convolution of a periodic impulse train with a time-invariant vocal-tract impulse response sequence. Segments of speech are selected at 10-msec intervals along the waveform. The window we have used is a Hamming window, which is specified by the equation

$$w(nT)=\begin{cases} 0.54-0.46\cos(2\pi nT/MT) & 0\leq nT\leq MT \\ 0 & \text{elsewhere.} \end{cases} \quad (8)$$

The duration of the window, MT, is four times the maximum of the previous two estimates of pitch period and is the same for pairs of segments. Symmetry proper-

ties of the discrete Fourier transforms allow the computation of two real transforms in one computation. To take advantage of this, it is most convenient to change the window duration only for pairs of segments. The choice of the duration of the time window is governed by two conflicting considerations. In order to obtain a strong peak in the cepstrum at the pitch period, it is necessary to have several periods of the waveform within the window. In contrast, in order to obtain strong formant peaks in the smoothed spectrum, only about two periods should be within the window—i.e., the formants should not have changed appreciably within the time interval spanned by the window. The choice of four times the pitch period represents a suitable compromise.

The first three blocks of Fig. 4 depict the computation of the cepstrum $c(nT)$. Since a digital computer is used to compute the cepstrum, the discrete Fourier transform (DFT) and the inverse discrete Fourier transform (IDFT) are used in place of the z-transform and the inverse z-transform. [The DFT and IDFT are computed using the fast Fourier transform (FFT) algorithm.[16]]

Since the logarithm of the magnitude of the DFT is a sampled version of the logarithm of the magnitude of the z-transform, the input sequence $x(nT)$ must be augmented with a number of zeros sufficient to ensure that the logarithm of the magnitude is sampled sufficiently often to avoid aliasing in the cepstrum. A value of $N=1024$ for the DFT's and IDFT has been used so that $(1024-M)$ zero samples must be appended to the windowed segment of speech samples.

The remainder of Fig. 4 depicts the estimation of pitch period and spectral envelope from the cepstrum. The cepstrum consists of two components. The component due primarily to the glottal wave and the vocal tract is concentrated in the region $|nT|<\tau$, whereas the component due to the pitch occurs in the region $|nT|\geq\tau$, where τ is the pitch period during the segment being analyzed. The pitch component consists mainly of sharp peaks at multiples of the pitch period. Thus, pitch period can be determined by searching the cepstrum for a strong peak in the region $nT>\tau_{min}$, where τ_{min} is the minimum expected pitch period. Noll[13] has given an algorithm that can be used for pitch-period estimation and voiced/unvoiced detection. The spectral envelope is obtained by low-pass filtering of the log magnitude of the discrete Fourier transform. This is accomplished by multiplying the cepstrum by a function $l(nT)$ of the form

$$l(nT)=\begin{cases} 1 & |nT|<\tau_1 \\ \frac{1}{2}\{1+\cos[\pi(nT-\tau_1)/\Delta\tau]\} & \tau_1\leq|nT|<\tau_1+\Delta\tau \\ 0 & |nT|\geq\tau_1+\Delta\tau, \end{cases} \quad (9)$$

[16] J. W. Cooley and J. W. Tukey, "An Algorithm for the Machine Calculation of Complex Fourier Series," Math. Computation 19, 297–301 (1965).

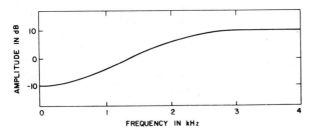

FIG. 5. Spectrum equalizing curve which is added to the smoothed spectral envelope.

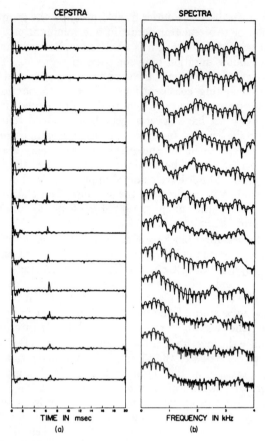

CEPSTRA   SPECTRA

TIME IN msec
(a)

FREQUENCY IN kHz
(b)

FIG. 6. (a) Cepstra for consecutive segments of speech separated by 20 msec. (b) Spectra and smoothed spectral envelopes corresponding to the cepstra on the left in (a).

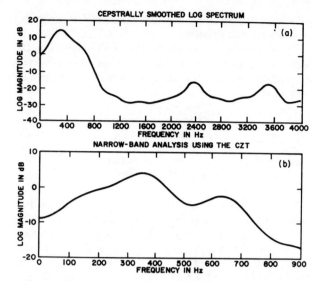

CEPSTRALLY SMOOTHED LOG SPECTRUM

NARROW-BAND ANALYSIS USING THE CZT

FIG. 7. (a) A smoothed spectral envelope in which F_1 and F_2 are too close to be resolved. (b) Analysis of the cepstrum over a narrow frequency band and on a contour inside the unit circle.

where $\tau_1 + \Delta\tau$ is less than the minimum pitch period that will be encountered. The sequence $e(nT)$ is added to the sequence $c(nT)l(nT)$. The purpose of adding this component to the cepstrum is to add the curve of Fig. 5 to the smoothed spectral envelope. The curve of Fig. 5 is an approximation to the frequency response of a spectral equalizer which has been used by Flanagan *et al.*[17] to equalize formant amplitudes. Comparison of Fig. 5 with Fig. 2 shows that the effect of the equalizer is to remove approximately the contribution of the glottal waveform and the radiation load. The sequence $e(nT)$ consists of the Fourier coefficients of the curve of Fig. 5, viewed as a real, even, periodic function. Three nonzero Fourier coefficients are used. The resultant sequence $c(nT)l(nT) + e(nT)$ is transformed to produce the equalized spectral envelope.

If pitch period information is not required, or if pitch period is independently estimated, then the logarithm of the magnitude of the z-transform can be filtered using either a direct convolution or a recursive digital filter. If a simple recursive filter is used, considerable saving in computation may result.

Figure 6(a) shows a series of cepstral plots. The cepstra correspond to consecutive segments of speech; the midpoint of each segment is displaced 20 msec from the midpoint of the previous segment. (In actual operation, the window is moved in 10-msec steps.) From Fig. 6(a), it can be seen that there is a distinct peak in the cepstrum that moves from slightly less than 6 msec to slightly more than 6 msec as time increases. It can also be seen that the cepstrum is large for small values of nT, then drops off rapidly before the peak at the pitch period.

Figure 6(b) shows the spectra corresponding to the same intervals of speech shown in Fig. 6a. Each of the rapidly varying curves is the unsmoothed spectrum corresponding to the cepstrum directly opposite to it in Fig. 6(a). The slowly varying curve is the corresponding smoothed spectrum. In the first curve, the first four formants are clearly in evidence. In the next three curves, F_2 has moved close to F_3, and in the third and fourth curves, F_2 and F_3 are not resolved. In the fifth through eighth curves, all the formants are clear, while in the last four curves, F_1 and F_2 are not resolved.

In cases where F_1, F_2, and F_3 are separated by more than about 300 Hz, there is no difficulty in resolving the corresponding peaks in the smoothed spectrum. However, when F_1 and F_2 or when F_2 and F_3 get closer than about 300 Hz the cepstral smoothing results in the peaks not being resolved. In these cases, a new spectral analysis algorithm called the chirp z-transform[18] (CZT) can be used to advantage. As discussed in Appendix A, the CZT permits the computation of samples of the z-transform at equally spaced intervals along a circular or spiral contour in the z-plane. In particular, if F_1 and F_2

[17] J. L. Flanagan, D. Meinhart, and P. Cummiskey, "Digital Equalizer and De-Equalizer for Speech," J. Acoust. Soc. Amer. 36, 1030(A) (1964).

[18] L. R. Rabiner, R. W. Schafer, and C. M. Rader, "The Chirp z-Transform Algorithm and its Application," Bell System. Tech. J. 48, 1249–1292 (1969).

The Journal of the Acoustical Society of America

are close, it is possible to compute the z-transform on a contour that passes closer to the pole locations than the unit-circle contour, thereby enhancing the peaks in the spectrum and improving the resolution. For example, Fig. 7(a) shows a smoothed spectral envelope in which F_1 and F_2 are unresolved. In this case, the parameters of the cepstral-window function $l(nT)$ were $\tau_1 = 2$ msec and $\Delta\tau = 2$ msec. Figure 7(b) shows the result of a CZT analysis along a circular contour of radius $e^{-0.0314}$ over the frequency range 0–900 Hz with a resolution of about 10 Hz. This analysis was achieved using only two 128-point FFTs. The effect of analysis along a contour that passes closer to the poles is evident in contrast to Fig. 7(a). Figure 8 shows an identical analysis for the case when F_2 and F_3 are close together. A discussion of how this technique is incorporated into the algorithm for choosing formants from the smoothed spectra is given in the next section. Discussions of the CZT algorithm itself and its application directly to the cepstrum are given in Appendixes A and B.

Oppenheim[15] has recently discussed a new speech analysis–synthesis system that is similar to the present analysis system. That is, a cepstrum is computed as in the previous discussion, and the pitch period is estimated from the cepstrum. However, instead of transforming to the smoothed spectrum at the analyzer, a small number of cepstral samples (32 or less) are sent to the synthesizer. The synthesizer converts these cepstral values into an impulse response that is then convolved with either a quasiperiodic impulse train (voiced sounds) or a random polarity equally spaced impulse train (unvoiced sounds). In contrast, the approach in the present system is to estimate formant frequencies and pitch period for a formant synthesizer rather than retain the cepstral values. No physical comparison of the two systems has been performed. However, it seems reasonable

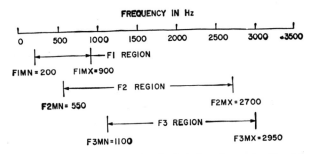

FIG. 9. Frequency ranges for the first three formants. (Empirically derived for male speech.)

to state that at least for voiced speech, the system discussed in this paper is related to that of Oppenheim in much the same way as a formant vocoder is related to a channel vocoder.

B. Estimation of Formant Frequencies from Cepstrally Smoothed Spectra

Before proceeding to the details of the process of estimating the formant frequencies from smoothed spectra, it is necessary to present some data relating to the properties of the speech spectrum. Figure 9 shows the frequency ranges of the first three formants. These ranges were determined from experimental data on male speakers, and it should be noted that these ranges are somewhat more restricted than ranges that would apply to both male and female speakers. On the other hand, individual speakers may have formant ranges that are even more restricted than those of Fig. 9, and, if known, these ranges could be used for that speaker.

It is important to note the high degree of overlap between regions in which the formants may be located. The first formant range is from 200 to 900 Hz, however, for half of this range (550–900 Hz), the second formant region can overlap the first. Similarly, the second and third formant regions overlap from 1100 to 2700 Hz. Thus, the estimation of the formants is not simply a matter of locating the peaks of the spectrum in nonoverlapping frequency bands.

Another property of speech pertinent to formant estimation is the relationship between formant frequencies and relative amplitudes of the formant peaks in the smoothed spectrum. It has previously been noted[1,19] that the form of the model imposes constraints on certain features of the spectral envelope. In particular, it is clear that, for the model of Fig. 1, given the formant frequencies and bandwidths, the relative levels of the peaks in the spectrum are completely specified. The relationships between the formant levels can be very useful in the process of selecting formants from the spectral peaks. In particular, considerable importance is placed on a measurement of the level of the F_2 peak

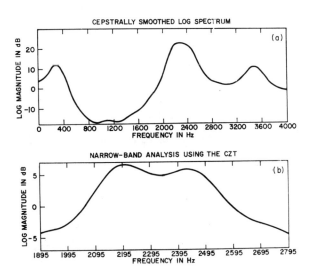

FIG. 8. (a) A smoothed spectral envelope in which F_2 and F_3 are too close to be resolved. (b) Analysis of the cepstrum over a narrow frequency band and on a contour inside the unit circle.

[19] K. N. Stevens and A. S. House, "An Acoustical Theory of Vowel Production and Some of its Applications," J. Speech Hearing Res. 4, 303–320 (1961).

relative to the level of the F_1 peak. The level measurement used Δ_{12} is defined as:

$$\Delta_{12} = \log |H(e^{j2\pi F_2 T})| - \log |H(e^{j2\pi F_1 T})|,$$

where F_1 and F_2 are the frequencies of the first and second formants and $|H(e^{j2\pi FT})|$ is the magnitude of the smoothed spectrum at frequency F hertz. Based upon the model of Fig. 1, a careful analysis shows that Δ_{12} depends primarily upon F_1 and F_2 and that it is fairly insensitive to the bandwidths of all the formants and to the higher formant frequencies. Figure 10 shows the dependence of Δ_{12} on F_2. The curve was derived from examination of a large number of spectra from several male speakers and from computations based on the model. This curve takes into account the equalization of the spectrum shown in Fig. 5 and served as a threshold against which the difference between the level of a possible F_2 peak and the level of the F_1 peak is compared. The dependence of Δ_{12} on F_1 is eliminated by assuming that F_1 is fixed at its lower limit, $F1MN$. If the F_1 dependence were to be accounted for, a family of curves, similar in shape but displaced vertically from the one in Fig. 10 would be required. For a value of F_1 greater than $F1MN$, the corresponding curve would be above the curve in Fig. 10. The shape of the curve is flat until 500 Hz, because F_2 is assumed to be above this minimum value. The curve then decreases until about 1500 Hz, reflecting the drop in F_2 level as it gets further away from F_1. However, above 1500 Hz, the curve rises again owing to the increasing proximity of F_2 and F_3. The curve continues to rise until F_2 gets to its maximum value $F2MX = 2700$ Hz, at which point F_2 and F_3 are maximally close (according to the simple model of fixed F_3).

The process of estimating formants from the smoothed spectral envelope is depicted in Fig. 11. The first step is of course the computation of the smoothed spectrum as discussed in the previous section. Once the spectrum is obtained, all the peaks (maxima) are located, and the location and amplitude level of each peak is recorded. This table of peak locations and peak levels contains all the spectral information that is used in the estimation of the formants.

C. Estimation of F_1

The formants are picked in sequence beginning with F_1. The process of estimating F_1 is depicted in Fig. 11(a). To start the process, the highest level of the spectrum in the frequency range 0 to $F1MX$ is found, where $F1MX$ is the upper limit of the F_1 region. This value of the spectrum is recorded as $FOAMP$. Generally, this value will occur at a peak in the F_1 region that will ultimately be chosen as the F_1 peak. However, sometimes there is an especially strong peak below $F1MN$, the lower limit of the F_1 region, which is due to the spectrum of the glottal-source waveform. In such cases, there may or may not be a clearly resolved F_1 peak

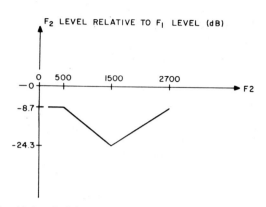

FIG. 10. Level of the F_2 peak relative to the F_1 peak for fixed F_1. (Derived from measurements and computations using the speech model.)

above $F1MN$. In order to avoid choosing a low-level spurious peak or possibly the F_2 peak for the F_1 peak, when in fact the F_1 peak and peak due to the source are not resolved, a peak in the F_1 region is required to be less than 8.7 dB (1.0 on a natural log scale) below $FOAMP$ to be considered as a possible F_1 peak. The frequency of the highest-level peak in the F_1 region which exceeds this threshold is selected as the first formant, F_1. The level of this peak is recorded as $F1AMP$. If no F_1 can be selected this way, the region 0–900 Hz is expanded and enhanced using the CZT algorithm, as discussed in the previous section and the appendixes. (This requires that about 40 values of the cepstrum be saved until after the formants are estimated.) This enhanced section of the spectrum is then searched for the highest-level peak in the F_1 region. The location of this peak is accepted as F_1. If the enhancement has failed to bring about a resolution of the source peak and the F_1 peak, F_1 is arbitrarily set equal to $F1MN$, the lower limit of the F_1 region.

The quantity $F1AMP$ is used in the estimation of F_2. If the F_1 peak is very low in frequency and is not clearly resolved from the lower-frequency peak due to the glottal waveform, $F1AMP$ is set equal to $(FOAMP - 8.7$ dB). This is done so as to effectively lower (because F_1 is very low) the threshold which is used in searching for F_2.

D. Estimation of F_2

The process of estimating F_2 is depicted in Fig. 11(b). The first step is to fix the frequency range to be searched for F_2. If F_1 has been estimated to be less than $F2MN$, the lower limit of the F_2 region, then only the region from $F2MN$ to $F2MX$ is searched. However, if F_1 has been estimated to be greater than $F2MN$, it is possible that the F_2 peak has in fact been chosen as the F_1 peak. Therefore, the combined F_1–F_2 region from $F1MN$ to $F2MX$ is searched so as to ensure that if this is the case, the F_1 peak will be found as the F_2 peak. After F_2 has been estimated, F_1 and F_2 are compared and their values are interchanged if F_2 is less than F_1.

The Journal of the Acoustical Society of America

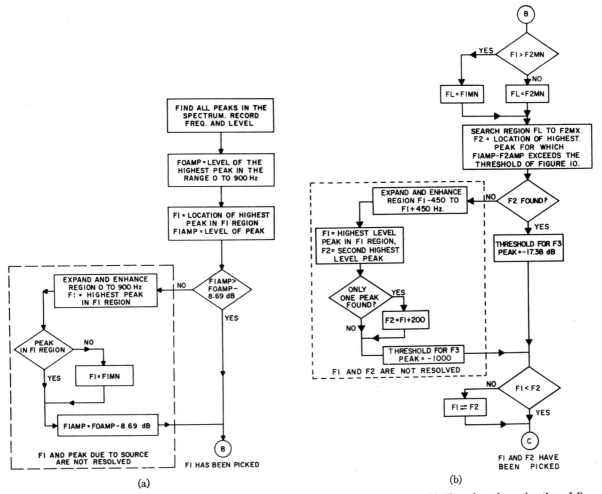

FIG. 11. (a) Flow chart depicting the process of estimating F_1 from the smoothed spectra. (b) Flow chart for estimation of F_2.

In deciding whether a particular spectral peak under investigation is a possible candidate for an F_2 peak, the threshold curve of Fig. 10 is used. The spectral peak is first checked to see if it is located in the proper frequency range. If so, the difference between the level of the peak under consideration and $F1AMP$ is computed. If this difference exceeds the threshold of Fig. 10, that peak is a possible F_2 peak; if not, that peak is not considered as a possible F_2 peak. The value of F_2 is chosen to be the frequency of the highest level peak to exceed the threshold. The level of this peak is recorded as $F2AMP$.

If not peaks are found that exceeded the threshold, further analysis is called for. The fact that no peaks are located has been found to be a reliable indication that F_1 and F_2 are close together as in Fig. 7(a). Therefore, the CZT algorithm is used to compute a high-resolution narrow-band spectrum over the frequency range (F_1-450) Hz to (F_1+450) Hz. (If $F_1<450$ Hz, the range is 0 to 900 Hz.) This spectrum is evaluated along a circular arc of radius $e^{-0.0314}$ in the z-plane. This analysis

generally produces a spectrum such as shown in Fig. 7(b) in which the two formants F_1 and F_2 are readily seen.

The value of F_1 is reassigned as the frequency of the highest-level peak in the F_1 region and F_2 is the frequency of the next highest peak. If only one peak is found, F_1 is arbitrarily set equal to the frequency of that peak and $F_2=(F_1+200)$ Hz.

In searching for F_3, a threshold on the difference in level between a possible F_3 peak and the F_2 peak is employed. In this case a fixed, frequency-independent threshold has been found satisfactory. If F_2 is located without the CZT analysis (i.e., F_2 is not extremely low), the threshold on the difference is set at -17.4 dB (-2.0 on a natural log scale). Otherwise, the threshold is effectively removed by setting it at -1000 dB.

E. Estimation of F_3

The estimation of F_3 from the smoothed spectrum is depicted in Fig. 11(c). Because of the equalization, there is a possibility of finding the F_3 peak as F_2. Thus, F_2 is

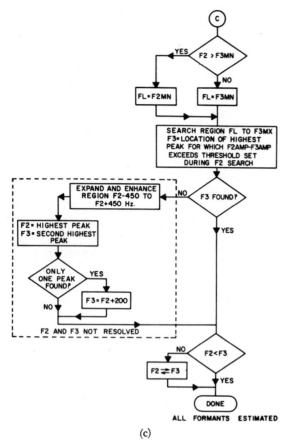

FIG. 11 (continued). (c) Flow chart for estimation of F_3.

considered for an F_3 peak and $F2AMP$ is computed. The highest-level peak that exceeds the threshold is chosen as the F_3 peak. If no peak is found for F_3, further analysis is again called for. It has been found that this situation is generally due to F_2 and F_3 being very close together as in Fig. 8(a). As before, an enhanced spectrum is computed using the CZT, in this case over the frequency range (F_2-450)–(F_2+450) Hz. The result is normally a spectrum such as shown in Fig. 8(b) where F_2 and F_3 are clearly resolved. F_2 is chosen to be the frequency of the highest peak and F_3 to be the frequency of the next highest peak. If only one peak is found, that peak is arbitrarily called the F_2 peak and F_3 is set to (F_2+200) Hz. (This may sometimes result in estimates of both F_2 and F_3 that are slightly high.) The final step in the process is to compare F_2 and F_3 and interchange their values if F_2 is greater than F_3.

F. Final Smoothing

As can be seen from the preceding discussion, the three formants are estimated entirely from a single com-

checked to see if it is greater than $F3MN$, the lower limit of the F_3 region. If so, the search for F_3 is extended to cover the combined F_2–F_3 region from $F2MN$ to $F3MX$. Otherwise, the frequency region $F3MN$ to $F3MX$ is searched. As before, a spectral peak is first checked to see if it is in the correct frequency range. Then, the difference between the level of the peak being

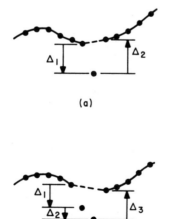

FIG. 12. Nonlinear smoothing applied to formant and pitch estimates. (a) One point "out of line." (b) Two points "out of line."

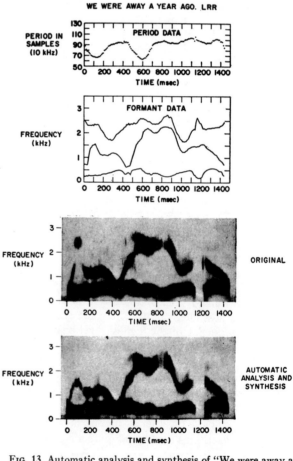

FIG. 13. Automatic analysis and synthesis of "We were away a year ago." Speaker LRR. (a) Pitch period and formant data as plotted by computer. (b) Wide-band spectrogram of original speech. (c) Wide-band spectrogram of synthetic speech generated from the data in (a).

The Journal of the Acoustical Society of America

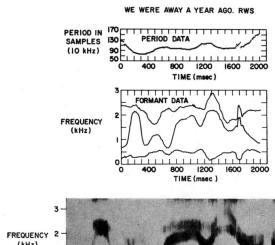

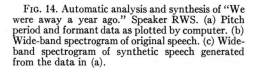

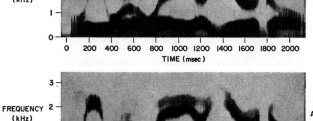

FIG. 14. Automatic analysis and synthesis of "We were away a year ago." Speaker RWS. (a) Pitch period and formant data as plotted by computer. (b) Wide-band spectrogram of original speech. (c) Wideband spectrogram of synthetic speech generated from the data in (a).

ORIGINAL

AUTOMATIC ANALYSIS AND SYNTHESIS

putation of the short-time cepstrum. No attempt has been made to take advantage of the fact that the formants must vary with time in a continuous manner. Simple schemes for using continuity constraints as an aid in searching for the formant peaks were tried. It was found that such schemes generally led to situations in which it was difficult to recover from an erroneous estimate of one of the formants.

For this reason, the estimate of the formants at a given time depends only on the spectrum computed at that time. It is inevitable that some gross errors are made in the estimation of the formants in this manner. The continuity constraint provides a means of correcting such gross errors, i.e., points which are clearly out of line. Continuity constraints are incorporated into the system through the use of a simple, nonlinear smoothing operation applied to both the formant and pitch period data. Figure 12 illustrates the two types of smoothing corrections that are applied. Figure 12(a) shows the case of one point out of line. Here both Δ_1 and Δ_2 are of opposite sign, and both are greater in magnitude than a fixed threshold Δ_T. The point out of line is reassigned the value of the average of the values of the preceding and following points. No other points in the region are altered. Figure 12(b) shows the case of two points out of line. Here both Δ_1 and Δ_3 are of opposite sign and both are greater in magnitude than Δ_T. In this case, the

points out of line are reassigned values on a straight line between the two end samples. No other type of smoothing is used. Values for Δ_T of 1 msec, 100 Hz, 150 Hz, and 200 Hz for the τ, F_1, F_2, and F_3 data, respectively, have been used.

II. RESULTS

An algorithm for estimating the three lowest formant frequencies of voiced speech has been described in considerable detail. The algorithm has been designed to perform well on vowels, glides, and semivowels. No attempt has been made to incorporate into the algorithm any special provisions for dealing with voiced stop consonants or nasal consonants.

One way of evaluating the performance of a formant estimation system is through synthesis of speech from the estimated formants and pitch period. The original speech and the synthetic speech can be compared aurally and through visual inspection of wideband spectrograms. Only informal listening tests have been performed, so that it is not possible to present detailed perceptual results. However, it is possible to present some results in spectrographic form. These results are shown in Figs. 13–16. Each figure consists of: (a) formant and pitch-period plots as obtained from the computer, (b) a wide-band spectrogram of the original speech, and (c) a wide-band spectrogram of speech

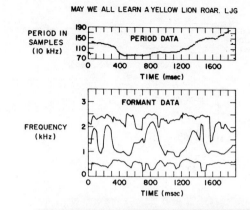

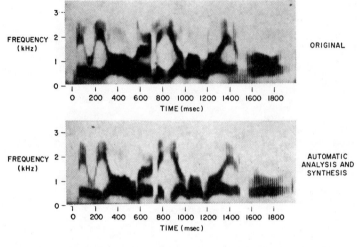

MAY WE ALL LEARN A YELLOW LION ROAR. LJG

ORIGINAL

AUTOMATIC
ANALYSIS AND
SYNTHESIS

FIG. 15. Automatic analysis and synthesis of "May we all learn a yellow lion roar." Speaker LJG. (a) Pitch period and formant data as plotted by computer. (b) Wide-band spectrogram of original speech. (c) Wide-band spectrogram of synthetic speech generated from the data in (a).

synthesized from the data shown in (a) of that figure. Before discussing these results, it is appropriate to discuss some of the details of the generation of the synthetic speech.

A. Synthesis

The synthesizer configuration is shown in Fig. 1. For the specific results presented here, the bandwidth parameters of all the formants were held fixed at the following values: $\alpha_1 = 60\pi$, $\alpha_2 = 100\pi$, $\alpha_3 = 120\pi$, and $\alpha_4 = 175\pi$. The frequency of the highest formant was fixed at the value $F_4 = 4000$ Hz. The fixed spectral shaping is as shown in Fig. 2, and the parameters a and b are, respectively, 400π and 5000π. The gain parameter A was computed from the original speech waveform. A new value of A was computed for each estimate of the formant frequencies and pitch period. The value of A is directly proportional to the rms value of the original speech waveform within the analysis interval. This causes the rms value of each period of synthetic speech to be approximately the same as a corresponding period of the real speech.

In using the system of Fig. 1 for synthesis, the parameters were supplied at 10-msec intervals. However, the system parameters are only allowed to change at a time

when an impulse is present at the output of the impulse generator, i.e., pitch synchronously.

B. Examples

Figure 13 shows the automatic analysis and synthesis of the utterance "We were away a year ago," spoken by Speaker LRR. Figure 14 shows the analysis and synthesis of the same utterance by Speaker RWS. Figure 15 shows the analysis and synthesis of the utterance "May we all learn a yellow lion roar," by Speaker LJG. Figure 16 shows the analysis and synthesis for "May we all . . ." by Speaker PDB. There are several comments on these examples and on our results in general that seem worthwhile.

● In all cases, it is clear that the spectrograms of original and synthetic speech compare favorably. As judged by informal listening, the intelligibility of the synthetic speech is equal to that of the original.

● The synthetic speech retains many of the qualities of the original speaker. However, in the case of Speakers LRR and LJG, the synthetic speech was judged by experienced listeners to sound more like the original than for the other two speakers. It is speculated that this is due to a better spectral balance for Speakers LRR

The Journal of the Acoustical Society of America

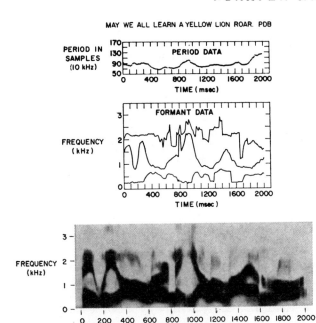

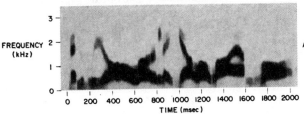

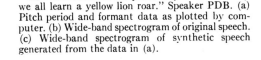

FIG. 16. Automatic analysis and synthesis of "May we all learn a yellow lion roar." Speaker PDB. (a) Pitch period and formant data as plotted by computer. (b) Wide-band spectrogram of original speech. (c) Wide-band spectrogram of synthetic speech generated from the data in (a).

and LJG, which can in turn be attributed to the fixed spectral balance network discussed earlier. It is conceivable that adjustment of the fixed parameters of this network would improve the spectral balance for other speakers.

● It is difficult to express quantitatively accuracy of the system in estimating formants. The synthetic speech was reanalyzed, and results were obtained that agreed with the synthesizer-control data to within 40 Hz for all formants. It can be seen in Fig. 15 and especially Fig. 16 that the F_3 data vary erratically in places. This did not cause much difficulty in the synthesis. It should be noted that the places where the automatic scheme is reliable are the same places where it is almost impossible to locate the formant by eye on the spectrogram of the original speech. At these places, the formant has a low spectra level and is perceptually unimportant.

● It is stressed that this system was not specially designed to handle nasal consonants. Figures 15 and 16 show the spectrograms of the utterance "*M*ay we all lear*n* a yellow lio*n* roar." By comparing the spectrograms, it can be seen that the system tends to estimate formants that produce a spectrum which matches the original reasonably well. In all cases except the /m/ in Fig. 16, the synthetic nasals are properly perceived even though the extra pole–zero pair called for by the acoustic theory has not been included. Since the results on nasals are at present limited, it is not appropriate to place much importance on this finding.

● Within the class of speech sounds for which the system was designed, its major limitation seems to be that results of the quality of Figs. 13–16 have only been obtained for male speakers. Using appropriate formant frequency ranges, we have tested the system on speech from a female speaker. The results were not as good as for male speech in the sense that the formant data was not very smooth. However, speech synthesized from these data was quite intelligible but contained some distracting sections due to the roughness of the data.

III. CONCLUSION

A new system for automatically estimating formant frequencies of voiced speech has been discussed in detail. This system, like many previous ones, attempts to obtain the short-time spectral envelope of the speech and estimates the formants by searching for peaks in this spectrum. Cepstral-analysis techniques and a new spectral-analysis algorithm as well as the theoretical properties of the spectral envelope have been used in the realization of this system.

The results obtained so far have been judged by experienced listeners to produce highly intelligible and, in some instances, very natural-sounding synthetic speech. It is anticipated that this approach may be extended to a wider class of speech sounds than it is presently used for.

A present limitation of the system is that high-quality results are produced only for speech from male speakers. The entire scheme has been programmed on a GE-635 computer and runs in about 120 times real time. That is, to estimate three formants and pitch period for 2 sec of speech and plot the result on microfilm requires about 4 min of computing time on a GE-635 computer. This cost is certainly not prohibitive if one is using the system as a tool in research on speech synthesis. Hardware realization of such a system is not out of the question given the existence of a special-purpose computer for computing the transforms.

Plans for future work primarily focus on extention to a wider class of speech sounds. This will require a reliable voiced/unvoiced detection and detection of different phoneme classes. It is felt that most of the analysis can be performed within essentially the present framework using a combination of the cepstrum, smoothed spectrum, and simple measurements on the acoustic waveform.

Appendix A. Chirp z-Transform Algorithm

The chirp z-transform algorithm[18] plays an important role in the method of estimating formant frequencies discussed in Sec. I. This Appendix discusses the algorithm and summarizes its important properties. Consider the z-transform of a finite sequence of samples $\{x_n, n=0, 1, \cdots, N-1\}$;

$$X(z) = \sum_{n=0}^{N-1} x_n z^{-n}. \quad \text{(A1)}$$

The CZT algorithm is an efficient means for evaluating Eq. A1 at the points

$$z_k = AW^{-k}, \quad k=0, 1, \cdots, M-1, \quad \text{(A2)}$$

where M is an arbitrary integer and A and W are arbitrary complex numbers of the form

$$A = A_0 e^{j2\pi\theta_0},$$
$$W = W_0 e^{j2\pi\phi_0}.$$

The case $A=1$, $M=N$, and $W=e^{j(2\pi/N)}$ corresponds to the discrete Fourier transform which, when N is a highly composite number, can be very efficiently evaluated using one of the so-called fast Fourier transform (FFT) algorithms.[16] The more general z-plane contour specified by Eq. A2 is shown in Fig. A-1, The contour begins at the point $z=A$, and depending on W_0, spirals in or out with respect to the origin. If $W_0=1$, the contour is an arc of a circle of radius A_0. The angular spacing of the samples along this contour is $2\pi\phi_0$. This z-plane contour can be related to an s-plane contour through the relation $z=e^{sT}$. Thus, the equivalent s-plane contour begins at the point

$$s_0 = \sigma_0 + j\omega_0 = (1/T)\ln A,$$

and the samples of the transform are evaluated at the points

$$s_k = s_0 + k(\Delta\sigma + j\Delta\omega) = (1/T)(\ln A - k \ln W)$$

for $k=0, 1, \cdots, M-1$. The CZT algorithm is an efficient algorithm for evaluating the transform on such contours and for our purposes affords the following advantages:

• The number of time samples N does not have to equal the number of frequency samples M.

• Neither M nor N need be a composite number.

• The starting point $z=A$ is arbitrary. ($A_0 \, \hat{} \, 1$ causes enhancement of the spectral resonances, and θ_0 is chosen so as to center the analysis on the frequency region of interest.)

• The frequency spacing of the spectral samples depends on ϕ_0, which is also arbitrary. Thus, a fine-grain

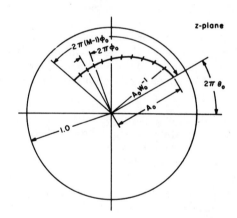

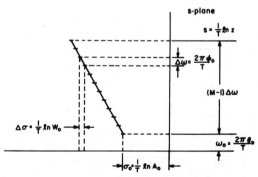

Fig. A-1. *Top*: z-plane contour for analysis using the chirp z-transform. *Bottom*: Corresponding s-plane contour.

The Journal of the Acoustical Society of America

frequency analysis can be performed over a narrow band beginning at some arbitrary frequency specified by θ_0.

Along the contour of Eq. A2, Eq. A1 becomes

$$X_k = \sum_{n=0}^{N-1} x_n A^{-n} W^{nk} \quad k=0, 1, \cdots, M-1, \quad \text{(A3)}$$

which seems to require $N \cdot M$ complex multiplications and additions. However, through the substitution[A1]

$$nk = [n^2 + k^2 - (k-n)^2]/2,$$

[A1] L. I. Bluestein, "A Linear Filtering Approach to the Computation of the Discrete Fourier Transform," 1968 NEREM Rec. 10, 218–219 (Nov. 1968).

Eq. A3 can be written

$$x_k = W^{k^2/2} \sum_{n=0}^{N-1} (x_n A^{-n} W^{n^2/2}) W^{-(k-n)^2/2},$$
$$k=0, 1, \cdots, M-1. \quad \text{(A4)}$$

This form of the equation can be evaluated with computation time roughly proportional to $(N+M) \log (N+M)$, since the convolution sum in Eq. A4 can be evaluated using the FFT.[A2] The steps in the programming of the algorithm are given in detail in Ref. 18.

[A2] T. G. Stockham, Jr., "High Speed Convolution and Correlation," 1966 Spring Joint Computer Conf. AFIPS Proc. 28, 229–233 (1966).

Appendix B. Application of the Chirp z-Transform to the Cepstrum

The purpose of this Appendix is to show that applying the CZT algorithm directly to the cepstrum $c(nT)$ leads to a meaningful enhancement of the resonances in the smoothed spectrum. The complex cepstrum, $\hat{x}(nT)$, is defined as the inverse transform of the *complex* logarithm of $X(z)$, where $X(z)$ is the z-transform of the input sequence $x(nT)$[14,B1]. It can be shown that the cepstrum $c(nT)$ (as defined in this paper) is just the even part of $\hat{x}(nT)$; i.e.,

$$c(nT) = [\hat{x}(nT) + \hat{x}(-nT)]/2.$$

Thus, $c(nT)$ and $\log|X(z)|$ are transforms of each other. A sequence $y(nT)$ whose z-transform $Y(z)$ is minimum phase (has no poles or zeros outside the unit circle) has a complex cepstrum $\hat{y}(nT)$ that is zero for $n < 0$.[14,B1] Furthermore, if

$$\log|Y(z)| = \log|X(z)|, \quad \text{(B1)}$$

then

$$\begin{aligned} \hat{y}(nT) &= 0 & n < 0 \\ &= c(nT) & n = 0 \\ &= 2c(nT) & n > 0. \end{aligned} \quad \text{(B2)}$$

[B1] A. V. Oppenheim, R. W. Schafer and T. G. Stockham, Jr., "Nonlinear Filtering of Multiplied and Convolved Signals," Proc. IEEE 56, 1264–1291 (1968).

Therefore, arguing backwards from Eq. B2, we can always compute a minimum phase sequence that has the same log magnitude as $X(z)$.

It can also be shown that if a sequence $y_1(nT)$ is defined by

$$y_1(nT) = A^n y(nT) \quad \text{(B3)}$$

with z-transform

$$Y_1(z) = \sum_{n=0}^{N-1} y(nT) A^n z^{-n} = Y(z/A), \quad \text{(B4)}$$

then

$$\hat{y}_1(nT) = A^n \hat{y}(nT). \quad \text{(B5)}$$

This computation of $\log|Y_1(e^{j\omega T})|$ is equivalent to evaluation of $\log|Y(A^{-1}e^{j\omega T})|$, which is in turn identical to $\log|X(A^{-1}e^{j\omega T})|$. Therefore, using the CZT algorithm to evaluate the transform of $\hat{y}(nT)$ as given in Eq. B2 on a circular arc of radius A^{-1}, the same result in the log magnitude is achieved as if the original evaluation of the z-transform had been made along that contour.

Received 2 April 1971; revised 21 April 1971

Speech Analysis and Synthesis by Linear Prediction of the Speech Wave

B. S. Atal and Suzanne L. Hanauer

Bell Telephone Laboratories, Incorporated, Murray Hill, New Jersey 07974

We describe a procedure for efficient encoding of the speech wave by representing it in terms of time-varying parameters related to the transfer function of the vocal tract and the characteristics of the excitation. The speech wave, sampled at 10 kHz, is analyzed by predicting the present speech sample as a linear combination of the 12 previous samples. The 12 predictor coefficients are determined by minimizing the mean-squared error between the actual and the predicted values of the speech samples. Fifteen parameters—namely, the 12 predictor coefficients, the pitch period, a binary parameter indicating whether the speech is voiced or unvoiced, and the rms value of the speech samples—are derived by analysis of the speech wave, encoded and transmitted to the synthesizer. The speech wave is synthesized as the output of a linear recursive filter excited by either a sequence of quasiperiodic pulses or a white-noise source. Application of this method for efficient transmission and storage of speech signals as well as procedures for determining other speech characteristics, such as formant frequencies and bandwidths, the spectral envelope, and the autocorrelation function, are discussed.

INTRODUCTION

Efficient representation of speech signals in terms of a small number of slowly varying parameters is a problem of considerable importance in speech research. Most methods for analyzing speech start by transforming the acoustic data into spectral form by performing a short-time Fourier analysis of the speech wave.[1] Although spectral analysis is a well-known technique for studying signals, its application to speech signals suffers from a number of serious limitations arising from the non-stationary as well as the quasiperiodic properties of the speech wave.[2] As a result, methods based on spectral analysis often do not provide a sufficiently accurate description of speech articulation. We present in this paper a new approach to speech analysis and synthesis in which we represent the speech waveform directly in terms of time-varying parameters related to the transfer function of the vocal tract and the characteristics of the source function.[3-5] By modeling the speech wave itself, rather than its spectrum, we avoid the problems inherent in frequency-domain methods. For instance, the traditional Fourier analysis methods require a relatively long speech segment to provide adequate spectral resolution. As a result, rapidly changing speech events cannot be accurately followed. Furthermore, because of the periodic nature of voiced speech, little information about the spectrum between pitch harmonics is available; consequently, the frequency-domain techniques do not perform satisfactorily for high-pitched voices such as the voices of women and children. Although pitch-synchronous analysis-by-synthesis techniques can provide a partial solution to the above difficulties, such techniques are extremely cumbersome and time consuming even for modern digital computers and are therefore unsuitable for automatic processing of large amounts of speech data.[6,7] In contrast, the techniques presented in this paper are shown to avoid these problems completely.

The speech analysis–synthesis technique described in this paper is applicable to a wide range of research problems in speech production and perception. One of the main objectives of our method is the synthesis of speech which is indistinguishable from normal human speech. Much can be learned about the information-carrying structure of speech by selectively altering the properties of the speech signal. These techniques can thus serve as a tool for modifying the acoustic properties of a given speech signal without degrading the speech quality. Some other potential applications of these techniques are in the areas of efficient storage and transmission of speech, automatic formant and pitch extraction, and speaker and speech recognition.

In the rest of the paper, we describe a parametric model for representing the speech signal in the time

Reprinted with permission from *J. Acoust. Soc. Am.*, vol. 50, pp. 637–655, Aug. 1971.

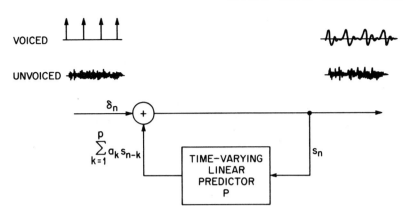

FIG. 1. Block diagram of a functional model of speech production based on the linear prediction representation of the speech wave.

domain; we discuss methods for analyzing the speech wave to obtain these parameters and for synthesizing the speech wave from them. Finally, we discuss applications for efficient coding of speech, estimation of the spectral envelope, formant analysis, and for modifying the acoustic properties of the speech signal.

The paper is organized such that most of the mathematical details are discussed in a set of appendixes. The main body of the paper is nearly complete in itself, and those readers who are not interested in the mathematical or computational aspects may skip the appendixes.

I. MODEL FOR PARAMETRIC REPRESENTATION OF THE SPEECH WAVE

In modern signal-processing techniques, the procedures for analyzing a signal make use of all the information that can be obtained in advance about the structure of that signal. The first step in signal analysis is thus to make a model of the signal.

Speech sounds are produced as a result of acoustical excitation of the human vocal tract. During the production of voiced sounds, the vocal tract is excited by a series of nearly periodic pulses generated by the vocal cords. In the case of unvoiced sounds, the excitation is provided by air passing turbulently through constrictions in the tract. A simple model of the vocal tract can be made by representing it as a discrete time-varying linear filter. If we assume that the variations with time of the vocal-tract shape can be approximated with sufficient accuracy by a succession of stationary shapes, it is possible to define a transfer function in the complex z domain for the vocal tract. The transfer function of a linear network can always be represented by its poles and zeros. It is well known that for nonnasal voiced speech sounds the transfer function of the vocal tract has no zeros.[8] For these sounds, the vocal tract can therefore be adequately represented by an all-pole (recursive) filter. A representation of the vocal tract for unvoiced and nasal sounds usually includes the antiresonances (zeros) as well as the resonances (poles) of the vocal tract. Since the zeros of the transfer function of the vocal tract for unvoiced and nasal sounds lie within the unit circle in the z plane,[9] each factor in the

numerator of the transfer function can be approximated by multiple poles in the denominator of the transfer function.[10] In addition, the location of a pole is considerably more important perceptually than the location of a zero; the zeros in most cases contribute only to the spectral balance. Thus, an explicit representation of the antiresonances by zeros of the linear filter is not necessary. An all-pole model of the vocal tract can approximate the effect of antiresonances on the speech wave in the frequency range of interest to any desired accuracy.

The z transform of the glottal volume flow during a single pitch period can also be assumed to have poles only and no zeros. With this approximation, the z transform of the glottal flow can be represented by

$$U_g(z) = \frac{K_1}{(1 - z_a z^{-1})(1 - z_b z^{-1})}, \qquad (1)$$

where K_1 is a constant related to the amplitude of the glottal flow and z_a, z_b are poles on the real axis inside the unit circle. In most cases, one of the poles is very close to the unit circle. If the radiation of sound from the mouth is approximated as radiation from a simple spherical source, then the ratio between the sound pressure at the microphone and the volume velocity at the lips is represented in the z-transform notation as $K_2(1 - z^{-1})$, where K_2 is a constant related to the amplitude of the volume flow at the lips and the distance from the lips to the microphone.[11] The contribution of the glottal volume flow, together with the radiation, can thus be represented in the transfer function by the factor

$$\frac{K_1 K_2 (1 - z^{-1})}{(1 - z_a z^{-1})(1 - z_b z^{-1})},$$

which, in turn, can be approximated as

$$\frac{K_1 K_2}{[1 + (1 - z_a) z^{-1}](1 - z_b z^{-1})}. \qquad (2)$$

The error introduced by this approximation is given by

$$-\frac{K_1 K_2 z^{-2}(1 - z_a)}{(1 - z_a z^{-1})[1 + (1 - z_a) z^{-1}](1 - z_b z^{-1})}.$$

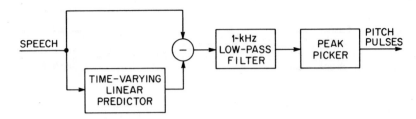

FIG. 2. Block diagram of the pitch pulse detector.

The contribution of this error to the transfer function in the frequency range of interest can be assumed to be small, since $z_a \approx 1$.

One of the important features of our model is that the combined contributions of the glottal flow, the vocal tract, and the radiation are represented by a single recursive filter. The difficult problem of separating the contribution of the source function from that of the vocal tract is thus completely avoided.

This representation of the speech signal is illustrated in sampled-data form in Fig. 1. The vocal-cord excitation for voiced sounds is produced by a pulse generator with adjustable period and amplitude. The noise-like excitation of unvoiced sounds is produced by a white-noise source. The linear predictor P, a transversal filter with p delays of one sample interval each, forms a weighted sum of the past p samples at the input of the predictor. The output of the linear filter at the nth sampling instant is given by

$$s_n = \sum_{k=1}^{p} a_k s_{n-k} + \delta_n, \qquad (3)$$

where the "predictor coefficients" a_k account for the filtering action of the vocal tract, the radiation, and the glottal flow; and δ_n represents the nth sample of the excitation.

The transfer function of the linear filter of Fig. 1 is given by

$$T(z) = 1/(1 - \sum_{k=1}^{p} a_k z^{-k}). \qquad (4)$$

The poles of $T(z)$ are the (reciprocal) zeros of the polynomial (in z^{-1}) in the denominator on the right side of Eq. 4. The linear filter thus has a total of p poles which are either real or occur in conjugate pairs. Moreover, for the linear filter to be stable, the poles must be inside the unit circle.

The number of coefficients p required to represent any speech segment adequately is determined by the number of resonances and antiresonances of the vocal tract in the frequency range of interest, the nature of the glottal volume flow function, and the radiation. As discussed earlier, two poles are usually adequate to represent the influence of the glottal flow and the radiation on the speech wave. It is shown in Appendix B that, in order to represent the poles of the vocal-tract transfer function adequately, the linear predictor memory must be equal to twice the time required for sound waves to

travel from the glottis to the lips (nasal opening for nasal sounds). For example, if the vocal tract is 17 cm in length, the memory of the predictor should be roughly 1 msec in order to represent the poles of transfer function of the vocal tract. The corresponding value of p is then 10 for a sampling interval of 0.1 msec. With the two poles required for the glottal flow and the radiation added, p should be approximately 12. These calculations are meant to provide only a rough estimate of p and will depend to some extent on the speaker as well as on the spoken material. The results based on speech synthesis experiments (see Sec. IV) indicate that, in most cases, a value of p equal to 12 is adequate at a sampling frequency of 10 kHz. p is, naturally, a function of the sampling frequency f_s and is roughly proportional to f_s.

The predictor coefficients a_k, together with the pitch period, the rms value of the speech samples, and a binary parameter indicating whether the speech is voiced or unvoiced, provide a complete representation of the speech wave over a time interval during which the vocal-tract shape is assumed to be constant. During speech production, of course, the vocal-tract shape changes continuously in time. In most cases, it is sufficient to readjust these parameters periodically, for example, once every 5 or 10 msec.

II. SPEECH ANALYSIS

A. Determination of the Predictor Parameters

Going back to Fig. 1, we see that, except for one sample at the beginning of every pitch period, samples of voiced speech are linearly predictable in terms of the past p speech samples. We now use this property of the speech wave to determine the predictor coefficients. Let us define the prediction error E_n as the difference between the speech sample s_n and its predicted value $\hat{s}_n$ given by

$$\hat{s}_n = \sum_{k=1}^{p} a_k s_{n-k}. \qquad (5)$$

E_n is then given by

$$E_n = s_n - \hat{s}_n = s_n - \sum_{k=1}^{p} a_k s_{n-k}. \qquad (6)$$

We define the mean-squared prediction error $\langle E_n{}^2 \rangle_{\mathrm{av}}$ as the average of $E_n{}^2$ over all the sampling instances n in the speech segment to be analyzed except those at the

The Journal of the Acoustical Society of America

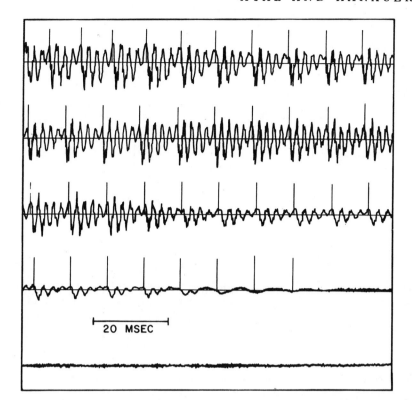

Fig. 3. Waveform of the speech signal together with the positions of the pitch pulses (shown by vertical lines).

20 MSEC

beginning of each pitch period, i.e.,

$$\langle E_n{}^2 \rangle_{\mathrm{av}} = \langle (s_n - \sum_{k=1}^{p} a_k s_{n-k})^2 \rangle_{\mathrm{av}}. \quad (7)$$

The predictor coefficients a_k of Eq. 3 are chosen so as to minimize the mean-squared prediction error $\langle E_n{}^2 \rangle_{\mathrm{av}}$. The same procedure is used to determine the predictor parameters for unvoiced sounds, too.

The coefficients a_k which minimize the mean-squared prediction error are obtained by setting the partial derivative of $\langle E_n{}^2 \rangle_{\mathrm{av}}$ with respect to each a_k equal to zero. It can then be shown[3] that the coefficients a_k are obtained as solutions of the set of equations

$$\sum_{k=1}^{p} \varphi_{jk} a_k = \varphi_{j0}, \quad j=1, 2, \cdots, p, \quad (8)$$

where

$$\varphi_{jk} = \langle s_{n-j} s_{n-k} \rangle_{\mathrm{av}}. \quad (9)$$

In general, the solution of a set of simultaneous linear equations requires a great deal of computation. However, the set of linear equations given by Eq. 8 is a special one, since the matrix of coefficients is symmetric and positive definite. There are several methods of solving such equations.[12,13] A computationally efficient method of solving Eq. 8 is outlined in Appendix C.

Occasionally, the coefficients a_k obtained by solving Eq. 8 produce poles in the transfer function which are outside the unit circle. This can happen whenever a pole of the transfer function near the unit circle appears out-

side the unit circle, owing to approximations in the model. The locations of all such poles must be corrected. A simple computational procedure to determine if any pole of the transfer function is outside the unit circle and a method for correcting the predictor coefficients are described in Appendix D.

B. Pitch Analysis

Although any reliable pitch-analysis method can be used to determine the pitch of the speech signal, we outline here briefly two methods of pitch analysis which are sufficiently reliable and accurate for our purpose.

In the first method,[14] the speech wave is filtered through a 1-kHz low-pass filter and each filtered speech sample is raised to the third power to emphasize the high-amplitude portions of the speech waveform. The duration of the pitch period is obtained by performing a pitch-synchronous correlation analysis of the cubed speech. The voiced–unvoiced decision is based on two factors, the density of zero crossings in the speech wave and the peak value of the correlation function. This method of pitch analysis is described in detail in Ref. 14.

The second method of pitch analysis is based on the linear prediction representation of the speech wave.[15] It follows from Fig. 1 that, except for a sample at the beginning of each pitch period, every sample of the voiced speech waveform can be predicted from the past sample values. Therefore, the positions of individual pitch pulses can be determined by computing the prediction error E_n given by Eq. 6 and then locating the

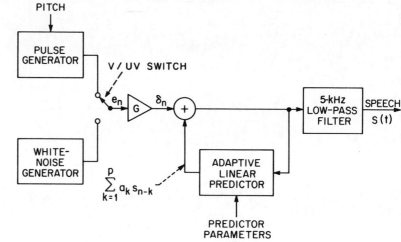

FIG. 4. Block diagram of the speech synthesizer.

samples for which the prediction error is large. The latter function is easily accomplished by a suitable peak-picking procedure. This procedure is illustrated in Fig. 2. In practice, the prediction error was found to be large at the beginning of the pitch periods and a relatively simple peak-picking procedure was found to be effective. The voiced–unvoiced decision is based on the ratio of the mean-squared value of the speech samples to the mean-squared value of the prediction error samples. This ratio is considerably smaller for unvoiced speech sounds than for voiced speech sounds—typically, by a factor of 10. The result of the pitch analysis on a short segment of the speech wave is illustrated in Fig. 3. The positions of the individual pitch pulses, shown by vertical lines, are superimposed on the speech waveform for easy comparison.

III. SPEECH SYNTHESIS

The speech signal is synthesized by means of the same parametric representation as was used in the analysis. A block diagram of the speech synthesizer is shown in Fig. 4. The control parameters supplied to the synthesizer are the pitch period, a binary voiced–unvoiced parameter, the rms value of the speech samples, and the p predictor coefficients. The pulse generator produces a pulse of unit amplitude at the beginning of each pitch period. The white-noise generator produces uncorrelated uniformly distributed random samples with standard deviation equal to 1 at each sampling instant. The selection between the pulse generator and the white-noise generator is made by the voiced–unvoiced switch. The amplitude of the excitation signal is adjusted by the amplifier G. The linearly predicted value $\hat{s}_n$ of the speech signal is combined with the excitation signal δ_n to form the nth sample of the synthesized speech signal. The speech samples are finally low-pass filtered to provide the continuous speech wave $s(t)$.

It may be pointed out here that, although for time-invariant networks the synthesizer of Fig. 4 will be equivalent to a traditional formant synthesizer with variable formant bandwidths, its operation for the time-varying case (which is true in speech synthesis) differs significantly from that of a formant synthesizer. For instance, a formant synthesizer has separate filters for each formant and, thus, a correct labeling of formant frequencies is essential for the proper functioning of a formant synthesizer. This is not necessary for the synthesizer of Fig. 4, since the formants are synthesized together by one recursive filter. Moreover, the amplitude of the pitch pulses as well as the white noise is adjusted to provide the correct rms value of the synthetic speech samples.

The synthesizer control parameters are reset to their new values at the beginning of every pitch period for voiced speech and once every 10 msec for unvoiced speech. If the control parameters are not determined pitch-synchronously in the analysis, new parameters are computed by suitable interpolation of the original parameters to allow pitch-synchronous resetting of the synthesizer. The pitch period and the rms value are interpolated "geometrically" (linear interpolation on a logarithmic scale). In interpolating the predictor coefficients, it is necessary to ensure the stability of the recursive filter in the synthesizer. The stability cannot, in general, be ensured by direct linear interpolation of the predictor parameters. One suitable method is to interpolate the first p samples of the autocorrelation function of the impulse response of the recursive filter. The autocorrelation function has the important advantage of having a one-to-one relationship with the predictor coefficients. Therefore, the predictor coefficients can be recomputed from the autocorrelation function. Moreover, the predictor coefficients derived from the autocorrelation function always result in a stable filter in the synthesizer.[16] The relationship between the predictor coefficients and the autocorrelation function can be derived as follows:

The Journal of the Acoustical Society of America

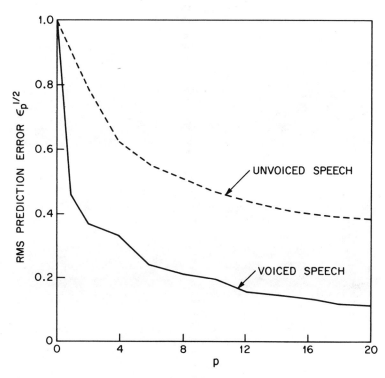

FIG. 5. Variation of the minimum value of the rms prediction error with p, the number of predictor coefficients. Solid line shows the curve for voiced speech. Dotted line shows the curve for unvoiced speech.

From Eq. 3, the impulse response of the linear recursive filter of Fig. 1 satisfies the equation

$$s_n = \sum_{k=1}^{p} a_k s_{n-k}, \quad n \geq 1, \tag{10}$$

with the initial conditions $s_0 = 1$ and $s_n = 0$ for $n < 0$. The autocorrelation function of the impulse response is, by definition, given by

$$r_{|i|} = \sum_{n=0}^{\infty} s_n s_{n+|i|}. \tag{11}$$

Let us multiply both sides of Eq. 10 by s_{n+i} and perform a sum over n from 0 to ∞. We then obtain

$$r_i = \sum_{k=1}^{p} a_k r_{|i-k|}, \quad i \geq 1, \tag{12}$$

and

$$r_0 = \sum_{k=1}^{p} a_k r_k + 1. \tag{13}$$

Equations 12 and 13 enable us to compute the samples of the autocorrelation function from the predictor coefficients, and the predictor coefficients from the autocorrelation function. A computational procedure for performing the above operations is outlined in Appendix E.

The gain of the amplifier G is adjusted to provide the correct power in the synthesized speech signal. In any speech segment, the amplitude of the nth synthesized speech sample s_n can be decomposed into two parts: one part q_n contributed by the memory of the linear predictor carried over from the previous speech segments and the other part v_n contributed by the excitation from the current speech segment. Thus, $s_n = q_n + v_n = q_n + g u_n$, where g is the gain of the amplifier G. Let us assume that $n=1$ is the first sample and $n=M$ the last sample of the current speech segment. The first part q_n is given by

$$q_n = \sum_{k=1}^{p} a_k q_{n-k}, \quad 1 \leq n \leq M, \tag{14}$$

where $q_0, q_{-1}, \cdots, q_{1-p}$ represent the memory of the predictor carried over from the previous synthesized speech segments. In addition, u_n is given by

$$u_n = \sum_{k=1}^{p} a_k u_{n-k} + e_n, \quad 1 \leq n \leq M, \tag{15}$$

where $u_n = 0$ for nonpositive values of n, and e_n is the nth sample at the output of the voiced–unvoiced switch as shown in Fig. 4. Let P_s be the mean-squared value of the speech samples. Then P_s is given by

$$P_s = \frac{1}{M} \sum_{n=1}^{M} (q_n + g u_n)^2 = \overline{(q_n + g u_n)^2}. \tag{16}$$

On further rearrangement of terms, Eq. 16 is rewritten as

$$g^2 \overline{u_n^2} + 2g \overline{q_n u_n} + \overline{q_n^2} - P_s = 0. \tag{17}$$

Equation 17 is solved for g such that g is real and non-

SYNTHETIC SPEECH

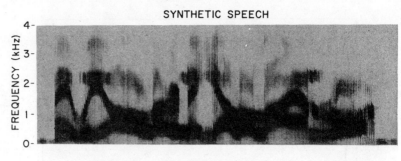

ORIGINAL SPEECH

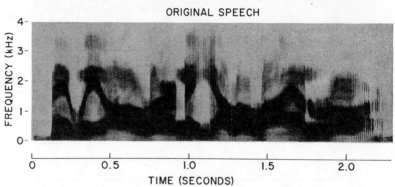

TIME (SECONDS)

FIG. 6. Comparison of wide-band sound spectrograms for synthetic and original speech signals for the utterance "May we all learn a yellow lion roar," spoken by a male speaker: (a) synthetic speech, and (b) original speech.

negative. In case such a solution does not exist, g is set to zero. The nth sample of the synthesized wave is finally obtained by adding q_n to $g u_n$.

IV. COMPUTER SIMULATION OF THE ANALYSIS–SYNTHESIS SYSTEM

In order to assess the subjective quality of the synthesized speech, the speech analysis and synthesis system described above was simulated on a digital computer. The speech wave was first low-pass filtered to 5 kHz and then sampled at a frequency of 10 kHz. The analysis segment was set equal to a pitch period for voiced speech and equal to 10 msec for unvoiced speech. The various parameters were then determined for each analysis segment according to the procedure described in Sec. II. These parameters were finally used to control the speech synthesizer shown in Fig. 4.

The optimum value for the number of predictor parameters p was determined as follows: The speech wave was synthesized for various values of p between 2 and 18. Informal listening tests revealed no significant differences between synthetic speech samples for p larger than 12. There was slight degradation in speech quality at p equal to 8. However, even for p as low as 2, the synthetic speech was intelligible although poor in quality. The influence of decreasing p to values less than 10 was most noticeable on nasal consonants. Furthermore, the effect of decreasing p was less noticeable on female voices than on male voices. This could be expected in view of the fact that the length of the vocal tract for female speakers is generally shorter than for male speakers and that the nasal tract is slightly longer

than the oral tract. From these results, it was concluded that a value of p equal to 12 was required to provide an adequate representation of the speech signal. It may be worthwhile at this point to compare these results with the objective results based on an examination of the variation of the prediction error as a function of p. In Fig. 5, we have plotted the minimum value of the rms prediction error as a function of several values of p. The speech power in each case was normalized to unity. The results are presented separately for voiced and unvoiced speech. As can be seen in the figure, the prediction error curve is relatively flat for values of p greater than 12 for voiced speech and for p greater than 6 for unvoiced speech. These results suggest again that p equal to 12 is adequate for voiced speech. For unvoiced speech, a lower value of p, e.g., p equal to 6, should be adequate. For those readers who wish to listen to the quality of synthesized speech at various values of p, a recording accompanies this article. Appendix A gives the contents of the record. The reader should listen at this point to the first section of the record.

In informal listening tests, the quality of the synthetic speech was found to be very close to that of the original speech for a wide range of speakers and spoken material. No significant differences were observed between the synthetic speech samples of male and female speakers. The second section of the record includes examples of synthesized speech for several utterances of different speakers. In each case, p was set to equal to 12. The spectrograms of the synthetic and the original speech for two of these utterances are compared in Figs. 6 and 7. As can be seen, the spectrogram of the synthetic speech closely resembles that of the original speech.

The Journal of the Acoustical Society of America

SYNTHETIC SPEECH

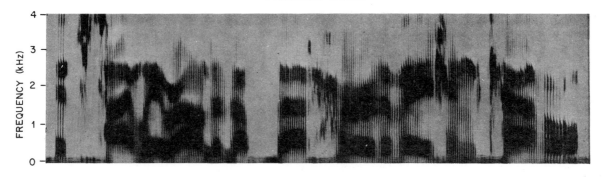

ORIGINAL SPEECH

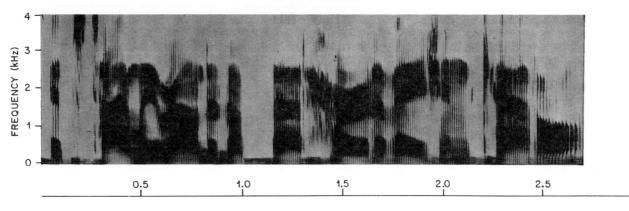

TIME (SEC)

FIG. 7. Comparison of wide-band sound spectrograms for synthetic and original speech signals for the utterance "It's time we rounded up that herd of Asian cattle," spoken by a male speaker: (a) synthetic speech, and (b) original speech.

V. APPLICATIONS

A. Digital Storage and Transmission of Speech

Methods for encoding speech at data rates considerably smaller than those needed for PCM encoding are important in many practical applications. For example, automatic answerback services can be practical if a sufficiently large vocabulary of words and phrases can be stored economically in a digital computer. Efficient speech coding methods can reduce, by a factor of 30 or more, the space needed for storing the vocabulary. We discuss in this section several procedures for efficient coding of the synthesizer control information.

The synthesizer control information includes 15 parameters for every analysis interval, i.e., the twelve predictor coefficients, the pitch period, the voiced–unvoiced parameter, and the rms value. The methods for proper encoding of this information, except the predictor coefficients, are relatively well understood.[17] On the other hand, the procedure for encoding the predictor coefficients must include provision for ensuring the

stability of the linear filter in the synthesizer. In general, to ensure stability, relatively high accuracy (about 8–10 bits per coefficient) is required if the predictor coefficients are quantized directly. Moreover, the predictor coefficients are samples of the inverse Fourier transform of the reciprocal of the transfer function. The reciprocal of the transfer function has zeros precisely where the transfer function has poles. Therefore, small errors in the predictor coefficients often can result in large errors in the poles. The direct quantization of the predictor coefficients is thus not efficient. One suitable method is to convert the 12 predictor coefficients to another equivalent set of parameters which possess well-defined constraints for achieving the desired stability. For example, the poles of the linear filter can be computed from the predictor coefficients. For stability of the filter, it is sufficient that the poles be inside the unit circle. The stability is therefore easily ensured by quantizing the frequencies and the bandwidths of the poles. The poles of the transfer function are by definition the

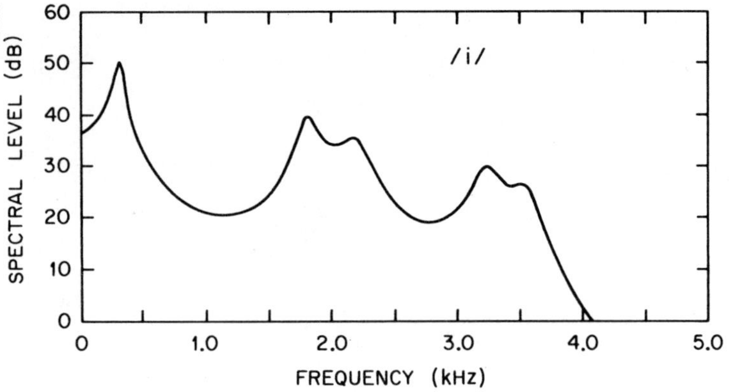

FIG. 8. Spectral envelope for the vowel /i/ in "we," spoken by a male speaker ($F_0 = 120$ Hz).

roots of the polynomial equation

$$\sum_{k=1}^{p} a_k z^{-k} = 1, \qquad (18)$$

where, as before, a_k are the predictor coefficients. Table I shows the precision with which each of the parameters is quantized. It was found that the frequencies and the bandwidths of the poles can be quantized within 60 bits without producing any perceptible effect on the synthesized speech. Adding this value to the bits needed for the pitch (6 bits), the rms value (5 bits), and the voiced–unvoiced parameter (1 bit), one arrives at a value of 72 bits ($60+6+5+1$) for each frame of analyzed data. The data rate in bits/sec is obtained by multiplying the number of bits used to encode each frame of data by the number of frames of data stored or transmitted per second. Thus, a bit rate of 7200 bits/sec is achieved if the parameters are sampled at a rate of 100/sec. The bit rate is lowered to 2400 bits/sec at a sampling rate of 33/sec.

At this point, the reader can listen to recorded examples of synthesized speech encoded at three different data rates, namely, 7200, 4800, and 2400 bits/sec, respectively, in the third section of the enclosed record.

The quantizing of the frequencies and the bandwidths of the poles is not the only method of encoding the predictor coefficients. For example, it can be shown (see Appendix F) that a transfer function with p poles is always realizable as the transfer function of an acoustic tube consisting of p cylindrical sections of equal length

with the last section terminated by a unit acoustic resistance. Moreover, the poles are always inside the unit circle if the cross-sectional area of each cylindrical section is positive. Thus, the stability of the synthesizer filter is easily achieved by quantizing the areas of the sections or any other suitable function of the areas.

No significant difference in speech quality was observed for the different quantizing methods outlined above at various bit rates above 2400 bits/sec. It is quite possible that at very low bit rates these different methods of coding may show appreciable differences. An example of speech synthesized using area quantization is presented in the fourth section of the record.

The data rates discussed in this paper are suitable for speech-transmission applications where large buffer storage is to be avoided. The efficiency of speech coding naturally can vary considerably from one application to another. For example, it has been assumed so far that the speech signal is analyzed at uniform time intervals. However, it may be more efficient to vary the analysis interval so that it is short during fast articulatory transitions and long during steady-state segments. Furthermore, in applications such as disk storage of voice messages, additional savings can be realized by choosing the quantization levels for each parameter around its mean value determined in advance over short time intervals. The mean value itself can be quantized separately.

B. Separation of Spectral Envelope and Fine Structure

It is often desirable to separate the envelope of the speech spectrum from its fine structure.[18] The representation of the speech signal shown in Fig. 1 is very suitable for achieving this decomposition. In this representation, the fine structure of the spectrum is contributed by the source while the envelope is contributed by the linear filter. Thus, the two are easily separated.[19] The spectral envelope is the power spectrum of the impulse response of the linear filter. In mathematical notation, the relationship between the spectral envelope $G(f)$ at the frequency f and the predictor coefficients is expressed by

$$G(f) = 1 / \left| 1 - \sum_{k=1}^{p} a_k e^{-2\pi j f k / f_s} \right|^2, \qquad (19)$$

TABLE I. Quantization of synthesizer control information.

Parameter	Number of levels	Bits
Pitch	64	6
V/UV	2	1
rms	32	5
Frequencies and bandwidths of the poles		60
	Total	72

The Journal of the Acoustical Society of America

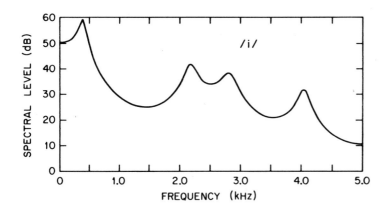

FIG. 9. Spectral envelope for the vowel /i/ in "we," spoken by a female speaker ($F_0 = 200$ Hz).

where a_k, as before, are the predictor coefficients and f_s is the sampling frequency. Two examples of the spectral envelope obtained in the above manner for the vowel /i/ belonging to the word "we" in the utterance "May we all learn a yellow lion roar" spoken by a male and a female speaker are illustrated in Figs. 8 and 9, respectively. We would like to add here that a spectral section obtained on a sound spectrograph failed to separate the third formant from the second formant for the female speaker both in the wide-band and the narrow-band analysis. The spectral section showed one broad peak for the two formants. On the other hand, the spectral envelope of Fig. 9 shows the two formants without any ambiguity. Of course, it is difficult to evaluate the accuracy of this method from results based on real speech alone. Results with synthetic speech, where the spectral envelope is known precisely, indicate that the spectral envelope is accurately determined over a wide range of pitch values (from 50 to 300 Hz).

It also follows from Eq. 19 that, although the Fourier transform of $G(f)$ is not time limited, the Fourier transform of $1/G(f)$ is time limited to $2p/f_s$ sec. Thus, spectral samples of $G(f)$, spaced $f_s/2p$ Hz apart, are sufficient for reconstruction of the spectral envelope. For $p=12$ and $f_s=10$ kHz, this means that a spacing of roughly 400 Hz between spectral samples is adequate.

In some applications, it may be desired to compute the Fourier transform of $G(f)$, namely, the autocorrelation function. The autocorrelation function can be determined directly from the predictor coefficients without computing $G(f)$. The relationship between the predictor coefficients and the autocorrelation function is given in Eqs. 12 and 13, and a computational method for performing these operations is outlined in Appendix E.

C. Formant Analysis

The objective of formant analysis is to determine the complex natural frequencies of the vocal tract as they change during speech production. If the vocal-tract configuration were known, these natural frequencies could be computed. However, the speech signal is influenced both by the properties of the source and by the vocal tract. For example, if the source spectrum has a zero close to one of the natural frequencies of the vocal tract, it will be extremely difficult, if not impossible, to determine the frequency or the bandwidth of that particular formant. A side-branch element such as the nasal cavity creates a similar problem. In determining formant frequencies and bandwidths from the speech signal, one can at best hope to obtain such information which is not obscured or lost owing to the influence of the source.

Present methods of formant analysis usually start by transforming the speech signal into a short-time Fourier spectrum, and consequently suffer from many additional problems which are inherent in short-time Fourier transform techniques.[5,6,20,21] Such problems, of course, can be completely avoided by determining the formant frequencies and bandwidths directly from the speech wave.[2]

In the representation of the speech wave shown in Fig. 1, the linear filter represents the combined contributions of the vocal tract and the source to the spectral envelope. Thus, the poles of the transfer function of the filter include the poles of the vocal tract as well as the source. So far, we have made no attempt to separate these two contributions. For formant analysis, however, it is necessary that the poles of the vocal tract be separated out from the transfer function. In general, it is our experience that the poles contributed by the source either fall on the real axis in the unit circle or produce a relatively small peak in the spectral envelope. The magnitude of the spectral peak produced by a pole can easily be computed and compared with a threshold to determine whether a pole of the transfer function is indeed a natural frequency of the vocal tract. This is accomplished as follows:

From Eq. 4, the poles of the transfer function are the roots of the polynomial equation

$$\sum_{k=1}^{p} a_k z^{-k} = 1. \tag{20}$$

Let there be n complex conjugate pairs of roots z_1, z_1^*; z_2, z_2^*; $\cdots$; z_n, z_n^*. The transfer function due to these

WE WERE AWAY A YEAR AGO

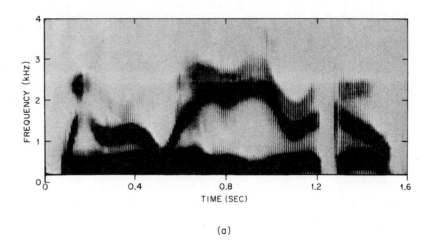

(a)

FIG. 10. Formant frequencies for the utterance "We were away a year ago," spoken by a male speaker ($F_0=120$ Hz). (a) Wideband sound spectrogram for the above utterance, and (b) formants determined by the computer program.

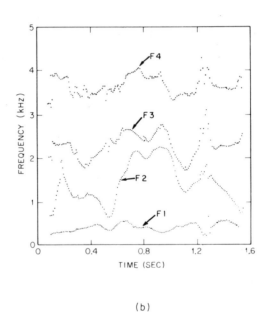

(b)

roots is given by

$$V(z)=\prod_{i=1}^{n}(1-z_i)(1-z_i^*)/\prod_{i=1}^{n}(z-z_i)(z-z_i^*), \quad (21)$$

where the additional factors in the numerator set the transfer function at dc ($z=1$) equal to 1. The spectral peak produced by the kth complex conjugate pole pair is given by

$$A_k=\left|\frac{(1-z_k)(1-z_k^*)}{(z-z_k)(z-z_k^*)}\right|^2, \quad (22)$$

where $z=\exp(2\pi jf_kT)$, $z_k=|z_k|\exp(2\pi jf_kT)$, and T is the sampling interval. The threshold value of A_k was set equal to 1.7. Finally, the formant frequency F_k and

the bandwidth (two-sided) B_k are related to the z-plane root z_k by

$$F_k=(1/2\pi T)\,\text{Im}(\ln z_k), \quad (23)$$

and

$$B_k=(1/\pi T)\,\text{Re}\left(\frac{1}{\ln z_k}\right). \quad (24)$$

Examples of the formant frequencies determined according to the above procedure are illustrated in Figs. 10–12. Each figure consists of (a) a wide-band sound spectrogram of the utterance, and (b) formant data as determined by the above method. The results are presented for three different utterances. The first utterance, "We were away a year ago," was spoken by a male speaker (average fundamental frequency $F_0=120$ Hz).

MAY WE ALL LEARN A YELLOW LION ROAR

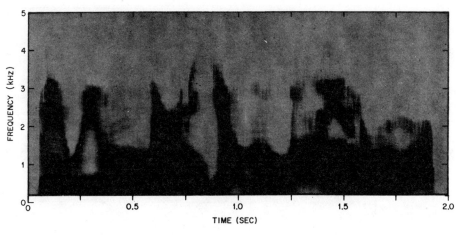

(a)

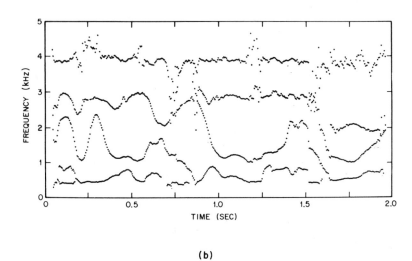

(b)

FIG. 11. Formant frequencies for the utterance "May we all learn a yellow lion roar," spoken by a female speaker ($F_0 = 200$ Hz). (a) Wide-band sound spectrogram for the above utterance, and (b) formants determined by the computer program.

The second utterance, "May we all learn a yellow lion roar," was spoken by a female speaker ($F_0 = 200$ Hz). The third utterance, "Why do I owe you a letter?" was spoken by a male speaker ($F_0 = 125$ Hz). Each point in these plots represents the results from a single frame of the speech signal which was equal to a pitch period in Figs. 10 and 11 and equal to 10 msec in Fig. 12. No

smoothing of the formant data over adjacent frames was done.

Again, in order to obtain a better estimate of the accuracy of this method of formant analysis, speech was synthesized with a known formant structure. The correspondence between the actual formant frequencies and bandwidths and the computed ones was found to be extremely close.

D. Re-forming the Speech Signals

The ability to modify the acoustical characteristics of a speech signal without degrading its quality is important for a wide variety of applications. For example, information regarding the relative importance of various acoustic variables in speech perception can be obtained by listening to speech in which some particular

TABLE II. Factor by which each parameter was scaled for simulating a female voice from parameters derived from a male voice.

Parameter	Scaling factor
Pitch period T	0.58
Formant frequencies F_i	1.14
Formant bandwidths B_i	$2 - F_i/5000$

WHY DO I OWE YOU A LETTER

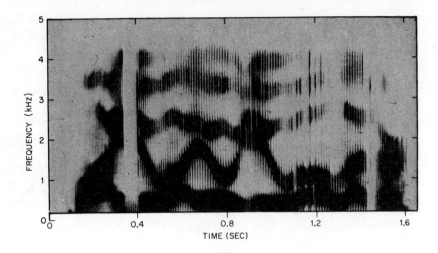

(a)

FIG. 12. Formant frequencies for the utterance "Why do I owe you a letter?" spoken by a male speaker ($F_0=125$ Hz). (a) Wide-band sound spectrogram for the above utterance, and (b) formants determined by the computer program.

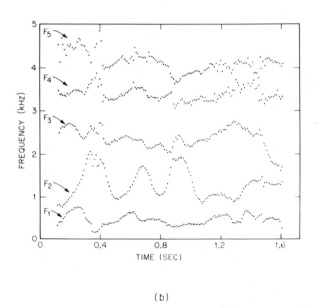

(b)

acoustic variables have been altered in a controlled manner. The speech analysis and synthesis techniques described in this paper can be used as a flexible and convenient method for conducting such speech-perception experiments. We would like to point out here that the synthesis procedure allows independent control of such speech characteristics as spectral envelope, relative durations, pitch, and intensity. Thus, the speaking rate of a given speech signal may be altered, e.g., for producing fast speech for blind persons or for producing slow speech for learning foreign languages. Or, in an application such as the recovery of "helium speech," the frequencies of the spectral envelope can be scaled, leaving the fundamental frequency unchanged. Moreover, in synthesizing sentence-length utterances from stored data about individual words, the method can be used to reshape the intonation and stress contours so that the speech sounds natural.

Examples of speech in which selected acoustical characteristics have been altered are presented in the fifth section of the enclosed record.* First, the listener can hear the utterance at the normal speaking rate. Next, the speaking rate is increased by a factor of 1.5. As the third item, the same utterance with the speaking rate reduced by a factor of 1.5 is presented. Finally, an example of a speech signal in which the pitch, the formant frequencies, and their bandwidths were changed from their original values, obtained from a male voice, to

*Not included in this reprint volume.

The Journal of the Acoustical Society of America

TABLE III. Computation times needed to perform various operations discussed in the paper on the GE 635 ($p=10$, $f_s=10$ kHz).

Operation	Computation time
Predictor coefficients from speech samples (No. of samples=100)	75 msec/frame
Spectral envelope (500 spectral samples) from predictor coefficients	250 msec/frame
Formant frequencies and bandwidths from predictor coefficients	60 msec/frame
p samples of autocorrelation function from predictor coefficients	10 msec/frame
Speech from predictor coefficients	8 times real time
Pitch analysis	10 times real time

simulate a "female" voice is presented. The factor by which each parameter was changed from its original value is shown in Table II.

VI. COMPUTATIONAL EFFICIENCY

The computation times needed to perform several of the operations described in this paper are summarized in Table III. The programs were run on a GE 635 computer having a cycle time of 1 μsec. As can be seen, this method of speech analysis and synthesis is computationally efficient. In fact, the techniques are about five to 10 times faster than the ones needed to perform equivalent operations by fast-Fourier-transform methods. For instance, both the formant frequencies and their bandwidths are determined in 135 msec for each frame of the speech wave 10 msec long. Assuming that the formants are analyzed once every 10 msec, the program will run in about 13 times real time; by comparison, fast-Fourier-transform techniques need about 100 times real time. Even for computing the spectral envelope, the method based on predictor coefficients is at least three times faster than the fast-Fourier-transform methods. The complete analysis and synthesis procedure was found to run in approximately 25 times real time. Real-time operation could easily be achieved by using special hardware to perform some of the functions.

VII. CONCLUSIONS

We have presented a method for automatic analysis and synthesis of speech signals by representing them in terms of time-varying parameters related to the transfer function of the vocal tract and the characteristics of the excitation. An important property of the speech wave, namely, its linear predictability, forms the basis of both the analysis and synthesis procedures. Unlike past speech analysis methods based on Fourier analysis, the method described here derives the speech parameters from a direct analysis of the speech wave. Consequently, various problems encountered when Fourier analysis is applied to nonstationary and quasiperiodic signals like speech are avoided. One of the main advantages of this method is that the analysis procedure requires only a short segment of the speech wave to yield accurate results. This method is therefore very suitable for following rapidly changing speech events. It is also suitable for analyzing the speech of speakers with high-pitched voices, such as women or children. As an additional advantage, the analyzed parameters are rigorously related to other well-known speech characteristics. Thus, by first representing the speech signal in terms of the predictor coefficients, other speech characteristics can be determined as desired without much additional computation.

The speech signal is synthesized by a single recursive filter. The synthesizer, thus, does not require any information about the individual formants and the formants need not be determined explicitly during analysis. Moreover, the synthesizer makes use of the formant bandwidths of real speech, in contrast to formant synthesizers, which use fixed bandwidths for each formant. Informal listening tests show very little or no perceptible degradation in the quality of the synthesized speech. These results suggest that the analyzed parameters retain all the perceptually important features of the speech signal. Furthermore, the various parameters used for the synthesis can be encoded efficiently. It was found possible to reduce the data rate to approximately 2400 bits/sec without producing significant degradation in the speech quality. The above bit rate is smaller by a factor of about 30 than that for direct PCM encoding of the speech waveform. The latter bit rate is approximately 70 000 bits (70 000 bits=7 bits/sample×10 000 samples/sec).

In addition to providing an efficient and accurate description of the speech signal, the method is computationally very fast. The entire analysis and synthesis procedure runs at about 25 times real time on a GE 635 digital computer. The method is thus well suited for analyzing large amounts of speech data automatically on the computer.

APPENDIX A: DESCRIPTION OF ENCLOSED RECORDED MATERIAL*

Side 1

Section 1. Speech analysis and synthesis for various values of p, the number of predictor coefficients:

(a) $p=2$,
(b) $p=6$,
(c) $p=10$,
(d) $p=14$,
(e) $p=18$,
(f) original speech.

Section 2. Comparison of synthesized speech with the original, $p=12$. Synthetic—original. Five utterances.

*Not included in this reprint volume.

Section 3. Synthesized speech encoded at different bit rates, the parameters quantized as shown in Table I, $p=12$. Original—unquantized—7200 bits/sec—4800 bits/sec—2400 bits/sec. Three utterances.

Section 4. Synthesized speech obtained by quantizing the areas of an acoustic tube, $p=12$. Bit rate$=7200$ bits/sec.

   (1) Frequencies and bandwidths quantized into 60-bit frames.
   (2) Areas quantized into 60-bit frames.

The rest of the parameters are quantized as shown in Table I.

Section 5. Fast and slow speech, $p=14$:

   (*a*) Original speech.
   (*b*) Speaking rate$=1.5$ times the original.
   (*c*) Speaking rate$=0.67$ times the original.

Section 6. Manipulation of pitch, formant frequencies, and their bandwidths, $p=10$:

   (*a*) Pitch, formant frequencies, and bandwidths altered as shown in Table II.
   (*b*) Original voice.

APPENDIX B: RELATIONSHIP BETWEEN THE LENGTH OF THE VOCAL TRACT AND THE NUMBER OF PREDICTOR COEFFICIENTS

Below about 5000 Hz, the acoustic properties of the vocal tract can be determined by considering it as an acoustic tube of variable cross-sectional area. The relationship between sound pressure P_g and volume velocity U_g at the glottis and the corresponding quantities P_l, U_l at the lips is best described in terms of the $ABCD$ matrix parameters (chain matrix) of the acoustic tube. These parameters are defined by the matrix equation (see Fig. B-1):

$$\begin{bmatrix} P_g \\ U_g \end{bmatrix} = \begin{bmatrix} A & B \\ C & D \end{bmatrix} \begin{bmatrix} P_l \\ U_l \end{bmatrix}. \qquad \text{(B1)}$$

We now prove that the inverse Fourier transforms of these parameters in the time domain have finite duration $\tau=2l/c$, where l is the length of the tube and c is the velocity of sound. Let $S(x)$ be the area function of the vocal tract, where x is the distance from the glottis to the point at which the cross-sectional area is specified. Consider a small element of tube of length dx at a distance x from the glottis. The $ABCD$ matrix parameters of the tube element dx are given by[B1]

$$A = D = \cosh \Gamma dx = 1/2(e^{\Gamma dx} + e^{-\Gamma dx}),$$
$$B = -Z_0 \sinh \Gamma dx = -Z_0(e^{\Gamma dx} - e^{-\Gamma dx})/2, \qquad \text{(B2)}$$
$$C = -\sinh \Gamma dx/Z_0 = -(e^{\Gamma dx} - e^{-\Gamma dx})/2Z_0,$$

where Z_0 is the characteristic impedance of the tube element $dx = \rho c/S(x)$, Γ is the propagation constant $= j\omega/c$, ρ is the density of air, c is the velocity of sound, and ω is the angular frequency in radians. The $ABCD$ matrix of the complete tube is given by the product of the $ABCD$ matrices of the individual tube elements of length dx spaced dx apart along the length of the tube. Let $l=ndx$. It is now easily verified that each of the $ABCD$ parameters of the tube can be expressed as a power series in $e^{\Gamma dx}$ of the form

$$\sum_{k=-n}^{n} \alpha_k e^{k\Gamma dx}.$$

The $ABCD$ parameters are thus Fourier transforms of functions of time each with duration $\tau=2n \cdot dx/c$. Taking the limit as $dx \to 0$, $n \to \infty$, and $n \cdot dx = l$, we obtain $\tau=2l/c$.

From Eq. B1, the relationship between the glottal and the lip volume velocities is expressed in terms of the $ABCD$ parameters by

$$U_g = CP_l + DU_l. \qquad \text{(B3)}$$

Since $P_l \cong j\omega K U_l$, K being a constant related to the mouth area, Eq. B3 is rewritten as

$$U_g \cong (j\omega KC + D)U_l. \qquad \text{(B4)}$$

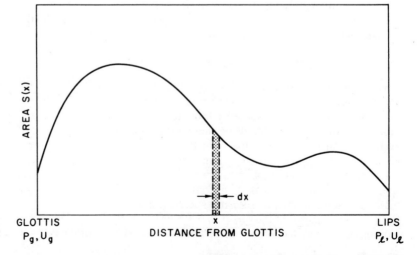

Fig. B-1. Nonuniform acoustic tube.

GLOTTIS P_g, U_g DISTANCE FROM GLOTTIS   LIPS P_l, U_l

The memory of the linear predictor (see Fig. 1) is by definition equal to the duration of the inverse Fourier transform of the reciprocal of the transfer function between the lip and the glottal volume velocities. Therefore, from Eq. B4, the memory of the linear predictor is equal to $\tau = 2l/c$.

APPENDIX C: DETERMINATION OF THE PREDICTOR PARAMETERS FROM THE COVARIANCE MATRIX Φ

Equation 8 can be written in matrix notation as

$$\Phi \mathbf{a} = \psi, \qquad (C1)$$

where $\Phi = [(\varphi_{ij})]$ is a positive definite (or positive semidefinite) symmetric matrix, and $\mathbf{a} = [(a_j)]$ and $\psi = [(\varphi_{j0})]$ are column vectors. Since Φ is positive definite (or semidefinite) and symmetric, it can be expressed as the product of a triangular matrix V with real elements and its transpose V^t. Thus,

$$\Phi = V V^t. \qquad (C2)$$

Equation C1 can now be resolved into two simpler equations:

$$V \mathbf{x} = \psi, \qquad (C3)$$

$$V^t \mathbf{a} = \mathbf{x}. \qquad (C4)$$

Since V is a triangular matrix, Eqs. C3 and C4 can be solved recursively.[C1]

Equations C3 and C4 provide a simple method of computing the minimum value of the prediction error $\langle E_n^2 \rangle_{av}$ as a function of p, the number of predictor coefficients. It is easily verified from Eqs. 7–9 that the minimum value of the mean-squared prediction error is given by

$$\epsilon_p = \varphi_{00} - \mathbf{a}^t \psi. \qquad (C5)$$

On substituting for $\mathbf{a}$ from Eq. C4 into Eq. C5, we obtain

$$\epsilon_p = \varphi_{00} - \mathbf{x}^t V^{-1} \psi,$$

which on substitution from Eq. C3 for ψ yields

$$\epsilon_p = \varphi_{00} - \mathbf{x}^t \mathbf{x}. \qquad (C6)$$

Thus, the minimum value of the mean-squared prediction error is given as

$$\epsilon_p = \varphi_{00} - \sum_{k=1}^{p} x_k^2. \qquad (C7)$$

The advantage of using Eq. C7 lies in the fact that a single computation of the vector x for one value of p is sufficient. After the vector $\mathbf{x}$ is determined for the largest value of p at which the error is desired, ϵ_p is calculated for smaller values of p from Eq. C7.

APPENDIX D: CORRECTION OF THE PREDICTOR COEFFICIENTS

Let us denote by $f(z)$ a polynomial defined by

$$f(z) = z^p - a_1 z^{p-1} - \cdots - a_p, \qquad (D1)$$

where the polynomial coefficients a_k are the predictor coefficients of Eq. 3. Associated with the polynomial $f(z)$, we define a reciprocal polynomial $f^*(z)$ by

$$f^*(z) = z^p f(z^{-1})$$
$$= -a_p z^p - a_{p-1} z^{p-1} - \cdots - a_1 z + 1. \qquad (D2)$$

Let us construct the sequence of polynomials $f_{p-1}(z)$, $f_{p-2}(z), \cdots, f_n(z), \cdots, f_1(z)$, where $f_n(z)$ is a polynomial of degree n, according to the formula

$$f_n(z) = k_{n+1} f_{n+1}^*(z) - l_{n+1} f_{n+1}(z), \qquad (D3)$$

where $f_p(z) = f^*(z)$, k_n is the coefficient of z^n in $f_n(z)$, and l_n is the constant term in $f_n(z)$. It can then be shown that the polynomial $f(z)$ has all its zeros inside the unit circle if and only if $|l_n| > |k_n|$ for each $n \le p$.[D1]

When one or more of the zeros of $f(z)$ are outside the unit circle, let us set

$$f(z) = \prod_{k=1}^{p} (z - z_k). \qquad (D4)$$

For every k for which $|z_k| > 1$, we replace z_k by $z_k/|z_k|$ in Eq. D4 and construct a new polynomial which has all of its zeros either inside or on the unit circle.

The above procedure is also suitable for testing that all the zeros of $f(z)$ are within any given circle $|z| = r$. In this case, we replace a_k by $r^{-k} a_k$ in Eq. D1 and proceed as before.

The roots of the polynomial $f(z)$ are determined by an iterative procedure based on the Newton–Raphson method.[D2] We start with a trial value of the root and then construct successively better approximations. The iteration formula has the form

$$z_k^{(n+1)} = z_k^{(n)} - \frac{f[z_k^{(n)}]}{f'[z_k^{(n)}]}, \qquad (D5)$$

where $z_k^{(n)}$ is the approximation of the kth root at the nth iteration. The iteration process is continued until either $f(z) = 0$ or the absolute difference between the roots in two successive iterations is less than a fixed threshold value. If convergence is not reached within 100 iterations, a new starting value is selected. The starting value is chosen randomly on the unit circle. Furthermore, the starting value never lies on the real axis.

APPENDIX E: DETERMINATION OF THE PREDICTOR COEFFICIENTS FROM THE AUTOCORRELATION FUNCTION AND THE AUTOCORRELATION FUNCTION FROM THE PREDICTOR COEFFICIENTS

We outline first a method of solving Eq. 12 for the predictor coefficients. Consider the set of equations

$$r_i = \sum_{k=1}^{n} a_k^{(n)} r_{|i-k|}, \quad \text{for} \quad n \ge i \ge 1. \qquad (E1)$$

Equation E1 is identical to Eq. 12 for $n=p$. In matrix form the above equation becomes

$$\begin{bmatrix} r_0 & r_1 & \cdots & r_{n-1} \\ r_1 & r_0 & \cdots & r_{n-2} \\ \vdots & \vdots & & \vdots \\ r_{n-2} & r_{n-3} & \cdots & r_1 \\ r_{n-1} & r_{n-2} & \cdots & r_0 \end{bmatrix} \begin{bmatrix} a_1^{(n)} \\ a_2^{(n)} \\ \vdots \\ a_{n-1}^{(n)} \\ a_n^{(n)} \end{bmatrix} = \begin{bmatrix} r_1 \\ r_2 \\ \vdots \\ r_{n-1} \\ r_n \end{bmatrix}. \quad (E2)$$

Let R_n be the $n \times n$ matrix on the left side of Eq. E2, $\mathbf{a}_m^{(n)}$ an m-dimensional vector whose kth component is $a_k^{(n)}$, and $\mathbf{r}_n$ an n-dimensional vector whose kth component is r_{n-k+1}. Let us define, for every vector, a reciprocal vector by the relationship

$$\mathbf{a}_m^{(n)*}\big|_k = \mathbf{a}_m^{(n)}\big|_{m-k+1}. \quad (E3)$$

Equation E2 can now be rewritten as

$$R_{n-1}\mathbf{a}_{n-1}^{(n)} + a_n^{(n)}\mathbf{r}_{n-1} = \mathbf{r}_{n-1}^*, \quad (E4)$$

and

$$\mathbf{r}_{n-1}^t \mathbf{a}_{n-1}^{(n)} + r_0 a_n^{(n)} = r_n. \quad (E5)$$

On multiplying Eq. E4 through by R_{n-1}^{-1} and rearranging terms, we obtain

$$\mathbf{a}_{n-1}^{(n)} = R_{n-1}^{-1}\mathbf{r}_{n-1}^* - a_n^{(n)}R_{n-1}^{-1}\mathbf{r}_{n-1}. \quad (E6)$$

It is easily verified from Eq. E2 that

$$R_{n-1}^{-1}\mathbf{r}_{n-1}^* = \mathbf{a}_{n-1}^{(n-1)}. \quad (E7)$$

Inserting Eq. E7 into Eq. E6 gives

$$\mathbf{a}_{n-1}^{(n)} = \mathbf{a}_{n-1}^{(n-1)} - a_n^{(n)}[\mathbf{a}_{n-1}^{(n-1)}]^*. \quad (E8)$$

Next, we multiply Eq. E8 through by $\mathbf{r}_{n-1}^t$ and insert the result in Eq. E5. After rearrangement of the terms, we find that

$$a_n^{(n)}\Big[r_0 - \sum_{k=1}^{n-1} r_k a_k^{(n-1)}\Big] = r_n - \sum_{k=1}^{n-1} r_{n-k} a_k^{(n-1)}. \quad (E9)$$

Equations E8 and E9 provide a complete recursive solution of Eq. E1. We start with $n=1$. The solution is obviously

$$a_1^{(1)} = r_1/r_0. \quad (E10)$$

Next, $a_n^{(n)}$ and $\mathbf{a}_{n-1}^{(n)}$ are computed for successively increasing values of n until $n=p$. Furthermore, if R_n is nonsingular, the expression inside the brackets on the left side of Eq. E9 is always positive. Therefore, $a_n^{(n)}$ is always finite.

To determine the autocorrelation function from the predictor coefficients, we proceed as follows: From Eq. E8,

$$[\mathbf{a}_{n-1}^{(n)}]^* = [\mathbf{a}_{n-1}^{(n-1)}]^* - a_n^{(n)}\mathbf{a}_{n-1}^{(n-1)}. \quad (E11)$$

Therefore, after eliminating $[\mathbf{a}_{n-1}^{(n-1)}]^*$ from Eqs. E8 and E11, one obtains

$$\mathbf{a}_{n-1}^{(n-1)} = \{\mathbf{a}_{n-1}^{(n)} + a_n^{(n)}[\mathbf{a}_{n-1}^{(n)}]^*\}/$$
$$\{1 - [a_n^{(n)}]^2\}. \quad (E12)$$

Starting with $n=p$, we compute $\mathbf{a}_n^{(n)}$ for successively smaller values of n until $n=1$. The autocorrelation function at the nth sampling instant is given from Eq. E1 by

$$r_n = \sum_{k=1}^{n} a_k^{(n)} r_{n-k}, \quad \text{for} \quad 1 \le n \le p. \quad (E13)$$

The samples of the autocorrelation function are computed recursively for successively larger values of n starting with $n=1$. Note that, on the right side of Eq. E13, only samples up to r_{n-1} appear in the sum. Thus, r_n can be computed recursively. Equation E13 is used to determine all the samples of the autocorrelation function with r_0 normalized to 1. The value of r_0 is finally determined from Eq. 13.

APPENDIX F: TRANSFER FUNCTION OF A NONUNIFORM ACOUSTIC TUBE

We consider sound transmission in an acoustic tube formed by cascading N uniform cylindrical sections, each of length Δ as shown in Fig. F-1. Let the cross-sectional area of the nth section be S_n. Let $p_n(t)$ and $v_n(t)$ be the components of the volume velocity due to the forward- and the backward-traveling waves, respectively, at the input of the nth section. Let us assume that there is a sound source of constant volume velocity at the input of the first section. Consider now the sound transmission between two adjacent sections, e.g., n and $n+1$. On applying the boundary conditions for the continuity of volume velocity and sound pressure across the junction, we obtain

$$p_n\Big(t-\frac{\Delta}{c}\Big) - v_n\Big(t+\frac{\Delta}{c}\Big) = p_{n+1}(t) - v_{n+1}(t), \quad (F1)$$

$$\Big[p_n\Big(t-\frac{\Delta}{c}\Big) + v_n\Big(t+\frac{\Delta}{c}\Big)\Big]\frac{\rho c}{S_n}$$

$$= [p_{n+1}(t) + v_{n+1}(t)]\frac{\rho c}{S_{n+1}}, \quad (F2)$$

where ρc is the characteristic impedance of air. Equations F1 and F2 can be solved for $p_{n+1}(t)$ and $v_{n+1}(t)$. We then obtain

$$p_{n+1}(t) = \frac{1}{1+r_n}\Big[p_n\Big(t-\frac{\Delta}{c}\Big) - r_n v_n\Big(t+\frac{\Delta}{c}\Big)\Big], \quad (F3)$$

$$v_{n+1}(t) = \frac{1}{1+r_n}\Big[-r_n p_n\Big(t-\frac{\Delta}{c}\Big) + v_n\Big(t+\frac{\Delta}{c}\Big)\Big], \quad (F4)$$

where

$$r_n = \frac{S_n - S_{n+1}}{S_n + S_{n+1}}. \quad (F5)$$

It is convenient to write Eqs. F3 and F4 in the z-trans-

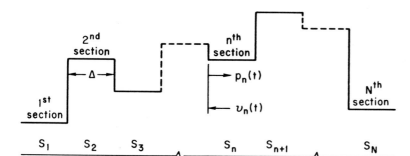

FIG. F-1. A nonuniform acoustic tube formed by cascading uniform cylindrical sections.

form notation as

$$\begin{bmatrix} \mathcal{P}_{n+1}(z) \\ \mathfrak{N}_{n+1}(z) \end{bmatrix} = \frac{1}{1+r_n} \begin{bmatrix} z^{-\frac{1}{2}} & -r_n z^{\frac{1}{2}} \\ -r_n z^{-\frac{1}{2}} & z^{\frac{1}{2}} \end{bmatrix} \begin{bmatrix} \mathcal{P}_n(z) \\ \mathfrak{N}_n(z) \end{bmatrix}, \quad \text{(F6)}$$

where $\mathcal{P}_n(z)$ and $\mathfrak{N}_n(z)$ are the z transforms of $p_n(t)$ and $\nu_n(t)$, respectively, with $z = \exp[j\omega(2\Delta/c)]$. Similarly as in Eq. F6, we have also the inverse relationship

$$\begin{bmatrix} \mathcal{P}_n(z) \\ \mathfrak{N}_n(z) \end{bmatrix} = \frac{1}{1-r_n} \begin{bmatrix} z^{\frac{1}{2}} & r_n z^{\frac{1}{2}} \\ r_n z^{-\frac{1}{2}} & z^{-\frac{1}{2}} \end{bmatrix} \begin{bmatrix} \mathcal{P}_{n+1}(z) \\ \mathfrak{N}_{n+1}(z) \end{bmatrix}, \quad \text{(F7)}$$

which can be written in matrix notation as

$$H_n(z) = Q_n(z)H_{n+1}(z). \quad \text{(F8)}$$

Moreover, from Eq. F8,

$$H_1(z) = \prod_{k=1}^{N} Q_k(z)H_{N+1}(z), \quad \text{(F9)}$$

$$= W_N(z)H_{N+1}(z). \quad \text{(F10)}$$

Let

$$W_n(z) = \prod_{k=1}^{n} Q_k(z) = \begin{bmatrix} w_{11}^{(n)}(z) & w_{12}^{(n)}(z) \\ w_{21}^{(n)}(z) & w_{22}^{(n)}(z) \end{bmatrix}. \quad \text{(F11)}$$

The matrix $W_n(z)$ satisfies the equation

$$W_{n+1}(z) = W_n(z)Q_{n+1}(z). \quad \text{(F12)}$$

It can be verified from Eq. F11 that

$$J[W_n^t(z^{-1})]^{-1}J = W_n(z), \quad \text{(F13)}$$

where

$$J = \begin{bmatrix} 1 & 0 \\ 0 & -1 \end{bmatrix}.$$

Equation F13 implies that

$$\begin{bmatrix} w_{11}(z) & w_{12}(z) \\ w_{21}(z) & w_{22}(z) \end{bmatrix} = \begin{bmatrix} w_{22}(z^{-1}) & w_{21}(z^{-1}) \\ w_{12}(z^{-1}) & w_{11}(z^{-1}) \end{bmatrix}, \quad \text{(F14)}$$

or

$$W_n(z) = \begin{bmatrix} w_{11}^{(n)}(z) & w_{21}^{(n)}(z^{-1}) \\ w_{21}^{(n)}(z) & w_{11}^{(n)}(z^{-1}) \end{bmatrix}. \quad \text{(F15)}$$

Let us assume that the tube is terminated in a unit acoustic resistance. We then have the terminal boundary condition

$$p_{N+1}(t) + \nu_{N+1}(t) = p_{N+1}(t) - \nu_{N+1}(t), \quad \text{(F16)}$$

from which it follows that $\nu_{N+1}(t) = 0$. The volume velocity at the input of the tube is given by $p_1(t) - \nu_1(t)$. Let

$$C_N(z) = \frac{\text{volume velocity at the input}}{\text{volume velocity at the output}}$$

$$= \frac{\mathcal{P}_1(z) - \mathfrak{N}_1(z)}{\mathcal{P}_{N+1}(z)}. \quad \text{(F17)}$$

It can now be easily verified from Eq. F10 that

$$C_N(z) = w_{11}^{(N)}(z) - w_{21}^{(N)}(z). \quad \text{(F18)}$$

Let us define for each n, between 1 and N,

$$C_n(z) = w_{11}^{(n)}(z) - w_{21}^{(n)}(z). \quad \text{(F19)}$$

On multiplying Eq. F12 by a vector $[1 \quad -1]$, and substituting for $W_n(z)$ from Eq. F15, we find that

$$[C_{n+1}(z) \quad -C_{n+1}(z^{-1})] = \frac{1}{1-r_{n+1}}[C_n(z) \quad -C_n(z^{-1})]$$

$$\times \begin{bmatrix} z^{\frac{1}{2}} & r_{n+1} z^{\frac{1}{2}} \\ r_{n+1} z^{-\frac{1}{2}} & z^{-\frac{1}{2}} \end{bmatrix}. \quad \text{(F20)}$$

Hence,

$$C_{n+1}(z) = \frac{1}{1-r_{n+1}}[z^{\frac{1}{2}}C_n(z) - z^{-\frac{1}{2}}r_{n+1}C_n(z^{-1})]$$

$$= \frac{z^{\frac{1}{2}}}{1-r_{n+1}}[C_n(z) - r_{n+1}C_n(z^{-1})z^{-1}]. \quad \text{(F21)}$$

Except for the factor $z^{n/2}$, each $C_n(z)$ is a polynomial of degree n. Thus, the transfer function, which is the reciprocal of $C_N(z)$, consists of a factor $z^{-N/2}$ divided by a polynomial of degree N. The factor $z^{-N/2}$ represents, of course, the transmission delay in the tube. The transfer function has N poles which are the zeros of $C_N(z)$. Furthermore, the poles are inside the unit circle, pro-

293

vided that r_n satisfies the condition[D1]

$$|r_n| < 1, \quad 1 \leq n \leq N, \quad \text{(F22)}$$

which, together with Eq. F5, implies that

$$S_n > 0, \quad 1 \leq n \leq N. \quad \text{(F23)}$$

We now show that every all-pole transfer function having poles inside the unit circle is always realizable, except for a constant multiplying factor and a delay, as the transfer function of an acoustic tube.

It follows from Eq. F20 that

$$C_n(z) = \frac{z^{-\frac{1}{2}}}{1 + r_{n+1}} [C_{n+1}(z) + r_{n+1} C_{n+1}(z^{-1})]. \quad \text{(F24)}$$

Furthermore, for each $C_n(z)$, the ratio of the coefficients of $z^{-n/2}$ and $z^{n/2}$ is r_n. Given $C_N(z)$, one can compute $C_n(z)$ for successively decreasing values of n starting with $n = N$ from Eq. F24. In each case, the coefficient r_n is always defined as the ratio of the coefficients of $z^{-n/2}$ and $z^{n/2}$. A sequence of numbers, $r_1, r_2, \cdots, r_N$, obtained in the above manner, defines a tube with areas $S_1, S_2, \cdots, S_N$ according to Eq. F5, provided that each of the areas is positive, i.e., $|r_n| < 1$ for $1 \leq n \leq N$. This is, however, assured if the original polynomial $C_N(z)$ has all its roots inside the unit circle (see Appendix D). Since the poles of the transfer function are inside the unit circle, it is indeed true.

[1] J. L. Flanagan, *Speech Analysis Synthesis and Perception* (Academic, New York, 1965), p. 119.
[2] E. N. Pinson, "Pitch-Synchronous Time-Domain Estimation of Formant Frequencies and Bandwidths," J. Acoust. Soc. Amer. **35**, 1264–1273 (1963).
[3] B. S. Atal and M. R. Schroeder, "Adaptive Predictive Coding of Speech Signals," Bell System Tech. J. **49**, 1973–1986 (1970).
[4] B. S. Atal, "Speech Analysis and Synthesis by Linear Prediction of the Speech Wave," J. Acoust. Soc. Amer. **47**, 65(A) (1970).
[5] B. S. Atal, "Characterization of Speech Signals by Linear Prediction of the Speech Wave," Proc. IEEE Symp. on Feature Extraction and Selection in Pattern Recognition, Argonne, Ill. (Oct. 1970), pp. 202–209.
[6] M. V. Mathews, J. E. Miller, and E. E. David, Jr., "Pitch Synchronous Analysis of Voiced Sounds," J. Acoust. Soc. Amer. **33**, 179–186 (1961).
[7] C. G. Bell, H. Fujisaki, J. M. Heinz, K. N. Stevens, and A. S. House, "Reduction of Speech Spectra by Analysis-by-Synthesis Techniques," J. Acoust. Soc. Amer. **33**, 1725–1736 (1961).
[8] G. Fant, *Acoustic Theory of Speech Production* (Mouton, The Hague, 1960), p. 42.
[9] B. S. Atal, "Sound Transmission in the Vocal Tract with Applications to Speech Analysis and Synthesis," Proc. Int. Congr. Acoust., 7th, Budapest, Hungary (Aug. 1971).
[10] Each factor of the form $(1 - az^{-1})$ can be approximated by $[1/(1 + az^{-1} + a^2z^{-2} + \cdots)]$ if $|a| < 1$, which is the case if the zeros are inside the unit circle.
[11] Ref. 1, p. 33.
[12] C. E. Fröberg, *Introduction to Numerical Analysis* (Addison-Wesley, Reading, Mass., 1969), 2nd ed., pp. 81–101.
[13] J. P. Ellington and H. McCallion, "The Determination of Control System Characteristics from a Transient Response," Proc. IEE **105**, Part C, 370–373 (1958).
[14] B. S. Atal, "Automatic Speaker Recognition Based on Pitch Contours," PhD thesis, Polytech. Inst. Brooklyn (1968).
[15] B. S. Atal, "Pitch-Period Analysis by Inverse Filtering" (to be published).
[16] U. Grenander and G. Szegö, *Toeplitz Forms and Their Applications* (Univ. California Press, Berkeley, 1958), p. 40.
[17] L. G. Stead and R. C. Weston, "Sampling and Quantizing the Parameters of a Formant-Tracking Vocoder System," Proc. Speech Commun. Seminar, R.I.T., Stockholm (29 Aug.–1 Sept. 1962).
[18] M. R. Schroeder, "Vocoders: Analysis and Synthesis of Speech," Proc. IEEE **54**, 720–734 (1966).
[19] The problem of separating the spectral envelope from the fine structure of the speech spectrum should be distinguished from the problem of separating the influence of the source from the speech spectrum. The latter problem is far more difficult and is discussed partially in the next subsection.
[20] R. W. Schafer and L. R. Rabiner, "System for Automatic Formant Analysis of Voiced Speech," J. Acoust. Soc. Amer. **47**, 634–648 (1970).
[21] J. P. Olive, "Automatic Formant Tracking by a Newton-Raphson Technique," J. Acoust. Soc. Amer. **50**, 661–670 (1971).
[B1] I. Malecki, *Physical Foundations of Technical Acoustics*, English transl. by I. Bellert (Pergamon, Oxford, England, 1969), p. 475.
[C1] D. K. Faddeev and V. N. Faddeeva, *Computational Methods of Linear Algebra*, English transl. by R. C. Williams (W. H. Freeman, San Francisco, 1963), pp. 144–147.
[D1] Ref. 16, pp. 40–41. See also L. Ya. Geronimus, *Orthogonal Polynomials* (Consultants Bureau, New York, 1961), p. 156.
[D2] Ref. 12, pp. 21–28.

A Statistical Method for Estimation of Speech Spectral Density and Formant Frequencies

Fumitada Itakura and Shuzo Saito, Members

Electrical Communication Laboratory
N.T.T., Musashino

SUMMARY

The extraction of spectral information of speech by means of the maximum-likelihood method is theoretically discussed. The method is applied to the analysis of actual speech, and its validity thus verified. The speech signal is first modeled to a stationary probability process of rational spectral density without null point, in consideration of the irregular fluctuations of the sound signal driving the vocal track and the pitch discrimination characteristics of hearing due to differences in spectral density. Next, to find an estimation of the maximum likelihood of unknown parameters contained in the assumed spectral density, the likelihood of a signal is given in the frequency domain. The result reveals that the estimation method of maximum likelihood is a kind of spectrum matching. Furthermore, the procedure of the estimation results in solving simultaneous linear equations. Finally, the method is applied to the analysis of actual speech. It is shown that several kinds of parameters (such as formant frequencies and bandwidths) contained in the spectral density are extracted with sufficient accuracy.

1. Introduction

For the machine recognition and efficient transmission of speech, it is one of the fundamental aspects that spectral information of short intervals of the speech should be accurately and efficiently extracted. Narrow-band filters have been utilized. However, the spectral components analyzed into the narrow bandwidths fluctuate greatly (which is the general case in nonperiodic signal analysis). It has been regarded as a difficult matter to extract meaningful information with sufficient accuracy and stability. Recently, K.N. Stevens et al. introduced a type of speech analysis based on the analysis-by-synthesis technique [1]. The method improved the analysis accuracy by introducing physical restrictions in the speech

generation process. On the other hand, not only the physical restrictions in the generation process but also the hearing characteristics as an ideal recognition process must be considered in case of the vocal sound elements.

This paper is an attempt to solve these questions. That is, the complex fluctuations contained in speech are modeled so that short-interval speech signals are taken as a sample of the stationary probability process. In consideration of the discrimination characteristics of the frequency spectrum in hearing, it is assumed that the power spectral density of the stationary probability process is approximated by the rational spectrum having poles only. On these assumptions, a maximum-likelihood method of estimating the unknown parameters contained in the spectral density in the probability process is theoretically obtained. Application to actual speech analysis is then shown.

2. A Model of Speech Signals

2.1 Speech Signals as a Probability Process

The sound source driving the vocal track is assumed to be noise in the case of a voiceless fricative sound or "whisper." On the other hand, a vocal-cords sound, that is, a voiced sound, is expressed by a pulse train which looks quite periodic, but various kinds of unknown fluctuation,* such as variation of the pulse interval [2] and change of the pulse shape, are seen in the precise analysis. Therefore, as far as the

---

*If it is assumed that the mean of the pitch period is 10 msec and that it distributes with the standard deviation of 0.5 msec without correlation, the harmonic construction in the spectral density of the pulse train is smoothed in the frequency range above 800 Hz [3].

Reprinted with permission from *Electron. and Commun.*, vol. 53-A, pp. 36–43, 1970.

macroscopic structure of the speech spectrum is concerned, it is more reasonable to treat the speech signals as those of a probability process with continuous spectra rather than as of periodic signals with line spectra.

2.2 Discrimination Characteristics of Speech Spectra in Hearing

Through experiments on tonal discrimination in hearing when frequency-response distortion of a peak or dip type is given to the speech signals, it is known that the discrimination threshold is much larger for the dip than for the peak [4]. This fact suggests that in the spectral analysis of speech, more attention must be paid to frequency response of the peak type, since it is more important in hearing.

2.3 A Mathematical Model of Speech Signals

For the simplification of the theoretical treatment, bearing in mind Sections 2.1 and 2.2 above, we assume that the speech signals under consideration satisfy the following conditions.

(1) The original speech signals are to be sampled with the constant period ΔT after proper low-pass filtering. A discrete time system is thus expressed as $\{\xi_i$, where $i = \cdots, -1, 0, 1, 2, \cdots \}$.

(2) The samples $x = (x_1, x_2, \cdots, x_N)$ which are extracted at short intervals from $\{\xi_i\}$ are assumed to be samples of a stationary Gaussian process with the spectral density $f(\lambda)$ (where $x_i = \xi_{j+i}$, $i = 1, \cdots, N$ and $j = $ fixed constant).

(3) The spectral density $f(\lambda)$ is expressed in terms of the rational spectral densities without null point; that is,

$$
\begin{aligned}
f(\lambda) &= \frac{\sigma_\epsilon^2}{2\pi} \frac{1}{\left| \prod_{i=1}^{p} \left(1 - \frac{z}{z_i}\right) \right|^2} \\
&= \frac{\sigma_\epsilon^2}{2\pi} \frac{1}{|1 + \alpha_1 z + \alpha_2 z^2 + \cdots + \alpha_p z^p|^2} \\
&= \frac{\sigma_\epsilon^2}{2\pi} \frac{1}{A_0 + 2 A_1 \cos\lambda + 2 A_2 \cos 2\lambda + \cdots + 2 A_p \cos p\lambda}
\end{aligned} \tag{1}
$$

where

$$
\begin{aligned}
&\lambda = \omega \Delta T \\
&z = e^{-j\lambda} \quad (-\pi \leq \lambda \leq \pi) \\
&z_i = e^{+\pi \Delta T B_i} e^{\pm j 2\pi \Delta T F_i} \\
&\quad (B_i : \text{3 dB bandwidth}, \\
&\quad\quad F_i : \text{pole frequency}) \\
&A_0 = 1 + \alpha_1^2 + \alpha_2^2 + \cdots + \alpha_p^2 \\
&A_1 = \alpha_1 + \alpha_1\alpha_2 + \cdots + \alpha_{p-1}\alpha_p \\
&A_2 = \alpha_2 + \alpha_1\alpha_3 + \cdots + \alpha_{p-2}\alpha_p \\
&\quad\vdots \\
&A_p = \alpha_p
\end{aligned} \tag{2}
$$

Quantity σ_ϵ^2 is a scale factor for the magnitude of the spectral density, and p is the number of poles within the bandwidth $[0, 1/2(\Delta T)]$ Hz which are necessary for the approximation of the actual speech spectral density (the conjugate poles of a pair are counted as two). The poles are caused by the vocal-cord vibration, the vocal track resonances, and the anti-resonances of the bypasses of the vocal track.

3. Maximum-Likelihood Method for Spectral Information

In Eq. (1) $(\sigma_\epsilon^2, z_1, z_2, \cdots, z_p), (\sigma_\epsilon^2, \alpha_1, \alpha_2, \cdots, \alpha_p)$ or $(\sigma_\epsilon^2, A_0, A_1, \cdots, A_p)$ are the parameters which define the probability distribution of the observed value x. This is called spectral information in the following and expressed by $\tilde{\omega}$. To extract the spectral information from the observed value x is, in other words, to estimate statistically the unknown parameter $\tilde{\omega}$ from the random variable, that is, the obtained value x.

In the present paper, the maximum-likelihood estimation method (it is called the maximum-likelihood method in the following) is employed among others. When $p(x|\tilde{\omega})$ is the probability density of the sample x for the parameter $\tilde{\omega}$, $p(x|\tilde{\omega})$ is called a likelihood function, or a function of $\tilde{\omega}$. The maximum-likelihood method is the estimation method in which, when the obtained value x is given, $\hat{\omega}$ which maximizes the likelihood function $p(x|\tilde{\omega})$ is taken as the estimate of the unknown parameter $\tilde{\omega}$.

The maximum-likelihood method provides the following merits [5] for certain frequently occurring conditions:

(1) The maximum-likelihood estimate is a consistent estimate.

(2) It is an unbiased estimate with an asymptotic character upon increases of the sample size.

(3) It is an asymptotic and efficient estimate with normal distribution.

(4) It is an immutable estimate. That is, if the maximum-likelihood estimate of the parameter $\tilde{\omega}$ is $\hat{\omega}$, the maximum likelihood estimate of $g(\tilde{\omega})$, that is, a single-valued function of $\tilde{\omega}$, is $g(\hat{\omega})$.

Condition (3) provides that when the sample size is large enough, the variance of the estimate is minimum. In this sense, the maximum-likelihood method is superior to others.

4. Probability Density of the Observed Value x, Logarithmic Likelihood and Its Approximation

Since x is assumed to be a sample of a stationary Gaussian process, the probability density of the sample $x = (x_1, x_2, \cdots, x_N)'$ is

$$
p(x|\tilde{\omega}) = \frac{1}{(2\pi)^{N/2} |V|^{1/2}} \exp\left\{ -\frac{1}{2} x' V^{-1} x \right\} \tag{3}
$$

where the prime mark indicates a transpose of the matrix and V indicates an $N \times N$ matrix consisting of the elements $E(x_ix_j)$, which means the expectation. Notation V^{-1} indicates the inverse matrix.

When the population spectral density of x is given by Eq. (1), $p(x|\tilde{\omega})$ is expressed as follows:

$$p(x|\tilde{\omega}) = \frac{C}{(2\pi\sigma_\epsilon^2)^{N/2}} \exp\left\{-\frac{Q(x)}{2\sigma_\epsilon^2}\right\} \qquad (4)$$

where C is a constant or $|\sigma_\epsilon^2 V^{-1}|^{1/2}$, which is defined by $(\alpha_1, \cdots, \alpha_p)$ independent of N, σ_ϵ^2 and x. Quantity Q(x) is of the second order with respect to x with the coefficients defined by $(\alpha_1, \alpha_2, \cdots, \alpha_p)$. That is [6],

$$\begin{aligned}
Q(x) = &A_0\sum_{i=1}^{N}x_i^2 + 2A_1\sum_{i=1}^{N-1}x_ix_{i+1} \\
&+ 2A_2\sum_{i=1}^{N-2}x_ix_{i-2} + \cdots + 2A_p\sum_{i=1}^{N-p}x_ix_{i-p} \\
&- [(\alpha_1^2 + \alpha_2^2 + \cdots + \alpha_p^2)(x_1^2 + x_N^2) \\
&\div (\alpha_2^2 + \alpha_3^2 + \cdots + \alpha_p^2)(x_2^2 + x_{N-1}^2) \\
&\div 2(\alpha_1\alpha_2 + \cdots + \alpha_{p-1}\alpha_p)(x_1x_2 + x_Nx_{N-1}) \\
&\div (\alpha_3^2 + \cdots + \alpha_p^2)(x_3^2 + x_{N-2}^2) \\
&+ 2(\alpha_2\alpha_3 + \cdots + \alpha_{p-1}\alpha_p)(x_2x_3 + x_{N-1}x_{N-2}) \\
&+ 2(\alpha_1\alpha_3 + \cdots + \alpha_{p-2}\alpha_p)(x_1x_3 + x_Nx_{N-2}) \\
&\div \cdots\cdots\cdots\cdots\cdots\cdots \\
&\div \alpha_p^2(x_p^2 + x_{N-p+1}^2) + \cdots \\
&+ 2\alpha_2\alpha_p(x_2x_p + x_{N-1}x_{N-p+1}) \\
&\div 2\alpha_1\alpha_p(x_1x_p + x_Nx_{N-p+1})]
\end{aligned} \qquad (5)$$

In the following, we employ, instead of $p(x|\tilde{\omega})$, the logarithmic likelihood function defined as follows:

$$\begin{aligned}
L(x|\tilde{\omega}) &\equiv \log p(x|\tilde{\omega}) \\
&= \log C - \frac{N}{2}\log 2\pi\sigma_\epsilon^2 - \frac{1}{2\sigma_\epsilon^2}Q(x)
\end{aligned} \qquad (6)$$

When the sample size N is large enough considering the number of poles p, the contribution of the terms inside the brackets in Eq. (5) is small in comparison with that of the first p + 1 terms. For Q(x) we can then approximately write

$$\begin{aligned}
Q(x) &\doteqdot A_0\sum_{i=1}^{N}x_i^2 + 2A_1\sum_{i=1}^{N-1}x_ix_{i-1} + \cdots + 2A_p\sum_{i=1}^{N-p}x_ix_{i+p} \\
&= N\sum_{s=-p}^{p}A_s\hat{v}_s
\end{aligned}$$

where

$$\hat{v}_s = \frac{1}{N}\sum_{i=1}^{N-s}x_ix_{i+s}, \quad (s = 0, 1, 2, \cdots, N-1) \qquad (8)$$
$$A_s = A_s, \quad \hat{v}_{-s} = \hat{v}_s$$

This $\hat{v}_s$ is the sample covariance in the time delay $s\Delta T$.

The first term in the second relation of Eq. (6), which $\log C$, is constant and independent of N, while the second and the third terms increase linearly with increase of N. Therefore, the

first term can be neglected for $N \gg p$. We then have approximately

$$L(x|\tilde{\omega}) \doteqdot -\frac{N}{2}\left[\log 2\pi\sigma_\epsilon^2 + \frac{1}{\sigma_\epsilon^2}\sum_{s=-p}^{p}A_s\hat{v}_s\right] \qquad (9)$$

The sign here indicating approximate equality is taken as full equality in the following.

5. Logarithmic Likelihood Function and Its Physical Meaning in Frequency Domain

In Eq. (1), A_0, A_1, $\cdots$, A_p are the coefficients of Fourier cosine terms of $\frac{\sigma_\epsilon^2}{2\pi}\frac{1}{f(\lambda)}$. Therefore,

$$A_i = \frac{\sigma_\epsilon^2}{(2\pi)^2}\int_{-\pi}^{\pi}\frac{\cos i\lambda}{f(\lambda)}d\lambda \quad (i = 0, 1, \cdots, p) \qquad (10)$$

On the other hand, the absolute value $|z_i|$ of every pole of $f(\lambda)$ is larger than 1. The integration of $\log f(\lambda)$ with respect to λ in the range of $[-\pi, \pi]$ gives

$$\int_{-\pi}^{\pi}\log f(\lambda)d\lambda = 2\pi\log\frac{\sigma_\epsilon^2}{2\pi} \qquad (11)$$
$$\frac{\sigma_\epsilon^2}{2\pi} = \exp\left\{\frac{1}{2\pi}\int_{-\pi}^{\pi}\log f(\lambda)d\lambda\right\} \qquad (11')$$

In other words, $\sigma_\epsilon^2/2\pi$ is a geometrical mean of $f(\lambda)$ in the range of $[-\pi, \pi]$. Substituting Eqs. (10) and (11') into Eq. (9), we have

$$\begin{aligned}
L(x|\tilde{\omega}) &= -\frac{N}{2}\left[\log(2\pi)^2 + \frac{1}{2\pi}\int_{-\pi}^{\pi}\log f(\lambda)d\lambda\right. \\
&\left.+ \frac{1}{(2\pi)^2}\int_{-\pi}^{\pi}\left(\sum_{s=-(N-1)}^{N-1}\hat{v}_s\cos s\lambda\right)\frac{d\lambda}{f(\lambda)}\right] \\
&= -\frac{N}{2}\left[2\log 2\pi + \frac{1}{2\pi}\right. \\
&\left.\cdot\int_{-\pi}^{\pi}\left(\log f(\lambda) + \frac{I_N(\lambda)}{f(\lambda)}\right)d\lambda\right]
\end{aligned} \qquad (12)$$

where

$$I_N(\lambda) = \frac{1}{2\pi}\sum_{s=-(N-1)}^{N-1}\hat{v}_s\cos s\lambda = \frac{1}{2\pi N}\left|\sum_{m=1}^{N}x_me^{-jm\lambda}\right|^2 \qquad (13)$$

which is a statistical value and is called the short-time spectral density or a periodogram. The logarithmic-likelihood function is thus expressed for the signal x given in the frequency domain.

Now, referring Eq. (12), we examine the physical meaning of the estimation of the spectral information by means of the maximum-likelihood method. In this equation $f(\lambda)$ is restricted in the same way as in Eq. (1). If this restriction is removed, the condition on which the right-hand side of Eq. (12) becomes maximum for given $I_N(\lambda)$ is $f(\lambda) = I_N(\lambda) (-\pi \leq \lambda \leq \pi)$. The maximum is

$$L_{max} = -\frac{N}{2}\left[2\log 2\pi + \frac{1}{2\pi}\int_{-\pi}^{\pi}\{\log I_N(\lambda) + 1\}d\lambda\right] \qquad (14)$$

Then, $E_1(f/I_N)$ defined as $8\pi/N \cdot (L_{max} - L(x|\tilde{\omega}))$ is as follows:

$$E_1(f/I_N) \equiv \int_{-\pi}^{\pi} 2\left\{ \log \frac{f(\lambda)}{I_N(\lambda)} + \frac{I_N(\lambda)}{f(\lambda)} - 1 \right\} d\lambda \qquad (15)$$

which is positive, but zero only when $f(\lambda) = I_N(\lambda) \, (-\pi \leq \lambda \leq \pi)$. Therefore, $E_1(f/I_N)$ is a measure of the matching error when the short-time spectral density is replaced by an assumed theoretical spectrum $f(\lambda)$. Furthermore, the estimation of the spectral information $\tilde{\omega}$ by means of the maximum-likelihood method is equivalent to the spectral matching which minimizes the matching-error measure $E_1(f/I_N)$. This is similar to the extraction of the spectral information by means of spectral matching in the analysis-by-synthesis method.

We now examine the characteristics of the matching error measure $E_1(f/I_N)$. If the integrand of $E_1(f/I_N)$ is expressed as a function of $d = \log[f(\lambda)/I_N(\lambda)] \doteqdot$ difference between $0.23 \times f(\lambda)$ and $I_N(\lambda)$ in dB, the matching error measure is

$$G_1(d) = 2(d + e^{-d} - 1) \qquad (16)$$

which is shown with the solid line in Fig. 1.

On the other hand, in case of spectrum matching by analysis-by-synthesis, the matching-error measure equivalent to $E_1(f/I_N)$ is

$$E_2(f/I_N) = \int_{-\pi}^{\pi} (\log f(\lambda) - \log I_N(\lambda))^2 d\lambda \qquad (17)$$

or a function in which the integrand of Eq. (17) is weighted on the frequency axis. In terms of d as the integrand of $E_2(f/I_N)$, the matching-error measure is

$$G_2(d) = d^2 \qquad (18)$$

which is shown with a dashed line in the same figure. It is seen that $G_1(d)$ and $G_2(d)$ are almost equal for $|d| < 1$, but $G_1(d)$ increases linearly with increase of d for $d > 1$ and increases exponentially with decrease of d for $d < -1$. On the other hand, $G_2(d)$ is quadratic and symmetrical with respect to $d = 0$. In case of spectrum matching by $E_2(f/I_N)$ for $\lambda = \lambda_0$ fixed, the matching error for $d = d_0 > 0$ (that is, $f(\lambda) > I_N(\lambda)$, overestimation) is equivalent to that for $d = -d_0$ (that is, underestimation). In case of the spectrum matching by $E_1(f/I_N)$, however, the former is evaluated to be larger than the latter. In other words, when the short-time spectrum $I_N(\lambda)$ is matched through an assumed theoretical spectrum $f(\lambda)$ by means of the maximum-likelihood method, the matching error when $I_N(\lambda)$ is replaced by a mean spectrum where a local dip is neglected, is evaluated to be smaller than the case when a spectral peak is neglected.

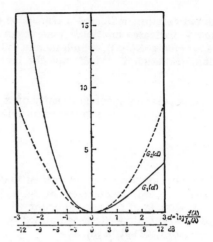

Fig. 1. Comparison of two matching-error measures used in the maximum-likehood method $G_1(d)$ and in the analysis-by-synthesis method $G_2(d)$.

The maximum likelihood is thus an estimation in which attention is paid to the spectral peak. This is a reasonable method with characteristics common to the human hearing, as discussed in Sect. 2.2.

6. Maximum-Likelihood Estimation of Spectral Information

To maximize the logarithmic likelihood function or Eq. (9) with respect to $\tilde{\omega}$, we treat the equation first with respect to σ_ϵ^2. That is,

$$\frac{\partial L(x|\tilde{\omega})}{\partial(\sigma_\epsilon^2)} = -\frac{N}{2}\left[\frac{1}{\sigma_\epsilon^2} - \frac{1}{(\sigma_\epsilon^2)^2} \right.$$
$$\left. \cdot (A_0 \hat{v}_0 + 2A_1 \hat{v}_1 + \cdots + 2A_p \hat{v}_p) \right] = 0 \qquad (19)$$

When

$$\sigma_\epsilon^2 = A_0 \hat{v}_0 + 2A_1 \hat{v}_1 + \cdots + 2A_p \hat{v}_p \qquad (19')$$

$L(x|\tilde{\omega})$ becomes maximum; that is,

$$\max_{\sigma_\epsilon^2} L(x|\tilde{\omega}) = -\frac{N}{2}$$
$$\cdot [\log 2\pi e(A_0 \hat{v}_0 + 2A_1 \hat{v}_1 + \cdots + 2A_p \hat{v}_p)]$$
$$= -\frac{N}{2}[\log 2\pi e \int_{-\pi}^{\pi} |1 + a_1 e^{-j\lambda} + \cdots$$
$$+ a_p e^{-jp\lambda}|^2 I_N(\lambda) d\lambda] \qquad (20)$$

Therefore, to obtain the maximum-likelihood estimation of $a_1, a_2, \cdots, a_p$ is equivalent to finding $a_1, a_2, \cdots, a_p$ which minimize the equation

$$J(a_1, a_2, \cdots, a_p) = \int_{-\pi}^{\pi} |1 + a_1 e^{-j\lambda} + \cdots$$
$$+ a_p e^{-jp\lambda}|^2 I_N(\lambda) d\lambda \qquad (21)$$

for given x or $I_N(\lambda)$.

298

To solve this equation, we define the following function consisting of the inner product of $g_1(\lambda)$ and $g_2(\lambda)$ with a weighting function $I_N(\lambda)$ (for $-\pi \leq \lambda \leq \pi$):

$$(g_1, g_2) = \int_{-\pi}^{\pi} \bar{g}_1(\lambda) g_2(\lambda) I_N(\lambda) d\lambda \qquad (22)$$

where $\bar{g}(\lambda)$ is the complex conjugate of $g(\lambda)$. With reference to Eq. (13), the inner product of an arbitrary pair out of the linearly independent function $\{\psi_m(\lambda) = e^{jm\lambda}, \ m = 0, 1, \cdots\}$ is

$$(\psi_m, \psi_n) = \int_{-\pi}^{\pi} e^{jm\lambda} e^{-jn\lambda} I_N(\lambda) d\lambda = \hat{v}_{m-n} \qquad (23)$$

Therefore, the normalized orthogonal function $\{\phi_n(\lambda), \ n = 0, 1, 2, \cdots\}$, which is obtained by the orthogonality of $\{\psi_m\}$ through the Schmidt procedure, is

$$\phi_n(\lambda) = \frac{D_n(\lambda)}{\sqrt{D_{n-1} D_n}} \qquad (24)$$

where

$$D_n(\lambda) = \begin{vmatrix} \hat{v}_0 & \hat{v}_1 & \cdots\cdots & \hat{v}_n \\ \hat{v}_1 & \hat{v}_0 & & \hat{v}_{n-1} \\ \vdots & & & \vdots \\ \hat{v}_{n-1} & \cdots & \hat{v}_1 & \hat{v}_0 & \hat{v}_1 \\ 1 & e^{j\lambda} & \cdots & e^{(n-1)j\lambda} & e^{nj\lambda} \end{vmatrix}, \quad D_0(\lambda) = 1 \qquad (25)$$

$$D_n = \begin{vmatrix} \hat{v}_0 & \hat{v}_1 & \cdots\cdots & \hat{v}_n \\ \hat{v}_1 & \hat{v}_0 & & \\ \vdots & & & \vdots \\ & & & \hat{v}_0 & \hat{v}_1 \\ \hat{v}_n & \hat{v}_{n-1} & \cdots & \hat{v}_1 & \hat{v}_0 \end{vmatrix}, \quad D_{-1} = 1 \qquad (26)$$

That is, $\phi_n(\lambda)$ is the n-th order polynomial with respect to $\zeta = e^{j\lambda}$, and the high-order coefficient is $(D_{n-1}/D_n)^{1/2}$. On the other hand, since λ in Eq. (21) is real,

$$|1 + \alpha_1 e^{-j\lambda} + \cdots + \alpha_p e^{-jp\lambda}|^2$$
$$= |e^{jp\lambda} + \alpha_1 e^{j(n-1)\lambda} + \cdots + \alpha_p|^2$$
$$= |\beta_p \phi_p(\lambda) + \beta_{p-1}\phi_{p-1}(\lambda) + \cdots + \beta_1\phi_1(\lambda) + \beta_0|^2 \qquad (27)$$

where $\beta_i (i = 0, 1, 2, \cdots, p)$ are the unknown constants. For the coefficient of ζ^p in the polynomial with respect to $\zeta = e^{j\lambda}$ inside of $|\ |^2$ in the last relation of Eq. (27) to be 1, $\beta_p = (D_p/D_{p-1})^{1/2}$. The, Eq. (21) becomes

$$J(\alpha_1, \alpha_2, \cdots, \alpha_p)$$
$$= \int_{-\pi}^{\pi} \left| \sqrt{\frac{D_p}{D_{p-1}}} \phi_p(\lambda) + \beta_{p-1}\phi_{p-1}(\lambda) + \cdots \right.$$
$$\left. + \beta_0 \right|^2 I_N(\lambda) d\lambda$$
$$= \frac{D_p}{D_{p-1}} + |\beta_{p-1}|^2 + |\beta_{p-2}|^2 + \cdots + |\beta_0|^2 \qquad (28)$$

Therefore, $\beta_0 = \beta_1 = \cdots = \beta_{p-1} = 0$ in $J(\alpha_1, \cdots, \alpha_p)$; that is, D_p/D_{p-1} becomes minimum, when

$$e^{jp\lambda} + \alpha_1 e^{j(p-1)\lambda} + \cdots + \alpha_p$$
$$= \sqrt{\frac{D_p}{D_{p-1}}} \phi_p(\lambda) = \frac{D_p(\lambda)}{D_{p-1}} \qquad (29)$$

By comparing the coefficients in both members of Eq. (29), we have the maximum-likelihood estimate $\hat{a}_1, \hat{a}_2, \cdots, \hat{a}_p$ as

$$\hat{a}_k = \frac{\Delta_p^{(k)}(\lambda)}{D_{p-1}} \quad (k = 1, \cdots, p) \qquad (30)$$

where $\Delta_p^{(k)}(\lambda)$ is a cofactor with respect to the element in the p-th row and the $p-k$-th column of the determinant in Eq. (25). Therefore, by means of the Cramer theorem, it is clear that $\hat{a}_k(k = 1, \cdots, p)$ is the solution of the following simultaneous equations of the p-th order;

$$\begin{pmatrix} \hat{v}_0 & \hat{v}_1 & \cdots\cdots & v_{p-1} \\ \hat{v}_1 & \hat{v}_0 & & \\ \vdots & & & \hat{v}_1 \\ \hat{v}_{p-1} & \cdots & \hat{v}_1 & \hat{v}_0 \end{pmatrix} \begin{pmatrix} \hat{a}_1 \\ \hat{a}_2 \\ \vdots \\ \hat{a}_p \end{pmatrix} = - \begin{pmatrix} \hat{v}_1 \\ \hat{v}_2 \\ \vdots \\ \hat{v}_p \end{pmatrix} \qquad (31)$$

By substituting $(\hat{a}_1, \hat{a}_2, \cdots, \hat{a}_p)$ given by Eq. (31) into Eq. (2), we obtain the maximum-likelihood estimate $A_0, A_1, \cdots, A_p$. This is an application of condition (4) of Sect. 3. Furthermore, the maximum-likelihood estimate of $\hat{\sigma}_\epsilon^2$ is also obtained through Eq. (19'). Finally, the maximum-likelihood estimate of the spectral density $f(\lambda)$ is established by substituting $\hat{A}_0, \hat{A}_1, \cdots, \hat{A}_p$ into Eq. (1).

7. Maximum-Likelihood Estimate of Formant Frequencies and Bandwidth

The estimate $\hat{z}_i$ of the pole z_i of $f(\lambda)$ in Eq. (1) is the root of the following algebraic equation of the p-th order with the coefficients $(\hat{a}_1, \hat{a}_2, \cdots, \hat{a}_p)$ which are the solution of Eq. (31):

$$\hat{a}_p z^p + \hat{a}_{p-1} z^{p-1} + \cdots + \hat{a}_1 z + 1 = 0 \qquad (32)$$

When $\hat{z}_i$ ($i = 1, 2, \cdots, p$) is expressed in polar coordinates, that is, $\hat{z}_i = \hat{r}_i e^{j\hat{\lambda}_i}$, the resonant frequency and the corresponding 3-dB bandwidth with respect to the pole $\hat{z}_i$ are

$$\hat{F}_i = |\hat{\lambda}_i|/2\pi\Delta T \qquad (33)$$
$$\hat{B}_i = \log \hat{r}_i / \pi\Delta T \qquad (34)$$

The speech formant is the region where the spectral components are concentrated. The resonant frequency $\hat{F}_i$ of a pole with a relatively narrow bandwidth among others means the formant frequency, and the corresponding bandwidth $\hat{B}_i$ is its bandwidth. In Fig. 2 is shown a block diagram of equipment for the maximum-likelihood method for spectral information.

8. Application to Speech Analysis

To examine the validity of this theoretical approach, the method has been applied to actual speech analysis. The original speech signals were filtered through a low-pass filter with the crossover frequency of 4 kHz, sampled at

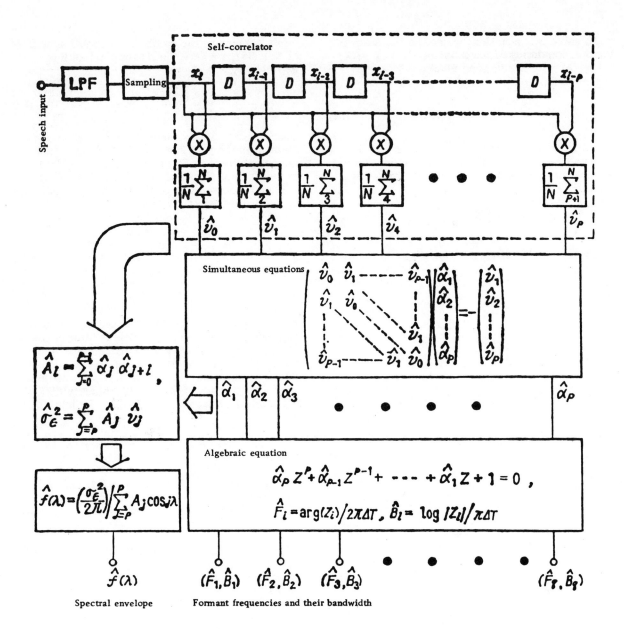

Fig. 2. Schematic diagram for extraction of spectral information based on the maximum-likehood method.

$1/\Delta T = 8000$ Hz and homogeneously digitalized in 10 bits including the sign. The signals thus processed were used for the analysis.

8.1 Variation of Estimate Due to Number of Poles Assumed

When speech is analyzed by this method, the estimate of the spectral information varies with the number of the poles assumed. Therefore, the assumption of the value of p is a question. In Fig. 3, the short-time spectral density $I_N(\lambda)$ of a male vowel (/a/ as in the English word "tar" and at 140 Hz fundamental) is shown in comparison with the spectral density of the maximum-likelihood estimates $\hat{f}(\lambda)$ for several pole

numbers p (p = 12, 10, 8 and 6). The same comparison was made for a female voice and the same vowel (at 258 Hz), and the data are shown in Fig. 4. It follows that:

(1) As expected from the theory, better matching is seen in the peak regions of $I_N(\lambda)$ than in the dip regions.

(2) The distinctive peaks in $I_N(\lambda)$ are almost perfectly reproduced in $\hat{f}(\lambda)$, if p is more than 10.

(3) Even when p is small, the general spectral distribution is extracted.

In Fig. 5, the variation of the estimate $\hat{F}_1$ of the poles of the spectral density for the male

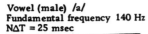

Vowel (male) /a/
Fundamental frequency 140 Hz
NΔT = 25 msec

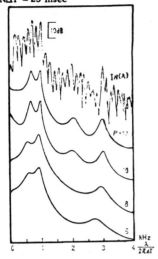

Fig. 3. Short-time spectrum
$I_N(\lambda)$ and the estimated
spectra $\hat{f}(\lambda)$.

Vowel (female) /a/
Fundamental frequency 258 Hz
NΔT = 25 msec

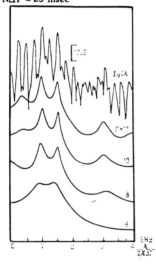

Fig. 4. Short-time spectrum
$I_N(\lambda)$ and the estimated
spectra $\hat{f}(\lambda)$.

vowel /i/ due to p is shown. The symbols in the
figure indicate the bandwidth of the poles arranged
into seven categories. It is seen that $\hat{F}_i$ with
relatively narrow bandwidth B_i is constant for
p = 10 to 14. The example shows that ten poles
are large enough for the assumption.

Vowel (male) /i/
Fundamental frequency 132 Hz

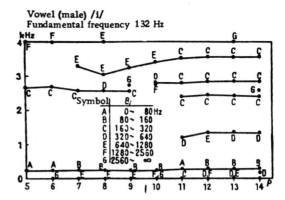

Fig. 5. The estimated spectrum
poles for various assumed numbers of poles.

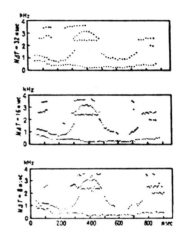

Fig. 6. Tracking of spectrum
poles of five continuously uttered vowels for various
analyzing intervals (ΔT
= 1/8000 sec).

8.2 Variation of Estimate Due to Observation Interval ΔT·N

If the speech signals are stationary, the variance of the estimate of the spectral information
naturally decreases with increase of the observation interval. In the case of actual speech,
however, the short-time spectrum varies with
time. Therefore, as long as the variance of the
estimate is within the limit, it is desirable to gain
time resolution for fluctuation of the spectrum by
employing an analytical interval ΔT·N as short
as possible. In Fig. 6 is shown the tracking of the
spectrum poles of five continuously uttered vowels
/aoiue/ (as in the English words, "tar" and
"only," the French "Isle de Cité, the English

"union" and "eight") for various analyzing intervals $\Delta T \cdot N$ = 32, 16 and 8 msec. We first obtain $(\hat{F}_i, \hat{B}_i)$; then $\hat{F}_i$ which satisfies $B_i < 640$ Hz is shown as a function of the interval. The results show that the formant frequencies can be stably extracted for the interval as short as that of the longest fundamental period (that is, about 8 msec).

9. Discussion of the Assumptions

The extraction of the spectral information in speech by the maximum-likelihood method discussed in Sections 3 through 8 provides the merits described in Sect. 3, as long as the conditions described in Sect. 2.3 are satisfied. In the case of actual speech, however, they are not always satisfied. We shall now examine these, referring to the experimental results obtained in Sect. 8.

The assumption that the input signal is stationary is reasonable because the spectral information is stably extracted for the short 8-msec interval. The assumption that the signal is Gaussian is questionable, particularly for voiced sounds, but it is adequate for the following reason. It is assumed that the extraction method gives the optimum solution by spectrum matching which has $E_1(f/I_N)$ as a matching-error measure, being independent of the probability distribution of the signal. This is proved by the experiments on the extraction of the vowel formants in Sect. 8.

Finally, the assumption that the speech spectrum can be approximated by the rational spectral density without null point is also adequate, not only from the spectrum discrimination characteristics in hearing described in Sect. 2.2, but also by the fact that an arbitrary continuous spectral density (as far as its reciprocal can be integrated) can be approximated to arbitrary accuracy by the rational spectra without null point for a large number of poles. The validity is also proved by the fact that the formant frequencies extracted on this assumption coincide with those obtained by the speech analyzer.

10. Conclusions

The maximum-likelihood method of obtaining spectral information on speech, as described above, has the following merits;

(1) The macroscopic spectral information can be obtained by the covariance of samples on a $(p+1)$ basis. Ten poles are sufficient for speech signal with 4-kHz bandwidth.

(2) This extraction method, like the analysis-by-synthesis method, is equivalent to spectrum matching by the theoretical spectral density $f(\lambda)$ against the short-time spectral density $I_N(\lambda)$. It

is not necessary, in practice, to obtain $I_N(\lambda)$, which would require laborious calculation. Furthermore, the procedure of matching gives the result of solving the simultaneous linear equations. Then, the solution can be uniquely given.

(3) In the matching-error measure of spectrum matching, like in the tonal discrimination characteristics of the spectral difference in hearing, the peak regions in the spectrum are more important than the dip regions.

This method is also available for the extraction of spectral information in audio pattern recognition and efficient transmission of speech. These applications are to be reported in due course.

Acknowledgement. The authors wish to express their gratitude to Professors Honda of Tohoku University and Ikeya and Fukumura of Nagoya University, and also to Mr. Oguchi and other colleagues at the Electrical Communication Laboratory, N.T.T.

REFERENCES

1. C.G. Bell, H. Fujisaki, J.M. Heinz, K.N. Stevens and A.S. House: Reduction of speech spectra by analysis-by-synthesis techniques, Jour. Acoust. Soc. Amer., 33, p. 1720 (1961).

2. Saito, Kato and Teranishi: On the characteristics of the fundamental frequencies of speech, Jour. of Acoust. Soc. of Japan, 14, 2, p. 111 (1958).

3. K. Udagawa and F. Itakura: Some properties of correlation function and spectral density of an impulse train, Jour. I.E.C.E., Japan, 50, 1, p. 99 (Jan. 1967); available in English in E.C.J., same date, p. 102.

4. R. Matsuda: Effects of the fluctuation characteristics of input signal on the tonal differential limen of a speech transmission system containing single dip in frequency response, Jour. I.E.C.E., Japan, 49, 10, p. 1865 (Oct. 1966); available in English in E.C.J., same date, p. 54.

5. H. Cramer: Mathematical Methods of Statistics, p. 497, Princeton University Press (1946).

6. Saito, Fukumura and Itakura: Theoretical consideration of the statistical optimum recognition of the spectral density of speech, Acoust. Soc. of Japan (Jan. 25, 1967).

Submitted June 30, 1969

Digital Inverse Filtering– A New Tool for Formant Trajectory Estimation

JOHN D. MARKEL

Speech Commun. Res. Lab., Inc.
Santa Barbara, Calif. 93101

Abstract

A new algorithm, based upon a digital inverse filter formulation, is presented and shown to be quite useful for estimating resonance or formant structure of voiced speech. The output of the algorithm is a set of raw data corresponding to peak frequencies versus time which is then used to estimate the first three and sometimes four continuously varying formant trajectories. Although an algorithm for automatically extracting the formants from the raw data is not presented here, for nearly 90 percent of the time an automatic decision algorithm is trivial, namely, the first three peaks of the reciprocal of the inverse filter spectrum define the first three formants.

I. Introduction

In 1966 Saito and Itakura [1] developed a new technique for time domain speech analysis based upon the maximum likelihood estimation method. A discussion in English was published in 1968 [2]. Also in 1968 Atal and Schroeder [3] published a method for linear prediction of the speech wave In 1970 Markel [4] observed that both of the basic analysis equations, independently developed, were of similar form and in fact, were derivable as special cases of Prony's method [5], [6] originally formulated in 1795 and extended to a least squares formulation at least as early as 1924 [7]. Prony's method in z-transform notation has been rediscovered at least twice within the past five years [8], [9]. From the analysis equations, moderate bit-rate speech transmission systems have been developed. The approach had, however, evidently been deemed unworkable as a tool for formant extraction. The purpose of this paper is to show that the basic analysis approach is transformable into a formant extraction algorithm and, moreover, to demonstrate that high quality formant trajectory estimation is possible even for the more difficult problems of closely spaced formants and fast transitions. The algorithm developed is linear, fast, and ac-

Manuscript received August 1971.

This work was supported by the Office of Naval Research under Contract N00014-67-0118

This paper is based largely upon a more detailed description in "Formant trajectory estimation from a linear least-squares inverse filter formulation," SCRL Monograph 7, Speech Commun. Res. Lab., Inc., Santa Barbara, Calif. 93101.

Reprinted from *IEEE Trans. Audio Electroacoust.*, vol. AU-20, pp. 129–137, June 1972.

curate. The raw data from which the formant trajectories are estimated consists only of a set of peak frequencies versus time. No formant amplitude or allowable formant frequency range information is necessary. On the average, for approximately 90 percent of the analysis frames, the first three formants can be uniquely defined as the first three peaks in the reciprocal of the inverse filter spectrum.

The approach relies heavily upon consideration of a frequency domain point of view, namely, inverse filtering for determining the necessary analysis conditions and parameter values.

II. Derivation of the Digital Inverse Filter

A digital filter of the form

$$A(z) = 1 + \sum_{i=1}^{M} a_i z^{-i}$$

is assumed where $M+1$ defines the filter length. Given an input sequence $\{x_n\}$ of length N we wish to determine the coefficients $\{a_i\}$ such that the total energy as measured at the filter output is minimized. Within a constant factor this formulation is equivalent to the problem of transforming an input sequence into the best least squares estimate of a unit pulse through the filter [10], [11]. Thus, the problem is essentially one of digital Wiener filtering [12].

The form of $A(z)$ is important in our development due to the fact that we are interested only in estimating the resonance structure of spectral data. Defining the leading term as unity instead of some arbitrary a_o has the following effects. 1) If the leading term is arbitrary, the error function must be the difference between a constant and the filter output instead of just the filter output—otherwise the optimum filter would be defined by setting $a_i=0$, $i=0, 1, \cdots, M$; and 2) the order of the equations which must be solved is reduced by one.

The solution to this digital inverse filter formulation is easily obtained as follows. The total energy ϵ of the output filter is calculated from the error function y_n by

$$\epsilon = \sum_{n=0}^{L} y_n^2 \qquad (1)$$

where

$$y_n = x_n + \sum_{i=1}^{M} a_i x_{n-i}$$

and

$$L = N + M - 1.$$

The total energy is minimized by taking the partial derivative of ϵ with respect to a_k, $k=1, 2, \cdots, M$, setting to zero, and solving for $\{a_k\}$. The result is

$$\sum_{i=1}^{M} a_i \sum_{n=0}^{L} x_{n-i} x_{n-k} = - \sum_{n=0}^{L} x_{n-k} x_n, \quad k=1, 2, \cdots, M. \quad (2)$$

By noting that $x_n = 0$, $n<0$, and $n \geq N$, (2) can be rewritten as

$$\sum_{i=1}^{M} a_i r_{i-k} = -r_k, \qquad k = 1, 2, \cdots, M \qquad (3)$$

where

$$r_k = \sum_{n=0}^{N-1-|k|} x_n x_{n+|k|}. \qquad (4)$$

The results are of similar form although not identical to the classical Wiener filter equations in discrete form [13]. These equations define the nucleus of the formant trajectory estimation algorithm which will be developed.

There is certainly nothing difficult about the development of the above equations. In various related forms they have existed for at least 50 years. The nontrivial and necessarily empirical part of the procedure is in determining various relationships between mathematical constants such as N, M, and the system sampling rate and the desired characteristics of the speech wave so that a useful formant analysis technique is developed.

III. Formant Extraction and the Inverse Filter

In essence, the inverse filter attempts to transform the input signal into a constant or white noise spectrum. If $M \rightarrow \infty$ the inverse filter will theoretically predict the exact inverse of the input signal spectrum, resulting in a constant for the output or error spectrum. For a finite M, it is no longer possible to span the input signal and thus the filter can only be designed to approximate the inverse of the signal characteristics.

Our hypothesis was that if M were properly chosen it would be possible to predict the inverse of the gross spectral structure corresponding to the resonance or formant behavior while ignoring the fine spectral structure corresponding to voice fundamental frequency F_o (at least for the case where F_o is in the range of a male voice). The estimate of the resonance behavior would then be determined as the reciprocal of the inverse filter spectrum. Figs. 1 and 2 illustrate the expected results for voiced and unvoiced sounds with proper choice of analysis conditions and parameters. Shown in Fig. 1(A) and (B) is a representative spectrum and its autocorrelation sequence, respectively. With the proper choice of analysis conditions log $|A(z)|^2$ evaluated along the unit circle gives the appearance shown in Fig. 1(C). The reciprocal of the inverse filter spectrum defines the estimate of the resonance structure of the input spectrum as shown in Fig. 1(D). The spectrum of the inverse filter output corresponding to the error in the representation is shown in Fig. 1(E). The effect of the inverse filter is to transform the input signal into the best estimate of white noise (in the least squares sense). It is seen that the result is roughly a white noise spectrum with a periodic component superimposed upon it. The autocorrelation sequence of the output shown in Fig. 1(F) is an alternate method of illustrating the effect of the inverse filter. The unit pulse at the time origin corresponds to the white noise or constant portion of the spec-

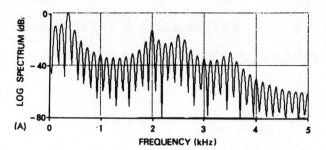

(A)

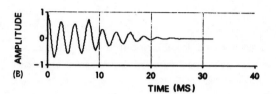

(B)

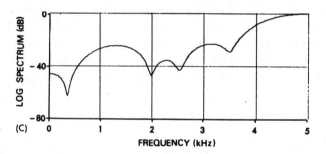

(C)

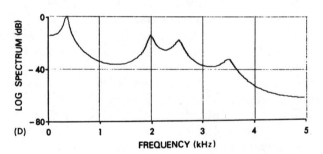

(D)

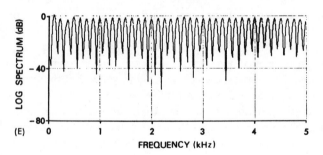

(E)

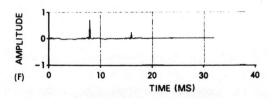

(F)

Fig. 1. Representative waveforms from the analysis of a voiced sound with proper choice of analysis conditions.

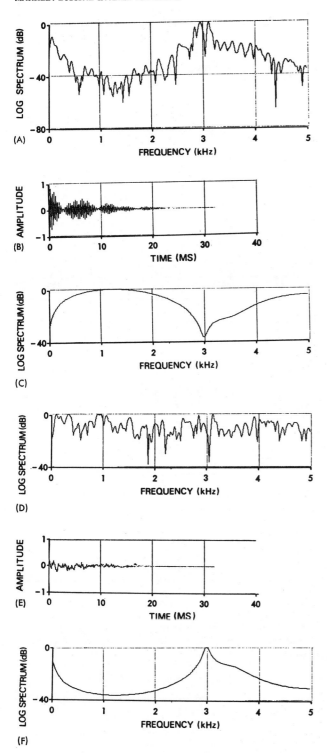

(A)

(B)

(C)

(D)

(E)

(F)

Fig. 2. Representative waveforms from the analysis of an unvoiced sound with proper choice of analysis conditions.

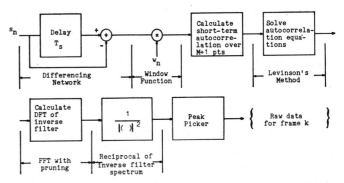

Fig. 3. Block diagram of the inverse filter algorithm for automatically extracting the raw data for use in formant trajectory estimation.

Fig. 2 presents corresponding results for the analysis of an unvoiced segment with proper analysis conditions. It can be seen that a quite reasonable estimate of the noise spectrum is obtained. The output autocorrelation sequence and spectrum illustrate the fact that the predictable (nonwhite) components of the input signal corresponding to the resonance structure have been accurately extracted.

The peak frequency locations in the spectrum shown in Fig. 1(D) (which can be obtained by simple peak peaking) define the "raw data" from which formant frequencies are estimated. For this synthetic example, the peak locations correspond precisely to the formant frequencies. The algorithm used for generating this raw data for continuous real speech will now be considered.

IV. The Inverse Filter Algorithm (IFA)

A block diagram of the IFA is shown in Fig. 3. Let s_k, $k = 0, 1, \cdots$, define the sampled data representation of the continuous speech wave $s(t)$, where

$$s_k = s(t) \big|_{t=kT_s}, \qquad k = 0, 1, \cdots,$$

and T_s is the sampling period with corresponding sampling frequency $F_s = 1/T_s$. Since speech is a continually time-varying process, short-term analysis of sets of contiguous data samples at some specified frame rate is needed. Each data frame is of duration T_f with corresponding frame rate $F_f = 1/T_f$.

For each frame the inverse filter input x_n is defined by $x_n = w_n(s_{k+n+1} - s_{k+n})$, $n = 0, 1, \cdots, N-1$ where k denotes the starting point of the particular frame being analyzed. The signal is differenced for two reasons. First, a 6 dB/octave pre-emphasis occurs which with windowing tends to emphasize the higher formants. In addition a troublesome low-frequency nonformant peak occasionally caused by a very strong fundamental frequency component is deemphasized. Secondly, if there is any bias or nonzero mean value in the frame, it will tend to cause the Fourier transform of the window function to appear in the low-frequency region of the discrete spectrum of the input sequence $\{x_n\}$. The

trum while the next highest amplitude spike and its diminished amplitude replications correspond to the periodic component of the spectrum. The application of the autocorrelation equations for obtaining high quality pitch information has previously been recognized by Itakura and Saito [2].

effect is to cause an increase in the filter length so that the peak at zero frequency along with the other resonances can be represented adequately.

If the N differenced speech samples are directly applied to the inverse filter equations, w_n is effectively defined as a rectangular window. Because of the properties of a rectangular window, zeros occur in the DFT of $\{x_n\}$ at the reciprocal of the window width. The effect of these zeros is so severe that often F_2 or F_3 can be completely disguised. A considerably more appropriate window function is the Hamming or Hanning window [14]. Somewhat arbitrarily we have chosen the Hamming window defined by

$$w_n = \begin{cases} 0.54 - 0.46 \cos (2\pi n/(N-1)], \\ \qquad\qquad\qquad n = 0, 1, \cdots, N-1 \\ 0, \quad \text{elsewhere.} \end{cases}$$

The necessity for a proper window function is shown in Fig. 4. Fig. 4(A) shows the spectrum of a 32-ms segment taken from a spoken phrase using a rectangular window. The inverse filter analysis with proper choice of conditions results in the spectral estimate shown in Fig. 4(B). In terms of extracting the apparent resonance structure of the spectrum, the analysis is reasonably good. At most, one resonance can be estimated.

However, by observing a spectrogram of the utterance from which this segment was taken, it is quite clear that there are two closely spaced low formants and two additional formants, one at about 2.2 kHz and the other at about 3.1 kHz. By applying a 320-point Hamming window to the input sequence, the spectral representation shown in Fig. 4(C) is obtained. By comparing Fig. 4(A) and (C) one can see the dramatic change in spectral character, due simply to the application of the Hamming window function.

In Fig. 4(A), F_1 is reasonably clear. However, it is not evident whether the single spike at about 0.6 kHz belongs to the first or second formant. In Fig. 4(C) it is clear that two separate peaks occur in the range (0, 1) kHz. Past 1 kHz, the effect of the rectangular window is to mask out the signal components. In Fig. 4(A), the peak at 2.2 kHz is barely perceivable, whereas it is quite distinct in Fig. 4(C). In Fig. 4(A), no resonances are observable past 3 kHz, whereas in Fig. 4(C) an additional resonance is apparent at 3.1 kHz. Since the inverse filter is designed to transform the input spectrum into a white noise or constant spectrum it should not be too surprising that the analysis result as shown in Fig. 4(D) is obtained. The four resonance frequencies can now be extracted by simple peak peaking.

The short term autocorrelation sequence $\{r_k\}$ is computed directly from (4) using the length N sequence $\{x_n\}$. Although r_k, $k=0, 1, \cdots, N-1$, is most efficiently calculated by applying two FFT's of length N (if N is highly composite), for speech analysis $M \ll N$ in general, and direct calculation of the $M+1$ autocorrelation coefficients will be somewhat faster.

Because of the special form of the autocorrelation equations it is possible to recursively solve for the unknown filter coefficients a_i, $i=1, 2, \cdots, M$, in the order of M^2 ($0(M^2)$)

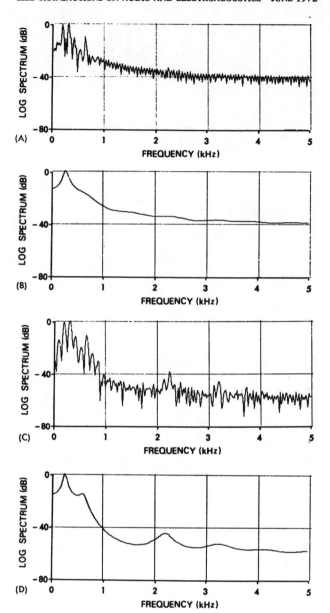

Fig. 4. Illustrations showing the effects of a rectangular window and a Hamming window on resonance estimates from the inverse filter algorithm.

operations as opposed to $0(M^3)$ operations for a general linear simultaneous equation solution. The solution was first developed by Levinson [13] and later derived in a somewhat different form using z transforms by Robinson [10].

From Robinson's development we obtain with only slight modifications the flow chart of Fig. 5 as the most efficient solution to (3). A Fortran program can be written directly from the flow chart by noting that the superscripts correspond to the iteration number (and are thus only implied) while the subscripts define the subscripted variables which must be dimensioned. With respect to (3), $a_n{}^{(M)} = a_n$ for $n=1, 2, \cdots, M$, as the coefficient solution set. One addi-

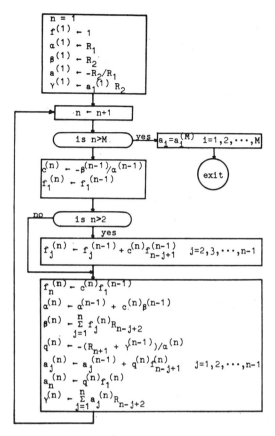

Fig. 5. Flow chart for determining the inverse filter coefficients a_i, $i = 1, 2, \cdots, M$ from the short-term autocorrelation coefficients $r_i = R_{i+1}$, $i = 0, 1, \cdots, M$ using Levinson's method.

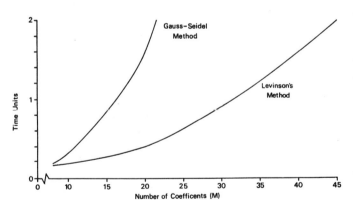

Fig. 6. Relative computational times for the $M \times M$ autocorrelation matrix inversion using Levinson's method and the general-purpose Gauss–Seidel procedure.

tional advantage of Levinson's method is that only $4M$ storage locations are required as opposed to M^2 for general linear simultaneous equation solution. The relative time saving possible from Levinson's method is shown in Fig. 6 where it is compared with the Gauss–Seidel method [15] versus M. The digital filter

$$A(z) = 1 + \sum_{i=1}^{M} a_i z^{-i}$$

is now determined for a particular frame. Since $A(z)$ is an inverse filter, $|D(z)| = |1/A(z)|$ must define the estimate of the input spectrum.

After some experimentation using a polynomial root solving program to calculate all the resonances, it became apparent that the roots which were possible candidates for formant parameters were of narrow enough bandwidth that the useful information could also be obtained from a frequency domain representation of the inverse filter.

The discrete frequency spectrum $D(z_k)$, where $z_k = \exp(j2\pi k/N')$, $k = 0, 1, \cdots, N'-1$, is most efficiently calculated by pruning the FFT. The input sequence is defined by

$$\{1, a_1, a_2, \cdots, a_M, \underbrace{0, \cdots, 0}_{N'-M-1 \text{ zeros}}\}.$$

An algorithm for pruning a radix-2 algorithm of length $2^{M'}$ where only $2^{L'}$ nonzero input values exist has recently been described [16]. With respect to a nonpruned FFT algorithm a time saving of $M'[L' + 2(1 - 2^{-\Delta})]^{-1} - 1$ where $\Delta = M' - L'$ is obtainable. If $M' = 9$ and $L' = 4$ (which means that $M \leq 16$), a time saving of nearly 60 percent is possible. Since the data are real, the computation time can be further reduced by one half by shuffling odd and even points into the real and imaginary arrays, applying an $N'/2$-point transform and then unshuffling.

The result of the FFT is $A_k = A(z_k)$. The magnitude spectrum corresponding to the estimate of the input spectrum is then computed from

$$|D_k|^2 = 1/[\text{Re}^2(A_k) + \text{Im}^2(A_k)]$$

where $\text{Re}(\cdot)$ and $\text{Im}(\cdot)$ denote the real and imaginary part, respectively. The magnitude spectrum is scanned and the L_k local maxima $p_k(l)$, $l = 1, 2, \cdots, L_k$ in frame k are recorded. The set of all local maxima defines the raw data from which the formant trajectories are to be estimated. (If there is no interest in displaying the resonance structure it should be noted that the most direct approach is to search for the local minima of $|A_k|^2$.)

V. Considerations in the Choice of Analysis Parameters

A study was performed to determine the relationship between the choice of filter length and the accuracy of resonance estimation. For a 10-kHz sampling frequency, typical results are illustrated in Fig. 7. The spectrum of the filter input sequence $\{x_n\}$ for a 32-ms portion of the spoken vowel /I/ is shown in Fig. 7(A). The spectra of the inverse filter are shown in Fig. 7(B)–(F). For $M = 6$, a very poor representation is obtained which might be expected since only three resonances are allowed for spanning the entire 5-kHz range. By inspection of Fig. 7(A) one can see that at least four formants are present. For $M = 10$ the representation improves somewhat and for $M = 14$ quite reasonable estimates of the formant frequencies are possible by simple peak peaking. For $M = 16$ the resonances are still accurately predicted. As M is increased still further, better and better ap-

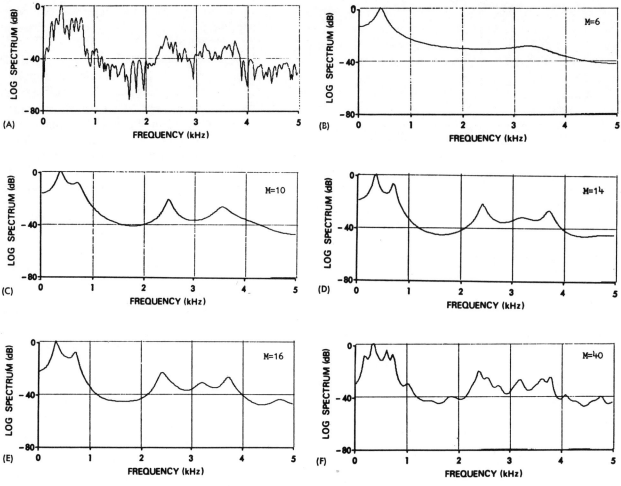

Fig. 7. Estimation of the resonance behavior of the input spectrum (shown at the top) for various filter lengths. A 10-kHz sampling rate was used for this example.

proximation to the input spectrum (as opposed to the resonance behavior) is obtained. This fact is illustrated for $M = 40$ which requires the solution of a 40×40 matrix of linear simultaneous equations.

Thus an M in the neighborhood of 14 to 16 would seem the logical choice for this example. Fortuitously it has been discovered that M is not a strong function of the particular speech sound. However, it is a strong function of the system sampling rate. In fact for $6 \leq F_s \leq 18$ kHz the equation $M = F_s + \gamma$ where $\gamma = 4$ or 5 has been found generally sufficient for the analysis. The physical interpretation of this result is simply that independent of the sampling rate, roughly one complex pole pair is required to span approximately every 700 Hz.

The choice of analysis window length is based upon consideration of two factors: 1) frequency resolution; and 2) spectral averaging. If the window is too short it will not be possible to resolve closely spaced formant structure. On the other hand if it is too long, strong formant peaks will not exist in the input spectrum due to the inherent frequency

averaging over the time interval of the window. Again, the window length has been determined to be a rather weak function of the particular speech sound but a strong function of the sampling rate. $N = \delta F_s$ where $\delta = 20$ to 35 defines reasonable limits on N.

VI. Experimental Results

In this paper, results will be presented for a constant sampling frequency of 10 kHz since nearly all significant spectral structure of speech (excluding possibly some voiceless fricatives and sibilants or aspiration noise) is contained below 5 kHz. From the Peterson–Barney study [17] it can be seen that the first three formants for vowels in a CVC environment are generally below 3 kHz. The same upper limit is also observed in voiced speech and has been used in the formant analysis algorithm as developed by Schafer and Rabiner [18].

Due to its being previously chosen as representative of a difficult form of voiced speech having both close first and second formants and close second and third formants and fast transitions, we will consider the voiced phrase "we were away" as a first example [17]. The results of the algorithm are shown in Fig. 8 for the parameter values $M = 14$ and $N = 256$.

The raw data are plotted on a scale of peak frequency location versus time. With the knowledge that formant trajectories must be continuous and cannot intersect, for voiced nonnasalized speech it is quite easy to estimate the first three formant trajectories by inspection. It can be seen that an occasional omission of a peak is obtained. There were no extraneous insertions (i.e., nonformant peaks) obtained for this example.

How easily the formant trajectories can be estimated is a strong function of the frame rate F_f. As F_f is increased, proportionally more data per unit time are obtained so that the effect of occasional omissions is minimized. In addition, more detailed behavior of the formant trajectories can be observed. To illustrate this point an expanded resolution analysis (ERA) was performed over the 32-ms time period shown in Fig. 8 by tripling F_f in this region. The results in the lower portion of the figure show the fast transitional second formant behavior in considerably more detail. The fastest rate of change of the trajectory is measured as -400 Hz/5 ms $= -80$ Hz/ms.

It is rather informative to consider the spectral displays from which these results were automatically obtained. Shown in Fig. 9 are the spectra corresponding to the inverse filter input on the left and the estimate of the resonance structure (obtained from the inverse of the resulting inverse filter spectra) on the right.

The inherent ability of the IFA to track closely spaced formants and fast transitions is clearly shown. In frame 1, F_2 and F_3 are separated by approximately 300 Hz. From the input spectra (frames 1 through 4) it is quite difficult to ascertain whether one or two formants exist in the region of 2 kHz. However, by invoking continuity it becomes clear that two formants must exist in the 2-kHz region. At frame 4, F_2 begins to break away from F_3 and move toward F_1. These input spectra are particularly good examples of the fact that formant extraction is not quite so simple as defining the three largest peaks of the speech spectrum in ascending order of frequency as the formants. This is necessarily the type of algorithm used in filter bank analysis of formant frequencies. In other words, peak picking of the input spectra will not generally produce correct results. However, peak picking of the inverse filter spectra, in general, will give correct results approximately 90 percent of the time.

From the lower portion of Fig. 8 and the inverse filter spectra it is seen that simple peak picking, namely $F_i(n) = p_i(n)$, $i = 1, 2, 3$, $n = 1, 2, \cdots, 7$, is 100 percent correct for these frames of data.

Frames 5 and 6 also illustrate the fact that correct results are not generally obtained by solving for the roots of $A(z)$ and then defining the three complex roots with smallest bandwidths as the first three formants. With this approach,

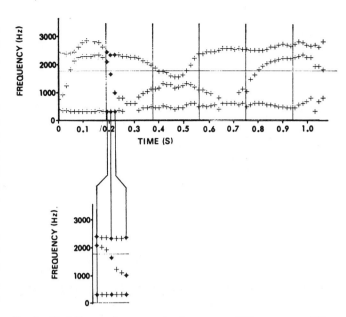

Fig. 8. (Top) The raw data output for the utterance: "We were away." (Bottom) An expanded resolution analysis (ERA) for the interval indicated to illustrate the tracking of a rapid F_2 transition.

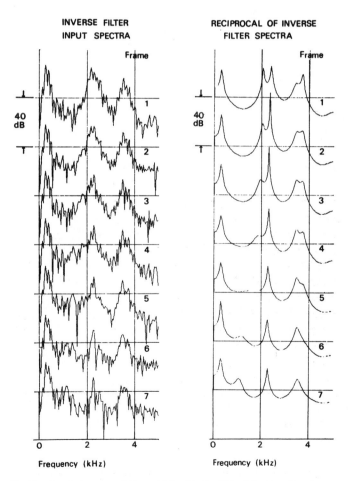

Fig. 9. Spectral representations obtained in the ERA of the transitional segment shown in Fig. 8. (Left) Inverse filter input spectra. (Right) Reciprocal of the resulting inverse filter spectra.

309

F_2 would be incorrectly defined as F_3, and F_3 would be incorrectly defined as F_4. Thus the IFA has an additional advantage besides computational efficiency over directly solving for the roots of $A(z)$. If a peak can be detected in $|A(e^{j\omega T})|^{-2}$ then it is a candidate for a formant frequency. Generally, only four or five peaks will be detected with peak picking whereas five to seven complex root pairs are usually obtained by directly solving the polynomial $A(z)$. (The extra roots generally have large bandwidths and are thus not detected by moving an analysis contour only along the unit circle in the z plane.)

It is believed that the results as illustrated here are unique in that: 1) the analysis is automatic; 2) the equations are linear, thus giving the results without recursion (in contradistinction to analysis-by-synthesis techniques [19]; 3) the formants are clearly and correctly obtained by simple peak picking of the inverse filter spectra (i.e., no decision criteria are required); and 4) the segment being tracked has formants separated by as little as 300 Hz and an F_2 transition with average slope of greater than -40 Hz/ms.

It should be emphasized that simple peak picking of the inverse filter spectra (more precisely the reciprocal of the inverse filter spectra) will uniquely define the formant trajectories only roughly 90 percent of the time. For the remaining 10 percent of the frames, some kind of decision criteria will be necessary for automatic formant trajectory extraction.

To illustrate the fact that analysis results are not dramatically changed for the suggested ranges of δ and γ, the same phrase was analyzed with $N=320$ and $M=15$. For this case several extraneous insertions are obtained as shown in Fig. 10(A), but the apparent merging of F_1 and F_2 at several locations in Fig. 8 has been eliminated. The first three formant trajectories are still easily definable by inspection using a "connect the dots" procedure. To illustrate this point a subject having no knowledge of acoustic phonetics was asked to draw three smooth continuous curves within the range (0, 3000) Hz that seemed most reasonable without any intersections.

The resulting curves were then superimposed upon a wideband spectrogram of the utterance for visual comparison as shown in Fig. 10(B). The trajectories are quite realistic with respect to what one experienced with spectrographic analysis would estimate. Note that on the wide-band spectrogram the closely spaced formants appear as a single very thick dark bar, and the fast transition and large portions of the F_3 trajectory appear quite faintly.

If an ERA is performed over the complete phrase with analysis conditions $N=320$ and $M=15$, results over the complete frequency range (0, $F_s/2$) are obtained as shown in Fig. 11. The first four formant trajectories are easily definable. The tradeoff is simply computation time. The ERA with 5-ms resolution is three times slower than the analysis using a 15-ms frame period.

Although the analysis system was strictly designed for formant trajectory estimation of nonnasalized voiced speech, the system works reasonably well with nasals and unvoiced sounds that contain formant structure.

The phrase: "Hello there, how are you?" was analyzed with parameter values somewhat arbitrarily chosen as

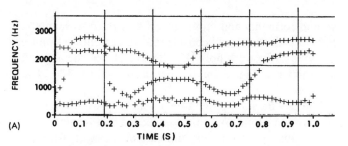
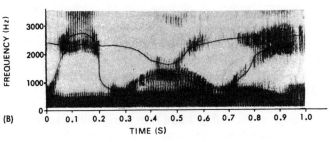

Fig. 10. Analysis of phrase: "We were away." (Top) Raw data from inverse filter algorithm. (Bottom) Spectrographic analysis of phrase with overlay of connected dots from raw data.

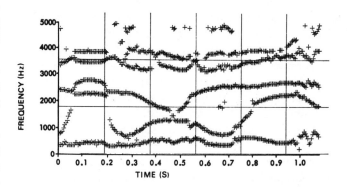

Fig. 11. Analysis of phrase: "We were away" using an expanded resolution analysis (ERA).

$N=256$ and $M=15$. The raw data is shown in Fig. 12(A) and an estimate of three nonintersecting continuous lines made by the same subject (superimposed on a spectrogram of the utterance for comparison) is shown in Fig. 12(B). Although there is a sharp transition in the region (0.24 s, 0.28 s), the raw data shows the formants to be continuously tracked. The spectrogram is used to demonstrate that they are correctly tracked.

The predominantly nasalized phrase: "I am now a man" was analyzed with the parameters $N=256$ and $M=15$. From the raw data as shown in Fig. 13(A) it can be seen that the first four formant trajectories are obtainable. The major difficulty is caused by the initial /m/. The coupling of the vocal tract to the nasal passage introduces zeros in the mathematical model of the physical system. The second formant in the time interval (0.22 s, 0.29 s) appears to have been cancelled by the nasal zero.

A comparison of a spectrogram of the phrase and four smooth continuous nonintersecting curves drawn by the same subject are shown in Fig. 13(B). Once again quite reasonable estimates appear to have been made.

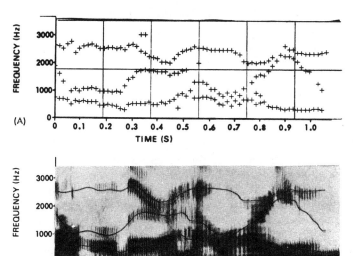

Fig. 12. Analysis of phrase: "Hello there how are you?" (Top) Raw data from inverse filter algorithm. (Bottom) Spectrographic analysis of phrase with overlay of connected dots from raw data.

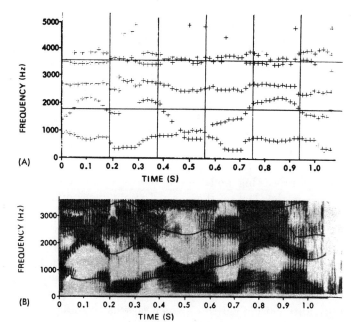

Fig. 13. Analysis of phrase: "I am now a man." (Top) Raw data from inverse filter algorithm. (Bottom) Spectrographic analysis of phrase with overlay of connected dots from raw data.

VII. Conclusion

A new application of the well-known inverse filter concept has been shown—namely, that it is a very useful tool for estimating formant trajectories from speech.

An inverse filter algorithm was presented for efficiently and automatically transforming voiced speech into a set of raw data from which the formant trajectories could then be easily estimated by inspection. Although an algorithm for automatically extracting the formant trajectories from the

raw data was not presented, it is believed tha[t it will] still be quite useful for those engaged in b[asic re]search along with applied research areas su[ch as] coding techniques. The predicted usefulnes[s from] the experimental results of the paper and in particular, the fact that the formant trajectories can be easily estimated from the raw data by a naive subject and the fact that simple peak picking of the raw data has been approximately 90 percent effective in estimating the formant trajectories.

Although it is not discussed here, the application of the inverse filter algorithm to the general problem of tracking resonance behavior of time-varying signals should be apparent. Techniques for automatically extracting formant trajectory estimates from the raw data are presently being investigated.

References

[1] S. Saito and F. Itakura, "The theoretical consideration of statistically optimum methods for speech spectral density" (in Japanese), Elec. Commun. Lab., N.T.T., Tokyo, Japan, Rep. 3107, Dec. 20, 1966.

[2] F. Itakura and S. Saito, "Analysis synthesis telephony based upon the maximum likelihood method," Rep. 6th Int. Congr. Acoust., Y. Konasi, Ed., Tokyo, Japan, Rep. C-5-5, Aug. 21–28, 1968.

[3] B. S. Atal and M. R. Schroeder, "Predictive coding of speech signals," Rep. 6th Int. Congr. Acoust., Y. Konasi, Ed., Tokyo, Japan, Rep. C-5-5, Aug. 21–28, 1968.

[4] J. D. Markel, "The Prony method and its application to speech analysis," J. Acoust. Soc. Amer., vol. 49, pt. 1, p. 105(A), Jan. 1971.

[5] R. Prony, "Essai experimental et analytique sur les lois de la dilatabilite des fluides elastiques et sur celles del la force expansive de la vapeur de l'eau et de la vapeur de l'alkool, a differentes temperatures," J. Ecole Polytech., vol. 1, no. 2, pp. 24–76, 1795.

[6] R. N. McDonough, "Matched exponents for the representation of signals," Ph.D. dissertation, Dep. Elec. Eng., the Johns Hopkins University, Baltimore, Md., Apr. 1963.

[7] C. Runge and H. Konig, Vorlesungen über Numerisches Rechnen, vol. 11 of Die Grundlehren der Mathematischen Wissenschaften. Berlin: Springer, 1924, p. 231.

[8] C. S. Burrus and T. W. Parks, "Time domain design of recursive digital filters," IEEE Trans. Audio Electroacoust., vol. AU-18, pp. 137–141, June 1970.

[9] J. L. Shanks, "Recursion filters for digital processing," Geophysics, vol. 32, pp. 33–51, Feb. 1967.

[10] E. A. Robinson, Statistical Communication and Detection. New York: Hafner, 1967.

[11] K. L. Peacock and S. Treitel, "Predictive deconvolution: Theory and practice," Geophysics, vol. 34, pp. 155–169, Apr. 1969.

[12] E. A. Robinson and S. Treitel, "Principles of digital Wiener filtering," Geophys. Prospect., vol. 15, pp. 311–333, Sept. 1967.

[13] N. Levinson, "The Wiener RMS (root mean square) error criterion in filter design and prediction," J. Math. Phys., vol. 25, no. 4, pp. 261–278, 1947; also in N. Wiener, Extrapolation Interpolation and Smoothing of Stationary Time Series. Cambridge, Mass.: M.I.T. Press, 1966.

[14] R. B. Blackman and J. W. Tukey, The Measurement of Power Spectra. New York: Dover, 1959.

[15] R. H. Pennington, Introductory Computer Methods and Numerical Analysis. Toronto, Canada: Macmillan, 1970, pp. 348–355.

[16] J. D. Markel, "FFT pruning," IEEE Trans. Audio Electroacoust., vol. AU-19, pp. 305–311, Dec. 1971.

[17] G. E. Peterson and H. L. Barney, "Control methods used in a study of the vowels," J. Acoust. Soc. Amer., vol. 24, pp. 175–184, Mar. 1952.

[18] R. W. Schafer and L. R. Rabiner, "System for automatic formant analysis of voiced speech," J. Acoust. Soc. Amer., vol. 47, pp. 634–648, Feb. 1970.

[19] C. G. Bell et al., "Reduction of speech spectra by analysis-by-synthesis techniques," J. Acoust. Soc. Amer., vol. 33, pp. 1725–1736, Dec. 1961.

An Algorithm for Automatic Formant Extraction Using Linear Prediction Spectra

STEPHANIE S. McCANDLESS

Abstract—An algorithm is presented which finds the frequency and amplitude of the first three formants during all vowel-like segments of continuous speech. It uses as input the peaks of the linear prediction spectra and a segmentation parameter to indicate energy and voicing. Ideally, the first three peaks are the first three formants. Frequently, however, two peaks merge, or spurious peaks appear, and the difficult part is to recognize such situations and deal with them. The general method is to fill formant slots with the available peaks at each frame, based on frequency position relative to an educated guess. Then, if a peak is left over and/or a slot is unfilled, special routines are called to decide how to deal with them. Included is a formant enhancement technique, analogous to a similar technique which has been implemented via the chirp-z transform [8], which usually succeeds in separating two merged formants. Processing begins at the middle of each high volume voiced segment, where formants are most likely to be correct, and branches outward from there in both directions in time, using the most recently found formant frequencies as the educated guess for the current frame.

The algorithm has been implemented at Lincoln Laboratory on the Univac 1219 and the Fast Digital Processor, a programmable processor [9], and has been tested on a large number of unrestricted sentences.

INTRODUCTION

THE SPEECH waveform can be modeled as the response of a resonator (the vocal tract) to a series of pulses (quasi-periodic glottal pulses during voiced sounds, or noise generated at a constriction during unvoiced sounds). The resonances of the vocal tract are called formants, and they are manifested in the spectral domain by energy maxima at the resonant frequencies.

The frequencies at which the formants occur are primarily dependent upon the shape of the vocal tract, which is determined by the positions of the articulators (tongue, lips, jaw, etc.). In continuous speech, the formant frequencies vary in time as the articulators change position.

The formant frequencies are an important cue in the characterization of speech sounds, and therefore, an automatic algorithm for reliably computing these frequencies would be useful for many aspects of speech research, such as speech synthesis, formant vocoder's, and speech recognition. Two basic approaches to the problem have been tried—analysis by synthesis and peak-picking from smoothed spectra.

In analysis by synthesis, an educated guess is made of the formant frequencies and bandwidths, and a spectrum

Manuscript received July 16, 1973; revised October 15, 1973. This work was sponsored by the Advanced Research Projects Agency of the Department of Defense.

The author is with Lincoln Laboratory, Massachusetts Institute of Technology, Lexington, Mass. 02173.

is generated based on the educated guess. The formant frequencies for the synthesized spectrum are varied systematically until the differences between it and the actual spectrum are minimal, according to some criterion [2]. Olive [6] has recently worked out a method for varying all three formant frequencies, using a Newton–Raphson technique to find a least-squares fit.

In peak-picking, certain rules are applied to select the appropriate peaks from a smoothed spectrum at each frame to be the first three formants. The challenge is in recognizing which peaks are spurious and/or whether two formants have merged into one peak. Schaefer and Rabiner [8] found the best candidate peak in a specified region for each formant, using cepstrally smoothed spectra. Markel [5] used peak-picking from linear prediction spectra. If there were exactly 3 peaks under 3 kHz, he assumed these were the first three formants. Otherwise, continuity constraints were applied to delete a peak or insert a formant.

Analysis by synthesis has certain advantages in that it incorporates the entire spectral shape rather than simply the spectral peaks. Hence, a small spurious peak would not grossly change the general spectral shape caused by the formants, and therefore, would not alter the results drastically. Its disadvantages are that it requires a great deal of processing and that it depends on an accurate speech model. Hence, the method might have difficulties with sounds other than nonnasalized vowels.

Peak-picking is a more tractable problem with linear prediction spectra than with other forms of spectral analysis because spurious peaks are rare. However, peak mergers are common, as well as peak cancellations due to nasalization effects. The method presented here is a systematic, fully automatic algorithm, which is usually successful in solving these problems. It yields the frequencies of the first three formants and the spectral amplitudes at their frequency positions during all sonorant sounds in continuous unrestricted speech. No attempt was made to extract formant frequencies during obstruent sounds because the acoustic characteristics of these sounds are not well represented through formants. In addition, the spectral characteristics of the noise source tend to mask the vocal tract resonances.

LINEAR PREDICTION

The following is a brief discussion of linear prediction analysis. A more detailed treatment can be found elsewhere in the literature [1], [4], [5].

Reprinted from *IEEE Trans. on Acoust., Speech, and Signal Process.*, vol. ASSP-22, pp. 135–141, Apr. 1974.

312

Approximate the sampled speech waveform $s(n)$ by another sequence $\hat{s}(n)$, by linearly predicting from the past p samples of $s(n)$:

$$\hat{s}(n) = \sum_{k=1}^{p} a_k s(n-k). \qquad (1)$$

The unknowns a_k in (1), can be determined by minimizing the mean squared difference, E, between $s(n)$ and $\hat{s}(n)$ over N samples of $s(n)$:

$$E = \frac{1}{N} \sum_{n=0}^{N-1} \left[s(n) - \hat{s}(n) \right]^2$$

$$= \frac{1}{N} \sum_{n} \left[s(n) - \sum_{k} a_k s(n-k) \right]^2. \qquad (2)$$

By setting $\partial E / \partial a_j$ to 0 for $j = 1,2,\cdots,p$, and simplifying, one obtains:

$$\sum_{k} a_k \phi_{jk} = x_j \qquad \begin{array}{l} j = 1,2,\cdots p \\ k = 1,2,\cdots p \end{array} \qquad (3)$$

where

$$\phi_{jk} = \sum_{n} s(n-j)s(n-k)$$

$$x_j = \phi_{j0}.$$

In the study discussed here, the speech waveform was sampled at 10 kHz after 6 dB/octave preemphasis. A new set of $p = 14$ coefficients a_k was computed every 5.0 ms on 25.6 ms of Hanning windowed speech, using the digital inverse filtering technique [5].

The choice of 14 predictor coefficients was arrived at through experimentation. It was found that, with fewer coefficients, the merging formants of certain sounds, such as ɜ and ɔ, were represented by only one complex pole-pair. With 14 coefficients the problem of spurious peaks is more common. However, the algorithm is capable of handling spurious peaks, whereas a missing pole-pair is an irrecoverable problem.

Once the coefficients a_k are available, it is an easy matter to obtain the approximated spectrum of $s(n)$. One simply evaluates the magnitude of the transfer function $H(z)$ of the filter represented by the coefficients a_k, at N equally spaced samples along the unit circle in the z-plane:

$$H(z) = a_0 / 1 - \sum_{k=1}^{p} a_k z^{-k} \qquad (4)$$

where (4) is evaluated at $z = \exp[j(2\pi n/N)]$ for $n = 0,1,\cdots,N-1$.

N can be chosen arbitrarily large to increase frequency resolution, at the expense of computation time. For our purposes, we have chosen $N = 256$, resulting in approximately 40 Hz spectral resolution. This means that 1) formant values are accurate to within 20 Hz and 2) any two spectral peaks which are within 80 Hz of each other

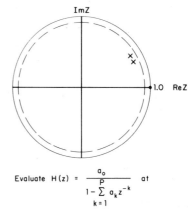

Evaluate $H(z) = \dfrac{a_0}{1 - \sum\limits_{k=1}^{P} a_k z^{-k}}$ at

equally spaced samples along a circle of radius <1, to enhance the peaks of the 2 poles that are close together.

(a)

(b)

Fig. 1. (a) Formant enhancement. (b) Linear prediction spectrum in $|r|$ of "there" before and after enhancement.

cannot be resolved. The accuracy is sufficient for our needs, and we found that the second constraint rarely causes problems.

Two closely spaced formants frequently merge into one spectral peak, and cannot be resolved on the unit circle even with infinite resolution. However, they can often be separated by simply recomputing the spectrum on a circle of radius less than 1. This amounts to reevaluating $H(z)$ at $z = re^{j}(2\pi n/N)$, $r < 1$. Because the contour comes in closer to the two poles, their peaks are enhanced, and a separation is effected (Fig. 1).

The method also frequently works to bring out a peak whose bandwidth was too wide due to pole zero interplay (as in nasalized vowels). Essentially, moving the circle inward is equivalent to moving the poles outward to a larger radius, and, therefore, to a narrower bandwidth.

PEAKS VS. POLES

Clearly, an obvious method for extracting formants from linear prediction would be to solve for the poles of the filter by setting the denominator in (6) to zero and solving for the roots of the resulting pth order polynomial in z. Some or none of the roots would be real, and the rest would be complex pole pairs which might or might not be formants. Out of those pole pairs, one would have to select three on the basis of frequency location, sufficiently narrow bandwidth, and some kind of formant continuity criterion, to be the first three formants.

Another technique, requiring much less computation, would be to simply pick the first three peaks in the spectrum and call those the first three formants, making the assumption that a pole strong enough to show up as a peak is necessarily a formant. Such a method works very well most of the time, but mistakes will occur during the following situations.

1) Often two poles show up as only one peak because they are close together in frequency.

2) Occasionally a pole due to frequency shaping will appear as a small peak, which would be incorrectly interpreted as a formant.

It was decided to use peak-picking rather than root extraction, and to develop an algorithm to solve cases 1) and 2) above.

NASALS AND NASALIZATIONS

Nasals present a special problem to any formant tracking algorithm because there are zeros in the transfer function in addition to the poles. In a nasal, the poles are resonances of the nasal tract and the oral tract is a closed side branch, which causes zeros. Frequently, F_2 is greatly reduced in amplitude, because of a nearby zero; and, in fact, often there is no peak corresponding to F_2.

Nasalization of a vowel is a problem of similar nature. In this case, the nasal cavity is an open side branch, causing extra zeros and extra poles. In a nasalized front vowel, typically, there is an extra small peak slightly above F_1 in frequency. In a nasalized back vowel, the apparent bandwidth of F_1 becomes quite wide, because of a nearby zero, and sometimes there is no peak for F_1.

Fig. 2 shows some examples of the problems discussed above.

HIGHLIGHTS OF THE ALGORITHM

Continuity is one of the strongest constraints that one can rely on in tracking formants. In general, one would expect the frequencies of F_1, F_2, and F_3 in the current frame to be near where they were in the previous frame, because the articulators cannot move too much in 5 ms. However, it is dangerous to rely too heavily on continuity for two reasons: 1) formant frequencies can change considerably within 5 ms, as at the boundary between a nasal and a vowel, and 2) if there is a single bad frame, for instance, a frame mistakenly labeled voiced, it might cause bad decisions in all of the following frames. Therefore, the algorithm uses continuity in an initial decision, but later applies another approach in situations where continuity has failed to yield reasonable results.

In order to lessen the possibility of getting off on the wrong track, it was decided to begin in a region where formants are most likely to be correct, and to branch from there towards the less certain areas. The approach is,

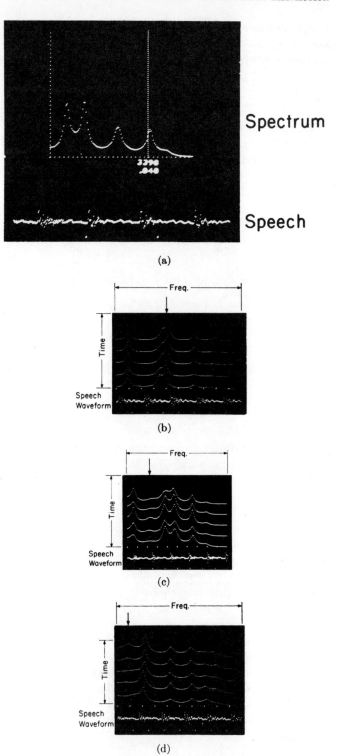

(a)

(b)

(c)

(d)

Fig. 2. (a) Typical linear prediction spectrum (in vowel | a |). (b) Five sequential spectral cross sections in | r | of "there" showing merger of F_2 with F_3. (c) Five sequential spectral cross sections in | ae | of "man" showing small extra peak between F_1 and F_2 due to nasalization. (d) Five sequential spectral cross sections in | ɔ | of "on" showing nasalization of F_1.

therefore, to find an "anchor point" in the middle of each vowel, and to branch from there in both directions in time, using the most recently found formant frequencies as a guide in determining the formants in the current frame.

Another feature of the algorithm is that, in the processing

at each frame, the formants are dealt with in parallel rather than in series. A typical peak-picking formant tracker would make a decision on F_1 and then eliminate that peak as a possible candidate for F_2. Then, after a peak was selected for F_2, that peak could not be later called F_3. The approach here is to fill available formant slots with available peaks, initially allowing each peak to fill more than one slot. Then in a later step, such duplicates could be dealt with, again in a symmetric way. Thus, if a peak met the criteria for F_1, but met even better the criteria for F_2, it would eventually be called F_2.

SEGMENTATION

Since the formants are tracked only in vowel-like sounds, and processing is begun in the middle of each vowel, it is necessary to have some form of segmentation of the speech waveform to determine which frames are voiced, and where to mark the anchor points.

The first step is to eliminate frames whose total spectral energy is below a threshold for silence. Then, the Gold–Rabiner pitch detector [3] and a ratio of the low frequency energy to the high frequency energy are used in combination to determine whether a frame is voiced. Each resulting voiced region is separated into "vowel" and "not vowel" on the basis of the total energy in the spectrum and the energy in the region from 640 to 2880 Hz. If either of these energy functions has a sufficiently deep valley between two peaks, then a boundary is marked between the valley and each surrounding peak at the place when the slope of the energy function is a maximum, thus dividing up the vowel-like regions into high energy voicing (vowels) and low energy voicing (intervocal is voiced consonants).

Fig. 3 shows a flow chart of the anchor point scheme. Processing of the backward branch is begun at the next anchor point, and continued until an unvoiced frame is encountered, or until a frame is encountered which had already been processed by the previous forward branch. Then the forward branch from the same anchor is begun, and continued until an unvoiced frame is encountered, or until a new vowel segment boundary is reached. At that point, processing jumps to the next anchor point, begins again with a backward branch, and so forth, until the sentence is complete.

THE PROCESSING OF EACH FRAME

At each frame one begins with four vacant formant slots, four estimates for the frequencies of the formants, and one, two, three, or four peaks. The task is to fill the slots with the peaks, based on the estimate frequencies, in such a way that spurious peaks and missing peaks can be recognized as such and dealt with. (No special attempt is made to fill the F_4 slot. It only exists to prevent F_4, when it exists, from competing with F_3 for the F_3 slot.)

The six steps of the peak mapping algorithm are listed in Fig. 4 and explained in greater detail below.

Step 1: Fetch Peaks. Find the frequencies and amplitude of up to four peaks in the region from 150 to 3400 Hz.

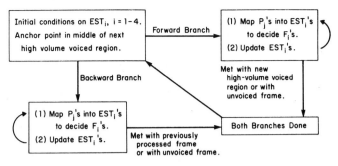

EST$_i$ = frequency estimates for four formants in current frame

P$_j$ = frequency locations of peaks in current frame

F$_i$ = formant frequencies decided in current frame

Fig. 3. Flow chart of anchor point scheme.

(1) FETCH PEAKS P_j IN NEXT FRAME.

(2) FILL FOUR FORMANT SLOTS S_i WITH PEAKS USING ESTIMATES EST$_i$ AS GUIDE.

(3) REMOVE DUPLICATE PEAKS.

(4) DEAL WITH UNASSIGNED PEAKS.

(5) DEAL WITH UNFILLED SLOTS.

(6) RECORD ANSWERS AS FORMANTS F_i FOR THIS FRAME AND AS ESTIMATES EST$_i$ FOR NEXT FRAME.

Fig. 4. Six steps to decide formants in each voiced frame.

Step 2: Fill Slots. Fill each formant slot S_i, $i = 1$ to 4, with the best candidate peak p_j, by the following rule. The peak p_j closest in frequency to estimate EST_i goes into slot S_i.[1]

The important thing to note is that every slot gets filled in Step 2. If there was only one peak, for instance, it would be put into all 4 slots.

Step 3. Remove Duplicates. If the same peak p_j fills more than one slot S_i keep it only in the slot S_k which corresponds to the estimate EST_k that it is closest to in frequency, and remove it from any other slots.

Step 4: Deal with Unassigned Peaks. If there are no unassigned peaks p_j, go to Step 5. Otherwise, try to fill empty slots with peaks not assigned in Step 2 as follows.

a) If there is a peak $p_{j=k}$ unassigned, and an $S_{i=k}$ unfilled, fill the slot with the peak and go to Step 5. Or if there is a peak $p_{j=k}$ unassigned, but slot $S_{i=k}$ is already filled, check the amplitude of p_k as follows: if amp $(p_k) < \frac{1}{2}$ amp (peak already assigned to S_k) throw p_k away and go to Step 5. Otherwise, go to (b).

b) If p_k is still unassigned, but $S_{i=k+1}$ is unfilled, move the peak in $S_{i=k}$ to $S_{i=k+1}$, and put p_k in S_k. Go to Step 5.

[1] The EST_i at the anchor point are set to initial conditions as follows:
  Male Voices—$EST_1 = 320$ Hz, $EST_2 = 1440$ Hz, $EST_3 = 2760$ Hz, $EST_4 = 3200$ Hz.
  Female Voices—$EST_1 = 480$ Hz, $EST_2 = 1760$ Hz, $EST_3 = 3200$ Hz, $EST_4 = 3520$ Hz.
These settings were determined empirically, and were found to be reasonable for most speakers. Some experimentation was done with speaker adaptation to determine these initial settings, and in most cases the resulting improvements were minimal.

c) If p_k is still unassigned, but $S_{i=k-1}$ is unfilled, move the peak in $S_{i=k}$ to $S_{i=k-1}$, and put p_k in S_k. Go to Step 5. If a), b), and c) all fail, throw p_k away.

Step 5: Deal with Unfilled Slots. If S_1, S_2 and S_3 are all filled, go to Step 6. (F_4 may or may not be filled.) *Otherwise:* Recompute the spectrum on a circle with radius less than one to enhance the formants and hopefully separate two merged peaks. Go to Step 1.

The enhanced spectrum is computed initially with $r = 0.98$. If the spectrum fails to yield a peak to fill the empty slot, then Steps 1–5 are repeated again with $r = r - 0.004$. The radius is shrunk repeatedly in this manner until a peak is finally found or until $r = 0.88$; at which point it is assumed that no peak exists to fill the empty slot.

Finally, whether or not enhancement has succeeded, the amplitudes of the peaks are reset to the amplitudes in the original spectrum. In addition, if the empty slot was S_3, and enhancement failed to yield a peak, then the peak in S_4 is moved down to S_3, assuming that F_3 was mistakenly called F_4.

Step 6: Record Answers. Accept formant slot contents as answers for this frame. Also, use formant slot contents as estimates for next frame. (If a slot is empty, keep the original formant estimate for that formant.)

Fig. 5(a) shows how the algorithm would work in a typical situation, as in a vowel. In Fig. 5(b), three pathological cases are illustrated. The frequency locations of the peaks and of the estimates are indicated by an x in the diagrams. An arrow from a peak to an estimate indicates that that peak would fill the formant slot corresponding to that estimate in Step 2. The double line through the arrow indicates that the peak was removed from the corresponding slot in Step 3. In the "Formant Merger" example, enhancement would be called upon in Step 5 to yield a new peak. In the "Rapid Formant Motion" example, Step 4 (b) would move peak 3 up into the vacant slot 3, and would put peak 2 into the now vacant slot 2. In the "Spurious Peak" example, even if peak 2 passed the amplitude test in Step 4 (a), it would still be thrown away, as no slot was available for it.

FINAL SMOOTHING

After Steps 1–6 above have been applied at each voiced frame in the sentence, to yield three formant tracks, each formant track should be smoothed separately in some way. The approach is to first correct any obvious gross errors, and to then send each track through a simple zero phase filter. However, each of these steps is done with caution because it is undesirable to 1) attempt to make smooth tracks in a region where they are very bumpy, as these tracks would convey false information (for instance, in a segment which was mistakenly labeled voiced), 2) smooth out sudden shifts in formant frequencies (for instance, at the junction of a vowel and a nasal), or 3) grossly alter good data by smoothing it with bad data that happen to be adjacent to it (for instance, at the

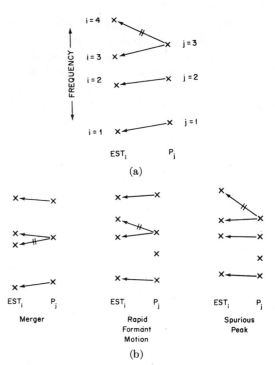

Fig. 5. (a) How the algorithm would work in a typical case. (b) Three pathological cases.

boundary between a vowel and a burst, if the onset of voicing had not been accurately determined).

Therefore, strong constraints are required for both the gross corrections and the smoothing filter. Unaligned frames are aligned by interpolation only in regions where the 4 frames surrounding the faulty frame(s) are relatively smooth. In addition, the output of the zero phase filter is not written over the original formant frequency in any frame when the output frequency is sufficiently different from the input frequency. The result is that the formant tracks will become very smooth where they were already fairly smooth; but sudden changes in formant frequency will be retained; and any region where formant tracks were too bumpy will remain untouched.

The following is a detailed discussion of the final smoothing algorithm.

1) If a formant is missing in a single frame, fill in its frequency and its amplitude with the average of the values in the previous and the following frames.

2) If a formant is grossly out of line or missing in one, two, or three frames, but well aligned in the two previous and two following frames, correct the misaligned frames by interpolation as follows.

Let the frequency location of formant F_i in the nth frame be L_n.

Define $D_{a,b} = L_a - L_b$, a measure of the alignment of a particular formant. θ = the threshold = 240 Hz. If $D_{n,n-1} < \theta$, frame n is considered smooth. If $D_{n,n-1} > \theta$, an attempt is made to smooth frame n, but only if either a), b) or c) is true.

a) If $D_{n-1,n-2} < \theta$, $D_{n+1,n-1} < \theta$, and $D_{n+2,n+1} < \theta$, then replace L_n with $(L_{n+1} + L_{n-1})/2$, and move to frame $n + 1$. (One frame out of line.)

b) If $D_{n-1,n-2} < \theta$, $D_{n+2,n-1} < \theta$, and $D_{n+3,n+2} < \theta$, then replace L_n with $(L_{n+2} + L_{n-1})/2$, and move to frame $n + 1$. (Two frames out of line.)

c) If $D_{n-1,n-2} < \theta$, $D_{n+3,n-1} < \theta$, and $D_{n+4,n+3} < \theta$, then replace L_n with $(L_{n+3} + L_{n-1})/2$, and move to frame $n + 1$. (Three frames out of line.) The new L_n is used in evaluating frame $n + 1$.

3) Smooth each formant track twice using the following filter:

$$F_i'(n) = \tfrac{1}{4}F_i(n-1) + \tfrac{1}{2}F_i(n) + \tfrac{1}{4}F_i(n+1),$$

but only at those frames where $|F_i'(n) - F_i(n)| < 100$ Hz.

RESULTS

Fig. 6 shows the results of the formant tracking algorithm for the phrase "average uranium lead ratio" spoken by a woman. In Fig. 6(a) the first three peaks are written over the spectrogram and also shown as three separate functions above the spectrogram. In Fig. 6(b), the first three formants as determined by the algorithm, are shown in a similar way for comparison. The three functions above are shown on a greatly constricted scale, and are useful mainly for determining which formant number was associated with each peak, and for identifying gross errors. It can be noted that in the $|r|$ of "uranium" and in the $|i|$ of "ratio," F_3 had merged with F_2, and was found by enhancement.

Fig. 7 shows a similar comparison for the sentence, "the box was thrown beside$\cdots$," spoken by a man. F_1 had merged with F_2 in the $|a|$ of "box," showing up as a discontinuity in the P_1 and P_2 curves, and a vacancy in the P_3 curve. The algorithm was able to recognize that it was F_1 that was missing and to find it by enhancement. Similarly, in the $|n|$ of "thrown," F_2 was missing and was recovered by the algorithm through enhancement.

The algorithm is very successful in recognizing peak merger problems and the missing formants are nearly always recovered by enhancement. However, the results for nasalized vowels and nasals are not always so predictable. In some nasalized back vowels, F_1 had to be recovered through enhancement. In those cases, F_1's frequency was often observed to be abnormally high. Occasionally in nasalized back vowels, an extra peak appeared between F_2 and F_3, which was sometimes tagged as F_3. In nasalized front vowels there was frequently an extra peak slightly above F_1. Sometimes this extra peak was called F_2 by the algorithm, and the actual second formant was called F_3. In nasals, enhancement had to be called upon quite often to recover F_2. In some nasals, enhancement failed to find a peak for F_2, but F_1 and F_3 were nearly always correctly identified.

A fully automatic implementation of the algorithm runs in 2 or 3 times real-time on a computer facility at Lincoln Laboratory consisting of a Univac 1219 and the Fast Digital Processor (FDP), a programmable processor [9] designed for real-time digital signal processing. The

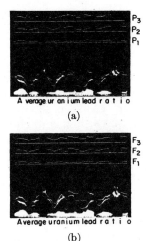

Fig. 6. (a) First three peaks in each voiced frame written over spectrogram and shown above it as three separate functions. (b) First three formants, as computed by algorithm, shown as in Fig. 6(a) for comparison.

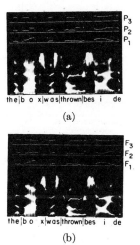

Fig. 7. (a) First three peaks in each voiced frame written over spectrogram and shown above it as three separate functions. (b) First three formants, as computed by algorithm, shown as in Fig. 7(a) for comparison.

linear prediction analysis is done entirely on the FDP in less than real-time. The time consuming part of the formant tracking algorithm is the iterative computation of enhanced spectra to find missing formants. We have used a conservative approach in shrinking the radius by very small increments, because the FDP is fast enough that time is not an issue. One could, to save time, use enhancement only at a few different radii, for instance, 0.96, 0.92, and 0.88, with the results being not as good as the results here, but still much better than no enhancement at all.

Statistics were collected for some 50 sentences on how often the various correction measures were necessary. The statistics showed that it is much more common in linear prediction spectra for a peak to be missing than for a spurious peak to exist. Although statistics varied considerably from sentence to sentence, on the average enhancement was tried in about 15 percent of the voiced frames. Out of these, a peak was found through enhancement in 9 out of 10 cases. In the remaining cases, either

IEEE TRANSACTIONS ON ACOUSTICS, SPEECH, AND SIGNAL PROCESSING, VOL. ASSP-22, NO. 2, APRIL 1974

the frame was mistakenly labelled voiced, or the formant was too strongly cancelled by a nearby zero (in nasals and nasalized vowels); or, rarely, a peak merger was not resolved.

In 1 percent of the voiced frames, F_3 was mistakenly callee F_4 initially, and was later moved to the F_3 slot after enhancement failed to yield a peak. In another 3 percent continuity constraints had failed in the initial slot-filling steps, and peaks had to be moved to new slots in Step 4 to accommodate a peak about to be thrown away. An equal number of peaks *were* thrown away in Step 4 either because they failed to pass the amplitude test or because there was no slot available for them. These extra peaks were usually due to nasalization effects.

About 3 percent of the time the output of the smoothing filter was not written over the original formant value, either because of a sharp shift in formant frequency or because of an irregular trajectory, as in a voiced fricative.

Second pass corrections of gross errors were rare, occurring only about 1.5 percent of the time.

SUMMARY

A completely automatic algorithm has been developed which yields the first three formants during all voiced sounds in continuous unrestricted speech. It uses the peaks of the linear prediction spectra as input, and resolves peak mergers and spurious peak problems in a systematic way.

It has been tested on a large number of sentences spoken by several different speakers. The algorithm was found to be extremely successful with nonnasalized sounds. The results in nasals and nasalized vowels were not as predictable, but were still quite good most of the time.

Work is now beginning on the application of the output of the formant tracking algorithm to both a speech understanding project and a formant vocoder.

REFERENCES

[1] B. S. Atal and S. L. Hanauer, "Speech analysis and synthesis by linear prediction of the speech wave," *J. Acoust. Soc. Amer.*, vol. 50, pp. 637–655, 1971.
[2] C. G. Bell *et al.*, "Reduction of speech spectra by analysis-by-synthesis techniques," *J. Acoust. Soc. Amer.*, vol. 33, pp. 1725–1736, 1961.
[3] B. Gold and L. R. Rabiner, "Parallel processing techniques for estimating pitch periods of speech in the time domain," *J. Acoust. Soc. Amer.*, vol. 46, pp. 442–448, 1969.
[4] J. Makhoul and J. Wolf, "Linear prediction and the spectral analysis of speech," Bolt, Baranek, and Newman, Inc., Cambridge, Mass., Rep. 2304, 1972.
[5] J. D. Markel, "Digital inverse filtering—a new tool for formant trajectory estimation," Speech Com. Res. Lab., Santa Barbara, Calif., Monograph 7, Oct. 1971.
[6] J. P. Olive, "Automatic formant tracking by a Newton–Raphson technique," *J. Acoust. Soc. Amer.*, vol. 50, pp. 661–670, 1971.
[7] G. E. Peterson and H. L. Barney, "Control methods used in a study of the vowels," *J. Acoust. Soc. Amer.*, vol. 24, pp. 175–184, 1952.
[8] R. W. Schaefer and L. R. Rabiner, "System for automatic formant analysis of voiced speech," *J. Acoust. Soc. Amer.*, vol. 47, pp. 637–648, 1970.
[9] B. Gold *et al.*, "The FDP, a fast programmable signal processor," *IEEE Trans. Comput.*, vol. C-20, pp. 33–39, Jan. 1971.

Modifications to Formant Tracking Algorithm of April 1974

STEPHANIE SENEFF

Abstract—This correspondence describes an improved version of the linear prediction formant tracking algorithm which was described in [1]. The new algorithm, like the original one, applies continuity constraints and branches out from an anchor point in the middle of each vowel. The changes are that the initial estimates for the formant

Manuscript received September 26, 1974. This work was sponsored by the Advanced Research Projects Agency of the Department of Defense.

The author is with the Lincoln Laboratory, Massachusetts Institute of Technology, Cambridge, MA 02173.

frequencies at the anchor are determined more carefully, and that the option of choosing a new anchor point near the original one is allowed if the original one caused problems.

The formant tracking algorithm which was described [1] found the first three formants in all voiced segments by choosing the appropriate peaks from the linear prediction spectrum. A peak was selected to be a given formant on the basis of its proximity to an estimated frequency for that formant. The estimated frequency for each formant in a given frame was defined to be the value found in the previous frame. At the anchor point, however, there is no previous frame from which to decide the estimates, and therefore some other method is needed.

The original version of the algorithm simply used four fixed speaker-dependent values for the formant estimates at the anchor, each essentially in the middle of the region for that formant. This method works well except when a formant is at an extreme of its region and a spurious peak is present at a more reasonable frequency location. Such is sometimes the case, for example, in a nasalized /i/, when $F2$ is high enough to be called $F3$, and a small spurious peak is present in the $F2$ region to fill the $F2$ slot.

The new method, as flow-charted in Fig. 1, uses the actual peaks in the enhanced spectrum ($r = 0.95$) at the anchor frame to determine initial conditions. The four EST_i slots are filled with the peaks p_j by choosing the best candidate peak in a region for each formant. If there are two peaks in the region for a given formant, then the one lower in frequency is se-

Reprinted from *IEEE Trans. on Acoust., Speech, and Signal Process.*, vol. ASSP-24, pp. 192–193, Apr. 1976.

319

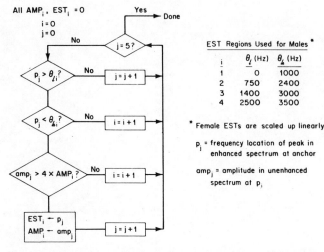

Fig. 1. Flow chart of algorithm to determine initial formant *EST*imates at anchor point.

	EST Regions Used for Males *	
i	θ_l (Hz)	θ_h (Hz)
1	0	1000
2	750	2400
3	1400	3000
4	2500	3500

* Female ESTs are scaled up linearly

p_j = frequency location of peak in enhanced spectrum at anchor

amp_j = amplitude in unenhanced spectrum at p_j

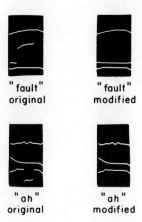

Fig. 2. Two examples in which the modified algorithm was successful where the original one had failed.

lected unless the other one has an amplitude at least four times as great. If a peak is in the overlap region for two formants, it is selected to be the lower formant, unless a sufficiently high-amplitude peak of lower frequency has already been selected to fill that slot. Any slot for which no peak can be found is filled with an initial fixed estimate. After all of the *EST* slots have been filled in this manner, the frame at the anchor point is subjected to the usual algorithm (as given in [1]) to yield the formants.

The other modification is the option of resetting the anchor point to a new frame if the original anchor was in error. If, at a frame within 25 ms of the anchor, the algorithm is unable to fill any of the first three formant slots, the decision is made that the original anchor had chosen a false track for that slot. This new frame is then used as the anchor, and analysis of the vowel is repeated.

The new version was tried on a large number of sentences, and was found to handle the problem of spurious peaks better than the original version, and the problem of peak mergers at least as well. Fig. 2 shows two examples of words in which

the original formant tracker was at fault, but the new one made the right decision. The first is in the ɔ of the word "default" where $F2$ is extremely low and a small amplitude spurious peak was at a frequency closer to the middle of the $F2$ range. The second example is the sound "ah" spoken by a female. $F1$ is extremely high, and a small amplitude peak is closer to the middle of the $F1$ frequency region. In both cases, the new algorithm was able to reject the spurious peak in favor of the stronger, correct peak.

The new algorithm also has the advantage that it is less speaker dependent. Good results have been obtained for females by a simple linear scaling upward of the formant regions. The only speaker dependent parameter, therefore, is the scale factor.

ACKNOWLEDGMENT

The author wishes to thank V. W. Zue for many fruitful discussions.

REFERENCES

[1] S. S. McCandless, "An algorithm for automatic formant extraction using linear prediction spectra," *IEEE Trans. Acoust., Speech, Signal Processing*, vol. ASSP-22, pp. 135–141, Apr. 1974.

Determination of the Vocal-Tract Shape from Measured Formant Frequencies

P. Mermelstein

Bell Telephone Laboratories, Incorporated, Murray Hill, New Jersey 07971

We model the vocal tract as a lossless acoustic tube and consider the relationship between the resonant frequencies and the cross-sectional area function. Empirical results show that if the logarithm of the area function is band limited preserving only $2n$ Fourier components, the lowest n pole and n zero frequencies of the admittance function measured at the lips uniquely determine the area coefficients. The formant frequencies determined from the speech signal, the normal resonant frequencies of the vocal tract, correspond to the admittance poles. They alone do not suffice for unique area determination unless the even area coefficients are constrained to specified values or some other physical contraints are imposed. The output-admittance zeros are not obtainable from the speech signal, as they correspond to resonant modes for closed-lip boundary conditions. The above results allow the synthesis of band-limited vocal-tract shapes from admittance functions that have only their low-frequency singularities specified. They can be generalized to any system exhibiting wave propagation primarily in one dimension only, for example, nonuniform transmission lines, and allow a low spatial-frequency synthesis of the system from two sets of low-order eigenvalues.

INTRODUCTION

THE generally accepted theory for production of the vocalic sounds of speech[1,2] considers the speech wave to be the result of the excitation of the vocal tract by a quasiperiodic source at the glottis. The vocal tract serves to modulate the excitation signal and thereby imparts linguistic character to the generated signal. The time-dependent positions of the various articulators, e.g., tongue, lips, velum, and jaw, are reflected in the short-time power spectrum of the speech signal, from which the formant frequencies (the resonant frequencies of the vocal tract) are determined. This paper considers to what extent the vocal-tract cross-sectional-area function is derivable from formant information. We anticipate that a representation of the speech event terms of a sequence of tract shapes more directly related to articulator positions will yield a simpler description of the event than one in terms of acoustic features only.

Detailed direct information regarding the shape of the entire vocal tract and the position of the articulators is available only through x-ray studies.[3] Three-dimensional information requires multiple sectional views, and time resolution is limited by exposure limitations. In view of the difficulties in obtaining direct articulatory data, an indirect approach of obtaining articulatory data from acoustic data deserves detailed consideration.

For a uniform cylindrical tube of given length closed at one end, the higher formant frequencies are odd multiples of the lowest formant value. The essential analytic relationship for deviations from these values, "when a pipe is constricted its resonance frequency becomes low or high according as the constricted point is near the maximum point of volume current [velocity] or of excess pressure," was enunciated by Chiba and Kajiyama[1] in their investigation of the generation of vowel sounds. Delattre[4] has identified measured formant patterns with specific cavity configurations formed by the articulators. Under the assumptions of only longitudinal wave propagation along the tract, the articulatory to acoustical mapping can be determined quantitatively by means of electrical analogs of the vocal tract[2,5,6] or digital simulation of the corresponding

---

[1] T. Chiba and M. Kajiyama, *The Vowel—Its Nature and Structure* (Tokyo-Kaiseikan Publ. Co., Tokyo, 1941).

[2] G. Fant, *Acoustic Theory of Speech Production* (Mouton & Company, The Hague, The Netherlands, 1960).

[3] A. S. Macmillan and G. Kelemen, Arch. Otolaryngol. **55**, 671–688 (1952).

[4] P. Delattre, "The Physiological Interpretation of Sound Spectrograms," Publ., Modern Language Assoc. Am. **66**, 864–875 (1951).

[5] H. K. Dunn, J. Acoust. Soc. Am. **22**, 740–753 (1950).

[6] K. N. Stevens, S. Kasowski, and C. G. M. Fant, J. Acoust. Soc. Am. **25**, 734–742 (1953).

Reprinted with permission from *J. Acoust. Soc. Am.*, vol. 41, pp. 1283–1294, May 1967.

behavior.[2,7] These methods generally require sampling the cross-sectional area function of the vocal tract every 0.5 cm, resulting in area specification by 30–40 parameters.

An articulatory model employing a set of three parameters in terms of which the articulation of vowel sounds can be simply described has been proposed by Stevens and House.[8] Their mapping from the three articulatory parameters to the first two formants of the tract takes the form of formant contours in sections of the parameter space. Over certain regions of this space the two formant contours have multiple intersections, showing the mapping to be one to many. Over other regions the formants turn out to be independent of one of the parameters, yielding a many-to-one mapping. We may ask, for what parameters is the mapping one to one?

A better insight into the nature of the cross-sectional-area to formant-frequency transformation may be gained from Ungeheuer,[9] who gave explicit approximate methods for determining the formant shifts exhibited by small area changes from the uniformly shaped tract. We extend Ungeheuer's work by formulating the formant-frequency shifts as first-order perturbations computable from the area changes. Within the limitations of first-order perturbation theory, each formant frequency is dependent on one and only one coefficient in the Fourier expansion of the logarithm of the cross-sectional area function. The even-order Fourier coefficients have no effect on the formant frequencies; hence, they cannot be determined from normal speech data.

For larger area changes, constraining the even coefficients to fixed values allows the computation of a set of odd coefficients equal in number to the specified formant values. A choice of different even-coefficient values results in different odd-coefficient values for the same formant frequencies. Complete area determination is made possible by measurement of the closed-lip resonant frequencies or by imposing appropriate physical constraints on the set of admissible area functions. The spatial resolution of the area data is directly dependent on the frequency range of the acoustic data. Information about higher-order formants contributes primarily to the specification of the higher spatial-frequency components of the area function.

Workers in the area of speech generation have long been looking for those elements of the vocal tract configuration which independently control the formant frequencies. The logarithmic Fourier coefficients play precisely this role. In the limiting case of small perturbations about a uniform tract, they independently determine each formant frequency. For larger distortions

of the tract, with the aid of the first-order formulas, they yield approximate formant-frequency values.

I. THEORY

Our model considers the vocal tract to be hard-walled, lossless, and to have a rate of change of cross-sectional area with distance x along the tract that is sufficiently small that the sound pressure $p(x)$ is representable by Webster's horn equation.[10] For sinusoidal time dependence, i.e., $P(x,t) = p(x)e^{i\omega t}$, we may write

$$\frac{d}{dx}\left[A(x)\frac{dp}{dx}\right] + \lambda A(x)p = 0, \quad \lambda = \frac{\omega^2}{c^2} \quad (1)$$

or its equivalent form

$$p''(x) + [A'(x)/A(x)]p'(x) + \lambda p(x) = 0, \quad (2)$$

where $A(x)$ is the cross-sectional area, λ is an eigenvalue, ω an eigenfrequency, c the velocity of sound, i the imaginary unit, and the primes denote differentiation.

The formant frequencies are defined as the frequencies of the normal modes of vibration of the vocal tract.[11] To first approximation, the glottal source acts as a constant volume velocity or high acoustic-resistance source. Therefore, the boundary condition at the glottis, $p'(x=0)=0$, is proper. The radiation load is best approximated in terms of the load of a piston in an infinite baffle. Its approximate effect is to lower the values of the imaginary parts of the formant frequencies by a factor $3\pi L/(3\pi L + 8a)$, where a is the lip radius and L the tract length.[12] Using suitable approximate values for the lip radius, an inverse correction can be applied to the measured formant frequencies to yield the appropriate values for zero lip loading conditions, i.e., $p(L)=0$. If $A(x)$, the uniform-tract configuration, is constant, we have $p'' + \lambda p = 0$, the eigenfunctions of which are

$$p_0^{(m)}(x) = \cos(2m-1)\pi x/2L, \quad m=1,2,\cdots \quad (3)$$

and the corresponding eigenvalues are

$$\lambda_0^{(m)} = [(2m-1)\pi/2L]^2, \quad m=1,2,\cdots, \quad (4)$$

where the subscript 0 denotes the uniform-tract condition.

Since the area ratios rather than their values directly affect the eigenfrequencies, following a suggestion of

[7] Y. Kadokawa and K. Nakata, J. Radio Res. Lab. Japan **11**, 99–112 (1964).

[8] K. N. Stevens and A. S. House, J. Acoust. Soc. Am. **27**, 484–493 (1955).

[9] G. Ungeheuer, *Elemente Einer Akustischen Theorie der Vokalartikulation* (Springer-Verlag, Berlin, 1962).

[10] A. G. Webster, Proc. Natl. Acad. Sci. (U.S.) **5**, 275–282 (1919).

[11] K. N. Stevens and A. S. House, J. Speech Hearing Res. **4**, 303–320 (1961).

[12] J. L. Flanagan, *Speech Analysis, Synthesis and Perception* (Academic Press Inc., New York, 1965).

Schroeder,[13] we examine the components of the logarithm of the area function. Anticipating the first-order perturbation theory result that

$$\delta\lambda^{(m)} = \int_0^L \delta \log A(x)[p_0^{(m)\prime}(x)p_0^{(m)}(x)]^\prime dx /$$
$$\int_0^L [p_0^{(m)}(x)]^2 dx, \quad (5)$$

we choose a representation for $\log A(x)$ in terms of the orthogonal set

$$[p_0^{(m)\prime}(x)p_0^{(m)}(x)]^\prime = \tfrac{1}{2}(2m-1)\pi\cos[(2m-1)\pi x/L]$$
$$= k_j \cos(j\pi x/L) \quad j=1,3,5,\cdots. \quad (6)$$

After adding the terms with j even to achieve completeness of the expansion,

$$\log A(x) = \log A_0 + \sum_{j=1}^{\infty} a_j \cos\frac{j\pi x}{L}, \quad (7)$$

the set of components is orthogonal and complete for all functions $A(x)$ for which Eq. 2 is valid. We may note that the representation does not provide for complete closure within the tract $[A(x)=0$ for some $x]$, but since under these conditions Webster's horn equation must be solved separately for the individual tube segments, the areas of segments having nonzero area values would be expanded separately. On substituting Eq. 7 into Eq. 2, we obtain

$$p''(x) - \frac{\pi}{L}\left(\sum_{j=1}^{\infty} ja_j \sin\frac{j\pi x}{L}\right)p'(x) + \lambda p(x) = 0. \quad (8)$$

Proceeding along lines suggested by Ungeheuer,[9] under the assumption that the tract is only slightly perturbed from a uniform shape, we can expand the eigenfunctions and eigenvalues in terms of the perturbation parameter ϵ to obtain

$$[p_0''(x) + \epsilon p_1''(x) + \cdots]$$
$$- \frac{\pi}{L}\sum_{j=1}^{\infty} ja_j \sin\frac{j\pi x}{L}[p_0'(x) + \epsilon p_1'(x) + \cdots]$$
$$+ (\lambda_0 + \epsilon\lambda_1 + \cdots)[p_0(x) + \epsilon p_1(x) + \cdots] = 0, \quad (9)$$

where the subscript 0 refers to the unperturbed (uniform-area) conditions. If the a_j are of order ϵ, we obtain by equating like powers of ϵ and invoking the ortho-

---

[13] M. R. Schroeder, personal communication. (See also Ref. 19).

gonality of the zero-order eigenfunctions $p_0^{(m)}$,

$$\lambda_1^{(m)} = -[(2m-1)\pi/2L]^2 a_{2m-1}, \quad (10)$$

where

$$\lambda^{(m)} \simeq \lambda_0^{(m)} + \lambda_1^{(m)}. \quad (11)$$

Thus, the first-order correction to the mth formant frequency is determined by the $(2m-1)$th Fourier coefficient of the area function. The even components of the Fourier expansion have no first-order effects on the formant frequencies.

If we were to consider a pipe closed at both ends, i.e.,

$$p'(0) = p'(L) = 0,$$

the corresponding eigenvalues for the uniform tract would be given by

$$\lambda_{0c}^{(m)} = [(2m)\pi/2L]^2 \quad m=0,1,2,\cdots \quad (12)$$

and the first-order perturbations by

$$\lambda_{1c}^{(m)} = -[m\pi/L]^2 a_{2m} \quad m=0,1,2,\cdots, \quad (13)$$

where the subscript c denotes the closed-lip boundary condition. Following Eq. 7, we can set $a_0 = \log A_0$, but we observe that this is of no consequence since $\lambda_{1c} = 0$; i.e., the zero eigenvalue is not subject to perturbation. Under these conditions, the odd Fourier coefficients have no first-order effects and the even coefficients uniquely specify the changes in the eigenvalues and the corresponding formant frequencies. As we see later, for area changes larger than first order, the respective eigenfrequencies are still strongly dependent on the corresponding Fourier components of the area function but weakly dependent, in general, on all others as well.

Now we consider the output admittance of the tract measured at the lips as a function of frequency,

$$Y_t(\omega) = \frac{-U(L,\omega)}{p(L,\omega)} \propto \frac{(\partial/\partial x)[p(L,\omega)]}{p(L,\omega)}, \quad (14)$$

where U is the volume velocity. The glottis boundary condition $p'(0)=0$ remains unchanged. The frequencies for which $Y_t(\omega)=0$ give the closed-lip boundary condition eigenfrequencies, and those for which $Y_t(\omega) \to \infty$ the open-lip boundary condition eigenfrequencies. The infinite sets of poles and zeros of the admittance function thus correspond to the eigenfrequencies under the two sets of boundary conditions, respectively. At least up to first-order perturbations from the uniform-tract shape, they uniquely determine the perturbing area Fourier components and, thereby, the complete function up to a multiplicative constant.

Let us now consider whether these results can be generalized to any tract shape. Webster's horn equation is a particular example of the general one-dimensional Sturm–Liouville equation. The general solution is given by the sum of two independent solutions, to one of which it may be always restricted by appropriate selection of the boundary conditions. Thus, the general solution is determined by two infinite sets of eigenvalues. Borg[14] has shown that knowledge of the two sets of eigenvalues corresponding to the two independent solutions uniquely specifies the distributed function of the system, the mass distribution with distance for the vibrating string, or, in this situation, the cross-sectional area of the tract. Thus, knowledge of the doubly infinite set of poles and zeros of the admittance function would be required for complete determination of the area function.

It is only for low frequencies that Webster's horn equation properly models the vocal tract; hence even if they could be measured, high-frequency poles and zeros could not be properly interpreted. Therefore, we restrict our attention to a continuous set of lowest-order singularities and consider the information they provide about the low-order spatial Fourier components of the area function. In view of the first-order perturbation-theory results, we expect the high-frequency area components to have only small effects on the low-order singularities. Hence, if one can find a band-limited area function from a given set of singularities, one can expect it to be a good representation for the exact function within the limitations implied by band limiting.

The most important practical question is the following:

For a tube of given length, does the set of n lowest-order poles and n lowest-order zeros (excluding the zero at $\omega \doteq 0$) uniquely determine the 2n lowest-order Fourier components of the logarithmic area function (a_j, $j=1,\cdots,2n$) under the constraint that $a_j=0$ for $j>2n$?

Although as yet we do not have a proof for the above statement, extensive empirical exploration by a computer of a six-dimensional Fourier-component space has led to unique results in all cases for a given set of six low-order poles and zeros. The expansion was limited to six components so that the three odd components would correspond to the normally measured first three formants of vowel articulations. Similar results are expected to hold for any 2n low-order coefficients and n low-order poles and n low-order zeros.

We may observe the dependence of the admittance singularities on the individual Fourier coefficients for nonuniform tracts, where the perturbation theory does not yield simple results, by experimentally introducing slight changes in the coefficients values. Using the methods outlined in Appendix A, the changes introduced in the respective singularities may be determined. In this manner, we obtain for every area configuration $\mathbf{A}(a_j, j=1,\cdots,6)$ a corresponding matrix $\mathbf{M}$ of approxi-

[14] G. Borg, Acta. Math. **78**, 1–96 (1946).

mations to the partial derivatives

$$m_{i,j}=\frac{\delta\omega_i/\omega_i}{\delta a_j},$$

where $\delta\omega_i/\omega_i$ are the proportional changes in the ordered set of open and closed lips boundary-condition eigenfrequencies that accompany small changes δa_j in the individual Fourier components. For the uniform tract, $\mathbf{M}\simeq-0.5\mathbf{I}$, where $\mathbf{I}$ is the unit matrix, but for nonuniform configurations the nondiagonal elements will be, in general, nonzero. Whenever $\mathbf{M}$ is nonsingular, every direction in the Fourier-coefficient space will be mapped into a unique direction in the singularity space and there will be no other articulation $\mathbf{A}'$ in the neighborhood of $\mathbf{A}$ that has the same low-order eigenfrequencies.

We have found empirically that, for δa_j of the order of 0.05, the Jacobian determinant $|\mathbf{M}|$ is always positive and therefore $\mathbf{M}$ is nonsingular. In fact, changing the articulation in the direction of the gradient of $|\mathbf{M}|$ by steepest-descent methods did not yield a sign change in $|\mathbf{M}|$ after more than 20 iterations from the uniform configuration, where each iteration would effect nominally a 10% change in eigenfrequencies. The final configuration had its poles and zeros located pairwise rather close together, leading us to believe that the same property of the system that forces the eigenfrequencies to take on nonidentical values may be responsible for the nonsingularity of $\mathbf{M}$ as well.

The nonsingularity of $\mathbf{M}$ allows us to approach a target point in singularity space iteratively from any starting point as closely as desired by mapping the desired path from the singularity space into the coefficient space and moving along that path by successive changes in the coefficient values. Appendix B gives further details on this procedure. Results are given in Table I for four different sets of singular-frequency data with iterative solutions in each case starting from seven different initial conditions. Computations were terminated whenever the frequency deviation from the target was less than 0.5% for all singularities. On the basis of first-order perturbation theory applied to a uniform shape, the maximum deviation in any area coefficient from the true value then should not exceed ±0.01, a range of 0.02. The maximum range in any coefficient in the terminating data was in fact 0.017.

Through similar methods we find that the Jacobian determinant $|\mathbf{M}|$ having elements

$$m_{ij}=\frac{\delta\omega_i/\omega_i}{\delta a_j}, \quad i=1,3,5$$

(the admittance pole frequencies) and $j=1,3,5$ (the odd Fourier coefficients) is always positive. Similarly, $|\mathbf{M}^e|$

TABLE I. Final area coefficient values as a function of initial coefficient values when approaching specified targets in admittance singularity space.

Target for admittance poles/zeros (Hz)						Initial values of area coefficients						Final values of area coefficients					
500	1000	1500	2000	2500	3000	0.0	0.0	0.0	0.0	0.0	0.0	0.000	0.000	0.000	0.000	0.000	0.000
500	1000	1500	2000	2500	3000	0.5	0.5	0.5	0.5	0.5	0.5	0.000	−0.002	−0.001	0.000	0.000	0.000
500	1000	1500	2000	2500	3000	−0.5	−0.5	−0.5	−0.5	−0.5	−0.5	0.000	0.000	0.000	0.000	0.000	0.000
500	1000	1500	2000	2500	3000	0.5	−0.5	0.5	−0.5	0.5	−0.5	−0.001	0.000	0.000	0.000	0.000	0.000
500	1000	1500	2000	2500	3000	−0.5	0.5	−0.5	0.5	−0.5	0.5	0.000	−0.001	0.000	0.000	0.000	0.000
500	1000	1500	2000	2500	3000	0.5	0.5	0.5	−0.5	−0.5	−0.5	0.000	−0.001	0.000	0.000	0.000	0.000
500	1000	1500	2000	2500	3000	−0.5	−0.5	−0.5	0.5	0.5	0.5	0.001	−0.001	0.002	−0.001	0.000	0.000
270	1800	2290	2600	3010	3300	0.0	0.0	0.0	0.0	0.0	0.0	−0.051	−1.689	−0.430	−0.080	−0.060	0.019
270	1800	2290	2600	3010	3300	0.5	0.5	0.5	0.5	0.5	0.5	−0.055	−1.691	−0.433	−0.082	−0.062	0.040
270	1800	2290	2600	3010	3300	−0.5	−0.5	−0.5	−0.5	−0.5	−0.5	−0.046	−1.689	−0.434	−0.082	−0.063	0.020
270	1800	2290	2600	3010	3300	0.5	−0.5	0.5	−0.5	0.5	−0.5	−0.053	−1.691	−0.433	−0.082	−0.062	0.021
270	1800	2290	2600	3010	3300	−0.5	0.5	−0.5	0.5	−0.5	0.5	−0.050	−1.689	−0.434	−0.083	−0.063	0.020
270	1800	2290	2600	3010	3300	0.5	0.5	0.5	−0.5	−0.5	−0.5	−0.051	−1.690	−0.433	−0.082	−0.062	0.020
270	1800	2290	2600	3010	3300	−0.5	−0.5	−0.5	0.5	0.5	0.5	−0.043	−1.686	−0.433	−0.083	−0.063	0.018
300	550	870	1500	2270	2600	0.0	0.0	0.5	0.5	0.0	0.0	0.048	0.109	0.521	0.728	0.517	0.544
300	550	870	1500	2270	2600	0.5	0.5	0.5	0.5	0.5	0.5	0.048	0.108	0.519	0.726	0.527	0.540
300	550	870	1500	2270	2600	−0.5	−0.5	−0.5	−0.5	−0.5	−0.5	0.049	0.107	0.518	0.728	0.526	0.541
300	550	870	1500	2270	2600	0.5	−0.5	0.5	−0.5	0.5	−0.5	0.053	0.108	0.519	0.725	0.531	0.537
300	550	870	1500	2270	2600	−0.5	0.5	−0.5	0.5	−0.5	0.5	0.049	0.108	0.520	0.727	0.522	0.542
300	550	870	1500	2270	2600	0.5	0.5	0.5	−0.5	−0.5	−0.5	0.049	0.108	0.521	0.728	0.519	0.543
300	550	870	1500	2270	2600	−0.5	−0.5	−0.5	0.5	0.5	0.5	0.049	0.108	0.521	0.728	0.520	0.543
730	900	1090	1700	2440	2800	0.0	0.0	0.0	0.0	0.0	0.0	−1.287	−0.224	0.350	0.472	0.275	0.322
730	900	1090	1700	2440	2800	0.5	0.5	0.5	0.5	0.5	0.5	−1.272	−0.216	0.354	0.468	0.268	0.319
730	900	1090	1700	2440	2800	−0.5	−0.5	−0.5	−0.5	−0.5	−0.5	−1.285	−0.223	0.351	0.471	0.274	0.322
730	900	1090	1700	2440	2800	0.5	−0.5	0.5	−0.5	0.5	−0.5	−1.279	−0.217	0.351	0.469	0.270	0.320
730	900	1090	1700	2440	2800	−0.5	0.5	−0.5	0.5	−0.5	0.5	−1.278	−0.219	0.353	0.469	0.270	0.320
730	900	1090	1700	2440	2800	0.5	0.5	0.5	−0.5	−0.5	−0.5	−1.289	−0.223	0.349	0.472	0.275	0.322
730	900	1090	1700	2440	2800	−0.5	−0.5	−0.5	0.5	0.5	0.5	−1.288	−0.223	0.350	0.472	0.275	0.322

having elements

$$m_{ij}{}^e = \frac{\delta \omega_i / \omega_i}{\delta a_j}, \quad i = 2,4,6$$

(the admittance zero frequencies) and $j = 2,4,6$, (the even Fourier coefficients) is always positive. Proceeding as before, we are led to the further result that if only the odd coefficients and not the even ones are variable, the set of admittance poles uniquely specifies the remaining odd coefficients and, thereby, the complete band-limited function. Similarly, if the odd coefficients are kept at some initial values, the set of admittance zeros determines the missing even coefficients. Of course, in each case the odd or even coefficients are functions of the specific values to which the even or odd coefficients, respectively, have been set.

Although exact results are unavailable for larger area deformations, on-line computer studies[15] have allowed us to state qualitatively the higher-order dependence of the formant frequencies on the Fourier coefficients of the cross-sectional area function. To first order, formant deviations from the nominal or uniform tract values are proportional to the odd Fourier coefficients. For area changes beyond the range of first-order perturbation theory, if, to first order, the formant frequency ω_n is linearly dependent on the coefficient a_k, then increasing $|a_j|$ shifts ω_n lower in frequency for

[15] P. Mermelstein, J. Acoust. Soc. Am. 39, 1219(A) (1966).

$j > k$ and higher in frequency for $j < k$. ω_n is still mostly dependent on a_k, decreasing with increasing a_k and increasing otherwise. The nonlinear effects decrease rapidly as the separation $|j-k|$ is increased.

II. APPLICATIONS OF THE THEORY

In order to demonstrate the applicability of these methods to real vocal-tract shapes, we have tested them on published quantized x-ray data of Fant[2] for six Russian vowels. The area functions were first modeled exactly, and the corresponding poles and zeros were determined. Next the band-limited area functions that satisfied these singularity data were computed, and they are compared to the original area data in Fig. 1. Since the poles and zeros are invariant to a uniform multiplicative change in area, the tract shapes are determined from the singularities only up to a multiplicative constant. Hence, all area data have been normalized to a zero mean logarithmic value.

Although the area plots of Fig. 1 compare well, some deviations remain. To demonstrate that the source of these deviations is the noninvariability of the low-order singularities to band limiting, the same x-ray-derived area functions were band limited to six harmonic components and the point-by-point area values newly determined. The corresponding singularities were again computed, and the area functions satisfying the new singularity data were redetermined. Table II contrasts the area data determined from the singularities of the original not-band-limited area function with those de-

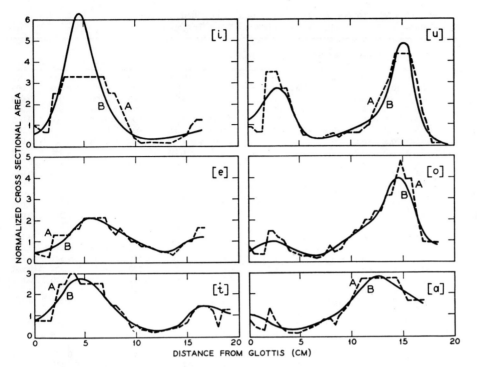

FIG. 1. Vocal-tract area functions band limited to six components determined from the first six admittance poles/zeros of the x-ray-derived area functions of six Russian vowels. A: X-ray derived area function (after Fant). B: Computed band-limited approximation.

termined from the singularities of the band-limited function and with the band-limited-function coefficients themselves. Band limiting to six Fourier coefficients was found to cause no more than a 5% error in the six singular frequencies and no more than a 3% error in the three formant frequencies. The coefficients determined from the singularities of the not-band-limited areas differ from those directly determined by Fourier

TABLE II. Singular frequency and area coefficient data for six Russian vowels.[a]

Vowel	Singularities for exact areas (Hz)						Six area coefficients determined from singularities at left					
ɑ	669	863	1139	2111	2487	3074	−0.925	0.107	0.560	0.098	0.143	0.032
o	523	689	911	2184	2350	3392	−0.753	0.246	0.696	0.224	0.003	−0.364
u	250	536	601	2291	2308	3575	0.101	0.207	0.951	−0.741	0.183	−0.552
ɫ	283	582	1733	2238	2319	3143	0.446	0.453	−0.714	−0.280	0.142	−0.215
i	224	784	2256	2287	3166	3549	1.056	−0.173	−0.942	0.310	−0.149	−0.096
e	421	1047	1971	2153	2908	3114	0.177	−0.338	−0.525	0.058	−0.196	0.088

Vowel	Singularities for band-limited areas (Hz)						Six area coefficients determined from singularities at left					
ɑ	696	916	1174	2156	2560	3217	−0.950	0.078	0.516	0.025	0.046	−0.089
o	536	709	922	2192	2364	3482	−0.801	0.203	0.625	−0.304	−0.069	−0.426
u	261	545	612	2332	2350	3663	0.023	0.177	0.830	−0.846	0.101	−0.596
ɫ	284	586	1774	2264	2354	3187	0.416	0.391	−0.780	−0.282	0.100	−0.246
i	224	796	2297	2331	3221	3668	1.006	−0.270	−0.984	0.273	−0.222	−0.156
e	424	1058	1993	2183	2988	3214	0.129	−0.390	−0.556	0.030	−0.229	0.048

Vowel	Tract length (cm)	Coefficients for band-limited approximations to exact areas					
ɑ	17.0	−0.956	0.076	0.518	0.028	0.048	−0.088
o	18.5	−0.800	0.204	0.624	−0.304	−0.070	−0.426
u	19.5	0.026	0.182	0.816	−0.856	0.106	−0.596
ɫ	19.0	0.418	0.390	−0.780	−0.282	0.100	−0.246
i	16.5	1.002	−0.272	−0.984	0.276	−0.220	−0.156
e	16.5	0.130	−0.388	−0.556	0.028	−0.230	0.048

[a] After Fant—see Ref. 2, p. 115.

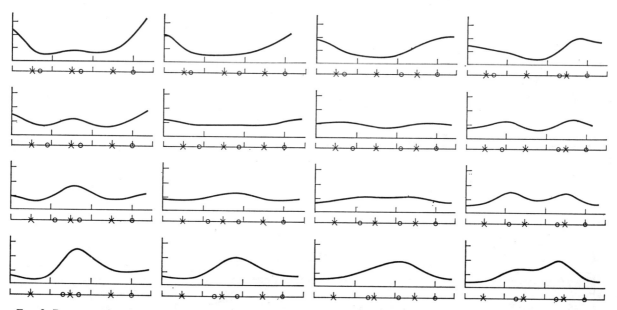

FIG. 2. Representative six-component band-limited vocal-tract area functions that have their formant frequencies equivalent to those of the uniform tract. Area values have been normalized to a zero mean logarithmic value and are in arbitrary units. Distance marks are 5 cm apart with the glottis at left. The output admittance pole–zero pattern is given below each area curve. Frequency marks are 500 Hz apart.

expansion of the log area function by no more than 0.1, i.e., a 10% ripple about the average area. Because Fant gives roughly quantized data, the high-frequency area components are exaggerated, and therefore the singularity shifts introduced by band-limiting are more extensive than would normally be expected. In fact, the coefficients determined from the singularities of the band-limited areas differ from those directly determined by less than 0.015.

Normal-speech spectral analysis yields only the formant frequencies, i.e., open-lip eigenvalues or only half the required information for unique area determination in terms of the low-spatial-frequency Fourier components. On an admittance basis, only the low-order poles and not the zeros are determined. To demonstrate that this information alone is insufficient for area determination, we have attempted to sample by means of examples the class of tract shapes that have their first three formant frequencies fixed at their corresponding values for the uniform tract but that have variable admittance zero frequencies. Let us assume an independent excitation source and frequency-dependent losses only. Then, except for the small effects of higher formant-frequency values on the vocal tract transfer function, signals generated from these tracts and low-pass filtered at 3 kHz are perceptually equivalent. In Fig. 2, we show 16 tract shapes having as first three formant values the formant frequencies of a uniform tract 17 cm long, namely, 500, 1500, and 2500 Hz. All possible combinations of the first admittance zero taking on values of 700, 900, 1100, and 1300 Hz and the second zero taking on values of 1700, 1900, 2100, and 2300 Hz are illustrated. The third zero is kept fixed

at 3000 Hz. It is not unreasonable to think that the vocal tract could assume many of these shapes.

In the absence of additional constraints, formant information only is evidently insufficient for unique area determination. Perhaps the physical constraints acting on the articulators can be invoked to limit the inherent ambiguities. Lacking such information, we have explored the effects of an arbitrary analytical constraint to demonstrate one method by which the ambiguity problem may be resolved. Restricting the admissible area functions to those whose logarithms are antisymmetric functions about the midpoint of the vocal tract (area representation in terms of odd coefficients only) yields unique areas for a set of formants. This constraint was found to be valid to a large extent for most vowels, as can be observed from Fig. 3, where the formants of the Fant x-ray-derived data were used to determine the corresponding antisymmetric area functions.[16] Area values have again been normalized to a zero mean logarithmic value. For the vowel /u/, the tract configuration tends to be almost symmetric, with the point of maximal constriction near the midpoint of the tract. Such a function cannot be represented in terms of antisymmetric components only. For the other vowels, however, the constraint is largely valid. In these cases, it appears to be a property of the anatomical system to vary primarily those components of the tract

[16] Figure 3 is taken from P. Mermelstein and M. R. Schroeder, "Determination of Smoothed Cross-sectional Area Functions of the Vocal Tract from Format Frequencies," Paper A24 in *Proceedings of the Fifth International Congress on Acoustics, 1965, Liege,* D. E. Commins, Ed. (Imprimerie Georges Thone, Liege, 1965), Vol. 1a.

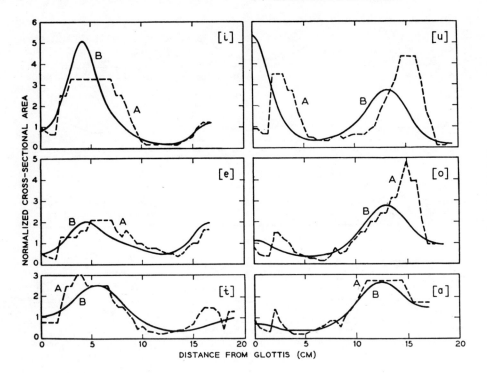

FIG. 3. Area functions anti-symmetric in their logarithms approximating x-ray-derived area functions for six Russian vowels and matching their first three formant frequencies. A: X-ray derived area function (after Fant.) B: Computed antisymmetric approximation.

area that have first-order effects on the formant frequencies of a uniform tract.

On the basis of the coarticulation model presented by Öhman,[17] the articulation for a stop in a vowel context can be represented by a vowel–vowel transition on which the appropriate stop constriction is superimposed. As a rough approximation, we may represent the articulatory transition between the two vowels as proceeding under the log-antisymmetric constraint by linear interpolation of the odd area coefficients. Any deviations between the formant tracks so generated and those experimentally measured can be considered to be manifestations of the stop articulation. A corrected composite area shape may be computed within the vowel-consonant transition region by applying increments to match the measured formant values at 10-msec intervals. The area-coefficient increments are taken in the direction in six-dimensional articulatory space that maximally reduces the formant frequency deviations with the least change in the sum of the squares of the area coefficients. The consonant articulation is taken to be the one computed from the last set of measurable formant frequencies as we proceed from the vowel to the consonant. Figure 4 illustrates the results of this procedure for the nonsense utterance /iba/. Apparently the assumptions are sufficiently valid to obtain the correct place of articulation for the stop.

To demonstrate a different application of the synthesis procedure and to shed light on certain aspects of articulatory compensation, we have synthesized tract shapes for five American vowels under the constraint

that lip area be constant at some fixed value $A(L)$. This constraint is imposed in addition to average log area normalization to an arbitrary value $\log \bar{A}$ and can be formulated as

$$\log A(L) = \log \bar{A} + \sum_{j=1}^{6} (-1)^j a_j, \qquad (15)$$

where the a_j are the logarithmic area coefficients. For this exercise the average vowel formants for men for the American vowels /i/, /ɛ/, /ɑ/, /ɔ/, and /u/ served as the acoustic criteria.[18] The second and third admittance zeros were arbitrarily fixed at $f_2 + (f_3 - f_2)/2$ and $f_3 + (f_3 - f_2)/2$, where f_2 and f_3 are the given second and third formants, respectively. The tract length was fixed at 17 cm, and for each vowel the first admittance zero z_1 was varied over the allowable range $f_1 < z_1 < f_2$ using the relationship $z_1 = f_1 + m(f_2 - f_1)$, $m = 0.1, 0.2, \cdots, 0.9$. For each set of three admittance zeros and three formant frequencies so obtained, the matching tract shape was computed to give some $A(L)$. By interpolation we have selected those configurations for which $A(L)/\bar{A} = 2.23$ and have plotted them in Fig. 5. With one exception, it appears quite possible that these articulations are generatable by the human articulatory apparatus, possibly with some additional training in the control of the pharyngeal musculature. The unusual shape obtained for /u/ is the result of using too short a tract length.

---

[17] S. E. C. Öhman, J. Acoust. Soc. Am. **41**, 310–320 (1967).

[18] G. E. Peterson and H. L. Barney, J. Acoust. Soc. Am. **24**, 175–184 (1952).

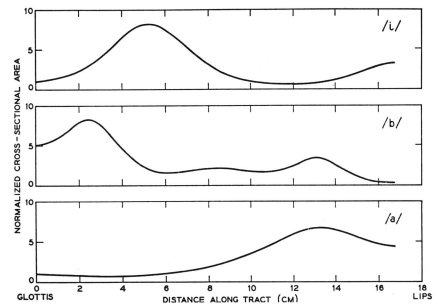

FIG. 4. Cross-sectional area functions approximating the initial, middle, and final articulations in the utterance /iba/.

To investigate the compensative effects between the area function and the tract length, we have synthesized areas for three vowels for tracts 16, 18, and 20 cm long in each case (Fig. 6). The sets of three curves for each vowel yield the identical values for the six lowest admittance poles/zeros, those listed as the band-limited singularities in Table II. The major effect of lengthening the tract appears to be a forward movement of the primary cavity. Minor effects of a strong dependence of the synthesized glottal area on the tract length, and the development of a second cavity in the pharyngeal region when the tract is lengthened are also noteworthy. It should not be implied that such changes normally accompany the lengthening of the human tract, for example, by lip rounding. It is quite unlikely that the formant values are maintained constant under such conditions.

III. DISCUSSION

It has long been known that formants do not completely specify the corresponding articulation. However, we can, in principle, determine the articulation uniquely from the doubly infinite set of admittance poles and zeros looking into the tract at the lips. The admittance poles correspond to the formant frequencies, but information regarding the admittance zeros is missing from speech signal.

We consider the important practical situation when the output admittance function is incompletely specified and only the low-frequency behavior is known. Under such conditions, we find that we can determine a unique approximate tract shape, one where the logarithm of the cross-sectional area function is band-limited to Fourier components equal in number to the given admittance poles and zeros. Although no theoretical proof for uniqueness is presently available, extensive empirical

computer explorations lead us to believe that such is in fact the case.

Our results can be generalized to any system exhibiting wave propagation in one dimension only, for example, nonuniform transmission lines or nonuniform vibrating beams. Whenever the vibrating system is specified in terms of the low-frequency output admittance singularities or equivalently by two independent sets of low-order eigenvalues corresponding to nonequivalent boundary conditions, we can synthesize the system in terms of a sequence of low-spatial-frequency components. The synthesis method is particularly applicable where it is important to avoid sharp changes in the characteristic impedance of the line or the cross-sectional area of the vibrator.

The results indicate precisely the manner and extent to which low-order formant specification falls short of

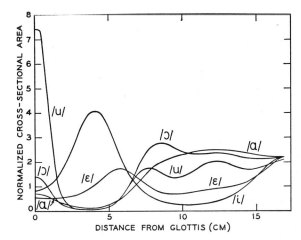

FIG. 5. Vocal-tract shapes with identical lip area values computed for five American vowels.

The Journal of the Acoustical Society of America

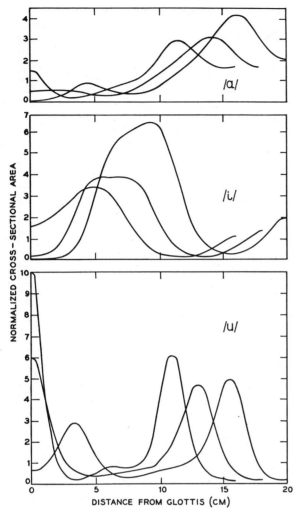

FIG. 6. Acoustically equivalent vocal-tract area functions of different lengths for three vowels. The lowest six admittance poles/zeros of each set of area functions are, respectively, equal.

complete cross-sectional area determination. The adjustment of the admittance zeros serves as a precise tool for the exploration of the classes of area functions having identical formant frequencies. A re-examination of normal articulatory movements in this light should serve to further limit the class of anatomically realizable configurations that have identical formant frequencies.

The results of the analysis presented here are in agreement with previous qualitative statements regarding the configurations of the vocal tract. It has been known that certain defects in the controlling mechanism of the articulators or in the articulatory mechanism itself can be overcome to a large extent by compensating movements at other places along the vocal tract. Our results indicate that a specific formant configuration may be generated by area functions ranging all the way from antisymmetric functions to those almost symmetric about the midpoint of the tract. Alternatively, if one half of the tract area is fixed, all vowel formant

configurations may be obtained by varying the shape of the other half only. By means of the methods outlined, we make explicit procedures available for the determination of such shapes.

Qualitative arguments based on the sampling theorem suggest that the low-frequency behavior of the vocal tract is determined by the gross shape distortions or low-spatial-frequency components of the cross-sectional area of the tract. As the phonemic quality of vowel utterances is at most slightly changed by low-pass filtering preserving only the first three formant frequencies, it is evident that highly localized distortions of small magnitude have no appreciable effects on the quality of the generated acoustic signal. This does not, however, justify the treatment of the vocal tract as two or three weakly coupled cavities having uniform cross-sectional areas. It should also be noted that due to the nature of the logarithmic transformation, the effect of localized constrictions is much exaggerated compared to local dilations of similar magnitude.

Tracts of different length can be distorted to yield the same formant frequencies. Hence, differences in the length of speakers' tracts do not necessarily manifest themselves in systematic formant differences. We may consider that the articulatory apparatus in attempting to attain a configuration under acoustic feedback control—the primary method of learning the vowel phonemes of a foreign language—may, within limits, vary the length as well as the shape of the tract. Small extensions or contractions, which by themselves vary in a certain sense only the average formant locations, can serve to reduce the additional shape distortion required.

The frequency dependent vocal-tract output-admittance function may be completely determined by exciting the tract at the lips from the outside. Independent knowledge of the direct and reflected sound waves can, in principle, be combined to compute the admittance function. Preliminary experiments with artificial shapes generally confirm the validity of the synthesis procedure.[19] Further experiments to measure the output admittance of the vocal tract as a function of time for speakers generating utterances without phonation are now in progress.

ACKNOWLEDGMENTS

The author is indebted to P. Denes, J. Flanagan, and O. Fujimura for helpful discussions during work on this project and for critical reading of the manuscript. This problem was suggested to the author by M. R. Schroeder, and without his unfailing encouragement and countless suggestions this work could not have been accomplished. H. J. Landau brought the Borg paper (Ref. 14) to the attention of the author. John Heinz, in reviewing the paper, suggested the given form for Eq. 5 leading to the particular identification of the area expansion terms given by Eq. 6.

[19] M. R. Schroeder, J. Acoust. Soc. Am. 41, 1002–1010 (1967)

Appendix A. Determination of the Admittance Poles and Zeros for a Given Tract Area Function

The continuous area function of the tract is approximated in our computational model by means of a cascade of segments of equal length and constant area (see Fig. A-1). In order for our representation to be valid up to a frequency of 4 kHz, we have chosen 0.5 cm as the length of the individual segments. The area values for each segment are taken to be those determined for segment midpoints from the expansion coefficients a_n by

$$A_i = \exp \sum_{n=1}^{6} a_n \cos\frac{n\pi(i-\frac{1}{2})h}{L}, \quad i = 1, \cdots, L/h.$$

Each segment may be described in terms of a T network of impedances as given by Dunn[5] or the equivalent two-terminal-pair network parameters $\mathcal{A}$, $\mathcal{B}$, $\mathcal{C}$, $\mathcal{D}$. Under lossless conditions, we obtain, for the matrix of the ith section,

$$\mathbf{K}_i(\omega) = \begin{bmatrix} \mathcal{A}_i(\omega) & \mathcal{B}_i(\omega) \\ \mathcal{C}_i(\omega) & \mathcal{D}_i(\omega) \end{bmatrix},$$

$$\mathcal{A}_i(\omega) = \cosh j\omega h/c = \cos\omega h/c,$$

$$\mathcal{B}_i(\omega) = \frac{\rho c}{A_i}\sinh j\frac{\omega h}{c} = j\frac{\rho c}{A_i}\sin\frac{\omega h}{c},$$

$$\mathcal{C}_i(\omega) = \frac{A_i}{\rho c}\sinh j\frac{\omega h}{c} = j\frac{A_i}{\rho c}\sin\frac{\omega h}{c},$$

$$\mathcal{D}(\omega) = \cosh j\omega h/c = \cos\omega h/c,$$

where ω is the angular frequency in radians per second, h is the length of the individual sections in centimeters, c is the velocity of sound in centimeters per second, ρ is the density of air in grams per cubic centimeter,

A_i is the cross-sectional area of the ith section in square centimeters, and j is the imaginary unit. For any frequency value ω, we compute the pressure and volume

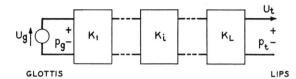

FIG. A-1. Network representation of the vocal tract.

velocity at the lips (p_t, U_t) from those at the glottis (p_g, U_g) by

$$\begin{bmatrix} p_t \\ U_t \end{bmatrix} = \prod_{i=1}^{L/h} \mathbf{K}_i(\omega) \begin{bmatrix} p_g \\ U_g \end{bmatrix}.$$

The source boundary condition forces us to set $Y_g = 0$, e.g., $p_g = 1$, $U_g = 0$, and the admittance poles and zeros are found as the frequencies for which $p_t = 0$ and $U_t = 0$, respectively. Now, for lossless networks,

$$-Y_t(\omega) = U_t(\omega)/p_t(\omega) = jB(\omega) \quad \text{and} \quad dB(\omega)/d\omega > 0;$$

thus changes in sign occur only at admittance zeros or poles.[A1] The algorithm employed determines $U_t(\omega)$ and $p_t(\omega)$ for the frequency range 0–4000 Hz with 25-Hz increments and interpolates over frequency ranges within which a change of sign is found.

By determining the zero crossings as a function of frequency for the two functions independently, we limit the situations where singularities may be missed to those where two poles or two zeros of $Y_t(\omega)$ are within 25 Hz of each other.

[A1] O. J. Zobel, Bell System Tech. J. 2, 1–46 (1923).

Appendix B. Determination of the Six-Coefficient Band-Limited Area Function of a Tract with Specified Six Low-Order Nonzero Admittance Poles and Zeros

Let an articulation $\mathbf{A}$ be represented as a vector of six logarithmic Fourier cosine coefficients a_i, $i = 1, \cdots, 6$, having wavelengths $2L/i$, respectively. For any $\mathbf{A}$, by methods of Appendix A, we may determine a vector of eigenfrequency ratios

$$\Omega(\mathbf{A}) = \begin{bmatrix} \omega_1/\omega_1^0 \\ \vdots \\ \omega_6/\omega_6^0 \end{bmatrix},$$

where the ω_1, ω_3, ω_5 are the three low-order admittance poles (open-lip eigenfrequencies); ω_2, ω_4, and ω_6 the low-order admittance zeros excluding $\omega = 0$ (closed-lip eigenfrequencies); and the ω^0 are the corresponding

values for a uniform tract of the same length. Consider a small perturbation in one of the articulatory coefficients,

$$\delta\mathbf{A}j = \begin{bmatrix} 0 \\ \vdots \\ \delta aj \\ \vdots \\ 0 \end{bmatrix}.$$

For the new articulation, $\mathbf{A}'_j = \mathbf{A} + \delta\mathbf{A}_j$,

$$\Omega(\mathbf{A}'_j) = \begin{bmatrix} \omega'_1/\omega_1^0 \\ \vdots \\ \omega'_6/\omega_6^0 \end{bmatrix} = \begin{bmatrix} (\omega_1+\delta\omega_1)/\omega_1^0 \\ \vdots \\ (\omega_6+\delta\omega_6)/\omega_6^0 \end{bmatrix} = \Omega(\mathbf{A}) + \delta\Omega(\mathbf{A}_j)$$

Let

$$m_{ij} = \frac{\delta\omega_i/\omega_i}{\delta a_j} = \frac{[\delta\Omega(A_j)]_i/[\Omega(A)]_i}{[\delta A_j]_j},$$

where the i subscript outside the braces denotes the ith element of the vector. m_{ij} represents an approximation to the partial derivative of the ith eigenfrequency ratio with respect to a change in the jth coefficient, all other coefficients kept constant. $M(A)$ then is the matrix of partial derivatives about the articulation A.

Let Ω_t be a target vector of eigenfrequency ratios for which the articulation is to be determined. If the articulation to eigenfrequency mapping were linear,

$$\delta A_n = M(A_n)^{-1}[\Omega_t - \Omega(A_n)]$$

would be exactly the required articulation change from an arbitrary articulation A_n that would satisfy Ω_t. Be-cause the above mapping is nonlinear, i.e., M is a function of A, we must proceed iteratively,

$$A_{n+1} = A_n + \delta A_n$$

being nearer to the target in the sense that

$$|\Omega_t - \Omega(A_{n+1})| < |\Omega_t - \Omega(A_n)|.$$

Iteration is terminated whenever no element of $[\Omega_t - \Omega(A_n)]$ exceeds some threshold δ in absolute value.

The use of logarithmic area coefficients constrains the synthesized area functions to positive values. The convergence of the iteration sequence, although not proven in general, has been demonstrated by numerous trials on a digital computer. The procedure is not re-stricted to six coefficients and six singularities but can be applied to any even number of coefficients and an equal number of singularities.

Direct Estimation of the Vocal Tract Shape by Inverse Filtering of Acoustic Speech Waveforms

HISASHI WAKITA

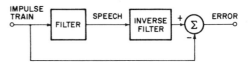

Fig. 1. Speech analysis model.

Abstract—This paper describes a new method for estimating the vocal tract area function directly from the acoustic speech waveform. Dynamic changes of the area functions and formants in voiced speech sounds are obtainable. The filtering processes of the inverse filter model and an acoustic tube model of speech are analyzed and they are shown to be identical, with the reflection coefficients in the acoustic tube model as a common factor, thus making possible the extraction of the reflection coefficients by the inverse filter processing of the speech signal. The discrete area function can easily be obtained from the set of reflection coefficients. Analysis examples for vowels, diphthongs, and consonants in vowel–consonant–vowel utterances are given.

I. Introduction

X-ray techniques have been used as direct methods for the determination of the human vocal tract shape [1], [2]. Although some improvements of the direct method have been tried [3], [4], there still remain some difficulties in the measurement of the lateral dimension, and there are strong limitations on safe dosages. Several indirect methods for computing the vocal tract area function from measured acoustic data that avoid the drawbacks of X-ray techniques have been published [5]–[8], and an attempt to estimate the vocal tract shape from the acoustic signal has been made [9]. This paper describes a new method for extracting a unique vocal tract area function directly from the acoustic speech wave. This method makes possible the simultaneous extraction of the vocal tract area function and its corresponding formant frequencies. It also makes possible the extraction of dynamic changes of the area function. The method is based on the inverse filter model [10]. Instead of directly solving a set of simultaneous linear equations

Manuscript received August 10, 1972; revised April 13, 1973. This work was supported by the Office of Naval Research, under Contract N00014-67-C-0118. This paper is based upon a more detailed description in "Estimation of the Vocal Tract Shape by the Optimal Inverse Filtering and Acoustic/Articulatory Conversion Methods," SCRL Monograph 9, Speech Communications Research Laboratory, Inc., Santa Barbara, Calif. 93109.

The author is with the Speech Communications Research Laboratory, Inc., Santa Barbara, Calif. 93109.

to obtain the inverse filter coefficients, the solution is observed as a recursive filtering process. It is then shown that a filtering process of identical form can be derived from a nonuniform acoustic tube model of the vocal tract. A set of reflection coefficients in the acoustic tube model is shown to be derivable by inverse filter processing of speech. Several analysis results for selected sounds are shown.

II. Speech Analysis Model

The speech analysis model employed in this study is shown schematically in Fig. 1. It is first assumed that the speech to be analyzed is limited to periodic nonnasalized voiced sounds so that the filter in Fig. 1 is driven by an impulse train. This implies that the filter includes all the contributions from the glottal wave, the vocal tract, and the radiation impedance at the lips. The purposes of this analysis are, first, to determine the filtering process of the inverse filter in such a way that the difference between the output of the inverse filter and the input impulse train attains the minimum for a certain error criterion, and second, to find an acoustic tube filter that is equivalent to the inverse filter so that the frequency domain behavior of the speech can be related to the vocal tract configuration.

The inverse filter is assumed to be a linear filter with only zeros in its transfer function, and the power spectral envelope of the speech is assumed to be approximated by poles only. The validity of this assumption has been demonstrated synthetically and perceptually by other studies [11]–[14].

Another filter that is equivalent to the inverse filter can be derived by modeling a nonuniform acoustic tube. The tube is divided into an arbitrary number of sections of equal length. The filtering process of this acoustic tube is determined in such a way that the continuity conditions for the volume velocity and the sound pressure are satisfied at each junction between two adjacent sections. It is then shown that the filtering process of the acoustic tube thus determined is entirely equivalent to that of the optimized inverse filter.

III. The Optimal Inverse Filtering Process

The transfer function of the inverse filter can be expressed in terms of z-transform notation as

$$A(z) = \sum_{i=0}^{M} a_i z^{-i}, \qquad a_0 = 1 \qquad (1)$$

Reprinted from *IEEE Trans. Audio Electroacoust.*, vol. AU–21, pp. 417–427, Oct. 1973.

where $z = \exp(j\omega T)$ and T is the sampling period. Since the speech sound is treated in sampled data form, z-transform notation is used hereafter. Here, a_0 affects only the gain of the system, so no generality is lost by setting $a_0 = 1$. The ordered set $\{a_i\} = \{a_0, a_1, \cdots, a_M\}$ defines the inverse filter coefficients. If the z transform of the input to the inverse filter $\{x_n\}$ [and the output of the inverse filter $\{y_n\}$] are denoted as $X(z)$ and $Y(z)$, respectively, then

$$A(z) = Y(z)/X(z). \qquad (2)$$

The inverse z transform of (2) is

$$\sum_{i=0}^{M} a_i x_{n-i} = y_n. \qquad (3)$$

Thus the error ϵ_n between the input excitation h_n and the output of the inverse filter y_n is given by

$$\epsilon_n = y_n - h_n = \sum_{i=0}^{M} a_i x_{n-i} - h_n \qquad (4)$$

where h_n defines the impulse train that is zero except for the beginning of each pitch period. Since this impulse train is an unknown quantity, some kind of assumption must be made in order to perform the comparison. Since the power spectral envelope of the speech sound is assumed to be approximated by poles only, the speech signal has the form

$$X(z) = \eta / A(z) \qquad (5)$$

where η is a constant. This assumption implies that the input impulse train can be replaced by an impulse of height η and that, in the z plane, the output of the inverse filter is compared with the constant η. Thus the analysis model in Fig. 1 is transformed equivalently to the model in Fig. 2.

Equation (4) can be rewritten as

$$\epsilon_n = \sum_{i=0}^{M} a_i x_{n-i} - \eta \delta_{n0} \qquad (6)$$

where δ_{n0} is zero for $n \neq 0$ and 1 for $n = 0$. The least mean square error technique is applied to (6) to obtain the optimum inverse filter. To do this, the sum E of the sequence of the squared errors ϵ_n^2 in (6) is taken, and this sum is minimized by setting its partial derivative with respect to each a_j equal to zero for $j = 1, 2, \cdots, M$. Any single frame of the sampled speech signal is assumed to be nonzero only over the interval from $0 \leqslant n \leqslant N - 1$. Thus $\{y_n\}$ is of length $N + M$. Then the derivative of E with respect to a_j is given by

$$\frac{\partial E}{\partial a_j} = 2 \sum_{i=0}^{M} a_i r_{i-j} - 2\eta \sum_{n=0}^{N+M-1} x_{n-j} \delta_{n0}, \quad j = 1, 2, \cdots, M \qquad (7)$$

where r_{i-j} is a short term autocorrelation function and is expressed as

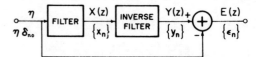

Fig. 2. Equivalent system of the analysis model in Fig. 1.

$$r_{i-j} = \sum_{i=0}^{N+M-1} x_{n-i} x_{n-j} = \sum_{n=0}^{N-1-|i-j|} x_n x_{n+|i-j|} \qquad (8)$$

since $x_n = 0$ for $n \geqslant N$ and $n < 0$. As the sampled speech signal is assumed to be zero for $n < 0$ and $n \geqslant N$, the second term of (7) is always zero as j goes from 1 to M. Thus the condition that minimizes E is given by

$$\sum_{i=0}^{M} a_i r_{i-j} = 0, \qquad j = 1, 2, \cdots, M \qquad (9)$$

where $a_0 = 1$.

It should be noted that the unspecified constant η does not appear in (9) and therefore the output $Y(z)$ of the inverse filter can be compared with an arbitrary constant. The set of M simultaneous linear equations in (9) is of a special form and can be efficiently solved as a special case of Robinson's method [15]. The interest in this study is not only in obtaining the filter coefficients in an efficient manner, but also in observing the process of how the filter coefficients are obtained in solving the set of linear equations. According to Robinson's method, the filter coefficients can be obtained in a recursive manner. The relations between the $\{a_i\}$ obtained in the passage between recursion steps m and $m + 1$ are given by

$$a_0^{(m+1)} = a_0^{(m)} = 1$$
$$a_1^{(m+1)} = a_1^{(m)} + k_m a_m^{(m)}$$
$$a_2^{(m+1)} = a_2^{(m)} + k_m a_{m-1}^{(m)}$$
$$\vdots$$
$$a_m^{(m+1)} = a_m^{(m)} + k_m a_1^{(m)}$$
$$a_{m+1}^{(m+1)} = k_m \qquad (10)$$

where parenthesized superscripts of the filter coefficients in (10) denote the recursion step and k_m is given by

$$k_m = - \frac{\displaystyle\sum_{i=0}^{m} a_i^{(m)} r_{m+1-i}}{\displaystyle\sum_{i=0}^{m} a_i^{(m)} r_i} \equiv - \frac{\beta_m}{\alpha_m}. \qquad (11)$$

Equation (10) can be transformed into a simple recursive matrix form. By multiplying by z^{-i}, $i = 0, 1, \cdots, m$ on both sides of (10), counting i from the top equation to the bottom equation, starting from

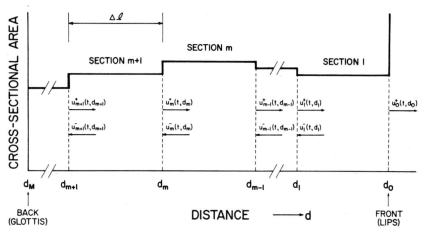

Fig. 3. A nonuniform acoustic tube model of the vocal tract.

$i = 0$, and summing up over all i, the following equation is obtained:

$$A_{m+1}(z) = A_m(z) - k_m B_m(z) \qquad (12)$$

where

$$A_m(z) = \sum_{i=0}^{m} a_i^{(m)} z^{-i} \qquad (13)$$

and

$$B_m(z) = -z^{-(m+1)} A_m(1/z). \qquad (14)$$

In the same fashion, by multiplying by $z^{-(m+1-i)}$ on both sides of (10) and summing up over all i,

$$B_{m+1}(z) = z^{-1} \{B_m(z) - k_m A_m(z)\}. \qquad (15)$$

Using matrix notation, (12) and (15) can be written as

$$\begin{bmatrix} A_{m+1}(z) \\ B_{m+1}(z) \end{bmatrix} = \begin{bmatrix} 1 & -k_m \\ -k_m z^{-1} & z^{-1} \end{bmatrix} \begin{bmatrix} A_m(z) \\ B_m(z) \end{bmatrix}. \qquad (16)$$

Initial values for $A_0(z)$ and $B_0(z)$ are given from (13) and (14) as

$$A_0(z) = 1 \qquad (17)$$

and

$$B_0(z) = -z^{-1} \qquad (18)$$

and k_0 is given from (11) as $k_0 = -r_1/r_0$. Then the quantities at steps $m = 1$ through $m = M$ are computed from (16), (11), and (10) in a recursive manner and $A_M(z)$ is defined as the inverse filter transfer function $A(z)$ in (1). The recursive relation in (16) is considered to represent the filtering process of the optimal inverse filter. It can be seen from (16) that $A_m(z)$ is also an inverse transfer function of order m.

In Section IV it will be shown that under certain conditions $A_M(z)$ is also an inverse transfer function of a nonuniform acoustic tube model of the all-pole vocal tract model, and thus that the filtering process of the acoustic tube can be equivalently replaced by the optimal inverse filter process.

IV. Filtering Process of the Acoustic Tube Model

A. A Solution to the Wave Equation

The vocal tract is now regarded as an acoustic tube with a varying cross-sectional area. The tube is divided into an arbitrary number, M, of sections with equal length Δl. The following assumptions are made for this model.

Assumption 1: The transverse dimension of each section is small enough compared with a wavelength so that the wave propagating through one section can be treated as a plane wave.

Assumption 2: The tube is rigid, and the losses in the sound wave due to viscosity and heat conduction are negligible. In the derivation of the transfer function of the acoustic tube, a procedure similar to that given by Atal and Hanauer [12] is used, though the formulation is different.

Let $u_m(t, d)$ and $p_m(t, d)$ be the volume velocity and the pressure, respectively, in section m where t is the time variable and d is the distance variable. The subscript m is taken from the lips to the glottis in an increasing order as shown in Fig. 3. The wave equation for the velocity potential $\phi_m(t, d)$ in section m is given by [16]

$$\frac{\partial^2 \phi_m(t, d)}{\partial d^2} - \frac{1}{c^2} \frac{\partial^2 \phi_m(t, d)}{\partial t^2} = 0 \qquad (19)$$

where c is sound velocity. The volume velocity $u_m(t, d)$ and the pressure $p_m(t, d)$ are given by [16]

$$u_m(t, d) = -S_m \frac{\partial}{\partial d} \{\phi_m(t, d)\} \qquad (20)$$

and

$$p_m(t, d) = \rho \frac{\partial}{\partial t} \{\phi_m(t, d)\} \qquad (21)$$

where S_m is the cross-sectional area of section m and ρ is the density of air. A solution to (19) for a sinusoidal time dependence of $\phi_m(t, d)$ is given by

$$\phi_m(t, d) = Ae^{j\omega(t-d/c)} + Be^{j\omega(t+d/c)} \qquad (22)$$

where A and B are constants. Then $u_m(t, d)$ is given by the difference of a component $u_m^+(t, d)$ of the volume velocity due to the sound wave traveling from the glottis to the lips and a component $u_m^-(t, d)$ due to the wave traveling toward the glottis in the section m, so that $u_m(t, d)$ and $p_m(t, d)$ are expressed as

$$u_m(t, d) = u_m^+(t, d) - u_m^-(t, d) \qquad (23)$$

$$p_m(t, d) = \frac{\rho c}{S_m}\{u_m^+(t, d) + u_m^-(t, d)\} \qquad (24)$$

where

$$u_m^+(t, d) = \frac{j\omega S_m A}{c} e^{j\omega(t-d/c)}$$

and

$$u_m^-(t, d) = \frac{j\omega S_m B}{c} e^{j\omega(t+d/c)}.$$

Now the volume velocity and the sound pressure must be continuous at the junction between section m and $m + 1$. Consequently, the following relations must hold:

$$u_{m+1}(t, d_m) = u_m(t, d_m) \qquad (25)$$

$$p_{m+1}(t, d_m) = p_m(t, d_m) \qquad (26)$$

where d_m is the distance from the glottis to the junction between sections m and $m + 1$ (see Fig. 3). Since no loss is assumed, the volume velocity component $u_{m+1}^+(t, d_m)$ is equal to that component of the volume velocity that started at d_{m+1} at time $\Delta l/c$ earlier, and the volume velocity component $u_{m+1}^-(t, d_m)$ is equal to that component of the volume velocity that will arrive at d_{m+1} at time $\Delta l/c$ later. Thus the solution of the continuous problem can be obtained by knowing only the values at each junction. Therefore, the notation can be simplified by eliminating the distance variable in the argument of the volume velocity components [e.g., $u_m^+(t, d_m) = u_m^+(t)$]. Then (23) and (24) can be expressed as

$$u_{m+1}^+(t - \Delta t) - u_{m+1}^-(t + \Delta t) = u_m^+(t) - u_m^-(t) \qquad (27)$$

$$\frac{\rho c}{S_{m+1}}\{u_{m+1}^+(t - \Delta t) + u_{m+1}^-(t + \Delta t)\}$$

$$= \frac{\rho c}{S_m}\{u_m^+(t) + u_m^-(t)\} \qquad (28)$$

where $\Delta t = \Delta l/c$. By rearranging (27) and (28),

$$u_{m+1}^+(t - \Delta t) = \frac{1}{1 - \mu_m}\{u_m^+(t) - \mu_m u_m^-(t)\} \qquad (29)$$

$$u_{m+1}^-(t + \Delta t) = \frac{1}{1 + \mu_m}\{-\mu_m u_m^+(t) + u_m^-(t)\} \qquad (30)$$

where

$$\mu_m = \frac{S_m - S_{m+1}}{S_m + S_{m+1}}. \qquad (31)$$

The term μ_m defines the reflection coefficient at the junction between sections m and $m + 1$. Taking the z transforms of (29) and (30),

$$\begin{bmatrix} U_{m+1}^+(z) \\ U_{m+1}^-(z) \end{bmatrix} = \frac{z^{1/2}}{1 + \mu_m} \begin{bmatrix} 1 & -\mu_m \\ -\mu_m z^{-1} & z^{-1} \end{bmatrix} \begin{bmatrix} U_m^+(z) \\ U_m^-(z) \end{bmatrix} \qquad (32)$$

where $U_m^+(z)$ and $U_m^-(z)$ are the z transforms of $u_m^+(t)$ and $u_m^-(t)$, respectively, and

$$z = \exp(j\omega 2\Delta t) = \exp(j\omega 2\Delta l/c). \qquad (33)$$

Although z is usually defined as $z = \exp(j\omega \Delta t)$, $z = \exp(j\omega 2\Delta t)$ was chosen here to be consistent with the results of the inverse filter model. It will be shown later that this relation is necessary for defining the identity of the filtering processes of the two models. Equation (32) gives the recursive relation of the volume velocity components between the two adjacent sections. Based upon (32), it is possible to define an acoustic tube inverse transfer function so that a comparison can be made to (16).

B. Derivation of an Acoustic Tube Inverse Transfer Function

As the boundary conditions, the front end of the tube that corresponds to the lips is assumed to be connected to another section with an infinite area so that $\mu_0 = 1$. Although the radiation effect should be taken into account, it is handled separately under the assumption of a linear system. At the back end, the tube is assumed to be connected to another section of the area S_{M+1} that is terminated with its characteristic impedance of $\rho c/S_{M+1}$. The tube is excited through this characteristic impedance by a source whose current is equal to the forward-going volume component $U_{M+1}^+(z)$.

By using the boundary condition at the front end of the tube, i.e., $\mu_0 = 1$, the following relations can be obtained from (32):

$$\begin{bmatrix} U_{m+1}^+(z) \\ U_{m+1}^-(z) \end{bmatrix} = z^{m+1/2} K_m \begin{bmatrix} D_m^+(z) \\ D_m^-(z) \end{bmatrix} \{U_0^+(z) - U_0^-(z)\} \qquad (34)$$

where

$$\begin{bmatrix} D_m^+(z) \\ D_m^-(z) \end{bmatrix} = \begin{bmatrix} 1 & -\mu_m \\ -\mu_m z^{-1} & z^{-1} \end{bmatrix} \begin{bmatrix} 1 & -\mu_{m-1} \\ -\mu_{m-1} z^{-1} & z^{-1} \end{bmatrix} \cdots \begin{bmatrix} 1 & -\mu_1 \\ -\mu_1 z^{-1} & z^{-1} \end{bmatrix} \begin{bmatrix} 1 \\ -z^{-1} \end{bmatrix} \qquad (35)$$

and

$$K_m = \prod_{i=0}^{m} \frac{1}{1 + \mu_i}. \qquad (36)$$

If $U_{m+1}^+(z)$ and $U_{m+1}^-(z)$ are normalized by K_m, then

$$\begin{bmatrix} \hat{U}_{m+1}^+(z) \\ \hat{U}_{m+1}^-(z) \end{bmatrix} = z^{m+1/2} \begin{bmatrix} D_m^+(z) \\ D_m^-(z) \end{bmatrix} \{U_0^+(z) - U_0^-(z)\} \qquad (37)$$

where

$$\hat{U}_{m+1}^+(z) = U_{m+1}^+(z)/K_m \qquad (38)$$

$$\hat{U}_{m+1}^-(z) = U_{m+1}^-(z)/K_m. \qquad (39)$$

Now the inverse transfer function of the acoustic tube model is defined as

$$C_M^+(z) = \frac{\text{forward-going volume velocity}}{\text{component at the back end}}$$
$$\frac{}{\text{volume velocity at the front end}}$$

$$= \frac{\hat{U}_{M+1}^+(z)}{U_0^+(z) - U_0^-(z)}. \qquad (40)$$

The inverse transfer function between section m and the front end is thus defined as

$$C_m^+(z) = \frac{\hat{U}_{m+1}^+(z)}{U_0^+(z) - U_0^-(z)}. \qquad (41)$$

Likewise, if the inverse transfer function between $U_0^+(z) - U_0^-(z)$ and $\hat{U}_{m+1}^-(z)$ is defined as

$$C_m^-(z) = \frac{\hat{U}_{m+1}^-(z)}{U_0^+(z) - U_0^-(z)}, \qquad (42)$$

then from (37)

$$\begin{bmatrix} C_m^+(z) \\ C_m^-(z) \end{bmatrix} = z^{m+1/2} \begin{bmatrix} D_m^+(z) \\ D_m^-(z) \end{bmatrix}. \qquad (43)$$

By replacing m with $m+1$ in (43), and from (35),

$$\begin{bmatrix} C_{m+1}^+(z) \\ C_{m+1}^-(z) \end{bmatrix} = z^{(m/2)+1} \begin{bmatrix} D_{m+1}^+(z) \\ D_{m+1}^-(z) \end{bmatrix} = z^{(m/2)+1} \begin{bmatrix} 1 & -\mu_{m+1} \\ -\mu_{m+1} z^{-1} & z^{-1} \end{bmatrix} \begin{bmatrix} D_m^+(z) \\ D_m^-(z) \end{bmatrix} \qquad (44)$$

The term $z^{(m/2)+1}$ is due to the transmission delay and the true inverse transfer function is expressed by $D_m^+(z)$ and $D_m^-(z)$. Thus, from (44), the recursive relation is given by

$$\begin{bmatrix} D_{m+1}^+(z) \\ D_{m+1}^-(z) \end{bmatrix} = \begin{bmatrix} 1 & -\mu_{m+1} \\ -\mu_{m+1} z^{-1} & z^{-1} \end{bmatrix} \begin{bmatrix} D_m^+(z) \\ D_m^-(z) \end{bmatrix}. \qquad (45)$$

It is easily shown from (35) that $D_m^+(z)$ is an mth order polynomial in z^{-1} with a leading term of unity and that

$$D_m^-(z) = -z^{-(m+1)} D_m^+(1/z). \qquad (46)$$

C. Results

By inspection of (45) and (16), it is seen that the filtering processes of the optimal digital inverse filter and of the acoustic tube model are equivalent under the condition in (33). In particular, since the inverse transfer function $A_M(z)$ in Section III can be set equal to the acoustic tube inverse transfer function $D_M^+(z)$, a proof by induction shows

$$\mu_m = k_{m-1} \qquad (47)$$

and thus the recursive expression in (45) becomes identical to (16). Consequently, it is possible to extract the reflection coefficients directly from the acoustic speech waveform.

There are two ways of introducing boundary conditions in this acoustic tube model.

Case 1: The front end of the tube is short-circuited, and the back end of the tube is terminated with the characteristic impedance of $\rho c/S_{M+1}$. The tube is excited by the forward-going volume velocity component at the back end.

Case 2: The front end of the tube is terminated with the characteristic impedance of $\rho c/S_0$, and the back end of the tube is completely closed. The tube is excited by a constant volume velocity at the back end.

The method corresponds to use of the boundary conditions (1) (referred to as Case 1), while the boundary conditions (2) (referred to as Case 2) were used by Atal and Hanauer [12]. The differences between these two boundary conditions are significant. For Case 1, the reflection coefficient μ_0 is assumed to be 1, whereas the reflection coefficient μ_M can take an arbitrary value between 0 and 1. Thus the transfer function is constructed in a recursive manner, starting from the front end of the tube. The analysis procedure for this case is identical to that of the optimal inverse filter method in Section III, as it has been shown in this section.

On the other hand, for Case 2, the back end of the tube is closed (which corresponds to $\mu_M = 1$), while the reflection coefficient μ_0 can take an arbitrary value between 0 and 1. Thus the transfer function is constructed in a recursive manner, starting from the back end of the tube. Generally, the transfer function of Case 1 is not equal to that of Case 2. For both cases they become identical only if the μ_M in Case 1 is equal to the μ_0 in Case 2. In this instance, however, the optimal inverse filter method cannot be applied to Case 2 to extract the reflection coefficients in a correct order. Reasonable results can be obtained

337

experimentally for Case 1, as will be shown later, while Case 2 does not lead to reasonable results.

V. Discussion

It should be noted that the identity of the filtering process of the acoustic tube to that of the optimum inverse filter is obtained under the condition $z = \exp(j\omega \, 2\Delta l/c) = \exp(j\omega T)$. Consequently, the sampling frequency $F_s = 1/T$ and the number of sections $M = l/\Delta l$ (where l is the assumed vocal tract length) is constrained by $F_s = Mc/2l$. As long as the sampling frequency is constant, the vocal tract length is assumed to be fixed. It is known, however, that the vocal tract length for the utterance of various sounds varies even for a single speaker. How the area function is affected by assuming a fixed vocal tract length is currently being studied. Methods for estimating the vocal tract length from the acoustic speech waveform are also being studied.

In this analysis model, the loss is introduced by the terminated resistance at the back end of the tube. This can be observed in the following way. The coefficient of the highest term of the inverse transfer function $A(z)$ [i.e., a_M of (1)] obtained from analysis is determined only from bandwidths since the polynomial $A(z)$ has only real or conjugate roots. Since the coefficient a_M is equal to the reflection coefficient μ_M, the loss pertaining to the vocal tract is known to be controlled by the μ_M. Indeed, the characteristic impedance $\rho c/S_{M+1}$ is controlled by the μ_M since it is related to the area S_{M+1} by (31). The opening area S_{M+1} at the back end of the tube is determined in such a way that the terminating characteristic impedance causes proper bandwidths for resonant frequencies. By the termination of the characteristic impedance $\rho c/S_{M+1}$, the system is in a matched state; no forward-going reflected velocity component exists in the $(M + 1)$th section unless $U_{M+1}^+(z)$ is generated by a forced excitation source.

It is interesting to note that the synthesis model based on the optimal inverse filter method and the acoustic tube model under the boundary conditions of Case 1 can be represented by a lossless network excited by a source with a matched impedance so that the power of the excitation source is transferred into the network in the most efficient manner, and thus that the speech production process can be approximated by such an efficient network model.

In applying this method to actual analysis, the losses due to the glottal source and the radiation impedance are equalized independently since the system is assumed to be linear. Even a simple equalization such as a 6 dB/octave equalization, which takes into account the conventional values of -12 dB/octave slope for the glottal wave spectral envelope and 6 dB/octave slope for the radiation impedance, was

found to be essential for fairly reasonable results, whereas unusual tract shapes were obtained without equalization. Although it is difficult to describe quantitatively the effect of equalization on the area function, it was observed that the poles of the input impedance at the lips varied markedly, whereas its zeros (corresponding to formants) were only slightly affected.

From the identity of the filtering processes of the two models, reflection coefficients can be computed from (11) based on the autocorrelation function of the sampled speech (defined as Method A). The reflection coefficients can also be obtained by introducing Itakura's method [17]. The inverse filter can then be realized by cascaded digital filters by using the relation in (16), and the value k_{m-1} (thus the reflection coefficient μ_m) is known to be the correlation coefficient of the two outputs $\epsilon_{m,n}^+$ and $\epsilon_{m,n}^-$ of the $(m - 1)$th digital filter (defined as Method B). The detailed structure of the inverse filter thus constructed is shown in Fig. 4.

Computationally, Method A is faster than Method B. However, Method B gives some physical insight into the filtering processes of the two models (see Appendix I). Furthermore, in case of hardware implementation, Method B allows us to process the sampled data time-serially, whereas Method A requires a window length of data to compute the autocorrelation function at the beginning of the analysis.

The transfer function obtained from a given positive area function is stable, and the area function obtained from a stable transfer function is also assured to be positive. The proof is given in Appendix II.

VI. Analysis Algorithm

The analysis procedures for extracting the reflection coefficients directly from the speech wave and for determining the discrete area function can be summarized as follows.

1) Let $\{w_n\}$ define the sampled speech data obtained by sampling the analog speech waveform $w(t)$ at a sampling rate of $F_s = Mc/2l$.

2) Equalization corresponding to the inverse of the glottal and radiation characteristics must be applied to $\{w_n\}$. For example, an approximate 6 dB/octave preemphasis via $\{x_n\} = \{w_{n+1} - w_n\}$ was used to obtain the analysis results shown later.

3) There are two ways to compute the reflection coefficients.

Method A: From the preprocessed N-length sample sequence $\{x_n\}$, the autocorrelation function is computed by the use of (8). Then, at step zero, $a_0 = 1$. At step 1, $\mu_1 = k_0 = -r_1/r_0$ is computed from (11), and $\{a_i^{(1)}\}$ can be computed from $a_0^{(0)}$ and k_0 by the use of (10). In the same fashion, at step M, $\mu_M = k_{M-1}$ is computed from (11), and the $\{a_i^{(M)}\}$ are computed from k_{M-1} and $\{a_i^{(M-1)}\}$ by the use of (10).

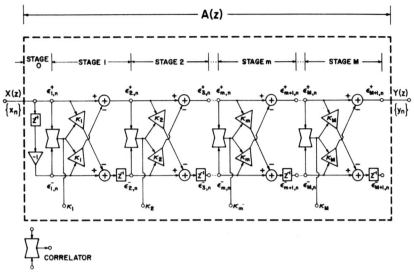

Fig. 4. Detailed structure of the optimum inverse filter ($K_m = k_{m-1}$).

Method B: The preprocessed sample sequence is processed by the digital inverse filter as shown in Fig. 4. The reflection coefficient μ_m is obtained at stage m for $m = 1, 2, \cdots, M$, by computing the correlation coefficient of the outputs of the previous filter via

$$\mu_m = k_{m-1} = \frac{\sum_{n=0}^{N+m-1} \epsilon_{m,n}^+ \epsilon_{m,n}^-}{\left\{ \sum_{n=0}^{N+m-1} \epsilon_{m,n}^{+2} \sum_{n=0}^{N+m-1} \epsilon_{m,n}^{-2} \right\}^{1/2}}. \quad (48)$$

After computing k_m for $m = 0, 1, 2, \cdots, M^{-1}$, $\{a_i^{(M)}\}$ is computed from (10).

4) The discrete area function can be computed from (31) as

$$S_m = \frac{1 + \mu_m}{1 - \mu_m} S_{m+1}, \quad m = M, M-1, \cdots, 1. \quad (49)$$

Since the area of each section is determined in a relative manner, the final area function is obtained, for example, by specifying $S_{M+1} = 1$.

5) From the filter coefficients, formant frequencies can be determined by applying Markel's method [10]. Thus the simultaneous extraction of the vocal tract area function and the formant frequencies is possible.

VII. Experimental Results

A program was written for a PDP-8 digital computer with 4096 12-b words of core. A sampling frequency of 7 kHz was used to digitize analog speech. An approximate equalization of +6 dB/octave spectral slope was used to account for the conventional values of -12 dB/octave slope for the glottal wave spectral envelope and +6 dB/octave slope for the radiation impedance. This was simply realized by differencing the original sampled speech. A 20-ms window length

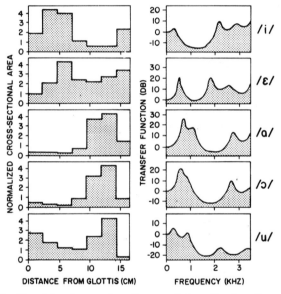

Fig. 5. Vocal tract area functions and transfer functions obtained for five American vowels.

of sampled speech was obtained and differenced and then a Hamming window was applied.

Five vowels uttered by a male American speaker were analyzed. The normalized area functions of these vowels are shown in Fig. 5 together with their corresponding transfer functions. Gross features of each vowel are extracted fairly well. However, we do not have enough data to check the validity of this method in a direct way at the moment. The synthesis of the area function from given acoustic data obtained by Fant [2] showed that this method seems reasonable.

As further examples, analysis results of a diphthong /aɪ/ are shown in Fig. 6. It should be noted that continuous changes of the area function are extracted quite stably and that the release of and the formation of each vowel constriction are depicted quite well. The changes of the area function can be visually com-

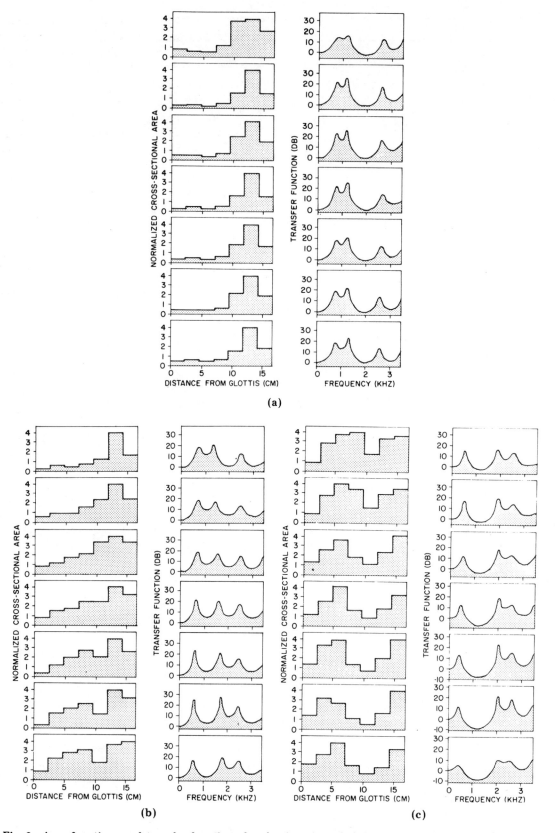

Fig. 6. Area functions and transfer functions for the American diphthong /aɪ/: window length 30 ms; window shift 20 ms.

pared with the changes of the transfer function. Figs. 7 and 8 show examples of the vowel-consonant-vowel utterances /ibɑ/ and /igɑ/, respectively.

VIII. Conclusion

Under the assumption of the linear speech production process, it was shown that the filtering process

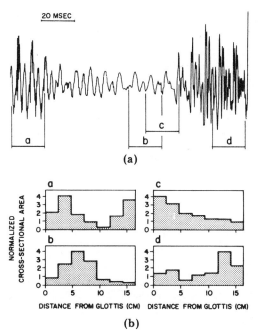

Fig. 7. Vocal tract area functions for the VCV utterance /iba/.
(a) The sound wave. (b) Area functions for the four segments specified in (a).

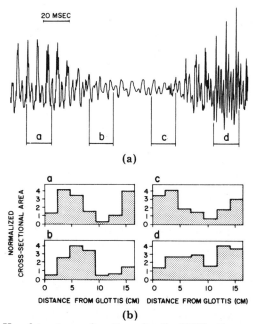

Fig. 8. Vocal tract area functions for the VCV utterance /iga/.
(a) The sound wave. (b) Area functions for the four segments specified in (a).

of the lossless nonuniform acoustic tube model of the vocal tract is identical to that of the optimal inverse filter model for proper boundary conditions at the glottis and the lips.

From the experimental results in the previous section, it is concluded that fairly reliable area functions for voiced sounds may be extracted by the present method. Although it is possible to obtain the dynamic description of the vocal tract configuration for vowel-consonant, consonant-vowel, or vowel-consonant-vowel utterances, it is not yet possible to obtain valid

configurations for tightly constricted vocal tract conditions. It is also difficult to derive isolated consonantal configurations for voiceless consonants. However, it may be possible to extract transitional configurations from or to voiced sounds reasonably well. Since this method does not include side branching, it is not well suited for nasal sounds, although an equivalent single tube representation for these sounds might be useful in the recognition problem. To obtain more reliable results, it is necessary to have better ways to account for the glottal wave shape and for losses involved in speech production. A study of effectiveness of this method by using a proper inverse glottal filter is in progress.

Even within the limitations mentioned above, the development of this analysis method should be of considerable importance in its application to major areas of speech research. In the area of basic study in articulatory and acoustic phonetics, it appears that although detailed studies of the acoustical and physiological features of various phone types have been pursued, there is still a need to know more about direct relationships between physiological and acoustical features. What might be called articulatory-acoustic phonetics seems to be necessary to bridge between physiological and acoustic phonetics, and the analysis method presented here may be particularly useful in this line of research. Especially in automatic speech recognition, the combination of articulatory and acoustic parameters will certainly raise the efficiency and the capability of recognition.

In application to the study of pathological speech, it may be possible to detect the site of alteration of the vocal tract shape due to obstruction in the vocal tract (e.g., a neoplasm) and evaluate the kind of speech problems that the patient will have after the surgery. Another potential application in this area is as an aid for the speech training of deaf persons. A visual display of the vocal tract shape might be a promising substitute for the display of speech spectra.

Appendix I

An Interpretation of the Filtering Process

In the acoustic tube model, the process between the right-hand side of the junction $d = d_{m+1}$, and the right-hand side of the junction $d = d_m$ (see Fig. 3) can be made clear by expressing the relation of the volume velocity components in (32) as

$$U_m^+(z) = z^{-1/2} \frac{K_{m-1}}{K_m} \{ U_{m+1}^+(z) + \mu_m U_m^-(z) \} \quad (50)$$

$$U_{m+1}^-(z) = z^{-1} \frac{K_m}{K_{m-1}} \{ -\mu_m U_m^+(z) + U_m^-(z) \}. \quad (51)$$

This process, which is shown in Fig. 9, can be interpreted as the speech production process at that por-

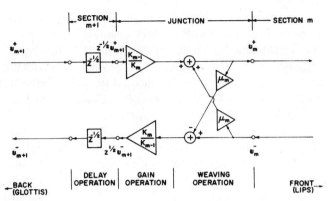

Fig. 9. Process at the junction between sections m and $m + 1$.

tion of the acoustic tube model. As indicated in the figure, the process consists of three operations: a delay operation, a gain operation, and a weaving operation. The latter two operations occur at the junction. The normalization of the volume velocity components $U_{m+1}^+(z)$ and $U_{m+1}^-(z)$ by K_m can be interpreted as the separation of the gain operation. Considering the identity of the reflection coefficient μ_m to the correlation coefficient of the outputs $\epsilon_{m,n}^+$ and $\epsilon_{m,n}^-$ of filter stage $m - 1$ at the junction d_m (see Fig. 4), the weaving operation can be interpreted as an addition of the correlation to the forward traveling wave, which is formed into the partial correlation between x_n and $x_{n-(m+1)}$ over all n in the output speech wave, and a subtraction of the correlation from the backward traveling wave. Thus the optimal inverse filtering of the speech wave by the least mean square error criterion is nothing more than the undoing of this intricate weaving operation.

Appendix II

Realizability

It is shown that a stable transfer function is realized from a given positive area function and that the positive area function is assured from a given stable transfer function.

1) For a given area function, and $|\mu_m| < 1$, let the unit circle contour be denoted as Γ and the domain outside Γ be denoted as Ω in the z plane. Then $D_m^+(z)$ and $D_m^-(z)$ in (45) are both analytic in the region Ω for $m = 1, 2, \cdots, M$. Now, from (45)

$$D_1^+(z) = D_0^+(z) - \mu_1 D_0^-(z) = 1 + \mu_1 z^{-1}. \quad (52)$$

Consequently, the root of $D_1^+(z)$, $-\mu_1$, is inside the unit circle. Assume that $D_m^+(z)$ has all its zeros inside the unit circle (and thus no zeros in the region Ω). Since $|\mu_m| < 1$,

$$|-\mu_{m+1} D_m^-(z)| < |D_m^+(z)| \quad (53)$$

for all z on the contour Γ for $m = 1, 2, \cdots, M$, since

$|D_m^+(z)| = |D_m^-(z)|$ on the contour Γ. Thus, by Roche's theorem [18], $D_m^+(z)$ and $D_{m+1}^+(z) = D_m^+ - \mu_{m+1} D_m^-(z)$ have the same number of zeros in the region Ω. By mathematical induction, $D_{m+1}^+(z)$ has no zeros in the region Ω.

2) If $D_{m+1}^+(z) = D_m^+(z) - \mu_{m+1} D_m^-(z)$ and $D_m^+(z)$ have no zeros in the region Ω, the following integral must be zero, according to the residue theorem:

$$\int_\Gamma \left[\frac{D_{m+1}^{+'}(z)}{D_{m+1}^+(z)} - \frac{D_m^{+'}(z)}{D_m^+(z)} \right] dz$$

$$= \int_\Gamma \frac{\left(1 + \dfrac{-\mu_{m+1} D_m(z)}{D_m^+(z)} \right)'}{1 + \dfrac{-\mu_{m+1} D_m^-(z)}{D_m^+(z)}} dz$$

$$= \log \left[1 + \frac{-\mu_{m+1} D_m^-(z)}{D_m^+(z)} \right] \Bigg|_\Gamma = 0 \quad (54)$$

where the primes denote differentiation. Since $\log z$ has a branch point at the origin and has a cut along the negative real axis in the z plane, the value of $1 + [-\mu_{m+1} D_m^-(z)/D_m^+(z)]$ must remain in the circle with center 1 and radius 1 in order to satisfy (54). Thus on the contour the following inequality holds:

$$|-\mu_{m+1} D_m^-(z)/D_m^+(z)| < 1. \quad (55)$$

Since $|D_m^+(z)| = |D_m^-(z)|$ on the contour Γ,

$$|\mu_{m+1}| < 1. \quad (56)$$

Thus, if $D_m^+(z)$ has all its zeros inside the unit circle, the absolute value of the reflection coefficients must be less than one, which assures the positive area from (31).

Appendix III

In the inverse filter analysis, four representations for (16) are possible, depending upon the definitions of k_m and $B_m(z)$.

(A)

$$\begin{bmatrix} A_{m+1}(z) \\ B_{m+1}(z) \end{bmatrix} = \begin{bmatrix} 1 & k_m \\ k_m z^{-1} & z^{-1} \end{bmatrix} \begin{bmatrix} A_m(z) \\ B_m(z) \end{bmatrix} \quad (57)$$

where

$$k_m = -\beta_m / \alpha_m$$

and

$$B_m(z) = z^{-(m+1)} A_m(1/z).$$

(B)

$$\begin{bmatrix} A_{m+1}(z) \\ B_{m+1}(z) \end{bmatrix} = \begin{bmatrix} 1 & -k_m \\ -k_m z^{-1} & z^{-1} \end{bmatrix} \begin{bmatrix} A_m(z) \\ B_m(z) \end{bmatrix} \quad (58)$$

where

$$k_m = -\beta_m/\alpha_m$$

and

$$B_m(z) = -z^{-(m+1)}A_m(1/z).$$

(C)

$$\begin{bmatrix} A_{m+1}(z) \\ B_{m+1}(z) \end{bmatrix} = \begin{bmatrix} 1 & -k_m \\ -k_m z^{-1} & z^{-1} \end{bmatrix} \begin{bmatrix} A_m(z) \\ B_m(z) \end{bmatrix} \quad (59)$$

where

$$k_m = \beta_m/\alpha_m$$

and

$$B_m(z) = z^{-(m+1)}A_m(1/z).$$

(D)

$$\begin{bmatrix} A_{m+1}(z) \\ B_{m+1}(z) \end{bmatrix} = \begin{bmatrix} 1 & k_m \\ k_m z^{-1} & z^{-1} \end{bmatrix} \begin{bmatrix} A_m(z) \\ B_m(z) \end{bmatrix} \quad (60)$$

where

$$k_m = \beta_m/\alpha_m$$

and

$$B_m(z) = -z^{-(m+1)}A_m(1/z).$$

On the other hand, in the acoustic tube analysis, two representations for (45) are possible, depending upon the definitions of the reflection coefficient μ_m and $D_m^-(z)$:

(a)

$$\begin{bmatrix} D_{m+1}^+(z) \\ D_{m+1}^-(z) \end{bmatrix} = \begin{bmatrix} 1 & -\mu_{m+1} \\ -\mu_{m+1} z^{-1} & z^{-1} \end{bmatrix} \begin{bmatrix} D_m^+(z) \\ D_m^-(z) \end{bmatrix} \quad (61)$$

where

$$\mu_m = \frac{S_m - S_{m+1}}{S_m + S_{m+1}}$$

and

$$D_m^-(z) = -z^{-(m+1)}D_m^+(1/z).$$

(b)

$$\begin{bmatrix} D_{m+1}^+(z) \\ D_{m+1}^-(z) \end{bmatrix} = \begin{bmatrix} 1 & \mu_{m+1} \\ \mu_{m+1} z^{-1} & z^{-1} \end{bmatrix} \begin{bmatrix} D_m^+(z) \\ D_m^-(z) \end{bmatrix} \quad (62)$$

where

$$\mu_m = \frac{S_{m+1} - S_m}{S_{m+1} + S_m}$$

and

$$D_m^-(z) = -z^{-(m+1)}D_m^+(1/z).$$

The representation in (B) corresponds to (a), as shown in Sections III and IV, and (D) corresponds to (b). The representation (A) was used in [19], and (C) was used in [17]. Thus care must be taken in comparison to other studies.

Acknowledgment

The author wishes to thank Dr. D. J. Broad, Dr. J. D. Markel, and Dr. A. H. Gray, Jr. for their valuable comments and discussions.

References

[1] T. Chiba and M. Kajiyama, *The Vowel, Its Nature and Structure.* Tokyo: Kaiseikan, 1941.
[2] G. Fant, *Acoustic Theory of Speech Production.* The Hague, The Netherlands: Mouton, 1960.
[3] O. Fujimura, H. Ishida, and S. Kiritani, "Computer controlled dynamic cineradiography," *Ann. Bull.* (Res. Inst. Logopedics and Phoniatrics), Univ. Tokyo, no. 2, pp. 6-10, 1968.
[4] P. Ladefoged, J. F. K. Anthony, and C. Riley, "Direct measurement of the vocal tract," *Univ. California, Los Angeles, Working Papers in Phonetics,* no. 19, pp. 4-13, June 1971.
[5] M. R. Schroeder, "Determination of the geometry of the human vocal tract," *J. Acoust. Soc. Amer.,* vol. 41, part 2, pp. 1002-1010, Apr. 1967.
[6] P. Mermelstein, "Determination of the vocal-tract shape from measured formant frequencies," *J. Acoust. Soc. Amer.,* vol. 41, pp. 1283-1294, May 1967.
[7] A. Paige and V. W. Zue, "Computation of vocal tract area functions," *IEEE Trans. Audio Electroacoust.,* vol. AU-18, pp. 7-18, Mar. 1970.
[8] B. Gopinath and M. M. Sondhi, "Determination of the shape of the human vocal tract from acoustical measurements," *Bell Syst. Tech. J.,* vol. 49, pp. 1195-1214, July-Aug. 1970.
[9] B. S. Atal, "Determination of the vocal tract shape directly from the speech wave," *J. Acoust. Soc. Amer.,* vol. 47 (A), p. 64, Jan. 1970.
[10] J. D. Markel, "Formant trajectory estimation from a linear least-squares inverse filter formulation," Speech Commun. Res. Lab., Inc., Santa Barbara, Calif., SCRL Monograph, Oct. 1971.
[11] F. Itakura and S. Saito, "Analysis synthesis telephony based on the maximum likelihood method," in *Rep. 6th Int. Congr. Acoust.,* Y. Kohashi, Ed., Tokyo, 1968, C-5-5.
[12] B. S. Atal and S. L. Hanauer, "Speech analysis and synthesis by linear prediction of the speech wave," *J. Acoust. Soc. Amer.,* vol. 50, part 2, pp. 637-655, Aug. 1971.
[13] R. Matsuda, "Tonal differential limen of the speech transmission system containing single dip in frequency-response," in *Rep. 6th Int. Congr. Acoust.,* Y. Kohashi, Ed., Tokyo, 1968, A-109.
[14] H. Wakita and S. Saito, "Tonal differential limen of music and speech transmitted through multi-resonance system," in *Rep. Meeting Acoust. Soc.,* Japan, Tokyo, 1965, 71, 1-2-18.
[15] E. A. Robinson, *Statistical Communication and Detection.* New York: Hafner, 1967, pp. 274-279.
[16] P. M. Morse and K. U. Ingard, *Theoretical Acoustics.* New York: McGraw-Hill, 1968, pp. 244-252.
[17] F. Itakura, "Extraction of feature parameters of speech by statistical method," in *Proc. 8th Symp. Speech Information Processing,* RIEC Tohoku Univ., Sendai, Japan, Feb. 1971, pp. II-5-1-II-5-12.
[18] G. A. Korn and T. M. Korn, *Mathematical Handbook for Scientists and Engineers.* New York: McGraw-Hill, 1961, p. 194.
[19] J. D. Markel and A. H. Gray, Jr., "Autocorrelation equations as applied to speech analysis," *IEEE Trans. Audio Electroacoust.,* vol. AU-21, pp. 69-79, Apr. 1973.

Part V
Analysis/Synthesis Systems

A major application of speech analysis techniques is in obtaining efficient representations of speech for transmission or storage.

The first paper in this part by Dudley, describes the first attempt at implementing a speech analysis/synthesis system. Dudley called his system a vocoder "because it operates on the principle of deriving voice codes." The basic idea of the channel vocoder was to represent the vocal tract response characteristics by a crude estimate of the magnitude of the short-time Fourier transform. This, together with a voiced/unvoiced classification and an estimate of the pitch period constitute the classical channel vocoder representation. The basic principles established by Dudley are still the basis for a wide range of speech representations and the term "vocoder" has come to mean any system in which speech is analyzed into a parametric representation and then reconstructed by using the parameters to control an appropriate synthsizer (i.e., model for speech production). The second paper, by Schroeder, is a tutorial review of the vocoder field through 1966. Although recent developments based on LPC methods are not covered, this paper summarizes many ideas that continue to surface in slightly different forms in the context of digital implementations.

The third paper in this section is a brief note by Flanagan which is concerned with estimates of the minimum bit-rate required to represent vowel sounds. Flanagan arrives at an estimate of 200–400 bps. Although this estimate ignores considerations of naturalness and quality, it never-the-less serves as an important bench mark in judging the efficiency of vocoder systems.

The fourth paper, by Gold and Rader, is a detailed exposition of the design of channel vocoders. Although the paper is written with analog implementation in mind, it contains useful information on vocoder filter design, digital coding of channel signals, and channel vocoder excitation. A worthwhile feature of this paper is a short section headed "Listening to Vocoders." The admonitions of this part section should be required reading for all those who are involved in the design of vocoders of any type.

A fundamental problem in vocoder analyzers is the estimation of pitch and voicing. The voice excited vocoder (VEV), as discussed in the fifth paper, by David et al., was proposed as a way around the pitch detection problem. In this scheme, the voice pitch is represented by a narrow lowpass band which retains the harmonic structure of voiced speech. At the vocoder synthesizer, a wideband flat spectrum signal is generated from the lowpass band by a nonlinear operation. This idea, which was originally proposed for channel vocoders, has also been used in linear predictive vocoders [1–3] and it could in principle be used in any scheme where excitation and vocal tract parameters are separated.

Another scheme designed to get around the pitch detection problem was the phase vocoder proposed by Flanagan and Golden in the sixth paper of this section. Their solution was to represent the speech signal by a complex short-time Fourier representation (actually magnitude and time derivative of phase). This approach was shown to be capable of high quality and considerable flexibility in manipulating speech parameters. The seventh paper, by Portnoff, shows how the FFT can be used to improve the computational efficiency of short-time Fourier analysis and synthesis. This paper summarizes and extends the results of an earlier paper by Schafer and Rabiner [4], in which the FFT was applied to analysis and it was shown that exact reconstruction of the speech signal from its complex short-time Fourier transform is possible under some conditions. This fact together with efficient digital implementations such as described in [5] offer the possibility of processing operations beyond the scope of this section.

The eighth paper, by Oppenheim, describes an analysis/synthesis system based on homomorphic filtering of the speech signal. In this system the vocal tract response is represented by the low-time portion of the short-time cepstrum. The homomorphic vocoder is of interest due to advances in integrated circuits which promise efficient implementation of discrete Fourier transforms [6].

The last four papers of this section are concerned with linear predictive vocoders, which are based on the linear predictive analysis techniques described in the papers of previous sections. The LPC representation can take many forms; e.g. predictor coefficients, polynominal roots, area function of a lossless tube, reflection coefficients, cepstrum, log area ratios, etc. Since it is relatively simple to transform between these different representations, there is considerable flexibility in choice of parameter set for quantization and in the choice of synthesizer form. The ninth paper, by Itakura and Saito, describes and introduces the notion of quantization of PARCOR (or reflection) coefficients so as to minimize a spectrum error measure. The next paper, by Markel, gives more detail on the implementation of a complete LPC vocoder in which reflection coefficients are quantized. The last two papers, by Viswanathan and Makhoul and Gray and Markel respectively, are concerned with a detailed study of quantization and bit allocation in LPC vocoders. These papers introduce transformations of the reflection coefficients that make the synthesized spectrum less sensitive to quantization of the LPC parameters.

References

1. B. S. Atal, M. R. Schroeder, and V. Stover, "Voice-excited predictive coding system for low bit-rate transmission of speech," *Proc. IEEE Internat. Conf. on Communications,* pp. 30–37, 30–40, San Francisco, 1975.

2. C. J. Weinstein, "A linear predictive vocoder with voice excitation," *Proc. EASCON,* Sept. 1975.

3. D. Estaban and C. Galand, "9.6/7.2 KBPS voice excited predictive coder (VEPC)," *1978 IEEE Internat. Conf. on Acoust., Speech, and Signal Proc.,* pp. 307–311, Tulsa, Apr. 1978.

4. R. W. Schafer and L. R. Rabiner, "Design and simulation of a speech analysis-synthesis system based on short-time fourier analysis," *IEEE Trans. Audio Electroacoust.,* vol. Au-21, pp. 165–174, June 1973.

5. J. B. Allen and L. R. Rabiner, "A unified theory of short-time spectrum analysis and synthesis," *Proc. IEEE,* vol. 65, pp. 1558–1564, Nov. 1977.

6. T. F. Quatieri, "CCD CZT spectral analysis applied to real time homomorphic speech analysis-synthesis," *1978 IEEE Internat. Conf. on Acoust., Speech, and Signal Proc.,* pp. 445–449, Tulsa, Apr. 1978.

The Vocoder

By HOMER DUDLEY
Circuit Research Department

AT THE World's Fairs in New York and San Francisco great interest was shown in the speech synthesizer in the Bell System exhibits. Known as the Voder, this device creates spoken sounds and combines them into connected speech. Its raw materials are two complex tones, a hiss and a buzz; selection of one or the other and its intensity and tone quality are controlled by an operator through a keyboard.*

The Voder is an offshoot of a more extensive system, first demonstrated† in its experimental stage some three years ago. That system analyzed

---

*RECORD, *Feb.* 1939, *p.* 170.
†RECORD, *Dec.* 1938, *p.* 98.

spoken sounds, and then used the information to control the synthesizing circuit. At the time World's Fair displays were under consideration, so it was naturally perceived that the synthesizer, manually controlled, could be made into a dramatic demonstration. Development was for a while concentrated in that field; as a successful Voder became assured, attention was shifted back to the broader and parent system. Shortly thereafter the system was given the name "Vocoder" because it operates on the principle of deriving voice codes to re-create the speech which it analyzes.

Figure 1 shows the over-all circuit for remaking speech; the analyzer is at the left and the synthesizer at the right. Electrical speech waves from a microphone are analyzed for pitch by the top channel and for spectrum by a group of channels at the bottom.

In the pitch analysis the fundamental frequency, which for simplicity will be called the pitch, is measured by a circuit containing a frequency-discriminating network for obtaining this frequency in reasonably pure form; a frequency meter for counting, by more or less uniform pulses, the current reversals therein; and a filter for eliminating the actual speech frequencies but retaining a slowly changing current that is a direct measure of the pitch. (Unvoiced sounds, whether in whispering or the unvoiced sounds of normal speech, have insufficient power to operate the frequency meter.) The output current of the pitch channel is then a pitch-defining signal with its current approximately proportional to the pitch of the voiced sound and equal to zero for the unvoiced sounds.

There are ten spectrum-analyzing channels,* the first handling the frequency range 0–250 cycles and the other nine, the bands, 300 cycles wide, extending from 250 cycles to 2950 cycles, a top frequency which is representative of commercial telephone circuits. Each spectrum-analyzing channel contains the proper band filter followed by a rectifier for measuring the power therein and a 25-cycle low-pass filter for retaining the current indicative of this power but eliminating any of the original speech frequencies.

The operation of the analyzer is illustrated in Figure 2 by a group of oscillograms taken in analyzing the sentence "She saw Mary." To insure that the same speech was analyzed in obtaining the various oscillograms, the sentence was recorded on a high-quality magnetic-tape recorder and reproductions therefrom supplied current to the analyzer. The speech-

---

*A 30-channel vocoder covering the wide range of speech frequencies required for high quality has also been built and is being used as a tool in laboratory investigations.

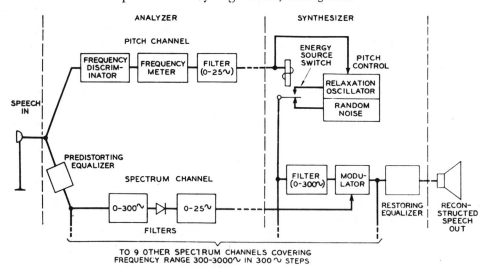

Fig. 1—*Simplified schematic of the Vocoder*

December 1939

wave input to the analyzer is shown in the line next to the bottom while the output is shown in the other oscillogram traces; the pitch-defining signal is at the bottom in the figure and the ten spectrum-defining signals in numerical order at the top. For convenient reference the oscillograms are lined up together whereas in the actual circuit the speech-defining signals lag about 17 milliseconds behind the speech-input wave. The inaudible speech-defining output signals contain all the essential speech information as to the input wave, but it is to be noted that they are slow-changing and in this way correspond to lip or tongue motions, as contrasted with the higher audible vibration rates of the rapid-changing speech wave itself. The dropping of the pitch to zero for the unvoiced sounds "sh" and "s" is also readily seen.

Figure 2 gives an idea also as to the synthesizing process. In the analyzer the speech wave is the input and the eleven speech-defining signals are the output; in the synthesizer the eleven speech-defining signals are the input and the speech wave the output.

The steps in speech synthesis are indicated at the right of Figure 1. The relaxation oscillator is the source of the buzz; and the random noise circuit the source of the hiss. The hiss is connected in circuit for unvoiced sounds and for quiet intervals. (In the latter case no sound output from the synthesizer results because there are no currents in the spectrum channels.) When a voiced sound is analyzed a pitch current other than zero is received with the result that the buzz is set for the current pitch by the "pitch control" on the relaxation oscillator; also, the relay marked "energy source switch" operates, switching from the hiss source to the buzz source.

December 1939

The outputs from the spectrum-analyzing channels are fed to the proper synthesizing spectrum controls with the band filters lined up to correspond. The power derived from the energy sources of the synthesizer in these various bands is then passed through modulators under the control of the spectrum-defining currents. The result is that the power output from the synthesizer is sensibly proportional in each filtered band to that measured by the analyzer in the original speech. From the loudspeaker comes, then, speech approximately the same in pitch and in spectrum as the original. This synthetic speech lags the original speech by about 17 milliseconds due to the inherent delay in electrical circuits of the types used.

In the present models of the Vocoder, control switches have been introduced which permit modifications in the operation of the synthesizer. Through the manipulation of these controls interesting effects are produced. Some of the possibilities of the Vocoder were recently demonstrated by the author and his associate, C. W. Vadersen, before the Acoustical Society of America and before the New York Electrical Society. In those presentations Mr. Vadersen supplied by his own voice the incoming speech which was picked up by a microphone as shown in the headpiece; and at the same time he manipulated the controls to produce desired effects. A remote-control switch was also provided through which, for purposes of comparison, the author could switch the microphone directly to the loudspeaker and so let the audience hear how the speech would sound if it had not been modified by the Vocoder.

In these demonstrations comparison is first made between direct speech and the best re-creation that the apparatus could make. Then by manipulation of dials and switches, speech is modified in various ways. Normal speech becomes a throaty whisper when the hiss is substituted for the buzz. Although the hiss is relatively faint, it is shown to be essential for discrimination as between "church" and "shirts."

Ordinarily the re-created pitch moves up and down with that of the original. If variation is prevented, the re-created speech is a monotone, like a chant. When the relative variation is cut in half, the voice seems flat and dragging; when the swings are twice normal, the voice seems more brilliant; when four times normal it sounds febrile, unnatural. The controls can be reversed so that high becomes low: the tune of a song is then unrecognizable, and speech has some of the lilting characteristics of Scandinavian tongues. Another control fixes the basic value of the re-created pitch; if this is "fluttered" by hand, the voice becomes that of an old person. By appropriate setting of the basic pitch, the voice may be anything from a low bass to a high soprano, and several amusing tricks can be performed. In one of these, the basic pitch is set to maintain a constant ratio of 5 to 4 to the original. This is a "major third" higher and harmonizes with the original. In two-part harmony, the demonstrator then sings a duet with himself. Connecting a spare synthesizer set for a 3 to 4 ratio he then sings one part in a trio, the others being taken by his electrical doubles. Finally, with the basic pitch-control of the apparatus, he becomes a father reprimanding his daughter; then the girl herself, and then becomes the grandfather interceding for the youngster.

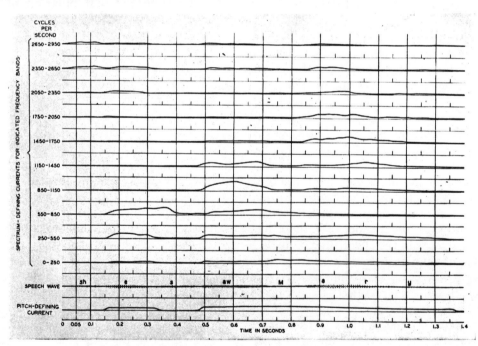

Fig. 2—The original speech wave and an analysis of its components, expressed as the variation of several direct currents

December 1939

350

For the vocal-cord tones of the original, the Vocoder substitutes the output of a relaxation oscillator. But any sound rich in harmonics can be used: an automobile horn, an airplane roar, an organ. In some demonstrations, the sound, taken from a phonograph record, replaces the buzz input from the oscillator. Keeping careful time with the puffs of a locomotive, the demonstrator can make the locomotive puff intelligibly "We're - start - ing - slow - ly - faster, faster, faster" as the puffs come closer together. Or a church bell may say "Stop - stop - stop - don't - do - that." A particularly striking effect is that of singing with an organ to supply the tones. Although the words may be spoken, the demonstrator usually sings them to hold the rhythm. It makes no difference whether his voice is melodious or not; the tonal quality comes only from the musical source.

These tricks and others have suggested uses for the Vocoder in radio and sound pictures. It appears to have possibilities as a tool in the investigation of speech, since by its numerous controls important variables in speech can be isolated for study. The engineering possibilities which may grow out of the application of the principles employed in this device are hard to predict at the present time. The speech-defining currents, however, do have features of simplicity and inaudibility which may open the way to new types of privacy systems or to a reduction in the range required for the transmission of intelligible telephonic speech.

Vocoders: Analysis and Synthesis of Speech

(A Review of 30 Years of Applied Speech Research)

M. R. SCHROEDER

Abstract—Techniques for analysis and synthesis of speech signals are reviewed with emphasis on vocoders and related devices for more efficient transmission and storage of speech. Selected applications of speech coding methods as sensory aids to the handicapped are described.

I. INTRODUCTION

IN OCTOBER, 1928, Homer Dudley of Bell Telephone Laboratories sketched in his technical notebook a device which subsequently became known as "vocoder"—a term derived from the words VOice and CODER.

Originally, the vocoder was conceived as a means for the efficient transmission of speech signals, especially over long and expensive telephone circuits. In ordinary telephone transmission, the bandwidth allotted for one talker is approximately 3000 Hz, from 200 Hz to 3200 Hz. This portion of the speech spectrum is sufficient to ensure adequate speech quality and intelligibility for many purposes. However, Dudley [1] has shown that speech signals can be transmitted over a fraction of that bandwidth if proper coding methods are used. The vocoder was the first device to realize the promised economy.

Dudley's demonstration implied that much of the natural speech signal is redundant (in the information theory sense) and that efficient speech coding methods are available both for transmission and storage of voice signals. Consequently, it is not surprising that, in the 37 years since its invention, the vocoder has blossomed into a great variety of speech coding devices with many useful applications in the transmission, storage, and encryption of speech signals.

Although the synthetic speech of early vocoders was plagued by an unpleasant "electrical accent," modern vocoders can sound surprisingly natural and are showing good promise for actually improving the quality of speech signals degraded by noise, nonlinear distortion, reverberation, and spectral distortion. A case in point is the "Donald Duck" speech from deep-sea divers, breathing a helium-oxygen mixture, which can be restored to high intelligibility by vocoder methods.

In addition, the vocoder and its relatives have found many unexpected applications as aides for the handicapped. Speech compression devices similar to the vocoder allow the blind to "speed hear" recorded books and the partially deaf better to understand speech. "Tactile vocoders" permit the deaf to "feel" the sounds of speech.

Vocoders also are finding increased use for secure transmission of speech signals—secure in accordance with the most exacting requirements of our government.

II. SPEECH PRODUCTION AND PERCEPTION

Articulation and Spectra

Speech sounds are produced by air escaping from the lungs. The steady (or "dc") air flow from the lungs is partially converted into pulsating (or "ac") energy by one or more of the following three mechanisms:

1) The action of the *vocal cords* (Fig. 1) which chops up the steady flow of air into short pulses.
2) Turbulence created at narrow constrictions in the *vocal tract.*
3) Sudden release of excess pressure following a complete closure of the vocal tract at some point along its length.

The acoustic ac-signal created in this manner, called the *excitation function* of speech, can take three distinct forms in accordance with these three modes of dc-to-ac conversion:

1) quasi-periodic pulses
2) continuous noise, and
3) a single pulse.

Most speech sounds are generated by only one of these excitation functions. Mode 1 provides energy for *voiced* speech sounds such as the vowels, *a*, *i*, *u*, etc. Mode 2 is active during *unvoiced* sounds such as the *fricatives*, *s*, *f*, etc. Mode 3 provides for the unvoiced *plosives*, *p*, *t*, and *k*. Some speech sounds are made from a mixture of two excitation functions, and a few English speech sounds utilize all three modes of excitation.

The spectra of the excitation functions cover a broad frequency range with significant spectral components over much of the audio frequency range. To produce the different speech sounds for each mode of excitation, the broadband excitation signals are "filtered" by the vocal tract. The frequency response of the vocal tract depends upon the positions of the tongue, the lips, and other articulatory organs (Fig. 2). The response of the vocal tract is characterized by a number of resonances or *formants* (typically three below 3000 Hz) which shape the spectrum of the excitation function, and give rise to the

Manuscript received March 7, 1966. The author is with Bell Telephone Laboratories, Inc., Murray Hill, N. J.

Reprinted from *Proc. IEEE*, vol. 54, pp. 720–734, May 1966.

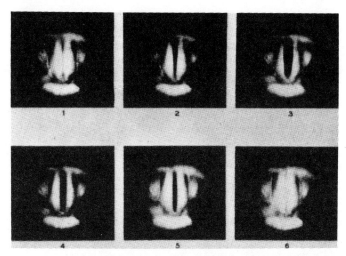

Fig. 1. Vocal cords at six different instants of a fundamental period from onset of parting (1), through maximum opening (3), back to complete closure (6). The pictures are from individual frames of a high-speed motion picture taken at 4000 frames per second [80].

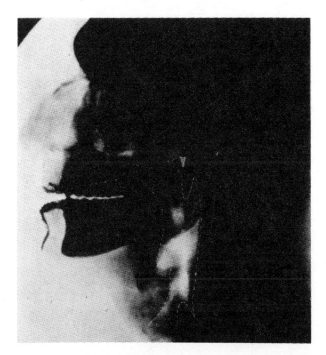

Fig. 2. X-ray picture of the human head showing the vocal tract (dashed outline) between the vocal cords (lower right) and the lips (left). The beginning of the nasal tract is also visible at the upper right. In this picture, it is nearly closed off by the soft palate or "velum" (from [19]).

quality or timbre characteristic of each speech sound.

When the vocal tract has uniform cross-sectional area along its entire length between the vocal cords and the lips, its formant frequencies fall near 500 Hz, 1500 Hz, and 2500 Hz. These frequencies correspond to $\lambda/4$, $3\lambda/4$, and $5\lambda/4$ resonances of a 17-cm long uniform pipe which is closed at one end and open at the other. This condition is approximated during the so-called *neutral vowel* (an unstressed "uh" sound as in "*above*"). For most vowels the cross-sectional area deviates significantly from uniformity, and the formant frequencies are shifted upward or downward from their neutral positions. In general, below about 5000 Hz, the vocal tract can be considered a nonuniform transmission line with variable terminal impedances: the driving impedance represented by the vocal cords and the radiation impedance of the mouth opening.[1] At higher frequencies, *transverse* acoustic modes are propagated in the vocal tract and the simple transmission line analogy ceases to hold.

A simplified block diagram for the production of vowels is shown in Fig. 3. The dc-air flow from the lungs is converted into ac-acoustic energy by the vocal cords whose spectrum is modified by the resonances of the vocal tract. The output speech signal $s(t)$ appearing at the lips is the convolution of the excitation function $e(t)$, representing the air flow at the vocal cords, with the impulse response of the filter representing the vocal tract:

$$s(t) = \int_{-\infty}^{t} e(\tau) \cdot h(t - \tau) \, d\tau. \qquad (1)$$

After taking Fourier transforms (designated by capital letters) on both sides of (1), the convolution turns into a multiplication,

$$S(f) = E(f) \cdot H(f). \qquad (2)$$

Thus, the spectrum of the speech signal is the product of the excitation spectrum $E(f)$ and the transfer function of the vocal tract $H(f)$.

By taking absolute values, one obtains the *amplitude spectrum* of the speech signal,

$$|S(f)| = |E(f)| \cdot |H(f)|. \qquad (3)$$

In actual speech, both the excitation spectrum and the transfer function vary with time. Thus, infinite-time spectral analysis has to be replaced by *short-time* spectral analysis [2], [3], employing a *time window* comparable in duration to the shortest speech sounds. In practice, to preserve adequate spectral resolution, time windows with a width of up to 40 ms are often used, although some speech sounds may be somewhat shorter.

[1] For some speech sounds, the transmission function of the vocal tract is characterized by zeros in addition to its poles. This is the case for plosive and fricative sounds where the excitation is not at the vocal cords but at a constriction somewhere between the vocal cords and the lips. Zeros in the transmission function also occur for *nasal* sounds (such as *m* and *n*), for which a side branch, the *nasal tract*, is coupled to the vocal tract at the velum (Fig. 2).

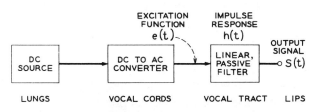

Fig. 3. Block diagram representing the production of voiced speech sounds.

The results of short-time analysis depend on running time; the spectra become functions of time. This is reflected in the notation

$$|S(f, t)| = |E(f, t)| \cdot |H_t(f)|, \qquad (4a)$$

where $|H_t(f)|$ is the transfer function of the vocal tract at time t. If the transfer function can be considered stationary during the analysis period, (4a) is an exact relation; otherwise it is only an approximation—the goodness of the approximation depending on the stationarity of $|H_t(f)|$. For normal speaking rates and analysis periods not exceeding 40 ms, the effects of time-varying transfer functions can usually be neglected.

Since spectral amplitudes are often measured in decibels, the following logarithmic form of (4a) is particularly convenient:

$$20 \log_{10} |S(f, t)| = 20 \log_{10} |E(f, t)|$$
$$+ 20 \log_{10} |H_t(f)|. \qquad (4b)$$

In this form, the effects of the excitation function and the transfer function are additive. This seemingly trivial conversion has some important consequences, as we shall see.

Figure 4(a) shows the short-time spectrum of the utterance "I triple E Proceedings" uttered by an adult male speaker of American English. The picture was obtained by a sound spectrograph [4], [5], an indispensable tool in speech research, using a time-window of about 3-ms duration. Time runs along the abscissa, frequency along the ordinate. The different shades of grey signify different spectral intensities, black corresponding to the highest value of $|S(f, t)|$ and white to the lowest. The curving black bands represent the formant frequencies. The irregularly stippled patches indicate aperiodic (noise-like) excitation for unvoiced speech sounds.

Figure 4(b) shows a *spectrogram* of the same utterance but with a longer analysis time (20 ms) and correspondingly higher spectral resolution ($\Delta f = 50$ Hz). As a result, the individual harmonics of voiced sounds become visible in the spectrogram (the nearly horizontal narrow lines).

For more detailed analyses of speech signals, the short-time spectrum at one instant in time or "section" may be obtained. Figure 5 is a section for the "EE" sound in "Proceedings." In Fig. 5, the abscissa is frequency (from right to left) and the ordinate is the logarithmic spectrum $20 \log_{10} |S(f, t_0)|$. The individual harmonics are visible as sharp spikes while the formants are represented by the smooth outline or "envelope."

Figure 5 suggests an alternative representation of the short-time spectrum, namely in terms of its *spectral envelope* $|G(f, t)|$ indicated by a dashed line, and the *spectral fine-structure* $|F(f, t)|$:

$$20 \log_{10} |S(f, t)| = 20 \log_{10} |F(f, t)|$$
$$+ 20 \log_{10} |G(f, t)|. \qquad (5)$$

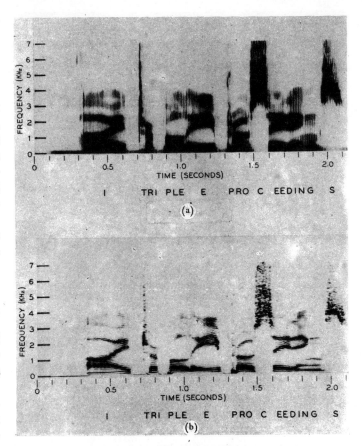

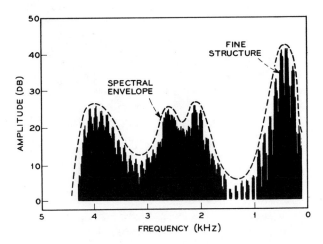

Fig. 4.   (a) Speech spectrogram of the utterance "I triple E Proceedings" (wide-band analysis). (b) Same as (a) but narrow-band analysis.

Fig. 5.   Logarithmic spectrum of "ee" sound in Proceedings. Spectrum envelope shows four peaks or formants. The fine structure corresponds to a fundamental frequency of about 110 Hz.

For voiced speech sounds, $|F(f, t)|$ has equidistant maxima at the fundamental frequency f_0 and its overtones or *harmonics*; for unvoiced sounds, $|F(f, t)|$ is a continuous function of frequency.

In spite of the formal similarity of the two representations of the short-time speech spectrum expressed in (4b) and (5), they are fundamentally different, and it is the latter representation, in terms of spectral fine-structure and envelope, that forms the basis of most spectral analysis and synthesis methods of speech. The reason is that speech spectra can often be separated into fine structure and envelope. By contrast, the excitation function is *not* directly accessible in a speech signal. In fact, recovery of the excitation function from a speech signal is one of the more difficult tasks in speech research [6]–[9].

Auditory Analysis and Speech

Three basic properties of human hearing bear on the analysis and synthesis of speech signals.

1) The ear performs a short-time spectral analysis.
2) For monaural perception, the ear is relatively insensitive to phase.
3) The ear is exceedingly sensitive to the periodicity (pitch) of speech signals.

The view of the ear as a spectrum analyzer insensitive to phase was first put forward by Ohm and von Helmholtz [10], who thought of the basilar membrane in the inner ear as an array of tuned resonators resembling the strings of a piano. This simplified view was later corrected by von Békésy [11], who demonstrated the existence of *traveling waves* on the basilar membrane. The model of the basilar membrane as a bank of simple resonators had to be abandoned in favor of a description as a nonuniform transmission line with limited spectral resolution. The acute frequency discrimination of the ear cannot be accounted for mechanically and has been assumed to occur in the neural processing [11].

The view that the ear is totally "phase deaf" (Ohm's law of Acoustics) has had to be qualified [12], [13]. However, the fact remains that, for speech signals, presented monaurally, phase is a relatively minor factor, having some influence on the quality of voiced speech sounds heard over earphones, but probably having no effect on intelligibility [14]. For listening in a reverberant environment, which randomizes the phase angles of the individual harmonic components, no perceptual effects due to phase have been reported. However, one important qualification should be kept in mind: phase distortions that correspond to delay distortions exceeding 50 milliseconds modify the *short-time amplitude* spectrum and are therefore audible—typically as a reverberant quality of the speech signal. In fact, speech can be made unintelligible by sending it through allpass networks with sufficiently large delay distortion.

The perceptual acuity for pitch or spectral fine structure is based on the powerful frequency discrimination of auditory perception. For example, for a frequency component near 1000 Hz, "difference limens" (just noticeable differences) as small as 3 Hz have been reported [15]. The exact mechanism of this astounding frequency discrimination (which seems to violate the "uncertainty relation" $\Delta f \cdot \Delta t \geq 1$) is still unknown. But it is clear that it must reside in the neural processing because the mechanical resolution of the ear is more than a magnitude poorer.

Other important perceptual effects are related to difference limens for formant frequencies and amplitudes [16], [17], spectral zeros, nonlinear distortions, frequency displacement [18], and other parameters. An excellent review of speech perception can be found in a recent book by J. L. Flanagan [19].

III. Spectral Analysis and Synthesis of Speech
The Spectrum Channel Vocoder

Most methods for analyzing and synthesizing speech are based on a parametric description of the short-time spectrum or an equivalent representation of the speech signal. The many different analysis and synthesis schemes are distinguished by different choices of parameters.

The oldest method for speech analysis-synthesis employing a parametric description of the short-time speech spectrum is the *spectrum-channel vocoder*. In it, the spectral envelope $|G(f, t)|$ (5) is represented typically by 10 to 20 samples spaced along the frequency axis. The spectral fine structure $|F(f, t)|$ is represented by one additional parameter which measures the fundamental frequency f_0 of voiced sounds and is equal to zero for unvoiced sounds or silence.

A block diagram of a spectrum channel vocoder is shown in Fig. 6. The speech signal is separated into 14 contiguous spectral bands with bandwidths between 100 Hz and 400 Hz covering the frequencies from 200 Hz to 3200 Hz. This frequency range, typical of telephone signals, permits high intelligibility and good quality. The output of each filter is connected to a rectifier and low pass filter whose output represents the time-varying average signal amplitude for each frequency band. Together, these 14 *channel signals* represent the envelope of the short-time spectrum of the speech signal.

Also shown in Fig. 6 are a voiced-unvoiced detector and a pitch detector which determine the fine structure of the speech signal and produce a corresponding narrow-band signal. These 15 narrow-band signals are combined into a single signal with a total bandwidth of 15 by 20 Hz = 300 Hz. Thus, the transmission bandwidth is only one-tenth of that required for the original speech signal. (In practice, some additional bandwidth is needed to avoid filters with unduly long delay for the separation of the transmitted signal into the individual channel signals.)

For digital transmission, the saving is even greater. For a sampling rate of 40 per second, allowing 3 bits per sample for the 14 channel signals and 6 bits per sample for the pitch signal, the vocoder analyzer output can be represented by a total bit rate of $40 \cdot (14 \cdot 3 + 6)$ bits/second = 1920 bits/second. This is less than one-twentieth of the bit rate required to represent the original speech signal (7000 samples/second times 7 bits/sample or approximately 50 000 bits per second); however, the voice quality of existing vocoders operating at such low bit rates is noticeably inferior.

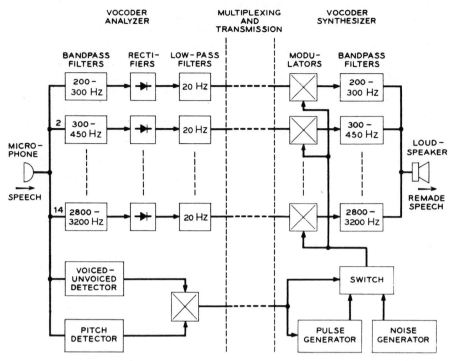

Fig. 6.   Block diagram of spectrum channel vocoder. A speech signal applied to the input at the left is represented by 15 narrow-band signals with a total bandwidth of 300 Hz or one tenth of its original bandwidth. The vocoder synthesizer on the right utilizes these narrow-band signals to synthesize a replica of the original speech signal.

At the synthesizer, the original channel signals are recovered and utilized to control the frequency response of a time-varying filter (consisting of modulators and narrow band-pass filters) to correspond to the spectral envelope measured at the analyzer. The input of this time-varying filter is supplied with a flat spectrum excitation signal of the proper spectral fine structure (quasi-periodic pulses for voiced speech sounds, or "white" noise for unvoiced sounds).

A spectrum-channel vocoder like the one just described was first built by H. W. Dudley. A mechanically operated speech synthesizer, an outgrowth of Bell Laboratories' vocoder work, was demonstrated at the New York World's Fair in 1939. During World War II, vocoders began to be used for the efficient transmission of encrypted speech.

After the war, it became apparent that speech processors based on the vocoder principle had great potential as sensory aids. By applying the spectrum channel signals of a vocoder to mechanical vibrators attached to the finger-tips, deaf persons can be made to "feel" speech [20], [21]. Spectral distortions, as in the speech of deep-sea divers breathing helium-oxygen mixtures, can be corrected by proper tailoring of filter pass bands and rescaling of frequencies in a vocoder synthesizer [22]. These are but some of the many applications that have resulted from the original invention of the vocoder.

More Parsimonious Descriptions of Speech Signals

The transmission of the spectral envelope information in terms of spectral samples, although leading to sub-stantial savings, does not represent the ultimate in economic speech transmission. It is known that spectral samples, especially adjacent channel signals of vocoders, are significantly correlated. Kramer and Mathews [23] have therefore suggested linear transformation of the channel signals into a smaller number of uncorrelated signals before transmission.

This method requires that the correlation matrix c_{ik} of the channel signals $g_k(t)$ first be determined:

$$c_{ik} = \overline{g_i(t)g_k(t)}, \qquad i, k = 1, 2, \cdots, K$$

where the bar indicates a long-time average. By definition, c_{ik} is a square $(K \times K)$ symmetric matrix. It has, therefore, K real eigenvalues $\lambda_1 \geq \lambda_2 \geq \cdots \geq \lambda_K$ and K orthonormal eigenvectors $h_k^{(1)}, h_k^{(2)}, \cdots, h_k^{(K)}$.

In order to achieve the desired economy, the channel signals are expanded in terms of R $(R < K)$ eigenfunctions. The selected eigenfunctions are those that have the R largest eigenvalues. The recovered approximate channel signals are

$$\tilde{g}_k(t) = \sum_{r=1}^{R} \alpha_r(t)h_k^{(r)}, \qquad k = 1, 2, \cdots, K, \qquad (6)$$

where

$$\alpha_r(t) = \sum_{k=1}^{K} g_k(t)h_k^{(r)}, \qquad r = 1, 2, \cdots, R \qquad (7)$$

are the transmitted signals.

The approximate channel signals $\tilde{g}_k(t)$, representable

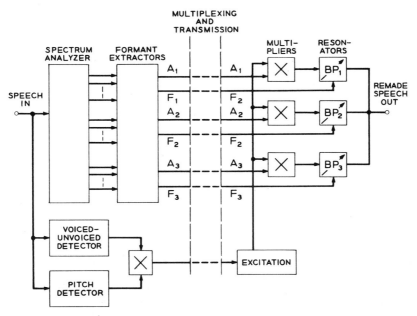

Fig. 7.   Formant vocoder using parallel synthesis. Formant amplitudes and frequencies are extracted in
the analyzer, on the left, and utilized to control modulators and variable parallel filters, on the right,
to produce an artificial speech signal.

by linear combinations of the first R eigenfunctions, are the best approximation (in the mean square error sense) to the original $g_k(t)$. The mean square error ϵ_R^2 is

$$\epsilon_R^2 = \sum_{k=R+1}^{K} \lambda_k^2. \tag{8}$$

For $R = K$ (i.e., no reduction in number of channel signals), the error is zero, as expected.

Reductions of about 2 to 1 in the number of channel signals have been realized in practice by this method. However, in spite of relatively small errors ($\epsilon_R^2 \ll 1$ for $R \geq K/2$), the quality of the synthetic speech recreated from such reduced representations has not been satisfactory. The reason is that our ears do not measure speech degradation in terms of mean square error in the amplitude spectrum. It has been surmised that an error criterion based on the logarithmic spectrum may be a better predictor. However, such error criteria attach too much weight to errors in the small-valued channel signal whose contribution to the output signal may be insignificant or inaudible because of masking effects [24].

Peak Picking

Another approach to reducing the number of channels to be transmitted is known as *peak picking* [25]. In its simplest form, it means transmitting only those channel signals that are larger than their neighbors. For independent or positively correlated channel signals, typically one third of their number are relative maxima at a given moment in time. Thus, a reduction of 3 to 1 in the number of signals to be transmitted can be achieved.

The resulting economy may be substantial, especially for digital transmission of vocoder signals which is particularly well suited for peak picking schemes. For a

15-channel digitized vocoder with a sampling rate of 40 per second and 3 bits per sample, the bit-rate for the channel signals would drop from 1800 bits/second to 600 bits/second. However, additional information capacity is required to transmit the channel *numbers* of the selected channels. Since there are fewer than 2^{11} possibilities of distributing 5 maxima over 15 channels, an additional 11 bits per sampling interval should be sufficient. Thus, the net reduction is from 1800 bits/second to 1040 bits/second.

In more ambitious schemes of peak picking, constraints reflecting the possible positions of the lower three formant frequencies are added in the selection of maxima. Thus, even greater economies are achieved. In fact, the analyzer of such a vocoder resembles that of formant vocoders which represent the next higher degree of abstraction in spectral analysis-synthesis of speech.

Formant Vocoders

The spectral envelopes of many speech sounds are characterized by several prominent maxima. These represent the resonances of the vocal tract called "formants"—a term derived from musicology. Below 3000 Hz, typically three formants are found in adult speech.

In a formant vocoder, the analyzer attempts to determine the frequency locations of the major formants. Signals corresponding to the formant locations are transmitted and utilized to control the resonances of a formant synthesizer consisting of three or more single-tuned resonant circuits. For vowels excited exclusively at the vocal cords, the formant frequencies (and bandwidths) suffice to specify the entire spectral envelope [26]. A preferred method of synthesis for this case is the *serial* synthesizer [27].

An alternative, the so-called parallel synthesizer, is

shown in Fig. 7. This arrangement is advantageous for consonant synthesis. Both formant amplitudes and frequencies are extracted from the speech signal and utilized at the synthesizer to control modulators and tuneable resonators. The excitation can be the same as in spectrum channel vocoders.

Formant synthesizers, when supplied with proper control signals, are capable of producing surprisingly natural speech [24], [28], [29]. However, the automatic extraction of sufficiently accurate control signals poses problems.

Measurement of Formant Frequencies

The simplest method of measuring a formant frequency is to separate, by means of filters, one formant from the others, and to measure the rate of axis crossings of the resulting "one-formant" speech signal. For a periodic speech signal, formant frequencies measured in this manner are necessarily multiples of the fundamental frequency. Thus, for a female voice with a fundamental frequency of 200 Hz, measured formant frequencies (200 Hz, 400 Hz, 600 Hz, etc.) may deviate from their actual values by as much as 100 Hz, which is several times larger than perceptual *difference limens* [16].

This inaccuracy can be avoided by frequency shifting the speech signal by single-sideband modulation. In this manner, an *anharmonic* signal can be created whose average axis-crossing rate represents the formant frequency more accurately than that of the original harmonic signal.

Another method of formant frequency measurement is based on spectral moments, such as the centroid of the signal spectrum in a formant frequency band. The centroid or mean frequency can be measured by subdividing the total speech band into several sub-bands and measuring the signal amplitude a_n in each. The desired mean frequency is then approximately

$$f_{mean} \approx \sum_n a_n f_n \bigg/ \sum_n a_n, \qquad (9)$$

when f_n is the center frequency of the nth sub-band [30].

Spectral moments can also be measured by operating on the signal in the time domain without the help of filters. It can be shown that [31]

$$f_{mean} \approx \frac{1}{2\pi} \overline{\left| \frac{d}{dt} s(t) \right|} \bigg/ \overline{|s(t)|}, \qquad (10)$$

where the horizontal bars indicate time averages and the vertical bars denote absolute values (full-wave rectification).

However, the methods of formant frequency measurement sketched here, and many others, do not cope with the most difficult problem: the separation of a speech signal into sub-bands containing one and only one formant each. The difficulty stems from the fact that formant frequency ranges overlap each other.

The problem can, in principle, be solved by a method called "analysis-by-synthesis" [32], in which artificial spectra are generated (for example, on a computer) and, by proper iteration, matched to the spectrum of a speech signal. The formant frequencies of the spectrum generator are then taken as those of the actual speech signal. Analysis-by-synthesis is an accurate method of measuring formant frequencies (and bandwidths). However, a fairly complicated analog computer is required to perform the necessary iterations in real time. In speech research, if real-time operation is not required, *digital* computers are used for analysis-by-synthesis.

An ingenious method which, like analysis-by-synthesis, avoids the problem of overlapping formant frequency ranges has recently been suggested [33]. In it, the largest peak of the logarithmic spectral envelope of a speech signal is located and the logarithmic spectrum of a formant centered at the largest peak is *subtracted* from the speech spectrum. The process is repeated four to five times with the largest peak of remaining spectrum playing the role of the original maximum. The bandwidths of the subtracted formants are chosen to equal the expected bandwidth for the frequency of the maximum. The successive absolute maxima are not necessarily all formants—nor must they occur in the order of increasing frequency. However, experience has shown that the three lowest admissible frequency values found by this method correspond to the frequencies of the first three formants.

Since the method avoids multiplication and other time-consuming operations, it is amenable to real-time processing even on smaller digital computers [34]. A computer controlled formant synthesizer has recently been demonstrated [35].

Pattern-Matching Vocoders

Pattern-matching vocoders [36] aim at abstraction of spectral information even greater than that represented by formant vocoders. At prescribed instants in time, the best match between the short-time speech spectrum and a set of stored spectral patterns is determined. A code representing the best match is transmitted to a vocoder synthesizer which produces a speech signal with the selected spectrum.

A crucial question for pattern matching vocoders concerns the number of discrete patterns required to represent the virtually unlimited variety of speech spectra. Digital data rates for the transmission of spectral patterns are estimated [37] to be on the order of 500 bits/second, corresponding to 1024 equi-probable spectral patterns at a sampling rate of 50 samples/second.

Correlation Vocoders

The autocorrelation function of a signal is the Fourier Cosine-Transform of its power spectrum and vice versa [38]. A similar relationship can be shown to hold for

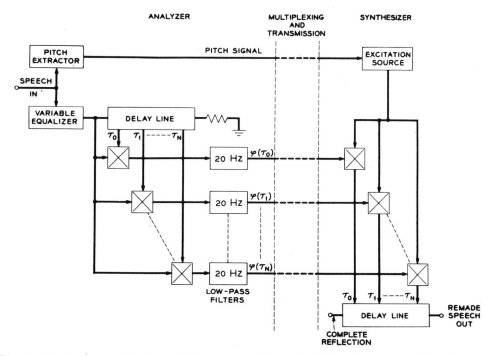

Fig. 8. Block diagram of autocorrelation vocoder. Narrow-band signals representing the short-time autocorrelation function of an equalized speech signal are derived in the analyzer on the left. The synthesizer is a time-varying symmetric transversal filter whose impulse response is controlled by the autocorrelation signals.

short-time spectra and autocorrelation functions [2], [3]. Thus, a speech signal can be represented by a time-varying short-time autocorrelation function instead of its short-time spectrum. This representation is the basis of *autocorrelation vocoders* [39], [40].

A block diagram of an autocorrelation vocoder is shown in Fig. 8. In the analyzer, an equalized speech signal is multiplied by itself delayed by various amounts $\tau_0, \tau_1, \cdots, \tau_n$ with a delay increment smaller than half the reciprocal bandwidth. The products are low-pass filtered to about 20 Hz to form correlation channel signals $\phi(\tau_0), \phi(\tau_1), \cdots, \phi(\tau_n)$.

The time-varying signals $\phi(\tau_n)$ represent a short-time autocorrelation function and can be used to synthesize speech in the time domain. The time-domain synthesizer shown in Fig. 8 consists of a time-varying symmetric transversal filter whose impulse response is a replica of the short-time autocorrelation function for delays between $-\tau_n$ and $+\tau_n$. The excitation signal applied to the synthesizer has a flat spectrum envelope and the proper fine-structure (quasi-periodic pulses for voiced speech sounds and "white" noise for unvoiced sounds). Hence, the spectrum envelope of the synthetic signal at the output of the synthesizer equals the spectrum of the autocorrelation function which in turn corresponds to the *power* spectrum of the input signal. Thus, without special precaution, autocorrelation vocoders produce output signals whose spectrum is the *square* of the spectrum of the input signal. While spectrum squaring does not destroy the intelligibility of speech, it does give rise to an unnatural "bouncy" quality. Also, all level differences in the original spectrum are doubled. Thus,

weaker formants are suppressed relative to strong formants.

To overcome the adverse effects of spectrum squaring, autocorrelation vocoders require special equalizers which perform a spectrum square-rooting operation. Such an equalizer is shown in Fig. 9. In it, the speech signal is divided into three broad frequency bands. For each band, the average amplitude is determined and square-rooted. Then the three signals are recombined to form an equalized signal which, after spectrum squaring, will have a spectrum that approximates that of the original speech signal.

The spectrum squaring inherent in autocorrelation analysis can also be avoided by cross-correlation analysis [41], [40]. A cross-correlation analyzer is illustrated in Fig. 10. It resembles the autocorrelation analyzer shown in Fig. 8. However, the speech signal is multiplied by delayed replicas of a *spectrally flattened* speech signal, i.e., a speech signal whose spectral envelope has been equalized to be nearly constant. The synthesizer is identical to the one shown in Fig. 8 for the autocorrelation vocoder. It produces signals whose spectral envelope approximates that of the original speech signal rather than its square.

A related approach to speech coding is the *harmonic vocoder* [42], in which the short-time spectral envelope is expanded into a Fourier series (by a resistance matrix, for example) whose coefficients are than transmitted to the synthesizer. Speech can then be synthesized either directly in the time domain, as shown in Fig. 8, or, after another Fourier transformation, by a filter-bank synthesizer such as the one illustrated in Fig. 6.

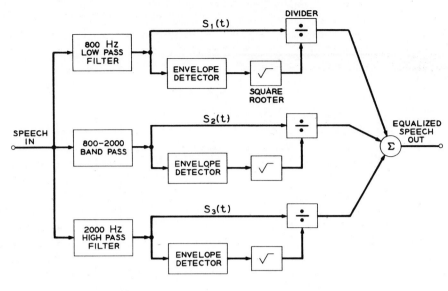

Fig. 9. Block diagram of spectrum square rooter used in autocorrelation vocoder.

CROSS–CORRELATION ANALYZER

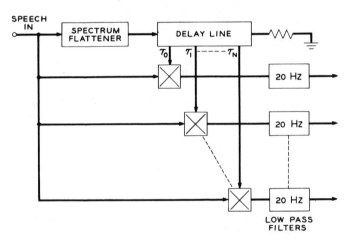

Fig. 10. Block diagram of cross-correlation analyzer. The spectrum
flattener makes the spectral envelope of the input speech signal
nearly independent of frequency and time in order to avoid
spectrum squaring effects. The corresponding synthesizer is the
same as that for an autocorrelation vocoder (see Fig. 8).

Correlation and harmonic vocoders as described here suffer from two major disadvantages.

1) Their channel signals, representing a time-domain description of the speech signal, require better signal-to-noise ratios for transmission over analog circuits or more bits per sample for digital transmission than corresponding spectrum-channel signals.

2) The equivalent spectral resolution of correlation vocoders is independent of frequency. Thus, they do not allow the progressive widening of analyzing filter bandwidth with increasing frequency that permits spectrum channel vocoders to cover the frequency scale by relatively few bands. In order to attain comparable qualities, the number of channel signals in correlation vocoders usually has to be considerably greater than that of spectrum channel vocoders.

Laguerre Expansion Vocoders and Beyond

In principle, speech signals or their spectra can be expanded according to any of a large number of orthogonal and complete systems of functions. The choice depends on the desired speech quality, available transmission facilities, and on the state of the instrumentation art.

Expansions in terms of orthogonalized exponentials [43] and Laguerre functions [44] are particularly attractive. The required filtering networks can be synthesized by cascading RC-circuits; inductances are not required. In addition, the Fourier transforms of the Laguerre function have decreasing frequency resolution with increasing frequency—a property they share with the basilar membrane, and which is believed to be advantageous for the efficient coding of speech spectra.

With smaller and cheaper solid-state circuits, especially integrated circuits [45], becoming available, many speech processing systems, previously forbiddingly complex, are now attracting attention. In addition, the new technology stimulates thinking along entirely new lines. The possibility of completely eliminating conventional filters in speech processing systems is one of the strongest motives for searching for fresh approaches and exploiting new technology.

The Excitation Problem in Speech Synthesis

Experience with vocoders and speaking machines, extending over several decades, has shown that the excitation function used in the synthesis of speech is very critical. Until fairly recently, vocoders of all descriptions spoke with an unpleasant "electrical accent," which seemed to defy correction. In the 1950's, it was finally established that the excitation function was primarily responsible for the unflattering quality of vocoder speech. It appeared that the human auditory system is extremely sensitive to errors in the excitation function, particularly the fundamental frequency (pitch) and the voiced-unvoiced dichotomy. Many years of concentrated efforts in speech analysis were required before a satisfactory solution could be found to the "pitch problem." This is the problem of determining, with the accuracy demanded by the ear, whether a speech signal is voiced or unvoiced and, if voiced, the pitch. Partial successes had been achieved in the laboratory with high-quality, noise-free speech signals. But the available methods were inadequate to cope with the large variety of speech signals encountered in telephony.

In principle, measurement of the fundamental frequency is simple. All that is required is a low-pass filter to reject higher harmonics and an axis-crossing counter [46]. This approach does indeed work—provided the signal contains a strong fundamental frequency component and is sufficiently noise-free. Otherwise, the axis-crossing intervals of the fundamental component have an additive random component. If these random fluctuations exceed 50 microseconds, they are audible as a "roughness" in the synthetic speech signal.

Another problem stems from the fact that fundamental frequencies range over more than an octave in frequency. In fact, fundamental frequencies in normal speech cover a range of more than 10 to 1, from below 50 Hz for low-pitched adult male speakers to above 500 Hz for children. Thus, fixed filters are not capable of suppressing the higher harmonics and isolating the fundamental. However, this difficulty has been overcome to some extent by filters automatically tracking the fundamental frequency—provided it is present in the signal.

In telephone signals, the lower portion of the speech spectrum, which contributes little to speech intelligibility but may contain the fundamental frequency, is often missing. Thus, the fundamental frequency has to be recreated from the available portion of the speech spectrum. Since the frequency difference between adjacent harmonics equals the fundamental frequency, nonlinear operations which create difference frequencies will, in general, give rise to frequency components at the fundamental frequency. The best-known processes for this purpose are rectification (half-wave or full-wave) or "envelope detection" (see Fig. 11). However, fundamental components so recreated have indeterminate phase angles. During transitions from one speech sound to the next, the phase of the recreated fundamental can change, leading to undesirable phase or frequency modulation of the fundamental frequency. Figure 11 shows a speech signal during such a transition. In spite of a constant fundamental frequency, time intervals between successive envelope peaks vary widely. This frequency modulation is easily detected by the ear in vocoded speech: the effect is that of a rather inhuman quaver [47].

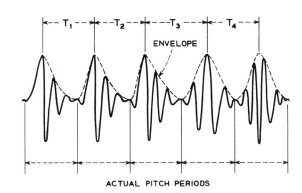

Fig. 11. Simplified speech waveform during phoneme transition. Spacing between envelope maxima varies although fundamental period remains constant.

Also, the presence of the fundamental frequency in the envelope cannot be assured. The amplitude of a fundamental frequency recreated from a wide-band (constant-amplitude) speech signal tends to be Rayleigh-distributed, the same distribution that governs radio multipath fading and sound propagation in concert halls. Thus, "fading" of the fundamental frequency component by as much as 40 dB, relative to its average intensity, is not uncommon. Given the fact that speech signals themselves vary considerably in intensity, the total amplitude range of the fundamental component exceeds the capabilities of most circuits unless exceedingly noise-free conditions prevail.

The problem is further aggravated by the extreme sensitivity of the ear to frequency mentioned above. Also, if only one out of 100 fundamental periods is incorrectly measured, the error *rate*, for a fundamental frequency of 100 Hz, will be one error per second. The resulting speech quality is unacceptable for many applications.

Perhaps the most valiant attack on the pitch problem was mounted by means of autocorrelation analysis [48]–[50], a technique which has proved its value for time interval measurements (range finding) in wartime radar [51].

The autocorrelation function of a signal has an absolute maximum for zero delay ($\tau = 0$). For a perfectly periodic signal, a like maximum occurs for a delay of one pitch period ($\tau = T$). However, for real speech and *short-time* analysis, the value of the correlation function for $\tau = T$ is usually considerably less than the absolute maximum; in fact, it can even be smaller than secondary maxima corresponding to the periodicities of the formants. This is true especially during fast pitch inflections or rapid formant glides in the transitions from one speech sound to the next—in general, when the signal lacks periodicity.

In an attractive variant of autocorrelation analysis for periodicity measurements, a speech signal is *subtracted* from itself delayed by various amounts. The difference signal, for a delay corresponding to the fundamental period, is zero [52]. For real speech, the amplitude of the difference signal will tend to be small but, during rapid transitions, it may become larger than the difference signal for other delays—again leading to erroneously measured periods [53].

Until recently, autocorrelation analysis and its variations have been the most sophisticated approach to the pitch problem. However, ultimately, autocorrelation analysis, like so many other approaches, failed because of the interaction and inseparability of formant frequencies (spectral envelope) and fundamental frequency (spectral fine structure). Solutions to this problem, so fundamental to all speech analysis, are discussed subsequently.

Over the years, there have been many more attempts to solve the pitch problem, including some rather ingenious failures. But the above discussion may suffice to illustrate the difficulties—technical and perceptual——inherent in the pitch problem. For further details, the reader may refer to a comprehensive review by McKinney [54].

The "High-Fidelity" Vocoder

In 1957, J. R. Pierce suggested the use of "semi-vocoders" [55] to transmit high-quality speech with a bandwidth of 10 kHz over regular telephone lines with a bandwidth of 3 kHz. (In a semi-vocoder, a portion of the speech spectrum, usually a low-frequency band, is transmitted without processing while the remaining portion of the speech spectrum is vocoded.) The practicality of such a "high-fidelity" vocoder was doubtful because, by intent, its quality was to be superior to that of an uncoded speech signal. As expected, the major difficulty was presented by the excitation problem aggravated by the requirement that the pitch of the vocoded portion of the signal match that of the original speech signal [56].

The solution of the excitation problem for the high-quality semi-vocoder led to a new principle of vocoder excitation called "voice excitation."

A *voice-excited vocoder* (VEV) is illustrated in Fig. 12. The excitation signal for the vocoder synthesizer is obtained from the uncoded "baseband" by a process called *spectrum-flattening* [57]. A spectrum-flattener performs two functions: first, the spectrum of the baseband signal is spread out, by nonlinear distortion, to cover the frequency band to be synthesized; then the frequency components generated by the nonlinear distortion are equalized to form a flat-spectrum excitation signal. The equalization is usually achieved "instantaneously" by means of a bank of contiguous band-pass filters, to which the signal is applied, followed by hard limiters ("infinite clippers") [58]. Alternatively, fast automatic gain controls can be used.

A spectrum flattener using clippers is shown in Fig. 13. In some voice-excited vocoder synthesizers, the level to which the output signal from each band-pass filter is clipped is made proportional to the corresponding spectral amplitude of the original speech signal. In this case, a synthetic speech signal appears at the output rather than a flat-spectrum signal. The second column of band-pass filters removes nonlinear distortion components introduced by the hard limiters.

With the high-fidelity vocoder and subsequent VEV's, vocoder speech lost much of its unnatural "buzzy" quality. The pitch inflection and voiced-unvoiced intervals of the original speech signal are reproduced with great fidelity. Talker identification, previously one of the weak points of vocoder speech, is almost as good as in natural speech of the same bandwidth [59], [60]. However, to accommodate the uncoded baseband, VEV's require a larger transmission bandwidth.

The success of the new excitation method stems from its avoidance of any decision-making processes which are always liable to error. The excitation signal in a VEV has inherently the correct periodicity; for an aperiodic input, the output of the spectrum-flattener is also aperiodic and, for a periodic input, the output will be periodic with the same periodicity.

Speech Coding by Frequency Division

In the early 1930's Miller [61] of Bell Laboratories proposed a bandwidth compression method in which the speech signal was divided into a large number of adjacent frequency bands by means of a bank of contiguous band-pass filters (see Fig. 14). The quasi-sinusoidal signal at the output of each of the band-pass filters is divided in frequency by a factor 2 (or more). After frequency division, the signals are recombined to form a signal of half the original bandwidth for transmission over a narrow bandwidth channel. At the receiver, the signal is again separated into many adjacent bands and the instantaneous frequency in each band is doubled.

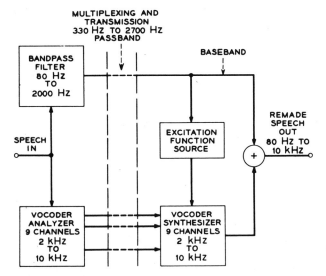

Fig. 12. Voice-excited vocoder for transmitting 10-kHz speech signals over 3-kHz telephone lines. The excitation signal at the synthesizer is derived from an uncoded baseband signal by means of a nonlinear "spectrum flattening" process.

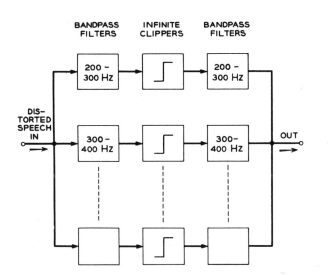

Fig. 13. Block diagram of spectrum flattener employing band-pass filters and hard limiters ("infinite clippers").

After recombination, a replica of the original signal is obtained. The proposal was put into practice in one form in the 1950's by Bogert [62]. Bogert's device, called "vobanc," used only three frequency bands, corresponding approximately to the frequency ranges of the first three formants. The resulting speech quality was judged to be rather poor and there was no distinct preference of the vobanc signal over a speech signal reduced to half its bandwidth by band-pass filtering. Other proposals for bandwidth compression by frequency division are due to Marcou and Daguet [63], [64], and Seki [65].

More recently, a 60-channel version of Miller's original proposal called "harmonic compressor," was *simulated* on a digital computer [66]. This was the first large-scale computer simulation of a speech processor em-

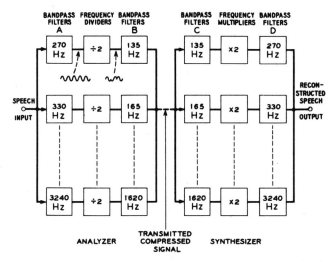

Fig. 14. Spectral envelope of voiced speech sound obtained by smoothing of logarithmic spectrum. Formant peaks and other features are clearly visible without interference from spectral fine structure.

ploying a total of 360 narrow band-pass filters. Although the computer running time for 3 seconds of speech was nearly one hour, the feasibility of exceedingly complex simulations was clearly established. In the intervening years, faster computers have reduced running time considerably. (See section on Digital Computer Simulation for additional details.)

It is interesting to note that by recording the output of the harmonic compressor analyzer and playing it back at twice the original speed, speaking rates can be doubled without changing fundamental and formant frequencies. The American Foundation for the Blind is presently exploring the possibilities of "speed hearing" for the blind in conjunction with the recorded book program of the U. S. Library of Congress.

The frequency doubler portion of the harmonic compressor can similarly be used to slow down speech to half the word rate [67]. This is of interest for teaching speech to mentally retarded children. Slowed-down speech may also be useful for speech therapy in general, and for learning foreign languages.

A related proposal, called "phase vocoder," was recently suggested by Flanagan [68]. In it, both amplitude and instantaneous frequency are measured for a number of adjacent frequency bands. Both amplitude and instantaneous frequency signals are transmitted over a reduced bandwidth channel. At the receiver, they are used to control the amplitudes and frequencies of sine-wave oscillators whose outputs are combined to form a synthetic speech signal. To date, bandwidth compression of 2 to 1 has been demonstrated with good quality. The phase vocoder (like the voice-excited vocoder, the vobanc, and the harmonic compressor) avoids the difficulties inherent in extracting the fundamental frequency and making voiced-unvoiced decisions.

Separation of Spectral Envelope and Fine Structure

One of the fundamental problems of speech analysis is the separation of spectral envelope and fine structure. The solution of this problem is crucial to the proper functioning of many speech processing systems, including automatic word and talker recognition schemes.

Reliable pitch and formant extraction, which is predicated on the separability of spectral envelope and fine structure, is required for many basic investigations on speech production, including the prosody of speech (intonation, duration, and stress patterns) and speech articulation (the dynamics of the articulator motions). Among the fruits of a better understanding of speech production are more reliable automatic word and talker recognizers [69], [70] and more human sounding speaking machines [71].

Much work on speech articulation is based on X-ray cinematography of the vocal tract, but recent results indicate that additional articulatory information can be gained from spectral analysis of the speech signal [72].

To date, the most successful schemes for separating spectral envelope and fine structure are based on the Fourier transform of the *logarithm* of the power spectrum (see Fig. 5). The fine structure of the logarithmic spectrum is characterized by a "short wavelength" ripple, while the spectral envelope is represented by a "long wavelength" modulation. Hence, Fourier transformation of the logarithmic spectrum will effect the desired separation. This double-spectrum method of analysis is known as "cepstrum" analysis which, in its original form, was conceived by Bogert and Tukey [73] for seismic signal analysis and elaborated for speech analysis by Schroeder and Noll [74]. A spectral envelope obtained by this method is shown in Fig. 15. Much detail is recognizable without interference from the fine structure. Pitch detectors based on cepstrum analysis have worked satisfactorily at signal-to-noise ratios approaching zero decibels. In fact, it has been possible to strip noise from speech signals and to improve their quality by cepstral analysis [75].

An alternative approach to ridding fundamental frequency analysis from spectral envelope influences is autocorrelation analysis of spectrally flattened speech signals. A particularly effective method of flattening is "center clipping" as suggested by Sondhi. (See [75] for further details.) The positive values of the autocorrelation function of a center clipped speech signal are shown in Fig. 16. The 8 different traces represent successive time intervals. The maxima near 5 ms delay correspond to the fundamental period. The secondary maxima near 10 ms delay correspond to twice the pitch period.

Digital Computer Simulation

The results illustrated in Figs. 15 and 16 were obtained by simulating the required operations on a digital

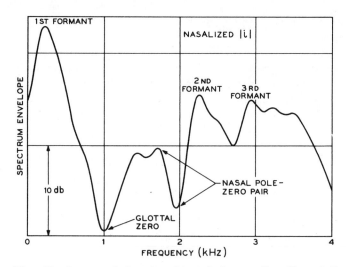

Fig. 15. Autocorrelation functions of "center-clipped" periodic speech signal. Peaks near 5-ms delay indicate fundamental periods. Secondary peaks hear 10-ms delay correspond to periodicity at twice the fundamental period. Each trace is advanced 10 ms in time with respect to the trace immediately above it.

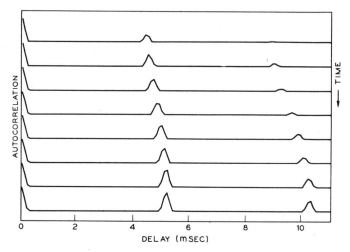

Fig. 16. Block diagram of harmonic compressor. Speech signal at input is separated into many adjacent spectral bands. Instantaneous frequencies for each band are halved and half-frequency signals are recombined for transmission over reduced-bandwidth channel. At receiver, frequencies in individual bands are doubled to form replica of original signal. Device can also be used to speed-up or slow-down speaking rates without changing fundamental and formant frequencies.

computer [76] making use of a special "Block Diagram Compiler" [77] and new programming techniques for the efficient simulation of complex filters [78]. With the advent of high-speed digital computers with large memories and sophisticated software, including special purpose compilers, the elapsed time between conception and testing of new ideas in speech processing has shrunk from months or even years to days or weeks. Digital simulation of complete vocoders [79] has answered many questions concerning filter design. Among many interesting new discoveries, a previous observation by A. J. Prestigiacomo was confirmed, namely, that the low-pass filters in a vocoder analyzer could give rise to an unpleasant reverberant quality if their impulse responses were too long.

Also, many seemingly ingenious proposals for speech compression have been shown to be, in fact, unworkable —thereby freeing people's minds and hands for more fruitful endeavors.

More recently, "on-line" computation, with a promise of even faster progress, has become available to speech researchers [34].

IV. Conclusion

Vocoders and related devices for efficient transmission and storage of speech signals have found many applications in communications between humans, and humans and machines. In addition, spectral coding schemes for speech signals have proved valuable for encrypting speech, for removing distortion and noise from speech signals, for improving intelligibility of degraded speech, and as sensory aids for the blind and the deaf.

Problems of naturalness of synthetic speech have been largely overcome although some devices continue to speak with a noticeable accent. As the quality of synthetic speech improves further—and continuing research justifies optimism—speech coding devices will find increasingly wider and significant application in modern communications.

References

[1] H. Dudley, "Remaking speech," J. Acoust. Soc. Am., vol. 11, pp. 169–177, 1939.

[2] R. M. Fano, "Short-time autocorrelation functions and power spectra," J. Acoust. Soc. Am., vol. 22, pp. 546–550, 1950.

[3] M. R. Schroeder and B. S. Atal, "Generalized short-time power spectra and autocorrelation functions," J. Acoust. Soc. Am., vol. 34, pp. 1679–1683, November 1962.

[4] A. J. Prestigiacomo, "Plastic tape sound spectrograph," J. Speech Hear. Disorders, vol. 22, pp. 321–327, September 1957.

[5] ——, "Amplitude contour display of sound spectrograms," J. Acoust, Soc. Am., vol. 34, pp. 1684–1688, November 1962.

[6] R. L. Miller, "Nature of the vocal cord wave," J. Acoust. Soc. Am., vol. 31, pp. 667–677, June 1959.

[7] G. Fant, "The acoustics of speech," Proc. Third Internat'l Congr. Acoust., Stuttgart, Germany, 1959.

[8] J. E. Miller and E. E. David, Jr., "An accurate estimate of the glottal waveshape," J. Acoust. Soc. Am., vol. 33, p. 843 (A), June 1961.

[9] J. N. Holmes, "An investigation of the volume velocity waveform at the larynx during speech by means of an inverse filter," Proc. Stockholm Speech Comm. Seminar, R.I.T., Stockholm, Sweden, September 1962.

[10] H. Helmholtz, On the Sensations of Tone. New York: Dover, 1954.

[11] G. v. Békésy, Experiments in Hearing. New York: McGraw-Hill, 1960.

[12] R. C. Mathes and R. L. Miller, "Phase effects in monaural perception," J. Acoust. Soc. Am., vol. 19, pp. 780–797, September 1947.

[13] M. R. Schroeder, "New results concerning monaural phase sensitivity," J. Acoust. Soc. Am., vol. 31, p. 1579 (A), November 1959.

[14] J. R. Pierce, "Some work on hearing," Am. Scientist, vol. 48, pp. 40–45, March 1960.

[15] E. G. Shower and R. Biddulph, "Differential pitch sensitivity of the ear," J. Acoust. Soc. Am., vol. 3, pp. 275–287, 1931.

[16] J. L. Flanagan, "A difference limen for vowel formant frequency," J. Acoust. Soc. Am., vol. 27, pp. 613–617, May 1955.

[17] ——, "Difference limen for formant amplitude," J. Speech Hear. Disorders, vol. 22, pp. 205–212, 1957.

[18] H. Fletcher, Speech and Hearing in Communication. Princeton, N. J.: Van Nostrand, 1953.

[19] J. L. Flanagan, Speech Analysis, Synthesis and Perception. New York: Springer-Verlag and Academic, 1965.

[20] J. M. Pickett, "Tactual vocoder as an aid for the deaf," Proc. Stockholm Speech Comm. Seminar, R.I.T., Stockholm, Sweden, September 1962.

[21] L. Piminow, "Coded speech and its application in aids for the deaf," Proc. Stockholm Speech Comm. Seminar, R.I.T., Stockholm, Sweden, September 1962.

[22] R. M. Golden, "Improving intelligibility and naturalness of helium-oxygen speech by vocoder techniques," J. Acoust. Soc. Am., to be published.

[23] H. P. Kramer and M. V. Mathews, "A linear coding for transmitting a set of correlated signals," IRE Trans. on Information Theory, vol. IT-2, pp. 41–46, September 1956.

[24] J. L. Flanagan, "Recent studies in speech research at Bell Telephone Laboratories (II)," presented at 5th Internat'l Congr. on Acoust., Liège, Belgium, paper A22, September 1965.

[25] E. Peterson and F. S. Cooper, "Peakpicker: a bandwidth compression device," J. Acoust. Soc. Am., vol. 29, p. 777 (A), June 1957.

[26] G. Fant, Acoustic Theory of Speech Production. 's-Gravenhage: Mouton & Co., 1960.

[27] J. L. Flanagan, "Note on the design of 'terminal analog' speech synthesizers," J. Acoust. Soc. Am., vol. 29, pp. 306–310, February 1957.

[28] S. J. Campanella, D. C. Coulter, and R. Irons, "Influence of transmission error on formant coded compressed speech signals," Proc. Stockholm Speech Comm. Seminar, R.I.T., Stockholm, Sweden, September 1962.

[29] J. N. Shearme, "Analysis of the performance of an automatic formant measuring system," Proc. Stockholm Speech Comm. Seminar, R. I. T., Stockholm, Sweden, September 1962.

[30] D. Gabor, "Lectures on communication theory," M.I.T. Res. Lab. of Electronics, Cambridge, Mass., Tech. Rept. 238, pp. 43, April 1952.

[31] M. R. Schroeder, "On the separation and measurement of formant frequencies," J. Acoust. Soc. Am., vol. 28, p. 159 (A), January 1956.

[32] C. G. Bell, H. Fujisaki, J. M. Heinz, K. N. Stevens, and A. S. House, "Reduction of speech spectra by analysis-by-synthesis techniques," J. Acoust. Soc. Am., vol. 33, pp. 1725–1736, December 1961.

[33] C. H. Coker, "Computer-simulated analyzer for a formant vocoder," J. Acoust. Soc. Am., vol. 35, p. 1911 (A), October 1963.

[34] P. B. Denes, "On-line computing in speech research," presented at 5th Internat'l Congr. on Acoust., Liège, Belgium, paper A23, September 1965.

[35] C. H. Coker, "Real-time formant vocoder, using a filter bank, a general-purpose digital computer, and an analog synthesizer," J. Acoust. Soc. Am., vol. 38, p. 940 (A), November 1965.

[36] H. Dudley and S. Balashek, "Automatic recognition of phonetic patterns in speech," J. Acoust. Soc. Am., vol. 30, pp. 721–732, 1958.

[37] C. P. Smith, "Voice-communications method using pattern matching for data compression," J. Acoust. Soc. Am., vol. 35, p. 805 (A), 1963.

[38] N. Wiener, The Extrapolation and Smoothing of Stationary Time Series with Engineering Applications. New York: Wiley, 1949.

[39] W. H. Huggins, "A note on autocorrelation analysis of speech sounds," J. Acoust. Soc. Am., vol. 26, pp. 790–792, September 1954.

[40] M. R. Schroeder, "Correlation techniques for speech bandwidth compression," J. Audio Eng. Soc., vol. 10, pp. 163–166, 1962.

[41] B. P. Bogert and W. E. Kock, "Narrowband transmission of speech," U. S. Patent 2 890 285, issued June 1959.

[42] A. A. Pirogov, "A harmonic system for compressing speech-spectra," Elektrosvyaz, no. 3, pp. 8–17, 1959; also, Telecommunications, no. 3, pp. 229–242, 1959.

[43] W. H. Huggins, "Representation and analysis of signals, Part I; the use of orthogonalized exponentials," The Johns Hopkins University, Baltimore, Md., Rept. AF'19, pp. 604, 1941; ASTIA AD 133741, September 1957.

[44] V. I. Kulya, "Application of Laguerre functions to parametric coding of speech signals," Elektrosvyaz, no. 7, pp. 33–39, 1962; also, "Telecommunications and Radio Engineering, pt. I," Telecommuncations, no. 7, pp. 34–41, 1962.

[45] W. C. Hittinger and M. Sparks, "Microelectronics," Scientific American, pp. 56–70, November 1965.

[46] M. Grützmacher and W. Lottermoser, "Über ein Verfahren zur

trägheitsfreien Aufzeichnung von Melodiekurven," *Akust. Z.*, vol. 2, pp. 242–248, 1937.
[47] R. L. Miller, "Improvements in the vocoder," *J. Acoust. Soc. Am.*, vol. 25, p. 832 (A), July 1953.
[48] G. Raisbeck, "Voice pitch determination." U. S. Patent 2 908 761, issued October 1959.
[49] J. S. Gill, "Automatic extraction of the excitation function of speech with particular reference to the use of correlation methods," *Proc. Third Internat'l Congr. Acoust.*, Stuttgart, Germany, September 1959.
[50] H. Fujisaki, "Automatic extraction of fundamental period of speech by autocorrelation analysis and peak detection," *J. Acoust. Soc. Am.*, vol. 32, p. 1518 (A), November 1960.
[51] P. M. Woodward, *Probability and Information Theory with Applications to Radar*, 2nd ed. New York: Pergamon, 1964.
[52] R. L. Miller and E. S. Weibel, "Measurement of the fundamental period of speech using a delay line," *J. Acoust. Soc. Am.*, vol. 28, p. 761 (A), July 1956.
[53] A. J. Prestigiacomo and B. F. Logan, personal communication.
[54] N. P. McKinney, "Laryngeal frequency analysis for linguistic research," Communication Sciences Lab., Univ. of Michigan, Ann Arbor, Rept. 14, September 1965.
[55] C. B. H. Feldman, U. S. Patent 2 817 711, issued December 24, 1957.
[56] M. R. Schroeder and E. E. David, Jr., "A vocoder for transmitting 10 kc/s speech over a 3.5 kc/s channel," *Acustica*, vol. 10, pp. 35–43, no. 1, 1960.
[57] M. R. Schroeder, "Band Compression System," U. S. Patent 3 030 450, issued April 17, 1962.
[58] A. J. Prestigiacomo and B. F. Logan, "Bandwidth Reduction System," U. S. Patent 3 139 487, issued June 30, 1964.
[59] M. R. Schroeder, B. F. Logan, and A. J. Prestigiacomo, "New applications of voice-excitation to vocoders," *Proc. Stockholm Speech Comm. Seminar*, R.I.T., Stockholm, Sweden, September 1962.
[60] E. E. David, Jr., M. R. Schroeder, B. F. Logan, and A. J. Prestigiacomo, "Voice-excited vocoders for practical speech bandwidth reduction," *Internat'l Symp. on Information Theory Proc.*, Brussels, Belgium, August 1962.
[61] R. L. Miller, "Signalling System," U. S. Patent 2 117 739, issued May 17, 1938.
[62] B. P. Bogert, "The vobanc—a two-to-one speech bandwidth reduction system," *J. Acoust. Soc. Am.*, vol. 28, pp. 399–404, May 1956.
[63] P. Marcou and J. Daguet, "New methods of speech transmission," *Proc. 3rd Symp. on Information Theory*, London, 1955; *Information Theory*, C. Cherry, Ed. London: Butterworths, 1956, pp. 231–244; and *Ann. Telecommun.*, vol. 11, pp. 118–126, 1956.
[64] J. Daguet, " 'Codimex' speech compression system," *Proc. Stockholm Speech Comm. Seminar*, R.I.T. Stockholm, Sweden, September 1962.
[65] H. Seki, "A new method of speech transmission by frequency division and multiplication," *J. Acoust. Soc. Japan*, vol. 14, pp. 138–142, 1958.

[66] M. R. Schroeder, B. F. Logan, and A. J. Prestigiacomo, "New methods for speech analysis-synthesis and bandwidth compression," *Proc. Stockholm Speech Comm. Seminar*, R.I.T., Stockholm, Sweden, September 1962.
[67] G. T. Gould, "Design of a speech stretcher, FM-TV" *J. Rad. Comm.*, vol. 11, pp. 30–36, 1951.
[68] J. L. Flanagan, D. I. S. Meinhart, R. M. Golden, and M. M. Sondhi, "Phase vocoder," *J. Acoust. Soc. Am.*, vol. 38, p. 939 (A), November 1965.
[69] P. B. Denes and M. V. Mathews, "Spoken digit recognition using time-frequency pattern matching," *J. Acoust. Soc. Am.*, vol. 32, pp. 1450–1455, November 1960.
[70] S. Pruzansky, "Pattern-matching procedure for automatic talker recognition," *J. Acoust. Soc. Am.*, vol. 35, pp. 354–358, March 1963.
[71] J. L. Kelly, Jr., and L. J. Gerstman, "An artificial talker driven from a phonetic input," *J. Acoust. Soc. Am.*, vol. 33, pp. 835 (A), June 1961.
[72] P. Mermelstein and M. R. Schroeder, "Determination of smoothed cross-sectional area functions of the vocal tract from formant frequencies," presented at 5th Internat'l Congr. on Acoust., Liège, Belgium, paper A24, September 1965.
[73] B. P. Bogert, M. J. R. Healy, and J. W. Tukey, in *Time Series Analysis*. New York: Wiley, 1963, ch. 15.
[74] A. M. Noll, "Short-time spectrum and 'cepstrum' techniques for vocal pitch detection," *J. Acoust. Soc. Am.*, vol. 36, pp. 296–302, February 1964.
[75] M. R. Schroeder and A. M. Noll, "Recent studies in speech research at Bell Telephone Laboratories (I)," presented at 5th Internat'l Cong. on Acoust., Liège, Belgium, paper A21, September 1965.
[76] E. E. David, Jr., "Computer-catalyzed speech research," *Proc. Fourth Internat'l Congr. Acoust.*, Copenhagen, Denmark, August 1962.
[77] J. L. Kelly, Jr., C. L. Lochbaum, and V. A. Vyssotsky, "A block diagram compiler," *Bell Sys. Tech. J.*, vol. 40, pp. 669–676, May 1961.
[78] R. M. Golden and J. F. Kaiser, "Design of wideband sampled-data filters," *Bell Sys. Tech. J.* (pt. II), vol. 53, pp. 1533–1546, July 1964.
[79] R. M. Golden, "Digital computer simulation of a sampled-data voice-excited vocoder," *J. Acoust. Soc. Am.*, vol. 35, pp. 1358–1366, September 1963.
[80] D. W. Farnsworth, "High-speed motion pictures of the human vocal cords," *Bell Labs. Rec.*, vol. 18, pp. 203–208, 1940.

Additional General References

E. E. David, Jr., "Signal theory in speech transmission," *IEEE Trans. on Circuit Theory*, vol. CT-3, pp. 232–244, December 1956.
E. E. David, Jr., "Digital simulation in research on human communication," *Proc. IEEE*, vol. 49, pp. 319–329, January 1961.
M. A. Sapozhkov, *The Speech Signal in Cybernetics and Communications*. Moscow: Svyaz'izdat, 1963.

Estimates of the Maximum Precision Necessary in Quantizing Certain "Dimensions" of Vowel Sounds

James L. Flanagan

Air Force Cambridge Research Center, Cambridge, Massachusetts

(Received February 7, 1957)

Results of psychoacoustic experiments are used to estimate the greatest precision necessary in quantizing narrow band-width data specifying the vowel sounds of speech.

RECENT developments in the theory and application of digital techniques have stimulated interest in applying these techniques to certain systems for reducing the band-width and channel capacity necessary to transmit speech. Such an application raises questions concerning the resolution necessary in quantizing (or digitalizing) the "compressed" speech data. It is apparent that employing a resolution in excess of that required would serve to nullify the saving in band-width and channel capacity that the compression system might afford, while, on the other hand, insufficient precision would obviously impair the usefulness of the communication link.

In a voice communication system the speech information usually originates and terminates with a human operator. The perceptual abilities of man, therefore, determine the precision with which the data must be transmitted and processed. It is the purpose of this note to summarize some experimental findings which permit quantitative estimates of the maximum precision necessary in quantizing certain useful "dimensions" of vowel sounds.

"Dimensions" of vowel sounds.—Experimental and theoretical investigations in speech production[1-3] have shown that the acoustic output of a speaker during vowel production can be specified reasonably accurately in a relatively simple fashion; namely, by specifying the frequencies of the normal modes of vibration of the vocal tract and the fundamental frequency of vibration of the glottis. In the production of vowel sounds the natural frequencies of the tract always are manifested as gross maxima, or formants, in the amplitude spectrum of the acoustic output. The relative amplitudes of the spectral maxima bear specific relationships to one another, uniquely determined by the values of the formant frequencies.[4] During speech the formant frequencies and the fundamental vocal frequency change relatively slowly with time and hence constitute a narrow band-width specification of vowel sounds. For this reason these quantities are useful as information-bearing signals in certain band-width compression systems, sometimes referred to as "formant-coding" system.[5]

In some types of formant-coding systems,[6] it has been found expedient not to make use of the fact that the relative amplitudes of the vowel formants are uniquely determined by the formant frequencies. In these cases additional narrow band-width signals representing the relative amplitudes of the formants usually are transmitted.

If the formant concept is extended to consonant sounds it is no longer true that the formant frequencies uniquely determine the formant amplitudes. For consonant sounds, therefore, data on the relative amplitudes of the spectral maxima are more important than for vowel sounds.

For the purpose of the following discussion let it be assumed that electrical signals representing the formant frequencies, formant amplitudes, and fundamental vocal frequency are to be used as information-bearing quantities in a compression system. In order to compute the channel capacity required for the transmission of such signals it is necessary to know the precision with which the signals must be transmitted.

Perception of speech sounds: differential versus absolute discrimination.—It is probable that the perception of speech by man corresponds more nearly to an absolute judgment of acoustic stimuli than to a differential discrimination. Furthermore, it also is probable that the differences which are differentially discriminable in the vowel dimensions are smaller when the sound exists in an isolated quasi-steady state than when it exists in the more dynamic state characterizing connected speech. If these assumptions are in fact true, it would appear that differential discrimination tests performed with relatively steady-state stimuli should lead to estimates of necessary precision that essentially represent maximum values or upper bounds. Such estimates based upon differential discriminations should be very conservative figures when compared to the accuracies necessary for proper identification of vowel sounds. Experimental evidence on absolute discriminations performed along frequency and amplitude dimensions[7, 8] indicates that the ability of man to make absolute discriminations is considerably less acute than his ability to make differential discriminations.

Results of psychoacoustic experiments.—On the basis of the foregoing assumptions, psychoacoustic experiments have been conducted to determine just discriminable differences (or difference limens) for certain of the vowel "dimensions." Most of the experiments have been pilot studies, considerably restricted in scope. In no respect can they be considered exhaustive. The experiments do provide, however, some quantitative data, albeit meager, in an area where none previously existed.

More specifically, experiments have been conducted on synthetic vowel sounds produced at conversational levels to determine difference limens (DL's) for the frequencies of the first and second formants[9]; the fundamental vocal frequency[10]; the amplitude of the second formant[11]; and the over-all vowel amplitude.[12] The gross results of these experiments are summarized as follows: (1) The DL's for formant frequency are of the order of $\pm3\%$ of the formant frequency; (2) The DL for fundamental frequency (or "pitch") is of the order of ±0.5 to $\pm1.0\%$ for a vowel having a fundamental frequency in the neighborhood of 120 cps; (3.) The DL for second formant amplitude is of the order of ±3 db, or

Reprinted with permission from *J. Acoust. Soc. Am.*, vol. 29, pp. 533–534, Apr. 1957.

TABLE I. Maximum number of levels of quantization and bits of information necessary to specify vowel parameters.

Parameter	Frequency			Amplitude		
	Size of levels (cps)	No. or levels	Bits	Size of levels (db)	No. of levels	Bits
$F1$	40	14	3.8	2	3	1.6
$F2$	100	14	3.8	6	3	1.6
$F3$	150	9	3.2	10	2	1.0
$F0$	2	40	5.3	...	...	...

±40% of the formant amplitude; (4.) The DL for over-all vowel amplitude is approximately ±1 db, or about ±12% of the over-all amplitude.

Since most of the sound energy of a vowel usually is contained in the first formant, the over-all amplitude DL might be used as a crude estimate of the DL for the amplitude of the first formant.

Quantization of vowel "dimensions".—Considerable data on the formant frequencies and amplitudes of natural vowels are available in the literature.[3] These data indicate that for adult male voices the average ranges occupied by the first three formants ($F1$, $F2$, and $F3$) are approximately: 250–800 cps for $F1$; 800–2300 cps for $F2$; and 1700–3000 cps for $F3$. The data also indicate that if the over-all amplitudes of the vowels in continuous speech are normalized approximately to the same value, the ranges of amplitudes covered by the formants of different vowels are about: 5 db for $F1$; 20 db for $F2$; and 20 db for $F3$.

Data also have been reported in the literature on the range of fundamental vocal frequency.[13] These data indicate that for adult males reading factual material the fundamental vocal frequency ($F0$) usually falls within the one octave frequency range 80–160 cps.

Assuming that the original hypothesis concerning differential discriminations is tenable and knowing the ranges associated with the vowel "dimensions" and the changes which are just discriminable, it is possible to make rough estimates of the maximum precision necessary in quantizing the "dimensions." The results of the psychoacoustic tests indicate that, to a first approximation, it should not be necessary to quantize formant frequency in steps smaller than about ±20 cps for $F1$, ±50 cps for $F2$, and ±75 cps for $F3$. Similarly, it should not be necessary to quantize formant amplitude in steps smaller than about ±1 db for $F1$, ±3 db for $F2$, and possibly ±5 db for $F3$. In a like manner it probably should not be necessary to quantize fundamental vocal frequency in steps smaller than about ±1 cps in the octave range 80–160 cps.

On the basis of these estimates, therefore, the maximum number of levels of quantization and bits of information (assuming uniform probability distributions) necessary to specify the frequencies and amplitudes of the first three formants and the fundamental frequency should not exceed the values shown in Table I.

For adult male voices the first three formants usually lie in the frequency range below 3000 cps and provide a reasonably accurate description of the acoustic output. Assuming, therefore, that vowels can be described and identified from a knowledge of the first three formant frequencies and the fundamental vocal frequency, the amount of information necessary to specify a vowel sound from an ensemble in which both phonemic and vowel-quality distinctions can be made should not exceed the sum of the bits associated with these frequency parameters, i.e., about 16 bits. If, however, in the development of automatic speech analysis and synthesis apparatus (such as a spectrum correlation or pattern-matching apparatus, or a speech compression system employing formant-coding principles) use is not made of the formant amplitude relations implicit in the formant frequency data, an additional amount of information of about 4 bits is necessary to specify the relative amplitudes of the formants, bringing the total to about 20 bits.

In normal conversational speech vowel sounds persist in a relatively "steady state" for durations of the order of 0.25 sec. However, the vowel formant transitions that occur between constants and vowels, or between two successive vowels, can take place in times as short as 50 msec, and sometimes shorter. If one wishes to resolve in time the transitions of the vowel formants, data on these "dimensions" should be specified at least 20 or 30 times per second.

Assuming that the vowel parameters are sampled once every 50 msec (i.e., 20 times per second) then the information rates connected with specification of the parameters are approximately the values shown in Table II. As the data in Table II show, the

TABLE II. Information rates associated with specification of vowel parameters.

Parameter	Bits/sec	
	Frequency	Amplitude
$F1$	76	32
$F2$	76	32
$F3$	64	20
$F0$	106	...

information rate associated with specification of the three formant frequencies is of the order of 200 bits/sec, while all of the frequency parameters are specified by a rate slightly greater than 300 bits/sec. The information rate for the formant amplitude data is of the order of 80 bits/sec, bringing the total rate for all the parameters to approximately 400 bits/sec.

It is interesting to note that the estimates of the information rates for the formant frequency parameters made here are in reasonably good agreement with estimates of these quantities that have been made from band-width and signal-to-noise ratio considerations.[14] Calculations of the band-widths and signal-to-noise ratios necessary for the transmission of analog signals representing the frequencies of the first three formants have been made using a criterion of accuracy based upon the formant frequency DL's discussed above. The information rate associated with these computed values of band-width and signal-to-noise ratio has been found to be of the order of 200 bits/sec.

[1] H. K. Dunn, J. Acoust. Soc. Am. **22**, 740–753 (1950).
[2] C. G. M. Fant, "Transmission properties of the vocal tract," Technical Report No. 12, Acoustics Laboratory, Massachusetts Institute of Technology (1952).
[3] G. E. Peterson and H. L. Barney, J. Acoust. Soc. Am. **24**, 175–184 (1952).
[4] J. L. Flanagan, J. Acoust. Soc. Am. **29**, 306–310 (1957).
[5] J. L. Flanagan and A. S. House, J. Acoust. Soc. Am. **28**, 1099–1106 (1956).
[6] C. R. Howard, J. Acoust. Soc. Am. **28**, 1091–1098 (1956).
[7] I. Pollack, J. Acoust. Soc. Am. **24**, 745–749 (1952).
[8] I. Pollack, and L. Ficks, J. Acoust. Soc. Am. **26**, 155–158 (1954).
[9] J. L. Flanagan, J. Acoust. Soc. Am. **27**, 613–617 (1953).
[10] J. L. Flanagan and M. L. Saslow, "Difference limen for the fundamental frequency of vowel sounds," Quarterly Reports, Acoustics Laboratory, Massachusetts Institute of Technology, (March, September, and December, 1956).
[11] J. L. Flanagan, "Difference limen for formant amplitude," Quarterly Report, Acoustics Laboratory, Massachusetts Institute of Technology, (September, 1956).
[12] J. L. Flanagan, J. Acoust. Soc. Am. **27**, 1223–1225 (1955).
[13] G. Fairbanks, J. Acoust. Soc. Am. **11**, 457–466 (1940).
[14] J. L. Flanagan, J. Acoust. Soc. Am. **28**, 592–596 (1956).

The Channel Vocoder

BERNARD GOLD, MEMBER, IEEE, AND CHARLES M. RADER, MEMBER, IEEE

Abstract—The channel vocoder is described. This device achieves bandwidth compression greater than that of the bandpass compressor but less than that of the formant vocoder. To date it has been much more widely used than any other kind of vocoder. The channel vocoder exploits the insensitivity of the aural mechanism to phase, and only attempts to reproduce the short time power spectrum of the speech waveform. The spectral envelope of the speech is measured with a bank of filters and ascribed wholly to the vocal tract filter, while the excitation is estimated to be either a quasi-periodic pulse train, or noise. There are several methods of combining these extracted parameters to reconstruct the speech. Several configurations of the channel vocoder are described and the factors which affect the specification of design parameters for channel vocoders are considered.

I. INTRODUCTION

THE CHANNEL vocoder is based on known properties of speech production and perception, or to say it another way, it bypasses some of the more difficult problems of imitating the human speech mechanism by taking advantage of the hearing mechanism. The resultant gain in system simplicity is achieved, however, at the loss of system bandwidth reduction; a formant vocoder intrinsically compresses the speech bandwidth more than does a channel vocoder.

Historically, the channel vocoder, invented by Dudley in the 1930's,[1]–[3] was the first analysis–synthesis system. It was not until after the second world war that research towards formant vocoders began. During the 1940's and 1950's, the notion grew that vocoders might play a useful role in digital speech communications systems. By the late 1950's enough experience had been gained that it seemed feasible to attempt to build vocoders for practical systems. The present paper summarizes more recent research and development which have led to these practical realizations.

We will see, in the next section, that there are quite a few electrical configurations, all of which are designated as channel vocoders. The principal idea behind the channel vocoder is that of the separation of vocal source and vocal tract. The vocal source during voicing is typified by a sequence of pulselike waves. In the frequency domain, this becomes the spectral fine structure. It is important to note that all the 'carriers' are harmonically related so that measurement of F_0 alone determines the fine structure. In the bandpass compressor, no use is made of this harmonic relation. In the channel vocoder, by contrast, the fine structure and the spectral envelope

Manuscript received September 14, 1967.
The authors are with Lincoln Laboratory, Massachusetts Institute of Technology, Cambridge, Mass. (Operated with support from the U. S. Air Force.)

are, to some extent, separated by the analyzer and put back together at the synthesizer. In addition, an indication of voicing is made at the analyzer so that it can be determined whether the source generator at the synthesizer is to be pulselike or noiselike.

II. CHANNEL VOCODER

A channel vocoder is shown in Fig. 1. The separation of the speech into voiced and unvoiced segments is accomplished by the voicing detector. During voicing, the frequency of vocal cord vibration, which is also the fundamental frequency in the harmonic representation of the voiced speech, is measured by the device labeled pitch extractor. Strictly speaking, the word 'pitch' denotes subjective perception of tones; its use here to denote the vocal cord vibration rate is in the interests of brevity; in the context of technologically oriented vocoder studies, this should not cause confusion. Psychophysically, pitch denotes a perceived entity whose acoustic correlates may be laryngeal frequency, speech intensity, or duration.

During all the speech, the spectral channels approximately measure the spectral envelope of the speech. During voicing, the speech spectrum can be crudely defined as a fine structure modulated by this spectral envelope. During unvoiced sounds, the spectrum is continuous rather than discrete, since the source functions introduced either by vocal tract constrictions (during fricatives) or occlusion (during plosives) tend to be noiselike rather than periodic. Spectral measurement may be erratic due to statistical fluctuations in short noise bursts, but otherwise it is reasonable to consider that the vocoder spectrum outputs during the unvoiced sounds are a good representation of the spectrum envelope of these sounds. For both the voiced and unvoiced sounds, then, the vocoder spectral measurement is a discrete sampling in frequency of a real or imagined continuous spectral envelope. Each of the n spectral channels contains a bandpass filter, rectifier, and lowpass filter, exactly as does the bandpass compressor analyzer. The bandpass filter bandwidths are arranged to continuously cover the speech bandwidth of interest. In a later section we will take up the question of choosing vocoder parameters, such as filter design, distribution of filter bandwidths, etc. In Section VI, various types of vocoder synthesizer configurations will be examined. We see plainly, now, the idea of the channel vocoder; the spectral envelope is analyzed and synthesized as in the bandpass compressor and the successful transmission of this information depends on human per-

Reprinted from *IEEE Trans. Audio Electroacoust.*, vol. AU–15, pp. 148–161, Dec. 1967.

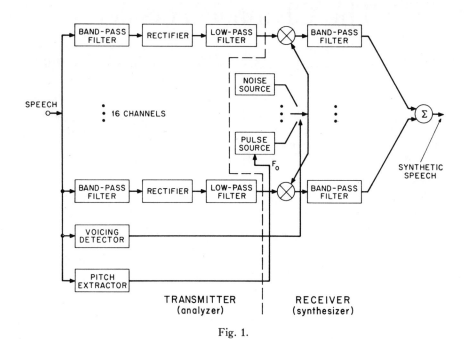

Fig. 1.

ception of short-time amplitude spectra. The separation, by means of the voicing indicator and pitch extractor and the use of pulse and noise generators in the synthesizers, follows closely the physiological speech production process.

III. Goals of Vocoder Research

The vocoder engineer, in writing about his subject, faces a problem as formidable as the writer of an unillustrated book on art criticism. No real insight into vocoders can be obtained without frequently listening to speech synthesized from many different band compression systems. Unhappily, it will be impossible in this work to avoid using poorly defined terms such as excellent, poor, and good, in referring to the speech quality in various system outputs. In this section we will describe some of the ground rules underlying our judgments. Unreferenced judgments about vocoder quality usually derive from informal listening by the authors and associates to various vocoder systems.

There exist at present a variety of speech communications systems which compress the speech bandwidth, one of which is the channel vocoder, which itself is quite varied. The four basic goals of the engineers who build these systems are:

1) to produce a system whose fidelity is acceptable to a large body of customers,
2) to produce a device of modest cost and size,
3) to reduce the transmission bandwidth, and
4) to make a device which is relatively insensitive to the input speech quality.

The first two items need no further explanation. An example of the third item is the use of vocoders on telephone lines. A typical telephone cable has a bandwidth of 3 kHz, sufficient for one speech signal. A vocoder which reduced the necessary transmission bandwidth to 600 Hz would make possible the simultaneous transmission of five conversations on one telephone cable, and thus be economically beneficial. For digitized vocoders, a rate of 2400 bits per second is presently desirable since data modems operating at these rates are commercially available and can be used with existing telephone systems. In this case, only one conversation per cable takes place but the users have the advantage of digital communications.

To explain the fourth item it is necessary to point out that most vocoders are very sensitive to the quality of the input speech. For example, a typical 2400-bit vocoder may produce acceptable synthesized speech if the input speech is obtained from a high quality moving coil microphone which is kept about six inches from the speaker's mouth. When a close-talking, dynamic microphone is installed in a telephone hand set so that it is within an inch or two of the speaker's mouth, degradation occurs in the vocoder. If a carbon button microphone is used, there is further degradation. If the speech is sent over an ordinary telephone system through several miles of cable before being vocoded, still more degradation occurs. These bad effects are caused primarily by the failure of the pitch extraction and voicing detection circuits when the input speech is sufficiently degraded.

In judging a speech compression system, it is necessary to ask which goals have been stressed. A modestly priced 2400-bit system may be preferable to an expensive 9600-bit system. The reader should, therefore, interpret our judgments cautiously; if we call one system superior to another we usually mean that it has greater fidelity but not necessarily that it is to be preferred in a practical system.

Listeners may be divided into three categories. First

there is the highly trained linguist who can perceive phonetic differences which other listeners will generally not hear. Second is the so-called trained listener, usually an engineer working on speech compression systems who has heard many different such systems over several years. Third is the naive listener, presumably everyone else who knows the language being spoken. The authors fall into the second class but we will have occasion to quote results from all three classes.

The range of speech quality from the different systems is very large. The authors have been subjected to synthetic speech which was completely unintelligible to them. At the other extreme, we have preferred some vocoder outputs to that of a telephone. The intelligibility (ability of the listener to understand what was said) is quite satisfactory for modern vocoders; there still exist sizeable variations in the naturalness of the speech and in the ability of the listener to identify the speaker. There seems little doubt that the first of the aforementioned goals can be achieved; vocoders can be made to produce very satisfactory speech.

Listening to Vocoders

When listening to vocoders, one should beware of the following.

1) A voice (usually male) with very good diction and speaking with little intensity and intonation changes will make many vocoders sound deceivingly good.
2) Listening to a loudspeaker rather than good earphones decreases greatly the perceptiveness of the listener to differences between two vocoders.
3) The reverberations in a large room will further mask vocoded speech degradations.
4) Knowing the sentence beforehand makes you think the vocoder is better. Ambitious inventors of new band compression devices have often unknowingly deluded themselves in this way.
5) It is much more difficult to judge quality absolutely than relatively. Thus, to compare two vocoders, or the same vocoder with two different parameters, the same sentence should be played sequentially to the listener. Even here, a bias appears; the sentence often sounds better the second time.
6) Different sentences and speakers will be differently affected by the vocoder. In order to judge a vocoder fairly, a variety of sentences and speakers should be listened to.

IV. VOCODER ANALYZERS

The use of a fixed filter bank to measure the speech spectrum is complicated by the fact that speech resembles either noise or a periodic signal of widely variable fundamental frequency. Additional complication arises from the time-variable nature of the speech spectrum. From steady-state analysis, one can deduce that sharp

cutoff filters will result in more accurate spectral measurements; however, in practice, such filters usually have long ringing times. Thus, their use would result in a smearing, in time, of rapid spectral changes and subsequent reverberation effects on the vocoded speech. Another manifestation of disturbing temporal effects arises if the bandpass filters have unequal time delays, such as might occur, for example, if different channels employed different bandwidths. In the latter case, careful design can insure uniform delay of the channel signals.

It is possible to design sharp cutoff bandpass filters having linear phase.[35] Provided that the positions of the poles are uniformly spaced, a bank of variable width, constant time delay filters can be designed. Although this design may be presently impractical to build economically, it is still of theoretical interest to study its effect in a vocoder. Idealizing the problem, we can imagine a bank of contiguous, rectangular filters narrow enough so that, during voicing, no more than a single harmonic enters any filter. Thus, each spectrum channel will be measuring either zero or the power in a given harmonic. At the synthesizer, the pulse generator will reproduce the correct harmonics. If each synthesizer channel includes a bandpass filter identical to that of the corresponding analyzer channel, then all harmonics receive exactly the correct modulation voltages and the original spectrum amplitude is reproduced. Furthermore, during unvoiced sounds, if the noise bandwidth (area under the amplitude versus frequency curve) of each analyzer bandpass filter is the same, the spectrum channel voltages would be the correct measure of the input spectrum, provided that no large spectral fluctuation occurred over a small frequency increment. Thus, voiced and unvoiced speech are correctly analyzed.

Disregarding practical design considerations, the disadvantage of such a filter bank would be that relatively little bandwidth compression results. If, for example, the lower bound on the fundamental frequency is chosen to be 60 Hz, then nearly 70 filters would be needed to analyze a 4-kHz speech signal. Assuming that a 25-Hz bandwidth of the low-pass filters is needed to faithfully reproduce the spectrum, a total vocoder spectrum bandwidth of 1750 Hz is called for. Considering that guard bands are needed to prevent undue crosstalk in any multiplexing scheme, it is clear that little saving results.

As the bandpass filter bandwidths are increased so that the total number of channels can be reduced, a spectral distortion during voicing becomes evident for voice fundamental frequencies sufficiently low that more than a single harmonic appears in a filter. If, for simplicity, we assume that the rectifiers are square law devices, then the measured spectral signal from a bandpass filter containing two equal harmonics is double the signal from a bandpass filter containing a single harmonic.

The resulting spectral distortion can be estimated for

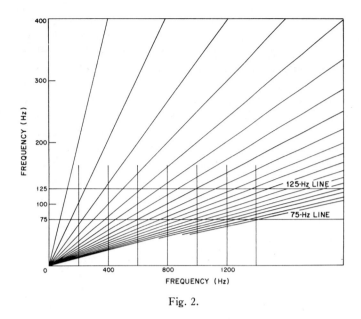

Fig. 2.

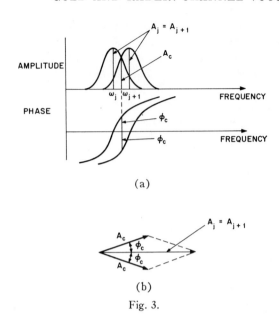

(a)

(b)

Fig. 3.

any fundamental frequency and filter bank using the construction shown in Fig. 2. The diverging lines are so arranged that any horizontal line, representing a given fundamental frequency, intersects these diverging lines at its harmonics. Vertical lines can be drawn representing filter boundaries and the number of harmonics in each filter can be determined. Clearly, if the fundamental is larger than the filter width, no distortion results. In Fig. 2 are shown filter widths of 200 Hz and several fundamentals. It is seen, for example, that a relatively large distortion results at a pitch of 125 Hz, compared to, say, 75 Hz since in the latter case the number of harmonics per filter varies between 2 and 3 while in the former case this number varies between 1 and 2. If the (voiced) input to the analyzer had a uniform spectral envelope, the spectrum as measured over the frequency band using 200-Hz-width filters at 125 Hz would contain 3 dB fluctuations. Although it is very difficult to deduce that such distortion degrades vocoder quality or intelligibility, it must be stressed that there are many causes of spectral distortion in a vocoder and ignoring any of them is dangerous.

V. Spectral Reproduction Capabilities of Vocoder Synthesizers

The synthesizer shown in Fig. 1 consists of n channels, generally of identical structure. While the overall configuration of vocoder analyzers has remained substantially constant, following Dudley's original conception, the synthesizer configuration has been the subject of much experimentation. In the following section, comparisons will be made between the various synthesizer configurations; in the present section, we will study how a given synthesizer reproduces the spectrum in certain idealized cases. Assume, for example, that each synthesizer channel contained a modulator and bandpass filter as shown in Fig. 1. Our main concern here is with the design of the bandpass filters and the consequent effect

on the spectrum of the vocoded speech.

Bandpass filters with long ringing times or unequal delays for different channels created the same problems, as discussed in Section IV, as would be created in the analyzer. Most vocoders have been designed using identical filters for the corresponding channels of both analyzer and synthesizer.

Let us assume that each synthesizer bandpass filter is a sharp cutoff linear phase filter. If all the modulation voltages shown in Fig. 1 were constant, then the transfer function of the entire synthesizer would be that of a flat-topped filter covering the entire frequency range. Thus, if all harmonic amplitudes were correctly measured at the analyzer during voicing, and if the noise spectrum were correctly analyzed during unvoiced sounds, the synthesizer would be distortionless.

To predict spectral distortion during synthesis when the bandpass filters are not sharp cutoff filters, the simple model illustrated in Fig. 3 can be utilized. We make the approximation, during voicing, that any harmonic of the excitation can appear in at most two adjacent filters. That harmonic can be represented as the vector sum of the two filter outputs. Now, as the harmonic frequency moves from w_j to w_{j+1}, we desire that this vector sum remain constant. This condition is approximately realized for well-behaved filters if it is stipulated that the vector sum at the filter crossover frequencies equal the vector sum at either of the filter center frequencies. Assuming that the contribution of a filter is negligible at the center frequency of the other filter and noting the vector diagram of Fig. 3 we can write

$$A_j = A_{j+1} = 2A_c{}^2 - 2A_c{}^2 \cos{(\pi - 2\phi_c)} \qquad (1)$$

where ϕ_c and $-\phi_c$ are the phases of the adjacent filters. Making the phase angles equal and opposite assumes that the bandpass filters are symmetric about their center frequency, which is valid until the center frequencies are quite low, perhaps 2 or 3 times the bandwidths.

Equation (1) leads to the relationship

$$\frac{A_c}{A_j} = \frac{1}{2 \cos \phi_c}, \tag{2}$$

thus yielding a design parameter, namely, the attenuation of the filters at crossover.

Consideration of Fig. 3(b) also leads to the result that the phase of the vocoded speech is approximately equal to the phase of the excitation signal. As we have stressed, a vocoder's successful operation depends on the relative insensitivity of the ear to a wide variety of phase distortions. However, there is evidence[4],[5] that the pulselike phase spectrum of a voiced excitation signal creates a subjective effect of roughness and causes the synthetic speech to be perceived as "less natural sounding."

VI. Vocoder Synthesizers Configurations

In Fig. 4 are shown several possible configurations of a synthesizer spectrum channel. Fig. 4(a) and (b) results in identical outputs [Fig. 4(a) is the same as shown in Fig. 1]; the disadvantage of the latter is in the linear modulator needed instead of the switch modulator of the former. Dudley[6] has commented that the channel of Fig. 4(c) proved in practice to yield more pleasant sounding speech than that of Fig. 4(a) and (b).

A significant departure from the synthesizer configurations of Fig. 4(a), (b), and (c) is that of Fig. 4(d), often referred to as spectral flattening. The introduction of an infinite clipper or "hard" limiter, with the property that its output is either +1 or −1 depending on the sign of the input, creates, at the input to all the modulators, an array of square waves, all having equal power.

A steady-state voiced excitation signal results in a set of square waves of frequencies which are approximately harmonics of the fundamental. Thus, the behavior of the spectrally flattened channel appears to be the same as that of Fig. 4(c), for example, in the simple case when only a single harmonic passes through the first bandpass filter; the third and higher harmonics produced by the hard limiter are filtered out by the final bandpass filter. Yet these two configurations do not yield the same sound even for high pitched voices where the approximation of no more than a single harmonic per filter is valid.

To explain this apparent discrepancy, it seems necessary to deal with situations wherein the glottal source spectrum is not constant but fluctuates with time. This fluctuation is caused both by variations in the glottal area from one period to the next and by changes in the vocal cord vibration rate. Both spectrographic inspection and analysis of laryngeal photographs[7] have revealed the strong effects of these fluctuations on the overall speech spectral envelope. In a vocoder, only the vocal cord vibration period, and not the wave shape, are

extracted. If it is assumed that observed fluctuations of the speech spectrum are created predominantly by glottal pulse wave shapes, then spectral flattening should not appreciably alter vocoded speech quality. The evidence[8]−[10] that synthetic speech quality is strongly affected by spectral flattening implies that spectral fluctuations in the speech are at least partly induced by the time variations between successive laryngeal pulses.

Short-time spectral fluctuations caused by variations in the excitation pulse periods can be examined quantitatively by computing the power spectrum of three pulses.[11] This computation gives

$$G(\omega) \sim \frac{\sin^2 \frac{1}{2}\omega\tau}{(\frac{1}{2}\omega\tau)^2} [3 + 4 \cos \Delta\omega \cos \omega T + 2 \cos 2\omega T] \tag{3}$$

where $\omega = 2\pi f$, $2T$ is the time between the first and third pulse, $T - \Delta$ is the time between the first and second pulse, and τ is the pulse width. If $\tau/T \ll 1$, we can assume that $\sin^2 \frac{1}{2}\omega\tau / (\frac{1}{2}\omega\tau)^2 \approx 1$ for all ω of interest. Equation (3) is plotted in Fig. 5 for a) $\Delta = 0$, b) $\Delta = 0.1\ T$.

If the preceding argument is accepted, then pitch-induced spectral fluctuations would be carried in both pitch and spectral analysis of the original speech. Spectral flattening effectively wipes out (for the case of no more than a single harmonic per filter) spectral variations in frequency carried by the excitation signal. The configurations of Fig. 4(a), (b), and (c) pass these variations, thereby introducing distortion of the vocoded speech.

When the fundamental frequency is low enough to allow two or more harmonics to pass through a filter, the configuration of Fig. 4(d) no longer completely flattens the excitation spectrum. This follows from the effect of the limiter on two harmonics; often the smaller harmonic is further suppressed. Also, listeners have sometimes commented adversely on the reproduction of unvoiced sounds. These difficulties can be substantially avoided by replacement of the limiter shown in Fig. 4(d) with the automatic volume control (AVC) shown in Fig. 6. The delayed narrow band signal is divided by its own average intensity. The delay τ of the low-pass filter is matched to the delay of the signal. As τ approaches zero, the output of the divider becomes proportional to the signal divided by its own magnitude, thus the limiting case of the AVC is the hard limiter; for moderate delays of, say 10 ms, very little spectral distortion occurs even if more than a single harmonic is present. In short, the AVC form of spectral flattening preserves intrafilter amplitude relations, while removing interfilter spectral fluctuations. Since little or no third harmonic distortion is created, the possibility (as yet untested) exists that the final bandpass filter bank is not needed, or at least can be made less complex.

Spectral flattening also makes possible speech-like phase modification of the excitation signal. The desired phase modifier network may be inserted between the

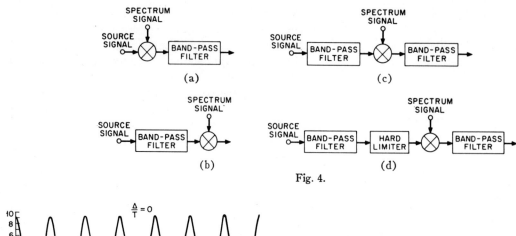

Fig. 4.

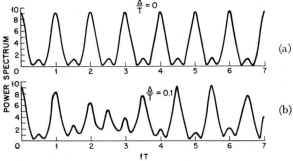

Fig. 5. (a) $\Delta/T=0$. (b) $\Delta/T=0.1$.

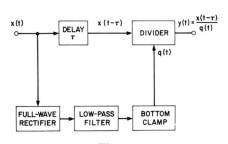

Fig. 6.

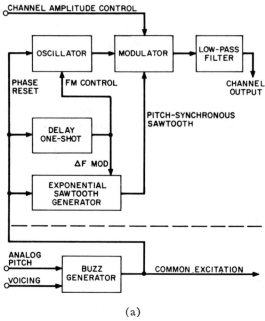

(a)

excitation pulses and the synthesizer. Since amplitude spectrum fluctuations are effectively eliminated if they take place before the spectral flattening, only the phase of the inserted network propagates through the synthesizer. Evidence exists, for example, that the insertion of four cascaded formant-like resonators, tuned to 500, 1500, 2500, and 3500 Hz, improves vocoded speech quality.[5]

The transition between voiced and unvoiced sounds is performed somewhat differently in the spectrally flattened synthesizer. A small noise source signal is always applied to the synthesizer. When voicing is present, the limiters suppress the noise sufficiently to render it inaudible but when voicing is absent, the noise "captures" the hard limiters. The resulting voiced–unvoiced transitions are smoother than in the configuration of Fig. 4(a), (b), and (c).

VII. VOCAL RESPONSE SYNTHESIZER

Another variation on the synthesizer configuration of a channel vocoder has been named the "vocal response synthesizer"[12] (VRS). The analyzer of a VRS is the same as that of a channel vocoder. A single channel of

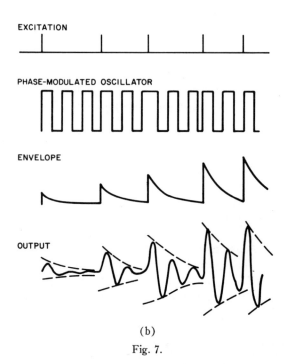

(b)

Fig. 7.

the synthesizer is shown in Fig. 7. A fixed frequency square wave generator is synchronized with incoming excitation pulses. This phase modulated square wave is then amplitude modulated by the output of an RC rundown circuit before being modulated by the spectral signals. The flexibility exists to force a different envelope decay characteristic when the glottis is open or closed, by means of a delay one-shot. The only change from channel to channel is in the frequency of the square wave generator. The outputs of each spectral modulator are passed through low-pass filters to remove third and higher harmonic distortion and all low-pass filter outputs are summed.

In a sense, the VRS is intermediate between the original vocoder configurations of Fig. 4(a), (b), and (c) and the spectrally flattened configuration of Fig. 4(d). When the RC rundown time constant is very small, the inputs to the spectral modulators are very much like the excitation pulses entering the modulator in Fig. 4(a). When the time constant is large, the square waves produced are very much like those exciting the modulators in Fig. 4(d).

Notice that there are no bandpass filters in Fig. 7. Thus, the VRS lends itself to microminiaturization techniques.

VIII. Bandpass Filter Design

As indicated in Section IV, vocoder bandpass filter characteristics must be a compromise between good spectral selectivity and fast transient response with little or no ringing. We shall limit the present discussion to standard filter designs, which may include Butterworth, Chebyshev, Bessel, Butterworth–Thomson, Elliptic, and Lerner filters. Several excellent books[13]–[15] and papers treat these filters.

Evidence[16] exists that Chebyshev and Elliptic filters, which are the filters with sharpest cutoff, are not suitable for vocoders. The long ringing times of these filters produce very noticeable reverberation effects in the vocoded speech. Butterworth filters with more than 3-pole pairs cause similar difficulties. The compromise between ringing time and selectivity seems to lie somewhere between 3-pole Butterworth filters and 3-pole Bessel filters, which corresponds to some intermediate parameter for the class of Butterworth–Thomson filters. Most vocoders have utilized 2-pole Butterworth filters. It is possible that the resultant poorer selectivity helps create some of the 'mechanical' quality often attributed to vocoded speech. It also appears[16] that a single pole pair is not an acceptable filter.[1]

Lerner filters,[17] like Bessel filters, have the attractive feature of a linear phase characteristic. For the same

total number of poles, the Lerner design, because it shares poles, gives greater selectivity.[18]

The number of filters used in the analysis and synthesis banks varies greatly depending on the application. The first vocoder built by Dudley had only ten equal bandwidth spectrum channels covering the speech band to 3 kHz. A later version had 30 channels over a 6-kHz band. To prevent distortion caused by the appearance of two voice harmonics in a single filter, about 40 filters would be required to cover the 3-kHz band. Often, frequencies above 3 kHZ are eliminated; this is perhaps unfortunate, since the spectral composition of the voiceless fricative and, to some extent, that the voiceless plosive consonants are primarily in the frequencies above 3 kHz.

Perhaps the most influential factor in determining the number of vocoder channels is the emphasis that has been put on using vocoders as part of digital communications channels. Since a speech signal can be coded and transmitted digitally with rates from 20 000 to 50 000 bits per second, the extra expense of using vocoders on a digital link must be compensated by appreciably lower bit rates. A commonly used vocoder rate is 2400 bits per second. This, or comparable requirements, indicates that since the spectral information is proportional to the number of channels, this number should be kept as low as possible. In most vocoders, for practical applications, the number of vocoder channels may vary between 14 and 20.

Another variable in bandpass filter design is the distribution of filter bandwidths. A common design feature is the use of constant bandwidth filters up to about 1000 Hz followed by bandwidths which are roughly proportional to the center frequencies. Justifying such a distribution is the argument[12] that the frequency perception ability of the ear follows this scale rather than a linear scale. The design of such a filter bank is complicated by the other requirements discussed in Section V, such as having amplitude response curves of adjacent filters cross properly and matching delays through different filters.

Additional difficulty is caused by unequal bandwidths for the vocoder configurations of Fig. 4(a), (b), and (c). Since each channel signal is a measure of the total energy bandwidth multiplied by energy density in that channel, wrong measurements occur for the noiselike, unvoiced sounds. These false measurements are not easily compensated by gain adjustments elsewhere in the channel because such compensation would then cause an error in the measurement of a single harmonic in that channel during voicing. This difficulty does not arise in the spectrally flattened configuration, Fig. 4(d), because increased energy measurement at the analyzer during unvoiced sounds is automatically compensated by decreased spectral density of the noise excitation in the synthesizer. The output of the hard limiter always has

---

[1] A recent paper presented by J. N. Holmes[24] indicates that single pole filters may, under certain conditions, be suitable for vocoder synthesis.

constant power; hence, the spectral density of the noise from the wider preclipping bandpass filter is decreased by roughly the same proportion that the analyzer output was increased.

IX. DESIGN OF ANALYZER LOW-PASS FILTERS

The major difficulty in correctly specifying a low-pass filter design arises because two harmonics appearing in a bandpass filter generate a ripple frequency from the rectifier equal to the voice fundamental. By contrast, if the input to any rectifier in Fig. 1 were a single sinusoid, the lowest ripple frequency would be equal to the frequency of that sinusoid (or twice that frequency, for a full wave rectifier). Since voice fundamental frequencies may be as low as 50 Hz, the low-pass filters need to be well attenuated at 50 Hz. Measurements of the average spectra of different channel signals[20] show that speech information is present within the bandwidth 0 through at least 25 Hz. If the further condition is attached that the low-pass filters have very little ringing to prevent reverberation effects, it is seen that the design is quite constrained.

There is some evidence that low-pass filters even wider than 25 Hz are desirable.[21] This can perhaps be explained by the transient nature of many portions of the speech, as discussed in the first paper of this series.

Given the above practical and theoretical constraints, a reasonable design is a low-pass filter having 3 dB attenuation at 25–35 Hz and an 18-dB-per-octave attenuation slope. Little is gained,[20] and design uniformity is hurt, by using low-pass filters of varying cutoff frequencies.

Dynamic Range Considerations

In a vocoder, as in other speech processing systems, provision must be made to handle the large amplitude variations of the input speech signal. The circuits must operate over more than a 60-dB range, unless the speech is first passed through an automatic volume control (AVC).

It is well known that AVC distorts the speech. Since the vocoder is a nonlinear device, it is not clear that amplitude expansion of the vocoded speech will compensate the distortion introduced by amplitude compression of the input speech. Fundamental frequency extraction and voicing detection may be hampered by AVC. In running vocoder experiments, it becomes difficult to separate audible effects caused by a vocoder parameter adjustment from audible effects caused by the AVC. For these reasons, wide dynamic range circuits are desirable. If the filters, rectifiers, modulators, and limiters (in a spectrally flattened vocoder) can operate within a few percent of linearity over a 60-dB range, the vocoder will be able to handle most sounds and speakers. To accommodate very loud and soft-spoken voices as well as movements away from the mouthpiece, a moderate amount of AVC may be added.

Due primarily to the vocal source, speech energy decreases quite rapidly with frequency. It is not uncommon for the speech spectral density at 3 kHz to be 30 or 40 dB below the spectral density at, say, 500 Hz. To prevent consequent further dynamic range difficulties, the high frequencies are always boosted before speech is processed by the vocoder. On the average, a 10-dB-per-octave boost above 500 Hz equalizes the speech spectrum in frequency.

X. TESTING OF VOCODERS

By applying a sine wave of constant amplitude and variable frequency to the vocoder input and measuring the amplitude of the resulting output sine wave, the overall vocoder frequency response may be determined. A constant amplitude versus frequency is the most desirable result, although, as discussed in Section IV, this does not necessarily demonstrate that the spectral reproduction of speech will be free of frequency distortion.

Vocoded speech is quite intelligible even if the synthesizer is excited wholly by either the noise source or pulses of constant repetition period within the range of voice fundamental frequency. In the former case, whispered speech is obtained and, in the latter case, expressionless "monotone" speech results. Listening to either mode often gives fresh insight into the vocoder performance.

A very useful test for spectrally flattened vocoders is to excite the synthesizer as well as the analyzer with the original speech. Both the spectral fine structure and the phase of the speech propagate through the synthesizer, while the amplitude spectrum is wiped out by the hard limiters. The result is vocoded speech which sounds almost as good as the original speech. Thus, the test affords a quick check on the operation of the vocoder spectrum channels and also serves as an excellent standard for comparison.

XI. VOCODERS FOR DIGITAL SPEECH COMMUNICATIONS

Most present-day vocoders have been designed for use with digital speech communications systems. There are many reasons for desiring digitized speech; for example, the greater ease of incorporating privacy into speech links and the affinity of certain communications channels for digital transmission.

A straightforward form of digitized vocoder is seen in Fig. 8. The spectrum and pitch channels are multiplexed, appearing serially at the analog–digital converter input where they are quantized before transmission. At the receiver, a digital–analog converter produces samples corresponding to each quantized signal; these samples are then filtered before application to the modulators and excitation circuits.

The new circuits and parameters introduced by digitization are the distribution of sampling rates and quan-

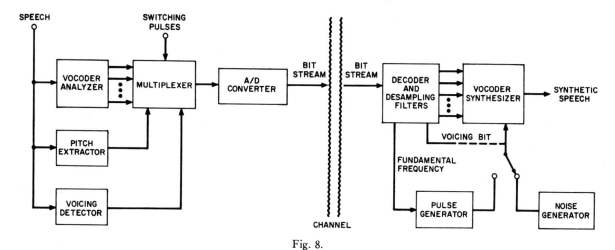

Fig. 8.

tization and the post-sampling low-pass filters. In many systems, the multiplexer switching is uniformly distributed over the frame interval (time during which all spectral parameters are sampled once), causing a skewing and a consequent time smearing of the spectral information. This can be prevented by sampling and serially quantizing all channels at a very fast rate and storing the bits in a buffer in order to transmit them at a uniform rate.

The minimum sampling rates and number of quantization levels needed to prevent degradation relative to the analog mode of a vocoder have not yet been determined.

The usual design begins with an overall rate specification such as 2400 bits per second or 4800 bits per second. Design then becomes a compromise between sampling rate and bits per sample. For the 2400 and 4800 rates, no digitized vocoder has yet been built which does not have a noticeable degradation relative to the analog mode. Despite this, even 2400-bit vocoded speech is highly intelligible and, for many practical purposes, very satisfactory.

XII. Quantization of Vocoder Spectrum Signals

There is presently no evidence that spectral signals from different channels should be quantized with different numbers of levels. The following remarks thus pertain to any channel.

It seems established that better results are obtained if successive quantization level differences be equal on a logarithmic rather than a linear scale. To an extent, this is theoretically justifiable on the ground that the probability distribution function of a spectral signal, on the average, is more nearly logarithmic than linear. It has been shown[22] that quantization levels, spaced so that each succeeding level adds an equal probability increment to the sample probability distribution, result in minimum mean-squared differences between the quantized and unquantized signals.

For convenience in coding, the number of levels is normally of the form 2^m, with m an integer. However, it is possible to code all the spectrum signals efficiently

even if the number of levels is not 2^m. Following is a procedure which efficiently codes n signals, each with an arbitrary number of levels.

Let the n quantized signals be $x_1, x_2, \cdots, x_n$ and let $M_1, M_2, \cdots, M_n$ be the number of quantization levels associated with each signal. Then, the single integer

$$S = x_1 + M_1x_2 + M_1M_2x_3 + M_1M_2M_3x_4 + \cdots$$
$$= x_1 + M_1(x_2 + M_2(x_3 + M_3(x_4 + \cdots))) \quad (4)$$

whose value is between zero and the product $M_1M_2 \cdots M_n$, represents a single set of combined quantization states. This integer is transmitted, for example, as a binary number. At the receiver, decoding takes place according to the following algorithm.

Divide the integer by M_1. The quotient is a new integer S' and the remainder is x_1. The new quotient is now divided by M_2, giving a new quotient S'' and remainder x_2. This process is continued until x_n is obtained.

Dynamic Encoding

Inspection of the amplitude variations of the spectrum channel signals shows large fluctuations with time. However, at any instant the amplitude as a function of the channel number fluctuates less rapidly. This is because all spectral signals tend to rise and fall proportionally to the overall speech level. One technique to take advantage of this redundancy is to code the signals relative to the maximum signal for any single frame. From computer simulation experiments, it has been ascertained that spectral signals which are more than 30 dB below the maximum signal can be given the value zero with no consequent loss in the vocoded speech quality. Assuming that the total system dynamic range is 64 dB, the maximum signal can be coded over the upper 32-dB range and the remaining signals coded relative to the maximum over a 32-dB range.

An estimate of the efficiency of coding relative to the maximum can be obtained from an example; assume that successive levels for both maximum and all sixteen other signals are separated by 2 dB; then 4 bits are needed for coding. In a 16-channel vocoder, $4 \times 17 = 68$ bits are needed. When the signals are coded directly rather than relative to the maximum, the codeword must specify levels over a 64-dB range; thus 5 bits are necessary to give the same fineness of quantization and $5 \times 16 = 80$ bits are needed.

Rather than coding relative to a maximum signal, one can obtain equivalent results by coding relative to an average signal.[1],[10],[23]

A modified delta-modulation scheme has also been used to advantage for coding the spectrum. In this scheme, one or more of the channel signals are coded in the usual way and the adjacent channels are coded by successively taking the logarithmic differences between the next channel and the previously coded channel. The coding takes place on a frame by frame basis; that is, the delta modulation is along the frequency dimension. Two such schemes are known to the authors, one of which is used for a 2400-bit vocoder[24] and the other to help reduce the bit rate to 1200.[25]

Redundancy Removing Coding Schemes

Considerations of the speech production mechanism show clearly that, at any instant, the samples of the spectral envelope, as measured by a vocoder spectrum analyzer, are to some extent redundant. For example, for the steady-state portion of a vowel, only the formants are sufficient to specify the spectral envelope; yet the 16-channel signals are transmitted. The discussion of speech sounds in the previous installment indicates that three or four parameters suffice to describe any sound.

Arguments of this sort have led many workers towards formant vocoders, but formidable theoretical and engineering problems still prevent concrete realization of operational formant vocoder systems. Furthermore, as digital techniques become more economic, there has been a tendency to try to eliminate channel vocoder spectral redundancy by means of digital coding. The dynamic encoding scheme and the delta-modulation schemes discussed in the previous section are examples of simple digital redundancy removal.

Approximate representation of the spectral envelope by means of a Fourier series has been used to reduce the digital bit rate.[26],[27] Presumably, many representations of the spectral envelope by means of orthogonal functions could lead to significant reduction in data rate; how to choose a representation with perceptual significance is not presently understood.

In the absence of suitable perceptual criteria for decreasing redundancy, a not unreasonable criterion is that of minimizing the mean-squared difference between 1) the input spectral envelope and 2) the restored spectral envelope, after transformation, redundancy removal, and inverse transformation. Such a transformation, if it is constrained to be linear, turns out to be the one which diagonalizes the correlation matrix of the input spectral samples,[27] and is found to be the solution

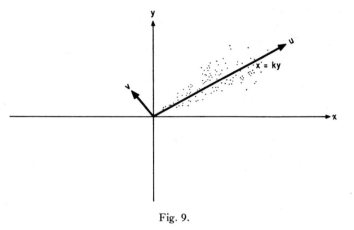

Fig. 9.

TABLE I

	Transformed Signals	Number of Levels
1	1	100
2	0.226	23
3	0.141	15
4	0.0795	8
5	0.0642	7
6	0.0572	6
7	0.042	5
8	0.0377	4
9	0.9327	4
10	0.0279	3
11	0.0261	3
12	0.0204	2
13	0.0191	2
14	0.0171	2
15	0.01318	1
16	0.0104	1

to a specific eigenvalue problem. Furthermore, when the mean-square values of the transformed signals are ordered, it turns out that for speech, there is a large range between the highest and lowest signals, indicating that sizeable correlations existed among the original spectral signals.

The results of the above linear transformation are perhaps more clearly understood by appealing to geometrical intuition. Let us consider two signals, $x(t)$ and $y(t)$, which at any instant are strongly correlated. Referring to Fig. 9, it is seen that the measurements (x, y) tend to fall near the straight line $x = ky$. Now, by introducing the new coordinates (n, v) as shown in Fig. 9, it is clear that a greater number of bits is needed for specifying the transformed signal n compared to specifying v. Furthermore, quantization of u and v are orthogonal, so that specification of one transformed variable appears to give little, if any, information about the other.

Computation of the transformation matrix for about 20 minutes of speech input leads to a list of root-mean-squared values as shown in Table I. Also shown are the number of levels used for quantizing the transformed signals. These were each chosen to be proportional to corresponding root-mean-squared value, the first entry in the right-hand column being chosen arbitrarily.

TABLE II

+1	+1	+1	+1	+1	+1	+1	+1	+1	+1	+1	+1	+1	+1	+1	+1
+1	+1	+1	+1	+1	+1	+1	+1	-1	-1	-1	-1	-1	-1	-1	-1
+1	+1	+1	+1	-1	-1	-1	-1	+1	+1	+1	+1	-1	-1	-1	-1
+1	+1	+1	+1	-1	-1	-1	-1	-1	-1	-1	-1	+1	+1	+1	+1
+1	+1	-1	-1	+1	+1	-1	-1	+1	+1	-1	-1	+1	+1	-1	-1
+1	+1	-1	-1	+1	+1	-1	-1	-1	-1	+1	+1	-1	-1	+1	+1
+1	+1	-1	-1	-1	-1	+1	+1	+1	+1	-1	-1	-1	-1	+1	+1
+1	+1	-1	-1	-1	-1	+1	+1	-1	-1	+1	+1	+1	+1	-1	-1
+1	-1	+1	-1	+1	-1	+1	-1	+1	-1	+1	-1	+1	-1	+1	-1
+1	-1	+1	-1	+1	-1	+1	-1	-1	+1	-1	+1	-1	+1	-1	+1
+1	-1	+1	-1	-1	+1	-1	+1	+1	-1	+1	-1	-1	+1	-1	+1
+1	-1	+1	-1	-1	+1	-1	+1	-1	+1	-1	+1	+1	-1	+1	-1
+1	-1	-1	+1	+1	-1	-1	+1	+1	-1	-1	+1	+1	-1	-1	+1
+1	-1	-1	+1	+1	-1	-1	+1	-1	+1	+1	-1	-1	+1	+1	-1
+1	-1	-1	+1	-1	+1	+1	-1	+1	-1	-1	+1	-1	+1	+1	-1
+1	-1	-1	+1	-1	+1	+1	-1	-1	+1	+1	-1	+1	-1	-1	+1

Coding the Logarithm of the Spectrum

Rather than reduce the mean-squared error of the transmitted spectrum, it seems intuitively preferable to try to reduce the error in the logarithm of the spectrum. This could presumably be accomplished by finding that linear transformation of the log-spectrum which diagonalizes the correlation matrix of the transformed log-spectrum, so that the technique reduces to that of the previous section once the log-spectrum is computed. A further simplification is possible by constraining the transformation matrix to contain only $+1$ or -1; such a system would be appreciably simpler to implement, and, interestingly, does not greatly increase the resultant spectral distortion. The actual matrix used [28] is shown in Table II and is known as a Hadamard matrix.[29] For example, the first linear combination is simply the sum of the channel signals and the second linear combination is the sum of the first eight-channel signals minus the sum of the last eight-channel signals. A major advantage of this transformation is the ease and economy of digital implementation.[28] Experiments have shown that the quality of vocoded speech is only slightly disturbed using a spectral transmission rate of 1650 bits per second (33 bits per 20 ms frame).

Pattern Matching

The set of vocoder spectrum signals may be viewed as a pattern at any instant of time. In particular, if we have an n channel vocoder and digitally code each channel with m bits, then the pattern obtained is one out of 2^{nm} possible patterns. For example, if $n = 18$ and $m = 4$, 2^{72} possible patterns can be generated. Obviously, this is a vastly greater number of patterns that can be generated by a vocoder analyzing human speech. From elementary considerations, a rough estimate can be made of the number of significantly different patterns obtainable. Assume that English is comprised of 1000 unique allophones (acoustic variants of the phonemes). Assume that there are 1000 different transition spectra between phonemes. In a channel vocoder, the spectral measurement is somewhat influenced by pitch, as discussed in Section V. Assume that a given spectral envelope has 10 pitch-caused variants. Also, let there be 10 variants of a given allophone to accommodate various speakers. The resulting number of patterns obtained is 200 000 or about 2^{18} patterns, at both the transmitter and receiver. Rather than transmitting the actual 72-bit pattern, as is normally done, the 18-bit address of the appropriate pattern is first found and transmitted to the receiver, which locates in its store the correct pattern from the received address. Given a 50-Hz sampling rate, it is seen that 900 bits per second is needed for transmission of the spectrum.

The above pattern matching concept is the basis of an experimental digital speech processing facility,[30],[31] wherein the resultant speech quality can be tested as functions of the number of stored patterns and the various strategies used to store and regenerate the patterns. The importance of the experimental setup lies in the ability to *perceptually* test the effect of parametric variations.

XIII. SAMPLING OF THE SPECTRUM SIGNALS

It can be reasonably argued that bit rate specifications of 2400 or even 4800 bits per second limit the sampling rate to too low a value. In general,

$$f_r = b_s/nq \tag{5}$$

where n is the number of channels, b_s is the total spectral bit rate, q is the number of quantization bits per channel, and f_r is the sampling frequency of any channel. For a 2400-bit vocoder, b_s is about 1800 bits per second, the remaining 600 being assigned to the excitation information. If $q = 3$, $f_r = 37.5$ samples per second. Transitions in the speech, especially during the plosive constants, generally occur over a time smaller than this sampling interval. Although the perceptual effects of such low sampling rates have not been systematically studied, it is possible that values of $f_r = 60$ Hz may be required for straight sampling, to avoid strong degradations. From (5), it is seen that q would be reduced to $1\frac{7}{8}$ bits to accommodate this increased rate, which, in turn, would cause unpleasant roughness of the speech. Clearly, the application of the techniques of Section

XII could be helpful for reducing the average number of quantization levels per channel, thus allowing a higher value of f_r for the same overall bit rate. In addition, however, more advantage can be taken of our knowledge of the speech process. We will now discuss some of these possibilities.

Although it is true that very rapid transitions occur in speech, there are other segments of a speech wave which change relatively slowly. An extreme illustration of a slowly varying speech spectrum is a sustained vowel. In theory, at least, to transmit a sustained vowel, only the formants and perhaps a parameter for the vocal source need be transmitted only once. An even more extreme example is a pause in the speech; during this pause, only the information that a pause exists needs to be transmitted. As a general rule, the information rate needed to transmit a speech signal varies greatly depending on the speech itself, that is, speech is a variable rate source. The problem of measuring this rate as a function of time remains to be solved.

The statistical distribution of the pauses in conversational English has been studied.[32] The use of a "pause detector," and buffer storage made it possible to experimentally determine the bit rate savings obtained by coding the pauses with the code bit zero. The graph in Fig. 10 shows the number of overflows versus percent saving for different buffer sizes corresponding to various delays.

When a spectral signal is sampled, the harmonics of the samples beat with the signal to create many new frequencies. Effectively, the original spectrum of any given spectral signal, which might have been confined to the frequencies 0 through f, is now repeated infinitely about the sampling frequency. This well-known phenomenon is called "alasing" or "folding" and has been treated extensively.[34]

At the vocoder synthesizer, the successive samples for any given channel must be reconverted to an analog signal before being applied to the modulators. This means that the samples must be passed through a low-pass filter which removes all the folding frequencies, conserving only the spectrum of the original signal. For example, if the sampling rate were 50 Hz, filters with 25-Hz cutoff frequencies are advisable, even though the analyzer low-pass filters ought to be appreciably wider, as indicated by the Cassel–Jurenko[21] experiment.

Measurements on the time averaged spectrum of any vocoder spectral channel signal show that about 99 percent of the energy lies within the band 0–25 Hz.[20] However, it is undesirable to use analyzer low-pass filters with sharp cutoff beyond 25 Hz, since much of the information about the rapid transitions during plosive consonants would thereby be lost. In practice, vocoder analyzer low-pass filters have about 3 dB of attenuation at 25–35 Hz and then roll off gradually to perhaps 40 dB of attenuation at 100 Hz.

Sampling rates must be kept as low as possible to

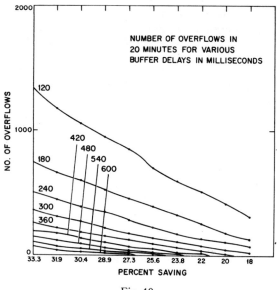

Fig. 10.

keep the overall bit rate low. In view of this, distortion created by overlap between the original and folded spectra occurs in most vocoders. The design of the post-sampling filters at the synthesizer must thus be stringently controlled to minimize the effects of this distortion. An additional requirement is that the post-sampling filters have very low delay distortion, otherwise reverberation effects become quite audible.

The sample-and-hold circuit is a very convenient and commonly used component of a post-sampling filter. Each incoming sample rapidly charges a capacitor whose charge is held until the next sample is applied. Such a circuit can be treated as a linear filter, with a rectangular impulse response and $\sin x/x$ frequency response. Thus, no spectral time dispersion occurs; however, folding frequencies are not sufficiently attenuated; therefore, it is advisable to follow the sample-and-hold circuit by something like a 3-pole Bessel filter with 25-Hz cutoff frequency.

XIV. VARIABLE SAMPLING RATE

The techniques described in Section XII take advantage of the redundancy across spectral channels at a given instant of time. But these spectral signals are also redundant in time; for example, during a sustained vowel, 100 ms may pass without any significant change versus time for all or most of these signals. However, during other portions of the speech, especially during transitions for one sound to the next, relatively rapid fluctuations occur in these signals. It is desirable, therefore, to have a measurement which gives a large answer when the spectrum is changing rapidly and a small answer when the spectrum is slowly varying. Such a measurement could then be used to control the vocoder spectral sampling rate.

The spectral derivative measurement proposed by Liljencrantz[36] for the automatic segmentation of

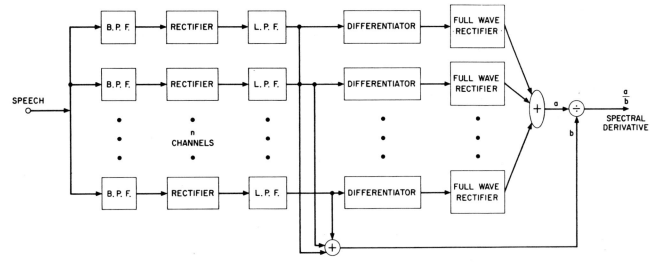

Fig. 11.

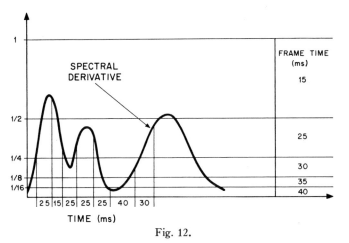

Fig. 12.

speech has the desired property. This measurement is defined as

$$S(t) = \frac{\sum_{i=1}^{N} | \dot{x}_i(t) |}{\sum_{i=1}^{N} x_i(t)}. \qquad (6)$$

In (6), $x_i(t)$ is the ith spectral signal and $\dot{x}_i(t)$ its time derivative. The numerator is the sum of the magnitudes of the derivatives for all N channels. The denominator normalizes the measurement so that it is more or less independent of the speech volume. Fig. 11 shows the block diagram of a vocoder analyzer which also generates the spectral derivative measurement.

One method of using $S(t)$ to control the spectral sampling rate is shown in Fig. 12. A set of thresholds are chosen and the time to the next sampling of the entire spectrum is determined by the value of $S(t)$ at the present sample. The functional dependence of the sampling intervals on $S(t)$ can be empirically adjusted to result in different average sampling rates.

Several aspects of this approach are worth noting. First, the entire spectrum is sampled together. It could be argued that an improvement could be effected by adjusting the sampling rate of *each* spectral signal in accordance with its own rate of change, since in many cases only a portion of the spectrum is changing rapidly. Such a scheme would, however, be very expensive to instrument. Another point is that since sampling is no longer uniform, the design of the post-sampling filters must be reconsidered. A solution which appeared to work well on a computer simulation experiment was to linearly interpolate between adjacent samples of signals from the same channel. It is possible that standard fixed parameter post-sampling filters may not be feasible for hardware realization of a variable sampling rate vocoder.

Experimental results, using a laboratory vocoder in conjucntion with the TX-2 computer, indicate that the rate of a 2400-bit vocoder may be reduced to about 1800 bits with little appreciable degradation of the synthetic speech. However, attempts to reduce the total rate to 1200 bits resulted in unacceptable degradation.

REFERENCES

[1] H. W. Dudley, "Remaking speech," *J. Acoust. Soc. Am.*, vol. 11, pp. 1969–1977, 1939a.
[2] ———, "The vocoder," *Bell Labs. Rec.*, vol. 17, pp. 122–126, 1939b.
[3] ———, "The carrier nature of speech," *Bell Sys. Tech. J.*, vol. 19, no. 4, October 1940.
[4] E. E. David, Jr., J. E. Miller, and M. V. Mathews, "Monaural phase effects in speech perception," *Proc. 3rd Internat'l Congress on Acoustics* (Stuttgart, 1959), vol. 1, L. Cremer, Eds. Amsterdam: Elsevier, 1961, p. 227.
[5] B. Gold, "Experiment with speechlike phase in a spectrally flattened pitch-excited channel vocoder," *J. Acoust. Soc. Am.*, vol. 36, pp. 1892–1894, 1964.
[6] H. W. Dudley, private communication.
[7] J. L. Flanagan, *Speech Analysis, Synthesis and Perception.* New York: Academic Press, 1965.
[8] J. Tierney, B. Gold, V. Sferrino, J. A. Dumanian, and E. Aho, "Channel vocoder with digital pitch extractor," *J. Acoust. Soc. Am.*, vol. 36, pp. 1901–1905, 1964.
[9] L. A. Yaggi, Jr., "Full-duplex digital vocoder, part one," Texas Instruments Incorporated, Final Rept. for AFCRL, June 10, 1963.
[10] L. E. Cassel, "Soft talk system (484L) vocoder improvement program," Philco Corp., Final Rept., vols. I and II, December 1963.
[11] B. Gold and J. Tierney, "Pitch-induced spectral distortion in channel vocoders," *J. Acoust. Soc. Am.*, vol. 35, pp. 730–731, 1963.

[12] C. P. Smith, "Vocal response synthesizer," *J. Acoust. Soc. Am.*, vol. 37, pp. 170–171, 1965.

[13] E. A. Guilleman, *Synthesis of Passive Networks*. New York: Wiley, 1957.

[14] J. E. Storer, *Passive Network Synthesis*. New York: McGraw-Hill, 1957.

[15] L. Weinberg, *Network Analysis and Synthesis*. New York: McGraw-Hill, 1962.

[16] C. M. Rader, "Study of vocoder filters by computer simulation," *J. Acoust. Soc. Am.*, vol. 36, p. 1023(A), 1964.

[17] R. M. Lerner, "Bandpass filters with linear phase," *Proc. IEEE*, vol. 52, pp. 249–268, March 1964.

[18] P. R. Drouilhet, Jr., and L. M. Goodman, "Pole-shared linear-phase band-pass filter bank," *Proc. IEEE*. (*Correspondence*), vol. 54, pp. 701–703, April 1966.

[19] W. Koenig, "A new frequency scale for acoustic measurements," *Bell Labs. Rec.*, August 1949.

[20] C. M. Rader, "Spectra of vocoder-channel signals," *J. Acoust. Soc. Am.*, vol. 35, p. 805(A), 1963.

[21] L. Cassel and D. Jurenko, "Improved vocoders," reprint of paper presented at Audio Engineering Society, 1964.

[22] J. Max, "Quantizing for minimum distortion," *IEEE Trans. Information Theory*, vol. IT-6, pp. 7–12, March 1960.

[23] C. P. Smith, "Normalization of the voice spectrum," *J. Acoust. Soc. Am.*, vol. 29, p. 777(A), 1957.

[24] J. N. Holmes, "Some recent research at the joint speech research unit of the British post office," presented at the IEEE Communications Convention, June 1966.

[25] L. E. Cassel, private communication.

[26] A. A. Pirogov, "A harmonic system for compressing speech spectra," *Elektrosviaz*, no. 3, pp. 8–17, 1959.

[27] H. P. Kramer and M. V. Mathews, "A linear coding for transmitting a set of correlated signals," *IRE Trans. Information Theory*, vol. IT-2, pp. 41–46, September 1956.

[28] C. M. Rader and W. R. Crowther, "Efficient coding of vocoder channel signals using linear transformation," *Proc. IEEE*, vol. 54, pp. 1494–1495, November 1966.

[29] S. W. Golomb, Ed., *Digital Communications with Space Applications*. Englewood Cliffs, N. J.: Prentice-Hall, pp. 53–58, 1964.

[30] C. P. Smith, "An approach to speech bandwidth compression," *Proc. of Seminar on Speech Compression and Processing*, vol. 2, pp. 28–30 (September 1959); sponsored by Electronics Research Directorate, Air Force Cambridge Research Center, Air Research and Development Command. (See also several other papers in this seminar.)

[31] ——, "Experiments with voice pattern matching," presented at the IEEE Communications Convention, June 1966.

[32] D. R. Ziemer, A. R. Aitken, R. L. Brueck, and A. E. Mason, Jr., "A study of the feasibility of multiplexing teletype data into nonspeech time of vocoded speech transmission," Texas Instruments Incorporated, Final Rept., pt. III, June 1963.

[33] W. R. Crowther and D. C. Walden, unpublished notes.

[34] J. R. Ragazzini and G. F. Franklin, *Sampled-Data Control Systems*. New York: McGraw-Hill, 1958.

[35] C. M. Rader and B. Gold, "Digital filter design techniques in the frequency domain," *Proc. IEEE*, vol. 55, pp. 149–171, February 1967.

[36] J. Liljencrantz, "A few experiments on voiced-voiceless identification and time segmentation of speech," Speech Transmission Laboratories, Stockholm, Sweden, Quart. Prog. Rept., October 15, 1962.

VOICE-EXCITED VOCODERS FOR PRACTICAL SPEECH BANDWIDTH REDUCTION

By

E. E. David, Jr., M. R. Schroeder, B. F. Logan, and A. J. Prestigiacomo
Bell Telephone Laboratories, Incorporated
Murray Hill, New Jersey

Summary

In spite of their great potential for bandwidth saving in long distance telephony, vocoders have not found wide-spread acceptance. Two major problems have retarded their application. First is their strong electrical accent. Second is the so-called "pitch problem;" namely, deducing the nature of the talker's vocal excitation from his speech waveform. The reliability of this deduction and measurement depends critically upon high input speech-to-noise ratio, particularly between 50 and 200 cps. In many communication situations, this requirement precludes satisfactory operation. This limitation can be removed by a new method known as "voice excitation," which eliminates the necessity for a decision-making pitch detector. The principal advantage of voice excitation is its insensitivity to input signal-to-noise ratio and equalization. A voice-excited vocoder (VEV) with a 720 cps (250-970 cps) baseband and 17 spectrum channels low-passed to 25 cps each, covering the band 970-3700 cps, has been built and evaluated. The test shows an average PB-word intelligibility of 86%, compared to 92% for input speech of the same bandwidth, both with an 18 db signal-to-noise ratio. Quality tests indicate that listeners rate VEV speech "as good as" the input in about 90% of the test utterances. Only 19% of conventional vocoder utterances were so considered. The vocoder performed about equally well for each of the 12 speakers in the quality test. Voice-discrimination tests indicate that voice identity is well preserved. Crucial factors influencing the remade speech quality are the accuracy of spectral flattening and the impulse response of the analyzer low-pass filters. These results indicate that the principle of voice excitation provides the key to practical speech bandwidth reduction.

Introduction

The vocoder principle for reduced bandwidth transmission of speech was invented some 30 years ago by H. W. Dudley.[1] He envisioned separating the low-rate phonetic information from the high-frequency acoustic excitation by analysis at the transmitter, coding each component into low-frequency descriptive signals for transmission, and reconstructing speech from the received description. The principle was first demonstrated in the middle 1930's. In spite of their great potential for bandwidth saving in long distance telephony, vocoders have been singularly unsuccessful in finding wide-spread acceptance.

Two major problems have retarded them. First is their strong electrical accent. Proverbially, vocoders put "marbles in the talker's mouth," eliminate a talker's individuality so that all speakers sound alike, and make speech sound inhuman. Such speech-correlated distortions are inadmissible in high-quality communication.

Second is the so-called "pitch problem". Vocoder analysis attempts to resolve the short-time speech spectrum into an envelope and a fine structure as indicated in Fig. 1. The latter consists of discrete harmonics of the voice fundamental for voiced sounds and a continuous spectrum for unvoiced sounds. The discrete structure results from excitation of the vocal tract by quasi-periodic vocal cord pulses. The continuous spectrum arises from turbulence-generated noise near points of constriction in the vocal tract.[2] Thus spectral fine-structure reflects the nature of the speech excitation, and to describe it for vocoder transmission calls for a voiced-unvoiced decision (based, for example, upon the amount of energy contained in a low frequency band) plus a measurement of the voice fundamental frequency (based usually upon a zero-crossing count of the voice fundamental).[3] The reliability of this decision and measurement depends critically upon the input speech quality, particularly speech-to-noise ratio and low-frequency equalization. In many practical instances, this sensitivity precludes satisfactory operation. (Variants of the classical scheme, based upon envelope detection, also fail because of the strong dependence of the envelope waveform on the shifting relative phases of the speech harmonics.)

In a voice-excited vocoder (see Fig. 2) these difficulties are avoided by generating the excitation signal required at the receiver-synthesizer from an uncoded sub-band (called the baseband) of the original speech. This band can be added directly to the output, but its principal function is to supply excitation for the synthesizer. Wide-band excitation is generated from the narrower baseband by nonlinear distortion, which produces appropriately either a flat spectrum of noise or harmonic frequency components. Thus the excitation is reproduced from the original voice and is not a result of

Reprinted from *IRE Trans. Inform. Theory*, vol. IT-8, pp. S101–S105, Sept. 1962.

any coding process. This method is quite insensitive to input conditions and so by-passes the pitch problem. A rather unexpected, but equally important dividend is that voice-excitation removes much of the vocoder's electrical accent. These benefits accrue at the expense of a wider transmission band since the classical pitch signal requires only a few tens of cycles for transmission while the baseband calls for several hundred.

Voice-Excitation

The most critical problem in voice-excitation is that of spectral flattening. A flat, time-invariant spectral envelope must be produced from the spectrally-varying baseband. In an early voice-excited vocoder,[4] the baseband was about 3000 cps wide; it was paired with spectrum channels covering the band 3000-10,000 cps. This so-called "high-fidelity" vocoder was intended to improve the intelligibility and quality of nominal 4-kc speech. With this 3000-cps baseband, a simple, zero-memory nonlinear circuit whose input-output relation is shown in Fig. 3, provided adequate flattening. Note that the effect of this network is to increase the frequency of zero-crossings in the output waveform. Thus the network tends to spread the baseband energy over the wider band. The output spectrum tends to be flat even though the baseband spectrum is fluctuating in shape since it covers several octaves.

In applying the voice-excitation principle for bandwidth reduction, the baseband must be narrower. The nominal minimum for a wide talker population without incurring some degradation is about 700 cps. For flattening such a band, a filter bank is necessary. As shown in Fig. 4, the baseband is first spread by rectification into a wider band whose shape fluctuates with the baseband spectral shape. This fluctuating spectrum is filtered into narrow bands; each one is then clipped to remove the fluctuation. Thus a flat excitation spectrum is obtained.

Note that if more than one voice harmonic falls in a particular band, the more intense one will be reinforced vis-a-vis the weaker one because of the well-known zero crossing "capture-effect." To avoid this form of distortion, the flattening bands should be narrow enough to preclude the two-harmonic case for the lowest pitch voice encountered. On the other hand, if a filter contains no harmonic, the noise in that band will be grossly amplified by the clipping process. This distortion can be avoided by making the filters wide enough to include at least one harmonic for the highest pitch talker. The conflict between these two requirements is happily resolved in the vocoder. Fluctuations in close-spaced harmonics do not

affect the gross overall spectral shape, and speech synthesized from such excitation seems to satisfy the ear. If there is no harmonic in a filter, its corresponding spectral channel signal will have a low value, and the flattening noise will be suppressed in the modulator.

Experimental Results

Several voice-excited vocoders (VEV's) yielding bandwidth reductions up to 4 or 5 have been built.[5,6] A comprehensive evaluation of one channel or filterbank model has been carried out. Its baseband covered 250 to 940 cps, and there were 17 vocoder channels covering 940 to 3650 cps. The first 14 of these took 150 cps slices of the input spectrum; the upper three were slightly wider. The transmission band totaled between 1000 and 1200 cps, yielding about a 3 to 1 bandwidth economy. To assure a realistic evaluation, the input speech for the tests originated from a carbon-button microphone; specifically, a production model of the Western Electric Type-500 telephone handset.

Phonetically-balanced word lists were used for testing intelligibility. Four male and four female talkers, and a crew of six listeners took part. The test compared intelligibility before and after the vocoder. The input handset speech was filtered to the same bandwidth as the vocoder output. As a precaution to keep all intelligibilities well below 100%, noise was added to the test materials to achieve a uniform 18-db speech-to-noise ratio. The results are shown in Fig. 5. Women are definitely less intelligible than men; the vocoder degradation, too, is somewhat greater for women. It should be noted that the intelligibility figures themselves hold little meaning; it is the differences that are significant. Absolute intelligibilities are subject to large variations depending upon test material, talker peculiarities, listener motivation, and the like. Differences in intelligibility between input and output are much more meaningful than a measurement of the output alone.

Overall speech quality was evaluated by having 8 male and 4 female talkers read sentences simultaneously into the carbon button and a high-quality dynamic microphone. These sentences were recorded and provided the source material for producing processed material for evaluation. One set of processed sentences was produced by playing the carbon-button sentences into the filter bank of a conventional 18-channel vocoder[3] whose voiced-unvoiced-pitch circuits were driven simultaneously from the dynamic microphone recording. Another set was produced by playing the carbon-button sentences over a long-distance carrier telephone loop (Murray Hill-Chicago-Murray Hill). Two other sets originated from this one; first by reproduction through the VEV, and second, through an 1800-cps low-pass filter. These four sets of sentences (the VEV, the 1800-cps low-pass, the conventional vocoder, and the carrier telephone) were intermixed and played one-by-one to 30 subjects, each listening over a single earphone. The subjects were asked to rate each sentence either "as good as normal telephone," or "worse than normal telephone." One way of looking at the results are shown in Fig. 6, where the percentages "as good as" (AGA) judgments are plotted for successive blocks of 12 trials for each sentence set. Clearly the VEV is closer to the originals than either the 1800-cps low-pass or the conventional vocoder. There is little or no learning effect and the average percentages are respectively 82% for the telephone, 72% VEV, 36% 1800-cps low-pass, and 17% conventional vocoder. Another way of looking at the data (Fig. 7) is to compare "as good as" (AGA) responses for each talker by all listeners on the VEV and the carrier telephone. For instance, talker 10's voice was judged as good as telephone on only some 30% of her sentences even on the telephone utterances, while some 40% of her VEV utterances were judged as good as telephone. Thus the VEV tends to improve her voice so far as the listeners are concerned. The points above the 45° line represent improvement by the vocoder, points below degradation. Roughly, talkers seem to be treated fairly uniformly by the vocoder since the points cluster about the diagonal.

Yet another way of looking at the data is shown in Fig. 8 where the individual judgments of each listener on all talkers are arranged on a similar plot. Some listeners liked the vocoder better than telephone; some disliked it heartily. Listeners were pretty well scattered in their opinions.

To test how well talker individuality was preserved by the VEV, a talker discrimination test was undertaken. Pairs of sentences were played to listeners who judged if the same talker or different talkers spoke the members[7] of each pair. Each pair was processed either by the VEV or the conventional vocoder, or came from the carrier telephone recording. Five talkers and 20 listeners took part. Two kinds of errors were possible--different talkers might be called the same or the same talker might be called different. If the vocoder tends to eradicate talker individuality, some vocoder pairs spoken by different talkers should be judged as spoken by the same talker. The results are shown in Fig. 9.[1] Clearly the VEV preserves talker individuality much better than the conventional vocoder and indeed seems to do as well as the telephone sentences. On the other hand, a significantly larger number of same-talker pairs were judged different after having been put through the VEV. This is a rather peculiar effect. It implies that over the VEV a talker may, on different utterances, not sound like himself although he will sound different from other talkers.

[1]) See page S 127.

Comment and Conclusion

It should be noted that these results do not hinge upon adding the baseband speech directly to the output. In other words, the entire speech band can be vocoded, the baseband used only for excitation, and very nearly the same quality maintained. This fact leads to the question, "Why is VEV quality so superior to conventional vocoders?" One possibility was pointed out in the 1959 Schroeder-David paper.[4] The mechanism of voice-excitation preserves the rapid pitch fluctuation which seem inherent in speech.[8,9] The conventional vocoder pitch circuit averages these so that they are absent from the reproduced speech. Another possibility involves the voiced-unvoiced decision in conventional vocoders. Their synthesizer excitation is either a quasi-periodic waveform or noise. In the VEV, a mixture (quasi-periodic for some frequencies, random noise for others) can be reproduced as appropriate. However, a firm answer to the above question is yet to be obtained.

While the VEV is superior to conventional vocoders with regard to quality, it yields less bandwidth reduction principally because of the wide baseband which must be transmitted intact. Recent work has shown that the baseband might be shaved to between 500 and 600 cps without adversely affecting quality. Apparently only 10-12 vocoder channels of some 30 cps (transmission band) each are needed. The total bandwidth of these signals is between 800 and 1000 cps, compared to some 400 cps for a conventional channel vocoder.

The actual transmission bandwidth for any vocoder depends, of course, on the method of modulation. To minimize this figure, the baseband should use single-sideband but the channel signals are not so simply disposed of. They have an important dc-component which must be preserved. Vestigial sideband is one possibility, but quadrature modulation is better.[10] Two signals are amplitude-modulated (double-sideband) onto a single carrier frequency, one onto $\cos W_c t$, the other onto $\sin W_c t$. At the receiver, coherent carriers and a product demodulator are required to disentangle the modulated signals. In the usual multiplex situation, for instance, two normal voice channels, carrier coherence cannot be assured to within the tolerances necessary for holding crosstalk between the channels within bounds. Vocoder channels are, however, highly correlated and the ear is not too fussy about spectral overlap. As a result, the crosstalk between adjacent vocoder channels need be held to within only some 20 decibels. This figure is well within the capabilities of a quadrature system. Using this plan, the actual transmission band need provide only for modest guard space between the various components. In all, a total band of 1000 to 1500 cps seems feasible, compared to 500 to 600 cps for conventional vocoders.

The optimum design of the VEV itself is still a subject of research, but two principles have emerged. First, the widths and shapes of the spectral analyzing filters are not critical. Second the impulse-response duration of the channel low-pass filters must be carefully tailored to prevent ringing.

In conclusion, our subjective evaluation enables us to say confidently that though the voice-excited vocoder introduces a measurable degradation, it is clearly superior to conventional vocoders. By overcoming the pitch problem and relieving the electrical accent, voice-excitation makes vocoders useful in a variety of contexts, particularly those where input conditions cannot be easily controlled and high-quality output speech is required.

The authors would like to acknowledge the assistance and advice of P. D. Bricker and H. K. Dunn in the VEV evaluation.

References

1. H. W. Dudley, "The carrier nature of speech," Bell Sys. Tech. J., Vol. 19, pp. 495-515, Oct., 1940.

2. C. G. M. Fant, Acoustic Theory of Speech Production, Mouton and Co, The Hague, Netherlands, 1960.

3. E. E. David, Jr., "Signal theory in speech transmission," IRE Trans. Circuit Theory, vol. CT-3, pp. 232-244, Dec., 1956.

4. M. R. Schroeder and E. E. David, Jr., "A vocoder for transmitting 10 kc/s speech over a 3.5 kc/s channel," Acustica, vol. 10, no. 1, pp. 35-43, 1960.

5. M. R. Schroeder, "Recent progress in speech coding at Bell Telephone Laboratories," Proc. III Int. Congress on Acoustics, pp. 201-210, Elsevier Publishing Co., Amsterdam, 1961.

6. J. L. Flanagan, "Resonance-vocoder and Baseband complement: hybrid speech transmission," IRE Wescon Conv. Record, Part 7, pp. 5-16, 1959.

7. The members of each pair were different sentences spoken by the same or different talkers.

8. E. E. David, Jr., L. G. Kersta, and P. D. Bricker, "Human or machine? A study of voice naturalness," J. Acoust. Soc. Am., vol. 32, 15-2(A), 1960.

9. P. Lieberman, "Perturbations in vocal pitch," J. Acoust. Soc. Am., vol. 33, pp. 597-603, May, 1961.

10. R. J. Halsey and J. Swaffield, "Analysis-synthesis telephony with special reference to the vocoder," J. of Inst. of Elec. Engrs., vol. 95, Part III, pp. 391-411, Sept., 1948.

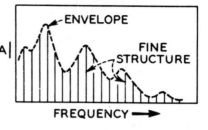

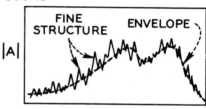

Figure 1 Speech Spectra

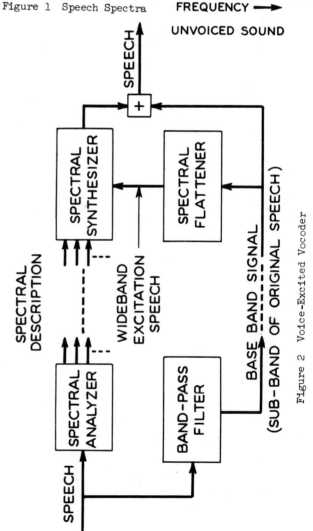

Figure 2 Voice-Excited Vocoder

386

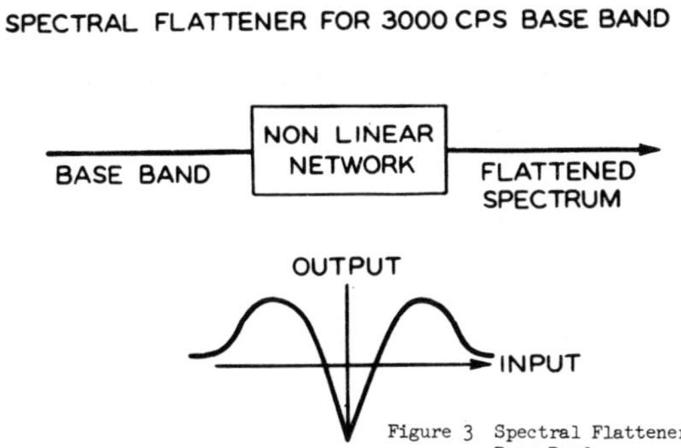

SPECTRAL FLATTENER FOR 3000 CPS BASE BAND

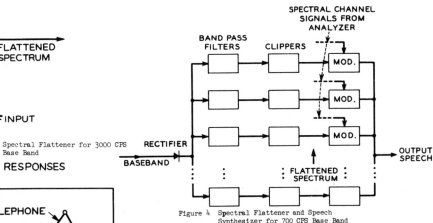

Figure 3 Spectral Flattener for 3000 CPS
Base Band

SPECTRAL FLATTENER AND SPEECH SYNTHESIZER
FOR 700 CPS BASE BAND

Figure 4 Spectral Flattener and Speech
Synthesizer for 700 CPS Base Band

THE TIME COURSE OF AGA RESPONSES

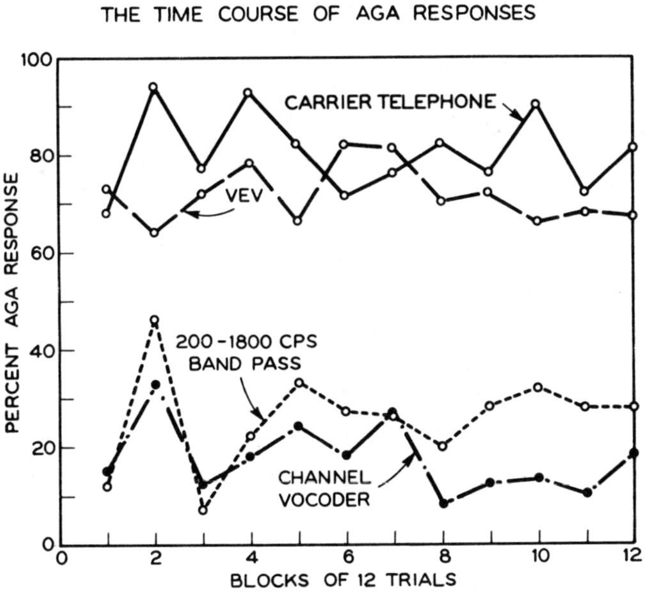

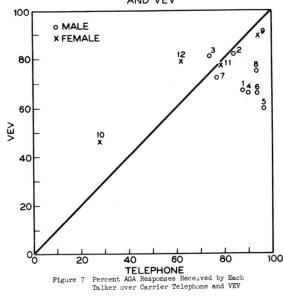

Figure 6 The Time Course of AGA Responses

INTELLIGIBILITY TESTS COMPARING VOICE-EXCITED VOCODER WITH CARBON-BUTTON MICROPHONE SPEECH OF THE SAME BANDWIDTH.

% PB-WORDS CORRECT
ADDED WHITE NOISE 18 DB BELOW AVG SPEECH LEVEL
6 LISTENERS

4 MALE SPEAKERS				4 FEMALE SPEAKERS			
CB		VEV		CB		VEV	
AVG.	DEV.	AVG.	DEV.	AVG.	DEV.	AVG.	DEV.
92.2	0.7	86.1	0.8	86.2	0.9	76.1	0.7

DIFF. 6.1 %   10.1 %

Figure 5 Intelligibility Tests Comparing Voice-
Excited Vocoder with Carbon-Button
Microphone Speech of the Same
Bandwidth

PERCENT AGA RESPONSES RECEIVED BY EACH TALKER OVER CARRIER TELEPHONE AND VEV

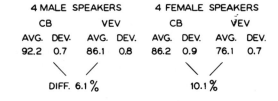

PERCENT AGA RESPONSES FOR EACH LISTENER TO CARRIER TELEPHONE AND VEV

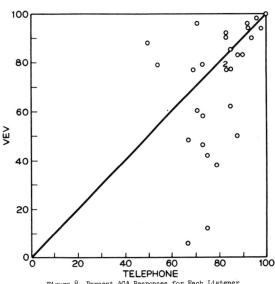

Figure 7 Percent AGA Responses Received by Each
Talker over Carrier Telephone and VEV

Figure 8 Percent AGA Responses for Each Listener
to Carrier Telephone and VEV

Phase Vocoder

By J. L. FLANAGAN and R. M. GOLDEN

(Manuscript received July 18, 1966)

A vocoder technique is described in which speech signals are represented by their short-time phase and amplitude spectra. A complete transmission system utilizing this approach is simulated on a digital computer. The encoding method leads to an economy in transmission bandwidth and to a means for time compression and expansion of speech signals.

I. INTRODUCTION

Analysis-synthesis methods for speech transmission aim at efficient encoding of voice signals. A customary approach is to represent separately the important features of vocal excitation and tract transmission.[1] The well-known channel vocoder of Dudley[2] derives signals which fall into this dichotomy. The tract transmission is described by values of the short-time amplitude spectrum measured at discrete frequencies, and the excitation is described in terms of the fundamental frequency of the voice and the voiced-unvoiced character of the signal. Efforts to solve the long-standing problem of good-quality synthesis from such representations have centered on adequate analysis and specification of the excitation data.

One advance in surmounting the difficulties connected with pitch and voiced-unvoiced extraction is the voice-excited vocoder (VEV).[3] This device relys on transmission of an unprocessed subband of the original speech to carry the excitation information. The spectral envelope information is transmitted as in the channel vocoder by a number of slowly-varying signals. Through accurate preservation of excitation details, a transmission of improved quality and modest bandsaving is achieved.

The present paper proposes another technique for encoding speech to achieve comparable bandsaving and acceptable voice quality. In addition, the technique provides a convenient means for compression and expansion of the time dimension. The method specifies the speech signal in terms of its short-time amplitude and phase spectra. For this reason, it is called phase vocoder. Like the VEV, the phase vocoder does not require the pitch tracking and voiced-unvoiced switching inherent in conventional channel vocoders. Elimination of these decision-making processes and the transmission of excitation information by phase-derivative signals contribute to improved quality in the synthesized signal.

II. PRINCIPLES

If a speech signal $f(t)$ is passed through a parallel bank of contiguous band-pass filters and then recombined, the signal is not substantially degraded. The operation is illustrated in Fig. 1, where BP_1---BP_N represent the contiguous filters. The filters are assumed to have relatively flat amplitude and linear phase characteristics in their pass bands. The output of the nth filter is $f_n(t)$, and the original signal is approximated as

$$f(t) \cong \sum_{n=1}^{N} f_n(t). \tag{1}$$

Let the impulse response of the nth filter be

$$g_n(t) = h(t) \cos \omega_n t, \tag{2}$$

where the envelope function $h(t)$ is normally the impulse response of a physically-realizable low-pass filter. Then the output of the nth filter is the convolution of $f(t)$ with $g_n(t)$,

$$
\begin{aligned}
f_n(t) &= \int_{-\infty}^{t} f(\lambda)h(t - \lambda) \cos [\omega_n(t - \lambda)]d\lambda \\
&= \mathrm{Re} \left[\exp (j\omega_n t) \int_{-\infty}^{t} f(\lambda)h(t - \lambda) \exp (-j\omega_n \lambda)d\lambda \right].
\end{aligned}
\tag{3}
$$

The latter integral is a short-time Fourier transform of the input signal $f(t)$, evaluated at radian frequency ω_n. It is the Fourier transform of that part of $f(t)$ which is "viewed" through the sliding time aperture

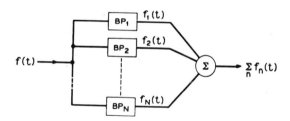

Fig. 1 — Filtering of speech by contiguous band-pass filters.

$h(t)$. If we denote the complex value of this transform as $F(\omega_n, t)$, its magnitude is the short-time amplitude spectrum $|F(\omega_n, t)|$, and its angle is the short-time phase spectrum $\varphi(\omega_n, t)$. Then

$$f_n(t) = \text{Re}[\exp(j\omega_n t)F(\omega_n, t)]$$

or

$$f_n(t) = |F(\omega_n, t)| \cos[\omega_n t + \varphi(\omega_n, t)]. \tag{4}$$

Each $f_n(t)$ may, therefore, be described as the simultaneous amplitude and phase modulation of a carrier $(\cos \omega_n t)$ by the short-time amplitude and phase spectra of $f(t)$, both evaluated at frequency ω_n.

Experience with channel vocoders shows that the magnitude functions $|F(\omega_n, t)|$ may be band-limited to around 20 to 30 Hz without substantial loss of perceptually-significant detail. The phase functions $\varphi(\omega_n, t)$, however, are generally not bounded; hence they are unsuitable as transmission parameters. Their time derivatives $\dot{\varphi}(\omega_n, t)$, on the other hand, are more well-behaved, and we speculate that they may be band-limited and used to advantage in transmission. To within an additive constant, the phase functions can be recovered from the integrated (accumulated) values of the derivatives. One practical approximation to $f_n(t)$ is, therefore,

$$\tilde{f}_n(t) = |F(\omega_n, t)| \cos[\omega_n t + \tilde{\varphi}(\omega_n, t)], \tag{5}$$

where

$$\tilde{\varphi}(\omega_n, t) = \int_0^t \dot{\varphi}(\omega_n, t)dt.$$

The expectation is that loss of the additive phase constant will not be unduly deleterious.

Reconstruction of the original signal is accomplished by summing the outputs of n oscillators modulated in phase and amplitude. The oscillators are set to the nominal frequencies ω_n, and they are simultaneously phase and amplitude modulated from band-limited versions of $\dot{\varphi}(\omega_n, t)$ and $|F(\omega_n, t)|$. The synthesis operations are diagrammed in Fig. 2.

These analysis-synthesis operations may be viewed in an intuitively appealing way. The conventional channel vocoder separates vocal excitation and spectral envelope functions. The spectral envelope functions of the conventional vocoder are the same as those described here by $|F(\omega_n, t)|$. The excitation information, however, is contained in a signal which specifies voice pitch and voiced-unvoiced (buzz-hiss) excitation. In the phase vocoder when the number of channels is reasonably

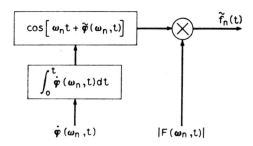

Fig. 2 — Speech synthesis based on the short-time amplitude and phase-derivative spectra.

large, the information about excitation is conveyed primarily by the $\dot{\varphi}(\omega_n, t)$ signals.* In the present technique, and if good quality and natural transmission are requisites, the indications are that the $\dot{\varphi}(\omega_n, t)$ signals may require about the same channel capacity as the spectrum-envelope information. This preliminary impression seems not unreasonable in view of our experience with voice quality in vocoders.

III. COMPUTER SIMULATION

We have simulated a complete phase vocoder analyzer and synthesizer on an IBM 7094 computer. The program, written in the BLODI-B language,[4,5] provides for the processing of any digitalized input speech signal. Flexibility built into the program permits examination of a number of design parameters such as number of channels, width of analyzing pass bands, band center frequencies, and band limitation of the phase and amplitude signals.

In the analyzer, the amplitude and phase spectra are computed by forming the real and imaginary parts of the complex spectrum

$$F(\omega_n, t) = a(\omega_n, t) - jb(\omega_n, t),$$

where

$$a(\omega_n, t) = \int_{-\infty}^{t} f(\lambda)h(t - \lambda) \cos \omega_n\lambda d\lambda$$

and

$$b(\omega_n, t) = \int_{-\infty}^{t} f(\lambda)h(t - \lambda) \sin {}_n\lambda d\lambda. \qquad (6)$$

---

* At the other extreme, with a small number of broad analyzing channels, the amplitude signals contain more information about the excitation, while the $\dot{\varphi}$ phase signals tend to contain more information about the spectral shape. Qualitatively, therefore, the number of channels determines the relative amounts of excitation and spectral information carried by the amplitude and phase signals.

Then,

$$| F(\omega_n , t) | = (a^2 + b^2)^{\frac{1}{2}}$$

and

$$\dot{\varphi}(\omega_n , t) = \left(\frac{\dot{a}b - \dot{b}a}{a^2 + b^2} \right) . \tag{7}$$

The computer, of course, must deal with sampled-data equivalents of these quantities. Transforming the real and imaginary parts of (6) into discrete form for programming yields

$$a(\omega_n , mT) = T \sum_{l=0}^{m} f(lT)[\cos \omega_n lT] h(mT - lT)$$

$$b(\omega_n , nT) = T \sum_{l=0}^{m} f(lT)[\sin \omega_n lT] h(mT - lT), \tag{8}$$

where T is the sampling interval. In the present simulation, $T = 10^{-4}$ sec. From these equations, the difference values are computed as

$$\Delta a = a[\omega_n , (m + 1)T] - a[\omega_n , mT]$$

and

$$\Delta b = b[\omega_n , (m + 1)T] - b[\omega_n , mT]. \tag{9}$$

The magnitude function and phase derivative in discrete form, are computed from (8) and (9) as,

$$| F[\omega_n , mT] | = (a^2 + b^2)^{\frac{1}{2}}$$

$$\frac{\Delta \varphi}{T} [\omega_n , mT] = \frac{1}{T} \frac{(b\Delta a - a\Delta b)}{a^2 + b^2} . \tag{10}$$

Fig. 3 shows a block diagram of a single analyzer channel as realized in BLODI-B. Since this block of coding is required for each channel, it is defined as a new block type and thereafter used as though it were a single block. A parameter associated with the block determines the center frequency for each channel. The time-window analyzing filter, labeled $h(lT)$, is itself a special block and can be changed simply by the substitution of a different block of coding.[6]

In the present simulation, a sixth-order Bessel filter is used for the $h(lT)$ window. Its amplitude, phase, and delay responses are plotted in Figs. 4(a), (b), and (c), respectively. Its impulse and step responses are given in Figs. 4(d) and (e). The present simulation uses 30 channels ($N = 30$) and $\omega_n = 2\pi n(100)$ rad/sec. The equivalent pass bands of the

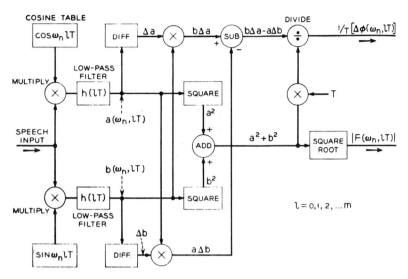

Fig. 3 — Programmed operations for extracting $|F(\omega_n, t)|$ and $\varphi(\omega_n, t)$.

analyzing filters overlap at their 6 dB down points and a total spectrum range of 50 to 3050 Hz is analyzed.

Programmed low-pass filtering of any desired form may be applied to the amplitude and phase difference signals as defined by Fig. 3. Simulation of the whole system is completed by the synthesis operations for each channel performed according to

$$\tilde{f}_n(mT) = |F(\omega_n, mT)| \cos\left(\omega_n mT + T \sum_{l=0}^{m} \frac{\Delta\varphi(\omega_n, lT)}{T}\right). \quad (11)$$

Adding the outputs of the n individual channels, according to (1), produces the synthesized speech signal.

IV. TYPICAL RESULTS

As part of the present simulation, identical (programmed) low-pass filters were applied to the $|F(\omega_n, lT)|$ and $(1/T)\Delta\varphi(\omega_n, lT)$ signals delivered by the coding block shown in Fig. 3. These low-pass filters are similar to the $h(lT)$ filters except they are fourth-order Bessel designs. Their response characteristics are shown in Fig. 5. The cut-off frequency is 25 Hz, and the response is -7.6 dB down at this frequency. This filtering is applied to the amplitude and phase signals of all 30 channels in the present simulation. The total bandwidth occupancy of the system is therefore 1500 Hz, or a band reduction of 2:1.

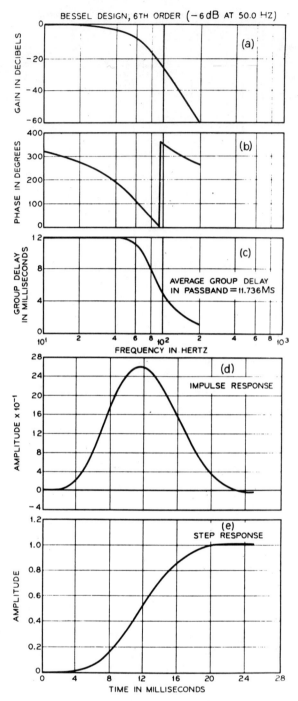

Fig. 4 — $h(t)$ analyzing function and its spectral transform used in one simulation of the phase vocoder. The function is a sixth-order Bessel filter having a −6 dB cut-off of 50 Hz.

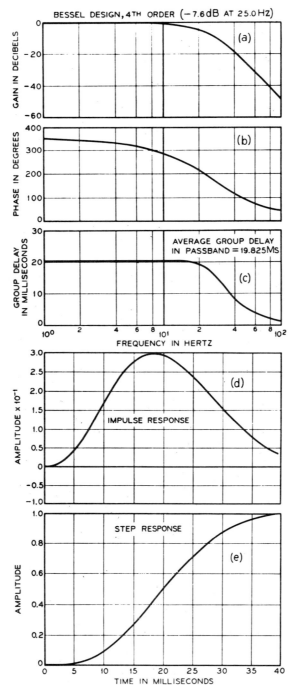

Fig. 5 — Fourth-order Bessel low-pass filter used to smooth the $|F_n|$ and $\dot{\varphi}_n$ signals.

After band-limitation, the phase and amplitude signals are used to synthesize an output according to (11). The result of processing a complete sentence through the programmed system is shown by the sound spectrograms in Fig. 6.* Since the signal band covered by the analysis and synthesis is 50 to 3050, the phase-vocoded result is seen to cut off at 3050 Hz. In this example, the system is connected in a "back-to-back" configuration, and the band-limited channel signals are not multiplexed.

Comparison of original and synthesized spectrograms reveals that formant details are well preserved and pitch and voiced-unvoiced features are retained to perceptually significant accuracy. The quality of the resulting signal considerably surpasses that usually associated with conventional channel vocoders.

V. MULTIPLEXING FOR TRANSMISSION

Besides conventional multiplexing methods for transmitting the band-limited phase and amplitude channel signals (that is, space-frequency or time-division multiplex), the coding technique suggests several other possibilities for transmission in a practicable communication system. As an example, suppose a limited-bandwidth analog channel is the available communication link. One advantageous procedure then is simply to divide (or scale down) all of the phase-derivative signals by some number, say 2 if the available channel has only one-half the conventional voice bandwidth. A synthetic signal of one-half the original bandwidth is then produced by modulating carriers of $\omega_n/2$ by the $\dot{\varphi}_n/2$ and $|F_n|$ signals. The synthetic analog signal now may be transmitted over the half-bandwidth channel.

At the receiver, restoration to the original bandwidth is accomplished by a second sequence of analysis and synthesis operations; namely, amplitude and phase analysis of the half-band signal, multiplication of the phase-derivative signals by a factor of 2, and modulation of ω_n carriers by the restored $\dot{\varphi}_n$ and reanalyzed $|F_n|$ signals. This "self-multiplexing" transmission is illustrated in Fig. 7. Spectrograms of the input signal, the half-band frequency divided signal, and the reanalyzed and resynthesized output are shown. It is clear that two trips through the process introduces measurable degradation, but the intelligibility and quality, particularly for high-pitched voices, remains reasonably good.

In effect, the greatest number q by which the ω_n and $\dot{\varphi}_n$'s may be

---

* The input speech signal is band limited to 4000 Hz. It is sampled at 10,000 Hz and quantized to 12 bits. It is called into the program from a digital recording prepared previously.

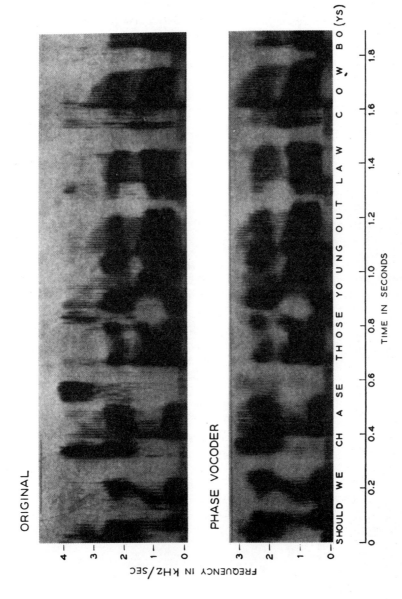

Fig. 6 — Spectrograms illustrating speech transmitted by the phase vocoder ($N = 30$). The band-pass analysis is by sixth-order Bessel filters of 100-Hz band-width. Low-pass filtering of $|F_n|$ and ϕ_n is by fourth-order Bessel filters with 25 Hz cut-off. Male speaker A. "Should we chase those young outlaw cowboys."

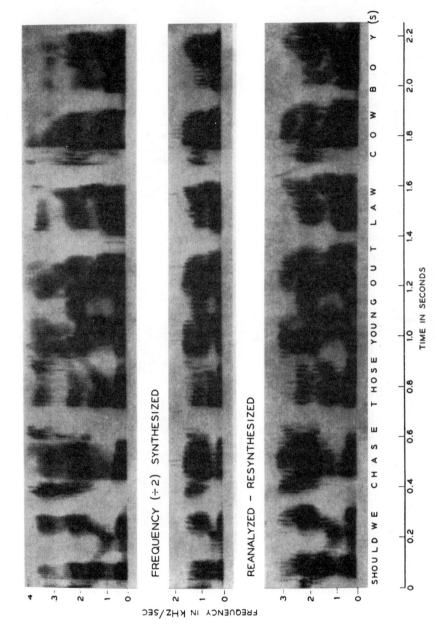

FREQUENCY (÷2) SYNTHESIZED

REANALYZED – RESYNTHESIZED

SHOULD WE CHASE THOSE YOUNG OUT LAW COW BOY (s)

TIME IN SECONDS

FREQUENCY IN KHZ/SEC

Fig. 7 – Self-multiplexing transmission for a bandwidth reduction of 2:1. (a) Original input; (b) Frequency-divided synthetic signal for analog transmission over one-half bandwidth channel; (c) Synthesized output from the reanalyzed, frequency-multiplied, half-band signal. Male speaker B.

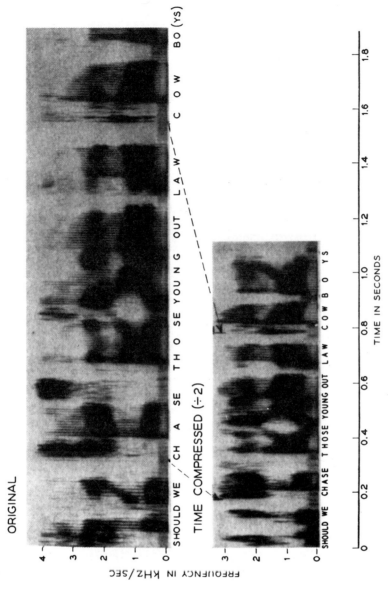

Fig. 8 — Time compression of speech by a factor of 2. Male speaker A. (a) Original input; (b) Time-compressed output.

divided is determined by how distinct the side-bands about each ω_n/q remain, and by how well each $\dot{\varphi}_n/q$ and $|F_n|$ may be retrieved from them.* Practically, the greatest number appears to be about 2 or 3 if transmission of acceptable quality is to be realized.

VI. COMPRESSION AND EXPANSION OF THE TIME SCALE

As mentioned above, a synthetic frequency-divided signal may be produced through division of $[\omega_n t + \int \dot{\varphi}_n dt]$ by some number q. This signal may be essentially restored to its original spectral position by a time speed-up of q. Such a speed-up can be accomplished by recording at one speed and replaying q-times faster. The result is that the time scale is compressed and the message, although spectrally correct, lasts $1/q$th as long as the original. An example of a 2:1 frequency division and time speed-up is shown by the sound spectrograms in Fig. 8. This feature of the phase vocoder is completely parallel to the time-compression feature of the "harmonic compressor" reported earlier.[7] However, the techniques for analysis and synthesis in the two cases are basically different, and the phase vocoder allows compression by non-integer factors.

Time-scale expansion is likewise possible by the frequency multiplication $q[\omega_n t + \int \dot{\varphi}_n dt]$; that is, by recording the frequency-multiplied synthetic signal and then replaying it at a speed q-times slower. An example of time-expanded speech is shown by the spectrograms in Fig. 9. The expansion feature provides an interesting "auditory microscope" for directing attention to the spectral properties of specific elements of speech sounds — such as rapidly articulated consonants. In both compression and expansion of the time scale, a perceptual limit exists, of course, to how greatly the time scale may be altered and still have the signal sound like human speech.

An attractive feature of the phase vocoder is that the operations for expansion and compression of the time and frequency scales can be realized by simple scaling of the phase-derivative spectrum. Since the frequency division and multiplication factors can be non-integers, and can be varied with time, the phase vocoder provides an attractive tool for studying non-uniform alterations of the time scale.[8]

* More precisely, the maximum divisor is determined by how closely

$$1/q \int_0^{qt} \dot{\varphi}_n dt$$

represents

$$\int_0^t \dot{\varphi}_n dt .$$

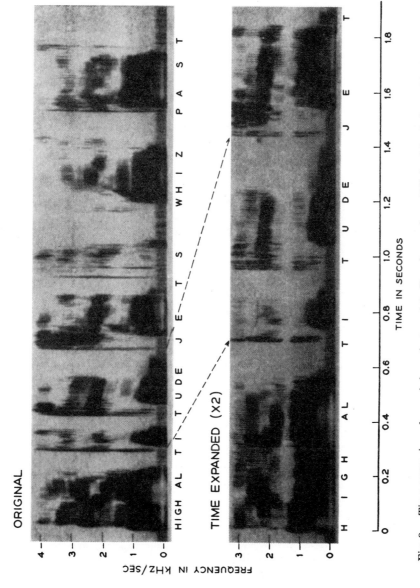

Fig. 9 — Time expansion of speech by a factor of 2. Female speaker. "High altitude jets whiz past screaming," (a) Original input; (b) Time-expanded output.

VII. FURTHER REMARKS ABOUT BAND OCCUPANCY

The possibilities of frequency division imply that the $|F_n|$ and $\dot{\varphi}_n$ signals are, in practical effect, band-limited. As described previously, modest bandwidth reduction of the order of 2:1 can be accomplished by a simple scaling of all the $\dot{\varphi}_n$ signals by $\frac{1}{2}$. (Overt low-pass filtering of the $\dot{\varphi}_n$ signals is not required.) Also, low-pass filtering the analyzed signals to a total band occupancy of one-half the original bandwidth results in relatively good speech quality upon synthesis (Fig. 6). If, however, some further trade between band saving and speech quality is desired, the control signals may be low-passed more severely, with concomitant loss in quality. The impairment resulting from low-passing the $\dot{\varphi}_n$ signals is a comb-filtering, reverberant effect in the reconstituted signals. Qualitatively, low-pass filtering of the $\dot{\varphi}_n$ signals apparently restricts the rate at which pitch changes can be duplicated, and "narrows" the sidebands produced about each ω_n-carrier at the synthesizer.

The discussion connected with (4) has pointed out that each bandpass signal in the phase vocoder may be considered as the simultaneous amplitude and phase modulation:

$$f_n(t) = |F_n| \cos(\omega_n t + \varphi_n),$$

where $|F_n|$ and φ_n are non-band limited, real-valued functions of ω_n and time. Practically, the bandwidth of $f_n(t)$ is confined to $2W$, where W is the cut-off frequency of the low-pass time aperture $h(t)$. This fact does not, however, suggest in an explicit way the band occupancy of the signals $|F_n|$ and φ_n. The experimental results of the present study indicate that each of the latter, at least for practical purposes, can be limited to around $W/2$ or less, but analytical treatment leading to explanation is difficult. Even the inverse problem, that is, calculation of the band occupancy of a simultaneously amplitude and phase modulated carrier, can only be bounded loosely.[9] To apply these bounds requires a precise description of the $|F_n|$ and $\dot{\varphi}_n$ signals. Although these parameters can be measured for a given speech signal, a general mathematical specification is not presently available. It is easy to indicate the difficulties involved. Consider the usual model of voiced speech sounds; that is, a periodic pulse source, whose frequency (pitch) may change with time, supplying excitation to a linear, passive, time-variable network. Variation of the network transmission represents the spectral changes both in the vocal sound source and the vocal tract transmission. For an analysis in terms of narrow pass-bands (large N), the $\dot{\varphi}_n$ signals depend primarily upon voice pitch. The $|F_n|$ signals, on the other hand, depend both upon source spectrum and vocal transmission at any given instant.

VIII. CONSIDERATIONS FOR DIGITAL TRANSMISSION

Applications of the phase vocoder technique to digital transmission are of course obvious. Given an acceptable band-limitation of the $|F_n|$ and $\dot{\varphi}_n$ signals, each may be sampled at its Nyquist rate, or higher, and quantized to an accuracy that is perceptually sufficient. At this writing, optimum parameters for sampling and quantizing the control signals have not been studied in detail. Based upon past experience, however, a nonuniform distribution of the pass bandwidths of the analyzing filters would appear advantageous. For example, center frequencies and bandwidths chosen according to the Koenig scale, the mel (pitch) scale, or the auditory critical-band function should yield dividends.*

All of these bandwidth tapers are characterized by widths which monotonically increase with frequency. In such cases, the low-pass filtering applied to the amplitude signals would have cut-off frequencies also increasing monotonically with frequency. On the other hand, the low-pass filters applied to the phase signals might have cut offs which decrease with frequency. As a result, sampling rates would increase with ω_n for amplitude signals and diminish for phase signals. In addition, quantization levels for all signals might be made more coarse (less numerous) with increasing channel frequency. This is indicated because the ability of the ear to perceive frequency and amplitude changes in the higher end of a complex spectrum is, in general, less acute than for the lower part.

Although detailed study is yet to be made of optimum digital formats, experience in this area with related vocoder devices suggests that transmission at bit rates somewhat less than ten kilobits/sec should be possible without impairment due to digitalization. This rate is several times less than that normally associated with comparable quality PCM encodings of the speech waveform. Besides the questions of design optimization and data format for digital transmission, the trade which may be effected between signal quality and total bit rate is also a subject for further investigation.

IX. CONCLUDING COMMENTS

Because the phase vocoder produces phase derivative signals, it pro-

---

* Preliminary tests along these lines indicate that a phase vocoder with as few as eight non-uniform channels is capable of relatively good transmission (J. J. Kalsalik, unpublished work).

vides a particularly convenient means for multiplying or dividing the frequency spectrum of a broadband signal. By the same token, it is a convenient method for compressing or expanding the time scale of a signal. Frequency division of speech appears to hold potential as a communication aid for persons with hearing deficient in the high frequencies. Time compression shows promise for auditory "speed-reading" by persons with impaired sight.

Psychoacoustic and physiological studies show that the human ear makes a type of short-time spectral analysis of acoustic signals. This analysis occurs at an early level in the auditory processing; in fact, at a preneural level. It is also clear that the auditory system utilizes information corresponding to smoothed values of the short-time amplitude and phase spectra. The phase vocoder aims to turn these facts to advantage by describing speech signals in terms of band-limited values of the short-time amplitude and phase-derivative spectra. Indications are that band-limited spectral samples, occupying a bandwidth on the order of one half that of the original signal, preserve perceptually-significant features of the signal. Further band conservation can be realized, but at the expense of signal quality. As in many other transmission systems, a continuum of band conservation (or bit rate) versus signal quality exists, and one may choose the point of operation to suit requirements.

REFERENCES

1. Flanagan, J. L., *Speech Analysis, Synthesis and Perception*, Springer Verlag and Academic Press, New York, 1965.
2. Dudley, H., The Vocoder, Bell Labs. Record, *17*, 1939, pp. 122–126.
3. David, E. E., Schroeder, M. R., Logan, B. F., and Prestigiacomo, A. J., New Applications of Voice-Excitation to Vocoders, Proc. Stockholm Speech Comm. Seminar, R.I.T., Stockholm, Sweden, September, 1962.
4. Karafin, B. J., The New Block Diagram Compiler for Simulation of Sampled-Data Systems, AFIPS Conf. Proc., *27*, Pt. 1, 1965, pp. 55–61, Fall Joint Computer Conference, Spartan Books, Washington, D. C.
5. Golden, R. M., Digital Computer Simulation of Sampled Data Communication Systems Using the Block Diagram Compiler, BLODI-B, BSTJ, *45*, March, 1966, pp. 345–358.
6. Golden, R. M. and Kaiser, J. F., Design of Wideband Sampled-Data Filters, BSTJ, *43*, Pt. 2, July, 1964, pp. 1533–1546.
7. Schroeder, M. R., Logan, B. F., and Prestigiacomo, A. J., Methods for Speech Analysis-Synthesis and Bandwidth Compression, Fourth International Congress on Acoustics, Copenhagen, August 21–28, 1962.
8. Hanover, S. L. and Schroeder, M. R., Nonlinear Time Compression and Time Normalization of Speech, 72nd Meeting Acoustical Society of America, November, 1966.
9. Kahn, R. E. and Thomas, J. B., Some Bandwidth Properties of Simultaneous Amplitude and Angle Modulation, IEEE Trans. Inform. Theor., *IT-11*, October, 1965, pp. 516–520.

Implementation of the Digital Phase Vocoder Using the Fast Fourier Transform

MICHAEL R. PORTNOFF, STUDENT MEMBER, IEEE

Abstract—This paper discusses a digital formulation of the phase vocoder, an analysis–synthesis system providing a parametric representation of a speech waveform by its short-time Fourier transform. Such a system is of interest both for data-rate reduction and for manipulating basic speech parameters. The system is designed to be an identity system in the absence of any parameter modifications. Computational efficiency is achieved by employing the fast Fourier transform (FFT) algorithm to perform the bulk of the computation in both the analysis and synthesis procedures, thereby making the formulation attractive for implementation on a minicomputer.

I. INTRODUCTION

THE REPRESENTATION of a speech signal by its short-time Fourier transform is of interest both as a means for data-rate reduction in communications and as a technique for manipulating the basic speech parameters. Systems based on this representation are often referred to as phase vocoders since the parameters obtained have traditionally been the magnitude and phase (or phase-derivative) of the short-time Fourier transform [1].

One difficulty in implementing such systems in digital form has been the rapid increase in the amount of computation required as the number of frequency bands is made large. Schafer and Rabiner [2] have shown how to greatly reduce

Manuscript received May 10, 1975; revised December 9, 1975. This work was supported by the Advanced Research Projects Agency, monitored by the ONR under Contract N00014-75-C-0951.

The author is with the Department of Electrical Engineering and Computer Science, Research Laboratory of Electronics, Massachusetts Institute of Technology, Cambridge, MA 02139.

the amount of computation required for the analysis procedure by formulating the system such that most of the computation is performed by the fast Fourier transform (FFT) algorithm. However, the computation required for the direct implementation of the synthesis procedure is at least as great as that required for the direct analysis, and it has, therefore, remained a problem.

In this paper, we present an analysis–synthesis system based on the discrete short-time Fourier transform. This system will be shown to be, mathematically, an identity system if no parameter modifications are introduced. The analysis procedure is a refinement of that proposed by Schafer and Rabiner in which the complex multiplies used to demodulate the channel signals are now eliminated. The synthesis procedure is new and is significantly more efficient than the direct procedure [2]. The computational savings is effected by reducing the number of interpolations required for each output value from N (where N is the number of frequency bands in the representation) to 1 and by performing the remaining computations using the FFT algorithm (a savings of approximately $\log_2 N$ versus N operations per output value).

II. FORMULATION

Let $x(n)$ represent samples of a speech waveform. The discrete short-time Fourier transform of $x(n)$ is defined by

$$X_k(n) = \sum_{r=-\infty}^{\infty} x(r) h(n-r) W_N^{-rk} \tag{1}$$

for $k = 0, 1, \cdots, N-1$, where $W_N = \exp [j(2\pi/N)]$ and $h(n)$

Reprinted from *IEEE Trans. Acoust., Speech, and Signal Processing*, vol. ASSP-24, pp. 243–248, June 1976.

is an appropriately chosen window. $X_k(n)$ may be interpreted as N samples of a time-varying spectrum with k the index associated with frequency and n the index associated with time. According to (1), $X_k(n)$ is obtained at each time sample n by weighting the sequence $x(r)$ by the window $h(n-r)$ and Fourier transforming the resulting sequence. In the next section it will be shown how to obtain $X_k(n)$ at a particular n by computing a single discrete Fourier transform (DFT) of a finite-duration sequence of length N.

By properly choosing $h(n)$, it can be guaranteed that the original sequence $x(n)$ is exactly recoverable from its short-time transform defined by (1). Furthermore, $x(n)$ is given in this case by

$$x(n) = \frac{1}{N} \sum_{k=0}^{N-1} X_k(n) W_N^{nk} \qquad \text{for all } n. \qquad (2)$$

Although the necessary and sufficient conditions for $x(n)$ to be given by (2) can be derived directly from (1), it is informative to interpret (1) and (2) in terms of a bank of digital bandpass filters with contiguous passbands. Consider a set of N complex bandpass filters $\{h_k(n)\}$ with passbands equally spaced about the unit circle and with unit-sample responses

$$h_k(n) = \frac{1}{N} h(n) W_N^{nk}, \qquad k = 0, 1, \cdots, N-1, \qquad (3)$$

where $h(n)$ is a prototype low-pass filter with real unit-sample response. If these filters are combined to form the structure shown in Fig. 1, then the output of the kth filter, denoted by $y_k(n)$, is given by the convolution

$$y_k(n) = \sum_{r=-\infty}^{\infty} x(r) h_k(n-r)$$

$$= \sum_{r=-\infty}^{\infty} x(r) \left[\frac{1}{N} h(n-r) W_N^{(n-r)k} \right]$$

$$= \frac{1}{N} W_N^{nk} \sum_{r=-\infty}^{\infty} x(r) h(n-r) W_N^{-rk}$$

$$= \frac{1}{N} W_N^{nk} X_k(n), \qquad (4)$$

where $X_k(n)$ is just the discrete short-time Fourier transform of $x(n)$ given by (1). From (1) and (4) a single channel of the filter bank is seen to be equivalent to the structure shown in Fig. 2.

The output of the filter bank $y(n)$ is given by the sum of the N channels $y_k(n)$, i.e.,

$$y(n) = \sum_{k=0}^{N-1} y_k(n)$$

$$= \frac{1}{N} \sum_{k=0}^{N-1} X_k(n) W_N^{nk}.$$

It is, therefore, clear that if $x(n)$ is to be recovered from $X_k(n)$ by means of (2), then $h(n)$ must be chosen in such a manner that the output $y(n)$ is identical to the input $x(n)$.

The filter-bank system depicted in Fig. 1 is linear and shift

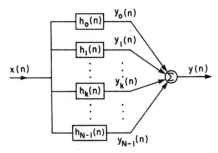

Fig. 1. Digital filter-bank analog for discrete short-time Fourier analysis.

Fig. 2. Representation of the kth filter-bank channel in terms of the prototype low-pass filter $h(n)$.

invariant and thus completely characterized by its unit-sample response. Let $\tilde{h}(n)$ represent the overall unit-sample response relating the output $y(n)$ of the filter bank to the input $x(n)$. Then

$$\tilde{h}(n) = \sum_{k=0}^{N-1} h_k(n)$$

$$= \sum_{k=0}^{N-1} \frac{1}{N} h(n) W_N^{nk}$$

$$= h(n) \left[\frac{1}{N} \sum_{k=0}^{N-1} W_N^{nk} \right]$$

$$= h(n) \left[\frac{1}{N} \frac{1 - W_N^{nN}}{1 - W_N^n} \right]$$

$$= h(n) \delta((n))_N,$$

where $\delta((n))_N = 1$ for all $n \equiv 0 \bmod N$ and is zero otherwise. Thus, $\tilde{h}(n)$ is simply the unit-sample response $h(n)$ of the prototype low-pass filter sampled every N samples, specifically

$$\tilde{h}(n) = \begin{cases} h(n) & \text{for } n = 0, \pm N, \pm 2N, \cdots \\ 0 & \text{otherwise.} \end{cases}$$

Now if $y(n)$ is to be identically equal to $x(n)$, then $\tilde{h}(n)$ must itself be a unit sample. Therefore, necessary and sufficient conditions for $y(n) = x(n)$ for all n are[1] as follows.

1) $h(0) = 1$.

[1] This result also follows directly from (1) by multiplying (1) by $(1/N) W_N^{nk}$ and summing over k for $0 \leqslant k \leqslant N-1$ to obtain

$$\frac{1}{N} \sum_{k=0}^{N-1} X_k(n) W_N^{nk} = \frac{1}{N} \sum_{k=0}^{N-1} \sum_{r=-\infty}^{\infty} x(r) h(n-r) W_N^{-rk} W_N^{nk}$$

$$= \sum_{r=-\infty}^{\infty} x(r) h(n-r) \left[\frac{1}{N} \sum_{k=0}^{N-1} W_N^{(n-r)k} \right]$$

$$= \sum_{q=-\infty}^{\infty} x(n+qN) h(-qN)$$

$$= x(n) \text{ iff (5).}$$

2) $h(n) = 0$ for $n = \pm N, \pm 2N, \pm 3N, \cdots$. (5)

These conditions are equivalent to the statement in the frequency domain that although each $h_k(n)$ is not necessarily an ideal bandpass filter, the sum of their N frequency responses is unity for all frequencies. Observe that the conditions (5) are precisely those constraints on the unit-sample response of a digital interpolating filter [3]. Moreover, if these conditions are not satisfied, then $\tilde{h}(n)$ will no longer be a unit sample, but a weighted sequence of unit samples with spacing N; hence $y(n)$ will not be identical to $x(n)$ and the resulting distortion will be perceived as reverberation in the output signal.

The most straightforward approach to designing the prototype low-pass filter $h(n)$ is by windowing [4]. Specifically, the unit-sample response

$$h_{i\text{deal}}(n) = \frac{\sin{(n\pi/N)}}{n\pi/N}$$

of an ideal low-pass filter with cutoff frequencies $\Omega_c = \pm(\pi/N)$ is multiplied by a smooth, finite-duration window (e.g., Hamming [5], Kaiser [6], Dolph–Chebyshev [7]) to obtain $h(n)$. The precise specifications of $h(n)$ are determined by the length and shape of the window; any $h(n)$ designed in this manner will satisfy conditions (5).

Alternatively, one might employ one of the recently proposed techniques for designing optimum (minimax) equiripple finite impulse response (FIR) interpolating filters [3], [8]. However, for a large number of frequency samples, the long length required for $h(n)$ tends to make these filters prohibitively expensive to design. Furthermore, the additional amount of computation incurred by using a suboptimum $h(n)$ designed by windowing is probably small compared with the total amount of computation in the overall system.

The short-time Fourier transform provides a parametric representation of the sequence $x(n)$ in terms of the parameters $X_k(n)$. If $X_k(n)$ is computed for $k = 0, 1, \cdots, N-1$ and for all n, then N complex parameters are required for each sample of $x(n)$. If $x(n)$ is real, then this represents an increase in complexity by a factor of $2N$. There are, however, properties of the discrete short-time Fourier transform that can be exploited to reduce the number of parameters required to represent $x(n)$ to an average of approximately one per sample of $x(n)$. First, if $X_k(n)$ is viewed for a particular value of n as N equally spaced samples of a Fourier transform, then, since $x(n)$ is assumed to be real, $X_k(n)$ is conjugate symmetric in k; that is,

$$X_k(n) = X^*_{((N-k))_N}(n)$$

where $((n))_N$ denotes the least residue of n modulo N. Thus, if N is even, $X_k(n)$ is completely specified by the values of $X_k(n)$ for $k = 0, 1, \cdots, N/2$, and only N real parameters are required (n.b., $X_k(n)$ is real for $k = 0$ and $k = N/2$). The second property of $X_k(n)$ that allows a further reduction in the number of parameters required to represent $x(n)$ is apparent when $X_k(n)$ is viewed for a particular value of k as a sequence in n. From Fig. 2 it can be seen that because it is the output of a low-pass filter with unit-sample response $h(n)$, each such sequence is approximately band-limited to the frequency range $-\pi/N < \Omega < \pi/N$. Thus, it follows from the sampling theorem that it is only necessary to compute $X_k(n)$

for every Rth value of n, where $R \leqslant N$. The sequences $X_k(n)$ can then be reconstructed by interpolation as part of the synthesis procedure.

If the sampling period R is chosen equal to N, which corresponds to the lowest sampling rate allowed by the sampling theorem, then the total number of real parameters in the short-time Fourier representation of $x(n)$ is exactly equal to the duration (total number of samples) of $x(n)$.[2] Although it is theoretically possible to reconstruct the sequences $X_k(n)$ if they are sampled every $R = N$ samples, in practice it is necessary to sample at a somewhat higher rate, because neither the low-pass filter nor the interpolator can be implemented ideally.

A procedure that is particularly well suited to designing interpolating filters for reconstructing the channel sequences is the algorithm proposed by Oetken et al. [9] for designing optimal FIR digital interpolating filters. This procedure is attractive because it is a simple and efficient procedure for designing filters of very high order. Furthermore, the design algorithm exploits the fact that the data to be interpolated can be oversampled to improve the performance of the filter.

III. Implementation of the Analysis System Using the FFT Algorithm

If the number of frequency bands N is chosen to be a highly composite number (usually an integral power of 2) then the FFT algorithm can be employed to compute efficiently the short-time Fourier transform $X_k(n)$ defined by (1). Observe that (1) does not have the form of a DFT and, therefore, cannot be computed directly with the FFT algorithm. The limits on the summation are given as infinite, but in practice are finite and determined by the length of $h(n)$. By recognizing $X_k(n)$ as samples, equally spaced in frequency, of the (continuous-valued) Fourier transform of $x(r)h(r-n)$, $X_k(n)$ can be expressed as the DFT of an N-point sequence obtained by time-domain aliasing of $x(r)h(n-r)$.

Substituting $s = r - n$ into (1) gives

$$X_k(n) = \sum_{s=-\infty}^{\infty} x(n+s)h(-s)W_n^{-(n+s)k}$$

$$= W_N^{-nk} \sum_{s=-\infty}^{\infty} x(n+s)h(-s)W_N^{-sk},$$

which can be rewritten as

$$X_k(n) = W_N^{-nk} \sum_{l=-\infty}^{\infty} \sum_{m=0}^{N-1} x(n+lN+m)h(-lN-m)$$
$$\cdot W_N^{-(lN+m)k}$$

by taking $s = lN + m$ for $m = 0, 1, \cdots, N-1$ and $l = -\infty, \cdots, -1, 0, +1, \cdots, \infty$. Interchanging the orders of summation and using $W_N^N = 1$ gives

$$X_k(n) = W_N^{-nk} \sum_{m=0}^{N-1} \sum_{l=-\infty}^{\infty} x(n+lN+m)h(-lN-m)W_N^{-mk}$$

or

---

[2]When this representation is used as a vocoder, data-rate reduction is achieved by quantizing the parameters $X_k(n)$ [2].

$$X_k(n) = W_N^{-nk} \sum_{m=0}^{N-1} \tilde{x}_m(n) W_N^{-mk}, \qquad (6)$$

where

$$\tilde{x}_m(n) = \sum_{l=-\infty}^{\infty} x(n + lN + m) h(-lN - m). \qquad (7)$$

The expression

$$\tilde{\tilde{X}}_k(n) = \sum_{m=0}^{N-1} \tilde{x}_m(n) W_N^{-mk}$$

is recognized as the DFT of the N-point (in m) sequence $\tilde{x}_m(n)$ for fixed n and can, therefore, be computed directly with the FFT algorithm once $\tilde{x}_m(n)$ has been formed.

In addition to the computational savings gained by computing the short-time Fourier transform using the FFT, further savings may be gained by avoiding the complex multiplications by W_N^{-nk} in (6). Observing that $X_k(n)$ is given by

$$X_k(n) = W_N^{-nk} \tilde{\tilde{X}}_k(n),$$

where $\tilde{\tilde{X}}_k(n)$ is the DFT of $\tilde{x}_m(n)$, we can exploit the property of the DFT that a circular shift in one domain corresponds to multiplication by a complex exponential in the other domain. Thus, by circularly shifting $\tilde{x}_m(n)$ prior to computing its DFT, the multiplications by W_N^{-nk} are avoided. Specifically, (6) can be rewritten as

$$X_k(n) = \sum_{m=0}^{N-1} \tilde{x}_{((m-n))_N}(n) W_N^{-mk}$$

or

$$X_k(n) = \sum_{m=0}^{N-1} x_m(n) W_N^{-mk} \qquad (8)$$

where

$$x_m(n) = \tilde{x}_{((m-n))_N}(n).$$

Based on the preceding analysis, the procedure for computing the discrete short-time Fourier transform coefficients $X_k(n)$ at a particular value of n is the following. Referring to Fig. 3, the input data sequence considered as a function of the dummy index r is multiplied by the window $h(n - r)$ (in practice $h(n)$ is often zero phase, in which case $h(n - r) = h(r - n)$). It is assumed that $h(n)$ is of finite duration and, in fact, chosen to have length equal to an even multiple of N, plus one. The resulting weighted sequence is partitioned into sections each of length N such that $x(r)|_{r=n}$ is the zeroth sample of one of the sections. The resulting N-point subsequences denoted by $x_m^{(l)}(n)$ for $0 \leqslant m \leqslant N - 1$ are then added together to form

$$\tilde{x}_m(n) = \sum_l x_m^{(l)}(n), \qquad m = 0, 1, \cdots, N - 1.$$

$\tilde{x}_m(n)$ is circularly shifted (in m) by n samples to obtain

$$x_m(n) = \tilde{x}_{((m-n))_N}(n),$$

and its DFT is computed by means of the FFT algorithm to give the desired $X_k(n)$, i.e.,

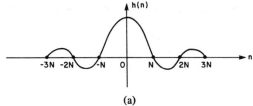

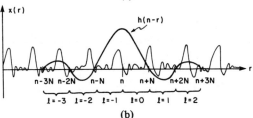

Fig. 3. (a) Typical unit-sample response for prototype low-pass filter $h(n)$. (b) $h(n)$ shifted and superimposed on input sequence $x(r)$.

$$X_k(n) = \sum_{m=0}^{N-1} x_m(n) W_N^{-mk} \qquad k = 0, 1, \cdots, N - 1.$$

IV. Implementation of the Synthesis System Using the FFT Algorithm

It has been shown that for any $h(n)$ satisfying conditions (5) the sequence $x(n)$ can be recovered from its discrete short-time Fourier transform by the relation

$$x(n) = \frac{1}{N} \sum_{k=0}^{N-1} X_k(n) W_N^{nk}. \qquad (2)$$

According to Fig. 2, this operation may be interpreted as modulating each of the N signals $X_k(n)$ to the center frequencies $\Omega_k = 2\pi k/N$ and summing the resulting signals. It was argued in Section II that it is only necessary to compute $X_k(n)$ for every Rth value of n where $R \leqslant N$. Hence, the parameters to the synthesizer will be assumed to be the samples $X_k(rR)$ and not $X_k(n)$.

Clearly, each of the N signals $X_k(rR)$ could be interpolated to get $X_k(n)$, which could then be used in (2) to compute $x(n)$ directly [2]. Unfortunately, since $X_k(n)$ depends on n, (2) does not have the form of an (inverse) DFT and is computationally intractable for large values of N.

A synthesis procedure will now be formulated which, for a highly composite number N, permits $x(n)$ to be computed from the samples $X_k(rR)$ using the FFT algorithm. In addition to the computational savings afforded by employing the FFT, the number of computations required to perform the $1:R$ interpolation is reduced by the factor N.

Let the input parameters to the synthesizer be denoted by $S_k(r)$, where

$$S_k(r) = X_k(rR) \qquad \text{for all } r \text{ and } k = 0, 1, \cdots, N - 1.$$

Let $f(n)$ represent the unit-sample response of a $1:R$ FIR interpolating filter with length $2QR + 1$. The interpolated signals $X_k(n)$ are, therefore, given by

$$X_k(n) = \sum_{r=L^-}^{L^+} f(n - rR) S_k(r), \qquad (9)$$

where the limits on the sum, determined by the length of $f(n)$, are

$$L^+(n) = \left[\frac{n}{R}\right] + Q$$

$$L^-(n) = \left[\frac{n}{R}\right] - Q + 1,$$

and where $[M]$ means "the largest integer contained in M." Substituting $X_k(n)$ given by (9) into the synthesis equation (2) gives

$$x(n) = \frac{1}{N} \sum_{k=0}^{N-1} \left\{ \sum_{r=L^-}^{L^+} f(n-rR) S_k(r) \right\} W_N^{nk}.$$

Since the limits on both sums are finite, the order of summation can be interchanged to give

$$x(n) = \sum_{r=L^-}^{L^+} f(n-rR) \left\{ \frac{1}{N} \sum_{k=0}^{N-1} S_k(r) W_N^{nk} \right\}$$

or

$$x(n) = \sum_{r=L^-}^{L^+} f(n-rR) s_n(r), \tag{10}$$

where

$$s_n(r) = \frac{1}{N} \sum_{k=0}^{N-1} S_k(r) W_N^{nk}. \tag{11}$$

Thus, for fixed values of r, $s_n(r)$ is the inverse DFT of $S_k(r)$ and can, therefore, be computed by the FFT algorithm. It is important to observe that $s_n(r)$ is periodic in n with period N. Since the FFT only computes values of $s_n(r)$ for one period $(n = 0, 1, \cdots, N-1)$, it is necessary to interpret the subscript n in (11) as reduced modulo N.

The synthesis procedure implied by (10) and (11) can be interpreted as follows. Consider the two-dimensional "net" shown in Fig. 4. The points on the net represent the discrete set of points on which $X_k(n)$ is defined. The horizontal direction represents time and the vertical frequency. The points corresponding to the values of $X_k(n)$ available to the synthesizer, i.e., every Rth column, are indicated by shading. Inverting (8) gives $x_m(n)$ as the inverse DFT of $X_k(n)$ for each n, i.e.,

$$x_m(n) = \frac{1}{N} \sum_{k=0}^{N-1} X_k(n) W_N^{mk}. \tag{12}$$

Furthermore, $x_m(n)$ is defined on the net shown in Fig. 5. Because $S_k(r) = X_k(rR)$, it follows that $s_m(r) = x_m(rR)$ and, therefore, $s_m(r)$ is defined on the shaded points in Fig. 5. By comparing (12) with (2), it can be seen that the values of $x(n)$ are given by the values of $x_m(n)|_{m \equiv n \bmod N}$, which correspond to the points in Fig. 5 on the "helical" path $m \equiv n \bmod N$. The operation defined by (10) is, therefore, interpreted as interpolating $s_m(r)$ to obtain the unknown values of $x_m(n)$, but only those values of $x_m(n)$ on the path $m \equiv n \bmod N$ that are the values of $x(n)$.

The implementation of the synthesis procedure is, therefore,

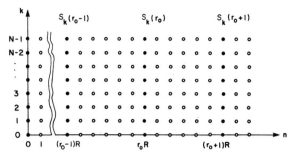

Fig. 4. Net on which $X_k(n)$ is defined. Shaded points represent values associated with $S_k(r) = X_k(rR)$.

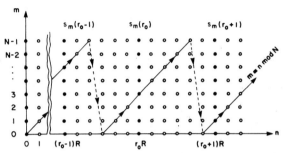

Fig. 5. Net on which $x_m(n)$ is defined. Shaded points represent values associated with $s_m(r) = x_m(rR)$. Values along path $m \equiv n \bmod N$ are $x(n) = x_n(n)$.

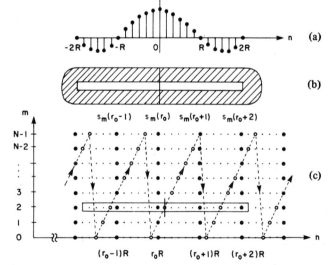

Fig. 6. (a) Typical unit-sample response for $1:R$ FIR digital interpolating filter. (b) Mask to extract values required for interpolation using $f(n)$. (c) Net associated with $x_m(n)$. ● indicates points representing $s_m(r) = x_m(rR)$. ○ indicates points representing $x(n) = x_n(n)$.

as follows. First, the values of $s_m(r)$ are obtained by inverse transforming $S_k(r)$ using the FFT (11). The values of $x(n)$ are then obtained by interpolating $s_m(r)$ according to (10). Notice that for each value of $x(n)$, $2Q$ values of $s_m(r)$ are required. In fact, for R consecutive values of $x(n)$, these values are obtained from the same $2Q$ columns. Thus, it is natural to compute $x(n)$ in records of length R. For each output value, imagine a mask that extracts $2Q$ values of $s_m(r)$, as shown in Fig. 6. These values are then processed according to (10) to compute $x(n)$. Successive output values are obtained by shifting the mask one sample at a time along the path $m \equiv n \bmod N$ and repeating the process.

V. Conclusions

We have discussed a new implementation of the digital phase vocoder, a system that provides a parametric representation of a sequence in terms of its discrete short-time Fourier transform. If no parameter modifications are introduced, the system has been shown to be, mathematically, an identity system. The bulk of the computation in both the analysis and synthesis procedures is performed by the FFT, thereby making the system attractive for implementation on a minicomputer (especially if a high-speed FFT processor is available).

The system described has been implemented on a PDP-9 computer using block floating-point arithmetic. The system is being used to modify certain parameters of speech signals and currently allows as many as 512 frequency channels. When operated as an identity system, the synthesized output differs in no perceptual or measurable way from the input speech.

Acknowledgment

The author wishes to thank his advisor, Prof. A. V. Oppenheim, who carefully read and commented on this manuscript during its preparation.

References

[1] J. L. Flanagan and R. M. Golden, "Phase vocoder," *Bell Syst. Tech. J.*, vol. 45, pp. 1493–1509, Nov. 1966.

[2] R. W. Schafer and L. R. Rabiner, "Design and simulation of a speech analysis–synthesis system based on short-time Fourier analysis," *IEEE Trans. Audio Electroacoust. (Special Issue on 1972 Conference on Speech Communication and Processing)*, vol. AU-21, pp. 165–174, June 1973.

[3] —, "A digital signal processing approach to interpolation," *Proc. IEEE*, vol. 61, pp. 692–702, June 1973.

[4] R. W. Schafer, L. R. Rabiner, and O. Herrmann, "FIR digital filter banks for speech analysis," *Bell Syst. Tech. J.*, vol. 54, pp. 531–544, Mar. 1975.

[5] A. V. Oppenheim and R. W. Schafer, *Digital Signal Processing*. Englewood Cliffs, NJ: Prentice-Hall, 1975.

[6] J. F. Kaiser, "Nonrecursive digital filter design using the I_0-sinh window function," in *Proc. 1974 IEEE Int. Symp. Circuits and Systems*, San Francisco, CA, Apr. 1974, pp. 20–23.

[7] H. D. Helms, "Nonrecursive digital filters: Design methods for achieving specifications on frequency response," *IEEE Trans. Audio Electroacoust. (Special Issue on Digital Filters: The Promise of LSI to Signal Processing)*, vol. AU-16, pp. 336–342, Sept. 1968.

[8] H. S. Hersey and R. M. Mersereau, "An algorithm to perform minimax approximation in the absence of the Haar condition," M.I.T. Res. Lab. Electron., Cambridge, MA, Quarterly Progress Rep. 114, pp. 157–160, July 15, 1974.

[9] G. Oetken, T. W. Parks, and H. W. Schüssler, "New results in the design of digital interpolators," *IEEE Trans. Acoust., Speech, Signal Processing (Special Issue on 1974 Arden House Workshop on Digital Signal Processing)*, vol. ASSP-23, pp. 301–309, June 1975.

Received 12 August 1968

Speech Analysis–Synthesis System Based on Homomorphic Filtering

ALAN V. OPPENHEIM

Lincoln Laboratory,* Massachusetts Institute of Technology, Lexington, Massachusetts 02173

A digital speech analysis–synthesis system based on a recently proposed approach to the deconvolution of speech is presented. The analyzer is based on a computation of the cepstrum considered as the inverse Fourier transform of the log magnitude of the Fourier transform. The transmitted parameters represent pitch and voiced–unvoiced information and the low-time portion of the cepstrum representing an approximation to the cepstrum of the vocal-tract impulse response. In the synthesis, the low-time cepstral information is transformed to an impulse response function, which is then convolved with a train of impulses during voiced portions or a noise waveform during unvoiced portions to reconstruct the speech. Since no phase information is retained in the analysis, phase must be regenerated during synthesis. Either a zero-phase or minimum-phase characteristic can be obtained by simple weighting of the cepstrum before transformation.

INTRODUCTION

MANY speech analysis–synthesis systems are directed toward a separation of the speech excitation function and the vocal-tract impulse response. Typically, the excitation function is characterized by a measurement of the pitch period, and the vocal-tract impulse response is characterized by samples of the spectral envelope, taken as the outputs of a filter bank with filter bandwidths on the order of several hundred hertz. This characterization of the spectral envelope is convenient, since it is obtained from a measurement of the coarse spectrum without the intermediate determination of a fine-grain spectrum.

The trend of present technology indicates the possibility of future speech-system realizations with digital components. This trend coupled with the use of recently discovered fast and efficient means for computing the spectrum digitally, suggests the possibility that speech systems in which an intermediate step involves the determination of a high-resolution spectrum may be practical. In this paper, a configuration for a speech analysis–synthesis system that requires the determination of a high-resolution spectrum is proposed and discussed. The system bases the measurement of the spectral envelope on a linear smoothing of the logarithm of the fine-grain spectrum, rather than on a linear smoothing of the complex spectrum, as in a conventional channel vocoder, or a linear smoothing of the

* Operated with support from the U. S. Air Force.

spectral energy as proposed by Freudberg *et al.*[1] In addition to providing what appears to be a good measurement of the spectral envelope, as judged by the quality of the synthesized speech obtained, this approach provides a simple mechanism for introducing into the synthesis a speechlike phase characteristic.

The basis for the system stems from a recently proposed approach to the deconvolution of speech.[2] In this approach, we consider the speech waveform to be modeled on a short-time basis as a convolution of the components representing the excitation function and the vocal-tract impulse response. Since we consider the processing to be digital, we represent the input speech in sampled form. Letting T denote the sampling period and $s(nT)$ the input speech weighted by a window $w(nT)$,

$$s(nT) = [p(nT) \otimes v(nT)]w(nT), \qquad (1)$$

where $p(nT)$ represents the excitation function and $v(nT)$ represents the vocal tract impulse response. If $w(nT)$ is a relatively smooth window, then Eq. 1 can be approximated as

$$s(nT) = p_1(nT) \otimes v(nT), \qquad (2)$$

[1] R. Freudberg, J. DeLellis, C. Howard, and H. Shaffer, "An All Digital Pitch Excited Vocoder Technique Using the FFT Algorithm," *1967 Conference on Speech Communication and Processing* (conference preprints) (November 1967), pp. 297–310.
[2] A. V. Oppenheim and R. W. Schafer, "Homomorphic Analysis of Speech," IEEE Trans. Audio Electroacoust. **AU-16**, No. 2, pp. 221–226 (1968).

where

$$p_1(nT) = p(nT)w(nT).$$

[The assumption that Eq. 1 can be replaced by Eq. 2 corresponds to assuming that $w(nT)$ is approximately constant over the duration of $v(nT)$. Results based on this assumption presented in Ref. 2 and in the present paper indicate that for the case of a 40-msec Hanning window, this assumption is justified.] Letting $P_1(\omega)$ represent the spectrum of $p_1(nT)$ and $V(\omega)$ represent the spectrum of the vocal-tract impulse response,

$$S(\omega) = P_1(\omega)V(\omega). \qquad (3)$$

The approach to recovering the vocal-tract impulse response by means of homomorphic filtering is based on the observation that in the logarithm of $S(\omega)$, the contributions of excitation and vocal tract are added. Furthermore, the contribution from the vocal tract tends to vary slowly with frequency, while the contribution from the excitation tends to vary more rapidly and periodically with frequency. Consequently, we may expect that to some approximation, each of these contributions can be separated by means of linear filtering. Specifically, if we consider the inverse transform of $\log S(\omega)$, we may expect the contribution due to the excitation to occur at multiples of the pitch period, while the contribution from the vocal-tract impulse response tends to occur near the origin. Thus, to recover the component $v(nT)$ we would retain those values in the inverse transform near the origin, corresponding to smoothing the log spectrum and then transform, exponentiate and inverse transform to obtain an impulse response function. The operations described above can be carried out either retaining phase information or discarding it. In the first of these the complex logarithm of the spectrum is obtained with the real part corresponding to the logarithm of the magnitude and the imaginary part corresponding to the phase. In the latter case, the imaginary part of the logarithm is taken to be zero.

The inverse transform of the logarithm of the transform has been termed the cepstrum when phase information is discarded, and the complex cepstrum when phase information is retained. Thus, the strategy for obtaining an impulse response function is to compute the cepstrum or complex cepstrum of a segment of the input speech, retain only that portion near the origin and transform the result by the inverse set of operations.

In considering the relation between the impulse response functions obtained using the cepstrum or the complex cepstrum, we note that they both have the same spectral magnitude and differ only in their phase characteristics. In particular, truncating the cepstrum in such a way that it remains an even function results in an impulse response function with zero phase. This can be seen by noting that if the cepstrum is an even function, its transform, and hence also the exponential of its transform, is a real function. As an alternative,

we may discard phase in the initial computation and generate a minimum phase characteristic from the spectral magnitude information. (We define a minimum phase sequence as one for which the phase is the Hilbert transform of the log magnitude. The properties of the cepstrum of minimum phase sequences and the use of the cepstrum in realizing the Hilbert transform are discussed in Ref. 3.) It has been argued previously that a minimum phase characteristic can be obtained by simple weighting of the cepstrum. We note that an impulse response function obtained in any of the three ways described will have identical spectral magnitudes and differ only in the phase associated with their Fourier transforms.

With a measurement of pitch and a voiced–unvoiced decision, an excitation function can be generated, which, when convolved with the impulse response function, will result in synthesized speech. During voicing, the excitation function consists of a train of unit impulses or unit samples with individual spacing corresponding to the pitch periods. During unvoiced intervals, a noiselike waveform with a flat spectrum is used, for example, a train of impulses with random polarity.

The above discussion outlines the basic strategy for the analysis and synthesis. In the next Sections, the analyzer and synthesizer configurations are described in more detail. The analysis is considered as the determination of the cepstrum and a measurement of the parameters of the excitation. The synthesis is considered as the conversion of this to an impulse response function and the generation of the synthesized speech.

I. ANALYZER CONFIGURATION

The analysis consists of a measurement of the cepstrum and a characterization of the excitation function by means of a voiced–unvoiced decision and a measurement of the pitch period during voicing. The parameters used to characterize the spectral envelope are samples of the cepstrum. Since the excitation function introduces into the cepstrum sharp peaks at multiples of a pitch period, we would generally choose the cutoff time to be less than the smallest expected pitch period.

Since we are considering digital processing, the input waveform and the cepstrum will be sampled functions. They will have the same sampling rate. This follows from the fact that the spectrum of a sampled function is periodic in frequency with a period equal to the reciprocal of the sampling rate. If the spectrum is periodic in frequency, then the logarithm of the spectrum is also, with the same period. Hence, the cepstrum is a sampled function with the same sampling rate as the original waveform. The parameters used to characterize the spectral envelope or vocal-tract impulse

[3] A. V. Oppenheim, R. W. Schafer, and T. G. Stockham, "Non-linear Filtering of Multiplied and Convolved Signals," IEEE Proc. **56**, No. 8, 1264–1291 (1968).

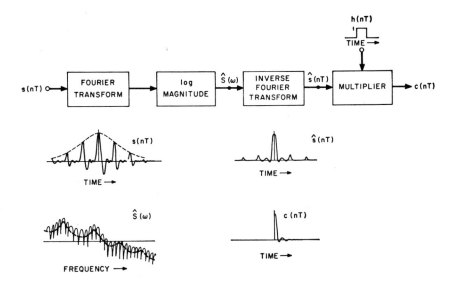

FIG. 1. Representation of the analyzer configuration.

response are taken as the first M samples of the cepstrum, where M represents the number of channels allotted to specifying spectral envelope information.

The cepstrum is obtained by weighting the input speech with a suitable window. Because the synthesis strategy is to excite an impulse response function with a train of constant amplitude impulses, then to within the accuracy of Eq. 2 the specific choice of the analysis window is not critical. For the specific system simulated, a Hanning window with a duration of 40 msec was used. With the speech waveform sampled at 10 kHz, the discrete Fourier transform (DFT) was computed for 512 points, followed by a computation of the log magnitude and the inverse DFT, resulting in samples of the cepstrum. A new cepstrum is obtained every T_c msec, where T_c is typically taken to be 10 or 20 msec.

Parameters characterizing the excitation function may be extracted by detecting the peak in the cepstrum which occurs at the pitch for voiced intervals and basing a voiced–unvoiced decision on its presence or absence. An alternative approach is to base a char-

acterization of the excitation function on measurements on the speech waveform that are independent of those used to characterize the spectral envelope, using any one of a variety of pitch and buzz–hiss detectors. Measurement of the excitation function from the cepstrum is perhaps the most reasonable if the excitation parameters are to be sampled at the same rate as the vocal-tract parameters. If the excitation parameters are to be sampled more rapidly, which is typically the case, then the use of other pitch-detection algorithms is very likely to be more practical. The analyzer configuration is summarized in Fig. 1.

II. SYNTHESIZER CONFIGURATION

Speech synthesis was accomplished by converting the results of the analysis to an impulse response function, which, when convolved with an excitation function, produced the synthetic speech. The excitation function was generated from a knowledge of the pitch period and a voiced–unvoiced decision. During voiced portions, the excitation function consists of a train of

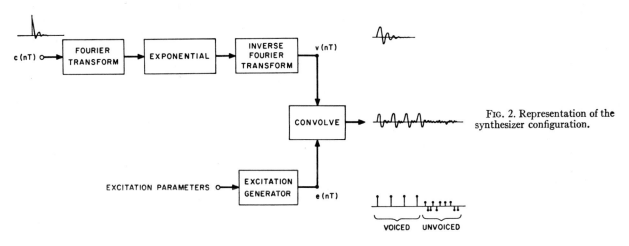

FIG. 2. Representation of the synthesizer configuration.

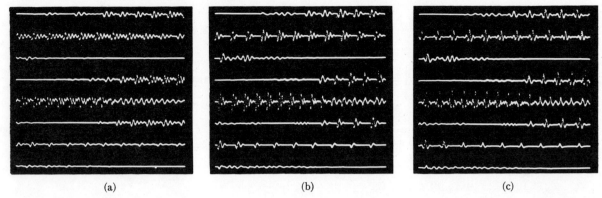

FIG. 3. Example of original and processed speech. (a) Sample of original speech. (b) Corresponding sample of processed speech with minimum-phase synthesis. (c) Corresponding sample of processed speech with zero-phase synthesis. Each sample corresponds to 819.2 msec with 102.4 msec per line. The sentence is "Your jumping thrilled him."

pulses with a spacing equal to the measured pitch period. During unvoiced portions, the excitation function consists of a train of equally spaced pulses with random polarity. The amplitudes of the pulses during hiss are adjusted to achieve a proper relationship in the relative energies during voicing and unvoicing.

The impulse response function is obtained from the cepstrum by computing the DFT of the cepstral values, followed by an exponential transformation and the inverse DFT. Thus, if C_n represents the nth channel, then the cepstrum $\hat{v}(nT)$ may be taken to be

$$\hat{v}(nT) = \hat{v}(-nT) = C_n, \qquad 0 \le n \le M-1,$$

and

$$\hat{v}(nT) = \hat{v}(-nT) = 0, \qquad M < n, \tag{4}$$

so that the cepstrum is taken to be an even function. The resulting impulse response function $v(nT)$ is then an even function.

An impulse response function obtained in this way is a zero-phase function, that is, it has a Fourier transform which is real. An alternative is to modify the cepstrum in such a way that a nonzero phase characteristic is introduced without altering the spectral magnitude. One specific means for accomplishing this is by forming the cepstrum from the channel signals as

$$\hat{v}(nT) = \begin{cases} 2C_n & 0 < n \le M-1 \\ C_n & n=0 \\ 0 & n<0 \end{cases}. \tag{5}$$

It is easily verified that the even part of the cepstrum defined either through Eq. 4 or 5 is the same, and consequently the magnitude of the spectrum of the impulse response function obtained from either is identical. However, the impulse response function obtained through Eq. 5 is not zero phase, since its Fourier transform has a nonzero imaginary part. In particular, reconstruction of the cepstrum by means of Eq. 5 corresponds to generating a minimum phase characteristic as defined through the Hilbert transform. Thus,

the impulse response function obtained in this way can be referred to as a minimum-phase impulse response function.

Synthesis of the speech is carried out by means of an explicit convolution of the impulse response function and the excitation function as depicted in Fig. 2.

III. COMPUTATIONAL CONSIDERATIONS

The system described above was simulated on an 18-bit digital computer with fixed-point arithmetic. The input speech was pre-emphasized, low-pass filtered at 5 kHz, and sampled at 10 kHz. The speech was digitized to 9 bits.

The analysis was carried out by weighting the input speech with a Hanning window having a duration of 40 msec. The spectral analysis consisted of a 512 point DFT corresponding to a spectral resolution of approximately 20 Hz. Similarly, the cepstrum was computed with a 512 point inverse transform. The channel signals consisted of the first 32 points of the cepstrum. A new cepstrum was computed at 20-msec intervals along the speech waveform, thus providing samples of the channel signals at 20-msec intervals.

In conventional channel vocoder systems in which transmission is digital, but for which the analyzer and synthesizer processing is analog, the channel signals are low-pass filtered and sampled before digitization and desampled by means of low-pass filtering at the receiver. In the system under discussion in this paper, we likewise interpolated the pitch information and the impulse response function information between sampling instants to avoid roughness that would be introduced into the synthesized speech due to sudden changes in pitch or spectral envelope information. While several means for implementing this interpolation suggest themselves, the most straightforward and the one incorporated in the system that was simulated, is a linear interpolation. Thus, in carrying out the synthesis, with a new impulse response computed at 20-msec intervals along the speech waveform, an im-

The Journal of the Acoustical Society of America

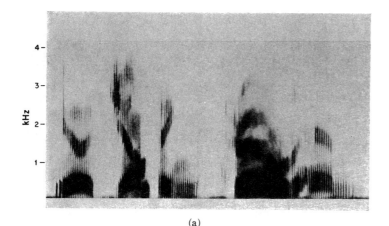

(a)

(b)

FIG. 4. Spectrograms of original and processed speech, for the sentence illustrated in Fig. 3. (a) Original speech. (b) Processed speech with minimum-phase synthesis. (c) Processed speech with zero-phase synthesis.

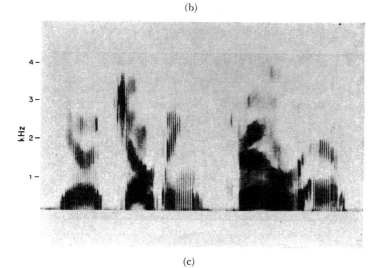

(c)

pulse response beginning at a time T into the interval would be computed as

$$f(nT) = f_1(nT) + [f_2(nT) - f_1(nT)]T/(20 \times 10^{-3}).$$

This is mathematically equivalent to carrying out a linear interpolation (in time) of the complex spectrum of the impulse response function.

The convolution of the excitation function and impulse-response functions requires that at the beginning of each pitch period the impulse response be added to the tail from the previous impulse response. An alternative that is considerably simpler is to truncate the previous impulse response at the beginning of the new pitch period. This can either be done for voiced portions only or for both voiced and unvoiced. Comparison of this method of synthesis indicates that if it is only carried out during voiced portions, there is no detectable effect as judged over a cross section of speakers and sentences. If it is also used during unvoiced synthesis, the effect is to reduce somewhat the quality of the noise excitation. This degradation is mild and might very well be justified in light of potential hardware simplicity.

The excitation parameters were obtained by means of cepstral pitch detection as described by Noll.[4] The long-time portion of the cepstrum was digitally interpolated to a sampling rate of 20 kHz and low-pass filtered. The interpolation was carried out by first generating a sequence consisting of the sequence to be interpolated alternating with samples of zero value. This new sequence was then low-pass filtered. Filtering was carried out using a recursive digital fourth-order Butterworth filter with a cutoff frequency of 2.5 kHz. The filtering was carried out forward and backward on the sequence to achieve an effective filter characteristic that has zero phase.

It was found that a particularly strong indication of the absence of voicing was a lack of correspondence between the location of a cepstral peak before and after interpolation and low-pass filtering. This coupled with a measurement of the input energy formed the basis for a voiced–unvoiced decision. The location of the peak during voicing was used as a measurement of pitch.

Measurement of the excitation parameters with the system described above led to errors in pitch consisting of pitch doubling and pitch halving. Errors in voiced–unvoiced decisions tended to occur primarily at boundaries, i.e., in transition from voiced to unvoiced. For the specific experiments described below, these errors in excitation were corrected by visual inspection and hand editing. The only changes made in pitch values were to correct errors of doubling or halving. The occurrence of errors of this type and algorithms for correcting them have been discussed by Noll.

IV. RESULTS AND DISCUSSION

An illustration of the synthesized speech is shown in Fig. 3. Figure 3(a) represents approximately 0.8 sec of original speech and Figs. 3(b) and (c) represent the same portion of the sentence after processing. Figure 3(b) corresponds to a minimum-phase synthesis and Fig. 3(c) corresponds to a zero-phase synthesis. Spectrograms of these sentences are shown in Figs. 4(a), (b), and (c).

The effect of introducing into synthesized speech a nonzero phase characteristic has been discussed by

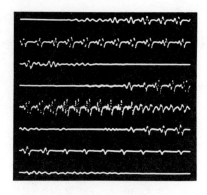

FIG. 5. Speech sample of Fig. 3(a) processed using maximum-phase synthesis.

David, Miller, and Mathews[5] and by Gold.[6] In the experiments reported in Ref. 5, a pitch synchronous analysis of the speech waveform was carried out and the individual pitch periods processed in an all-pass manner followed by resynthesis of the speech. Their results were phrased in terms of the peak factor of the synthesized speech. They reported that speech samples with a higher peak factor tended to have "raucous" quality, while a lower peak factor sounded more tonal. They comment, however, that the effect seemed highly variable to the observers with the magnitude of the effect varying considerably between speakers and sentences.

Gold describes a set of experiments that are directed toward introducing into speech generated by means of a spectrally flattened channel vocoder a speechlike phase characteristic. In his system, the channel vocoder synthesizer was preceded by a formant synthesizer based on the notion that after spectral-flattening the effect of the formant synthesizer is to introduce a phase characteristic into the synthesized speech without affecting the spectral magnitude characteristics. Since a set of formant networks is a minimum-phase network, this system can be considered to generate an approximation to a minimum phase characteristic. Gold hypothesizes that ". . . this improvement occurs because a formant-tracking vocoder more faithfully reproduces the phase of the actual speech than does a channel vocoder."

On the basis of these two sets of experiments, we may expect that within the context of the present system the minimum-phase synthesis is preferable to the zero-phase synthesis both because it has a lower peak factor and because it is closer to the phase of the original speech. Informal listening tests were conducted using an AB forced-choice preference test with experienced listeners. With careful listening over headphones a preference for minimum-phase speech was

[4] A. M. Noll, "Cepstrum Pitch Determination," J. Acoust. Soc. Amer. **41**, 293–309 (1967).

[5] E. E. David, J. E. Miller, and M. V. Mathews, "Monaural Phase Effects in Speech Perception," Proc. Third Int. Congr. Acout., 3rd, Stuttgart, 1959, **1**, 227 (1961).

[6] B. Gold, "Experiment with Speechlike Phase in a Spectrally Flattened Pitch-Excited Channel Vocoder," J. Acoust. Soc. Amer. **36**, 1892–1894 (1964).

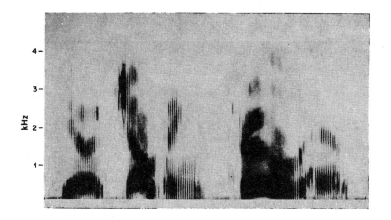

FIG. 6. Spectrogram of processed speech with maximum-phase synthesis.

given in roughly 75% of the pairs. Consistent with the results of David *et al.*, the effect was subtle, being evident for some sentences and speakers and not all evident for others. It was generally agreed among the listeners that the effect was not first order.

To help focus the question of whether a minimum-phase characteristic was preferable to other phase characteristics with the same peak factor, speech was synthesized with a different phase characteristic that was chosen to maintain the same peak factor as in the minimum-phase case. Specifically, a minimum-phase impulse response function was obtained, and prior to convolution with the excitation function, was reversed in time. That is, if $v_1(nT)$ denotes a minimum-phase impulse response, and $v_2(nT)$ represents the impulse-response function used in the synthesis, then

$$v_2(nT) = v_1(-nT).$$

The phase characteristic associated with $v_2(nT)$ is the negative of the phase associated with $v_1(nT)$. The magnitude of the spectrum is the same in both cases. If $v_1(nT)$ is a minimum-phase function, that is, it has all its poles and zeros in its z transform inside the unit circle, then $v_2(nT)$ has all its poles and zeros outside the unit circle and could consequently be referred to as maximum phase. We would expect that speech based on a maximum-phase synthesis would have the same peak factor as with minimum phase. Figure 5 shows the same segment of speech displayed in Fig. 3, but using maximum phase synthesis. In Fig. 6 is shown a spectrogram for comparison with Fig. 4. Again, informal listening tests were conducted with experienced listeners using an AB forced-choice format. Maximum-phase synthesis was compared with minimum-phase synthesis and with zero-phase synthesis. Minimum-phase synthesis was preferred to maximum phase in approximately 85% of the pairs and zero phase was preferred to maximum phase in approximately 85% of the pairs. Maximum phase has a noticeably rougher quality with the effect being con-

siderably more evident than in the comparison between minimum phase and zero phase.

V. SUMMARY AND CONCLUSIONS

A speech analysis–synthesis system has been described that requires a digital computation of a high-resolution spectrum and is based on a recently proposed method for carrying out a deconvolution of waveforms. In effect, the system analyzer computes the cepstrum and uses samples near the origin to characterize the spectral envelope or equivalently the vocal-tract impulse response. In the synthesizer, the cepstral samples are converted to an impulse-response function and an explicit convolution carried out with an excitation function. Either zero-phase or minimum-phase impulse-response functions may be obtained. The system was simulated and informal tests were carried out using a cross section of sentences and speakers. Minimum phase was slightly preferred over zero phase, although the difference was subtle and both speaker and sentence dependent. This result is consistent with those reported by David *et al.* and by Gold. In contrast, maximum-phase speech, which has the same peak factor as minimum-phase speech, had a markedly rougher quality, supporting the hypothesis that a speechlike phase is preferable in synthetic speech.

In general, comments from experienced listeners were that this system produced very high quality, natural-sounding speech. There are three primary aspects in which this system differs from conventional channel vocoder systems. One difference is in the means for obtaining spectral envelope information. In the present system, this information is obtained by linear smoothing of the log spectrum. A conventional channel vocoder is more nearly equivalent to carrying out a linear smoothing of the complex Fourier transform of a weighted sample of speech. The second difference lies in the phase characteristics of the synthesized speech. The phase associated with the equivalent impulse response in a conventional channel vocoder is introduced by the phase characteristics of the synthesizer filter bank and is essentially constant phase. The third major difference lies in the method of synthesis.

For the experiments discussed above, the system was considered to be operating in an analog mode, that is no additional quantization was imposed on the channel signals beyond the 18-bit quantization imposed by the finite register length of the computer. In a separate experiment, it was ascertained that the number of channel signals could be reduced to 26 (that is, the upper six channels discarded) and quantized to six bits per channel corresponding to 7800 bits/sec for the channel signals without noticeable degradation in the quality of the synthesized speech. It is anticipated that a further reduction in the bit rate can be accomplished.

ON THE OPTIMUM QUANTIZATION OF FEATURE PARAMETERS
IN THE PARCOR SPEECH SYNTHESIZER

Fumitada Itakura and Shuzo Saito

Musashino Electrical Communication Laboratory, N.T.T.
Musashino, Tokyo, Japan

This paper describes a new method of speech analysis and synthesis, in which the spectral features are expressed in terms of the partial autocorrelation (PARCOR) coefficients, and also presents a techinique for the optimum quantization of PARCOR coefficients to keep the spectrum quantization error miminum by allocating different bits to different PARCOR coefficients, using the dynamic programming algorithm.

Introduction

Time series obtained by sampling a speech signal shows a significant autocorrelation between adjacent samples. The short-time autocorrelation function is related with the running spectrum, which plays the most important role in speech perception. The autocorrelation vocoder is a speech analysis and synthesis method, in which the spectral features are expressed in terms of the short-time autocorrelation, but it has several problems to be solved, such as to unsquare the spectrum intensity level, to reduce the quantization bits without noticeable degradation of speech quality.

PARCOR coefficients are a new set of spectral parameters, which permits concise description of the short time speech spectrum.

Definition and Derivation of PARCOR Coefficients

Let $(x_t, t = .., -2, -1, 0, 1, 2, ..)$ be a discrete time series obtained by sampling a speech waveform every ΔT seconds, where the time spacing ΔT should be chosen according to the formula $\Delta T = 1/2f_N$, where f_N is the maximum frequency present in the speech signal. In the followings, ΔT is fixed to $1/8000$ seconds. The autocovariance $v_\tau = \langle x_t x_{t-\tau} \rangle$, or the autocorrelation coefficient defined by

$$\rho_\tau = v_\tau / v_0 \qquad (1)$$

can be regarded as a measure of linear dependency for the time shift τ, but a set of ρ_τ is still redundant because there are significant dependency among $\{\rho_\tau\}$. The notion of partial autocorrelation is introduced to reduce the redundancy using linear prediction techniques.

Definition

Suppose $(x_{t-\tau}, x_{t-\tau+1}, ..., x_{t-1}, x_t)$ is $(\tau+1)$-dimensional random variables taken from a stochastic process, which is stationary within a short interval, for example 20 to 30 msec. Let $e_{ft}^{(\tau-1)}$ ($\tau \geq 2$) be the residual of the least squares forward prediction, when x_t is predicted from ($x_{t-\tau+1}, ..., x_{t-1}$), and similarly $e_{bt}^{(\tau-1)}$ ($\tau \geq 2$) the residual of the least squares backward prediction, when $x_{t-\tau}$ is predicted from the same samples. If $\tau = 1$, we assume $e_{ft}^{(0)} = x_t$, and $e_{bt}^{(0)} = x_{t-1}$. The PARCOR coefficient k_τ ($\tau = 1, 2, 3, ...$) between $x_{t-\tau}$ and x_t, is defined as the cross correlation coefficient between two residuals:

$$k_\tau = \langle e_{ft}^{(\tau-1)} e_{bt}^{(\tau-1)} \rangle / [\langle e_{ft}^{(\tau-1)2} \rangle \langle e_{bt}^{(\tau-1)2} \rangle]^{1/2} \quad (2)$$

Derivation

In order to show how PARCOR coefficients are derived from $\{x_t\}$, we introduce two linear operators, the forward and backward residual operators, defined by,

$$e_{ft}^{(\tau)} = (\sum_{i=0}^{\tau} \alpha_i^{(\tau)} D^i) x_t = A_\tau(D) x_t, \quad \alpha_0^{(\tau)} = 1 \qquad (3)$$

$$e_{bt}^{(\tau)} = (\sum_{i=1}^{\tau+1} \beta_i^{(\tau)} D^i) x_t = B_\tau(D) x_t, \quad \beta_{\tau+1}^{(\tau)} = 1 \qquad (4)$$

where D is the shift operator for unit time, $D^n x_t = x_{t-n}$, and $\alpha_i^{(\tau)}$ and $\beta_i^{(\tau)}$ are weighting coefficients for prediction. Then it can be shown that the residual operators satisfy the following recursive relations: 1),2)

$$A_\tau(D) = A_{\tau-1}(D) - k_\tau B_{\tau-1}(D) \qquad (5)$$

$$B_\tau(D) = D[B_{\tau-1}(D) - k_\tau A_{\tau-1}(D)] \qquad (6)$$

Equations (5) and (6) indicates that the τ-th residual operators are uniquely determined from the $(\tau-1)$-th residual operators and k_τ, which is determined by Equation (2) if the $(\tau-1)$-th residual operators are known. In this way, all the PARCOR coefficients k_τ are recursively determined.

A blockdiagram of the PARCOR analyzer is shown in Fig.1, which is composed of lattice type digital filters, whose coefficients k_τ's are controlled by the output of the short-time cross correlators. 3)

Reprinted from The *IEEE 1972 Conf. on Speech Commun. and Process.*, April 24-26, 1972, pp. 434-437.

Extraction of Source Parameters

As the input signal $\{x_t\}$, passes through the PARCOR analyzer, auto-correlations between adjacent samples are gradually removed. If the number of sections, p , is chosen sufficiently large, the spectral features of the input signal are extracted almost completly, and the spectrum envelope of the residual is nearly flattend. Thus,

only characteristics related to the excitation source, such as signal amplitude, voicing and pitch, are contained in it. The signal amplitude is the root mean squares value of the residual,

$$A = [\langle e_{ft}^{(p)2} \rangle]^{\frac{1}{2}} \qquad (7)$$

In order to detect the periodicity and to determine pitch period, autocorrelation coefficients of the residual, $\mathcal{E}_{ft}^{(p)}$ are computed, and the lag time, T, indicating the maximum autocorrelation is picked up. If the maximum value is greater than a preset threshold, the input speech may be judged to be voiced sound with pitch period T, if not, unvoiced. Some additional logics, however ,are required to prevent errors, such as pitch period doubling.

Speech Synthesis from PARCOR Coefficients

Speech synthesis from PARCOR coefficients and excitation source parameters is just an inverse process of speech analysis described above. The excitation source is generated by controlling the impulse generator and the white noise generator by pitch period, voicing and amplitude. The resulting signal with flat spectrum envelope excites a time varying filter composed of p identical sections of lattice type, as shown in Fig.2. The transfer function of the filter is exactly inverse to the residual operator $A_p(D)$. Therefore, the output from the filter have nearly the same spectrum as the input speech.

Tonal quality of synthesized speech depends upon the information rate of control parameters. The information rate R_T is given by

$$R_T = (\sum_{i=1}^{p} N_i + N_T + N_V + N_A)/T_T \quad (bits/sec)(8)$$

where p is the number of PARCOR coefficients, T_T (seconds) is the frame period to readjust all the parameters, and N_i, N_T, N_V, N_A are the numbers of quantization bits of PARCOR k_i, pitch period, voicing and signal amplitude, respectively.

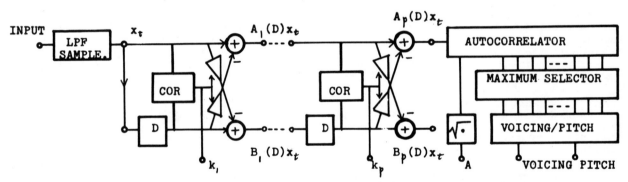

Fig. 1. Blockdiagram for extraction PARCOR coefficients and excitation source parameters

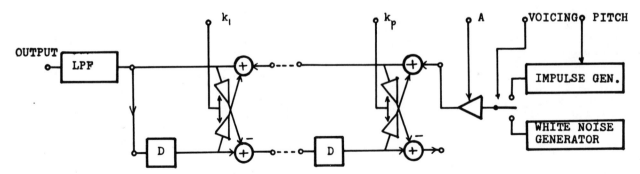

Fig. 2. Block diagram of speech synthesizer from PARCOR coefficients and excitation source parameters

Listenig test shows that the number of PARCOR coefficients, p, should not be less than 8, and no remarkable improvement is observed over 12. In the followings, we fixed p to 10.

Minimization of Spectrum Quantization Error

The frequency transfer function $T(z)$ of the synthesizer filter is expressed by

$$T(z) = 1 \Big/ \left| \sum_{i=0}^{P} \alpha_i^{(P)} z^i \right|^2 \quad , \quad z = \exp(-j\omega\Delta T)$$

where $\{\alpha_i^{(P)}\}$ are recursively determined from k_τ by using Equations (5) and (6). If PARCOR coefficients k_τ are quantized to finite binary digits, $T(z)$ deviates from the original transfer function, and resulting synthesized speech suffers some impairments in quality.

Our aim is to allocate binary digits to obtain the best quality under the constraint of fixed total bits. As the object function for optimization, mean squares (m.s.) spectrum error averaged over both frequency and time domains, was chosen:

$$F_p(N_1,\ldots,N_P) = \left\langle \left(10 \log \left| T'(z)/T(z) \right|^2 \right)^2 \right\rangle_{\omega,t}$$
$$(dB) \quad (9)$$

where $T'(z)$ is the transfer function with quantized k_τ's. Experimental studies have revealed that $F_p(N_1,\ldots,N_P)$ is approximated by

$$F_p(N_1,N_2,\ldots,N_P) = \sum_{i=1}^{P} f_i(N_i) \quad (dB^2) \quad (10)$$

where $f_i(N_i)$ is m.s. spectrum error when only k_i is quantized to N_i bits and k_j's ($j \neq i$) are not quantized. By this formula, $F_p(N_1,N_2,\ldots,N_P)$ is estimated from $f_i(N_i)$, which is easy to measure.

Thus, the problem is formulated as follows: minimize a function $F_p(N_1,\ldots,N_P)$

subject to constraint

$$N = \sum_{i=1}^{P} N_i \quad (11)$$

This problems is solved using Dynamic Programming algorithm. We define $\widetilde{F}_p(N)$ by

$$\widetilde{F}_p(N) = \min_{N_1,N_2,\ldots,N_P} F_p(N_1,N_2,\ldots,N_P) \quad (12)$$

Then recurrence formula for $\widetilde{F}_n(N)$ follows

$$\widetilde{F}_n(N) = \min_{N_n} [f_n(N_n) + \widetilde{F}_{n-1}(N-N_n)] \quad (13)$$

From this formula, given N, the optimum allocation $(N_1,N_2,\ldots,N_P)$ and minimum m.s. spectrum error is determined as a function of N.

Objective Evaluation

The m.s. spectrum errors $f_i(N_i)$, $i=1,2,\ldots,p=10$, $N_i=3,4,\ldots,10$ were measured on an utterance of 10 seconds long by a female speaker. In Fig.3 (a),(b), $F(N)$ is plotted against N, together with $F_{10}(N/10,\ldots,N/10)$, which is the m.s. spectrum error when all the PARCOR coefficients are quantized to N/10 bits, uniformly. As is evident from Fig.3, it is possible to reduce the number of total bits with the m.s. spectrum error held constant.

If the amplitude of the higher frequencies is emphasized before extraction of PARCOR coefficients, a substantial decrease of the m.s. spectrum error is observed by uniform allocation of quantization bits, but the improvements by the opitmum allocation is slight, as shown in Fig.3. (b).

Subjective Evaluation

In order to examine the subjective effects of the optimum bit allocation, we conducted paired comparision experiments.

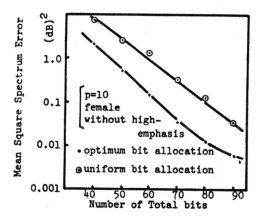

Fig. 3. (a)

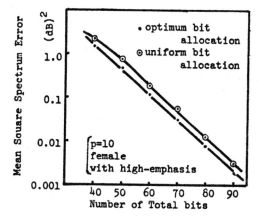

Fig. 3. (b)

421

Speech samples synthesized under 10 conditions are presented in pairs to 9 subjects,through headphones. The number of paired comparisions is 324 for each experiment. The measure of relative quality is expressed in terms of the number of preferences scored by each condition. The preference scores are plotted against N, in Fig. 5 and 6, on two cases(without and with high emphasis). We can see from these Figures that, in the case of without-emphasis, 42 bits with optimization is equivalent to 60 bits without optimization. In the case of with-emphasis, 53 bits is equivalent to 60 bits. These results are consistent with the objective evaluation qualitatively, but the effects of the optimum bit allocation is more evidently observed subjectively.

Conclusions

In this paper, we have reported a new speech analysis and synthesis system based on partial autocorrelation(PARCOR) coefficients for efficient coding of speech into digital form.

By using the fact that the m.s. spectrum errors caused by quantization of PARCOR coefficients are different from one to another, we can allocate the fixed number of total bits optimally. From objective and subjective evaluation, it has been shown that nearly 30 % of information rate is reduced by the optimization without further degradation of the quality.

Authors wish to acknowledge to the invaluable advice of Dr.Unotoro, the director of the Research Division, E.C.L., N.T.T..

References

1) F.Itakura, S.Saito,"Speech Analysis-Synthesis System based on the Partial Autocorrelation Coefficient", Acoust. Soc. of Japan Meeting, Oct. 1969.
2) B.S. Atal,S.L. Hanauer,"Speech Analysis and Synthesis by Linear Prediction of the Speech Signal", J.A.S.A. 50, NO.2,1971
3) F. Itakura, S.Saito,"Digital Filtering Techniques for Speech Analysis and Synthesis", The 7th ICA, 25C1, Aug. 1971

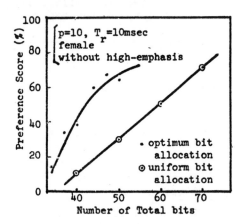

Fig. 5.

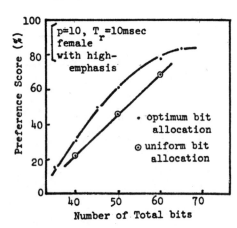

Fig. 6.

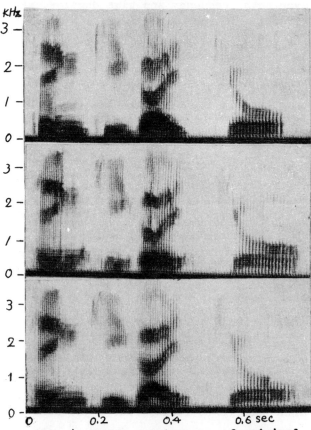

Fig. 4. Sound spectrogram of original speech(top) and synthesized speech when N=40,and T_r=10msec and $N_T+N_\gamma+N_A$ =15, uniform bit allcation(middle) and optimum allocation(bottom).

A Linear Prediction Vocoder Simulation Based upon the Autocorrelation Method

JOHN D. MARKEL, MEMBER, IEEE, AND AUGUSTINE H. GRAY, JR., MEMBER, IEEE

Abstract—A detailed discussion of the computer simulation of a linear prediction vocoder system is presented. The basic technique used for analysis is the autocorrelation method of linear prediction. New results include modifications to the simplified inverse filter tracking (SIFT) algorithm for more efficient pitch extraction, coding algorithms for low-bit rate transmission, a simplified synthesizer gain calculation, and a bias correction for the synthesizer driving function. Experimental results are presented which illustrate both the capabilities and limitations of linear prediction vocoders.

I. INTRODUCTION

ALTHOUGH the term linear prediction has been widely used to describe a new approach to speech analysis and synthesis, there are at least two different techniques which can be considered in the category of linear prediction. These are referred to as the covariance method, developed in detail by Atal and Hanauer [1], and the autocorrelation method, developed in detail by Itakura and Saito [2]–[4], and Markel and Gray [5]–[7]. The relationships between these two methods have been discussed in some detail by Makhoul and Wolf [8].

A complete speech analysis/synthesis system has been developed and discussed for the covariance method. The purpose of this paper is to present the details of the autocorrelation method in the form of a digital computer simulation of a vocoder system. For the sake of brevity, portions of the total system which have already been discussed in readily available literature will simply be mentioned and referenced.

Although the very important finite word length problem is not solved in this paper (that is, what is the minimal computer fixed point word length necessary to implement the system without degradation), integer arithmetic is used in the simulation in many places, and the parts which appear most sensitive to finite word length computation are mentioned.

In terms of system components, our version of the complete vocoder system is shown in Fig. 1. The *transmitter* input is a continuous speech signal $s(t)$.

The purpose of the *coefficient analysis* is to extract a set of inverse filter coefficients [5], [6] that contain the smoothed spectral behavior and gain of the particular frame of data being analyzed. The purpose of the *pitch extraction* is to make a voicing decision and to determine a pitch period for the particular frame of data being analyzed.

After the above-described parameters have been extracted, they are quantized and applied to the *coding* which transforms them into an acceptable format for transmission. These components make up the transmitter. The transmission *channel* could be represented by additive noise superimposed upon the transmission parameters, but for simplicity, the channel is assumed to be error free in this paper. The first component of the *receiver* performs the *decoding* of the received parameters into a best estimate of the analysis parameters. The *synthesis* is then performed using these parameters to reconstruct an estimate $\hat{s}(t)$ of the original signal for the duration of time represented by the parameters. Each of the system components will now be discussed in detail, then experimental results obtained from the system will be presented.

II. TRANSMITTER SIMULATION

A. Coefficient Analysis

A detailed block diagram of the coefficient analysis method is shown in Fig. 2. A low-pass filter (usually referred to as a prefilter) that forces negligible energy to exist above the half-sampling frequency $F_s/2$ is inserted to prevent aliasing of the continuous signal. In most speech processing applications the filter cutoff (the 3 or 6 dB bandwidth) is somewhat less than $F_s/2$. For the autocorrelation method of linear prediction, the filter should have extremely sharp cutoff characteristics and a 6 dB bandwidth approximately equal to $F_s/2$. The autocorrelation method forces the inverse filter coefficients to be adjusted so that the flatness of the output spectrum is maximized [9] over the range of frequencies spanning $0 \leq f \leq F_s/2$. Thus, if a great amount of spectral attenuation (with respect to low frequencies) exists near $F_s/2$ from the filter rolloff characteristic, many of the coefficients will be used in representing the reciprocal of this behavior. In other words, the least significant amplitudes in the prefiltered spectrum are the most significant amplitudes in the inverse filter spectrum. Analog elliptic filters are readily available which have a maximum out of band ripple of 40 dB down at 1.06 times the 3 dB cutoff frequency. Since extremely sharp rolloff and linear phase are incompatible, the phase and group delay characteristics

Manuscript received May 14, 1973; revised October 15, 1973. This research was supported under ONR Contract N00014-67-C-0118.

J. D. Markel is with Speech Communications Research Laboratory, Santa Barbara, Calif. 93109.

A. H. Gray, Jr. is with the Speech Communications Research Laboratory, Santa Barbara, Calif. 93109 and the Department of Electrical Engineering and Computer Science, University of California, Santa Barbara, Calif. 93106.

Reprinted from *IEEE Trans. Acoust., Speech, and Signal Process.*, vol. ASSP-22, pp. 124–134, Apr. 1974.

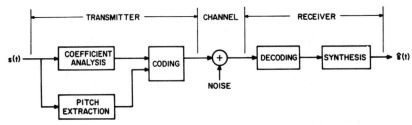

Fig. 1. Block diagram of linear prediction autocorrelation vocoder.

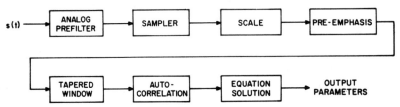

Fig. 2. Detailed block diagram of the coefficient analysis method.

of this type of filter will be rather nonlinear; in addition, some amount of aliasing must be introduced since the cutoff at $F_s/2$ is not infinite. Nonetheless, this approach is, in our opinion, the preferable one to use.

The prefiltered signal is then sampled at the rate F_s by an analog-to-digital converter and stored in data blocks using a fixed-point computer word format. Analysis is performed on the data blocks of length N every $1/F_r$ units of time where F_r is the analysis frame rate. Since F_r is chosen as a constant, the analysis is asynchronous with respect to the actual pitch period behavior. For maximum precision, the peak amplitude $\hat{x}$ in the present block is found and then all samples are scaled upward by λ where

$$\lambda = [[(2^{\beta-1})/\hat{x}]]$$

and β is the fixed-point computer word length in bits (not including the sign bit) and the brackets $[[\cdot]]$ are used to indicate the integer result obtained by truncation. The integer λ is stored for use later in the gain term calculation.

The scaled data block sequence $\{s_n\} = \{s_0, s_1, \cdots, s_{N-1}\}$ is then applied to the preemphasis filter

$$P(z) = 1 - \mu z^{-1}.$$

The digital frequency spectrum of this filter for constant μ is given by

$$|P(\exp[j\omega T])|^2 = 1 + \mu^2 - 2u \cos \omega T.$$

For μ close to ± 1, $P(z)$ acts as an approximate ± 6 dB/octave preemphasis filter. For $\mu = \pm 1$ a maximum error of 3.9 dB at the half-sampling frequency is obtained. For μ near zero, $P(z)$ leaves the spectrum nearly unchanged. Considerations in the choice of the preemphasis coefficient have been discussed in detail elsewhere [5], [9]. Optimal preemphasis has the advantage of guaranteeing that the output spectrum of the data block is as flat as possible (in the sense of maximizing the spectral–flatness measure [9]). Under these conditions, numerical problems in the analysis will be decreased considerably. A disadvantage of this approach is the need for slightly more computation; that is, μ must be computed for each block by

$$\mu = -\sum_{n=0}^{N-2} s_n s_{n+1} \Big/ \sum_{n=0}^{N-1} s_n^2 \qquad (s_n = 0, n < 0).$$

In addition, it must be considered as a transmission parameter.

If a constant μ is chosen, it should be near unity so that the higher formant structure will be accentuated [5]. Values between 0.90 and 0.95 are reasonable choices. This simplification has the disadvantage, however, that the synthesized fricative sounds will have some amount of erroneous low frequency noise inserted. One-bit optimal preemphasis experimentally appears to solve this problem. The term μ is calculated and reset to zero if $\mu < 0.6$ or reset to 0.9 if $\mu \geq 0.6$. Thus only F_r bits/s are necessary for transmitting the preemphasis information.

The benefits derived by properly windowing data are well known. Two of the simplest and most effective windows are the Hamming and Hanning windows. For the autocorrelation method of linear prediction, proper windowing is quite important since the overall effect is to produce more distinct resonance structure, narrower band width estimations, and thus more realistic sounding synthetic speech. Computationally, for the Hamming window, the inverse filter input sequence $\{x_n\}$ is computed from the scaled data block sequence $\{s_n\}$ by

$$x_n = c(0.54 - 0.46 \cos(2\pi n/N))(s_n - \mu s_{n-1})$$

$$n = 0, 1, \cdots, N - 1$$

where $c = 1.5863$ and $s_{-1} = 0$. The constant c is determined by forcing the rms value of the window to unity. The 4 dB gain increase is necessary to retain an approximate overall absolute system gain factor of unity since windowing is not applied as part of the synthesis procedure.

Next, the normalized autocorrelation $v_j = r_j/r_0$ is computed where

$$r_j = \sum_{n=0}^{N-1-j} x_n x_{n+j} \qquad j = 0, 1, \cdots, M.$$

Since by far the greatest percentage of computation time is the coefficient analysis is spent in determining the autocorrelation coefficients, it is well worth while to write the autocorrelation program in assembler language. If the implementation is done in fixed-point arithmetic, considerable care must be applied since the resulting analysis parameters are extremely sensitive to errors in calculating r_j.

The analysis coefficients which are coded for transmission are calculated from a recursive procedure which has been previously described and presented as a Fortran computer program [7] using floating-point arithmetic.

The parameters chosen for coding are the k-parameters (also referred to as the reflection coefficients and the *parcor* parameters), and the gain term σ which is the square root of the inverse filter output energy. The importance of the k-parameters (which are related by a simple recursive transformation to the inverse filter coefficients a_i, $i = 1,2,\cdots,M$) will be discussed in the next section. Representative choices of other constant parameter values such as N and M are discussed in the experimental results section.

B. Pitch Extraction

Most published results on linear prediction have shown the pitch extraction and coefficient analysis blocks to be intimately related; i.e., after the coefficients are obtained, an error signal is computed from the inverse filter; then, pitch extraction is performed on this new signal which has the formant structure removed. This point of view is overly restrictive since with the linear prediction techniques it is not necessary to obtain it from the error signal. In fact, there are at least two important reasons for considering the two processes independently: 1) computation can be done in parallel, which may be significant for approaching real time computation, and 2) pitch extraction can be accomplished at a lower sampling rate than is necessary for the coefficient analysis at considerable computational time savings. The simplified inverse filter tracking (SIFT) algorithm [10] is used in this study. Since it has been discussed in detail, only a few modifications which appear to make the algorithm more optimal in the sense of simplicity and accuracy will be presented. In this study a 6.5 kHz sampling rate was used so the down-sampling factor was chosen at 3.0. In addition, a simpler interpolation formula (linear interpolation) was used for choosing the peak location and slightly more complex decision rules were used. The two most important modifications are incorporation of preliminary tests and filtering of the error signal.

Preliminary Tests: There are at least three preliminary tests which should be performed on the data before extracting pitch and making a voiced–unvoiced decision. First, a threshold should be set corresponding to the lower limit of the dynamic range allowed in the system. Otherwise it is possible that very low amplitude 60 cycle hum will cause 16–17 ms pitch indications. Second, a test should be made for the zero-crossing density of the signal. If the zero-crossing density exceeds 2 zero-crossings/ms, for example, the frame should immediately be defined as unvoiced. Finally, before performing any correlations, the mean of the data should be extracted. Although speech is a zero mean process over long intervals, considerable bias can exist during a single frame. In addition, if low frequency background or room noise has sufficient amplitude, the threshold may be crossed. Since the autocorrelation of a rectangle (the form of a constant bias term in a frame) is a triangle, it is possible to either: 1) cross the pitch amplitude threshold defining the highest fundamental frequency of the system, or, 2) increase a noisy amplitude portion of the autocorrelation so that it exceeds the true pitch period amplitude indicator to the right of it. The order of implementation should be: 1) zero mean extraction, 2) threshold test, and then 3) zero crossing detection. It is also important to note that all of these could easily be implemented approximately with analog circuitry.

The fixed system parameters are: 1) analysis window length 40 ms, 2) down-sampling factor $D = 3$, 3) sampling frequency = 6500 Hz, 4) cutoff frequency of down-sampling prefilter = 900 Hz, 5) minimum value for peak searching 2.5 ms, and 6) maximum value 20 ms.

Filtering the Error Signal: A rather important discovery has recently been made with respect to the error signal and its usage for pitch extraction. The fact that the input autocorrelation can be used for very accurate voiced–unvoiced decisions and also for determination of pitch period of nasal and voiced plosive sounds has been previously discussed [10]. Unfortunately, the formant-fundamental frequency interaction is often sufficient to render it useless for the pitch period estimation. The error signal eliminates the interaction problem, but because of the fact that harmonic structure in the spectrum exists only for the first 300–600 Hz with nasal and voiced plosive sounds, it generally fails in these cases for voicing decision and pitch period estimation. If the error signal is filtered with $1 - \mu z^{-1}$, where $u = 0.4$, the optimum properties of both input and output autocorrelation are retained while the undesirable features are eliminated. In the preliminary testing of the simulation system, good pitch and voicing decisions are being obtained by using only the filtered error signal autocorrelation.

Final Comments on Pitch: After the autocorrelation, a peak-picker is applied to the corresponding range of 2.5–20 ms. This interpolated peak value and location are then obtained by parabolic interpolation of the adjacent peak values. Decision logic is then applied to determine the integer pitch and voicing code. The pitch extractor has a delay of two frames (excluding the present frame being analyzed) before pitch is transmitted. This delay allows error correction to be applied to the values obtained by peak-picking. The logic for testing threshold crossings and error correction from previous frames consists of ten IF statements in the Fortran subroutine.

Presently, the desirability of incorporating a "running average" of pitch is being tested, based upon the physical constraint that excluding infrequent, exceptional circumstances, during voiced intervals the pitch period values will move in a smoothly varying fashion. Based upon this running average, pitch doubling and halving problem tests are then performed using 5 "IF" statements. From the data analyzed thus far, there has been almost complete success in using this procedure to eliminate gross errors.

C. Coding

There are three parameters or parameter groups which are coded for transmission in addition to the 1-bit parameter for μ already mentioned: 1) the k-parameters, 2) the pitch period and voiced/unvoiced (V/UV) decision, and 3) the gain term σ. For a minimal bit rate representation (while retaining maximum synthesis quality), each of these must be considered separately and coded according to desired or inherent properties of the parameter.

Coding of the k-Parameters: The k-parameters determine the estimated smooth resonance structure of the inverse filter input signal averaged over the number of samples in the data block. Properties of the k-parameters relevant to the coding problem are as follows.

1) $|k_m| < 1 \quad m = 0,1,\cdots,M-1$ is a necessary and sufficient condition for stability of the synthesis filter.
2) k_m, $m = 0,1,\cdots,M-1$ values are independent of signal gain.
3) Parameter sensitivity is highest for the lowest ordered parameter.
4) The k-parameters are generally nonuniformly distributed over the interval $[-1,1]$.

The first property (proven in [7]) guarantees that parameter quantization will not affect the synthesis filter $1/\hat{A}(z)$ stability where $\hat{A}(z)$ is the inverse filter based upon decoded parameters. In the coefficient analysis, it is possible to obtain $|k_m| \geq 1$ if insufficient word length is used in either the autocorrelation coefficient determination or the recursive solution for k_m. For coding purposes, if $|k_m| \geq 1, k_i, i = m,m+1,\cdots,M-1$ is reset to zero. The corresponding synthesis filter then becomes a stable m-length filter. If the filter coefficients $\{a_i\}$ are directly quantized, stability of $1/\hat{A}(z)$ can no longer be assured.

Since the k_m parameters carry only spectral shape, not gain information, these parameters can be coded in the best respective way. For example, it is known that the probability density function of speech peak amplitudes is approximately exponential, and therefore logarithmic coding is preferred for peak amplitudes.

Itakura and Saito have demonstrated experimentally that nonuniform bit allocation on the k-parameters results in fewer total bits, without degradation of synthetic speech quality when compared to uniform bit allocation [11]. For most voiced speech, it has been observed that k_0 has a skewed distribution near -1, while k_1 is skewed near $+1$. The other k parameters are usually bounded by $\simeq 0.7$ in magnitude and are more evenly distributed near zero value. A simple Taylor series expansion in the Appendix

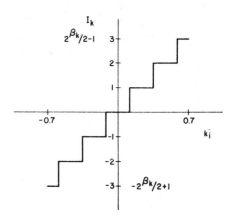

Fig. 3. Illustration of $\beta_k = 3$ bit quantization with rounding.

demonstrates theoretically that the k_0 and k_1 distributions are to be expected for voiced speech (where the first few samples of the autocorrelation are near unity). It is also possible to show that the inverse filter spectrum sensitivity is largest for k-parameter magnitudes near unity. Thus, the k_0 and k_1 parameters should have the most accurate representation.

A coding algorithm which has been successfully applied to the k-parameters is as follows. First the k-parameters are linearly shifted and transformed into the interval $[-0.7,0.7]$ by

$$
k_i' = \begin{cases} (k_0 + 0.3)q(k_0) & i = 0 \\ (k_1 - 0.3)q(k_1) & i = 1 \\ k_i q(k_i) & i = 2,3,\cdots,M-1 \end{cases}
$$

where

$$
q(\alpha) = \begin{cases} \alpha & |\alpha| \leq 0.7 \\ 0.7\ \text{sgn}\ (\alpha) & |\alpha| > 0.7 \end{cases}
$$

and

$$
\text{sgn}\ (\alpha) = \begin{cases} 1 & \alpha \geq 0 \\ -1 & \alpha < 0. \end{cases}
$$

To obtain accurate representation for a given number of bits with linear quantization, symmetrical quantization with rounding, as indicated in Fig. 3, is used. The quantizer input range consists of the real numbers from $[-0.7,0.7]$. The possible quantizer output values are the $2^{\beta_k} - 1$ integers I_k,

$$
I_k = 0,\pm 1,\cdots,\pm 2^{\beta_k}/2 - 1
$$

where

$$
I_k = [[k_i'\Delta k + \text{sgn}\ (k_i')/2]
$$

$$
\Delta_k = (2^{\beta_k}/2 - 1)/0.7,
$$

and β_k defines the number of bits used in representing k_i. For notational simplicity, the index on k is suppressed on I_k and β_k. Direct linear quantization of the k-parameters,

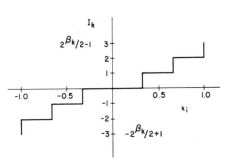

Fig. 4. Illustration of $\beta_k = 3$ bit quantization with truncation.

as illustrated in Fig. 4, is certainly easier to implement since the quantizer output for this case is

$$I_k = [\![k_i(2^{\beta_k}/2 - 1)]\!].$$

The tradeoff is coding efficiency versus simplicity of implementation. The logarithmic coding with roundoff, results in greater than 30 percent coding efficiency on the k-parameters.

Coding of Pitch Period and V/UV: For each frame of data, an integer i_p is calculated that is related to the pitch period average, P, within the frame by

$$i_p = [\![PF_s + 1]\!].$$

Since the range 2.5 to 20 ms includes the pitch period values for nearly all male speakers and most female speakers, i_p is required to lie within

$$i_{mi} \leq i_p \leq i_{ma}$$

where

$$i_{mi} = [\![2.5F_s + 1.5]\!]$$

$$i_{ma} = [\![22F_s + 1]\!]$$

and the term 1.5 introduces upward rounding.

The chosen criterion for quantization error is the approximate minimization of the relative fundamental frequency error over the complete range of interest for a given number of bits. Although the authors are not aware of any perceptual studies that indicate that this criterion is optimum over the wide range chosen, there is at least some evidence that fundamental frequency discrimination is relative, as opposed to absolute [12]. Logarithmic coding of i_p satisfies this criterion. For example, with five-bit log coding, the relative percentage quantization errors are around six percent maximum over the complete range. With linear quantization on i_p, the relative percent error increases from approximately zero percent near i_{mi} to 35 percent near i_{ma}. Coding for the data block pitch value is performed as follows. If $i_p > i_{mi}$ define

$$a_1 = 1/i_{ma}$$

$$a_2 = 1/i_{mi}$$

$$a_p = 1/i_p$$

and $C_p = (2^{\beta_p} - 2)/(ln a_2 - ln a_1)$ where β_p is the total number of bits allocated for pitch and V/UV, then

$$Ip = [\![A_p + 0.5]\!]$$

where $A_p = C_p ln(a_p - a_1) + 1$ and $Ip = 1, 2, \cdots, 2^{\beta_p} - 1$. If $i_p = 0$, indicating that the data block is unvoiced, $I_p = 0$.

Coding of Gain Parameter σ: Theoretically, σ^2 (the inverse filter output energy for the data block) can have a much larger dynamic range than the input energy r_0 since σ^2 must satisfy the relation $\sigma^2 \leq r_0$. Practically, a dynamic range equal to that necessary for coding r_0 is sufficient. When low amplitude fricative sounds such as /f/ in fish or /θ/ in think are analyzed, σ^2 is only slightly less in amplitude than r_0. When voiced sounds are analyzed with relatively high r_0, $\sigma^2 \ll r_0$, in general. Thus, it has been perimentally determined that if R is the maximum input energy expected within any data block,

$$\sigma_2^2 = 0.3R$$

is a reasonable choice for the maximum energy expected from the inverse filter output. It is necessary to define a lower nonzero limit on σ since logarithmic coding is applied. Also, it has been found important to set this lower limit above the operating system noise level. Otherwise, extraneous low frequency sounds can be perceived in the synthesis. A lower limit σ_1^2 for energy output has been defined by

$$\sigma_1^2 = \sigma_2^2/9 \times 10^4$$

which allows for a 46 dB dynamic range. The probability density function for the gain term appears to be roughly exponential. Therefore, if $ln\sigma$ is linearly coded, approximately equal probability of occurrence is expected within each quantization interval. If β_g bits are allocated for the gain factor, the transmission parameter I_g is given by

$$I_g = [\![C_g(ln\sigma - ln\sigma_2) + 0.5]\!]$$

where

$$C_g = \frac{2^{\beta_g} - 1}{ln\sigma_2 - ln\sigma_1}$$

and

$$0 \leq I_g \leq 2^{\beta_g} - 1.$$

Bit Rate Calculation: Based upon these coded parameters and constant frame rate analysis, the transmission bit rate B in bits/s can be calculated by

$$B = (\sum_{i=0}^{M-1} K(i) + K_p + K_g + 1)F_r (\text{Hz})$$

where $K(i)$, K_p, and K_g correspond to the number of bits used to represent k_i, I_p, and I_g, respectively. The constant 1 is for one-bit optimal preemphasis.

III. RECEIVER

A. Decoder

The synthesis parameters are decoded from the transmission parameters by approximately inverse operations.

In particular, if $\hat{i}_p$ is the estimate of i_p based upon reception of $\hat{I}_p$, the corrupted value of I_p ($\hat{I}_p = I_p$ in the noiseless channel case), then

$$\hat{i}_p = a_1^{-1} \exp[-(\hat{I}_p - 1)/C_p]$$

where $a_1 = 1/i_{ma}$. If $\hat{I}_g$ is the corrupted value of I_g, the gain estimate $\hat{\sigma}$ is

$$\hat{\sigma} = \exp(\hat{I}_g/C_g + ln\sigma_2).$$

The k-parameters must be treated differently due to the fact that when $\hat{k}_i$ is coded into one of the $\pm(2^{\beta k} - 1)$ levels, inverse operations would decode the parameter to unity for $i = 0,1$. For these conditions, $\hat{k}_i$ is set to 0.98 sgn $(\hat{k}_i')$. Thus,

$$\hat{k}_i = \begin{cases} \hat{k}_0' - 0.3 & i = 0 & k_0 \neq -0.7 \\ \hat{k}_1' + 0.3 & i = 1 & k_1 \neq 0.7 \\ \hat{k}_i' & i = 2,3,\cdots,M-1 \end{cases}$$

where $\hat{k}_i' = \hat{I}_k(i)/\Delta_k$. If $\hat{k}_i' = 0.7$, $i = 0,2$, $\hat{k}_i = 0.98$ sgn $(\hat{k}_i)$.

B. Synthesizer

The synthesizer can take on many different forms depending upon such tradeoffs as complexity, accuracy, and speed of computation. Assuming that numerical accuracy is sufficient, probably the two most important requirements for good synthesis quality are pitch synchronous synthesis and interpolation. Implementation of these only moderately increases the system complexity while greatly increasing the quality of the synthesis, particularly at lower bit rates.

Flow Chart: A flow chart of the basic synthesizer operation (ignoring the setup of initial conditions) is shown in Fig. 5. A counter KK is tested to see if IP, the count before the next parameter update, is exceeded. If $KK \leq IP$, without further testing, control is passed to the calculation of the driving function sample. For example, if the present frame corresponds to an unvoiced frame, a sample from a pseudo-random number generator is extracted. A cascaded filter mathematically having the reciprocal form of the inverse filter is then used to compute a single output sample. This sample is then applied to a postemphasis filter having the reciprocal form of the analysis preemphasis filter.

If the synthesis is not yet completed, the counter KK is incremented and KK is tested against IP once more. If $KK > IP$, a second counter LL is tested against LP, the number of integer samples corresponding to the length of the analysis frame. Thus, when the counter LL exceeds the count LP, the snythesis parameters must be updated. To perform pitch synchronous synthesis and interpolation, parameter values at two adjacent analysis frame periods must be known. The vector which stores the various parameter sets is denoted by Ω. The synthesis parameters for two adjacent frames are referred to as Ω_L and Ω_R, mnemonically referring to the left and right-hand frames, respectively. During the update procedure, Ω_R is shifted

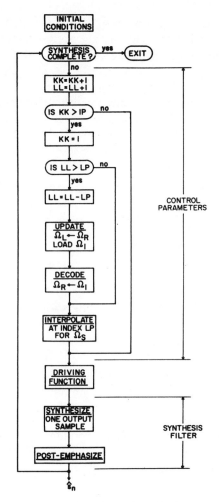

Fig. 5. Flow chart of synthesizer.

into Ω_L and the newest input parameter set Ω_I is obtained. This vector is decoded according to the equations of the previous section and then stored as the new Ω_R. Interpolation is performed between Ω_L and Ω_R at point LL where $1 \leq LL \leq LP$ and $LL = 1$ corresponds to the left-hand frame and $LL = LP$ corresponds to the right-hand frame. The interpolated parameters are stored in Ω_s and used as the cascaded filter synthesis control parameters until KK exceeds IP.

Finally, if KK exceeds IP but $LL \leq LP$, a new interpolated parameter set Ω_s is computed from the present Ω_L and Ω_R sets based upon the index LL, without any update. The important details of the system will now be considered.

Control Parameters: To initialize the synthesize procedure, the first received vector Ω_I is decoded and stored as Ω_L. The second decoded input vector is stored as Ω_R. A synthesizer parameter vector Ω_S is defined as Ω_L, with the exception that $IP = \hat{i}_p$ where $\hat{i}_p$ equals the number of pitch period samples if $IP_L > 0$, and $\hat{i}_p$ equals the frame interval IP when $IP_L = 0$ (the subscripts L and R for left and right, respectively, are used whenever necessary for clarification). Since two received frames are necessary before synthesis can begin, the synthesizer has an inherent delay or memory of at least $1/F_R$ with respect to the received parameters, even if computations are performed in real time. The pitch period counter KK and the parameter frame update counter LL are initially set to zero.

For the first IP sample output calculations, $KK \leq IP$; thus, IP output samples are computed from the parameters Ω_S essentially without interruption.

When $KK = IP + 1$, the next pitch period initiation time has been reached. At this point, the output sample calculation is interrupted so that an update of new parameters and/or a pitch synchronous interpolation at location LL can be performed. The linear gain parameter interpolation is performed by

$$\sigma = (\sigma_R - \sigma_L)\Delta + \sigma_L$$

where $\Delta = (LL - 1)/(LP - 1)$, the k-parameter interpolation is

$$CK(i) = (CK_R(i) - CK_L(i))\Delta + CK_L(i)$$
$$i = 1,2,\cdots,M,$$

and $CK(i)$, $i = 1,2,\cdots,M$ defines the decoded k-parameter set. The length of the pitch period over which these parameters will be used is then computed as

$$IP = (IP_R - IP_L)\Delta + IP_L.$$

Driving Function: The synthesizer gain is calculated in a simple manner, yet it appears to produce results which on an absolute scale compare favorably with the original signal. When Ω_L is voiced, the following approach is used. In the analysis, a data block of length N results in energy σ^2. If the synthesizer is driven by unit samples separated by the pitch period IP, each unit sample should then be multiplied by $(IP/N)^{1/2}$ so that, on the average, the inverse filter output energy and the synthesizer input signal energy are approximately equal over a window length N. This result is due to the fact that if the actual error signal (having gain σ) is used to drive the synthesizer, the actual input signal is reconstructed (with the exception of generally small errors due to transition effects between data frames).

In the postemphasis (discussed in the next section), the filter acts as an integrator if μ is near unity. During voicing, each period has a driving sequence $G_{KK} = C\delta_{KK,1}$, $KK = 1,2,\cdots,IP$ where C is some constant and thus positive bias equal to $C/(IP - 1)$ exists. The effect of this bias is to introduce annoying low frequency "thumps" in synthetic speech having high fundamental frequency voiced-unvoiced transitions since the pseudo-random number generator (RNG) has an expected zero bias. The solution to this problem is to modify the voiced driving sequence from the start of each count IP so that

$$G_{KK} = \begin{cases} C & KK = 1 \\ -C/(IP-1) & KK = 2,3,\cdots,IP. \end{cases}$$

When Ω_L is unvoiced, it is necessary to drive the synthesizer with samples from the RNG such that

```
      SUBROUTINE SYN(Y,CK,B,M)
      DIMENSION Y(1),CK(1),B(1)
      DO 1 II=1,M
      I = M+1-II
      Y(I) = -CK(I)*B(I)+Y(I+1)
1     B(I+1) = Y(I)*CK(I) + B(I)
      B(1) = Y(1)
      RETURN
      END
```

Fig. 6. Fortran subroutine for implementing the synthesis filter $1/A(z)$ as a two-multiplier model.

$$\frac{G_{KK}}{x} = \frac{\sigma/N^{1/2}}{\sigma_x}$$

where $\sigma_x = 4a^2/12$ is the variance of the RNG with uniform distribution over the interval $[-a,a]$. Thus, if x is a sample output at KK, G_{KK} is computed by

$$G_{KK} = x\sigma 3^{1/2}/N^{1/2}a.$$

Note that it is only necessary to perform one multiplication to obtain G_{KK} in the main loop for V/UV = 0 and none for V/UV = 1, by computing and storing the necessary constants at an appropriate location in the control loop.

Synthesis Filter and Postemphasis: The synthesis filter should mathematically implement the reciprocal of the inverse filter $A(z)$. Implementation of $1/A(z)$ is quite simple; however, the transmission parameters are the k-parameters, not the inverse filter coefficients. It is possible to either recursively transform the k-parameters into the filter coefficients $\{a_i\}$ or to directly implement $1/A(z)$ using the k-parameters [13]. A direct solution results in the form referred to as a two-multiplier model, while additional manipulation results in a one-multiplier model. A Fortran implementation of the two-multiplier model called SYN is presented in Fig. 6. The output sample $Y(1)$ is computed in response to the driving sample $Y(M + 1) = G_{KK}$ for the M coefficient synthesis filter which is mathematically equivalent to $1/A(z)$. The filter coefficients are defined from $CK(I) = \hat{k}_{I-1}$, $I = 1,2,\cdots,M$. The temporary subscripted variable B is used for retaining the M-length filter memory.

The postemphasis is performed by implementing the reciprocal of the preemphasis filter as

$$\frac{1}{P(z)} = \frac{1}{1 - \mu z^{-1}}.$$

The synthetic speech sample $\hat{s}_n$ at index n is then computed as

$$\hat{s}_n = Y(1) + \mu\hat{s}_{n-1} \qquad \hat{s}_n = 0, \quad n < 0.$$

In terms of simulation efficiency, by far the greatest amount of computation time is spent performing the synthesis of each output sample. By leaving all programming in a higher level language such as Fortran, for ease of modification and programming the subroutine SYN in machine or assembler language, dramatic reductions in computation time are obtained.

IV. DISCUSSION

One of the most important potential applications of linear prediction is for low-bit rate (2,400–3,600 bits/s) secure voice transmission over telephone-type bandwidths. Due to the fact that single channel high-quality speech transmission requires from 40,000 to 200,000 bits/s [14], it should be obvious that certain characteristics of speech must be incorporated into the system model along with other tradeoffs in order to reduce the bit rate by more than an order of magnitude. It is important to understand these considerations so that realistic judgments of the inherent capabilities and limitations of linear prediction vocoder systems can be obtained. Several of these realities are presented below.

1) Fixed frame analysis is the only practical technique for transmitting analysis parameters. Thus, one can directly trade off bit rate for frame rate. Perceptually, as the frame rate is increased, "cleaner and crisper" representations of transient sounds (such as tick) are obtained.

2) An explicit pitch extraction value must be estimated for each frame (no voicing implies $P = 0$). It is this feature alone that accounts for by far the greatest reduction in bit rate. If it is done well, a surprisingly small loss in "naturalness" occurs in the synthesized speech. Because of the explicit extraction, however, background noise must be kept to a minimum—music, dog barking, or multiple speakers will degrade the system almost completely. In addition, only a limited range of fundamental frequency is allowable, depending on how complex the pitch extraction rules are allowed to be.

3) Generally in the pitch extraction process, each frame is classified as all voiced (V/UV = 1) or all unvoiced (V/UV = 0). There are obviously speech sounds that would be more accurately classified as something in between, such as V/UV $\simeq$ 0.7 for the /V/ as in thieves. The binary decision is usually made because of practical considerations. It is difficult to automatically compute the proper ratio of periodic component to turbulent (noise) component and synthesis quality is often not greatly improved.

4) Given that explicit pitch extraction is used, the allowable bit rate cannot be lowered beyond a fairly sharp cutoff, in the neighborhood of 1,200 to 1,400 bits/s. With the techniques described in this paper, the highest possible synthesis quality (no coding, quantization, or finite word length calculation) can be maintained down to around 3,300 bits/s with essentially negligible degradation in quality. From around 1,400 to 3,300 bits/s, the degradation may be negligible to significant depending upon the particular speech sounds and speaker characteristics. Below 1,400 bits/s, almost complete degradation of synthesis quality is obtained.

In the following section, examples processed by the vocoder system simulation are presented. An attempt is made to present an unbiased point of view that realistically shows both the capabilities and limitations of linear prediction vocoder systems.

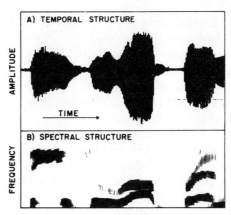

Fig. 7. Temporal and spectral structure of original utterance, "thieves who rob friends deserve jail."

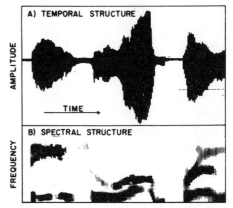

Fig. 8. Temporal and spectral structure of synthetic utterance, "thieves who rob friends deserve jail."

V. EXPERIMENTAL RESULTS

A. Example 1

The first example shows the accuracy with which the simulation represents both spectral (frequency) and temporal (time) structure in the utterance, "thieves who rob friends deserve jail." The acoustic waveform is presented on the same time scale with a spectrogram in Fig. 7(a) and (b), respectively. Analysis was performed with the following parameters: $F_s = 6.5$ kHz, $N = 128$, $M = 10$, $F_r = 51$ Hz. In addition, optimal one-bit preemphasis was used. The transmission parameters were quantized and coded as follows: $\{K(i), i = 1,10; K_p, K_g\} = \{7,7,5,\cdots,5; 5,4\}$ bits. The bit rate, therefore, is $B = (54 + 5 + 4 + 1)51 = 3,264$ bits/s. The synthetic speech corresponding to Fig. 7 is shown in Fig. 8.

Comparison of the spectrograms shows that the spectral structure is represented very accurately over the voiced regions. The only notable difference is in the representation of the /v/ of thieves where, as previously stated, a forced error must be made. It is very important in the system to be able to represent abrupt changes such as the transition from the /a/ to /b/ in rob and the /ε/ to /n/ in friends. It is seen that these are fairly well represented, with the most error in the synthesis of friends. This illustrates a necessary tradeoff not present in the theory; namely, interpolation is necessary to effect good synthesis quality with a 50 Hz frame rate, but it will also cause a slight amount of "smearing" in situations such as these. The effect of choosing the simple synthesizer gain calculation for voiced and unvoiced frames is shown more clearly in the acoustic waveforms of Figs. 7(a) and 8(a). The temporal representation is not as accurate as the spectral representation. The desirable feature of the system is that the accuracy of the temporal and spectral structure correlates with perception. Namely, during voiced sounds, it is far more important to have an accurate envelope behavior. If the envelope of Fig. 8(a) were forced to be a best match to Fig. 7(a), only a slight difference would be perceivable. If the same percentage changes were introduced in the location of the spectral peaks, the perceived difference would be substantial. Overall, the perceived quality and naturalness of this example is informally judged to be good.

B. Example 2

The class of plosive sounds is very difficult to accurately analyze because their duration is often times less than or close to the analysis frame duration.

A rather critical test of the simulation system is illustrated by a spectrographic comparison in Fig. 9. The utterance, "open the crate but don't break the glass," was spoken by a male speaker with a high average fundamental frequency of approximately 200 Hz. It can be seen that the original [Fig. 9(a)] and the synthetic [Fig. 9(b)] are quite similar in spectral appearance. Close inspection, however, shows slight differences in the intensity and timing of the plosive sounds. These differences are due to the fixed frame analysis. If the first half of the frame has silence and the last half contains the plosive /p/, for example, the synthesizer will produce pseudorandom samples from the first of the frame with a constant lower gain factor. The frame rate for this example was only 34 Hz. In addition, only eight analysis coefficients were used with a coding of $\{K(i);K_p,K_g\} = \{7,7,3,\cdots,3;5;4\}$. Therefore, the bit rate is only $(32 + 5 + 4 + 1)34 = 1428$ bits/s. This represents approximately the lower bound of system capability. The significant result is that the degradation (both as observed from the spectrogram and as perceived in the synthesis) is not severe. It must be noted, however, that at this bit rate, the synthetic results are highly dependent upon both the particular utterance and speaker.

C. Example 3

Synthetic results have been presented elsewhere [1] that indicate an almost negligible decrease in quality and naturalness when compared to the original utterance. In general, those results illustrate the upper bound attainable by having very accurate pitch extraction with a particular speaker and utterance that just happen to match the analysis model closely. These facts can be illustrated by studying the approximation process via the error signal $\{e_n\}$ obtained by passing the inverse filter (or linear pre-

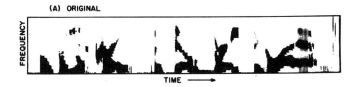
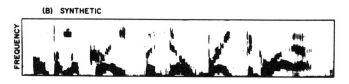

Fig. 9. Spectrograms of utterance, "open the crate, but don't break the glass."

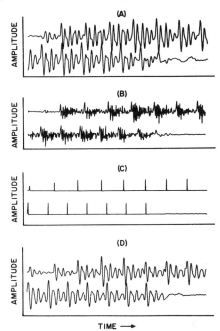

Fig. 10. Various waveforms from segment, "oak." (a) original, (b) error signal, (c) synthesizer driving function, and (d) synthetic.

diction filter) input through the filter. In Fig. 10(a)–(d) various waveforms corresponding to the portion, "oak," spoken by a low-pitched male in the context "oak is strong···," are presented in detail. Fig. 10(a) shows the original acoustic waveform. Fig. 10(b) shows the actual error signal which has approximately flat spectral character with nearly all resonance structure removed. Fig. 10(c) shows the actual synthesizer driving signal [on the same scale as Fig. 10(b)] reconstructed from interpolation of the transmitted gain parameters obtained during the fixed frame analysis. Finally, Fig. 10(d) shows the synthesized speech based upon the driving sequence, Fig. 10(c), and five interpolated k-parameter sets. Fig. 10(d) was thus constructed from a total of 205 bits of information ($F_r = 34$ Hz). Even with this very small amount of information, a realistic approximation to both the temporal (time) and spectral stucture of the original signal can be obtained. This result is obtained in spite of the rather dramatic difference in temporal character of the actual error

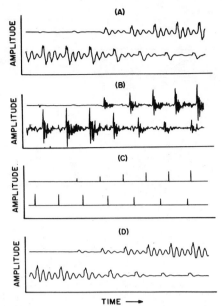

Fig. 11. Various waveforms from segment, "is." (a) original, (b) error signal, (c) synthesizer driving function, and (d) synthetic.

signal and the synthesizer driving signal. The quality is good, but there is a substantial difference in the "timbre" when compared directly to the original. If the actual error signal is used to drive the synthesizer, the resulting synthetic speech is essentially indistinguishable from the original speech in temporal and spectral appearance and perception. This, however, should not be overly surprising since transmission of the error signal requires at least 26 000 bits/s (4 bit log coding at a 6.5 kHz sampling rate). The corresponding synthesizer driving signal based upon explicit pitch, voicing decision, and gain requires 305 bits/s $F_r(B_p + B_g) = 6500(5 + 4)/192 = 305$—a reduction of nearly two orders of magnitude.

During the utterance, "oak," the actual spoken sound does not closely fit the classical speech model [15] of an all-pole vocal tract $V(s)$, times a glottal and radiation shaping term $s/(s + a)^2$ driven by a periodic impulse train. If synthetic speech is generated by this model, the error signal will look very similar to Fig. 10(c). It is important to note that the closeness between the error signal and the synthesizer driving signal is dependent not only upon the particular speaker, but also upon the particular sound. Consider the wave-forms for the same speaker from the utterance, "is," in Fig. 11(a)–(d). The error signal has very distinct spikes at the initiation of each pitch period with only a small residue between the pitch period spikes. Thus, the similarity between error signal and synthesizer driving signal is much stronger in this portion of the utterance. For these conditions, the perceivable differences between the original sound and the synthetic sound are very small.

D. Example 4

The utterance, "it's time we rounded up that herd of Asian cattle," from Atal and Hanauer [1] was analyzed for comparative purposes. The same conditions as in

Example 1 were used, thus also resulting in a 3264 bits/s rate. The spectrograms of the original and synthetic utterance are shown in Fig. 12(a) and (b), respectively. The results compare quite favorably. Close inspection shows an error in the pitch extraction for the portion "cattle" and an averaging of the sharp onset of "cattle" due to the fixed frame analysis. For this example, the synthesis is perceived as very natural and compares closely to the original in quality and "timbre."

VI. SUMMARY

The details of a computer simulation of a linear prediction vocoder based upon the autocorrelation method were presented. Experimental results were then presented to illustrate both the capabilities and limitations of linear prediction vocoder systems.

Although primary interest during this study was in fundamental frequencies in the range of 50 to 250 Hz (as illustrated in the examples), the techniques can be applied to very high fundamental frequency voices. Success is highly dependent upon how accurately the pitch extraction is performed.

The theoretical and practical considerations in implementing the vocoder system in fixed-point arithmetic are presently being studied.

APPENDIX

Expected Skewness Property of k_0 and k_1 for Voiced Speech

If $x(t)$ is a continuous time function, and its first few derivatives are continuous, then it is known that the autocorrelation function of $x(t)$ can be approximated for small time behavior in terms of the first few terms of the Taylor series, which involves only even powers of time. In particular, $r(t)$ can be expanded as

$$r(t) \simeq r(0) - \frac{t^2}{2}a + \frac{b}{4!}t^4$$

where $r(0)$ is the mean square of $x(t)$, a is the mean square of the derivative of $x(t)$, and b is the mean square of the second derivative of $x(t)$. If we assume that the correlation sequence r_n approximates samples taken of the true correlation (within a multiplicative constant c) for $n = 0,1,2$, then

$$r_0 \simeq cr(0)$$

$$r_1 \simeq c\left[r(0) - \frac{(\Delta t)^2}{2}a + \frac{b}{4!}(\Delta t)^4\right]$$

$$r_2 \simeq c[r(0) - 2a(\Delta t)^2 + \tfrac{2}{3}b(\Delta t)^4]$$

where Δt represents the sample time.

A direct calculation [7] shows that the first two reflection coefficients are given by

$$k_0 = -\frac{r_1}{r_0}$$

$$k_1 = \frac{r_1{}^2 - r_2 r_0}{r_0{}^2 - r_1{}^2}.$$

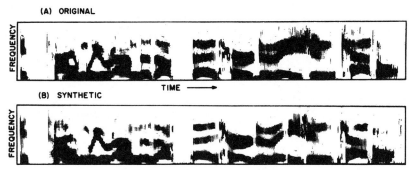

Fig. 12. Spectrogram of utterance, "it's time we rounded up that herd of Asian cattle."

If the approximations just found are utilized, and only terms up to the second power of Δt are retained, then

$$k_0 \simeq -1 + \frac{a}{r(0)} \frac{(\Delta t)^2}{2}$$

$$k_1 \simeq 1 - \frac{2b}{3a} (\Delta t)^2.$$

As a result of these approximations, one can note that for small sample times and reasonably smooth signals, k_0 will lie slightly above -1, while k_1 will lie slightly below $+1$.

REFERENCES

[1] B. S. Atal and S. L. Hanauer, "Speech analysis and synthesis by linear prediction of the speech wave," *J. Acoust. Soc. Amer.*, vol. 50, pp. 637–655, 1971.

[2] F. Itakura and S. Saito, "Analysis synthesis telephony based upon the maximum likelihood method," in *Proc. 6th Int. Cong. Acoust.*, Tokyo (Edited by Y. Kohasi), C-5-5, August 21–28, 1968.

[3] F. Itakura, "Speech analysis and synthesis systems based on statistical method," (in Japanese), Ph.D. Dissertation, Dept. of Engineering, Nagoya University, Nagoya, Japan, Mar. 1972.

[4] F. Itakura *et al.*, "An audio response unit based on partial autocorrelation," *IEEE Trans. Commun.*, vol. COM-20, pp. 792–797, Aug. 1972.

[5] J. D. Markel, "Formant trajectory estimation from a linear least-squares inverse filter formulation," Speech Comm. Res. Lab., Santa Barbara, Calif., Monograph 7, Oct. 1971.

[6] ——, "Digital inverse filtering, a new tool for formant trajectory estimation," *IEEE Trans. Audio Electroacoust.*, vol AU-20, pp. 129–137, June 1972.

[7] J. D. Markel and A. H. Gray, Jr., "On autocorrelation equations as applied to speech analysis," *IEEE Trans. Audio Electroacoust.*, vol. AU-21, pp. 69–79, Apr. 1973.

[8] J. I. Makhoul and J. J. Wolf, "Linear prediction and the spectral analysis of speech," Bolt, Beranek, and Newman, Inc., Cambridge, Mass., Rep. 2304, Aug. 1972.

[9] A. H. Gray, Jr. and J. D. Markel, "Linear prediction and a spectral-flatness measure," to be published in *IEEE Trans. Acoustic., Speech, and Signal Processing.*

[10] J. D. Markel, "The SIFT algorithm for fundamental frequency estimation," *IEEE Trans. Audio Electroacoust.*, vol. AU-20, pp. 367–377, Dec. 1972.

[11] F. Itakura and S. Saito, "On the optimum quantization of feature parameters in the PARCOR speech synthesizer," presented at the 1972 Conf. Speech Communications and Processing, Paper L4, New York, N Y.

[12] J. L. Flanagan, "Digital representation of speech signals," presented at the Bell Telephone Laboratory Symp. Digital Techniques in Communication, Nov. 12–13, 1970.

[13] F. Itakura and S. Saito, "Digital filtering techniques for speech analysis and synthesis," presented at the 7th Int. Conf. on Acoust., Budapest, Hungary, 1971, Paper 25 C 1.

[14] J. L. Flanagan, *Speech Analysis Synthesis and Perception* (2nd Edition). New York: Springer, 1972.

[15] C. G. M. Fant, *Acoustic Theory of Speech Production.* 'S-Gravenhage: Mouton and Co., 1960.

Quantization Properties of Transmission Parameters in Linear Predictive Systems

R. VISWANATHAN, MEMBER, IEEE, AND JOHN MAKHOUL, MEMBER, IEEE

Abstract—Several alternate sets of parameters that represent the linear predictor are investigated as transmission parameters for linear predictive speech compression systems. Although each of these sets provides equivalent information about the linear predictor, their properties under quantization are different. The results of a comparative study of the various parameter sets are reported. Specifically it is concluded that the reflection coefficients are the best set for use as transmission parameters. A more detailed investigation of the reflection coefficients is then carried out using a spectral sensitivity measure. A method of optimally quantizing the reflection coefficients is derived using a minimax spectral error criterion and the sensitivity analysis. The method consists of transforming the reflection coefficients to the so-called log area ratios and linearly quantizing them. A qualitative study on changes in pole locations due to quantization serves to corroborate the use of this optimal quantization. An optimal bit allocation strategy for the transmission parameters is also presented.

The use of another spectral sensitivity measure renders logarithms of the ratios of normalized errors associated with linear predictors of successive orders as the optimal quantization parameters. Informal listening tests indicate that the use of log area ratios for quantization leads to better synthesis than the use of log error ratios.

I. INTRODUCTION

IN RECENT years the method of linear prediction has been quite successfully used in speech compression systems [1]–[5]. In this method, speech is modeled by an all-pole filter $H(z)$ as shown in Fig. 1.

Manuscript received February 1, 1974; revised November 25, 1974. This work was supported by the Information Processing Techniques Branch of the Advanced Research Projects Agency.

The authors are with Bolt Beranek and Newman, Inc., Cambridge, Mass. 02138.

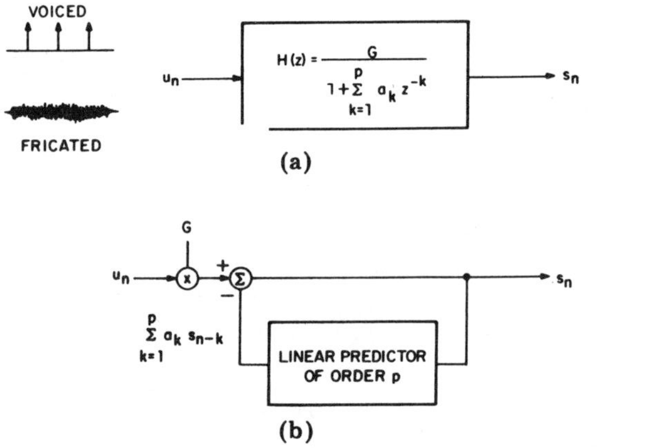

Fig. 1. Discrete model of speech production as employed in linear prediction. (a) Frequency-domain model. (b) Time-domain model.

The input to the filter is either a sequence of pulses separated by the pitch period for voiced sounds, or white noise for fricated (or unvoiced) sounds. The parameters a_k, $1 \leq k \leq p$, are known as the predictor coefficients, and G is the filter gain. For a particular speech segment the filter parameters are obtained by passing the speech signal through the inverse filter $A(z)$ (as in Fig. 2) and then minimizing the total-squared prediction error

$$E = \sum_n e_n^2 = \sum_n \left(s_n + \sum_{k=1}^{p} a_k s_{n-k} \right)^2 \qquad (1)$$

with respect to a_k. If the signal s_n is assumed to be zero for $n < 0$ and $n > N$ (e.g., by multiplying it by a finite window), the error minimization results in the

Reprinted from *IEEE Trans. Acoust., Speech, and Signal Process.*, vol. ASSP-23, pp. 309–321, June 1975.

434

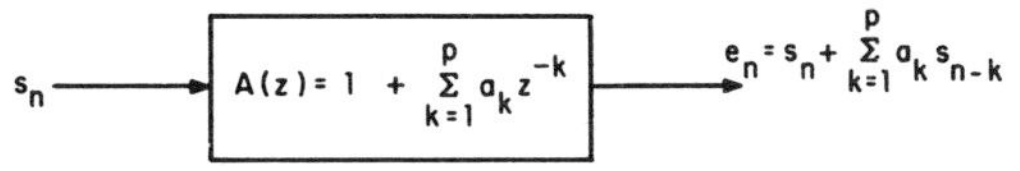

$$s_n \longrightarrow \boxed{A(z) = 1 + \sum_{k=1}^{p} a_k z^{-k}} \longrightarrow e_n = s_n + \sum_{k=1}^{p} a_k s_{n-k}$$

Fig. 2. The error sequence e_n as the output of an inverse filter $A(z)$.

set of equations

$$\sum_{k=1}^{p} a_k R_{|i-k|} = -R_i, \qquad 1 \leqslant i \leqslant p \tag{2}$$

where

$$R_i = \sum_{n=0}^{N-|i|} s_n s_{n+|i|} \tag{3}$$

is the autocorrelation function of the signal s_n. The set of equations (2) can be recursively solved for the predictor coefficients a_k as follows:

$$E_0 = R_0 \tag{4a}$$

$$k_i = -\left(R_i + \sum_{j=1}^{i-1} a_j^{(i-1)} R_{i-j} \right) \Big/ E_{i-1} \tag{4b}$$

$$a_i^{(i)} = k_i$$

$$a_j^{(i)} = a_j^{(i-1)} + k_i a_{i-j}^{(i-1)}, \qquad 1 \leqslant j \leqslant i-1 \tag{4c}$$

$$E_i = (1 - k_i^2) E_{i-1}. \tag{4d}$$

Equations (4b)–(4d) are solved recursively for $i = 1, 2, \cdots, p$. The final solution is given by

$$a_j = a_j^{(p)}, \qquad 1 \leqslant j \leqslant p. \tag{4e}$$

The filter $H(z)$ with the predictor coefficients obtained from (4) is always stable, i.e., the poles of $H(z)$ lie inside the unit circle in the z plane. Since $H(z)$ is an all-pole filter, stability also implies that $H(z)$ is minimum phase.

The intermediate quantities k_i, $1 \leqslant i \leqslant p$, in (4) are called the reflection coefficients (or partial correlation coefficients [3], [10]). Reflection coefficients occur naturally in the treatment of the vocal tract as an acoustic tube with p sections, each with a different cross-sectional area [2], [9]. An important result that will be used in the sequel is that the conditions

$$-1 < k_i < 1, \quad 1 \leqslant i \leqslant p \tag{5}$$

are both necessary and sufficient for the stability of $H(z)$:

The quantity E_p obtained from (4) is the minimum value of the prediction error given in (1). By expanding the squared terms in (1) and using (2), it can be shown that the minimum error is given by

$$E_p = R_0 + \sum_{k=1}^{p} a_k R_k. \tag{6}$$

Of interest also is the normalized error V_p which is the ratio of the minimum error to the energy of the input speech signal, i.e.,

$$V_p = E_p / R_0. \tag{7}$$

From (4a), (4d), and (7) we obtain

$$V_p = \prod_{j=1}^{p} (1 - k_j^2). \tag{8}$$

The gain G of the filter $H(z)$ is obtained by conserving the total energy between the speech signal and the impulse response of $H(z)$. The gain can be shown to satisfy [6]

$$G^2 = E_p = R_0 V_p = R_0 + \sum_{k=1}^{p} a_k R_k. \tag{9}$$

Equations (2), (3), and (9) completely specify the filter parameters. It can be shown that (for a well chosen p) the resulting linear prediction all-pole spectrum is a good match to the envelope of the signal spectrum [6].

Above we assumed that the speech signal was multiplied by a finite window. The shape of the window is of importance if the signal spectrum is to approximate the transfer function of the vocal tract. This issue is discussed in detail elsewhere [7]. A smooth window such as the Hamming or Hanning window is adequate.

When applying the linear prediction method to speech compression, the model parameters—predictor coefficients, gain and pitch frequency for voiced sounds—have to be extracted, quantized and transmitted to the receiver. The rate of such parameter extraction is usually on the order of 50–100 Hz to follow the time-varying overall characteristics of the input speech signal. At the receiver, speech is reconstructed (or synthesized) using the speech production model given in Fig. 1.

The optimal choice and quantization of transmission parameters is of prime importance if the resulting synthesized speech is to be of good quality. In this paper, several alternate sets of transmission parameters are considered and their quantization properties are compared.[1] This comparative study has indicated that the reflection coefficients possess many desirable quantization properties. An optimal method of quantizing the reflection coefficients is derived using a spectral sensitivity measure and a minimax spectral error criterion. The sensitivity measure is also used for allocating a fixed number of bits among the various parameters in an optimal manner (in a minimax sense). Finally, the use of a second spectral sensitivity measure for the optimal quantization of the reflection coefficients is investigated.

II. ALTERNATE TRANSMISSION PARAMETER SETS

The all-pole model used in a linear predictive system has a transfer function

---

[1] As the quantization properties of pitch and gain are well understood we have not considered them in this study.

$$H(z) = \frac{G}{A(z)} = \sum_{n=0}^{\infty} h_n z^{-n} \qquad (10)$$

where the inverse filter $A(z)$ is given by

$$A(z) = 1 + \sum_{n=1}^{p} a_n z^{-n}. \qquad (11)$$

Given below is a list of possible sets of parameters for characterizing uniquely the linear prediction filter $H(z)$.

1) Impulse response of the inverse filter $A(z)$, i.e., predictor coefficients a_n, $1 \leqslant n \leqslant p$.

2) Impulse response of the all-pole model h_n, $0 \leqslant n \leqslant p$, which are easily obtained by long division. Note that the first $p + 1$ coefficients uniquely specify the filter.

3) Autocorrelation coefficients of $\{a_n/G\}$,

$$b_i = \frac{1}{G^2} \sum_{j=0}^{p-|i|} a_j a_{j+|i|}, \quad a_0 = 1, \quad 0 \leqslant i \leqslant p. \qquad (12)$$

4) Autocorrelation coefficients of $\{h_n\}$

$$r_i = \sum_{j=0}^{\infty} h_j h_{j+|i|}, \qquad 0 \leqslant i \leqslant p. \qquad (13)$$

It can be shown that r_i is equal to R_i in (3) for $0 \leqslant i \leqslant p$ [6], [7].

5) Spectral coefficients of $A(z)/G$, P_i, $0 \leqslant i \leqslant p$, (or equivalently spectral coefficients of $H(z)$, $1/P_i$)

$$P_i = b_0 + 2 \sum_{j=1}^{p} b_j \cos \frac{2\pi ij}{2p+1}, \qquad 0 \leqslant i \leqslant p \qquad (14)$$

where b_j are as defined in (12). In words, $\{P_i\}$ is obtained from $\{b_i\}$ through a discrete Fourier transform (DFT). Traditionally, vocoders that transmit the spectrum at selected frequencies have been known as channel vocoders. Thus, use of the spectral coefficients as transmission parameters leads to a *linear prediction channel vocoder*. While in the classical channel vocoder different channel signals are derived from contiguous bandpass filters, in the linear prediction channel vocoder a selected set of $p + 1$ points from the all-pole spectrum constitute the "channel outputs." The main advantage of the linear prediction channel vocoder, however, is that we are able to regenerate exactly the all-pole spectrum from a knowledge of the $p + 1$ spectral coefficients, unlike in the classical channel vocoder.

6) Cepstral coefficients of $A(z)$, c_n, $1 \leqslant n \leqslant p$, (or equivalently cepstral coefficients of $H(z)/G$, $-c_n$)

$$c_n = \frac{1}{2\pi} \int_{-\pi}^{\pi} \log A(e^{j\omega}) e^{jn\omega} \, d\omega.$$

Since $A(z)$ is minimum phase, we obtain using the results given in [8, p. 246]

$$c_1 = a_1$$

$$c_n = a_n - \sum_{m=1}^{n-1} \frac{m}{n} c_m a_{n-m}, \qquad 2 \leqslant n \leqslant p. \qquad (15)$$

7) Poles of $H(z)$ [or equivalently zeros of $A(z)$].

8) Reflection coefficients k_i, $1 \leqslant i \leqslant p$, or simple transformations thereof, e.g., area coefficients [2], [9]. The area coefficients are given by

$$A_i = A_{i+1} \frac{1 + k_i}{1 - k_i}, \; A_{p+1} = 1, \qquad 1 \leqslant i \leqslant p. \qquad (16)$$

Although the reflection coefficients are obtained as a byproduct of the solution in (4), they can also be computed directly from the predictor coefficients using the following recursive relations:

$$k_i = a_i^{(i)}$$

$$a_j^{(i-1)} = \frac{a_j^{(i)} - a_i^{(i)} a_{i-j}^{(i)}}{1 - k_i^2}, \qquad 1 \leqslant j \leqslant i - 1, \qquad (17)$$

where the index i takes values $p, p - 1, \cdots, 1$ in that order. Initially, $a_j^{(p)} = a_j$, $1 \leqslant j \leqslant p$.

Some of the above sets of parameters have $p + 1$ coefficients while others have only p coefficients. However, for the latter sets the signal energy (or gain G) needs to be transmitted as well, thus keeping the total number of parameters as $p + 1$ for all the cases. Although the above sets provide equivalent information about the linear predictor, their properties under quantization are different. Certain aspects of the sets (1), (4), (7), and (8) have been studied in the past [2], [10]. Our purpose in this paper is to investigate the relative quantization properties of all these parameters with a particular emphasis on the reflection coefficients.

It should be emphasized that the predictor coefficients can be recovered from any of the various sets of parameters listed above. The required transformations for such a recovery are given below only for the sets (3), (5), (6), and (8) since they are well-known for the others.

The sequence $\{b_i\}$ is transformed through an FFT after appending it with an appropriate number of zeros to achieve sufficient resolution in the resulting spectrum of the filter $A(z)/G$. The spectrum of the all-pole filter $H(z)$ is then obtained by simply inverting the amplitudes of the computed spectrum. Inverse Fourier transformation of the spectrum of $H(z)$ yields autocorrelation coefficients $\{r_i\}$ defined in (13). The first $p + 1$ autocorrelation coefficients r_i, $0 \leqslant i \leqslant p$, are then used to compute the predictor coefficients via the normal equations (2) with $R_i = r_i$, $0 \leqslant i \leqslant p$.

The predictor coefficients are recovered from the spectral coefficients $\{P_i\}$ by first taking the inverse DFT of the sequence $\{P_i\}$ to get the autocorrelation sequence $\{b_i\}$. The process of getting the predictor coefficients from $\{b_i\}$ has been discussed above.

Rearranging (15) provides the necessary transformation from cepstral coefficients to predictor coefficients.

$$a_1 = c_1$$

$$a_n = c_n + \sum_{m=1}^{n-1} \frac{m}{n} c_m a_{n-m}, \qquad 2 \leqslant n \leqslant p. \qquad (18)$$

The predictor coefficients can be recovered from the reflection coefficients using the relations (4c) with $i = 1, 2, \cdots, p$, then (4e).

III. Preprocessing Methods

Before we discuss the quantization properties of the different parameters we should mention that such properties can be improved by proper preprocessing, which is later undone at the synthesizer. For each set of parameters (1–8 above) we have observed that the short-time spectral dynamic range of the speech signal is the single most important factor that affects the quantization properties. We use two methods of preprocessing to reduce the spectral dynamic range and thereby to improve the quantization properties [11].

The first method, called *preemphasis*, reduces the spectral dynamic range by decreasing the general slope of the spectrum. This is done by passing the speech signal through a single-zero filter of the form $1 + az^{-1}$. The new signal is given by

$$s_n' = s_n + a s_{n-1}. \qquad (19)$$

An optimal value for a is obtained by solving for the preemphasis filter that "whitens" (spectrally flattens) the signal [7], [11], [15]. This is given by the first-order linear predictor, where

$$a = -\frac{R_1}{R_0}. \qquad (20)$$

R_1 and R_0 are autocorrelation coefficients of the signal s_n.

In the second method, which we shall call the *bandwidth expansion method*, reduction in the spectral dynamic range is achieved by increasing the pole bandwidths of the linear predictor. This is accomplished by multiplying the impulse response of the inverse filter $A(z)$ by a decaying exponential.[2] The new predictor coefficients are given by

$$a_n' = a_n e^{-\sigma n}, \quad \sigma > 0, \quad 1 \leqslant n \leqslant p. \qquad (21)$$

Preprocessing by either of these methods can be done after the linear prediction analysis, so that it can be viewed as part of the encoding process.

IV. Quantization Properties

For the purpose of quantization, two desirable properties for a parameter set to have are: 1) filter stability upon quantization and 2) a natural ordering

---

[2] If, however, an appropriate growing exponential is used, many of the pole bandwidths decrease thus enhancing the formant peaks in the spectrum and facilitating better formant tracking [6], [7].

of the parameters. Property 1) means that the poles of $H(z)$ continue to be inside the unit circle even after parameter quantization. By 2) we mean that the parameters exhibit an inherent ordering, e.g., the predictor coefficients are ordered as $a_1, a_2, \cdots, a_p$. If a_1 and a_2 are interchanged then $H(z)$ is no longer the same in general, thus illustrating the existence of an ordering. The poles of $H(z)$, on the other hand, are not naturally ordered since interchanging the order of any two poles does not change the filter. When such an ordering is present, a statistical study on the distribution of individual parameters can be used to develop better encoding schemes (e.g., Huffman coding [16]). Only the poles and the reflection coefficients ensure stability upon quantization, while all the sets of parameters except the poles possess a natural ordering. Thus, only the reflection coefficients possess both of these properties.

We have investigated experimentally the quantization properties of the sets of parameters discussed in Section II, with and without preprocessing of the speech signal. The absolute error between the log power spectra of the unquantized and the quantized linear predictors was used as a criterion in this study, since we believe that a good spectral match is necessary for synthesizing speech with good quality. A summary of the results is provided in the following.

The impulse responses $\{a_n\}$ and $\{h_n\}$ are highly susceptible to causing instability of the filter upon quantization. This is well known from discrete filter analysis. Positive definiteness of autocorrelation coefficients $\{b_i\}$ and $\{r_i\}$ is not ensured under quantization, which also leads to instabilities in the linear prediction filter. An attempt to synthesize speech with quantized autocorrelation coefficients $\{r_i\}$ resulted in distinctly perceivable "clicks" in the synthesized speech. Our conclusion is that the impulse responses and autocorrelation coefficients can be used only under minimal quantization, in which case the transmission rate would be excessive.

In the experimental investigation of the spectral and cepstral parameters, we found that the quantization properties of these parameters are generally superior to those of the impulse responses and autocorrelation coefficients. The spectral parameters often yield results comparable to those obtained by quantizing the reflection coefficients. However, for the cases when the spectrum consists of one or more very sharp peaks (narrow bandwidths), the effects of quantizing the spectral coefficients often result in the autocorrelation coefficients $\{b_i\}$ being nonpositive definite and hence cause certain regions in the reconstructed spectrum (see Section II) to become negative. This in turn causes the autocorrelation coefficients $\{r_i\}$ to be nonpositive definite, which leads to instability of the filter. Preprocessing the speech signal by the bandwidth expansion method (see Section III) remedies this situation, but the spectral deviation in these regions can be relatively large. Quantization of cepstral parameters can also lead to instabilities, where the predictor coefficients are computed from (18). As before, with proper preprocessing stability is restored, but at the expense of increased spectral deviation.

As mentioned earlier, the stability of the filter $H(z)$ is guaranteed under quantization of the poles. This makes the poles potentially a good set of parameters for transmission. Unfortunately, the poles do not possess a natural ordering: a property that is necessary if a low transmission rate is desired. Traditionally, poles have been ordered in terms of vocal tract resonances (formants). Since the ranges of frequencies for the various formants have been well established, their quantization can be done with improved accuracy. In addition, the formant bandwidths may be quantized less accurately than formant frequencies, which leads to further savings in transmission rate. However, experience has shown that the problem of identifying the poles as ordered formants is computationally complex and involves a fair amount of decision making which is not completely reliable. In addition, computing the poles requires finding the roots of a pth-order polynomial ($p \sim 12$): not a straightforward task.

Based on the results of our experimental study of the spectral deviation due to quantization, on computational considerations, and on stability and natural ordering properties, we conclude that the reflection coefficients are the best set for use as transmission parameters. In addition to these advantages, the values of the reflection coefficients k_i, $i < p$, do not change as p is varied, unlike any of the other parameters.

The question now is, what is an optimal quantization scheme for the reflection coefficients which gives the best results in terms of the quality of the synthesized speech? First, however, we need to establish a suitable criterion with respect to which we shall develop an optimal quantization scheme. It is known that an utterance that has been synthesized perfectly but for one or two "glitches" (segments involving large errors of some sort) would invariably be rated by a human subject as having a relatively poor quality. In other words, these glitches mask the perception giving an impression that the utterance has been poorly synthesized. Thus, the quality of the synthesized speech is a function of the "maximum perceptual error" between the synthesized and the original speech. Therefore, a reasonable criterion is to minimize the maximum perceptual error. We shall assume that an accurate representation of the power spectrum is necessary for synthesizing good quality speech. Thus, our criterion for optimal quantization is to minimize the maximum spectral error due to quantization.

To use the minimax spectral error criterion in de-

veloping an optimal scheme for quantizing the reflection coefficients, it is necessary first to investigate the sensitivity of the all-pole model spectrum to small changes in the values of the reflection coefficients. This spectral sensitivity analysis is carried out in the next section. The results of this study are then used in Section VI to develop an optimal scheme for the quantization of the reflection coefficients.

V. SENSITIVITY ANALYSIS OF REFLECTION COEFFICIENTS

If ΔS is the deviation in the all-pole model spectrum due to a change Δk_i in the reflection coefficient k_i, then we define the spectral sensitivity for the coefficient k_i as

$$\frac{\partial S}{\partial k_i} = \lim_{\Delta k_i \to 0} \left| \frac{\Delta S}{\Delta k_i} \right|. \tag{22}$$

Note that the spectral sensitivity in (22) is defined to have nonnegative values always. The definition of spectral deviation ΔS can be arbitrary, but for it to be useful it must somehow relate in a proportional manner to the corresponding effect on perception of the synthesized speech. Here we employ a measure of spectral deviation that has been found to be useful in speech research, namely, the average of the absolute value of the difference between the two log spectra under consideration. Thus the spectral sensitivity is defined by

$$\frac{\partial S}{\partial k_i} = \lim_{\Delta k_i \to 0} \left| \frac{1}{\Delta k_i} \left[\frac{1}{2\pi} \int_{-\pi}^{\pi} \left| \log P(k_i, \omega) \right. \right. \right.$$

$$\left. \left. \left. - \log P(k_i + \Delta k_i, \omega) \right| d\omega \right] \right|,$$

or

$$\frac{\partial S}{\partial k_i} = \lim_{\Delta k_i \to 0} \left| \frac{1}{\Delta k_i} \left[\frac{1}{2\pi} \int_{-\pi}^{\pi} \right. \right.$$

$$\left. \left. \cdot \left| \log \frac{P(k_i, \omega)}{P(k_i + \Delta k_i, \omega)} \right| d\omega \right] \right|, \tag{23}$$

where

$$P(\cdot, \omega) = |H(e^{j\omega})|^2$$

is the spectrum of the all-pole model $H(z)$. The quantity between brackets in (23) is the spectral deviation ΔS due to a perturbation in the ith reflection coefficient. Experimentally, $(\partial S / \partial k_i)$ is computed by replacing the integral by a summation, and by using a sufficiently small value for Δk_i.

Typical sensitivity curves are shown in Fig. 3. (We have used $10 \log_{10}$ instead of the natural logarithm in evaluating (23), and second for display purposes we have plotted $10 \log_{10} (\partial S / \partial k_i)$ in decibels.) These curves were obtained from a 12-pole linear predictive analysis of a 20 ms frame from a 10 kHz sampled speech signal. Each curve in Fig. 3 is a plot of the

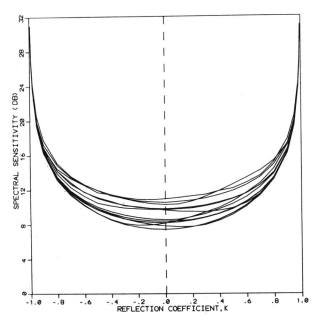

Fig. 3. Typical spectral sensitivity curves for the reflection coefficients of a 12-pole analysis of a 20 ms speech frame.

spectral sensitivity for one of the 12 reflection coefficients as its value is varied over the range (-1, 1) while the other 11 reflection coefficients are kept constant at their respective values obtained for that frame. We have performed this type of sensitivity analysis for a large number of different sounds, both voiced and unvoiced, recorded from different male and female speakers. The resulting sensitivity curves were similar to those shown in Fig. 3. The sensitivity curves have the following properties in common.

1) Each sensitivity curve ($\partial S/\partial k_i$) versus k_i has the same *general shape*, irrespective of the index i and irrespective of the values of the other coefficients k_n, $n \neq i$, at which the sensitivity is computed.

2) Each sensitivity curve is U-shaped. It is even-symmetric about $k_i = 0$, and has large values when the magnitude of k_i is close to 1 and small values when the magnitude of k_i is close to zero.

It must be emphasized that property 1) refers only to the *shape* of the sensitivity curve. The actual value of the sensitivity for a particular reflection coefficient does, in general, depend on the values of the other reflection coefficients.

Although the above sensitivity properties were derived experimentally by perturbing, one at a time, the magnitudes of the reflection coefficients that corresponded to different speech sounds, these properties should be viewed as inherent to the reflection coefficients themselves and not to the particular speech sounds. Thus, voiced sounds generally have a higher spectral sensitivity than unvoiced sounds because some of the reflection coefficients for voiced sounds have magnitudes close to 1. Also, in general, preemphasis reduces the spectral sensitivity of voiced

sounds by reducing the magnitudes of the reflection coefficients which are close to 1.

The sensitivity properties given above strongly suggest the existence of a prototype sensitivity function which would apply approximately to every reflection coefficient and for different speech sounds. Such a prototype function could then be used in developing an optimal quantization scheme that would apply to all reflection coefficients all the time. Due to the above sensitivity properties, it is meaningful to obtain this prototype sensitivity function as the simple average of the sensitivity curves over different reflection coefficients and for a large number of different speech sounds. Such an averaged sensitivity function is defined below.

$$\frac{\overline{\partial S}}{\partial k} = \frac{1}{pN} \sum_{t=1}^{N} \sum_{i=1}^{p} \frac{\partial S}{\partial k_i}\bigg|_{k_i=k} \tag{24}$$

where t refers to the number of the analysis frame (time averaging). The averaged sensitivity function for a representative number of sentences spoken by males and females is shown plotted as the solid curve in Fig. 4. In this plot the sensitivity values are given in decibels relative to the sensitivity at $k = 0$. In the next section, we develop an optimal quantization scheme for the reflection coefficients using the averaged sensitivity function in Fig. 4.

VI. Optimal Quantization of Reflection Coefficients

In view of the sensitivity properties of the reflection coefficients discussed in the previous section and depicted in Figs. 3 and 4, it is clear that linear quantization of the reflection coefficients is not satisfactory, especially when some of them take values close to 1 in magnitude. What is needed is a nonlinear quantization scheme that is much more sensitive (has more steps) near 1 than near 0. A nonlinear quantization of a reflection coefficient is equivalent to a linear quantization of a different parameter that is related to the reflection coefficient by a nonlinear transformation. It is not difficult to show that linear quantization of the transformed parameter is optimal (in the sense of minimizing the maximum spectral error due to quantization) if and only if the transformed parameter has a flat or constant spectral sensitivity behavior. The sufficiency of the condition is evident from the fact that with a flat sensitivity behavior and linear quantization, the maximum spectral error is constant over the entire range of variation of the parameter (see subsection on optimal bit allocation below), which trivially leads to a minimum equal to that constant value. The necessity of the condition can be established by using the proof by contradiction method as follows. If the transformed parameter

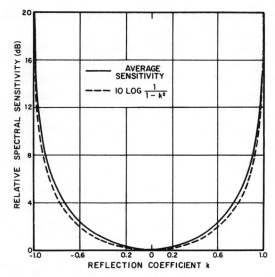

Fig. 4. Averaged spectral sensitivity curve for the reflection coefficients (solid line) and an analytical function that approximates it (dashed line).

does not have a flat sensitivity behavior, then a suitable nonlinear quantization leading to a smaller maximum spectral error can be found by assigning smaller quantization steps in regions where the parameter has high sensitivity and vice versa. This is clearly a contradiction to the fact that linear quantization is optimal. Thus, the search for the optimal quantization scheme for the reflection coefficients reduces to the search for a nonlinear transformation that results in a flat spectral sensitivity behavior for the transformed parameters.

Denoting the transformed parameter as g, we have

$$g = f(k) \tag{25}$$

where $f(\cdot)$ is the underlying nonlinear mapping. The optimal mapping is one where the transformed parameter g has constant spectral sensitivity, i.e.,

$$\frac{\partial S}{\partial g} = L = \text{a constant} \tag{26}$$

where the sensitivity is defined in a manner analogous to (23). Writing formally,

$$\frac{\partial S}{\partial g} = \frac{\partial S}{\partial k} \frac{dk}{dg} = \frac{\partial S}{\partial k} \bigg/ \frac{df(k)}{dk}. \tag{27}$$

Thus, from (26) and (27) we have

$$\frac{df(k)}{dk} = \frac{1}{L} \frac{\partial S}{\partial k}. \tag{28}$$

Equation (28) provides the condition for a mapping to be optimal. The optimal mapping $f(k)$ is obtained by simply integrating (28). It is clear that (28) may be applied to each reflection coefficient separately. However, for the reasons mentioned in the last section we shall consider the averaged sensitivity function in Fig. 4 and derive the mapping that is optimal *on the average* for all the reflection coefficients.

Although it is possible to obtain the optimal transformation by integrating the solid curve in Fig. 4 directly, we have found it simpler and ultimately more useful to approximate the averaged sensitivity curve by a well specified mathematical function which could then be integrated to obtain an approximately optimal $f(k)$. An experimental fitting of the averaged sensitivity curve in Fig. 4 has revealed that the function $1/(1 - k^2)$ approximates the sensitivity function reasonably well (to within a multiplicative constant), as shown by the dashed curve in Fig. 4 (note that the plot is given in decibels). Thus, from (28), the approximately optimal transformation is given by

$$\frac{df(k)}{dk} = \frac{1}{L(1 - k^2)}. \tag{29}$$

Integrating (29) we obtain

$$f(k) = \frac{1}{2L} \log \frac{1 + k}{1 - k}. \tag{30}$$

As L is arbitrary, an interesting transformation is obtained by substituting $L = \frac{1}{2}$:

$$f(k) = \log \frac{1 + k}{1 - k}. \tag{31}$$

From (16), the ratio of consecutive area coefficients is given by

$$\frac{A_i}{A_{i+1}} = \frac{1 + k_i}{1 - k_i}, \quad A_{p+1} = 1, \quad 1 \leqslant i \leqslant p. \tag{32}$$

Therefore, the transformation in (31) is simply the logarithm of the area ratios. Thus, we have shown that the logarithms of the area ratios (henceforth called *log area ratios*) provide an approximately optimal set of coefficients for quantization.

Fig. 5 shows sensitivity curves for the log area ratios using the same example as in Fig. 3. A comparison of Figs. 3 and 5 shows that the sensitivity curves are relatively flat for the log area ratios. Our experimental investigations into the quality of the synthesized speech also indicate that the log area ratios possess good quantization properties. The log area ratios were first used in a linear predictive speech compression system by Haskew et al. [4]. In this paper, we have demonstrated that linear quantization of the log area ratios indeed provides optimal quantization results based on the spectral sensitivity measure in (23).

Fig. 6 shows a plot of the log area ratio as a function of the reflection coefficient. We have also plotted in Fig. 6 a linear characteristic that passes through the intersection of a vertical line at $k = 0.7$ and the log area ratio curve. For values of k less than 0.7 in magnitude, the log area ratio curve is almost linear. Thus, if a certain reflection coefficient takes

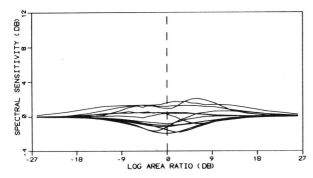

Fig. 5. Spectral sensitivity curves using the log area ratios for the same case as in Fig. 3.

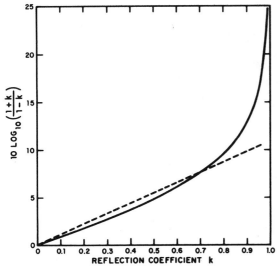

Fig. 6. Log area ratio plotted as a function of the reflection coefficient (solid line) and a linear characteristic that intersects it at $k = 0.7$ (dashed line).

values always less than 0.7 in magnitude, one could quantize it linearly to obtain approximately flat sensitivity characteristics. In practice it is found that the reflection coefficients k_i, $i > 3$, have in general magnitudes less than 0.7. However, use of the log area ratios automatically leads to the desired quantization irrespective of the reflection coefficient and the range of values it spans.

We note from (5) and (31) that, for a stable filter, the log area ratios take on values in the region $-\infty < g_i < \infty$, for all i. The filter becomes unstable if any of the log area ratios becomes unbounded. The potential unboundedness of the log area ratios means that the range over which they need to be quantized can be very large, which can lead to an excessive number of quantization bits or else to very coarse quantization. However, in practice, the range is often limited by the types of signals that are processed. For example, we have not found the range to be very large for speech signals, especially when preemphasis is used. The problem could still arise, however, as a result of computations with a small word length. In that case, the range could be limited artificially. This is good practice because otherwise very narrow band-

width filters would result, which, in general, is not a good thing in speech synthesis.

Interpretation in terms of Pole Locations

While the spectral sensitivity measure given by (23) is useful in quantifying the overall deviation in the spectrum due to perturbations in the reflection coefficients or the log area ratios, it does not, however, explain corresponding deviations in the pole locations of the linear prediction filter. Much is known about the relations between the accuracy of pole (or formant) locations and the corresponding effects on speech quality. Therefore, it would be useful to examine the pole deviations due to quantization of the transmission parameters. Unfortunately, the problem is quite untractable, in general. However, some insight can still be gained by examining a 2-pole model. Although it is possible to examine this model in mathematical terms, here we shall take a graphical approach due to Kitawaki and Itakura [12].

For the second-order linear predictor, the inverse filter is given by

$$A(z) = 1 + k_1(1 + k_2)z^{-1} + k_2 z^{-2}. \tag{33}$$

The zeros of $A(z)$ are the poles of our model filter $H(z)$. We shall restrict our discussion to the cases where the zeros form complex conjugate pairs. From (33) we see that $A(z)$ has a complex zero when

$$k_1 \in (-1, 1)$$
$$k_2 \in \left(\frac{2 - k_1^2 - 2\sqrt{1 - k_1^2}}{k_1^2}, 1 \right). \tag{34}$$

Fig. 7 shows a plot of only the complex zeros as k_1 is varied uniformly in the interval $[-0.99, 0.99]$ in equal steps of 0.01 while k_2 is varied uniformly in the interval $[0, 0.99]$ also in equal steps of 0.01. Let

$$g_i = \log \frac{1 + k_i}{1 - k_i}, \qquad i = 1, 2 \tag{35}$$

be the log area ratios corresponding to k_1 and k_2. Fig. 8 depicts the complex zeros of $A(z)$ when g_1 is varied over $[-\log 199, \log 199]$ and g_2 over $[0, \log 199]$ uniformly and in equal steps. The total number of steps is kept the same as in the previous case. Relative to Fig. 7, Fig. 8 shows that there is denser clustering of the zeros near the unit circle and for angles close to 0 and π. This means that in these regions, quantization errors in the log area ratios lead to a smaller deviation in the position of zeros of $A(z)$ than that obtained by the quantization of the reflection coefficients, assuming the same number of quantization levels in both cases. Fig. 9 shows the complex roots obtained by a second-order linear predictive analysis of several sentences of speech material sampled at 10 kHz. An inspection of Figs. 8 and 9 reveals that the roots of the second-order linear predictor for continuous speech occur mainly in the areas where

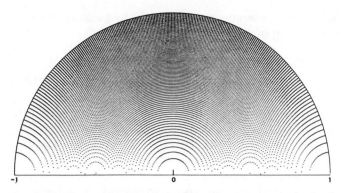

Fig. 7. Root loci for a second order all-pole system obtained by varying the two reflection coefficients in equal steps. (After Kitawaki and Itakura [12].)

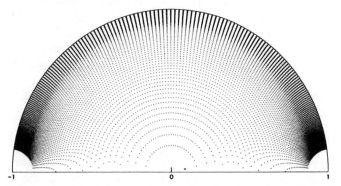

Fig. 8. Root loci for a second order all-pole system obtained by varying the two log area ratios in equal steps (the total number of steps being the same as in Fig. 7). (After Kitawaki and Itakura [12].)

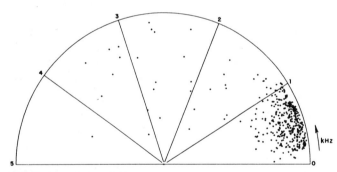

Fig. 9. Complex roots obtained by the second order linear predictive analysis of about 30 seconds of continuous speech sampled at 10 kHz.

there is a dense clustering of zeros in Fig. 8. We view this as further independent evidence supporting our earlier findings of the desirable quantization properties of the log area ratios for the purpose of speech compression.

Kitawaki and Itakura considered still other non-linear mappings of the reflection coefficients but concluded that the log area ratios lead to the best overall quantization accuracy [12]. Our results make the stronger statement that the log area ratios are actually optimal in the sense discussed earlier.

Optimum Bit Allocation

In the following we investigate the use of the spectral sensitivity measure for allocating a fixed number of bits among the various parameters. Let q_1, $q_2, \cdots, q_p$ be the parameters chosen for quantization. These may be the reflection coefficients or the log area ratios or any other set of parameters. Given the total number of bits for quantization as M, the problem is to distribute this among the p parameters as M_i, $1 \leqslant i \leqslant p$, in some optimal manner. In terms of quantization levels, the above problem may be restated as the allocation of $N = 2^M$ levels among the p parameters as N_i, $1 \leqslant i \leqslant p$, in some optimal manner. Therefore, we have

$$\sum_{i=1}^p M_i = \sum_{i=1}^p \log_2 N_i = M$$

$$\prod_{i=1}^p N_i = N, \quad N_i = 2^{M_i}, \quad 1 \leqslant i \leqslant p. \tag{36}$$

We derive the optimal bit allocation by minimizing the maximum spectral deviation due to quantization. The total spectral deviation ΔS due to changes Δq_i in the parameters q_i, $1 \leqslant i \leqslant p$, is given approximately by

$$\Delta S = \sum_{i=1}^p \left| \frac{\partial S}{\partial q_i} \Delta q_i \right|. \tag{37}$$

Define the quantization step size for q_i as

$$\delta_i = \frac{\bar{q}_i - \underline{q}_i}{N_i} \tag{38}$$

where $\bar{q}_i$ and $\underline{q}_i$ are the upper and lower bounds on q_i, respectively. Then, for a linear quantization of q_i using round-off arithmetic, the maximum quantization error is equal to half the quantization step size:

$$|\Delta q_i|_{\max} = \tfrac{1}{2} \delta_i.$$

Thus,

$$(\Delta S)_{\max} = \sum_{i=1}^p \left| \frac{\partial S}{\partial q_i} \right| \frac{\bar{q}_i - \underline{q}_i}{2N_i}. \tag{39}$$

Let

$$K_i = \frac{\bar{q}_i - \underline{q}_i}{2} \left| \frac{\partial S}{\partial q_i} \right|, \quad 1 \leqslant i \leqslant p. \tag{40}$$

Then

$$(\Delta S)_{\max} = \sum_{i=1}^p \frac{K_i}{N_i}. \tag{41}$$

We wish to minimize $(\Delta S)_{\max}$ with respect to $\{N_i\}$ subject to the constraint

$$\sum_{i=1}^p \log_2 N_i = M. \tag{42}$$

This is a simple problem in constrained minimization [13] and its solution is given by

$$N_1 = K_1 \left[\frac{2^M}{\prod\limits_{i=1}^{p} K_i} \right]^{1/p}$$

$$N_i = \frac{K_i}{K_1} N_1, \quad 2 \leqslant i \leqslant p. \tag{43}$$

The bit allocation strategy given in (43) is thus optimal in a minimax sense since it minimizes the maximum spectral deviation due to quantization. Note that if truncation arithmetic is used, the constants K_i in (40) will be doubled, but that will not affect the bit allocation results from (43).

The optimal bit allocation in (43) effectively says that the contributions of the different parameters to the maximum spectral deviation in (41) must be equal. We know that for the log area ratios the spectral sensitivity $(\partial S / \partial q_i)$ is approximately constant and is approximately the same for all the coefficients. From (38), (40), and (43), this implies that the quantization step size δ_i should be the same for all the log area ratios. For this case, the bit allocation can be done as follows. Compute the constant step size δ from

$$\delta = \left[\frac{\prod\limits_{i=1}^{p} (\overline{q}_i - \underline{q}_i)}{2^M} \right]^{1/p}. \tag{44}$$

Then the number of levels N_i for each coefficient is computed from (38). We have found it convenient and useful to begin with a particular step size. That automatically determines the total number of bits needed, as well as the maximum spectral deviation which, in turn, determines the resulting speech quality. One can then study the change in speech quality as a function of only one variable, namely the step size.

VII. Comments on Another Spectral Sensitivity Measure

In Section V we introduced a spectral sensitivity measure to study the quantization properties of the reflection coefficients. Other types of sensitivity measures may also be used. In particular we have considered a measure which is similar to the total-square error used for minimization in linear predictive analysis. By using Parseval's theorem in (1), the total-square error is given by

$$E = \frac{G^2}{2\pi} \int_{-\pi}^{\pi} \frac{P_0(\omega)}{P(\omega)} \, d\omega \tag{45}$$

where $P_0(\omega)$ is the power spectrum of the input speech signal and $P(\omega)$ is the power spectrum of the all-pole filter;

$$P(\omega) = |H(e^{j\omega})|^2 = \frac{G^2}{|A(e^{j\omega})|^2}. \tag{46}$$

The gain G is given by (9).

Properties of the error measure E have been studied in detail elsewhere [6], [7], [14]. In particular, the minimization of E results in an all-pole model spectrum $P(\omega)$ that is a good approximation to the envelope of the signal spectrum $P_0(\omega)$. Because of this property, it seemed reasonable to study the use of this error E as a measure of the deviation between the two spectra. For the sake of normalization we have chosen to work with an error measure E' obtained from (45) by eliminating the factor G^2:

$$E' = \frac{1}{2\pi} \int_{-\pi}^{\pi} \frac{P_1(\omega)}{P_2(\omega)} \, d\omega \tag{47}$$

where $P_1(\omega)$ and $P_2(\omega)$ are now any two spectra. Also, the two spectra are normalized such that they have equal total energy.

For our study of spectral sensitivity we let $P_1(\omega) = P(k_i, \omega)$ and $P_2(\omega) = P(k_i + \Delta k_i, \omega)$, where $P(\cdot, \omega)$ is given by (46). The error between the two spectra is then given by

$$E'(\Delta k_i) = \frac{1}{2\pi} \int_{-\pi}^{\pi} \frac{P(k_i, \omega)}{P(k_i + \Delta k_i, \omega)} \, d\omega. \tag{48}$$

We define the spectral deviation, then, as

$$\Delta S' = \log E'(\Delta k_i). \tag{49}$$

The definition of the new measure of spectral sensitivity follows from (22), (49), and (48) as

$$\frac{\partial S'}{\partial k_i} = \lim_{\Delta k_i \to 0} \left| \frac{1}{\Delta k_i} \log \right.$$
$$\left. \cdot \left[\frac{1}{2\pi} \int_{-\pi}^{\pi} \frac{P(k_i, \omega)}{P(k_i + \Delta k_i, \omega)} \, d\omega \right] \right|. \tag{50}$$

The spectral sensitivity in (50) can be derived analytically, without the need to resort to experimental data as was the case for the study of $(\partial S / \partial k_i)$ in (23). This is done below.

Substituting (9) and (46) in (50), we obtain

$$\frac{\partial S'}{\partial k_i} = \left| \lim_{\Delta k_i \to 0} \frac{1}{\Delta k_i} \log \frac{V_p(k_i)}{V_p(k_i + \Delta k_i)} + \lim_{\Delta k_i \to 0} \frac{1}{\Delta k_i} \right.$$
$$\left. \cdot \log \left[\frac{1}{2\pi} \int_{-\pi}^{\pi} \left| \frac{A(k_i + \Delta k_i, e^{j\omega})}{A(k_i, e^{j\omega})} \right|^2 \, d\omega \right] \right|. \tag{51}$$

It is shown in Appendix I that the second term in the right-hand side of (51) is zero for all k_i, $1 \leqslant i \leqslant p$. Thus, we have

$$\frac{\partial S'}{\partial k_i} = \left| \lim_{\Delta k_i \to 0} \frac{\log V_p(k_i) - \log V_p(k_i + \Delta k_i)}{\Delta k_i} \right|$$

or

$$\frac{\partial S'}{\partial k_i} = \left| \frac{\partial [\log V_p(k_i)]}{\partial k_i} \right|. \tag{52}$$

Using (8) in (52) we obtain the desired result

$$\frac{\partial S'}{\partial k_i} = \frac{2|k_i|}{1 - k_i^2}. \tag{53}$$

It is important to note that this is an exact result and it is true for each reflection coefficient, independent of the values of the other coefficients. A plot of $(\partial S'/\partial k)$ versus k also gives a U-shaped curve. Therefore, the spectral sensitivity in (53) has the same general properties as the spectral sensitivity $(\partial S/\partial k)$ obtained experimentally in Section V. The only difference between the two is the actual shape of the sensitivity curve.

Substituting (53) in the optimality condition (28) and integrating it with $L = 1$, we obtain the following optimal mapping for the sensitivity measure (50):

$$f'(k) = \text{sign}(k) \log \frac{1}{1 - k^2} \tag{54}$$

where sign (k) is +1 if k is positive and -1 if k is negative. From (8) and (54), it is interesting to observe that $|f'(k_i)|$ is equal to the logarithm of the ratio of the normalized errors (or *log error ratio*) associated with the linear predictors of orders $i - 1$ and i,

$$f'(k_i) = \text{sign}(k_i) \log \frac{V_{i-1}}{V_i}. \tag{55}$$

We have experimentally investigated the quantization properties resulting from the mappings given by (31) and (55). Through informal listening tests we have found that the use of the log area ratios for quantization leads to uniformly better speech quality than that obtained using the log error ratios. This points out the important fact that not all reasonable spectral sensitivity measures lead to good results; the measure must somehow relate to perception. Our conclusion is that the spectral sensitivity measure in (23) relates more to perception than the measure in (50) since it produces better results in terms of speech quality.

It is of interest to understand the difference between the two sensitivity measures given by (23) and (50). For small Δk_i, the logarithm of the average of the spectral ratio in (50) can be approximated by the average of the logarithm of the spectral ratio, i.e.,

$$\log E'(\Delta k_i) \cong \frac{1}{2\pi} \int_{-\pi}^{\pi} \log \frac{P(k_i, \omega)}{P(k_i + \Delta k_i, \omega)} d\omega. \tag{56}$$

The approximation improves as Δk_i decreases, and becomes exact in the limit as $\Delta k_i \to 0$. Thus,

$$\frac{\partial S'}{\partial k_i} = \lim_{\Delta k_i \to 0} \left| \frac{1}{\Delta k_i} \left[\frac{1}{2\pi} \int_{-\pi}^{\pi} \right.\right.$$
$$\left.\left. \cdot \log \frac{P(k_i, \omega)}{P(k_i + \Delta k_i, \omega)} d\omega \right] \right|. \tag{57}$$

Note that the only difference between the two sensitivity measures given by (23) and (57) is the lack of an absolute value sign inside the integral in (57). This makes the sensitivity measure in (57) less powerful, because spectral deviations when $P(k_i, \omega) > P(k_i + \Delta k_i, \omega)$ can cancel deviations when $P(k_i + \Delta k_i, \omega) > P(k_i, \omega)$. Note that both of these cases contribute to the total spectral deviation in (23). This is another reason why (23) is to be preferred over (57) or (50) as a definition of spectral sensitivity, and therefore why the log area ratios are to be preferred over the log error ratios as transmission parameters. [See [14] for further comparison of the spectral deviations in (23) and (50).]

VIII. Conclusions

We have dealt with the problem of quantization of transmission parameters in linear predictive speech compression systems. Several alternate sets of transmission parameters were considered and their relative quantization properties were presented. The results of this study have shown that the reflection coefficients are the best set for use as transmission parameters. Specifically, the reflection coefficients preserve the stability of the linear predictor under quantization, and possess a natural ordering property which can be used in the design of better encoding schemes. The quantization of the reflection coefficients was then examined in more detail using a spectral sensitivity measure.

The spectral sensitivity of a given reflection coefficient was defined in terms of the absolute spectral deviation due to a small perturbation in the reflection coefficient. Experimental study of this spectral sensitivity measure has shown that reflection coefficients have a high sensitivity for magnitudes close to 1 and a low sensitivity near 0. Further, all the reflection coefficients have approximately the same sensitivity behavior, irrespective of the particular speech sound to which they correspond. A prototype sensitivity function was obtained experimentally by averaging the sensitivity values over the various reflection coefficients and over a large number of speech sounds. We then developed an optimal quantization procedure for the reflection coefficients. This consisted in finding a suitable mapping that transforms the reflection coefficients to a set of parameters having a flat or constant sensitivity behavior. Using an analytical function that well approximates the averaged sensitivity of the reflection coefficients, we demonstrated that the logarithms of the ratios of area coefficients (or log area ratios) possess approximately optimal quantization properties.

An optimal solution was then derived for the problem of bit allocation among the different parameters. This was done by minimizing the maximum spectral deviation due to quantization. For the log area ratios, this optimal solution reduces to using equal quantization steps for all the parameters.

Finally, motivated to use an error measure similar to the one used in linear predictive analysis, we provided an alternate definition of spectral sensitivity. An analytical evaluation of this spectral sensitivity for the reflection coefficients has shown that the logarithms of the ratios of normalized errors of linear predictors of successive orders (or log error ratios) exhibit optimal quantization properties. However, informal listening tests have indicated that the use of log area ratios for quantization leads to better synthesis than the use of log error ratios. This further implies that the definition of spectral sensitivity that resulted in the log area ratios gives a superior measure of spectral sensitivity for the purpose of quantization studies.

Appendix I

We want to show that the partial derivative

$$
\frac{\partial J(k_i)}{\partial k_i} \triangleq \lim_{\Delta k_i \to 0} \frac{1}{\Delta k_i}
$$

$$
\cdot \log \left[\frac{1}{2\pi} \int_{-\pi}^{\pi} \left| \frac{A(k_i + \Delta k_i, e^{j\omega})}{A(k_i, e^{j\omega})} \right|^2 d\omega \right] \quad (58)
$$

is equal to zero for $1 \leq i \leq p$. It is more instructive to consider the vector partial derivative

$$
\frac{\partial J(k)}{\partial k} = \left(\frac{\partial J(k)}{\partial k_1}, \frac{\partial J(k)}{\partial k_2}, \cdots, \frac{\partial J(k)}{\partial k_p} \right)^T \quad (59)
$$

where superscript T denotes transpose and $k = (k_1, k_2, \cdots, k_p)^T$. The partial derivative in (59) can be rewritten in terms of $a = (a_1, a_2, \cdots, a_p)^T$ as

$$
\frac{\partial J(k)}{\partial k} = \left(\frac{\partial k}{\partial a} \right)^T \frac{\partial J(a)}{\partial a}. \quad (60)
$$

The elements of the matrix $(\partial k / \partial a)$ can be computed from (17). It can be shown that all these elements are bounded for a stable filter. Thus, our problem reduces to showing that $(\partial J(a)/\partial a) = 0$.

Consider the deviation term

$$
\Delta J(a) = \log \left[\frac{1}{2\pi} \int_{-\pi}^{\pi} \left| \frac{A(a + \Delta a, e^{j\omega})}{A(a, e^{j\omega})} \right|^2 d\omega \right]. \quad (61)
$$

Multiplying and dividing the integral in (61) by $G^2 = E_p$ from (9) and substituting $P(\omega)$ from (46), there results

$$
\Delta J(a) = \log \left\{ \frac{1}{E_p} \left[\frac{1}{2\pi} \int_{-\pi}^{\pi} P(\omega) \right. \right.
$$

$$
\left. \left. \cdot \left| A(a + \Delta a, e^{j\omega}) \right|^2 d\omega \right] \right\}. \quad (62)
$$

The error E_p can be written from (1) in matrix notation as

$$
E_p = E(a) = R_0 + 2a^T r + a^T R a \quad (63)
$$

where $r = (R_1, R_2, \cdots, R_p)^T$, and R is the $p \times p$ autocorrelation matrix

$$
R = [R_{i-j}], \quad i, j = 1, 2, \cdots, p. \quad (64)
$$

If we think of $P(\omega)$ as the spectrum of some signal s_n, then the term within the square brackets in (62) is equal to the total error $E(a + \Delta a)$ obtained by passing the signal s_n through the inverse filter $A(a + \Delta a, z)$ (see Fig. 2). Therefore, (62) reduces to

$$
\Delta J(a) = \log E(a + \Delta a) - \log E(a) \quad (65)
$$

and

$$
\frac{\partial J(a)}{\partial a} = \frac{\partial [\log E(a)]}{\partial a}. \quad (66)
$$

From (63) and (66)

$$
\frac{\partial J(a)}{\partial a} = \frac{1}{E(a)} \frac{\partial E(a)}{\partial a} = \frac{2}{E(a)} (r + Ra). \quad (67)
$$

Since (2) can be rewritten as $Ra = -r$, we conclude from (67) that $(\partial J(a)/\partial a) = 0$. From (60), $(\partial J(k)/\partial k) = 0$.

Note that the above derivation depended on evaluating the partial derivative of the prediction error at its minimum, which is of course zero.

Acknowledgment

The authors would like to thank F. Itakura for bringing his work [12] to their attention.

References

[1] F. Itakura and S. Saito, "Analysis synthesis telephony based upon the maximum likelihood method," in *Rep. 6th Int. Congr. on Acoustics*, Kohasi, Ed. Tokyo, Japan Aug. 21–28, 1968, C-5-5.

[2] B. S. Atal and S. L. Hanauer, "Speech analysis and synthesis by linear prediction of the speech wave," *J. Acoust. Soc. Amer.*, vol. 50, pp. 637–655, 1971.

[3] F. Itakura *et al.*, "An audio response unit based on partial autocorrelation," *IEEE Trans. Commun.*, vol. COM-20, pp. 792–797, Aug. 1972.

[4] J. R. Haskew, J. M. Kelly, and T. H. McKinney, "Results of a study of the linear prediction vocoder," *IEEE Trans. Commun.*, vol. COM-21, pp. 1008–1014, Sept. 1973.

[5] J. D. Markel and A. H. Gray, Jr., "A linear prediction vocoder simulation based upon the autocorrelation method," *IEEE Trans. Acoust., Speech, Signal Processing*, vol. ASSP-22, pp. 124–134, Apr. 1974.

[6] J. Makhoul, "Spectral analysis of speech by linear prediction," *IEEE Trans. Audio Electroacoust.*, vol. AU-21, pp. 140–148, June 1973.

[7] J. I. Makhoul and J. J. Wolf, "Linear prediction and the spectral analysis of speech," Bolt Beranek and Newman, Inc., Cambridge, Mass., NTIS No. Ad-749066, BBN Rep. 2304, Aug. 1972, 237 pp.

[8] B. Gold and C. M. Rader, *Digital Processing of Signals*. New York: McGraw-Hill, 1969.

[9] H. Wakita, "Direct estimation of the vocal tract shape

by inverse filtering of acoustic speech waveforms," *IEEE Trans. Audio Electroacoust.*, vol. AU-21, pp. 417–427, Oct. 1973.

[10] F. Itakura and S. Saito, "On the optimum quantization of feature parameters in the PARCOR speech synthesizer," in *Conf. Rec., 1972 Conf. Speech Communications and Processing*, Newton, Mass., Apr. 1972, pp. 434–437.

[11] J. Makhoul and R. Viswanathan, "Adaptive preprocessing for linear predictive speech compression systems," Presented at the 86th meeting of the Acoustical Society of America, Los Angeles, Oct. 30–Nov 2, 1973.

[12] N. Kitawaki and F. Itakura, "Nonlinear coding of PARCOR Coefficients," in *Meeting of the Acoustic*

Society of Japan (in Japanese), Oct. 1973, pp. 449–450.

[13] A. E. Bryson, Jr. and Y. C. Ho, *Applied Optimal Control.* Waltham, Mass.: Blaisdell, 1969.

[14] J. Makhoul, "Spectral linear prediction: Properties and applications," *IEEE Trans. Acoust., Speech, Signal Processing*, this issue, pp. 283–296.

[15] A. H. Gray Jr. and J. D. Markel, "A spectral-flatness measure for studying the autocorrelation method of linear prediction of speech analysis," *IEEE Trans. Acoust., Speech, Signal Processing*, vol. ASSP-22, pp. 207–217, June 1974.

[16] R. Viswanathan and J. Makhoul, "Current issues in linear predictive speech compression," in *Proc. 1974 EASCON Conf.*, Washington, D.C., Oct. 1974, pp. 577–585.

Quantization and Bit Allocation in Speech Processing

AUGUSTINE H. GRAY, JR., MEMBER, IEEE, AND JOHN D. MARKEL, MEMBER, IEEE

Abstract—The topic of quantization and bit allocation in speech processing is studied using an L_2 norm. Closed-form expressions are derived for the root mean square (rms) spectral deviation due to variations in one, two, or multiple parameters. For one-parameter variation, the reflection coefficients, log area ratios, and inverse sine coefficients are studied. It is shown that, depending upon the criterion chosen, either log area ratios or inverse sine quantization can be viewed as optimal. From a practical point of view, it is shown experimentally that very little difference exists among the various quantization methods beyond the second coefficient.

Two-parameter variations are studied in terms of formant frequency and bandwidth movement and in terms of a two-pair quantization scheme. A lower bound on the number of quantization levels required to satisfy a given maximum spectral deviation is derived along with the two-pair quantization scheme which approximately satisfies the bound. It is shown theoretically that the two-pair quantization scheme has a 10-bit superiority over other above-mentioned quantization schemes in the sense of theoretically assuring that a maximum overall log spectral deviation will not be exceeded.

Manuscript received January 12, 1976; revised June 7, 1976. This work was supported by the Department of Defense under Contract MDA904-76-C-0259.

A. H. Gray, Jr. is with the Department of Electrical Engineering, University of California, Santa Barbara, CA 93106 and the Speech Communications Research Laboratory, Inc., Santa Barbara, CA 93109.

J. D. Markel is with the Speech Communications Research Laboratory, Inc., Santa Barbara, CA 93109.

I. INTRODUCTION

THE QUANTIZATION properties of transmission parameters in linear prediction speech compression systems have been discussed in a recent paper by Viswanathan and Makhoul [1] on the basis of a spectral sensitivity analysis using an L_1 norm on log spectral differences. The emphasis was on sensitivity to the reflection coefficient parameter set, $\{k_1, k_2, \cdots, k_M\}$, which can define an all-pole filter model. The reflection coefficients have the desirable property of retaining stability under quantization. Spectral sensitivity curves were numerically obtained and used to show that log area quantization of the reflection coefficients was optimal in the sense of minimizing a maximum spectral error over the entire range of possible values for the reflection coefficients, -1 to $+1$. In addition, based upon the assumption that total spectral deviation due to changes in all the parameters can be approximated by the sum of individual deviations, a bit-allocation scheme was proposed for minimizing the total spectral deviation.

The topic of quantization and bit allocation is also studied here, but using an L_2 as opposed to the L_1 norm. This seemingly minor change has a significant effect in that tractable

Reprinted from *IEEE Trans. Acoust., Speech, and Signal Process.*, vol. ASSP-24, pp. 459–473, Dec. 1976.

447

analytical results can be used without approximations or frequency-domain calculations. Within this framework, the results of Viswanathan and Makhoul [1] are reinterpreted and a number of new or previously unpublished results are shown. In terms of single-parameter variations which cover all possible values of each reflection coefficient from -1 to $+1$, it is shown that the log area quantization of [1] theoretically results from the choice of a gain term which normalizes the all-pole model energies. If the log spectral means are normalized, then inverse sine quantization becomes optimal in the above-defined sense. In a practical sense it is shown that with the exception of the first two-reflection coefficients, simple linear quantization produces essentially equivalent results and, in fact, slightly superior results over the range of reflection coefficients measured from actual speech.

II. THEORY

Assume a linear prediction all-pole model $H(z, \lambda)$ of the form

$$H(z, \lambda) = \sigma(\lambda)/A(z, \lambda), \tag{1}$$

where λ is a parameter row vector

$$\lambda = (\lambda_1, \lambda_2, \cdots, \lambda_L). \tag{2}$$

The inverse filter polynomial $A(z, \lambda)$ has the form

$$A(z, \lambda) = \sum_{i=0}^{M} a_i z^{-i} \quad \text{with} \quad a_0 = 1, \tag{3}$$

where $\sigma(\lambda)$ is a gain term. Both the gain terms $\sigma(\lambda)$ and the filter coefficients $a_1, a_2, \cdots, a_M$ may be functions of the parameter vector λ. It is assumed that $A(z, \lambda)$ has all of its roots within the unit circle so that $H(z, \lambda)$ is minimum phase. Analogously, a model $H(z, \lambda + \Delta\lambda)$ is defined by replacing λ with $\lambda + \Delta\lambda$ where

$$\Delta\lambda = (\Delta\lambda_1, \Delta\lambda_2, \cdots, \Delta\lambda_L). \tag{4}$$

It is assumed that the elements of $\Delta\lambda$ are sufficiently small to insure that $H(z, \lambda + \Delta\lambda)$ remains a minimum-phase function.

The log spectral difference between $H(z, \lambda)$ and $H(z, \lambda + \Delta\lambda)$ is defined as

$$\Delta V(\theta) = \ln |H(e^{j\theta}, \lambda + \Delta\lambda)|^2 - \ln |H(e^{j\theta}, \lambda)|^2$$
$$= \ln |H(e^{j\theta}, \lambda + \Delta\lambda)/H(e^{j\theta}, \lambda)|^2, \tag{5}$$

where θ is the normalized frequency (the angle on the unit circle in the z plane). A distance between the log spectra, Δd, or equivalently, the length of $\Delta V(\theta)$, can be defined in terms of an L_p norm as

$$\Delta d = \left(\int_{-\pi}^{\pi} |\Delta V(\theta)|^p \frac{d\theta}{2\pi} \right)^{1/p}, \tag{6}$$

where p is a positive integer.

Viswanathan and Makhoul [1] used the L_1 norm, $p = 1$, so that Δd represented the mean absolute value of $\Delta V(\theta)$. It has been noted [2] that when analyzing real speech, the choice of p is not a major consideration in terms of the end results. Although the L_p norms increase monotonically with p, they are all highly correlated for differences in all-pole model log spectra over reasonable ranges expected in speech processing. As a result, we shall restrict ourselves to the value of $p = 2$, so that the norm is a root mean square (rms) value. This leads to mathematically tractable results which can be numerically evaluated without frequency-domain calculations.

For the remainder of this study, unless otherwise stated, $p = 2$ and L_2 norms are implied. The rms log spectral deviation Δd will be called the spectral deviation. The norm square $(\Delta d)^2$ will be called the mean-square deviation. When only one parameter is being considered, independent of the others $(L = 1)$, the parameter row vector λ will be replaced by the scalar λ. For more general values of p other than $p = 2$, Δd of (6) can only be estimated by using discrete Fourier transforms (DFT's) and numerical approximations of the integral. For $p = 2$ and incremental changes in the parameters, known properties of analytic functions can be used to evaluate Δd in terms of finite summations without approximations.

A. Spectral Deviation Evaluation

Equation (5) can be rewritten using (1) as

$$\Delta V(\theta) = 2 \ln [\sigma(\lambda + \Delta\lambda)/\sigma(\lambda)] - \Delta G(e^{j\theta}) - \Delta G^*(e^{j\theta}), \tag{7}$$

where

$$\Delta G(z) = \ln [A(z, \lambda + \Delta\lambda)/A(z, \lambda)], \tag{8}$$

and the asterisk denotes a complex conjugate. As $A(z, \lambda)$ and $A(z, \lambda + \Delta\lambda)$ are minimum phase, $\Delta G(1/z)$ is analytic on and within the unit circle. This fact can be used with (6) and (7) to yield

$$(\Delta d)^2 = 4 \left\{ \ln [\sigma(\lambda + \Delta\lambda)/\sigma(\lambda)] \right\}^2 + 2 \int_{-\pi}^{\pi} |\Delta G(e^{j\theta})|^2 \frac{d\theta}{2\pi}. \tag{9}$$

The mean-square deviation is thus expressed as the sum of the mean-square deviation arising from the gain term $\sigma(\lambda)$, and the integral of $|\Delta G(e^{j\theta})|^2$. The effects of the gain term are seen to be additive in the mean-square deviation, and will be considered separately later. For purposes of the present discussion, the gain term is defined by

$$\sigma(\lambda) = 1,$$

which minimizes the mean-square deviation and normalizes the log spectra [2] so that

$$\int_{-\pi}^{\pi} \ln |H(e^{j\theta}, \lambda)|^2 \frac{d\theta}{2\pi} = 0. \tag{10}$$

Discussion of other gain normalizations is found elsewhere [2].

By defining an incremental polynomial

$$\Delta A(z) = A(z, \lambda + \Delta\lambda) - A(z, \lambda)$$

and substituting for $A(z, \lambda + \Delta\lambda)$ in (8), the approximation $\ln (1 + \delta) \cong \delta$ for small δ gives

$$\Delta G(z) = \Delta A(z)/A(z,\lambda) \qquad (11)$$

for sufficiently small incremental parameter changes. The incremental polynomial $\Delta A(z)$ can be evaluated by expanding $A(z, \lambda + \Delta\lambda)$ in a Taylor series and retaining only first-order terms as

$$\Delta A(z) = \sum_{i=1}^{L} \Delta\lambda_i \frac{\partial A(z,\lambda)}{\partial \lambda_i} \qquad (12)$$

with unity gain. The mean-square deviation can be expressed from (9) and (11) as twice a total-squared integral in the form

$$(\Delta d)^2 = 2 \int_{\pi}^{\pi} \left| \frac{\Delta A(e^{j\theta})}{A(e^{j\theta},\lambda)} \right|^2 \frac{d\theta}{2\pi}. \qquad (13)$$

The polynomial $\Delta A(z)$ contains at most the powers z^{-1} through z^{-M} based upon the form of (3). The integral of (13) can be evaluated as a summation involving no more than M terms by two different methods. First, one can use a stepdown approach [4] utilizing a set of orthogonal polynomials. The polynomials $\{B_0(z), B_1(z), \cdots, B_M(z)\}$ used for the backwards prediction error which are defined by

$$B_0(z) = z^{-1} \qquad (14a)$$

and

$$B_m(z) = z^{-1} B_{m-1}(z) + k_m z^{-(m+1)} B_{m-1}(1/z) \qquad (14b)$$

for $m = 1, 2, \cdots, M$, form an orthogonal set. As shown in Appendix A, these can be used to expand $\Delta A(z)$ in the form

$$\Delta A(z) = \sum_{m=0}^{M-1} \nu_m B_m(z), \qquad (15)$$

leading to the mean-square deviation

$$(\Delta d)^2 = 2 \sum_{m=0}^{M-1} \nu_m^2 \alpha_m / \alpha_M, \qquad (16)$$

where the coefficients ν_m are defined in Appendix A, and

$$\alpha_m = (1 - k_m^2) \alpha_{m-1} \quad \text{for } m = 1, 2, \cdots, M. \qquad (17)$$

When using the autocorrelation method of linear prediction [which is assumed here based upon the minimum-phase requirement for $H(z,\lambda)$], α_m is the minimum prediction error energy obtainable with an mth-order predictor, so that α_0 is the input signal energy.

An alternate approach to the evaluation of (13) is similar to that used in the evaluation of likelihood ratios [2]. Let the autocorrelation sequence $\{r_x(n)\}$ represent the autocorrelation sequence for the unit sample response of a filter $\sqrt{\alpha_M}/A(z, \lambda)$. In the autocorrelation method, this sequence is also the autocorrelation sequence for the input data used in calculating $A(z, \lambda)$ [3]. Let the autocorrelation sequence $\{r_\Delta(n)\}$ represent the autocorrelation sequence for the polynomial coefficients of $\Delta A(z)$. Applying the discrete form of Parseval's Theorem to the integral of (13) then gives

$$(\Delta d)^2 = \frac{2}{\alpha_M} \sum_{n=-\infty}^{\infty} r_x(n) r_\Delta(n).$$

As $\Delta A(z)$ contains at most the powers z^{-1} through z^{-M}, $r_\Delta(n)$ must be zero for $|n| > M - 1$. In addition, the autocorrelation sequences are even, so that a second closed-form expression for the mean-square deviation is

$$(\Delta d)^2 = \frac{2}{\alpha_M} \left[r_x(0) r_\Delta(0) + 2 \sum_{n=1}^{M-1} r_x(n) r_\Delta(n) \right]. \qquad (18)$$

Either (16) or (18) can be used to evaluate the mean-square deviation, once the incremental polynomial $\Delta A(z)$ is found. The former expression appears to be most useful for theoretical discussions while the latter expression appears most useful for numerical evaluation using the autocorrelation method of linear prediction since the autocorrelation sequence $\{r_x(n)\}$ is part of the analysis.

B. Single-Parameter Variations (L = 1)

Let λ represent either a linear or nonlinear transformation of the single-filter coefficient a_l in (3). From (12),

$$\Delta A(z) = (\Delta\lambda) \frac{\partial A(z, \lambda)}{\partial \lambda} = (\Delta\lambda) \frac{\partial a_l}{\partial \lambda} z^{-l}, \qquad (19)$$

so that the autocorrelation coefficients corresponding to

$$R_\Delta(z) = [\Delta A(z)] [\Delta A(1/z)]$$

are then

$$r_\Delta(n) = (\Delta\lambda)^2 (\partial a_l/\partial \lambda)^2 \delta_{n,0},$$

where $\delta_{n,k}$ is the Kronecker delta. Therefore, from (18), the mean-square deviation is

$$(\Delta d)^2 = 2 [r_x(0)/\alpha_M] (\Delta\lambda)^2 (\partial a_l/\partial \lambda)^2. \qquad (20)$$

The ratio $r_x(0)/\alpha_M$ is the ratio of the input signal energy to the prediction error energy and can be expressed in several forms [3] as

$$r_x(0)/\alpha_M = \alpha_0/\alpha_M = \int_{-\pi}^{\pi} \frac{1}{|A(e^{j\theta},\lambda)|^2} \frac{d\theta}{2\pi}$$

$$= \prod_{i=1}^{M} (1 - k_i^2)^{-1}. \qquad (21)$$

For the case where λ equals the filter coefficient a_l, (20) and (21) show that the spectral deviation due to a change in the coefficient a_l is proportional to the magnitude of the change as

$$\Delta d = \sqrt{2\alpha_0/\alpha_M} \, |\Delta a_l|.$$

The proportionality constant, $\sqrt{2\alpha_0/\alpha_M}$, is the square root of twice the energy of the unit sample response for the all-pole model, $1/A(z, \lambda)$. As any reflection coefficient approaches unity magnitude (21) becomes unbounded. This result illustrates what has been experimentally known for some time— quantizing the filter coefficients for parameter transmission is unadvisable [4], independent of stability problems.

When λ is a linear or nonlinear function of a single reflection coefficient, k_l, then from (19),

$$\Delta A(z) = (\Delta\lambda) \frac{\partial A(z,\lambda)}{\partial\lambda} = (\Delta\lambda)(\partial k_l/\partial\lambda)[\partial A(z,\lambda)/\partial k_l].$$

$$(22)$$

The polynomial $A(z,\lambda)$ can be recursively generated from the reflection coefficients using a step-up procedure [3] which effectively corresponds to the solution for the recursive filter coefficients with unnecessary steps removed. Each individual reflection coefficient appears only once in the recursion, in a linear manner. Starting with

$$A_0(z) = 1, \ B_0(z) = z^{-1}, \tag{23a}$$

the recursion is specified by

$$A_m(z) = A_{m-1}(z) + k_m B_{m-1}(z) \tag{23b}$$

and

$$B_m(z) = z^{-1}[k_m A_{m-1}(z) + B_{m-1}(z)] \tag{23c}$$

for $m = 1, 2, \cdots, M$, terminating with

$$A(z,\lambda) = A_M(z). \tag{23d}$$

Thus $A(z,\lambda)$ is a linear function of each individual reflection coefficient.

Using the recursion relationships of (23), closed-form results can be obtained for $\partial A(z,\lambda)/\partial k_l$ which increase in complexity as l decreases. For example,

$$\frac{\partial A(z,\lambda)}{\partial k_M} = B_{M-1}(z) \tag{24a}$$

$$\frac{\partial A(z,\lambda)}{\partial k_{M-1}} = B_{M-2}(z) + k_M z^{-1} A_{M-2}(z) \tag{24b}$$

$$\frac{\partial A(z,\lambda)}{\partial k_{M-2}} = (k_{M-1} z^{-1} + k_M z^{-2}) A_{M-3}(z)$$
$$+ (1 + k_M k_{M-1} z^{-1}) B_{M-3}(z). \tag{24c}$$

Since $A(z,\lambda)$ is a linear function of each individual reflection coefficient, the partial derivative of $A(z)$ can be numerically obtained directly from the difference between two polynomials. Let $A(z,\lambda')$ be another polynomial generated from the reflection coefficient set, but with k_l replaced by $k_l + 1$,

$$k_l(\lambda') = k_l(\lambda) + 1,$$

with all other reflection coefficients unchanged. Therefore,

$$\frac{\partial A(z,\lambda)}{\partial k_l} = A(z,\lambda') - A(z,\lambda). \tag{25}$$

For $l = M$ and $l = M - 1$, convenient closed-form results can be obtained for the mean-square deviation $(\Delta d)^2$ by using (24), as shown in Appendix B. These results are presented in Table I. For $l = M - 2$, the closed form results is quite complex in general, and is thus shown in the table only for the case $M = 3$. A common characteristic of the mean-square deviation is that for any l, the mean-square deviation has the form

TABLE I
MEAN-SQUARE DEVIATIONS DUE to k_1 QUANTIZATION

Restrictions		$(\Delta d)^2$
$l = M,$	$M > 0$	$2(\Delta\lambda)^2 (\partial k_M/\partial\lambda)^2 \dfrac{1}{1 - k_M^2}$
$l = M - 1,$	$M > 2$	$2(\Delta\lambda)^2 (\partial k_{M-1}/\partial\lambda)^2 \left[\dfrac{1 + 2k_M k_{M-2} + k_M^2}{(1 - k_{M-1}^2)(1 - k_M^2)}\right]$
$l = M - 1 = 1,$	$M = 2$	$2(\Delta\lambda)^2 (\partial k_1/\partial\lambda)^2 \left[\dfrac{1 + k_2}{(1 - k_1^2)(1 - k_2)}\right]$
$l = M - 2 = 1,$	$M = 3$	$2(\Delta\lambda)^2 (\partial k_1/\partial\lambda)^2 \left[\dfrac{(1 - 2k_1 k_3 + k_3^2)(1 + k_2)}{(1 - k_1^2)(1 - k_2)(1 - k_3^2)}\right]$

$$(\Delta d)^2 = (\Delta\lambda)^2 (\partial k_l/\partial\lambda)^2 f_l(k_1, k_2, \cdots, k_M)/(1 - k_l^2), \tag{26}$$

where $f_l(\cdot)$ is a well-behaved function of k_l (it does not go to infinity). It is shown in Appendix C that (26) is a general result. Although $f_l(\cdot)$ does not depend upon k_l for the first three entries in Table I, it is a function of k_l for the last entry. The importance of this relation is that it shows how to define a transformation which removes the singular characteristic at $k_l = \pm 1$.

In order to remove the singularity at $k_l = \pm 1$, it is necessary that $(\partial k_l/\partial\lambda)^2$ be proportional to $(1 - k_l)^2$ near $k_l = \pm 1$. This is accomplished if λ is proportional to the inverse sine of k_l, i.e.,

$$\lambda = c_l \sin^{-1} k_l, \tag{27a}$$

for then

$$k_l = \sin(\lambda/c_l), \tag{27b}$$

and

$$(\Delta d)^2 = (\Delta\lambda/c_l)^2 f_l(k_1, k_2, \cdots, k_M).$$

The inverse sine quantization suggested by (27) differs from the log area ratio quantization of [1] because of the gain normalization. In [1] the gain was normalized to yield unity energy

$$\int_{-\pi}^{\pi} |H(e^{j\theta}, \lambda)|^2 \frac{d\theta}{2\pi} = 1. \tag{28}$$

Therefore, from (1) and (21),

$$\sigma(\lambda) = \sqrt{\alpha_M/\alpha_0} = \prod_{i=1}^{M} (1 - k_i^2)^{1/2}. \tag{29}$$

From (9) we see that there is an additive effect from the gain term, which for incremental variations is given by

$$4\{\ln[\sigma(\lambda + \Delta\lambda)/\sigma(\lambda)]\}^2 = (\Delta\lambda)^2 \left\{\frac{\partial}{\partial\lambda}[\ln\sigma^2(\lambda)]\right\}^2.$$

Using this result with (29) gives the additional term in the mean-square deviation as

$$4\{\ln\left[\sigma(\lambda+\Delta\lambda)/\sigma(\lambda)\right]\}^2 = (\Delta\lambda)^2\,(\partial k_l/\partial\lambda)^2\,\frac{4k_l^2}{(1-k_l^2)^2}.$$

When this result is added to (26), the mean-square deviation takes on the form

$$(\Delta d)^2 = (\Delta\lambda)^2\,(\partial k_l/\partial\lambda)^2\,g_l(k_1,k_2,\cdots,k_M)/(1-k_l^2)^2,$$

$$(30)$$

where $g_l(\cdot)$ is a well-behaved function of k_l.

Following the same logic leading to the inverse sine quantization of (27), we find that to eliminate the singularities at $k_l = \pm 1$ in (30), λ must be proportional to the log area ratio

$$\lambda = c_l \ln\,[(1+k_l)/(1-k_l)] \qquad (31)$$

near the extremes $k_l = \pm 1$. If k_l is allowed to cover the full range from -1 through $+1$, then the singularities from the denominators of (26) and (30) predominate in the behavior of Δd, leading to either the inverse sine or log area quantization schemes as being optimal. The difference in the two results lies in the choice of the gain terms, not in the choice of a norm (L_1 or L_2).

It should be noted that the "optimality" of either the log area of inverse sine quantization is specifically addressed to finding elementary nonlinear transformations of variables which depend only upon individual reflection coefficients. These transformations remove any singular behavior at the end points, where the magnitudes of the reflection coefficients approach unity.

We prefer to use the gain normalization $\sigma(\lambda) = 1$ which normalizes the log spectra (10), so that the gain term is treated as an independent parameter, as is customary in most speech compression systems. Using this choice, inverse sine quantization is superior to log area quantization when the full range of values for k_l from -1 to $+1$ is covered. In Section III we present experimental results which show that when the reflection coefficients are restricted to more practical ranges, particularly for $l > 2$, the choice of quantization makes little difference, for the singularities at $k_l = \pm 1$ are never approached. We shall see that with the exception of k_1 and k_2, uniform quantization is quite adequate (and, in fact, is slightly superior!). For k_1 and k_2, the inverse sine quantization or the log area quantization results are very similar and slightly superior to uniform quantization.

C. Two Parameter Variations (L = 2)

Assume that $A(z,\lambda)$ is factored into a product of first-order terms representing real roots and second-order terms representing complex root pairs or pairs of real roots. If parameter variations occur within only a single product term, then all other factors of $A(z,\lambda)$ and $A(z,\lambda+\Delta\lambda)$ will be equal, and will thus cancel in (8). To study such parameter changes, it is, therefore, sufficient to look at first- and second-order polynomials only. First-order polynomials can be treated by applying the first entry in Table I, with $M = 1$. Following the results of the preceding section, it can be seen that the maximum spectral deviation for a first-order polynomial is minimized with inverse sine quantization of $k_1 = a_1$.

The second-order polynomials which can represent either complex or real root pairs are given by

$$A(z,\lambda) = 1 + a_1 z^{-1} + a_2 z^{-2}$$

$$= 1 + k_1(1+k_2)z^{-1} + k_2 z^{-2}. \qquad (32)$$

When the roots are complex conjugates occurring at $re^{\pm j\phi}$, then

$$a_1 = -2r\cos(\phi), \qquad a_2 = r^2, \qquad (33a)$$

and

$$k_1 = -2r\cos(\phi)/(1+r^2), \qquad k_2 = r^2. \qquad (33b)$$

Assuming that the row vector λ has elements λ_1 and λ_2, all spectral deviations can be expressed in terms of Δk_1 and Δk_2 as

$$\Delta k_1 = (\partial k_1/\partial\lambda_1)(\Delta\lambda_1) + (\partial k_1/\partial\lambda_2)(\Delta\lambda_2) \qquad (34a)$$

and

$$\Delta k_2 = (\partial k_2/\partial\lambda_1)(\Delta\lambda_1) + (\partial k_2/\partial\lambda_2)(\Delta\lambda_2). \qquad (34b)$$

From (12) and (32), with the reflection coefficients as parameters, the incremental polynomial is found to be

$$\Delta A(z) = (\Delta k_1)(1+k_2)z^{-1} + (\Delta k_2)(k_1 z^{-1} + z^{-2}).$$

In terms of the orthogonal polynomials defined by (14), the incremental polynomial has the form

$$\Delta A(z) = (1+k_2)\,B_0\,(z)(\Delta k_1) + B_1(z)(\Delta k_2).$$

As in the derivation of (16), the orthogonality of the polynomials $B_m(z)$ leads to a mean-square deviation given by

$$(\Delta d)^2 = 2(1+k_2)^2\,(\Delta k_1)^2\,(\alpha_0/\alpha_2) + 2(\Delta k_2)^2\,(\alpha_1/\alpha_2).$$

By applying (17), this expression takes on the form

$$(\Delta d)^2 = 2\,\frac{1+k_2}{1-k_2}\,\frac{(\Delta k_1)^2}{1-k_1^2} + 2\,\frac{(\Delta k_2)^2}{1-k_2^2}. \qquad (35)$$

This result can be used to study the effect of pole location quantization in terms of resultant spectral deviation, and to obtain an incremental lower bound on the minimum number of bits needed to quantize any pole pair for a maximum allowable spectral deviation.

D. Formant Movement and Spectral Deviation

A problem of basic research interest is to know how the spectral deviation is related to formant movement. Equation (35) can be directly applied to solve this problem for single-formant movement. The frequency F and bandwidth B of a formant is defined in terms of a complex pole pair $r\exp(\pm j\phi)$ with sampling frequency f_s as

$$r = e^{-\pi B/f_s}, \qquad \phi = 2\pi F/f_s. \qquad (36)$$

Equations (33b) and (34) can be used with (35) to express the mean-square deviation in terms of the pole location incremental changes. After some tedious trigonometric manipulations, the mean-square deviation takes on the form

$$(\Delta d)^2 = [u_{rr}(\Delta r)^2 - 2u_{r\phi}(\Delta r)(\Delta\phi)$$
$$+ [u_{\phi\phi}(\Delta\phi)^2]/[(1 - k_1^2)(1 - k_2^2)]$$

where

$$u_{rr} = [(r^2 - 1)^2 + (3r^2 - 1)\sin^2\phi]/(1 + r^2),$$

$$u_{r\phi} = r\sin(\phi)\cos(\phi)(1 - r^2)/(1 + r^2),$$

$$u_{\phi\phi} = r^2\sin^2\phi,$$

and

$$(1 - k_1^2)(1 - k_2^2) = [(1 - r^2)^2$$
$$+ 4r^2\sin^2\phi](1 - r^2)/(1 + r^2)^2.$$

As the formant behavior is highly resonant [5], $B << F$ and the above expressions can easily be approximated by using the assumption

$$(1 - r^2) = 2\pi B/f_s << \sin(\phi) = \sin(2\pi F/f_s), \tag{37}$$

giving

$$(\Delta d)^2 \cong \frac{2f_s}{\pi B}[(r\Delta\phi)^2 + (\Delta r)^2], \tag{38a}$$

or

$$\Delta d \cong |\Delta z_p|\sqrt{2f_s/\pi B}, \tag{38b}$$

where $|\Delta z_p|$ is the actual incremental distance in the z plane for pole motion resulting from incremental parameter changes.

In terms of single-formant movement, the spectral deviation is found to be related to changes in formant movement ΔF and formant bandwidth ΔB by

$$(\Delta d)^2 = \frac{8\pi}{Bf_s}[(\Delta F)^2 + (\Delta B/2)^2]. \tag{39}$$

From (38) it is seen that the spectral deviation resulting from an incremental change in a narrow bandwidth pole location is directly proportional to the distance moved and to the square root of the ratio of sampling frequency to bandwidth. Increasing the sampling frequency while holding the bandwidth fixed increases Δd, a result which can intuitively be seen by noting that the poles are closer to the unit circle. From (39) it can be noted that for a fixed bandwidth $\Delta B = 0$, Δd is proportional to the absolute change in formant frequency $|\Delta F|$. This result can be compared to the perceptual experiments of Stevens [5] where distance limens (values of ΔF which resulted in barely perceptible changes in sounds) were essentially constant for one formant synthesis models. Using Stevens' bandwidths of 130 Hz and a difference limen of 20 Hz, a typical spectral deviation for a 6.5-kHz sampling frequency corresponding to one distance limen is 4.34 (Δd) = 0.47 dB.

While (38) and (39) lend insight into how formant movement relates to spectral deviation, it must be kept in mind that the results are based upon the assumption of (37). In considering general pole-pair quantization where wide bandwidth shaping terms are used, for example, it is theoretically preferable to

return to (35) and the reflection coefficients, and to use the two-parameter coding scheme which is now described.

E. Minimum Bits to Implement a Pole Pair

Let $\Delta\overline{d}$ represent an upper limit to be allowed on the spectral deviation arising from quantization errors in a single pole pair. We wish to determine how to quantize the pole pair of (32) so that the range of reflection coefficients

$$-1 \leqslant k_1 \leqslant 1, \quad -1 \leqslant k_2 \leqslant \overline{k}_2$$

is covered by the smallest number of quantization points, without exceeding a maximum spectral deviation $\Delta\overline{d}$ due to quantization error, where $\overline{k}_2$ is the maximum allowable value of k_2 based upon values observed from speech. For complex pole pairs, $\overline{k}_2$ is the square of the maximum pole magnitude, and is related to a minimum allowable bandwidth $\underline{B}$ by

$$\overline{k}_2 = e^{-2\pi\underline{B}/f_s}.$$

If β is the number of bits used for quantization, we shall show that an incremental lower bound, valid for very small $\Delta\overline{d}$, is given by

$$2^\beta \geqslant \pi\frac{\ln[2/(1 - \overline{k}_2)]}{(\Delta\overline{d})^2}. \tag{40}$$

In addition, a quantizing scheme which approximately satisfies the lower bound is derived.

The first step is to change variables using inverse sine transformations

$$\psi_i = \sin^{-1}k_i \quad \text{for } i = 1, 2, \tag{41}$$

so that (35) can be rewritten as

$$(\Delta d)^2 = 2\frac{1 + \sin(\psi_2)}{1 - \sin(\psi_2)}(\Delta\psi_1)^2 + 2(\Delta\psi_2)^2. \tag{42}$$

Using this transformation, we see that (42) describes incremental ellipses. The locus of points which satisfies the inequality $\Delta d \leqslant \Delta\overline{d}$ is then given by the interiors of the ellipses, centered at ψ_1, ψ_2. Two such ellipses are shown in Fig. 1. Their principal axes are parallel to the coordinate axes. The heights of the ellipses are equal to $\sqrt{2}(\Delta\overline{d})$. The ellipse widths depend upon the vertical coordinate of the ellipse centers, and are given by

$$w = \sqrt{2}(\Delta d)\{[1 - \sin(\psi_2)]/[1 + \sin(\psi_2)]\}^{1/2}.$$

These ellipses are assumed to be incrementally small, so that the value of ψ_2 used in determining the width can be taken as the center value, since it differs only incrementally within the ellipse. More precise curves would taper towards the top, giving an egg-shaped appearance. Using more precise curves only slightly modifies the end results while substantially increasing the complexity of the derivation.

In order that the rms deviation due to quantization error be less than $\Delta\overline{d}$, it is necessary that every point in the range

$$-\pi/2 \leqslant \psi_1 \leqslant \pi/2, \quad -\pi/2 \leqslant \psi_2 \leqslant \sin^{-1}(\overline{k}_2) \tag{43}$$

lie within at least one such ellipse, centered at a quantization

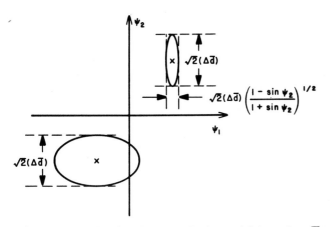

Fig. 1. Illustration showing the locus of points satisfying $\Delta d \leqslant \Delta \overline{d}$ in the ψ_1, ψ_2 plane.

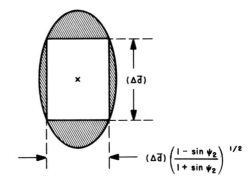

Fig. 2. Illustration showing the largest rectangle fitting within an ellipse.

point. As the ellipses do not have rectangular boundaries, there will be some overlap, effectively wasting area. To minimize the waste, we obtain the largest possible rectangle (in terms of area) within an ellipse. This maximization problem leads to rectangles with dimensions as shown in Fig. 2. All numerical values that fall within the rectangle are represented by the single numerical value corresponding to its center. The shaded region between the rectangle and the ellipse indicates the wasted area that could be assigned to more than one quantization point.

To cover the full range of ψ_1 and ψ_2, values by quantization points without exceeding a spectral deviation of $\Delta \overline{d}$, we can divide the plane into horizontal strips with heights not less than the rectangle height $\Delta \overline{d}$ of Fig. 2. From the range of ψ_2 value of (43), it is seen that at least N_s strips are required where

$$N_s = [\sin^{-1} (\overline{k}_2) + \pi/2]/(\Delta \overline{d}). \qquad (44)$$

Within each strip, numbered $n = 1, 2, \cdots, N_s$, the vertical ordinate for the quantization points (or rectangle centers) is given by

$$\psi_2(n) = -\frac{\pi}{2} + \left(n - \frac{1}{2}\right)(\Delta \overline{d}), \quad \text{for } n = 1, 2, \cdots, N. \qquad (45)$$

From (43), the width of each strip is π. With reference to Fig. 2, the number of quantization points along a strip, $N(n)$, must at least equal the strip width divided by the rectangle width, so that $N(n)$ must at least equal

$$N(n) = \frac{\pi}{\Delta \overline{d}} \left[\frac{1 + \sin [\psi_2(n)]}{1 - \sin [\psi_2(n)]}\right]^{1/2}.$$

The horizontal ordinate for the quantization points is then given by

$$\psi_1(n, l) = -\frac{\pi}{2} + \left(l - \frac{1}{2}\right)\frac{\pi}{N(n)} \quad \text{for } l = 1, 2, \cdots, N(n). \qquad (46)$$

The total number of quantization points must at least equal the sum

$$N = \sum_{n=1}^{N_S} N(n) = \frac{\pi}{\Delta \overline{d}} \sum_{n=1}^{N_S} \left[\frac{1 + \sin [\psi_2(n)]}{1 - \sin [\psi_2(n)]}\right]^{1/2}. \qquad (47)$$

From the incremental nature of $\Delta \overline{d}$, this summation can be approximated by an integral, or by slightly changing the limits, (47) can be bounded by an integral. Using (45) to define

$$\Delta \psi_2 = \psi_2(n + 1) - \psi_2(n) = \Delta \overline{d},$$

(47) can be rewritten as

$$N = [\pi/(\Delta \overline{d})^2] \sum_{n=1}^{N_S} g [\psi_2(n)] \Delta \psi_2,$$

where

$$g(\psi) = \left[\frac{1 + \sin (\psi)}{1 - \sin (\psi)}\right]^{1/2}.$$

The integral approximation to the summation is then

$$\sum_{n=1}^{N_S} g [\psi_2(n)] \Delta \psi_2 \cong \int_{-\pi/2}^{\sin^{-1} (\overline{k}_2)} g(\psi) \, d\psi$$

$$= \ln [2/(1 - \overline{k}_2)].$$

This result can be combined with (48) to give the bound of (40) where $N = 2^\beta$. It is a bound, because in each step of the derivation the minimum number of quantization levels was used. If, for example, (44) specifies 23.7 strips, then at least 24 strips must be used.

The transformation that approximately attains equality in (40) is given by uniform quantization along the ψ_2 axis and nonuniform quantization along the ψ_1 axis, where the nonuniformity is specified by Fig. 2. Equivalently, the transformation is given by uniform quantization of

$$\lambda_2 = \sin^{-1} (k_2) \qquad (48a)$$

$$\lambda_1 = \left[\frac{1 + k_2}{1 - k_2}\right]^{1/2} \sin^{-1} (k_1). \qquad (48b)$$

This end result has apparently also been developed by Itakura from the likelihood function of an all-pole stochastic signal [6].

453

III. Experimental Results

The sentences "Thieves who rob friends deserve jail," "Open the crate but don't break the glass," "Oak is strong and also gives shade," and "It's time we rounded up that herd of Asian cattle," each spoken by a different person, were analyzed by the autocorrelation method of linear prediction. The fundamental frequency ranged from 50 Hz to 220 Hz. The analysis windows of 100 samples (15.38 ms) moved every 10 ms for a total of 912 analysis frames (9.12 s). A constant preemphasis coefficient of 0.9 was applied to all frames.

A. Single-Parameter Variations

For determining bit allocation based upon single-parameter variations, the following approach was used. For each frame a set of 10 reflection coefficients was obtained. Histograms were made of the frequency of occurrence of the reflection coefficient over all reflection coefficients for determining reasonable ranges for each coefficient value. The histograms incorporate all of the speech sounds but silence. The bit-allocation procedure to be described can be directly applied to finding efficient quantization for the separate categories of voiced and unvoiced sounds at the cost of additional storage for quantization tables. The results are shown in Fig. 3 for the 10 reflection coefficients. The first two coefficients show a very strong skewing effect towards -1 and $+1$, respectively. This characteristic has been theoretically shown for voiced sounds having high correlation [7]. The bimodal distribution of k_2 is due to the inclusion of unvoiced sounds which results in a high frequency of occurrence near $k_2 = 0$. The remaining histograms are reasonably well modeled by Gaussian probability density curves as shown. The maxima and minima of these parameter distributions are shown in Table II, along with means and standard deviations. By combining (12), (13), and (25), the expression for $(\Delta d)^2$ and $L = 1$ can be written in a normalized form:

$$I_l = 2 \int_{-\pi}^{\pi} \left| \frac{A(e^{j\theta}, \lambda') - A(e^{j\theta}, \lambda)}{A(e^{j\theta}, \lambda)} \right|^2 \frac{d\theta}{2\pi}$$

$$= \frac{[\Delta d(l)]^2 (\partial \lambda / \partial k_l)^2}{(\Delta \lambda)^2} \tag{49}$$

where $\Delta d(l)$ defines the spectral deviation due to a single-parameter variation. The normalized spectral deviation is computed from (49) using the computer program in Appendix D. The transformations and partial derivatives for the three cases of interest here are as follows:

reflection coefficient quantization:

$$\lambda = k_l, \qquad \partial k_l / \partial \lambda = 1;$$

log area quantization:

$$\lambda = \ln \left(\frac{1 + k_l}{1 - k_l} \right), \qquad \partial k / \partial \lambda = (1 - k_l^2)/2; \text{ and}$$

inverse sine quantization:

$$\lambda = \sin^{-1}(k_l), \qquad \partial k_l / \partial \lambda = \sqrt{1 - k_l^2}.$$

Given the min–max values $\underline{k}_l, \overline{k}_l$ from Table II, $\underline{\lambda}_l$ and $\overline{\lambda}_l$ are

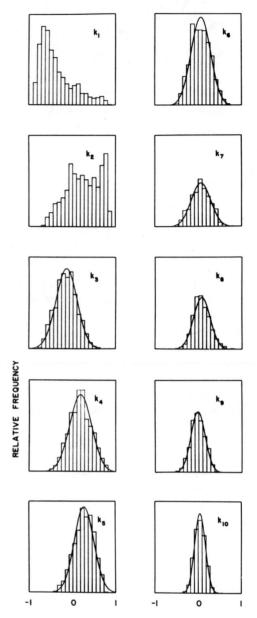

Fig. 3. Histograms of reflection coefficients.

computed from the above expressions. Linear quantization of the parameter λ into N_l levels (or $\log_2 (N_l)$ bits) produces a maximum quantization error of $\Delta \overline{\lambda} = (\overline{\lambda}_l - \underline{\lambda}_l)/2N_l$ assuming that rounding is used. Therefore, the maximum value of the mean-square spectral deviation is given by

$$[\Delta d(l)]^2 = \left(\frac{\overline{\lambda}_l - \underline{\lambda}_l}{2N_l} \right)^2 \left(\frac{\partial k_l}{\partial \lambda} \right)^2 I_l.$$

The resultant scatter plots of normalized spectral deviation versus k_l for the above quantization methods are presented in Fig. 4. Each graph shows the quantity $2(4.34 \, \Delta d(l)) N_l$ (decibels) versus k_l over the range -1 to 1. For each index the corresponding plots are scaled identically. For discussion purposes, the graphs will be referenced in the form of matrix elements as G_{ij} where $i = 1, 2, \cdots, 10$ defines the coefficient index and $j = 1, 2, 3$ corresponds to reflection coefficient, log

TABLE II
REFLECTION COEFFICIENT DISTRIBUTION

l	Minimum Reflection Coefficient $\underline{k}_l$	Maximum Reflection Coefficient $\overline{k}_l$	Mean	Standard Deviation
1	−0.9729	0.9243	−0.40630	0.4334
2	−0.7288	0.9503	0.26920	0.4219
3	−0.8774	0.6411	−0.17430	0.2721
4	−0.5789	0.8622	0.18550	0.2819
5	−0.5237	0.7200	0.05539	0.2470
6	−0.4762	0.8539	0.28130	0.2517
7	−0.6444	0.8049	0.05886	0.2487
8	−0.5146	0.8562	0.07080	0.2121
9	−0.5876	0.4532	−0.02784	0.1801
10	−0.3972	0.5099	0.03665	0.1366

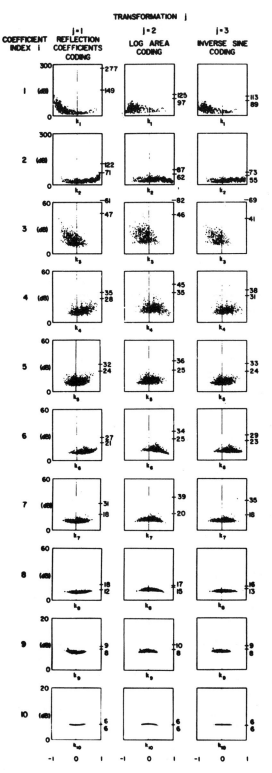

Fig. 4. Scatter plots for normalized spectral deviation.

area, and inverse sine quantization, respectively. On the right side of each graph two numbers are shown. The top number is the largest value computed for G_{ij} over all 912 frames (rounded to an integer value). Only one percent of the frames produce values which exceed the lower number.

In G_{11} a u-shaped characteristic is easily seen for k_1 near −1. The peak deviation is $4.34\Delta d = 277/(2N)$ dB. To insure that the spectral deviation over all frames in the data base does not exceed 0.3 dB due to quantization of k_1 requires $N_1 = 462$ or 9 bits. If it is required that the spectral deviation not exceed 0.3 dB more than one percent of the time, then $N_1 \geqslant 248$ or 8 bits. In G_{12} and G_{13}, the peak spectral deviation is substantially reduced. Although G_{12} shows a greater reduction of spectral deviation near $|k_1| = 1$ than G_{13}, it does so at the expense of slightly increased errors away from these regions. Both spectral deviation values are slightly less for G_{13}. By quantizing with $j = 2$ or $j = 3$ for either a peak or one percent exceeded criterion, it is seen that the quantization requirements are reduced by approximately one bit for the first coefficient, with respect to reflection coefficient coding.

For $i = 2$, G_{21} shows a moderate amount of u-shaped behavior near $k_2 = 1$. Again G_{22} shows a substantial reduction in spectral deviation near the boundaries $|k_2| = 1$, but slightly higher peak and one percent values than for G_{23}. For $i > 2$ the possibly surprising result is seen that log area and inverse sine quantization are theoretically inferior to direct reflection coefficient quantization. For example, to insure that the spectral deviation due to quantization of k_3 does not exceed 0.3 dB, log area quantization requires $N_3 \geqslant 136$ or 7.08 bits whereas reflection coefficient quantization requires $N_3 \geqslant 102$ or 6.67 bits. For inverse sine quantization, $N_3 \geqslant 115$ or 6.84 bits. The reason for this behavior is that for G_{i2} or G_{i3}, higher resolution is guaranteed as $|k_i|$ increases towards unity at the expense of less resolution for $|k_i|$ near zero. A graph of $(\lambda/\overline{\lambda})$ versus k for $0 \leqslant k \leqslant \overline{k}$ will show that log area quantization has the most extreme curvature from the $\lambda = k$ line and, therefore, the highest resolution for $|k|$ near one and lowest resolution for $|k|$ near zero. From a practical viewpoint, it can be seen that for $i > 2$, very little difference exists among the quantization schemes.

It is interesting to note that beyond $i = 6$, a deterministic trend begins to appear in each respective graph G_{ij}. At the final coefficient $i = M = 10$, the variations of the data become deterministic. This behavior was predicted by the first entry of Table I as

$$[\Delta d(M)]^2 = 2(\Delta\lambda)^2 (\partial k_M/\partial\lambda)^2 (1 - k_M^2)^{-1}.$$

Therefore,

$$[\Delta d(M)]^2 = \begin{cases} \sqrt{2}\left(\dfrac{\overline{\lambda}_M - \lambda_M}{2N_M}\right)(1 - k_M^2)^{-1/2} \\ \qquad \text{reflection coefficient quantization} \\ \sqrt{2}\left(\dfrac{\overline{\lambda}_M - \lambda_M}{4N_M}\right)(1 - k_M^2)^{1/2} \\ \qquad \text{log area quantization} \\ \sqrt{2}\left(\dfrac{\overline{\lambda}_M - \lambda_M}{2N_M}\right) \\ \qquad \text{inverse sine quantization.} \end{cases}$$

Whereas $\Delta d(M)$ becomes unbounded as k_M approaches unity for reflection coefficient quantization, it approaches zero for log area quantization and is constant for inverse sine quantization. The constant line for inverse sine quantization intersects the convex and concave functions from the reflection coefficient and log area quantization.

Specific bit allocations are obtained from Fig. 4 by the following procedure. First, a maximum decibel rms spectral deviation max (Δd) is chosen along with a criterion of 1) never being exceeded (or more precisely for the number of frames of data, approximately 0.1 percent of the time) or 2) being exceeded 1.0 percent of the time. Applying the triangle inequality, we know that the overall maximum spectral deviation satisfies

$$\max(\Delta d) \leqslant \sum_{l=1}^{M} \Delta \overline{d}(l).$$

The minimum spectral deviation for a given number of levels or bits is obtained by choosing each of the $\Delta \overline{d}(l)$ terms to be equal. Therefore, choose

$$\Delta \overline{d}(l) = \max(\Delta d)/M.$$

If an overall maximum spectral deviation of 3 dB is desired, with 10 coefficients, then $\Delta \overline{d}(l) = 0.3$ dB. The number of levels N_i for each coefficient is defined by the peak or one percent number for the specified G_{ij} divided by $2\Delta d(l)$. The required bit allocations for each quantization method based upon peak values and max $(\Delta d) = 3$ dB and Fig. 4 are given in Table III. The number of levels, fractional bits and integer number of bits obtained by arbitrarily rounding upward if the fraction exceeds 0.25, are presented. Beyond $l > 2$ all three quantization methods are essentially equivalent, although for a detailed comparison the direct reflection coefficient quantization is superior for $l > 2$. For $l = 1$ and 2, one additional bit is saved by using either log area or inverse sine quantization. The inverse sine quantization for $l \leqslant 2$ is seen to be slightly superior to log area quantization and significantly superior to the reflection coefficient quantization.

It is important to note that a halving of the spectral deviation requires one additional bit per parameter or M total bits. Conversely, a reduction of one bit per parameter (for example, a reduction to 49 bits) will double the decibel spectral deviation.

It should be emphasized that the results presented are for sampling frequencies in the vicinity of 6.5 kHz and analysis using the autocorrelation method with preemphasis near 0.9. The normalized bit allocations described can be used directly to find the bit allocation and necessary number of bits to guarantee that no frames or one percent of the frames analyzed (statistically speaking) will exceed a specified maximum spectral deviation. If no preemphasis is used, somewhat different results are obtained due to the fact that a significant percentage of the first few reflection coefficients will lie closer to unity magnitude. An important practical implication is that for the same maximum rms spectral deviation, a larger number of bits will generally be necessary and, in addition, a larger percentage of the available bits will have to be allocated to the first few coefficients.

Similar statements hold for higher sampling frequencies. For a maximum desired spectral deviation, a larger (although possibly not significant) number of bits will have to be allocated. The bit allocation will also change in the direction of requiring a larger percentage of the total bits to be used for the first few coefficients. For any desired analysis condition it is only necessary to analyze a reasonably long segment of data such as 5–10 s with representative speech behavior, and then perform the same straightforward computation for N_l based upon the maximum overall allowable rms spectral deviation.

B. Two-Parameter Variations

In this section, the two-parameter quantization scheme is compared with quantizing methods of the previous section. For each of the 912 frames of data, the polynomial roots z_i, $i = 1, 2, \cdots, M$, were obtained from $A(z)$. Since M is even ($M = 10$), second-order polynomial pairs can be constructed from the real and imaginary parts of the roots in terms of reflection coefficients. Assuming $z_i = x_i + jy_i$,

$$\left. \begin{array}{l} k_2 = (x_i)^2 + (y_i)^2 \\ k_1 = -2x_i/(1 + k_2) \end{array} \right\} z_i \text{ complex}$$

$$\left. \begin{array}{l} k_2 = x_i x_j \\ k_1 = -(x_i + x_j)/(1 + k_2) \end{array} \right\} z_i, z_j \text{ real,}$$

or every frame of analysis data, each pair is ordered from highest to lowest k_2. Since $k_2 = \exp(-2\pi B/f_s)$ for complex conjugate root pairs, the ordering corresponds to ranking pairs in order of increasing bandwidth. The parameter transformation used is

$$\lambda_2 = \sin^{-1}(k_2)$$

$$\lambda_1 = \left[\frac{1 + k_2}{1 - k_2}\right]^{1/2} \sin^{-1}(k_1).$$

For a given maximum $\Delta \overline{d}$, this transformation will result in the minimum number of quantization levels over all possible two-parameter transformations. Scatter plots of the root pairs, reflection coefficient pairs (k_1, k_2), and two-parameter quantization pairs (λ_1, λ_2) for each second-order polynomial are shown in Fig. 5(a)–(c), respectively. For $l = 1, 2$ in Fig. 5(a), the roots are seen to cluster near the unit circle. For $l = 4, 5$, the samples appear to be somewhat randomly scattered around

Index l	Reflection Coefficient Quantization			Log Area Quantization			Inverse Sine Quantization		
	N_l	β (exact)	β (rounded)	N_l	β (exact)	β (rounded)	N_l	β (exact)	β (rounded)
1	462	8.85	9	208	7.70	8	188	7.55	8
2	203	7.66	8	145	7.18	7	121	6.92	7
3	101	6.66	7	136	7.09	7	115	6.84	7
4	58	5.86	6	75	6.23	6	63	5.98	6
5	53	5.73	6	60	5.91	6	55	5.78	6
6	45	5.49	6	56	5.81	6	48	5.58	6
7	51	5.67	6	65	6.02	6	58	5.86	6
8	30	4.91	5	28	4.81	5	26	4.70	5
9	15	3.91	4	16	4.00	4	15	3.91	4
10	10	3.32	4	10	3.32	4	10	3.32	4
Total		58.0	61		58.1	59		56.4	59

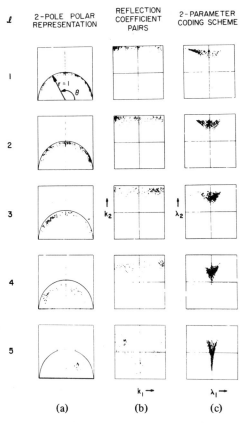

Fig. 5. Scatter plots of parameters for two-pair quantization. (a) Pole pairs, (b) reflection coefficients, and (c) two-parameter quantization pairs λ_1, λ_2.

the interior of the unit circle. In Fig. 5(b), the values along the k_1 axis appear somewhat randomly distributed over the range $-1 < k_1 < 1$. The k_2 axis values, however, tend to lie within restricted ranges of k_2 with largest values of k_2 occurring for the first few ordered pairs. For the first pair ($l = 1$), there is a concentration of samples near $k_2 = +1$ and $k_1 = -1$. In this region, $k_1 \cong -\cos(\phi)$ for complex pole pairs and $k_1 = -(z_i + z_j)$ for real pole pairs. This concentration is thus primarily due to the large number of narrow bandwidth terms at, or near, zero frequency. For $-1 < k_1 < 1$, the points indicated correspond to the narrowest bandwidth formant along the warped fre-

quency scale $\cos(\phi)$ for $0 < \phi < f_s/2$. Without preemphasis, very few samples would exist beyond $k_1 = 0$ (corresponding to $f_s/4$) since the narrowest bandwidths will usually be attributed to the highest energy terms. For the remaining pairs, there do not appear to be any particularly clustered regions along the warped frequency axis.

In Fig. 5(c) the data seem to lie approximately within horizontal strips bounded by a wedge. Since $|k_1| < 1$, the wedge is defined by

$$\lambda_1 = \pm \frac{\pi}{2} \left[\frac{1 + \sin \lambda_2}{1 - \sin \lambda_2} \right]^{1/2}.$$

If the λ_1, λ_2 plane is uniformly quantized in both dimensions with quantization intervals of length Δd, we are assured that the spectral deviation due to quantization of any second-order polynomial (using this quantization scheme) will not exceed $4.34 \Delta d$ (decibels). These figures illustrate the important fact that as k_2 decreases (the bandwidths increase) fewer quantization levels are necessary to represent the log spectrum with the same degree of accuracy. As λ_2 approaches unity (zero-bandwidth), the necessary number of levels becomes unbounded. It is interesting to note that the tightly clustered samples about $k_1 = -1$ and $k_1 = 1$ in Fig. 5(b) (for $l = 1$) are spread out over a fairly wide range in Fig. 5(c). From Section II, the necessary number of levels to insure that $\Delta \bar{d}$ is not exceeded is easily generalized to allow for a maximum range of $\underline{k} \leqslant k_2 \leqslant \overline{k}$ with the result

$$N \geqslant \frac{\pi}{(\Delta \bar{d})^2} \ln \left[\frac{1 - \underline{k}}{1 - \overline{k}} \right] \quad \text{for } \underline{k} \leqslant k_2 \leqslant \overline{k}.$$

Using the same criterion of choosing extrema values for $\underline{k}$ and $\overline{k}$ as in the previous section, and a specified maximum overall spectral deviation, we can compare the different quantization methods theoretically. For a maximum total spectral deviation of 3 dB, $\Delta \bar{d}$ for each pair must not exceed 0.6 dB or $\Delta \bar{d} = 0.1382$. Using the above expression and the k_2 extrema measured from the data, results are summarized in Table IV. If 45 bits are uniformly allocated over the five ordered pairs with their corresponding extrema ranges, by making use of the triangle inequality, we are assured that the total rms log spectral deviation between the original spectrum and the spectrum

TABLE IV
BIT ALLOCATION FOR ORDERED PAIRS USING TWO-PARAMETER
QUANTIZATION METHOD

l	$\overline{k}_2$	$\underline{k}_2$	N	Bits	[Bits]
1	0.976	0.7	417	8.70	9
2	0.960	0.6	379	8.57	9
3	0.930	0.3	379	8.57	9
4	0.920	−0.3	462	8.85	9
5	0.710	−0.8	300	8.23	9
Totals				42.92	45

reconstructed from quantized parameters will not exceed 3 dB. If the total range $\underline{k} \leqslant k_2 \leqslant \overline{k}$ were quantized for each pair without ordering terms, the required number of bits would increase to 50. From (40) it can be seen that if the maximum spectral deviation $\Delta \overline{d}$ is doubled, the required number of bits per pole pair is reduced by two. In the one-parameter quantization methods, the required number of bits was only reduced by one per parameter. However, since only $M/2$ pairs are quantized, all methods described have the same overall decibel versus max (Δd) behavior.

The improvement of this quantization method over reflection, inverse sine or log area coefficient quantization is significant. For the same maximum overall rms log spectral deviation of 3 dB, the other methods all require approximately 59 bits. Assume representative values for a linear prediction vocoder as 5 bits for pitch, 5 bits for gain, and a fixed transmission frame rate of 50 Hz, with 10 coefficients. Using a criterion of quality as not exceeding an rms log spectral deviation of 3 dB, with all else equal, reflection coefficient, log area, or inverse sine quantization require 3500 bits/s whereas the two-parameter quantization scheme required only 2800 bits/s. When the quantization efficiency of only the quantized 10 coefficients is considered, a savings of 14 bits per frame can be obtained without any sacrifice in quality. The price paid for this increased efficiency is the requirement of polynomial root solving. Although encoding/decoding details have not been presented here, they are relatively straightforward and do not require complex numerical operations or excessive computer storage.

C. Bit Allocation for Fixed Bandwidth Formant Vocoders

Based upon the theoretical developments of Section II, we can also determine the necessary number of levels or bits for satisfying a maximum spectral deviation in formant vocoders. The procedure is illustrated here for the fixed bandwidth case. For fixed bandwidths, $\Delta B_n = 0$ so that (39) reduces to

$$\Delta d = \sqrt{\frac{8\pi}{B_n f_s}} |\Delta F_n|.$$

Now if F_n is restricted to the range $(\underline{F}_n, \overline{F}_n)$ and N_n levels are used to quantize F_n, the maximum frequency error ΔF_n will be

$$\Delta F_n = \frac{\overline{F}_n - \underline{F}_n}{2N_n}.$$

The maximum spectral deviation is then

$$\Delta \overline{d} = \sqrt{\frac{8\pi}{B_n f_s} \left[\frac{\overline{F}_n - \underline{F}_n}{2N_n}\right]}.$$

Typical ranges for F_n $n = 1, 2, 3$ are given in Table IV. To guarantee less than 3 dB total maximum spectral deviation,

$$\max(\Delta d) < \Delta d(1) + \Delta d(2) + \Delta d(3) = 0.690775$$

or $\Delta \overline{d} = 0.23026$. Therefore, the necessary number of levels is

$$N_n \geqslant \frac{1}{\Delta \overline{d}} \sqrt{\frac{8\pi}{B_n f_s} \left[\frac{\overline{F}_n - \underline{F}_n}{2}\right]}.$$

The assumed min–max range of formant frequencies and fixed bandwidth values, along with the minimum number of bits $\log_2(N_1 N_2 N_3)$ and integer number of bits for each parameter to insure that $4.34 \max(\Delta d) < 3$ dB, is shown in Table V. When rounded, the allocation corresponds to five bits per parameter. Assuming a 50-Hz frame rate and pitch and gain quantized to 6 bits and 5 bits, respectively, the formant vocoder bit rate would be 1300 bits/s for the same quality, as the other systems. The subjective quality, however, will be considerably less than that of the other systems simply because of the fixed bandwidth definition and implied fixed spectral slope for glottal driving function and lip radiation characteristics.

IV. CONCLUSIONS

A theoretical basis for studying the effects of quantization and bit-allocation methods in speech processing has been developed and applied to speech data. The three most widely used parameters in linear prediction vocoder systems are the reflection coefficients, log area coefficients, and inverse sine coefficients. It was shown that in the sense of minimizing a maximum spectral deviation, either the log area ratios or inverse sine coefficients could be considered optimal, depending on the definition of a particular gain term. Although either of these quantization methods is superior to direct reflection coefficient quantization for the first two coefficients, the surprising result is shown that reflection coefficients are either nearly equal or superior to log-area coefficients or inverse sine coefficients beyond the first two terms. Using the number of levels as specified in the section on experimental results for insuring against a specified overall maximum spectral deviation, it was informally verified that the synthesized speech using each quantization method was of approximately the same perceived quality.

A two-pair quantization method was derived which approximately satisfies a lower bound on the necessary number of levels to insure that a specified maximum spectral deviation is not exceeded. Based upon use of the triangle inequality, the two-pair quantization scheme was shown to be significantly better than the reflection coefficient, log area, or inverse sine quantization at the expense of root solving.

In all of the quantization methods discussed, it is necessary to apply the triangle inequality for insuring against an overall maximum spectral deviation since only one-parameter or two-parameter variations can be theoretically studied in a useful manner. Presently, we are performing analysis/synthesis ex-

TABLE V
BIT ALLOCATION FOR FIXED BANDWIDTH FORMANT VOCODING

n	$\underline{F}_n$	$\overline{F}_n$	N_n (min)	Bits
1	2.000	1.200	19.11	5
2	5.000	2.400	30.23	5
3	1.500	3.000	22.67	5
			13.67 bits	15 bits

periments to test how conservative the results are for the one-parameter and two-parameter variations based upon quantization of all parameters. Preliminary studies indicate that it is quite conservative, with the two-parameter results being much more conservative than the one-parameter results.

APPENDIX A

Evaluation of Mean-Square Spectral Deviation

This Appendix summarizes the relations needed to evaluate the mean-square deviation (16) from $\Delta A(z)$ and $A(z, \lambda)$. Details may be found elsewhere [3]. For notational convenience we define the inner product of two functions of z by the integral

$$\langle F(z), G(z) \rangle = \alpha_M \int_{-\pi}^{\pi} \frac{F(e^{j\theta}) G^*(e^{j\theta})}{|A(e^{j\theta}, \lambda)|^2} \frac{d\theta}{2\pi}, \quad \text{(A1)}$$

so that (13) can be written in the form of an inner product

$$(\Delta d)^2 = \frac{2}{\alpha_M} \langle \Delta A(z), \Delta A(z) \rangle. \quad \text{(A2)}$$

The polynomials $B_m(z)$ defined by (14) are each of the form

$$B_m(z) = \sum_{i=1}^{m+1} b_{mi} z^{-i} \quad \text{with} \quad b_{m,m+1} = 1, \quad \text{(A3)}$$

and are orthogonal to each other, so that

$$\langle B_m(z), B_n(z) \rangle = \delta_{mn} \alpha_m. \quad \text{(A4)}$$

As $\Delta A(z)$ contains at most the powers z^{-1} through z^{-M}, it can be expressed as a linear combination of the $B_m(z)$ for $m = 0, 1, \cdots, M - 1$. This expansion is readily carried out by using the fact that the coefficient of $z^{-(m+1)}$ in $B_m(z)$ is unity. Thus if we define

$$\Delta A(z) = P_{M-1}(z), \quad \text{(A5a)}$$

$$P_m(z) = \sum_{i=1}^{m+1} p_{mi} z^{-i}, \quad \text{(A5b)}$$

and

$$P_{m-1}(z) = P_m(z) - p_{m,m+1} B_m(z), \quad \text{(A5c)}$$

for $m = M - 1, M - 2, \cdots, 0$, we obtain

$$A(z) = P_{M-1}(z) = \sum_{m=0}^{M-1} p_{m,m+1} B_m(z), \quad \text{(A6)}$$

which is identical to (18) with $\nu_m = p_{m,m+1}$. Equation (16) follows from (15), (A2), and the orthogonality relation of (A3).

APPENDIX B

Evaluation of Mean-Square Deviations in Table I

The derivation of the results in Table I is most efficiently carried out by using (24) and the inner product notation of Appendix A. In addition to the use of (17), one must use other properties derived elsewhere [3], but summarized as follows:

$$A_m(z) = z^{-(m+1)} B_m(1/z) = \sum_{i=0}^{m} a_{mi} z^{-i}$$

$$\text{with } a_{m0} = 1 \quad \text{(B1)}$$

$$\langle A_m(z), z^{-l} \rangle = \langle B_m(z), z^{-l} \rangle = 0$$

$$\text{for } l = 1, \cdots, m, \quad \text{(B2)}$$

$$\langle A_m(z), A_m(z) \rangle = \langle B_m(z), B_m(z) \rangle = \alpha_m, \quad \text{(B3)}$$

$$\langle A_m(z), B_m(z) \rangle = -k_{m+1} \alpha_m, \quad \text{(B4)}$$

$$\langle z^{-l} F(z), z^{-l} G(z) \rangle = \langle F(z), G(z) \rangle. \quad \text{(B5)}$$

Furthermore, if $F(z)$ and $G(z)$ are polynomials with only real coefficients, then the order is immaterial, i.e.,

$$\langle F(z), G(z) \rangle = \langle G(z), F(z) \rangle. \quad \text{(B6)}$$

Using (A1) and (24) along with the properties given, the results of Table I follow directly.

APPENDIX C

The General Form of the Mean-Square Deviation

Using the reflection coefficients, the polynomials $A_m(z)$ can be recursively generated through (23). The coefficients of these polynomials a_{mi} of (B1), can be used to recursively generate the autocorrelation sequence $\{r_x(n)\}$ used in the summation of (18) for the evaluation of mean-square deviations. From [3], this recursion has the form

$$r_x(0) = \alpha_0, \quad \text{(C1a)}$$

$$r_x(n) = -\sum_{k=1}^{n} a_{nk} r_x(n - k) \quad \text{for } n = 1, 2, \cdots, M. \quad \text{(C1b)}$$

If a reflection coefficient is allowed to approach plus or minus unity, it can be seen from the relations generating both the autocorrelation sequences, $\{r_x(n)\}$ and $\{r_\Delta(n)\}$, that these sequences remain well behaved and bounded, so that the bracketed summation of (18) will approach some finite limit. It is only the effect of the α_M in the denominator of (18) that lends a singular behavior to the mean-square deviation as a reflection coefficient approaches unity. From (21) it is seen that the singularity is of the nature of a simple pole as a reflection coefficient approaches either plus or minus one, hence (26) follows directly.

APPENDIX D

Computer Program for Evaluating Spectral Deviation

The evaluation of the spectral deviation due to changes in filter coefficients and reflection coefficients is carried out by the Fortran subroutine SENS of Fig. 6. The approach is quite

```
01300                 SUBROUTINE SENS(M,R,SM,RC)
01600                 DIMENSION R(1),SM(1),RC(1)
01700                 DIMENSION A(21),AQ(21),RAQ(21),RQ(21)
01900                 DATA DBFAC/4.342944819/
02000                 MP=M+1
02100                 A(1)=1.
03500                 AQ(1)=1.
03600                 A(2)=-R(2)/R(1)
03700                 RC(1)=A(2)
03800                 ALPHA=R(1)*(1.-A(2)*A(2))
03900                 DO 450 J=2,M
04000                 MH=J/2
04100                 JM=J-1
04200                 Q=R(J+1)
04300                 DO 420 L=1,JM
04400                 LB=J+1-L
04500          420    Q=Q+A(L+1)*R(LB)
04600                 Q=-Q/ALPHA
04700                 RC(J)=Q
04800                 DO 430 K=1,MH
04900                 KB=J-K+1
05000                 AT=A(K+1)+Q*A(KB)
05100                 A(KB)=A(KB)+Q*A(K+1)
05200          430    A(K+1)=AT
05300                 A(J+1)=Q
05400                 ALPHA=ALPHA*(1.-Q*Q)
05500        C        KILL JOB IF UNSTABLE FILTER
05600          450    IF(ALPHA.LE.0.) CALL EXIT
05700        C        ..............
05900                 DO 600 I=1,M
06000                 DO 460 K=1,M
06100          460    RQ(K)=RC(K)
06200                 RQ(I)=RC(I)+1.
06300                 AQ(2)=RQ(1)
06400                 DO 480 J=2,M
06500                 MH=J/2
06600                 JM=J-1
06700                 DO 470 K=1,MH
06800                 KB=J-K+1
06900                 AT=AQ(K+1)+RQ(J)*AQ(KB)
07000                 AQ(KB)=AQ(KB)+RQ(J)*AQ(K+1)
07100          470    AQ(K+1)=AT
07200          480    AQ(J+1) =RQ(J)
07300        C        EVALUATION OF POLYNOMIAL AUTOCORRELATION
07400                 DO 500 L=1,MP
07500                 K=MP+L-1
07600                 RAQ(L)=0.
07700                 DO 500 J=1,K
07800                 JL=L+J-1
07900          500    RAQ(L)=RAQ(L)+AQ(J)*AQ(JL)
08000                 DEL=R(1)*RAQ(1)
08100                 DO 590 J=2,MP
08200          590    DEL=DEL+2.*R(J)*RAQ(J)
08300          600    SM(I)=DBFAC*SQRT(2.*DEL/ALPHA-2.)
08400                 SM(MP)=DBFAC*SQRT(2.*R(1)/ALPHA)
08600                 RETURN
08900                 END
```

Fig. 6. Fortran subroutine SENS for computing spectral deviations.

similar to that used for the Fortran evaluation of likelihood measures [2]. Many of the lines of the programs are identical and have the same statement numbers. Inputs to the subroutine SENS are the filter order, M, and the dimensioned array $R(\cdot)$, which contains the autocorrelation sequence for the data being analyzed, where

$$R(n) = r_x(n-1) \quad \text{for } n = 1, 2, \cdots, M+1.$$

The outputs are the dimensioned array $RC(\cdot)$ containing the reflection coefficients

$$RC(n) = k_n \quad \text{for } n = 1, 2, \cdots, M,$$

and the array $SM(\cdot)$ containing the sensitivities or normalized spectral deviations given by

$$SM(n) = 4.34294418 \cdot \Delta d,$$

where Δd is based upon the change in a single-reflection coefficient

$$\Delta k_n = 1 \quad \text{for } n = 1, 2, \cdots, M.$$

The final array element based upon a unit change in a single-filter coefficient is computed as

$$SM(M+1) = 4.34294418 \sqrt{2 \cdot [r_x(0)/\alpha_M]},$$

as indicated by (20). All outputs are in units of decibels.

As in the subroutine FIND of [2], the subroutine SENS begins by solving the autocorrelation equations within DO LOOP 450, and terminates for the case of unstable model filters. A step-up procedure [3] is then followed to generate the polynomial $A(z, \lambda')$ as required for the evaluation of $\partial A(z, \lambda)/\partial k_l$ in (25). Since Δk_l is chosen as unity, the incremental polynomial $A(z)$ needed in (13) can be expressed as

$$\lambda A(z) = \frac{\partial A(z, \lambda)}{2k_l} A(z, \lambda') - A(z, \lambda). \tag{D1}$$

The orthogonality of $A(z, \lambda)$ and the powers $z^{-1}, z^{-2}, \cdots, z^{-M}$ are used to note that

$$\int_{-\pi}^{\pi} \left| \frac{\Delta A(e^{j\theta})}{A(e^{j\theta}, \lambda)} \right|^2 \frac{d\theta}{2\pi} = \int_{-\pi}^{\pi} \left| \frac{A(e^{j\theta}, \lambda')}{A(e^{j\theta}, \lambda)} \right|^2 \frac{d\theta}{2\pi} - 1. \tag{D2}$$

460

```
C        TEST FOR PROGRAM
         DIMENSION R(5),SM(9),RC(4)
         DATA R/2.,1.6,.776,.15568006,-.0098079/
         M=4
         MP=M+1
         CALL SENS(M,R,SM,RC)
         WRITE(5,50)(SM(J),J=1,MP)
         WRITE(5,50)(RC(J),J=1,M)
50       FORMAT(5F10.5)
         CALL EXIT
         END


 17.74352   15.62195    9.88957    6.43840   18.78245
 -0.80000    0.70000   -0.60000    0.30000
```

Fig. 7. Sample test program for subroutine SENS with output results.

Therefore, the integral of (13) can be evaluated by taking a likelihood ratio minus one. The portions of FIND in [2] which evaluate the likelihood ratio are then used to obtain (D2).

A sample test program is shown in Fig. 7. The input test data are identical to an autocorrelation sequence used in [2]. The output data give the normalized spectral deviations in decibels that would arise from reflection coefficient variations

$k_n = 1$ for $n = 1, 2, 3, 4$, and that which would arise for a unity filter coefficient variation.

REFERENCES

[1] R. Viswanathan and J. Makhoul, "Quantization properties of transmission parameters in linear predictive systems," *IEEE Trans. Acoust., Speech, Signal Processing (Special Issue on 1974 Arden House Workshop on Digital Signal Processing)*, vol. ASSP-23, pp. 309–321, June 1975.

[2] A. H. Gray, Jr. and J. D. Markel, "Distance measures for speech processing," *IEEE Trans. Acoust., Speech, Signal Processing*, vol. ASSP-24, pp. 380–391, Oct. 1976.

[3] J. D. Markel and A. H. Gray, Jr., *Linear Prediction of Speech*. Berlin, Germany: Springer-Verlag, 1976.

[4] B. S. Atal and S. L. Hanauer, "Speech analysis and synthesis by linear prediction of the speech wave," *J. Acoust. Soc. Amer.*, vol. 50, pp. 637–644, 1971.

[5] K. N. Stevens, "The perception of sounds shaped by resonant circuits," Sc.D. dissertation, Massachusetts Inst. Technol., Cambridge, 1952.

[6] F. Itakura, "Optimal nonlinear transformation of LPC's to improve quantization properties," *J. Acoust. Soc. Amer.*, vol. 56 (supplement), Paper H14, p. S16.

[7] J. D. Markel and A. H. Gray, Jr., "A linear prediction vocoder simulation based upon the autocorrelation method," *IEEE Trans. Acoust., Speech, Signal Processing*, vol. ASSP-22, pp. 124–134, Apr. 1974.

Author Index

A

Atal, B. S., 276

B

Barney, H. L., 45
Bell, C. G., 98

C

Cheng, M. J., 196
Cherry, L., 74
Cohen, A., 158

D

David, E. E., Jr., 110, 383
Dudley, H., 347
Dunn, H. K., 31, 241

F

Fant, G., 17
Flanagan, J. L., 4, 74, 232, 367, 388
Freudberg, R., 158
Fujimura, O., 55
Fujisaki, H., 98

G

Gold, B., 146, 369
Golden, R. M., 388
Gray, A. H., Jr., 423, 447

H

Hanauer, S. L., 276
Heinz, J. M., 66, 98
Holmes, J. N., 227
House, A. S., 98

I

Itakura, F., 295, 419

L

Logan, B. F., 383

M

Makhoul, J., 124, 434
Manley, H. J., 158
Markel, J. D., 168, 303, 423, 447
Mathews, M. V., 110
McCandless, S., 312
McGonegal, C. A., 196
Mermelstein, P., 321
Miller, J. E., 110
Miller, R. L., 216

N

Noll, A. M., 179

O

Oppenheim, A. V., 118, 411

P

Peterson, G. E., 45
Pinson, E. N., 251
Portnoff, M. R., 405
Prestigiacomo, A. J., 383

R

Rabiner, L. R., 82, 146, 196, 261
Rader, C. M., 369
Rosenberg, A. E., 196
Ross, M. J., 158

S

Saito, S., 295, 419
Schafer, R. W., 82, 118, 261
Schroeder, M. R., 352, 383
Seneff, S., 319
Shaffer, H. L., 158
Sondhi, M. M., 153
Stevens, K. N., 66, 98

V

Viswanathan, R., 434

W

Wakita, H., 333

Subject Index

467

EDITORS' BIOGRAPHIES

Ronald W. Schafer (S'62-M'67-SM'74-F'77) received the B.S.E.E. and M.S.E.E. degrees from the University of Nebraska, Lincoln, in 1961 and 1962, and a Ph.D. degree in electrical engineering from the Massachusetts Institute of Technology, Cambridge, in 1968.

From 1964 to 1968 he served as instructor of electrical engineering at M.I.T. During that period he did extensive teaching in graduate and undergraduate courses in the areas of circuits and linear systems. At the same time, he was a member of the Research Laboratory of Electronics where he was involved in signal processing research.

In 1968 he became a member of the Technical Staff in the Acoustics Research Department of Bell Laboratories, Murray Hill, New Jersey. Subsequently he became a supervisor in that department. From 1968 to 1974, he carried out research and supervised research in speech analysis and synthesis, digital signal processing techniques, and digital waveform coding.

Since 1974, he has been on the faculty of the Georgia Institute of Technology as a John O. McCarty/Audichron Professor of Electrical Engineering. At Georgia Tech, he has been involved in developing a program of teaching and research in the general area of digital signal processing. He is co-author, with A. V. Oppenheim, of the textbook *Digital Signal Processing,* and he is co-author, with L. R. Rabiner, of the recently published textbook, *Digital Processing of Speech Signals.* He is also author or co-author of over 50 technical publications and is the coholder of four patents.

He has been very active in the affairs of The IEEE Transactions on Acoustics, Speech, and Signal Processing (ASSP) Society during the past ten years, having been elected to the Administrative Committee of ASSP for the term 1974–76 and serving as Vice-President from 1975 to 1977. He has served on the Technical Committees for Digital Signal Processing and Speech Processing, and he was Associate Editor of The IEEE Transactions on Acoustics, Speech, and Signal Processing from 1974 to 1976. He presently serves as President of the ASSP Society.

Dr. Schafer is a Fellow of IEEE and of the Acoustical Society of America. He is a member of Eta Kappa Nu, Phi Eta Sigma, and Sigma Xi.

John D. Markel (M'72-SM'77) was born in Wichita, Kansas, on January 20, 1943. He received the B.S.E.E. degree from Kansas State University, Manhattan, in 1965, the M.S.E.E. degree from Arizona State University, Tempe, in 1968, and the Ph.D. degree from the University of California, Santa Barbara, in 1970.

From 1965 to 1969, he was employed at Motorola Government Electronics Division, Scottsdale, Arizona. In 1969, he joined Speech Communications Research Laboratory (SCRL) in Santa Barbara, CA. He was actively involved in various speech research topics and became Vice President in 1972. During this period, he also consulted for government and commercial organizations and developed speech and signal processing short courses.

In 1977, he founded Signal Technology, Inc. (STI), where he is also President. He has remained active in speech processing research and in industrial consulting. Drs. Markel and A. H. Gray, Jr., are co-authors of the book "Linear Prediction of Speech" (New York: Springer–Verlag, 1976) and have received several awards including the 1977 IEEE ASSP Achievement Award for their contributions to the development of linear prediction techniques.

Dr. Markel has served as the first book reviews editor for the IEEE Acoustics, Speech and Signal Processing Society and is presently a member of its Administrative Committee.